PN 1998 .N78 1991

Nowlan, Robert A.

The films of the eighties

The Films of the Eighties

The Films
of the Eighties

*A Complete, Qualitative Filmography
to Over 3400 Feature-Length English
Language Films, Theatrical and Video-
Only, Released between January 1, 1980,
and December 31, 1989*

by
ROBERT A. NOWLAN
GWENDOLYN WRIGHT NOWLAN

McFarland & Company, Inc., Publishers
Jefferson, North Carolina, and London

British Library Cataloguing-in-Publication data are available

Library of Congress Cataloguing-in-Publication Data

Nowlan, Robert A.
  The films of the eighties : a complete, qualitative filmography to
over 3400 feature-length English language films, theatrical and
video-only, released between January 1, 1980, and December 31, 1989
/ by Robert A. Nowlan and Gwendolyn Wright Nowlan.
    p. cm.
  Includes index.
  ISBN 0-89950-560-0 (lib. bdg. : 40# alk. paper) ∞
  1. Motion pictures — Catalogs. I. Nowlan, Gwendolyn Wright, 1945- .
II. Title.
PN1998.N78 1991
016.79143'75 — dc20   90-53516
                                                    CIP

Manufactured in the United States of America

McFarland & Company, Inc., Publishers
 Box 611, Jefferson, North Carolina 28640

For our children and friends

and

Robert De Niro *as Jake La Motta*
Harrison Ford *as Indiana Jones*
F. Murray Abraham *as Antonio Salieri*
Julie Walters *as Rita*
Daniel Day-Lewis *as Christy Brown*
Dustin Hoffman *as Raymond Babbitt*
Robert Preston *as Toddy*
Burt Lancaster *as Lou*
Susan Sarandon *as Annie Savoy*
Morgan Freeman *as Hoke Colburn*
Richard Dreyfuss *as BB*
Danny DeVito *as Ernest Tilley*
Tom Hanks *as Josh Baskin*
Maggie Smith *as Charlotte Bartlett*
Barbara Hershey *as Ruth Sullivan*
Ian Bannen *as Grandfather George*
Tina Turner *as Aunty Entity*
Sean Connery *as Jim Malone*
Kathleen Turner *as Matty Walker*
Olympia Dukakis *as Rose Castorini*
Don Ameche *as Mortimer Duke*
Meryl Streep *as Sophie Zawistowska*
Jack Nicholson *as Francis Phelan*
Glenn Close *as Alex Forrest*
Michael Douglas *as Gordon Gekko*
John Cusack *as Walter 'Gib' Gibson*
Joan Cusack *as Cyn*
Sigourney Weaver *as Dian Fossey*
Woody Allen *as Danny Rose*
M. Emmet Walsh *as Private Detective Visser*
Frances McDormand *as Mrs. Pell*
Andie MacDowell *as Ann Millaney*
Bob Hoskins *as Owney Madden*
Hector Elizondo *as Arthur Willis*
Robin Williams *as Adrian Cronauer*

Table of Contents

Introduction

This book contains more than 3400 English language films released during the 1980s, arranged in alphabetical order by title. For each film we provide its year of release, the production or releasing company, country of origin if other than the United States, running time, whether it is in color or black and white, the leading performers and the names of their characters, production credits including producers, directors, screenwriters, basis of story, photographer, musical composer, editor, and production director, and other credits which seem appropriate. This information is followed by a brief description of the film, our own review of it, and an evaluation of the movie, its entertainment value, and its cinematic values if any.

A number of these movies never made it to a theater, going instead directly to prosperous or dusty lives on the shelves of video stores. For differing reasons we have not included documentary, experimental or pornographic movies. That there are some films we have missed which would meet our criteria for inclusion is a certainty. However, we believe that we have captured just about all that were deemed worthy of being reviewed by some critic in some periodical.

The eighties saw the emergence of some notable new film stars: Rosanna Arquette, Kevin Bacon, Ellen Barkin, Kim Basinger, Matthew Broderick, Nicolas Cage, Chevy Chase, Glenn Close, Kevin Costner, Tom Cruise, Billy Crystal, Jamie Lee Curtis, John Cusack, Willem Dafoe, Geena Davis, Daniel Day-Lewis, Laura Dern, Danny De Vito, Matt Dillon, Emilio Estevez, Harrison Ford, Michael J. Fox, Mel Gibson, Whoopi Goldberg, Jeff Goldblum, Melanie Griffith, Tom Hanks, Daryl Hannah, Gregory Hines, Paul Hogan, Bob Hoskins, Holly Hunter, William Hurt, Anjelica Huston, Timothy Hutton, Jeremy Irons, Amy Irving, Michael Keaton, Nastassja Kinski, Kevin Kline, Shelley Long, Rob Lowe, Ralph Macchio, Andie MacDowell, John Malkovich, Steve Martin, Mary Stuart Masterson, Kelly McGillis, Bette Midler, Eddie Murphy, Bill Murray, Judd Nelson, Sean Penn, Michelle Pfeiffer, Lou Diamond Phillips, River Phoenix, Dennis Quaid, Molly Ringwald, Julia Roberts, Mickey Rourke, Meg Ryan, Charlie Sheen, Lori Singer, Eric Stoltz, Patrick Swayze, Meg Tilly, Kathleen Turner, Tracey Ullman, Denzel Washington, Sigourney Weaver, Dianne Wiest, Robin Williams, Bruce Willis, Debra Winger, James Woods, and Sean Young.

In the eighties, the film industry paid final farewells to such luminaries as Mary Astor, Fred Astaire, Lucille Ball, Anne Baxter, John Belushi, Ingrid Bergman, Irving Berlin, Gunnar Bjornstrand, Mel Blanc, Beulah Bondi, Louise Brooks, Yul Brynner, Luis Bunuel, Richard Burton, James Cagney, Yakima Canutt, John Carradine, John Cassavetes, Rene Clair, Jackie Coogan, Broderick Crawford, George Cukor, Bette Davis, Dolores Del Rio, Divine (Harris Glenn Millstead), Melvyn Douglas, Allan Dwan, Stepin Fetchit (Lincoln Perry), Henry Fonda, Carl Foreman, Bob Fosse, Janet Gaynor, Jackie Gleason, Ruth Gordon, Gloria Grahame, Cary Grant, Joan Greenwood, Margaret Hamilton, Ann Harding, Henry Hathaway, Sterling Hayden, Rita Hayworth, Edith Head, Lillian Hellman, Alfred Hitchcock, William Holden, Trevor Howard, Rock Hudson, John Huston, Sam Jaffe, Celia Johnson, Danny Kaye, Grace Kelly, Henry King, Alan Jay Lerner, Mervyn LeRoy, Silvana Mangano, James Mason, Raymond Massey, Jessie Matthews, Steve McQueen, Ethel Merman, Lewis Milestone, Ray Milland, Vincente Minnelli, Mary Miles Minter, Robert Montgomery, Colleen Moore, Anna Neagle, Pola Negri, David Niven, Pat O'Brien, Laurence Olivier, Geraldine Page, George Pal, Lilli Palmer, John Payne, Sam Peckinpah, Eleanor Powell, William Powell, Otto Preminger, Robert Preston, George Raft, Michael Redgrave, Donna Reed, Ralph Richardson, Simone Signoret, Dore Schary, Randolph Scott, Peter Sellers, Norma Shearer, Sam Spiegel, Lee Strasberg, Gloria Swanson, Jacques Tati, François Truffaut, King Vidor, Hal Wallis, Raoul Walsh, Robert Penn Warren, Johnny Weissmuller, Orson Welles, Mae West, Cornel Wilde, Tennessee Williams, Natalie Wood and William Wyler.

Although many, too many, of the films of the eighties fell into the slasher and sexploitation subgenres in which gross violence was visited on nubile and scantily clad young women by a variety of maniacs, the decades had its share of memorable films and performances.

It was the time when just about every performance of Meryl Streep or Glenn Close was honored with an Oscar nomination. Jack Nicholson, on the other hand, chose to appear in just enough stinkers to hurt his chances of being named male actor of the decade. The same may be said for intense Robert De Niro, who started the decade on its way with his masterful interpretation of the life of boxer Jake LaMotta in *Raging Bull,* a film many hail as the best of the 1980s. Audiences discovered that Barbara Seagull, back to calling herself Barbara Hershey, was an exceptional actress, that Susan Sarandon looked only better as she aged, that Richard Dreyfuss was not finished as it had once seemed, and that Woody Allen was the most inventive filmmaker around, with young Spike Lee coming up fast on the outside.

Dustin Hoffman derailed his career with *Ishtar,* but saved it with his moving performance in *Rain Man.* Shirley MacLaine moved nicely into character roles. Oliver Stone refused to allow us to forget the Vietnam war and the sacrifices of the men who fought, died, or were crippled there mentally, physically or emotionally. Director Martin Scorsese discovered for himself why moviemakers had usually made movies with a religious theme both extremely reverent and boring.

Daniel Day-Lewis, an actor of remarkable range, topped his decade of brilliance with arguably the best performance by a male in the ten year span, as Irish writer and cerebral palsy victim Christy Brown in *My Left Foot*. British actor, director and writer Kenneth Branagh risked comparison to the great Laurence Olivier, and came out a winner with his version of *Henry V*. With his 1989 performances in *Driving Miss Daisy* and *Glory*, Morgan Freeman served notice that he had to be considered among the best actors of the decade.

John Cusack wins our vote for the most appealing new young male (his sister Joan is to be held in high regard also), but Matt Dillon is probably a better actor. Molly Ringwald delighted us with her perky high school princess good looks, but by the end of the decade, found what so many other youngsters have learned to their sorrow, that moving into adult roles is very difficult for a child star.

Harrison Ford, Mel Gibson and Kevin Costner came on like gangbusters, making us believe that someday they will be the Humphrey Bogarts, Clark Gables and Gary Coopers for a younger generation. Michael Douglas did something his illustrious father Kirk Douglas never did, win an Oscar and practically own Hollywood. Burt Lancaster found a home in roles of rascally old fellows. Beautiful Jane Greer came back to the movies, even appearing in *Against All Odds,* a remake of one of her most successful films, 1947's *Out of the Past*.

Kathleen Turner proved that wholesome beauty can be very sexy, while Michelle Pfeiffer's great good looks, so different and delightful in each of her roles, would win many votes as the most beautiful of all actresses of the eighties. Sigourney Weaver not only stands tall in stature but in the quality of her work as well, while little Jodie Foster is a giant talent.

George Burns, Jessica Tandy, Hume Cronyn, Ralph Bellamy and Don Ameche are among the many senior citizen performers who proved they just get better with age. At the other end of the age spectrum, we tip our hats to Christian Bale of *Empire of the Sun,* Hugh O'Conor in *My Left Foot,* and Lukas Haas in *The Wizard of Loneliness.*

As far as films were concerned, the eighties weren't particularly kind to the likes of Jacqueline Bisset, Linda Blair, James Caan, Julie Christie, James Coburn, Tony Curtis, Faye Dunaway, Elliott Gould, David Hemmings, Kris Kristofferson, Ali MacGraw, Marsha Mason, Al Pacino, Oliver Reed, George Segal and John Travolta, each of whom were unable to match their earlier successes. Paul Newman and Michael Caine finally won Academy Awards, but not for performances which most deserved the prize. Sean Connery and Geraldine Page, however, did.

Bo Derek spent the decade trying to hide her lack of talent by constantly exposing her remarkable body. Burt Reynolds began the decade as number one at the box office. By the end of the period he acted as if he was bored and didn't need to act to succeed. Dudley Moore discovered in 1988 with *Arthur on the Rocks* that he was roasted for repeating the drunken act that so endeared him to fans in 1981 with *Arthur*.

We are sure we are just two among a large number of movie fans who have grown tired of Sylvester Stallone's two roles, left profile for Rocky and right profile for Rambo. We've also had our fill of little guys such as Ralph Macchio and Michael J. Fox pretending they have found the fountain of youth and playing the same teen role over and over again. Will any others join us in the sincere hope that before the 90s are out, series such as *Back to the Future, Friday the 13th, Halloween, The Karate Kid, Nightmare on Elm Street, Police Academy, Rambo, Rocky, Star Trek, Superman,* and *The Toxic Avenger* will be sent to the island of lost movies.

Still, all in all it was a very good ten years for movies.

Robert A. Nowlan, Ph.D.
Gwendolyn Wright Nowlan, Ed.D.

Acknowledgments

We are pleased to express our thanks to our many contributors, whose reactions, opinions and evaluations of the movies of the eighties have been incorporated in our reviews. We also acknowledge a great debt to the many individuals who have made our work a bit easier due to their interest and support. These include:

Esther Anderson, Robert Aubrey, Mackey Barron, Claire Bennett, George Bick, Arlene Bielefield, Mariellen Black, Sonja Blanchard, Newell Bliss, Lorena Brown, David Brownell, David Burke, Emil Capatoni, Roberta Carlson, Johnny Chambers, Roland Chamblee, Tom Clarie, Heather Corcoran, Jim Countryman, Spud Crank, Jerry Davidson, Sonny Deatherage, Laura DeMartino, Ann Demsky, Ron DeNardo, John Derwent, Karen Dunbar, Dick Eberhardt, John Evans, Suzanne Farrell, Richard Galligan, Eustace Galois, Rachel Garcia, K.F. Gauss, Kim Golis, Bodh Gulati, John Haggerty, Jane Hamilton-Merritt, Barbara Hanscom, Bill Hickey, Ann Hickman, Frances Hughes, Milko Jeglic, Stevie Johnson, Gaylen Kelley, John Kennedy, Ruth Kindersley, Lynn Kohrn, Mary Jane Kunde, Louis Kuslan, Eve Kyberg, King Kwok, Rod Lane, Bert Latil, Ray Lawson, Tom Lawson, Annabel Lee, Tom Leeson, Florence Lowe, Ron Malooley, Tom McCann, Ann McCleery, Jimmy McGoon, Joel Meisel, Wayne Miller, Larry Montgomery, Marilyn Montlick, Billy Mulligan, Gilbert Noble, Timothy O'Meara, Pete Olsen, Rocco Orlando, Dan Ort, Rocco Pannella, Evelyn Peters, Walter Petroskey, Kathy Pettit, Phil Poffenberger, Tom Porter, Elnora Potter, Timmy Powell, Jeanette Ray, Gus Reynolds, Tara Roberts, Tim Rodd, Elisa Roller, Harold Ross, Tony Rother, Ted Sands, Dorothy Schrader, Bruce Shattuck, Michael Shea, John Sheehan, Jeanette Shields, Jim Shilokowski, Robert Smith, John Splaine, James Stasheff, Bud Stone, Don Sutherland, Ronald Swanson, George Telecki, Tom Therriault, Robert Vogen, Robert Washburn, James While, Winnie Wu, Kelly Yakamoko, David Young, Dick Zimmerman.

We are greatly in the debt of the friendly staff of McFarland & Company, Inc. It is a pleasure to deal with a company knowing that whenever we have a question, it will be promptly answered, that whenever a decision must be made, it will be made.

We also are pleased to express our fond memories of our beloved mothers Marian Shields Nowlan and Gertrude Evans Lawson, our gratitude to our fathers Robert A. Nowlan, Sr., and Dr. Ray N. Lawson, his wife Dr. Anne Lawson, our children, Robert, Philip, Edward, his wife Amy, their daughter and our granddaughter Alexandra, and Jennifer Nowlan; and Evan and Andrew Wright. Additional thanks goes to our dear brothers and sisters, Marty and Steve Johnson, Mary Nowlan, Michael and Kitty Nowlan, Steve Nowlan, Danny and Lynne Nowlan, Mary and Bill Corcoran, Ray E. and Mollie Lawson, Joseph Lawson and Peter Lawson, our numerous nieces and nephews, and a special thanks to Howard and Marian Wright.

R.A.N.
G.W.N.

Key to Abbreviations

Title Section

* — Academy Award Winner
† — Academy Award Nominee
aka — also known as
b&w — black and white
c — color
GB — Great Britain
m — minutes
3-D — three Dimensional

Cast and Production Credits

* — Academy Award Winner
† — Academy Award Nominee
AD — art director
ANIM — animation
ANIM D — animation director
CH — choreographer
COS — costume designer
D — director
ED — film editor
LP — leading performers
M — musical composer of score
MD — musical director
MK — makeup
P — producer
PD — production designer
PH — photographer
SD — set director
SE — special effects
SO — sound editing
ST — stunts
VE — visual effects
W — screenwriter

The Films, A–Z

1. *About Last Night...* (1986, Tri-Star, 113m, c). P Jason Brett & Stuart Oken, D Edward Zwick, W Tim Kazurinsky & Denise DeClue (based on the play *Sexual Perversity in Chicago* by David Mamet), PH Andrew Dintenfass, M Miles Goodman, ED Harry Keramidas, PD Ida Random.

LP Rob Lowe (Danny), Demi Moore (Debbie), Jim Belushi (Bernie), Elizabeth Perkins (Joan), George DiCenzo (Mr. Favio), Michael Alldredge (Mother Malone), Robin Thomas (Steve Carlson), Donna Gibbons (Alex).

Rob Lowe and Demi Moore fall into lust and then into bed before they have much more than a chance to exchange names. Moore is looking for something more permanent than the "going nowhere" relationship she has with her boss. Lowe finds it difficult to make a commitment. The film makes the bar scene seem dreary and demeaning. Elizabeth Perkins, as Moore's disapproving friend, steals the show.

2. *Above the Law* (1988, Warner, 104m, c). P Steven Seagal & Andrew Davis, D Davis, W Steven Pressfield & Ronald Shusett (based on a story by Davis & Seagal), PH Robert Steadman, M David Frank, ED Michael Brown, PD Maher Ahmad.

LP Steven Seagal (Nico Toscani), Pam Grier (Delores Jackson), Sharon Stone (Sara), Daniel Faraldo (Salvano), Henry Silva (Zagon), Ronnie Barron (Bartender), Nicholas Kusenko (Agent Neely), Ron Dean (Lukich), Joe V. Greco (Father Gennaro).

Tough Chicago cop and one time CIA agent Steven Seagal goes to war with his former associates in "the company" who in order to finance their covert activities have stooped to becoming murdering drug traffickers. The main baddie is Henry Silva, who has his back broken by Seagal in the climactic battle of a very brutal movie.

3. *Absence of Malice* (1981, Columbia, 116m, c). P&D Sydney Pollack, W Kurt Luedtke†, PH Owen Roizman, M Dave Grusin, ED Sheldon Kahn, PD Terence Marsh.

LP Paul Newman† (Michael Gallagher), Sally Field (Megan Carter), Bob Balaban (Rosen), Melinda Dillon† (Teresa), Luther Adler (Malderone), Barry Primus (Waddell), Josef Sommer (McAdam), John Harkins (Davidck), Don Hood (Quinn), Wilford Brimley (Wells).

Miami newspaper reporter Sally Field's stories make it appear that honest businessman Paul Newman is behind the disappearance of a Hispanic longshoremen's union leader. Even a budding romance between Field and Newman doesn't temper her reporter's zeal. When the spotlight on his activities drives his friend Melinda Dillon to suicide, Newman takes steps to get even.

4. *Absolute Beginners* (1986, Orion, GB, 111m, c). P Stephen Woolley & Chris Brown, D Julien Temple, W Christopher Wicking, Richard Burridge & Don MacPherson (based on the novel by Colin MacInnes), PH Oliver Stapleton, M Gil Evans, Clive Langer & Alan Winstanley, ED Michael Bradsell, Gerry Hambling, Richard Bedford & Russell Lloyd, PD John Beard, CH David Toguri.

LP Eddie O'Connell (Colin), Patsy Kensit (Suzette), David Bowie (Vendice Partners), James Fox (Henley of Mayfair), Ray Davies (Arthur), Mandy Rice-

Davies (Mum), Eve Ferret (Big Jill), Anita Morris (Dido Lament), Steven Berkoff (The Fanatic), Sade Adu (Athene Duncannon).

Set in 1958 London, this original musical features alienated youths rocking to a pulsating score in the midst of racial tensions and riots. Finding more pluses than minuses for the film requires ignoring the flat characterizations and concentrating on the music and youthful energy.

5.   *Absolution* (1988, Trans World, GB, 95m, c). P Danny O'Donovan & Elliott Kastner, D Anthony Page, W Anthony Shaffer, PH John Coquillon, M Stanley Myers, ED John Victor Smith, PD Natasha Kroll.

LP Richard Burton (Fr. Goddard), Dominic Guard (Benjie), Dai Bradley (Arthur), Billy Connolly (Blakey), Andrew Keir (Headmaster), Willoughby Gray (Brig. General Walsh), Preston Lockwood (Fr. Hibbert).

Richard Burton didn't enhance his acting reputation with this dreary story of a priest teaching at a British Catholic public school. He is easily manipulated by students Dominic Guard and Dai Bradley. Burton favors Guard, whom he considers a bright but mischievous boy. But Guard's predilection for practical jokes gets way out of hand. The film went to video almost immediately after its delayed release in theaters. Burton didn't live to see the film released nine years after its 1979 completion.

6.   *The Abyss* (1989, 20th Century-Fox, 140m, c). P Gale Anne Hurd, D&W James Cameron, PH Mikael Salomon† & Al Giddings (underwater camera), M Alan Silvestri, ED Joel Goodman, PD Leslie Dilley, SOUND Blake Leyh†, AD Peter Childs†, SD Anne Kuljian†, VE John Bruno, Hoyt Yeatman, Dennis Muren, Robert Skotak & Gene Warren, Jr.*

LP Ed Harris (Bud Brigman), Mary Elizabeth Mastrantonio (Lindsey Brigman), Michael Biehn (Lt. Coffey), George Robert Klek (Wilhite), John Bedford Lloyd ("Jammer" Willis), Christopher Murphy (Seal Schoenick), J.C. Quinn ("Sonny" Dawson), Kimberly Scott (Lisa "One-Night" Standing), Capt. Kidd Brewer, Jr. (Lew Finler), Leo Burmester ("Catfish" De Vries), Todd Graff (Alan "Hippy" Carnes).

James Cameron's last two films were *The Terminator* and *Aliens*. This $50 million-plus underwater adventure story was meant to be his masterpiece. Well, everyone must deal with shattered dreams. An American nuclear submarine is mysteriously rendered powerless some 2,000 feet below the ocean's surface. The only hope for rescue is to utilize a prototype manned underwater oil-drilling habitat, a huge spidery-looking rig called Deepcore which sits on the ocean floor. Its designer is tough engineer Mary Elizabeth Mastrantonio and its foreman is her estranged husband Ed Harris. The crew of Deepcore is recruited to work with a group of Navy SEALS to attempt the rescue. To add to the rescue team's problems, the SEALS leader, Michael Biehn, develops a raging case of High Pressure Nervous Syndrome which transforms him into a fanatic, imagining Soviets to be behind every problem. His solution is to nuke 'em.

7.   *Acceptable Levels* (1983, Enterprise Pictures, GB, 103m, c). P&D John Davies, W Gordon Hann, Ellin Hare, Alastair Herron, Robert Smith, Kate McManus & Davies, PH Robert Smith, M Nick Garvey, ED Ellin Hare.

LP Kay Adshead (Sue), Andy Rashleigh (Simon), Patrick Higgins (Tony McAteer), Tracey Lynch (Roisin McAteer), Sally McCaffery (Kathleen McAteer), George Shane (Frank McAteer), Paul Jesson (Major Green).

While interviewing a Belfast family, one of whose sons was killed by a stray plastic bullet, fired by a British soldier, British TV reporter Kay Adshead becomes politically and emotionally involved. When the crew returns to London, her producer, Andy Rashleigh destroys her most indicting film footage.

8.   *The Accidental Tourist*† (1988, Warner, 122m, c). P&D Lawrence Kasdan, W Frank Galati & Kasdan† (based on the novel by Anne Tyler), PH John Bailey, M John Williams†, ED Carol Littleton, PD Bo Welch.

LP William Hurt (Macon Leary), Kathleen Turner (Sarah Leary), Geena Davis† (Muriel Pritchett), Amy Wright

(Rose Leary), David Ogden Stiers (Porter Leary), Ed Begley, Jr. (Charles Leary), Bill Pullman (Julian), Robert Gorman (Alexander).

The film has much to recommend it, but it's not the cinematic masterpiece that some critics would have us believe. William Hurt, an unemotional man from an unusual family of eccentrics, stoically suffers the death of his child and his wife Kathleen Turner walking out on him. He seems intent on shunning life even when he meets lively and somewhat kooky Geena Davis, whose attraction to and for him is a bit difficult to fathom. In the end Hurt must choose between Davis and Turner. Davis wins out in what appears to be a mental flip of the coin. The book is better.

9. *The Accused* (1988, Paramount, 110m, c). P Stanley R. Jaffe & Sherry Lansing, D Jonathan Kaplan, W Tom Topor, PH Ralf D. Bode, M Brad Fiedel, ED Jerry Greenberg & O. Nicholas Brown, PD Richard Kent Wilcox.

LP Kelly McGillis (Kathryn Murphy), Jodie Foster* (Sarah Tobias), Bernie Coulson (Kenneth Joyce), Ann Hearn (Sally Frazer), Steve Antin (Bob Joiner), Tom O'Brien (Larry), Allan Lysell (Asst. D.A. Al Massi), Leo Rossi (Cliff Albrecht), Carmen Argenziano (Paul Rudolph), Terry David Mulligan (Det. Duncan), Woody Brown (Danny Rudkin), Peter Van Norden (Ted Paulson).

In the most powerful way imaginable this film makes the point that even if a woman is not as pure as the driven snow, she doesn't deserve to be raped and brutalized by male animals. Jodie Foster gives a shattering performance as a tiny young woman who visits a roadhouse to have some fun, drinks too much, smokes a little pot and, becomes overly friendly and encouraging to a couple of the regulars. When she puts on a sexy dance, she is thrown on top of a pinball machine and raped by three men, as others shout and cheer them on, even though she's yelling for them to stop. Assistant D.A. Kelly McGillis, not believing Foster will make a creditable witness against the rapists because of her behavior and reputation, allows the three defendants to plea bargain to a lesser

charge. Foster is outraged. McGillis has a change of heart and brings members of the cheering throng to trial for the crime of encouraging a person to commit rape. Bernie Coulson, whose best friend was one of the rapists, sickened by his own feelings of guilt in doing nothing to help the rape victim, finally gets up the nerve to tell what really happened. In flashbacks during the trial, the audience is treated to the rape in all of its brutality. The cheerers are convicted and Foster leaves the courtroom with a bit of her dignity restored. Some have argued that in showing the rape sequence so graphically, the filmmakers are actually exploiting what they are so rightly condemning. The argument has some merit.

10. *The Act* (1984, Film Ventures, 94m, c, aka *Bless 'Em All*). P David Greene & Sig Shore, D Shore, W Robert Lipsyte, PH Benjamin Davis, M John Sebastian & Phil Goldston, ED Ron Kalish, PD Steve Wilson.

LP Robert Ginty (Don), Sarah Langenfeld (Leslie), Nick Surovy (Julian), John Aprea (Ron), John Tripp (Dixie), Eddie Albert (Harry), James Andronica (Mickey), John Cullum (President), Pat Hingle (Frank).

Lawyer Robert Ginty finds himself involved with union politics when he accepts a large fee to defend a crooked union leader. He wins the case, but the union wants the fee back and they aren't too particular how they get it.

11. *Action Jackson* (1988, Lorimar, 93m, c). P Joel Silver, D Craig R. Baxley, W Robert Reneau, PH Matthew F. Leonetti, M Herbie Hancock & Michael Kamen, ED Mark Helfrich, PD Virginia Randolph.

LP Carl Weathers (Jericho "Action" Jackson), Craig T. Nelson (Peter Dellaplane), Vanity (Sydney Ash), Sharon Stone (Patrice Dellaplane), Thomas F. Wilson (Officer Kornblau), Bill Duke (Capt. Armbruster), Robert Davi (Tony Moretti), Jack Thibeau (Det. Kotterwell).

Former *Rocky* co-star Carl Weathers stars as a cop, with a Harvard law degree, who is too tough for his bosses' tastes, as well as for the Detroit underworld. He's out to stop a power-mad automobile executive whose henchmen are killing off automobile union leaders. There are plenty of car chases, and violence, and for those who have the time, there's sexy Vanity to ogle.

12.   Action U.S.A. (1989, Stewart & Berger, 89m, c, aka *A Handful of Trouble*). P Alan Stewart & Susan Stewart, D John Stewart, W David Reskin (based on a story by Reskin & John Stewart), PH Thomas L. Callaway, M Del Casher, ED Gabrielle Gilbert.

LP Barri Murphy (Carmen), Gregory Scott Cummins (Osborn), William Hubbard Knight (McKinnon), Hoke Howell (Hitch), William Smith (Conover), Cameron Mitchell (Frankie Navarro), Ross Hagen (Drago).

When her boyfriend is rubbed out for executing a diamond heist that she witnessed, Barri Murphy must go on the lam to escape gangsters intent on eliminating her.

13.   Adventure of the Action Hunters (1987, Troma, 80m, c). P Mary Holland, D Lee Bonner, W Bonner & Leif Elsmo, PH David Insley, M John Pallumbo, ED Bonner.

LP Ronald Hunter (Walter), Sean Murphy (Betty), Joseph Cimino (1st Gangster), Art Donovan (2nd Gangster), Steve Beauchamp (Skipper), Peter Walker (Oliver).

Set in Baltimore of the 1950s, this action film, shot in 1982, consists of a series of chases, explosions and shoot-'em-ups. Ronald Hunter and Sean Murphy search for a cache of $500,000 hidden by an old sailor before he's killed by gangsters who are also after the loot.

14.   Adventures in Baby Sitting (1987, Touchstone, 99m, c). P Debra Hill & Lynda Obst, D Chris Columbus, W David Simkins, PH Ric Waite, M Michael Kamen, ED Fredric & William Steinkamp, PD Todd Hallowell.

LP Elisabeth Shue (Chris Parker), Maia Brewton (Sara Anderson), Keith Coogan (Brad Anderson), Anthony Rapp (Daryl Coopersmith), Calvin Levels (Joe Gipp), Vincent Phillip D'Onofrio (Dawson), Penelope Ann Miller (Brenda), George Newbern (Dan), John Ford Noonan (John Pruitt).

Cute teen Elisabeth Shue drags her three babysitting charges with her when a chum calls for help from downtown Chicago. A tire on their station wagon blows and they discover that no one thought to bring any money with them. The four have plenty of dangerous and comical adventures, tangling with street people and gangsters. In a black blues club they are required to perform before being allowed to leave. Young teens Keith Coogan and Anthony Rapp are charming gangly nerds. Little brat Maia Brewton scores by resisting being too precocious and Shue as the little lady in charge is a delight.

Adventures in the Creep Zone see Spacehunter: Adventures in the Forbidden Zone

15.   The Adventures of Baron Munchausen (1989, Columbia, GB, 126m, c). P Thomas Schuhly, D Terry Gilliam, W Charles McKeown & Gilliam, PH Giuseppe Rotunno, M Michael Kamen, ED Peter Hollywood, PD Dante Ferretti†, SE Richard Conway†.

LP John Neville (Baron Munchausen), Eric Idle (Desmond/Berthold), Sarah Polley (Sally Salt), Oliver Reed (Vulcan), Charles McKeown (Rupert/Adolphus), Winston Dennis (Bill/Albrecht), Jack Purvis (Jeremy/Gustavus), Valentina Cortesa (Queen Ariadne/Violet), Jonathan Pryce (Horatio Jackson), Uma Thurman (Venus/Rose), Sting (Heroic Officer), Ray D. Tutto [Robin Williams] (King of the Moon).

This delightful loony spectacular stars John Neville as an 18th century Baron, and most notorious liar, who protects his city from the advance of the Turks. In the company of ten-year-old Sarah Polley, Neville traces his way backwards and forwards in time to locate his friends, Winston Dennis, the strongest man in the world; Eric Idle, the fastest; Charles McKeown, with the eyes of an eagle, and Jack Purvis, who can blow harder than a typhoon. Neville and the other actors are good, but most of the credit for the success of director Terry Gilliam's enjoyable film goes to cameraman Giuseppe Rotunno, production designer Dante Ferretti and special effects expert Richard Conway.

16.   The Adventures of Buckaroo Banzai: Across the 8th Dimension (1984,

20th Century–Fox, 103m, c). P Neil Canton & W.D. Richter, D Richter, W Earl Mac Rauch, PH Fred J. Koenekamp, M Michael Boddicker, ED Richard Marks & George Bowers, PD J. Michael Riva, SE Michael Fink.

LP Peter Weller (Buckaroo Bonzai), John Lithgow (Dr. Emilio Lizardo/Lord John Whorfin), Ellen Barkin (Penny Priddy), Jeff Goldblum (New Jersey), Christopher Lloyd (John Bigboote), Lewis Smith (Perfect Tommy), Rosalind Cash (John Emdall), Robert Ito (Prof. Hikita).

Nuclear physicist, brain surgeon and rock 'n' roll singer Peter Weller is called upon to save the world from aliens who landed on Earth on Halloween in 1939 (Orson Welles' report of their landing wasn't a hoax after all). An additional adversary is crazy scientist John Lithgow, who like Weller has succeeded in crashing into the 8th dimension.

Adventures of Hercules see Hercules I

17. *Adventures of Mark Twain* (1985, Atlantic, 90m, Claymation, c). P&D Will Vinton, W Susan Shadburne, M Billy Scream, Character designer Barry Bruce, Clayanimators Bruce, William L. Fiesterman, Tom Gasek, Mark Gustafson, Craig Bartlett & Bruce McKean, ED Kelley Baker, Michael Gall, Will Vinton, Ed Ghis & Skeets McGrew.

LP VOICES James Whitmore (Mark Twain), Chris Ritchie (Tom Sawyer), Gary Krug (Huck Finn), Michele Mariana (Becky Thatcher/The Mysterious Stranger), John Morrison (Adam), Carol Edelman (Eve).

Filmed in the Claymation animation process, Mark Twain is joined by Tom Sawyer, Huck Finn and Becky Thatcher for a balloon ride, heading for Halley's Comet.

Aerobicide see Killer Workout

18. *Aerodrome* (1983, BBC TV Release, GB, 91m, c). P Kenith Trodd, D Giles Foster, W Robin Chapman (based on the novel by Rex Warner), PH Kenneth McMillan, M Carl Davis, ED Clare Douglas, PD Geoff Powell & Tim Harvey.

LP Peter Firth (Roy), Richard Johnson (Air Commander), Richard Briers (The Rector), Dominic Jephcott (Mark), Natalie Ogle (Bess), Jill Bennett (Eustasia), Mary MacLeod (Mary), Mary Peach (Florence).

Stuck with a very complicated plot, this film attempts to adapt Rex Warner's 1941 novel, similar to *Things to Come* in showing Britain's future. Twenty-one year-old Peter Firth contends with a fascist airforce which builds a mysterious aerodrome near his home. The invaders make all the rules by which the locals must live. The film has a quaint, old-fashioned feel to it.

19. *After Hours* (1985, Warner, 97m, c). P Amy Robinson, Griffin Dunne & Robert F. Colesberry, D Martin Scorsese, W Joseph Minion, PH Michael Ballhaus, M Howard Shore, ED Thelma Schoonmaker, PD Jeffrey Townsend.

LP Griffin Dunne (Paul Hackett), Rosanna Arquette (Marcy), Verna Bloom (June), Thomas Chong (Pepe), Linda Fiorentino (Kiki), Teri Garr (Julie), John Heard (Tom the Bartender), Cheech Marin (Neil).

Computer operator Griffin Dunne spends a nightmarish but funny night in the Soho region of downtown Manhattan. He's seduced and horrified by the likes of Rosanna Arquette, Linda Fiorentino and Teri Garr. Dunne is the only normal person in the film and that makes his problems seem all the worse.

20. *After Midnight* (1989, MGM/United Artists, 90m, c). P Ken & Jim Wheat, Richard Arlook & Peter Greene, D&W Ken & Jim Wheat, PH Phedon Papamichael, M Marc Donahue, ED Philip Linson & Quinnie Martin, Jr., AD Chris Henry.

LP Jillian McWhirter (Allison), Pamela Segall (Cheryl), Ramy Zeda (Professor Derek), Nadine van der Velde (Joan), Marc McClure (Kevin), Marg Helgenberger (Alex), Billy Ray Sharkey (Ray).

The setting is a college campus where nutty professor Ramy Zeda teaches a course in fear. One night a cuddle of coeds meet at the professor's house to tell scary stories to each other, which are much too familiar and too violent for most potential viewers.

21. *After School* (1989, Moviestore, 89m, c). P Hugh Parks & William Olsen, D Olsen, W Parks, John Linde, Rod Mc-Brien & Joe Tankersley, PH Austin Mc-Kinney, M David C. Williams, ED John David Allen.

LP Sam Bottoms (Father Michael Mc-Carren), Renee Coleman (September Lane), Edward Binns (Monsignor Barrett), James Farkas (First Leader), Page Hannah (Annie), Don Harvey (Nathan), Robert Lansing (C.A. Thomas), Dick Cavett (Himself).

Young cleric Sam Bottoms is chosen to debate ex-priest Robert Lansing on the Dick Cavett show, the topic being the existence of God. Bottoms is having his own questions of faith, intensified when he falls in love with student Renee Coleman. The film intercuts its main story with flashbacks to primitive man, apparently so it can include scenes of topless cavewomen.

22. *Against All Odds* (1984, Columbia, 128m, c). P Taylor Hackford & William S. Gilmore, D Hackford, W Eric Hughes (based on the screenplay *Out of the Past* by Daniel Mainwaring and the novel *Build My Gallows High* by William Morrow), PH Donald Thorin, M Michel Colombier & Larry Carlton, ED Fredric Steinkamp & William Steinkamp, song "Against All Odds (Take a Look at Me Now)" by Phil Collins.

LP Rachel Ward (Jessie Wyler), Jeff Bridges (Terry Brogan), James Woods (Jake Wise), Alex Karras (Hank Sully), Jane Greer (Mrs. Wyler), Richard Widmark (Ben Caxton), Swoosie Kurtz (Edie), Saul Rubinek (Steve Kirsch).

Elusive heiress Rachel Ward is the hypotenuse of a dangerous romantic triangle whose other sides are disgruntled football player Jeff Bridges and tough bookie James Woods. The plot of this remake of the excellent film noir *Out of the Past* (1947), starring Robert Mitchum, Jane Greer and Kirk Douglas, has Bridges hired by Woods to locate his runaway mistress Ward. When Bridges and Ward connect, he forgets about Woods, but is Ward trustworthy?

23. *Agency* (1981, Jensen Farley, Canada, 94m, c). P Robert Lantos & Stephen J. Roth, D George Kaczender, W Noel Hynd (based on the novel by Paul Gottlieb), PH Miklos Lente, M Lewis Furey, ED Kirk Jones, PD Bill Brodie.

LP Robert Mitchum (Ted), Lee Majors (Philip), Valerie Perrine (Brenda), Saul Rubinek (Sam), Alexandra Stewart (Mimi), Hayward Morse (Tony), Anthony Parr (Charlie), Michael Kirby (Peters).

Robert Mitchum plants subliminal messages in TV ads to enhance his political chances. This story of power struggles in the advertising world is not credible or interesting. Sleepy-looking Mitchum doesn't appear to be an ambitious man.

24. *Agent on Ice* (1986, Shapiro Entertainment, 97m, c). P Louis Pastore, D Clark Worswick, W Worswick & Pastore, PH Erich Kollmar, M Ian Carpenter, ED Bill Freda.

LP Tom Ormeny (John Pope), Clifford David (Kirkpatrick), Louis Pastore (Frank Matera), Matt Craven (Joey), Debra Mooney (Secretary), Donna Forbes (Jane), Jennifer Leak (Helen Pope).

Ex-CIA agent Tom Ormeny is on the hit list of both the CIA and the Mafia. He must find out who is after him and do unto them before they do unto him.

25. *Agnes of God* (1985, Columbia, 98m, c). P Patrick Palmer & Norman Jewison, D Jewison, W John Pielmeier (from his play), PH Sven Nykvist, M Georges Delerue†, ED Antony Gibbs, PD Ken Adam.

LP Jane Fonda (Dr. Martha Livingston), Anne Bancroft† (Sister Miriam Ruth), Meg Tilly† (Sister Agnes), Anne Pitoniak (Dr. Livingston's Mother), Winston Rekert (Detective Langevin), Gratien Gelinas (Father Martineau), Janine Fluet (Sister Marguerite).

Novice Quebec nun Meg Tilly is accused of giving birth and killing her baby. Court-appointed psychiatrist Jane Fonda is brought in to determine if Tilly is sane. The latter seems to be a naive innocent, unaware of the ways of the world and without any apparent opportunity to encounter a man. Is this another Immaculate Conception? Sounds like heresy to some and bull to Fonda. The film ends without clearing up the mysteries of the father's identity and if Tilly killed her baby.

26. *Airplane!* (1980, Paramount, 88m, c). P Jon Davison, D&W Jim Abrahams, David & Jerry Zucker, PH Joseph Biroc, M Elmer Bernstein, ED Patrick Kennedy, SE Bruce Logan.

LP Robert Hays (Ted Striker), Julie Hagerty (Elaine), Kareem Abdul-Jabbar (Murdock), Lloyd Bridges (McCroskey), Peter Graves (Captain Oveur), Leslie Nielsen (Dr. Rumack), Lorna Patterson (Randy), Robert Stack (Kramer), Stephen Stucker (Johnny), Barbara Billingsley (Jive Lady), Joyce Bulifant (Mrs. Davis), Maureen McGovern (Nun), Ethel Merman (Lt. Hurwitz).

The film is delightful lunacy, filled with outrageous verbal and sight puns. It's a satire of air flight disaster films such as *Airport,* but pays tribute to numerous other movies, including *Saturday Night Fever, Star Wars* and *From Here to Eternity.* The jokes are nonstop and childish, but fun nevertheless. Each character's behavior is weird, but not to them or those around them.

27. *Airplane II: The Sequel* (1982, Paramount, 85m, c). P Howard Koch, D&W Ken Finkleman, PH Joseph Biroc, M Elmer Bernstein, ED Dennis Virkler.

LP Robert Hays (Ted Striker), Julie Hagerty (Elaine), Lloyd Bridges (McCroskey), Peter Graves (Capt. Oveur), William Shatner (Murdock), Chad Everett (Simon), Stephen Stucker (Jacobs), Oliver Robins (Jimmie), Sonny Bono (Bomber), Raymond Burr (Judge), Chuck Connors (Sarge), John Dehner (Commissioner), Rip Torn (Kruger), Kent McCord (Unger), James A. Watson, Jr. (Dunn), John Vernon (Dr. Stone).

Robert Hays, Julie Hagerty and an assortment of rejects from "Love Boat" episodes are back in an outrageous sequel to *Airplane!* with more of the tasteless jokes and puns, delivered without any hint of shame. Unfortunately, what was fresh and amusing in 1980, had worn thin two years later. The basic joke of Hays' fear of flying is growing old, even with the setting changed from a jet liner to a space shuttle.

28. *Alamo Bay* (1985, Tri-Star, 98m, c). P Louis & Vincent Malle, D Louis Malle, W Alice Arlen, PH Curtis Clark, M Ry Cooder, ED James Bruce, PD Trevor Williams.

LP Amy Madigan (Glory), Ed Harris (Shang), Ho Nguyen (Dinh), Donald Moffat (Wally), Truyen V. Tran (Ben), Rudy Young (Skinner), Cynthia Carle (Honey), Martino LaSalle (Luis), William Frankfather (Mac).

Louis Malle disappoints by giving us one-dimensional characters in this unexceptional film about Texas fishermen who resort to Ku Klux Klan activities when they find themselves unable to compete commercially with Vietnamese refugees. The Americans are all beastly rednecks while the Vietnamese are models of decency and hard work.

29. *The Alchemist* (1985, Empire, 84m, c). P Lawrence Applebaum, D James Amante (Charles Band), W Alan J. Adler.

LP Robert Ginty, Lucinda Dooling, John Sanderford, Viola Kate Stimpson, Robert Glaudini.

Filmed in 1981, the movie is set in 1955. A century earlier Robert Ginty was cursed by Robert Glaudini to live as an animal. He is saved by Lucinda Dooling, a look-alike of the woman who came between the men years before.

30. *Alexa* (1989, Platinum Pictures, 80m, c). P Peggy Bruen, D Sean Delgado, W Bruen & Delgado, PH Joey Forsyte, M Gregory Alper, ED James Davalos.

LP Christine Moore (Alexa Avery), Kirk Baily (Tony), Ruth Collins (Marshall Newhouse), Joseph P. Giardina (Jan), Tom Voth (Tommy), Adam Michenner (March).

After eight years of hooking, high-priced call girl Christine Moore considers her friend Ruth Collins' suggestion of quiting the business and opening a restaurant. Things get nasty when Moore falls for playwright Kirk Baily, who interviews her for a show he's writing about prostitution. Moore's pimp Joseph P. Giardina disapproves and interferes with fatal results.

Alien Dead see It Fell from the Sky

31. *The Alien Factor* (1984, Cinemagic, 80m, c). D&W Donald M. Dohler, PH Britt McDonough, M Kenneth Walker, ED Dave Ellis, SE Larry Schlechter.

LP Don Leifert (Ben), Tom Griffith (Sheriff), Richard Dyszel (Mayor), Mary Martens (Edie), Richard Geiwitz (Pete), George Stover (Steven), Eleanor Herman (Mary Jane), Anne Frith (Dr. Sherman).

When a spaceship crashes near a rural community, four aliens step out. Only one is good, the others terrorize the locals. Ho-hum.

32. ***Alien from L.A.*** (1988, Cannon, 87m, c). P Menahem Golan & Yoram Globus, D Albert Pyun, W Debra Ricci, Regina Davis & Albert Pyun, PH Tom Fraser, M James Saad, ED Daniel Loewenthal, PD Pamela Warner, SE John Hartigan.

LP Kathy Ireland (Wanda Saknussemm), Thom Mathews (Charmin), Don Michael Paul (Robbie), Linda Kerridge (Auntie Pearl/Freki), Richard Haines (Professor Arnold Saknussemm), William R. Moses (Guten "Gus" Edway).

Mousy valley girl Kathy Ireland wins the title appellation by dint of going to Africa to search for her missing explorer father and falling with him into a pit that opens up in a lost city in the center of the earth. More ho-hum.

33. ***Alien Nation*** (1988, 20th Century–Fox, 94m, c). P Gale Ann Hurd & Richard Kobritz, D Graham Baker, W Rockne S. O'Bannon, PH Adam Greenberg, M Curt Sobel, ED Kent Beyda, PD Jack T. Collis.

LP James Caan (Matthew Sykes), Mandy Patinkin (Sam Francisco), Terence Stamp (William Harcort), Kevin Major Howard (Kipling), Leslie Bevis (Cassandra), Peter Jason (Fedorchuk), George Jenesky (Quint).

Mandy Patinkin is one of a group of "Newcomers," called "slags" by racists, some 100,000 aliens whose space ship landed in the Mojave desert in the late 1980s and were given American citizenship. This new minority replaces all others as despised members of society. Some rise to prominent positions while others turn to criminal activities. Patinkin is the first cop. He's teamed with alcoholic James Caan who hates the aliens but wishes to use Mandy in his search for the Newcomer murderers of his former partner, a black man. The premise is interesting, the execution is faulty.

34. ***Alien Predator*** (1987, Trans World, 90m, c). P Deran Sarafian, Carlos Aured & Michael Sourapas, D&W Sarafian (based on screenplay "Massacre at R.V. Park" by Noah Blogh), PH Tote Trenas, M Chase/Rucker Productions, ED Dennis Hill & Peter Teschner, SE John Balandin, James Cummins, Bill Sturgeon, Margaret Bessara & Mark Shoftrom.

LP Dennis Christopher (Damon), Martin Hewitt (Michael), Lynn-Holly Johnson (Samantha), Luis Prendes (Prof. Tracer), J.O. Bosso (Capt. Wells), Yousaf Bokhari (Mr. Bodi), Yolanda Palomo (Mrs. Bodi), Christina Augustin (Baby Bodi).

When a spacelab falls to Earth near a small Spanish village, aliens are attached. The latter kill the inhabitants and take over their bodies. Three young touring Americans Dennis Christopher, Martin Hewitt and Lynn-Holly Johnson stumble into town at about the same time. Confrontation time!

35. ***Alien Seed*** (1989, Action Intl., 88m, c). P Mark Paglia, D Bob James, W Ken Carmack, M John Standish, ED Douglas K. Grimm & Tom Matthies, PD Kari Stewart.

LP Heidi Paine (Lisa Jordan), Steven Blade (Mark Timmons), Erik Estrada (Dr. Stone), Shellie Block (Mary Jordan), David Hayes (Rev. Bolam), Terry Phillips (Gen. Dole), Michael Ford (Col. Hobbs).

This sci-fi film went directly to video. Steven Blade portrays a writer obsessed with UFO incidents since childhood, when his family was involved in one. His sisters Heidi Paine and Shellie Block are kidnapped and impregnated by aliens. Time for a space ray gun wedding, we suppose.

36. ***Alienator*** (1989, Amazing Movies, 92m, c). P Jeffrey C. Hogue, D Fred Olen Ray, W Paul Garson, PH Gary Graver, M Chuck Cirino, ED Chris Roth, AD Lindah Lauderbaugh.

LP Jan-Michael Vincent (Commander), John Phillip Law (Ward), Ross Hagen (Kol), Dyana Ortelli (Orrie), Jesse Dabson (Benny), Dawn Wildsmith (Caroline), P.J. Soles (Tara), Teagan Clive (Alienator).

This tongue-in-cheek sci-fi thriller is meant for the home video market. Ross Hagen is a rebel leader who escapes execution on a remote prison planet and travels to Earth. Muscular female Teagan Clive is sent to destroy his Earthling youngsters.

37. *Aliens* (1986, 20th Century–Fox, 137m, c). P Gale Anne Hurd, D James Cameron, W Cameron, Walter Hill & David Giler (based on characters created by Dan O'Bannon & Ronald Shusett), PH Adrian Biddle, M James Horner†, ED Ray Lovejoy†, PD Peter Lamont, AD/SD Lamont & Crispian Sallis†, VE Robert Skotak, Stan Winston, John Richardson & Suzanne Benson*, SOUND Graham V. Hartstone, Nicholas Le Messurier, Michael A. Carter & Roy Charman†, SOUND EFFECTS ED Don Sharpe*.

LP Sigourney Weaver† (Ripley), Carrie Henn (Newt), Michael Biehn (Corporal Hicks), Paul Reiser (Burke), Lance Henriksen (Bishop), Bill Paxton (Pvt. Hudson), William Hope (Lt. Gorman), Jenette Goldstein (Pvt. Vasquez), Al Matthews (Sgt. Apone), Mark Rolston (Pvt. Drake).

Sigourney Weaver, the sole survivor of the space team in *Alien,* returns to the planet Acheron with a new team and encounters more horrible creatures. The movie, the special effects, Weaver's performance and the pace of action are all top notch if one doesn't mind becoming a bit queasy in the stomach.

38. *All Dogs Go to Heaven* (1989, United Artists, animated, 84m, c). P Sullivan Bluth Studios Ireland, D Don Bluth, W David N. Weiss (based on a story by Bluth, Ken Cromar, Gary Goldman, Larry Leker, Linda Miller, Monica Parker, John Pomeroy, Guy Schulman, David Steinberg & Weiss), ANIM D Lisa Dorney, M Ralph Burns, Charles Strouse & T.J. Kuenster, ED John K. Carr, PD Bluth & Leker.

VOICES Dom DeLuise (Itchy), Burt Reynolds (Charlie), Charles Nelson Reilly (Killer), Vic Tayback (Carface), Melba Moore (Whippet Angel), Judith Barsi (Anne-Marie), Loni Anderson (Flo).

Burt Reynolds speaks and sings (badly) for a German shepherd named Charlie and Dom DeLuise for a dachshund called Itchy in this marginal animated picture whose theme is that dogs unlike people are kind and trustworthy. So what else is new? It's a debatable pleasure to only hear Reynolds and DeLuise without seeing them. Strangely, the same thing can't be said about Loni Anderson.

39. *All Night Long* (1981, Universal, 88m, c). P Leonard Goldberg & Jerry Weintraub, D Jean-Claude Tramont, W W.D. Richter, PH Philip Lathrop, M Ira Newborn & Richard Hazard, ED Marion Rothman, PD Peter Jamison.

LP Gene Hackman (George Dupler), Barbra Streisand (Cheryl Gibbons), Diane Ladd (Helen Dupler), Dennis Quaid (Freddie Dupler), Kevin Dobson (Bobby Gibbons), William Daniels (Richard H. Copleston), Hamilton Camp (Buggams), Terry Kiser (Ultra-Sav Day Manater).

In an offbeat comedy which could be a lot funnier, executive Gene Hackman is reduced to running a drugstore. He rebels against everything when he falls for married housewife Barbra Streisand, who is having an affair with his son Dennis Quaid.

40. *All of Me* (1984, Universal, 93m, c). P Stephen Freidman, D Carl Reiner, W Phil Alden Robinson & Henry Olek (based on the novel *Me Too* by Ed Davis), PH Richard H. Kline, M Patrick Williams, ED Bud Molin, PD Edward Carfagno.

LP Steve Martin (Roger Cobb), Lily Tomlin (Edwina Cutwater), Victoria Tennant (Terry Hoskins), Madolyn Smith (Peggy Schuyler), Richard Libertini (Prahka Lasa), Dana Elcar (Burton Schuyler), Jason Bernard (Tyrone Wattell), Selma Diamond (Margo).

Wealthy but dying Lily Tomlin plans to leave her soul to Victoria Tennant, but instead it gets injected into the body of her lawyer Steve Martin. Both Tomlin and Martin want to enter Tennant's body — by different means of course. The jokes are predictable and wear thin very quickly.

41. *...All the Marbles* (1981, MGM/United Artists, 112m, c, aka *The California Dolls*). P William Aldrich, D Robert

Aldrich, W Mel Frohman, PH Joseph Biroc, M Frank De Vol, ED Irving C. Rosenblum, PD Carl Anderson.

LP Peter Falk (Harry), Vicki Frederick (Iris), Laurene Landon (Molly), Burt Young (Eddie Cisco), Tracy Reed (Diane), Ursaline Bryant-King (June), Claudette Nevins (Solly), Richard Jaeckel (Reno Referee).

Peter Falk is the manager of a sexy tag team, Vicki Frederick and Laurene Landon, in a supposed comedy about the nonsport of professional wrestling. It's dreadful, featuring nudity, profanity and violence and even this doesn't help.

42.   *All the Right Moves* (1983, 20th Century-Fox, 91m, c). P Stephen Deutsch, D Michael Chapman, W Michael Kane, PH Jan De Bont, M David Campbell, ED David Garfield.

LP Tom Cruise (Stef Djodjevic), Craig T. Nelson (Nickerson), Lea Thompson (Lisa), Charles Cioffi (Pop), Gary Graham (Greg), Paul Carafotes (Salvucci), Christopher Penn (Brian), Sandy Faison (Suzie).

Blue collar class high school athlete Tom Cruise hopes to win a football scholarship and escape his Pennsylvania mill town. He's encouraged by girl friend Lea Thompson, but has lots of problems with his overbearing coach, Craig T. Nelson. The film rates an R for sex, nudity and profanity.

43.   *Allan Quatermain and the Lost City of Gold* (1987, Cannon, 99m, c). P Menahem Golan & Yoram Globus, D Gary Nelson & Newt Arnold, W Gene Quintano & Lee Reynolds (based on the novel *Allan Quatermain* by H. Rider Haggard), PH Alex Phillips & Frederick Elmes, M Michael Linn & Jerry Goldsmith, ED Alain Jakubowicz, Gary Griffen & Dan Loewenthal, PD Trevor Williams & Leslie Dilley.

LP Richard Chamberlain (Allan Quatermain), Sharon Stone (Jesse Huston), James Earl Jones (Umslopogaas), Henry Silva (Agon), Robert Donner (Swarma), Doghmi Larbi (Nasta), Aileen Marson (Nyleptha), Cassandra Peterson (Sorais).

Richard Chamberlain appears as a cardboard Indiana Jones in this follow-up to his version of *King Solomon's Mines*. In both he inadequately mas-

querades as H. Rider Haggard's adventurer. This time he's seeking a lost city of gold and his brother. In case any one asks, he finds both.

44.   *Alley Cat* (1984, Film Ventures, 82m, c). P Robert E. Waters & Victor Ordonez, D Edward Victor (Eduardo Palmos, Al Valletta & Ordonez), W Waters, PH Howard Anderson III, M Quinto Colayco, ED Robert Ernst, PD Robert Lee.

LP Karin Mani (Billie), Robert Torti (Johnny), Britt Helfer (Hooker), Michael Wayne (Scarface), Jon Greene (Boyle), Jay Fisher (Charles), Claudie Decea (Rose), Tim Cutt (Thomas), Jay Walker (Judge Taylor).

Karin Mani is attacked by a street gang. She has them arrested, but the judge releases them on a technicality and sends her to a vicious female prison. When she gets out, she uses martial arts skills to get revenge.

45.   *Alligator* (1980, Group 1, 94m, c). P Brandon Chase, D Lewis Teague, W John Sayles, PH Joseph Mangine.

LP Robert Forster (David Madison), Robin Riker (Marisa), Michael Gazzo (Police Chief), Perry Lang (Kelly), Jack Carter (Mayor), Henry Silva (Col. Brock), Dean Jagger (Tycoon), Sue Lyon (Reporter), Angel Tompkins (Reporter).

The title character was flushed down a toilet as a baby and has grown to monstrous size. It's up to cop Robert Forster and scientist Robin Riker to postpone their romance long enough to track down the giant alligator, menacing L.A. The comedy-thriller is filled with good sight gags and in-jokes about other movies.

46.   *The Allnighter* (1987, Universal, 108m, c). P Tamar Simon Hoffs & Nancy Israel, D&W Tamar Simon Hoffs, PH Joseph Urbanczyk, M Charles Bernstein, ED Dan M. Rich, PD Cynthia Sowder.

LP Susanna Hoffs (Molly), Dedee Pfeiffer (Val), Joan Cusack (Gina), John Terlesky (C.J.), James Anthony Shanta (Killer), Michael Ontkean (Mickey Leroi), Pam Grier (Sgt. MacLeish), Phil Brock (Brad).

Director Tamar Simon Hoffs and her daughter Susanna, leading singer of the rock group The Bangles, conspire to produce another worthless youth exploitation film. Hoffs the younger and her two college chums Dedee Pfeiffer and Joan Cusack, having spent four years without any major romance (make that getting laid), decide to do something about it on the eve of their graduation.

47. *All's Fair* (1989, Moviestore, 89m, c). P Jon Gordon, D Rocky Lane, W Randee Russell, John Finegan, Tom Rondinella & William Pace (based on a story by Finegan & Watt Tyler), PH Peter Lyons Collister, M Bill Myers, ED Maryann Brandon.

LP George Segal (Colonel), Sally Kellerman (Florence), Robert Carradine (Mark), Jennifer Edwards (Ann), Jane Kaczmarek (Linda), John Kapelos (Eddie), Lou Ferrigno (Klaus).

Candy bar manufacturer George Segal is obsessed with weekend war games in which participants track each other, shooting paint pellets at their victims. Hardworking Jennifer Edwards, excluded from this activity, because of her sex, finds her advancement in the company blocked. She forms her own war-game team with the wives of the men of the company and takes on the good ole boys.

48. *Almost You* (1984, 20th Century–Fox, 96m, c). P Mark Lipson, D Adam Brooks, W Mark Horowitz (based on a story by Brooks), PH Alexander Gruszynski, M Jonathan Elias, ED Mark Burns.

LP Brooke Adams (Erica Boyer), Griffin Dunne (Alex Boyer), Karen Young (Lisa Willoughby), Marty Watt (Kevin Danzig), Christine Estabrook (Maggie), Josh Mostel (David), Laura Dean (Jeannie).

Griffin Dunne and his wife Brooke Adams are a thirtyish couple bored with their life and each other. Dunne tries to break the monotony by taking up with Karen Young. It's a trite story, done often before and better.

49. *Aloha Summer* (1988, Spectrafilm, 97m, c). P Mike Greco, D Tommy Lee Wallace, W Grego & Bob Benedetto, PH Steven Poster, M Jesse Frederick & Bennett Salvay, ED James Coblentz, Jack Hofstra & Jay Cassidy.

LP Chris Makepeace (Mike Tognetti), Yuji Okumoto (Kenzo Konishi), Don Michael Paul (Chuck Granville), Tia Carrere (Lani Kepoo), Andy Bumatai (Kimo Kepoo), Lorie Griffin (Amanda Granville), Scott Nakagawa (Scott Tanaka), Blaine Kia (Jerry Kahani), Warren Fabro (Kilarney).

The film visits Hawaii of 1959, in which six lads of different nationalities and races become fast surfing friends, lust after each other's sisters and have trouble making their dads understand — like how they feel. Don't expect anything of the quality of *Beach Blanket Bingo*.

50. *Alone in the Dark* (1982, New Line Cinema, 92m, c). P Robert Shaye, D&W Jack Sholder, PH Joseph Mangine, M Renato Serio, ED Arline Garson.

LP Jack Palance (Frank Hawkes), Donald Pleasence (Dr. Leo Bain), Martin Landau (Bryon "Preacher" Sutcliff), Dwight Schultz (Dan Potter), Erland Van Lidth (Ronald "Fatty" Elster), Deborah Hedwall (Nell Potter).

Escaped psychopaths Jack Palance, Martin Landau and Erland Van Lidth terrorize Donald Pleasence and his family. The only interesting thing in this typical slasher film is the work of the once big-time heavies.

51. *Alphabet City* (1984, Atlantic, 85m, c). P Andrew Braunsberg, D Amos Poe, W Gregory K. Heller, Poe & Robert Seidman (based on a novel by Heller), PH Oliver Wood, M Nile Rodgers, ED Grahame Weinbren & Lois Freeman, PD Nord Haggerty.

LP Vincent Spano (Johnny), Kate Vernon (Angie), Michael Winslow (Lippy), Jami Gertz (Sophia), Zohra Lampert (Mama), Ray Serra (Gino), Kenny Marino (Tony), Daniel Jordano (Juani), Laura Carrington (Louisa).

Vincent Spano, a "sympathetic" drug dealer, works the seedy environs of Manhattan's lower East side between Avenues A and D. If you fancy bizarre street characters, this film has them in spades.

52. *Altered States* (1980, Warner, 102m, c). P Howard Gottfried, D Ken Russell, W Sidney Aaron (Paddy Chayefsky) (based on the novel by Chayefsky), PH Jordan Cronenweth, M John Corigliano†, ED Eric Jenkins, SE Bran Ferren,

SOUND Arthur Piantadosi, Les Fresholtz, Michael Minkler & Willie D. Burton†.

LP William Hurt (Eddie Jessup), Blair Brown (Emily Jessup), Bob Balaban (Arthur Rosenberg), Charles Haid (Mason Parrish), Thaao Penghlis (Eccheverria), Miguel Godreau (Primal Man), Dori Brenner (Sylvia Rosenberg), Peter Brandon (Hobart), Drew Barrymore (Margaret Jessup).

Psychophysiologist William Hurt uses himself as a guinea pig in a sensory deprivation tank. He hallucinates himself back into primitive states of evolution. Hurt reverts to a killing prehuman beast. It's a cult film most noted for Hurt's sincere acting.

53. *Always* (1985, Samuel Goldwyn, 105m, c). P,D&W Henry Jaglom, PH Hanania Baer, ED Jaglom.

LP Henry Jaglom (David), Patrice Townsend (Judy), Amnon Meskin (The Notary), Bud Townsend (Judy's Father), Joanna Frank (Lucy), Alan Rachins (Eddie), Melissa Leo (Peggy), Jonathan Kaufer (Maxwell).

Henry Jaglom films his own divorce of Patrice Townsend. One can see why the marriage failed; the couple and their friends talked the union to death. Despite this, it has its moments.

54. *Always* (1989, Universal, 121m, c). P Steven Spielberg, Frank Marshall & Kathleen Kennedy, D Spielberg, W Jerry Belson & Diane Thomas (based on the 1943 film *A Guy Named Joe,* screenplay by Dalton Trumbo, adaptation by Frederick Hazlitt Brennan, story by Chandler Sprague & David Boehm), PH Mikael Salomon, M John Williams, ED Michael Kahn, PD James Bissell.

LP Richard Dreyfuss (Pete Sandich), Holly Hunter (Dorinda Durston), John Goodman (Al Yackey), Brad Johnson (Ted Baker), Audrey Hepburn (Hap), Roberts Blossom (Dave), Keith David (Powerhouse), Ed Van Nuys (Nails), Marg Helgenberger (Rachel).

Updated to the present, this reworking of the 1943 movie *A Guy Named Joe,* starring Spencer Tracy, Irene Dunne and Van Johnson, is set in Montana and Wyoming where men and women fly aircraft and helicopters to fight forest fires. Fire-fighter Richard Dreyfuss meets a firey death, but returns to earth as a sort-of guardian angel for co-worker Brad Johnson, a real dud who also provides romantic comfort for Dreyfuss' bereaved girl friend Holly Hunter. There's a lot of talent here, so why isn't the film great? The fantasy just doesn't work anymore.

55. *Amadeus** (1984, Orion, 158m, c). P Saul Zaentz, D Milos Forman*, W Peter Shaffer* (from his play), PH Miroslav Ondricek†, M Wolfgang Amadeus Mozart, Antonio Salieri & others, ED Nena Danevic†, Michael Chandler MD Neville Marriner, PD Patrizia Von Brandenstein, AD/SD Von Brandenstein & Karel Cerny†, CH Twyla Tharp, COS Theodor Pistek*, SOUND Mark Berger, Tom Scott, Todd Beokelheide & Chris Newman*, MK Paul LeBlanc & Dick Smith*.

LP F. Murray Abraham* (Antonio Salieri), Tom Hulce† (Wolfgang Amadeus Mozart), Elizabeth Berridge (Constanze Mozart), Simon Callow (Emanuel Schikaneder), Roy Dotrice (Leopold Mozart), Christine Ebersole (Katerina Cavalieri), Jeffrey Jones (Emperor Joseph II), Charles Kay (Count Orsini-Rosenberg), Kenny Baker (Parody Commendatore), Lisabeth Bartlett (Papagena), Barbara Byrne (Frau Weber), Roderick Cook (Count Von Strack), Patrick Hines (Kappelmeister Bonno), Richard Frank (Father Vogler).

Director Milos Foreman magnificently brings Peter Shaffer's fascinating play to the screen. Although Tom Hulce in the title role as an *enfant terrible* genius is excellent, it is F. Murray Abraham as Mozart's jealous rival Salieri who is most memorable. The film repeats the unsubstantiated claim that Salieri sabotaged young composer Mozart at every turn, preventing him from receiving the fame and fortune in his lifetime which he so richly deserved. The claim that Salieri poisoned Mozart is not actually made in the film. Mozart's music featured includes brilliantly presented excerpts from *The Magic Flute, The Marriage of Figaro* and *Don Giovanni.* Besides Abraham and Hulce, the work of the outstanding supporting cast is led by bravo performances by Roy Dotrice as Mozart's father and Jeffery Jones as the musically-illiterate emperor.

56. *Amanda* (1989, Independent, 120m, c). P,D,W&E Jeff Meyer & Gail Kappler Rosella, PH Mark Shapiro.

LP Jeff Meyer (Jason), Gail Kappler Rosella (Amanda), William Mitchell (Bill Bettman), Ann Bowden (Trudy), Claire Janell (Patricia), Drew Forsythe (Nelson), Vern Taylor (Elliot Tanner).

Down and out Seattle photographer Jeff Meyer meets beautiful Gail Kappler Rosella who helps him get his book of photographs published. Then it appears that it was all a dream—but then he meets Rosella again. Nothing here! Go back to sleep!

57. *The Amateur* (1982, 20th Century–Fox, 111m, c). P Joel B. Michaels & Garth H. Drabinsky, D Charles Jarrott, W Robert Littell & Diana Maddox (based on Littell's novel), PH John Coquillon, M Ken Wannberg, ED Richard Halsey.

LP John Savage (Charles Heller), Christopher Plummer (Prof. Lakos), Marthe Keller (Elizabeth), Arthur Hill (Brewer), Nicholas Campbell (Schraeger), George Coe (Rutledge), John Marley (Molton), Jan Rubes (Kaplan), Ed Lauter (Anderson), Graham Jarvis (Porter).

After the murder of his girl friend in a hostage encounter, computer expert John Savage blackmails the U.S. government into training him as a professional killer so he can sneak into East Berlin and take revenge on the responsible international terrorists. Savage is over-matched by the role. He shouldn't have given up his amateur standing.

58. *Amateur Hour* (1985, Kaufman, 85m, c). P Susan Kaufman, D Stanford Singer, W Singer & Kevin McDonough, PH Lisa Rinzler, M Cengiz Yaltkaya, ED Richard King.

LP Adam Nathan (Paul Pierce), Julie Hanlon (Donna Rose), John MacKay (Billy Reid), Walt Willey (Bill Johnson), Saul Alpiner (Frank Romance), Mikhail Druhan (Miss Murphy), Michael Griffith (Marcel Pederewsky).

After Adam Nathan and Julie Hanlon steal a video camera from their former high school, they are hired by Nathan's father to work for his nothing TV station.

They rip-off the station's storeroom to add to their equipment. Don't set the timer on your VCR to catch this loser.

59. *Amazing Grace and Chuck* (1987, Tri-Star, 115m, c). P&W David Field, D Mike Newell, PH Robert Elswit, M Elmer Bernstein, ED Peter Hollywood, PD Dena Roth.

LP Jamie Lee Curtis (Lynn Taylor), Alex English (Amazing Grace Smith), Gregory Peck (President), William L. Petersen (Russell Murdock), Joshua Zuehlke (Chuck Murdock), Dennis Lipscomb (Johnny B. Goode).

Young American Joshua Zuehlke is able to convince the leaders of the US and USSR to do away with nuclear weapons by getting the world's athletes, starting with Alex English, the star basketball player for the Boston Celtics, to join him in a boycott of all sport contests until a nuclear disarmament agreement is signed. It's not as naive as it sounds, but sincerity in acting is not enough to make an interesting film.

60. *Amazon Women on the Moon* (1987, Universal, 85m, c/b&w). P Robert K. Weiss, D Joe Dante, Carl Gottlieb, Peter Horton, John Landis & Robert K. Weiss, W Michael Barrie & Jim Mulholland, PH Daniel Pearl, ED Bert Lovitt, Marshall Harvey & Malcolm Campbell, PD Ivo Cristante.

LP Rosanna Arquette (Karen), Michelle Pfeiffer (Brenda), Ralph Bellamy (Mr. Gower), Carrie Fisher (Mary Brown), Griffin Dunne (Doctor), Steve Guttenberg (Jerry), Sybil Danning (Queen Lara), Kelly Preston (Violet), Russ Meyer (Video Salesman), Steve Forrest (Capt. Nelson), Joey Travolta (Butch), Arsenio Hall (Apartment Victim), Ed Begley, Jr. (Griffin), Howard Hesseman (Rupert King), Mike Mazurki (Dutch).

The film consists of 20 different comedy sketches lampooning late-night TV fare, local commercials, horrible movies, etc. The cast includes many more than those listed above, with no one on camera for very long. The titles of the sketches include: "Amazon Women on the Moon," "Roast Your Loved One," "Blacks Without Soul," "Video Pirates," "Mondo Condo" and "Hospital." If you are in a silly mood, this can be fun.

61. *Amazons* (1987, MGM/United Artists, 76m, c). P Hector Olivera, D Alex Sessa, W Charles Saunders, PH Leonard Solis, M Oscar Camp, ED Edward Lowe, SE Willy Smith.

LP Windsor Taylor Randolph (Dyala), Penelope Reed (Tashi), Joseph Whipp (Kalungo), Danitza Kingsley (Tashinge), Wolfram Hoechst (Martin), Jacques Arndt (High Priest), Charles Finch (Timar), Annie Larronde (Emerald Queen).

In studying about Amazons, we were led to believe that they cut off their bosom in order to better use a bow and arrow. In this sword and sorcery fantasy, Amazons Windsor Taylor Randolph and Penelope Reed bare their breasts often enough to put that rumor to rest. Their quest is to recover an ancient sword that will allow them to defeat evil Joseph Whipp.

62. *The Ambassador* (1984, Cannon, 90m, c, aka *Peacemaker*). P Menahem Golan, Yoram Globus & Issac Kol, D J. Lee Thompson, W Max Jack (based on the novel *52 Pick-Up* by Elmore Leonard), PH Adam Greenberg, M Dov Seltzer, ED Mark Goldblatt, PD Yoram Barzilai.

LP Robert Mitchum (Peter Hacker), Ellen Burstyn (Alex Hacker), Rock Hudson (Frank Stevenson), Fabio Testi (Mustapha Hashimi), Donald Pleasence (Minister Eretz), Michael Bat-Adam (Tova), Ori Levy (Abe).

Controversial Ambassador Robert Mitchum is attempting to solve the Palestinian question. In his last film role, Rock Hudson portrays a security officer whose assignment is to prevent Mitchum from being assassinated by radicals on all sides. Mitchum's wife Ellen Burstyn complicates matters when her affair with a PLO leader is revealed.

63. *America* (1986, ASA Communications, 83m, c). P Paul A. Leeman, D&W Robert Downey, PH Richard Price, M Leon Pendarvis, ED C. Vaughn Hazell, PD Elliott Schwartz.

LP Zack Norman (Terrance Hackley), Tammy Grimes (Joy Hackley), Michael J. Pollard (Bob Jolly), Richard Belzer (Gypsy Beam), Monroe Arnold (Floyd), Liz Torres (Dolores Frantico), Pablo Ferro (Hector Frantico).

The nutzy operators of a New York cable TV station gain world renown when their signal is accidentally bounced off the moon and beamed all over the world. Amateur rot!

64. *America 3000* (1986, Cannon, 92m, c). P Menahem Golan & Yoram Globus, D&W David Engelbach, PH David Gurfinkel, M Tony Berg, ED Alain Jakubowicz, PD Kuli Sander & Stephen Dane.

LP Chuck Wagner (Korvis), Lauren Landon (Vena), William Wallace (Gruss), Sue Giosa (Mohra), Victoria Barrett (Lakella), Galyn Gorg (Lynka), Camilla Sparv (Reya), Karen Lee Shepherd (Keva).

Nine hundred years after a nuclear war, blonde female warrior Lauren Landon assumes the leadership of her fighting clan. Enslaved men come across weapons and wrest control from the ladies.

65. *American Anthem* (1986, Columbia, 100m, c). P Robert Schaffel & Doug Chapin, D Albert Magnoli, W Evan Archerd & Jeff Benjamin (based on a story by Archerd, Benjamin & Susan Williams), PH Donald E. Thorin, M Alan Silvestri, ED James Oliver, PD Ward Preston.

LP Mitch Gaylord (Steve Tevere), Janet Jones (Julie Lloyd), Michelle Phillips (Linda Tevere), R.J. Williams (Mikey Tevere), Michael Pataki (Coach Soranhoff), Patrice Donnelly (Danielle).

This love story between gymnastics champion Mitch Gaylord and beautiful, talented gymnast Janet Jones is just about what one might expect — boring! Give it a 4.2.

66. *American Blue Note* (1989, Vested Interests, 97m, c). P&D Ralph Toporoff, W Gilbert Girion (based on a story by Toporoff & Girion), PH Joey Forsyte, M Larry Shanker, ED Jack Haigis, PD Charles Lagola.

LP Peter MacNicol (Jack), Carl Capotorto (Jerry), Tim Guinee (Bobby), Bill Christopher-Myers (Lee), Jonathan Walker (Tommy), Charlotte d'Amboise (Benita), Trini Alvarado (Lorraine).

Peter MacNicol, the leader of a struggling 1961 jazz quintet, is as tentative in that role as is he in his relationship with ballet instructor Charlotte d'Amboise.

He needs to grow up some and more realistically view his future.

67. *American Boyfriends* (1989, Alliance, Canada, 100m, c). P Steve De Nure, D&W Sandy Wilson, PH Benton Spencer, M Terry Frewer, ED Lara Mazur, PD Philip Schmidt.

LP Margaret Langrick (Sandy Wilcox), John Wildman (Butch), Jason Blicker (Marty), Lisa Ropo Martell (Julie), Michele Bardeaux (Thelma), Dela Brett (Lizzie), Scott Andersen (Daryl), Troy Mallory (Spider).

This sequel to *My American Cousin* is not as charming as the original. The time is the mid-60s in British Columbia. Margaret Langrick has been invited to the wedding of her hunk of an American cousin John Wildman. She convinces three friends to travel with her to Portland for the event. After the ceremony, the girls take Wildman's bright red Cadillac for a cruise down the coast, hoping to meet some surfer boys, but only come across Canadians, black UCLA student Troy Mallory and Jason Blicker, his Jewish friend from the Bronx. The latter two turn on the girls to opposing America's undeclared war in Vietnam.

68. *American Dreamer* (1984, Warner, 105m, c). P Doug Chapin, D Rick Rosenthal, W Jim Kouf & David Greenwalt (based on a story by Ann Biderman), PH Giuseppe Rotunno, M Lewis Furey, ED Anne Goursaud, PD Brian Eatwell.

LP JoBeth Williams (Cathy Palmer), Tom Conti (Alan McMann), Giancarlo Giannini (Victor Marchand), Coral Browne (Margaret McMann), James Staley (Kevin Palmer), C.B. Barnes (Kevin Palmer, Jr.), Huckleberry Fox (Karl Palmer), Jean Rougerie (Don Carlos Dominguez).

Housewife JoBeth Williams wins a trip to Paris in a writing contest. While in the City of Lights, she suffers a blow to the head. On awakening, she believes she's the heroine of the trashy novels she reads. It doesn't get much better than this—unfortunately.

69. *American Flyers* (1985, Warner, 114m, c). P Gareth Wigan & Paula Weinstein, D John Badham, W Steve Tesich, PH Don Peterman, M Lee Ritenour &

Greg Mathieson, ED Frank Morriss, Dallas Puett & Jeff Jones, PD Lawrence G. Paull.

LP Kevin Costner (Marcus Sommers), David Grant (David Sommers), Rae Dawn Chong (Sarah), Alexandra Paul (Becky), Janice Rule (Mrs. Sommers), Luca Bercovici (Muzzin), Robert Townsend (Jerome), John Amos (Dr. Conrad), Jennifer Grey (Leslie).

Steve Tesich who scored with *Breaking Away* is back with another bicycle-racing story. Kevin Costner and David Grant are estranged brothers who learn to care for each other during a grueling three-day overland race. Too bad one of the boys must die of an incurable disease.

70. *American Gigolo* (1980, Paramount, 117m, c). P Jerry Bruckheimer, D&W Paul Schrader, PH John Bailey, M Giorgio Moroder, ED Richard Halsey.

LP Richard Gere (Julian Kay), Lauren Hutton (Michelle), Hector Elizondo (Sunday), Nina Van Pallandt (Anne), Bill Duke (Leon James), Brian Davies (Charles Stratton), K. Callan (Lisa Williams), Tom Stewart (Mr. Rheiman), Patti Carr (Judy Rheiman), David Cryer (Lt. Curtis).

Male prostitute Richard Gere makes his living servicing Beverly Hills matrons (it must be his staying power that has him in such demand, it sure isn't his charm and sparkling personality—he's dry as dust). He's set up for the murder of one of his clients in a kinky sex murder. His married nonclient lover Lauren Hutton can provide him with an alibi, but it'll cause such a scandal.

71. *American Gothic* (1988, Vidmark, GB/Canada, 90m, c). P John Quested & Christopher Harrop, D John Hough, W Bert Wetanson & Michael Vines, PH Harvey Harrison, M Alan Parker, ED John Victor Smith, PD David Hiscox.

LP Rod Steiger (Pa), Yvonne De Carlo (Ma), Sarah Torgov (Cynthia), Michael J. Pollard (Woody), Fiona Hutchinson (Lynn), William Hootkins (Teddy), Janet Wright (Fanny), Terry Kelly (Psychiatrist).

Old pros Rod Steiger and Yvonne De Carlo apparently have fallen on hard times, agreeing to appear in this ridiculous horror story. They are the parents of a trio of loonies. Guffawing at these two who have seen much better days seems cruel, but their work is laughable.

72. *American Justice* (1986, The Movie Store, 95m, c). P Jack Lucarelli & Jameson Parker, D Gary Grillo, W Dennis A. Pratt, PH Steve Yaconelli, M Paul Chihara, ED Steve Mirkovich, PD Anita Terrian.

LP Jack Lucarelli (Joe Case), Jameson Parker (Dave Buchanon), Gerald McRaney (Jake Wheeler), Jeannie Wilson (Jess Buchanon), Wilford Brimley (Sheriff Mitchell), Dennis A. Pratt (Connie Baldwin), Danielle Hand (Angelica).

Jameson Parker and Gerald McRaney, the stars of TV's "Simon and Simon," try their hands at the big screen in a story of a vicious killer knocking off illegal aliens in a border town. Back to the small screen boys!

73. *American Ninja* (1985, Cannon, 95m, c). P Menahem Golan & Yoram Globus, D Sam Firstenberg, W Paul de Mielche (based on a story by Avi Kleinberger & Gideon Amir), PH Hanania Baer, M Michael Linn, ED Andrew Horvitch, Marcus Manton, Marcel Mindlin, Peter Lee-Thompson & Daniel Wetherbee, SE Danilo Dominguez.

LP Michael Dudikoff (Joe Armstrong), Guich Koock (Hickock), Judie Aronson (Patricia), Steve James (Jackson), John Fujioka (Shinyuki), Don Stewart (Ortega), Tadashi Yamashita (Black Star Ninja).

While stationed in the Philippines, American soldier Michael Dudikoff fights off an army of martial arts mercenaries. For films featuring slapping people silly, we prefer The Three Stooges.

74. *American Ninja 2: The Confrontation* (1987, Cannon, 89m, c). P Menahem Golan & Yoram Globus, D Sam Firstenberg, W Gary Conway & James Booth (based on a story by Conway from characters created by Avi Kleinberger & Gideon Amir), PH Gideon Porath, M George S. Clinton, ED Michael J. Duthie, PD Holger Gross.

LP Michael Dudikoff (Joe Armstrong), Steve James (Curtis Jackson), Larry Poindexter (Sgt. Charlie McDonald), Gary Conway (Leo "The Lion" Burke), Jeff Weston (Col. "Wild Bill"

Woodward), Michelle Botes (Alicia Sanborn).

The sequel to *American Ninja* is superior but that's not necessarily high praise. Michael Dudikoff is back as an army ranger who gets a kick out of his work. He must deal with Gary Conway who is abducting Marines stationed on a small Caribbean island to clone their strong cells into a mindless force of Ninja killers.

75. *American Ninja 3: Blood Hunt* (1989, Cannon, 90m, c). P Harry Alan Towers, D&W Cedric Sundstrom (based on a story by Gary Conway and characters created by Avi Kleinberger & Gideon Amir), PH George Bartels, M George S. Clinton, ED Michael J. Duthie, PD Ruth Strimling.

LP David Bradley (Sean), Steve James (Curtis Jackson), Marjoe Gortner (Cobra), Michele Chan (Chan Lee), Yehuda Erfoni (Andreas), Calvin Jung (Izumo), Evan J. Klisser (Dexter), Grant Preston (Minister of Interior).

Top international martial arts combatants gather on a tropical island for a tournament. Not too surprisingly there's an evil joker in the deck, in the person of Marjoe Gortner who is on the verge of perfecting a virus as a terrorist weapon. There's the usual chop-sock action against black-hooded baddies.

76. *American Pop* (1981, Columbia, animated, 97m, c). P Martin Ransohoff, D Ralph Bakshi, W Ronni Kern, M Lee Holdridge, ED David Ramirez.

VOICES Ron Thompson (Tony/Pete), Marya Small (Frankie), Jerry Holland (Louie), Lisa Jane Persky (Bella), Jeffrey Lippa (Zalmie), Roz Kelly (Eva Tanguay), Frank DeKova (Crisco), Richard Singer (Benny).

Director Ralph Bakshi's attempt to tell the history of American pop music from the turn of the century to new wave rock through animation fails on too many counts to enumerate.

77. *The American Success Company* (1980, Columbia, 94m, c). P Daniel H. Blatt & Edgar J. Scherick, D William Richert, W Richert & Larry Cohen (based on a story by Cohen), PH Anthony Richmond, M Maurice Jarre, ED Ralph E. Winters.

LP Jeff Bridges (Harry), Belinda Bauer (Sarah), Ned Beatty (Mr. Elliot), Steven Keats (Rick Duprez), Bianca Jagger (Corinne), John Glover (Ernst), Mascha Gonska (Greta), Michael Durrell (Herman).

Wimpish failure Jeff Bridges grows weary of being reminded of his shortcomings by his boss and his shrewish wife Belinda Bauer. He adopts the behavior of a gangsterish tough guy, hires prostitute Bianca Jagger to turn him into a great lover, and is transformed into the man he always dreamed of becoming.

78. *American Taboo* (1984, Lustgarten, 87m, c). P Sali Borchman, Steve Lustgarten & Ron Schmidt, D Lustgarten, W Lustgarten, Jay Horenstein & Nicole Harrison, PH Lustgarten, Eric Edwards, Mark Whitney & Lee Nesbit, M Dana Libonati & Dan Brandt, ED Schmidt & Lustgarten.

LP Jay Horenstein (Paul Wunderlich), Nicole Harrison (Lisa), Mark Rabiner (Michael), Katherine King (Maggie), Ki Skinner (1st Model), Suzette Taylor (2nd Model), Dorothy Anton (Lisa's Mother).

Loser Jay Horenstein allows himself to be seduced by Nicole Harrison, a nymphet who lives next door. Just another male fantasy film.

79. *An American Tail* (1986, Universal, animated, 80m, c). P Don Bluth, John Pomeroy & Gary Goldman, D Bluth, W Judy Freudberg, Tony Geiss & David Kirschner, M James Horner, ED Dan Molina, PD Bluth, SONG "Somewhere Out There" by Horner, Barry Mann & Cynthia Weil†.

VOICES Erica Yohn (Mama Mouskewitz), Nehemiah Persoff (Papa Mouskewitz), Amy Green (Tanya Mouskewitz), Phillip Glasser (Fievel Mouskewitz), Christopher Plummer (Henri), John Finnegan (Warren T. Rat), Madeline Kahn (Gussie Mausheimer), Dom DeLuise (Tiger).

The animated Mouskewitz family makes the journey from Russia to the United States at the end of the 19th century after their home is destroyed in a pogrom. During the voyage, little Fievel is thrown overboard and from here on the movie concentrates on his efforts to find

his family. None of the Disney cuteness here, just boring sentimentality.

80. *The American Way* (1987, Miramax, 92m, c, aka *Riders of the Storm*). P Laurie Keller & Paul Cowan, D Maurice Phillips, W Scott Roberts, PH John Metcalfe, M Brian Bennett, ED Tony Lawson, PD Evan Hercules.

LP Dennis Hopper (Captain), Michael J. Pollard (Tesla), Eugene Lipinski (Ace), James Aubrey (Claude), Al Matthews (Ben), William Armstrong (Jerry), Michael Ho (Minh), Nigel Pegram (Mrs. Westinghouse).

Vietnam vets run a pirate radio station, jamming broadcasts of right-wingers as well as opposing a female presidential candidate they don't fancy.

81. *An American Werewolf in London* (1981, Universal, 97m, c). P George Folsey, Jr., D&W John Landis, PH Robert Paynter, M Elmer Bernstein, ED Malcolm Campbell, SE Effects Associates, Rick Baker, MK Rick Baker†.

LP David Naughton (David Kessler), Jenny Agutter (Alex Price), Griffin Dunne (Jack Goodman), John Woodvine (Dr. Hirsch), Brian Glover (Chess Player), David Schofield (Dart Player), Lila Kaye (Barmaid), Paul Kember (Sgt. McManus), Don McKillop (Inspector Villiers).

When American backpackers David Naughton and Griffin Dunne are attacked by a wolf on the English Moors, Dunne is torn to pieces but Naughton survives. As he recovers, he falls in love with Jenny Agutter who nurses him in a hospital. He becomes a werewolf who terrorizes modern-day London. The film is interesting and at times even humorous, but the gore is hard to take.

82. *Americana* (1981, Sherwood, 91m, c). P David Carradine & Skip Sherwood, D Carradine, W Richard Carr, PH Michael Stringer, M Craig Hundley & Carradine, ED David Kern.

LP David Carradine (Soldier), Barbara Hershey (Girl), Michael Greene (Garage Man), Bruce Carradine, John Barrymore III, Frank Ryan.

Vietnam vet David Carradine's obsessive attempts to rebuild a merry-go-round in a rural Kansas town are met with resistance by the locals who mistrust strangers. The film is an allegory of America's treatment of Vietnam veterans.

Amin — The Rise and Fall see The Rise and Fall of Idi Amin

83. *Amityville II: The Possession* (1982, Orion, 104m, c). P Ira N. Smith & Stephen R. Greenwald, D Damiano Damiani, W Tommy Lee Wallace (based on a book by Hans Holzer), PH Franco Digiacomo, M Lalo Schifrin, ED Sam O'Steen, PD Pierluigi Basile, SE Glen Robinson.

LP Burt Young (Anthony Montelli), Rutanya Alda (Deloris Montelli), James Olson (Fr. Adamski), Jack Magner (Sonny Montelli), Diane Franklin (Patricia Montelli), Andrew Prine (Fr. Tom), Moses Gunn (Det. Turner).

In a prequel to *The Amityville Horror,* Burt Young and his family of six move into an eerie Long Island home. The eldest son Jack Magner becomes possessed and ultimately hacks his family to death.

84. *Amityville 3-D* (1983, Orion, 105m, c). P Stephen F. Kesten, D Richard Fleischer, W William Wales [David E. Ambrose], PH Fred Schuler, M Howard Blake, ED Frank J. Urioste, SE Michael Wood.

LP Tony Roberts (John Baxter), Tess Harper (Nancy Baxter), Robert Joy (Elliot West), Candy Clark (Melanie), John Beal (Harold Caswell), Leora Dana (Emma Caswell), Lori Loughlin (Susan Baxter), Meg Ryan (Lisa).

Reporter Tony Roberts and photographer Candy Clark won't listen when warned about the infamous Amityville, New York house. They end up its victims in one of the worst movies of the decade.

85. *Among the Cinders* (1985, New World, New Zealand, 103m, c). P John O'Shea, D Rolf Haedrich, W Haedrich & O'Shea (based on the novel by Maurice Shadbolt), PH Rory O'Shea, M Jan Preston, ED Inge Behrens & John Kiley, PD Gerry Luhman.

LP Paul O'Shea (Nick Flinders), Derek Hardwick (Hubert Flinders), Yvonne Lawley (Beth Flinders), Rebecca Gibney (Sally), Amanda Jones (Glenys Appleby), Bridget Armstrong (Helga Flinders), Maurice Shadbolt (Frank Flinders), Ricky Duff (Sam Waikai).

Sixteen-year-old New Zealander Paul O'Shea feels guilty about a hunting accident which wounded him and left his boyhood friend, Maori, dead. He goes to live with his grandparents, but suffers a relapse when his grandmother dies. It's up to grandpa to put him back on the road to recovery.

86. *Amy* (1981, Buena Vista, 100m, c). P Jerome Courtland, D Vincent McEveety, W Noreen Stone, PH Leonard J. South, M Robert F. Brunner, ED Gregg McLaughlin.

LP Jenny Agutter (Amy Medford), Barry Newman (Dr. Ben Corcoran), Kathleen Nolan (Helen Gibbs), Chris Robinson (Elliot Medford), Lou Fant (Lyle Ferguson), Margaret O'Brien (Hazel Johnson), Nanette Fabray (Malvina), Otto Rechenberg (Henry Watkins).

In 1913 Jenny Agutter arrives at an Appalachian school to teach deaf students to speak. She and Barry Newman teach the handicapped children to play football. The climax is a football game between their special kids and the "normal" children of the area. The film has several moving moments.

87. *And God Created Woman* (1988, Vestron, 100m, c). P George G. Braunstein & Ron Hamady, D Roger Vadim, W R.J. Stewart, PH Stephen M. Katz, M Thomas Chase & Steve Rucker, ED Suzanne Pettit, PD Victor Kempster.

LP Rebecca De Mornay (Robin Shay), Vincent Spano (Billy Moran), Frank Langella (James Tiernan), Donovan Leitch (Peter Moran), Judith Chapman (Alexandra Tiernan), Jaime McEnnan (Timmy Moran), Benjamin Mouton (Blue), David Shelley (David).

Roger Vadim remakes his 1957 shocker, but Rebecca De Mornay is no Brigitte Bardot and the times, they are a-changing. De Mornay's casual attitudes towards sex are not sexy. Prison inmate De Mornay is paroled with the aid of politician Frank Langella, because she is able to convince carpenter Vincent Spano to marry her. Once the knot is tied, she has no use for him in bed anymore. She doesn't suffer from sexual deprivation as she pursues her goal of becoming a rock 'n' roll singer.

And Nothing But the Truth see Giro City

And Once Upon a Love see Fantasies

88. Android (1982, New World, 80m, c). P Mary Ann Fisher, D Aaron Lipstadt, W James Reigle & Don Opper (Based on an idea by Reigle), PH Tim Suhrstedt, M Don Preston, ED Andy Horvitch.

LP Klaus Kinski (Dr. Daniel), Brie Howard (Maggie), Norbert Weisser (Keller), Crofton Hardester (Mendes), Kendra Kirchner (Cassandra), Don Opper (Max 404).

In a lonely space station fanatical scientist Klaus Kinski strives to create the perfect female android. The station is invaded by escaped convicts and sensitive simple robot Don Opper falls for one of the female convicts.

89. Angel (1982, Motion Picture Co. of Ireland, Irish, 92m, c). P Barry Blackmore, D&W Neil Jordan, PH Chris Menges, M Paddy Meegan, ED Pat Duffner.

LP Stephen Rea (Danny), Alan Devlin (Bill), Veronica Quilligan (Annie), Peter Caffrey (Ray), Honor Heffernan (Deirdre), Ray McAnally (Bloom).

Saxaphone player Stephen Rea is obsessed with the notion of finding the killers involved in a murder he has witnessed. In the process he becomes a murderer.

90. Angel (1984, New World, 92m, c). P Roy Watts & Donald P. Borchers, D Robert Vincent O'Neil, W O'Neil & Joseph Cala, PH Andy Davis, M Craig Safan, ED Charles Bornstein & Wilt Henderson.

LP Donna Wilkes (Angel/Molly), Cliff Gorman (Lt. Andrews), Susan Tyrrell (Mosler), Dick Shawn (Mae), Rory Calhoun (Kit Carson), John Diehl (Billy Boy), Robert Acey (Driver/John), David Anthony (Howie).

"High school honor student by day, Hollywood hooker by night" Donna Wilkes and her street people family, Susan Tyrrell, Dick Shawn and Rory Calhoun are determined to bring to justice sickie John Diehl who picks up hookers and kills them. It's a surprisingly enjoyable film. Wilkes is so thumb-sucking little-girl looking that watching her lustfully will seem almost incestuous for any man who has a daughter.

91. Angel of H.E.A.T. (1983, Studios Pan Imago, 93m, c). P&D Myrl A. Schreibman, W Helen Sanford, PH Jacques Haitkin, M Guy Sobell, ED Barry Zetlin.

LP Marilyn Chambers (Angel Harmony), Stephen Johnson (Mark), Mary Woronov (Samantha), Milt Kogan (Harry), Remy O'Neill (Andrea), Dan Jesse (Albert), Harry Townes (Peter), Gerald Okamura (Hans).

Former porno star Marilyn Chambers *(Behind the Green Door)* is a female Derek Flint working for Harmony's Elite Attack Team. Her mission: to save the world from destruction at the hands of an evil genius who possesses the ultimate weapon. And what might that be, do you suppose?

92. Angel Heart (1987, Tri-Star, 113m, c). P Alan Marshall & Elliott Kastner, D&W Alan Parker (based on the novel *Falling Angel* by William Hjortsberg), PH Michael Seresin, M Trevor Jones, ED Gerry Hambling, PD Brian Morris.

LP Mickey Rourke (Harry Angel), Robert De Niro (Louis Cyphre), Lisa Bonet (Epiphany Proudfoot), Charlotte Rampling (Margaret Krusemark), Stocker Fontelieu (Ethan Krusemark), Brownie McGhee (Toots Sweet), Michael Higgins (Dr. Fowler), Elizabeth Whitcraft (Connie).

One needs a strong stomach to get through this gory film. In 1955 cheap private eye Mickey Rourke is hired by sinister Robert De Niro to find a 1940s singer who reneged on a contract. Wherever Rourke's investigation leads him, he encounters some gruesome murder. The trail of the singer leads Rourke to New Orleans where a few more horrible killings take place before Rourke realizes that he's the missing singer demon-like De Niro has been seeking.

Angel of Vengeance see Ms. 45

93. Angel Three: The Final Chapter (1988, New World, 99m, c). P Arnold Orgolini, D&W Tom DeSimone (based on characters created by Joseph M. Cala & Robert Vincent O'Neil), PH Howard

Wexler, M various artists, ED Warren Chadwick.

LP Maud Adams (Nadine), Mitzi Kapture (Angel), Mark Blankfield (Spanky), Kin Shriner (Neal), Emile Beaucard (Shahid), Richard Roundtree (Lt. Doniger), Tawny Fere (Michelle), Anna Navarro (Gloria).

When we left Molly, aka Angel in *Avenging Angel,* she was just finishing law school. Apparently she didn't pursue a career as an attorney, because now as Mitzi Kapture (previously played by Donna Wilkes and Betsy Russell) she's a photographer shooting pictures of street people in Hollywood for a planned book. She encounters her mother Anna Navarro who had abandoned her 14 years earlier. The reunion isn't long as mom is blown up by a car bomb, but not before telling her darling daughter that she has a half-sister Tawny Fere who's in trouble. With the help of some of the street people, Kapture rescues Fere from the clutches of white slaver Maud Adams and dope pusher Emile Beaucard, avenging her mother's death in the process. The first two films in the series titillated without getting down right pornographic. This production has no apparent dramatic goal.

94. *Angelo My Love* (1983, Cinecom International, 115m, c). P,D&W Robert Duvall, PH Joseph Friedman, ED Stephen Mack.

LP Angelo Evans, Michael Evans, Ruthie Evans, Tony Evans, Debbie Evans, Steve "Patalay" Tsigonoff, Millie Tsigonoff, Frankie Williams, George Nicholas (each plays himself or herself).

Director Robert Duvall films the alien community of gypsies, featuring charismatic 11-year-old Angelo Evans, an expert hustler and clown.

95. *Angels of the City* (1989, Raedon/ PM Entertainment, 89m, c). P Richard Pepin & Joseph Merhi, D Lawrence-Hilton Jacobs, W Raymond Martino, Merhi & Jacobs, PH Pepin, M Jastereo Coviare, John Gonzalez & Jacobs, ED Paul Volk.

LP Kelly Galindo (Catherine), Cynthia Cheston (Wendy), Michael Ferrare (Gold), Renny Stroud (Lee), Jastereo Coviare (Tavares), Lawrence-Hilton Jacobs (Det. Jon Chance), Brian Ochse (Mick).

College coeds Kelly Galindo and Cynthia Cheston, posing as streetwalkers as part of a sorority initiation, witness a bloody shootout between rival pimps, and hit the streets running for the rest of the film.

96. *Angry Earth* (1989, Bloom Street, GB, 106m, c). P Ruth Kenley, D&W Karl Francis, PH Roger Pugh Evans, M Ken Howard, ED Christopher Lawrence, PD Francis Pugh.

LP Sue Roderick, Mark Lewis Jones, Maria Pride, Dafydd Hywell, Jack Shephard, Phyllis Logan, Robert Pugh.

An 110-year-old Welsh women recalls the oppression of the coal miners in Wales in the 19th century. They were treated as virtual slaves by laissez-faire capitalism. As a girl the centenarian survived by washing miners' corpses, disemboweling them and laying them out for burial. Apparently there was plenty of work for her due to the unsafe conditions in the mines.

97. *Animal Behavior* (1989, Millimeter Films, 85m, c). P Kjehl Rasmussen, D H. Anne Riley (Jenny Bowen & Rasmussen), W Susan Rice, PH David Spellvin, M Cliff Eidelman, ED Joseph Weintraub, PD Jeannine Claudia Oppewall.

LP Karen Allen (Alex Bristow), Armand Assante (Mark Mathias), Holly Hunter (Coral Grable), Josh Mostel (Mel Gorsky), Richard Libertini (Dr. Parrish), Alexa Kenin (Sheila Sandusky), Michael (Michael).

In an attempt to film what they consider a screwball comedy, the filmmakers have music professor Armand Assante and absent-minded psychology professor Karen Allen fall in love. The third member of the triangle is not Holly Hunter who has what amounts to a cameo role, but Michael, Allen's chimpanzee.

98. *Anna* (1987, Vestron, 95m, c). P Yurek Bogayevicz & Zanne Devine, D Bogayevicz, W Agnieszka Holland (based on a story by Bogayevicz Holland), PH Bobby Bukowski, M Greg Hawkes, ED Julie Sloane, PD Lester Cohen.

LP Sally Kirkland† (Anna), Robert Fields (Daniel), Paulina Porizkova (Krystyna), Gibby Brand (Director #1), John

Robert Tillotson (Director #2), Joe Aufiery (Stage Manager), Charles Randall (Agent).

Sally Kirkland is sort of a Joan Crawford to Paulina Porizkova's Ann Blyth (see *Mildred Pierce*) in this story of former Czech movie star Kirkland. Reduced to insulting auditions for New York stage productions, she turns her only fan, Porizkova, from an ugly duckling into a beautiful swan, and sees her protegée become a spoiled brat.

99.   Anne Devlin (1984, Aeon Films, Ireland, 121m, c). P Pat Murphy & Tom Hayes, D&W Murphy, PH Thaddeus O'Sullivan, M Robert Boyle, ED Arthur Keating, PD John Lucas.

LP Brid Brennan (Anne Devlin), Bosco Hogan (Robert Emmett), Des McAleer (James Hope), Gillian Hackett (Rose Hope), David Kelly (Dr. Trevor), Ian McElhinney (Major Serr), Chris O'Neill (Thomas Russell).

In 1798 Ireland, Brid Brennan becomes housemaid to a Republican leader. She is jailed as a rebel, resists her captors and eventually is pardoned.

100.   Annie (1982, Columbia, 130m, c). P Ray Stark, D John Huston, W Carol Sobieski (based on the stage production book by Thomas Meehan, Charles Strouse & Martin Chamin, and the comic strip "Little Orphan Annie" by Harold Gray), PH Richard Moore, M Ralph Burns†, ED Michael A. Stevenson, PD Dale Hennesy, AD/SD Hennesy & Marvin March†.

LP Albert Finney (Daddy Warbucks), Carol Burnett (Miss Hannigan), Bernadette Peters (Lily), Ann Reinking (Grace Farrell), Tim Curry (Rooster), Aileen Quinn (Annie), Geoffrey Holder (Punjab), Roger Minami (Asp), Edward Herrmann (FDR), Lois DeBanzie (Eleanor Roosevelt).

Once again Hollywood demonstrates that a slew of talent can't make a big screen success of a fantasy-like stage musical. Little Aileen Quinn is cute as the comic strip character who charms munitions millionaire Albert Finney and appeals to FDR for all the unemployed and homeless, but almost everyone else is a caricature of a caricature.

101.   Annie's Coming Out (1985, Universal, Australia, 93m, c, aka *Test of Love*). P Don Murray, D Gil Brealey, W John Patterson & Chris Borthwick (Annie's narration by Anne McDonald; based on the true story "Annie's Coming Out" by Rosemary Crossley McDonald), PH Mick Van Bornemann, M Simon Walker, ED Lindsay Frazer.

LP Angela Punch-McGregor (Jessica Hathaway), Drew Forsythe (David Lewis), Liddy Clark (Sally Clements), Monica Maughan (Vera Peters), Philippa Baker (Sister Waterman), Tina Arhondis (Annie O'Farrell), Mark Butler (Dr. John Monroe), John Frawley (Harding).

Based on a true story, Angela Punch-McGregor joins the staff of a home for disabled children and encounters Tina Arhondis, a child afflicted with cerebral palsy, receiving only caretaker care. McGregor believes the child has a brain which can be developed. McGregor eventually must go to court to prove Arhondis can function in society.

102.   The Annihilators (1985, New World, 87m, c). P Allan C. Pedersen & Thomas C. Chapman, D Charles E. Sellier, Jr., W Brian Russell, PH Henning Schellerup, M Bob Summers, ED Dan Gross.

LP Gerrit Graham (Ray Track), Lawrence Hilton-Jacobs (Garrett Floyd), Paul Koslo (Roy Boy Jagger), Christopher Stone (Bill Esker), Andy Wood (Woody), Sid Conrad (Louie Wace), Dennis Redfield (Joey Wace).

The good folks of a southern town hire a group of Vietnam vets to protect them from local youth gangs. Typical violent vigilante fare which won't make anyone think of *The Magnificent Seven*.

103.   Another Country (1984, Orion Classics, GB, 90m, c). P Alan Marshall, D Marek Kanievska, W Julian Mitchell (based on his novel), PH Peter Biziou, M Michael Storey, ED Gerry Hambling, PD Brian Morris.

LP Rupert Everett (Guy Bennett), Colin Firth (Tommy Judd), Michael Jenn (Barclay), Robert Addie (Delahay), Anna Massey (Imogen Bennett), Betsy Brantley (Julie Schofield), Rupert Wainwright (Devenish), Tristan Oliver (Fowler), Cary

Elwes (Harcourt), Frederick Alexander (Menzies).

The film is loosely based on the careers of British traitors Burgess and Maclean who spied for the Soviet Union. According to this film, Rupert Everett (as Burgess) developed his hatred for his country and a desire to get even, when his sexual preferences for males at school, lost him the chance to join a group of underclassmen known as "The Gods." The purpose of the latter group was to ensure that their members were taken care of in business and government upon graduation.

104.   *Another Time, Another Place* (1984, Goldwyn, GB, 101m, c). P Simon Perry, D&W Michael Radford (based on the novel by Jessie Kesson), M John McLeod, ED Tom Priestley.

LP Phyllis Logan (Janie), Giovanni Mauriello (Luigi), Gian Luca Favilla (Umberto), Claudio Rosini (Paolo), Paul Young (Dougal), Gregor Fisher (Beel), Tom Watson (Finlay), Jennifer Piercey (Kirsty).

Bored Scottish housewife Phyllis Logan has an affair with Giovanni Mauriello, an Italian prisoner of war, who fills her head with visions of sunny Naples while all he has on his mind is sex.

105.   *Another Woman* (1988, Orion, 88m, c). P Robert Greenhut, D&W Woody Allen, PH Sven Nykvist, ED Susan E. Morse, PD Santo Loquasto.

LP Gena Rowlands (Marion), Mia Farrow (Hope), Ian Holm (Ken), Blythe Danner (Lydia), Gene Hackman (Larry), Betty Buckley (Kathy), Martha Plimpton (Laura), John Houseman (Marion's Father), Sandy Dennis (Claire), Philip Bosco (Sam), Harris Yulin (Paul).

Having just turned 50, intelligent, beautiful esteemed professor of philosophy Gena Rowlands re-exams her life. She's an emotionally fastidious person and she notes that something important is missing from her life. Director Woody Allen has brought together an outstanding cast headed by Rowlands who gives a superb performance.

106.   *Anti-Clock* (1980, International Film Exchange, 107m, b&w). P Jack Bond, D Jane Arden & Bond, W Arden, M Arden.

LP Sebastian Saville (Prof. Zanof/ Joseph Sapha), Susan Cameron (Sapha's Mother), Liz Saville (Sapha's Sister), Louise Temple (Madame Aranovitch).

Sebastian Saville waxes philosophically in this terrible nuclear comedy about the raising of one's consciousness.

107.   *Any Which Way You Can* (1980, Warner, 116m, c). P Fritz Manes, D Buddy Van Horn, W Stanford Sherman (based on characters created by Jeremy Joe Kronsberg), PH David Worth, ED Ferris Webster & Ron Spang, MD Snuff Garrett.

LP Clint Eastwood (Philo Beddoe), Sondra Locke (Lynne Halsey-Taylor), Geoffrey Lewis (Orville), William Smith (Jack Wilson), Harry Guardino (James Beekman), Ruth Gordon (Ma), Michael Cavanaugh (Patrick Scarfe).

This sequel to *Every Which Way But Loose* continues the adventures of bare-knuckle fighter Clint Eastwood, his friend the orangutan Clyde and his country-and-western singer girlfriend Sondra Locke. It's a fairly funny film with Clyde showing more emotional range than Locke.

108.   *Apartment Zero* (1989, Skouras, 124m, c). P Martin Donovan & David Koepp, D Donovan, W Donovan & Koepp (based on the story by Donovan), PH Miguel Rodriguez, M Elia Cmiral, ED Conrad M. Gonzalez, PD Miguel Angel Lumaldo.

LP Hart Bochner (Jack Carney), Colin Firth (Adrian LeDuc), Dora Bryan (Margaret McKinney), Liz Smith (Mary Louise McKinney), Fabrizio Bentivoglio (Carlos Sanchez-Verne), James Telfer (Vanessa), Mirella D'Angelo (Laura Werpachowsky), Juan Vitali (Alberto Werpachowsky).

In a bizarre odd-couple saga, Colin Firth is an Anglophile Argentinian movie nut who runs a dying revival house in Buenos Aires. His lifestyle is suddenly enriched and contaminated when he rents a room to bisexual Hart Bochner, who apparently will sleep with anyone. Bochner is not what he seems in this very dark comedy.

109.   *The Apple* (1980, Cannon, 90m, c). P Menahem Golan & Yoram Globus,

D&W Golan, PH David Gurfinkle, M Coby & Iris Recht, ED Alain Jakubowicz, PD Jurgen Kiebach.

LP Catherine Mary Stewart (Bibi), George Gilmour (Alphie), Grace Kennedy (Pandi), Allan Love (Dandi), Joss Ackland (Topps), Vladek Sheybal (Boogalow), Ray Shell (Snake), Miriam Margolyes (Landlady).

Set in 1994, devilish record producer Vladek Sheybal seduces young folk-singing duo Catherine Mary Stewart and George Gilmour into becoming part of his stable of musical stars kept in line by sex and drugs.

110. *Appointment with Death* (1988, Cannon, 102m, c). P&D Michael Winner, W Anthony Shaffer, Peter Buckman & Winner (based on the novel by Agatha Christie), PH David Gurfinkel, M Pino Donaggio, Rafi Kadishzon, Frank Barber & DeWolfe, ED Arnold Crust, PD John Blezard.

LP Peter Ustinov (Hercule Poirot), Lauren Bacall (Lady Westholme), Carrie Fisher (Nadine Boynton), John Gielgud (Col. Carbury), Piper Laurie (Mrs. Emily Boynton), Hayley Mills (Miss Quinton), Jenny Seagrove (Dr. Sarah King), David Soul (Jefferson Cope), Nicholas Guest (Lennox Boynton), Valerie Richards (Carol Boynton).

Peter Ustinov makes his sixth movie appearance as Christie's Belgian sleuth Hercule Poirot. While travelling in Jerusalem, he's called upon to solve the murder of shrewish widow Piper Laurie. As is the custom in these mysteries, there is a long list of suspects with good reasons to wish her dead.

111. *Appointment with Fear* (1985, Galaxy, 98m, c). P Tom Boutross, D Ramzi Thomas, W Thomas & Bruce Meade, PH Nicholas Von Sternberg, M Andrea Saparoff, ED Paul Jasiukonis.

LP Michele Little (Carol), Michael Wyle (Bobby), Kerry Remsen (Heather), Douglas Rowe (Det. Kowalski), Garrick Dowhen (The Man), Deborah Sue Voorhees (Ruth), Pamela Bach (Samantha).

This story of police detective Douglas Rowe tracking down a serial killer is so bad the director disowned it.

112. *Apprentice to Murder* (1988, New World, 94m, c). P Howard K.

Grossman, D R.L. Thomas, W Alan Scott & Wesley Moore, PH Kelvin Pike, M Charles Gross, ED Patrick McMahon, PD Gregory Bolton.

LP Donald Sutherland (John Reese), Chad Lowe (Billy Kelly), Mia Sara (Alice Spangler), Knut Husebo (Lars Hoeglin), Rutanya Alda (Elma Kelly), Eddie Jones (Tom Kelly), Mark Burton (Clay Meyers).

In rural Pennsylvania, circa 1927, pleasant small-town doctor Donald Sutherland, who has supernatural powers, battles Knut Husebo, a mysterious neighbor who may well be Satan incarnate.

113. *April Fool's Day* (1986, Paramount, 90m, c). P Frank Mancuso, Jr., D Fred Walton, W Danilo Bach, PH Charles Minsky, M Charles Bernstein, ED Bruce Green, PD Randolph F. Cheveldave.

LP Jay Baker (Harvey), Pat Barlow (Clara), Lloyd Berry (Ferryman), Deborah Foreman (Muffy/Buffy), Deborah Goodrich (Nikki), Tom Heaton (Constable Potter/Uncle Frank), Mike Nomad (Buck).

In a spoof of the holiday horror films, dumb college students are systematically bumped off on a deserted island.

114. *Aria* (1988, Warner, US/GB, 98m, c). P Don Boyd, D&W Nicolas Roeg, Charles Sturridge, Jean-Luc Godard, Julien Temple, Bruce Beresford, Robert Altman, Franc Roddam, Ken Russell, Derek Jarman, Bill Bryden, PH various photographers, M various artists, ED various editors, PD various designers.

LP John Hurt (Searcher for a lost love), Theresa Russell (King Zog), Buck Henry (Preston), Beverly D'Angelo (Gilda), Anita Morris (Phoebe), Julie Hagerty (Lover), Bridget Fonda (Lover), Stephanie Lane (Baroness), Nicola Swain (Marie), Jackson Kyle (Travis), Gary Kasper (Jake), Elizabeth Hurley (Marietta), Peter Birch (Paul).

Ten directors take turns creating a story based on arias by Verdi, Lully, Korngold, Rameau, Wagner, Puccini, Charpentier & Leoncavallo. As might be expected, the results vary widely in quality and dramatic effect. The best seems to be by Charles Sturridge based on the Verdi aria "La Vergine degli Angeli" from *La*

Forza del Destino and Franc Roddam's melodrama based on Wagner's "Liebestod" from *Tristan und Isolde.*

115. *Arizona Heat* (1988, Spectrum, 91m, c). P&D John G. Thomas, W Daniel M. Colmerauer, PH Howard Wexler, M Gary Stockdale, ED Thomas.

LP Michael Parks (Larry Kapinski), Denise Crosby (Jill Andrews), Hugh Farrington (Capt. Samuels), Ron Briskman (Toad), Dennis O'Sullivan (Paul Murphy), Renata Lee (Lisa).

Tough Arizonian cop Michael Parks has an attitude problem, a lesbian partner Denise Crosby, and an assignment to bring in a serial killer. This went straight to video.

116. *Armed and Dangerous* (1986, Columbia, 88m, c). P Brian Grazer & James Keach, D Mark L. Lester, W Harold Ramis & Peter Torokvei (based on a story by Ramis, Grazer & Keach), PH Fred Schuler, M Bill Myers, ED Michael Hill, Daniel Hanley & Gregory Prange, PD David L. Snyder.

LP John Candy (Frank Dooley), Eugene Levy (Norman Kane), Robert Loggia (Michael Carlino), Kenneth McMillan (Clarence O'Connell), Meg Ryan (Maggie Cavanaugh), Brion James (Anthony Lazrus), Jonathan Banks (Clyde Klepper), Don Stroud (Sgt. Rizzo), Steve Railsback (The Cowboy).

Bungling nightwatchmen John Candy and Eugene Levy redeem themselves by exposing corruption in the security guard business. Moderately funny.

117. *Arrogant* (1988, Cannon, 87m, c). P,D&W Phillipe Blot, PH Claude Agostini, M Paul Erickson, ED Ken Bornstein.

LP Sylvia Kristel (Julie), Gary Graham (Giovanni), Leigh Wood (Leticia), Joe Condon (Senator), Brian Strom, Michael Justin, J.R. Zdvorak, Dale Segal.

Shot in 1986, this pretentious road picture had brief theater release before going to video and the Playboy Channel. The story, what there is of one, has Gary Graham fleeing his brothers-in-laws, after having killed his father-in-law. He picks up hitchhiking Emmanuelle star Sylvia Kristel and they head for nowhere.

118. *Arthur* (1981, Orion/Warner, 117m, c). P Robert Greenhut, D&W Steve Gordon† (for screenplay), PH Fred Schuler, M Burt Bacharach, ED Susan E. Morse, PD Stephen Hendrickson, SONG "Arthur's Theme (Best That You Can Do)" by Burt Bacharach, Carole Bayer Sager, Christopher Cross & Peter Allen*.

LP Dudley Moore† (Arthur Bach), Liza Minnelli (Linda Marolla), John Gielgud† (Hobson), Geraldine Fitzgerald (Martha Bach), Jill Eikenberry (Susan Johnson), Stephen Elliott (Burt Johnson), Ted Ross (Bitterman), Barney Martin (Ralph Marolla), Thomas Barbour (Stanford Bach), Anne DeSalvo (Gloria).

Dudley Moore gets an opportunity to do his drunk act, and play it, and play it for two hours. He's a wealthy ne'er-do-well, ordered to marry Jill Eikenberry by grandmother Geraldine Fitzgerald who controls the purse strings — or else. Trouble is he's fallen in love with wisecracking Liza Minnelli. Will he have enough strength of character to follow his heart? The best performance is given by John Gielgud, who is quite a droll comedian.

119. *Arthur 2 on the Rocks* (1988, Warner, 112m, c). P Robert Shapiro, D Bud Yorkin, W Andy Breckman, PH Stephen H. Burum, M Burt Bacharach, ED Michael Kahn, PD Gene Callahan.

LP Dudley Moore (Arthur Bach), Liza Minnelli (Linda Bach), Geraldine Fitzgerald (Martha), Stephen Elliott (Bert Johnson), Cynthia Sikes (Susan), John Gielgud (Hobson), Paul Benedict (Fairchild), Kathy Bates (Mrs. Canby), Barney Martin (Ralph).

Why anyone would think audiences would want another serving of Dudley Moore's drunk act is beyond us. Even resurrecting John Gielgud, whose character died in the original can't help this dog with fleas. The story deals with Moore and Liza Minnelli's problems trying to adopt a baby and the plans of the father of the girl Moore jilted to blackmail the souse into leaving Liza.

120. *Ascendancy* (1983, British Film Institute, GB, 92m, c). P Penny Clark & Ian Elsey, D Edward Bennett, W Bennett & Nigel Gearing, PH Clive Tickner, M Ronnie Leahy, ED Charles Rees & George Akers.

LP Julie Covington (Connie), Ian Charleson (Ryder), John Phillips (Wintour), Susan Engel (Nurse), Phillip Locke (Dr. Strickland), Kieran Montague (Dr. Kelso).

In 1920 Belfast, Julie Covington, the daughter of a Protestant shipyard owner, loses the use of her right arm soon after her brother is killed on the battlefield. As the tension grows between the Protestants and Catholics she becomes mute. The more the unrest the more she retreats into catatonia.

121. *The Assam Garden* (1985, Moving Picture Company, GB, 92m, c). P Nigel Stafford-Clark, D Mary McMurray, W Elizabeth Bond, PH Bryan Loftus, M Richard Harvey, ED Rodney Holland.

LP Deborah Kerr (Helen), Madhur Jaffrey (Ruxmani), Alec McCowen (Mr. Philpott), Zia Mohyeddin (Mr. Lal), Anton Lesser (Mr. Sutton), Iain Cuthbertson (Arthur), Tara Shaw (Sushi), Dev Sagoo (Raju).

In her first film appearance in fifteen years, Deborah Kerr stars as an Englishwoman refurbishing her garden in her husband's memory with the help of Indian woman Madhur Jaffrey.

122. *Assassination* (1987, Cannon, 88m, c). P Pancho Kohner, D Peter Hunt, W Richard Sale, PH Hanania Baer, M Robert O. Ragland & Valentine McCallum, ED James Heckert, PD William Cruise.

LP Charles Bronson (Jay Killian), Jill Ireland (Laramie Royce Craig), Stephen Elliott (Fitzroy), Jan Gan Boyd (Charlotte Chang), Randi Brooks (Tyler Loudermilk), Erik Stern (Reno Bracken), Michael Ansara (Sen. Hector Bunsen), James Staley (Briggs).

Secret Service agent Charles Bronson is assigned to protect free-spirited First Lady Jill Ireland who has only a marriage of convenience to the president. Political pro Michael Ansara, believes that his candidate will have a better chance of being re-elected if he's a widower. Bronson must prevent Ireland's assassination.

Assault Force see *ffolkes*

123. *Assault of the Killer Bimbos* (1988, Titan/Empire, 80m, c). P David De Coteau & John Schouweiler, D Anita Rosenberg, W Ted Nicolaou (based on a story by Rosenberg, Patti Astor & Nicolaou), PH Thomas Callaway, M Fred Lapides & Marc Ellis, ED Barry Zetlin, PD Royce Mathew.

LP Christina Whitaker (Peaches), Elizabeth Kaitan (LuLu), Tammara Souza (Darlene), Nick Cassavetes (Wayne-O), Griffin O'Neal (Troy), Jamie Bozian (Billy), Mike Muscat (Vinnie), Patti Astor (Poodles).

As all things are relative, this dopey comedy about go-go girls on the lam from the police, after being wrongly accused of murder, is far better than the usual sexploitation subgenre to which it belongs. Oh sure, there's plenty of flesh to be seen, but the leads Christina Whitaker, Elizabeth Kaitan and Tammara Souza are more than just pieces of meat — but not a lot more.

124. *Assault of the Party Nerds* (1989, Check Entertainment, 79m, c). P Richard Gabai & M. Alex Becker, D Gabai, PH Howard Wexler, M Larry Berliner, ED Richard Deckard, PD Royce Mathew.

LP Michelle Bauer (Muffin), Linnea Quigley (Bambi), Troy Donahue (Sid Witherspoon), Richard Gabai (Ritchie), Deborah Roush (Diane), Joe Whyte (T.K.), Marc Silverberg (Scott), C. Paul Dempsey (Bud).

This low-budget, direct-to-video comedy is a so-so knock-off of *Revenge of the Nerds*. Lambda Alpha Eta is down to four members, all seniors at State U. The president, Richard Gabai, plans a major rush party to corral new members, but must deal with their natural adversaries, the jocks.

125. *Assault with a Deadly Weapon* (1983, Aquarius, 94m, c). D Walter Gaines, W William Dyer, M Paul Fox.

LP Richard Holliday, Sandra Foley, Lamont Jackson, Rinaldo Rincon.

Richard Holliday is a cop guilty of the title crime, but his assault is on a society soft on criminals.

Assignment: Kill Castro see *Sweet Dirty Tony*

126. *The Assisi Underground* (1985, Golan-Globus, 178m, c). P Menahem Golan & Yoram Globus, D&W Alexander Ramati (based on his documentary novel), PH Giuseppe Rotunno, M Dov Seltzer, ED Michael Duthie, PD Luciano Spadoni.

LP Ben Cross (Padre Rufino), James Mason (Bishop Nicolini), Irene Papas (Mother Giuseppina), Maximilian Schell (Col. Mueller), Karl-Heinz Hackl (Capt. Von Velden), Riccardo Cucciolla (Luigi Brizzi), Angelo Infanti (Giorgio Kropf), Paolo Malco (Paolo Josza).

Franciscan priest Ben Cross is part of the Jewish liberation network in World War II in this fact-based movie. The film is poorly edited and one loses interest as the three hours drag on.

127. *Astonished* (1988, Dream Bird, 103m, c). P Sydney & Herman Kahn, D Jeff Kahn & Travis Preston, W J. Kahn, PH Peter Fernberger & Rob Draper, M Michael Urbaniak, ED Peter Friedman & Bill Daughton.

LP Liliana Komorowski (Sonia), Ken Ryan (Det. Jonah Wylee), Rock Dutton, Theresa Merritt, Fred Neuman, Tommy Hollis.

In this version of Dostoyevski's *Crime and Punishment,* impoverished Liliana Komorowski kills her landlord when she catches him brutally beating a prostitute.

128. *At Close Range* (1986, Orion, 111m, c). P Elliott Lewitt & Don Guest, D James Foley, W Nicholas Kazan, PH Juan Ruiz Anchia, M Patrick Leonard, ED Howard Smith, PD Peter Jamison.

LP Sean Penn (Brad Whitewood, Jr.), Christopher Walken (Brad Whitewood, Sr.), Mary Stuart Masterson (Terry), Christopher Penn (Tommy), Millie Perkins (Julie), Eileen Ryan (Grandmother), Alan Autry (Ernie), Candy Clark (Mary Sue).

Rural gang leader Christopher Walken returns to his Pennsylvania home after many years of absence. His two sons Sean and Christopher Penn try to prove themselves worthy of joining his gang. There is a brutal showdown between father and sons in this story based on a true case.

129. *Atlantic City†* (1981, Paramount, Canada/Fr., 104m, c, aka *Atlantic City, USA*). P Denis Heroux, D Louis Mallet†, W John Guare†, PH Richard Ciupka, M Michel Legrand, ED Suzanne Baron, PD Anne Pritchard.

LP Burt Lancaster† (Lou), Susan Sarandon† (Sally), Kate Reid (Grace), Michel Piccoli (Joseph), Hollis McLaren (Chrissie), Robert Joy (Dave), Al Waxman (Alfie), Moses Znaimer (Felix), Angus MacInnes (Vinnie), Sean Sullivan (Buddy).

Burt Lancaster and Susan Sarandon are a great team. He is an aging small-time hood; she's an apprentice blackjack dealer for an Atlantic City casino. Sarandon's former husband has ripped off a cache of drugs from the mob. Hit men rub him out, but the drugs fall into the hands of Lancaster. Burt protects Sarandon from the hit men, killing both. He also beds Susan, before he allows her to leave with the major part of the money he's received for the drugs.

Atlantic City, U.S.A. see Atlantic City

Ator the Invincible see The Blade Master

130. *The Aurora Encounter* (1985, New World, 90m, c). P Jim McCullough, Jr., & Jim McCullough, Sr., D McCullough, Sr., W McCullough, Jr.

LP Jack Elam (Charlie), Peter Brown (Sheriff), Carol Bagdasarian (Alain), Dottie West (Irene), Will Mitchel (Ranger), Charles B. Pierce (Preacher), Mickey Hays (Aurora Spaceman), Spanky McFarland (Governor).

Delightful character actor Jack Elam shines in this enjoyable science fiction story about aliens visiting a small Texas town in the late 1800s.

131. *Author! Author!* (1982, 20th Century–Fox, 110m, c). P Irwin Winkler, D Arthur Hiller, W Israel Horovitz, PH Victor J. Kemper, M Dave Grusin, ED William Reynolds, PD Gene Rudolf.

LP Al Pacino (Travalian), Dyan Cannon (Alice Detroit), Tuesday Weld (Gloria), Alan King (Kreplich), Bob Dishy (Finestein), Bob Elliott (Patrick Dicker), Eric Gurry (Igor), Elva Leff (Bonnie).

Playwright Al Pacino's wife Tuesday Weld walks out on him, leaving behind their children and hers from three previous marriages. Pacino must finish his newest play, take care of his large brood and deal with his new lady love Dyan Cannon, an actress totally unsuitable for her role in his new drama. Frankly, it's a drag.

132. *Avenging Angel* (1985, New World, 93m, c). P Sandy Howard & Keith Rubinstein, D Robert Vincent O'Neil, W O'Neil & Joseph M. Cala, PH Peter Lyons Collister & Bryan England, M Chris Young, ED John Bowey.

LP Betsy Russell (Angel/Molly Stewart), Rory Calhoun (Kit Carson), Robert F. Lyons (Det. Andrews), Susan Tyrrell (Solly Mosler), Ossie Davis (Capt. Moradian), Barry Pearl (Johnny Glitter), Ross Hagen (Ray Mitchell), Tim Rossovich (Teddy Butts), Estee Chandler (Cindy), Steven M. Porter (Yo-Yo Charlie).

Lolita-like high school honor student and Hollywood Strip hooker Donna Wilkes has grown up to become sexy law student Betsy Russell. She returns to the streets when the detective who helped get her off them is murdered by four assassins. The killers also gun down an undercover female cop, posing as a hooker, and her parents. Russell and delightful Rory Calhoun break the case with Betsy stalking the murders with a .357 magnum.

133. *Avenging Force* (1986, Cannon, 103m, c). P Menahem Golan & Yoram Globus, D Sam Firstenberg, W James Booth, PH Gideon Porath, M George S. Clinton, ED Michael J. Duthie, PD Marcia Hinds.

LP Michael Dudikoff (Matt Hunter), Steve James (Larry Richards), James Booth (Adm. Brown), John P. Ryan (Glastenbury), Bill Wallace (Delaney), Karl Johnson (Wallace), Mark Alaimo (Lavall), Allison Gereighty (Sara Hunter).

Former Secret Service agent Michael Dudikoff is called back into action when an ex-colleague is threatened by a right-wing extremist group called the Pentacle. Hunter Dudikoff becomes the hunted in this decent action adventure yarn.

134. *The Aviator* (1985, MGM/United Artists, 96m, c). P Mace Neufeld & Thomas H. Brodek, D George Miller, W Marc Norman (based on the novel by Ernest K. Gann), PH David Connell, M Dominic Frontiere, ED Duane Hartzell, PD Brenton Swift.

LP Christopher Reeve (Edgar Anscombe), Rosanna Arquette (Tillie Hansen), Jack Warden (Moravia), Sam Wanamaker (Bruno Hansen), Scott Wilson (Jerry Stiller), Tyne Daly (Evelyn Stiller), Marcia Strassman (Rose Stiller).

During the early years of air travel, aviator Christopher Reeve and his passenger Rosanna Arquette don't get along until their plane crashes. Then a romance develops. Miss this flight.

135. *The Awakening* (1980, Orion/Warner, 102m, c). P Robert Solo, Andrew Scheinman & Martin Shafer, D Mike Newell, W Allan Scott, Chris Bryant & Clive Exton (based on the novel *The Jewel of Seven Stars* by Bram Stoker), PH Jack Cardiff, M Claude Bolling, ED Terry Rawlings, PD Michael Stringer.

LP Charlton Heston (Matthew Corbeck), Susannah York (Jane Turner), Jill Townsend (Anne Corbeck), Stephanie Zimbalist (Margaret Corbeck), Patrick Drury (Paul Whittier), Bruce Myers (Dr. Khalid).

Egyptologist Charlton Heston's daughter Stephanie Zimbalist is possessed by the spirit of vengeful Queen Kara, dead for over 2000 years. When the bodies begin to mount, Heston starts putting two and two together.

136. *Axe* (1983, New American Films, 67m, c). P J.G. Patterson, Jr., D&W Frederick R. Friedel, PH Austin McKinney, M George Newman Shaw, ED Friedel & Patterson.

LP Leslie Lee (Lisa), Jack Canon (Steele), Ray Green (Lomax), Frederick R. Friedel (Billy), Douglas Powers (Grandfather), Frank Jones (Aubrey).

Three killers lurk in a secluded home waiting for their victims to return. After slaughtering the couple, they flee but are followed by the wife who takes her revenge with a well-sharpened axe.

137. *Babar: The Movie* (1989, New Line Cinema, Canada/France, animated, 70m, c). P Patrick Loubert, Michael Hirsh & Clive A. Smith, D Alan Bunce, W Peter Sauder, J.D. Smith, John De Klein, Raymond Jafelice & Bunce (based on a story by Sauder, Loubert & Bunce, and on characters created by Jean & Laurent de Brunhoff), ANIM D John Laurence Collins, M Milan Kymlicka, PD Ted Bastien.

VOICES Gordon Pinsent (King Babar, the elder), Gavin Magrath (Boy Babar), Elizabeth Hanna (Queen Celeste), Sarah Polley (Young Celeste), Chris Wiggins (Cornelius), Stephen Ouimette (Pompadour), John Stocker (Zephir), Charles Kerr (Rataxes).

Although the storyline is as minimal as the animation, this picture should please youngsters. Elephantland is attacked by rhinoceroses who enslave the peaceful pachyderms. Never fear, Babar prevails, with a little help from his friends.

138. Baby Boom (1987, United Artists/MGM, 103m, c). P Nancy Meyers, D Charles Shyer, W Meyers & Shyer, PH William A. Fraker, M Bill Conti, ED Lynzee Klingman, PD Jeffrey Howard.

LP Diane Keaton (J.C. Wiatt), Harold Ramis (Steven Buchner), Sam Wanmaker (Fritz Curtis), Sam Shepard (Dr. Jeff Cooper), James Spader (Ken Arrenberg), Pat Hingle (Hughes Larrabee), Britt Leach (Vern Boone), Kristina & Michelle Kennedy (Elizabeth Wiatt), Linda Ellerbee (Narrator).

Hard-driving Yuppie career woman Diane Keaton finds her life hopelessly complicated when she is forced to take custody of a relative's baby. Her live-in lover Harold Ramis moves out, and when caring for the child causes her to slip while climbing the corporate ladder, she retreats to the country in upper New England. She initially finds that she's not equipped to live in such a rustic setting until she falls in love with veterinarian Sam Shepard. She becomes an overnight success manufacturing gourmet baby food. She is offered the opportunity to return to New York and the fast lane in triumph, but decides she prefers her Norman Rockwell–like family life in the sticks. We suppose there is a feminist message here, but it's garbled.

139. Baby, It's You (1983, Paramount, 105m, c). P Griffin Dune & Amy Robinson, D&W John Sayles (based on a story by Robinson), PH Michael Ballhaus, ED Sonya Polonsky, PD Jeffrey Townsend.

LP Rosanna Arquette (Jill), Vincent Spano (Sheik), Joanna Merlin (Mrs. Rosen), Jack Davidson (Dr. Rosen), Leora Dana (Miss Vernon), Sam McMurray (Mr. McManus), Dolores Messina (Mrs. Capadilupo), Nick Ferrari (Mr. Capadilupo).

In a 1960s slice-of-life film, Jewish girl Rosanna Arquette is the object of affection of Italian Catholic Vincent Spano. The boy gets, loses, gets girl theme is one of the oldest, and this film adds no new twists.

140. Baby . . . Secret of the Lost Legend (1985, Buena Vista/Disney, 93m, c). P Jonathan T. Taplin, D B.W.L. Norton, W Clifford & Ellen Green, PH John Alcott, M Jerry Goldsmith, ED Howard Smith & David Bretherton, PD Raymond G. Storey, SE Peter Anderson, DINOSAURS CREATED BY Isidoro Raponi & Roland Tantin.

LP William Katt (George Loomis), Sean Young (Susan Mathews-Loomis), Patrick McGoohan (Dr. Erick Kiviat), Julian Fellowes (Nigel Jenkins), Kyalo Mativo (Cephu), Hugh Quarshie (Kenge Obe), Olu Jacobs (Col. Nsogbu), Eddie Tagoe (Sgt. Gambwe), Edward Hardwicke (Dr. Pierre Dubois).

Paleontologists William Katt and Sean Young discover a family of live dinosaurs in the jungles of Africa. It's a Disney movie, so of course the baby dinosaur is cute and appealing. The movie is less so.

141. Babylon (1980, Diversity Music Production, GB, 95m, c). P Gavrik Losey, D Franco Rosso, W Martin Stellman & Rosso, PH Chris Menges, M Denis Bovell, ED Thomas Schwalm.

LP Brinsley Forde (David Blue), Karl Howman (Ronnie), Trevor Laird (Beefy), Brian Bovell (Spark), Victor Romero Evans (Lover), David N. Haynes (Errol), Archie Pool (Dreadhead), T. Bone Wilson (Wesley).

Black youth Brinsley Forde turns to murder and mayhem when racists destroy his reggae sound system.

142. Bachelor Party (1984, 20th Century–Fox, 106m, c). P Ron Moler & Bob Israel, D Neal Israel, W Neal Israel & Pat Proft (based on a story by Bob Israel), PH Hal Trussel, M Robert Folk, Tom Jenkins & Barry Schleifer, ED Tom Walls.

LP Tom Hanks (Rick Gassko), Tawny Kitaen (Debbie Thompson), Adrian

Zmed (Jay O'Neill), George Grizzard (Mr. Thompson), Robert Prescott (Cole Whittier), William Tepper (Dr. Stan Gassko), Wendie Jo Sperber (Dr. Tina Gassko), Barry Diamond (Rudy), Gary Grossman (Gary), Michael Dudikoff (Ryko).

It's understandable that father George Grizzard isn't thrilled that his darling daughter Tawny Kitaen is marrying unambitious and bizarre Tom Hanks, but it's not credible that he would prefer nerdy Robert Prescott as a son-in-law. Most of the action takes place at Hanks' bachelor party, where hired hookers are augmented by the arrival of a suspicious Kitaen and her girlfriends. With this tasteless film Hanks is still struggling to find his comedy place in the sun.

143. *Back Roads* (1981, Warner, 94m, c). P Ronald Shedlo, D Martin Ritt, W Gary Devore, PH John A. Alonzo, M Henry Mancini, ED Sidney Levin, PD Walter Scott Herndon.

LP Sally Field (Amy Post), Tommy Lee Jones (Elmore Pratt), David Keith (Mason), Miriam Colon (Angel), Michael Gazzo (Tazio), Dan Shor (Spivey), M. Emmet Walsh (Arthur), Barbara Babcock (Rickey's Mom), Nell Carter (Waitress).

Southern prostitute Sally Field teams up with stumble-bum prize fighter Tommy Lee Jones to head for California and a hoped-for better life. This road picture isn't worth the trip.

144. *Back to School* (1986, Orion, 96m, c). P Chuck Russell, D Alan Metter, W Steven Kampmann, Peter Torokvei & Harold Ramis, PH Thomas E. Ackerman, M Danny Elfman, ED David Rawlins, PD David L. Snyder.

LP Rodney Dangerfield (Thornton Melon), Sally Kellerman (Diane), Burt Young (Lou), Keith Gordon (Jason Melon), Robert Downey, Jr. (Derek), Paxton Whitehead (Philip Barbay), Terry Farrell (Valerie), M. Emmet Walsh (Coach Turnbull), Adrienne Barbeau (Vanessa), Ned Beatty (Dean Martin), Sam Kinison (Prof. Terguson).

Rodney Dangerfield, the self-made millionaire owner of the "Tall and Fat" chain of men stores, decides to attend school with his son Keith Gordon. At first

he tries to buy success in his classes but when he sees how this disgusts his son and threatens his relationship with one of his professors, Sally Kellerman, he hits the books, and succeeds on his own merits. It's moderately funny.

145. *Back to the Beach* (1987, Paramount, 92m, c). P Frank Mancuso, Jr., D Lyndall Hobbs, W Peter Krikes, Steve Meerson & Christopher Thompson (based on a story by James Komack from characters created by Lou Rusoff), PH Bruce Surtees, M Steve Dorff, ED David Finfer, PD Michael Helmy.

LP Annette Funicello (Annette), Frankie Avalon (The Big Kahuna), Connie Stevens (Connie), Lori Loughlin (Sandi), Tommy Hinkley (Michael), Demian Slade (Bobby), John Calvin (Troy), Joe Holland (Zed), David Bowe (Mountain).

My how time flies. Who would believe there would be an audience yearning nostalgically to find out what happened to the characters in the 60s beach-party movies? You say this story of fortyish Annette Funicello and Frankie Avalon, trying to rekindle their marriage with a Hawaiian vacation, is a satire? Guess we missed that.

146. *Back to the Future* (1985, Universal, 116m, c). P Bob Gale & Neil Canton, D Robert Zemeckis, W Zemeckis & Gale†, PH Dean Cundey, M Alan Silvestri, ED Arthur Schmidt & Harry Keramidas, PD Lawrence G. Paull, SOUND Bill Varney, B. Tennyson Sebastian II, Robert Thirlwell & William B. Kaplan†, SOUND EFFECTS ED Charles L. Campbell & Robert Rutledge*, SONG "The Power of Love" by Chris Hayes, Johnny Colla & Huey Lewis†.

LP Michael J. Fox (Marty McFly), Christopher Lloyd (Dr. Emmett Brown), Lea Thompson (Lorraine Baines), Crispin Glover (George McFly), Thomas F. Wilson (Biff Tannen), Claudia Wells (Jennifer Parker), George DiCenzo (Sam Baines), James Tolkan (Mr. Strickland), Jeffrey Jay Cohen (Skinhead).

Michael J. Fox is transferred back thirty years in time in a specially equipped DeLorean-like automobile, designed by zany scientist Christopher Lloyd. Fox finds his own mother, Lea Thompson, developing romantic feelings for him. His unintentional beating of his father's (Crispin Glover) time with Mom will result in his never having been born. Fortunately Fox is able to help his Dad develop some backbone and stand up to a bully and win Fox's mother. Then Lloyd helps Fox make it back to the future. The end of the blockbuster film promises the following sequel.

147.   *Back to the Future Part II* (1989, Universal, 107m, c). P Bob Gale & Neil Canton, D Robert Zemeckis, W Gale (based on a story by Zemeckis & Gale and the characters they created for *Back to the Future*), PH Dean Cundey, M Alan Silvestri, ED Arthur Schmidt, PD Rick Carter, AD Margie Stone McShirley, VE Industrial Light & Magic†.

LP Michael J. Fox (Marty McFly/ Marty McFly, Jr./Marlene McFly), Christopher Lloyd (Dr. Emmett Brown), Lea Thompson (Lorraine), Thomas F. Wilson (Biff Tannen/Griff), Harry Waters, Jr. (Marvin Berry), Charles Fleischer (Terry), Flea (Needles), Elizabeth Shue (Jennifer), James Tolkan (Strickland), Jeffrey Weissman & Crispin Glover (George McFly), Casey Siemaszko (3-D).

Few sequels of hit movies have been more eagerly awaited by fans, perhaps too young or ignorant of film history to realize that sequels seldom live up to expectations. (For further evidence of this, see our book *Cinema Sequels and Remakes,* McFarland, 1989.) Michael J. Fox, a bit too old to be convincing as a teen, is even less so as himself later in life, his own son, and most especially as his daughter. The story is quite similar to the original. This time, eccentric inventor Christopher Lloyd transports Fox to the future, where he is supposed to save his children from a terrible fate. Instead, the kids get lost in the shuffle as Fox and Lloyd find themselves in a time chase after Thomas F. Wilson who absconds with the flying DeLorean and a sports almanac and heads back to his 1955 self with plans to become rich betting on the known outcomes of sporting events. The film did only moderately well at the box-office, recouping its reported $35-million price tag. It was not as well received because it

doesn't have the heart and emotional impact of the original. Stay tuned for *Back to the Future III* in 1990.

148.   *Backfire* (1989, ITC/Vidmark, 90m, c). P Danton Rissner, D Gilbert Cates, W Larry Brand & Rebecca Reynolds, PH Tak Fujimoto, M David Shire, ED Melvin Shapiro, PD Daniel Lomino.

LP Karen Allen (Mara), Keith Carradine (Reed), Jeff Fahey (Donnie), Bernie Casey (Clint), Dean Paul Martin (Jake), Dinah Manoff (Jill), Virginia Capers (Maxine), Philip Sterling (Dr. Creason), Frances Flanagan (Claire).

Jeff Fahey and Karen Allen are a rich, young and attractive couple. What few suspect is that Vietnam vet Fahey suffers through a recurring nightmare about trying to save a buddy back in Nam. What Fahey doesn't suspect is that Allen with the help of Carradine is trying to drive him to suicide and when that doesn't work, they have murder on their minds.

149.   *Backlash* (1987, Goldwyn, Australia, 90m, c). P,D&W Bill Bennett, PH Tony Wilson, M Michael Atkinson, ED Denise Hunter.

LP David Argue (Trevor Darling), Gia Carides (Nikki Iceton), Lydia Miller (Kath), Brian Syron (Lyle), Anne Smith (Mrs. Smith), Don Smith (Mr. Smith), Jennifer Cluff (Waitress).

Cops David Argue and Lydia Miller escort female murderer Gia Carides across the Australian desert. Sand and heat raise passions.

150.   *Bad Blood* (1989, Platinum Pictures, 103m, c, aka *Son*). P&D Chuck Vincent, W Craig Horrall, PH Larry Revene, M Joey Mennonna, ED James Davalos.

LP Ruth Raymond [Georgina Spelvin] (Arlene Billings), Gregory Patrick (Ted Barnes), Troy Donahue (Jack Barnes), Carolyn Van Bellinghen (Wanda), Linda Blair (Evie Barnes), Harvey Siegel (Jasper), Scott Baker (Henry).

Georgina Spelvin, the star of the porno movie *The Devil in Miss Jones* (among others), plays a wealthy artist, reunited with her long lost son Gregory Patrick, when the latter and his wife Linda Blair visit her Long Island mansion. Blair is poisoned and Spelvin puts a move on her son, believing him to be the reincarnation of her late husband.

151. Bad Boys (1983, EMI/Universal, 123m, c). P Robert Solo, D Richard Rosenthal, W Richard Dilello, PH Bruce Surtees & Donald Thorin, M Bill Conti, ED Antony Gibbs, PD J. Michael Riva.

LP Sean Penn (Mick), Reni Santoni (Pramon Herrea), Esai Morales (Paco), Jim Moody (Gene Daniels), Eric Gurry (Horowitz), Clancy Brown (Viking), Ally Sheedy (J.C. Walenski), Robert Lee Rush (Tweety).

Chicago hoodlum Sean Penn is sent to a prison where he establishes himself as top dog until his life-long enemy Esai Morales is sent to the same slammer for raping Penn's girlfriend. The two swear to kill each other. Ally Sheedy makes her film debut in this overly long violent film.

152. Bad Dreams (1988, 20th Century-Fox, 84m, c). P Gale Anne Hurd, D Andrew Fleming, W Fleming & Steven E. de Souza (based on a story by Fleming, Michael Dick, Yuri Zeltser & P.J. Pettiette), PH Alexander Gruszynski, M Jay Ferguson, ED Jeff Freeman, PD Ivo Cristante.

LP Jennifer Rubin (Cynthia), Bruce Abbott (Dr. Alex Karmen), Richard Lynch (Harris), Dean Cameron (Ralph), Harris Yulin (Dr. Berrisford), Susan Barnes (Connie), John Scott Clough (Victor), E.G. Daily (Lana).

If you feel the need to be nauseated, rush to a video store and rent this story of Jennifer Rubin awakened from a 13-year coma, only to be haunted and hunted by Richard Lynch, the maniacal leader of a hippie cult.

153. Bad Manners (1984, New World, 85m, c). P Kim Jorgensen, D Bobby Houston, W Houston & Joseph Kwong, PH Jan De Bont, M Sparks "Ron and Russell Mael" & Michael Lewis, ED Barry Zetlin.

LP Karen Black (Gladys Fitzpatrick), Martin Mull (Warren Fitzpatrick), Anne De Salvo (Sister Serena), Murphy Dunne (Kurtz), Pamela Segall (Girl Joey), Georg Olden (Piper), Michael Hentz (Mouse), Joey Coleman (Whitey).

Orphans attempt to abduct Michael Hentz from his wealthy adoptive parents, Karen Black and Martin Mull, and return him to the miserable orphanage run by sadistic nun Anne De Salvo and her electrified cattle-prod using assistant Murphy Dunne.

154. Bad Medicine (1985, 20th Century-Fox, 97m, c). P Alex Winitsky, Arlene Sellers & Jeffrey Ganz, D&W Harvey Miller (based on the novel *Calling Dr. Horowitz* by Steven Horowitz & Neil Offen), PH Kelvin Pike, M Lalo Schifrin, ED O. Nicholas Brown, John Jympson & Keith Palmer, PD Les Dilley.

LP Steve Guttenberg (Jeff Marx), Alan Arkin (Dr. Madera), Julie Hagerty (Liz Parker), Bill Macy (Dr. Gerald Marx), Curtis Armstrong (Dennis Gladstone), Julie Kavner (Cookie Katz), Joe Grifasi (Gomez), Robert Romanus (Carlos), Taylor Negron (Pepe), Candi Milo (Maria Morales).

"Ugly Americans" Steve Guttenberg and Julie Hagerty, attending a fourth-rate medical school in Central America, steal drugs from the school's pharmacy to set up a clinic in a nearby village with serious health problems. The film won't endear the producers to Central Americans.

155. Bad Taste (1987, Blue Dolphin, New Zealand, 93m, c). P,D&W Peter Jackson, W Tony Hiles, Ken Hammon, PH Jackson, M Michelle Scullion, ED Matt Noonan, AD Caroline Girdlestone.

LP Mike Minett (Frank), Terry Potter (Ozzie), Peter O'Herne (Barry), Peter Jackson (Derek), Craig Smith (Giles), Doug Wren (Crumb, the Alien Leader).

The Alien Investigations & Defense Service are called in to explore a seemingly deserted small town. They find a blood-thirsty band of aliens intent on selling human flesh to an intergalactic fast food chain.

156. Bad Timing: A Sensual Obsession (1980, Rank, GB, 123m, c). P Jeremy Thomas, D Nicolas Roeg, W Yale Udoff, PH Anthony Richmond, M Richard Hartley, ED Tony Lawson.

LP Art Garfunkel (Dr. Alex Linden), Theresa Russell (Milena Flaherty), Harvey Keitel (Insp. Netusil), Denholm Elliott (Stefan Vognic), Daniel Massey (Fop), Dana Gillespie (Amy), William Hootkins (Col. Taylor).

Psychologist Art Garfunkel falls in love with Theresa Russell in Vienna. They engage in a stormy, passionate sexual relationship which ends with Russell's suicide attempt. Among others, she has alcoholic and drug abuse problems.

157. *The Ballad of Gregorio Cortéz* (1983, Embassy Pictures, 104m, c). P Michael Hausman, D Robert M. Young, W Victor Villasenor (based on the novel *With His Pistol in His Hands* by Americo Paredes), PH Ray Villalobos & Young, M W. Michael Lewis & Olmos, ED Richard Soto.

LP Edward James Olmos (Gregorio Cortéz), Tom Bower (Boone Choate), Bruce McGill (Bill Blakely), James Gammon (Sheriff Fly), Alan Vint (Sheriff Trimmell), Tim Scott (Sheriff Morris), Pepe Serna (Romaldo Cortéz), Brion James (Capt. Rogers), Barry Corbin (Abernethy).

Due to a language misunderstanding, Mexican cowboy Edward James Olmos kills a sheriff in self-defense. His flight from the law occasions one of the most famous manhunts in Texas history. Olmos is forced to surrender when he learns that his family is being held in custody.

158. *The Baltimore Bullet* (1980, Avco Embassy, 103m, c). P John F. Brascia, D Robert Ellis Miller, W Brascia & Robert Vincent O'Neil, PH James A. Crabe, M Johnny Mandel, ED Jerry Brady, PD Herman Blumenthal.

LP James Coburn (Nick Casey), Omar Sharif (The Deacon), Bruce Boxleitner (Billie Joe Robbins), Ronee Blakley (Carolina Red), Jack O'Halloran (Max), Calvin Lockhart (Snow White), Michael Lerner (Paulie), Paul Barselou (Cosmo), Cissie Cameron (Sugar).

Pool shark James Coburn takes Bruce Boxleitner under his wing. They know they must one day go head-to-head across a green-felt table, but Coburn reminds Boxleitner that he taught the younger man all Bruce knows about the game, but not all that Coburn does. The film features ten of the greatest pool players in the world, including Willie Mosconi, Irving Crane and Steve Mizerak.

159. *Band of the Hand* (1986, Tri-Star, 109m, c). P Michael Rauch, D Paul

Michael Glaser, W Leo Garen & Jack Baran, PH Reynaldo Villalobos, M various artists, ED Jack Hofstra, PD Gregory Bolton.

LP Stephen Lang (Joe), Mitchell Carmine (Ruben), Lauren Holly (Nikki), John Cameron Mitchell (J.L.), Daniele Quinn (Carlos), Leon Robinson (Moss), Al Shannon (Dorcey), Danton Stone (Aldo), Paul Calderon (Tito), Larry Fishburne (Cream), James Remar (Nestor).

Vietnam vet Stephen Lang turns a group of incorrigible Florida teens into a crack antidrug squad. Once reformed the five take on a powerful drug lord.

160. *The Banker* (1989, Westwind, 95m, c). P&D William Webb, W Dana Augustine (based on a story by Webb, Augustine & Richard Brandes), PH John Huneck, M Sam Winans & Reg Powell, ED Patrick Dodd, PD James R. Shumaker.

LP Robert Forster (Sgt. Dan Jefferson), Duncan Regehr (Spalding Osbourne), Shanna Reed (Sharon Maxwell), Jeff Conaway (Cowboy), Leif Garrett (Fowler), Richard Roundtree (Lt. Lloyd Hughes).

Following some South American Indian practice, banker Duncan Regehr paints his face and uses a crossbow to slaughter call girls, after which he mutilates their bodies. Yeah, that sounds like your typical banker.

161. *Banzai Runner* (1987, Montage, 86m, c). P&D John G. Thomas, W Phillip L. Harange, PH Howard A. Wexler, M Joel Goldsmith, ED Drake Silliman, SE Tom Callway & Stephen Stanton.

LP Dean Stockwell (Billy Baxter), John Shepherd (Beck Baxter), Charles Dierkop (Traven), Dawn Schneider (Shelley), Ann Cooper (Maysie), Barry Sattles (Osborne), Billy Drago (Syszek), Rick Fitts (Winston).

California highway patrolman Dean Stockwell's special obsession is hit and run drivers. For those who like that kind of thing, there's a lot of meaningless chases in souped-up autos.

162. *The Barbarians* (1987, Cannon, 88m, c, aka *The Barbarians and Co.*). P John Thompson, D Ruggero Deodato, W James R. Silke, PH Gianlorenzo Battaglia, M Pino Donaggio, ED Eugenio Alabiso, PD Giuseppe Mangano.

LP David Paul (Kutchek), Peter Paul (Gore), Richard Lynch (Kadar), Eva La Rue (Ismena/Cara), Virginia Bryant (Canary), Sheeba Alahani (China), Michael Berryman (Dirtmaster), Tiziana Di Gennaro (Kara).

David & Peter Paul, billed as "The Bad Boys of Bodybuilding," stink up the screen in this putrid sword-and-sorcery tale of two muscular lads who must recover the ruby that belongs in the navel of the virgin queen who protects their people.

The Barbarians & Co. see ***The Barbarians***

The Barbaric Beast of Boggy Creek see ***Boggy Creek II***

163. ***Barbarosa*** (1982, Universal, 90m, c). P Paul N. Lazarus III & William D. Wittliff, D Fred Schepisi, W Wittliff, PH Ian Baker, M Bruce Smeaton, ED Don Zimmerman & David Ramirez.

LP Willie Nelson (Barbarosa), Gary Busey (Karl), Isela Vega (Josephina), Gilbert Roland (Don Braulio), Danny De La Paz (Eduardo), Alma Martinez (Juanita), George Voskovec (Herman), Sharon Compton (Hilda).

Country singer Willie Nelson portrays an aging, legendary bandit who, because of a long-standing family feud, must constantly be on the look-out for assassination attempts on his life by his wife's family.

164. ***Barfly*** (1987, Cannon, 100m, c). P Barbet Schroeder, Fred Roos & Tom Luddy, d Schroeder, W Charles Bukowski, PH Robby Muller, ED Eva Gardos, PD Bob Ziembicki.

LP Mickey Rourke (Henry Chinaski), Faye Dunaway (Wanda Wilcox), Alice Krige (Tully Sorenson), Jack Nance (Detective), J.C. Quinn (Jim), Frank Stallone (Eddie), Gloria LeRoy (Grandma Moses).

Mickey Rourke stands in for poet/novelist Charles Bukowski who writes about the gutter existence he shares with other barflies and lowlifes of a L.A. subculture. Rourke is a revelation as the boozy macho young writer as is Faye Dunaway as his bar stool companion.

165. ***Basket Case*** (1982, Analysis Releasing, 90m, c). P Edgar Levins, D&W Frank Henenlotter, PH Bruce Torbet, M Gus Russo, ED Henenlotter, SE Kevin Haney & John Caglione.

LP Kevin Van Hentryck (Duane Bradley), Terri Susan Smith (Sharon), Beverly Bonner (Casey), Lloyd Pace (Dr. Harold Needleman), Diana Browne (Dr. Judith Kutter), Bill Freeman (Dr. Julius Lifflander), Joe Clarke (Brian "Mickey" O'Donovan).

Kevin Van Hentryck wanders around Times Square carrying a basket in which lives his deformed Siamese twin. The boys are out to avenge their botched surgical separation. And you thought you'd heard everything.

166. ***Basic Training*** (1985, Movie Store/Playboy Prods., 88m, c). P Otto Salamon & Gil Adler, D Andrew Sugerman, W Bernard M. Kahn, PH Stephen W. Gray, M Michael Cruz, ED Larry Bock.

LP Ann Dusenberry (Melinda), Rhonda Shear (Debbie), Angela Aames (Cheryl), Will Nye (Lt. Cranston), Walter Gotell (Ambassador Gotell).

In this raunchy comedy, buxom Ann Dusenberry fights sexual harassment and lax national security in the Pentagon by destroying the careers of the lechers among the top brass who drool over her and her fellow well endowed co-workers. Dusenberry is so successful, she's named Secretary of State. It's the type of jiggle and bounce and pandering nudity one would expect from Playboy productions.

167. ***Bat 21*** (1988, Tri-Star, 105m, c). P David Fisher, Gary Neill & Michael Balson, D Peter Markle, W William C. Anderson & George Gordon (based on the book by Anderson), PH Mark Irwin, M Christopher Young, ED Stephen E. Rivkin, PD Vincent Cresciman.

LP Gene Hackman (Lt. Col. Iceal Hambleton), Danny Glover (Capt. Bartholomew Clark), Jerry Reed (Col. George Walker), David Marshall Grant (Ross Carver), Clayton Rohner (Sgt. Harley Rumbaugh), Erich Anderson (Maj. Jake Scott), Joe Dorsey (Col. Douglass).

"Bat 21" is the radio signal code of Gene Hackman, a 53-year-old Air Force strategist who is shot down over Vietnam while flying a reconnaissance mission. The story deals with his attempts to survive until Danny Glover can rescue him. Hackman gives a bravo performance as a decent, frightened, non-macho man.

168. *Batman* (1989, Warner, 126m, c). P Jon Peters & Peter Guber, D Tim Burton, W Sam Hamm & Warren Skaaren (from a story by Hamm based on characters created by Bob Kane appearing in DC Comics), PH Roger Pratt, M Danny Elfman, SONGS Prince, ED Ray Lovejoy, PD Anton Furst*, AD Les Tomkins, Terry Ackland-Snow & Nigel Phelps, SD Peter Young*, COS Bob Ringwood & Linda Henrikson, SE Derek Meddings, MK Paul Engelen & Nick Dudman.

LP Michael Keaton (Batman/Bruce Wayne), Jack Nicholson (Joker/Jack Napier), Kim Basinger (Vicki Vale), Robert Wuhl (Alexander Knox), Pat Hingle (Commissioner Gordon), Billy Dee Williams (Harvey Dent), Michael Gough (Alfred), Jack Palance (Grissom), Jerry Hall (Alicia).

No 1980s film since *Star Wars* in 1977 has hit the theaters with more accompanying hype and commercial tie-ins than the current version of *Batman*. There even was a pre-release controversy. How could Michael Keaton be Batman? His forte seemed to be weird comedies, with looks suggesting a future in villainous roles. It hardly matters, the film is making a mint, and the fact that Jack Nicholson as the Joker overshadows Keaton hasn't prevented fans from flocking to showings. It's not the camp version of the 60s with Adam West as Batman and Burt Ward as Robin, in fact there is no Robin. The role of the Caped Crusader's sidekick is taken by beautiful Kim Basinger, even though the scenes between her and Keaton are the weakest in the film. The story isn't much, but the technical aspects of the movie make it work. The style is heavily influenced by film noir (and of course film noir was heavily influenced by the comics). Will there be a sequel? Are you kidding?

169. *Batteries Not Included* (1987, Universal, 106m, c). P Ronald L. Schwary, D Matthew Robbins, W Robbins, Brad Bird, Brent Maddock & S.S. Wilson (based on a story by Mick Garris and an uncredited TV script by Steven Spielberg), PH John McPherson, M James Horner, ED Cynthia Scheider, PD Ted Haworth, SE Industrial Light & Magic.

LP Hume Cronyn (Frank Riley), Jessica Tandy (Faye Riley), Frank McRae (Harry Noble), Elizabeth Pena (Marisa), Michael Carmine (Carlos), Dennis Boutsikaris (Mason), Tom Aldredge (Sid), Jane Hoffman (Muriel), John DiSanti (Gus), John Pankow (Kovacs), MacIntyre Dixon (DeWitt), Michael Greene (Lacey).

Whether you will enjoy this "feel-good" movie about down-and-out New York tenement dwellers, threatened with eviction by unfeeling developers and aided by some cute hardware from Outer Space, may depend upon whether you are up for a pathetic fairy tale with a Star Wars bent.

170. *Battle Beyond the Stars* (1980, New World, 104m, c). P Ed Carlin, D Jimmy T. Murakami, W John Sayles (based on a story by Sayles & Ann Dyer), PH Daniel Lacambre, M James Horner, ED Allan Holzman & Bob Kizer, SE C. Comisky & Ken Jones.

LP Richard Thomas (Shad), Robert Vaughn (Gelt), Darlanne Fluegel (Sador), George Peppard (Cowboy), Sybil Danning (St. Exmin), Sam Jaffe (Dr. Hephaestus), Morgan Woodward (Cayman), Steve Davis (Quopeg).

When a peaceful planet is attacked by invaders, the inhabitants hire George Peppard and others to come to their aid à la *The Seven Samurai* and *The Magnificent Seven*. The film is often funny and the special effects are interesting.

171. *Battletruck* (1982, New World, 91m, c, aka *Warlords of the 21st Century*). P Lloyd Phillips & Rob Whitehouse, D Harley Cokliss, W Irving Austin, Cokliss & John Beech, PH Chris Menges, M Kevin Peek, ED Michael Horton, PD Gary Hansen.

LP Michael Beck (Hunter), Annie McEnroe (Carlie), James Wainwright (Straker), John Ratzenberger (Rusty), Randolph Powell (Judd), Bruno Lawrence (Willie), Diana Rowan (Charlene), John Bach (Bone).

Sometime after WWIII, there is no fuel to be found, but an outlaw army led by James Wainwright does have a massive truck and the gasoline to run it. His daughter Annie McEnroe teams with Michael Beck to ensure that good triumphs over evil. You've seen it all before.

172. Bay Boy (1984, Orion, Canada, 107m, c). P John Kemeny & Denis Heroux, D&W Daniel Petrie, PH Claude Agostini, M Claude Bolling, ED Susan Shanks, Petrie & Peter Wintonick, PD Wolf Kroeger.

LP Liv Ullmann (Jennie Campbell), Kiefer Sutherland (Donald Campbell), Alan Scarfe (Sgt. Tom Coldwell), Mathieu Carrière (Father Chaisson), Peter Donat (Will Campbell), Leah Pinsent (Saxon Coldwell), Jane McKinnon (Dianna Coldwell), Kathy McGuire (Sister Roberta).

Kiefer Sutherland, a 17-year-old growing up in a Cape Breton village in 1937, is torn between the desire of his parents, Liv Ullmann and Peter Donat, that he become a priest and his active libido. He's attracted to young nun Kathy McGuire and has to fight off the advances of homosexual priest Mathieu Carrière. He also has adolescent fantasies about Leah Pinsent and Jane McKinnon. To make his moral dilemma worse, Sutherland sees their sadist father Alan Scarfe, the local constable, murdering an aged Jewish couple. He denies having seen the murders, but his conscience bothers him.

173. Beach Balls (1988, Concorde, 77m, c). P Matt Leipzig, D Joe Ritter, W David Rocklin, PH Anthony Cobbs, M Mark Governor, ED Carol Oblath, PD Stephen Greenberg.

LP Phillip Paley (Charlie Harrison), Heidi Helmer (Wendy), Amanda Goodwin (Toni), Steven Tash (Scully), Todd Bryant (Doug), Douglas R. Starr (Keith), Leslie Danon (Kathleen), Morgan Englund (Dick).

The barest plot of hapless teen Phillip Paley pursuing dreamgirl Heidi Helmer is used as an excuse to show a lot of curvy girls in the briefest of swimming suits.

174. Beach Girls (1982, Crown International, 91m, c). P Marilyn J. Tenser & Michael D. Castle, D Pat Townsend, W

Patrick Duncan & Phil Groves, PH Michael Murphy, M Michael Lloyd, ED George Bowers.

LP Debra Blee (Sarah), Val Kline (Ginger), Jeana Tomasina (Ducky), James Daughton (Scott), Adam Roarke (Uncle Carl).

This soft-core teenage trash is the bawdy story of a prim teenager Debra Blee who shares her uncle's beach house with two friends during summer vacation.

175. Beach House (1982, New Line, 76m, c). P Marino Amoruso, D John Gallagher, W Amoruso & Gallagher, PH Peter Stein, M C.P. Rith, ED Victor Kanefsky & John Bloomgarden.

LP Kathy McNeil (Cindy), Richard Duggan (Jimmy), Ileana Seidel (Cecile), John Cosola (Anthony), Spence Waugh (Kathy), Paul Anderson (Baby), Adam Roth (Googie), Chris Phillips (Nudge), Jonathan Paley (Drake).

In a nothing movie, teens frolic on the beach, get drunk and listen to rock 'n' roll.

176. Beaches (1988, Buena Vista/Disney, 123m, c). P Bonnie Bruckheimer-Martell, Bette Midler & Margaret Jennings South, D Garry Marshall, W Mary Agnes Donoghue (based on the novel by Iris Rainer Dart), PH Dante Spinotti, M Georges Delerue, ED Richard Halsey, PD Albert Brenner, AD Brenner†, SD Garrett Lewis†.

LP Bette Midler (CC Bloom), Barbara Hershey (Hillary Whitney Essex), John Heard (John Pierce), Spalding Gray (Dr. Richard Milstein), Lainie Kazan (Leona Bloom), James Read (Michael Essex), Grace Johnston (Victoria Essex), Mayim Bialik (CC age 11), Marcie Leeds (Hillary age 11).

The friendship between lower class Bronx Jew Bette Midler and San Francisco blueblood Barbara Hershey stretches from childhood to beyond the grave. It begins when two 11-year-olds, played delightfully by Mayim Bialik and Marcie Leeds, meet by chance one day under the Atlantic City boardwalk. Midler grows up to become a renowned singer and Hershey a successful lawyer. They both bed John Heard, and although he marries one, he ends up with neither.

One becomes terminally ill and wants her friend to take care of her child, but the youngster and the friend have their problems getting along. It's a grand old soap opera. Midler has a couple of fine songs, notably, "Wind Beneath My Wings (You're My Hero)."

177. *The Bear* (1984, Embassy Pictures, 110m, c). P Larry G. Spangler, D Richard Sarafian, W Michael Kane, PH Laszlo George, M Bill Conti, ED Robert Florio, PD George Costello.

LP Gary Busey (Paul "Bear" Bryant), Cynthia Leake (Mary Harmon Bryant), Carmen Thomas (Mae Martin Bryant), Cary Guffey (Grandson Marc), Harry Dean Stanton (Coach Thomas), Jon-Erik Hexum (Pat Trammell), Pat Greenstein (Joe Namath), Michael McGrady (Gene Stallings), William Wesley Neighbors, Jr. (Billy Neighbors), Brett Rice (Don Hutson), Buddy Farmer (Herman Ball).

This film all but confirms sainthood on the legendary Alabama college football coach, Paul "Bear" Bryant, portrayed with flair by Gary Busey. Unfortunately, the production is short on drama and the football scenes are no great shakes either.

178. *The Bear* (1989, Tri-Star, Fr./Canada, 93m, c). P Claude Berri, D Jean-Jacques Annaud, W Gerard Brach (based on "The Grizzly King" by James Oliver Curwood, PH Philippe Rousselot, M Philippe Sarde, ED Noelle Boisson†.

LP Bart (Kaar), Douce (Youk), Jack Wallace (Bill), Tcheky Karyo (Tom), Andre Lacombe (The Dog Handler).

The story isn't much, but the stars are excellent in their interpretations of their roles, considering they are amateurs. Douce is a Kodiak bear, orphaned when his mother is killed in a rockslide. Douce is befriended by Bart, a huge adult male bear. Except possibly for an explicit mating scene between bears, the film is something for the entire family.

179. *Bear Island* (1980, Columbia, GB-Canada, 118m, c). P Peter Snell, D Don Sharp, W Sharp, David Butler & Murray Smith (based on the novel by Alistair MacLean), PH Alan Hume, ED Tony Lower.

LP Donald Sutherland (Frank Lansing), Vanessa Redgrave (Hedi Lindquist), Richard Widmark (Otto Gerran), Christopher Lee (Lechinski), Barbara Parkins (Judith Ruben), Lloyd Bridges (Smithy), Lawrence Dane (Paul Hartman), Patricia Collins (Inge Van Zipper), Michael Reynolds (Heyter).

A United Nations expedition to the Polar region comes up against a group of Nazis, attempting to retrieve a sunken U-boat filled with gold bullion. This thrilless thriller lost a bundle.

180. *Bearskin: An Urban Fairytale* (1989, Film Four Intl./Cinema Action IPC, GB/Portuguese, 95m, c). P Leontine Ruette & Eduardo Guedes, D&W Ann and Eduardo Guedes, PH Michael Coulter, M Michael McEvoy, ED Edward Marnier, AD Jock Scott & Luis Monterio.

LP Tom Waits (Silva), Damon Lowry (Johnny Fortune), Charlotte Coleman (Kate), Julia Britton (Laura), Bill Paterson (Jordan), Isabel Ruth (Mrs. J.), Ian Dury (Barman), David Grant (Broker).

In this self-indulgent blend of chase-thriller and philosophical mish-mash, Damon Lowry, on run from casino hoods, hides out in a Punch and Judy show run by Tom Waits, a man with a past. Lowry's job is to prowl around the show dressed in a bearskin. Somehow or other the hoods get onto him. Waits saves Lowry's life.

181. *The Beast* (1988, Columbia, 109m, c). P John Fiedler, D Kevin Reynolds, W William Mastrosimone (based on his play *Nanawatai*), PH Douglas Milsome, M Mark Isham, ED Peter Boyle, PD Kuli Sander.

LP George Dzundza (Daskal), Jason Patric (Koverchenko), Steven Bauer (Taj), Stephen Baldwin (Golikov), Don Harvey (Kaminski), Kabir Bedi (Akbar), Erick Avari (Samad), Shosh Marciano (Moustafa).

Set in 1981 during the second year of the Soviet occupation of Afghanistan, the film provides an informative look at the Soviet-Afghan conflict, rather than the jingoistic nonsense presented in Sylvester Stallone's *Rambo III*.

182. *The Beast Within* (1982, MGM/United Artists, 90m, c). P Harvey Bernhard & Gabriel Katzka, D Philippe Mora,

W Tom Holland (based on the novel by Edward Levy), PH Jack L. Richards, M Les Baxter, ED Robert Brown & Bert Livitt, PD David M. Haber.

LP Ronny Cox (Eli MacCleary), Bibi Besch (Caroline MacCleary), Paul Clemens (Michael MacCleary), Dan Gordon (Judge Curwin), R.G. Armstrong (Doc), Kitty Moffat (Amanda), L.Q. Jones (Sheriff), Ramsay King (Edwin).

Raped on her honeymoon by a deformed maniac in a Southern swamp, Bibi Besch gives birth to a son who 17 years later has become weird-behaving Paul Clemens. When Mom and Dad take the lad back to the place of his conception, he is transformed into a slimy monster.

183. *The Beastmaster* (1982, MGM/United Artists, 118m, c). P Paul Pepperman & Sylvio Tabet, D Don Coscarelli, W Coscarelli & Pepperman, PH John Alcott, M Lee Holdridge, ED Ray Watts, PD Conrad E. Angone.

LP Marc Singer (Dar), Tanya Roberts (Kiri), Rip Torn (Maax), John Amos (Seth), Josh Milrad (Tal), Rod Loomis (Zed), Ben Hammer (Young Dar's father), Ralph Strait (Sacco), Billy Jacoby (Young Dar).

Because his mother was a cow (yeah, that's what we said), Marc Singer, a Conan with a sense of humor, has a special affinity with animals, which serves him well in his struggles with the evil Rip Torn in an ordinary sword and fantasy film.

184. *The Beat* (1987, Vestron, 98m, c). P Julia Phillips, Jon Klik & Nick Wechsler, D&W Paul Mones, PH Tom DiCillo, M Carter Burwell, ED Elizabeth Kling, PD George Stoll.

LP John Savage (Frank Ellsworth), David Jacobson (Rex Voorhaus Ormine), William McNamara (Billy Kane), Kara Glover (Kate Kane), Stuart Alexander (Doug), Marcus Flanagan (Vis), David McCarthy (Dirt).

David Jacobson, a new kid in a street gang–dominated New York City high school, is at first viewed as a weird nerd, because he spouts beat poetry and lives in his imagination, but somehow he gets through to his classmates. That's more than can be said for the movie with audiences.

185. *Beat Street* (1984, Orion, 105m, c). P David V. Picker & Harry Belafonte, D Stan Lathan, W Andy Davis, David Gilbert & Paul Golding (based on a story by Steven Hager), PH Tom Priestley, Jr., M Belafonte & Arthur Baker, ED Dov Hoenig, PD Patrizia Von Brandenstein.

LP Rae Dawn Chong (Tracy), Guy Davis (Kenny), Jon Chardiet (Ramon), Leon W. Grant (Chollie), Saundra Santiago (Carmen), Mary Alice (Cora), Shawn Elliot (Domingo), Jim Borrelli (Monte), Dean Elliott (Henry).

Trying to cash-in on the Break-dance phenomenon, the film is merely a series of musical numbers with just enough plot to get from one number to the next.

186. *Beauty and the Beast* (1987, Cannon, 93m, c). P Menahem Golan & Yoram Globus, D Eugene Marner, W Carole Lucia Satrina (based on the story by Madame De Villeneuve), PH Avi Karpick, M Lori McKelvey, ED Tova Ascher, PD Marek Dobrowolski.

LP Rebecca DeMornay (Beauty), John Savage (Beast/Prince), Yossi Graber (Father), Michael Schneider (Kuppel), Carmela Marner (Bettina), Ruth Harlap (Isabella), Joseph Bee (Oliver).

Geared towards the kiddies, this version of the classic story isn't in the league of Jean Cocteau's 1946 masterpiece and won't impress viewers as much as the romantic TV series starring Linda Hamilton as Beauty and Ron Perlman as a New York Beast.

187. *Bedroom Eyes* (1986, Canada, Aquarius Releasing, 90m, c). P Robert Lantos & Stephen J. Roth, D William Fruet, W Michael Alan Eddy, PH Miklos Lente, ED Tony Lower.

LP Kenneth Gilman (Harry), Dayle Haddon (Alixe), Barbara Law (Jobeth), Cristine Cattell (Kit).

Voyeur Kenneth Gilman must prove his innocence when the beautiful woman he watches from his window each night is murdered.

188. *The Bedroom Window* (1987, DEG, 112m, c). P Martha Schumacher, D&W Curtis Hanson (based on the novel *The Witnesses* by Anne Holden), PH Gil Taylor, M Michael Shrieve, Patrick

Gleeson & Felix Mendlessohn, ED Scott Conrad, PD Ron Foreman.

LP Steve Guttenberg (Terry Lambert), Elizabeth McGovern (Denise), Isabelle Huppert (Sylvia Wentworth), Paul Shenar (Collin Wentworth), Frederick Coffin (Detective Jessup), Wallace Shawn (Defense Attorney).

Yuppie architect Steve Guttenberg tries to do the gentlemanly thing when his boss' wife sees a murder—from his window. He reports to the police that he has seen the murder and immediately becomes the number one suspect. Despite the presence of Guttenberg, it's not a comedy, but it's not much of a thriller either.

189. *Beetlejuice* (1988, Warner, 92m, c). P Michael Bender, Larry Wilson & Richard Hashimoto, D Tim Burton, W Michael McDowell & Warren Skaaren (based on a story by McDowell and Larry Wilson), PH Thomas Ackerman, M Danny Elfman, ED Jane Kurson, PD Bo Welch, MK Ve Neill, Steve LaPorte & Robert Short*.

LP Michael Keaton (Betelgeuse), Alec Baldwin (Adam), Geena Davis (Barbara), Jeffrey Jones (Charles Deetz), Catherine O'Hara (Delia Deetz), Winona Ryder (Lydia Deetz), Sylvia Sidney (Juno).

Married New England ghosts Alec Baldwin and Geena Davis live happily in their house until a family of New York yuppies, Jeffrey Jones, Catherine O'Hara and Winona Ryder, move in and start redecorating. Unable to scare the tasteless family away, they ask the dangerously evil Michael Keaton for help. But the new tenants are unmovable and even plan to charge admission to their haunted home.

190. *Beginner's Luck* (1986, New World, 85m, c). P Caroline Mouris, D Frank Mouris, W Caroline & Frank Mouris, PH Ayne Coffey, M Richard Lavsky, ED Ray Anne School.

LP Sam Rush (Hunter), Riley Steiner (Tech), Charles Homet (Aris), Kate Talbot (Bethany), Mickey Coburn (Babs), Phil Kilbourne (Willem), Stephen Weagle (Don/Ronnie), Cynthia Weagle (Stella/Bonnie).

Sam Rush, an uptight virgin law student, has that little problem ironed-out by his sexy upstairs neighbors Riley Steiner and Charles Homet, who introduce him to a funny ménage à trois.

191. *The Being* (1983, BFV, 79m, c). P William Osco, D&W Jackie Kong, PH Robert Ebinger, M Don Preston, ED David Newhouse.

LP Martin Landau (Garson Jones), Jose Ferrer (Mayor), Ruth Buzzi (Mayor's Wife), Dorothy Malone (Marge), Rexx Coltrane (Mortimer), Marianne Gordon Rogers (Laurie), Kent Perkins (Dudley).

Strange occurrences are happening in Pottsville, Idaho. They all seem to date from the time a nuclear dump-site was established just outside of town. Would the U.S. government place its citizens in danger? Of course not, but watch out for the bug-eyed monsters.

192. *The Believers* (1987, Orion, 114m, c). P John Schlesinger, Michael Childers & Beverly Camhe, D Schlesinger, W Mark Frost (based on the novel *The Religion* by Nicholas Conde), PH Robby Muller, M J. Peter Robinson, ED Peter Honess, PD Simon Holland.

LP Martin Sheen (Dr. Cal Jamison), Helen Shaver (Jessica Halliday), Harley Cross (Chris Jamison), Robert Loggia (Lt. Sean McTaggert), Elizabeth Wilson (Kate Maslow), Richard Masur (Marty Wertheimer).

While investigating the ritual stabbings of young boys in New York City, recently widowed psychologist Martin Sheen discovers that it's the work of a voodoo sect. Sheen's son Harley Cross has been targeted for their next victim and they expect Sheen to deliver Cross to them. The film contains graphic violence, gory effects and, oh yes, sexual situations.

193. *Belizaire the Cajun* (1986, Skouras Pictures, 103m, c). P Allan L. Durand & Glen Pitre, D&W Pitre, PH Richard Bowen, M Michel Doucet, ED Paul Trejo, PD Randall LaBry.

LP Armand Assante (Belizaire Breaux), Gail Youngs (Alida Thibodaux), Michael Schoeffling (Hypolite Leger), Stephen McHattie (James Willoughby), Will Patton (Matthew Perry), Nancy Barrett (Rebecca), Loulan Pitre (Sheriff), Andre DeLaunay (Dolsin), Robert Duvall (Preacher).

Armand Assante, faith healer and medicine man, lives in the Louisiana Cajun country in the years following the Civil War. It's an interesting but not totally successful attempt to examine one of the country's least understood minorities.

194. *Bell Diamond* (1987, Light, 96m, c). P,D,W&PH Jon Jost, M Jon English & Jost, ED Jost.

LP Marshall Gaddis (Jeff Dolan), Sarah Wyss (Cathy Dolan), Terrilyn Williams (Hailey), Scott Andersen (Scott), Pat O'Connor (The Boss), Kristi Jean Hager (Laura), Hal Waldrup (Mick), Dan Cornell (Danny).

Unemployed Butte, Montana, mine worker Marshall Gaddis, left sterile by exposure to Agent Orange in Vietnam, loses his wife Sarah Wyss because she wants a baby. After she leaves him, he does nothing but sit in front of the TV and drink beer. He contemplates suicide, but when without warning Wyss returns, obviously pregnant, he's happy.

195. *Bellman and True* (1988, GB, 118m, c). P Michael Wearing, D Richard Loncraine, W Desmond Lowden & Loncraine (based on a novel by Lowden), PH Ken Westbury, M Colin Towns, ED Paul Green, PD John Bunker.

LP Bernard Hill (Hiller), Kieran O'Brien (The Boy), Richard Hope (Salto), Frances Tomelty (Anna), Derek Newark (Guv'nor), John Kavanagh (Donkey), Ken Bones (Gort), Arthur Whybrow (Peterman), Peter Howell (Bellman).

Computer expert Bernard Hill and his son Kieran O'Brien are kidnapped by gangsters planning an elaborate bank heist. He's to break the bank's alarm system.

Bells see Murder by Phone

196. *The Belly of an Architect* (1987, Hemdale, GB/Italy, 108m, c). P Colin Callender & Walter Donohue, D&W Peter Greenaway, PH Sacha Vierny, M Wim Mertens & Glenn Branca, ED John Wilson.

LP Brian Dennehy (Stourley Kracklite), Chloe Webb (Louisa Kracklite), Lambert Wilson (Caspasian Speckler), Vanni Corbellini (Frederico), Sergio Fantoni (Io Speckler), Stefania Casini (Flavia Speckler), Alfredo Varelli (Julio Ficcone), Geoffrey Copleston (Caspetti).

When architect Brian Dennehy arrives in Rome where he's to curate an exhibition, he notices the mutual interest between his pregnant wife Chloe Webb and his co-director Lambert Wilson. Dennehy becomes concerned not only that Wilson is having an affair with his wife but is also poisoning him. Wilson is such a swine, it's a treat for the audience when Dennehy finally slugs him.

197. *Below the Belt* (1980, Atlantic, 91m, c). P&D Robert Fowler, W Fowler & Sherry Sonnett (based on the novel *To Smithereens* by Rosalyn Drexler), PH Alan Metzger, M Jerry Fielding, ED Steven Zaillian.

LP Regina Baff (Rosa Rubinsky), Mildred Burke (Herself), John C. Becher (Promoter), Annie McGreevey (The Beautiful Boomerang), Jane O'Brien (Terrible Tommy), Sierra Pecheur (Verne Vavoom), Shirley Stoler (Trish).

It took six years for this film to attain a modest release in 1980. New York waitress Regina Baff looks for her place in the sun by joining the grunt and groan female wrestling circuit. It's no more ridiculous as entertainment than the World Wrestling Federation.

198. *Benji the Hunted* (1987, Buena Vista, 88m, c). P Ben Vaughn, D&W Joe Camp, PH Don Reddy, M Euel & Betty Box, ED Karen Thorndike.

LP Benji (Himself), Red Steagall (Hunter), Nancy Francis (Newscaster), Mike Francis (TV Cameraman), Frank Inn (Himself).

As dog movies goes, this is no mongrel. When talented Benji is separated from his trainer Frank Inn after a fishing accident, the cute mutt swims ashore and finds himself in mountain wilds where he becomes a protector of orphaned cougar cubs. Benji endures the hardships of the wilderness and takes good care of his adopted charges. The best part: after the first 10 minutes there are no humans in the movie.

Berry Gordon's the Last Dragon see The Last Dragon

199. *Berserker* (1988, Shapiro, 85m, c). P Jules Rivera, D&W Jef Richard, PH Henning Schellerup, ED Marcus Manton, M Chuck Francour & Gary Griffin.

LP Joseph Alan Johnson, Valerie Sheldon, Greg Dawson, George Flower.

Teens arriving at a lonely site for a weekend camping trip of sex and drugs are menaced by the spirits of a "berserker," a Viking warrior so strong that he took on bears in hand-to-paw combat and had to be chained in the bow of his longboat because he was so fierce.

200. *Bert Rigby, You're a Fool* (1989, Warner, 95m, c). P George Shapiro, D&W Carl Reiner, PH Jan De Bont, M Ralph Burns, ED Bud Molin, PD Terrence Marsh.

LP Robert Lindsay (Bert Rigby), Cathryn Bradshaw (Laurel), Robbie Coltrane (Sid Trample), Jackie Gayle (I.I. Perlestein), Anne Bancroft (Mrs. Perlestein), Corbin Bernsen (Jim Shirley), Bruno Kirby (Kyle De Forrest).

Robert Lindsay, the original star of Broadway's *Me and My Gal,* a music-loving mineworker, is forced to seek his fortune elsewhere after a strike closes down the coal mine. He enters a talent contest, where he hopes to wow them with his singing, but a nosebleed makes him a comedy triumph who wins first prize. He makes it to California, but becomes infamous rather than famous for his performing talent when he sets fire to Impressionist paintings.

201. *Best Defense* (1984, Paramount, 94m, c). P Gloria Katz, D Willard Huyck, W Katz & Huyck (based on the novel *Easy and Hard Ways Out* by Robert Grossbach), PH Don Peterman, M Patrick Williams, ED Sidney Wolinsky & Michael A. Stevenson, PD Peter Jamison.

LP Dudley Moore (Wylie Cooper), Eddie Murphy (Landry), Kate Capshaw (Laura), George Dzundza (Loparino), Helen Shaver (Claire Lewis), Mark Arnott (Brank), Peter Michael Geotz (Frank Joyner), Tom Noonan (Holtzman).

Dudley Moore and Eddie Murphy's bizarre talents can't save this absurd story of engineer Moore's attempt to pass off the plans for a "DYP gyro" as his. Murphy, an American lieutenant, chosen to test the weapon, accidentally drives his tank into the middle of a war between Iraq and Kuwait. The audience's best defense is to avoid this bomb at all costs.

202. *Best Friends* (1982, Warner, 116m, c). P Norman Jewison & Patrick Palmer, D Jewison, W Valerie Curtin & Barry Levinson, PH Jordan Cronenweth, M Michel Legrand, ED Don Zimmerman, SONG "How Do You Keep the Music Playing?" by Michel Legrand, Alan Bergman & Marilyn Bergman†.

LP Burt Reynolds (Richard Babson), Goldie Hawn (Paula McCullen), Jessica Tandy (Eleanor McCullen), Barnard Hughes (Tim McCullen), Audra Lindley (Ann Babson), Keenan Wynn (Tom Babson), Ron Silver (Larry Weisman), Richard Libertini (Jorge Medina).

After years of living and working together, screenwriters Burt Reynolds and Goldie Hawn decide to marry. They find their collaboration and relationship falling apart as they make a cross-country pilgrimage to meet their respective in-laws.

203. *The Best Little Whorehouse in Texas* (1982, Universal, 114m, c). P Thomas Miller, Edward Milkis & Robert Boyett, D Colin Higgins, W Larry L. King, Peter Masterson, Higgins (based on the play), PH William A. Fraker, ED Pembroke J. Herring, David Bretherton, Jack Hofstra, Nicholas Eliopoulous & Walter Hanneman, CH Tony Stevens, M/L Carol Hall, Dolly Parton & Pat Williams.

LP Burt Reynolds (Sheriff Ed Earl Dodd), Dolly Parton (Mona Strangely), Dom DeLuise (Melvin), Charles Durning† (Governor), Jim Nabors (Deputy Fred), Robert Mandan (Senator Wingwood), Lois Nettleton (Dulcie Mae), Theresa Merritt (Jewel), Noah Beery (Edsel), Raleigh Bond (Mayor).

Since the musical-play wasn't any great shakes, how could the producers think the story would make a successful movie-musical? Burt Reynolds is his usual boring good-ole boy, Dolly Parton busts out all over, Dom DeLuise is a disgusting faggish parody of himself and only Charles Durning does himself credit, singing and dancing to a politician's theme song "Sidestep."

204. *Best of the Best* (1989, Taurus, 95m, c). P Phillip Rhee & Peter E. Strauss, D Bob Radler, W Paul Levine (based on a story by Rhee & Levine), PH Doug Ryan, M Paul Gilman, ED William Hoy.

LP Eric Roberts (Alex), James Earl Jones (Coach Couzo), Sally Kirkland (Catherine Wade), Phillip Rhee (Tommy), Christopher Penn (Travis), John Dye (Virgil), David Agresta (Sonny).

Phillip Rhee, who co-produced and wrote the story of this dull martial arts film (perhaps a bit of redundancy there), is a Korean-American member of the American martial arts team which is headed for a competition in Korea. While there Rhee plans to settle a score with the Korean champ who killed Rhee's brother.

205. *The Best of Times* (1986, Universal, 105m, c). P Gordon Carroll, D Roger Spottiswoode, W Ron Shelton, PH Charles F. Wheeler, M Arthur B. Rubinstein, ED Garth Craven, AD Anthony Brockliss.

LP Robin Williams (Jack Dundee), Kurt Russell (Reno Hightower), Pamela Reed (Gigi Hightower), Holly Palance (Elly Dundee), Donald Moffat (The Colonel), Margaret Whitton (Darla), M. Emmet Walsh (Charlie), Kathleen Freeman (Rosie), Tony Plana (Chico), Kirk Cameron (Teddy).

After living for 15 years with the shame of having fumbled the pass which cost his high school victory against their archrivals, Robin Williams decides the only way to win the self-respect of his townspeople is to replay the game. Somehow he arranges for the belated rematch — but who really cares about the outcome, or for that matter, a game which happened 15 years earlier? Football fans, that's who!

206. *Best Seller* (1987, Orion, 110m, c). P Carter De Haven, D John Flynn, W Larry Cohen, PH Fred Murphy, M Jay Ferguson, ED David Rosenbloom, PD Gene Rudolf.

LP James Woods (Cleve), Brian Dennehy (Det. Lt. Dennis Meechum), Victoria Tennant (Roberta Gillian), Allison Balson (Holly Meechum), Paul Shenar (David Madlock), George Coe (Graham), Anne Pitoniak (Mrs. Foster), Mary Carver (Cleve's Mother), Sully Boyar (Monks), Kathleen Lloyd (Annie).

Violent psychopathic former hit man James Woods teams up with cop turned author Brian Dennehy to tell Woods'

story of his work for prominent businessman Shenar whose underworld ties have been covered-up. It's a violent movie, but Woods and Dennehy, two outstanding character actors, give credible performances.

207. *Betrayal* (1983, 20th Century-Fox, GB, 95m, c). P Sam Spiegel, D David Jones, W Harold Pinter† (based on his play), PH Mike Fash, M Dominic Muldowney, ED John Bloom, PD Eileen Diss.

LP Jeremy Irons (Jerry), Patricia Hodge (Emma), Ben Kingsley (Robert), Avril Edgar (Mrs. Banks), Ray Marioni (Waiter), Caspar Norman (Sam).

The story of book publisher Ben Kingsley, his wife Patricia Hodge and her lover Jeremy Irons is told backwards. The acting is superb, but one must note that the ending, which of course is the beginning, is anticlimactic — or would that be postclimactic?

208. *Betrayed* (1988, MGM/United Artists, 123m, c). P Irwin Winkler, D Constantin Costa-Gavras, W Joe Eszterhas, PH Patrick Blossier, M Bill Conti, ED Joele Van Effenterre, PD Patrizia Von Brandenstein.

LP Debra Winger (Katie Phillips/Cathy Weaver), Tom Berenger (Gary Simmons), John Heard (Michael Carnes), Betsy Blair (Gladys Simmons), John Mahoney (Shorty), Ted Levine (Wes), Jeffrey DeMunn (Flynn), Albert Hall (Al Sanders), David Clennon (Jack Carpenter), Robert Swan (Dean), Richard Libertini (Sam Kraus), Maria Valdez (Rachel Simmons), Brian Bosak (Joey Simmons).

FBI agent Debra Winger is sent to the Farm Belt to investigate the murder of a controversial Chicago radio personality by far right extremists. The trail leads the undercover agent to farmer Tom Berenger. Unfortunately, she falls in love with him (even murdering bigots have their tender sides). Through him she encounters all the far-right crazies that anyone would wish to avoid, KKK members, Nazi survivalists, and other White Power fanatics. When Berenger is appointed the hit man of a presidential candidate, Winger is forced to gun down her man, but another gunman gets the politician. This political thriller is pretty strong stuff from relentless director Costa-Gavras, but the most frightening point is that these good ole boys exist in large numbers in the U.S., and except when involved in their struggles against blacks, Jews and liberals, they appear to be decent hard-working folks.

209. *Better Late Than Never* (1983, Warner, 87m, c). P Jack Haley, Jr. & David Niven, Jr., D&W Bryan Forbes, PH Claude Lecomte & Gerry Fisher, M Henry Mancini, ED Phillip Shaw, PD Peter Mullins.

LP David Niven (Nick), Art Carney (Charley), Maggie Smith (Anderson), Kimberley Partridge (Bridget), Catherine Hicks (Sable), Lionel Jeffries (Hargreaves), Melissa Prophet (Marlene).

David Niven and Art Carney are two aging scamps trying to convince ten-year-old poor-little-rich-girl Kimberley Partridge into choosing one of them as her grandfather. Her grandmother slept with both of them years ago to produce Partridge's parent, but which of them was the father was never established. The performances of Niven, Carney and Maggie Smith are better than the movie.

210. *Better Off Dead* (1985, Warner, 98m, c). P Michael Jaffe, D&W Savage Steve Holland, PH Isidore Mankofsky, M Rupert Hine, ED Alan Balsam, PD Herman Zimmerman.

LP John Cusack (Lane Myer), David Ogden Stiers (Al Myer), Diane Franklin (Monique Junet), Kim Darby (Jenny Myer), Amanda Wyss (Beth Truss), Curtis Armstrong (Charles De Mer), Vincent Schiavelli (Mr. Kerber).

Poor John Cusack has just lost the girl of his dreams Amanda Wyss to a jock and he feels he's better off dead. However, he finds happiness with French exchange student Diane Franklin and beats the jock in a ski race. The film has little sketches of great hilarity interspersed with the usual teenage exploitation nonsense.

211. *Between Wars* (1985, Satori, Australia, 97m, c). P&D Michael Thornhill, W Frank Moorhouse, PH Russell Boyd, M Bill Hasler, Ramola Constantina & Adrian Ford, ED Max Lemon, PD Bill Hutchinson.

LP Corin Redgrave (Dr. Edward Trenbow), Arthur Dignam (Dr. Peter Avante), Judy Morris (Deborah Trenbow), Patricia Leahy (Marguerite Saunders), Gunter Meisner (Dr. Karl Schneider), Brian James (Father), Jan Winchester (Mother).

Made 11 years earlier, this undistinguished film from Down Under details the travails of pioneering Australian psychoanalyst Dr. Edward Trenbow, played by Corin Redgrave. Redgrave treats his first patients, shellshocked soldiers of World War I, learns from Gunter Meisner, who has studied with Freud, and has as his first patient nymphomaniac Patricia Leahy, who always dresses in red.

212. *Beverly Hills Brats* (1989, Taurus, 91m, c). P Terry Moore & Jerry Rivers, D Dimitri Sotirakis, W Linda Silverthorn (based on a story by Moore & Rivers), PH Harry Mathias, M Barry Goldberg, ED Jerry Frizell, PD George Costello.

LP Burt Young (Clive), Martin Sheen (Jeffrey Miller), Terry Moore (Veronica Miller), Peter Billingsley (Scooter), Ramon Sheen (Sterling), Cathy Podewell (Tiffany).

Eminent plastic surgeon Martin Sheen lives in luxury with his wife Terry Moore and three kids in opulent Beverly Hills. One of the kids, Peter Billingsley, feels unloved, and arranges for would-be burglar Burt Young to pretend to kidnap him so he'll get some attention. Meant to be a comedy, the film provides almost no laughs.

213. *Beverly Hills Cop* (1984, Paramount, 105m, c). P Don Simpson & Jerry Bruckheimer, D Martin Brest, W Daniel Petrie, Jr. (based on a story by Petrie & Danilo Bach†), PH Bruce Surtees, M Harold Faltermeyer, ED Billy Weber & Arthur Coburn, PD Angelo Graham.

LP Eddie Murphy (Axel Foley), Judge Reinhold (Billy Rosewood), John Ashton (Sgt. Taggart), Lisa Eilbacher (Jenny Summers), Ronny Cox (Lt. Bogomil), Steven Berkoff (Victor Maitland), James Russo (Mikey Tandino), Jonathan Banks (Zack), Stephen Elliott (Chief Hubbard).

Eddie Murphy is a very funny fellow, right? Would you believe that Sylvester

Stallone was originally scheduled to make the picture? Jive-talking engaging Detroit cop Murphy traces the killers of a friend to Beverly Hills, where he teams with an Abbott and Costello-like police team of Judge Reinhold and John Ashton. The three nearly destroy all of California before putting away evil British crime czar Steven Berkoff. Murphy's language is too raw for children, titillating for the immature, and tiresome for adults for whom profanity is not knee-slapping humor.

214. *Beverly Hills Cop II* (1987, Paramount, 102m, c). P Don Simpson & Jerry Bruckheimer, D Tony Scott, W Larry Ferguson & Warren Skaaren (based on a story by Eddie Murphy & Robert D. Wachs from characters created by Danilo Bach & Daniel Petrie), PH Jeffrey L. Kimball, M Harold Faltermeyer, ED Billy Weber, Chris Lebenzon & Michael Tronick, PD Ken Davis, SONG "Shakedown" by Harold Faltermeyer, Keith Forsey & Bob Seger†.

LP Eddie Murphy (Axel Foley), Judge Reinhold (Billy Rosewood), Jurgen Prochnow (Maxwell Dent), Ronny Cox (Andrew Bogomil), John Ashton (John Taggart), Brigitte Nielsen (Karla Fry), Allen Garfield (Harold Lutz), Dean Stockwell (Charles "Chip" Cain), Paul Reiser (Jeffrey Friedman).

Eddie Murphy acts like he's Michael Jordan. He expects everyone to clear out so he can score. His enemies, villains Jurgen Prochnow and Dean Stockwell, as well as stupid police chief Allen Garfield, are merely pawns for him to outsmart. Murphy is back in Beverly Hills, as profane as ever and with Brigitte Nielsen on the scene, he's able to add rapid fire sexist remarks to his repertoire. We must remember that Murphy is very young and very successful. Hopefully he will get back to being funny.

215. *Beverly Hills Vamp* (1989, American-Independent Prods., 89m, c). P Grant Austin Waldman, D Fred Olen Ray, W Ernest D. Farino, PH Stephen Ashley Blake, M Chuck Cirino, ED Chris Roth.

LP Eddie Deezen (Kyle Carpenter), Britt Ekland (Madam Cassandra), Tim Conway, Jr. (Brock), Jay Richardson (Aaron Pendleton), Tom Shell (Russel), Debra Lamb (Jessica), Jillian Kesner (Claudia), Ralph Lucas (Balthzar).

This spoof of vampire horror movies is filled with in-jokes parodying low-budget filmmaking. Somehow nerdish Eddie Deezen survives a night with vampire call girls which takes the life of two of his friends.

216. *Beyond Evil* (1980, Score III, 94m, c). P David Baughn & Herb Freed, D Freed, W Paul Ross & Freed (based on a story by Baughn), PH Ken Plotin, ED Rick Westover.

LP John Saxon (Larry Andrews), Lynda Day George (Barbara Andrews), Michael Dante (Del), Mario Milano (Albanos), Janice Lynde (Alma Martin), David Opatoshu (Dr. Solomon), Anne Marisse (Leia), Zitto Kazaan (Esteban).

John Saxon and his wife Lynda Day George arrive on a tropical island for a working honeymoon. They are put up in a luxurious haunted mansion by George's ex-husband. Ghost Janice Lynde has plans on possessing George.

217. *Beyond Reasonable Doubt* (1980, Endeavour, New Zealand, 127m, c). P John Barnett, D John Laring, W David Yallop, PH Alun Bollinger, M Dave Fraser, ED Michael Horton.

LP David Hemmings (Insp. Hutton), John Hargreaves (Arthur Allen Thomas), Martyn Sanderson (Lem Dembler), Tony Barry (Det. John Hughes), Grant Tilly (David Morris), Diana Rowan (Vivien Thomas), Ian Watkin (Kevin Ryan).

It's a chilling true story of a murder mystery which divides New Zealand over the innocence or guilt of farmer John Hargreaves, the only suspect in a double murder.

218. *Beyond the Doors* (1989, Omni-Leisure, 116m, c). D&W Larry Buchanan, PH Nicholas Joseph von Sternberg, M Jeffrey Danna & David Shorey, ED uncredited, AD Shay Austin.

LP Gregory Allen Chatman (Jimi Hendrix), Riba Meryl (Janis Joplin), Bryan Wolf (Jim Morrison), Sandy Kenyon (Alex Stanley), Susanne Barnes (She-Morrison's Girl Friend), Steven Tice (Frank Stanley), Toni Sawyer (Mrs.

Stanley), Jennifer Wilde (Ellen), Richard Kennedy (J. Edgar Hoover).

Did you know that the government put "hits" out on rock singers Jimi Hendrix, Janis Joplin and Jim Morrison? Well that's the conspiracy theory of director-writer Larry Buchanan in his 1983-made film, which headed direct to video. The story goes that like Socrates, the trio were ordered killed because of their great influence on young people.

219. *Beyond the Fog* (1981, International, GB, 86m, c, aka *Tower of Evil; Horror on Snape Island*). P Richard Gordon, D&W Jim O'Connolly (based on a story by George Baxt), PH Desmond Dickinson, M Ken Jones, ED Henry Richardson.

LP Bryant Haliday (Brent), Jill Haworth (Rose), Anna Palk (Nora), Jack Watson (Hamp), Mark Edwards (Adam), Derek Fowlds (Dan), John Hamill (Gary), Candace Glendenning (Penny), Dennis Price (Bakewell).

Archaeologists exploring an island are murdered by a mad lighthouse keeper. The acting is horrible in this sleazy movie.

Beyond the Gate* see *Human Experiments

220. *Beyond the Limit* (1983, Paramount, 102m, c, aka *The Honorary Consul*). P Norma Heyman, D John MacKenzie, W Christopher Hampton (based on the novel *The Honorary Consul* by Graham Greene), PH Phil Meheux, M Stanley Myers & Richard Harvey, ED Stuart Baird.

LP Michael Caine (Charlie Fortnum), Richard Gere (Dr. Plarr), Bob Hoskins (Col. Perez), A. Martinez (Aquino), Geoffrey Palmer (Ambassador), Elpidia Carrillo (Clara), Joaquim De Almeida (Leon), Domingo Ambriz (Diego).

Richard Gere helps revolutionaries kidnap the British Consul Michael Caine who they mistake for the American Ambassador. Gere is responsible for the pregnancy of Caine's wife as well. It just isn't Caine's day, the revolutionaries promise to execute him if the usual political prisoners aren't released, even if he is the wrong hostage. Dumb!

221. *Beyond the Reef* (1981, Universal, 91m, c). P Raffaella DeLaurentiis, D

Frank C. Clark, W Louis LaRusso II & Jim Carabatsos (based on Clement Richer's novel *Tikoyo and His Shark*), PH Sam Martin, M Francis Lai, ED Ian Crafford & John Jympson.

LP Dayton Ka'ne (Tikayo), Maren Jensen (Diana), Kathleen Swan (Milly), Keahi Farden (Jeff), Oliverio Maciel Diaz (Manidu), George Tapare (Hawaiian), David Nakuna (Mischima), Robert Atamu (Maku).

South Seas youngsters Dayton Ka'ne and Maren Jensen make friends with a man-eating shark that guards a cache of sacred black pearls. Ka'ne and Jensen aren't quite as good actors as were Jon Hall and Dorothy Lamour, who might have made the movie some 40 years ago. It's a pretty stupid flick.

222. *Beyond Therapy* (1987, New World, 93m, c). P Steven M. Haft, D Robert Altman, W Christopher Durang & Altman (based on the play by Durang), PH Pierre Mignot, M Gabriel Yared, ED Steve Dunn & Jennifer Auge, PD Stephen Altman.

LP Julie Hagerty (Prudence), Jeff Goldblum (Bruce), Glenda Jackson (Charlotte), Tom Conti (Dr. Stuart Framingham), Christopher Guest (Bob), Genevieve Page (Zizi), Cris Campion (Andrew, Waiter), Sandrine Dumas (Cindy), Bertrand Bonvoison (Le Gerant).

Robert Altman fails with this farce about the absurdity of psychotherapy. Bisexual Jeff Goldblum, tiring of his flaming faggot boyfriend Christopher Guest, puts an ad in a personal column and meets uptight Julie Hagerty. They don't communicate and each goes to their respective shrinks to find out why not. Nothing is resolved in a series of dull episodes.

223. *Biddy* (1983, Sands Film Productions, GB, 86m, c). P Richard Goodwin, D&W Christine Edzard, PH Alec Mills, M Michael Sanvoisin.

LP Celia Bannerman (Biddy), Patricia Napier (Mother), Sam Ghazoros (Tom), Luke Duckett (Tom), David Napier (Tom), Kate Elphick (Mathilde), Sabine Goodwin (Mathilde), Emily Hone (Mathilde), Sally Ashby (Susan).

It's the dull and uneventful story of a

children's nanny during the Victorian era.

224. *Big* (1988, 20th Century–Fox, 104m, c). P James L. Brooks & Robert Greenhut, D Penny Marshall, W Gary Ross & Anne Spielberg†, PH Barry Sonnenfeld, M Howard Shore, ED Barry Malkin, PD Santo Loquasto.

LP Tom Hanks† (Josh Baskin), Elizabeth Perkins (Susan Lawrence), Robert Loggia ("Mac" MacMillan), John Heard (Paul Davenport), Jared Rushton (Billy Kopeche), David Moscow (Young Josh Baskin), Mercedes Ruehl (Mrs. Baskin), Josh Clark (Mr. Baskin), Kimberlee M. Davis (Cynthia Benson), Oliver Block (Freddie Benson).

Tom Hanks comes of age both as a comedian and an actor in his sensitive and charming portrayal of a 30-year-old in the body of a 13-year-old. The notion of body-switches has been done to death recently, but this one works. Hanks is just a larger version of his other self, David Moscow, but he has the maturity of the youngster which causes Elizabeth Perkins no end of trouble when she becomes romantically interested in Hanks. Hanks is a guileless delight. Excellent performances are also given by the very talented character actor Robert Loggia as Hanks' boss and Jared Rushton as his 13-year-old friend.

225. *Big Bad Mama II* (1987, Concorde, 83m, c). P Roger Corman, D Jim Wynorski, W R.G. Robertson & Wynorski, PH Robert C. New, M Chuck Cirino, ED Noah Blough & Nancy Nuttall.

LP Angie Dickinson (Wilma McClatchie), Robert Culp (Daryl Pearson), Danielle Brisebois (Billie Jean McClatchie), Julie McCullogh (Polly McClatchie), Bruce Glover (Crawford), Jeff Yagher (Jordon Crawford), Jacque Lynn Colton (Alma).

Angie Dickinson reprises her 1974 role as a tough-talking, machine-gun toting Texas bandit of the 30s. When villain Bruce Glover has Dickinson's husband murdered, she and her two buxom daughters, Danielle Brisebois and Julie McCullogh, set out to get revenge. There's plenty of violence and skin in this one.

226. *The Big Blue* (1989, Angelika, 100m, c). P Yoram Mandel, D Andrew Horn, W Jim Neu (based on a story by Andrew Horn), PH Carl Teitelbaum, M Jill Jaffe, ED Ila von Hasperg, AD Ann Stuhler.

LP David Brisbin (Jack Kidd), Taunie VreNon (Carmen), John Erdman (Max), Jim Neu (Howard Monroe), Sheila McLaughlin (Myrna Monroe), Bill Rice (Arthur Murray), Jose Rafael Arango (Ramone).

The film fails in its attempt to resurrect the film noir subgenre. Sheila McLaughlin hires private eye David Brisbin to tail her husband Jim Neu, whom she suspects of infidelity. No way, he's only involved in a drug deal; but this leads Brisbin to bed with Taunie VreNon, girl friend of drug dealer John Erdman. Everyone betrays everyone else until the final showdown between Brisbin and Erdman.

227. *The Big Brawl* (1980, Warner, 95m, c). P Fred Weintraub & Terry Morse, Jr., D&W Robert Clouse (based on a story by Clouse & Weintraub), PH Robert Jessup, M Lalo Schifrin, ED George Greenville.

LP Jackie Chan (Jerry), Jose Ferrer (Dominici), Kristine De Bell (Nancy), Mako (Herbert), Ron Max (Leggetti), David Sheiner (Morgan), Rosalind Chao (Mae), Lenny Montana (John), Pat Johnson (Carl).

In the Chicago of the 30s, Jose Ferrer hires martial-arts expert Jackie Chan to fight in a Big Brawl, with the winner taking all. This kick and yell movie has the benefit of some humor.

228. *Big Business* (1988, Buena Vista, 94m, c). P Steve Tisch & Michael Peyser, D Jim Abrahams, W Dori Pierson & Marc Rubel, PH Dean Cundey, M Lee Holdridge, ED Harry Keramidas, PD William Sandell.

LP Bette Midler (Sadie Shelton/Sadie Ratliff), Lily Tomlin (Rose Shelton/Rose Ratliff), Fred Ward (Roone Dimmick), Edward Herrmann (Graham Sherbourne), Michele Placido (Fabio Alberici), Daniel Gerroll (Chuck), Barry Primus (Michael), Michael Gross (Dr. Jay Marshall).

In another casting of the irrepressible Divine Miss Bette Midler with an actress as different from her as possible, the producers thought a mix-up with Lily Tomlin might be fun. They believed having two

Midlers and two Tomlins would be even a bigger kick. They were wrong. Playing two sets of twins mixed-up at birth, Midler and Tomlin are given opportunities to show two different comedy characters. None of the four in this ridiculous comedy of errors is the least bit funny. Only the sassy Midler, fans have come to expect, is even close to being an amusing personality. Tomlin seems a big zero in both her parts.

229.   *The Big Chill*†   (1983, Columbia, 103m, c). P Michael Shamberg, D Lawrence Kasdan, W Kasdan & Barbara Benedek†, PH John Bailey, ED Carol Littleton, PD Ida Random.

LP Glenn Close† (Sarah), Tom Berenger (Sam), William Hurt (Nick), Jeff Goldblum (Michael), Mary Kay Place (Meg), Kevin Kline (Harold), Meg Tilly (Chloe), Don Galloway (Richard), Jo-Beth Williams (Karen), James Gillis (Minister), Ken Place (Peter).

The superb cast of this film gathers together to reminisce and comfort each other after the suicide of one of their closest college-age friends. There is a fine balance of humor and sentiment, even though one has a feeling that the parts are greater and better than the whole. The film meant a great deal to those who came to age in the 60s, but it's not quite clear what exactly it means. Kevin Costner was cast as the one who commits suicide but his part ended-up on the cutting room floor.

230.   *The Big Easy*   (1987, Columbia, 108m, c). P Stephen Friedman, D Jim McBride, W Daniel Petrie, Jr. & Jack Baran, PH Affonso Beato, M Brad Fiedel, ED Mia Goldman, PD Jeannine Claudia Oppewall.

LP Dennis Quaid (Remy McSwain), Ellen Barkin (Anne Osborne), Ned Beatty (Jack Kellom), Ebbe Roe Smith (Det. Dodge), John Goodman (Det. DeSoto), Lisa Jane Persky (Det. McCabe), Charles Ludlam (Lamar), Thomas O'Brien (Bobby), David Petitjean (Uncle Sal).

Dennis Quaid is a Cajun New Orleans cop from a long line of Cajun cops in The Big Easy (New Orleans). Quaid's bend-the-rules ways annoy straight-arrow Ellen Barkin, an assistant district attorney, looking into possible police corruption. A series of underworld murders make it appear that a gang war has broken out between the Mafia and black racketeers. Instead Quaid and Barkin discover that the killers are cops covering up the fact that they have been skimming off huge caches of heroine from the mobsters.

231.   *Big Man on Campus*   (1989, Vestron, 105m, c). P Arnon Milchan, D Jeremy Paul Kagan, W Allan Katz, PH Bojan Bazelli, M Joseph Vitarelli, ED Howard Smith.

LP Allan Katz (Bob), Corey Parker (Alex), Cindy Williams (Diane Girard), Melora Hardin (Cathy), Tom Skerritt (Dr. Webster), Jessica Harper (Dr. Fisk), Gerrit Graham (Stanley Hoyle), John Finnegan (Judge Ferguson).

It was planned to call this woefully weak melodrama *The Hunchback of UCLA* but UCLA objected. Troll-like Allan Katz lives in a campus bell tower from which he descends to defend Melora Hardin whom he has admired from his lofty perch. Katz is placed in the custody of psychology professor Tom Skerritt who arranges for him to move in with Hardin's boy friend Corey Parker, so he may be observed.

232.   *Big Meat Eater*   (1984, New Line Cinema, Canada, 82m, c). P Laurence Keane, D Chris Windsor, W Keane, Windsor & Phil Savath, PH Doug McKay, M J. Douglas Dodd, ED Keane, Windsor, Lilla Pederson, SE Michael Dorsey, Iain Best & Jim Bridge.

LP George Dawson (Bob), Andrew Gillies (Jan), Big Miller (Abdulla), Stephen Dimopoulous (Josef), Georgina Hegedos (Rosa), Ida Carnevali (Babushka), Howard Taylor (Mayor).

In this occasionally hilarious sci-fi spoof, aliens arrive to gather radioactive meat waste that forms in the septic tank below George Dawson's butcher shop. Hero Andrew Gillies destroys the aliens' mother ship and saves the world from the meat-eating invaders. The climactic scene fails because of the cheaply produced special effects.

233.   *The Big Picture*   (1989, Columbia, 99m, c). P Michael Varhol, D Christopher Guest, W Guest & Varhol, PH Jeff Jur, M David Nichtern, ED Marty Nicholson, PD Joseph Garrity.

LP Kevin Bacon (Nick Chapman), Emily Longstreth (Susan Rawlings), J.T. Walsh (Allen Habel), Jennifer Jason Leigh (Lydia Johnson), Martin Short (Neil Sussman), Michael McKean (Emmet Sumner), Kim Miyori (Jenny Sumner), Teri Hatcher (Gretchen).

Insiders in Hollywood will try to decide whom the various motion picture personalities the characters in this movie represent. For outsiders, the in-jokes may well go over their heads. Still there is a certain nice humor to the film and the performances are pleasant. Kevin Bacon stars as a film student, more than willing to sell out to Hollywood when the movies beckon. Martin Short who gets no screen credit steals the show as an agent in this likeable comedy.

234. *The Big Red One* (1980, United Artists, 113m, c). P Gene Corman, D&W Samuel Fuller, PH Adam Greenberg, M Dana Koproff, ED Morton Tubor.

LP Lee Marvin (Sergeant), Mark Hamill (Griff), Robert Carradine (Zab), Bobby DiCicco (Vinci), Kelly Ward (Johnson), Siegfried Rauch (Schroeder), Stephane Audran (Walloon), Serge Marquand (Rensonnet), Charles Macaulay (General/Captain), Alain Doutey (Broban), Maurice Marsac (Vichy Colonel).

The title refers to the First Infantry Division. Battle-hardened sergeant Lee Marvin leads a platoon of green kids into battle during World War II. The settings are in Europe and Africa. Marvin is smashing in this flag-waver.

235. *The Big Score* (1983, Almi, 85m, c). P Michael S. Landes & Albert Schwartz, D Fred Williamson, W Gail Morgan Hickman, PH Joao Fernandes, M Jay Chattawy, ED Dan Loewenthal.

LP Fred Williamson (Frank Hooks), John Saxon (Davis), Richard Roundtree (Gordon), Ed Lauter (Parks), Nancy Wilson (Angie Hooks), D'Urville Martin (Easy), Michael Dante (Jackson), Bruce Glover (Koslo).

Private eye Fred Williamson is fed up with drug pushers getting off scot free and the cops getting the horse laughs. He may

have to bend a few rules but he's going to do something about it. Dirty Harry he is not.

236. *Big Shots* (1987, 20th Century-Fox, 90m, c). P Joe Medjuck & Michael C. Gross, D Robert Mandel, W Joe Eszterhas, PH Miroslav Ondricek, M Bruce Broughton, ED Sheldon Kahn, William Anderson & Dennis Virkler, PD Bill Malley.

LP Rickie Busker (Obie), Darius McCrary (Jeremy "Scam" Henderson), Robert Joy (Dickie), Robert Prosky (Keegan), Jerzy Skolimowski (Doc), Paul Winfield (Johnnie Red), Brynn Thayer (Obie's Mom), Bill Hudson (Obie's Dad).

When his father dies of a heart attack, 12-year-old suburban kid Rickie Busker rides his bike into a Chicago ghetto where he is befriended by young black Darius McCrary, who teaches Busker how to survive on the streets.

237. *Big Top Pee-Wee* (1988, Paramount, 82m, c). P Paul Reubens & Debra Hill, D Randal Kleiser, W Reubens & George McGrath, PH Steven Poster, M Danny Elfman, ED Jeff Gourson, PD Stephen Marsh.

LP Pee-Wee Herman (Himself), Penelope Ann Miller (Winnie), Kris Kristofferson (Marc Montana), Valeria Golino (Gina Piccolapupula), Wayne White (Voice of Vance the Pig), Susan Tyrrell (Midge Montana).

We recognize that Pee-Wee Herman is an acquired taste. Not believing he will last long in movies, we have chosen not to acquire the taste. In this one Herman is an agricultural scientist who has invented a hot dog tree.

238. *The Big Town* (1987, Columbia, 109m, c). P Martin Ransohoff & Don Carmody, D Ben Bolt, W Robert Roy Pool (based on the novel *The Arm* by Clark Howard), PH Ralf D. Bode, M Michael Melvoin, ED Stuart Pappe, PD Bill Kenney.

LP Matt Dillon (J.C. Cullen), Diane Lane (Lorry Dane), Tommy Lee Jones (George Cole), Bruce Dern (Mr. Edwards), Lee Grant (Ferguson Edwards), Tom Skerritt (Phil Carpenter), Suzy Amis (Aggie Donaldson), David Marshall Grant (Sonny Binkley), Don Francks (Carl Hooker).

Matt Dillon, a small town crapshooter with a "golden arm," arrives in Chicago to clean up. He has a lot to learn and with the help of stripper Diane Lane, he does. In the end he leaves the big city with unwed mother Suzy Amis to start a new life.

239.   *Big Trouble* (1986, Columbia, 93m, c). P Michael Lobell, D John Cassavetes, W Warren Bogle (Andrew Bergman), PH Bill Butler, M Bill Conti, ED Donn Cambern & Ralph Winters, PD Gene Callahan.

LP Peter Falk (Steve Rickey), Alan Arkin (Leonard Hoffman), Beverly D'Angelo (Blanche Rickey), Charles Durning (O'Mara), Paul Dooley (Noozel), Robert Stack (Winslow), Valerie Curtin (Arlene Hoffman), Richard Libertini (Dr. Lopez), Steve Alterman (Peter Hoffman).

Alan Arkin needs money to send his gifted triplet boys to Yale. He allows Beverly D'Angelo to talk him into helping her kill her zany husband Peter Falk and collect his insurance money. It's an outrageous parody of *Double Indemnity*.

240.   *Big Trouble in Little China* (1986, 20th Century–Fox, 100m, c). P Larry J. Franco, D John Carpenter, W W.D. Richter, Gary Goldman & David Z. Weinstein, PH Dean Cundey, M Carpenter, ED Mark Warner, Steve Mirkovich & Edward A. Warschilka, PD John J. Lloyd.

LP Kurt Russell (Jack Burton), Kim Cattrall (Gracie Law), Dennis Dun (Wang Chi), James Hong (Lo Pan), Victor Wong (Egg Shen), Kate Burton (Margo), Donald Li (Eddie Lee), Carter Wong (Thunder), Peter Kwong (Rain).

Kurt Russell is only occasionally effective as a modern Indy Jones, a truck driver who helps rescue his buddy's fiancée from an evil 2000-year-old Chineses magician.

241.   *A Bigger Splash* (1984, Buzzy Enterprises, 105m, c). P&D Jack Hazan, W Hazan & David Mingay, PH Hazan, M Patrick Gowers & Greg Bailey, ED Mingay.

LP David Hockney (Painter), Peter Schlesinger (Painter's Friend), Ossie Clark (Dress Designer), Celia Birtwell (Designer's Wife), Mo McDermott

(Friend), Henry Geldzahler (Collector), Kasmin (Dealer).

Made in 1974 and put on the shelf, the film is essentially fiction with the actors portraying themselves. David Hockney is a painter whose male lover Peter Schlesinger has left him, which gives the artist painter's block. It doesn't give the audience much of anything.

242.   *Biggles: Adventures in Time* (1985, UIP, GB, 108m, c). P Kent Walwin & Pam Oliver, D John Hough, W John Groves & Walwin (based on characters created by Capt. W.E. Johns), PH Ernest Vincze, M Stanislas, ED Richard Trevor, PD Terry Pritchard.

LP Neil Dickson (Biggles), Alex Hyde-White (Jim Ferguson), Fiona Hutchison (Debbie), Peter Cushing (Col. Raymond), Marcus Gilbert (Von Stalheim), William Hootkins (Chuck).

In this sci-fi adventure, Alex Hyde-White travels back from 1986 to World War II where he helps rescue his time twin, British fighter pilot Neil Dickson.

243.   *The Bikini Shop* (1987, Int. Film Marketing, 99m, c, aka *The Malibu Bikini Shop*). P Gary Mehlman & J. Kenneth Rotcop, D&W David Wechter, PH Tom Richmond, M Don Perry, ED Jean-Marc Vasseur, AD Dian Perryman.

LP Michael David Wright (Alan), Bruce Greenwood (Todd), Barbra Horan (Ronnie), Debra Blee (Jane), Jay Robinson (Ben), Gayln Gorg (Cindy), Ami Julius (Kathy), Frank Nelson (Richard J. Remington).

Knowledgeable viewers seeing a title like this one anticipate horny guys, scantily clad girls, lots of T & A and no story. They won't be disappointed.

244.   *Bill & Ted's Excellent Adventure* (1989, Orion, 90m, c). P Scott Kroopf, Michael S. Murphey & Joel Soisson, D Stephen Herek, W Chris Matheson & Ed Solomon, PH Timothy Suhrstedt, M David Newman, ED Larry Bock & Patrick Rand, PD Roy Forge Smith.

LP Keanu Reeves (Theodore "Ted" Logan), Alex Winter (Bill S. Preston), George Carlin (Rufus), Terry Camilleri (Napoleon), Dan Shor (Billy the Kid), Tony Steedman (Socrates), Rod Loomis

(Sigmund Freud), Al Leong (Genghis Khan), Jane Wiedlin (Joan of Arc), Robert V. Barron (Abraham Lincoln), Bernie Casey (Mr. Ryan), Amy Stock-Poynton (Missy).

The release of this film was delayed, probably to see if anything of value could be salvaged. The answer would seem to be no, but it was released anyway. Keanu Reeves and Alex Winter are two high school buddies who are able to visit great moments in history via a magic phone booth. Enough people answered their ring in theaters to get producers dialing up a 1990 sequel. As someone once said, there's no accounting for taste.

245. *Billy Galvin* (1986, Vestron, 94m, c). P Sue Jett & Tony Mark, D&W John Gray, PH Eugene Shlugleit, ED Lou Kleinman, PD Shay Austin.

LP Karl Malden (Jack Galvin), Lenny Von Dohlen (Billy Galvin), Joyce Van Patten (Mae Galvin), Toni Kalem (Nora), Keith Szarabajka (Donny), Alan North (George), Paul Guilfoyle (Nolan), Barton Heyman (Kennedy).

Crusty Boston construction worker Karl Malden wants his son Lenny Von Dohlen to go to college. The lad wants a construction career like his old man. The sparks fly in an all too obvious story.

246. *Biloxi Blues* (1988, Universal, 106m, c). P Ray Stark, D Mike Nichols, W Neil Simon (based on the play by Simon), PH Bill Butler, M Georges Delerue, ED Sam O'Steen, PD Paul Sylbert.

LP Matthew Broderick (Eugene Morris Jerome), Christopher Walken (Sgt. Merwin J. Toomey), Michael Dolan (James Hennesey), Markus Flanagan (Roy Selridge), Mark Evan Jacobs (Anthony Pinelli), Penelope Ann Miller (Daisy), Matthew Mulhern (Joseph Wykowski), Park Overall (Rowena), Corey Parker (Arnold Epstein), Casey Siemaszko (Donald Carney).

In 1943, Matthew Broderick (impersonating Neil Simon in this autobiographical story), who has never been far from his home in Brooklyn, is drafted and is sent to basic training in Biloxi, Mississippi. He and his fellow green recruits survive the rigors of the training and the rough treatment of insane drill instructor Christopher Walken to become men and soldiers.

247. *Bird* (1988, Warner, 163m, c). P&D Clint Eastwood, W Joel Oliansky, PH Jack N. Green, M Lennie Niehaus, ED Joel Cox, PD Edward C. Carfagno, SOUND Les Frescholtz, Dick Alexander, Vern Poore & Willie D. Burton*.

LP Forest Whitaker (Charlie "Bird" Parker), Diane Venora (Chan Richardson Parker), Michael Zelniker (Red Rodney), Samuel E. Wright (Dizzy Gillespie), Keith David (Buster Franklin), Michael McGuire (Brewster).

Forest Whitaker gives a first-rate performance as the legendary jazz musician Charlie "Bird" Parker, whose excesses with women, drugs and alcohol finished his career and his life when he was only 34. Director Clint Eastwood handles his subject with great sensitivity and a sure hand.

248. *Birds of Prey* (1987, Shapiro, Canada, 90m, c). P Peter Haynes & Jorge Montesi, D Montesi, W Haynes & Montesi, PH Gary Armstrong, M Paul Zsa Zsa, ED Montesi.

LP Jorge Montesi (Carlos Solo), Joseph Patrick Finn (Harry Card), Linda Elder (The Woman), Maurice Brand (Fence), Suzanne Tessier (Cheryl), Jennifer Keene (Thelma), Sam Mottrich (Levre), Deryck Hazel (Deryck).

When a pimp is found crucified and disemboweled, detective Jorge Montesi is assigned to the case. The prime suspect is Joseph Patrick Finn, an old friend of Montesi. Finn is on the run with vicious hit woman Linda Elder on his trail. Finn confronts the real murderer Maurice Brand who is shot down by Elder. She tosses her gun to Finn, just before Montesi arrives. Montesi guns down Finn.

249. *Birdy* (1984, Tri-Star, 120m, c). P Alan Marshall, D Alan Parker, W Sandy Kroopf & Jack Behr (based on the novel by William Wharton), PH Michael Seresin, M Peter Gabriel, ED Gerry Hambling, PD Geoffrey Kirkland.

LP Matthew Modine (Birdy), Nicolas Cage (Al Columbato), John Harkins (Dr. Weiss), Sandy Baron (Mr. Columbato), Karen Young (Hannah Rourke), Bruno Kirby (Renaldi), Nancy Fish (Mrs. Prevost), Robert L. Ryan (Joe Sagessa).

Vietnam vet Matthew Modine, who has always had an affinity for birds, is in a military hospital for the insane. He sits stark naked in his room, acting like a caged bird. His friend, Nicolas Cage, whose wounds in Vietnam were merely physical is determined to help his shell-shocked friend. It's a heavy-going feature, difficult to like.

250.   *The Black Cauldron* (1985, Buena Vista/Disney, animated, 82m, c). P Joe Hale, D Ted Berman & Richard Rich, W David Jonas, Vance Gerry, Hale, Rich, Al Wilson, Roy Morita, Peter Young, Art Stevens, Rosemary Anne Sisson & Roy Edward Disney (based on the five novels of the series *The Chronicles of Prydainby* by Lloyd Alexander), M Elmer Bernstein, ED James Melton, Jim Koford & Armetta Jackson, KEY ANIMATOR Walt Stanchfield.

LP VOICES Grant Bardsley (Taran), Susan Sheridan (Eilonwy), Freddie Jones (Dallben), Nigel Hawthorne (Fflewddur), Arthur Malet (King Eidileg), John Byner (Gurgi/Doli).

In an animated sword and sorcery story, medieval hero Taran combats magic swords, wicked witches and the evil Horned King who wishes to gain control of the black cauldron, the source of supernatural powers.

251.   *Black Eagle* (1989, Taurus Entertainment, 94m, c). P Shimon Arama, D Eric Karson, W A.E. Peters & Michael Gonzales (based on a story by Arama), PH George Koblasa, M Terry Plumeri, ED Michael Kelly.

LP Sho Kosugi (Ken Tani), Jean-Claude Van Damme (Andrei), Doran Clark (Patricia Parker), Bruce French (Father Joseph Bedelia), Vladimir Skontarovsky (Vladimir Klimenko), William H. Bassett (Dean Richert).

Belgian martial-arts ace Jean-Claude Van Damme, cast as a Russian heavy, goes up against hard-hitting hero Sho Kosugi.

252.   *Black Jack* (1980, Kestrel Films, GB, 110m, c). P Tony Garnett, D&W Kenneth Loach (based on the novel by Leon Garfield), PH Chris Menges, M Bob Pegg, ED William Shapter.

LP Stephen Hirst (Bartholomew Pick-

ering), Louise Cooper (Belle Carter), Jean Franval (Black Jack), Phil Askham (Hangman), Pat Wallis (Mrs. Gorgandy), John Young (Dr. Hunter), Doreen Mantle (Mrs. Carter).

In York, England in 1750, French sailor Jean Franval escapes hanging and helps save Louise Cooper from a private madhouse.

253.   *The Black Marble* (1980, Avco Embassy, 113m, c). P Frank Capra, Jr., D Harold Becker, W Joseph Wambaugh (based on his novel), PH Owen Roizman, M Maurice Jarre, ED Maury Winetrobe, PD Alfred Sweeney.

LP Robert Foxworth (Sgt. Valnikov), Paula Prentiss (Sgt. Natalie Zimmerman), James Woods (Fiddler), Harry Dean Stanton (Philo Skinner), Barbara Babcock (Madeline Whitfield), John Hancock (Clarence Cromwell), Raleigh Bond (Capt. Hooker), Judy Landers (Pattie Mae).

Drunken Russian-American cop Robert Foxworth redeems himself when teamed with policewoman Paula Prentiss, who is less cynical about their work than he. The cases they are investigating are child murders and dog torturing. Sure hate to see those dogs suffer.

254.   *Black Moon Rising* (1986, New World, 100m, c). P Joel B. Michaels & Douglas Curtiss, D Harley Cokliss, W John Carpenter, Desmond Nakano & William Gray. PH Misha Suslov, M Lalo Schifrin, ED Todd Ramsay, PD Bryan Ryman.

LP Tommy Lee Jones (Quint), Linda Hamilton (Nina), Robert Vaughn (Ryland), Richard Jaeckel (Earl Windom), Lee Ving (Ringer), Bubba Smith (Johnson), Dan Shor (Billy Lyons), William Sanderson (Tyke Thayden), Keenan Wynn (Iron John), Don Opper (Frenchie).

In this absurd action film, professional thief Tommy Lee Jones, in the pay of the U.S. government, hides an important tape in the back of a super-high-powered car, stolen by a sophisticated gang of car thieves. It's a high-tech caper filled with plenty of violent action but disappoints nevertheless.

255.   *Black Rain* (1989, Paramount, 126m, c). P Stanley R. Jaffe & Sherry

Lansing, D Ridley Scott, W Craig Bolotin & Warren Lewis, PH Jan De Bont, M Hans Zimmer, ED Tom Rolf, PD Norris Spencer, SOUND Keith A. Webster & James J. Sabat†.

LP Michael Douglas (Nick), Andy Garcia (Charlie), Ken Takakura (Masahiro), Kate Capshaw (Joyce), Yusaku Matsuda (Sato), Shigeru Koyama (Ohashi), John Spencer (Oliver), Guts Ishimatsu (Katayama), Yuya Uchida (Nashida), Tomisaburo Wakayama (Sugai), Miyuki Ono (Miyuki).

In this atmospheric action film, hardboiled, reckless and somewhat corrupt New York cop Michael Douglas and his partner Andy Garcia have escorted *yakuza* (i.e. Japanese gangster) hood Yusaku Matsuda to Osaka, Japan. Douglas loses his prisoner and watches helplessly as Garcia is murdered. From then on it's Douglas trying to bring Matsuda and the others to some form of justice and finding strange are the ways of the Japanese. The title is explained when crime boss Tomisaburo Wakayama tells Douglas that with the World War II fire bombings by American pilots of Japanese cities, making "black rain," an enduring climate for crime was created. Director Ridley Scott, author of *Alien* and *Blade Runner,* provides an intense modern-day film noir.

256. *Black Rainbow* (1989, Goldcrest, GB, 113m, c). P John Quested & Geoffrey Helman, D&W Mike Hodges, PH Gerry Fisher, M John Scott, ED Malcolm Cooke, PD Voytek.

LP Rosanna Arquette (Martha Travis), Jason Robards (Walter Travis), Tom Hulce (Gary Wallace), Mark Joy (Lloyd Harley), Ron Rosenthal (Lt. Weinberg), John Bennes (Ted Silas).

Spiritualist Rosanna Arquette and her alcoholic father Jason Robards take her clairvoyant act on the road in rural North Carolina. She receives a message from a murdered man for his wife. The wife is understandably upset, because her husband isn't dead. However that night he's murdered. Reporter Tom Hulce wants to learn more about the case.

257. *Black Roses* (1989, Rayvan/Shapiro Glickenhaus, 83m, c). P John Fasano & Ray Van Doorn, D Fasano, W Cindy Sorrell, PH Paul Mitchnick, M Elliot Solomon, ED Fasano, Van Doorn & James K. Ruxin, AD Nick White.

LP John Martin (Matthew Moorhouse), Ken Swofford (Mayor Farnsworth), Sal Viviano (Damian), Julia Adams (Mrs. Miller), Frank Dietz (Johnny), Carla Ferrigno (Priscilla Farnsworth), Carmine Appice (Vinny Apache).

In the small town of Mill Basin, teenagers are pitted against their parents with the arrival of a heavy metal band, Black Roses. The group turns out to be disciples of the Devil. The film, which seems to be taking itself seriously may be a horror spoof—but it's hard to tell.

258. *The Black Stallion Returns* (1983, MGM/United Artists, 93m, c). P Tom Sternberg, Fred Roos & Doug Claybourne, D Robert Dalva, W Richard Kletter & Jerome Kass (based on the book by Walter Farley), PH Carlo DiPalma & Caleb Deschanel, M Georges Delerue, ED Paul Hirsch.

LP Kelly Reno (Alec), Vincent Spano (Raj), Allen Goorwitz (Kurr), Woody Strode (Meslar), Ferdinand Mayne (Abu Ben Ishak), Teri Garr (Alec's Mother), Jodi Thelen (Tabari), Doghmi Larbi (The Little Man).

While *The Black Stallion* is a brilliant little gem, the sequel is a phony stone. Kelly Reno, now a teenager, loses his stallion in Morocco, but gets him back after a series of daredevil adventures.

259. *Black Widow* (1987, 20th Century-Fox, 103m, c). P Harold Schneider, D Bob Rafelson, W Ronald Bass, PH Conrad L. Hall, M Michael Small, ED John Bloom, PD Gene Callahan.

LP Debra Winger (Alexandra Barnes), Theresa Russell (Catharine), Sami Frey (Paul Nuytten), Dennis Hopper (Ben Dumers), Nicol Williamson (William Macauley), Terry O'Quinn (Bruce), James Hong (Shin), Diane Ladd (Etta), D.W. Moffett (Michael), Lois Smith (Sara), Leo Rossi (Ricci).

This is an excellent suspense thriller, starring Theresa Russell as a beautiful, elusive murderess, fond of marrying rich men and then killing them, after they have adjusted their wills, naming her as their benefactor. Justice Department investigator Debra Winger is hot on Russell's trail. The two play a lovely cat-and-mouse game, before Winger brings Russell to justice.

260.   *The Blade Master*   (1984, New Line, Ital., 92m, c, aka *Ator the Invincible*). P John Newman, D David Hills, W Hills (uncredited), PH Federico Slonisco, M Carlo Rustichelli, ED David Framer.

LP Miles O'Keeffe (Ator), Lisa Foster (Raines) (Mila), Charles Borromel (Akronas), David Cain Haughton (Zor), Chen Wong (Thong).

Filmed in Europe in 1982, this incredibly dull fantasy adventure has its beefcake prehistoric hero Miles O'Keeffe hang-gliding. Muscular O'Keeffe, surely among the worst incompetent actors of all time, battles the power hungry evil tyrant David Cain Haughton.

261.   *Blade Runner*   (1982, Warner, 114m, c). P Michael Deeley, D Ridley Scott, W Hampton Fancher & David Peoples (based on the novel *Do Androids Dream of Electric Sheep?* by Philip K. Dick), PH Jordan Cronenweth, M Vangelis, ED Terry Rawlings, AD/SD Lawrence G. Paull, David Snyder & Linda DeScenna†, SE Douglas Trumbull, Richard Yuricich & David Dryer†.

LP Harrison Ford (Deckard), Rutger Hauer (Roy Batty), Sean Young (Rachael), Edward James Olmos (Gaff), M. Emmet Walsh (Bryant), Daryl Hannah (Pris), William Sanderson (Sebastian), Brion James (Leon), Joe Turkel (Tyrell), Joanna Cassidy (Zhora).

In physically decayed Los Angeles, circa A.D. 2019, Harrison Ford is a licensed-to-kill cop who tracks down and destroys a gang of intelligent robots, led by superhuman android Rutger Hauer. The latter has hijacked a space shuttle and returned to earth. Wonder how Jack Webb as Joe Friday would have handled the assignment?

262.   *Blake Edward's That's Life!*   (1986, Columbia, 102m, c, aka *That's Life*). P Tony Adams & Edwards, D Blake Edwards, W Milton Wexler & Edwards, PH Anthony Richmond, M Henry Mancini, ED Lee Rhoads, "Life in a Looking Glass" by Henry Mancini & Leslie Bricusse.

LP Jack Lemmon (Harvey Fairchild), Julie Andrews (Gillian Fairchild), Sally Kellerman (Holly Parrish), Robert Loggia (Father Baragone), Jennifer Edwards (Megan Fairchild Bartlet), Rob Knepper (Steve Larwin), Matt Lattanzi (Larry Bartlet), Chris Lemmon (Josh Fairchild).

This personal home-movie was shot at Edwards' and wife Julie Andrews' Malibu home. Employing loads of family members, it explores the concerns of family man Lemmon as he turns 60 and his wife Andrews' fear that she has cancer.

263.   *Blame It on Rio*   (1984, 20th Century–Fox, 110m, c). P&D Stanley Donen, W Charlie Peters & Larry Gelbart (based on the screenplay *Un Moment d'Egarement* by Claude Berri), PH Reynaldo Villalobos, M Ken Wannberg, ED George Hively & Richard Marden.

LP Michael Caine (Matthew Hollis), Joseph Bologna (Victor Lyons), Valerie Harper (Karen Hollis), Michelle Johnson (Jennifer Lyons), Demi Moore (Nicole Hollis), Jose Lewgoy (Eduardo Marques), Lupe Gigliotti (Signora Botega), Michael Menaugh (Peter), Tessy Callado (Helaine).

Best friends Michael Caine and Joseph Bologna and their respective daughters, Demi Moore and Michelle Johnson, are vacationing in Rio. Bologna beds every woman in sight, but teenage Johnson, her libido no doubt heated-up by the climate, takes a reluctant Caine for a lover. If Moore sleeps with anyone, we are not informed. Bologna enlists Caine in helping discover who the bastard is who has deflowered his little darling. By the time Bologna learns the truth, Caine discovers that Bologna has had a long-standing affair with Valerie Harper, Caine's wife. It's a stupid sex farce, but one could waste two hours in worse ways.

264.   *Blame It on the Night*   (1984, Tri-Star, 85m, c). P&D Gene Taft, W Len Jenkin (based on a story by Taft & Michael Philip "Mick" Jagger), PH Alex Phillips, M Ted Neeley, ED Tony Lombardo, PD Ted Haworth.

LP Nick Mancuso (Chris Dalton), Byron Thames (Job Dalton), Leslie Ackerman (Shelly), Dick Bakalyan (Manzini), Leeyan Granger (Melanie),

Rex Ludwick (Animal), Michael Wilding (Terry), Dennis Tufano (Leland).

Rock star Nick Mancuso is forced to take in Byron Thames, the 13-year-old son who he's never seen. The story of their adjustment to each other is not compelling drama.

265. *Blaze* (1989, Touchstone, 120m, c). P Gil Friesen & Dale Pollock, D&W Ron Shelton (based on the book *Blaze Starr: My Life as Told to Huey Perry* by Blaze Starr and Huey Perry), PH Haskell Wexler†, M Bennie Wallace, ED Robert Leighton, PD Armin Ganz.

LP Paul Newman (Earl Long), Lolita Davidovich (Blaze Starr), Jerry Hardin (Thibodeaux), Gailard Sartain (La-Grange), Jeffrey DeMunn (Tuck), Garland Bunting (Doc Ferriday), Richard Jenkins (Times-Picayune Reporter), Brandon Smith (Arvin Deeter), Robert Wuhl (Red Snyder), Jay Chevalier (Wiley Braden), Blaze Starr (Lily).

This is not a great movie. It may not even be a good movie. Lolita Davidovich, lovely as she is, doesn't stack up to the superlative figure of Blaze Starr, one of the country's premier strippers. Add to this that the story makes Starr out as some kind of sexy Girl Scout. Her widely publicized affair with married Louisiana politician Earl Long is presented as fantasy land. But ole Paul Newman is deliciously delightful as ole Earl Long, brother of Louisiana's infamous Kingfish, and an eccentric corrupt politician with his own demerits. Newman injects the role with peppery humor. If he isn't careful, he'll give Earl Long, three times governor of a state noted for its corrupt governors, a good name.

Bless 'Em All see The Act

266. *Bless Their Little Hearts* (1984, Black Ind. Features, 80m, c). P&D Billy Woodberry, W&PH Charles Burnett, M Archie Shepp & Little Esther Phillips, ED Woodberry.

LP Nate Hardman (Charlie Banks), Kaycee Moore (Andais Banks), Angela Burnett, Ronald Burnett, Kimberly Burnett (Banks Children), Eugene Cherry.

Shot in the Watts section of L.A., the film is an impressive low-budget production about an unemployed black married man who drifts into an affair with a welfare mother.

267. *Blind Date* (1984, New Line, 99m, c). P&D Nico Mastorakis, W Mastorakis & Fred C. Perry, PH Andreas Bellis, M Stanley Myers, ED George Rosenburg, PD Anne Marie Papadelis.

LP Joseph Bottoms (Jonathan Ratcliffe), Kirstie Alley (Claire Parker), James Daughton (David), Lana Clarkson (Rachel), Keir Dullea (Dr. Steiger).

Blind Joseph Bottoms has a computer implanted in his brain in order to track down a psychopathic killer in Athens.

268. *Blind Date* (1987, Tri-Star, 93m, c). P Tony Adams, D Blake Edwards, W Dale Launer, PH Harry Stradling, Jr., M Henry Mancini, ED Robert Pergament, PD Rodger Maus.

LP Kim Basinger (Nadia Gates), Bruce Willis (Walter Davis), John Larroquette (David Bedford), William Daniels (Judge Harold Bedford), George Coe (Harry Gruen), Mark Blum (Denny Gordon), Phil Hartman (Ted Davis), Stephanie Faracy (Susie Davis), Alice Hirson (Muriel Bedford).

Kim Basinger's drinking problem is, if she has just one drink she causes problems. Bruce Willis, the unhappy recipient of her jinx, falls in love with her nevertheless, and must fight off Night Court's John Larroquette to win her, and keep her sober ever after, we suppose. It's meant to be funny, but Basinger isn't much of a comedienne and Willis tries too hard.

269. *Blind Fear* (1989, Cineplex Odeon, Canada, 90m, c). P Pierre David & Franco Battista, D Tom Berry, W Sergio Alteri, PH Rodney Gibbons, M Michael Malvoin, ED Battista & Yves Langlois, PD Richard Tasse.

LP Shelley Hack (Erika Breen), Jack Langedijk (Bo), Kim Coates (Ed), Heidi Von Palleske (Maria), Ron Lea (Cal), Jan Rubes (Lasky), Geza Kovacs (Heinemann).

Blind Shelley Hack is trapped in an abandoned country lodge where she is hunted by three psycho robbers, including trigger-happy killer Kim Coates. It's not *Wait Until Dark* and Hack isn't Audrey Hepburn, but still it's entertainingly suspenseful.

270. *Blind Fury* (1989, Tri-Star, Australia, 85m, c). P Daniel Grodnik & Tim Matheson, D Phillip Noyce, W Charles Robert Carner (based on a screenplay by Ryozo Kasahara), PH Don Burgess, M J. Peter Robinson, ED David Simmons, PD Peter Murton.

LP Rutger Hauer (Nick Parker), Brandon Call (Billy Deveraux), Terrance O'Quinn (Frank Deveraux), Lisa Blount (Annie Winchester), Noble Willingham (MacCready), Meg Foster (Lynn Devereaux), Rick Overton (Tector Pike), Randall "Tex" Cobb (Slag), Sho Kosugi (Japanese Swordsman).

Rutger Hauer's character, a blind Vietnam veteran who wields a samurai sword with great skill, is based on the Japanese character Zatoichi, played in several movies in the 60s and early 70s by Shintaru Katsu. Twenty years after losing his sight and picking up his new skill, Hauer is in Miami, where he comes to the aid of old army buddy Terrance O'Quinn, who's in trouble with the mob.

271. *Bliss* (1985, Window III, Australia, 111m, c). P Anthony Buckley, D Ray Lawrence, W Lawrence & Peter Carey (based on the novel by Carey), PH Paul Murphy, M Peter Best, ED Wayne LeClos.

LP Barry Otto (Harry Joy), Lynette Curran (Bettina Joy), Helen Jones (Honey Barbara), Miles Buchanan (David Joy), Gia Carides (Lucy Joy), Tim Robertson (Alex Duval), Jeff Truman (Joel), Paul Chubb (Mr. Des).

This bizarre, disgusting satirical comedy won the Australian Academy Award. Successful advertising executive Barry Otto drops dead, but during the four minutes it takes for the paramedics to revive him, he learns there is a heaven and decides that earth is hell. He wakes up to new perceptions about life and discovers that his wife and adult children are no-goods.

272. *The Blob* (1988, Tri-Star, 92m, c). P Jack H. Harris & Elliott Kastner, D Chuck Russell, W Russell & Frank Darabont, PH Mark Irwin, M Michael Hoenig, ED Tod Feuerman & Terry Stokes, PD Craig Stearns.

LP Shawnee Smith (Meg Penny), Donovan Leitch (Paul Taylor), Ricky Paull Goldin (Scott Jeskey), Kevin Dillon (Brian Flagg), Billy Beck (Can Man), Jeffrey DeMunn (Sheriff Herb Geller), Candy Clark (Fran Hewitt), Del Close (Rev. Meeker), Michael Kenworthy (Kevin Penny), Joe Seneca (Dr. Meddows).

Writer-director Chuck Russell has improved on the 1958 science-fiction classic. The lives of the residents of a small town are altered considerably when a meteor from outer space crash lands in a nearby woods. An old man is the first victim of a glutinous substance which grows with each victim. High school cheerleader Shawnee Smith and leather jacket–clad delinquent boyfriend Kevin Dillon team up to finally put an end to the Blob. It's actually a scientific experiment headed by Joe Seneca, gone wrong.

273. *Blood Beach* (1981, Gross Organization, 89m, c). P Steven Nalevansky, D&W Jeffrey Bloom (based on a story by Bloom & Nalevansky), PH Steve Poster, M Gil Melle, ED Gary Griffen.

LP David Huffman (Harry Caulder), Mariana Hill (Catherine), John Saxon (Pearson), Otis Young (Piantadosi), Stefan Gierasch (Dimitros), Burt Young (Royko), Darrell Fetty (Hoagy).

Seven people are sucked beneath the sand at a Santa Monica beach and cops John Saxon and Otis Young must find out why. Why?

274. *Blood Diner* (1987, Vestron, 90m, c). P Jimmy Maslon & Jackie Kong, D Kong, W Michael Sonye, PH Jorg Walthers, M Don Preston, ED Thomas Meshelski, PD Ron Petersen.

LP Rick Burks (Michael Tutman), Carl Crew (George Tutman), Roger Dauer (Mark Shepard), LaNette La France (Sheba Jackson), Lisa Guggenheim (Connie Stanton), Max Morris (Chief Miller), Roxanne Cybelle (Little Michael).

There must be audiences for trash like this, but we don't care to meet any of them. The brain of their uncle orders Rick Burks and Carl Crew to prepare a blood banquet, serving up certain juicy parts of nubile females. Other parts will be sewn together to serve as the home for an ancient goddess, Sheetar. Must we go on?

275. *Blood Hook* (1987, Troma, 95m, c). P David Herbert, D James Mallon, W Larry Edgerton & John Galligan (based on a story by Gail Anderson, Herbert, Mallon & Douglas Rand), PH Marsha Kahm, M Thomas A. Naunas, ED Kahm.

LP Mark Jacobs (Peter Van Clease), Don Cosgrove (Roger Swain), Patrick Danz (Rodney), Paul Drake (Wayne Duerst), Dale Dunham (Denny Dobyns), Donald Franke (Grandfather), Ryan Franke (Young Peter).

In another in the seemingly unending films about mad killers preying on teenagers, this film's demented one snags his victims with a muskie fishing lure in the woods outside a Wisconsin fishing town. What do these movies say about those who flock to rent their videos? We're afraid of the answer.

276. *Blood Link* (1983, Zadar, US/Italy, 94m, c). P Robert Palaggi, D Alberto de Martino, W Theodore Apstein (based on a story by Max de Rita & de Martino), PH Romano Albani, M Ennio Morricone, ED Russell Lloyd, AD Uberto Bertacca.

LP Michael Moriarty (Dr. Craig Mannings/Keith Mannings), Penelope Milford (Dr. Julie Warren), Cameron Mitchell (Bud Waldo), Sarah Langenfeld (Christine Waldo), Martha Smith (Hedwig), Geraldine Fitzgerald (Mrs. Thompson).

Physician Michael Moriarty's nightmares plague him during the day as well, when he discovers he has an evil twin brother. Cameron Mitchell does some nice work in an interesting if predictable film.

Blood Mad see The Glove

Blood on the Moon see Cop

277. *Blood Simple* (1984, River Road, 97m, c). P Ethan Coen, D Joel Coen, W Ethan & Joel Coen, PH Barry Sonnenfeld, M Carter Burwell, ED Roderick Jaynes, Don Wiegmann & Peggy Connolly, PD Jane Musky.

LP John Getz (Ray), Frances McDormand (Abby), Dan Hedaya (Julian Marty), M. Emmet Walsh (Private Det. Visser), Samm-Art Williams (Maurice), Deborah Neumann (Debra), Raquel Gavia (Landlady).

Jealous husband Dan Hedaya hires seedy private eye M. Emmet Walsh to kill his unfaithful wife Frances McDormand

and her lover John Getz, but Walsh kills Hedaya instead. Getz helps the murderer when he discovers the body, trying to cover up the crime because he believes that McDormand did in her hubby. The strangely appealing picture doesn't take many survivors.

278. *Blood Sisters* (1987, Reeltime, 86m, c). P Walter E. Sear, D,W&PH Roberta Findlay, M Sear & Martin Litovsky, ED Sear & Findlay.

LP Amy Brentano (Linda), Shannon McMahon (Alice), Dan Erickson (Russ), Maria Machart (Marnie), Elizabeth Rose (Bonnie), Cjerste Thor (Cara), Patricia Finneran (Diana), Gretchen Kingsley (Ellen).

A group of sorority pledges are forced to spend a night in a spooky deserted house which once was a house of prostitution. The pledges begin disappearing one by one, killed by an apparition dressed in a prostitute's negligee. The murderer is no ghost, just a transvestite who lives in the house and hates the invasion of his domain.

279. *Blood Tide* (1982, 21st Century-Fox, 82m, c, aka *The Red Tide*). P Nico Mastorakis & Donald Langdon, D Richard Jeffries, W Jefferies, Langdon & Mastorakis, PH Ari Stavrou, M Jerry Moseley, ED Robert Leighton.

LP James Earl Jones (Frye), Jose Ferrer (Nereus), Lila Kedrova (Sister Anna), Mary Louise Weller (Sherry), Martin Kove (Neil), Deborah Shelton (Madeline), Lydia Cornell (Barbara).

When a treasure hunter blows up an underwater grotto, a monster is released who is madder than hell. A lot of people are killed for daring to disturb the rest of the creature, including several bikini-clad lovelies. It's a disturbing sickness that infects fans of such movies, who apparently enjoy seeing beautiful, sexy women killed.

280. *Bloodbath at the House of Death* (1984, Columbia, GB, 92m, c). P Ray Cameron & John Downes, D Cameron, W Cameron & Barry Cryer, PH Brian West, M Mike Moran, ED Brian Tagg.

LP Kenny Everett (Dr. Lucas Mandeville), Pamela Stephenson (Dr. Barbara Coyle), Vincent Price (Sinister Man), Gareth Hunt (Elliott Broome), Don Warrington (Stephen Wilson), John Fortune (John Harrison).

In a horror-comedy, a team of inept scientists investigate multiple ritual murders at the former site of a gory massacre. Trying to scare them away is an equally inept coven of devil-worshipers.

281. *Bloodeaters* (1980, CM Productions, 84m, c, aka *Forest of Fear*). P,D&W Chuck McCrann, PH David Sperling, ED McCrann & Sperling.

LP Charles Austin (Cole), Beverly Shapiro (Polly), Dennis Heffend (Hermit), Paul Haskin (Briggs), John Amplas (Phillips).

When the government dumps chemicals on a marijuana field, the herbicide turns everyone who comes into contact with it into a murdering zombie-like creature. See: smoking pot is bad for you.

282. *Bloodfist* (1989, Concorde/New Horizons, 85m, c). P Roger Corman, D Terence H. Winkless, W Robert King, PH Ricardo Jacques Gale, M Sasha Matson, ED Karen Horn.

LP Joe Mari Avellana (Kwong), Michael Shaner (Baby), Riley Bowman (Nancy), Rob Kaman (Raton), Billy Blanks (Black Rose), Kris Aguilar (Chin Woo), Vic Diaz (Detective), Don "The Dragon" Wilson (Jake).

Real-life kickboxing champion Don "The Dragon" Wilson portrays a kickboxing champion in this film whose plot is remarkably similar to several others in the sub-sub-subgenre.

283. *Bloodhounds of Broadway* (1989, Vestron, 101m, c). P&D Howard Brookner, W Brookner & Colman de Kay (based on short stories "The Bloodhounds of Broadway," "A Very Honorable Guy," "Social Error" & "The Brain Goes Home" by Damon Runyon), PH Elliot Davis, M Jonathan Sheffer.

LP Julie Hagerty (Harriet MacKyle), Randy Quaid (Feet Samuels), Madonna (Hortense Hathaway), Esai Morales (Handsome Jack Maddigan), Ethan Phillips (Basil Valentine), Matt Dillon (Regret), Jennifer Grey (Lovey Lou), Josef Sommer (Waldo Winchester), Anita Morris (Miss Missouri Martin), Rutger Hauer (The Brain).

Four Damon Runyon stories are interwoven into a film about New Year's Eve on Broadway in 1928. While it doesn't quite work, there are some decent performances. Julie Hagerty is appealing as a rich dame throwing a big party who invites some gangsters for some spice. Randy Quaid is good as a none-too-bright street person, madly in love with Madonna. Rutger Hauer is a powerful gangster with a knife in his stomach looking for some help.

284. *Bloodspell* (1988, Vista Street-Feifer/Miller, 88m, c). P Jessica Rains, D Deryn Warren, W Gerry Daly, PH Ronn Schmidt, M Randy Miller, ED Tony Miller, PD Peter Kanter.

LP Anthony Jenkins (Daniel), Aaron Teich (Charlie), Alexandra Kennedy (Debbie), John Reno (Luther), Edward Dloughy, Jacque J. Coon, Kimble Jemison.

In this ultra-low budget rip-off of *Nightmare on Elm Street 3,* Anthony Jenkins is a telekinetic teen sent to an institution for his own protection. His dangerous father has vowed to get his son. When other patients start dying, we wonder who's responsible.

285. *Bloodsport* (1988, Cannon, 92m, c). P Mark DiSalle, D Newt Arnold, W Sheldon Lettich, Christopher Crosby & Mel Friedman (based on a story by Lettich), PH David Worth, M Paul Hertzog, ED Carl Kress, PD David Searl.

LP Jean-Claude Van Damme (Frank Dux), Donald Gibb (Ray Jackson), Leah Ayres (Janice), Norman Burton (Helmer), Forest Whitaker (Rawlins), Roy Chiao (Senzo "Tiger" Tanaka), Philip Chan (Capt. Chen).

Jean-Claude Van Damme is trained by Roy Chiao, a former Kumite champion, to become the first Westerner to dominate the brutal martial arts competition, held clandestinely every five years in Hong Kong. The film is based on true events in the life of American special forces commando Frank Dux, but that doesn't make it any more interesting.

286. *Bloodstone* (1989, Omega Pictures, 91m, c). P Nico Mastorakis, D Dwight Little, W Curt Allen (based on a story by Mastorakis), PH Eric Anderson, M Jerry J. Grant, ED Mastorakis.

LP Brett Stimely (Sandy McVey), Rajni Kanth (Shyam Sabu), Anna Nicholas (Stephanie McVey), Charlie Brill (Inspector Ramesh), Jack Kehler (Paul Lorre), Christopher Neame (Van Hoeven), Laura Albert (Kim Chi).

While on his honeymoon with heiress Anna Nicholas, ex-cop Brett Stimely becomes involved in the chase for a huge, cursed ruby when a bad guy hides it in Nicholas' tennis bag.

287. *Bloodsuckers from Outer Space* (1987, Reel Movies Int., 79m, c). P Gail Boyd Latham, D&W Glen Coburn, PH Chad D. Smith, ED Karen D. Latham, MK Tim McDowell & J.P. Joyce.

LP Thom Meyers (Jeff Rhodes), Laura Ellis (Julie), Dennis Letts (Gen. Sanders), Chris Heldman (Sam), Robert Bradeen (Uncle Joe), Billie Keller (Aunt Kate), John Webb (Dr. Pace), Rick Garlington (Maj. Hood).

After an alien substance descends on a small Texas farming community, good honest folk become bloodsucking monsters.

288. *Bloodsucking Freaks* (1982, Troma, 88m, c, aka *The Incredible Torture Show*). P Alan Margolin, D&W Joel M. Reed, PH Gerry Toll, M Michael Sahl, ED Victor Kanefsky.

LP Seamus O'Brien (Sardu), Louie De-Jesus (Ralphus), Niles McMaster (Tom), Viju Krim (Natasha), Alan Dellay (Crazy Silo), Dan Fauci (Det. Sgt. Tucci).

Set your VCR to play in the bathroom, so you won't have far to go when this gross picture makes you sick. It's a base sado-masochistic film and can only appeal to those who are whippers or whippees.

289. *Bloody Birthday* (1986, Judica Productions, 85m, c). P Gerald T. Olson, D Ed Hunt, W Hunt & Barry Pearson, PH Stephen Posey, M Arlon Ober, ED Ann E. Mills, SE Roger George.

LP Jose Ferrer (Doctor), Susan Strasberg (Mrs. Davis), Lori Lethin (Joyce), Melinda Cordell (Mrs. Brody), Julie Brown (Beverly), Joe Penny (Harding), Billy Jacoby (Curtis), Andy Freeman (Steven).

Under the spell of a total solar ellipse, three women in the same small town simultaneously give birth to seemingly angelic children. They don't stay that way. They become lethal killers.

The Bloody Bushido Blade see The Bushido Blade

290. *Bloody Pom Poms* (1988, Atlantic, 88m, c, aka *Cheerleader Camp*). P Jeffrey Prettyman & John Quinn, D Quinn, W David Lee Fein & R.L. O'Keefe, PH Bryan England, M Murielle Hodler-Hamilton & Joel Hamilton, ED Jeffrey Reiner, PD Keith Barrett.

LP Betsy Russell (Alison Wentworth), Leif Garrett (Brent Hoover), Lucinda Dickey (Cory Foster), Lorie Griffin (Bonnie Reed), Buck Flower (Pop), Travis McKenna (Timmy Moser), Teri Weigel (Pam Bently).

Mean-looking sexy Betsy Russell, a troubled cheerleader, suffers from horrible nightmares. She and six of her cheerleading teammates are enrolled in a cheerleading camp. When loads of these rah-rahing cuties start dying, Russell is the obvious choice as the villain, but that would be too easy.

291. *Bloody Wednesday* (1987, Visto International, 96m, c). P Philip Yordan, Mark G. Gilhuis, Robert Ryan & Susan Gilhuis, D Mark G. Gilhuis, W Yordan, PH Ryan, M Al Sendry.

LP Raymond Elmendorf (Harry), Pamela Baker (Dr. Johnson), Navarre Perry (Ben Curtis), Teresa Mae Allen (Elaine Curtis), Jeff O'Haco (Animal), John Landthoop (Bellman).

Auto mechanic Raymond Elmendorf slowly loses touch with reality. He machine-guns a crowd of people in a diner. The massacre is shot in slow-motion so it can be savored by blood-thirsty audiences.

292. *Blow Out* (1981, Filmways, 108m, c). P George Litto, D&W Brian De Palma, PH Vilmos Zsigmond, M Pino Donaggio, ED Paul Hirsch, PD Paul Sylbert.

LP John Travolta (Jack), Nancy Allen (Sally), John Lithgow (Burke), Dennis Franz (Karp), Peter Boyden (Sam), Curt May (Frank), Ernest McClure (Jim), Davie Roberts (Anchor Man), Maurice Copeland (Jack), Claire Carter (Anchor Woman), John Aquino (Detective).

Sound man John Travolta stumbles into the secret behind a political candidate's death. Prostitute Nancy Allen is caught up in a seedy plot that nearly costs Travolta's life. John's not the only one to stumble in this Brian De Palma nearmiss.

293. *Blowing Hot and Cold* (1989, Chancom, Australia, 85m, c). P Rosa Colosimo, D Marc Gracie, W Colosimo, Reg McLean, Luciano Vincenzoni & Sergio Donati, PH James Grant, M Joe Dolce, ED Nicolas Lee.

LP Peter Adams (Jack Phillips), Joe Dolce (Nino), Kate Gorman (Sally Phillips), Elspeth Ballantyne (Shelagh McBean), Bruce Kane (Jeff Lynch).

Con-man Joe Dolce, a salesman of porno magazines and sexual aids, befriends beer swilling Aussie mechanic Peter Adams, when the latter's daughter Kate Gorman runs away with her druggie boyfriend Bruce Kane. It's a fairly typical male bonding road film and nothing to get up off the couch to go to a theater to see.

294. *Blue City* (1986, Paramount, 83m, c). P William Hayward & Walter Hill, D Michelle Manning, W Lukas Heller & Hill (based on the novel by Ross MacDonald), PH Steven Poster, M Ry Cooder, ED Ross Albert, PD Robert Latham Brown.

LP Judd Nelson (Billy Turner), Ally Sheedy (Anne Rayford), David Caruso (Joey Rayford), Paul Winfield (Luther Reynolds), Scott Wilson (Perry Kerch), Anita Morris (Malvina Kerch), Luis Conteras (Lt. Ortiz).

Ross MacDonald's 1946 story is set in the 80s in this film. Judd Nelson, estranged from his family, returns to his hometown to discover his father, the former mayor, has been murdered. Nelson goes on a destructive spree against the local crime boss to get revenge.

295. *Blue Heaven* (1985, Five Points Films, 111m, c). P Elaine Sperber & Kathleen Dowdey & Jed Dannenbaum, D&W Dowdey, PH Kees Van Oostrum, M Fonda Feingold, ED Dowdey.

LP Leslie Denniston (Carol Sabella), James Eckhouse (Tony Sabella), Lisa Sloan, Marsha Jackson, Bruce Evers, Brenda Byrum, Merwin Goldsmith.

In a dullish, plotless film, TV executive James Eckhouse's problems with alcohol lead him to brutally beat his wife Leslie Denniston, who leaves him. It's an important subject, poorly handled.

296. *Blue Iguana* (1988, Paramount, 90m, c). P Steven Golin & Sigurjon Sighvatsson, D&W John Lafia, PH Rodolfo Sanchez, M Ethan James, Glen Mont & Freddie Ramos, ED Scott Chestnut, PD Cynthia Sowder.

LP Dylan McDermott (Vince Holloway), Jessica Harper (Cora), James Russo (Reno), Pamela Gidley (Dakota), Tovah Feldshuh (Det. Vera Quinn), Dean Stockwell (Det. Carl Strick), Katia Schkolnik (Mona), Flea (Floyd).

Modern day bounty-hunter Dylan McDermott, in hock to the IRA, is given an assignment to go South of the border and recover millions of dollars in laundered drug money on which no taxes have been paid. Everyone double-crosses everyone in this sloppy salute to earlier movies.

297. *The Blue Lagoon* (1980, Columbia, 102m, c). P&D Randal Kleiser, W Douglas Day Stewart (based on the novel by Henry Devere Stacpoole), PH Nestor Almendros†, M Basil Poledouris, ED Robert Gordon.

LP Brooke Shields (Emmeline), Christopher Atkins (Richard), Leo McKern (Paddy Button), William Daniels (Arthur LeStrange), Elva Josephson (Young Emmeline), Glenn Kohan (Young Richard), Alan Hopgood (Captain).

This remake of a 1949 film of the same name starring Jean Simmons and Donald Houston is beautiful to look at, but a boring story of two youngsters shipwrecked on a deserted island. As they grow up, they fall in love and have a child. Other than a little nudity, nothing much happens. Young actors Brooke Shields and Christopher Atkins aren't actors.

298. *Blue Monkey* (1987, Spectrafilm, 98m, c, aka *Green Monkey*). P Martin Walters, D William Fruet, W George Goldsmith, PH Brenton Spencer, M Patrick Coleman & Paul Novotny, ED Michael Fruet.

LP Steve Railsback (Det. Jim Bishop), Gwynyth Walsh (Dr. Rachel Carson), Susan Anspach (Dr. Judith Glass), John Vernon (Roger Levering), Joe Flaherty (George Baker), Robin Duke (Sandra Baker), Don Lake (Elliot Jacobs), Sandy Webster (Fred Adams), Helen Hughes (Marwella Harbison).

A patient in a small hospital is infected

by an unknown insect which causes terminal gangrene as it gestates eggs. One insect becomes mutated and grows to huge proportions, having the head of a wasp, the eyes of a dragonfly, the stomach of a scorpion, the back of a beetle and the arms of a praying mantis. Steve Railsback saves the day when he blinds the monster with a laser — but did he get all the eggs?

299. *Blue Movies* (1988, Skouras, 92m, c). P Maria Snyder, D&W Paul Koval & Ed Fitzgerald, PH Vance Piper, M Patrick Gleeson & Michael Shrieve, ED John Currin.

LP Steve Levitt (Buzz), Larry Poindexter (Cliff), Lucinda Crosby (Randy Moon), Darian Mathias (Kathy), Christopher Stone (Brad), Don Calfa (Max), Larry Linville (Dr. Gladding).

Losers Steve Levitt and Larry Poindexter decide to make some money by making a porno movie. They do, but the mob gets mad, believing the boys are moving in on their turf.

300. *Blue Skies Again* (1983, Warner, Samuel Bronston, 96m, c). P Arlene Sellers & Alex Winitsky, D Richard Michaels, W Kevin Sellers, PH Don McAline, ED Danford B. Greene, M John Kander.

LP Harry Hamlin (Sandy), Mimi Rogers (Liz), Kenneth McMillan (Dirk), Robyn Barto (Paula), Dana Elcar (Lou), Joey Gian (Calvin), Doug Moeller (Carroll), Tommy Lane (The Boy), Andy Garcia (Ken).

Robyn Barto wants to be a major league baseball player. She can hit, so she gets her wish. It's a pleasant bit of sports fluff.

301. *Blue Thunder* (1983, Columbia, 108m, c). P Gordon Carroll, D John Badham, W Dan O'Bannon & Don Jakoby, PH John Alonzo, M Arthur B. Rubenstein, ED Frank Morriss & Edward Abroms†, SE Chuck Gaspar, Jeff Jarvis & Peter Albiez.

LP Roy Scheider (Murphy), Malcolm McDowell (Cochrane), Candy Clark (Kate), Warren Oates (Braddock), Daniel Stern (Lymangood), Paul Roebling (Icelan), David Sheiner (Fletcher), Ed Berhard (Short), Jason Bernard (Mayor).

L.A. police pilot Roy Scheider is given the opportunity to test the government's new ultimate surveillance/attack weapon, code name "Blue Thunder." The "heliocopter" is to be used to combat terrorists at the 1984 Olympics. It's a high-tech thriller.

302. *Blue Velvet* (1986, De Laurentiis Entertainment Group, 120m, c). P Fred Caruso, D&W David Lynch† (as director), PH Frederick Elmes, M Angelo Badalamenti, ED Duwayne Dunham, PD Patricia Norris.

LP Kyle MacLachlan (Jeffrey Beaumont), Isabella Rossellini (Dorothy Vallens), Dennis Hopper (Frank Booth), Laura Dern (Sandy Williams), Hope Lange (Mrs. Williams), Dean Stockwell (Ben), George Dickerson (Det. Williams), Priscilla Pointer (Mrs. Beaumont), Frances Bay (Aunt Barbara), Jack Harvey (Mr. Beaumont), Ken Stovitz (Mike), Brad Dourif (Raymond).

Director David Lynch received an Oscar nomination for this voyeur-like investigation into sado-masochism, sexual obsession and murder. Dennis Hopper is excellent as the almost unearthly evil villain, Isabella Rossellini is laid bare in more than one way. This bizarre film has already become a cult classic, highly praised by most critics.

303. *Blueberry Hill* (1988, MGM, 87m, c). P Mark Michaels, D Strathford Hamilton, W Lonon Smith, PH David Lewis, M Ira Ingber, ED Marcy Hamilton, PD John Sperry Wade.

LP Margaret Avery (Hattie Cale), Carrie Snodgress (Becca Dane), Matt Lattanzi (Denny Logan), Jennifer Rubin (Ellie Dane), Tommy Swerdlow (Ray Porter), Dendrie Allynn Taylor (Rachel), Ian Patrick Williams (Owen Shackleford).

In this slow-paced coming-of-age film, Matt Lattanzi is an aspiring young mechanic whose girlfriend Jennifer Rubin has a troubled relationship with her mother Carrie Snodgress. Margaret Avery, a piano teacher who befriends Rubin, sings a number of 50s jazz numbers.

304. *The Blues Brothers* (1980, Universal, 133m, c). P Robert K. Weiss, D

John Landis, W Landis & Aykroyd, PH Stephen M. Katz, M Ira Newborn, ED George Folsey, Jr.

LP John Belushi (Joliet Jake Blues), Dan Aykroyd (Elwood Blues), James Brown (Rev. Cleophus James), Cab Calloway (Curtis), Ray Charles (Ray), Carrie Fisher (Mystery Woman), Aretha Franklin (Soul Food Cafe Owner), Henry Gibson (Nazi Leader), John Candy (Burton Mercer), Murphy Dunne (Murph), Steve Cropper (Steve "The Colonel" Cropper), Willie Hall (Willie "Too Big" Hall), Tom Malone ("Boots" Malone), Lou Marini ("Blue" Lou Marini), Matt Murphy (Matt "Guitar" Murphy), Donald "Duck" Dunn (Himself), Kathleen Freeman (Sister Mary Stigmata).

John Belushi, just out of Joliet Prison, is met by his brother Dan Aykroyd. They accept a mission from God to come up with the tax money to save the orphanage where they grew up. They put together their old band to get the money. This gives the film the opportunity to feature some real jazz musicians and allow for cameo appearances of the likes of James Brown, Ray Charles and Aretha Franklin. They almost ruin every police vehicle in Chicago before they pay their debt and go back to jail.

305.   *BMX Bandits* (1983, Nilsen Premiere Pty., Australia, 90m, c). P Tom Broadbridge & Paul Davies, D Brian Trenchard-Smith, W Patrick Edgeworth (based on the screenplay by Russell Hagg), PH John Seale, M Colin Stead & Frank Strangio, ED Alan Lake, PD Ross Major.

LP David Argue (Duane), John Ley (Povic), James Lugton (Goose), Brian Marshall (The Boss), Nicole Kidman (Judy), Angelo d'Angelo (PJ).

BMX Australian bikers find a stash of two-way radios belonging to bank robbers. They sell the radios tuned to the police frequency to their friends. The gangsters want the radios back and the kids rubbed out. The chase is on.

306.   *Body and Soul* (1981, Cannon, 109m, c). P Menahem Golan & Yoram Globus, D George Bowers, W Leon Isaac Kennedy, PH James Forrest, M Webster Lewis, ED Sam Pollard & Skip Schoolnick.

LP Leon Isaac Kennedy (Leon Johnson), Jayne Kennedy (Julie Winters), Perry Lang (Charles Golphin), Nikki Swassy (Kelly Johnson), Mike Grazzo (Frankie), Kim Hamilton (Mrs. Johnson), Muhammad Ali (Himself), Peter Lawford (Big Man).

This is a black version of the 1947 classic boxing drama starring John Garfield. Warning! It is a mistake. The people involved in making the movie have little talent. Rent the video of the earlier film rather than gag on this one.

307.   *Body Beat* (1988, Vidmark, 96m, c, aka *Dance Academy*). P Jef Richard & Aldo U. Passalacqua, D Ted Mather, W Mather (based on a story by Mather & Guido De Angelis, PH Dennis Peters, M De Angelis & Maurizio De Angelis, ED Rebecca Ross.

LP Tony Dean Fields (Moon), Galyn Gorg (Jana), Scott Grossman (Tommy), Eliska Krupka (Patrizia), Steve La Chance (Vince), Paula Nichols (Paula), Julie Newmar (Miss McKenzie).

In a film trying to be another *Fame*, Julie Newmar runs a classical ballet academy. Student Tony Dean Fields would like to enliven the curriculum with some jazz numbers. Julie was better as the Catwoman in Batman.

308.   *Body Count* (1988, Manson International, 93m, c). P,D&W Paul Leder (based on a story by William W. Norton, Sr.), PH Francis Grumman, M Bob Summers, ED Leder.

LP Bernie White (Robert Knight), Marilyn Hassett (Joanne Knight), Dick Sargent (Charles Knight), Greg Mullavey (Ralph Duris), Thomas Ryan (Lt. Chernoff), Haunani Minn (Kim), Steven Ford (Tom Leary).

In another straight to video feature, murderous psychopath Bernie White breaks out of a mental institution vowing revenge against his greedy uncle, Dick Sargent, who had him committed.

309.   *Body Double* (1984, Columbia, 109m, c). P&D Brian De Palma, W De Palma & Robert Avrech (based on a story by De Palma), PH Stephen H. Burum, M Pino Donaggio, ED Jerry Greenberg & Bill Pankow, PD Ida Random.

LP Craig Wasson (Jake), Melanie

Griffith (Holly), Gregg Henry (Sam), Deborah Shelton (Gloria), Guy Boyd (Jim McLean), Dennis Franz (Rubin), Rebecca Stanley (Kimberly), Al Israel (Corso), B.J. Jones (Douglas).

Out-of-work actor Craig Wasson is drawn into a nightmare when he falls for a married woman who he spies on with a telescope as she does a sexy striptease. He's unable to save her from being killed by an "Indian" with an electric drill. He then discovers that he's been used to put the cops off the trail of the real killer. Melanie Griffith is convincing as a porno star in this trite voyeuristic Brian De Palma film.

310. Body Heat (1981, Warner/Ladd, 113m, c). P Fred T. Gallo, D&W Lawrence Kasdan, PH Richard H. Kline, M John Barry, ED Carol Littleton.

LP William Hurt (Ned Racine), Kathleen Turner (Matty Walker), Richard Crenna (Edmund Walker), Ted Danson (Peter Lowenstein), J.A. Preston (Oscar Grace), Mickey Rourke (Teddy Lewis), Kim Zimmer (Mary Ann), Jane Hallaren (Stella), Lanna Saunders (Roz Kraft), Michael Ryan (Miles Hardin).

Sexy femme fatale Kathleen Turner wraps wimpy Florida lawyer William Hurt around her body. She has him panting to do her bidding to eliminate Turner's husband Richard Crenna. Turner is so hot, it's a wonder that wooden Hurt doesn't burst into flames while making love to her. It's a technicolor clone of film noir classic *Double Indemnity,* although credit is not given to the earlier film.

311. Body Rock (1984, New World, 93m, c). P Jeffrey Schechtman, D Marcelo Epstein, W Desmond Nakano, PH Robby Muller, M Sylvester Levay, ED Richard Halsey, PD Guy Comtois.

LP Lorenzo Lamas (Chilly D), Vicki Frederick (Claire), Cameron Dye (E.Z.), Michelle Nicastro (Darlene), Ray Sharkey (Terrence), Grace Zabriskie (Chilly's Mother), Carole Ita White (Carolyn), Joseph Whipp (Donald).

Son of Fernando Lamas and Esther Williams, neither of whom were noted for their acting, Lorenzo Lamas comes by his lack of talent (except, we suppose for being a "hunk") naturally. This stupid break-dance movie shouldn't advance the career of any of the nonmusical "stars" who make up its cast.

312. Body Slam (1987, De Laurentiis, 89m, c). P Shel Lytton & Mike Curb, D Hal Needham, W Lytton & Steve Burkow (based on a story by Lytton), PH Mike Shea, M Michael Lloyd & Jon D'Andrea, ED Randy Thornton, AD Pamela Warner.

LP Dirk Benedict (Harry Smilac), Tanya Roberts (Candace Van Der Vegen), Rowdy Roddy Piper (Rick Roberts), Capt. Lou Albano (Capt. Lou Milano), Barry Gordon (Sheldon), Charles Nelson Reilly (Vic Carson).

Unscrupulous rock 'n' roll promoter Dirk Benedict makes it big in the wrestling business. Look for a lot of familiar wrestling figures—that is if you are familiar with wrestling figures—and if not what the hell are you watching this turkey for?

313. Boggy Creek II (1985, Howco, 91m, c, aka *The Barbaric Beast of Boggy Creek*). P,D&W Charles B. Pierce, PH Shirah Kojayan, M Frank McKelvey, ED Kojayan.

LP Charles B. Pierce (Prof. Lockhart), Cindy Butler (Leslie Ann Walker), Serene Hedin (Tanya), Chuck Pierce (Tim Thorn), Jimmy Clem (Crenshaw), Fabus Griffin (Adult Creature), Victor Williams (Young Creature).

First came *The Legend of Boggy Creek,* a 1973 docudrama about a Bigfoot-like creature in Arkansas. Then in 1977, there was an unofficial sequel, *Return to Boggy Creek,* in which a hairy creature helps some kids lost in a storm. Finally in 1985, the monster has been spotted again. He falls in a trap when a small scale monster is used for bait, but Charles B. Pierce lets them both go, mumbling something or other about not tampering with nature.

314. Bolero (1984, Cannon, 106m, c, aka *Bolero: An Adventure in Ecstasy*). P Bo Derek, D,W&PH John Derek, M Peter Bernstein & Elmer Bernstein, PD Alan Roderick-Jones.

LP Bo Derek (Ayre McGillvary), George Kennedy (Cotton Grey), Andrea Occhipinti (Angel Contreras), Ana

Obregon (Catalina Terry), Olivia d'Abo (Paloma), Greg Bensen (The Sheik), Ian Cochran (Robert Stewart).

More trash from the Dereks. Young college grad Bo Derek is off on a world-wide quest to lose her virginity. How difficult can it be?

Bolero: An Adventure in Ecstasy see Bolero

315. ***Bon Voyage, Charlie Brown (And Don't Come Back)*** (1980, Paramount, animated, 75m, c). P Lee Mendelson & Bill Melendez, D Melendez, W Charles M. Schultz (based on his "Peanuts" characters), PH Nick Vasu, M Ed Bogas & Judy Munson, ANIM Sam Jaimes, Hank Smith, Al Pabian, Joe Roman, Ed Newmann, Bill Littlejohn, Bob Carlson, Dale Baer, Spencer Peel, Larry Leichliter & Sergio Bertolli.

VOICES Daniel Anderson, Scott Beach, Casey Carlson, Debbie Fuller, Patricia Patts, Laura Planting, Arrin Skelley, Bill Melendez, Annalisa Bortolin, Roseline Rubens, Pascale De Bardlet.

In their fourth feature-length animated movie, the cartoon characters from "Peanuts," Charlie Brown, Linus, Peppermint Patty, Marcie, Snoopy, etc., become exchange students in Europe.

316. ***The Boogens*** (1982, Sunn Classic, 95m, c). P Charles E. Sellier, Jr., D James L. Conway, W David O'Malley & Bob Hunt, PH Paul Hipp, M Bob Summers, ED Michael Spence.

LP Rebecca Balding (Trish), Fred McCarren (Mark), Anne-Marie Martin (Jessica), Jeff Harlan (Roger), John Crawford (Brian), Med Flory (Dan), Jon Lormer (Blanchard), Peg Stewart (Victoria), Scott Wilkinson (Deputy), Marcia Reider (Martha).

When locals reopen a long-closed Utah silver mine, mysterious creatures (not seen until the very end of the picture) go on a killing rampage.

317. ***The Boogey Man*** (1980, Jerry Gross, 79m, c). P,D&W Ulli Lommel, PH David Sperling, M Tim Krog, ED Terrell Tannen.

LP Suzanna Love (Lacey), Ron James (Jake), John Carradine (Doctor), Michael Love, Raymond Boyden.

Suzanna Love is haunted by the spirit of her mother's lover, killed years go by her now mute brother. She goes back to the place of the murder and sees the dead man in a piece of broken mirror. The mirror avenges murders it has witnessed.

318. ***Boogeyman II*** (1983, New West Films, 79m, c). P Ulli Lommel, D Lommell & Bruce Starr, PH Philippe Carr-Foster & David Sperling, M Tim Krog, Wayne Love & Craig Hundley, ED Terrell Tannen.

LP Suzanna Love (Lacey), Ulli Lommel (Mickey), Bob Rosenfarb (Bernie), Shannah Hall (Bonnie), Shoto von Douglas (Joseph), Ahley DuBay, Rhonda Aldrich, Sarah Jean Watkins, David D'Arnel.

There's a lot of flashbacks to *The Boogey Man* in this perfectly horrible excuse for a horror film. Lots of gore and attempts at black humor, but no new ground is broken. If there was, this film could be buried in the hole.

319. ***The Boost*** (1988, Hemdale, 95m, c). P Daniel H. Blatt, D Harold Becker, W Darryl Ponicsan (based on the book *Ludes* by Benjamin Stein), PH Howard Atherton, M Stanley Myers, ED Maury Winetrobe, PD Waldemar Kalinowski.

LP James Woods (Lenny Brown), Sean Young (Linda Brown), John Kapelos (Joel), Steven Hill (Max), Kelle Kerr (Rochelle), John Rothman (Ned Lewis), Amanda Blake (Barbara), Grace Zabriskie (Sheryl).

James Woods and Sean Young are a young couple, very much in love. Smooth operator Woods gets his golden opportunity from Steven Hill to move from New York to L.A. to sell tax shelters. Woods is a big success, and he and his beloved become social cocaine users. When his balloon pops due to Congressional action, Woods steals from Hill and is dismissed from his position, deeply in debt and hooked on cocaine. One naturally notes the similarity to *Days of Wine and Roses,* where alcohol was the preferred means of destroying the lives of a young couple.

320. ***The Border*** (1982, Universal, 107m, c). P Edgar Bronfman, D Tony Richardson, W Deric Washburn, Walon

Green & David Freeman, PH Ric Waite & Vilmos Zsigmond, M Ry Cooder, ED Robert K. Lambert.

LP Jack Nicholson (Charlie), Harvey Keitel (Cat), Valerie Perrine (Marcy), Warren Oates (Red), Elpidia Carrillo (Maria), Shannon Wilcox (Savannah), Manuel Viescas (Juan), Jeff Morris (J.J.), Mike Gomez (Manuel).

Border cop Jack Nicholson's sympathies go out to the wretchedly poor Mexicans he's paid to keep out of the country. His grasping shrewish wife Valerie Perrine and his corrupt fellow officers encourage him to rip off the wetbacks and earn extra money. He does, but his conscience bothers him. Young Mexican mother Elpidia Carrillo comforts him.

321. *Borderline* (1980, Associated Film Distribution, 97m, c). P James Nelson, D Jerrold Freedman, W Freedman & Steve Kline, PH Tak Fujimoto, M Gil Melle, ED John Link.

LP Charles Bronson (Jeb Maynard), Bruno Kirby (Jimmy Fante), Bert Remsen (Carl Richards), Michael Lerner (Henry Lydell), Kenneth McMillan (Malcolm Wallace), Ed Harris (Hotchkiss), Karim Murcelo (Elena Morales), Wilford Brimley (Scooter Jackson).

Dedicated border officer Charles Bronson clashes with the FBI as he goes after flesh smuggler Ed Harris who runs Latinos across the Mexican border near San Diego.

322. *B.O.R.N.* (1989, Movie Outfit, 92m, c). P Claire Hagen, D Ross Hagen, W Hoke Howell & R. Hagen, PH Gary Graver, M William Belote, ED Diana Friedberg, AD Shirley Thompson.

LP Ross Hagen (Buck Cassidy), P.J. Soles (Liz), Hoke Howell (Charlie), William Smith (Dr. Farley), Russ Tamblyn (Hugh), Amanda Blake (Rosie), Rance Howard, Clint Howard, Claire Hagen.

In this *Coma*-like movie (the title is an acronym for "Body Organ Replacement Network") Ross Hagen finds himself in a struggle with evil doctors who have kidnapped his daughters to obtain organ parts for lucrative black market transplants. In her last screen role, Amanda Blake helps Hagen take on the bad guys,

one of whom is vicious heavy Russ Tamblyn (which for fans who remember when he was called Rusty, this is difficult to imagine).

323. *Born American* (1986, Cinema Group, US/Finland, 96m, c). P Markus Selin, D Renny Harlin, W Harlin & Selin, PH Henrik Paerchs, M Richard Mitchell, ED Paul Martin Smith.

LP Mike Norris (Savoy), Steve Durham (Mitch), David Coburn (K.C.), Thalmus Rasulala (Admiral), Albert Salmi (Drane), Piita Vusosalmi (Nadja), Vesa Vierikko (Kapsky), Ismo Kallio (Zarkov), Laura Heimo (Irina).

Three vacationing American college boys, Mike Norris, Steve Durham and David Coburn, accidentally stumble across the Finnish border into the Soviet Union. They elude the Red Army, cause havoc in a small Ukrainian town, are accused of raping a girl, survive torture at the hands of the KGB and finally escape. It's escapism, all right.

324. *Born in East L.A.* (1987, Universal, 84m, c). P Peter MacGregor-Scott, D&W Richard "Cheech" Marin, PH Alex Phillips, M Lee Holdridge, ED Donald Brochu.

LP Cheech Marin (Rudy Robles), Paul Rodriguez (Javier), Daniel Stern (Jimmy), Kamala Lopez (Dolores), Jan-Michael Vincent (McCalister), Neith Hunter (Marcie), Alma Martinez (Gloria), Tony Plana (Feo).

This spoof of Bruce Springsteen's hit "Born in the USA" features Cheech Marin, a third generation Mexican-American, rounded up with some illegal aliens. Because he hasn't any identification on him, he is sent back across the border where he has no money and is unable to speak Spanish. It's a serious comedy study which was a surprising hit.

325. *Born in Flames* (1983, First Run Features, 80m, c). P&D Lizzie Borden, W Hisa Tayo (based on story by Borden), PH Ed Bowes & Al Santana.

LP Honey (Herself), Adele Bertei (Isabel), Jeanne Satterfield (Adelaide), Flo Kennedy (Zella), Hillary Hurst, Sheila McLaughlin & Marty Pottenger (Army Women).

Set in New York, sometime in the

future, the new women's army has gone underground after the death of its leader Jeanne Satterfield. It plans to overthrow the established ruling party.

326.   *Born of Fire* (1987, IFEX-Vidmark, 84m, c). P Jamil Dehlavi & Therese Pickard, D Dehlavi, W Raficq Abdulla, PH Bruce McGowan.

LP Peter Firth, Susan Crowley, Stefan Kalipha, Oh-tee, Nabil Shaban.

Concert flautist Peter Firth journeys to the Middle East to discover the reason for his father's death. Instead he comes under the spell of the "Master Musician" who intends to use his music to consume the earth with fire. Firth saves the day in this confusing and generally boring occult film.

327.   *Born on the Fourth of July†* (1989, Universal, 145m, c). P A. Kitman Ho & Oliver Stone, D Stone*, W Stone & Ron Kovic† (based on Kovic's book), PH Robert Richardson†, M John Williams†, ED David Brenner*, PD Bruno Rubeo, SOUND Todd A. Maitland†.

LP Tom Cruise† (Ron Kovic), Bryan Larkin (Young Ron), Kyra Sedgwick (Donna), Jessica Prunell (Young Donna), Raymond J. Barry (Mr. Kovic), Caroline Kava (Mrs. Kovic), Jerry Levine (Steve Boyer), Frank Whaley (Timmy), Willem Dafoe (Charlie), Josh Evans (Tommy Kovic), Tom Berenger & Richard Haus (Recruiting Sergeants), Ed Lauter (American Legion Commander), Abbie Hoffman (Strike Organizer), Cordelia Gonzalez (Maria Elena), Holly Marie Combs (Jenny).

Tom Cruise gives the performance of his young career in this true story of All-American boy Ron Kovic, who upon graduating from high school joined the Marine corps to fight the communist menace. The film brilliantly examines how a gung-ho, patriotic kid becomes one of the leading spokesmen for Vietnam Veterans Against the war. He returns to an unhappy home after he sees civilians — men, women and children — slaughtered in a dog-fight, he accidentally kills a fellow gyrene, and a sniper bullet makes him a paraplegic. Oliver Stone wins his second directorial Oscar for proving that audiences are not yet ready to put Vietnam and the many questions the war raised behind them.

328.   *Born to Race* (1988, MGM—United Artists, 98m, c). P Andrew Bullians & Jean Bullians, D James Fargo, W Dennis McGee & Mary Janeway Bullians (based on a story by M.J. Bullians), PH Bernard Salzmann, M Ross Vannelli, ED Tony Lombardo & Thomas Stanford, PD Katherine G. Vallin.

LP Joseph Bottoms (Al Pagura), Marc Singer (Kenny Landruff), George Kennedy (Vincent Duplain), Marla Heasley (Andrea Lombardo), Antonio Sabato (Enrico Lombardo), Robert F. Logan (Theo Jennings), Dirk Blocker (Bud).

When villains Marc Singer and George Kennedy kidnap race-car designer Marla Heasley, stealing her plans for a car which will revolutionize auto racing, it falls to her new love, driver Joseph Bottoms, to rescue her.

329.   *The Boss' Wife* (1986, Tri-Star, 83m, c). P Thomas H. Brodek, D&W Ziggy Steinberg, PH Gary P. Thieltges, M Bill Conti, ED John A. Martinelli, PD Brenton Swift.

LP Daniel Stern (Joel), Arielle Dombasle (Louise), Fisher Stevens (Carlos), Melanie Mayron (Janet), Lou Jacobi (Harry), Martin Mull (Tony), Christopher Plummer (Roalvang), Diane Stilwell (Suzy).

Young married stockbroker Daniel Stern competes with Martin Mull for a promotion in Christopher Plummer's company. The latter's nymphomaniac wife Arielle Dombasle assures Stern his chances will improve if he goes to bed with her.

330.   *The Bostonians* (1984, Almi, GB, 120m, c). P Ismail Merchant, D James Ivory, W Ruth Prawer Jhabvala (based on the novel by Henry James), PH Walter Lassally, M Richard Robbins, ED Katherine Wenning & Mark Potter, PD Leo Austin, COS Jenny Beavan & John Bright†.

LP Christopher Reeve (Basil Ransom), Vanessa Redgrave† (Olive Chancellor), Madeleine Potter (Verena Tarrant), Jessica Tandy (Miss Birdseye), Nancy Marchand (Mrs. Burrage), Wesley Addy (Dr. Tarrant), Linda Hunt (Dr. Prance), Wallace Shawn (Mr. Pardon).

In 19th century Boston, faith healer Wesley Addy's daughter Madeleine Potter is forced to choose between the affections of militant suffragette Vanessa Redgrave and young lawyer Christopher Reeve. The film is beautiful to look at, but is unfortunately a boring production of Henry James' novel.

331. *The Bounty* (1984, Orion, GB, 132m, c). P Bernard Williams, D Roger Donaldson, W Robert Bolt (based on the novel *Captain Bligh and Mr. Christian* by Richard Hough), PH Arthur Ibbetson, M Vangelis, ED Tony Lawson, PD John Graysmark.

LP Mel Gibson (Fletcher Christian), Anthony Hopkins (Lt. William Bligh), Sir Laurence Olivier (Adm. Hood), Edward Fox (Capt. Greetham), Daniel Day-Lewis (Fryer), Bernard Hill (Cole), Philip Davis (Young), Liam Neeson (Churchill), Wi Kuki Kaa (King Tynah), Tevaite Vernette (Mauatua), Philip Martin Brown (Adams), Malcolm Terris (Dr. Huggan).

This version of the infamous *Bounty* mutiny in 1789 doesn't make Captain Bligh out to be an unfeeling monster. In fact he's a close friend of Fletcher Christian, perhaps with feelings of more than a mere friend. The captain has his character flaws but he's no worse than most british skippers of the time. It's only after his crew hits the beach at Tahiti and mates with the ever-willing native girls, that Bligh has trouble getting them to toe the line on the voyage back to England. Christian moons for the love he left behind and isn't much help. Bligh's means to instill discipline become more severe and along with the longing for Tahiti and its obvious advantages, the crew is driven to take the ship, setting Bligh adrift with loyal seamen. Bligh proves his seamanship by taking the small boat 4,000 miles in 40 days to land. Anthony Hopkins completely dominates the proceedings while Mel Gibson almost sleep-walks his way through his part.

332. *Bounty Hunter* (1989, Action Intl., 90m, c). P Fritz Matthews, D Robert Ginty, W Thomas Baldwin, PH Robert Baldwin, M Tim James, Steve McClintock & Tim Heintz, ED David Campling & Jonathan Shaw.

LP Robert Ginty (Duke Evans), Bo Hopkins (Sheriff Bennett), Loeta Waterdown (Marion Foot), Melvin Holt (Kevin Foot), John White (Barnes), Robert Knott (Jimmy Gibbons).

Like some latter-day Spencer Tracy at Bad Rock, Robert Ginty heads for a small Oklahoma town to avenge the death of an Indian with whom he served in Vietnam. Ginty's skills as a bounty hunter seem to have little to do with the main portion of the story.

333. *Boxoffice* (1982, Bogdanovich Prod., 93m, c). P Josef Bogdanovich & Bruce Chastain, D Bogdanovich, PH Eric Saarinen, M Omette Coleman, ED Bonnie Kozek & Edward Salier.

LP Robin Clarke (Peter Malloy), Monica Lewis (Francesca), Eddie Constantine (Hugh Barren), Aldo Ray (Lew), Edie Adams (Carolyn), Carol Cortne (Eve Chandler), Peter Hurkos (Himself), Chuck Mitchell (Mr. Joy).

Josef Bogdanovich attempts to show the sleazy aspects of show business as young Carol Cortne strives to become a Hollywood star. Give him an F for failure.

334. *The Boy in Blue* (1986, 20th Century Fox, Canada, 98m, c). P John Kemeny, D Charles Jarrott, W Douglas Bowie, PH Pierre Mignot, M Roger Webb, ED Rit Wallis, PD William Beeton.

LP Nicolas Cage (Ned), Cynthia Dale (Margaret), Christopher Plummer (Knox), David Naughton (Bill), Sean Sullivan (Walter), Melody Anderson (Dulcie), James B. Douglas (Collins), Walter Massey (Mayor).

Nicolas Cage, an actor of very little range and less appeal, is miscast. He muddies the water in his portrayal of the real-life Canadian rowing champ of the late 19th century. Cage acts as if he believes the film is set in contemporary Philadelphia.

335. *The Boy Who Could Fly* (1986, Lorimar, 114m, c). P Gary Adelson, D&W Nick Castle, PH Steven Poster & Adam Holender, M Bruce Broughton, ED Patrick Kennedy, PD Jim Bissell.

LP Lucy Deakins (Milly), Jay Underwood (Eric), Bonnie Bedelia (Charlene),

Fred Savage (Louis), Colleen Dewhurst (Mrs. Sherman), Fred Gwynne (Uncle Hugo), Mindy Cohn (Geneva), Janet MacLachlan (Mrs. D'Gregario).

After his parents are killed in a plane crash, Jay Underwood becomes autistic but exhibits evidence of being able to fly. When Lucy Deakins moves next door, the young couple form a relationship which slowly brings Underwood out of his shell. They still must deal with bureaucrats who want to institutionalize the lad.

336.   The Boys in Blue (1983, Rank, GB, 91m, c). P Greg Smith, D Val Guest, W Guest & Sid Green (based on the story "Ask a Policeman" by Sidney Gilliat), PH Jack Atheler, M Ed Welch, ED Peter Weatherley.

LP Tommy Cannon (Sgt. Cannon), Bobby Ball (PC Ball), Suzanne Danielle (Kim), Roy Kinnear (Hector Lloyd), Eric Sykes (Chief Constable), Jack Douglas (Superintendent), Edward Judd (Hilling).

In this British comedy, inefficient country policemen Tommy Cannon and Bobby Ball pursue and catch painting thieves.

337.   The Boys Next Door (1985, New World—Republic, 88m, c). P Keith Rubinstein & Sandy Howard, D Penelope Spheeris, W Glen Morgan & James Wong, PH Arthur Albert, M George S. Clinton, ED Andy Horvitch.

LP Maxwell Caulfield (Roy Alston), Charlie Sheen (Bo Richards), Christopher McDonald (Det. Woods), Hank Garrett (Det. Hanley), Patti D'Arbanville (Angie), Paul C. Dancer (Chris).

Just about to graduate from high school, desperate and hopeless, Maxwell Caulfield and Charlie Sheen, go on a murderous spree, but what motivates them isn't quite clear.

338.   Braddock: Missing in Action III (1988, Cannon, 101m, c). P Menahem Golan & Yoram Globus, D Aaron Norris, W James Bruner & Chuck Norris (based on characters created by Arthur Silver, Larry Levinson & Steve Bing), PH Joao Fernandes, M Jay Chattaway, ED Michael J. Duthie, PD Ladislav Wilheim.

LP Chuck Norris (Braddock), Aki Aleong (General Quoc), Roland Harrah 3d (Van Tan Cang), Miki Kim (Lin Tan Cang), Yehuda Erfoni (Rev. Polanski), Ron Barker (Mik), Floyd Levine (Gen. Duncan), Melinda Betron (Thuy).

Chuck Norris makes yet another trip to Vietnam, this time to get his Vietnamese wife whom he was forced to leave behind at the fall of Saigon. It's not POWs and MIAs which he brings out, but Amerasian children, including a son he didn't know he had.

339.   Brady's Escape (1984, Satori, US/Hungary, 96m, c). P Robert Halmi, Jr., D Pal Gabor, W William W. Lewis (based on a story by Gabor), PH Elemer Ragayli, M Charles Gross, ED Norman Gay & Eva Karmento.

LP John Savage (Brady), Kelly Reno (Miki), Ildiko Bansagi (Klara), Laszlo Mensaros (Dr. Dussek), Ferenc Bacs (Wortman), Dzsoko Rosic (Csorba).

World War II U.S. bomber pilot John Savage is forced to bail out over Nazi-occupied Hungary. With the help of nomads, Savage is able to make it to Yugoslavia and joins Tito's partisans.

340.   Brain Damage (1988, Henenlotter/Ievins/Palisades, 87m, c). P Edgar Ievins, D&W Frank Henenlotter, PH Bruce Torbet, M Gus Russo & Clutch Reiser, ED James Y. Kwei & Henenlotter, SE Al Magliochetti.

LP Rick Herbst (Brian), Gordon MacDonald (Mike), Jennifer Lowry (Barbara), Theo Barnes (Morris Ackerman), Lucille Saint-Peter (Martha Ackerman), Vicki Darnell (Blonde in Hell Club), Kevin Van Hentenryck (Man with Basket).

We don't wish to give away the plot of this gory, violent, profane film. Suffice it to say that Rick Herbst's life is changed when a 1,000-year-old brain-eating parasite named Elmer slithers under his apartment door.

341.   Brainstorm (1983, MGM/United Artists, 106m, c). P&D Douglas Trumbull, W Robert Statzel & Phillip Frank Messina (based on a story by Bruce Joel Rubin), PH Richard Yuricich, M James Horner, ED Edward Warschilka & Freeman Davies, PD John Vallone.

LP Christopher Walken (Michael Brace), Natalie Wood (Karen Brace),

Louise Fletcher (Lillian Reynolds), Cliff Robertson (Alex Terson), Georgianne Walken (Wendy), Bill Morey (James Zimbach), Joe Dorsey (Hal).

In Natalie Wood's last film (near the end of production, she drowned off Catalina Island), she appears in support of Louise Fletcher, who with fellow scientist Christopher Walken has developed a headphone-like machine that can record any human sensation, dream or nightmare and transmit it to the wearer. Fletcher manages to see her own death with the machine. She and Walken don't want their work to be used as a weapon by the government.

Brainwash see Circle of Power

342. *Brainwaves* (1983, Motion Picture Marketing, 81m, c). P&D Ulli Lommel, W Lommel & Suzanna Love, PH Jon Kranhouse, M Robert O. Ragland, ED Richard Brummer, SE N.H.P. Inc.

LP Keir Dullea (Julian), Suzanna Love (Kaylie), Percy Rodrigues (Dr. Robinson), Vera Miles (Marian), Tony Curtis (Dr. Clavius), Paul Wilson (Dr. Shroder), Ryan Seitz (Danny), Nicholas Love (Willy).

After an auto accident puts her in a coma, Suzanne Love's husband Keir Dullea and mother Vera Miles allow Tony Curtis to try a new surgical procedure for giving her the brain waves of a murdered girl. Love recovers, but she also inherits the dead girl's memory and when the killer learns this, he's out to put Love in a permanent trance.

343. *The Brave Little Toaster* (1987, Hyperion-Kushner-Locke, animated, 80m, c). P Donald Kushner & Thomas L. Wilhite, D Jerry Rees, W Rees & Joe Ranft (based on a story by Rees, Ranft & Brian McEntee from the novella by Thomas M. Disch), M David Newman.

LP VOICES Jon Lovitz (Radio), Tim Stack (Lampy), Timothy E. Day (Blanky), Thurl Ravencroft (Kirby), Deanna Oliver (Toaster), Phil Hartman (Air Conditioner, Hanging Lamp), Jonathon Benair (B&W TV), Joe Ranft (Elmo St. Peters).

Five household appliances led by the Toaster leave their home to search for their former master "Rob." They ulti-mately find happiness in an urban junkyard. It's cute.

The Brave Men of Wernberg see Up the Academy

344. *Brazil* (1985, Universal, GB, 131m, c). P Arnon Milchan, D Terry Gilliam, W Gilliam, Tom Stoppard & Charles McKeown†, PH Roger Pratt, M Michael Kamen, ED Julian Doyle, PD Norman Garwood, AD/SD Norman Garwood & Maggie Gray†.

LP Jonathan Pryce (Sam Lowry), Robert De Niro (Tuttle), Katherine Helmond (Ida Lowry), Ian Holm (Kurtzmann), Bob Hoskins (Spoor), Michael Palin (Jack Lint), Ian Richardson (Warren), Peter Vaughn (Helpmann), Kim Greist (Jill Layton), Jim Broadbent (Dr. Jaffe).

Former Monty Python member Terry Gilliam has produced an eccentric fantasy about hapless government official Jonathan Pryce wandering through a totalitarian society seeking his "dream" woman. The plot's not the thing in this savagely visual and chaotic but enjoyable film which updates Orwell's *1984*.

345. *Break Out* (1985, Eyeline, GB, 63m, c). P Harold Orton & Frank Godwin, D Godwin, W Ranald Graham (based on the novel *A Place to Hide* by Bill Gillham), PH Ray Orton, M Harry Robinson, ED Gordon Grimward.

LP David Jackson (Donny), Ian Bartholomew (Keith), John Bowler (Phil), Simon Nash (David), John Hasler (Stephen), Ian Rattray (Inspector), Brian Binns (PC), Stephen Jacobs (PC), Barry Norman (PC).

A group of bird-watching children are captured by escaped convicts.

Breakdance see Breakin'

Breakdance 2 – The Electric Boogaloo see Breakin' 2: Electric Boogaloo

Breakdown see The Freeway Maniac

346. *Breaker Morant* (1980, New World, Australia, 107m, c). P Matt Carroll, D Bruce Beresford, W Jonathan Hardy, David Stevens & Beresford† (based on a play by Kenneth Ross), PH Don McAlpine, M Phil Cunneen, ED William Anderson.

LP Edward Woodward (Lt. Harry Morant), Jack Thompson (Major J.F. Thomas), John Waters (Capt. Alfred Taylor), Bryan Brown (Lt. Peter Handcock), Rod Mullinar (Maj. Charles Bolton), Lewis Fitz-Gerald (Lt. George Witton), Charles Tingwell (Lt. Col. Denny), Vincent Ball (Lt. Ian Hamilton), Frank Wilson (Dr. Johnson), Terence Donovan (Capt. Simon Hunt), Russell Kiefel (Christian Botha), Alan Cassell (Lord Kitchener).

Here's another film preaching that when the military high command blunders, scapegoats are found among the fighting men. This is the true story of Harry "Breaker" Morant, who with two other Aussie soldiers, Peter Handcock and George Witton, is chosen to take the heat of World condemnation off the British high command during the Boer War. They are put on trial for murdering guerrilla prisoners of wars. They don't deny it, but insist they were acting on orders from higher up because of the unusual nature of the war. The three are convicted, with Morant and Handcock going before a firing squad the morning after their conviction. Edward Woodward is superb in the title role, as is Jack Thompson as the frustrated defense attorney who is defeated by the lies of those who could have saved his clients. Since Nuremberg, many have dismissed the defense of merely following orders, but it is a shame the ones who gave the damnable orders get off scot-free.

347. The Breakfast Club (1985, Universal, 97m, c). P Ned Tanen & John Hughes, D&W Hughes, PH Thomas Del Ruth, M Keith Forsey & Gary Chang, ED Dede Allen, PD John W. Corso.

LP Molly Ringwald (Claire Standish), Emilio Estevez (Andrew Clark), Judd Nelson (John Bender), Ally Sheedy (Allison Reynolds), Anthony Michael Hall (Brian Johnson), Paul Gleason (Richard Vernon), John Kapelos (Carl).

Older members of the audience get a chance to watch adolescents being pretty much themselves as pretty Molly Ringwald, a high school princess; Emilio Estevez, a wrestling jock; Judd Nelson, a hoodish rebel; Anthony Michael Hall, a brainy nerd; and Ally Sheedy, an intro-

verted loner, are punished for various infractions with a Saturday detention. Before the day is over, the five completely different kids have learned to communicate and appreciate their differences. It's a nonpreachy lesson that all ages could benefit from learning.

348. Breakin' (1984, Cannon/MGM/United Artists, 87m, c, aka *Breakdance*). P Allen DeBevoise & David Zito, D Joel Silberg, W Charles Parker, DeBevoise & Gerald Scaife (based on a story by Parker & DeBevoise), PH Hanania Baer, M Gary Remal & Michael Boyd, ED Larry Bock, Gib Jaffe & Vincent Sklena, PD Ivo G. Christante.

LP Lucinda Dickey (Kelly), Adolfo "Shabba-Doo" Quinones (Ozone), Michael "Boogaloo Shrimp" Chambers (Turbo), Phineas Newborn III (Adam), Christopher McDonald (James), Ben Lokey (Franco), Tracey "Ice-T" Morrow (Rap Talker).

If you felt the break-dance fad was fun, get down and spin with this film. Chorus girl Lucinda Dickey teams up with a group of breakers to further their careers. Frankly, it doesn't take many spins on the floor to lose our interest.

349. Breakin' 2: Electric Boogaloo (1984, Cannon/Tri-Star, 94m, c, aka *Breakdance 2—Electric Boogaloo; Electric Boogaloo "Breakin' 2"*). P Menahem Golan & Yoram Globus, D Sam Firstenberg, W Jan Ventura & Julia Reichert (based on characters created by Charles Parker & Allan DeBevoise), PH Hanania Baer, M Russ Regan, ED Sally Allen, Bertl Glatstein, Bob Jenkis & Barry Zetlin, PD Joseph T. Garrity.

LP Lucinda Dickey (Kelly), Adolfo "Shabba-Doo" Quinones (Ozone), Michael "Boogaloo Shrimp" Chambers (Turbo), Susie Bono (Rhonda), Harry Caesar (Byron), Jo de Winter (Mrs. Bennett), John Christy Ewing (Mr. Bennett).

The sequel to *Breakin'* was released within seven months of the original and is just more of the same. We've now seen all the break dancing we will ever require for the rest of our lives.

350. Breaking All the Rules (1985, New World, 91m, c). P Pieter Kroonenburg, David Patterson & Pierre David, D

James Orr, W Orr & James Cruikshank (based on a story by Edith Rey &Rafal Zielinski), PH Rene Verzier, M Paul Zaza, ED Nick Rotundo & Janet Lazare, PD Sandra Kybartas.

LP Carl Marotte (Jack), Thor Bishopric (David), Carolyn Dunn (Debbie), Rachel Hayward (Angie), Michael Rudder (Harry), Papusha Demitro (Patty), Pierre Andre Larocoque (Babyface), Walter Massey (Charlie).

Looking for a little sex on the last day of summer vacation, four lusty teenagers find it at an amusement park, where they also become mixed-up with jewel thieves.

351. Breaking Glass (1980, Paramount, GB, 104m, c). P Davina Belling & Clive Parsons, D&W Brian Gibson, PH Stephen Goldblatt, M Tony Visconti, ED Michael Bradsell.

LP Phil Daniels (Danny), Hazel O'Connor (Kate), Jon Finch (Woods), Jonathan Pryce (Ken), Peter-Hugo Daly (Mick), Mark Wingett (Tony), Gary Tibbs (Dave), Charles Wegner (Campbell).

In this New Wave version of an oft-told showbusiness story, Hazel O'Connor is a young singer who moves from working in small clubs to superstardom, but doesn't find happiness.

352. Breaking In (1989, Samuel Goldwyn, 91m, c). P Harry Gittes, D Bill Forsyth, W John Sayles, PH Michael Coulter, M Michael Gibbs, ED Michael Ellis, PD Adrienne Atkinson & John Wollett.

LP Burt Reynolds (Ernie Mullins), Casey Siemaszko (Mike Lefebb), Sheila Kelley (Carrie), Lorraine Toussaint (Delphine), Albert Salmi (Johnny Scat), Harry Carey, Jr. (Shoes).

Burt Reynolds portrays a graying, 61-year-old, professional burglar, who teams with young Casey Siemaszko so as to have someone to pass on his bag of tricks to. There's not much action in this gentle comedy, but the two leads hit it off rather well.

353. Breathless (1983, Orion, 100m, c). P Martin Erlichman, D Jim McBride, W McBride & L.M. Kit Carson (based on a screenplay by Jean-Luc Godard and story by François Truffaut), PH Richard H. Kline, M Jack Nitzsche, ED Robert Estrin, PD Richard Sylbert.

LP Richard Gere (Jesse), Valerie Kaprisky (Monica), Art Metrano (Birnbaum), William Tepper (Paul), John P. Ryan (Lt. Parmental), Lisa Persky (Salesgirl), Gary Goodrow (Berrutti), Robert Dunn (Sgt. Enright).

Jean-Luc Godard's 1959 New Wave production of François Truffaut's story is a classic with Jean-Paul Belmondo and Jean Seberg as two characters lost in existentialism. The remake with Richard Gere and Valerie Kaprisky is transported to Los Angeles, where Gere gets into all kinds of trouble, stealing cars and shooting people. It's not a classic.

354. A Breed Apart (1984, Orion, 101m, c). P John Daly & Derek Gibson, D Philippe Mora, W Paul Wheeler, PH Geoffrey Stephenson, M Maurice Gibb, ED Chris Lebenzon.

LP Rutger Hauer (Jim Malden), Powers Boothe (Michael Walker), Kathleen Turner (Stella Clayton), Donald Pleasence (J.P. Whittier), John Dennis Johnston (Charles Peyton), Brion James (Huey Miller).

Crazy millionaire Donald Pleasence, whose hobby is collecting rare bird eggs, hires expert mountain climber Powers Boothe to scale the cliffs on Rutger Hauer's remote island to pilfer specimens of a new bald eagle. Hauer would just as soon kill intruders as dally with Kathleen Turner. Does that ever show his intensity.

355. Breeders (1986, Empire Pictures, 77m, c). P Cynthia DePaula, D&W Tim Kincaid, PH Arthur D. Marks, M Tom Milano & Don Great, ED Barry Zetlin.

LP Teresa Farley (Dr. Gamble Pace), Lance Lewman (Det. Dale Andriotti), Frances Raines (Karinsa Marshall), Natalie O'Connell (Donna), Amy Brentano (Gail), Leeanne Baker (Kathleen), Ed French (Dr. Ira Markum), Owen Flynn (Monster).

Six beautiful girls have been brutally raped and beaten. Detective Lance Lewman and physician Teresa Farley suspect a "serial" rapist, but the real link between these violent crimes are alien horrors called breeders.

356. Brenda Starr (1989, New World, 87m, c). P Myron A. Hyman, D Robert Ellis Miller, W Noreen Stone, James

David Buchanan & Jenny Wolkind (based on a story by Stone & Buchanan and on the comic strip by Dale Messick), PH Freddie Francis, M Johnny Mandel, ED Mark Melnick.

LP Brooke Shields (Brenda Starr), Timothy Dalton (Basil St. John), Tony Peck (Mike Randall), Diana Scarwid (Libby "Lips" Lipscomb), Charles Durning (Newspaper Editor), Eddie Albert (Police Chief), Ed Nelson (President Truman).

This film, shot in 1986, was shown at the Cannes Film Festival in 1989. To date it's not been released to U.S. theaters and perhaps it never will. Many of a certain age fondly recall the beautiful redhead with great legs who appeared in the comic pages of newspapers in the 40s, 50s and 60s and beyond, Others will admit that Brooke Shields is nicely making the transition from a beautiful child to a beautiful woman. If she were a good newspaper reporter, Shields would be forced to report that in this film, the writing, directing and acting is not up to comic page quality.

357. *Brewster's Millions* (1985, Universal, 101m, c). P Lawrence Gordon & Joel Silver, D Walter Hill, W Herschel Weingrod & Timothy Harris (based on the novel by George Barr McCutcheon), PH Ric Waite, M Ry Cooder, ED Freeman Davies & Michael Ripps, PD John Vallone.

LP Richard Pryor (Montgomery Brewster), John Candy (Spike Nolan), Lonette McKee (Angela Drake), Stephen Collins (Warren Cox), Jerry Orbach (Charley Pegler), Pat Hingle (Edward Roundfield), Tovah Feldshuh (Marilyn), Hume Cronyn (Rupert Horn).

This chestnut has been filmed many times, starring the likes of Fatty Arbuckle, Jack Buchanan, Dennis O'Keefe and even, once, for a change of pace and gender, Bebe Daniels. Richard Pryor doesn't do himself proud as a broken-down baseball pitcher who is shocked to discover that Hume Cronyn has left him $300 million if he can spend $30 million in 30 days without having anything to show for it at the end of the period. The 1945 film with O'Keefe was only a "B" picture, but is more entertaining.

358. *The Bride* (1985, Columbia, 119m, c). P Victor Drai, D Franc Roddam, W Lloyd Fonvielle (based on the novel *Frankenstein* by Mary Shelley), PH Stephen H. Burum, M Maurice Jarre, ED Michael Ellis, PD Michael Seymour.

LP Sting (Frankenstein), Jennifer Beals (Eva), Anthony Higgins (Clerval), Clancy Brown (Viktor), David Rappaport (Rinaldo), Geraldine Page (Mrs. Baumann), Alexei Sayle (Magar), Phil Daniels (Bela), Veruschka (Countess), Quentin Crisp (Dr. Zalhus), Cary Elwes (Josef).

Those who recall Colin Clive's creation of Elsa Lanchester to be the bride of his monster in *The Bride of Frankenstein* may observe that this time the bad doctor (Sting) gets things right with beautiful naked Jennifer Beals. He treats her as a sort of spare-parts Eliza Doolittle to his Professor Henry Higgins. If it seems that Frankenstein has forgotten to give her the spark of life, it's not his fault. Beauteous actress Beals is about as capable of expressing emotion as is a folding chair. As for the monster (giant actor Clancy Brown), he's hit the road and taken up with dwarf David Rappaport. Brown and Rappaport have sort of a Lenny-and-George relationship as in *Of Mice and Men*. The film is an interesting failure.

359. *Bright Lights, Big City* (1988, United Artists, 110m, c). P Mark Rosenberg & Sydney Pollack, D James Bridges, W Jay McInerney (based on his novel), PH Gordon Willis, M Donald Fagen, ED John Bloom, PD Santo Loquasto.

LP Michael J. Fox (Jamie Conway), Kiefer Sutherland (Tad), Phoebe Cates (Amanda), Swoosie Kurtz (Megan), Frances Sternhagen (Clara), Tracy Pollan (Vicky), Charlie Schlatter (Michael), Dianne Wiest (Mother).

Michael J. Fox's life is coming apart. His mother has died and his wife has left him to pursue a modeling career in Paris. Trying to escape his problems, he turns to drink, sex and drugs in the New York club scene. Only when he hits the bottom, does he finally realize that he's not handling his problems with maturity.

360. *Brighton Beach Memoirs* (1986, Universal, 108m, c). P Ray Stark, D Gene Saks, W Neil Simon (based on his stage play), PH John Bailey, M Michael Small, ED Carol Littleton, PD Stuart Wurtzel.

LP Blythe Danner (Kate), Bob Dishy (Jack), Brian Drillinger (Stanley), Stacey Glick (Laurie), Judith Ivey (Blanche), Jonathan Silverman (Eugene), Lisa Waltz (Nora), Fyvush Finkel (Mr. Greenblatt), Kathleen Doyle (Mrs. Laski), Alan Weeks (Andrew).

Neil Simon reminisces about his adolescence, having Jonathan Silverman impersonating him. It has its moments, but only if you can stomach a chokingly loving extended family.

361. *Brimstone and Treacle* (1982, United Artists Classics, GB, 87m, c). P Kenith Trodd, D Richard Loncraine, W Dennis Potter, PH Peter Hannan, M Sting, ED Paul Green.

LP Sting (Martin Taylor), Denholm Elliott (Thomas Bates), Joan Plowright (Norma Bates), Suzanna Hamilton (Patricia Bates), Mary McLeod (Valerie Holdsworth), Benjamin Whitrow (Businessman), Dudley Sutton (Stroller).

In his first major movie role, Sting, the lead singer of the rock group Police, is an angelic-diabolical young drifter who insinuates himself into a middle-class British family. He does vile things to their handicapped daughter Suzanna Hamilton, an almost vegetable-like creature, who can't communicate with anyone. Sting is a real sadistic bastard.

362. *Brittania Hospital* (1982, Columbia-EMI-Warner, GB, 116m, c). P Davina Belling & Clive Parsons, D Lindsay Anderson, W David Sherwin, PH Mike Fash, M Alan Price, ED Michael Ellis.

LP Leonard Rossiter (Vincent Potter), Brian Pettifer (Briles), John Moffatt (Greville Figg), Fulton Mackay (Supt. Johns), Vivian Pickles (Matron), Barbara Hicks (Miss Tinker), Graham Crowden (Prof. Millar), Jill Bennett (Macmillan), Marsha Hunt (Amanda Persil).

In this black comedy, a head-transplanting mad professor and terrorists causes chaos during a hospital's 500th anniversary. It's a lampoon of the state of the British empire which doesn't quite make the grade despite some enjoyable sequences.

363. *Broadcast News†* (1987, 20th Century–Fox, 131m, c). P James L. Brooks & Penney Finkelman Cox, D&W Brooks† (as screenwriter), PH Michael Ballhaus†, M Bill Conti, ED Richard Marks†, PD Charles Rosen.

LP William Hurt† (Tom Grunick), Albert Brooks† (Aaron Altman), Holly Hunter† (Jane Craig), Robert Prosky (Ernie Merriman), Lois Chiles (Jennifer Mack), Joan Cusack (Blair Litton), Peter Hackes (Paul Moore), Christian Clemenson (Bobby), Robert Katims (Martin Klein), Ed Wheeler (George Wein), Jack Nicholson (Bill Rorich).

Director-writer-producer James L. Brooks delves into the struggles of TV news pros Holly Hunter and Albert Brooks to prevent their service media from playing by the rules of the entertainment world. The entire cast is outstanding, headed by Oscar nominees William Hurt as a good-looking empty-headed future anchor man, Hunter as a hot-shot producer who has all the answers, but gets fired all the same, and Albert Brooks as the brilliant correspondent, not considered sexy enough for on-camera work. This bitter, funny, touching and engrossing film is solid entertainment.

364. *Broadway Danny Rose* (1984, Orion, 86m, b&w). P Robert Greenhut, D&W Woody Allen† (for both directing and writing), PH Gordon Willis, ED Susan E. Morse, PD Mel Bourne.

LP Woody Allen (Danny Rose), Mia Farrow (Tina Vitale), Nick Apollo Forte (Lou Canova), Sandy Baron, Corbett Monica, Jackie Gayle, Morty Gunty, Will Jordan, Howard Storm, Jack Rollins, Joe Franklin, Howard Cosell & Milton Berle (Themselves), Craig Vandenburgh (Ray Webb), Herb Reynolds (Barney Dunn).

Two-bit New York talent agent Woody Allen specializes in off-beat acts that no one else will handle and no one will employ. His one potential winner is Lounge singer Nick Apollo Forte, an overweight lush who's cheating on his wife with Mia Farrow. Allen has to pretend that he's Farrow's boyfriend which gets him in trouble with the mob because loud-mouth, uncouth Mia is the bride-to-be of a "soldier." As for Forte, he turns out to be a class–A louse and ingrate who dumps Allen when he gets his big chance. Somehow we know this blow won't prevent Allen from continuing to try and place his blind xylophonist, bird lady and incompetent hypnotist.

365. *Broken English* (1981, Lorimar, 93m, c). P Keith Rothman & Burt Schneider, D Michie Gleason, W Gleason, PH Elliot Davis, M Georges Delerue, ED Suzanne Fenn.

LP Beverly Ross (Sarah), Jacques Martial (Maas), Greta Rannigen (Leslie), Mansour Sy (Cheekh), Oona Chaplin (Sarah's Mother), Frankie Stein (Cecile), Sandy Whitelaw (Arms Dealer), Assane Fall (Amidau).

The only thing noteworthy about this miscegenation film involving white woman Beverly Ross and black African Jacques Martial is the appearance of Oona Chaplin as Ross' mother.

Broken Hearts and Noses* see *Crimewave

366. *Broken Victory* (1988, Double Helix, 79m, c). P David Carstens & Jonathan Smith, D Gregory Strom, W Smith & Strom (based on a story by Smith), PH Brett Webster & Carstens, M Tom Howard, ED Pat Edmondson, PD Heather Roseborough.

LP Jeannette Clift (Sarah Taylor), Ken Letner (Matthew Taylor), John Sharp (Colonel), Jonathan Turner Smith (Joshua Taylor), John Shepherd (Kevin Taylor), Bonnie Hawley (Elizabeth), Elias McCabe (Nathanael).

New world leader Jon Sharp insists that peace and prosperity can only exist if everyone denounces their religious beliefs. The Taylor family refuses and must pay the consequences, which include being forced to wear gray uniforms and live in a ghetto.

367. *Bronco Billy* (1980, Warner, 119m, c). P Dennis Hackin & Neal Bobrofsky, D Eastwood, W Hackin, PH David Worth, M Snuff Garrett, ED Ferris Webster & Joel Cox.

LP Clint Eastwood (Bronco Billy), Sondra Locke (Antoinette), Geoffrey Lewis (John Arlington), Sam Bottoms (Leonard), Scatman Crothers (Doc Lynch), Bill McKinney (Lefty LeBow),

Dan Vadis (Chief Big Eagle), Sierra Pecheur (Lorraine Running Water), Tanya Russell (Doris Duke).

Back in the days when the former mayor of Carmel, California, and his main squeeze Sondra Locke were happy together, Clint Eastwood directed himself as the owner and chief attraction of a shoddy traveling Wild West show. Other than main attraction Clint as a sharpshooting, knife-throwing expert, the performers are all losers. Eastwood has trouble keeping pretty girls as assistants for his act. At first runaway heiress Locke doesn't want the job either, but she comes to love her work and Clint. The film is entertaining but the public stayed away.

368. *The Brother from Another Planet* (1984, Cinecom, 110m, c). P Peggy Rajski & Maggie Renzi, D&W John Sayles, PH Ernest Dickerson, M Mason Daring, ED Sayles, PD Nora Chavooshian.

LP Joe Morton (The Brother), Darryl Edwards (Fly), Steve James (Odell), Leonard Jackson (Smokey), Bill Cobbs (Walter), Maggie Renzi (Noreen), Tom Wright (Sam), Ren Woods (Bernice), Reggie Rock Bythewood (Rickey), David Strathairn & John Sayles (Men in Black), Dee Dee Bridgewater (Malverne).

Mute Joe Morton is an escaped slave from an unnamed planet. He lands on Ellis Island and makes his way to Harlem, looking like a street bum. He is pursued by two bounty hunters David Strathairn and John Sayles. While trying to look out for himself, Morton takes time out to have a brief affair with Dee Dee Bridgewater and thwart a businessman who deals heroin to poor black kids.

369. *Brothers* (1984, Areflex, Australia, 99m, c). P,D&W Terry Bourke (based on the book *Reflex* by Roger Ward), PH Ray Henman, M Bob Young, ED Ron Williams.

LP Chard Hayward (Adam Wild), Ivar Kants (Kevin Wild), Margaret Laurence (Lani Aveson), Jennifer Cluff (Allison Levis), Alyson Best (Jenine Williams), Joan Bruce (Mrs. Williams), Les Foxcroft (Jim Williams).

Philandering brute Chard Hayward upsets his brother Ivar Kants' New Zealand domestic life, causes a prostitute to attempt suicide when he dumps her for an attractive widow, and is finally killed in a car wreck.

370. *Brothers and Sisters* (1981, British Film Institute, GB, 96m, c). P Keith Griffiths, D Richard Woolley, W Woolley & Tammy Walker, PH Pascoe MacFarlane, M Trevor Jones, ED Mickey Audsley.

LP Carolyn Pickles (Theresa & Jennifer Collins), Sam Dale (David Barratt), Robert East (James Barratt), Elizabeth Bennett (Sarah Barratt), Jennifer Armitage (Tricia Snow), Barry McCarthy (Pete Gibson).

Set in Leeds, England, this crime story ticks off the events leading up to the murder of a prostitute. Carolyn Pickles plays the unfortunate whore and her sister.

Brothers in Arms see Slow Burn

371. *Brothers in Arms* (1989, Ablo, 94m, c). P Mark R. Gordon & Christopher Meledandri, D George Jay Bloom 3d, W D. Shone Kirkpatrick, PH Kim Haun, M Alan Howarth, ED Chuck Weiss.

LP Todd Allen (Joey), Charles Grant (Dallas), Jack Starrett (Father), DeDee Pfeiffer (Stevie), Mitch Pileggi (Caleb).

Charles Grant drags his naive younger brother Todd Allen into the Big Bear region of California to take revenge on religious fanatic Jack Starnett and his family, who literally crucified a friend of Grant.

372. *Brown Bread Sandwiches* (1989, Eagle Pictures, Canada, 92m, c). P Nellie Zucker & Carlo Liconti, D&W Liconti, PH Paul van der Linden, M Lawrence Shragge & Raymond Pennal, ED Ron Wisman.

LP Daniel DeSanto (Michelangelo), Lina Sastri (Giulia), Kim Cattrall (Aunt Eva), Giancarlo Giannini (Alberto), Kim Coates, Tony Nardi, Peter Boretski.

This film about learning to live in a strange land, features Daniel DeSanto as a young Italian boy struggling to be assimilated into Canadian culture in Toronto around 1957. His alter-ego narrator is the grown-up boy commenting on what's happening to the lad.

373. *Brubaker* (1980, 20th Century-Fox, 132m, c). P Ron Silverman, D Stuart Rosenberg, W W.D. Richter† (based on a story by Richter & Arthur Ross), PH Bruno Nuytten, M Lalo Schifrin, ED Robert Brown.

LP Robert Redford (Brubaker), Yaphet Kotto (Dickie Coombes), Jane Alexander (Lillian), Murray Hamilton (Deach), David Keith (Larry Lee Bullen), Morgan Freeman (Walter), Matt Clark (Purcell), Tim McIntire (Huey Rauch), Richard Ward (Abraham), Albert Salmi (Rory Poke).

About an hour into this movie, Robert Redford, a convict in a brutal Southern prison whose trustees keep the discipline with whips, straps and other assorted means of torture, reveals that he's the new warden. He wished to get a firsthand impression of how bad things really are. He makes efforts to improve conditions, but even after finding the unmarked graves of dozens of prisoners, he learns the state has no intention of changing things, and Redford leaves dejectedly.

374. *Buddies* (1983, PTY Ltd., Australia, 99m, c). P John Dingwall, D Arch Nicholson, W Dingwall, PH David Eggby, M Chris Neal, ED Martyn Down.

LP Colin Friels (Mike), Kris McQuade (Stella), Harold Hopkins (Johnny), Dennis Miller (Andy), Simon Chilvers (Alfred), Norman Kaye (George), Lisa Peers (Jennifer), Bruce Spence (Ted), Andrew Sharp (Peter), Dinah Shearing (Merle).

Close friends Colin Friels and Harold Hopkins are scratching out a living in Queensland mining diamonds with Kris McQuade and Dennis Miller, when claim-jumpers interfere with their work, changing their lives.

375. *Buddy, Buddy* (1981, MGM/United Artists, 96m, c). P Jay Weston, D&W Billy Wilder (based on the play and story by Francis Veber), PH Harry Stradling, Jr., M Lalo Schifrin, ED Argyle Nelson.

LP Jack Lemmon (Victor Clooney), Walter Matthau (Trabucco), Paula Prentiss (Celia Clooney), Klaus Kinski (Dr. Zuckerbrot), Dana Elcar (Capt. Hubris), Miles Chapin (Eddie the Bellhop), Michael Ensign (Assn't Manager), Joan Shawlee (Receptionist).

There's a lot of talent associated with this film. Too bad it is so poorly used. Walter Matthau is an aging hit man, holed up in a hotel room, waiting to fulfill a contract. Next door is Jack Lemmon, intent on committing suicide. Both die as does director-writer Billy Wilder's hopes to produce a successful black comedy.

376. *The Buddy System* (1984, 20th Century–Fox, 110m, c). P Alain Chammas, D Glenn Jordan, W Mary Agnes Donoghue, PH Matthew F. Leonetti, M Patrick Williams, ED Arthur Schmidt, PD Rodger Maus.

LP Richard Dreyfuss (Joe), Susan Sarandon (Emily), Nancy Allen (Carrie), Jean Stapleton (Mrs. Price), Wil Wheaton (Tim), Edward Winter (Jim Parks), Keene Curtis (Dr. Knitz), Tom Lacy (The Man Who Gives Emily the Test).

Living in Venice, California, struggling author Richard Dreyfuss has a brief affair with single parent Susan Sarandon. Eventually, they both agree it's not what they want; so they choose to be just friends. The film borrows from *The Goodbye Girl,* even to the point of having Wil Wheaton as a wise-beyond-his-years son of Sarandon, delivering all the funny foul-mouthed lines.

377. *Bugs Bunny's Third Movie—1001 Rabbit Tales* (1982, Warner, animated, 90m, c). P Friz Freleng, D David Detiege, Art Davis & Bill Perez, W John Dunn, Detiege & Freleng, PH Nick Vasu, M Rob Walsh, Milt Franklyn, Bill Lava & Carl Stalling, ANIM Warren Batchelder, Bob Bransford, Marcia Fertig, Terrence Lennon, Bob Matz, Norm McCabe, Tom Ray & Virgil Ross.

LP VOICES Mel Blanc.

For those who enjoy Bugs Bunny, Daffy Duck, Tweety Bird, Sylvester and Elmer Fudd (and you know you do, even if you're too adult to admit it), watch this complication of classic Looney Tunes with a youngster and let yourself laugh. It'll do you both good.

378. *Bull Durham* (1988, Orion, 108m, c). P Thom Mount & Mark Burg, D&W Ron Shelton† (for screenplay), PH Bobby Byrne, M Michael Convertino, ED Robert Leighton & Adam Weiss, PD Armin Ganz.

LP Kevin Costner (Crash Davis), Susan Sarandon (Annie Savoy), Tim Robbins (Ebby Calvin "Nuke" LaLoosh), Trey Wilson (Joe "Skip" Riggins), Robert Wuhl (Larry Hockett), Jenny Robertson (Millie), Max Patkin (Himself), William O'Leary (Jimmy), David Neidorf (Bobby), Danny Gans (Deke).

It used to be that baseball movies were enjoyed only by the most uncritical fans of the game. But with *The Natural* and *Bull Durham,* things have changed. Journeyman catcher Kevin Costner has spent most of his adult life riding the buses in the minor leagues. He's sent to Durham of the Carolina League to try to teach Tim Robbins, who has a big league arm and the brain of a pea, how to become a successful pitcher. Susan Sarandon is a knowledgeable lover of the game, who each season picks out one of the Bull Durham players to become her pet project. She will teach him things about life as well as things in bed. She is about to choose between Costner and Robbins, when the former takes himself out of the competition. Robbins learns enough from both Costner and Sarandon to make it in to "The Show" (i.e. the major leagues) while Kevin and Susan get each other. Sort-of reminds one of *Trapeze* with Burt Reynolds, Gina Lollobrigida and Tony Curtis, doesn't it?

Bulldance see Forbidden Sun

379. *Bulletproof* (1987, Cinetel, 85m, c). P Paul Hertzberg, D Steve Carver, W Carver & T.L. Lankford (based on a story by Lankford & Fred Olen Ray), PH Frances Grumman, ED Jeff Freeman.

LP Gary Busey (Frank "Bulletproof" McBain), Darlanne Fluegel (Lt. Devon Shepard), Rene Enríquez (Gen. Brogado), Henry Silva (Col. Kartiff), Bill Smith (Russian Major), Thalmus Rasulala (Billy Dunbar).

Ex-CIA agent Gary Busey singlehandedly sets out to rescue a secret weapon and sexy lieutenant Darlanne Fluegel who was in charge of it, from terrorists led by Mexican general Rene Enríquez, and Libyan colonel Henry Silva.

380. *Bullies* (1986, Universal, Canada, 95m, c). P Peter Simpson, D Paul Lynch, W John Sheppard & Bryan

McCann, PH Rene Verzier, M Paul Zaza, ED Nick Rotundo, PD Jack McAdam.

LP Jonathan Crombie (Matt Morris), Janet-Laine Green (Jenny Morris), Stephen B. Hunter (Clay Morris), Dehl Berti (Will Crow), Olivia D'Abo (Becky), Bill Croft (Ben), Bernie Coulson (Jimmy), Adrien Dorval (Judd).

When the Morris clan, headed by wimpish stepfather Stephen B. Hunter, Mom Janet-Laine Green and teen Jonathan Crombie, move to rural British Columbia, they suffer at the hands of the loutish Cullen clan, consisting of Bill Croft and his three brutal sons. After experiencing beatings, slashings, torture and rape, the Morrises fight back à la *Straw Dogs*.

381. *Bullshot* (1983, Handmade Films, GB, 85m, c). P Ian La Frenais, D Dick Clement, W Ron House, Alan Shearman & Diz White, PH Alex Thomson, M John Du Prez, ED Allan Jones.

LP Alan Shearman (Bullshot Crummond), Diz White (Rosemary Fenton), Ron House (Count Otto von Bruno), Frances Tomelty (Fraulein Lenya von Bruno), Ron Pember (Dobbs), Mel Smith (Crouch), Michael Aldridge (Rupert Fenton).

Bullshot is a spoof of the old Bulldog Drummond movies, but how many people in 1983 remember them or will admit to remembering them? The plot isn't the thing, it's the antics of the caricatures which count, with Alan Shearman looking forward to one last encounter with Ron House, his World War I adversary.

Bump in the Night *see* ***The Final Terror***

382. *The 'burbs* (1989, Universal, 102m, c). P Michael Finnell & Larry Brezner, D Joe Dante, W Dana Olsen, PH Robert Stevens, M Jerry Goldsmith, ED Marshall Harvey, PD James Spencer.

LP Tom Hanks (Roy Peterson), Bruce Dern (Mark Rumsfield), Carrie Fisher (Carol Peterson), Rick Ducommun (Art Weingartner), Corey Feldman (Ricky Butler), Henry Gibson (Dr. Werner Klopek), Brother Theodore (Uncle Reuben Klopek), Courtney Gains (Hans Klopek).

Tom Hanks, so good in his Academy Award–nominated role in *Big,* follows up that marvelous performance with this silly story of nervous and nosey suburban neighbors who decide they better investigate the strange nocturnal behavior of some newcomers. Nothing very funny occurs.

383. *Burglar* (1987, Warner, 102m, c). P Kevin McCormick & Michael Hirsh, D Hugh Wilson, W Joseph Loeb III, Matthew Weisman & Wilson (based on books by Lawrence Block), PH William A. Fraker, M Sylvester Levay, ED Fredric Steinkamp & William Steinkamp, PD Todd Hallowell.

LP Whoopi Goldberg (Bernice Rhodenbarr), Bob Goldthwait (Carl Hefler), G.W. Bailey (Ray Kirschman), Lesley Ann Warren (Dr. Cynthia Sheldrake), James Handy (Carson Verrill), Anne DeSalvo (Detective Todras), John Goodman (Det. Nyswander).

Burglar is not the worst film of the year, but it is a serious contender. Stand-up comedians Whoopi Goldberg and Bob Goldthwait make the mistake of moving around. Goldberg is a cat burglar who accidentally witnesses a murder and is forced to solve the case to clear herself. Where have we heard that plot before, and before, and before...?

384. *Burke & Wills* (1985, Hoyts Edgley, Australia, 140m, c). P Graeme Clifford & John Sexton, D Clifford, W Michael Thomas, PH Russell Boyd, M Peter Sculthorpe, ED Tim Wellburn, PD Ross Major.

LP Jack Thompson (Robert O'Hara Burke), Nigel Havers (William John Wills), Greta Scacchi (Julia Matthews), Matthew Fargher (John King), Ralph Cotterill (Charley Gray), Drew Forsythe (William Brahe).

Jack Thompson is impressive in this historical epic about the doomed expedition of the first men to attempt to cross the Australian continent in 1860.

385. *The Burning* (1981, Filmways, 90m, c). P Harvey Weinstein, D Tony Maylam, W Peter Lawrence & Weinstein (based on a story by Weinstein, Maylam & Brad Grey), PH Harvey Harrison, M Rick Wakeman, ED John Sholder.

LP Brian Matthews (Todd), Leah Ayres (Michelle), Brian Backer (Alfred),

Larry Joshua (Glazer), Jason Alexander (Dave), Ned Eisenberg (Eddie), Carrick Glenn (Sally), Carolyn Houlihan (Karen), Lou David (Cropsey).

A counselor whose face was burned by bratty campers five years earlier is back in the woods looking for revenge. The fact that the kids who made his face look like a pocked moonscape are no longer in attendance doesn't matter to our villain. Look for a bit of gratuitous nudity and Holly Hunter in a minor role in her film debut.

386. *Burning an Illusion* (1982, British Film Institute, GB, 101m, c). P Vivien Pottersman, D Menelik Shabbazz, W Shabbazz, PH Roy Cornwall, M Seyoum Nefta, ED Judy Seymour.

LP Cassie MacFarlane (Pat Williams), Victor Romero (Del Bennett), Beverley Martin (Sonia), Angela Wynter (Cynthia), Malcolm Fredericks (Chamberlain), Chris Tummings (Scotty), Trevor Laird (Pest).

In this low-budgeted sociodrama, Cassie MacFarlane, a young black woman from the Caribbean living in London, is in love with Victor Romero, but he goes astray after losing his job and is jailed for violence.

387. *Burning Secret* (1988, Vestron, GB/US/W. Ger., 106m, c). P Norma Heyman, Eberhard Junkersdorf & Carol Lynn Greene, D Andrew Birkin, W Birkin (based on a short story "Brennendes Geheimnis" by Stefan Zweig), PH Ernest Day, M Hans Zimmer, ED Paul Green, PD Bernd Lepel.

LP Faye Dunaway (Sonya), Klaus Maria Brandauer (The Baron), David Eberts (Edmund), Ian Richardson (The Father), John Nettleton (Dr. Weiss), Martin Obernigg (Concierge), Vaclav Stekl (Assn't Concierge).

Set in World War I Austria, the film views the near-adultery of Faye Dunaway with Klaus Maria Brandauer through the eyes of impressionable 12-year-old David Eberts. The story by Stefan Zweig, more famous for "Letter from an Unknown Woman," was first filmed in 1933 Germany, starring Willi Forst, Hilde Wagener and Ernst Joachim Schaufus.

388. *Bush Christmas* (1983, Hoyts Release, Australia, 91m, c). P Gilda Baracchi & Paul Barron, D Henri Safran, W Ted Roberts (based on the 1947 film version by Ralph Smart), PH Malcolm Richards & Ross Berryman, M Mike Perjanik, ED Ron Williams.

LP John Ewart (Bill), John Howard (Sly), Nicole Kidman (Helen), Mark Spain (Michael), Vineta O'Malley (Mother), James Wingrove (Johnny), Peter Sumner (Father), Manalpuy (Manalpuy).

While on holiday at Christmas time, Australian children help their father's servant, the Aborigine Manalpuy, catch horse thieves. It's a remake of a 1947 British film starring Chips Rafferty.

389. *The Bushido Blade* (1982, Aquarius/Trident, GB/US, 92m, c, aka *The Bloody Bushido Blade*). P Arthur Rankin, Jr., D Tom Kotani, W William Overgard, PH Shoji Ueda, M Maury Laws, ED Yoshitami Huroiwa.

LP Richard Boone (Matthew Perry), Sonny Chiba (Prince Edo), Frank Converse (Capt. Hawk), Laura Gemser (Edo's Cousin), James Earl Jones (Harpooner), Mako (Friend), Toshiro Mifune (Shogun's Commander), Tetsuro Tamba (Lord Yamato), Mayumi Atano (Yuki).

The only thing missing from this action-packed samurai adventure thriller is Richard Chamberlain. Oh, what the heck, it's boring enough without him.

390. *Busted Up* (1987, Shapiro, 90m, c). P Damian Lee & David Mitchell, D Conrad E. Palmisano, W Lee, PH Ludek Bogner, M Charles Barnett, ED Gary Zubeck.

LP Irene Cara (Simone), Paul Coufos (Earl Bird), Stan Shaw (Angie), Tony Rosato (Irving Drayton), Frank Pellegrino (Nick Sevins), Gordon Judges (Tony Tenera).

Gym instructor Irene Cara and barefisted boxer Paul Coufos must stand up to the mob as they attempt to establish a health club.

391. *Buster* (1988, Tri-Star, GB, 102m, c). P Norma Heyman, D David Green, W Colin Shindler, PH Tony Imi, M Anne Dudley, ED Lesley Walker, PD Simon Holland, SONG "Two Hearts" by Lamont Dozier & Phil Collins†.

LP Phil Collins (Buster Edwards), Julie Walters (June Edwards), Larry Lamb (Bruce Reynolds), Stephanie Lawrence

(Franny Reynolds), Ellen Beaven (Nicky Edwards), Michael Attwell (Harry), Ralph Brown (Ronnie).

Rock star Phil Collins plays a "lucky thief," a small-time crook, who has spent only two weeks in jail for all of his crimes. His wife Julie Walters wishes he would get a real job, but instead he falls in with some boys who have big plans. Collins becomes a member of the gang which pulls off the Great Train Robbery in 1963 and gets away with 2.6 million pounds. Collins escapes with his family to Mexico but the cultural shock proves too great and he heads back to London where he is soon arrested, tried, convicted and sentenced to 15 years in prison. He gets out in nine and the film ends with him reduced to being a street flower vendor.

392. *Bustin' Loose* (1981, United Artists, 94m, c). P Richard Pryor & Michael S. Glick, D Oz Scott, W Roger L. Simon (based on an adaptation by Lonne Elder III of a story by Pryor), PH Dennis Dalzell, M Mark Davis & Roberta Flack, ED David Holden.

LP Richard Pryor (Joe Braxton), Cicely Tyson (Vivian Perry), Alphonso Alexander (Martin), Kia Cooper (Samantha), Edwin DeLeon (Ernesto), Jimmy Hughes (Harold), Edwin Kinter (Anthony), Tami Luchow (Linda).

In this slightly sloppy sentimental comedy, Richard Pryor is a paroled thief hired to drive a bus load of maladjusted kids across the country. The bus breaks down frequently and Pryor has to deal with several other types of emergencies including an encounter with the KKK.

393. *Butcher Baker (Nightmare Maker)* (1982, International Films, 91m, c, aka *Night Warning; Nightmare Maker*). P Stephen Breimer & Eugene Mazzola, D William Asher, W Breimer, Alan Jay Glueckman & Boon Collins.

LP Jimmy McNichol (Billy Lynch), Bo Svenson (Lt. Carlson), Susan Tyrrell (Susan).

Accused of both murder and being the third side in a homosexual love triangle, Jimmy McNichol tries to convince cop Bo Svenson of his innocence.

394. *Butterfly* (1982, Analysis, 107m, c). P&D Matt Cimber, W John Goff & Cimber (based on the novel by James M. Cain), PH Eddy van der Enden, M Ennio Morricone, ED Brent Schoenfeld.

LP Stacy Keach (Jeff Tyler), Pia Zadora (Kady), Orson Welles (Judge Rauch), Lois Nettleton (Belle Morgan), Edward Albert (Wash Gillespie), James Franciscus (Moke Blue), Stuart Whitman (Rev. Rivers).

Everyone tries to blame poor Pia Zadora for this turkey. That's totally unfair. She can't act, that's true, but all the others associated with this backwoods story of a 17-year-old sexpot, incest and murder deserve equal condemnation.

The Butterfly Revolution see Summer Camp Nightmare

395. *Buy & Cell* (1989, Altar/Empire, 91m, c). P Frank Yablans, D Robert Boris, W Neal Israel & Larry Siegel, PH Daniele Nannuzzi, M Mark Shreeve, ED Bert Glatstein, PD Giovanni Natalucci.

LP Malcolm McDowell (Warden Tennant), Robert Carradine (Herbie Altman), Michael Winslow (Sly), Randall "Tex" Cobb (Wolf), Ben Vereen (Shaka), Lise Cutter (Dr. Ellen Scott).

The film takes a comical look at the greed and corruption in the U.S. prison system and the dishonesty of some brokers and players on Wall Street.

396. *Buying Time* (1989, MGM/United Artists, Canada, 97m, c). P Richard Gabourie, D Mitchell Gabourie, W The Gabouries, PH Manfred Guthe, M David Krystal, ED Michael Todd.

LP Jeff Schultz (Jabber), Page Fletcher (Curtis King), Laura Cruickshank (Jessie), Leslie Toth (Reno), Martin Louis (Dez), Dean Stockwell (Detective Novak).

Carwash employee Jeff Schultz would be a good kid except for his feelings of obligation to Leslie Toth and Martin Louis. When Toth has trouble with a bookie, Schultz helps him pull a robbery to make good what he owes. The police catch them and blackmail Schultz into helping them get the goods on the killers of Louis.

397. *By Design* (1982, BDF Alpha, Canada, 90m, c). P Werner Aellen & Beryl Fox, D Claude Jutra, W Joe Weisenfeld, Jutra & David Eames, PH Jean

Boffety, M Chico Hamilton, ED Tony Trow.

LP Patty Duke Astin, Sara Botsford, Saul Rubinek, Sonia Zimmer, Mina Mina, Alan Durusissean, Clare Coulter, Robert Benson, Jeannie Elias, Anya Best.

The picture examines the plan of two lesbian lovers to adopt a child. When this fails, one seeks sexual relations with a man in order to become pregnant.

398. *Bye Bye Blues* (1989, Festival, Canada, 118m, c). P Anne Wheeler & Arvi Litmatainen, D&W Wheeler, PH Vic Sarin, M George Blondheim, ED Christopher Tate, PD John Blackie.

LP Rebecca Jenkins (Daisy Cooper), Michael Ontkean (Teddy Cooper), Luke Reilly (Max Gramley), Stuart Margolin (Slim Godfrey), Robyn Stevan (Frances Cooper), Kate Reid (Mary Wright), Leslie Yeo (Arthur Wright).

When her husband is posted to some secret base during World War II, Rebecca Jenkins and her two children return to her Alberta farmland. She becomes the singer for a dance band after hearing nothing from her husband (her letters have been returned, unopened). Just as the band is getting its big break, her husband returns, having been a prisoner-of-war in Singapore. Jenkins leaves the band and the clarinetist who had befriended her, and goes home to be a wife and mother once again.

399. *Caboblanco* (1981, Avco Embassy, 87m, c). P Lance Hool & Paul A. Joseph, D J. Lee Thompson, W Mort Fine & Milton Gelman, PH Alex Phillips, Jr., M Jerry Goldsmith, ED Michael F. Anderson.

LP Charles Bronson (Giff Hoyt), Jason Robards, Jr. (Gunther Beckdorff), Dominique Sanda (Marie Claire Allesandri), Fernando Rey (Tereda), Simon MacCorkindale (Lewis Clarkson), Camilla Sparv (Hira), Denny Miller (Horst), Gilbert Roland (Dr. Ramirez).

In this lame ripoff of *Casablanca,* set in Peru after World War II, Charles Bronson is a saloon owner who has a run-in with former Nazi Jason Robards and beautiful Dominique Sanda searching for her missing lover. Sacrilege!

400. *Cactus* (1986, Spectrafilm, Australia, 95m, c). P Jane Ballantyne & Paul Cox, D Cox, W Cox, Norman Kaye & Bob Ellis, PH Yuri Sokol, ED Tim Lewis, PD Asher Bilu.

LP Isabelle Huppert (Colo), Robert Menzies (Robert), Norman Kaye (Tom), Monica Maughan (Bea), Banduk Marika (Banduk), Sheila Florance (Martha), Peter Aanensen (George).

Frenchwoman Isabelle Huppert is partially blinded in a car accident and must face the very real possibility of completely losing her sight. She becomes romantically involved with Robert Menzies, a totally blind young man. He studies cacti, thus the title.

401. *Caddyshack* (1980, Orion/Warner, 99m, c). P Douglas Kenney, D Harold Ramis, W Brian Doyle-Murray, Ramis & Kenney, PH Stevan Larner, M Johnny Mandel, ED William Carruth, PD Stan Jolley.

LP Chevy Chase (Ty), Rodney Dangerfield (Al), Ted Knight (Judge), Michael O'Keefe (Danny), Bill Murray (Cal), Sarah Holcomb (Maggie), Scott Colomby (Tony), Cindy Morgan (Lacey), Dan Resin (Dr. Beeper), Henry Wilcoxon (Bishop), Albert Salmi (Noonan), Ann Ryerson (Grace).

What little plot there is in this slapstick comedy has to do with caddy Michael O'Keefe trying to win a college scholarship by winning a golf match. Generally speaking the film is a showcase for the respective hammy comedy routines of Chevy Chase, Rodney Dangerfield, Ted Knight and Bill Murray.

402. *Caddyshack II* (1988, Warner, 103m, c). P Neil Canton, Jon Peters & Peter Guber, D Allan Arkush, W Harold Ramis & Peter Torokvei, PH Harry Stradling, Jr., M Ira Newborn, ED Bernard Gribble, PD Bill Matthews.

LP Jackie Mason (Jack Hartounian), Robert Stack (Chandler Young), Dina Merrill (Cynthia Young), Dyan Cannon (Elizabeth Pearce), Randy Quaid (Peter Blunt), Jessica Lundy (Kate Hartounian), Chevy Chase (Ty Webb), Dan Aykroyd (Capt. Tom Everett), Chynna Phillips (Miffy Young).

For those who have waited patiently eight years for a sequel to the not very funny *Caddyshack,* our condolences for your disappointment. Rodney Danger-field pulled out of the film at the last moment and Jackie Mason was brought in to impersonate a loud-mouth, self-made millionaire. He tries to break into society for his daughter's sake by joining a very snooty country club. His attempts are resisted with extreme prejudice by Robert Stack, Dina Merrill and the other blue-blooded members. We wouldn't want to belong to any club that included any of the jerks in this flop.

403. Cage (1989, New Century/Vista, 101m, c). P&D Lang Elliott, W Hugh Kelley, PH Jacques Haitkin, M Michael Wetherwax, ED Mark S. Westmore, PD Joseph M. Altadonna.

LP Lou Ferrigno (Billy Thomas), Reb Brown (Scott Monroe), Michael Dante (Lucky), Mike Moroff (Dominic), Marilyn Tokuda (Morgan Garrett), Al Leong (Tiger Joe), James Shigeta (Tim Lum Yin).

The film is the boring story of "cage fighters" who engage in a gladiatorial sport in which two men are locked in a cage and fight until one dies.

404. Caged Fury (1980, Saturn Intl., 84m, c). P Emily Blas, D Cirio H. Santiago, W Bobby Greenwood, M Ernani Cuenco.

LP Bernadette Williams, Jennifer Laine, Taaffe O'Connell, Catherine Barch, S.P. Victoria, Mari Karen Ryan, Ken Metcalf.

Female American POWs being held captive in Southeast Asia are brainwashed into becoming walking time bombs.

405. Caged Women (1984, MPM, 96m, c). D Vincent Dawn (Bruno Mattei), W P. Molteni & Oliver LeMat, PH Luigi Ciccarese, M Luigi Ceccarelli, ED Bruno Mattei.

LP Laura Gemser (Laura/Emanuelle), Gabriele Tinti (Dr. Moran), Lorraine de Selle (Warden), Marie Romano, Ursula Flores, Raul Cabrera.

An undercover journalist enters a women's prison to get a story. She gets more than she bargained for.

406. Cal (1984, Warner, Ireland, 102m, c). P Stuart Craig & David Putt-nam, D Pat O'Connor, W Bernard Mac-Laverty (based on his novel), PH Jerzy Zielinski, M Mark Knopfler, ED Michael Bradsell, PD Craig.

LP Helen Mirren (Marcella), John Lynch (Cal), Donal McCann (Shamie), John Kavanagh (Skeffington), Ray Mc-Anally (Cyril Dunlop), Stevan Rimkus (Crilly), Kitty Gibson (Mrs. Morton), Louis Rolston (Dermot Ryan), Tom Hickey (Preacher).

Nineteen-year-old Catholic John Lynch falls in love with older Protestant Helen Mirren, despite the fact that as an IRA member he was involved in the murder of her policeman husband. It's an intelligent handling of a love story complicated by the Catholic-Protestant conflict in Northern Ireland.

Calhoun see Nightstick

The California Dolls see All the Marbles

407. Caligula (1980, Penthouse Films, US/Ital., 156m, c). P Bob Guccione & Franco Rossellini, D Piernico Solinas, W Gore Vidal, PH Silvano Ippoliti & Tinto Brass, M Paul Clemente, Khatchaturian, Prokofiev, ED Nino Baragli, Guccione & Rossellini, AD Danilo Donati.

LP Malcolm McDowell (Caligula), Teresa Ann Savoy (Drusilla), Guido Mannari (Macro), John Gielgud (Nerva), Peter O'Toole (Tiberius), Giancarlo Badessi (Claudius), Bruno Brive (Gemellus), Adriana Asti (Ennia), Leopoldo Trieste (Charicles), Helen Mirren (Caesonia), Lori Wagner (Agrippina), Anneka DiLorenzo (Messalina).

Penthouse publisher Bob Guccione is responsible for this tasteless piece of soft porn, showing all the decadence and adebauchery of Caligula's Rome in sickening detail. Hold out for a rerun of Public TV's "I, Claudius."

408. Call Me (1988, Vestron, 97m, c). P John E. Quill & Kenneth F. Martel, D Sollace Mitchell, W Karyn Kay, PH Zoltan David, M David Frank, ED Paul Fried, PD Stephen McCabe.

LP Patricia Charbonneau (Anna), Patti D'Arbanville (Cori), Sam Freed (Alex), Boyd Gaines (Bill), Stephen Mc-Hattie (Jellybean), Steve Buscemi (Switch Blade), John Seitz (Pressure), David Strathairn (Sam).

One night dumb-dumb Patricia Charbonneau gets an obscene phone call and is really turned on. This leads the naive ding-a-ling into a world of drugs, dishonest cops and assorted other creeps.

The Calling see Murder by Phone

409. Came a Hot Friday (1985, Orion Classics, New Zealand, 100m, c). P Larry Parr, D Ian Mune, W Mune & Dean Parker (based on the novel by Ronald Hugh Morrieson), PH Alun Bollinger, M Stephen McCurdy, ED Ken Zemke.

LP Peter Bland (Wesley Pennington), Philip Gordon (Cyril Kidman), Billy T. James (The Tainuia Kid), Michael Lawrence (Don Jackson), Marshall Napier (Sel Bishop), Don Selwyn (Norm Cray), Marise Wipani (Esmerelda).

In 1949 New Zealand, con men Peter Bland and Philip Gordon have an unusual, slightly illegal, means of picking winners at the races. Run out of the cities by the bookies they have cheated, they find a smaller town with a racetrack but have the tables turned on them by the wacky locals.

410. Cameron's Closet (1989, Smart Egg Pictures, 86m, c). P Luigi Cingolani, D Armand Mastroianni, W Gary Brandner (based on his novel), PH Russell Carpenter, M Harry Manfredini, SE Carlo Rambaldi.

LP Cotter Smith (Det. Sam Talliaferro), Mel Harris (Nora Haley), Scott Curtis (Cameron Lansing), Chuck McCann (Ben Majors), Leigh McCloskey (Det. Pete Groom), Kim Lankford (Dory Lansing), Tab Hunter (Owen Lansing).

Scott Curtis' father Tab Hunter experiments with his son, combining psychokinesis and demonology. The result is that he unleashes a monster in the boy's closet which kills Dad and several others in hellish ways.

Campsite Massacre see The Final Terror

411. Campus Man (1987, RKO/Paramount, 94m, c). P Peggy Fowler & Jon Landau, D Ron Casden, W Matt Dorff, Alex Horvat & Geoffrey Baere (based on a story by Dorf & Horvat), PH Francis Kenny, M James Newton Howard, ED Steven Polivka, PD David Gropman.

LP John Dye (Todd Barrett), Steve Lyon (Brett Wilson), Kim Delaney (Dayna Thomas), Kathleen Wilhoite (Molly Gibson), Miles O'Keeffe (Cactus Jack), Morgan Fairchild (Katherine Van Buren).

Arizona State student John Dye needs tuition money. He convinces diver Steve Lyon to pose for a beefcake calender to raise the money. He has to borrow seed money from loan shark Miles O'Keeffe. Everything goes wrong, before it goes right.

412. Can She Bake a Cherry Pie? (1983, Jagfilm, 90m, c). P M.H. Simonsons, D&W Henry Jaglom, PH Bob Fiore, M/L Karen Black.

LP Karen Black (Zee), Michael Emil (Eli), Michael Margotta (Larry), Frances Fisher (Louise), Martin Harvey Friedberg (Mort), Paul Williams (Zee's Husband), Ariela Nicole (Eli's Daughter), Larry David (Philosopher).

In this slow-moving comedy, after Karen Black's husband leaves her, she takes up with confirmed bachelor Michael Emil. They talk a lot and finally decide to be in love.

413. Cannery Row (1982, United Artists/MGM, 120m, c). P Michael Phillips, D&W David S. Ward (based on *Cannery Row* and *Sweet Thursday* by John Steinbeck), PH Sven Nykvist, M Jack Nitzsche, ED David Bretherton.

LP Nick Nolte (Doc), Debra Winger (Suzy), Audra Lindley (Fauna), Frank McRae (Hazel), M. Emmet Walsh (Mack), Tom Mahoney (Hughie), John Malloy (Jones), James Keane (Eddie), Sunshine Parker (The Seer), Santos Morales (Joseph and Mary), Sharon Ernster (Agnes).

Nick Nolte and Debra Winger give decent performances as a marine biologist and would-be hooker, respectively, but the material is Steinbeck at his corniest. The film is slow-paced and uneven. One bright spot is Frank McRae as a loveable half-wit.

414. The Cannonball Run (1981, 20th Century-Fox, 95m, c). P Albert S. Ruddy, D Hal Needham, W Brock Yates, PH Michael Butler, M Al Capps, ED Donn Cambern & William D. Gordean.

LP Burt Reynolds (J.J. McClure), Roger Moore (Seymour), Farah Fawcett (Pamela), Dom DeLuise (Victor), Dean Martin (Jamie Blake), Sammy Davis, Jr. (Fenderbaum), Jack Elam (Doctor), Adrienne Barbeau (Marcie), Terry Bradshaw (Terry), Jamie Farr (Sheik), Peter Fonda (Chief Biker).

Burt Reynolds and friends put together this mediocre chase comedy based on the illegal Cannonball Sea-to-Shining-Sea Memorial Trophy dash which is held every two years. It just goes to show that one doesn't have to make a good movie to make money. This moronic waste of celluloid was one of the top grossing films of the year.

415. *Cannonball Run II* (1984, Warner, 108m, c). P Albert S. Ruddy, D Hal Needham, W Needham, Ruddy & Harvey Miller (based on characters created by Brock Yates), PH Nick McLean, M Al Capps, ED William Gordean & Carl Kress.

LP Burt Reynolds (J.J. McClure), Dom DeLuise (Victor/Chaos), Shirley MacLaine (Veronica), Marilu Henner (Betty), Dean Martin (Blake), Sammy Davis, Jr. (Fenderbaum), Susan Anton (Jill), Catherine Bach (Marcie), Ricardo Montalban (King), Jim Nabors (Homer), Charles Nelson Reilly (Don Don), Telly Savalas (Hymie), Jamie Farr (Sheik), Jack Elam (Doc), Richard Kiel (Arnold), Frank Sinatra (Himself), Henry Silva (Slim).

The producers of *Cannonball Run* apparently wished to prove there is no way to underestimate the taste of certain sections of the movie-going public, by bringing out this tasteless and offensive sequel. The race is merely an excuse to gather a group of over-the-hill and out-of-work friends of Burt Reynolds and Hal Needham for an outing where everyone makes a fool of himself or herself.

416. *Can't Buy Me Love* (1987, Buena Vista, 94m, c). P Thom Mount, D Steve Rash, W Michael Swerdlick, PH Peter Lyons Collister, M Robert Folk, ED Jeff Gourson, PD Donald L. Harris.

LP Patrick Dempsey (Ronald Miller), Amanda Peterson (Cindy Mancini), Courtney Gains (Kenneth Wurman), Tina Caspary (Barbara), Seth Green (Chuckie Miller), Sharon Farrell (Mrs. Mancini), Darcy De Moss (Patty).

In this film originally entitled *Boy Rents Girl,* nerdish high school student Patrick Dempsey spends all his hard-earned savings to rent the girl next door, Amanda Peterson, an unattainable blonde beauty and the queen of the in-crowd, as his girl friend for a month. She reluctantly accepts his offer because she has ruined an $1000 suede outfit belonging to her mother. It takes Dempsey's becoming a cool-cat, in love with his own new found popularity, and his to-be-expected downfall, before he becomes a normal kid and earns Peterson's love by being himself.

417. *Can't Stop the Music* (1980, Associated Film Distribution, 118m, c). P Allan Carr, Jacques Morali & Henri Belolo, D Nancy Walker, W Bronte Woodward & Carr, PH Bill Butler, M Morali, ED John F. Burnett.

LP Village People: Ray Simpson (Policeman), David Hodo (Construction Worker), Felipe Rose (Indian), Randy Jones (Cowboy), Glenn Hughes (Leatherman), Alex Briley (GI), Valerie Perrine (Samantha Simpson), Bruce Jenner (Ron White), Steve Guttenberg (Jack Morell), Paul Sand (Steve Waits), Tammy Grimes (Sydney Channing), June Havoc (Helen Morell), Barbara Rush (Norma White).

By the time this silly movie featuring the disco singing group The Village People was released, their moment in the sun had passed. What jokingly is called the plot has Valerie Perrine trying to get the Village People to sing songs written by Steve Guttenberg. It ought to be the kiss of death for a songwriter.

418. *Cappuccino* (1989, Ronin Films, Australia, 84m, c). P Andrew Bowman & Sue Wild, D&W Bowman, PH Danny Batterham, M William Motzing, ED Richard Hindley, PD Darrell Lass.

LP John Clayton (Max), Rowena Wallace (Anna French), Jeanie Drynan (Maggie Spencer), Barry Quin (Larry), Cristina Parker (Celia), Ritchie Singer (Bollinger), Simon Matthew (Nigel).

A group of middle-aged actors and actresses hang out at a cafe where cappuccino is the preferred beverage. They drift into and out of relationships with each other as easily as they assume roles.

419. *Captive Hearts* (1987, MGM/ United Artists, 97m, c). P John A. Kuri, D Paul Almond, W Pat Morita & Kuri (based on a story by Sargon Tamimi), PH Thomas Vamos, M Osamu Kitajima, ED Yurij Luhovy, PD Steve Sardanis & Francois DeLucy.

LP Noriyuki "Pat" Morita (Fukushima), Chris Makepeace (Robert), Mari Sato (Miyoko), Michael Sarrazin (Sgt. McManus), Seth Sakai (Takayama), Denis Akiyama (Masato).

During World War II, bomber crewman Chris Makepeace is shot down over Japan; he is adopted by village elder Noriyuki Morita and falls in love with Mari Sato. The film barely made it to the theaters. The simplistic plot is not the sole reason. It's dreary!

420. *Captive Rage* (1988, The Movie Group-OKA, 92m, c). P Harry Alan Towers, Barry Wood & Keith Rosenbaum, D Cedric Sundstrom, W Rick Marx & Sundstrom (based on a story by Peter Welbeck [Towers]), PH George Bartels, M Mark Mitchell & Mick Hope Bailie, ED Allan Morrison, PD George Canes.

LP Oliver Reed (Gen. Belmondo), Robert Vaughn (Edward Delacorte), Claudia Udy (Chiga), Lisa Rinna (Lucy Delacorte), Maureen Kedes, Sharon Schaffer, Diana Tilden-Davis.

Oliver Reed is the psychopathic dictator of a mythical South American country. When his son is arrested for trafficking in controlled substances by the U.S. Drug Enforcement Agency, Reed hijacks a planeload of college coeds, including Lisa Rinna, the daughter of DEA chief Robert Vaughn. Reed threatens all kinds of bodily harm to the coeds unless his son is returned to him within 72 hours. However the girls escape and turn the tables on Reed.

421. *Carbon Copy* (1981, Avco Embassy, 92m, c). P Carter DeHaven III & Stanley Shapiro, D Michael Schultz, W Shapiro, PH Fred Koenekamp, M Bill Conti, ED Marion Segal.

LP George Segal (Walter Whitney), Susan St. James (Vivian Whitney), Jack Warden (Nelson), Denzel Washington (Roger), Paul Winfield (Bob), Dick Martin (Victor), Vicki Dawson (Marie-Ann), Tom Poston (Rev. Hayworth), Macon McCalman (Tubby).

White executive George Segal loses his wife Susan St. James and his job when it is revealed that he has a black illegitimate son, Denzel Washington, from a fling nearly two decades earlier. Segal is forced to take menial labor jobs. He and Washington find ways to appreciate each other.

422. *The Care Bears Adventure in Wonderland* (1987, Cineplex Odeon, Canada, animated, 75m, c). P Michael Hirsh, Patrick Loubert & Clive A. Smith, D Raymond Jafelice, W Susan Snooks & John De Klein (based on a story by Peter Sauder), M Trish Cullen, ED Rob Kirkpatrick.

VOICES Bob Dermer (Grumpy Bear), Eva Almos (Swift Heart Rabbit), Dan Hennessey (Brace Heart Lion/Dum), Jim Henshaw (Tenderheart Bear), Maria Lukofsky (Good Luck Bear), Luba Goy (Lots-a-Heart Elephant), Keith Knight (White Rabbit), Tracey Moore (Alice), Colin Fox (Wizard).

Produced for the little tykes, this animated feature sees the Care Bears trying to persuade Lewis Carroll's Alice to stand in for a princess who's been abducted by an evil wizard.

423. *The Care Bears Movie* (1985, Goldwyn, Canada, animated, 75m, c). P Michael Hirsh, Patrick Loubert & Clive Smith, D Arna Selznick, W Peter Sauder, M John Sebastian, Walt Woodward & Trish Cullen, ED Robert Fitzpatrick, John Broughton, Jim Erickson, Tom Joerin, Gordon Kidd, Stephan Mitchell, Sheila Murray, Steve Westlake & Michael O'Farrell, PD Charles Bonifacio.

VOICES Mickey Rooney (Mr. Cherrywood), Georgia Engel (Love-a-Lot Bear), Harry Dean Stanton (Brave Heart Bear).

This cute story for the three- to six-year-old group is a 75-minute advertisement for the Care Bears, who help some orphaned kids threatened by an evil spirit.

424. *Care Bears Movie II: A New Generation* (1986, Columbia, Canada, animated, 77m, c). P Michael Hirsh,

Patrick Loubert & Clive A. Smith, D Dale Schott, W Peter Sauder (based on a story by Nelvana), M Patricia Cullen, ED Evan Landis, PD Charles Bonifacio.

VOICES Hadley Kay (Dark Heart/ The Boy), Chris Wiggins (Great Wishing Star), Cree Summer Francks (Christy), Alyson Court (Dawn), Maxine Miller (True Heart Bear), Pam Hyatt (Noble Heart Horse), Dan Hennessey (Brave Heart Lion), Billie Mae Richards (Tender Heart Bear), Eva Almos (Friend Bear), Bob Dermer (Grumpy Bear), Patrice Black (Share Bear).

The cute little buttinsky bears intervene when Dark Heart indoctrinates young campers with a bad attitude about the importance of winning at all costs.

425. *Careful He Might Hear You* (1984, 20th Century–Fox, Australia, 116m, c). P Jill Robb, D Carl Schultz, W Michael Jenkins (based on the novel by Sumner Locke Elliott), PH John Seale, M Ray Cook, ED Richard Francis-Bruce, PD John Stoddart.

LP Nicholas Gledhill ("P.S." Bill), Wendy Hughes (Vanessa), Robyn Nevin (Lila), Peter Whitford (George), John Hargreaves (Logan), Isabelle Anderson (Agnes), Geraldine Turner (Vere), Colleen Clifford (Ettie), Julie Nihill (Diana), Beth Child (Mrs. Grindel), Pega Williams (Winnie Grindel).

This winner of eight Australian Oscars is the story of a bitter custody fight for 6-year-old Nicholas Gledhill. The young actor is a joy to behold and one can't help but becoming emotionally involved and concerned about what is to become of him. Those fighting for custody of the boy also get audience's juices going, particularly Wendy Hughes as a beautiful, wealthy, malicious and unstable aunt.

426. *The Carhops* (1980, NMD, 88m, c). P Jim Buckley, D Peter Locke, W Paul Ross & Michael Blank, PH Colin Campbell, M Ronald Frangipane, ED Rick Jackson & Wes Craven, AD Michael Sullivan & Peter Bramley.

LP Kitty Carl (Kitty), Lisa Farringer (Cindy), Fay de Witt (Kitty's Mother), Pamela Miller (Vicki), Marcie Barkin (Sherry), Jack DeLeon (MacGregor), Walter Wanderman (Albert).

The film is just another mindless, plotless excuse for displaying well-endowed young women in revealing attire. You say that's what you're looking for? Well, you've found it.

427. *Caribe* (1987, Miramax, Canada, 89m, c). P Nicolas Stiliadis, D Michael Kennedy, W Paul Donovan, PH Ludek Boner, ED Stan Cole & Michael McMahon, AD Bronwen Hughes.

LP John Savage (Jeff Richardson), Kara Glover (Helen Williams), Stephen McHattie (Whitehale), Paul Koslo (Mercenary), Maury Chaykin (Capt. Burdoch), Sam Makin (Roy Forbes), Zack Nesis (Tommy Goff).

CIA agent Kara Glover's partner is killed by arms smuggler Stephen McHattie when the two federal agents arrange a weapons sale for their own profit. It's a routine thriller with excellent photography of the Belize jungles and mountains.

428. *Carny* (1980, United Artists, 105m, c). P Robbie Robertson, D Robert Kaylor, W Thomas Baum (based on a story by Phoebe Taylor, Kaylor & Robertson), PH Harry Stadling, Jr., M Alex North, ED Stuart Pappe.

LP Gary Busey (Frankie), Jodie Foster (Donna), Robbie Robertson (Patch), Meg Foster (Gerta), Kenneth McMillan (Heavy), Elisha Cook (On-Your-Mark), Theodore Wilson (Nails), John Lehne (Skeet), Tina Andrews (Sugaree), Bert Remsen (Delno), Craig Wasson (Mickey).

The friendship of carnival pros Gary Busey and Robbie Robertson is disrupted when runaway Jodie Foster seeks shelter with them. Foster sure is a sexy, promiscuous, little waif.

429. *The Carpenter* (1989, Cinepix/ Capstone, Canada, 87m, c). P Pierre Grise, D David Wellington, W Doug Taylor, PH David Franco, M Pierre Bundock, ED Roland Pollack, SD Sylvain Gendron.

LP Wings Hauser (Ed), Lynne Adams (Alice), Pierre Lenoir (Martin), Barbara Jones (Rachel).

The lives of young couple Lynne Adams and Pierre Lenoir are disrupted by the arrival of Wings Hauser, the ghost of the previous resident of their house, a carpenter. Then again he may be a figment of Adams' terrified imagination.

430.   *The Carrier* (1988, Swan, 99m, c). P Jeffrey Dougherty, D&W Nathan J. White, PH Peter Deming, M Joseph Lo Duca, ED White.

LP Gregory Fortesque (Jake), Steve Dixon (Dr. Anthony King), N. Paul Silverman (The Reverend), Paul Urbanski (Joshua), Patrick Butler (Tim), Stevie Lee (Treva).

Cut off from the outside world by a devastating flood, the inhabitants of a small community must deal with the fact that one of their number is the carrier of a fatal contagious disease.

431.   *Castaway* (1987, Cannon, 118m, c). P Rick McCallum, D Nicolas Roeg, W Allan Scott (based on the book by Lucy Irvine), PH Harvey Harrison, M Stanley Myers, ED Tony Lawson, PD Andrew Sanders.

LP Oliver Reed (Gerald Kingsland), Amanda Donohoe (Lucy Irvine), Tony Rickards (Jason), Todd Rippon (Rod), Georgina Hale (Sister Saint Margaret), Frances Barber (Sister Saint Winnifred).

Scruffy Oliver Reed advertises for a "wife" to spend a year with him on a deserted island. Amanda Donohoe is the adventure seeker who takes him up on his offer.

432.   *Casual Sex?* (1988, Universal, 87m, c). P Ilona Herzberg & Sheldon Kahn, D Genevieve Robert, W Wendy Goldman & Judy Toll (based on the play by Goldman & Toll), PH Rolf Kestermann, M Van Dyke Parks, ED Kahn & Donn Cambern, PD Randy Ser.

LP Lea Thompson (Stacy), Victoria Jackson (Melissa), Stephen Shellen (Nick), Jerry Levine (Jamie), Andrew Dice Clay (Vinny), Mary Gross (Ilene), Valeri Breiman (Megan), Peter Dvorsky (Matthew), David Sargent (Frankie).

Lea Thompson and Victoria Jackson are long time friends. Thompson has had a busy, enjoyable sex life, usually falling in bed with artistic types who end up failing to meet her standards of sensitivity after the one-night stands. Jackson has had very few sexual experiences, none of which have been satisfying. The fear of AIDS and other diseases has slowed

down Thompson to a point where she hasn't had sex for a year. The two friends head for a vacation at a health spa, hoping to find some Mr. Rights or at least some Mr. Tonights. They do but not the ones they first thought filled the bill. While mourning the death of the romantic notion of grand passion bringing on sex, one can still enjoy this comedy in which sex is just another appetite to be fed.

433.   *Casualties of War* (1989, Columbia, 120m, c). P Art Linson, D Brian De Palma, W David Rabe (based on the book by Daniel Lang), PH Stephen H. Burum, M Ennio Morricone, ED Bill Pankow, PD Wolf Kroeger.

LP Michael J. Fox (Eriksson), Sean Penn (Meserve), Don Harvey (Clark), John C. Reilly (Hatcher), John Leguizamo (Diaz), Thuy Thu Le (Oahn), Erik King (Brown), Jack Gwaltney (Rowan), Ving Rhames (Lt. Reilly), Dan Martin (Hawthorne), Dale Dye (Capt. Hill).

The night before Sean Penn and the four men under his command are to go on a dangerous mission, they kidnap young Vietnamese woman Thuy Thu Le, bind and gag her, and take her with them on the mission. In the days that follow they gang rape her and when threatened with exposure, they stab and shoot her to death. Only Michael J. Fox refuses to take part in the brutality, although he does nothing to try and stop it. When he gets back, against the advice of officers, Fox turns in his buddies, even though he is rightfully petrified that they will retaliate against him. Up to and including the court martials, everyone treats Fox as if his action is that of a disloyal cowardly tattle-tale; as if he had reported the other four for taking an extra cookie from mother's cookie jar. Penn as the barely-literate, foul-mouthed sergeant, totally devoid of any moral standards, is superb. His deranged character represents the bad side of the American character in its orgy of destruction in Vietnam. Fox, who usually plays an All-American boy that mothers can love, represents the thoughtless innocence that some brought to a conflict which so split the nation.

434.   *The Cat and the Canary* (1981, Grenadier, GB, 98m, c). P Richard Gordon, D&W Radley Metzger (based on the play by John Willard), PH Alex Thomson, M Steven Cagen, ED Roger Harrison.

LP Honor Blackman (Susan Sillsby), Michael Callan (Paul Jones), Edward Fox (Hendricks), Wendy Hiller (Allison Crosby), Olivia Hussey (Cicily Young), Beatrix Lehmann (Mrs. Pleasant), Carol Lynley (Anabelle West), Daniel Massey (Harry Blythe), Peter McEnery (Charlie Wilder), Wilfrid Hyde-White (Cyrus West).

It's a routine production of the oft-filmed mystery-horror story of a hooded killer trying to drive an heiress mad.

435. *Cat Chaser* (1989, Vestron, 90m, c). P Peter Davis & William Panzer, D Abel Ferrara, W Elmore Leonard, Jim Borelli & Alan Sharp (based on a novel by Leonard), PH Anthony Richmond, M Chick Corea, ED Kim Kennedy, PD Dan Leigh.

LP Peter Weller (George Moran), Kelly McGillis (Mary de Boya), Charles Durning (Jiggs Scully), Frederic Forrest (Nolan Tyner), Thomas Milian (Andres de Boya), Juan Fernandez (Rafi).

Kelly McGillis is a femme fatale married to Thomas Milian, the former head of the secret police of Santo Domingo, but her heart belongs to Miami hotel owner Peter Weller who fought during the American intervention in Santo Domingo. The latter-day film noir is a wordy production of a successful racy novel. It will probably make its mark in home video.

436. *Cat People* (1982, Universal/RKO, 118m, c). P Charles Fries, D Paul Schrader, W Alan Ormsby (based on the story by DeWitt Bodeen), PH John Bailey, M Giorgio Moroder, TITLE THEME BY David Bowie, ED Jacqueline Cambas, SE Albert Whitlock.

LP Nastassja Kinski (Irena Gallier), Malcolm McDowell (Paul Gallier), John Heard (Oliver Yates), Annette O'Toole (Alice Perrin), Ruby Dee (Female), Ed Begley, Jr. (Joe Creigh), Scott Paulin (Bill Searle), Frankie Faison (Det. Brandt), John Larroquette (Bronte Judson).

New Orleans virgin Nastassja Kinski is warned by her brother Malcolm McDowell that people in their family turn into panthers after making love with nonrelatives and kill their lover. Somehow zookeeper John Heard bravely solves Kinski's problem.

437. *Catch Me If You Can* (1989, MCEG, 105m, c). P Jonathan D. Krane & Don Schain, D&W Stephen Sommers, PH Ronn Schmidt, M Tangerine Dream, ED Bob Ducsay, AD Stuart Blatt.

LP Matt Lattanzi (Dylan), Loryn Locklin (Melissa), Grant Heslov (Nevil), Billy Morrissette (Monkey), Geoffrey Lewis (Mr. Johnson), M. Emmet Walsh (Johnny Phantmun), Dan Bell (Manney).

The plot of this first effort by Helmer Stephen Sommers has teenagers staging drag races to raise funds to prevent the closing of Cathedral High.

438. *Catch the Heat* (1987, Trans World, 87m, c, aka *Feel the Heat*). P Don Van Atta, D Joel Silberg, W Stirling Silliphant, PH Nissim Leon Nitcho & Frank Harris, M Thomas Chase & Steve Rucker, ED Christopher Holmes & Darren Holmes, PD Jorge Marchegiani.

LP David Dukes (Waldo), Tiana Alexandra (Checkers Goldberg), Rod Steiger (Jason Hannibal), Brian Thompson (Danny), Jorge Martinez (Raul), John Hancock (Ike), Brian Libby (Brody), Jessica Schultz (Maria).

Tiana Alexandra is a U.S. narcotics agent sent to Buenos Aires to infiltrate the operations of drug dealer Rod Steiger. The latter smuggles his goods into the United States by implanting them in the breasts of exotic dancers.

Catholic Boys see Heaven Help Us

439. *Cat's Eye* (1985, MGM/United Artists, 93m, c). P Martha Schumacher, D Lewis Teague, W Stephen King (based on his short stories "Quitters Inc.," "The General" and "The Ledge"), PH Jack Cardiff, M Alan Silvestri, ED Scott Conrad, PD Giorgio Postiglione, SE Jeff Jarvis.

LP Drew Barrymore (Girl), James Woods (Morrison), Alan King (Dr. Donatti), Kenneth McMillan (Cressner), Robert Hays (Norris), Candy Clark (Sally Ann), James Naughton (Hugh), Tony Munafo (Junk), Court Miller (Mr. McCann), Russell Horton (Mr. Milquetoast), Patricia Benson (Mrs. Milquetoast), Mary D'Arcy (Cindy).

This is an anthology of three of horror writer Stephen King's stories. In the first, wacky physician Alan King has a sadistic cure for smoking. He shoots electricity through his subject's wife every time the smoker takes a puff. In the second, gambler Kenneth McMillan forces his wife's lover Robert Hays out on the ledge of the 20th floor of a hotel. If Hays can make it all around the building he gets McMillan's wife and money. In the third installment, Drew Barrymore is harrassed in her bedroom by a hideous troll which her parents believe to be only in the child's imagination.

440.   *Cattle Annie and Little Britches* (1981, Universal, 97m, c). P Rupert Hitzig & Allan King, D Lamont Johnson, W David Eyre & Robert Ward (based on a story by Ward from his novel), PH Larry Pizer, M Sanh Berti & Tom Slocum, ED Robbe Roberts & William Haugse, PD Stan Jolley.

LP Burt Lancaster (Bill Doolin), John Savage (Bittercreek Newcomb), Rod Steiger (Tighman), Diane Lane (Jenny), Amanda Plummer (Annie), Scott Glenn (Bill Dalton), Redmond Gleason (Red Buck), William Russ (Little Dick Raidler), Ken Call (George Weightman).

Diane Lane and Amanda Plummer, thrilled by Ned Buntline's dime novels, ride off to join the Doolin gang of Oklahoma, led by crusty Burt Lancaster. The outlaws pull off several semicomic heists, all the time pursued by relentless lawman Rod Steiger.

441.   *Caught* (1987, World Wide Pictures, 113m, c). P Jerry Ballew, D&W James F. Collier, PH Eddy Van Der Enden, M Ted Neely, PD J. Michael Hooser.

LP John Shepherd (Tim Devon), Amerjit Deu (Rajam Prasad), Jill Ireland (Janet Devon), Alex Tetteh-Lartey (Abraham Abimue), Frederik DeGroot (Jacques), Marnix Kappers (Erik de Bie), Kimberly Simms (Aimee Lynn).

Made by evangelist Billy Graham's production company, the film is the story of Indian evangelist Amerjit Deu who befriends American junkie John Shepherd, eventually converting the latter to Christianity.

442.   *Cave Girl* (1985, Crown International, 86m, c, aka *Cavegirl*). P,D, W&PH David Oliver (based on a screenplay by Phil Groves), M Jon St. James, ED Robert Field.

LP Daniel Roebuck (Rex), Cindy Ann Thompson (Eba), Saba Moor (Saba), Jeff Chayette (Argh), Darren Young (Dar), Charles Mitchell (Char), Cynthia Rullo (Aka), Tom Hamil (Casey), Bill Adams (Bill, Old Man).

Nerdy anthropology student Daniel Roebuck is transported back to prehistoric times where he encounters yummy Cindy Ann Thompson and her family. He is eventually accepted by the cave dwellers when he saves Thompson from a lion and the whole clan from a group of cannibals. It's meant to be a comedy, but it's terribly juvenile.

Cavegirl see Cave Girl

443.   *Caveman* (1981, United Artists, 91m, c). P Lawrence Turman & David Foster, D Carl Gottlieb, W Gottlieb & Rudy De Luca, PH Alan Hume, M Lalo Schifrin, ED Gene Fowler, Jr.

LP Ringo Starr (Atouk), Dennis Quaid (Lar), Shelley Long (Tala), Jack Gilford (Gog), John Matuszak (Tonda), Barbara Bach (Lana), Cork Hubbert (Ta), Mark King (Ruck), Paco Morayta (Flok), Evan Kim (Nook).

Ringo Starr invents rock 'n' roll with real rocks in this prehistoric spoof. The film is blessed by a charming scene-stealing dinosaur.

444.   *Cease Fire* (1985, CineWorld, 97m, c). P William Grefe, D David Nutter, W George Fernandez (based on his play *Vietnam Trilogy*), PH Henning Schellerup, M Gary Fry, ED Julio Chaves, Nutter & Ralph R. Clemente.

LP Don Johnson (Tim Murphy), Lisa Blount (Paula Murphy), Robert F. Lyons (Luke), Richard Chaves (Badman), Rick Richards (Robbs), Chris Noel (Wendy), Jorge Gil (Sanchez), John Archie (Rafer), T.R. Durphy (Hartz), Buddy Bolan (Benny).

Fifteen years after the fact, Vietnam vet Don Johnson begins to have flashbacks to the horror he faced in Indochina. He can't keep any job, and spends much of his time drinking with another vet, Robert F. Lyons. Johnson's wife Lisa Blount gets him to attend veterans meetings, but it isn't until after Lyons' suicide that Johnson is able to snap back to reality. It's a sensitive telling of an ex-soldier's problems in putting his war behind him.

445. *Cellar Dweller* (1988, Dove/Empire, 77m, c). P Bob Wynn, D John Carl Buechler, W Kit DuBois, PH Sergio Salvati, M Carlo Dante, ED Barry Zetlin.

LP Pamela Bellwood (Amanda), Deborah Mullowney (Whitney Taylor), Brian Robbins (Philip), Cheryl-Ann Wilson (Lisa), Vince Edwards (Mr. Shelski), Yvonne De Carlo (Mrs. Briggs), Michael S. Deak (Cellar Dweller).

Cartoonist Michael S. Deak finds a work called "The Curses of the Ancient Dead" which allows him to draw a killing by monsters and have his creations come to life and carry out the crime for real.

446. *Cemetery High* (1989, Titan, 80m, c). P Gorman Bechard & Kristine Covello, D Bechard, W. Bechard & Carmine Capobianco, PH Patrick J. Donoghue, ED Frank Christopher.

LP Debi Thibeault (Kate), Karen Nielsen (Kathy), Lisa Schmidt (Michelle), Simone (Dianne), Ruth Collins (Lisa), Tony Kruk, David Coughlin, Frank Stewart.

Four very angry Connecticut women, just graduated from high school, band together to become vigilantes to wipe out male "slimeballs" after each has been assaulted.

447. *The Census Taker* (1984, Argentum/Borde, 95m, c). P Robert Bealmer, D Bruce Cook, W Cook & Gordon Smith, PH Tom Jewett, M Jay Seagrave, ED Cook.

LP Garrett Morris (Harvey McGraw), Greg Mullavey (George), Meredith MacRae (Martha), Austen Taylor (Eva), Timothy Bottoms (Pete).

Census taker Garrett Morris' questions into the private lives of Greg Mullavey and wife Meredith MacRae prove too personal, so they kill him and then try to hide the body from weird detective Timothy Bottoms. By the end of this mildly amusing black comedy, Mullavey and Bottoms are both dead, with MacRae collecting their life insurance.

448. *Certain Fury* (1985, New World, 87m, c). P Gilbert Adler, D Stephen Gyllenhaal, W Michael Jacobs, PH Kees Van Oostrum, M Bill Payne, Russell Kunkel & George Massenburg, ED Todd Ramsay, PD Beala Neel.

LP Tatum O'Neal (Scarlet), Irene Cara (Tracy), Nicholas Campbell (Sniffer), George Murdock (Lt. Speier), Moses Gunn (Dr. Freeman), Peter Fonda (Rodney), Rodney Gage (Superman), Jonathan Pallone (Barker).

In this trashy film, middle-class Irene Cara and illiterate streetwise Tatum O'Neal are in a courtroom awaiting the hearing of the cases against them when two lesbian hookers grab a policeman's gun and proceed to shoot the place up. The cops believe Cara and O'Neal are part of the break, so they are forced to flee. Their flight takes them into all the sleazy parts of the city where they encounter society's worst. Like *The Defiant Ones,* they learn to depend upon each other. Unfortunately, that's where the similarities end.

449. *The Chain* (1985, Rank, GB, 96m, c). P Victor Glynn, D Jack Gold, W Jack Rosenthal, PH Wolfgang Suschitzky, M Stanley Myers, ED Bill Blunden, PD Peter Murton.

LP Herbert Norville (Des), Denis Lawson (Keith), Rita Wolf (Carrie), Maurice Denham (Grandpa), Nigel Hawthorne (Mr. Thorn), Billie Whitelaw (Mrs. Andreos), Judy Parfitt (Deirde), Leo McKern (Thomas), Anna Massey (Betty), Charlotte Long (Rosemary), John Rowe (Alex), David Troughton (Dudley), Phyllis Logan (Alison).

Like a La Ronde of house moves, this amusing film traces the moving days of various people, starting with Herbert Norville setting up housekeeping with his girlfriend in a flat from which young couple Denis Lawson and Rita Wolf leave to take up residence in Willesden. The latter apartment is being vacated by David Troughton and Phyllis Logan, who are buying their first house, currently the residence of miserly Nigel Hawthorne and his wife Anna Massey. They are supposed to move into the home of Billie Whitelaw, who sees no reason to move, as it was her recently deceased husband who sold the place. Next in the chain is Judy Parfitt and John Rowe who are about to move into a rich neighborhood, from which self-made millionaire Leo McKern is leaving to move back to the neighborhood of his youth, to take up residency in the place where the film began.

450. Chain Reaction (1980, Palm Beach Pictures/Hoyt, Australia, 87m, c). P David Elfick, D&W Ian Barry, PH Russell Boyd (underwater photography by George Greenough), M Andrew Thomas Wilson, ED Tim Wellburn.

LP Steve Bisley (Larry), Arna-Maria Winchester (Carmel), Ross Thompson (Heinrich), Ralph Cotterill (Gray), Patrick Ward (Oates), Laurie Moran (Police Sgt. McSweeney), Richard Moir (Junior Constable Piggott).

In another nuclear whistle-blower film, Steve Bisley is an employee of a contaminated plant whose officials want to get rid of him before he can spread the alarm to the public.

451. Chained Heat (1983, Jensen/Farley, 95m, c). P Billy Fine, D Paul Nicholas, W Vincent Mongol & Nicholas, PH Mac Ahlberg, M Joseph Conlon, ED Nino di Marco.

LP Linda Blair (Carol), John Vernon (Warden Backman), Sybil Danning (Ericka), Tamara Dobson (Duchess), Stella Stevens (Capt. Taylor), Sharon Hughes (Val), Henry Silva (Lester).

Linda Blair portrays the familiar innocent young girl sent to a brutal women's prison where she is violently courted by busty lesbians. One doesn't know whether to be amused or outraged by this gross sexploitation film.

452. The Chair (1989, Urban/Angelika, 94m, c, aka *Hot Seat*). P Anthony Jones, D Waldemar Korzeniowsky, W Carolyn Swartz, PH Steven Ross, M Eddie Reyes, ED Swartz, PD Robert Pusilo.

LP James Coco (Dr. Harold Woodhouse Langer), Trini Alvarado (Lisa Titus), Paul Benedict (Warden Edward Dwyer), John Bentley (Warden Callahan), Clark Morgan (Power Inspector), Jack Betts (Detective).

James Coco died shortly after most of the filming of *The Chair* was completed in

1986. He is a psychiatrist who sets up a "psychosupport" unit in a prison haunted by prisoners who died there during a 60s riot.

453. The Challenge (1982, Embassy Pictures, 110m, c). P Robert L. Rosen & Ron Beckman, D John Frankenheimer, W Richard Maxwell & John Sayles, PH Kozo Okazaki, M Jerry Goldsmith, ED John W. Wheeler, PD Yoshiyuki Ishida.

LP Scott Glenn (Rick), Toshiro Mifune (Yoshida), Donna Kei Benz (Akiko), Atsuo Nakamura (Hideo), Calvin Jung (Ando), Clyde Kusatsu (Go), Sab Shimada (Father of Yoshida), Yoshio Inaba (Instructor).

American drifter Scott Glenn finds himself in the middle of a longstanding feud between two Japanese brothers Toshiro Mifune and Atsuo Nakamura over possession of a treasured sword.

Challenge to Survive see **The Land of No Return**

454. Chameleon Street (1989, Prismatic One-Filmworld, 98m, c). P Dan Lawton, D&W Wendell B. Harris, Jr., PH Daniel S. Noga, M Peter S. Moore, ED Matthew Mallinson, AD Tim Alvaro.

LP Wendell Harris (William Douglas Street), Angela Leslie, Aminaa Fakir, Paula McGee, Anthony Ennis, David Kiley.

Told in flashback, Afro-American imposter Wendell Harris tells the mostly true story of his life as a convincing phony to a prison psychiatrist. Rather than take the time to go to medical school, he manufactures a phony Harvard résumé and convinces a hospital staff that he's a hot-shot surgeon. He also poses as a reporter for *Time* magazine to interview an Amazon-like female basketball player. He later will pose as an African exchange student at Yale. It's a witty film which will of course be compared to the work of Spike Lee and found wanting, but not by much.

455. Champions (1984, Embassy, GB, 115m, c). P Peter Shaw, D John Irvin, W Evan Jones (based on the book *Champion's Story* by Bob Champion & Jonathan Powell), PH Ronnie Taylor, M Carl Davis, ED Peter Honess.

LP John Hurt (Bob Champion), Gregory Jones (Peter), Mick Dillon (Snowy), Ann Bell (Valda Embiricos), Jan Francis (Jo), Peter Barkworth (Nick Embiricos), Edward Woodward (Josh Gifford), Ben Johnson (Burly Cocks), Kirstie Alley (Barbara), Alison Steadman (Mary Hussey).

In this true story, jockey John Hurt triumphs over the ravages of cancer and torturous chemotherapy to win the Grand National. His horse Aldaniti (playing himself) overcame a broken leg before his victory.

456. *Chan Is Missing* (1982, New Yorker, 80m, b&w). P&D Wayne Wang, W Wang, Isaac Cronin & Terrel Seltzer, PH Michael Chin, M Robert Kikuchi, ED Wang.

LP Wood Moy (Jo), Marc Hayashi (Steve), Laureen Chew (Amy), Judi Nihei (Lawyer), Peter Wang (Henry the Cook), Presco Tabios (Presco), Frankie Alarcon (Frankie), Ellen Yeung (Mrs. Chan), Emily Yamasaki (Jenny).

Filmed in San Francisco's Chinatown, this amusing film is the story of two cab drivers, Wood Moy and Marc Hayashi, who have their savings stolen by Chan Hung, whom they track down during the remainder of the film. The missing Chan is never seen.

457. *Chances Are* (1989, Tri-Star Pictures, 108m, c, aka *Unforgettable*). P Mike Lobell, D Emile Ardolino, W Perry Howze & Randy Howze, PH William A. Fraker, M Maurice Jarre, ED Harry Keramidas, PD Dennis Washington, SONG "After All"†.

LP Cybill Shepherd (Corinne Jeffries), Robert Downey, Jr. (Alex Finch), Ryan O'Neal (Philip Train), Mary Stuart Masterson (Miranda Jeffries), Christopher McDonald (Louie Jeffries), Josef Sommer (Judge Fenwick), Joe Grifasi (Omar), Henderson Forsythe (Ben Bradlee).

Cybill Shepherd dearly loves her husband, Christopher McDonald, which makes Ryan O'Neal sad, because he loves Shepherd. On their first wedding anniversary McDonald is killed but not forgotten. Shepherd mourns for him for 23 years, with O'Neal waiting patiently. Shepherd's daughter Mary Stuart Masterson meets Robert Downey, Jr., who is a

reincarnation of her father. She falls for him, but when Downey sees Momma, it's as if 23 years never happened. This improbable film has its amusing moments. Too bad there aren't more of them.

458. *Chanel Solitaire* (1981, United Film Distribution, US/France, 120m, c). P Larry Spangler, D George Kaczender, W Julian More (based on the book by Mme. Claude Delay), PH Ricardo Aronovich, M Paul Jabara & Jean Musy, ED Georges Klotz.

LP Marie-France Pisier (Gabrielle Chanel), Timothy Dalton (Boy Capel), Rutger Hauer (Etienne De Balsan), Karen Black (Emilienne D'Alencon), Brigitte Fossey (Adrienne), Leila Frechet (Coco Chanel as a Child).

It's a not very interesting treatment of poor orphan Coco Chanel overcoming her background to conquer the fashion world.

459. *A Change of Seasons* (1980, 20th Century–Fox, 102m, c). P Martin Ransohoff, D Richard Lang, W Erich Segal, Fred Segal & Ronni Kern (based on a story by Ransohoff & E. Segal), PH Philip Lathrop, M Henry Mancini, ED Don Zimmerman.

LP Shirley MacLaine (Karen Evans), Anthony Hopkins (Adam Evans), Bo Derek (Lindsey Rutledge), Michael Brandon (Pete Lachapelle), Marybeth Hurt (Kasey Evans), Ed Winter (Steven Rutledge), Paul Regina (Paul DiLisi), K. Callan (Alice Bingham).

College professor Anthony Hopkins beds willing student Bo Derek. To get even Shirley MacLaine has an affair with Michael Brandon. The four very civilized people go on a ski trip together with predictable results.

460. *The Changeling* (1980, Associated Film Distributors, Canada, 107m, c). P Joel B. Michaels & Garth H. Drabinsky, D Peter Medak, W William Grey & Diana Maddox (based on a story by Russell Hunter), PH John Coquillon, M Rick Wilkins, ED Lilla Ledersen, SE Gene Grigg.

LP George C. Scott (John Russell), Trish Van Devere (Claire Norman), Melvyn Douglas (Sen. Joe Carmichael), John Colicos (DeWitt), Jean Marsh

(Joanna Russell), Barry Morse (Dr. Pemberton), James Douglas (Eugene Carmichael), Madeleine Thornton-Sherwood (Mrs. Norman).

Widower music professor George C. Scott moves into a historic Seattle mansion haunted by the spirit of a dead child who lived 70 years earlier. It's an eerie and frightening film.

461.   *The Chant of Jimmie Blacksmith* (1980, Filmhouse, Australia, 108m, c). P,D&W Fred Schepisi (based on the novel by Thomas Keneally), PH Ian Baker, M Bruce Smeaton, ED Brian Kavanaugh.

LP Tommy Lewis (Jimmie Blacksmith), Freddy Reynolds (Mort), Angela Punch (Gilda), Ray Barrett (Constable Farrell), Steve Dodds (Tabidgi), Jack Thompson (Rev. Neville), Julie Dawson (Mrs. Neville), Tim Robertson (Healy), Jane Harders (Mrs. Healy).

Half-white Aborigine Tommy lewis has been raised by a Methodist minister. When he leaves the squalor of his native village, he is abused and used by the whites. His resentment grows to such a point that he massacres some whites and then is chased like a dog into the outback.

462.   *Chariots of Fire* (1981, 20th Century-Fox, GB, 123m, c). P David Puttnam, D Hugh Hudson†, W Colin Welland*, PH David Watkin, M Vangelis Papathanassiou*, ED Terry Rawlings†, COS Milena Canonero*.

LP Ben Cross (Harold Abrahams), Ian Charleson (Eric Liddell), Nigel Havers (Lord Andrew Lindsay), Nicholas Farrell (Aubrey Montague), Ian Holm† (Sam Mussabini), John Gielgud (Master of Trinity), Lindsay Anderson (Master of Caius), Nigel Davenport (Lord Birkenhead), Cheryl Campbell (Jennie Liddell), Alice Krige (Sybil Gordon), Dennis Christopher (Charles Paddock), Brad Davis (Jackson Scholtz), Patrick Magee (Lord Cadogan), Peter Egan (Duke of Sutherland).

Ben Cross as Harold Abrahams, a wealthy Jew, paranoid about prejudice hires his own private coach, Ian Holm, to train him to become an Olympic champion in the 1924 Games in Paris. The late Ian Charleson is serious Scottish Christian missionary Eric Liddell who believes that he runs for the glory of Jesus. Be-

cause of his convictions he will not compete on Sunday, but nevertheless wins a gold medal, as does Abrahams. The latter ultimately was knighted and served as the spokesman for English amateur athletics, even though it could be argued that hiring a coach made him something of a pro. Liddell went to China as a missionary, dying in a Japanese prisoner-of-war camp. It's a lovely looking, feel-good movie, with inspiring theme music by Vangelis, almost worthy of all the praise and awards it received.

463.   *Charlie Chan and the Curse of the Dragon Queen* (1981, American Cinema, 97m, c). P Jerry Sherlock, D Clive Donner, W Stan Burns & David Axelrod (based on a story by Sherlock), PH Paul Lohmann, M Patrick Williams, ED Walt Hannemann & Phil Tucker.

LP Peter Ustinov (Charlie Chan), Lee Grant (Mrs. Lupowitz), Angie Dickinson (Dragon Queen), Richard Hatch (Lee Chan, Jr.), Brian Keith (Police Chief), Michelle Pfeiffer (Cordelia Farrington III), Roddy McDowall (Gillespie), Rachel Roberts (Mrs. Dangers).

Peter Ustinov and Lee Grant act like no-talent amateurs in this horrible spoof of the Oriental detective films of the 30s and 40s. For all those who enjoyed the Charlie Chan films with Warner Oland and even Sidney Toler, this tasteless embarrassment is irritating. It's a cliché-ridden story concentrating on Richard Hatch, Chan's half-Jewish, half-Chinese grandson, and his bungling attempts to follow in Ustinov's footsteps as a detective. Beautiful people Angie Dickinson and Michelle Pfeiffer are just plain misused in this stinker.

464.   *Chasing Dreams* (1989, Nascent, 94m, c). P David G. Brown, Therese Conte & Marc Schwartz, D Sean Roche & Conte, W Brown, PH Connie Holt, M Gregory Conte, ED Jerry Weldon & Robert Sinise, PD Bobbi Peterson Hunter.

LP David G. Brown (Gavin), John Fife (Parks), Jim Shane (Father), Matthew Clark (Ben), Lisa Kingston (Sue), Claudia Carroll (Mother), Cecilia Bennett, Kelly McCarthy, Don Margolin, Kevin Costner.

The only apparent reason this nostalgic

baseball story, filmed in 1981, was released in 1989 is because of the brief appearance of star Kevin Costner. David G. Brown portrays a youngster whose attempts to become a baseball star are complicated by his father's insistence that he spend his time on farm chores and caring for his wheelchair-bound younger brother Matthew Clark.

465. *Chattahoochie* (1989, Hemdale, 103m, c). P Aaron Schwab, D Mick Jackson, W James Hicks, PH Andrew Dunn, M John Keane, ED Don Fairservice, AD Patrick Tagliaferro.

LP Gary Oldman (Emmett Foley), Dennis Hopper (Walker), Frances McDormand, Pamela Reed, Ned Beatty, M. Emmet Walsh.

Korean veteran Oldman returns to the deep South in the 50s as a hero. He can't deal with life and finds himself a brutalized patient in a hospital for the criminally insane (Chattahoochie) after he goes berserk.

466. *Chattanooga Choo Choo* (1984, April Fools, 102m, c). P George Edwards & Jill Griffith, D Bruce Bilson, W Robert Mundy & Steven Phillip Smith, PH Gary Graver, M Nelson Riddle, ED Bud S. Isaacs.

LP Barbara Eden (Maggie), George Kennedy (Bert), Melissa Sue Anderson (Jenny), Joe Namath (Newt), Bridget Hanley (Estelle), Christopher McDonald (Paul), Clu Gulager (Sam), Tony Azito (Lucky Pierre).

In order to collect a million dollar inheritance, football team owner George Kennedy must restore a vintage train and take it on one final trip from Tennessee to New York.

467. *Cheaper to Keep Her* (1980, American Cinema, 92m, c). P Lenny Isenberg, D Ken Annakin, W Timothy Harris & Herschel Weingrod, PH Roland "Ozzie" Smith, M Dick Halligan, ED Edward Warschilka.

LP Mac Davis (Bill Dekkar), Tovah Feldshuh (K.D. Locke), Art Metrano (Tony Turino), Ian McShane (Dr. Alfred Sunshine), Priscilla Lopez (Theresa), Rose Marie (Ida Bracken), Jack Gilford (Stanley Bracken).

American Cinema took an early lead in the race to capture the market for the most tasteless sexist and racist films with this disgusting movie. Mac Davis is an alimony attorney who takes advantage of his female client's confused mental state. He's a sleaze and so is the movie.

468. *Checking Out* (1989, Handmade Films, 93m, c). P Ben Myron & Garth Thomas, D David Leland, W Joe Eszterhas, PH Ian Wilson, M Carter Burwell, ED Lee Percy, PD Barbara Ling.

LP Jeff Daniels (Ray Macklin), Melanie Mayron (Jenny), Michael Tucker (Harry), Kathleen York (Diana), Ann Magnuson (Connie), Allan Havey (Pat), Jo Harvey Allen (Barbara), Felton Perry (Dr. Duffin).

After the sudden death of his best friend from a heart attack, jittery businessman Jeff Daniels believes he's going to be the next to go. Near the end of the film is a vision of heaven, which doesn't look like a place anyone would wish to go to. The treatment of the story does in the decent cast.

469. *Checkpoint* (1987, New Film Group-MTA, 91m, c). P,D&W Parviz Sayyad, PH Michael Davis, M Ahmad Pejman, ED Sayyad.

LP Mary Apick (Firouzeh), Houshang Touzie (Kazem), Peter Spreague (Mike), Mark Nichols (Bob), Buck Kartalian (Frank), Michael Zand (Farhad), Mayeva Martin (Kate), Ali Poutash (Hatam), Ali F. Dean (Ali).

This talky film is based on an incident which took place at the height of the Iranian hostage crisis in 1980. A bus holding Michigan college students returning from a field trip to Ontario is stopped at the border. The eight Iranian students are denied entry until their visas can be checked. Their U.S. friends refuse to leave them, and all spend the night arguing the pros and cons of Iran's actions.

470. *Cheech and Chong's Next Movie* (1980, Universal, 99m, c). P Howard Brown, D Thomas Chong, W Chong & "Cheech" Marin, PH King Baggot, M Mark Davis, ED Scott Conrad, PD Fred Harpman.

LP Richard Marin (Cheech), Thomas Chong (Chong), Evelyn Guerrero (Donna), Betty Kennedy (Candy), Sy Kramer (Neatnik), Rikki Marin (Gloria), Bob McClurg (Chicken Charlie), Edie

McClurg (Gloria's Mother), Paul Reubens (Pee-Wee Herman/Desk Clerk).

Cheech and Chong follow up their gross dope film *Up in Smoke* with a plotless movie about one day and night in the life of two sophomoric idiots who live only for "grass," sex and hanging out.

471. *Cheech and Chong's Nice Dreams* (1981, Columbia, 88m, c). P Howard Brown, D Thomas Chong, W Chong & "Cheech" Marin, PH Charles Correll, M Harry Betts, ED Scott Conrad, PD James Newport.

LP Thomas Chong (Chong), Cheech Marin (Cheech), Stacy Keach (The Sarge), Dr. Timothy Leary (Himself), Evelyn Guerrero (Donna), Paul Reubens (Howie Hamburger), Michael Masters (Willard "Animal" Bad).

Perhaps members of the subculture who make it worth the time and money to produce these idiotic movies, starring two of the least talented "comedians" on screen, are so stoned that they see something that the rest of us, unaided by chemicals, miss. This time Cheech and Chong sell drugs from ice cream trucks.

Cheech and Chong's Still Smokin'* see *Still Smokin'

472. *Cheech and Chong's the Corsican Brothers* (1984, Orion, 90m, c). P Peter MacGregor-Scott, D Thomas Chong, W Chong & "Cheech" Marin, PH Harvey Harrison, M Geo, ED Tom Alvidsen.

LP Richard "Cheech" Marin & Thomas Chong (Corsican Brothers), Roy Dotrice (Evil Fuckaire/Ye Old Jailer), Shelby Fiddis (Princess No. 1), Rikki Marin (Princess No. 2), Edie McClurg (The Queen), Robbi Chong (Princess No. 3), Rae Dawn Chong (The Gypsy), Simono (The Waiter).

Cheech and Chong have here dropped their drug-related jokes but their gutter language, scatological jokes, raucous sexual gags and homophobic humor makes their treatment of Alexandre Dumas' familiar story of two brothers who feel each other's pain just as distasteful as their earlier works. Consider this trash as unsophisticated Mel Brooks material.

Cheerleader Camp* see *Bloody Pom Poms

473. *Cherry 2000* (1988, Orion, 93m, c). P Edward R. Pressman & Caldecot Chubb, D Steve de Jarnatt, W Michael Almereyda (based on a story by Lloyd Fonvielle), PH Jacques Haitkin, M Basil Poledouris, ED Edward Abroms & Duwayne Dunham, PD John J. Moore.

LP Melanie Griffith (E. Johnson), David Andrews (Sam Treadwell), Ben Johnson (Six Finger Jake), Tim Thomerson (Lester), Brion James (Stacy), Pamela Gidley (Cherry 2000), Harry Carey, Jr. (Snappy Tom), Cameron Milzer (Ginger), Michael C. Gwynne (Slim).

Filmed in 1985 before Melanie Griffith became a star, this science-fiction piece is set in the year 2017. Earth has squandered most of its natural resources. Diseased paranoia is such that safe sex means making love to robots. When David Andrews short-circuits his sex toy, he hires tough broad Griffith to scavenge for the needed parts to repair the robot-lover. Instead, Andrews and Griffith discover the fun of sex the old-fashioned way.

474. *Cheetah* (1989, Disney, 83m, c). P Robert Halmi, D Jeff Blyth, W Erik Tarloff, John Cotter & Griff Du Rhone (based on the novel *The Cheetahs* by Alan Caillou), PH Tom Burstyn, M Bruce Rowland, ED Eric Albertson, PD Jane Cavedon.

LP Keith Coogan (Ted), Lucy Deakins (Susan), Collin Mothupi (Morogo), Timothy Landfield (Earl Johnson), Breon Gorman (Jean Johnson).

Two L.A. teens, Keith Coogan and Lucy Deakins, spend six months in the Rift Valley of Kenya, where their dad works at a space tracking station. They become friends with Masai boy Collin Mothupi. With him as a guide they venture into the bush, where they adopt a cheetah cub left orphaned when its mother is killed by a poacher. The three will have to save the grown cheetah, which they name Duma, from the same poacher and an unscrupulous Englishman who wishes to race the animal against greyhounds.

475. *The Children* (1980, World-Northal, 90m, c). P Max Kalmanowicz & Carlton J. Albright, D Kalmanowicz, W Albright & Edward Terry, PH Barry

Abrams, M Harry Manfredini, ED Nikki Wessling.

LP Martin Shakar (John Freemont), Gil Rogers (Sheriff Billy Hart), Gale Garnett (Cathy Freemont), Jessie Abrams, Tracy Griswold, Joy Glaccum, Suzanne Barnes.

Radioactive kids turn their parents to ashes on contact in this silly horror film.

476. *Children of a Lesser God*† (1986, Paramount, 119m, c). LP Burt Sugarman & Patrick Palmer, D Randa Haines, W Hesper Anderson & Mark Medoff† (based on the stage play by Medoff), PH John Seale, M Michael Convertino, ED Lisa Fruchtman, PD Gene Callahan.

LP William Hurt† (James), Marlee Matlin* (Sarah), Piper Laurie† (Mrs. Norman), Philip Bosco (Dr. Curtis Franklin), Allison Gompf (Lydia), John F. Cleary (Johnny), Philip Holmes (Glen), Georgia Ann Cline (Cheryl), William D. Byrd (Danny), Frank Carter, Jr. (Tony).

The acting in this award-winning theatrical piece is laudable. William Hurt is a dedicated teacher obsessed with making proud, deaf Marlee Matlin cope with the hearing world. For a brief time after the filming of the movie Hurt and Matlin were an item but the romance cooled.

477. *Children of Babylon* (1980, Rainbow, Jamaica, 122m, c). P,D&W Lennie Little-White, PH Franklyn St. Juste, M Harold Butler, ED Little-White.

LP Tobi (Penny), Don Parchment (Rick), Bob Andy (Luke), Leonie Forbes (Dorcas), Elizabeth de Lisser (Laura), Keith Walker (Hitchhiker).

If one is a voyeur, this Marxist message reggae film about a girl, Tobi, who falls in love with whomever she's with, might be enjoyed for the scenes in which she bares her breasts. If not, we can't think of any other reason to see it.

478. *Children of the Corn* (1984, New World, 93m, c). P Donald P. Borchers & Terence Kirby, D Fritz Kiersch, W George Goldsmith (based on the short story "Night Shift" by Stephen King), PH Raoul Lomas, M Jonathan Elias, ED Harry Keramidas, SE Max W. Anderson.

LP Peter Horton (Dr. Burt Stanton), Linda Hamilton (Vicky Baxter), R.G.

Armstrong (Diehl), John Franklin (Isaac), Courtney Gains (Malachai), Robby Kiger (Job), Annemarie McEvoy (Sarah), Julie Maddalena (Rachel), Jonas Marlowe (Joseph), John Philbin (Amos).

In this slow-moving horror film, newly minted doctor Peter Horton and his wife Linda Hamilton, find themselves at the mercy of some Nebraska kids, led by John Franklin. The youngsters belong to a strange cult which worships a deity in the corn fields. They have killed all of the adults in their small town and are on the verge of crucifying Hamilton, when she is rescued by Horton and two dissident kids, Robby Kiger and Annemarie McEvoy.

479. *Child's Play* (1988, MGM/United Artists, 88m, c). P David Kirschner, D Tom Holland, W Don Mancini, John Lafia & Holland, PH Bill Butler, M Joe Renzetti, ED Edward Warschilka & Roy E. Peterson, PD Daniel A. Lomino.

LP Catherine Hicks (Karen Barclay), Chris Sarandon (Mike Norris), Alex Vincent (Andy Barclay), Brad Dourif (Charles Lee Ray), Dinah Manoff (Maggie Peterson), Tommy Swerdlow (Jack Santos), Jack Colvin (Dr. Ardmore).

When murderer Brad Dourif is trapped by detective Chris Sarandon in a toy store, he is shot and killed, but not before he is able to transfer his soul to a three-foot talking doll. The doll is purchased for six-year-old Alex Vincent, who must match wits with his menacing, murdering plaything.

480. *Chillers* (1988, Big Pictures/Raedon, 87m, c). P,D&W Daniel Boyd, PH Bill Hogan, M Michael Lipton.

LP Jesse Emery, Marjorie Fitzsimmons, Laurie Pennington, Jim Wolff, David Wohl, Gary Brown, Jesse Johnson, Thom Delventhal, Bradford Boll.

In this low-budget horror anthology, passengers waiting in a bus station tell each other macabre tales.

481. *Chilly Scenes of Winter* (1982, United Artists Classic, 92m, c, aka *Head Over Heels*). P Mark Metcalf, Amy Robinson & Griffin Dunne, D&W Joan Micklin Silver (based on the novel *Head Over Heels* by Ann Beattie), PH Bobby Byrne, M Ken Lauber, ED Cynthia Scheider, PD Peter Jamison.

LP John Heard (Charles), Marybeth Hurt (Laura), Peter Riegert (Sam), Kenneth McMillan (Pete), Gloria Grahame (Clara), Nora Heflin (Betty), Jerry Hardin (Patterson), Tarah Nutter (Susan), Mark Metcalf (Ox), Allen Joseph (Blind Man), Frances Bay (Mrs. Delilo), Griffin Dunne (Dr. Mark).

This touching comedy of John Heard's love for married Marybeth Hurt, who cares for Heard but is still attached to her husband, evokes the pain of unrequited love which most everyone has felt at one time or another. When the film was released as *Head Over Heels,* it had a different ending. The one now shown may leave viewers somewhat disappointed.

482.   China Girl (1987, American-Vestron, 88m, c). P Michael Nozik, D Abel Ferrara, W Nicholas St. John, PH Bojan Bazelli, M Joe Delia, ED Anthony Redman, PD Dan Leigh.

LP James Russo (Alberto "Alby" Monte), Richard Panebianco (Tony Monte), Sari Chang (Tyan-Hwa), David Caruso (Johnny Mercury), Russell Wong (Yung-Gan), Joey Chin (Tsu-Shin), Judith Malina (Maria), James Hong (Gung-Tu), Robert Miano (Perito), Paul Hipp (Nino).

Richard Panebianco and Sari Chang appear in a modern-day Manhattan Italian-Chinese version of Romeo and Juliet, which owes a great deal to *West Side Story.* A single bullet fired by her cousin, gang leader Joey Chin, passes through Chang's heart into Panebianco's body, killing them both. Chin is then killed by an angry Chinese mob.

483.   Chinese Boxes (1985, Road Movies, GB/Germany, 87m, c). P Chris Sievernich, D Christopher Petit, W Petit & L.M. Kit Carson, PH Peter Harvey, M Gunther Fischer, ED Fred Srp.

LP Will Patton (Langdon Marsh), Gottfried John (Zwemmer), Adelheid Arndt (Sarah), Robbie Coltrane (Harwood), Beate Jensen (Donna), Susanne Meierhofer (Eva), Jonathan Kinsler (Alan), L.M. Kit Carson (Crewcut).

A Berlin heroin smuggler gets mixed up in a girl's murder.

484.   The Chipmunk Adventure (1987, Goldwyn, animated, 76m, c). P Ross Bagdasarian, Jr., D Janice Karman, W Karman & Bagdasarian, M Randy Edelman, PD Carol Holman Grosvenor.

VOICES Ross Bagdasarian, Jr., Janice Karman, Dody Goodman, Susan Tyrrell, Anthony DeLongis, Frank Welker, Nancy Cartwright, Ken Sansom, Charles Adler, Philip Clark.

Ross Bagdasarian, Sr., came up with a money-making idea when he speeded up the voices on a record and created the singing chipmunks. Now that Sr. is dead, his son is carrying on. In this movie the chipmunks are rock musicians, conned by a female diamond smuggler into participating in an around-the-world balloon race.

485.   The Chocolate War (1989, MCEG Inc., 103m, c). P Jonathan D. Krane, D&W Keith Gordon, PH Tom Richmond, M various artists, ED Jeff Wishengrad.

LP John Glover (Brother Leon), Ilan Mitchell-Smith (Jerry), Wally Ward (Archie), Doug Hutchinson (Obie), Corey Gunnestad (Goober), Bud Cort (Brother Jacques), Adam Baldwin (Carter).

At St. Trinity's boy's high school, malevolent and overzealous John Glover and the Vigils, a secret society of solemn inquisitors, use the annual fund-raising event, selling chocolate, as a means to control students. Ilan Mitchell-Smith is one boy who resists conforming to peer pressure.

486.   Choke Canyon (1986, United Film, 94m, c, aka *On Dangerous Ground*). P Ovidio G. Assonitis, D Chuck Bail, W Sheila Goldberg, Assonitis & Alfonso Brescia, PH Dante Spinotti, M Sylvester Levay, ED Roberto Silvi, PD Frank Vanorio.

LP Stephen Collins (David Lowell), Janet Julian (Vanessa), Lance Henriksen (Brook), Bo Svenson (Captain), Victoria Racimo (Rachel), Nicholas Pryor (John), Robert Hoy (Buck), Michael Gates, Mark Baer.

The only chance of saving earth's energy supply is if a sound-energy experiment can be carried out at Choke Canyon, the exact moment Halley's comet passes over.

487.   Choose Me (1984, Island Alive, 114m, c). P Carolyn Pfeiffer & David

Blocker, D&W Alan Rudolph, PH Jan Kiesser, ED Mia Goldman, PD Steven Legler, M/L "Choose Me" by Luther Vandross, Marcus Miller & Michael Masser.

LP Keith Carradine (Mickey), Lesley Ann Warren (Eve), Genevieve Bujold (Ann/"Dr. Nancy Love"), Patrick Bauchau (Zack Antoine), Rae Dawn Chong (Pearl Antoine), John Larroquette (Billy Ace), Edward Ruscha (Ralph Chomsky), Gailard Sartain (Mueller).

Free-loving, talk-toughing, but frightened bar owner Lesley Ann Warren gets advice about her love life from radio expert Genevieve Bujold, who is hopelessly maladjusted herself. By chance Bujold becomes Warren's roommate without either knowing their other relationship. Keith Carradine is a nutty but brilliant truth-teller who enters their lives, and those of others who hang out at the bar, having affairs with each other.

488.   *Chopping Mall* (1986, Concorde, 76m, c, aka *Killbots*). P Julie Corman, D Jim Wynorski, W Wynorski & Steve Mitchell, PH Tom Richmond, M Chuck Cirino, ED Leslie Rosenthal, Killbots created by Robert Short, SE Roger George.

LP Kelli Maroney (Allison Parks), Tony O'Dell (Ferdy Meisel), John Terlesky (Mike Brennan), Russell Todd (Rick Stanton), Karrie Emerson (Linda Stanton), Barbara Crampton (Suzie Lynn), Nick Segal (Greg Williams), Suzee Slater (Leslee Todd), Mary Woronov (Mrs. Bland).

Killbots are security robots working in a shopping mall. When they malfunction, they attack a group of teenagers who are trapped overnight in the mall.

489.   *A Chorus Line* (1985, Columbia, 113m, c). P Cy Feuer & Ernest Martin, D Richard Attenborough, W Arnold Schulman (based on the stage play *A Chorus Line,* conceived, choreographed and directed by Michael Bennett), PH Ronnie Taylor, M/L Marvin Hamlisch & Edward Kleban, ED John Bloom†, PD Patrizia Von Brandenstein, CH Jeffrey Hornaday, SONG "Surprise, Surprise" by Marvin Hamlisch & Edward Kleban†, SOUND Donald O. Mitchell, Michael Minkler, Gerry Humphreys & Chris Newman†.

LP Michael Douglas (Zach), Alyson Reed (Cassie), Vicki Frederick (Sheila), Cameron English (Paul), Yamil Borges (Morales), Gregg Burge (Richie), Audrey Landers (Val), Pam Klinger (Maggie), Blane Savage (Don), Michael Blevins (Mark), Jan Gan Boyd (Connie), Sharon Brown (Tricia), Janet Jones (Judy), Michelle Johnston (Bebe).

Seeing *A Chorus Line* on a Broadway stage and seeing it in a movie theater are experiences in no way comparable. The music and dancing is still great, but the magic of the auditions of boys and girls for the chorus of a new Broadway show is sadly missing.

490.   *A Chorus of Disapproval* (1989, South Gate, GB, 100m, c). P&D Michael Winner, W Winner & Alan Ayckbourn (based on Ayckbourn's play), PH Alan Jones, M John DuPrez, ED Chris Barnes.

LP Jeremy Irons (Guy Jones), Anthony Hopkins (Dafydd Llewellyn), Prunella Scales (Hannah Llewellyn), Jenny Seagrove (Fay), Sylvia Syms (Rebecca), Gareth Hunt (Ian), Lionel Jeffries (Jarvis), Alexandra Pigg (Bridget), Patsy Kensit (Linda), Barbara Ferris (Enid).

This screening of Alan Ayckbourn's play is credible, but not inspired. Jeremy Irons is excellent as a shy young widower who joins a local amateur group to meet people. The director, Anthony Hopkins, is a seedy solicitor who has a passion for theater and theater people. Irons has an affair with Hopkins' lonely wife Prunella Scales, but she's not the only one with whom he becomes involved.

491.   *The Chosen* (1982, Contemporary, 108m, c). P Edie & Ely Landau, D Jeremy Paul Kagan, W Edwin Gordon (based on the novel by Chaim Potok), PH Arthur Ornitz, M Elmer Bernstein, ED David Garfield.

LP Maximilian Schell (David Malter), Rod Steiger (Reb Saunders), Robby Benson (Danny Saunders), Barry Miller (Reuven Malter), Hildy Brooks (Mrs. Saunders), Ron Rifkin (Baseball Coach), Val Avery (Teacher).

The Chaim Potok story depicts the problems of a growing friendship during the 40s of Hassidic Jew Robby Benson and Orthodox Jew Barry Miller. Miller is a typical American kid while Benson is ruled by his father Rod Steiger, a powerful rabbi. The two youngsters' friendship is brought to an end over the creation of the Jewish state of Israel. Miller's father Maximilian Schell, a Zionist, is all for it, while traditionalist Steiger is dead set against it.

492.   *Christine* (1983, Columbia, 116m, c). P Richard Kobritz, D John Carpenter, W Bill Phillips (based on the novel by Stephen King), PH Donald M. Morgan, M Carpenter & Alan Howarth, ED Marion Rothman, SE Roy Arbogast.

LP Keith Gordon (Arnie Cunningham), John Stockwell (Dennis Guilder), Alexandra Paul (Leigh Cabot), Robert Prosky (Will Darnell), Harry Dean Stanton (Rudolph Junkins), Christine Belford (Regina Cunningham), Roberts Blossom (George LeBay), William Ostrander (Buddy).

Stephen King has a money machine. There are millions who will buy anything he writes and other millions who will rush to any theater showing a film version of his work, no matter how weak and ridiculous the story. And this one about a killer Plymouth Fury automobile is surely weak and ridiculous.

493.   *A Christmas Carol* (1984, Entertainment Pictures, GB, 101m, c). P William Storke & Alfred Kelman, D Clive Donner, W Roger Hirson (based on the novel by Charles Dickens), PH Tony Imi, M Nick Bicat, ED Peter Tanner.

LP George C. Scott (Ebenezer Scrooge), Frank Finlay (Jacob Marley), Angela Pleasence (Christmas Past), Edward Woodward (Christmas Present), Michael Carter (Christmas Future), David Warner (Bob Cratchit), Susannah York (Mrs. Cratchit), Anthony Walters (Tiny Tim), Roger Rees (Fred Holywell), Caroline Langrishe (Janet Holywell), Lucy Gutteridge (Belle), Mark Strickson (Scrooge as a boy), Joanne Whalley (Fan), Timothy Bateson (Fezziwig), Peter Woodthorpe (Old Joe).

Although George C. Scott won't make fans of Scrooge forget Alastair Sim, he does give a very decent portrayal of the miserly old man who reforms after visits from the ghosts of Christmas Past, Present and Future.

494.   *Christmas Evil* (1983, Pressman, 100m, c, aka *You Better Watch Out*). P Burt Kleiner & Peter Kameron, D&W Lewis Jackson, PH Ricardo Aronovich, ED Corky O'Hara & Linda Leeds, PD Lorenzo Jodie Harris.

LP Brandon Maggart (Harry), Dianne Hull (Jackie), Scott McKay (Fletcher), Joe Jamrog (Frank), Peter Friedman (Grosch), Ray Barry (Gleason), Bobby Lesser (Gottleib), Sam Gray (Grilla).

Toy maker Brandon Maggart goes over the edge and becomes a Santa Claus who knows who's been good and who's been bad. He rewards the good and punishes the bad in this modest body-count horror film.

495.   *A Christmas Story* (1983, MGM/United Artists, 98m, c). P Rene Dupont & Bob Clark, D Clark, W Jean Shepherd, Leigh Brown & Clark (based on the novel *In God We Trust, All Others Pay Cash* by Shepherd), PH Reginald H. Morris, M Carl Ziffer & Paul Zaza, ED Stan Cole.

LP Melinda Dillon (Mother), Darren McGavin (Old Man), Peter Billingsley (Ralphie), Ian Petrella (Randy), Scott Schwartz (Flick), R.D. Robb (Schwartz), Teddi Moore (Miss Shields), Yano Anaya (Grover), Zack Ward (Scot), Jeff Gillen (Santa Claus), Colin Fox (Ming), Paul Hubbard (Flash Gordon).

In this very funny episodic comedy, humorist Jean Shepherd narrates the story, set in the 40s, of a Christmas in which he (played very well by young Peter Billingsley) wants nothing more than a Red Ryder BB gun for Christmas (ah, every boy's dream at that time), but his mother has vetoed the request, fearing he'll shoot out his eyes.

496.   *Chronicle of a Death Foretold* (1988, Island, 89m, c). P Francis Von Buren & Yves Gasser, D Francesco Rosi, W Rosi & Tonino Guerra (based on the novel by Gabriel Garcia Marquez).

LP Ornella Muti, Rupert Everett, Gian Maria Volonte, Irene Papas.

On his wedding night in a sleepy Colombian village, Rupert Everett discovers that his bride Ornella Muti isn't a virgin. The next day he returns her to her brothers, who force her to name her seducer, whom they then kill. Whether the victim is to blame is left to the audience to decide.

497. *Chu Chu and the Philly Flash* (1981, 20th Century–Fox, 100m, c). P Jay Weston, D David Lowell Rich, W Barbara Dana (based on a story by Henry Barrow), PH Victor J. Kemper, M Pete Rugolo, ED Argyle Nelson.

LP Alan Arkin (Flash), Carol Burnett (Emily), Jack Warden (Commander), Danny Aiello (Johnson), Adam Arkin (Charlie), Danny Glover (Morgan), Sid Haig (Vince), Vincent Schiavelli (B.J.), Ruth Buzzi (Consuelo).

In this moronic comedy, former Philadelphia Phillies relief pitcher Alan Arkin has been on a 20-year drunk when he and failed street entertainer Carol Burnett each spot a briefcase and both claim it. From then on the film shows the couple falling in love, keeping him sober and returning the briefcase. It wouldn't have made a moderately funny sketch on the old Carol Burnett Show.

498. *C.H.U.D.* (1984, New World, 110m, c). P Andrew Bonime, D Douglas Cheek, W Parnell Hall, PH Peter Stein, M Cooper Hughes, ED Dennis O'Connor, PD William Bilowit.

LP Laure Mattos (Flora Bosch), John Heard (George Cooper), Kim Greist (Lauren Daniels), Brenda Currin (Francine), Christopher Curry (Capt. Bosch), Justin Hall (Justine), Michael O'Hare (Fuller).

C.H.U.D. stands for Cannibalistic Humanoid Underground Dwellers, creatures that live in the sewers, coming up to street level at night to feast on human flesh. Originally, they were the city's homeless who took to the sewers for warmth, but have been changed into monsters by toxic wastes dumped into the sewers. Only devoted horror fans will find anything to like about these sewer scum.

499. *C.H.U.D. II: Bud the Chud* (1989, Vestron, 84m, c). P Jonathan D. Krane, D David Irving, W "M. Kane Jeeves" Ed Naha, PH Arnie Sirlin, M Nicholas Pike, ED Barbara Pokras, PD Randy Moore.

LP Brian Robbins (Steve), Bill Calvert (Kevin), Tricia Leigh Fisher (Katie), Gerrit Graham (Bud the Chud), Robert Vaughn (Masters), Larry Cedar (Graves),

Bianca Jagger, Larry Linville, Norman Fell.

When the government cancels a research project, the cannibalistic ghouls of the title are slated for destruction. High school students Brian Robbins and Bill Calvert snitch the last ghoulish corpse, belonging to Gerrit Graham, and accidentally revive him. Each time Graham bites someone, he has a new ghoul friend.

500. *Circle of Power* (1981, Mehlman, 97m, c, aka *Mystique; Brainwash; The Naked Weekend*). P Gary L. Mehlman & Jeffrey White, D Bobby Roth, W Beth Sullivan & Stephen Bello (based on the book by Gene Church & Conrad D. Carnes), PH Affonso Beato, M Richard Markowitz, ED Gail Yasunaga.

LP Yvette Mimieux (Bianca Ray), Christopher Allport (Jack Nisson), Cindy Pickett (Lyn Nilsson), John Considine (Jordon Carelli), Scott Marlowe (Ted Bartel), Walter Olkewitz (Buddy Gordon).

In this film supposedly based on actual executive training services, sadistic Yvette Mimieux runs EDT (Executive Development Training) sessions, in which aspiring top executives and their wives make fools of themselves in a series of humiliating rituals. How this will make them more productive is not made clear.

501. *Circle of Two* (1980, Film Consortium of Canada, Canada, 105m, c). P Henk Van der Kolk, D Jules Dassin, W Thomas Hedley (based on a story "A Lesson in Love" by Marie Terese Baird), PH Lazlo George, M Paul Hoffert, ED David Nochols.

LP Richard Burton (Ashley St. Clair), Tatum O'Neal (Sarah Norton), Nuala FitzGerald (Claudia Aldrich), Robin Gammell (Mr. Norton), Patricia Collins (Mrs. Norton), Kate Reid (Dr. Emily Reid).

Richard Burton is a 60-year-old artist who hasn't painted in ten years. He encounters 16-year-old Tatum O'Neal in a porno theater. A friendship develops which blossoms into a romance. She gets Burton painting again. He encourages Tatum to write. Their relationship is discovered. Burton is held up to ridicule and O'Neal is made almost a prisoner by her parents. They escape to New York, where they decide they have no future.

502.   *The City Girl*   (1984, Moon, 85m, c). P&D Martha Coolidge, W Judith Thompson & Leonard-John Gates (based on a story by John MacDonald & Coolidge), PH Daniel Hainey, M Scott Wilk & Marc Levinthal, ED Linda Leeds & Eva Gardos.

LP Laura Harrington (Anne), Joe Mastroianni (Joey), Carole McGill (Gracie), Peter Riegert (Tim), Jim Carrington (Steve), Lawrence Phillips (The Stripper), Geraldine Baron (Monica), Colleen Camp (Rose).

Young photographer Harrington has several unsatisfactory relationships with men as she attempts to advance her career. The film sat on the shelf from 1981 until director Martha Coolidge became marketable after her success with *Valley Girl.*

503.   *City Heat*   (1984, Warner, 97m, c). P Fritz Manes, D Richard Benjamin, W Sam O. Brown "Blake Edwards" & Joseph C. Stinson (based on a story by Brown), PH Nick McLean, M Lennie Niehaus, ED Jacqueline Cambas, PD Edward Carfagno.

LP Clint Eastwood (Lt. Speer), Burt Reynolds (Mike Murphy), Jane Alexander (Addy), Madeline Kahn (Caroline Howley), Rip Torn (Primo Pitt), Irene Cara (Ginny Lee), Richard Roundtree (Dehl Swift), Tony Lo Bianco (Leon Coll), William Sanderson (Lonnie Ash).

Original director-screenwriter Blake Edwards' disagreements with Clint Eastwood and Burt Reynolds led him to walk off the set of the production to be called *Kansas City Blues.* Richard Benjamin was brought in and the result is this mishmash. It is set in Kansas City of the 30s where Eastwood is a police detective and Reynolds, his former partner, is a private eye. The two dance through their roles, asking audiences to take them seriously at the same time we're supposed to laugh at them. We don't feel like doing either.

504.   *City Limits*   (1985, Atlantic, 85m, c). P Rupert Harvey & Barry Opper, D Aaron Lipstadt, W Don Opper (based on a story by Lipstadt & James Reigle), PH Tim Suhrstedt, M Mitchell Froom, ED R.J. Kizer.

LP John Stockwell (Lee), Darrell Larson (Mick), Rae Dawn Chong (Yogi), James Earl Jones (Albert), Kim Cattrall (Wickings), John Diehl (Whitey), Don Opper (Sammy), Danny De La Paz (Ray), Pamela Ludwig (Frankie), Tony Plana (Ramos), Robby Benson (Carver).

After a plague decimates the world, killing most adults, various kid motorcycle gangs battle for supremacy.

505.   *City News*   (1983, Cinecom International, 65m, c). P,D,W&ED David Fishelson & Zoe Zinman, PH Jonathan Sinaiko, M various artists.

LP Elliot Crown (Tom), Nancy Cohen (Daphne), Thomas Trivier (Frenchy), Richard Schlesinger (Lou), Valerie Felitto (DeeDee), Tony Mangis (Tony), Gail Gibney (Gail), David Fishelson (Punch), Zoe Zinman (Judy).

In this stream-of-consciousness comedy piece, underground newspaper publisher and editor Elliot Crown creates a comic strip based on his relationship with Nancy Cohen, whom he meets in a Greenwich Village bar.

506.   *The Clan of the Cave Bear*   (1986, Warner, 100m, c). P Gerald I. Isenberg, D Michael Chapman, W John Sayles (based on the novel by Jean M. Auel), PH Jan De Bont, M Alan Silvestri, ED Wendy Greene Bricmont, PD Anthony Masters, MK Michael G. Westmore & Michele Burke†.

LP Daryl Hannah (Ayla), Pamela Reed (Iza), James Remar (Creb), Thomas G. Waites (Broud), John Doolittle (Brun), Curtis Armstrong (Goov), Martin Doyle (Grod), Adel C. Hammoud (Vorn), Karen Austin (Aba).

Daryl Hannah, who looks wild even when dressed to the teeth, is perfectly cast as a caveperson feminist outsider who joins a band of Neanderthals and raises their consciousness. Other than that it's a rather dumb and dull film.

507.   *Clara's Heart*   (1988, Warner, 108m, c). P Martin Elfand, D Robert Mulligan, W Mark Medoff (based on the novel by Joseph Olshan), PH Freddie Francis, M Dave Grusin, ED Sidney Levin, PD Jeffrey Howard.

LP Whoopi Goldberg (Clara Mayfield), Michael Ontkean (Bill Hart),

Kathleen Quinlan (Leona Hart), Neil Patrick Harris (David Hart), Spalding Gray (Dr. Peter Epstein), Beverly Todd (Dora), Hattie Winston (Blanche Loudon), Fred Strother (Bundy).

Whoopi Goldberg makes her first dramatic appearance since *The Color Purple,* appearing as a Jamaican maid caring for 15-year-old Neil Patrick Harris, the son of Michael Ontkean and Kathleen Quinlan, a Baltimore couple whose marriage is breaking up. While Goldberg does quite well, the production and story is nothing to get excited about and the other performers are almost cardboard characters.

508.   *Clarence and Angel* (1981, Gardner, 75m, c). P,D&W Robert Gardner, PH Doug Harris.

LP Darren Brown (Clarence), Mark Cardova (Angel), Cynthia McPherson (Teacher), Louise Mike (Claree's Mother), Lolita Lewis (Robert's Mother), Robert Leroy Smith & Ellwoodson Williams (Men in barbershop).

Kung-fu crazy, street-wise Mark Cardova befriends shy illiterate Darren Brown who has just arrived in Harlem from South Carolina and teaches him how to read.

509.   *Clash of the Titans* (1981, MGM/United Artists, GB, 120m, c). P Ray Harryhausen & Charles H. Schneer, D Desmond Davis, W Beverley Cross, PH Ted Moore, M Laurence Rosenthal, ED Timothy Gee, SE Harryhausen.

LP Laurence Olivier (Zeus), Claire Bloom (Hera), Maggie Smith (Thetis), Ursula Andress (Aphrodite), Jack Gwillim (Poseidon), Susan Fleetwood (Athena), Pat Roach (Hephaestus), Harry Hamlin (Perseus), Judi Bowker (Andromeda), Burgess Meredith (Ammon), Sian Phillips (Cassiopeia), Tim Pigott-Smith (Thallo), Neil McCarthy (Calibos).

Some important show business names were well paid to enact cameo roles in this otherwise laughable mythic tale. The real "star" is Harry Hamlin who spends his time running after Judi Bowker and fighting off all kinds of horrific monsters and dangers. The special effects are generally wonderful but that's the only thing stylish about the picture.

510.   *Class* (1983, Orion, 100m, c). P Martin Ransohoff, D Lewis John Carlino, W Jim Kouf & David Greenwalt, PH Ric Waite, M Elmer Bernstein, ED Dennis Dolan.

LP Jacqueline Bisset (Ellen), Rob Lowe (Skip), Andrew McCarthy (Jonathan), Cliff Robertson (Burroughs), Stuart Margolin (Balaban), John Cusack (Roscoe), Alan Ruck (Roger), Rodney Pearson (Allen), Remak Ramsay (Kennedy), Virginia Madsen (Lisa), Deborah Thalberg (Susan), Fern Parsons (Headmistress).

Looking all of an immature 13, prep school student Andrew McCarthy is nearly raped on an elevator by Jacqueline Bisset, who pretends to buy his story of being 20-something. She's the mother of McCarthy's roommate Rob Lowe. The affair between the unlikely pair puts a serious strain on the friendship of McCarthy and Lowe. It would seem Bisset has some sort of male–Lolita complex.

511.   *Class of 1984* (1982, United Film Distribution, Canada, 96m, c). P Arthur Kent, D Mark Lester, W John Saxton, Tom Holland & Lester (based on a story by Holland), PH Albert Dunk, M Lalo Schifrin, ED Howard Kunin.

LP Perry King (Andy Norris), Timothy Van Patten (Peter Stegman), Merrie Lynn Ross (Diane Norris), Roddy McDowall (Terry Corrigan), Al Waxman (Stewiski), Lisa Langlois (Patsy), David Gardner (Morganthau).

In an updated version of *Blackboard Jungle,* Perry King is a new music teacher in a high school terrorized by a gang of hoods, headed by Timothy Van Patten, who runs a drug and prostitution ring from the school. When King breaks up a drug deal, the authorities take no action against the punks, and King is rewarded by having his car vandalized and his wife Merrie Lynn Ross kidnapped and gang-raped. King tracks down and kills each of his wife's assailants in this violent, sadistic and bloody exploitation movie.

512.   *Class of Nuke 'em High* (1986, Troma, 92m, c). P Lloyd Kaufman & Michael Herz, D Richard W. Haines & Samuel Weil [Lloyd Kaufman], W Haines, Mark Rudnitsky & Kaufman, PH Michael Mayers & Jim Grib, M Clive

Burr, David Barreto & David Behennah, ED Haines, SE Scott Coulter & Brian Quinn, ANAMATRONIC CREATURES Ton Lauten.

LP Janelle Brady (Chrissy), Gilbert Brenton (Warren), Robert Prichard (Spike), R.L. Ryan (Paley), James Nugent Vernon (Eddie), Brad Dunker (Gonzo), Gary Schneider (Pete), Theo Cohan (Muffey), Gary Rosenblatt (Greg), Mary Taylor (Judy), Rick Howard (Spud).

When high school students are exposed to nuclear waste from a power plant, a girl gives birth to a lizard which becomes a monster. Other teenagers are transformed into sadistic cretins. Just typical teens in some of the more violent and out-of-control schools in this country.

513. *Clean and Sober* (1988, Warner, 124m, c). P Tony Ganz, Deborah Blum & Jay Daniel, D Glenn Gordon Caron, W Tod Carroll, PH Jan Kiesser, M Gabriel Yared, ED Richard Chew, PD Joel Schiller.

LP Michael Keaton (Daryl Poynter), Kathy Baker (Charlie Standers), Morgan Freeman (Craig), M. Emmet Walsh (Richard Dirks), Brian Benben (Martin Laux), Luca Bercovici (Lenny), Tate Donovan (Donald Towle).

Michael Keaton is a hot-shot real estate salesman who has a costly cocaine and alcohol problem. He "borrows" $92,000 from his company's escrow account and loses it in the stock market. In order to avoid the police, he checks into a detoxification program, where he finally realizes the seriousness of his addictions. Keaton plays against type in an understated manner, but the film didn't do well in the theaters, although it is a hot ticket at the video stores.

514. *Cleo/Leo* (1989, Platinum Pictures, 94m, c). P,D&W Chuck Vincent, PH Larry Revene, M Joey Mennonna, ED "Martha Ubell" (Vincent), PD Chip Lambert.

LP Jane Hamilton [Veronica Hart] (Cleo Clock), Scott Baker (Leo Blockman), Alan Naggar (Marvin Blockman), Ginger Lynn Allen (Karen), Kevin Thomsen (Bob Miller), Ruth Collins (Sally).

Sexist businessman Scott Baker falls into a river after being chased by an irate female who doesn't like his insulting comments. He emerges from the water as Jane Hamilton, foul-mouthed and unaware that a sex transformation has taken place. Hamilton — or is it Baker's consciousness? — is raised as he/she must put up with guys coming on to her.

515. *Cloak and Dagger* (1984, Universal, 101m, c). P Allan Carr, D Richard B. Franklin, W Tom Holland (based on the short story "The Boy Cried Murder" by Cornell Woolrich, PH Victor J. Kemper, M Brian May, ED Andrew London, PD William Tuntke.

LP Henry Thomas (Davey Osborne), Dabney Coleman (Jack Flack/Hal Osborne), Michael Murphy (Rice), Christina Nigra (Kim Gardener), John McIntire (George MacCready), Jeanette Nolan (Eunice MacCready), Eloy Casados (Alvarez), Tim Rossovich (Haverman), Bill Forsythe (Morris).

Highly imaginative youngster Henry Thomas plays pretend games of espionage with imaginary friend Dabney Coleman (who also portrays Thomas' father). He finds himself involved with the real thing when he stumbles across a plot to smuggle top secret information out of the United States. The only trouble is, only the bad guys believe him.

516. *Clockwise* (1986, Universal, GB, 105m, c). P Michael Codron, D Christopher Morahan, W Michael Frayn, PH John Coquillon, ED Peter Boyle, PD Roger Murray-Leach.

LP John Cleese (Brian Stimpson), Alison Steadman (Gwenda Stimpson), Penny Leatherbarrow (Teacher), Howard Lloyd-Lewis (Ted), Jonathan Bowater (Clint), Stephen Moore (Mr. Jolly), Mark Bunting (Studious Boy), Robert Wilkinson (Streaker).

In his best Fawltyesque manner, John Cleese is a punctilious comprehensive headmaster en route to make a speech at a teacher's convention. When he misses a train he hijacks a student's car and he's off on a series of predictable but hilarious adventures.

517. *Cloud Dancer* (1980, Blossom, 108m, c). P&D Barry Brown, W William Goodhart (based on a story by Brown,

Goodhart & Daniel Tamkus), PH Travers Hill, M Fred Karlin, ED Marshall Borden.

LP David Carradine (Bradley Randolph), Jennifer O'Neill (Helen St. Clair), Joseph Bottoms (Tom Loomis), Colleen Camp (Cindy), Albert Salmi (Ozzie Randolph), Salome Jens (Jean Randolph), Nina Van Pallandt (Caroline Sheldon).

David Carradine and Joseph Bottoms are competing stunt flyers. Because his brother Albert Salmi is simple-minded, Carradine resists marriage and having children. Apparently it never occurred to him when he had an affair with photographer Jennifer O'Neill that a child might result. One did and she just doesn't know if she should tell him. Antihero Carradine finally becomes strong enough to perform well on the ground as he does in the air. He straightens out the drug problem of his protégé Bottoms and settles down with O'Neill and their baby.

518. *The Club* (1980, Roadshow, Australia, 99m, c). P Matt Carroll, D Bruce Beresford, W David Williamson (based on his play), PH Don McAlpine, M Mike Brady, ED William Anderson.

LP Jack Thompson (Laurie), Graham Kennedy (Ted), Frank Wilson (Jock), Harold Hopkins (Danny), John Howard (Geoff), Alan Cassell (Gerry), Maggie Doyle (Suzy).

Jack Thompson is excellent as a former star soccer player, now a failing coach, angry over the off-field politics he feels is ruining the game and his team.

519. *Club Life* (1987, Troma Team, 92m, c). P,D&W Norman Thaddeus Vane (based on a story by Vane & Bleu McKenzie), PH Joel King, M Jack Conrad, ED David Kern.

LP Tom Parsekian (Cal), Michael Parks (Tank), Jamie Barrett (Sissy), Tony Curtis (Hector), Dee Wallace [Stone] (Tilly Francesca), Ron Kuhlman (The Doctor), Pat Ast (Butch), Bruce Reed (Punk), Kristine Debell (Fern), Sal Landi (Sonny), Robert Miano (Ferd).

Motorcyclist Tom Parsekian shows up in Hollywood with hopes of becoming an actor, but instead ends up as a bouncer in a seedy club owned by Tony Curtis. When Curtis and another bouncer,

Michael Parks, are both killed by the mob, Parsekian and his girl Jamie Barrett climb aboard his "hog" and hit the road.

520. *Club Paradise* (1986, Warner, 104m, c). P Michael Shamberg, D Harold Ramis, W Ramis & Brian Doyle-Murray (based on a story by Ed Roboto, Tom Leopold, Chris Miller & David Standish), PH Peter Hannan, M David Mansfield, ED Marion Rothman, PD John Graysmark.

LP Robin Williams (Jack Moniker), Peter O'Toole (Gov. Anthony Croyden Hayes), Rick Moranis (Barry Nye), Jimmy Cliff (Ernest Reed), Twiggy (Phillipa Lloyd), Adolph Caesar (Prime Minister Solomon Gundy), Eugene Levy (Barry Steinberg), Joanna Cassidy (Terry Hamlin), Andrea Martin (Linda White), Brian Doyle-Murray (Voit Zerbe).

It's as if writer-director Harold Ramis and the cast challenged each other to do the worst work of which they were individually and collectively capable. All their talent is wasted in a story of retired Chicago fireman Robin Williams trying to turn a ramshackled beachfront property on a West Indian island into a going resort. The lack of laughs makes this an embarrassment for those in it who lay claim to being comics.

Club Sandwich see Last Resort

521. *Clue* (1985, Paramount, 87m, c). P Debra Hill, D&W Jonathan Lynn (based on a story by John Landis, Lynn and the Parker Bros. board game), PH Victor J. Kemper, M John Morris, ED David Bretherton & Richard G. Haines, PD John Lloyd.

LP Eileen Brennan (Mrs. Peacock), Tim Curry (Wadsworth), Madeline Kahn (Mrs. White), Christopher Lloyd (Professor Plum), Michael McKean (Mr. Green), Martin Mull (Col. Mustard), Lesley Ann Warren (Miss Scarlet), Colleen Camp (Yvette), Lee Ving (Mr. Boddy), Howard Hesseman (FBI Agent).

Clue has long been a popular board game in which players are to solve a murder by deducing the name of the killer, the weapon used and the particular room where the murder takes place. The producers of the movie filmed three endings, which were shown in different theaters. We must have seen the worst.

522. *Coal Miner's Daughter* (1980, Universal, 125m, c). P Bernard Schwartz, D Michael Apted, W Tom Rickman† (based on the autobiography of Loretta Lynn with George Vescey), PH Ralf D. Bode†, M Owen Bradley, ED Arthur Schmidt†, PD John Corso†, SD John M. Dwyer†, M/L Loretta Lynn, Shel Silverstein & Bob Montgomery.

LP Sissy Spacek* (Loretta Lynn), Tommy Lee Jones (Doolittle "Mooney" Lynn), Levon Helm (Ted Webb), Phyllis Boyens (Clara Webb), Beverly D'Angelo (Patsy Cline), Robert Elkins (Bobby Day), Bob Hannah (Charlie Dick), Ernest Tubb (Himself).

Sissy Spacek is remarkably good in this rag-to-riches true story of a 13-year-old girl who marries, has a brood of kids by the time she's 19, and then moves on to become one of the biggest stars of country music. Spacek sings the Loretta Lynn songs and does quite well by them. The same can be said of Beverly D'Angelo doing the Patsy Cline numbers. It's a bit long, but still a treat for country-and-western fans and those who appreciate good performances.

523. *Coast to Coast* (1980, Paramount, 95m, c). P Steve Tisch & Jon Avnet, D Joseph Sargent, W Stanley Weiser, PH Mario Tosi, M Charles Bernstein, ED George Jay Nicholson.

LP Dyan Cannon (Madie Levrington), Robert Blake (Charlie Callahan), Quinn Redeker (Benjamin Levrington), Michael Lerner (Dr. Froll), Maxine Stuart (Sam Klinger), Bill Lucking (Jules), David Moody (Chester).

Blabbermouth Dyan Cannon, just escaped from an asylum, where her husband has put her to avoid a costly divorce, hitches a ride with surly trucker Robert Blake, who's also on the run from those who wish to repossess his truck. During the cross-country trip, the two fall in love.

Coastwatcher* see *The Last Warrior

524. *Cobra* (1986, Warner, 87m, c). P Menahem Golan & Yoram Globus, D George P. Cosmatos, W Sylvester Stallone (based on the novel *Fair Game* by Paula Gosling), PH Ric Waite, M Sylvester Levay, ED Don Zimmerman & James Symons, PD Bill Kenney.

LP Sylvester Stallone (Marion Cobretti), Brigitte Nielsen (Ingrid), Reni Santoni (Gonzales), Andrew Robinson (Det. Monte), Brian Thompson (Night Slasher), John Herzfeld (Cho), Lee Garlington (Nancy Stalk), Art LaFleur (Capt. Sears), Marco Rodriguez (Supermarket Killer).

Killing machine Sylvester Stallone is a cop who handles cases no one else wants. This time he's on the trail of a group of ax-wielding serial killers. Stallone and then wife Brigitte Nielsen wear jeans so tight their genes are showing.

525. *The Coca Cola Kid* (1985, Cinecom International, Australia, 94m, c). P David Roe & Sylvia Le Clezio, D Dusan Makavejev, W Frank Moorhouse (based on his short story collections "The Americans," "Baby" & "The Electrical Experience"), PH Dean Semler, M William Motzing, ED John Scott, PD Graham [Grace] Walker.

LP Eric Roberts (Becker), Greta Scacchi (Terri), Bill Kerr (T. George McDowell), Chris Haywood (Kim), Kris McQuade (Juliana), Max Gilles (Frank), Tony Barry (Bushman), Paul Chubb (Fred).

Intense American adman Eric Roberts will stop at nothing to saturate Australia with the world's most popular soft drink. He discovers one region of the continent down under totally void of coke, because there is a local soft drink made by eccentric Bill Kerr. The latter is determined to keep out any competition. Roberts' trouble-shooting efforts are made more difficult as well as pleasurable by Greta Scacchi, who radiates sexuality and is intent on bedding him. She certainly is among the things that go better with coke.

526. *Cocaine Wars* (1985, Concorde, 83m, c). P Roger Corman & Alex Sessa, D Hector Olivera, W Steven M. Krauzer (based on a story by Olivera & David Vinas), PH Victor Kaulen, M George Brock, ED Edward Lowe, PD Julie Bertotto.

LP John Schneider (Cliff), Kathryn Witt (Janet), Royal Dano (Bailey), Federico Luppi (Gonzalo Reyes), Rodolfo Ranni (Gen. Lwan), Ivan Grey (Klausman), Richard Hamlin (Wilhelm), Edgar Moore (Rikki).

Former "Dukes of Hazard" TV figure John Schneider stars in this exploitation film produced by drive-in king Roger Corman. There's the all to be expected violence and soft-core sex scenes in a Mexican drug-trafficking story.

527. *Cocktail* (1988, Buena Vista, 103m, c). P Ted Field & Robert W. Cort, D Roger Donaldson, W Heywood Gould (based on his book), PH Dean Semler, M J. Peter Robinson, ED Neil Travis, PD Mel Bourne.

LP Tom Cruise (Brian Flanagan), Bryan Brown (Doug Coughlin), Elisabeth Shue (Jordan Mooney), Lisa Banes (Bonnie), Laurence Luckenbill (Mr. Mooney), Kelly Lynch (Kerry Coughlin), Gina Gershon (Coral), Ron Dean (Uncle Pat), Robert Donley (Eddie).

Tom Cruise portrays a shallow Manhattan bartender who sacrifices the love of a good woman, Elisabeth Shue, so he may be kept by a rich one, Lisa Banes. His older Aussie friend Bryan Brown, who taught him everything about hustling behind a bar, is no more successful in life or business. Cruise, who has succeeded in other films playing dislikable pretty boys or charming creeps, can't carry this soggy bar towel.

528. *Cocoon* (1985, 20th Century–Fox, 117m, c). P Richard D. Zanuck, David Brown & Lili Fini Zanuck, D Ron Howard, W Tom Benedek, PH Don Peterman & Jordan Klein, M James Horner, ED Michael Hill & Daniel Hanley, PD Jack T. Collis.

LP Don Ameche* (Art Selwyn), Wilford Brimley (Ben Luckett), Hume Cronyn (Joe Finley), Brian Dennehy (Walter), Jack Gilford (Bernie Lefkowitz), Steve Guttenberg (Jack Bonner), Maureen Stapleton (Mary Luckett), Jessica Tandy (Alma Finley), Gwen Verdon (Bess McCarthy), Herta Ware (Rose Lefkowitz), Tahnee Welch (Kitty), Barret Oliver (David), Linda Harrison (Susan), Tyrone Power, Jr. (Pillsbury).

This lighthearted comedy is most enjoyable. The credit goes to the cast of delightful old folks who prove they are no wiser for having lived a long time, but who still have life in them. When Don Ameche, Wilford Brimley and Hume Cronyn sneak into an indoor swimming pool on the property rented by some kindly aliens, led by Brian Dennehy, they find the water revitalizes them, making them feel and think young once more. When the aliens, who have returned to earth to pick up some of their comrades left behind centuries ago, prepare to depart, the young-at-heart lads and their ladies, Gwen Verdon, Maureen Stapleton and Jessica Tandy, are invited to go along to a planet where their life expectancy is almost endless. They leave but it is a foregone conclusion that they will return. See the next entry.

529. *Cocoon: The Return* (1988, 20th Century–Fox, 116m, c). P Richard D. Zanuck, David Brown & Lili Fini Zanuck, D Daniel Petrie, W Stephen McPherson (based on a story by Petrie & Elizabeth Bradley), PH Tak Fujimoto, M James Horner, ED Mark Roy Warner, PD Lawrence G. Paull.

LP Don Ameche (Art Selwyn), Wilford Brimley (Ben Luckett), Hume Cronyn (Joe Finley), Jack Gilford (Bernie Lefkowitz), Steve Guttenberg (Jack Bonner), Maureen Stapleton (Mary Luckett), Jessica Tandy (Alma Finley), Gwen Verdon (Bess McCarthy Selwyn), Elaine Stritch (Ruby), Courteney Cox (Sara), Tahnee Welch (Kitty), Tyrone Power, Jr. (Pillsbury).

No one can be surprised that the sequel to *Cocoon* is not as charming as the original. That seems to be the way with sequels. Unfortunately, the director and screenwriter fail to allow these fine senior citizens the same sense of liveliness and dignity that made audiences believe that old age and its infirmities are manageable as long as the mind and spirit maintains their youth. The space travelers to a world where illness and death are almost nonexistent have returned to earth for a visit with their friends and families. They go through another bout of soul-searching questioning to decide if they did the right thing when they left their home planet and whether they should go or stay this time. Director Daniel Petrie holds the cast in check and allows things to become maudlin and weighted down with bathos.

530. *C.O.D.* (1983, Lone Star, 94m, c). P&D Chuck Vincent, W Vincent, Rick

Marx & Jonathan Hannah (based on a story by Wolfgang von Schiber), PH Larry Revene, M Jonathan Hannah, ED James Macreading.

LP Chris Lemmon (Albert), Olivia Pascal (Holly), Jennifer Richards (Lydia), Teresa Ganzel (Lisa), Corrine Alphen (Cheryl), Marilyn Joi (Debbie), Carol Davis (Countess), Dolly Dollar (Christina).

In this snickering, giggly film, two competing advertising executives must come up with a winning campaign for the Beaver Bra Company.

531. *Code Name: Emerald* (1985, MGM/United Artists, 93m, c). P&D Martin Starger, W Ronald Bass (based on his novel *The Emerald Illusion*), PH Freddie Francis, M John Addison, ED Stu Linder, PD Gerard Viard.

LP Ed Harris (Gus Lang), Max von Sydow (Jurgen Brausch), Horst Buchholz (Walter Hoffman), Helmut Berger (Ernst Ritter), Cyrielle Claire (Claire Jouvet), Eric Stoltz (Andy Wheeler), Patrick Stewart (Col. Peters), Graham Crowden (Sir Geoffrey Macklin).

During World War II, American agent Ed Harris is in occupied Paris, posing as a German officer so he can get close to young American officer Eric Stoltz, just captured by the Nazis. Stoltz has information about the planned invasion and Harris is to use any means to prevent him from talking.

Code Name: The Soldier see The Soldier

532. *Code Name Vengeance* (1989, Action International, 96m, c). P&D David Winters, W Anthony Palmer, PH Keith Dunkley, M Tim James, Steve McClintock & Mark Mancina, ED Brian G. Frost.

LP Robert Ginty (Monroe Bieler), Shannon Tweed (Sam), Cameron Mitchell (Dutch), Don Gordon (Harry Applegate), Kevin Brophy (Chuck), James Ryan (Tabrak).

Ex-CIA agent Robert Ginty is sent to North Africa to rescue a kidnapped Middle Eastern magnate's wife and son.

533. *Code Name Zebra* (1987, Trans World, 94m, c). P Joseph Lucchese, D Joe Tornatore, W Robert Leone, PH Bill

Dickson & Tom Denove, M Louis Febre & Peter Rotter, ED Ed Hansen.

LP Jim Mitchum (Frank Barnes), Mike Lane (Carmine Longo), Timmy Brown (Cougar), Joe Dante (Voce), Chuck Morrell (Lt. Dietrich), Deana Jurgens (Julie), Lindsay Crosby (Police Sergeant), Chris Costello (Mrs. Noble), Frank Sinatra, Jr. (Koslo), Charles Dierkop (Crazy).

The sons of Robert Mitchum, Jim Brown and Frank Sinatra form an elite group of Vietnam vets who combat crime throughout the world. The boys have their troubles with vengeance-seeking hitman Mike Lane.

534. *Code of Silence* (1985, Orion, 101m, c). P Raymond Wagner, D Andrew Davis, W Michael Butler, Dennis Shryack & Mike Gray (based on a story by Butler & Shryack), PH Frank Tidy, M David Frank, ED Peter Parasheles & Christopher Holmes, PD Maher Ahmed.

LP Chuck Norris (Eddie Cusack), Henry Silva (Luis Comacho), Bert Remsen (Cmdr. Kates), Mike Genovese (Tony Luna), Nathan Davis (Felix Scalese), Ralph Foody (Cragie), Alan Hamilton (Pirelli), Ron Henriquez (Victor Comacho), Joseph Guzaldo (Nick Kopalas), Molly Hagan (Diana Luna).

Tough cop Chuck Norris takes on warring mob families and corrupt cops alike. Norris is all-business in his first film with good production values.

535. *Cohen and Tate* (1989, Tri-Star, 85m, c). P Antony Rufus Isaacs & Jeff Young, D&W Eric Red, PH Victor J. Kemper, M Bill Conti, ED Ed Abroms, PD David M. Haber.

LP Roy Scheider (Cohen), Adam Baldwin (Tate), Harley Cross (Travis Knight), Cooper Huckabee, Suzanne Savoy.

Hit men Scheider and Baldwin kill nine-year-old Harley Cross' family and kidnap him. Cross' family had been hiding under FBI protection ever since he witnessed a mob hit. The two hit men hate each other, which makes the trip to Houston and their boss with the boy, interesting.

536. *Cold Comfort* (1989, Norstar, Canada, 90m, c). P Ilana Frank & Ray

Sager, D Vic Sarin, W Richard Beattie & L. Elliott Simms, PH Sarin, M Jeff Danna & Mychael Danna, ED Nick Rotundo, AD Jo-Ann Chorney.

LP Maury Chaykin (Floyd), Margaret Langrick (Dolores), Paul Gross (Stephan).

Set in the cold and comfortless prairies of Manitoba, mentally deranged Maury Chaykin kidnaps travelling salesman Paul Gross to present to his daughter Margaret Langrick as a birthday present.

537. *Cold Feet* (1984, Cinecom International, 96m, c). P Charles Wessler, D&W Bruce van Dusen, PH Benjamin Blake, M Todd Rundgren, ED Sally Joe Menke.

LP Griffin Dunne (Tom Christo), Marissa Chibas (Marty Fenton), Blanche Baker (Leslie Christo), Mark Cronogue (Bill), Kurt Knudson (Louis), Joseph Leon (Harold Fenton).

Griffin Dunne and Marissa Chibas meet and, before hitting the old bed, wittily discuss their previous bad relationships.

538. *Cold Feet* (1989, Avenue Pictures, 94m, c). P Cassian Elwes, D Robert Dornhelm, W Tom McGuane & Jim Harrison, PH Brian Duggan, M Tom Bahler, ED David Rawlins & Debra McDermott, PD Bernt Capra.

LP Keith Carradine (Monte Latham), Sally Kirkland (Maureen), Tom Waits (Kenny), Bill Pullman (Buck), Rip Torn (Sheriff), Kathleen York (Laura), Tom McGuane (Cowboy in Bar), Jeff Bridges (Bartender).

Keith Carradine, a small time thief in Montana, wishes to maintain his bachelor status, while his silly girlfriend Sally Kirkland has plans to change her name to his. The third member of a trio of antiheroes who smuggles emeralds into the United States in the leg of a champion stallion is hilarious hitman Tom Waits, inept at everything except his profession.

539. *Cold Front* (1989, Shapiro Glickenhaus, Canada, 96m, c). P Ed Richardson & Sean Allan, D "Paul Bnarbic" (Allan S. Goldstein), W Sean Allan & Stefan Arngrim, PH Thomas Burstyn, M Braun Farnon & Craig Zurba, ED Martin Hunter, PD Sarina Rothstein-Cheikes.

LP Martin Sheen (John Hyde), Michael Ontkean (Derek MacKenzie), Kim Coates (Mantha), Beverly D'Angelo (Amanda), Yvan Ponton (Inspector Duchesne), Shelagh McLeod (Jeannie), Joshua Murray (Matthew), Kate Murray (Katie), Doug McGrath (Jackie Clearly).

U.S. Drug Enforcement agent Martin Sheen teams with Royal Canadian Mounted Police Criminal Intelligence agent Michael Ontkean to track down a terrorist who always kills the female partners of his male targets before assassinating the men. Ladies first, we suppose.

540. *Cold Steel* (1987, Cinetel, 90m, c). P Lisa M. Hansen, D Dorothy Ann Puzo, W Michael Sonye & Moe Quigley (based on stories by Sonye, Puzo & Hansen), PH Tom Denove, M David A. Jackson, ED David Bartlett.

LP Brad Davis (Johnny Modine), Sharon Stone (Kathy Connors), Jonathan Banks (Iceman), Jay Acovone (Cookie Manero), Adam Ant (Mick), Eddie Egan (Lt. Hill), Sy Richardson (Rashid), Anne Haney (Anna Modine).

Cop Brad Davis is out to avenge the brutal murder of his father. The killer, Jonathan Banks, hideously scarred, must speak through a voice-box in his throat. He blames Davis for his condition, suffered when they both were police cadets attacked by a vicious gang.

541. *The Color of Money* (1986, Buena Vista/Touchstone, 119m, c). P Irving Axelrad & Barbara DeFina, D Martin Scorsese, W Richard Price (based on the novel by Walter Tevis), PH Michael Ballhaus, M Robbie Robertson, ED Thelma Schoonmaker, PD Boris Leven.

LP Paul Newman* (Eddie Felson), Tom Cruise (Vincent), Mary Elizabeth Mastrantonio (Carmen), Helen Shaver (Janelle), John Turturro (Julian), Bill Cobbs (Orvis), Robert Agins (Earl), Alvin Anastasia (Kennedy), Elizabeth Bracco (Diane), Vito D'Ambrosio (Lou).

Paul Newman is rewarded for a career of fine movies by being given an Oscar for a performance not as good as others for which he was passed over. The film is sort of a sequel to *The Hustler*. Newman is an aging pool champion who makes cocky snooker player Tom Cruise his protégé. The story is a cliché and very predictable, but it's still entertaining with fine performances by the principals.

542. *The Color Purple†* (1985, Warner, 152m, c). P Steven Spielberg, Kathleen Kennedy, Frank Marshall, Quincy Jones, Jon Peters & Peter Guber, D Spielberg, W Menno Meyjes† (based on the novel by Alice Walker), PH Allen Daviau†, M Jones, ED Michael Kahn, PD J. Michael Riva, AD Robert W. Welch†, SD Linda DeScenna†, COS Aggie Guerard Rodgers†, MK Steve LaPorte, Richard Alonzo & Michael Laudati†, SONG "Miss Celie's Blues (Sister)" by Jones, Rod Temperton & Lionel Richie†.

LP Danny Glover (Albert), Whoopi Goldberg† (Celie), Margaret Avery† (Shug Avery), Oprah Winfrey (Sofia)†, Willard Pugh (Harpo), Akosua Busia (Nettie), Adolph Caesar (Old Mister), Rae Dawn Chong (Squeak), Desreta Jackson (Young Celie), Dana Ivey (Miss Millie), Leonard Jackson (Pa), Bennet Guillory (Grady), John Patton, Jr. (Preacher), Carl Anderson (Rev. Samuel), Susan Beaubian (Corrine).

Nominated for 11 Academy Awards, *Purple* became one of the all-time greatest losers when it received no awards. After raising so many expectations, it is probably natural that some associated with the movies believed that the losses were the result of resentment and jealousy of Steven Spielberg with some racial overtones. This may be a part of the story, but the movie, story and the performances just aren't as outstanding as all the nominations would seem to suggest. The story traces the miserable life of black woman Whoopi Goldberg from 1909 to 1947 in a small Southern town where her mistreatment is mostly the responsibility of insensitive and mean-spirited black men in her life. Despite everything, she grows in dignity, maturity and independence.

543. *Colors* (1988, Orion, 120m, c). P Robert H. Solo & Paul Lewis, D Dennis Hopper, W Michael Schiffer (based on a story by Schiffer & Richard DiLello), PH Haskell Wexler, M Herbie Hancock, ED Robert Estrin, PD Ron Foreman.

LP Sean Penn (Danny McGavin), Robert Duvall (Bob Hodges), Maria Conchita Alonso (Louisa Gomez), Randi Brooks (Ron Delaney), Grand Bush (Larry Sylvester), Don Cheadle (Rocket), Gerrardo Mejia (Bird), Glenn Plummer (High Top), Trinidad Silva (Frog).

In another one of the young cop–old cop pictures, brash young police officer Sean Penn is teamed with cagey veteran Robert Duvall, as part of a special crime unit trying to contain gang violence in Los Angeles. Even though they become friends, they are constantly at odds and they don't do much to ease the gang problem either.

544. *Combat Shock* (1986, Troma Team, 96m, c). P,D&W Buddy Giovinazzo, PH Stella Varveris, M Ricky Giovinazzo & ED Giovinazzo.

LP Ricky Giovinazzo (Frankie Dunlan), Veronica Stork (Cathy Dunlan), Mitch Maglio (Paco), Aspah Livni (Labo), Nick Nasta (Morbe), Mike Tierno (Mike), Mary Cristadoro (Mary).

Vietnam veteran Ricky Giovinazzo has difficulty coping with his deformed child, whose plight has been caused because of his father's exposure to Agent Orange.

Come 'n' Get It see Lunch Wagon

545. *Come Back to the 5 & Dime, Jimmy Dean, Jimmy Dean* (1982, Viacom, 109m, c). P Scott Bushnell, D Robert Altman, W Ed Graczyck (based on his play), PH Pierre Mignot, ED Jason Rosenfield, PD David Gropman.

LP Sandy Dennis (Mona), Cher (Sissy), Karen Black (Joanne), Sudie Bond (Juanita), Marta Heflin (Edna Louise), Kathy Bates (Stella May), Mark Patton (Joe Qualley), Caroline Aaron (Martha), Ruth Miller (Clarissa).

Five women who have grown up fans of the late actor James Dean gather in the small Texas town's 5 & Dime store to discuss their lives. Sandy Dennis finally has her illusion shattered that Dean was the father of her illegitimate child. It's really only a filming of Ed Graczyck's play but the performances are impressive.

546. *The Comeback* (1982, Lone Star, GB, 100m, c, aka *The Day the Screaming Stopped*). P&D Pete Walker, W Murray Smith, PH Peter Jessop, M Stanley Myers, ED Alan Brett, PD Denis Johnson.

LP Jack Jones (Nick Cooper), Pamela Stephenson (Linda Everett), David Doyle (Webster Jones), Bill Owen (Mr. B), Sheila Keith (Mrs. B), Holly Palance (Gail Cooper), Peter Turner (Harry), Richard Johnson (Dr. Macauley).

Singer Jack Jones is mixed up in a series of gruesome murders. He also must deal with the ghost of his estranged wife while he's staying at a spooky English country mansion.

547. *The Comeback Trail* (1982, Dynamite Entertainment, 76m, c). P,D&W Harry Hurwitz (based on a story by Roy Frumkes, Robert J. Winston & Hurwitz), PH Victor Petrashevitz, M Igo Kantor, ED Hurwitz.

LP Chuck McCann (Enrico Kodac), Buster Crabbe (Duke Montana), Robert Staats (E. Eddie Eastman), Ina Balin (Julie Thomas), Jara Kahout (German Producer), Henny Youngman, Irwin Corey.

This film was shot ten years earlier and had only a very limited theater run. Shady producers Chuck McCann and Robert Staats hire washed-up star Buster Crabbe for a movie, hoping he will die during production so they can collect enough insurance to get started again on another project. But Buster proves to be healthier than they thought.

548. *Comfort and Joy* (1984, Universal, GB, 106m, c). P Davina Belling & Clive Parsons, D&W Bill Forsyth, PH Chris Menges, M Mark Knopfler, ED Michael Ellis, PD Adrienne Atkinson.

LP Bill Paterson (Alan "Dickie" Bird), Eleanor David (Maddy), C.P. Grogan (Charlotte), Alex Norton (Trevor), Patrick Malahide (Colin), Rikki Fulton (Hilary), Roberto Bernardi (Mr. McCool), George Rossi (Bruno), Billy McElhaney (Renato), Gilly Gilchrist (Rufus).

Scottish filmmaker Bill Forsyth *(Local Hero* and *Gregory's Girl)* comes up with another delightful comedy about disc jockey Paterson whose life is falling apart. His live-in kleptomaniac lover Eleanor David is moving out and he finds himself in the midst of a gang war between two Glasgow Mafia families who are seeking to control the local ice cream business.

549. *Comin' at You* (1981, Filmways, 91m, c). P Tony Anthony, D Ferdinando Baldi, W Lloyd Battista, Wolf Lowenthal & Gene Quintano (based on a story by Tony Pettito), PH Fernando Arribas, M Carlo Savina, ED Franco Fraticelli.

LP Tony Anthony (H.H. Hart), Gene Quintano (Pike), Victoria Abril (Abilene), Ricardo Palacios (Polk), Lewis Gordon (Old Man).

In this rare 80s 3-D movie, Tony Anthony seeks his kidnapped fiancée Victoria Abril, who is being held hostage by white slaver Gene Quintana.

Coming Attractions see Loose Shoes

550. *Coming to America* (1988, Paramount, 116m, c). P George Folsey, Jr. & Robert D. Wachs, D John Landis, W David Sheffield & Barry W. Blaustein (based on a story by Murphy and an idea by Art Buchwald according to the courts), PH Woody Omens, M Nile Rodgers, ED Malcolm Campbell & Folsey, PD Richard MacDonald, COS Deborah Nadoolman†, MK Rick Baker†.

LP Eddie Murphy (Prince Akeem), Arsenio Hall (Semmi), James Earl Jones (The King of Zamonda), John Amos (Mr. McDowell), Madge Sinclair (The Queen of Zamonda), Shari Headley (Lisa McDowell), Eriq LaSalle (Darryl Jenks), Allison Dean (Patrice McDowell), Paul Bates (Oha), Louie Anderson (Maurice), Clint Smith (Sweets), Vanessa Bell (Imani Izzi).

Rather than his usual scatological jive-talking persona, Eddie Murphy is an African prince, speaking perfect if stilted English, who has come to the United States with his lackey Arsenio Hall to find a bride who will love him for himself. Once in New York, the pair disappear into Queens, where they encounter hookers, hustlers and deadbeats. Murphy also falls in love with Shari Headley, the daughter of John Amos who gives the two menial jobs in his fast food restaurant. Murphy and Hall portray many of the characters they encounter in cameo roles. Also in cameo roles are Don Ameche and Ralph Bellamy in their Mortimer and Randolph Duke roles from *Trading Places.*

551. *Commando* (1985, 20th Century–Fox, 90m, c). P Joel Silver, D Mark

L. Lester, W Steven E. De Souza (based on a story by Joseph Loeb III, Matthew Weisman & De Souza), PH Matthew F. Leonetti, M James Horner, ED Mark Goldblatt, John F. Link & Glenn Farr, PD John Vallone.

LP Arnold Schwarzenegger (Col. John Matrix), Rae Dawn Chong (Cindy), Dan Hedaya (Arius), Vernon Wells (Bennett), James Olson (Gen. Kirby), David Patrick Kelly (Sully), Alyssa Milano (Jenny), Bill Duke (Cooke), Drew Snyder (Lawson), Sharon Wyatt (Leslie).

Ex-commando Arnold Schwarzenegger fights an evil South American despot who has kidnapped the muscular one's daughter. There's all the violence and dying that any Rambo fan could hope for. Rae Dawn Chong has the best line when she tells the rampaging bull, "I'm tired of your macho bullshit."

552. *Commando Squad* (1987, Trans-World, 89m, c). P Alan Amiel & Fred Olen Ray, D Ray, W David A. Jackson, James Saad, Tom Riparetti & Steve Le Gassick, PH Gary Graver, ED Kathie Weaver.

LP Kathy Shower (Kat Withers), Brian Thompson (Clint Jensen), William Smith (Morgan Denny), Robert Quarry (Milo), Sid Haig (Iggy), Mel Welles (Quintano), Marie Windsor (Casey), Benita Martinez (Anita).

Former *Playboy* Playmate of the Year Kathy Shower is the toughest drug agent around. She's sent to Mexico to investigate the disappearances of other narcotics agents investigating a cocaine factory, including old boyfriend Brian Thompson. The operation is run by William Smith, another former colleague gone bad. The latter gets his when he is stabbed with a special knife with a break-off handle filled with sulphuric acid.

553. *Communion* (1989, Vestron, 109m, c). P Philippe Mora, Whitley Strieber & Dan Allingham, D Mora, W Strieber (based on his book), PH Louis Irving, M Eric Clapton & Alan Zavod, ED Lee Smith, PD Linda Pearl.

LP Christopher Walken (Whitley Strieber), Lindsay Crouse (Anne Strieber), Joel Carlson (Andrew Strieber), Frances Sternhagen (Dr. Janet Duffy), Andreas Katsulas (Alex), Terri Hanauer (Sara), Basil Hoffman (Dr. Friedman).

Self-absorbed novelist Christopher Walken and his family visit their mountain cabin for a vacation, but are greeted by noises, bright lights, commotion and, at least to Walken, strange creatures. It will take hypnosis to make Walken recall what really happened in his encounter with aliens.

554. *The Company of Wolves* (1985, Cannon, GB, 95m, c). P Chris Brown & Stephen Woolley, D Neil Jordan, W Angela Carter & Jordan (based on a collection of short stories by Carter), PH Bryan Loftus, M George Fenton, ED Rodney Holland, PD Anton Furst.

LP Angela Lansbury (Granny), David Warner (Father), Graham Crowden (Old Priest), Kathryn Pogson (Young Bride), Stephen Rea (Young Groom), Tusse Silberg (Mother), Sarah Patterson (Rosaleen), Georgia Slowe (Alice).

Angela Lansburg rattles off eerie tales and fills her granddaughter Sarah Patterson's head with scary stories full of warnings and dread regarding men who are turned into wolves. Patterson becomes the original Little Red Riding Hood in this fascinating and perplexing psychological fable, which combines sexual symbolism, mysterious occurrences, violence and gore.

555. *The Competition* (1980, Columbia, 129m, c). P William Sackheim, D&W Joel Oliansky (based on a story by Oliansky and Sackheim), PH Richard H. Kline, M Lalo Schifrin, ED David Blewitt, PD Dale Hennesy.

LP Richard Dreyfuss (Paul Dietrich), Amy Irving (Heidi Schoonover), Lee Remick (Greta Vandemann), Sam Wanamaker (Erskine), Joseph Cali (Jerry DiSalvo), Ty Henderson (Michael Humphries), Vickie Kriegler (Tatiana Baronov), Adam Stern (Mark Landau), Bea Silvern (Mme. Gorshev).

Classical pianists Richard Dreyfuss and Amy Irving fall in love while competing for top honors in a prestigious piano competition. It's ninety-nine and forty-four one-hundredths percent pure soap opera.

556. *Compo* (1989, Sunrise, Australia, 82m, c). P Nigel Buesst, Joanne Bell & Matthew Lovering, D Buesst, W

Abe Pogos (based on his play *Claim No. Z84*), PH Vladimir Oscherov, M Iain Mott, ED Nubar Ghazarian.

LP Jeremy Stanford (Paul Harper), Bruce Kerr (David Bartlett), Cliff Neate (Dale Bradley), Christopher Barry (Carlo Garbanzo), Elizabeth Crockett (Gina), Rowan Woods (Tom Little), Peter Hosking (Vince Caruana), Leo Regan (Eddie).

"Compo" is Australian slang for "worker's compensation." In this low-key comedy, the state compensation office's employees are shown to be a group of uncivil servants who offer only apathy and no hope to their clients.

557. Compromising Positions (1985, Paramount, 98m, c). P&D Frank Perry, W Susan Isaacs (based on her novel), PH Barry Sonnenfeld, M Brad Fiedel, ED Peter Frank, PD Peter Larkin.

LP Susan Sarandon (Judith Singer), Raul Julia (David Suarez), Edward Herrmann (Bob Singer), Judith Ivey (Nancy Miller), Marybeth Hurt (Peg Tuccio), Anne De Salvo (Phyllis Fleckstein), Deborah Rush (Brenda Dunck), Josh Mostel (Dicky Dunck), Joe Mantegna (Bruce Fleckstein).

Susan Sarandon is special in this comedy-mystery, which sees her as an amateur sleuth looking into the death of a highly successful periodontist Joe Mantegna, who treats, beds and photographs in S&M gear a series of wealthy, bored Long Island housewives.

558. Computer Beach Party (1988, Vestron, 97m, c). P,D,W&ED Gary Troy, PH Robert E. Poimbeauf.

LP Hank Amigo (Andy), Andre Chimene (Dennis), Stacey Nemour (Allison).

Filmed in 1985, this beach party movie is set in Galveston where nerdish computer expert Hank Amigo fights to prevent beachfront property from being converted to a tourist attraction by the ambitious mayor.

559. Comrades (1989, Gavin Film, GB, 180m, c). P Simon Relph, D&W Bill Douglas, M Hans Werner Henze & David Graham, ED Mick Audsley, PD Michael Pickwoad.

LP Robin Soans (George Loveless), William Gaminara (James Loveless), Stephen Bateman (Old Tom Stanfield), Philip Davis (Young Stanfield), Patrick Field (John Hammett), Keith Allen (James Hammett), Jeremy Flynn (Brine), Robert Stephens (Frampton), Michael Hordern (Pitt), Freddie Jones (Vicar), Vanessa Redgrave (Mrs. Carlyle), James Fox (Norfolk).

In 1834 England, the Tolpuddle farmers, who had formed a union to protect their rights, were convicted of administering "illegal oaths" and sent to Australia to serve seven-year sentences. Their case became a cause célèbre, with their being pardoned two years later. The movie uses their plight to make a comment about the low state to which the labor movement has fallen in the present Tory government of Margaret Thatcher.

560. Conan the Barbarian (1982, Universal, 115m, c). P Buzz Feitshans & Raffaella De Laurentiis, D John Milius, W Milius & Oliver Stone (based on the character created by Robert E. Howard), PH Duke Callaghan & John Cabrera, M Basil Poledouris, ED C. Timothy O'Meara & Fred Stafford, PD Ronn Cobb.

LP Arnold Schwarzenegger (Conan), James Earl Jones (Thulsa Doom), Max Von Sydow (King Orsic), Sandhal Bergman (Valeria), Ben Davidson (Rexor), Cassandra Gaviola (The Witch), Gerry Lopez (Subotai), Mako (The Wizard), Valerie Quinnessen (The Princess).

Arnold Schwarzenegger stars in this raunchy sword and sorcery epic as a muscular young gladiator who seeks to avenge the death of his parents, killed when he was but a lad. It's a sexist film and not much fun.

561. Conan the Destroyer (1984, Universal, 103m, c). P Raffaella De Laurentiis, D Richard Fleischer, W Stanley Mann (story by Roy Thomas & Gerry Conway, based on the character created by Robert E. Howard), PH Jack Cardiff, M Basil Poledouris, ED Frank J. Urioste, PD Pier Luigi Basile.

LP Arnold Schwarzenegger (Conan), Grace Jones (Zula), Wilt Chamberlain (Bombaara), Mako (Akjiro, "The Wizard"), Tracey Walter (Malak), Sarah Douglas (Queen Taramis), Olivia D'Abo (Princess Jehnna), Pat Roach (Man Ape/Thoth-Amon), Jeff Corey (Grand Vizier), Sven Ole Thorsen (Togra).

The sequel to *Conan the Barbarian* is superior because it doesn't take itself as seriously as its predecessor. It allows for some welcome humor as Arnold Schwarzenegger accepts the assignment of transporting virgin princess Olivia D'Abo (who tries to entice Arnie to change her status), along with her massive bodyguard Wilt Chamberlain, on a quest to find a mystical gem. Along the way, they pick up wild woman Grace Jones, who steals the picture.

562.   *Concrete Angels* (1987, Shapiro-Academy Ent., Canada, 97m, c). P Anthony Kramreither & Carlo Liconti, D Liconti, W Jim Purdy, PH Karol Ike, M Various artists, ED John Harding.

LP Joseph Dimambro (Bello Vecchio), Luke McKeehan (Sean), Omie Craden (Ira), Dean Bosacki (Jessie), Derrick Jones (Bullet), Rosemary Varnese (Carla), Simon Craig (Mick), Dion Farentino (Gigi).

In 1964, all of Toronto is excited about the forthcoming appearance of the Beatles. To add to the anticipation, there is to be a battle-of-the-bands contest, with the winner opening the show for the Fab Four. Fourteen-year-old Italian kid Joseph Dimambro puts together a band which makes the semifinals but loses out to a more experienced group. The night of the concert, Diamambro and his friends join a local hood to burglarize the hospital where Dimambro works.

563.   *The Concrete Jungle* (1982, Pentagon, 99m, c). P Billy Fine, D Tom DeSimone, W Alan J. Adler, PH Andrew W. Friend, M Joe Conlan, ED Nina DiMarco.

LP Jill St. John (Warden Fletcher), Tracy Bregman (Elizabeth Demming), Barbara Luna (Cat), June Barrett (Icy), Peter Brown (Danny), Aimee Eccles (Spider), Sondra Currie (Katherine), Susan Mechsner (Breaker).

Framed for smuggling cocaine, naive Tracy Bregman is given a year in prison where she is at the mercy of warden Jill St. John and the obligatory lesbian Barbara Luna, who lusts after the sweet young thing.

564.   *Condorman* (1981, Disney/Buena Vista, GB, 90m, c). P Jan Williams, D Charles Jarrott, W Marc Stirdirant, Glen Caron & Mickey Rose (based on the novel *The Game of X* by Robert Sheckley), PH Charles F. Wheeler, M Henry Mancini, ED Gordon D. Brenner, PD Albert Witherick.

LP Michael Crawford (Woody), Oliver Reed (Krokov), Barbara Carrera (Natalia), James Hampton (Harry), Jean-Pierre Kalfon (Morovich), Dana Elcar (Russ), Vernon Dobtcheff (Russian Agent), Robert Arden (CIA Chief).

The Disney studios try for a spoof of the James Bond spy movies, but neither they nor their hero Michael Crawford is up to the job.

565.   *Consuming   Passions* (1988, Goldwyn, US/GB, 98m, c). P William P. Cartlidge, D Giles Foster, W Paul D. Zimmerman & Andrew Davis (based on a play by Michael Palin & Terry Jones), PH Roger Pratt, M Richard Hartley, ED John Grover, PD Peter Lamont.

LP Tyler Butterworth (Ian Littleton), Jonathan Pryce (Farris), Vanessa Redgrave (Mrs. Garza), Freddie Jones (Graham Chumley), Sammi Davis (Felicity), Prunella Scales (Ethel), Thora Hird (Mrs. Gordon), William Rushton (Big Teddy), John Wells (Dr. Forrester).

Bungler Tyler Butterworth has dreams of making it to the top of the corporate ladder at Chumley's Chocolates. He studies success tapes constantly. When he accidentally dumps three workers into a vat of chocolate, he creates a new taste sensation. Evil manager Jonathan Pryce gives Butterworth a promotion and urges him to keep the new recipe secret.

566.   *Continental Divide* (1981, Universal, 103m, c). P Bob Larson, D Michael Apted, W Lawrence Kasdan, PH John Bailey, M Michael Small, ED Dennis Virkler, PD Peter Jamison.

LP John Belushi (Ernie Souchak), Blair Brown (Nell), Allen Goorwitz (Howard), Carlin Glynn (Sylvia), Tony Ganios (Possum), Val Avery (Yablonowitz), Liam Russell (Deke), Everett Smith (Fiddle).

Hard-nosed Chicago newspaper columnist John Belushi is sent to the Rockies to interview reclusive and wacky ornithologist Blair Brown. What follows is an unlikely love story which could use more humor.

567.   *Contract Kill* (1982, New American, 86m, c). P Edgar Oppenheimer, D Claude Mulot, W Albert Kantof & Mulot.

LP Bruno Pradal, Patti D'Arbanville, Gabrielle Tinti, Eva Swan, Charles Southwood, Sydney Chaplin, Francoise Prevost.

There's nothing new or startling in this story of murder for hire.

568. *Cookie* (1989, Warner, 93m, c). P Laurence Mark, D Susan Seidelman, W Nora Ephron & Alice Arlen, PH Oliver Stapleton, ED Andrew Mondshein, M Thomas Newman, PD Michael Haller.

LP Peter Falk (Dominick "Dino" Capisco), Dianne Wiest (Lenore), Emily Lloyd (Carmella "Cookie" Voltecki), Michael V. Gazzo (Carmine Taratino), Brenda Vaccaro (Bunny Capisco), Adrian Pasdar (Vito), Lionel Stander (Enzo Della Testa), Jerry Lewis (Arnold Ross), Bob Gunton (Segretto), Ben Rayson (Henry Solomon), Ricki Lake (Pia).

We must resist the urge to make cookie-like comments about this half-bak ... no, no ... this modest comedy about mobster Falk, just out of prison after serving 13 years. He's intent on getting even with his former partner Michael V. Gazzo. He's not aided and abetted very much by his wife Brenda Vaccaro, mistress Diane Wiest, daughter Emily Lloyd (in the title role) or by the cameo-like appearances of Lionel Stander and Jerry Lewis.

569. *Cop* (1988, Atlantic, 110m, c, aka *Blood on the Moon*). P James B. Harris & James Woods, D Harris, W Harris (based on the novel *Blood on the Moon* by James Ellroy), PH Steve Dubin, M Michel Colombier, ED Anthony Spano, PD Gene Rudolf.

LP James Woods (Lloyd Hopkins), Lesley Ann Warren (Kathleen McCarthy), Charles Durning (Dutch), Charles Haid (Whitey Haines), Raymond J. Barry (Gaffney), Randi Brooks (Joanie), Steven Lambert (Bobby Franco).

Bad/good-guy James Woods is a maverick cop out to get a serial killer no one else believes exists. Woods is good as the hard-boiled detective, but the plot is so idiotic that it's difficult to enjoy it as a thriller.

570. *Corrupt* (1984, New Line Cinema, US/Ital., 99m, c, aka *Order of Death*). P Elda Ferri, D Roberto Faenza, W Ennio De Concini, Faenza & Hugh Fleetwood (based on the novel *The Order of Death* by Fleetwood), PH Giuseppe Pinori, M Ennio Morricone.

LP Harvey Keitel (Lt. Fred O'Connor), John Lydon (Leo Smith), Sylvia Sidney (Margaret Smith), Nicole Garcia (Lenore), Leonard Mann (Bob).

Policeman Harvey Keitel uses illegal means to trap a killer.

571. *The Cotton Club* (1984, Orion, 127m, c). P Robert Evans, D Francis Coppola, W William Kennedy & Coppola (based on a story by Kennedy, Coppola, Mario Puzo, inspired by a pictorial history by James Haskins), PH Stephen Goldblatt, M John Barry, ED Barry Malkin & Robert Q. Lovett†, PD Richard Sylbert, AD/SD Sylbert, George Gaines & Les Bloom†.

LP Richard Gere (Dixie Dwyer), Gregory Hines (Sandman Williams), Diane Lane (Vera Cicero), Lonette McKee (Lila Rose Oliver), James Remar (Dutch Schultz), Nicolas Cage (Vincent Dwyer), Allen Garfield (Abbadabba Berman), Bob Hoskins (Owney Madden), Fred Gwynne (Frenchy Demange), Gwen Verdon (Tish Dwyer), Lisa Jane Persky (Frances Flegenheimer), Maurice Hines (Clay Williams).

The story of the famous Harlem hot spot reportedly cost $47 million to make. The picture follows the careers of white horn player Richard Gere and tap-dancer Gregory Hines. Gere's association with mobsters such as Dutch Schultz (James Remar) leads to movie roles as gangsters (à la George Raft). Hines stars at the club where the only blacks allowed are employees. Gere's main squeeze is lovely Diane Lane, who also serves as Remar's mistress when his wife Lisa Jane Persky isn't around. Hines lucks out with lovely songbird Lonette McKee. It's entertaining, but not worth the price.

572. *The Couch Trip* (1988, Orion, 97m, c). P Lawrence Gordon, D Michael Ritchie, W Steven Kampmann, Will Porter & Sean Stein (based on a novel by Ken Kolb), PH Donald E. Thorin, M Michel Colombier, ED Richard A. Harris, PD Jimmie Bly.

LP Dan Aykroyd (John Burns), Walter Matthau (Donald Becker), Charles Grodin (George Maitlin), Donna Dixon (Laura Rollins), Richard Romanus (Harvey Michaels), Mary Gross (Vera Maitlin), David Clennon (Lawrence

Baird), Arye Gross (Perry Kovin), Victoria Jackson (Robin).

When successful Los Angeles radio sex therapist Charles Grodin has a nervous breakdown, prison psychiatrist David Clennon is asked to fill in for him. Instead mental patient Dan Aykroyd gets the job. His direct and profane approach makes him an overwhelming success. Walter Matthau, in a small role as a loony street preacher, wastes his time and talent. Donna Dixon, as Grodin's beautiful assistant, may distract males in the audience, but not enough to prevent them from seeing the glaring weaknesses in this not very funny movie.

573. *Country* (1984, Buena Vista, 105m, c). P William D. Wittliff, Jessica Lange & William Beaudine, Jr., D Richard Pearce, W Wittliff, PH David M. Walsh & Roger Shearman, M Charles Gross, ED Bill Yahraus, PD Ron Hobbs.

LP Jessica Lange† (Jewell Ivy), Sam Shepard (Gil Ivy), Wilford Brimley (Otis), Matt Clark (Tom McMullen), Therese Graham (Marlene Ivy), Levi L. Knebel (Carlisle Ivy), Jim Haynie (Arlon Brewer), Sandra Seacat (Louise Brewer), Alex Harvey (Fordyce), Stephanie-Stacie Poyner (Missy Ivy), Jim Ostercamp (Cowboy).

After a huge tornado hits the area, Sam Shepard and Jessica Lange, as well as other farm families in the region, are faced with losing their land. Shepard looks for an answer in a bottle, but the threat makes Lange as strong as steel. This excellent look at the difficult times of modern farmers never resorts to soap opera excesses. It's somber but really quite a wonderful film.

574. *The Country Girls* (1984, London Films, GB, 108m, c). P Aida Young, D Desmond Davis, W Edna O'Brien (based on her novel), PH Denis Lewiston, M Francis Shaw, ED Martin Crane.

LP Sam Neill (Me Gentleman), Maeve Germaine (Kate), Jill Doyle (Baba Brennan), John Olahan (Hickey), Britta Smith (Lil), Patricia Martin (Martha), Des Nealon (Brennan), John Kavanagh (James).

In Ireland in 1955, a drunken farmer's daughter goes to a convent school and falls in love with a married lawyer.

Courage *see* ***Raw Courage***

575. *Courage Mountain* (1989, Trans-World, US/France, 96m, c, aka *The Further Adventures of Heidi*). P Stephen Ujlaki, D Christopher Leitch, W Weaver Webb (based on a story by Fred & Mark Brogger), PH Jacques Steyn, M Sylvester Levay, ED Martin Walsh, PD Robb Wilson King.

LP Juliette Caton (Heidi), Jan Rubes (Grandfather), Charlie Sheen (Peter), Leslie Caron (Jane Hillary), Yorgo Voyagis (Signor Bonelli), Laura Betti (Signora Bonelli).

This follow-up to the classic Heidi story by Johanna Spyri has the Swiss Miss entering an exclusive Italian boarding school on the eve of World War I. She's sad to leave her boyfriend Peter (Charlie Sheen), who is off to join the Swiss army. At school our heroine, Juliette Caton, is treated like a country bumpkin by her snotty classmates; but the worst comes when Italian soldiers take over the school and send the girls to work as slave laborers in an orphanage. Plucky Heidi and four others make a daring escape across the Alps to safety in Switzerland.

576. *The Courier* (1989, Vestron, Ireland, 85m, c). P Hilary McLoughlin, D Frank Deasy & Joe Lee, W Deasy, PH Gabriel Beristain, M Declan MacManus, ED Annette D'Alton, PD Dave Wilson.

LP Padraig O'Loingsigh (Mark), Cait O'Riordan (Colette), Gabriel Byrne (Val), Ian Bannen (McGuigan), Patrick Bergin (Christy), Andrew Connelly (Danny), Michelle Houlden (Sharon).

Former drug addict Padraig O'Loingsigh discovers that he has been innocently carrying drugs and money for dealer Gabriel Byrne. When this results in O'Loingsigh's best friend Andrew Connelly's dying of an overdose, he goes after the vicious and sinister gangster.

577. *Cousins* (1989, Paramount, 111m, c). P William Allyn, D Joel Schumacher, W Stephen Metcalfe, PH Ralf Bode, M Angelo Badalamenti, ED Robert Brown, PD Mark S. Freeborn.

LP Ted Danson (Larry Kozinski), Isabella Rossellini (Maria Hardy), Sean Young (Tish Kozinski), William Petersen (Tom Hardy), Lloyd Bridges (Vince Kozinski), Norma Aleandro (Edie Costello), Keith Coogan (Mitch Kozinski).

This remake of Jean-Charles Tac- chella's charming 1976 romantic comedy *Cousin, Cousine* is less appealing than the original because of the different atti- tudes of the French and Americans about infidelity. The French film treated adultery with a matter-of-factness which is still unacceptable in American societies. Ted Danson and Isabella Rossellini are drawn to each other at a wedding, after being left alone by their respective spouses Sean Young and William Petersen, who are having some of their own hanky-panky in a car. Danson's and Rossellini's resulting affair leads to a great deal of unpleasant- ness with Young and Petersen.

578. *Covergirl* (1984, New World, Canada, 93m, c, aka *Dreamworld*). P Claude Heroux, D Jean-Claude Lord, W Charles Dennis, PH Rene Verzier, M Christopher L. Stone, ED Christopher Holmes.

LP Jeff Conaway (T.C. Sloane), Irena Ferris (Kit Paget), Cathie Shirriff (Tessa), Roberta Leighton (Dee), Deborah Wake- ham (Avril), Kenneth Welsh (Harrison), William Hutt (Cockridge), Charles Den- nis (Blitzstein), Paulle Clark (Eva Ran- dall), Tiiu Leek (Zara).

Jeff Conaway, best known for his role as an aspiring actor in TV's "Taxi," has made a fortune in the high-tech industry. When he meets beautiful model Irena Ferris, he temporarily puts aside all of his electronic gadgets to help her become "The Dreamworld Girl—the face of the 80's." As is usual in these climb-to-fame movies, Ferris has to roll around in the gutter some to make it to the top.

579. *Crack House* (1989, 21st Cen- tury–Fox, 90m, c). P Jim Silverman & Joan Weidman, D Michael Fischa, W Blake Schaefer (based on a story by Jack Silverman), PH Arledge Armenaki, M Michael Piccirillo, ED Claudia Finkle, PD Keith Barrett.

LP Jim Brown (Steadman), Anthony Geary (Dockett), Richard Roundtree (Lt. Johnson), Cheryl Kay (Melissa), Gregg Gomez Thomsen (Rick Morales), Angel Tompkins (Mother), Clyde R. Jones (B.T.).

This rip-off of *Colors* is a violent and loathsome examination of gang violence, featuring feuds between blacks and Chi- canos.

580. *Crackers* (1984, Universal, 92m, c). P Edward Lewis & Robert Cortes, D Louis Malle, W Jeffrey Fiskin (based on the movie *Big Deal on Madonna Street* by Suso Cecchi D'Amico, Mario Monicelli, Agenore Incrocci & Furio Scarpelli), PH Laszlo Kovacs, M Paul Chihara, ED Suzanne Baron, PD John J. Lloyd.

LP Donald Sutherland (Weslake), Jack Warden (Garvey), Sean Penn (Dil- lard), Wallace Shawn (Turtle), Larry Riley (Boardwalk), Trinidad Silva (Ramon), Christine Baranski (Maxine), Charlaine Woodard (Jasmine), Tasia Valenza (Maria), Irwin Corey (Lazzarelli).

Louis Malle invites audiences to a Thanksgiving dinner. He supplies the turkey with this unfunny caper comedy about down-on-their-luck San Francisco misfits who turn to crime to better their lot. It's based on *Big Deal on Madonna Street,* but has none of the charm of the 1956 movie.

Cracking Up see Smorgasbord

581. *Crazy Fat Ethel II* (1987, West- ern-World, 60m, c). P,D,W&ED Nick Phillips.

LP Priscilla Alden (Ethel), Jane Lam- bert (Hope Bartholomew), Michael Flood, Robert Copple.

Here's a sure cult film. It's a belated se- quel to Phillips' 1974 bizarre romp, *Criminally Insane.* In the latter film, Priscilla Alden is a gross, eating-machine psycho. By the end of the movie she is justifiably put into a nut-house. Now due to drastic state budget cuts, she's been released to a half-way house—but she's not half-way improved.

Crazy Horse see Friends, Lovers and Lunatics

Crazy Legs see Off the Mark

582. *Crazy Moon* (1986, Miramax, Canada, 90m, c). P&W Tom Berry & Stefan Wodoslawsky, D Allan Eastman, PH Savas Kalogeras, M Lou Forestieri, ED Franco Battista, AD Guy Lalande.

LP Kiefer Sutherland (Brooks), Va- nessa Vaughan (Anne), Peter Spence (Cleveland), Ken Pogue (Alec), Eve Na- pier (Mimi), Sean McCann (Anne's Fa- ther), Bronwen Mantel (Anne's Mother).

Gentle, withdrawn, alienated teen Kiefer Sutherland finds himself in a romance with a much older deaf sales-woman, Vanessa Vaughan.

583. *Creator* (1985, Universal, 108m, c). P Stephen Friedman, D Ivan Passer, W Jeremy Leven (based on his novel), PH Robbie Greenberg, M Sylvester Levay, ED Richard Chew.

LP Peter O'Toole (Dr. Harry Wolper), Mariel Hemingway (Meli), Vincent Spano (Boris Lapkin), Virginia Madsen (Barbara Spencer), David Ogden Stiers (Dr. Sid Kulenbeck), John Dehner (Paul), Karen Kopins (Lucy), Kenneth Tigar (Pavlo).

Scientist Peter O'Toole has been trying for 30 years to bring his wife, who died in childbirth, back to life. He is oblivious to the interest in him of nymphomaniac un-dergraduate Mariel Hemingway. When his lab assistant Vincent Spano pleads with O'Toole to help him bring his lady love Virginia Madsen out of a coma, Peter instructs the lad that love alone will do the trick. Sure enough, Madsen awakens. O'Toole gives up his crusade and turns his attention to Hemingway.

584. *Creature* (1985, TransWorld, 97m, c, aka *Titan Find*). P William G. Dunn, Jr. & William Malone, D Malone, W Malone & Alan Reed, PH Harry Mathias, M Thomas Chase & Steve Rucker, ED Bette Cohen, PD Bob Sko-tak, SE L.A. Effects Group.

LP Stan Ivar (Mike Davison), Wendy Schaal (Beth Sladen), Lyman Ward (David Perkins), Robert Jaffe (Jon Fennel), Annette McCarthy (Dr. Oliver), Diane Salinger (Melanie Bryce), Marie Laurin (Susan Delambre), Klaus Kinski (Hans Rudy Hofner).

In this *Alien* imitator, set on Saturn's moon Titan, an American expedition led by Lyman Ward is investigating the dis-appearance of a previous spaceship. They discover what the earlier expedition found, a creature who sucks the life from its victims, turning them into zombies who do its bidding.

The Creature Wasn't Nice* see *Spaceship

585. *The Creeper* (1980, Coast, Can-ada, 100m, c, aka *Rituals*). P Lawrence Dane, D Peter Carter, W Ian Sutherland.

LP Hal Gammell, Lawrence Dane, Robin Gammell, Ken James, Gary Reineke, Peter Carter.

In this cheap version of *Deliverance,* four physicians take a vacation in the woods and are terrorized by some nasty locals.

586. *Creepozoids* (1987, Urban Clas-sics, 71m, c). P David De Coteau & John Showalter, D De Coteau, W Buford Hau-ser & De Coteau, PH Thomas Callaway, ED Miriam Preissel, M Guy Moon.

LP Linnea Quigley (Bianca), Ken Abraham (Butch), Michael Aranda (Jesse), Richard Hawkins (Jake), Kim McKamy (Kate), Joi Wilson (Scientist).

Seeking to avoid acid rain, five army deserters take refuge in a scientific lab, becoming the victims of a mutated mon-ster lurking there.

587. *Creepshow* (1982, Warner, 129m, c). P Richard P. Rubinstein, D George A. Romero, W Stephen King, PH Michael Gornick, M John Harrison, ED Michael Spolan, Pasquale Buba, Romero & Paul Hirsch, PD Cletus Anderson.

LP Hal Holbrook (Henry), Adrienne Barbeau (Wilma), Fritz Weaver (Dexter), Leslie Nielsen (Richard), Carrie Nye (Sylvia), E.G. Marshall (Upson), Viveca Lindfors (Aunt Bedelia), Ed Harris (Hank), Ted Danson (Harry), Stephen King (Jordy).

Director George A. Romero and screenwriter Stephen King make their homage to the E.C. comic books of the 50s such as "Tales of the Crypt." The film consists of five vignettes, each with a comic book format. The results are decidedly mixed.

588. *Creepshow 2* (1987, New World, 89m, c). P David Ball, D Michael Gor-nick, W George A. Romero (based on stories by Stephen King), PH Dick Hart & Tom Hurwitz, M Les Reed & Rick Wakeman, ED Peter Weatherly, PD Bruce Miller.

LP Lois Chiles (Annie Lansing), George Kennedy (Ray Spruce), Dorothy Lamour (Martha Spruce), Tom Savini (The Creep), Domenick John (Boy Billy), Frank S. Salsedo (Ben Whitemoon), Holt McCallany (Sam Whitemoon), David Holbrook (Fatso Gribbens), Tom Wright (The Hitchhiker), Dan Kamin (Indian), Stephen King (Truck Driver).

None of the three Stephen King stories save this boring horror film. The first episode, "Old Chief Wood'nhead," is about a cigar-store Indian that comes to life to avenge the deaths of general store proprietors George Kennedy and Dorothy Lamour. In the second take, "The Raft," four pot-smoking college students are attacked by a carnivorous oil slick. The final story, "The Hitchhiker," has Lois Chiles as a cheating wife who is forced to kill black hitchhiker Tom Wright over and over again.

Cries in the Night see Funeral Home

589. *Crime of Honor* (1987, Academy Home Entertainment, Germany, 95m, c). D John Goldschmidt, W Peter Prince, PH Wolfgang Treu, M Carl Davis, ED Richard Key.

LP David Suchet (Stephen Dyer), Maria Schneider (Madeline Dyer), Anne-Marie Blanc (Meman), Reinhard Glemnitz (Weipel), Georges Claisse (Dulourd), Dietmar Schonherr (Junger), Robert Freitag (Meser), Michael Gempart (Ehrill), Jurgen Brugger (Dr. Bauer).

David Suchet, a high ranking official with an international pharmaceutical company, is about to retire to become a pig farmer in Italy. He has seen so many ethical violations by his company that he blows the whistle. His reward is losing everything, culminating in the death of his wife Maria Schneider, driven to suicide by Suchet's revenge-seeking former employer.

590. *Crime Zone* (1988, Concorde, 93m, c). P&D Luis Llosa, W Daryl Haney, PH Cusi Barrio, M Rick Conrad, ED William Flicker, SE Fernando Vasquez de Velasco.

LP David Carradine (Jason), Peter Nelson (Bone), Sherilyn Fenn (Helen), Michael Shaner (Creon), Orlando Sacha (Alexi), Don Manor (J.D.), Alfredo Calder (Cruz), Jorgo Bustamante (Hector).

In some postwar futuristic society, Peter Nelson and Sherilyn Fenn are subgrades induced to turn to a life of crime by "first tier" bigshot David Carradine. The latter is in reality a government operative who recruits criminals to give the police something to do. Nelson and Fenn, however, seem to have a talent for crime, and give the cops all the practice in their craft that they could hope for.

591. *Crimes and Misdemeanors* (1989, Orion, 104m, c). P Robert Greenhut, D&W Woody Allen† (for both directing and original screenplay), PH Sven Nykvist, M Various Artists, ED Susan E. Morse, PD Santo Loquasto.

LP Martin Landau† (Judah Rosenthal), Anjelica Huston (Dolores Paley), Woody Allen (Cliff Stern), Alan Alda (Lester), Mia Farrow (Halley Reed), Jerry Orbach (Jack Rosenthal), Claire Bloom (Miriam Rosenthal), Joanna Gleason (Wendy Stern), Sam Waterston (Ben), Caroline Aaron (Barbara), Martin Bergmann (Prof. Louis Levy), Jenny Nichols (Jenny), Stephanie Roth (Sharon Rosenthal), David S. Howard (Sol Rosenthal), Daryl Hannah (Lisa), Anna Berger (Aunt May).

Woody Allen has come up with another winner in this dramatic comedy, featuring Martin Landau as a successful Manhattan ophthalmologist, honored for his work in behalf of science and humanity. He has a little problem. His long-time mistress Anjelica Huston hysterically insists that he divorce his wife Claire Bloom and marry her. She threatens to go to his wife Bloom and not only reveal his infidelities but also some embezzlement activities. His black sheep brother Jerry Orbach suggests that his underworld connections can be useful in getting rid of Huston. Interspersed with Landau's story is that of a gloomy producer of unseen documentaries, Allen, who is in love with would-be television producer Mia Farrow, but loses her to TV big shot Alan Alda, wonderful in a role of an egotistical phony. The picture belongs to Landau, who gives an award-worthy performance as a selfish man who becomes increasingly corrupt and even learns to live with his guilt and the evil he has condoned and arranged. Allen provides the comical side of the film with numerous wonderful zingers. The film should have been nominated for an Academy Award.

592. *Crimes of Passion* (1984, New World, 102m, c). P Barry Sandler & Donald P. Borchers, D Ken Russell, W Sandler, PH Dick Bush, M Rick Wakeman, ED Brian Tagg, PD Richard MacDonald.

LP Kathleen Turner (Joanna Crane/

China Blue), Anthony Perkins (Rev. Peter Shayne), John Laughlin (Bobby Grady), Annie Potts (Amy Grady), Bruce Davison (Hopper), Norman Burton (Bateman), James Crittenden (Tom), Peggy Feury (Adrian).

By day Kathleen Turner is a highly paid fashion designer. By night, she's a costly prostitute whose specialty is providing the kinky for an assortment of weird "johns." Anthony Perkins is a street-corner evangelist who becomes obsessed with Turner. The film itself is another example of director Ken Russell's self-indulgence and is pretty disgusting.

593. *Crimes of the Heart* (1986, De Laurentiis, 105m, c). P Freddie Fields, D Bruce Beresford, W Beth Henley (based on her play), PH Dante Spinotti, M Georges Delerue, ED Anne Goursaud, PD Ken Adam.

LP Diane Keaton (Lenny Magrath), Jessica Lange (Meg Magrath), Sissy Spacek (Babe Magrath), Sam Shepard (Doc Porter), Tess Harper† (Chick Boyle), David Carpenter (Barnette Lloyd), Hurt Hatfield (Old Granddaddy), Beeson Carroll (Zachery Botrelle), Jean Willard (Lucille Botrelle), Tom Mason (Uncle Watson), Gregory Travis (Willie Jay).

This Southern Gothic black comedy allows four very fine actresses to have a field day. Jessica Lange, who has a failed marriage and failed career as a singer, returns home when her sister Sissy Spacek is accused of attempting to murder her husband. He had gotten in the way of her planned affair with 15-year-old black boy Gregory Travis. She shoots hubby and goes off to the kitchen to make lemonade, even offering some to the poor man writhing in agony on the floor. Third sister Diane Keaton is a 40-year-old spinster, whose wardrobe, laugh, makeup and attitude likely will keep her one for the rest of her life. Spacek has a thing for suicide, but she's as inept at killing herself as she was in eliminating her husband. Lange takes time out to explore the possibility of revising a romance with married ex-boyfriend Sam Shepard. They decide not to but that doesn't prevent them from having a grand old blast with a whiskey bottle. Then there's Tess Harper, superb

as the disapproving cousin of the three sisters.

594. *Crimewave* (1985, Embassy, 83m, c, aka *The XYZ Murders: Broken Hearts and Noses*). P Robert Tapert, D Sam Raimi, W Joel Coen, Ethan Coen & Raimi, PH Claudia Sills, M Arlon Ober, ED Michael Kelly.

LP Louise Lasser (Mrs. Trend), Paul L. Smith (Crush), Brion James (Coddish), Sheree J. Wilson (Nancy), Edward R. Pressman (Ernest Trend), Bruce Campbell (The Heel), Reed Birney (Vic), Hamid Dana (Donald Odegard).

When Louise Lasser witnesses the murder of her business partner by Brion James and Paul L. Smith, the two add her to the list of people to be exterminated. They had been hired by Lasser's husband Edward R. Pressman. In the end, both he and Lasser are gleefully assassinated in some slapstick killings.

595. *Criminal Act* (1988, Film Ventures, 93m, c, aka *Tunnels*). P Daniel Yost, D Mark Byers, W Yost, PH Roxanne di Santo, M Wayne Coster, ED M. Kathryn Campbell, PD Cole Lewis.

LP Catherine Bach (Pam Weiss), Charlene Dallas (Sharon Fields), Nicholas Guest (Ron Bellard), John Saxon (Herb), Cork Hubbert, Victor Brandt, Luis Avalos, Ray Tillotson, Rick Zumwalt, Vic Tayback.

Newspaper reporter Catherine Bach and photographer Charlene Dallas believe that there are humanoid rats in the tunnels under their apartment building. No, it's just some nasty real estate guys kidnapping and killing bums to pave the way for a multimillion-dollar redevelopment scheme.

596. *Criminal Conversation* (1980, BAC Films, Ireland, 61m, c). D Kieran Hickey, W Hickey & Philip Davison, PH Sean Corcoran, ED J. Patrick Duffner.

LP Emmet Bergin (Frank), Deirdre Donnelly (Margaret), Peter Caffrey (Charlie), Leslie Lalor (Bernadette), Kate Thompson (Susan), Garrett Keogh (Student).

Having had a wee bit too much to drink at a Christmas Eve party, an Irishman tells all present that he's been having an affair with his friend's wife. The title refers to the Irish legal term describing the illicit activity. A cuckolded husband may sue the other man for damages.

597. *Criminal Law* (1989, Hemdale Film Corp., 112m, c). P Robert Maclean & Hilary Heath, D Martin Campbell, W Mark Kasdan, PH Philip Meheux, ED Christopher Wimble, PD Curtis Schnell.

LP Gary Oldman (Ben Chase), Kevin Bacon (Martin Thiel), Karen Young (Ellen Faulkner), Joe Don Baker (Det. Mesel), Tess Harper (Det. Stillwell), Ron Lea (Gary Hull), Karen Woolridge (Claudia Curwen).

The day after Boston lawyer Gary Oldman gains an acquittal for babyfaced Kevin Bacon on a murder and rape charge, another woman suffers the same fate. The modus operandi is the same as in the case involving Bacon. Sure enough Oldman has set free a psychotic killer. What can he do about it?

598. *Critical Condition* (1987, Paramount, 99m, c). P Ted Field & Robert Cort, D Michael Apted, W Denis Hamill & John Hamill (based on a story by Denis Hamill, John Hamill & Alan Swyer), PH Ralf D. Bode, M Alan Silvestri, ED Robert K. Lambert, PD John Lloyd.

LP Richard Pryor (Eddie), Rachel Ticotin (Rachel), Ruben Blades (Louis), Joe Mantegna (Chambers), Bob Dishy (Dr. Foster), Sylvia Miles (Maggie), Joe Dallesandro (Stucky), Randall "Tex" Cobb (Box), Bob Saget (Dr. Joffe), Garrett Morris (Helicopter Junkie).

In this underinteresting mish-mash, Richard Pryor is a hustler in trouble both with the law and the mob. If he is sent to prison, he knows that the gang has plans to eliminate him. To forestall this possibility he feigns insanity and is assigned to a mental hospital. During a blackout, Pryor is mistaken for a physician. He wins over everyone at the hospital with his behavior, becoming a hero when he captures escaped killer Joe Dallesandro. The script and jokes are feeble and predictable. Where, oh where, did funnyman Pryor go?

599. *Critters* (1986, New Line Cinema, 86m, c). P Rupert Harvey, D Stephen Herek, W Herek, Domonic Muir & Don Opper, PH Tim Suhrstedt, M David Newman, ED Larry Bock, PD Gregg Fonseca, Critters Effects Chiodo Brothers Prods.

LP Dee Wallace Stone (Helen Brown), M. Emmet Walsh (Harv), Billy Green Bush (Jay Brown), Scott Grimes (Brad Brown), Nadine Van Der Velde (April Brown), Don Opper (Charles McFadden), Billy Zane (Steve Elliot).

Eight very hungry creatures escape from a distant planet and head for earth. They set down in rural Kansas, where they whiz around at high speed, biting everything in sight. It's a hilarious horror film with cult pretensions.

600. *Critters 2: The Main Course* (1988, New Line, 87m, c). P Barry Opper, D Mick Garris, W D.T. Twohy & Garris, PH Russell Carpenter, M Nicholas Pike, ED Charles Bornstein, PD Philip Dean Foreman, SE Chiodo Brothers, Marty Bresin.

LP Scott Grimes (Brad Brown), Liane Curtis (Megan Morgan), Don Opper (Charlie McFadden), Barry Corbin (Harv), Tom Hodges (Wesley), Sam Anderson (Mr. Morgan), Lindsay Parker (Cindy Morgan), Herta Ware (Nana), Terrence Mann (Ug), Roxanne Kernohan (Lee).

The disgusting little creatures are back and are as hungry as ever. Scott Grimes needs the help of bounty hunters Terrence Mann and Roxanne Kernohan to rout them.

601. *"Crocodile" Dundee* (1986, Paramount, Australia, 105m, c). P John Cornell, D Peter Faiman, W Paul Hogan, Ken Shadie & Cornell (based on a story by Hogan), PH Russell Boyd, M Peter Best, ED David Stiven, PD Graham Grace Walker.

LP Paul Hogan (Mick "Crocodile" Dundee), Linda Kozlowski (Sue Charlton), John Meillon (Walter Reilly), David Gulpilil (Neville Bell), Ritchie Singer (Con), Maggie Blinco (Ida), Steve Rackman (Donk), Gerry Skilton (Nugget), Terry Gill (Duffy), Mark Blum (Richard Mason).

Paul Hogan could be a Capra hero, a hick from the sticks (this time the outback of Australia), arriving in the big city (New York) where his naive innocence is more than a match for the corrupt city slickers. The crocodile poacher is quite a free spirit, always ready to take a "walk-about." He proves irresistible to lovely

New York journalist Linda Kozlowski and, judging by the box-office receipts, to the entire movie-going world as well.

602. *"Crocodile" Dundee II* (1988, Paramount, 110m, c). P John Cornell & Jane Scott, D Cornell, W Paul Hogan & Brett Hogan, PH Russell Boyd, M Peter Best, ED David Stiven, PD Lawrence Eastwood.

LP Paul Hogan (Mick "Crocodile" Dundee), Linda Kozlowski (Sue Charlton), John Meillon (Walter Reilly), Ernie Dingo (Charlie), Hechter Ubarry (Rico), Juan Fernandez (Miguel), Charles Dutton (Leroy), Kenneth Welsh (Brannigan).

The huge success of *"Crocodile" Dundee* guaranteed a sequel, but as is too often the case, it didn't guarantee a film as amusing and charming as the first. Paul Hogan is living with Linda Kozlowski in Manhattan, but when his slinky playmate is menaced by Colombian drug dealers, the still fancy dresser is able to pick off the thugs one-by-one after they pursue Paul and Linda back to Australia.

603. *Cross Country* (1983, MGM/United Artists, Canada, 95m, c). P Pieter Kroonenburg & David J. Patterson, D Paul Lynch, W Logan N. Danforth & William Gray (based on a novel by Herbert Kastle), PH Rene Verzier, M Chris Rea, ED Nick Rotundo, PD Michel Proulx.

LP Richard Beymer (Evan Bley), Nina Axelrod (Lois Hayes), Michael Ironside (Det. Sgt. Ed Roersch), Brent Carver (John Forrest), Michael Kane (Harry Burns), August Schellenberg (Glen Cosgrove).

When a call girl is savagely murdered, suspicion falls on Richard Beymer. As he flees across Canada, just ahead of cop Michael Ironside, Beymer picks up some kinky hitchhikers.

604. *Cross Creek* (1983, Universal, 127m, c). P Robert B. Radnitz, D Martin Ritt, W Dalene Young (based on the book by Marjorie Kinnan Rawlings), PH John A. Alonzo, M Leonard Rosenman, ED Sidney Levin, PD Walter Scott Herndon.

LP Mary Steenburgen (Marjorie Kinnan Rawlings), Rip Torn (Marsh Turner), Peter Coyote (Norton Baskin), Dana Hill (Ellie Turner), Alfre Woodard (Geechee), Joanna Miles (Mrs. Turner), Ike Eisenmann (Paul).

Possessor of one of the most appealing faces in movies today, Mary Steenburgen nicely plays the real life role of author Marjorie Kinnan Rawlings *(The Yearling),* who in an attempt to "find herself" leaves her home in a big city to live in the Florida Everglades with simple folk.

605. *Cross My Heart* (1987, Universal, 96m, c). P Lawrence Kasdan, D Armyan Bernstein, W Bernstein & Gail Parent, PH Thomas del Ruth, M Bruce Broughton, ED Mia Goldman, PD Lawrence G. Paull.

LP Martin Short (David), Annette O'Toole (Kathy), Paul Reiser (Bruce), Joanna Kerns (Nancy), Jessica Puscas (Jessica), Lee Arenberg (Parking Attendant), Corinne Bohrer (Susan), Michael D. Simms (Stud).

Martin Short and Annette O'Toole both have lied about themselves to the other. They are having their third date, which will determine if they will become a sexual couple. Short lies about his job: he's been fired; his car and apartment belong to Paul Reiser. She hasn't mentioned her seven-year-old daughter or the fact she's been around the block a few times. It all works out for them as they learn the truth about each other. Only audiences lose in this fumbling comedy attempt.

606. *Crossing Delancey* (1988, Warner, 97m, c). P Michael Nozik, D Joan Micklin Silver, W Susan Sandler (based on her play), PH Theo Van de Sande, M Paul Chihara, ED Rick Shaine, PD Dan Leigh.

LP Amy Irving (Isabelle "Izzy" Grossman), Reizl Bozyk (Bubbie Kantor), Peter Riegert (Sam Posner), Jeroen Krabbe (Anton Maes), Sylvia Miles (Hannah Mandelbaum), Suzzy Roche (Marilyn), George Martin (Lionel), John Bedford Lloyd (Nick), Claudia Silver (Cecilia Monk).

In sort of a Jewish answer to the romantic comedy *Moonstruck,* Amy Irving is an attractive, intelligent Jewish woman in her 30s. Her grandmother, delightfully played by Reizl Bozyk, employs gloriously grotesque Sylvia Miles as a marriage broker to find a husband for Irving. Her choice is pickle merchant Peter Riegert. Irving is having none of this old-fashioned means of marriage making. But as things work out, she comes to realize that this very decent and loving man is the right one for her after all.

607. *Crossover Dreams* (1985, Miramax, 86m, c). P Manuel Arce, D Leon Ichaso, W Arce & Ichaso, PH Claudio Chea, M Mauricio Smith, ED Gary Karr, PD Octavio Soler.

LP Ruben Blades (Rudy Veloz), Shawn Elliot (Orlando), Elizabeth Pena (Liz Garcia), Virgilio Marti (Chico Rabala), Tom Signorelli (Lou Rose), Frank Robles (Ray Soto), Joel Diamond (Neil Silver).

The film tells the familiar story of the high price which must be paid to become a star. Talented Latino musician Ruben Blades goes for the big time by crossing over to popular music. With success he cuts himself off from his East Harlem ties and friends. Things don't go according to plan and he finds himself returning to his roots.

608. *Crossroads* (1986, Columbia, 98m, c). P Mark Carliner, D Walter Hill, W John Fusco, PH John Bailey, M Ry Cooder, ED Freeman Davies.

LP Ralph Macchio (Eugene Martone), Joe Seneca (Willie Brown), Jami Gertz (Frances), Joe Morton (Scratch's Assistant), Robert Judd (Scratch), Steve Vai (Jack Butler), Dennis Lipscomb (Lloyd), Tim Russ (Robert Johnson).

Ambitious bluesman Ralph Macchio "goes down to the crossroads" to make a deal with the devil for fame and fortune. Veteran blues singer and harp player Joe Seneca is his mentor. The score by Ry Cooder featuring the harmonica playing of Sonny Terry makes this film special.

609. *Cruising* (1980, United Artists, 106m, c). P Jerry Weintraub, D&W William Friedkin (based on the novel by Gerald Walker), PH James Contner, M Jack Nitzsche, ED Bud Smith, PD Bruce Weintraub.

LP Al Pacino (Steve Burns), Paul Sorvino (Capt. Edelson), Karen Allen (Nancy), Richard Cox (Stuart Richards), Don Scardino (Ted Bailey), Joe Spinell (Patrolman DiSimone), Jay Acovone (Skip Lee), Randy Jurgensen (Det. Lefransky), Barton Heyman (Dr. Rifkin), Gene Davis (Da Vinci).

Al Pacino makes far too few movies to waste his considerable talents on such zeroes as this story about a New York undercover cop looking for a homosexual killer in the slimy, sick gay S&M world. It's disgusting voyeurism, intent on repulsively presenting all the perversions that the movie makers can imagine.

610. *Crusoe* (1989, Island Pictures, 95m, c). P Andrew Braunsberg, D Caleb Deschanel, W Christopher Logue & Walon Green (based on the novel by Daniel Defoe and the memoirs of Alexander Selkirk), PH Tom Pinter, M Michael Kamen, ED Humphrey Dixon, PD Velco Despotovic.

LP Aidan Quinn (Robinson Crusoe), Ade Sapara (The Warrior), Warren Clarke (Capt. Lee), Hepburn Graham (Lucky), Jimmy Nail (Tarik), Tim Spall (Rev. Milne), Shane Rimmer (Mr. Mather).

In this version of the Crusoe story Aidan Quinn is an early 19th century Virginia slavetrader who is shipwrecked while en route to West Africa to pick up more slaves. He doesn't run into anyone he calls Friday. He does encounter two cannibals, one whom he calls "Lucky" and the other who is not given a name. The tropical scenery is beautiful, but Quinn, director Caleb Deschanel and screenwriter Walon Green don't seem to have anything to say.

611. *Cry Freedom* (1987, Universal, GB, 154m, c). P Sir Richard Attenborough, Norman Spencer & John Briley, D Attenborough, W Briley (based on the books *Biko* and *Asking for Trouble* by Donald Woods), PH Ronnie Taylor, M George Fenton & Jonas Gwangwa†, ED Lesley Walker, PD Stuart Craig, M/L "Cry Freedom" by Fenton & Gwangwa†.

LP Denzel Washington† (Stephen Biko), Kevin Kline (Donald Woods), Penelope Wilton (Wendy Woods), Kate Hardie (Jane Woods), John Thaw (Kruger), Zakes Mokae (Father Kani), John Hargreaves (Bruce), Alec McCowen (Acting High Commissioner), Kevin McNally (Ken), Ian Richardson (State Prosecutor), Timothy West (Capt. de Wet).

Told through the eyes and ears of white South African journalist Kevin Kline, the film is based on the true story of South African activist and leader of the Black Consciousness Movement, Stephen Biko, brilliantly played by Denzel Washington.

Biko died from beatings while in police custody in 1977.

612. *A Cry in the Dark* (1988, Warner, 121m, c). P Verity Lambert, D Fred Schepisi, W Robert Caswell & Schepisi (based on the book *Evil Angels* by John Bryson), PH Ian Baker, M Bruce Smeaton, ED Jill Bilcock, PD Wendy Dickson & George Liddle, AD Brian Edmonds.

LP Meryl Streep† (Lindy Chamberlain), Sam Neill (Michael Chamberlain), Bruce Myles (Barker), Charles Tingwell (Justice Muirhead), Nick Tate (Charlwood), Neil Fitzpatrick (Phillips), Maurie Fields (Barritt), Lewis Fitz-Gerald (Tipple).

In this true story, Meryl Streep portrays the humorless wife of Seventh Day Adventist pastor Sam Neil. In 1980, while on a visit to the monumental Ayers Rock in the outback, Australia's most popular tourist attraction, Streep's nine-week-old baby is apparently carried off by a dingo with no trace of the infant ever found. Sentiment grows, spread by rumor and a news media which can't leave the story alone, that Streep murdered the child. She is charged with murder, and her husband is named an accessory after the fact. Streep is found guilty and sentenced to life imprisonment. The controversy surrounding the actual case raged on for eight years.

613. *Cry Wilderness* (1987, Visto International, 95m, c). P Philip Yordan & Jay Schlossberg-Cohen, D Schlossberg-Cohen, W Yordan, PH Joseph D. Urbanczyk, M Fritz Heede.

LP Eric Foster (Paul Cooper), Maurice Grandmaison (Will Cooper), Griffin Casey (Morgan), John Tallman (Jim), Faith Clift (Dr. Helen Foster).

Eric Foster has befriended Bigfoot and must prevent his hairy pal from being slaughtered by a gun-happy trio.

614. *Crystal Heart* (1987, New World, 103m, c). P Carlos Vasallo, D Gil Bettman, W Linda Shayne (based on a story by Alberto Vazquez-Figueroa), PH Alexander [Alejando] Ulloa, M Joel Goldsmith, ED Nicholas Wentworth, PD Jose Maria Alarcon.

LP Lee Curreri (Christopher Newley), Tawny Kitaen (Alley Daniels), Lloyd Bochner (Frank Newley), May Heatherly (Diana Newley), Simon Andreu (Jean-Claude), Marina Saura (Justine), LaGena Lookabill (Jasper), Emiliano Redondo (Dr. Navarro).

Lee Curreri is confined to a sterilized environment due to a genetic inability to produce natural immunization. His parents are quite wealthy and surround him with electronic equipment. He develops his musical talent and corresponds with rising rock singer Tawny Kitaen. They meet and fall in love. Before the movie ends Curreri breaks out of his glass prison. The young lovers have a brief idyllic interlude before our hero expires.

615. *Crystalstone* (1988, TMS, 103m, c). P John Williams & Britt Lomond, D&W Antonio Pelaez, PH John Stephens, M Fernando Uribe, ED Arnold Baker, PD George Costello.

LP Kamlesh Gupta (Pablo), Laura Jane Goodwin (Maria), Frank Grimes (Captain), Edward Kelsey (Hook), Sydney Bromley (Old Man), Terence Bayler (Policeman), Ann Way (Housekeeper), Helen Ryan (Aunt).

Rather than be separated when their mother dies, at the turn of the century, ten-year-old Kamlesh Gupta and six-year-old Laura Jane Goodwin run away from their home in Spain to seek the fabled Crystalstone. They have run-ins with pirate Edward Kelsey along the way.

Cuba Crossing see Sweet Dirty Tony

616. *Cujo* (1983, Warner, 91m, c). P Daniel H. Blatt & Robert Singer, D Lewis Teague, W Don Carlos Dunaway & Lauren Currier (based on the novel by Stephen King), PH Jan De Bont, M Charles Bernstein, ED Neil Travis.

LP Dee Wallace (Donna), Danny Pintauro (Tad), Daniel Hugh-Kelly (Vic), Christopher Stone (Steve), Ed Lauter (Joe), Kaiulani Lee (Charity), Billy Jacoby (Brett), Mills Watson (Gary), Sandy Ward (Bannerman).

Stephen King's story of a mother and her son terrorized by a rabid Saint Bernard bitten by bats is bound to keep viewers on the edge of their seats. Still the humans are not particularly sympathetic and the poor dog is unwillingly turned into a snarling, drooling monster.

617. *Curfew* (1989, New World, 84m, c). P Julia Philips, D Gary Winick, W Kevin Kennedy, PH Makoto Watanabe,

M Cengiz Yaltkaya, ED Carole Kravetz.

LP Kyle Richards (Stephanie Davenport), Wendell Wellman (Ray Perkins), John Putch (Bob Perkins), Jean Brooks (Megan), Frank Miller (Walter), Peter Nelson, Nori Morgan, Bert Remsen, Christopher Knight.

Wendell Wellman and John Putch are escaped prisoners who take hostage the family of the D.A. who sent them up. Kyle Richards is the D.A.'s sexy daughter who must be home by 10 p.m. according to her strict parent's rules. The brothers psychologically and physically torture their captives, who in turn try to turn the siblings against each other.

618. *The Curse* (1987, TransWorld, 90m, c, aka *The Farm*). P Ovidio G. Assonitis, D David Keith, W David Chaskin, PH Robert D. Forges, M Franco Micalizzi, ED Claudio M. Cutry, PD Frank Vanorio, SE Kevin Erham & Mark Moller.

LP Wil Wheaton (Zachary Hayes), Claude Akins (Nathan Hayes), Malcolm Danare (Cyrus), Cooper Huckabee (Dr. Alan Forbes), John Schneider (Carl Willis), Amy Wheaton (Alice Hayes), Steve Carlisle (Charley Davidson), Kathleen Jordan Gregory (Frances Hayes).

In this nauseating horror story, young Wil and Amy Wheaton live on a lonely Tennessee farm with their sexually frustrated mother Kathleen Jordan Gregory, their religious fanatic and ultraconservative stepfather Claude Akins, and his cruel son Malcolm Danare. A strange meteorite lands on the farm, melts into the ground, contaminating the food and water and turning all except the youngsters into pus-oozing homicidal monsters.

619. *Curse II: The Bite* (1989, Viva/Towa, US/Italy/Japan, 98m, c). P Ovidio Assonitis, D Fred Goodwin, W Susan Zelouf & Federico Prosperi, PH Roberto D'Ettore Piazzoli, M Carlo Maria Cordio, ED Claudio Cutry, PD William Jett.

LP Jill Schoelen (Lisa), J. Eddie Peck (Clark), Jamie Farr (Harry), Savina Gersak (Iris), Bo Svenson (Sheriff), Marianne Muellerleile (Big Flo), Al Fann (Gas jockey), Sidney Lassick (George).

While driving to Albuquerque along a short-cut, J. Eddie Peck is bitten by a snake. He is given the wrong antidote by Jamie Farr, a traveling salesman, who happens along and for some reason poses as a physician. Due to nuclear testing and waste dumping in the area, Peck's arm mutates into a giant snake's head that attacks people. It's not a subtle story.

620. *Curse of the Pink Panther* (1983, MGM/United Artists, 110m, c). P Blake Edwards & Tony Adams, D Edwards, W Blake Edwards & Geoffrey Edwards, PH Dick Bush, M Henry Mancini, ED Ralph E. Winters & Bob Hathaway, PD Peter Mullins.

LP David Niven (Sir Charles Litton), Ted Wass (Clifton Sleigh), Robert Wagner (George Litton), Herbert Lom (Dreyfus), Joanna Lumley (Chandra), Capucine (Lady Litton), Robert Loggia (Bruno), Harvey Korman (Prof. Balls), Leslie Ash (Juleta Shane), Peter Arne (Col. Bufoni).

Blake Edwards should be ashamed of himself. This tasteless movie is a ghoulish series of outtakes from earlier Pink Panther movies starring the deceased Peter Sellers. Not content with one act of grave robbing, Edwards had Rich Little dub David Niven's voice when the actor died.

621. *Curtains* (1983, Simcom, Canada, 90m, c). P Peter R. Simpson, D Jonathan Stryker, W Robert Guza, Jr., PH Robert Paynter & Fred Guthe, M Paul Zaza, ED Michael MacLaverty, PD Roy Forge Smith.

LP John Vernon (Jonathan), Samantha Eggar (Samantha), Linda Thorson (Brooke), Anne Ditchburn (Laurian), Lynne Griffin (Patti O'Connor), Sandra Warren (Tara), Lesleh Donaldson (Christie).

Actress Samantha Eggar gets herself committed to a mental institution to research her next role. Her producer and husband John Vernon sees that she stays committed. He brings in six young starlets to his home, subjecting them to various forms of sexual harassment, promising them that they will replace Eggar. A mad slasher shows up and knocks off the girls one by one.

622. *Cutter and Bone* (1981, United Artists, 105m, c, aka *Cutter's Way*). P

Paul R. Gurian, D Ivan Passer, W Jeffrey Alan Fiskin (based on the novel by Newton Thornburg), PH Jordan Cronenweth, M Jack Nitzsche, ED Caroline Ferriol.

LP Jeff Bridges (Richard Bone), John Heard (Alex Cutter), Lisa Eichhorn (Mo Cutter), Ann Dusenberry (Valerie Duran), Stephen Elliott (J.J. Cord), Arthur Rosenberg (George Swanson), Nina Van Pallandt (Woman in Hotel), Patricia Donahue (Mrs. Cord), Geraldine Baron (Susie Swanson).

Vulgar, crippled Vietnam vet John Heard, pretty boy Jeff Bridges, a man of no convictions, and Heard's wife Lisa Eichhorn, who has repressed sexual urgings for Bridges, are the main characters in this uncompromising story of friendship and heroes. Heard prods Bridges into action when the latter thinks he catches sight of a murderer, guilty of killing a girl, a crime for which Bridges almost takes the rap.

Cutter's Way see Cutter and Bone

623. *Cutting Class* (1989, Republic/ Gower Street, 90m, c). P Rudy Cohen & Donald R. Beck, D Rospo Pallenberg, W Steve Slavkin, PH Avi Karpick, M Jill Fraser, ED Natan Zahavi & Bill Butler, PD Richard Sherman.

LP Donovan Leitch (Brian Woods), Jill Schoelen (Paula Carson), Brad Pitt (Dwight Ingalls), Roddy McDowall (Dr. Dante), Brenda Lynn Klemme (Colleen), Mark Barnet, Robert Glaudini, Eric Boles, Dirk Blocker.

This film satirizes slasher films at the same time it ensures enough killings take place to satisfy real fans of the subgenre.

624. *Cyborg* (1989, Cannon, 85m, c). P Menahem Golan & Yoram Globus, D Albert Pyun, W Kitty Chalmers, PH Philip Alan Waters, M Kevin Bassinson, ED Rozanne Zingale & Scott Stevenson, PD Douglas Leonard, SE Joey DiGaetano & R.J. Hohman.

LP Jean-Claude Van Damme (Gibson Rickenbacker), Deborah Richter (Nady Simmons), Vincent Klyn (Fender Tremolo), Alex Daniels (Marshall Strat), Dayle Haddon (Pearl Prophet), Blaise Loong (Furman Vox), Rolf Muller (Brick Bardo), Haley Peterson (Haley), Terrie Batson (Mary).

In an unimaginative post-apocalypse film, Jean-Claude Van Damme takes on superevil Vincent Klyn for domination of an already devastated society, in a predictable and stupid revenge plot.

625. *Cyclone* (1987, Cinetel Films, 83m, c). P Paul Hertzberg, D Fred Olen Ray, W Paul Garson & T.L. Lankford (based on a story by Ray), PH Paul Elliot, M David A. Jackson & James Saad, AD Maxine Shepard, SE Kevin McCarthy.

LP Heather Thomas (Teri Marshall), Jeffrey Combs (Rick Davenport), Ashley Ferrare (Carla Hastings), Dar Robinson (Rolf), Martine Beswicke (Waters), Robert Quarry (Knowles), Martin Landau (Bosarian), Huntz Hall (Long John), Troy Donahue (Bob Jenkins), Michael Reagan (McCardy).

Jeffrey Combs gives his life trying to deliver his super motorcycle. Its "transformer" device provides an ultimate inexhaustible free energy source. His girlfriend Heather Thomas attempts to honor his dying request and deliver the transformer to the right people, but she is threatened by a slew of bad guys, all of whom get killed. Thomas throws the transformer away, figuring it only causes trouble.

626. *Da* (1988, Filmdallas Pictures, 102m, c). P Julie Corman, D Matt Clark, W Hugh Leonard (based on the play *Da* and novel *Home Before Night* by Leonard), PH Alar Kivilo, M Elmer Bernstein, ED Nancy Nuttal Beyda, PD Frank Conway.

LP Barnard Hughes (Da), Martin Sheen (Charlie), William Hickey (Drumm), Karl Hayden (Young Charlie), Doreen Hepburn (Mother), Hugh O'Conor (Boy Charlie), Ingrid Craigie (Polly), Joan O'Hara (Mrs. Prynne), Peter Hanly (Young Oliver).

Barnard Hughes beautifully recreates his Tony award-winning performance as the meddling father to Martin Sheen, who even in death isn't through interfering with his son's life or in giving unsought sage advice. Sheen has returned to Ireland to bury his father, and everything triggers remembrances of his platitude-spouting, maddening "Da" with whom he has always had a love-hate relationship.

While Sheen, Doreen Hepburn as his mother and William Hickey as young Charlie's employer are excellent, it's still a one-man's triumph—Hughes.

627. Dad (1989, Universal, 117m, c). P Joseph Stern & Gary David Goldberg, D&W Goldberg (based on the novel by William Wharton), PH Jan Kiesser, M James Horner, ED Eric Sears, PD Jack DeGovia, MK Dick Smith†.

LP Jack Lemmon (Jake Tremont), Ted Danson (John Tremont), Olympia Dukakis (Bette Tremont), Kathy Baker (Annie), Kevin Spacey (Mario), Ethan Hawke (Billy), Zakes Mokae (Dr. Chad), J.T. Walsh (Dr. Santana).

Loveable old Jack Lemmon is 78 years old. He and his wife Olympia Dukakis are infirmed. Senility is creeping up on them and they aren't putting up much of a fight against it. Ted Danson portrays their somewhat estranged son who sees it as his responsibility to move in with them and take care of them in what he assumes to be their final days. In doing so, he finds new meaning in his relationship with his own college-aged son, Ethan Hawke. Despite the cloying sweetness of the story, it's hard not to be moved by Lemmon and his performance, even though he's better than his material. Even more impressive is Danson in the first role where he really demonstrates dramatic acting ability. If you like sweet syrup, this comedy-drama is just the thing for your pancakes.

628. Daddy's Boys (1988, Concorde, 85m, c). P Roger Corman, D Joe Minion, W Daryl Haney, PH David G. Stump, M Sasha Matson, ED Norman Hollyn, PD Gabrielle Petrissans.

LP Daryl Haney (Jimmy), Laura Burkett (Christie), Raymond J. Barry (Daddy), Dan Shor (Hawk), Christian Clemenson (Otis), Ellen Gerstein (Mme. Wang), Robert V. Barron (Axelrod), Paul Linke (Traveling Salesman).

Psycho widower Raymond J. Barry and his three morose and retarded sons go on a Midwestern bank-robbing spree while he looks for a woman willing to be Mama to his brood. His son Daryl Haney teams up with hooker Laura Burkett, who may have to play more than one role in the unhappy family.

629. Daddy's Deadly Darling (1984, Aquarius, 83m, c, aka *Daddy's Girl; The Pigs*). P&D Marc Lawrence, W F.A. Foss (Lawrence), PH Glenn Roland, Jr., M Charles Bernstein, ED Irvin Goodnoff.

LP Toni Lawrence (Lynn Webster), Marc Lawrence (Zambrini), Jesse Vint (Sheriff Dan Cole), Walter Barnes (Doctor), Katherine Ross (Miss Macy), Jim Antonio, Erik Holland, Paul Hickey.

This film was shot in 1972. Why was it taken from the shelf to be released now, you may ask. We haven't the foggiest. Marc Lawrence runs a roadside cafe where he serves his customers to his pigs. He is helped in this noble endeavor by escaped mental patient Toni Lawrence. The film is garbage pigs wouldn't touch.

Daddy's Girl see Daddy's Deadly Darling

Daddy's Little Girl see She's Out of Control

630. Daffy Duck's Movie: Fantastic Island (1983, Warner, animated, 78m, c). P&D Friz Freleng, W John Dunn, David Detiege & Freleng, ED Jim Champin, PD Bob Givens & Michael Mitchell.

LP VOICES Mel Blanc, June R. Foray, Les Tremayne.

Warner Bros. has re-edited a number of their cartoons to serve as a spoof of TV's "Fantasy Island." Pull down the shades and have a good laugh while no one can see you acting so childish.

631. Daffy Duck's Quackbusters (1989, Warner, animated, 80m, c). P Steven S. Greene, D&W Greg Ford, PH Nick Vasu, Inc., M Carl Stalling, Milt Franklyn & Bill Lava, PD Robert Givens.

VOICES Mel Blanc, Mel Torme, Roy Firestone, B.J. Ward.

This enjoyable compilation film features the many vintage horror-movie spoofs. Daffy Duck inherits a fortune and forms a "ghostbusting" firm with partners Bugs Bunny and Porky Pig.

632. Daisy and Simon (1989, Falcon/Barron-Executive Prods., Australia/Hong Kong, 106m, c). P Pamela Borain & Paul Barron, D Stasch Radwanski, Jr., W Anthony Wheeler, PH John McLean, M Andrew Hagan & Morton Wilson, ED Mark Norfolk, PD Kelvin Sexton.

LP Jan Adele (Daisy), Sean Scully

(Simon), Colin McEwan (Vince), Loith Taylor (Susie), Shaunna O'Grady (Joan), Tony Wager (Cuthbert).

Dirty, self-loathing old hag Jan Adele has cared about nothing since her husband died. Sean Scully arrives on the scene from Perth. He tries to shame her into cleaning up and returning to life. Things become complicated in this fine comedy when Adele's daughter Shaunna O'Grady shows up with plans of putting away her daffy 70-year-old mother.

633.   *Dakota* (1988, Miramax, 96m, c). P Darryl J. & Frank J. Kuntz, D Fred Holmes, W Lynn & Darryl Kuntz, PH Jim Wrenn, M Chris Christian, ED Leon Seith, AD Pat O'Neill.

LP Lou Diamond Phillips (Dakota), Herta Ware (Aunt Zard), DeeDee Norton (Molly), Jordan Burton (Casey), Eli Cummins (Walt), Steven Ruge (Bo), John Hawkes (Rooster), Tom Campitelli (Rob).

Lou Diamond Phillips, who also serves as associate producer, made this film prior to *La Bamba*. He's a youth on the run who takes a job on a Texas ranch, relating to various people.

Dance Academy see Body Heat

634.   *Dance of the Damned* (1989, Concorde, 83m, c). P Andy Ruben, D Katt Shea Ruben, W Andy & Katt Shea Ruben, PH Phedon Papamichael, M Gary Stockdale, ED Carole Kravetz, PD Stephen Greenberg.

LP Starr Andreeff (Jodi Kurtz), Cyril O'Reilly (Vampire), Deborah Ann Nassar (La Donna), Maria Ford (Teacher), Athena Worthey (Ray Gun Girl), Tom Ruben (Cabby).

Stripper Starr Andreeff, despondent because a court order prevents her from visiting her young son, contemplates suicide. She gets a better offer from vampire Cyril O'Reilly, who propositions her into spending the night with him with the promise he'll kill her in the morning.

635.   *Dance or Die* (1988, City Lights, 81m, c). P Richard Pepin & Joseph Merhi, D&W Richard Munchkin, PH Peter Jensen, M John Gonzalez, ED Paul Volk, SE Judy Yonemoto & Kerby Brothers, CH Minnie Madden.

LP Ray Kieffer (Jason Chandler),

Rebecca Barrington, Georgia Neu, Jerry Cleary, Jim Williams, Jerry Tiffe, Jack Zavorak.

Released straight to video this film features Ray Kieffer as a man with but two dreams, to stay off drugs and choreograph a musical like *Flashdance*. He accomplishes both but still must deal with the death of his drug-dealing roommate and the fact that the older woman with whom he's fallen in love is a "narc."

636.   *Dance with a Stranger* (1985, 20th Century–Fox, GB, 102m, c). P Roger Randall-Cutler, D Mike Newell, W Shelagh Delaney, PH Peter Hannan, M Richard Hartley, ED Mick Audsley, PD Andrew Mollo.

LP Miranda Richardson (Ruth Ellis), Rupert Everett (David Blakely), Ian Holm (Desmond Cussen), Matthew Carroll (Andy), Tom Chadbon (Anthony Findlater), Jane Bertish (Carole Findlater), David Troughton (Cliff Davis), Paul Mooney (Clive Gunnell), Stratford Johns (Morrie Conley).

Ex-prostitute Miranda Richardson, infatuated with worthless upper-class rotter Rupert Everett, plugs him dead rather than lose him. For her crime, on July 13, 1955, she became the last woman to hang in Great Britain. One is hard pressed to feel any sympathy for anyone in this muddled movie, although the acting of Richardson, Everett and Ian Holm is excellent.

637.   *Dancers* (1987, Cannon, 99m, c). P Menahem Golan & Yoram Globus, D Herbert Ross, W Sarah Kernochan, PH Ennio Guarnieri, M Adolphe Adam & Pino Donaggio, ED William Reynolds, PD Gianni Quaranta.

LP Mikhail Baryshnikov (Anton "Tony" Sergoyev), Alessandra Ferri (Francesca), Leslie Browne (Nadine), Thomas Rall (Patrick), Lynn Seymour (Muriel), Victor Barbee (Wade), Julie Kent (Lisa), Mariangela Melato (Contessa).

Mikhail Baryshnikov is in southern Italy making a film of the ballet *Giselle*. He's quite a Don Juan, engaged to jetsetter Mariangela Melato, has had affairs with Alessandra Ferri and Leslie Browne of the dance troupe and is now inviting 17-year-old Julie Kent into his spider's web. Director Herbert Ross is not in the least subtle in making parallels between the story of the ballet and the actions of his movie characters.

638. *Dancing in the Dark* (1986, New World, Canada, 98m, c). P Anthony Kramreither, D&W Leon Marr (based on the novel by Joan Barfoot), PH Vic Sarin, M Erik Satie, ED Tom Berner.

LP Martha Henry (Edna), Neil Munro (Henry), Rosemary Dunsmore (Nurse), Richard Monette (Doctor), Elena Kudaba (Edna's Roommate), Brenda Bazinet (Susan).

Martha Henry gives a chilling performance as a housewife totally devoted to satisfying her husband's every whim and need. When he strays, she has a mental breakdown and goes to great extremes to pull him back in line.

639. *The Danger Zone* (1987, Skouras, 89m, c). P Jason Williams & Tom Friedman, D Henry Vernon, W Williams, Friedman & Karen Levitt, PH Daniel Yarussi, M Robert Etoll, ED Louis George & Susan Medaglia.

LP Robert Canada (Reaper), Jason Williams (Wade), Kris Braxton (Judy), G. Cervi (Simon), Dana Dowell (Kim), Mickey Elders (Reptile), James Ferreira (Jamie), Daniel Friedman (Needles), Cynthia Gray (Linda).

Bikers led by Robert Canada hold hostage and terrorize a group of girls. They become stranded when their car breaks down on their way to Las Vegas and a chance to appear in a talent show. Jason Williams, an undercover narcotics agent, eventually is able to rescue the girls.

640. *Danger Zone II: Reaper's Revenge* (1989, Skouras, 95m, c). P Jason Williams & Tom Friedman, D Geoffrey G. Bowers, W Dulany Ross Clements (based on a story by Williams & Friedman), PH Daniel Yarussi, M Robert Etoll, ED Susan Medaglia.

LP Jason Williams (Wade Olson), Robert Random (Reaper), Jane Higginson (Donna), Alisha Das (Francine), Walter Cox (Doug), Barne Wms. Subkoski (Rainmaker).

In this sequel to the 1987 release, taciturn biker Williams' nemesis Robert Random is released from prison on a legal technicality. The latter kidnaps Williams' girlfriend Jane Higginson, and the wheelies through the desert begin.

641. *Dangerous Curves* (1989, Lightning Pictures, 95m, c). P Mark Borde & Kenneth Raich, D David Lewis, W Michael Dugan, Michael Zand & Paul Brown, PH Lewis, M John D'Andrea, ED Bob Bring, PD Elliot Gilbert.

LP Tate Donovan (Chuck), Danielle Von Zerneck (Michelle West), Grant Heslov (Wally), Valeri Breiman (Blake Courtland), Karen Lee Scott (Shawn Brooks), Leslie Nielsen, Elizabeth Ashley, Robert Stack, Robert Klein.

Nerds Tate Donovan and Grant Heslov are off for a weekend's adventure, driving a new red Porsche. The car is stolen and the boys track it to a beauty contest in San Diego where the automobile has been put up as the grand prize. Even with several "guest stars," 'tain't funny.

642. *Dangerous Davies—The Last Detective* (1981, Maidenhead, GB, 111m, c). P Greg Smith, D Val Guest, W Guest & Leslie Thomas (based on a novel by Thomas), PH Frank Watts, M Ed Welch, ED Bill Lennie.

LP Bernard Cribbins (Dangerous Davies), Bill Maynard (Mod Lewis), Joss Ackland (Chief Inspector Yardbird), Bernard Lee (Sgt. Ben), Frank Windsor (Fred Fennell), John Leyton (Dave Boot), Maureen Lipman (Ena Lind).

Bumbling police detective Bernard Cribbins' crime detection methods are outdated, but still he tracks down the murderer in a long-unsolved killing of a teenage girl.

643. *Dangerous Liaisons*† (1988, Warner, 120m, c). P Norma Heyman, D Stephen Frears, W Christopher Hampton* (based on his play, adapted from the novel *Les Liaisons Dangereuses* by Choderlos de Laclos), PH Philipe Rousselot, M George Fenton†, ED Mick Audsley, PD Stuart Craig, AD Stuart Craig*, SD Gerard James*, COS James Acheson*.

LP Glenn Close† (Marquise de Merteuil), John Malkovich (Vicomte de Valmont), Michelle Pfeiffer† (Madame de Tourvel), Swoosie Kurtz (Madame de Volanges), Keanu Reeves (Chevalier

Danceny), Mildred Natwick (Madame de Rosemonde), Uma Thurman (Cecile de Volanges).

Glenn Close and John Malkovich devote themselves to the pursuit of sexual liaisons, not necessarily for the pleasure, but because of the power it gives them over their lovers. Close wishes Malkovich to seduce young convent girl Uma Thurman, engaged to one of Glenn's former lovers. She wishes to punish the rascal, knowing he insists on marrying a virgin. Malkovich accommodates Close, but his real target is the virtuous wife, Michelle Pfeiffer, whom he wishes to surrender to him without abandoning her high principles. Each of the major performers are excellent, but it's clearly Close's picture, giving the finest performance of her career in a film that is not only good to look at, but good-looking as well.

644. *Dangerous Love* (1988, Concorde, 94m, c). P Brad Krevoy & Steven Stabler, D&W Marty Ollstein, PH Nicholas Von Sternberg, ED Tony Lanza, PD Michael Clousen.

LP Lawrence Monoson (Gabe), Brenda Bakke (Chris), Peter Marc (Jay), Elliott Gould (Rick), Anthony Geary (Mickey).

Detective Elliott Gould is on the trail of a serial killer who videotapes the death of his pretty female victims.

645. *Dangerously Close* (1986, Cannon, 95m, c). P Harold Sobel, D Albert Pyun, W Scott Fields, John Stockwell & Marty Ross (based on a story by Ross), PH Walt Lloyd, M Various Artists, ED Dennis O'Connor, PD Marcia Hinds.

LP John Stockwell (Randy), J. Eddie Peck (Donny), Carey Lowell (Julie), Bradford Bancroft (Krooger), Don Michael Paul (Ripper), Thom Mathews (Brian), Jerry Dinome (Lang), Madison Mason (Corrigan).

In a poorly done film, rich kids in a Northern California high school decide to put some uppity poor kids in their place. The result is death and disaster.

646. *Daniel* (1983, Paramount, 130m, c). P Burtt Harris, D Sidney Lumet, W E.L. Doctorow (based on his novel *The Book of Daniel*), PH Andrzej Bartkowiak, M Bob James, ED Peter Frank, PD Philip Rosenberg.

LP Timothy Hutton (Daniel Isaacson), Edward Asner (Jacob Ascher), Mandy Patinkin (Paul Isaacson), Lindsay Crouse (Rochelle Isaacson), Joseph Leon (Selig Mindish), Amanda Plummer (Susan Isaacson), Ellen Barkin (Phyllis Isaacson), Tovah Feldshuh (Linda Mindish), John Rubinstein (Robert Lewin).

The movie cuts back and forth between the events leading up to the execution of the "Isaacsons" (The Rosenbergs, played bravely by Mandy Patinkin and Lindsay Crouse) for passing atomic secrets to the Russians, and the fate of their grown children. Their daughter, radical Radcliffe student Amanda Plummer, shows signs of madness while their guilt-ridden son, grad student Timothy Hutton, is filled with unfocussed anger. There's nothing wrong with the technique of switching from the present to the past and back again, but director Sidney Lumet seems confounded by it.

647. *Danny Boy* (1982, Triumph, Ireland, 92m, c). P Barry Blackmore, D&W Neil Jordan, PH Chris Menges, M Paddy Meegan, ED Pat Duffner.

LP Veronica Quilligan (Annie), Stephen Rea (Danny), Alan Devlin (Bill), Peter Caffrey (Ray), Honor Heffernan (Deirdre), Lise-Ann McLaughlin (Bride), Ian McElhinney (Groom), Derek Lord (Best Man).

Filled with symbolism to represent the troubles and hostilities in present-day Northern Ireland, this grim film tells the story of young saxophonist Stephen Rea who after witnessing a brutal double murder, goes on a vengeance mission.

648. *Dark Age* (1988, RKO-FGH, US/Australia, 90m, c). P Basil Appleby, D Arch Nicholson, W Sonia Borg (based on the novel *Numunwari* by Grahame Webb), PH Andrew Lesnie, M Danny Beckerman, ED Adrian Carr, PD David Copping.

LP John Jarratt (Steve), Nikki Coghill (Cathy), Max Phipps (John), Burnham Burnham (Oondabund), David Gulpilil (Adjaral), Ray Meagher (Rex), Jeff Ashby (Mac), Paul Bertram (Jackson).

When a 25-foot-long crocodile, revered by natives, is washed downstream by heavy rains, a government ranger and two Aborigines track down the animal to save it from poachers.

649. Dark Before Dawn (1988, PSM, 95m, c). P Ben Miller, D Robert Totten, W Reparata Mazzola, PH Steve M. Mc-Williams, M Ken Sutherland, ED Ron Hanthaner & Tom Boutross.

LP Sonny Gibson (Jeff Parker), Doug McClure (James Kirkland), Reparata Mazzola (Jessica Stanton), Ben Johnson (Sheriff), Billy Drago (Cabalistas Leader), Rance Howard (Glen Logan), Buck Henry (Charlie Stevens).

Released only in Kansas where it was filmed, this farm thriller depicts the efforts to prevent a giant agribusiness conglomerate from manipulating the wheat market. The firm plans to make millions as the price of wheat products jumps hundreds of percent.

650. The Dark Crystal (1982, Universal, 94m, c). P Jim Henson & Gary Kurtz, D Henson & Frank Oz, W David Odell (based on a story by Henson), PH Oswald Morris, M Trevor Jones, ED Ralph Kemplen, PD Harry Lange.

LP PUPPET OPERATORS/CHARACTER VOICES Jim Henson/Stephen Garlick (Jen), Kathryn Mullen/Lisa Maxwell (Kira), Frank Oz/Billie Whitelaw (Aughra), Dave Goelz/Percy Edwards (Fizzgig), Frank Oz/Barry Dennen (Chamberlain), Dave Goelz/Michael Kilgarriff (General).

The late Jim Henson and Frank Oz, creators of the Muppets, present a lavish fantasy about a world ruled by monstrous flesh-eating Skeksis, who rule because the Dark Crystal has been broken. Prophecy has it that the evil rule of the Skeksis will end when the crystal is mended by a Gelfling, but only two are left.

651. The Dark End of the Street (1981, First Run Features, 89m, c). P Dian K. Miller, D&W Jan Egelson, PH D'Arcy Marsh, M Marion Gillon & Tyrone Johnson, ED Jerry Bloedow.

LP Laura Harrington (Donna), Henry Tomaszewski (Billy), Michelle Green (Marlene), Lance Henriksen (Jimmy), Pamela Payton-Wright (Mary Ann), Terence Grey (Ethan), Al Eaton (Brian), Gustave Johnson (Reynolds).

Shot in Cambridge, Massachusetts, the film is a story of two white teenagers, Laura Harrington and Henry Tomaszewski, who witness the accidental death of a black friend and are afraid to say anything about it until the deceased's girlfriend Michelle Green is suspected of murder.

652. Dark Enemy (1984, Children's Film Foundation, GB, 82m, c). P Colin Finbow, W Finbow & The Children's Film Unit, PH Amos Richardson, M David Hewson.

LP Rory Macfarquhar (Aron), Martin Laring (Barnaby), Chris Chescoe (Garth), David Haig (Ash), Douglas Storm (Ezra), Jennifer Harrison (Ruth), Helen Mason (Rosemary), Cerian Van Doorninck (Beth).

In a post-nuclear holocaust age, most adults are dead. Farm boy Rory Macfarquhar seeks answers to what brought the world to this state. It's a depressing film which forces children to think about unpleasant things.

Dark Eyes see Satan's Mistress

Dark of Night see Mr. Wrong

653. Dark Tower (1989, Spectrafilm, 91m, c). P John R. Bowey & David M. Witz, D "Ken Barnett" (Freddie Francis), W Robert J. Avrech, Ken Wiederhorn & Ken Blackwell (based on a story by Avrech), PH Gordon Hayman, M Stacy Widelitz, ED Tom Merchant.

LP Michael Moriarty (Dennis Randall), Jenny Agutter (Carolyn Page), Carol Lynley (Tilly Ambrose), Theodore Bikel (Dr. Max Gold), Anne Lockhart (Elaine), Kevin McCarthy (Sergie), Patch Mackenzie (Maria).

A Barcelona skyscraper, under construction, is the scene of a rash of murders. Security chief Michael Moriarty comes to the conclusion that the culprit is the ghost of the deceased husband of the building's architect, Jenny Agutter.

654. D.A.R.Y.L. (1985, Paramount, 99m, c). P John Heyman, Burtt Harris & Gabrielle Kelly, D Simon Wincer, W David Ambrose, Allan Scott & Jeffrey Ellis, PH Frank Watts, M Marvin Hamlisch, ED Adrian Carr, PD Alan Cassie.

LP Marybeth Hurt (Joyce Richardson), Michael McKean (Andy Richardson), Kathryn Walker (Ellen Lamb), Colleen Camp (Elaine Fox), Josef Sommer (Dr. Jeffrey Stewart), Ron Frazier (Gen. Graycliffe), Steve Ryan (Howie Fox), Barret Oliver (Daryl), Danny Corkill (Turtle Fox).

After an automobile accident, sole survivor 10-year-old Barret Oliver can only tell authorities his name, Daryl. He is taken in by childless couple Marybeth Hurt and Michael McKean. Oliver proves to be the perfect son — too perfect. After awhile a couple appears claiming to be the boy's real parents. He is whisked to a secret military base where it is revealed that he's actually a robot, Data Analyzing Robot Youth Lifeform. A general orders the D.A.R.Y.L. project terminated, which translates into destroying the prototype Oliver. You don't think Hurt and McKean will allow this, do you?

655. Date with an Angel (1987, De Laurentiis, 105m, c). P Martha Schumacher, D&W Tom McLoughlin, PH Alex Thomson, M Randy Kerber, ED Marshall Harvey, PD Craig Stearns.

LP Michael E. Knight (Jim Sanders), Phoebe Cates (Patty Winston), Emmanuelle Beart (Angel), David Dukes (Ed Winston), Phil Brock (George), Albert Macklin (Don), Pete Kowanko (Rex), Vinny Argiro (Ben Sanders), Bibi Besch (Grace Sanders).

Angel Emmanuelle Beart, on a mission to pick up a dying man, has a collision with a communications satellite and falls to earth, landing in the swimming pool of the man she seeks, Michael E. Knight. Beart has a broken wing and is unable to complete her mission. When Knight's fiancée Phoebe Cates gets a look at the beautiful Beart, she assumes they have spent the night together and walks out on Knight. The remainder of the film concentrates on Knight and Beart falling in love and finding a heavenly solution so they can be together.

656. Dawn of the Mummy (1981, Harmony Gold, 88m, c). P&D Frank Agrama, W Daria Price, Ronald Dobrin & Agrama, PH Sergio Rubini, M Shuki Y. Levy, ED Jonathon Braun.

LP Brenda King, Barry Sattels, George Peck, John Salvo, Joan Levy, Diane Beatty.

A mummy awakes to kill the desecrators of a pharoah's tomb — four beautiful American models.

657. The Dawning (1988, TVS, GB, 97m, c). P Sarah Lawson, D Robert Knights, W Noira Williams (based on the novel *The Old Jest* by Jennifer Johnston), PH Shaun O'Dell, M Simon May.

LP Anthony Hopkins (Cassius), Rebecca Pidgeon (Nancy), Jean Simmons (Aunt Mary), Trevor Howard (Grandfather), Tara MacGowran (Maeve), Hugh Grant (Harry), Ronnie Masterson (Bridie), Mark O'Regan (Joe Mulhare).

In this film set in 1920 in southern Ireland, orphan Rebecca Pidgeon lives with her doddering old grandfather Trevor Howard (in his final screen appearance) and her aunt Jean Simmons. The naive, romantic teenager meets stranger Anthony Hopkins on the beach, befriends him and names him Cassius. She agrees to take a message from Hopkins to Mark O'Regan in Dublin. She's shocked when she realizes the message is an order to murder 12 British officers. Nevertheless she warns Hopkins of a patrol coming for him, and is present when he is gunned down.

658. The Day After Halloween (1981, Group 1, Australia, 90m, c, aka *Snapshot*). P Anthony I. Ginnane, D Simon Wincer, W Chris & Everett DeRoche, PH Vincent Monton, M Brian May, ED Philip Reid.

LP Chantal Contouri (Madeline), Sigrid Thornton (Angela), Robert Bruning (Elmer), Hugh Keays-Byrne (Linsey), Vincent Gil (Daryl), Denise Drysdale (Lilly).

The plot of this obscure crime film has nothing to do with the smash hit *Halloween*. Model Chantal Contouri is menaced by her ex-boyfriend, her mother and sister, and several dirty old men.

659. Day of the Dead (1985, Laurel/ UFDC, 102m, c). P Richard P. Rubinstein, D&W George A. Romero, PH Michael Gornick, M John Harrison, ED Pasquale Buba, PD Cletus Anderson.

LP Lori Cardile (Sarah), Terry Alexander (John), Joseph Pilanto (Capt. Rhodes), Jarlath Conroy (McDermott), Antone DiLeo, Jr. (Miguel), Richard Liberty (Dr. Logan), Howard Sherman (Bub), Gary Howard Klar (Steel).

This is the last chapter in director George A. Romero's *Living Dead* trilogy (*Night of the Living Dead* and *Dawn of the Dead* having preceded it). Scientists labor to develop a solution to the epidemic which has brought the dead back to life as zombies. The latter now outnumber normal humans 400,000 to one. Richard Liberty tries to domesticate them. This talky horror piece is not for everyone.

660. Day of the Panther (1988, Virgo Prods., Australia, 84m, c). P Damien Parer, D Brian Trenchard-Smith, W Peter West (based on a story by West & David Groom), PH Simon Atkerman, M Gary Hardman, ED David Jaeger & Kerry Regan.

LP Edward John Stazak (Jason Blade), John Stanton (William Anderson), Jim Richards (Jim Baxter), Paris Jefferson (Gemma Anderson), Michael Carmine (Damien Zukor), Zale Daniel (Colin), Matthew Quartermaine (The Constable).

Trained by the Chinese cult "The Panthers," Edward John Stazak travels from Hong Kong to Perth on a secret mission against drug king Michael Carmine. When his partner is killed, Stazak recruits the deceased's cousin Paris Jefferson to help him. The film builds to the usual bloody gladiatorial battle.

Day of the Woman see I Spit on Your Grave

The Day the Screaming Stopped see The Comeback

661. The Day Time Ended (1980, Compass Intl., 79m, c). P Wayne Schmidt, Steve Neill & Paul W. Gentry, D John "Bud" Cardos, W Schmidt, J. Larry Carroll & David Schmoeller (based on a story by Neill), PH John Morrill, M Richard Band, ED Ted Nicolaou, AD Rusty Rosene.

LP Jim Davis (Grant), Chris Mitchum (Richard), Dorothy Malone (Ana), Marcy Lafferty (Beth), Natasha Ryan (Jenny), Scott Kolden (Steve).

Strange and terrifying things happen in a house that is slipping into a different dimension.

662. D.C. Cab (1983, Universal, 104m, c). P Topper Carew & Cassius Vernon Weathersby, D&W Joel Schumacher (based on a story by Carew & Schumacher), PH Dean Cundey, M Giorgio Moroder, ED David Blewitt, PD John J. Lloyd.

LP Adam Baldwin (Albert), Charlie Barnett (Tyrone), Irene Cara (Herself), Anne DeSalvo (Myrna), Max Gail (Harold), Gloria Gifford (Miss Floyd), DeWayne Jessie (Bongo), Bill Maher (Baba), Whitman Mayo (Mr. Rhythm), Mr. T. (Samson).

It's a likeable and lively comedy about the antics of a ragtag Washington cab company staffed by an assortment of weird types and misfits, who show their mettle when it's needed to save the brattish kids of an ambassador from a kidnapping plot.

663. The Dead (1987, Vestron, 83m, c). P Wieland Schulz-Keil & Chris Sievernich, D John Huston, W Tony Huston† (based on the short story from "The Dubliners" by James Joyce), PH Fred Murphy, M Alex North, ED Roberto Silvi, PD Stephen Grimes & Dennis Washington, COS Dorothy Jeakins†.

LP Anjelica Huston (Gretta Conroy), Donal McCann (Gabriel Conroy), Rachael Dowling (Lily), Cathleen Delany (Aunt Julia Morkan), Helena Carroll (Aunt Kate Morkan), Ingrid Craigie (Mary Jane), Dan O'Herlihy (Mr. Browne), Frank Patterson (Bartell D'Arcy), Donal Donnelly (Freddy Malins).

In a magnificent final film, John Huston seems to be communicating from beyond the grave. The James Joyce–inspired story is adapted by his son Tony Huston and stars his daughter Anjelica Huston as one of three women who give a party for their dearest friends. During the evening the conversation turns to those people, who have passed on to their rewards, who have had the most influence on the hostesses and their guests.

664. Dead and Buried (1981, Avco Embassy, 92m, c). P Ronald Shusett & Robert Fentress, D Gary A. Sherman, W Shusett & Dan O'Bannon (based on a story by Jeff Millar & Alex Stern), PH Steve Poster, M Joe Renzetti, ED Alan Balsam, SE Stan Winston.

In his last movie role Jack Albertson plays a small town mortician and zombie master. Everyone except stupid sheriff James Farentino can figure out who's coming up with all those reconstructed corpses.

Dead and Married* see *She's Back

665. *Dead Bang* (1989, Warner, 105m, c). P Steve Roth, D John Frankenheimer, W Robert Foster, PH Gerry Fisher, M Gary Chang, ED Robert F. Shugrue, PD Ken Adam.

LP Don Johnson (Jerry Beck), Penelope Ann Miller (Linda), William Forsythe (Arthur Kressler), Bob Balaban (Elliot Webly), Frank Military (Bobby Burns), Tate Donovan (John Burns), Tim Reid (Chief Dixon).

Frustrated L.A. detective Don Johnson is on the trail of black motorcyclists who have killed a cop. His investigation leads him to a confrontation with white supremacists. There must be a few more hate-groups to throw into the movie.

666. *Dead Calm* (1989, Warner, Australia, 95m, c). P Terry Hayes, Doug Mitchell & George Miller, D Phillip Noyce, W Terry Hayes (based on the novel by Charles Williams), PH Dean Semler, M Graeme Revell, ED Richard Francis-Bruce, PD Graham (Grace) Walker.

LP Nicole Kidman (Rae Ingram), Sam Neill (John Ingram), Billy Zane (Hughie Warringer), Rod Mullinar (Russell Bellows), Joshua Tilden (Danny), George Shevtsov (Doctor), Michael Long (Specialist Doctor).

Husband and wife Sam Neill and Nicole Kidman are alone on a yacht after their small son is killed in an automobile accident. They are joined by a repugnant and mysterious stranger Billy Zane. Is he a sadistic murderer? Is the president of the United States left-handed?

667. *Dead End City* (1989, Action International, 85m, c). P&D Peter Yuval, W Yuval & Michael Bogert, PH Paul Maibaum, M Brian Bennett, ED David Khachatorian.

LP Dennis Cole (Chief Felker), Greg

Cummins (Jack Murphy), Christine Lunde (Opal Brand), Robert Zdar (Max), Durrell Nelson (Brett), Aleana Downs (Nancy), Johnny Venocur (Paul).

The government is behind a plan to use city neighborhood gangs fighting each other to destroy sections of the city in line for urban renewal.

668. *Dead End Drive-In* (1986, New World, Australia, 92m, c). P Andrew Williams, D Brian Trenchard-Smith, W Peter Smalley (based on the short story "Crabs" by Peter Carey), PH Paul Murphy, M Frank Strangio, ED Alan Lake & Lee Smith, PD Lawrence Eastwood.

LP Ned Manning (Crabs), Natalie McCurry (Carmen), Peter Whitford (Thompson), Wilbur Wilde (Hazza), Dave Gibson (Dave), Sandie Lillingston (Beth), Ollie Hall (Frank), Lyn Collingwood (Fay), Nikki McWatters (Shirl).

In 1990 after the economic collapse of the world, misfits and other undesirables the government has no further use for are sent to a futuristic prison camp where they are subjected to a steady and inescapable barrage of exploitation films. Now that's really cruel and unusual punishment.

669. *Dead Heat* (1988, New World, 86m, c). P Michael Meltzer & David Helpern, D Mark Goldblatt, W Terry Black, PH Robert D. Yeoman, M Ernest Troost, ED Harvey Rosenstock, PD Craig Stearns.

LP Treat Williams (Roger Mortis), Joe Piscopo (Doug Bigelow), Lindsay Frost (Randi James), Darrin McGavin (Dr. Ernest McNab), Vincent Price (Arthur P. Loudermilk), Claire Kirkconnell (Rebecca Smythers), Keye Luke (Mr. Thule).

Meant to be a comedy-horror spoof of the living-dead subgenre, this dud features Treat Williams and Joe Piscopo as two L.A. police detectives trying to learn the identity of the mastermind behind a series of robberies committed by criminals brought back from the dead.

Dead Kids* see *Strange Behavior

670. *Dead Man Walking* (1988, Metropolis-Hit, 90m, c). P Gregory Brown & Craig Thurman Suttle, D Brown, W John Weidner & Rick Marx, PH Paul Desatoff, M Claude Cave Powell, ED Kert Vander Meulen, PD Rick Wiggington.

LP Wings Hauser (John Luger), Brion

James (Decker), Pamela Ludwig (Lelia), Sy Richardson (Snake), Leland Crooke (Nomad Farmer), Jeffrey Combs (Chaz), Joseph d'Angerio (Gordon), Tasia Valenza (Rika), John Walter Davis (The Body Counter).

Only to be found in video stores, this film is set in the year 2004 after a plague has wiped out half the world's population. UNITUS, the ruling worldwide corporation, has assigned those infected with the disease into plague zones. Others, infected with a fatal but noncontagious strain, are allowed to live freely, but the life expectancy of these Zero Men is only one or two years. One of the Zero Men, Brion James, tries to rouse the dying against the fat cats that control everything. He's pursued by another Zero Man, Wings Hauser.

671. *Dead Man's Float* (1980, Andromeda, Australia, 75m, c). P Tom Broadbridge, D Pete Sharp, W Roger Carr (based on his novel), PH David Eggby, ED Clifford Hayes.

LP Sally Boyden (Anne), Greg Rowe (Johnny), Jacqui Gordon (Sue), Rick Ireland (Pete), Bill Hunter (Eddie Bell), Sue Jones (Shirley Bell), John Heywood (Capt. Collins), Gus Mercurio (Mr. Dobraski), Brian Hannan (Rex Coates).

Australian beach bunnies Sally Boyden and Jacqui Gordon fall for visiting American surfer Rick Ireland. If this isn't enough to get your interest, the entire crew get mixed up with drug dealers.

672. *Dead Men Don't Wear Plaid* (1982, Universal, 89m, b&w). P David V. Picker & William E. McEuen, D Carl Reiner, W George Gipe, Reiner & Steve Martin, PH Michael Chapman, M Miklos Rozsa (from earlier films), ED Bud Molin, PD John De Cuir.

LP Steve Martin (Rigby Reardon), Rachel Ward (Juliet Forrest), Carl Reiner (Field Marshall Von Kluck), Reni Santoni (Carlos Rodriguez), George Gaynes (Dr. Forrest), Frank McCarthy (Waiter), Adrian Ricard (Mildred).

Action of Steve Martin as an inept 1940s private eye is edited in with old film clips from movies starring Humphrey Bogart, Alan Ladd, James Cagney, Ava Gardner, et al. This rip-off must have seemed like a good idea at the time but it

would have been better to have a compilation film of old detective movies and left out the junk involving Martin and his modern co-actors.

673. *Dead of Winter* (1987, MGM/United Artists, 100m, c). P John Bloomgarden & Marc Shmuger, D Arthur Penn, W Shmuger & Mark Malone, PH Jan Weincke, M Richard Einhorn, ED Rick Shaine, PD Bill Brodie.

LP Mary Steenburgen (Katie McGovern), Roddy McDowall (Mr. Murray), Jan Rubes (Dr. Joseph Lewis), William Russ (Rob Sweeney), Mark Malone (Roland McGovern), Ken Pogue (Officer Mullavy), Wayne Robson (Officer Huntley).

Clearly patterned after *My Name Is Julie Ross,* actress Mary Steenburgen is hired by eccentric Roddy McDowall to appear in a movie to be produced in his eerie old mansion. After awhile Steenburgen realizes that she is being held prisoner, but for what reason she does not know—but she'll find out.

674. *Dead Pit* (1989, Cornerstone/Skouras, 92m, c). P Gimel Everett, D Brett Leonard, W&ED Leonard & Everett, PH Marty Collins, M Dan Wyman.

LP Jeremy Slate (Dr. Gerald Swan), Danny Gochnauer (Dr. Colin Ramzi), Cheryl Lawson (Jane Doe), Steffen Gregory Foster (Christian Myers).

In this moderately scary horror pictures, deranged scientist Danny Gochnauer, killed by Jeremy Slate 20 years earlier and sealed in a chamber in the subbasement of a mental institute, is somehow revived by the arrival of lovely young amnesiac Cheryl Lawson.

675. *Dead Poets Society*† (1989, Touchstone Pictures, 128m, c). P Steven Haft, Paul Junger Witt & Tony Thomas, D Peter Weir†, W Tom Schulman*, PH John Seale, M Maurice Jarre, ED William M. Anderson, PD Wendy Stites.

LP Robin Williams† (John Keating), Robert Sean Leonard (Neil Perry), Ethan Hawke (Todd Anderson), Josh Charles (Knox Overstreet), Gale Hansen (Charles Dalton), Norman Lloyd (Mr. Nolan), Dylan Kussman (Richard Cameron), Allelon Ruggiero (Steven Meeks).

Robin Williams' Mr. Keating is no Mr. Chips. He doesn't drill his students. His indoctrination is that they shouldn't allow themselves to be indoctrinated. He wants his students to feel they can soar intellectually, follow their own drummer and discover their personal life-long passions. "Seize the Moment" and "Suck the Marrow from Life" are to be their mottos. Were this only possible. Instead they discover the clay feet of their parents, their instructors and themselves. One even must die. The problem in many schools is not the absence of caring teachers like Williams, but the scarcity of students who can be convinced that reading, let alone poetry and literature, is enjoyable and important. As a fantasy which would have had more currency in the 50s, the decade in which is set, this is an enjoyable film. Williams gives a fine performance as the odd master out in a private boy's preparatory school. The young actors portraying the seven members of the Dead Poet's Society, especially Robert Sean Leonard, Ethan Hawke and Gale Hansen, are well cast in their respective roles, but unfortunately they represent types rather than multidimensional teens.

676. The Dead Pool (1988, Warner, 91m, c). P David Valdes, D Buddy Van Horn, W Steve Sharon (based on a story by Sharon, Durk Pearson & Sandy Shaw from characters created by Harry Julian & R.M. Fink), PH Jack N. Green, M Lalo Schifrin, ED Ron Spang, PD Edward C. Carfagno.

LP Clint Eastwood (Harry Callahan), Patricia Clarkson (Samantha Walker), Evan C. Kim (Al Quan), Liam Neeson (Peter Swan), David Hunt (Harlan Rook), Michael Currie (Capt. Donnelly), Michael Goodwin (Lt. Ackerman), Darwin Gillett (Patrick Snow), Anthony Charnota (Lou Janero).

Looking all of his 58 years, Clint Eastwood is still entertaining in his portrayal of Dirty Harry. He's put out to discover that not only has a mobster hired hit men to eliminate him but his name appears on a bettor's list of celebrities whom the player believes will die within the year. Some nut is eliminating those on movie director Liam Neeson's list. Clint is forced to play nice with cute, tiny, TV reporter Patricia Clarkson. He towers over the well-built nuisance. As one might expect, he comes to respect and bed her. Oh, by the way, he settles things with the imprisoned mobster and the homicidal maniac.

677. Dead Ringers (1988, 20th Century–Fox, Canada, 115m, c). P David Cronenberg & Marc Boyman, D Cronenberg, W Cronenberg & Norman Snider (based on *Twins* by Bari Wood & Jack Geasland), PH Peter Suschitzky, M Howard Shore, ED Ronald Sanders, PD Carol Spier.

LP Jeremy Irons (Beverly & Elliot Mantle), Genevieve Bujold (Claire Niveau), Heidi Von Palleske (Cary), Barbara Gordon (Danuta), Shirley Douglas (Laura), Stephen Lack (Anders Wolleck), Nick Nichols (Leo), Lynn Cormack (Arlene).

Besides the book *Twins,* this poignant spectacle owes inspiration to the story of doctors Cyril and Stewart Marcus, who died in 1975. Strangely, Jeremy Irons did not receive an Academy Award nomination for his not one but two outstanding performances as identical-twin Toronto gynecologists who share an obsessively close relationship. These experts on infertility pass women back and forth until one falls in love with film star Genevieve Bujold and wishes to keep her for himself. His brother can't tolerate this betrayal and the result in this psychological thriller is tragedy. It's easier to admire this film than like it.

678. The Dead Zone (1983, Paramount, 103m, c). P Debra Hill, D David Cronenberg, W Jeffrey Boam (based on the novel by Stephen King), PH Mark Irwin, M Michael Kamen, ED Ronald Sanders, PD Carol Spier.

LP Christopher Walken (Johnny Smith), Brooke Adams (Sarah Bracknell), Tom Skerritt (Sheriff Bannerman), Herbert Lom (Dr. Sam Welzak), Anthony Zerbe (Roger Stuart), Colleen Dewhurst (Henrietta Dodd), Martin Sheen (Greg Stillson), Nicholas Campbell (Frank Dodd).

After an accident which leaves him in a coma for five years, shy teacher Christopher Walken awakens to discover he possesses psychic powers. He uses them to prevent multiple murders and the destruction of the earth. Seems a noble use of his gift.

679. *Deadhead Miles* (1982, Paramount, 93m, c). P Vernon Zimmerman & Tony Bill, D Zimmerman, W Terence Malick, PH Ralph Woolsey, M Tom T. Hall, ED Bud Smith.

LP Alan Arkin (Cooper), Paul Benedict (Tramp), Hector Elizondo (Bad Character), Charles Durning (Red Ball Rider), Barnard Hughes (Old Man), Loretta Swit (Woman with Glass Eye), Allen Garfield (Juicy Brucey), George Raft (Himself), Bruce Bennett (Johnny Mesquitero), Ida Lupino (She).

This movie was made 10 years earlier, which explains George Raft's relatively healthy-looking appearance even though he died two years before its release. Former truck driver Alan Arkin steals a rig, picks up hitchhiking bum Paul Benedict, and drives across country. Sure makes a trucker's life look tedious and uneventful.

680. *Deadline* (1987, Skouras, GB/Ger./Israel, 99m, c). P Elisabeth Wolters-Alfs, D Nathaniel Gutman, W Hanan Peled, PH Amnon Salomon & Thomas Mauch, M Jacques Zwart & Hans Jansen, ED Peter Przygodda.

LP Christopher Walken (Don Stevens), Marita Marschall (Linda Larson), Hywel Bennett (Mike Jessop), Arnon Zadok (Hamdi Abu-Yussuf), Amos Lavie (Yessin Abu-Riadd), Ette Ankri (Samira), Martin Umbach (Bernard).

Globe-trotting, detached journalist Christopher Walken is changed by the events he covers in Lebanon. While interviewing Amos Lavie, a disgruntled PLO leader, the latter denounces terrorism and recommends peace talks with Israel. For his stand Lavie is assassinated. From then on Walken is in the middle of a four-way war.

681. *Deadly Blessing* (1981, United Artists, 102m, c). P Micheline and Max Keller & Pat Herskovic, D Wes Craven, W Glenn M. Benest, Matthew Barr & Craven, PH Robert Jessup, M James Horner, ED Richard Bracken.

LP Maren Jensen (Martha), Susan Buckner (Vicky), Sharon Stone (Lana), Jeff East (John Schmidt), Lisa Hartman (Faith), Lois Nettleton (Louisa), Ernest Borgnine (Isaiah), Coleen Riley (Melissa), Doug Barr (Jim).

Maren Jensen, living near a mysterious religious cult, "The Hittites," led by Ernest Borgnine, finds her husband, a former member, slain under strange circumstances. Jensen invites two beautiful friends Susan Buckner and Sharon Stone to live with her. From that point the weird events and the bodies really begin to pile up.

682. *Deadly Breed* (1989, P/M Entertainment Group, 83m, c). P Richard Pepin & Joseph Merhi, D&W Charles T. Kanganis, PH Rick Lamb, M John Gonzalez, ED Paul Volk.

LP William Smith (Captain), Addison Randall (Kilpatrick), Blake Bahner (Jake), Joe Vance (Vincent), Michelle Berger (Lana), Rhonda Grey (Alex).

Parole officer Blake Bahner finds his clients being killed. He traces the murders to local police captain William Smith, with the actual killings being carried out by Addison Randall and his gang of right-wing Skinheads.

683. *Deadly Dreams* (1988, Concorde, 79m, c). P Matt Leipzig, D Kristine Peterson, W Thom Babbes, PH Zoran Hochstatter, M Todd Boekelheide, ED Bernard Caputo, PD Stephen Greenberg, SE Deborah Zoeller.

LP Mitchell Anderson (Alex), Juliette Cummins (Maggie), Xander Berkeley (Jack), Thom Babbes (Danny), Timothy Austin (Young Alex).

We won't give away the ending of this well-done, low-budget horror film. Suffice it to say, there are several twists in the story of Mitchell Anderson's descent into madness from nightmares brought on by the murders of his parents ten years earlier.

684. *Deadly Embrace* (1989, Arcade, 83m, c). P David DeCoteau & Richard Gabai, D Ellen Cabot, W Gabai, PH Thomas Callaway, M Del Casher, ED Tony Malanowski, PD Royce Mathew.

LP Jan-Michael Vincent (Stewart Morland), Ty Randolph (Charlotte Morland), Linnea Quigley (Michelle Arno), Ken Abraham (Chris Thompson), Jack Carter (Evan Weiss), Michelle Bauer (Female Spirit of Sex), Ruth Collins (Dede Magnolia).

Ty Randolph, neglected wife of Jan-Michael Vincent, has an affair with houseman Ken Abraham. Their games are disrupted when Abraham's young girlfriend Linnea Quigley comes to live with him. It's an awkward film noir which badly uses the flashback device.

685. *Deadly Eyes* (1982, Golden, 93m, c, aka *The Rats*). P Paul Kahnert & Charles Eglee, D Robert Clouse, W Eglee (from the novel by James Herbert), PH Rene Verzier, ED Ron Wisman, SE Allan Apone.

LP Sam Groom (Paul Harris), Sara Botsford (Kelly Leonard), Scatman Crothers (George Fask), Lisa Langlois (Trudy White), Cec Linder (Dr. Luis Spenser), James B. Douglas (Mel Dederick), Lesleh Donaldson (Martha).

For those who feel uncomfortable when they see rodents of any kind, it's best to avoid this film about rats who get into some steroids and grow so bold that they will attack anyone and anything in New York City.

686. *Deadly Force* (1983, Embassy, 95m, c). P Sandy Howard, D Paul Aaron, W Ken Barnett, Barry Schneider & Robert Vincent O'Neil, PH Norman Leigh & David Myers, M Gary Scott, ED Roy Watts, PD Alan Roderick-Jones.

LP Wings Hauser (Stoney Cooper), Joyce Ingalls (Eddie Cooper), Paul Shenar (Joshua Adams), Al Ruscio (Sam Goodwin), Arlen Dean Snyder (Ashley Maynard), Lincoln Kilpatrick (Otto Hoxley), Bud Ekins (Harvey).

Vile cop Wings Hauser tries to juggle tracking down a mass murderer and patching things up with his estranged wife Joyce Ingalls, a TV news reporter covering the murder case. It's hard to have any more sympathy for Hauser than for the psychopath.

687. *Deadly Friend* (1986, Warner, 99m, c). P Robert M. Sherman, D Wes Craven, W Bruce Joel Rubin (based on the novel *Friend* by Diana Henstell), PH Philip Lathrop, M Charles Bernstein, ED Michael Eliot, PD Daniel Lomino, SE Peter Albiez.

LP Matthew Laborteaux (Paul), Kristy Swanson (Samantha), Michael Sharrett (Tom), Anne Twomey (Jeannie), Anne Ramsey (Elvira), Richard Marcus (Harry), Russ Martin (Dr. Johanson), Lee Paul (Sgt. Volchek).

Brilliant teen Matthew Laborteaux implants the computer-chip brain of his

robot into the body of Kristy Swanson, the pretty girl next door, who has been beaten to death by her drunken father. Swanson is no longer the demure, shy young thing, a fact some local thugs learn to their sorrow.

688. *Deadly Illusion* (1987, Cinetel, 87m, c). P Irwin Meyer, D William Tannen & Larry Cohen, W Cohen, PH Daniel Pearl, M Patrick Gleason, ED Steve Mirkovich & Ronald Spang.

LP Billy Dee Williams (Hamberger), Vanity (Rina), Morgan Fairchild (Jane/ Sharon), Joe Cortese (Det. Lefferts), Dennis Hallahan (Fake Burton), Jenny Cornuelle (Gloria Reid), Michael Wilding, Jr. (Costillion).

Unlicensed private eye Billy Dee Williams is on the trail of a murderer who has set him up. He finds himself involved with Morgan Fairchild both as a brunette and a blonde, as well as with a drug-smuggling ring which she heads. And then there's Vanity...

689. *Deadly Obsession* (1989, Distant Horizon, 95m, c). P Anant Singh, D Jeno Hodi, W Hodi, Paul Wolansky & Brian Cox (based on a story by Hodi & Wolansky), PH Zoltan David, M Marty Dunayer, ED Wolansky, PD Kimberly von Brandenstein.

LP Jeffrey R. Iorio (Dino Andretti), Joe Paradise (John Doe), Darnell Martin (Denise), Martin Haber (Lt. Walsh), Monica Breckenridge (Pamela).

Heroine Darnell Martin barely escapes death when she eats ice cream dosed with rat poison by animal-rights advocate Joe Paradise. Others are not so fortunate.

690. *Deadly Passion* (1985, UIP/ Warner, South Africa, 98m, c). P Anant Singh, D Larry Larson, W Larson & Curt Allen, PH Vincent Cox, M Jay Ferguson, ED Bill Blunden.

LP Brent Huff (Sam Black), Ingrid Boulting (Martha Greenwood), Harrison Coburn (Andy Andrews), Lynn Maree (Marsha), Eric Flynn (Robert Chandler), Erica Rogers (Abigail Marx).

Brent Huff sees beautiful Ingrid Boulting and immediately falls in love with her. She agrees to meet him and tells Huff of her late husband's multimillion-dollar legacy that is being blocked by the deceased's business manager. Huff agrees to help, then finds himself accused of murder with Boulting nowhere to be found.

691. *Deadly Prey* (1987, Action International, 88m, c). P Peter Yuval, D&W David A. Prior, PH Stephen A. Blake, M Steve McClintock, Tim James & Tim Heintz, ED Brian Evans.

LP Cameron Mitchell (Jaimy's Dad), Troy Donahue (Don Michaelson), Ted Prior (Michael Danton), Fritz Matthews (Lt. Thornton), David Campbell (Col. Hogan), Dawn Abraham (Sybil), Suzzane Tara (Jaimy).

In an absurd ripoff of *The Most Dangerous Game,* David Campbell runs a mercenary camp located in Southeast L.A. He kidnaps citizens to be prey for his trainees to track in a jungle setting. But like Joel McCrea earlier, Ted Prior proves to be too much for his pursuers, picking them off one-by-one.

692. *Deadly Reactor* (1989, Action International, 88m, c, aka *Reactor*). P Fritz Matthews, D David Heavener, W Heavener (based on a story by Thomas Baldwin), PH David Hue, M Brian Bennett, ED Brian Evans.

LP Stuart Whitman (Duke), David Heavener (Cody), Darwyn Swalve (Hog), Allyson Davis (Shawna), Barbara Kerek, Arvid Holmberg, Ingrid Vold.

David Heavener portrays a preacher-styled gunslinger in a post–nuclear war West. This Sergio Leone–Clint Eastwood-like antihero is appointed sheriff, charged with defending the peace-loving citizens from marauding bike gangs.

693. *The Deadly Spawn* (1983, 21st Century, 78m, c). P Ted Bohus, D&W Douglas McKeown & Tim Sullivan (based on a story by McKeown, Bohus & John Dods), PH Harvey Birnbaum, M Michael Perlstein, Ken Walker & Paul Cornell, SE Dods.

LP Charles George Hildebrandt (Charles), Tom DeFranco (Tom), Richard Lee Porter (Frankie), Jean Tafler (Ellen), Karen Tighe (Kathy), Ethel Michelson (Aunt Millie), John Schmerling (Uncle Herb).

A meteor shower unleashes hundreds of aliens on New Jersey. No it's not Orson Welles' "War of the Worlds" broadcast made into a film. It's not that credible.

694. *Deadly Spygames* (1989, Sell/Double Helix, 86m, c). P Jack M. Sell & Adrianne Richmond, D Sell, W Sell & Richmond, PH Wayne Kohlar, M Hutch Deloach, ED Maurits Guepin, AD Jim Bandsuh.

LP Troy Donahue (Python), Jack M. Sell (Stephen Banner), Tippi Hedren (Chastity), Adrianne Richmond (Jacqueline), Joni Le Goddessa (Ling Choy), Bob McDonald (Russian General), Kathlyn Miles (Karlov).

There was a time when Troy Donahue and Tippi Hedren would attract certain movie fans. But neither were known for their acting, and age hasn't changed things in this spoof of James Bond movies. Jack M. Sell is a government spy who may be the only one who can prevent a possible World War III.

695. *Deadly Twins* (1988, Prism, 92m, c). P&D Joe Oaks, PH Jim Banks, ED Warren Banks.

LP Audrey Landers, Judy Landers, Harry Wolf, Joe Martinez, James McCartney, Wayne Allison, Gus Wood.

For those who take note of such things, Audrey and Judy Landers were the first twins featured as Playmates of the Month for *Playboy* magazine. Here they appear as horrible singers who are raped and beaten in Cologne by the son of a local mob boss and his buddy. Finding they can get no justice with the authorities, the girls decide to take their own revenge.

696. *Deadly Weapon* (1989, Empire, 90m, c). P Peter Manoogian, D Michael Miner, W Miner (based on a story by George Lafia & Miner), PH James L. Carter, M Guy Moon, ED Peter Teschner.

LP Rodney Eastman (Zeke), Kim Walker (Traci), Gary Frank (Dalton), Michael Horse (Indian Joe), Gary Kroeger, Barney Martin, Sam Melville.

Fifteen-year-old Arisonian Rodney Eastman imagines himself an alien awaiting the return of his mother ship. He comes across the army's antimatter pistol with which he blasts his enemies, including his nasty father. Eastman goes joy riding in a Cadillac with thrillseeker Kim Walker, but is heading for a tragic end, courtesy of the U.S. Army.

697. *Deadtime Stories* (1987, Scary Stuff Productions, 81m, c). P Bill Paul, D

Jeffrey Delman, W Delman & Charles F. Shelton (based on a story by Delman), PH Daniel B. Canton, M Taj, ED William Szarka, SE Bryant Tausek & Edward French.

LP Michael Mesmer (Uncle Mike), Brian DePersia (Little Brian), Scott Valentine (Peter), Phyllis Craig (Hanagohl), Anne Redfern (Florinda), Lesley Sank (Reviving Magoga), Lisa Cain (Living Magoda), Fran Lopate (Grandma), Cathryn DePrume (Goldi Lox), Robert Trimboli (Lt. Jack B. Nimble).

Michael Mesmer is miffed because he is missing the Nude Miss World contest on cable TV due to his duties as babysitter for his nephew Brian DePersia. Mesmer tells the lad, who can't sleep because he imagines monsters in his room, three bizarre, ghoulish versions of fairy tales: "Peter and the Witches," "Little Red Runninghood" and "Goldi Lox and the Three Bears."

698. *Deal of the Century* (1983, Warner, 98m, c). P Bud Yorkin, D William Friedkin, W Paul Brickman, PH Richard H. Kline, M Arthur B. Rubinstein, ED Bud Smith, Ned Humphreys & Jere Huggins, PD Bill Malley.

LP Chevy Chase (Eddie Muntz), Sigourney Weaver (Mrs. De Voto), Gregory Hines (Ray Kasternak), Vince Edwards (Frank Stryker), William Marquez (Gen. Cordosa), Eduardo Ricard (Col. Salgado), Wallace Shawn (Harold De Voto).

This disappointing black comedy stars Chevy Chase as a two-bit gunrunner, who sells an ultrasophisticated superweapon to a Central American dictator. The piece is just too heavy-going to have any real chuckles.

699. *Dealers* (1989, Euston/Rank, GB, 95m, c). P William P. Cartlidge, D Colin Bucksey, W Andrew MacLear, PH Peter Sinclair, M Richard Hartley, ED Jon Costelloe, PD Peter J. Hampton.

LP Paul McGann (Daniel Pascoe), Rebecca DeMornay (Anna Schuman), Derrick O'Connor (Robby Barrell), John Castle (Frank Mallory), Paul Guilfoyle (Lee Peters), Rosalind Bennett (Bonnie), Adrian Dunbar (Lennox Mayhew).

When one of the traders of the London branch of American bank Whitney Payne blows out his brains, star trader Paul McGann figures to fill the vacant spot. But he must compete with American hotshot Rebecca DeMornay for the job. The adversaries enter into a wary romance.

700. *Death Before Dishonor* (1987, New World, 95m, c). P Lawrence Kubik, D Terry J. Leonard, W John Gatliff & Kubik (based on a story by Gatliff & Kubik), PH Don Burgess, M Brian May, ED Steve Mirkovich, PD Kuli Sandor.

LP Fred Dryer (Sgt. Jack Burns), Joey Gian (Ramirez), Sasha Mitchell (Ruggieri), Peter Parros (James), Brian Keith (Col. Halloran), Paul Winfield (Ambassador), Joanna Pacula (Elli), Kasey Walker (Maude), Muhamad Bakri (Gavril).

The battle lines are drawn. On one side is Fred Dryer and his troop of reconnaissance marines. On the other is a Lebanese rebel leader and the two international terrorists Kasey Walker and Muhamad Bakri who have kidnapped Dryer's old buddy Brian Keith. Doing his Rambo imitation, Dryer kills every Arab in sight.

Death Bite see Spasms

701. *Death Chase* (1988, Action International, 88m, c). P Peter Yuval & Yakov Bentsvi, D David A. Prior, W James L. Hennessy, Jr., Craig L. Hyde & Prior, PH Keith Holland, M Tim James, Steve McClintick & Mark Mancina, ED Brian Evans.

LP Paul Smith (Steele), Jack Starrett (Lt. MacGrew), William Zipp (Steven Chase), Bainbridge Scott (Diana Lewis), Reggie DeMorton (Eddie), Paul Bruno (Sgt. Boone), C.T. Collins (Chairman).

Innocent bystander William Zipp gets pulled into a deadly game of tag organized by a malevolent businessman, C.T. Collins, when Zipp's sister is caught in the cross-fire.

702. *Death Hunt* (1981, 20th Century-Fox, 96m, c). P Murray Shostak, D Peter Hunt, W Michael Grais & Mark Victor, PH James Devis, M Jerrold Immel, ED Allan Jacobs & John F. Burnett, PD Ted Haworth.

LP Charles Bronson (Johnson), Lee Marvin (Millen), Andrew Stevens (Alvin), Carl Weathers (Sundog), Ed Lauter (Hazel), Scott Hylands (Pilot), Angie Dickinson (Vanessa), Henry Beckman

(Luce), William Sanderson (Ned Warren), Jon Cedar (Hawkins).

Reclusive 1930s trapper Charles Bronson kills a man in self-defense, but is accused of murder. When he flees, he is mercilessly tracked by a tough-as-nails Mountie, Lee Marvin, who would put Inspector Javert to shame.

703. *Death of a Soldier* (1986, Scotti Bros., Australia, 93m, c). P David Hannay & William Nagle, D Philippe Mora, W Nagle, PH Louis Irving, M Alan Zavod, ED John Scott.

LP James Coburn (Maj. Patrick Dannenberg), Reb Brown (Edward J. Leonski), Bill Hunter (Det. Sgt. Adams), Maurie Fields (Det. Sgt. Martin), Belinda Davey (Margot Saunders), Max Fairchild (Maj. William Fricks), Jon Sidney (Gen. MacArthur), Michael Pate (Maj. Gen. Sutherland).

In 1942, when hundreds of thousands of American servicemen were stationed in Australia, psychopathic Reb Brown kills three Melbourne women. He is tried for his crimes and ordered hanged by General MacArthur even though his military lawyer, James Coburn, doesn't feel Brown is sane enough even to stand trial.

704. *Death of an Angel* (1985, 20th Century-Fox, 92m, c). P Peter Burrell, D&W Petru Popescu, PH Fred Murphy, M Peter Myers, ED Christopher Lebenzon, PD Linda Pearl.

LP Bonnie Bedelia (Grace), Nick Mancuso (Father Angel), Pamela Ludwig (Vera), Alex Colon (Robles), Abel Franco, Irma Garcia.

Female Episcopal priest Bonnie Bedelia follows her wheelchair bound daughter Pamela Ludwig to a Mexican mission run by a mystic, Nick Mancuso, who seems to be courting martyrdom. Bedelia and Mancuso's faith are stretched to the limit in this preachy movie. It was made with the financial assistance of Robert Redford's Sundance Institute.

705. *Death on Credit* (1980, Green, 81m, c). P Victor Petrashevich & Fred I. Jasons, D Petrashevich, W Inese L. Apelis, PH Petrashevich, M Chuck Mymit, ED Debbie Brownstein.

LP Linda Boyce (Linda), Kent Bateman (Ken), Caesar Cordova (Caesar), Joseph Lewis (Chauffeur), Lucky Kargo, Billy Jackson.

Murder is to be paid C.O.D. because the victim will be D.O.A.

706. *Death Screams* (1982, United Film, 88m, c). P Chuck Ison & Ernest Bouskos, D David Nelson, W Paul C. Elliott, M Dee Barton.

LP Susan Kiger, Jody Kay, Martin Tucker, William T. Hicks, Jennifer Chase, Andria Savio, Monica Boston.

A machete-wielding maniac hacks to death a group of lovely coeds who have gotten together for a party.

707. *Death Ship* (1980, Avco Embassy, Canada, 91m, c). P Derek Gibson & Harold Greenberg, D Alvin Rakoff, W John Robins, PH Rene Verzier, ED Mike Campbell, SE Mike Albrechtsen.

LP George Kennedy (Ashland), Richard Crenna (Trevor Marshall), Nick Mancuso (Nick), Sally Ann Howes (Margaret Marshall), Kate Reid (Sylvia), Victoria Burgoyne (Lori), Jennifer McKinney (Robin), Danny Higham (Ben), Saul Rubinek (Jackie).

An ocean liner is suddenly rammed by a freighter. Nine survivors seek refuge on the freighter, where they encounter a power so evil and deadly that to stay alive they must deal with the devil. It's so dumb it's almost funny.

708. *Death Valley* (1982, Universal, 87m, c). P Elliot Kastner, Richard Rothstein & Stanley Beck, D Dick Richards, W Rothstein, PH Stephen H. Burum, M Dana Kaproff, ED Joel E. Cox, SE Roy L. Downey & Bill Nicholson.

LP Paul Le Mat (Mike), Catherine Hicks (Sally), Stephen McHattie (Hal), A. Wilford Brimley (Sheriff), Peter Billingsley (Billy), Edward Herrmann (Paul), Jack O'Leary (Earl), Mary Steelsmith (Babysitter).

While driving with his divorced mother and her new boyfriend through the Southwest, youngster Peter Billingsley witnesses a vicious murder. As often happens in such stories, the only one who believes our young hero is the murderer. He has similar plans for Billingsley.

709. *Death Vengeance* (1982, EMI Productions, 96m, c). P D. Constantine Conte, D Lewis Teague, W Tom Hedley

& David Z. Goodman, PH Franco DiGiacomo, M Piero Piccioni, ED John J. Fitzstephens.

LP Tom Skerritt, Patti LuPone, Michael Sarrazin, Yaphet Kotto, David Rasche, Donna DeVarona, Gina DeAngelis, Jonathan Adam Sherman, Pat Cooper.

Fed-up Tom Skerritt organizes an urban neighborhood vigilante group to combat the pimps and punks terrorizing the area. It's all old hat. See Charles Bronson and *Death Wish I, II, 3...Infinity*.

710.   *Death Wish II* (1982, Columbia/EMI/Warner, 93m, c). P Menahem Golan & Yoram Globus, D Michael Winner, W David Engelbach (based on characters created by Brian Garfield), PH Richard H. Kline & Tom Del Ruth, M Jimmy Page, ED Arnold Crust & Julian Semilian, PD William Hiney.

LP Charles Bronson (Paul Kersey), Jill Ireland (Geri Nichols), Vincent Gardenia (Frank Ochos), J.D. Cannon (New York D.A.), Anthony Franciosa (L.A. Police Commissioner), Ben Frank (Lt. Mankiewicz), Robin Sherwood (Carol Kersey), Silvana Gillardo (Rosario), Michael Prince (Elliott Cass).

Urban vigilante Charles Bronson is back in this sequel to 1974's *Death Wish*, this time in L.A., where there are just as many punks deserving to be blown away as in the Big Apple, at least according to the morality of our "hero." The creeps who killed his wife and raped his daughter, sending the latter into an eight-year coma, go after the youngster again, raping her again. In addition they impale her on an iron-spiked fence. Bronson shoots anyone who looks vaguely suspicious until he gets the ones who killed his daughter.

711.   *Death Wish 3* (1985, Cannon, 90m, c). P Menahem Golan & Yoram Globus, D Michael Winner, W Michael Edmonds (based on characters created by Brian Garfield), PH John Stanier, M Jimmy Page, ED Arnold Crust, PD Peter Mullins.

LP Charles Bronson (Paul Kersey), Deborah Raffin (Kathryn Davis), Ed Lauter (Richard Striker), Martin Balsam (Bennett), Gavan O'Herlihy (Fraker), Kirk Taylor (Giggler), Alex Winter (Hermosa), Tony Spiridakis (Angel).

Plug-ugly vigilante Charles Bronson is up to his old tricks, wiping out a gang of thugs terrorizing an apartment block. The killings are routine by now and the film offers nothing new. Wouldn't it be wonderful if we all had a license to eliminate everyone we felt deserved it? No, we guess not.

712.   *Death Wish 4: The Crackdown* (1987, Cannon, 99m, c). P Pancho Kohner, D J. Lee-Thompson, W Gail Morgan Hickman (based on characters created by Brian Garfield), PH Gideon Porath, M Paul McCallum, Valentine McCallum & John Bisharat, ED Peter Lee-Thompson.

LP Charles Bronson (Paul Kersey), Kay Lenz (Karen Sheldon), John P. Ryan (Nathan White), Perry Lopez (Ed Zacharias), George Dickerson (Det. Reiner), Soon-Teck Oh (Det. Nozaki), Dana Barron (Erica Sheldon).

Ho-hum. Avenging angel Charles Bronson is back on his beat killing lawbreakers. This time his targets are drug dealers. Bronson is financed by millionaire John P. Ryan, who turns out to be the real drug king-pin, only using Bronson to knock off the competition. Boy, is Charley pissed.

713.   *Deathstalker* (1984, New World, 80m, c). P James Sbardellati, Hector Olivera & Alex Sessa, D John Watson, W Howard Cohen, Ph Leonardo Rodriguez Solis, M Oscar Cardozo Ocampo, ED John Adams & Silvia Ripoll.

LP Richard Hill (Deathstalker), Richard Brooker (Oghris), Victor Bo (Kang), August Larreta (Salmaron), Marcos Woinsky (Gargit), George Sorvic (King Tulak), Barbi Benton (Codille), Lana Clarkson (Kaira), Bernard Erhard (Munkar).

Filmed in Argentina, this tacky movie presents a ridiculous sword and fantasy story, featuring lots of female nudity. Warrior Richard Hill is always on the lookout for lands to conquer and women to ravage. He combines his two ambitions when he goes after the magic amulet worn by Bernard Erhard, who holds princess Barbi Benton captive. Little Barbi's one talent, which she demonstrates repeatedly, seems to be taking off her clothes.

714. *Deathstalker II: Duel of the Titans* (1988, New Horizon, 78m, c). P Frank Isaac, Jr., D Jim Wynorski, W Neil Ruttenbery & R.J. Robertson (based on a story by Wynorski), PH Leonardo Solis, M Chuck Cirino, Christopher Young & Oscar Cardoza.

LP John Terlesky (Deathstalker), Monique Gabrielle (Evie), John La Zar (Jarek), Toni Naples (Sultana), Maria Socas (Amazon Queen), Marcos Wolinsky (One Eye), Deanna Booher (Gargol).

This tongue-in-cheek sword 'n' sorcery saga, overflowing with dumb jokes, isn't taken seriously by the performers or the directors, nor should it be by the audience. Showing all the acting talent of black-and-white blue movies of the 40s and professional wrestlers, fearless swordsman John Terlecky and exiled princess Monique Gabrielle fight to restore her to her throne.

715. *Deathstalker and the Warriors from Hell* (1989, Concorde, 86m, c). P Alfonso Corona & Antonio De Noreiga, D Corona, W Howard R. Cohen, PH Xavier Cruz, M Israel Torres.

LP John Allen Nelson (Deathstalker), Carla Herd (Carissa/Elezena), Terri Treas (Camisarde), Thom Christopher (Troxartas), Aaron Hernan (Nicias), Roger Cudney (Inares), Agustin Salvat (Makut).

The third in Concorde's "Deathstalker" series has John Allen Nelson treking through a mythical medieval land searching for the secret treasure city of Erendor. He's accompanied by Princess Carla Herd, who is seeking the matching stone to her big diamond. She's killed, but Nelson runs into her sister (also Herd) and the other stone. The performance of the cast is to acting as a kindergarten pageant is to Masterpiece Theater.

716. *Deathrow Gameshow* (1987, Crown International, 83m, c). P Brian J. Smith, D Mark Pirro, W Pirro & Alan Gries, PH Craig Bassuk, M Gregg Gross, ED Tim Shoemaker, PD Mark Simon.

LP John McCafferty (Chuck Toedan), Robin Blythe (Gloria Sternvirgin), Beano (Luigi Pappalardo), Mark Lasky (Momma), Darwyn Carson (Trudy), Debra Lamb (Shanna Shallow), Paul Farbman (Dinko).

Rather than a rating, idiotic movies like this should be accompanied with the location of the sections of the country where it is popular, so normal people can be forewarned about visiting those regions. John McCafferty is the host of a TV gameshow in which condemned prisoners compete for prizes for their surviving relatives before they are put to death on camera.

717. *Deathtrap* (1982, Warner, 115m, c). P Burtt Harris, D Sidney Lumet, W Jay Presson Allen (based on the stage play by Ira Levin), PH Andrzej Bartkowiak, M Johnny Mandel, ED John J. Fitzstephens, PD Tony Walton.

LP Michael Caine (Sidney Bruhl), Christopher Reeve (Clifford Anderson), Dyan Cannon (Myra Bruhl), Irene Worth (Helga ten Dorp), Henry Jones (Porter Milgrim), Joe Silver (Seymour Starger).

Things aren't what they seem in this screen version of Ira Levin's hit play. Michael Caine, a playwright in need of one more hit, is encouraged by his wealthy but ailing wife Dyan Cannon to collaborate with young playwright Christopher Reeve, who seems to idolize Caine. But what is the relationship between these two literary men that causes poor Cannon to suffer a fatal heart attack? There are a lot of twists and turns before everything is straightened out.

718. *The Deceivers* (1988, Cinecom, GB/India, 112m, c). P Ismail Merchant & Tim Van Rellim, D Nicholas Meyer, W Michael Hirst (based on the novel by John Masters), PH Walter Lassally, M John Scott, ED Richard Trevor, PD Ken Adam.

LP Pierce Brosnan (William Savage), Saeed Jaffrey (Hussein), Shashi Kapoor (Chandra Singh), Helena Michell (Sarah Wilson), Keith Michell (Col. Wilson), David Robb (George Angelsmith), Tariq Yunus (Feringea), Jalal Agha (Nawab).

Set in India in 1825, Pierce Brosnan portrays a character based on William Sleeman, an officer of the British East India Company, who took up the crusade of ridding the subcontinent of the Thugee, a secret cult of murderers responsible for the death of some two million people. These "deceivers," also featured in the classic black and white adventure yarn *Guna Din,* worshipped Kali, a six-armed goddess of death and destruction. Their modus operandi was to weasel their way into the confidence of wealthy travelers and then strangle them.

719. *Deep in the Heart* (1983, EMI/Warner, 101m, c, aka *Handgun*). P,D&W Tony Garnett, PH Charles Stewart, M Mike Post, ED William Shapter, PD Lily Kilvert.

LP Karen Young (Kathleen Sullivan), Clayton Day (Larry Keeler), Suzie Humphreys (Nancy), Helena Humann (Miss Davis), Ben Jones (Chuck).

Passive Bostonian Karen Young turns to guns and violence after a rape attempt by macho Texas lawyer Clayton Day. It's a simplistic and confused story.

720. *Deep Space* (1988, TransWorld, 90m, c). P Alan Amiel, D Fred Olen Ray, W Ray & T.L. Lankford, PH Gary Graver, M Robert O. Ragland & Alan Oldfield, ED Natan Zahavi.

LP Charles Napier (Detective Macliamor), Ann Turkel (Carla Sanborn), Bo Svenson (Captain Robertson), Ron Glass (Jerry), Julie Newmar (Elaine Wentworth), James Booth (Dr. Forsyth), Norman Burton (Gen. Randolph).

The alien that goes on a killing spree after escaping from the crash-landing of a space vehicle on earth is revealed to be the product of a top-secret project of the U.S. government.

721. *Deepstar Six* (1989, Tri-Star Pictures, 99m, c). P Sean S. Cunningham & Patrick Markey, D Cunningham, W Lewis Abernathy & Geof Miller (based on a story by Abernathy), PH Mac Ahlberg, M Harry Manfredini, ED David Handman, PD John Reinhart.

LP Taurean Blacque (Laidlaw), Nancy Everhard (Joyce Collins), Greg Evigan (McBride), Miguel Ferrer (Snyder), Nia Peeples (Scarpelli), Matt McCoy (Richardson).

All the oceanographers address each other by their last names in this nautical junket set six miles under the sea. They are experimenting with underseas colonization, and some couples are into introductory breeding. The underseas lab is attacked by a prehistoric monster who is unhappy with the way the neighborhood is deteriorating. It's a flat, unsuspenseful, horrible horror film.

722. *Def-Con 4* (1985, New World, 85m, c). P B.G. Gillian, Maura O'Connell & Paul Donovan, D&W Donovan, PH Doug Connell & Les Krizsan, M Chris Young, ED Todd Ramsay, PD J.W. Walch & Emanuel Jannasch.

LP Lenore Zann (J.J.), Maury Chaykin (Vinny), Kate Lynch (Jordan), Kevin King (Gideon Hayes), John Walsch (Walker), Tim Choate (Howe), Jeff Pustil (Lacey), Donna King (Alice), Allan MacBillivray (Boomer).

Three astronauts, Tim Choate, Kate Lynch and John Walsch, return to post–nuclear holocaust earth to find the survivors to be inhuman renegades and modern savages, led by Donna King.

723. *Defence of the Realm* (1985, Rank-Warner, GB, 96m, c). P Robin Douet & Lynda Myles, D David Drury, W Martin Stellman, PH Roger Deakins, M Richard Hartley, ED Michael Bradsell, PD Roger Murray-Leach.

LP Gabriel Byrne (Nick Mullen), Greta Scacchi (Nina Beckman), Denholm Elliott (Vernon Bayliss), Ian Bannen (Dennis Markham), Fulton Mackay (Victor Kingsbrook), Bill Paterson (Jack Macleod), David Calder (Harry Champion).

Reporter Gabriel Byrne tries to check the relationship between Ian Bannen, a prominent Member of Parliament and the military attaché of the East German embassy, who share the same very expensive lover. It's an efficient conspiracy thriller.

724. *Defense Play* (1988, TransWorld, 93m, c). P Wolf Schmidt, D Monte Markham, W Aubrey Solomon & Steven Greenberg (based on a story by Schmidt & Stan Krantman), PH Tim Galfas, M Arthur B. Rubinstein, ED James Ruxin, PD Petko Kadiev.

LP David Oliver (Scott Denton), Susan Ursitti (Karen Vandemeer), Monte Markham (Col. Mark Denton), Eric Gilliom (Starkey), William Frankfather (Gen. Philips), Jamie McMurray (Norm Beltzer).

Teens David Oliver and Susan Ursitti come to the rescue when her scientist father is killed and his Army colonel dad's career seems at an end when a secret high-tech project goes wrong. They discover dirty-rotten Soviet agents are responsible.

725. *Defiance* (1980, American International, 102m, c). P William S. Gilmore, Jr. & Jerry Bruckheimer, D John Flynn, W Thomas Michael Donnelly (based on a story by Donnelly & Mark Tulin), PH Ric Waite, M Basil Poledouris, ED David Finfer, PD Bill Malley.

LP Jan-Michael Vincent (Tommy), Theresa Saldana (Marsha), Fernando Lopez (Kid), Danny Aiello (Carmine), Art Carney (Abe), Santos Morales (Paolo), Don Blakely (Abbie Jackson), Frank Pesce (Herbie), Rudy Ramos (Angel Cruz).

Like a latter-day Bogie, blue collar outsider Jan-Michael Vincent reluctantly and single-handedly takes on a vicious New York street gang which is terrorizing his neighborhood.

726. *Deja Vu* (1985, Cannon, GB, 90m, c). P Menahem Golan & Yoram Globus, D Anthony Richmond, W Ezra D. Rappaport, Arnold Schmidt & Richmond (adapted by Joane A. Gil, based on a book by Trevor Meldal-Johnson), PH David Holmes, M Pino Donaggio, ED Richard Trevor, PD Tony Woollard.

LP Jaclyn Smith (Maggie Rogers/Brooke Ashley), Nigel Terry (Gregory Thomas/Michael Richardson), Claire Bloom (Eleanor Harvey), Shelley Winters (Olga Nabokov), Richard Kay (William Tanner in 1935), Frank Gatliff (William Tanner in 1984).

Lovers Jaclyn Smith and Nigel Terry learn that they are the reincarnations of a couple who perished in a fire fifty years earlier.

727. *The Delinquents* (1989, Greater Union/Warner, Australia, 101m, c). P Alex Cutler & Michael Wilcox, P Chris Thomson, W Clayton Frohman & Mac Gudgeon (based on a novel by Criena Rohan), PH Andrew Lesnie, M Miles Goodman, ED John Scott, PD Lawrence Eastwood.

LP Kylie Minogue (Lola Lovell), Charlie Schlatter (Brownie Hansen), Angela Punch-McGregor (Mrs. Lovell), Bruno Lawrence (Bosun), Desiree Smith (Mavis), Todd Boyce (Lyle), Melissa Jaffer (Aunt Westbury).

Set in a small town in Queensland in the late 50s, the film tells the story of the passionate love affair of teens Kylie Minogue and Charlie Schlatter. While still in school she becomes pregnant. Their plans to elope are thwarted by her mother, who forces Minogue to have an abortion. The lovers are separated for years but accidentally meet again. The spark is still there, but their problems aren't over.

728. *Delivery Boys* (1984, New World, 94m, c). P Craig Horrall & Per Sjostedt, D&W Ken Handler, PH Larry Revene, ED Gary Karr.

LP Joss Marcano (Max), Tom Sierchio (Joey), Jim Soriero (Conrad), Nelson Vasquez (Izzie), Victor Colicchio (Tony), Naylon Mitchell (Jazz Mace), Ralph Cole, Jr. (Wild Man), Jody Oliver (Angelina).

In this predictable, inane comedy, three pizza delivery boys, Joss Marcano, Tom Sierchio and Jim Soriero, enter a breakdance contest, hoping to win the top prize of $10,000.

729. *The Delos Adventure* (1987, American Cinema, 99m, c). P&D Joseph Purcell, W Purcell & Roger Kern, PH William Meurer, M Richard DeLabio & Kenny Kotwitz, SE Paul Staples.

LP Roger Kern (Bard Clemens), Jenny Neumann (Deni Trion), Kurtwood Smith (Arthur McNeil), E.J. Castillo (Luis Vasquez), Kevin Brophy (Greg Bachman), Al Mancini (Koutsavaki), Charles Lanyer (Dr. James DeKalb).

In this dullish action film, a team of scientists believe that they are planting seismic sensors on the bottom of the ocean off the coast of Chile to monitor earthquake activity. When they are attacked by Russian frogmen, they catch on that the sensors are actually to pick up Soviet submarine activity.

730. *The Delta Force* (1986, Cannon, 129m, c). P Menahem Golan & Yoram Globus, D Golan, W James Bruner & Golan, PH David Gurfinkel, M Alan Silvestri, ED Alain Jakubowicz, PD Luciano Spadoni.

LP Chuck Norris (Major Scott McCoy), Lee Marvin (Col. Nick Alexander), Martin Balsam (Ben Kaplan), Joey

Bishop (Harry Goldman), Robert Forster (Abdul), Lainie Kazan (Sylvia Goldman), George Kennedy (Father O'Malley), Hanna Schygulla (Ingrid), Susan Strasberg (Debra Levine), Robert Vaughn (Gen. Woolbridge), Shelley Winters (Edie Kaplan).

Avenging angel Chuck Norris teams up with Lee Marvin to lead a rescue mission of kidnapped passengers whose airplane has been hijacked by a group of Middle East terrorists.

731. *Delta Pi* (1985, Pegasus, 90m, c, aka *Mugsy's Girls*). P Leonard Shapiro & Kevin Brodie, D&W Brodie, PH Paul Lohmann, M Nelson Kole, ED Bill Parker.

LP Ruth Gordon (Mugs), Laura Brannigan, Joanna Dierek, Estrelita, Rebecca Forstadt & Candace Pandolfo (The Girls), Eddie Deezen (Lane), James Marcel (Shaun).

Ruth Gordon is her usual crusty but appealing self as a sorority house mother who enters her girls into a mud-wrestling contest to raise enough money to pay the mortgage. The story is just an excuse to show some beautiful girls scantily clothed.

Delusion see The House Where Death Lives

Demon Rage see Satan's Mistress

732. *Demonoid* (1981, American Panorama, 78m, c, aka *Macabra*). P&D Alfred Zacharias, W David Lee Fein, Zacharias & E. Amos Powell (based on a story by Zacharias), PH Alex Phillips, Jr., M Richard Gillis, ED Sandy Nervig, SE Bob Burns.

LP Samantha Eggar (Jennifer Baines), Stuart Whitman (Father Cunningham), Roy Cameron Jenson (Mark Baines), Narciso Busquets (Dr. Julian Rivkin), Erika Carlsson (Nurse Morgan), Lew Saunders (Sgt. Leo Matson).

In this inane story, Samantha Eggar and her husband Roy Cameron Jenson are in Mexico searching for silver. Instead they uncover a box containing the hand of the devil. The hand possesses anyone it comes in contact with, compelling them to perform acts of gory violence. They can only escape by destroying their own hands.

733. *Demonwarp* (1988, Vidmark-Design, 91m, c). P Richard L. Albert, D Emmett Alston, W Jim Bertges & Bruce Akiyama (based on a story by John Buechler), PH R. Michael Stringer, M Dan Slider, ED W. Peter Miller & John Travers.

LP George Kennedy (Bill Crafton), David Michael O'Neill (Jack), Pamela Gilbert (Carrie), Billy Jacoby (Tom), Colleen McDermott (Cindy), Hank Stratton (Fred), Michelle Bauer (Betsy), Shannon Kennedy (Tara).

When a Bigfoot creature menaces a group of teenage campers, shotgun-toting George Kennedy becomes their protector. He had lost his daughter to the creature some time before.

734. *Deranged* (1987, Platinum Pictures, 81m, c). P&D Chuck Vincent, W Craig Horrall, PH Larry Revene, M Bill Heller, ED James Davalos.

LP Jane Hamilton [Veronica Hart] (Joyce), Paul Siederman (Frank), Jennifer Delora (Mary Ann), Jill Cumer (Mother), James Gillis (Father), Gary Goldman (Nick), John Brett (Darren), Loretta Palma, Jessica Rose.

Jane Hamilton, on the verge of a nervous breakdown, goes over the edge when she is forced to kill an intruder in her apartment. Rather than call the police, she imagines visits from various unwelcome people, both living and dead. Hamilton [Veronica Hart] and her husband, Chuck Vincent, veterans of the porno movie business, are trying to make it in straight cinema, without much apparent success.

735. *Desert Bloom* (1986, Columbia, 106m, c). P Michael Hausman, D&W Eugene Corr (based on a story by Linda Remy & Corr), PH Reynaldo Villalobos, M Brad Fiedel & Michael Melvoin, ED David Garfield, John Currin & Cari Coughlin.

LP Annabeth Gish (Rose Chismore), Jon Voight (Jack), JoBeth Williams (Lily), Ellen Barkin (Starr), Jay D. Underwood (Robin), Desiree Joseph (Dee Ann), Dusty Balcerzak (Barbara Jo), Allen Garfield (Mr. Mosol).

The time is 1951, the place is Nevada, the background is the dawn of the Atomic age, and the heroine is lovely 13-year-old

Annabeth Gish, who suffers through a chaotic homelife with a brutish drunken stepfather, Jon Voight, and a loving but ineffectual mother, JoBeth Williams. Along comes sexy aunt Ellen Barkin to give the girl some of the female insights she desperately needs.

736. *Desert Hearts* (1985, Goldwyn, 96m, c). P&D Donna Deitch, W Natalie Cooper (based on the novel *Desert of the Heart* by Jane Rule), PH Robert Elswit, ED Robert Estrin, PD Jeannine Oppewall.

LP Helen Shaver (Vivian Bell), Patricia Charbonneau (Cay Rivvers), Audra Lindley (Frances Parker), Andra Akers (Silver), Gwen Welles (Gwen), Dean Butler (Darell), James Staley (Art Warner), Katie La Bourdette (Lucille).

New York college professor Helen Shaver is temporarily in Reno to fulfill the state residency laws so she may get a divorce. Living at the same ranch is casino worker Patricia Charbonneau. The two become friends and ultimately lovers. The subject is well-handled without any appeal to sensationalism.

737. *Desert Warrior* (1985, Concorde/Rodeo, 85m, c, aka *Vindicator; Wheels of Fire*). P&D Cirio H. Santiago, W Frederick Bailey, PH Richard Remias, M Chris Young, ED George Saint.

LP Gary Watkins (Trace), Laura Banks (Stinger), Lynda Wiesmeier (Harley), Linda Grovenor (Spike).

In this violent rip-off of Mad Max movies, tough Gary Watkins is joined by lady bounty hunter Laura Banks and psychic Linda Grovenor is rescuing Watkins' sister Lynda Wiesmeier from a post-nuclear gang of ruthless outlaws.

738. *Deserters* (1983, Exile, Canada, 93m, c). P Tom Braidwood & Jack Darcus, D&W Darcus, PH Tony Westman, M Michael Conway Baker, ED Darcus.

LP Alan Scarfe (Sgt. Ulysses Hawley), Jon Bryden (Peter), Barbara March (Val), Dermot Hennelly (Noel), Ty Haller (Army Captain), Bob Metcalfe, Robin Mossley.

When hard-nosed drill instructor Alan Scarfe is shown up by two trainees in front of an officer, he tracks them down when they go AWOL. The deserters become antiheroes to liberals as victims of the oppressive American government.

739. *Desperately Seeking Susan* (1985, Orion, 104m, c). P Sarah Pillsbury & Midge Sanford, D Susan Seidelman, W Leora Barish, PH Ed Lachman, M Thomas Newman, ED Andrew Mondshein, PD Santo Loquasto.

LP Rosanna Arquette (Roberta), Madonna (Susan), Aidan Quinn (Dez), Mark Blum (Gary), Robert Joy (Jim), Laurie Metcalf (Leslie), Anna Levine (Crystal), Will Patton (Nolan), Peter Maloney (Ian).

Bored New Jersey housewife Rosanna Arquette follows the personal ads in the newspaper and becomes intrigued by a periodically appearing heading *Desperately Seeking Susan.* Arquette goes into New York City and locates the mysterious Susan (Madonna). By a series of Hollywood-like coincidences and circumstances, Arquette believes she is Susan, and so do some dangerous types who worked for a murdered mobster. Despite the fact that neither pop queen Madonna nor wide-eyed Arquette know much about acting, this is an enjoyable piece of fluff.

740. *Destiny to Order* (1989, Cineplex Odeon, Canada, 97m, c). P Seaton McLean, Jonathan Goodwill & John Kramer, D&W Jim Purdy, PH Ludek Bogner, M Dave Gray, ED Ian Webster, PD Richard Harrison.

LP Stephen Ouimette (J.D. Baird), Alberta Watson (Thalia), Michael Ironside (Kenrick), Victoria Snow (Anne).

The trick beginning of this film has a young author working at his wordprocessor when he runs out of ideas for his biker, sex and drug story. His computer is hit by lightning, flinging the author into the world of his characters, where he becomes his own hero.

741. *Destroyer* (1988, Moviestore, 94m, c). P Peter Garrity & Rex Hauck, D Robert Kirk, W Garrity & Hauck, PH Chuy Elizondo, M Patrick O'Hearn, ED Mark Rosenbaum, PD Paul Staheli.

LP Deborah Foreman (Susan Malone), Clayton Rohner (David Harris), Lyle Alzado (Ivan Moser), Anthony Perkins (Director Edwards), Tobias Anderson

(Russell), Lannie Garrett (Sharon Fox), Jim Turner (Rewire).

Former real-life pro football star Lyle Alzado appears as a condemned con, sentenced to fry in the electric chair for murdering 25 people. He goes to the hot seat but it doesn't take. He returns to his speciality, picking on members of a film crew at the prison to film a women-in-the-pen special.

742.   *Detective School Dropouts* (1986, Cannon, 90m, c, aka *Dumb Dicks*). P Menahem Golan & Yoran Globus, D Philip Ottoni, W Lorin Dreyfuss & David Landsberg, PH Giancarlo Ferrando, M G. and M. De Vangelis, ED Cesare D'Amico, PD Antonello Geleng.

LP Lorin Dreyfuss (Paul Miller), Donald Landsberg (Donald Wilson), George Eastman (Bruno), Christian DeSica (Carlo), Valeria Golino (Caterina), Annette Meriweather (Carlotta), Mario Brega (Don Lombardi).

If you enjoy slapstick and consistently low humor this little comedy should grab you. Aspiring detective Donald Landsberg seeks instructions in detection from private eye Lorin Dreyfuss. The two become involved with star-crossed lovers Christian DeSica and Valeria Golino, members of warring Mafia families.

743.   *The Devil and Max Devlin* (1981, Buena Vista, 96m, c). P Jerome Courtland, D Steven Hilliard Stern, W Mary Rodgers (based on a story by Rodgers & Jimmy Sangster), PH Howard Schwartz, M Buddy Baker, ED Raymond A. de Leuw.

LP Elliott Gould (Max Devlin), Bill Cosby (Barney Satin), Susan Anspach (Penny Hart), Adam Rich (Toby Hart), Julie Budd (Stella Summers), David Knell (Nerve Nordlinger), Sonny Shroyer (Big Billy).

Sent to Hell after he is run over by a bus-load of Hari Krishnas, mean landlord Elliott Gould is given a chance by Satan (Bill Cosby) to save himself from eternal damnation if he returns to earth and within three months collects three "unsullied" souls for Hell. Every good movie should have a beginning, a middle and an end. This one only has a beginning.

Devil's Odds see ***The Wild Pair***

744.   *The Devonsville Terror* (1983, MPM/New West, 84m, c). P&D Ulli Lommel, W Lommel, George T. Lindsey & Suzanna Love, PH Lommel, M Ray Colcord & Ed Hill, ED Richard Brummer, SE Matthew Mungle, George Rogers, David Hewitt & Donald Flick.

LP Suzanna Love (Jenny), Donald Pleasence (Dr. Warley), Deanna Haas (Monica), Mary Walden (Chris), Morrigan Hurt, Leslie Smith, Barbara Cihlar (Witches).

As they are executed in 1683, witches Morrigan Hurt, Leslie Smith and Barbara Cihlar utter a curse on their host New England town. Three hundred years later to the day, mysterious Suzanna Love appears in the town to wreak havoc.

745.   *Diamond Skulls* (1989, Film Four Intl., GB, 87m, c, aka *Dark Obsession*). P Tim Bevan, D Nick Broomfield, W Tim Rose Price, PH Michael Coulter, M Hans Zimmer, ED Rodney Holland, PD Jocelyn James.

LP Gabriel Byrne (Sir Hugo Buckton), Amanda Donohoe (Lady Virginia Buckton), Michael Hordern (Hugo's Father), Judy Parfitt (Hugo's Mother), Douglas Hodge (Jamie), Sadie Frost (Rebecca), Ian Carmichael (Exeter).

Extremely jealous businessman Gabriel Byrne is driving someone else's car after a drunken dinner. He hits a young woman, fatally injuring her. He and his friends leave her to die. When Douglas Hodge, who is having an affair with Byrne's sister Sadie Frost, threatens to expose Byrne, the latter and his friends silence Hodge permanently.

746.   *Die Hard* (1988, 20th Century–Fox, 131m, c). P Lawrence Gordon & Joel Silver, D John McTiernan, W Jeb Stuart & Steven de Souza (based on the novel by Roderick Thorp), PH Jan De Bont, M Michael Kamen, ED Frank J. Urioste & John F. Link†, PD Jackson DeGovia, SOUND Don Bassman, Kevin F. Cleary, Richard Overton & Al Overton†, SOUND EFFECTS EDITING Stephen H. Flick & Richard Shorr†, VE Richard Edlund, Al DiSarro, Brent Boates & Thaine Morris†.

LP Bruce Willis (John McClane), Bonnie Bedelia (Holly Gennaro McClane), Reginald Veljohnson (Sgt. Al Powell),

Paul Gleason (Dwayne T. Robinson), De'voreaux White (Argyle), William Atherton (Thornburg), Hart Bochner (Ellis), James Shigeta (Takagi), Alan Rickman (Hans Gruber), Alexander Godunov (Karl).

While in L.A. to see his estranged wife Bonnie Bedelia at a Christmas party held in the skyscraper where she works, New York cop Bruce Willis is forced to become a Rambo-like commando. One-by-one he picks off the 12 German thieves, posing as terrorists, who have occupied the building, taking Bedelia and 30 others as hostages. Everything is a bit too pat in this action-adventure yarn, with only Willis, Bedelia and a fat black desk cop Reginald Veljohnson wearing white hats. Besides the murderous invaders, the other cops, the FBI, the media and some of the hostages are shown as insensitive, unthinking, interfering fools.

747. Die Laughing (1980, Orion/Warner, 108m, c). P Mark Canton & Robby Benson, D Jeff Werner, W Benson, Jerry Segal & Scott Parker (based on a story by Parker), PH David Myers, M Benson & Segal, ED Neil Travis, PD James H. Spencer.

LP Robby Benson (Pinsky), Linda Grovenor (Amy), Charles Durning (Arnold), Elsa Lanchester (Sophie), Bud Cort (Mueller), Marty Zagon (Friend), Rita Taggart (Thelma), Larry Hankin (Bock), Samuel Krachmalnick (Zhukov).

In this pitiful black comedy, would-be rock star Robby Benson is pitted against a scar-faced assassin, a mad computer genius and a whole circus of Russian spies.

748. Dim Sum: A Little Bit of Heart (1985, Orion Classics, 88m, c). P Tom Sternberg, Wayne Wang & Danny Yung, D Wang, W Terrel Seltzer (based on an idea by Laureen Chew, Seltzer & Wang), PH Michael Chin, M Todd Boekelheide, ED Ralph Wikke & David Lindblom.

LP Laureen Chew (Geraldine Tam), Kim Chew (Mrs. Tam), Victor Wong (Uncle Tam), Ida F.O. Chung (Auntie Mary), Cora Miao (Julia), John Nishio (Richard), Amy Hill (Amy Tam), Keith Choy (Kevin Tam).

This gentle comedy explores the universal problems of a grown woman living with her widowed mother. Thirty-year-old San Francisco Chinese-American Laureen Chew is torn between her desire to marry her boyfriend and her duty to her mother Kim Chew. Although the latter has lived in America for a long time, she refuses to become assimilated.

749. Diner (1982, MGM/United Artists, 110m, c). P Jerry Weintraub, D&W Barry Levinson† (for writing), PH Peter Sova, M Bruce Brody & Ivan Kral, ED Stu Linder, AD Leon Harris, SD R. Chris Westlund.

LP Steve Guttenberg (Eddie), Daniel Stern (Shrevie), Mickey Rourke (Boogie), Kevin Bacon (Timothy Fenwick), Timothy Daly (Billy), Ellen Barkin (Beth), Paul Reiser (Modell), Kathryn Dowling (Barbara), Michael Tucker (Bogel), Colette Blonigan (Carol Heathrow), Kelle Kipp (Diane).

This very witty, original comedy-drama is set in 1959 where an all-nite Baltimore diner is the gathering spot for a group of five lifelong buddies, Steve Guttenberg, Daniel Stern, Timothy Daly, Mickey Rourke and Kevin Bacon. They are trying to make sense out of their lives. Just out of college, they are beginning to drift apart, but still cling to the group rituals they have shared since childhood. Writer-director Barry Levinson remembers his youth with a sure eye and audiences are the beneficiaries.

750. The Dirt Bike Kid (1985, Concorde, 90m, c). P Julie Corman, D Hoite C. Caston, W David Brandes & Lewis Colick (based on a story by J. Halloran), PH Daniel Lacambre, M Bill Bowersock & Phil Shenale, ED Jeff Freeman.

LP Peter Billingsley (Jack Simmons), Stuart Pankin (Mr. Hodgkins), Anne Bloom (Janet Simmons), Patrick Collins (Mike), Sage Parker (Miss Clavell), Chad Sheets (Bo), Gavin Allen (Max), Danny Breen (Flaherty).

In a strictly formula teenage film, young Peter Billingsley becomes a white knight on a very unusual Yamaha bike. He takes on unscrupulous banker Stuart Pankin and some very nasty bikers.

751. Dirty Dancing (1987, Vestron, 97m, c). P Linda Gottlieb & Eleanor Bergstein, D Emile Ardolino, W Bergstein, PH Jeff Jur, M John Morris, ED

Peter C. Frank, PD David Chapman, ML "The Time of My Life" by Frank Previte, Donald Markowitz & John DeNicola*, Performed by Bill Medley & Jennifer Warnes.

LP Jennifer Grey (Frances "Baby" Houseman), Patrick Swayze (Johnny Castle), Jerry Orbach (Dr. Jake Houseman), Cynthia Rhodes (Penny Johnson), Jack Weston (Max Kellerman), Jane Brucker (Lisa Houseman), Kelly Bishop (Marjorie Houseman), Lonny Price (Neil Kellerman), Max Cantor (Robbie Gould).

Joel Grey's darling daughter, Jennifer Grey, and Patrick Swayze hit the heights with this delightful film. It is set in the early 60s at a Catskill Mountains–like resort, to which middle-class Jewish Gray, her doctor father, her mother and older sister come for the summer. It was a time when one could get away with calling an almost grown woman, "Baby." Grey meets, falls in love with and becomes the dancing partner of resort entertainer employee Swayze. Before completing their climactic exotic and erotic dance number, Swayze has to survive being suspected of both getting his previous partner pregnant and stealing from the guests.

752. *Dirty Laundry* (1987, Skouras, 79m, c). P William Webb & Monica Webb, D William Webb, W Brad Munson (based on a story by William Webb), PH John Huneck, M Sam Winans & Elliot Solomon, ED Richard Casey.

LP Leigh McCloskey (Jay), Jeanne O'Brien (Trish), Frankie Valli (Macho Marty Benedictine), Sonny Bono (Maurice), Nicholas Worth (Vito), Robbie Rist (Oscar), Johnny B. Frank (Ricky Savoy).

In this embarrassing comedy, Leigh McCloskey, washing his clothes at a laundromat, mixes up his laundry with a drug dealer's drop, and walks off with $1 million. Naturally the drug dealer is anxious to get his loot back.

753. *Dirty Rotten Scoundrels* (1988, Orion, 110m, c). P Bernard Williams, D Frank Oz, W Dale Launer, Stanley Shapiro & Paul Henning, PH Michael Ballhaus, M Miles Goodman, ED Stephen A. Rotter & William Scharf, PD Roy Walker.

LP Steve Martin (Freddy Benson), Michael Caine (Lawrence Jamieson), Glenne Headly (Janet Colgate), Anton Rodgers (Inspector Andre), Barbara Harris (Fanny Eubanks), Ian McDiarmid (Arthur), Dana Ivey (Mrs. Reed).

Steve Martin and Michael Caine star in a remake of the 1964 comedy *Bedtime Story,* starring Marlon Brando and David Niven. Caine is a suave con-man who lives off the money of rich women who visit the Riviera. Martin is a slob American con-man who also makes his living taking money from women. He has invaded Caine's hunting grounds. A contest involving wealthy young Glenne Headly is arranged to determine who will have the region as his private preserve.

754. *Dirty Tricks* (1981, Avco Embassy, Canada, 91m, c). P Claude Heroux, D Alvin Rakoff, W William Norton, Sr., Eleanor Elias Norton, Thomas Gifford & Camille Gifford (based on a novel by Thomas Gifford), PH Richard Ciupka, M Hagood Hardy, ED Alan Collins.

LP Elliott Gould (Colin Chandler), Kate Jackson (Polly Bishop), Arthur Hill (Bert Prosser), Rich Little (Robert Brennan), Nick Campbell (Bill Darcy), Angus McInnes (FBI Jones), Michael Kirby (FBI Wicklow).

Harvard history professor Elliott Gould gets mixed up in a government plot to cover up some documents which implicate George Washington in a political scandal. The film is absurd and there's not even any academic humor worth noting, and we all know how truly hilarious academicians are.

755. *The Disappearance* (1981, World Northal, GB/Canada, 88m, c). P David Hemmings & Gerry Arbeid, D Stuart Cooper, W Paul Mayersberg (based on the novel *Echoes of Celandine* by Derek Marlow), PH John Alcott, M Robert Farnon, PD Anne Pritchard.

LP Donald Sutherland (Jay), Francine Racette (Celandine), Christopher Plummer (Deverell), David Hemmings (Edward), David Warner (Burband), Virginia McKenna (Catherine), John Hurt, Peter Bowles, Michelle Magny.

Hit man Donald Sutherland accepts an assignment in Britain, but is preoccupied with the break-up of his marriage and the disappearance of his wife. So much talent, so little demonstrated.

756. *Disorderlies* (1987, Warner, 96m, c). P Michael Schultz, George Jackson & Mitchell Jaffe, D Schultz, W Mark Feldberg & Mitchell Klebanoff, PH Rolf Kesterman, ED Ned Humphreys.

LP Damon Wimbley (Kool Rock), Darren Robinson (Buffy), Mark Morales (Markie), Ralph Bellamy (Albert Dennison), Tony Plana (Miguel), Anthony Geary (Winslow Lowry), Marco Rodriguez (Luis Montana), Troy Beyer (Carla).

Hoping to push his ancient uncle Ralph Bellamy into the grave so he may collect his millions, Anthony Geary hires Damon Wimbley, Darren Robinson and Mark Morales, known collectively as the Rap group "The Fat Boys" to care for Bellamy, hoping their incompetency will do the old man in. However their energy actually rejuvenates Bellamy.

757. *Disorganized Crime* (1989, Touchstone Pictures, 98m, c). P Lynn Bigelow, D&W Jim Kouf, PH Ron Garcia, M David Newman, ED Frank Morriss & Dallas Puett, PD Waldemar Kalinowski.

LP Hoyt Axton (Sheriff Henault), Corbin Bernsen (Frank Salazar), Ruben Blades (Carlos Barrios), Fred Gwynne (Max Green), Ed O'Neill (George Denver), Lou Diamond Phillips (Ray Forgy), Daniel Roebuck (Bill Lonigan).

It's a bank-heist story involving four mismatched gang members and a pair of dumb detectives who interfere with their plans.

758. *Distant Thunder* (1988, Paramount, US/Canada, 114m, c). P Robert Schaffel, D Rick Rosenthal, W Robert Stitzel (based on a story by Stitzel & Deedee Wehle), PH Ralf D. Bode, M Maurice Jarre, ED Dennis Virkler.

LP John Lithgow (Mark Lambert), Ralph Macchio (Jack Lambert), Kerrie Keane (Char), Reb Brown (Harvey Nitz), Janet Margolin (Barbara Lambert), Dennis Arndt (Larry), Jamey Sheridan (Moss), Tom Bower (Louis).

Vietnam veteran John Lithgow attempts to have some kind of relationship with his son, Ralph Macchio, who he abandoned along with the boy's mother when Ralph was only three. The duo's attempts to work out their anger, resentment, frustrations and pain is made more difficult by a more deranged member of Lithgow's group of Vietnam veteran dropouts.

759. *Distant Voices, Still Lives* (1989, BFI/Film Four, GB, 85m, c). P Jennifer Howarth, D&W Terence Davies, PH William Diver & Patrick Duval, ED William Diver, AD Miki van Zwanenberg & Jocelyn James.

LP Freda Dowie (Mother), Peter Postlethwaite (Father), Angela Walsh (Eileen), Lorraine Ashbourne (Maisie), Dean Williams (Tony), Sally Davies (Eileen as a chile), Nathan Walsh (Tony as a child).

It's a bittersweet look at the lives of a working class family in postwar Liverpool.

760. *Distortions* (1988, Cori, 96m, c). P Jackelyn Giroux, D Armand Mastrioanni, W John Goff, PH John Dirlam, M David Morgan, ED Jack Tucker.

LP Steve Railsback (Scott), Olivia Hussey (Amy), Piper Laurie (Margot), June Chadwick (Kelly), Rita Gam (Mildred), Terence Knox (Paul Elliot), Edward Albert (Jason), Tom J. Castronova (Det. Harry Cory).

The film is meant to be a sizzling, sexy and surprising tale of double, triple and quadruple crosses. Olivia Hussey, whose face has been burnt beyond recognition in a car crash which kills her husband, becomes the victim of a plot to drive her insane and steal her insurance money. Rent the video and decide if they succeeded.

761. *The Distribution of Lead* (1989, Zeno Films, 77m, c). P,D,W&ED Charles Libin, PH Paul A. Cameron, M John Zorn.

LP Katherine Rose (Maude), Ely Rowe (Fred), Ghasem Ebrahimian (Gus), Derek Lynch (Albert), Corey Shaff (Dylan), Pouran Esrafily (Paula), Mindel Goldstein (Joanne Ford), Paul Libin (Duke West).

In this claustrophobic picture, five intense young Wall Street types, led by ruthless Pouran Esrafily, take over and hold captive the inhabitants of a working-class apartment building. The urban terrorists had botched an attempt to take over the firm where they worked, killing a board member in the process. One by one stray bullets into the apartment pick off members of the gang.

762.   *Do the Right Thing*   (1989, Universal, 120m, c). P,D&W Spike Lee† (for original screenplay), PH Ernest Dickerson, M Bill Lee, ED Barry Alexander Brown, PD Wynn Thomas.

LP Danny Aiello† (Sal), Ossie Davis (Da Mayor), Ruby Dee (Mother Sister), Richard Edson (Vito), Giancarlo Esposito (Buggin Out), Spike Lee (Mookie), Bill Nunn (Radio Raheem), John Turturro (Pino), Paul Benjamin (ML), Frankie Faison (Coconut Sid), Robin Harris (Sweet Dick Willie), Joie Lee (Jade), John Savage (Clifton).

Thirty-two-year-old auteur Spike Lee's film is seeped in controversy. It's the story of a day of racism in Brooklyn's Bedford-Stuyvesant neighborhood. An argument between decent, hard-working pizzeria owner Danny Aiello and Bill Nunn over the volume of the latter's giant boom box, leads to Nunn's being killed by police and Aiello's place being destroyed by black rage. The polemics aside, the performances are outstanding, and there is little doubt that Lee is a multithreat talent in the league of Woody Allen. There were many who were surprised and outraged that the film was not nominated for a Best Picture Academy Award, but then controversial pictures frequently are overlooked.

763.   *D.O.A.*   (1988, Touchstone, 93m, c). P Ian Sander & Laura Ziskin, D Rocky Morton & Annabel Jankel, W Charles Edward Pogue (based on a story by Pogue, Russell Rouse & Clarence Greene), PH Yuri Neyman, M Chaz Jankel, ED Michael R. Miller, PD Richard Amend.

LP Dennis Quaid (Dexter Cornell), Meg Ryan (Sydney Fuller), Daniel Stern (Hal Petersham), Charlotte Rampling (Mrs. Fitzwaring), Jane Kaczmarek (Gail Cornell), Robin Johnson (Cookie Fitzwaring), Christopher Neame (Bernard).

Cynical professor Dennis Quaid has been poisoned with a slow-acting toxin that will soon kill him. He and student Meg Ryan pursue his "killer." The film originally was made in 1949 as a black-and-white thriller starring Edmond O'Brien. It was also made in 1969 with Tom Tryon, under the name *Color Me Dead*. None of the three are much to get excited about.

764.   *Dr.   Alien*   (1989, Phantom Prods., 87m, c). P Dave DeCoteau & John Schouweiler, D DeCoteau, W Kenneth J. Hall, PH Nicholas Von Sternberg, M Reg Purcell & Sam Winans, ED Tony Malanurski, PD Royce Mathew.

LP Billy Jacoby (Wesley Littlejohn), Judy Landers (Ms. Xenobia), Olivia Barash (Leanne), Stuart Fratkin (Marvin), Raymond O'Connor (Drax), Arlene Golonka (Mom), Bobby Jacoby (Bradford Littlejohn), Julie Gray (Lynn), Troy Donahue (Dr. Ackerman).

Nerdish college freshman Billy Jacoby has been chosen for an experiment by new biology professor Judy Landers. She actually is an alien from another planet who has killed biology professor Troy Donahue and taken his job. The original title of the film will give you an idea of the nature of the experiment: *I Was a Teenage Sex Mutant*.

765.   *The Doctor and the Devils*   (1985, 20th Century–Fox, GB, 93m, c). P Jonathan Sanger, D Freddie Francis, W Ronald Harwood (based on the original screenplay by Dylan Thomas), PH Gerry Turpin & Norman Warwick, M John Morris, ED Laurence Mery-Clark, PD Robert Laing.

LP Timothy Dalton (Dr. Thomas Rock), Jonathan Pryce (Robert Fallon), Twiggy (Jenny Bailey), Julian Sands (Dr. Murray), Stephen Rea (Timothy Broom), Phyllis Logan (Elizabeth Rock), Beryl Reid (Mrs. Flynn), Patrick Stewart (Prof. Macklin), Sian Phillips (Annabella Rock).

Dedicated Victorian scientist Timothy Dalton doesn't ask any questions when his suppliers of cadavers, Jonathan Pryce and Stephen Rea (based on real-life graverobbers and murderers Burke and Hare), keep him well stocked with freshly deceased corpses.

766. *Dr. Caligari* (1989, Steiner Films, Canada, 80m, c). P Joseph F. Robertson, D Stephen Sayadian, W Jerry Stahl & Sayadian, PH Ladi von Jansky, M Mitchell Froom, ED G. Martin Steiner, PD Sayadian.

LP Madeleine Reynal (Dr. Caligari), Fox Harris, Laura Albert, Jennifer Balgobin, John Durbin, Gene Zerna.

The difference in this production of the famous horror story (other than it's not worth seeing) is that the doctor is a sadomasochistic, metal breast-plated woman (Madeleine Reynal) who runs experiments in pain at her CIA (Caligari Insane Asylum) establishment.

767. *Doctor Detroit* (1983, Universal, 91m, c). P Robert K. Weiss, D Michael Pressman, W Carl Gottlieb, Robert Boris & Bruce Jay Friedman (based on Friedman's novel *Detroit Abe*), PH King Baggot, M Lalo Schifrin, ED Christopher Greenbury, PD Lawrence G. Paull.

LP Dan Aykroyd (Clifford Skridlow), Howard Hesseman (Smooth Walker), Donna Dixon (Monica), Lydia Lei (Jasmine), T.K. Carter (Diavolo), Lynn Whitfield (Thelma), Franc Drescher (Karen), Kate Murtagh (Mom), Andrew Duggan (Harmon).

Dan Aykroyd is occasionally a very funny movie personality. This wretched film is not an example of his comedy talent. He stars as a nerd's nerd, a professor who innocently finds himself the pimp for five beautiful high-price call girls. This entangles him in a deadly struggle for control of the girl's careers with disgustingly mean and evil Kate Murtagh. The film is totally moronic and should only be watched by those undergoing punishment for some serious infraction.

768. *Dr. Hackenstein* (1989, Vista Street Prods., 88m, c). P Reza Mizbani & Megan Barnett, D Richard Clark, W Clark, PH Jens Sturup, M Randy Miller, ED Tony Miller, PD Leon King.

LP David Muir (Dr. Elliot Hackenstein), Stacey Travis (Melanie Victor), Catherine Davis Cox (Leslie), Dyanne DiRosario (Wendy), John Alexis (Alex), Catherine Cahn (Yolanda).

Doctor David Muir plans to bring his wife back to life with the aid of spare body parts unwillingly contributed by three pretty girls. The latter have been forced to take refuge in the doctor's manor after their car crashes.

769. *Dr. Heckyl and Mr. Hype* (1980, Cannon, 99m, c). P Menahem Golan & Yoram Globus, D&W Charles B. Griffith, PH Robert Carras, M Richard Band, ED Skip Schoolnik, PD Maxwell Mendes.

LP Oliver Reed (Dr. Heckyl/Mr. Hype), Sunny Johnson (Coral Careen), Maia Danziger (Miss Fineburn), Mel Welles (Dr. Vince Hinkle), Virgil Frye (Lt. MacDruck "Il Topo"), Kedrick Wolfe (Dr. Lew Hoo), Jackie Coogan (Sgt. Fleacollar), Corinne Calvet (Pizelle Puree).

Oliver Reed stars in this comedy as a repulsive-looking podiatrist who attempts suicide by drinking a potion and becomes an incredibly handsome murderer. The film was made "with apologies to Robert Louis Stevenson," as well it should have been.

770. *Dr. Jekyll's Dungeon of Death* (1982, New American, 88m, c). P&D James Wood, W James Mathers, PH Wood, M Marty Allen, ED Wood.

LP James Mathers (Dr. Jekyll), John Kearney, Tom Nicholson, Dawn Carver Kelly, Nadine Kalmes.

Apparently no money was wasted (or spent) on this stinker shot in Nevada and telling the story of Dr. Jekyll's grandson who injects his captives with an aggression serum. The result is torture and sadism. It apparently bothers no one that the virtuous Dr. Jekyll died before he could wed and sire a child, let alone have a grandson.

771. *Dogs in Space* (1987, Skouras, Australia, 108m, c). P Glenys Rowe, D&W Richard Lowenstein, PH Andrew De Groot, M Ollie Olsen, ED Jill Bilcock, AD Jody Borland.

LP Michael Hutchence (Sam), Saskia Post (Anna), Nique Needles (Tim), Deanna Bond (The Girl), Tony Helou (Luchio), Chris Haywood (Chainsaw Man), Peter Walsh (Anthony), Laura Swanson (Clare), Adam Briscomb (Grant).

Michael Hutchence, the lead singer of

the Australian rock group INXS, stars in this film about the Haight-Asbury–like pop culture community of Melbourne in 1978. The almost nonexistent plot is merely a device to introduce the songs.

Dogs of Hell see Rotweiler: Dogs of Hell

772. ***The Dogs of War*** (1980, United Artists, GB, 122m, c). P Larry DeWaay, D John Irvin, W Gary DeVore & George Malko (based on the novel by Frederick Forsyth), PH Jack Cardiff, M Geoffrey Burgon, ED Antony Gibbs, PD Peter Mullins, SE Larry Cavanaugh, Rudi Liszczak, Steve Lombardi & Mike Collins.

LP Christopher Walken (Shannon), Tom Berenger (Drew), Colin Blakely (North), Hugh Millais (Endean), Paul Freeman (Derek), Jean-Francois Stevenin (Michel), JoBeth Williams (Jessie), Robert Urquhart (Capt. Lockhart), Winston Ntshona (Dr. Okoye), Pedro Armendariz (Major).

Mercenary Christopher Walken is hired to overthrow an African dictator. He and his fellow soldiers-of-fortune make an impressive raid on the country. The special effects are the best thing in this slickly made action film.

773. ***Doin' Time*** (1985, Warner, 80m, c). P Bruce Mallen & George Mendeluk, D Mendeluk, W Franelle Silver, Ron Zwang & Dee Caruso (based on a story by Silver, Zwang, Mendeluk & Peter Wilson), PH Ronald V. Garcia, M Charles Fox, ED Stanford C. Allen, PD Jack McAdam.

LP Jeff Altman (Duke Jarrett), Dey Young (Vicki Norris), Richard Mulligan (Mongo Mitchell), John Vernon (Big Mac), Colleen Camp (Nancy Catlett), Melanie Chartoff (Linda Libel), Judy Landers (The Bride).

Meant to be a comedy about the antics of the amusing convicts in the John Dillinger Memorial Penitentiary, the film is only a foul-mouthed, bathroom-humor, unfunny flip side of *Police Academy*.

774. ***Doin' Time on Planet Earth*** (1988, Cannon, 85m, c). P Menahem Golan & Yoram Globus, D Charles Matthau, W Darren Star (based on a story by Star, Andrew Licht & Jeffrey A. Mueller), PH Timothy Suhrstedt, M Dana Kaproff, ED Alan Balsam & Sharyn L. Ross, PD Curtis A. Schnell.

LP Nicholas Strouse (Ryan Richmond), Andrea Thompson (Lisa Winston), Hugh Gillin (Fred Richmond), Hugh O'Brian (Richard Camalier), Timothy Patrick Murphy (Jeff Richmond), Candice Azzara (Edna Pinsky), Roddy McDowall (Minister), Adam West (Charles Pinsky), Maureen Stapleton (Harriett).

Nicholas Strouse feels so alienated from his family, he wonders if he isn't from another planet. Wackos Candice Azzara and Adam West, who may or may not be from another planet themselves, encourage his fantasy.

775. ***Dolls*** (1987, Empire, 77m, c). P Brian Yuzna, D Stuart Gordon, W Ed Naha, PH Mac Ahlberg, M Fuzzbee Morse, ED Lee Percy, SE John Brunner.

LP Ian Patrick Williams (David Bower), Carolyn Purdy-Gordon (Rosemary Bower), Carrie Lorraine (Judy Bower), Guy Rolfe (Gabriel Hartwicke), Hilary Mason (Hilary Hartwicke), Bunty Bailey (Isabel Prange).

Assorted people take refuge on a dark and rainy night in a spooky old house, whose owners make murderous dolls. It lacks any new ideas for this sub-subgenre.

776. ***Dominick and Eugene*** (1988, Orion, 111m, c). P Marvin Minoff & Mike Farrell, D Robert M. Young, W Alvin Sargent & Corey Blechman (based on a story by Danny Porfirio), PH Curtis Clark, ED Arthur Coburn, PD Doug Kraner.

LP Tom Hulce (Dominick Luciano), Ray Liotta (Eugene Luciano), Jamie Lee Curtis (Jennifer Reston), Todd Graff (Larry Higgins), Bill Cobbs (Jesse Johnson), Mimi Cecchini (Mrs. Gianelli), Jacqueline Knapp (Mrs. Vinson), David Strathairn (Martin Chernak).

Tom Hulce and Ray Liotta are fraternal twins living together in Pittsburgh. Mentally retarded Hulce works as a garbage collector, putting Liotta through medical school. When Liotta begins dating fellow medical student Jamie Lee Curtis, he considers leaving home to study at Stanford University. Hulce is terrified that his well-ordered world is falling apart. This is a beautifully acted and very skillfully directed film.

777. ***Don't Answer the Phone*** (1980, Scorpion/Crown, 94m, c, aka *The Hollywood Strangler*). P&D Robert Hammer, W Hammer & Michael Castle, PH James Carter, M Byron Allerd, ED Joseph Fineman.

LP James Westmoreland (Chris), Flo Gerrish (Dr. Gale), Ben Frank (Hatcher), Nicholas Worth (Kirk), Stan Haze (Adkins), Gary Allen (Feldon), Pamela Bryant (Sue), Ted Chapman (Bald Man), Denise Galick (Lisa).

Nicholas Worth is an obese Vietnam vet, an obsessed weightlifter, a porno photographer, a rapist and a strangler. He calls a L.A. radio psychiatrist to vent his anger for a larger audience. This wretched sick movie is loosely based on the Hillside Strangler murders of the 70s.

778. ***Don't Change My World*** (1983, Enfield, 89m, c). P George P. Macrenaris, D,W&ED Robert Rector.

LP Roy Tatum (Eric), Ben Jones (Jake), George Macrenaris (Mike), Edie Kramer.

In order to preserve the beauty of the north woods, a nature photographer must thwart a villainous land developer and a reckless poacher.

779. ***Don't Cry, It's Only Thunder*** (1982, Sanrio Communications, 108m, c). P Walt deFarla, D Peter Werner, W Paul Hensler, PH Don McAlpine, M Maurice Jarre, ED Jack Woods & Barbara Pokras, PD Robert Checchi.

LP Dennis Christopher (Brian), Susan Saint James (Katherine), Roger Aaron Brown (Moses), Robert Englund (Tripper), James Whitmore, Jr. (Maj. Flaherty), Lisa Lu (Sister Marie), Thu Thuy (Sister Hoa).

Vietnam drug-dealing medic Dennis Christopher is blackmailed by Army doctor Susan Saint James into helping a group of Vietnamese war orphans. Together they use the black market to buy or steal supplies to run the orphanage.

780. ***Don't Go In the House*** (1980, Film Ventures, 82m, c). P Ellen Hammill, D Joseph Ellison, W Hammill, Ellison & Joseph Masefield, PH Oliver Wood,

M Richard Einhorn, ED Jane Kurson.

LP Dan Grimaldi (Donny), Robert Osth (Bobby), Ruth Dardick (Mrs. Kohler), Charlie Bonet (Ben), Bill Ricci (Vito), Dennis M. Hunter, John Hedberg, Johanna Brushay.

Maniac incinerator operator Dan Grimaldi, burned by his mother as a child, scours discos for victims whom he roasts. He then sets their charred bodies around his house to keep his mother company, having cremated her to a crisp when she died. The bodies come alive and take their revenge.

781. ***Don't Go Into the Woods Alone*** (1982, Borde, 88m, c). P&D James Bryan, W Garth Eliassen, PH Henry Zinman, M H. Kingsley Thurber.

LP Nick McClelland, James P. Hayden, Mary Gail Artz, Angie Brown, Tom Drury.

Four young campers, looking for a relaxing weekend in the wilderness, are stalked by Tom Drury, a crazed monster.

782. ***Don't Mess with My Sister*** (1988, Vidamerica-Shotwed, 84m, c). P,D&W Meir Zarchi, PH Phil Gries, M Todd Rice, ED Zarchi.

LP Joe Perce (Steven), Jeannie Lemay (Wife), Jack Gurci & Peter Sapienza (Brothers-in-law), Laura Lanfranchi (Annika).

When accounting student Joe Perce falls for the belly dancer his wife hired to entertain at his surprise birthday, his wife's Italian-American brothers plan to teach the unfaithful husband a lesson.

783. ***Don't Open Till Christmas*** (1984, 21st Century–Fox, GB, 86m, c). P Dick Randall & Steve Minasian, D Edmund Purdom, W Derek Ford & Al McGoohan, PH Alain Pudney, M Des Dolan, ED Ray Selfe.

LP Edmund Purdom (Inspector Harris), Alan Lake (Giles), Belinda Mayne (Kate), Gerry Sundquist (Cliff), Mark Jones (Sgt. Powell), Caroline Munro (Herself), Kevin Lloyd (Gerry), Kelly Baker (Experience Girl).

In a dreary, dull film, police inspector Edmund Purdom is assigned the case of tracking down the maniac who kills various people he finds dressed as Father Christmas (Santa Claus).

Don't Turn Out the Light see Skull: A Night of Terror

784. Doom Asylum (1988, Filmworld, 78m, c). P Steve Menkin, D Richard Friedman, W Rick Marx (based on a story by Friedman, Menkin & Marx), PH Larry Revene, M Jonathan Stuart & Dave Erlanger, ED Ray Shapiro, PD Kosmo Vinyl.

LP Patty Mullen (Judy/Kiki), Ruth Collins (Tina), Kristin Davis (Jane), William Hay (Mike), Kenny L. Price (Dennis), Harrison White (Darnell).

The killer in this straight-to-video movie walked away from his own autopsy ten years earlier. He's a maniac terrorizing teenagers like all the others in slasher films, but at least he has a sense of humor — not, however, that his victims have an opportunity to appreciate it.

785. Door to Door (1984, Shapiro, 88m, c). P Ken Wales, D Patrick Bailey, W Peter Baloff & Dave Wollert.

LP Ron Leibman (Larry Price), Arliss Howard (Leon Spencer), Jane Kaczmarek (Katherine Holloway), Alan Austin (Jimmy Lupus).

Con-man vacuum cleaner salesman Ron Liebman is being blackmailed by Alan Austin, a detective for the vacuum cleaner company. While on the road, Liebman passes on his various swindling tricks to young Arliss Howard. The film could take lessons from *The Flim Flam Man* (1967).

786. The Dorm That Dripped Blood (1983, New Image/Wescom, 84m, c). P Jeffrey Obrow, D Obrow & Stephen Carpenter, W Obrow, Carpenter & Stacey Giachino, PH Carpenter, M Chris Young, ED Obrow.

LP Laurine Lapinski, Stephen Sachs, David Snow, Pamela Holland, Daphne Zuniga.

A seven-story dorm is ruled unsafe and must be torn down. Five college students volunteer to close the dorm. Mysteriously all phone lines are cut and the lights fail, plunging the building into darkness. One by one the students disappear. As the terror mounts, the survivors realize they are up against a psychopathic killer.

787. Dot and the Bunny (1983, Yoram Gross Film Studio, Australia, animated, 80m, c). P&D Yoram Gross, W John Palmer (based on a story by Gross), PH John Shaw, Jenny Ochse & Graham Sharp (animation), M Bob Young, ED Christopher Plowright, ANIM D Athol Henry.

VOICES Drew Forsythe, Barbara Frawley, Ron Haddrick, Anne Haddy, Ross Higgins, Robyn Moore.

This creative children's film goes from live-action sequences of animals to animated characters. Dot searches for Joey, a kangaroo through the back bush of Australia. Also on the hunt is the bunny who wishes to become a kangaroo and take Joey's place.

Double Down see Stacy's Knights

788. Double Exposure (1982, Crown, 95m, c). P,D&W William Byron Hillman, PH R.M. Stringer, M Jack Goga, PD Ron Talsky.

LP Michael Callan, Joanna Pettet, James Stacy, Pamela Hensley, Cleavon Little, Seymour Cassel, Misty Rowe, Joey Forman, Terry Moore.

A photographer's friend is revealed to be a psychopathic killer who cannot resist his urges. Audiences can easily resist this trash despite the familiar names in the cast.

789. Double Exposure (1987, Omega, 103m, c, aka *Terminal Exposure*). P&D Nico Mastorakis, W Mastorakis & Kirk Ellis (based on a story by Mastorakis), PH Cliff D. Ralke, ED Hans Zimmer, M Mastorakis & Roger Tweten, PD Patricia Hall.

LP Mark Hennessy (Lenny), Scott King (Bruce), Hope Marie Carlton (Christie), Steve Donmyer (Skip), Ted Lange (Fantastic), John Vernon (Karrothers), Joe Phelan (Eskanazy).

Aimless buddies Mark Hennessy and Scott King decide to take photos of the lovely bottoms of the beach bunnies who hang out at Venice Beach, California, so they can put together a calendar to sell. As in *Blow-Up,* they accidentally photograph a murder. The woman holding a gun can be identified by a rose tattoo on her derriere.

790. Double Negative (1980, Quadrant, Canada, 96m, c). P Jerome Simon, D George Bloomfield, W Thomas Hedley, Jr., Charles Dennis & Janis Allen (based on the novel *The Three Roads* by

Ross MacDonald), PH Rene Verzier, M Paul Hoffert, ED George Appleby.

LP Michael Sarrazin (Michael Taylor), Susan Clark (Paula West), Anthony Perkins (Lawrence Miles), Howard Duff (Lester Harlan), Kate Reid (Mrs. Swanscott), Al Waxman (D'Allasandro), Elizabeth Shepherd (Frances).

After the murder of his wife, journalist Michael Sarrazin, accused of the crime, is confined to a mental institution. His lover Susan Clark springs him from the loony bin, hoping she can help him find the real killer, before he goes off the deep end again.

791. *Down and Out in Beverly Hills* (1986, Touchstone, 103m, c). P&D Paul Mazursky, W Mazursky & Leon Capetanos (based on the play *Bondu Sauvé des Eaux* by René Fauchois), PH Donald McAlpine, M Andy Summers, ED Richard Halsey, PD Pato Guzman.

LP Nick Nolte (Jerry Baskin), Richard Dreyfuss (Dave Whiteman), Bette Midler (Barbara Whiteman), Little Richard (Orvis Goodnight), Tracy Nelson (Jenny Whiteman), Elizabeth Pena (Carmen), Evan Richards (Max Whiteman), Donald F. Muhich (Dr. Von Zimmer), Paul Mazursky (Sidney Waxman).

Rescued from drowning in the Beverly Hills swimming pool of nouveau-riche Richard Dreyfuss and his wife Bette Midler, bum Nick Nolte is the catalyst for some humorous and startling changes in the lives of everyone in the household. While amusing in spots, the slick comedy is too obvious to be considered great comedy.

792. *Down by Law* (1986, Island Pictures, 107m, b&w). P Alan Kleinberg, D&W Jim Jarmusch, PH Robby Muller, M John Lurie, ED Melody London.

LP Tom Waits (Zack), John Lurie (Jack), Roberto Benigni (Roberto), Nicoletta Braschi (Nicoletta), Ellen Barkin (Laurette), Billie Neal (Bobbie), Rockets Redglare (Gig), Vernel Bagneris (Preston).

In this dour comedy, director-screenwriter Jim Jarmusch trails three losers who make a break from a New Orleans jail and trudge through the Bayou looking for a way to make good their escape. The star of the movie is Italian comic Roberto Benigni. John Lurie and Tom Waits' characters are unusually solemn for a comedy. Still, many find the film to be hilarious at least part of the time. It has been described as drolly understated.

Down on Us see Beyond the Doors

793. *Down Twisted* (1989, Cannon, 97m, c). P Menahem Golan & Yoram Globus, D Albert Pyun, W Gene O'Neill & Noreen Tobin (based on a story by Pyun), PH Walt Lloyd, M Berlin Game, ED Dennis O'Connor, PD Chester Kaczenski.

LP Carey Lowell (Maxine), Charles Rocket (Reno), Trudi Dochtermann (Michelle), Thom Mathews (Damalas), Norbert Weisser (Deltoid), Linda Kerridge (Soames), Nicholas Guest (Brady), Gaylyn Gorg (Blake).

In a hopelessly convoluted mess, industrialist Norbert Weisser hires international jewel thieves to steal a gold religious relic. All hell breaks loose, with murder, double-crosses, explosions, military attacks and numerous chases being just some of the Marx Brothers–like substitutes for a plot.

794. *The Dozens* (1981, First Run/Calliope, 78m, c). P&D Christine Dall & Randall Conrad, W Dall, Conrad & Marian Taylor, PH Joe Vitagliano, ED Dall & Conrad.

LP Debra Margolies (Sally), Edward Mason (Sonny), Marian Taylor (Russel), Jessica Hergert (Jessie), Ethel Michelson (Mother), Genevieve Reale (Debbie), Sumru Tekin (Nivia), Catherine DeLeon (Gypsy).

In this film based on a true story, Debra Margolies is a volatile young woman who tries to put her life back in order after being released from prison.

Dracula's Last Rites see Last Rites

795. *Dracula's Widow* (1988, De Laurentiis, 86m, c). P Stephen Traxler, D Christopher Coppola, W Kathryn Ann Thomas & Coppola, PH Giuseppe Macari, M James Campbell, ED Tom Siiter, PD Alexandra Kicenik.

LP Sylvia Kristel (Vanessa), Josef Sommer (Lt. Lannon), Lenny Von Dohlen (Raymond Everett), Marc Coppola (Brad), Stefan Schnabel (Von Helsing), Rachel Jones (Jenny), Traver Burns, Rick Warner, Candice Sims.

Sylvia Kristel, as the infamous count's widow, arrives in L.A. where she is informed by Lenny Von Dohlen that her husband was killed by the legendary Professor Von Helsing. The latter's grandson, Stefan Schnabel, is out to put an end to Kristel's neck-nibbling ways. The spoof is neither funny nor frightening.

796. *Dragnet* (1987, Universal, 106m, c). P David Permut & Robert K. Weiss, D Tom Mankiewicz, W Aykroyd, Alan Zweibel & Mankiewicz, PH Matthew F. Leonetti, M Ira Newborn, ED Richard Halsey & William D. Gordean, PD Robert F. Boyle.

LP Dan Aykroyd (Sgt. Joe Friday), Tom Hanks (Pep Streebek), Christopher Plummer (Rev. Whirley), Harry Morgan (Capt. Bill Gannon), Alexandra Paul (The Virgin Connie Swail), Jack O'Halloran (Emil Muzz), Elizabeth Ashley (Police Commissioner Jane Kirkpatrick), Dabney Coleman (Jerry Caesar).

Dan Aykroyd does a first-rate imitation of Jack Webb, a monosyllabic, crisp-talking star of the radio, TV and movie *Dragnet*. Aykroyd plays the nephew of the late Sgt. Friday and he carries the latter's love of the city of L.A. and all of its laws to almost idiotic but comical proportions. The story hardly matters. Dan and his new irreverant partner Tom Hanks stumble onto a conspiracy involving sinful evangelist Christopher Plummer and corrupt Police Commissioner Elizabeth Ashley. Other than the exchanges between Aykroyd and Hanks, and the times Aykroyd does his Webb impersonations, the film drags.

Dragon Lady see The G.I. Executioners

797. *Dragonslayer* (1981, Disney/Paramount, 108m, c). P Hal Barwood, D Matthew Robbins, W Barwood & Robbins, PH Derek Vanlint, M Alex North, ED Tony Lawson, PD Elliot Scott, SE Brian Johnson, Dennis Muren, Phil Tippett & Ken Ralston†.

LP Peter MacNicol (Galen), Caitlin Clarke (Valerian), Ralph Richardson (Ulrich), John Hallam (Tyrian), Peter Eyre (Casidorus Rex), Albert Salmi (Greil), Sydney Bromley (Hodge), Chloe Salaman (Princess Elspeth), Emrys James (Simon).

In an Arthurian-type legend, young apprentice sorcerer Peter MacNicol goes on a quest to vanquish an evil dragon terrorizing the countryside. He comes across a corrupt king who gives the beast his realm's virgins in return for protection. This one is worth seeing.

798. *The Draughtsman's Contract* (1983, United Artists, GB, 108m, c). P David Payne, D&W Peter Greenaway, PH Curtis Clark, M Michael Nyman, ED John Wilson.

LP Anthony Higgins (Mr. Neville), Janet Suzman (Mrs. Herbert), Anne Louise Lambert (Mrs. Talmann), Hugh Fraser (Mr. Talmann), Neil Cunningham (Mr. Noyles), Dave Hill (Mr. Herbert), David Gant (Mr. Seymour).

In 1694 Wiltshire, England, artist Anthony Higgins is hired by Janet Suzman, an aristocrat's wife, to make 12 drawings of the estate to surprise her husband Dave Hill. The latter is abroad, wenching. Higgins agrees on the terms that Suzman have sex with him daily. His terms are accepted. When Hill is found dead, floating in a moat, Higgins' sketches contain clues to his murder. Most intriguing.

799. *Dream a Little Dream* (1989, Vestron, 99m, c). P D.E. Eisenberg, D Marc Rocco, W Daniel Jay Franklin, Rocco & Eisenberg (based on a story by Franklin), PH King Baggot, M John William Dexter, ED Russell Livingstone, PD Matthew C. Jacobs.

LP Corey Feldman (Bobby Keller), Corey Haim (Dinger), Jason Robards (Coleman Ettinger), Piper Laurie (Gena Ettinger), Harry Dean Stanton (Ike Baker), Meredith Salenger (Lainie Diamond), Alex Rocco (Gus Keller).

We believe this is a reincarnation movie. Corey Feldman and Meredith Salenger have an accident and may or may not take on the personas of older Jason Robards and Piper Laurie. We'll wager the director and screenwriters aren't any more certain than we are.

800. *Dream Lover* (1986, MGM/United Artists, 104m, c). P Alan J. Pakula & Jon Boorstin, D Pakula, W Boorstin, PH Sven Nykvist, M Michael Small, ED Trudy Ship & Angelo Corrao, PD George Jenkins.

LP Kristy McNichol (Kathy Gardner), Ben Masters (Michael Hansen), Paul Shenar (Ben Gardner), Justin Deas (Kevin McCann), John McMartin (Martin), Gayle Hunnicutt (Claire), Joseph Culp (Danny), Matthew Penn (Billy).

Flautist Kristy McNichol attempts to expunge recurring nightmares from her mind through "dream therapy." McNichol does a decent job, but she doesn't get much help from the director or the screenwriter. The film doesn't work either as drama or as a thriller.

801. *Dream One* (1984, NEF/Columbia, Fr./GB, 97m, c). P Claude Nedjar & John Boorman, D Arnaud Selignac, W Selignac, Jean-Pierre Esquenazi & Telshe Boorman, PH Philippe Rousselot, M Gabriel Yared, ED Tom Priestley.

LP Seth Kibel (Nemo as a child), Jason Connery (Nemo as a teen), Mathilda May (Alice), Nipsey Russell (Mr. Rip/Benjamin), Harvey Keitel (Mr. Legend), Carole Bouquet (Rals-Akrai), Michel Blanc (Boris).

The boy Nemo, named after Jules Verne's famous character in *20,000 Leagues Under the Sea,* is the son of a well-to-do Manhattan couple. An elevator containing him fails to stop at the ground floor and burrows through the earth, falling into space. When the lad finally lands on another planet, he comes across the famous *Nautilus* and the only survivor of Capt. Nemo's crew, his monkey. Various mythical visitors arrive soon after. It's a rather charming childhood fantasy.

802. *The Dream Team* (1989, Universal, 113m, c). P Christopher W. Knight, D Howard Zieff, W Jon Connolly & David Loucka, PH Adam Holender, M David McHugh, ED C. Timothy O'Meara, PD Todd Hallowell.

LP Michael Keaton (Billy Caulfield), Christopher Lloyd (Henry Sikorsky), Peter Boyle (Jack McDermott), Stephen Furst (Albert Ianuzzi), Dennis Boutsikaris (Dr. Weitzman), Lorraine Bracco (Riley), Milo O'Shea (Dr. Newald), Philip Bosco (O'Malley).

Four hospitalized mental patients, Michael Keaton, Christopher Lloyd, Peter Boyle and Stephen Furst, are on their way to a baseball game in New York City.

Their doctor-chaperone Dennis Boutsikaris steps in an alley to relieve himself and witnesses a murder by a pair of corrupt cops. They beat him senseless, but before they can kill him they are interrupted and their victim is taken to a hospital in a coma. His patients are forced to fend for themselves and ultimately foil the murderer's attempt to finish the job of killing Boutsikaris. Keaton's character is given to murderous rages. Lloyd's is a neat-freak, who tries single-handedly to clean up Manhattan's litter. Boyle believes he's Jesus Christ and Furst only speaks in baseball clichés, not always pertinent to the conversation. As in *Rain Man,* one is uncomfortable laughing at people with mental problems. It's worse here because the film is not as sensitively handled as the Dustin Hoffman triumph.

803. *Dreamaniac* (1987, Taryn, 82m, c). P&D David DeCoteau, W Helen Robinson, PH Howard Wexler, ED Peter Teschner, PD Rozanne Taucher.

LP Thomas Bern (Adam), Kim McKamy (Pat), Sylvia Summers (Lily), Lauren Peterson (Jodi), Bob Pelham (Jamie), Cynthia Crass (Frances), Brad Laughlin (Brad), Linda Watts (Jan), Matthew Phelps (Foster), Michael Warren (Ace).

Young writer Thomas Bern conjures up a succubus who goes on a murdering spree at a sorority party—or was it all a story he made up?

804. *Dreamchild* (1985, Universal, GB, 94m, c). P Rick McCallum & Kenith Trodd, D Gavin Millar, W Dennis Potter, PH Billy Williams M Stanley Myers & Max Harris, ED Angus Newton, PD Roger Hall.

LP Coral Browne (Mrs. Alice Hargreaves), Ian Holm (Rev. Charles Dodgson), Peter Gallagher (Jack Dolan), Caris Corfman (Sally Mackeson), Nicola Cowper (Lucy), Jane Asher (Mrs. Liddell), Amelia Shankley (Little Alice), Imogen Boorman (Lorina), Emma King (Edith).

Coral Browne stars as the elderly Alice Liddell, brought to New York in 1932 for the centenary of Lewis Carroll/Charles Dodgson's birth. Now 80 years old, the inspiration for the precious little girl in blue recalls her idyllic childhood and the love felt for her by the repressed clergyman, mathematician and writer.

805. *Dreamscape* (1984, 20th Century–Fox, 95m, c). P Bruce Cohn Curtis & Jerry Tokofsky, D Joseph Ruben, W David Loughery, Chuck Russell & Ruben (based on a story by Loughery), PH Brian Tufano, M Maurice Jarre, ED Richard Halsey.

LP Dennis Quaid (Alex Gardner), Max von Sydow (Paul Novotny), Christopher Plummer (Bob Blair), Eddie Albert (The President), Kate Capshaw (Jane Devries), David Patrick Kelly (Tommy Ray Glatman), George Wendt (Charlie Prince), Larry Gelman (Mr. Webber).

Telepath Dennis Quaid is part of a scientific experiment that involves projecting him and others with like powers into other people's nightmares, supposedly for therapeutic purposes. But the real purpose of the experiment, unknown to Quaid, is to assassinate the president, Eddie Albert.

Dreamworld see Covergirl

806. *Dressed to Kill* (1980, Filmways, 105m, c). P George Litto, D&W Brian De Palma, PH Ralf Bode, M Pino Donaggio, ED Jerry Greenberg, PD Gary Weist.

LP Michael Caine (Dr. Robert Elliott), Angie Dickinson (Kate Miller), Nancy Allen (Liz Blake), Keith Gordon (Peter Miller), Dennis Franz (Detective Marino), David Margulies (Dr. Levy), Ken Baker (Warren Lockman), Brandon Maggart (Cleveland Sam), Susanna Clemm (Bobbi).

This film has all the ingredients to be a heart-stopping suspense thriller: a disturbed woman adrift in sexual fantasy . . . a New York psychiatrist who has one patient too many . . . a call girl caught between cops and a razor-wielding madman . . . and the killer herself, a tall elusive blonde psycho. Too bad it didn't have Alfred Hitchcock to direct it.

807. *The Dresser*† (1983, Columbia, GB, 118m, c). P&D Peter Yates† (for directing), W Ronald Harwood† (based on his play), PH Kelvin Pike, M James Horner, ED Ray Lovejoy, PD Stephen Grimes.

LP Albert Finney† (Sir), Tom Courtenay† (Norman), Edward Fox (Oxenby), Zena Walker (Her Ladyship), Eileen Atkins (Madge), Michael Gough (Frank Carrington), Cathryn Harrison (Irene), Betty Marsden (Violet Manning).

This filmed play, featuring Albert Finney as the senile boozing head of a Shakespearean acting troupe touring England during World War II and his homosexual dresser Tom Courtenay, who looks after him, is almost but not quite as effective as the stage version.

808. *The Dressmaker* (1989, Euro-American Films, GB, 92m, c). P Ronald Shedlo, D Jim O'Brien, W John McGrath (based on the novel by Beryl Bainbridge), PH Michael Coulter, M George Fenton, ED William Diver.

LP Joan Plowright (Nellie), Billie Whitelaw (Margo), Jane Horrocks (Rita), Peter Postlethwaite (Jack), Tim Ransom (Wesley), Rosemary Martin (Mrs. Manders).

In 1944 Liverpool, the very proper Joan Plowright is not pleased with the invasion of all the Yank soldiers and the ease with which they make time with British girls. This spinster seamstress shares a grim little house with her slightly younger, long-ago-married sister Billie Whitelaw and their 17-year-old niece Jane Horrocks. The youngster falls in love with American soldier Tim Ransom, who is after only one thing. How this romance develops and its influence on Plowright and Whitelaw makes for an interesting if not outstanding cinema experience.

809. *The Drifter* (1988, Concorde, 90m, c). P Ken Stein, D&W Larry Brand, PH David Sperling, M Rick Conrad, ED Stephen Mark.

LP Kim Delaney (Julia), Timothy Bottoms (Arthur), Al Shannon (Kriger), Miles O'Keeffe (Trey), Anna Gray Garduno (Matty), Loren Haines (Willie Munroe), Larry Brand (Morrison), Thomas Wagner (Capt. Edwards).

The defects of this low-budget thriller are too many to enumerate. Kim Delaney has a one-night stand with drifter Miles O'Keeffe, despite being engaged to lawyer Timothy Bottoms. O'Keeffe wants to continue the affair, so he keeps after her. When Anna Gray Garduno, living in the same apartment building as Delaney, is killed, everyone except the audience believe O'Keeffe is the killer. He must save our not-so-lily-white heroine from the real murderer.

810. *Driving Force* (1989, J&M Entertainment, Australian, 91m, c). P D. Howard Grigsby & S.M. Confesor, D A.J. Prowse, W Patrick Edgeworth, PH Richard Michalak, M Paul Schutze, ED Prowse, PD Toto Castillo.

LP Sam Jones (Steve), Catherine Bach (Harry), Don Swayze (Nelson), Stefanie Mason (Becky), Angel Cook (Surf).

Headed quickly to the home-video market, this routine action picture, set in the near future features rival tow-truck operators who cause often fatal pile-ups to generate business.

811. *Driving Miss Daisy** (1989, Warner, 99m, c). P Richard D. Zanuck & Lili Fini Zanuck, D Bruce Beresford, W Alfred Uhry* (based on his play), PH Peter James, M Hans Zimmer, ED Mark Warner†, PD Bruno Rubeo†, COS Elizabeth McBride†, MK Manlio Rocchetti*.

LP Morgan Freeman† (Hoke Colburn), Jessica Tandy* (Daisy Werthan), Dan Aykroyd† (Boolie Werthan), Patti LuPone (Florine Werthan), Esther Rolle (Idella), Joann Havrilla (Miss Mc-Clatchey), William Hall, Jr. (Oscar).

Having reached the age of 70, Jessica Tandy has all of her faculties, but her car tends to misbehave. Over her furious objections, her son Dan Aykroyd hires Morgan Freeman, a black widower in his 60s and a man of infinite patience and tact, to drive for her. Although stage plays, even Pulitzer prize winners, often fail to make the transformation to the screen, Alfred Uhry's work is a delightful exception. The film has the best of both worlds. It has a theatrical light touch, even as it successfully opens up a lovely cinematic treatment. The two main characters make a superb team. Despite her constant complaints about Freeman, she teaches him to read. Freeman, who originated the role on Broadway, teaches her something just as valuable. Before their 25 years together comes to an end, theirs is a friendship of equals. Tandy at 80 became the oldest Oscar winner and if it weren't for

Daniel Day-Lewis in *My Left Foot,* Morgan Freeman, one of the best actors in America, would have made a worthy recipient of the Academy Award.

812. *Drugstore Cowboy* (1989, Avenue, 100m, c). P Nick Wechsler & Karen Murphy, D Gus Van Sant, Jr., W Van Sant & Daniel Yost (based on a novel by James Fogle), PH Robert Yeoman, M Elliot Goldenthal, ED Curtiss Clayton, PD David Brisbin.

LP Matt Dillon (Bob Hughes), Kelly Lynch (Dianne Hughes), James Le Gros (Rick), Heather Graham (Nadine), James Remar (Gentry), William S. Burroughs (Tom the Priest), Grace Zabriskie (Bob's Mother), Max Perlich (David).

Set in Portland, Oregon, in the early 70s, the film stars Matt Dillon as a drug fiend with no excuses. He takes drugs because he likes them. To maintain his happy habit, he robs drugstores, He is assisted in these ventures by his tough wife Kelly Lynch and his best friend James Le Gros and the latter's weepy girlfriend Heather Graham. When the latter dies of an overdose, Dillon's world begins to fall apart.

813. *A Dry White Season* (1989, MGM/United Artists, 97m, c). P Paula Weinstein, D Euzhan Palcy, W Colin Welland & Palcy (based on the novel by Andre Brink), PH Kelvin Pike & Pierre-William Glenn, M Dave Grusin, ED Sam O'Steen & Glenn Cunningham, PD John Fenner.

LP Donald Sutherland (Ben du Toit), Winston Ntshona (Gordon Ngubene), Zakes Mokae (Stanley), Jurgen Prochnow (Captain Stolz), Susan Sarandon (Melanie Bruwer), Marlon Brando† (Ian McKenzie), Janet Suzman (Susan du Toit), Thoko Ntshinga (Emily Ngubene), Susannah Harker (Suzette du Toit), Leonard Maguire (Mr. Bruwer), Rowen Elmes (Johan du Toit).

Black director-writer Euzhan Palcy makes the important point that the problems in South Africa are not likely to be resolved by one race alone. Set in 1976, the film offers no false hope, showing the brutality of police and troops who beat and tear-gas demonstrators, opening fire on children as they flee. Donald Sutherland is a decent white man, but one who doesn't question his country's policies too closely. Sutherland undergoes a crisis of conscience when the son of his gardener, Winston Ntshona, is arrested, killed and buried in an unmarked grave. This is shortly followed by the torture and murder of the gardener by Jurgen Prochnow, a sadistic captain of the police. Sutherland persuades human rights attorney Marlon Brando to bring Prochnow up on murder charges. Brando loses the case in a courtroom presided over by a judge who makes no pretense of impartiality. Brando moves on, but Sutherland, now completely radicalized, works with a political activist in Soweto to build a new case against the police.

814.   *Dudes* (1988, New Century/ Vista, 89m, c). P Herb Jaffe & Miguel Tejada-Flores, D Penelope Spheeris, W J. Randal Johnson, PH Robert Richardson, M Charles Bernstein, ED Andy Horvitch, PD Robert Ziembicki.

LP Jon Cryer (Grant), Daniel Roebuck (Biscuit), Flea [Michael Balzary] (Milo), Lee Ving (Missoula), Catherine Mary Stewart (Jessie), Billy Ray Sharkey, Glenn Withrow, Michael Melvin.

The story of three punk rockers being harassed by redneck killers in the Southwest is thoroughly disgusting and incomprehensible.

815.   *Duel* (1983, Universal, 90m, c). P George Eckstein, D Steven Spielberg, W Richard Matheson (based on his story), PH Jack A. Marta, M Billy Goldenberg, ED Frank Morriss, AD Robert E. Smith.

LP Dennis Weaver (David Mann), Eddie Firestone (Cafe Owner), Gene Dynarski (Man in Cafe), Tim Herbert (Gas Station Attendant), Charles Seel (Old Man), Alexander Lockwood (Old Man in Car), Amy Douglass (Old Woman in Car).

What starts out as an ordinary business trip becomes a life and death struggle for Dennis Weaver who is tailgated by a menacing psychopath.

816.   *Duet for Four* (1982, Burstall, Australia, 97m, c, aka *Partners*). P Tom & Tim Burstall, D Tim Burstall, W David Williamson, PH Dan Burstall.

LP Mike Preston, Wendy Hughes, Diane Cilento, Michael Pate, Gary Day, Vanessa Leigh, Sigrid Thornton, Rod Mullinar.

Melbourne toy manufacturer Mike Preston is sad to learn that his wife is having an affair. His own mistress is pressing him to marry. Oh, what deceit! It's a very familiar romantic quadrilateral.

817.   *Duet for One* (1987, Cannon, GB, 108m, c). P Menahem Golan & Yoram Globus, D Andrei Konchalovsky, W Tom Kempinski, Jeremy Lipp & Konchalovsky (based on the play by Kempinski), PH Alex Thomson, M Various Artists, ED Henry Richardson, PD John Graysmark.

LP Julie Andrews (Stephanie Anderson), Alan Bates (David Cornwallis), Max von Sydow (Dr. Louis Feldman), Rupert Everett (Constantine Kassanis), Margaret Courtenay (Sonia Randvich), Cathryn Harrison (Penny Smallwood), Sigfrit Steiner (Leonid Lefimov), Liam Neeson (Totter).

Julie Andrews portrays a talented violinist stricken with multiple sclerosis. What worked brilliantly on the stage seems quite ordinary on the big screen.

Dumb Dicks see *Detective School Dropouts*

818.   *Dune* (1984, Universal, 140m, c). P Rafaella De Laurentiis, D David Lynch, W Lynch, Eric Bergren & Christopher De Vore (based on the novel by Frank Herbert), PH Freddie Francis, M Toto, Marty Paich, Brian Eno, Roger Eno & Daniel Lanois, ED Antony Gibbs, PD Anthony Masters, SOUND Bill Varney, Steve Maslow, Kevin O'Connell & Nelson Stoll†.

LP Kyle MacLachlan (Paul Atreides), Francesca Annis (Lady Jessica), Leonardo Cimino (the Baron's Doctor), Brad Dourif (Piter De Vries), Jose Ferrer (Padishah Emperor Shaddam IV), Linda Hunt (Shadout Mapes), Freddie Jones (Thufir Hawat), Richard Jordan (Duncan Idaho), Virginia Madsen (Princess Irulan), Silvano Mangano (Reverend Mother Ramallo).

Two warring families, the honorable Atreides and the sinister Harkonnens, battle for control of the desert planet, Dune. On this mysterious planet, giant sand worms produce a mind-expanding spice that prolongs life and facilitates space travel.

819. *Dungeonmaster* (1985, Empire, 73m, c). P Charles Band, D Band, Rosemarie Turko, John Carl Buechler, David Allen, Steve Ford, Peter Manoogian & Ted Nicolaou, W Allen Actor, PH Mac Ahlberg, M Richard Band & Shirley Walker, ED Marc Lief, PD Julie Stroh.

LP Jeffrey Byron (Paul Bradford), Richard Moll (Mestema), Leslie Wing (Gwen), Blackie Lawless (Heavy Metal), Danny Dick (Slasher), W.A.S.P. (Heavy Metal Band).

In an imbecilic sword-and-sorcery thriller, an evil wizard wanders the galaxies in search of a worthy opponent to play his brutal and deadly game.

820. *Dutch Treat* (1987, Cannon, 84m, c). P Menahem Golan & Yoram Globus, D Boaz Davidson, W Lorin Dreyfuss & David Landsberg, M Steve Bates, ED Bruria Davidson.

LP David Landsberg (Jerry), Lorin Dreyfuss (Norm), The Dolly Dots (Themselves), Terry Camilleri, Linda Lutz, Robert Sella.

David Landsberg and Lorin Dreyfuss are knife-throwing entertainers on a cruise ship. When a couple of officers are put away via knife punctures, our heroes become the main suspects. When they reach port, they find themselves in a Dutch prison.

821. *Earth Girls Are Easy* (1989, Vestron, 100m, c). P Tony Garnett, D Julien Temple, W Julie Brown, Charlie Coffey & Terrence E. McNally, PH Oliver Stapleton, M Nile Rodgers, ED Richard Halsey, PD Dennis Gassner.

LP Geena Davis (Valerie Dale), Jeff Goldblum (Mac), Jim Carrey (Wiploc), Damon Wayans (Zeebo), Julie Brown (Candy Pink), Michael McKean (Woody), Charles Rocket (Dr. Ted Gallagher), Larry Linville (Dr. Bob), Rick Overton (Dr. Rick).

When three hairy aliens from Jhazzala land in manicurist Geena Davis' swimming pool, she and her boss Julie Brown shave them. The red one becomes Jim Carrey, the yellow one, Damon Wayans, and Mr. Blue, none other than Jeff Goldblum. It's a spoof which parodies just about everything from science-fiction to old Hollywood musicals. The film is outrageous and a real hoot, worth seeing — once.

822. *Earthbound* (1981, Taft Intl., 94m, c). P&W Michael Fisher, D James L. Conway.

LP Burl Ives (Ned Anderson), Christopher Connelly (Zef), Meredith MacRae (Lara), Joseph Campanella (Conrad), Todd Porter (Tommy), Marc Gilpin (Dalem), Elissa Leeds (Teva), John Schuck (Sheriff).

This nothing little sci-fi film features a dull alien family whose spaceship breaks down over a small American town. If the army doesn't kill them, they'll fit right in.

823. *The Earthling* (1980, Filmways/Roadshow, 97m, c). P Elliot Schick & John Strong, D Peter Collinson, W Lanny Cotler, PH Don McAlpine, M Dick DeBenedictis, ED Nick Beauman & Frank Morriss, PD Bob Hilditch.

LP William Holden (Patrick Foley), Ricky Schroder (Shawn Daley), Jack Thompson (Ross Daley), Olivia Hamnett (Bettina Daley), Alwyn Kurts (Christian Neilson), Redmond Phillips (Bobby Burns).

Dying of cancer, William Holden returns to his native Australia to live out his final days. He teaches young Ricky Schroder what he knows about survival before passing on.

824. *Easy Money* (1983, Orion, 100m, c). P John Nicolella, D James Signorelli, W Rodney Dangerfield, Michael Endler, P.J. O'Rourke & Dennis Blair, PH Fred Schuler, M Laurence Rosenthal, ED Ronald Roose, PD Eugene Lee.

LP Rodney Dangerfield (Monty), Joe Pesci (Nicky), Geraldine Fitzgerald (Mrs. Monahan), Candy Azzara (Rose), Val Avery (Louie), Tom Noonan (Paddy), Taylor Negron (Julio), Lili Haydn (Belinda), Jeffrey Jones (Clive), Tom Ewell (Scrappleton), Jennifer Jason Leigh (Allison).

All overweight, heavy-smoking, boozing, gambling, girl-chasing Rodney Dangerfield has to do to inherit millions from his mother-in-law Geraldine Fitzgerald is lose weight, quit smoking, stop drinking, make no bets and put on blinders where females are concerned. Might as well ask him to give up breathing.

825. *Easy Wheels* (1989, New Star Entertainment, 90m, c). P Dmitri Villard,

Robby Wald & Jake Jacobson, D David O'Malley, W O'Malley, Celia Abrams & Ivan Raimi, PH James Lemmo, ED John Currin, M John Ross, PD Helen Dersjam.

LP Paul Le Mat (Bruce), Eileen Davidson (She-Wolf), Marjorie Bransfield (Wendy), Jon Menick (Prof), Mark Holton (Animal), Karen Russell (Candy), Jami Richards (Merilee), Roberta Vasquez (Tondaleyo).

Raised by wolves, man-hater Eileen Davidson, the leader of a tough female motorcycle gang, wishes to create a world run by women. To this end, she and her followers ride through the Midwest kidnapping baby girls to be raised in the woods by wolves. The opposing force is a bunch of scuffy male bikers led by Paul Le Mat. The battle of the sexes never saw anything like this before, but that's not meant to be taken as a recommendation.

826.   *Eat a Bowl of Tea* (1989, Columbia, 102m, c). P Tom Sternberg, D Wayne Wang, W Judith Rascoe (based on the novel by Louis Chu), PH Amir Mokri, M Mark Adler, ED Richard Candib, PD Bob Ziembicki.

LP Cora Miao (Mei Oi), Russell Wong (Ben Loy), Victor Wong (Wah Gay), Lee Sau Kee (Bok Fat), Eric Tsiang Chi Wai (Ah Song).

After World War II, New York Chinese gambling club owner Victor Wong sends his son Russell Wong to China to marry the daughter of his best friend. When the young couple returns to the States, deeply in love, the father gives his son a restaurant as a present. The pressures of running a business prove more than the younger man can handle and to add to his problems he's impotent. Wife Cora Miao takes Eric Tsiang Chi Wai as a lover and becomes pregnant. When her husband's family learns their son isn't the baby's father, meat axes swing.

827.   *Eat and Run* (1987, New World, 85m, c). P Jack Briggs, D Christopher Hart, W Stan Hart & Christopher Hart, PH Dyanna Taylor, M Donald Pippin, ED Pamela S. Arnold.

LP Ron Silver (Mickey McSorley), Sharon Schlarth (Judge Cheryl Cohen), R.L. Ryan (Murray Creature), John F. Fleming (Captain), Derek Murcott (Sor-

ley McSorley), Robert Silver (Pusher), Mimi Cecchini (Grandmother).

This sci-fi spoof features R.L. Ryan as a 300-pound alien who eats Italian — the people, not the food.

828.   *Eat the Peach* (1987, Skouras, GB, 95m, c). P John Kelleher, D Peter Ormrod, W Ormrod & Kelleher, PH Arthur Wooster, M Donal Lunny, ED J. Patrick Duffner, PD David Wilson.

LP Stephen Brennan (Vinnie), Eamon Morrissey (Arthur), Catherine Byrne (Nora), Niall Toibin (Boots), Joe Lynch (Boss Murtagh), Tony Doyle (Sean Murtagh), Takashi Kawahara (Bunzo), Victoria Armstrong (Vicky).

Inspired by an old Elvis Presley movie, laid-off Irish factory workers Stephen Brennan and Eamon Morrissey build a "Wall of Death," a giant cylinder in which motorcyclists can ride parallel to the ground with the aid of centrifugal force. They steal materials needed for the wall and become smugglers to finance their project. It's based on an actual incident.

829.   *Eat the Rich* (1988, New Line, GB, 88m, c). P Tim Van Rellim, D Peter Richardson, W Richardson & Peter Richens, PH Witold Stok, ED Chris Risdale, AD Caroline Amies.

LP Ronald Allen (Commander Fortune), Robbie Coltrane (Jeremy), Sandra Dorne (Sandra), Jimmy Fagg (Jimmy), Lanah Pellay (Alex), Nosher Powell (Nosher), Fiona Richmond (Fiona), Ron Tarr (Ron).

After being fired from a trendy London restaurant for the rich called Bastards that serves such dishes as fried baby panda, transsexual Lanah Pellay starts a people's uprising. He gathers around him a small group of dedicated Red Guards. They take over the restaurant and put their rich patrons on the menu.

830.   *Eating Raoul* (1982, 20th Century-Fox, 90m, c). P Anne Kimmel, D Paul Bartel, W Bartel & Richard Blackburn, PH Gary Thieltges, M Arlon Ober, ED Alan Toomayan, PD Robert Schulenberg.

LP Mary Woronov (Mary Bland), Paul Bartel (Paul Bland), Robert Beltran (Raoul), Buck Henry (Mr. Leech), Richard Paul (Mr. Kray), Susan Saiger (Doris the Dominatrix), Ed Begley, Jr. (Hippy), Dan Barrows (Bobbie R.).

You will either hate this weird black comedy or consider it among the campiest things you have ever seen. Paul Bartel and his wife Mary Woronov need to raise money to start a restaurant they've always dreamed of. When they accidentally kill a swinger who tries to make it with Woronov, they find he has a lot of money in his wallet. The enterprising couple come up with a plan of advertising for others of his ilk and take these "johns" for whatever they have on them. They eventually are forced to take on Robert Beltran as a partner, but he goes too far after seducing Woronov, suggesting they do away with Bartel. Instead Beltran ends up "a friend they have for dinner."

831. *Echo Park* (1986, Atlantic, US/ Austria, 93m, c). P Walter Shenson, D Robert Dornhelm, W Michael Ventura, PH Karl Kofler, M David Rickets, ED Ingrid Koller.

LP Susan Dey (May), Thomas Hulce (Jonathan), Michael Bowen (August), Christopher Walken (Henry), Shirley Jo Finney (Gloria), Heinrich Schweiger (August's Father), John Paragon (Hugo), Richard Marin (Sid).

Susan Dey, Thomas Hulce and Michael Bowen live in a seedy L.A. neighborhood, hoping for fame and fortune in show business. It's a likeable episodic film.

832. *Echoes* (1983, Continental, 89m, c). P George R. Nice & Valerie Y. Belsky, D Arthur Allan Seidelman, W Richard J. Anthony, PH Hanania Baer, M Gerard Bernard Cohen & Stephen Schwartz, ED Dan Perry.

LP Richard Alfieri (Michael Durant/ Dream Michael), Nathalie Nell (Christine), Ruth Roman (Michael's Mother), Gale Sondergaard (Mrs. Edmunds), Mercedes McCambridge (Lillian Gerben), Mike Kellin (Sid Berman), Barbara Monte-Britton (Dream Woman), Duncan Quinn (Dream Man).

The present of such talents as Ruth Roman, Gale Sondergaard and Mercedes McCambridge can't salvage this film, which does have an interesting premise, long on promise, short on delivery.

Richard Alfieri has a recurring dream that his twin who died at birth is out to kill him.

833. *Echoes of Paradise* (1989, Quartet Films, 92m, c). P Jane Scott, D Phillip Noyce, W Jan Sharp & Anne Brooksbank, PH Peter James, M Bill Motzing, ED Frans Vandenburg, PD Clarissa Patterson.

LP Wendy Hughes (Maria), John Lone (Raka), Steven Jacobs (George), Peta Toppano (Judy), Rod Mullinar (Terry), Gillian Jones (Mitty), Claudia Karvan (Julia).

Wendy Hughes is bored, bored, bored. She's also furious with her husband Steven Jacobs. Needing adventure in her life while in Thailand, she has an affair with exotic, long-haired Balinese dancer John Lone. It makes her feel better, but doesn't teach her anything. It's pretty, but boring.

834. *Eddie and the Cruisers* (1983, Embassy, 92m, c). P Joseph Brooks & Robert K. Lifton, D Martin Davidson, W Martin & Arlene Davidson (based on the novel by P.F. Kluge), PH Fred Murphy, M John Cafferty, ED Priscilla Nedd.

LP Tom Berenger (Frank), Michael Pare (Eddie), Joe Pantoliano (Doc), Matthew Laurance (Sal), Helen Schneider (Joann), David Wilson (Kenny), Michael "Tunes" Antunes (Wendell), Ellen Barkin (Maggie), Kenny Vance (Lew), John Stockwell (Keith), Joe Cates (Lois), Barry Sand (Barry).

The music in this film is better than the acting. Michael Pare, the lead singer of a successful rock group, apparently was killed in an automobile accident, but his body was never found. Years later, the missing tapes of the group's last recordings resurface and so it seems does Eddie—or could we be wrong? See below.

835. *Eddie and the Cruisers II: Eddie Lives* (1989, Scotti Bros., Canada, 100m, c). P Stephanie Reichel, D Jean-Claude Lord, W Charles Zev Cohen & Rick Doehring (based on characters created by P.F. Kluge), PH Rene Verzier, M John Cafferty and the Beaver Brown Band, ED Jean-Guy Montpetit.

LP Michael Pare (Eddie Wilson/Joe West), Marina Orsini (Diane Armani), Bernie Coulson (Rick De Sal), Matthew

Laurance (Sal Amato), Michael Rhoades (Dave Pagent), Anthony Sherwood (Hilton), Mark Holmes (Quinn), David Matheson (Stewart), Paul Markle (Charlie).

In the 1983 film *Eddie and the Cruisers,* a Jim Morrison/Bruce Springsteen–like working-class rock star Michael Pare disappeared in 1964 at the height of his career when he drove his car off the Raritan Bridge. There were plenty of clues at that time that the charismatic singer hadn't really died, but had arranged the accident to get away from all the hullabaloo. In this film for no more apparent reason than when he turned his back on his career, he sheds his Montreal construction worker's role 18 years later and picks up where he left off, just as popular as before. Hard to believe? Try impossible to believe.

836. *Eddie Macon's Run* (1983, Universal, 95m, c). P Louis J. Stroller, D&W Jeff Kanew (based on the novel by James McLendon), PH James A. Contner, M Norton Buffalo, ED Kanew, PD Bill Kenney.

LP Kirk Douglas (Marzack), John Schneider (Eddie Macon), Lee Purcell (Jilly Buck), Leah Ayres (Chris), Lisa Dunsheath (Kay Potts), Tom Noonan (Daryl Potts), J.C. Quinn (Shorter), Gil Rogers (Logan), Jay O. Sanders (Rudy Potts).

"Dukes of Hazard" star John Schneider is another in a long line of TV big shots who fell on their faces when they moved to the big screen. Falsely imprisoned, he escapes, and with lawman Kirk Douglas on his trail, tries to make it to Mexico and freedom.

837. *Edgar Allan Poe's Masque of the Red Death* (1989, Concorde, 85m, c, aka *Masque of the Red Death*). P Roger Corman, D Larry Brand, W Daryl Haney & Brand (based on the story by Edgar Allan Poe), PH Edward Pei, M Mark Governor, ED Stephen Mark, AD Troy Meyers.

LP Patrick Macnee (Machiavel), Adrian Paul (Prospero), Clare Hoak (Julietta), Jeff Osterhage (Claudio), Tracy Reiner (Lucrecia).

We have a theory that when a movie's name is preceded by the author of the work on which it is based, it is because the film is weak and the filmmakers hope to draw customers on the basis of the famous author. This film is offered as evidence of that premise. Roger Corman produced a 1964 version of "Masque" which makes this bomb totally unnecessary. Bring back Vincent Price.

The Edge of Hell see Rock 'n' Roll Nightmare

838. *Edge of Sanity* (1989, Allied Vision, GB, 90m, c). P Edward Simons & Harry Alan Towers, D Gerard Kikoine, W J.P. Felix & Ron Raley (based on the novel *Dr. Jekyll and Mr. Hyde* by Robert Louis Stevenson), PH Tony Spratling, M Frederic Talgorn, ED Malcolm Cooke, PD Jean Charles Dedieu.

LP Anthony Perkins (Dr. Jekyll/Mr. Hyde), Glynis Barber (Elizabeth Jekyll), Sarah Maur Thorp (Susannah), David Lodge (Underwood), Ben Cole (Johnny), Ray Jewers (Newcomen), Jill Melford (Flora), Lisa Davis (Maria), Noel Coleman (Egglestone).

Robert Louis Stevenson's novel is uncredited, and if he saw the film, he might prefer it that way. Would you believe (would anyone believe?) that Anthony Perkins' pet monkey accidentally invents crack, which results in a Mr. Hyde who is a cokehead Jack the Ripper–like slasher. Dr. Jekyll, as played by Perkins, is just about as nutzoid as Mr. Hyde.

839. *Educating Rita* (1983, Columbia, GB, 110m, c). P&D Lewis Gilbert, W Willy Russell† (based on his play), PH Frank Watts, M David Hentschel, ED Garth Craven.

LP Michael Caine† (Dr. Frank Bryant), Julie Walters† (Rita), Michael Williams (Brian), Maureen Lipman (Trish), Jeananne Crowley (Julia), Malcolm Douglas (Denny), Godfrey Quigley (Rita's Father), Dearbhla Molloy (Elaine), Pat Daly (Bursar), Kim Fortune (Collins), Philip Hurdwood (Tiger), Hilary Reynolds (Lesley).

Michael Caine probably won his Oscar for *Hannah and Her Sisters* because he didn't win for his brilliant performance in this film. He's a failed writer and drunken British don, who takes on lower-class London hairdresser Julie Walters as a student. Desperate for an education, Walters proves the best of all students, one who's curiosity is insatiable and whose joy of learning is the dream of any teacher. Walters is about as appealing as any actress making her film debut.

840. *Effects* (1980, International Harmony, 87m, c). P John Harrison & Pasquale Buba, D&W Dusty Nelson (based on a novel by William H. Mooney), PH Carl Augenstein, ED Buba.

LP John Harrison (Lacy), Susan Chapek (Celeste), Joseph Pilato (Dom), Bernard McKenna (Barney), Debra Gordon (Rita), Tom Savini (Nicky), Chuck Hoyes (Lobo), Blay Bahnsen (Scratch).

In another horror movie within a horror movie, the cast of the film within a film doesn't know that the director is actually shooting a film about a mad killer murdering the cast and crew of a movie. Confused? It's not worth sorting out.

841. *Eight Men Out* (1988, Orion, 120m, c). P Sarah Pillsbury, D&W John Sayles (based on the book by Eliot Asinof), PH Robert Richardson, M Mason Daring, ED John Tintori, PD Nora Chavooshian.

LP John Cusack (Buck Weaver), Clifton James (Charles Comiskey), Michael Lerner (Arnold Rothstein), Christopher Lloyd (Bill Burns), John Mahoney (Kid Gleason), Charlie Sheen (Hap Felsch), David Strathairn (Eddie Cicotte), D.B. Sweeney (Shoeless Joe Jackson), Gordon Clapp (Ray Schalk), Michael Rooker (Chick Gandil).

Fans of baseball often forget that the men they admire on the field are usually mere boys without much sophistication or intelligence, easily led into temptation. Consider the various drug cases, the Wade Boggs scandal involving his roadie, and Pete Rose's gambling illness. If this is the case with today's greatly over-paid players, how much more so of the farm boys who toiled for peanuts for owners like tight-fisted Charles Comiskey in 1919. This film purports to tell the story of the eight players who were banned from baseball for life for their involvement in throwing the 1919 World Series at the behest of gamblers.

842. *8 Million Ways to Die* (1986, Tri-Star, 115m, c). P Steve Roth, D Hal Ashby, W Oliver Stone & David Lee Henry (based on books by Lawrence Block), PH Stephen H. Burum, M James Newton Howard, ED Robert Lawrence & Stuart Pappe, PD Michael Haller.

LP Jeff Bridges (Scudder), Rosanna Arquette (Sarah), Alexandra Paul (Sunny), Randy Brooks (Chance), Andy Garcia (Angel), Lisa Sloan (Linda Scudder), Christa Denton (Laurie), Vance Valencia (Quintero).

This brutal, cynical film stars Jeff Bridges as an ex-cop who becomes involved with a gang war over drugs, a high-priced call girl, her friends and sadistic pimp Andy Garcia. Considering the talent, it should have been better.

843. *18 Again!* (1988, New World, 99m, c). P Walter Coblenz, D Paul Flaherty, W Josh Goldstein & Jonathan Prince, PH Stephen M. Katz, M Billy Goldenberg, ED Danford B. Greene, PD Dena Roth.

LP George Burns (Jack Watson), Charlie Schlatter (David Watson), Tony Roberts (Arnold Watson), Anita Morris (Madelyn), Miriam Flynn (Betty), Jennifer Runyon (Robin), Red Buttons (Charlie).

In another of the body-switch (or is it mind-switch) films, George Burns at 92, plays a younger man, only 81. He makes the switcheroo with his 18-year-old grandson Charlie Schlatter. The boy, now with Burns' mind, makes short shrift of the college students who had been giving him a hard time, and easily wins over the comely young Miriam Flynn. Burns also learns that his live-in love Anita Morris isn't interested in him for himself—seems his money is the attraction. Surprisingly, this surprises Burns.

844. *84 Charing Cross Road* (1987, Columbia, 97m, c). P Geoffrey Helman, D David Jones, W Hugh Whitemore (based on a book by Helene Hanff), PH Brian West, M George Fenton, ED Chris Wimble, PD Eileen Diss & Edward Pisoni.

LP Anne Bancroft (Helene Hanff), Anthony Hopkins (Frank Doel), Judi Dench (Nora Doel), Jean De Baer (Maxine Bellamy), Maurice Denham (George Martin), Eleanor David (Cecily Farr), Mercedes Ruehl (Kay), Daniel Gerroll (Brian), Wendy Morgan (Megan Wells).

Struggling New York writer Anne Bancroft and married Anthony Hopkins, who oversees an antiquarian bookshop in London at the title address, develop first a friendship, and then a love affair by letter, over the course of a 20-year correspondence, although they never meet.

845. *84 Charlie Mopic* (1989, New Century/Vista, 95m, c). P Michael Nolin & Jill Griffith, D&W Patrick Duncan, PH Alan Caso, ED Stephen Purvis.

LP Jonathan Emerson (LT), Nicholas Cascone (Easy), Jason Tomlins (Pretty Boy), Christopher Burgard (Hammer), Glenn Morshower (Cracker), Richard Brooks (OD), Byron Thames (Mopic).

"84 Charlie" is military slang for combat cameraman and "mopic" means motion picture. Vietnam vet Patrick Duncan presents an intimate portrayal of war by filming a documentary-like production in which a military cameraman Byron Thames accompanies a six-man patrol on a jungle reconnaissance mission. He films them in action and interviews them during lulls in the fighting.

Electric Boogaloo "Breakin' 2" see Breakin' 2: Electric Boogaloo

846. *Electric Dreams* (1984, MGM/United Artists, 95m, c). P Rusty Lemorande & Larry De Waay, D Steve Barron, W Lemorande, PH Alex Thomson, M Giorgio Moroder, ED Peter Honess, PD Richard MacDonald.

LP Lenny Von Dohlen (Miles), Virginia Madsen (Madeline), Maxwell Caulfield (Bill), Bud Cort (Edgar), Don Fellows (Ryley), Alan Polonsky (Frank), Wendy Miller (Computer Clerk), Harry Rabinowitz (Conductor).

We've heard of romantic triangles, but one involving a man, a woman and a computer is fairly rare. The home computer composes love songs for its beloved, Virginia Madsen, while at the same time making life miserable for its human competition Lenny Von Dohlen.

847. *Eleni* (1985, Warner, 114m, c). P Nick Vanoff, Mark Pick & Nicholas Gage, D Peter Yates, W Steve Tesich (based on the book by Gage), PH Billy Williams, M Bruce Smeaton, ED Raymond Lovejoy, PD Roy Walker.

LP Kate Nelligan (Eleni), John Malkovich (Nick), Linda Hunt (Katina), Oliver Cotton (Katis), Ronald Pickup (Spiro), Rosalie Crutchley (Grandmother), Glenne Headly (Joan), Dimitra Arliss (Ana), Steve Plytas (Christos), Peter Woodthorpe (Grandfather), John Rumney (Lukas).

Kate Nelligan is terribly miscast as the Greek peasant woman, executed by a Communist guerrilla firing squad during the occupation of post–World War II Greece. Only marginally better is John Malkovich as her grown son, an investigative reporter for the *New York Times* obsessed with finding the man who ordered her execution for no other reason than it would be an object lesson to others.

848. *The Elephant Man†* (1980, Paramount, GB, 125m, b&w). P Jonathan Sanger, D David Lynch†, W Christopher DeVore, Eric Bergren & Lynch† (based on *The Elephant Man: A Study in Human Dignity* by Ashley Montagu & *The Elephant Man and Other Reminiscences* by Sir Frederick Treves), PH Freddie Francis, M John Morris†, ED Anne V. Coates†, PD Stuart Craig, AD/SD Craig, Bob Cartwright & Hugh Scaife†, COS Patricia Norris†.

LP Anthony Hopkins (Dr. Frederick Treves), John Hurt† (John Merrick), Anne Bancroft (Mrs. Kendal), John Gielgud (Carr Gomm), Wendy Hiller (Mothershead), Freddie Jones (Bytes), Michael Elphick (Night Porter), Hannah Gordon (Mrs. Treves), Helen Ryan (Princess Alex).

In 1884 London, John Hurt, a penniless man deformed by a rare illness, is rescued from a freak show by prominent physician Anthony Hopkins. He becomes a member of fashionable society. Hurt gives a sensitive performance as the poor suffering creature.

849. *Eliminators* (1986, Empire, 96m, c). P Charles Band, D Peter Manoogian, W Paul De Meo & Danny Bilson, PH Mac Ahlberg, M Charles Band, ED Andy Horvitch, PD Phillip Foreman.

LP Andrew Prine (Harry Fontana), Denise Crosby (Nora Hunter), Patrick Reynolds (Mandroid), Conan Lee (Kuji), Roy Dotrice (Abbott Reeves), Peter

Schrum (Ray), Peggy Mannix (Bayou Betty).

A female scientist, a jungle guide, a ninja and a man-droid team up to battle a mad-genius scientist with plans to take over the world.

850. *Ella* (1988, Orion, 113m, c, aka *Monkey Shines: An Experiment in Terror*). P Charles Evans, D&W George A. Romero (based on the novel by Michael Stewart), PH James A. Contner, M David Shire, ED Pasquale Buba, PD Cletus Anderson.

LP Jason Beghe (Allan Mann), Kate McNeil (Melanie Parker), John Pankow (Geoffrey Fisher), Joyce Van Patten (Dorothy Mann), Christine Forrest (Maryanne Hodges), Stephen Root (Dean Burbage), Stanley Tucci (Dr. John Wiseman).

When law student Jason Beghe is accidentally paralyzed, he is given a trained monkey. He names her Ella; she learns to feed him, turn the pages of his law books, and dial his phone. Before long Ella starts carrying out her master's subconscious evil wishes.

851. *Ellie* (1984, Film Ventures, 88m, c). P Francine Roudine, D Peter Wittman, W Glenn Allen Smith, PH George Tirl, M Bob Pickering, ED John Davis.

LP Sheila Kennedy (Ellie), Shelley Winters (Cora), Edward Albert (Tom), Pat Paulsen (Sheriff), George Gobel (Preacher).

In this cornpone black comedy, Shelley Winters marries wealthy old geezers and dispatches them to their eternal reward after they have altered their wills in her favor. Sheila Kennedy, daughter of one of the old codgers, takes her revenge on Shelley and her three lustful sons.

852. *Elvira, Mistress of the Dark* (1988, New World, 96m, c). P Eric Gardner & Mark Pierson, D James Signorelli, W Sam Egan, John Paragon & Cassandra Peterson, PH Hanania Baer, M James Campbell, ED Battle David, PD John De Cuir, Jr.

LP Cassandra Peterson (Elvira), Edie McClurg (Chastity Pariah), Pat Crawford Brown (Mrs. Meeker), William Duell (Mr. Meeker), Susan Kellermann (Patty), Daniel Greene (Bob Redding), W.W. Morgan Sheppard (Uncle).

Cassandra Peterson portrays an outrageously, almost undressed vampira-like host on many TV horror movie programs. Now she appears in her own comedy horror film, which no one should take seriously—neither she nor does the rest of the cast nor the production crew do. The predictable plot about small town conservatives and a magic book compliment the dumb off-color jokes, usually about the star's ponderous breasts.

853. *Emanon* (1987, Paul Enterprizes, 94m, c). P Hank Paul & Dorothy Koster-Paul, D&W Stuart Paul, PH John Lambert, M Lennie Niehaus, ED Richard Meyer & Janet Riley.

LP Stuart Paul (Emanon), Cheryl M. Lynn (Molly Ballentine), Patrick Wright (Max), Jeremy Miller (Jason Ballentine), Tallie Cochrane (Laura Lowe), William F. Collard (Masora), Robert Hackman (Barnie).

Writer-director Stuart Paul appears as the Messiah. He arrives in New York City wearing rags and chooses to live with bums. He's ignored by everyone except crippled boy Jeremy Miller, who asks Paul to perform a miracle which will help his mother's dress business. What starts as an interesting premise breaks down into an unintentional comedy.

854. *Emmanuelle in Soho* (1981, Roldvale, GB, 67m, c). P John M. East, D David Hughes, W East & Brian Daly, PH Don Lord, M Barry Kirsch, ED David Woodward.

LP Mandy Miller (Emmanuelle), Julie Lee (Kate Benson), John M. East (Bill Anderson), Keith Fraser (Paul Benson), Gavin Clare (Cole), Tim Blackstone (Derek), Geraldine Hooper (Jill), Anita Desmarais (Sheila Burnett).

Sex-obsessed French girl Mandy Miller wants to become a porn star. She finds there are many anxious to help her achieve her objective.

855. *Emerald City* (1989, Greater Union, Australia, 93m, c). P Joan Long, D Michael Jenkins, W David Williamson (based on his play), PH Paul Murphy, M Chris Neal, ED Neil Thumpston, PD Owen Williams.

LP John Hargreaves (Colin Rogers), Robyn Nevin (Kate Rogers), Chris

Haywood (Mike McCord), Nicole Kidman (Helen Davey), Ruth Cracknell (Elaine Ross), Dennis Miller (Malcolm Bennett), Ella Scott (Penny Rogers), Hayden Samuels (Sam Rogers), Michelle Torres (Kath Mitchell).

Screenwriter David Williamson explores his own mixed feelings about the conflict Aussie writers face; whether to concentrate on "serious" Australian projects, which means only modest recompense and fame, or go for the big bucks and produce Americanized versions of Aussie screenplays. John Hargreaves as Williamson is contrasted with Chris Haywood as Mike McCord, a writer who will do anything for the almighty dollar.

856.   *The Emerald Forest* (1985, Embassy, 113m, c). P John Boorman & Michael Dryhurst, D Boorman, W Rospo Pallenberg, PH Philippe Rousselot, M Junior Homrich & Brian Gascoigne, ED Ian Crafford, PD Simon Holland.

LP Powers Boothe (Bill Markham), Meg Foster (Jean Markham), William Rodriquez (Young Tommy), Yara Vaneau (Young Heather), Estee Chandler (Heather), Charley Boorman (Tomme), Dira Paes (Kachiri), Eduardo Conde (Uwe Werner), Ariel Coelho (Padre Leduc), Peter Marinker (Perreira).

In this marvelous film based on an actual event, Powers Boothe is an American engineer helping to build a dam in the Amazon jungle. His five-year-old son is kidnapped by the "Invisible People," a jungle tribe of Indians whose use of camouflage is exceptionally effective. Boothe searches for his son for ten years and when he does find the youngster, he realizes he has lost him forever to an age-old civilization which in its innocence knows instinctly that the rain forest is more important for the world than a dam which will adversely affect the production of oxygen. Boothe agrees and blows up the dam — or perhaps it was the prayers of his son and the Indians that did the deed.

857.   *The Emperor's New Clothes* (1987, Cannon, 80m, c). P Menahem Golan & Yoram Globus, D David Irving, W Anna Mathias, Len Talan & David Irving (based on the story by Hans Christian Andersen), PH David Gurfinkel, M David Krivoshei, ED Tova Neeman, PD Marek Dobrowlski.

LP Robert Morse (Henry), Jason Carter (Nicholas), Lysette Anthony (Gilda), Clive Revill (Prime Minister), Julian Joy-Chagrin (Duke), Eli Gorenstein (Sergeant), Israel Gurion (Wenceslas), Susan Berlin-Irving (Christine), Sid Caesar (Emperor).

Legendary funny man Sid Caesar is the vainglorious ruler who doesn't want anyone to know that he's not smart enough to see the fine suit crooked tailors have made for him. The music is nothing very special.

858.   *Empire of the Sun* (1987, Warner, 152m, c). P Steven Spielberg, Kathleen Kennedy & Frank Marshall, D Spielberg, W Tom Stoppard (based on the novel by J.G. Ballard), PH Allen Daviau†, M John Williams†, ED Michael Kahn†, PD Norman Reynolds, AD/SD Reynolds & Harry Cordwell†, COS Bob Ringwood†, SOUND Robert Knudson, Don Digrolamo, John Boyd & Tony Dawe†.

LP Christian Bale (Jim Graham), John Malkovich (Basie), Miranda Richardson (Mrs. Victor), Nigel Havers (Dr. Rawlins), Joe Pantoliano (Frank Demerest), Leslie Phillips (Maxton), Masato Ibu (Sgt. Nagata), Emily Richard (Jim's Mother), Rupert Frazer (Jim's Father), Peter Gale (Mr. Victor), Takatoro Kataoka (Kamikaze Boy Pilot), Ben Stiller (Dainty), David Neidorf (Tiptree).

Arguably the best picture of 1987, *Empire of the Sun* was virtually ignored by voters for the Motion Picture Academy Awards, supposedly because of a dislike for producer-director Steven Spielberg — or is it just a case of jealousy? The story follows 11-year-old Christian Bale, a British subject born and raised in Shanghai who is separated from his parents during the Japanese takeover, shortly after the bombing of Pearl Harbor. He is befriended by survivor John Malkovich; both are interned in a prison camp. Bale survives the war, adapting to the harsh conditions and environment, and is finally reunited with his parents.

859.   *Empire State* (1987, Vidmark, GB, 104m, c). P Norma Heyman, D Ron Peck, W Peck & Mark Ayres, PH Tony

Imi, M Various Artists, ED Chris Kelly, PD Adrian Smith.

LP Cathryn Harrison (Marion), Jason Hoganson (Pete), Elizabeth Hickling (Cheryl), Jamie Foreman (Danny), Emily Bolton (Susan), Ian Sears (Paul), Martin Landau (Chuck), Lorcan Cranitch (Richard).

The film looks at the intersection of the lives of various characters at a London club called Empire State. Nothing much happens.

860. *The Empire Strikes Back* (1980, 20th Century-Fox, 124m, c). P Gary Kurtz, D Irvin Kershner, W Leigh Brackett & Lawrence Kasdan (based on a story by George Lucas), PH Peter Suschitzky, M John Williams†, ED Paul Hirsch, PD Norman Reynolds, AD/SD Reynolds, Leslie Dilley, Harry Lange, Alan Tomkins & Michael Ford†, SE Brian Johnson, Richard Edlund, Dennis Muren & Bruce Nicholson, SOUND Bill Varney, Steve Maslow, Gregg Landaker & Peter Sutton*.

LP Mark Hamill (Luke Skywalker), Harrison Ford (Han Solo), Carrie Fisher (Princess Leia), Billy Dee Williams (Lando Calrissian), Anthony Daniels (C-3PO), David Prowse (Darth Vader), James Earl Jones (Vader's voice), Peter Mayhew (Chewbacca), Kenny Baker (R2-D2), Frank Oz (Yoda), Alec Guinness (Ben Kenobi), Jeremy Bulloch (Boba Fett).

Audiences are enchanted with more exhilarating adventures of Mark Hamill, Harrison Ford and Carrie Fisher, who must take refuge from Darth Vader on a frozen planet. Many consider the sequel an improvement on the original. They both seem to be mindless escapism with great special effects and a certain amount of welcome humor to season the feast for the eyes.

861. *The Empty Beach* (1985, Jethro, Australia, 89m, c). P Timothy Read & John Edwards, D Chris Thomson, W Keith Dewhurst (based on the book by Peter Corris), PH John Seale, M Martin Armiger & Red Symons, ED Lindsay Frazer, PD Lawrence Eastwood.

LP Bryan Brown (Cliff Hardy), Anna-Maria Monticelli [Anna Jemison] (Anne Winter), Ray Barrett (MacLeary), John Wood (Parker), Nick Tate (Brian Henneberry), Belinda Giblin (Marion Singer), Peter Collingwood (Fred Ward), Kerry Mack (Hildegard).

The film details the exploits of Peter Corris' somber, tough and sardonic private eye Cliff Hardy (Bryan Brown). He's hired by wealthy widow Belinda Giblin who wants to know if her husband's disappearance in a boating accident two years earlier was on the level or if he's still alive.

862. *The End of August* (1982, Quartet, 105m, c). P Warren Jacobson & Sally Sharp, D Bob Graham, W Eula Seaton, Leon Heller, Anna Thomas & Gregory Nava (based on the novel *The Awakening* by Kate Chopin), PH Bob Elswit, M Shirley Walker, ED Jay Lash Cassidy, PD Jacobson, Erin Jo Jurow & Fred Baldwin.

LP Sally Sharp (Edna), Lilia Skala (Mlle. Reisz), David Marshall Grant (Robert), Kathleen Widdoes (Adele), Paul Roebling (Leonce), Paul Shenar (Arobin), John McLiam (Colonel), Mark Linn-Baker (Victor).

In 1900 New Orleans, bored young wife Sally Sharp takes a lover below her station. It's a nice looking film but doesn't have much of a story.

863. *End of the Line* (1988, Orion Classics, 105m, c). P Lewis Allen & Peter Newman, D Jay Russell, W Russell & John Wohlbruck, PH George Tirl, M Andy Summers, ED Mercedes Danevic, PD Neil Spisak.

LP Wilford Brimley (Will Haney), Levon Helm (Leo Pickett), Mary Steenburgen (Rose Pickett), Barbara Barrie (Jean Haney), Henderson Forsythe (Thomas Clinton), Bob Balaban (Warren Gerber), Kevin Bacon (Everett), Michael Beach (Alvin), Holly Hunter (Charlotte).

The film is sabotaged by Jay Russell & John Wohlbruck's stereotyped notion of how country folk think and talk. Wilford Brimley and all the other inhabitants of Clifford, Arkansas, are deeply concerned when the town's main employer, the Southland Railroad decides to shut down its operation. Brimley heads for Chicago to change the company's boss' mind.

864. *The End of the World Man* (1985, Irish Film Board, Ireland, 85m, c). P

Marie Jackson, D Bill Miskelly, W Jackson & Miskelly, PH Seamus Deasy, M John Anderson, ED Maurice Healey, PD Diane Menaul.

LP John Hewitt (Johnson), Maureen Dow (Mrs. D'Arcy), Michael Knowles (Sir George), Leanne O'Malley (Paula), Ian Morrison (Noel), Rowan Moore (Joe), Anthony McClelland (Colm), Eoin O'Callaghan (Pete).

In Belfast, Ireland, tomboy Leanne O'Malley and her friends rally to prevent local officials from turning a forest preserve into a shopping mall.

865.   *Endangered Species* (1982, MGM/United Artists, 97m, c). P Carolyn Pfeiffer, D Alan Rudolph, W Rudolph & John Binder (based on a story by Judson Klinger & Richard Woods), PH Paul Lohmann, M Gary Wright, ED Tom Walls, PD Trevor Williams.

LP Robert Urich (Ruben Castle), JoBeth Williams (Harriet Purdue), Paul Dooley (Joe Hiatt), Hoyt Axton (Ben Morgan), Peter Coyote (Steele), Marin Kanter (Mackenzie Castle), Dan Hedaya (Peck), Harry Carey, Jr. (Dr. Emmer), John Considine (Burnside).

New York detective Robert Urich is out west to investigate the mutilation of cattle. He uncovers a germ warfare research project involving—who else?—the CIA, unscrupulous businessmen and government agents.

866.   *Endless Love* (1981, Universal, 115m, c). P Dyson Lovell, D Franco Zeffirelli, W Judith Rascoe (based on the novel by Scott Spencer), PH David Watkin, M Jonathan Tunick, ED Michael J. Sheridan, PD Ed Wittstein, SONG "Endless Love" by Lionel Richie†.

LP Brooke Shields (Jade), Martin Hewitt (David), Shirley Knight (Anne), Don Murray (Hugh), Richard Kiley (Arthur), Beatrice Straight (Rose), Jimmy Spader (Keith), Ian Ziering (Sammy), Robert Moore (Dr. Miller).

Nominated as one of the worst films of all times, *Endless Love* bores audiences with the obsessive love of 17-year-old Martin Hewitt and 15-year-old Brooke Shields, two handsome youngsters with absolutely no acting ability. They are aided and and abetted by all the adults associated with the film, be they members of the cast or part of the production staff.

867.   *Enemies, A Love Story* (1989, 20th Century–Fox, 118m, c). D&P Paul Mazursky, W Mazursky & Roger Simon† (based on a novel by Isaac Bashevis Singer), PH Fred Murphy, M Maurice Jarre, ED Stuart Pappe, PD Pato Guzman.

LP Anjelica Huston† (Tamara), Ron Silver (Herman), Lena Olin† (Masha), Margaret Sophie Stein (Yadwiga), Alan King (Rabbi Lembeck), Judith Malina (Masha's Mother), Rita Karin (Mrs. Schreier), Phil Leeds (Pesheles), Elya Baskin (Yasha Kotik), Paul Mazursky (Leon Tortshiner).

This love story is more than the sum of its parts. Set in Brooklyn in 1949, Ron Silver appears as a Holocaust survivor who suddenly discovers that he has three "wives" to contend with: Anjelica Huston, the one he thought had died in the death camps, Margaret Sophie Stein, the one he married soon after the war and brought with him to America, and Lena Olin, the sly mistress with whom he shares a second residence in the Bronx. It's a story to make audiences both laugh and cry. The performances by the four main characters are superb. Olin is the apparent heir to Greta Garbo and Ingrid Bergman as a talented import from Sweden.

868.   *Enemy Mine* (1985, 20th Century–Fox, 114m, c). P Stephen Friedman, D Wolfgang Petersen, W Edward Khmara (based on a story by Barry Longyear), PH Tony Imi, M Maurice Jarre, ED Hannes Nikel, PD Rolf Zehetbauer.

LP Dennis Quaid (Davidge), Louis Gossett, Jr. (Jeriba, the Drac), Brion James (Stubbs), Richard Marcus (Arnold), Carolyn McCormick (Morse), Bumper Robinson (Zammis), Jim Mapp (Old Drac), Lance Kerwin (Wooster).

Acting like science-fiction versions of Tony Curtis and Sidney Poitier in *The Defiant Ones,* futuristic foes Dennis Quaid, an Earthman, and Lou Gossett, Jr., a reptilian alien, are stranded on a hostile planet where they must learn to depend upon each other to survive. The brotherhood message is lost in a very poor production and hampered by a weak story development.

869. *Enemy Territory* (1987, Empire, 90m, c). P Cynthia DePaula & Tim Kincaid, D Peter Manoogian, W Stuart M. Kaminsky & Bobby Liddell (based on a story by Kaminsky), PH Ernest Dickerson, M Sam Winans & Richard Koz Kosinaki, ED Peter Teschner, PD Medusa Studios, Marina Zurkow.

LP Gary Frank (Barry), Ray Parker, Jr. (Jackson), Jan-Michael Vincent (Parker), Frances Foster (Elva Briggs), Tony Todd (The Count), Stacey Dash (Toni Briggs), Deon Richmond (Chet), Tiger Haynes (Barton).

White insurance agent Gary Frank is sent by his boss to collect some money from a resident of a ghetto high rise. While there he innocently makes enemies of the building's street gang, The Vampires, and spends the rest of the night trying to escape from them.

870. *Enigma* (1983, Embassy, GB/ Fr., 101m, c). P Peter Shaw, Ben Arbeid & Andre Pergament, D Jeannot Szwarc, W John Briley (based on the novel *Enigma Sacrifice* by Michael Barak), PH Jean-Louis Picavet, M Marc Wilkinson & Douglas Gamley, ED Peter Weatherley & Peter Culverwell.

LP Martin Sheen (Alex Holbeck), Sam Neill (Dimitri Vasilkov), Brigitte Fossey (Karen), Derek Jacobi (Kurt Limmer), Michel Lonsdale (Bodley), Frank Finlay (Canarsky), David Baxt (Melton), Kevin McNally (Bruno).

Borrowing the plot of *Notorious,* CIA agent Martin Sheen enlists ex-lover Brigitte Fossey to make nice with Sam Neill, the head of an assassination squad of five KGB agents out to eliminate five Soviet dissidents.

871. *Enormous Changes at the Last Moment* (1985, ABC, 115m, c). P Mirra Bank, D Bank, Ellen Hovde & Muffie Meyer, W John Sayles & Susan Rice (based on short stories by Grace Paley), PH Tom McDonough.

LP Ellen Barkin (Virginia), David Strathairn (Jerry), Ron McLarty (John), Sudie Bond (Mrs. Raftery), Lynn Milgrim (Faith), Jeffrey DeMunn (Ricardo), Zvee Scooler (Pa), Eda Reiss Merin (Ma), Maria Tucci (Alexandra), Kevin Bacon (Dennis), John Wardwell (Doc).

Three of Grace Paley's stories have been adapted by screenwriter John Sayles, showing three women, Ellen Barkin, Lynn Milgrim and Maria Tucci, at crossroads in their lives. Each segment is sensitively presented and for the most part workable.

872. *Enter the Ninja* (1982, Cannon, 99m, c). P Judd Bernard & Yoram Globus, D Menahem Golan, W Dick Desmond, Golan & Bernard, PH David Gurfinkel, M W. Michael Lewis & Laurin Rinder, ED Mark Goldblatt.

LP Franco Nero (Cole), Susan George (Mary-Ann Landers), Sho Kosugi (Hasegawa), Alex Courtney (Frank Landers), Will Hare (Dollars), Zachi Noy (The Hook), Constantin de Goguel (Parker), Dale Ishimoto (Komori), Christopher George (Charles Venarius).

After graduating from Ninja school Franco Nero goes to the Philippines to help his buddy Alex Courtney save his plantation from Christopher George and his gang of nasties.

873. *The Entity* (1982, 20th Century-Fox, 125m, c). P Harold Schneider, D Sidney J. Furie, W Frank DeFelitta (based on his novel), PH Stephen H. Burum, M Charles Bernstein, ED Frank J. Urioste, PD Charles Rosen.

LP Barbara Hershey (Carla Moran), Ron Silver (Phil Schneidermann), David Labisoa (Billy), George Coe (Dr. Weber), Margaret Blye (Cindy Nash), Jacqueline Brooks (Dr. Cooley), Richard Brestoff (Gene Kraft).

Suburban single mother Barbara Hershey finds herself being sexually molested by an invisible, sex-crazed demon. You'll have to love rape and degradation of women to enjoy this horrid film, reportedly based on an actual possession case which took place in L.A.

874. *Equalizer 2000* (1987, Concorde, 79m, c). P Leonard Hermes, D Cirio H. Santiago, W Frederick Bailey (based on a story by Bailey & Joe Mari Avellana), PH Johnny Araojo, ED Pacifico Sanchez, Jr., PD Avellana.

LP Richard Norton (Slade), Corinne Wahl (Karen), William Steis (Lawton), Robert Patrick (Deke), Frederick Bailey (Hayward), Rex Cutter (Dixon), Warren McLean (Fletcher), Peter Shilton (MacLaine).

This *Mad Max* ripoff by Filipino action director Cirio H. Santiago is set in Alaska after a "nuclear winter" which has left the state a desert. The major conflict of the movie is over control of oil. It has plenty of sex, violence and car crashes.

875. *Erik* (1989, SC/Creswin, Canada, 90m, c). P Nicolas Stiliadis, D&W Michael Kennedy, PH Ludek Bogner, M Mychael Danna, ED Nick Rotundo, PD John Dondertman.

LP Stephen McHattie (Erik), Deborah Van Valkenburgh (Liliana), Aharon Ipale (The General), Ismael Carlo, Michael Champion, Dennis A. Pratt.

A lot of shooting and dying takes place as Vietnam vet Stephen McHattie, suffering from war nightmares, plies his trade as a mercenary in some unnamed South American country. He sells his services to the highest bidder.

876. *Erik the Viking* (1989, Orion, GB, 103m, c). P John Goldstone, D&W Terry Jones, PH Ian Wilson, M Neil Innes, ED George Akers, PD John Beard.

LP Tim Robbins (Erik), Gary Cady (Keitel), Mickey Rooney (Erik's Grandfather), Eartha Kitt (Freya), Terry Jones (King Arnulf), Imogen Stubbs (Princess Aud), John Cleese (Halfdan the Black), John Gordon Sinclair (Ivor the Boneless), Samantha Bond (Helga).

Viking Tim Robbins figures there must be more to life than pillaging and raping. He travels the world looking for a way to bring to a close the era of fighting and killing.

877. *Ernest Goes to Camp* (1987, Buena Vista, 93m, c). P Stacy Williams, D John R. Cherry, III, W Cherry & Coke Sams, PH Harry Mathias & Jim May, M Shane Keister, ED Marshall Harvey.

LP Jim Varney (Ernest P. Worrell), Victoria Racimo (Nurse St. Cloud), John Vernon (Sherman Krader), Iron Eyes Cody (Old Indian Chief), Lyle Alzado (Bronk Stinson), Gailard Sartain (Jake), Daniel Butler (Eddy), Patrick Day (Bobby Wayne), Scott Menville (Crutchfield).

Commercial spokesman Jim Varney as the moronic Ernest P. Worrell wants to become a counselor at Camp Kikakee, but instead is made a janitor. When a counselor has an accident, Varney is put in charge of the camp's misfits. The film is filled with sight gags which were old in silent one-reelers. Varney's character is as irritating as he is in his commercials, where the theory seems to be, people will buy anything to get away from the product's aggravating spokesman.

878. *Ernest Saves Christmas* (1988, Buena Vista, 89m, c). P Stacy Williams & Doug Claybourne, D John Cherry, W B. Kline & Ed Turner, PH Peter Stein, M Mark Snow, ED Sharyn L. Ross.

LP Jim Varney (Ernest P. Worrell), Douglas Seale (Santa Claus), Oliver Clark (Joe Carruthers), Noelle Parker (Harmony), Robert Lesser (Marty), Gailard Sartain (Chuck), Billie Bird (Mary Morrissey), Bill Byrge (Bobby).

Disaster-prone, well-meaning bungling Florida cab driver Jim Varney as Ernest picks up an old man, who turns out to be Santa Claus. At 151 the jolly old elf is losing his magical powers and must find a successor. No, it's not to be Varney, but he'll help, as will a runaway teen, the beguiling and tough-talking Noelle Parker. Maybe it's the season, but Varney's performance is more appealing this time.

879. *The Escape Artist* (1982, Orion/ Warner, 93m, c). P Doug Claybourne & Buck Houghton, D Caleb Deschanel, W Melissa Mathison & Stephen Zito (based on a novel by David Wagoner), PH Stephen H. Burum, M Georges Delerue, ED Arthur Schmidt, PD Dean Tavoularis.

LP Raul Julia (Stu Quinones), Griffin O'Neal (Danny Masters), Desiderio Arnaz (Mayor Quinones), Teri Garr (Arlene), Joan Hackett (Aunt Sybil), Gabriel Dell (Uncle Burke), John P. Ryan (Vernon), Elizabeth Daly (Sandra), M. Emmet Walsh (Fritz), Jackie Coogan (Magic Shop Owner).

In his film debut Ryan O'Neal's son Griffin does a mighty fine job. The teenager attempts to learn all the tricks of the trade of his famous escape artist father in order to avenge the latter's death at the hands of local politicians.

880. *Escape from New York* (1981, Avco Embassy, 99m, c). P Debra Hill & Larry Franco, D John Carpenter, W Carpenter & Nick Castle, PH Dean Cundey,

M John Carpenter & Alan Howarth, ED Todd Ramsay, PD Joe Alves.

LP Kurt Russell (Snake Plissken), Lee Van Cleef (Bob Hauk), Ernest Borgnine (Cabby), Donald Pleasence (The President), Isaac Hayes (Duke of New York), Season Hubley (Girl in Chock Full O'Nuts), Harry Dean Stanton (Brain), Adrienne Barbeau (Maggie), Tom Atkins (Rehme).

It's 1997 and New York City has become a maximum security prison fortress, walling in untold numbers of criminals and madmen. When the president's plane is hijacked by revolutionaries who crash it into the middle of Manhattan, former war hero and now renegade Kurt Russell has 24 hours to get the president out.

Escape to Victory see Victory

Escape 2000 see Turkey Shoot

881. *Escapes* (1987, Prism Entertainment, GB, 72m, c). P David Steensland & Angela Sanders, D&W Steensland, PH Gary Tomsic, M Todd Popple, ED Dane Westvic & Kiplan Hall.

LP Vincent Price (Mailman), Todd Fulton (Matt Wilson), Jerry Grishaw (Fisherman), Michael Patton-Hall (Delivery Driver), John Mitchum (Mr. Olson), Lee Cranfield & Roelle Mitchell (Young Couple), Ken Thorley (Jogger), Jeff Boudov (Scientist), Shirley O'Key (Mary Tucker).

In this low-budget "Twilight Zone"-like anthology Vincent Price hosts six bizarre stories: "A Little Fishy," "Coffee Break," "Hall of Faces," "Who's There?," "Jonah's Dream" and "Think Twice."

882. *E.T. The Extra-Terrestrial*† (1982, Universal, 115m, c). P Steven Spielberg & Kathleen Kennedy, D Spielberg†, W Melissa Mathison†, PH Allen Daviau†, M John Williams*, ED Carol Littleton†, PD James D. Bissell, SOUND Robert Knudson, Robert Glass, Don Digrolamo & Gene Cantamessa*, E.T. CREATED BY Carlo Rambaldi, VE Carlo Rambaldi, Dennis Muren & Kenneth F. Smith*, SOUND EFFECTS ED Charles L. Campbell & Ben Burtt*.

LP Dee Wallace (Mary), Henry Thomas (Elliott), Peter Coyote (Keys), Robert MacNaughton (Michael), Drew Barrymore (Gertie), K.C. Martel (Greg), Sean Frye (Steve), Tom Howell (Tyler), Erika Eleniak (Pretty Girl), David O'Dell (Schoolboy), Richard Swingler (Science Teacher).

In one of the all-time blockbuster box-office hits, Steven Spielberg and Melissa Mathison combine to give audiences a splendid fantasy tale of the friendship between earth children and a young visitor from another planet, accidentally left behind by its parents. The bad guys are earth adults who nearly are responsible for the death of E.T. But young Henry Thomas outsmarts them and reunites his friend with his alien parents. One just can't help but care for the odd-looking little alien creature, an innocent in a corrupt world — or at least that's how he's presented.

883. *Eternal Evil* (1988, New Century, US/Canada, 85m, c). P Pieter Kroonenburg, D George Mihalka, W Robert Geoffrion, PH Paul van der Linden, M Marvin Dolgay, ED Yves Langlois & Nick Rotundo.

LP Winston Rekert (Paul Sharpe), Karen Black (Janus), John Novak (Det. Kaufman), Andrew Bednarski (Matthew), Patty Talbot (Jennifer Sharpe), Lois Maxwell (Monica), Vlasta Varna (Scott), Walter Massey (John Westmore).

Made in 1985 the film headed to the video stores in 1988. Winston Rekert, a director of TV commercials, becomes a suspect in a murder case because of his "channeling" activities, which allow him to make psychic trips. During one such trip he witnesses a murder. The police figure he must be the murderer because he knows so much about the killing.

884. *Eureka* (1983, United Artists, GB, 129m, c). P Jeremy Thomas, D Nicolas Roeg, W Paul Mayersberg (based on the book *Who Killed Sir Harry Oakes?* by Marshall Houts), PH Alex Thomson, M Stanley Myers, ED Tony Lawson, PD Michael Seymour.

LP Gene Hackman (Jack McCann), Theresa Russell (Tracy), Rutger Hauer (Maillot van Horn), Jane Lapotaire (Helen McCann), Ed Lauter (Perkins), Mickey Rourke (Aurelio), Joe Pesci

(Mayakofsky), Helena Kallianiotis (Frieda).

Having made a fortune in gold, prospector Gene Hackman buys an isolated island. He's obsessed with the fear that someone will steal his money. He loses his daughter, Theresa Russell, to adventurer Rutger Hauer and his life to Joe Pesci's minions when he refuses the use of his island for a gambling resort.

885.   *The Everlasting Secret Family* (1989, Intl. Film Exchange, Australia, 93m, c). P&D Michael Thornhill, W Frank Moorhouse (based on his collection of short stories), PH Julian Penney, ED Pam Barnetta, AD Peta Lawson.

LP Arthur Dignam (The Senator), Mark Lee (The Youth), Heather Mitchell (Senator's Wife), John Meillon (The Judge), Dennis Miller (Eric), Paul Goddard (Son).

Mark Lee, a student at an exclusive Australian boy's school, becomes the kept lover of a prominent male politician, Dignam. The film explores the power that comes from shared sex.

886.   *Every Picture Tells a Story* (1984, Flamingo, GB, 82m, c). P Christine Oestreicher, D James Scott, W Shane Connaughton, PH Adam Barker-Mill, M Michael Storey, ED Chris Kelly, PD Louise Stjernsward.

LP Phyllis Logan (Agnes Scott), Alex Norton (William Scott, Sr.), Leonard O'Malley (William, age 15–18), John Docherty (William, age 11–14), Mark Airlie (William, age 5–8), Paul Wilson (Tocher), Willie Joss (Grandfather), Natasha Richardson (Miss Bridle).

Director James Scott pays tribute to his real-life father and grandfather in this story of World War I veteran Alex Norton, who moves his family to Northern Ireland where he earns a living as a sign painter. He encourages his son's artistic interests. When he dies the townspeople take up a collection to send the son to art school. The young man becomes a successful painter and director Scott's father.

887.   *Everybody's All American* (1988, Warner, 122m, c). P Taylor Hackford, Laura Ziskin & Ian Sander, D Hackford, W Tom Rickman (based on the novel by Frank Deford), PH Stephen Goldblatt, M James Newton Howard, ED Don Zimmerman, PD Joe Alves.

LP Dennis Quaid (Gavin Grey), Jessica Lange (Babs Rogers Grey), Timothy Hutton (Donnie [Cake]), John Goodman (Edward Lawrence), Raymond Baker (Bolling Kiely), Savannah Smith Boucher (Darlene Kiely), Carl Lumbly (Narvel Blue), Patricia Clarkson (Leslie).

The film spans 25 years in the lives of Louisiana football hero Dennis Quaid and Magnolia Queen Jessica Lange, who becomes his wife. Lange grows, but Quaid seems content to rest on past glory, but as the years go by, he finds that few are still interested. What happens to the two is meant to reflect changes in the South and succeeds without hitting audiences in the face with the symbolism.

888.   *Everytime We Say Goodbye* (1986, Tri-Star, Israel, 97m, c). P Jacob Kotzky & Sharon Harel, D Moshe Mizrahi, W Mizrahi, Rachel Fabien & Leah Appet (based on a story by Mizrahi), PH Giuseppe Lanci, M Philippe Sarde, ED Mark Burns.

LP Tom Hanks (David), Cristina Marsillach (Sarah), Benedict Taylor (Peter Ross), Anat Atzmon (Victoria), Gila Almagor (Lea), Monny Moshanov (Nessin), Avner Hizkiyahu (Raphael), Caroline Goodall (Sally).

Set in Israel during World War II, American officer Tom Hanks falls in love with Spanish Jew Cristina Marsillach, whose family ancestors settled in the Holy Land centuries ago. Her folks are very protective of their customs and their daughter. This soaper sank at the box-office.

889.   *Evil Altar* (1989, Ryan Rao, 87m, c). P Robert A. Miller & George L. Briggs, D Jim Winburn, Ryan Rao, W Brend Friedman, Scott Rose & Jon Geilfuss, PH Peter Wolf, M Bruce Lowe & Briggs, ED Rick Mitchell.

LP William Smith (Reed Weller), Pepper Martin (Collector), Robert Zdar (Sheriff O'Connell), Theresa Cooney (Teri Connors), Tal Armstrong (Daley Long).

William Smith sells his soul in order to become powerful enough to run a little town. He's sent by Pepper Martin to collect 103 souls for sacrifice.

890. *The Evil Below* (1989, Gibraltar/ Legend, 92m, c). P Barrie Saint Clair, D Jean-Claude Dubois, W Art Payne, PH Keith Dunkley, M Julian Laxton, ED Ettie Feldman.

LP Wayne Crawford (Max Cash), June Chadwick (Sarah Livingstone), Sheri Able (Tracy), Ted Le Platt (Adrian Barlow), Gordon Mulholland, Brian O'Shaughnessy.

In a routine adventure film going directly to video, Wayne Crawford and June Chadwick dive for the treasure to be found in a ship that sank in 1683. They dredge up competition, shark attacks, rumors of a local devil and bizarre nightmares.

891. *The Evil Dead* (1983, New Line, 85m, c). P Robert G. Tapert, D&W Sam Raimi, PH Tim Philo & Joshua M. Becker, M Joe LoDuca, ED Edna Ruth Paul, SE Bar Pierce.

LP Bruce Campbell (Ash), Ellen Sandweiss (Cheryl), Betsy Baker (Linda), Hal Delrich (Scott), Sarah York (Shelly).

Five college students find a strange book and a cassette tape (nice modern touch) in a remote cottage in a woods. The tape explains that the book is an ancient Sumerian Book of the Dead. When the kids call back the spirits of some of the not-so-dearly-departed, one by one their bodies, minds and souls are taken over, leaving only Bruce Campbell to battle the evil ones.

892. *Evil Dead 2: Dead by Dawn* (1987, Rosebud, 85m, c). P Robert G. Tapert, D Sam Raimi, W Raimi & Scott Spiegel, PH Peter Deming & Eugene Shlugleit, M Joseph LoDuca, ED Kaye Davis, SE Vern Hyde & Doug Beswick Prods.

LP Bruce Campbell (Ash), Sarah Berry (Annie), Dan Hicks (Jake), Kassie Wesley (Bobby Joe), Theodore Raimi (Possessed Henrietta), Denise Bixler (Linda), Richard Domeier (Ed), John Peaks (Prof. Raymond Knowby), Lou Hancock (Henrietta).

In this sequel to the 1983 horror hit, Bruce Campbell is besieged by assorted spirits in a mountain cabin. He's forced to dismember his own hand when it turns on him and then the damn thing scampers away. Various individuals become possessed and attack Campbell and Berry, the resourceful daughter of the archeologist who unleashed the cabin's fiends in the first place.

893. *Evil Laugh* (1989, Cinevest, 87m, c). P Dominick Brascia & Steven Baio, D Brascia, W Baio & Brascia, PH Stephen Sealy, M David Shapiro, ED Brian McIntosh & Michael Scott.

LP Steven Baio (Johnny), Kim McCamy (Connie), Tony Griffin (Sammy), Jody Gibson (Tina), Johnny Venocur (Freddy), Jerold Pearson (Barney).

The masked slasher in this low-budget film has an evil cackle. The young people who are his victims are medical students and interns spending a weekend at an abandoned orphanage.

894. *Evil Spawn* (1987, American Indp. Prods., 73m, c). P Anthony Brewster & Frank Bresee, D&W Kenneth J. Hall, PH Christopher Condon, M Paul Natzke, ED William Shaffer, SE Dan Bordona & Christopher Ray.

LP Bobbie Bresee (Lynn Roman), Drew Godderis (Ross Anderson), John Terrence (Brent Price), Donna Shock [Dawn Wildsmith] (Evelyn), Jerry Fox (Harry Fox), Pamela Gilbert (Elaine Talbot), John Carradine (Dr. Zeitman), Mark Anthony (Mark Randall).

Aging starlet Bobbie Bresee submits to a treatment by evil scientist Donna Shock. Shock's care makes her look younger, but it turns her into a hideous insect monster, hungering for human blood.

895. *The Evil That Men Do* (1984, Tri-Star, 90m, c). P Pancho Kohner, D J. Lee Thompson, W David Lee Henry & John Crowther (based on the novel by R. Lance Hill), PH Javier Ruvalcaba Cruz, M Ken Thorne, ED Peter Lee-Thompson.

LP Charles Bronson (Holland), Theresa Saldana (Rhiana), Joseph Maher (Mulloch), Jose Ferrer (Lomelin), Rene Enriquez (Max), John Glover (Briggs), Raymond St. Jacques (Randolph), Antoinette Bower (Claire).

Retired professional hitman Charles Bronson is called back to work to eliminate a doctor—and torture specialist—

who has been hiring himself out to various regimes in Latin American countries. Bronson, as ever, is an effective avenging angel of death.

896. *Evil Town* (1987, TransWorld Ent., 82m, c). P Peter S. Traynor & William D. Sklar, D Edward Collins, Traynor, Larry Spiegel & Mardi Rustam, W Spiegel & Richard Benson (based on a story by Royce Applegate), PH Bill Mann & Bob Ioniccio, M Michael Linn, ED Jess Mancilla, David G. Blangsted & Peter Parasheles.

LP James Keach (Dr. Chris Fuller), Michele Marsh (Julie), Doria Cook (Linda), Robert Walker (Mike), Dean Jagger (Dr. Schaeffer), Keith Hefner, Dabbs Greer, Scott Hunter, Lurene Tuttle, Regis Toomey.

Mad scientist Dean Jagger requires human organs for his research. His neighbors oblige him by luring unsuspecting visitors to their town and then turning them over to the tender mercies of the bad doctor. One such couple is physician James Keach and his girlfriend Michele Marsh. When they escape, they free other unwilling donors, who kill Jagger.

897. *Evil Under the Sun* (1982, EMI/ Universal, GB, 102m, c). P John Brabourne & Richard Goodwin, D Guy Hamilton, W Anthony Shaffer (based on the novel by Agatha Christie), PH Christopher Challis, M Cole Porter, ED Richard Marden, PD Elliot Scott.

LP Peter Ustinov (Hercule Poirot), Colin Blakely (Sir Horace Blatt), Jane Birkin (Christine Redfern), Nicholas Clay (Patrick Redfern), Maggie Smith (Daphne Castle), Roddy McDowall (Rex Brewster), Sylvia Miles (Myra Gardener), James Mason (Odell Gardener), Denis Quilley (Kenneth Marshall), Diana Rigg (Arlena Marshall), Emily Hone (Linda Marshall).

Peter Ustinov, as Poirot, must discover who among the various guests of an isolated island retreat did in obnoxious stage star Diana Rigg. As Agatha Christie's hero, he sifts through the various alibis, and as is his custom, reveals the culprit in a room containing all the suspects.

898. *Evils of the Night* (1985, Shapiro, 98m, c). P&D Mardi Rustam, W

Rustam & Phillip Dennis Connors, PH Don Stern, M Robert O. Ragland, ED Henry Chapro.

LP Neville Brand (Kurt), Aldo Ray (Fred), Tina Louise (Cora), John Carradine (Dr. Kozmar), Julie Newmar (Dr. Zarma), Karrie Emerson (Nancy), Bridget Holloman (Heather), G.T. Taylor (Connie).

Teenage campers are missing. Villainous extraterrestrials are responsible, keeping their victims hostage in order to sap their bodily fluids. Pretty awful stuff.

899. *Evilspeak* (1982, Leisure Investment/Coronet, 89m, c). P Sylvio Tabet & Eric Weston, D Weston, W Joseph Garofalo & Weston, PH Irv Goodnoff, M Roger Kellaway, Charles Tetoni, SE Harry Woolman & John Carter.

LP Clint Howard (Coopersmith), R.G. Armstrong (Sarge), Charles Tyner (Col. Kinkaid), Joseph Cortese (Rev. Jameson), Claude Earl Jones (Coach), Lynn Hancock (Miss Freidermyer), Lenny Montana (Jake).

In this absurdity, military school cadet Clint Howard uses his computer to conjure up a devil-worshipping medieval Spanish priest. Howard plans to employ the evil Padre to get even with his classmates who constantly bait him. The film should only appeal to those who are looking for nudity, violence and sickening gore. We guess you know who you are.

900. *Excalibur* (1981, Orion/Warner, 140m, c). P&D John Boorman, W Rospo Pallenberg & Boorman (based on the novel *Le Morte d'Arthur* by Thomas Malory), PH Alex Thomson†, M Trevor Jones, ED John Merritt, PD Anthony Pratt, AD Tim Hutchinson, COS Bob Ringwood, SE Peter Hutchinson & Alan Whibley.

LP Nigel Terry (King Arthur), Nicol Williamson (Merlin), Nicholas Clay (Lancelot), Helen Mirren (Morgana), Cherie Lunghi (Guenevere), Paul Geoffrey (Perceval), Robert Addie (Mordred), Gabriel Byrne (Uther), Keith Buckley (Uryens), Katrine Boorman (Igrayne), Liam Neeson (Gawain), Corin Redgrave (Cornwall).

The visual effects of this presentation of the Arthurian legend are impressive. So is the maintenance of the mythic qualities of the familiar story of a trusting king, his magician mentor Merlin, and his betrayal by his queen Guenevere and his beloved friend Lancelot.

901. *The Executioner Part II* (1984, 21st Century, 85m, c). P Renee Harmon, D James Bryant.

LP Christopher Mitchum (Lt. O'Malley), Aldo Ray (Police Commissioner), Antoine John Mottet (Mike), Renee Harmon (Celia Amherst), Dan Bradley, Jim Draftfield.

In a hopelessly amateurish thriller, homicide cop Christopher Mitchum is on the trail of a vigilante murderer.

902. *The Expendables* (1989, Concorde, 95m, c). P Anna Roth & Christopher Santiago, D Cirio H. Santiago, W Phillip Alderton, PH Ricardo Remias, MD Jaime Fabregas, ED Edgar Viner.

LP Anthony Finetti (Capt. Rosello), Peter Nelson (Sterling), Loren Haynes (Lord), Kevin Duffs (Jackson), William Steis (Col. Ridamann), Vic Diaz (Col. Tran Um Phi), David Light (Cabrini), Leah Navarro (Phu Ling).

Filipino director Cirio H. Santiago provides a well-made action film about gung-ho American captain Anthony Finetti. The latter leads a band of misfits on a mission to capture a Vietnamese colonel, Vic Diaz, for questioning. The ending is very grim.

903. *Experience Preferred...But Not Essential* (1983, Goldwyn, GB, 80m, c). P Chris Griffin, D Peter Duffell, W June Roberts, PH Phil Meheux, M John Scott, ED John Shirley.

LP Elizabeth Edmonds (Annie), Sue Wallace (Mavis), Geraldine Griffith (Doreen), Karen Meagher (Paula), Maggie Wilkinson (Arlene), Ron Bain (Mike), Alun Lewis (Hywel), Robert Blythe (Ivan), Roy Heather (Wally).

In this delightful and charming film Elizabeth Edmonds falls in love with a cook during her first summer job at a small Welch coastal hotel. She arrives insecure and frumpy-looking, but leaves self-assured and sexy.

904. *The Experts* (1989, Paramount, 83m, c). P James Keach, D Dave Thomas, W Nick Thiel, Steven Greene & Eric Alter (based on a story by Greene & Alter), PH Ronnie Taylor, M Marvin Hamlisch, ED Bud Molin, PD David Fischer.

LP John Travolta (Travis), Ayre Gross (Wendell), Kelly Preston (Bonnie), Deborah Foreman (Jill), James Keach (Yuri), Charles Martin Smith (Cameron Smith), Jan Rubes, Brian Doyle Murray, Mimi Maynard.

Gotham hipster John Travolta and nightclub owner Ayre Gross are drugged and kidnapped by KGB agent Charles Martin Smith, who takes them to Russia. They are to serve as up-to-date experts on America for a KGB run village, whose inhabitants are studying to be Americans so they can infiltrate U.S. communities as spies. According to this Soviet-bashing comedy, the Russians' notion of American culture is about 30 years out of date.

905. *Explorers* (1985, Paramount, 109m, c). P Edward S. Feldman & David Bombyk, D Joe Dante, W Eric Luke, PH John Hora, M Jerry Goldsmith, ED Tina Hirsch & John Wright, PD Robert F. Boyle, SE Industrial Light & Magic.

LP Ethan Hawke (Ben Crandall), River Phoenix (Wolfgang Muller), Jason Presson (Darren Woods), Amanda Peterson (Lori Swenson), Dick Miller (Charles Drake), Robert Picardo (Starkiller/Wak/Father of Wak and Neek), Leslie Rickert (Neek).

Youngsters Ethan Hawke, River Phoenix and Jason Presson build their own spaceship with which they travel to distant galaxies, encountering some loveable aliens, but also plenty of danger.

906. *Exposed* (1983, MGM/United Artists, 100m, c). P,D&W James Toback, PH Henri Decae, M Georges Delerue, ED Robert Lawrence & Annie Charvein, PD Brian Eatwell.

LP Nastassja Kinski (Elizabeth Carlson), Rudolf Nureyev (Daniel Jelline), Harvey Keitel (Rivas), Ian McShane (Greg Miller), Bibi Andersson (Margaret), Ron Randell (Curt), Pierre Clementi (Vic).

Small town girl Nastassja Kinski travels to the big city where she becomes a top model. She also gets mixed up in the plans of concert violinist Rudolf Nureyev to kill terrorist Harvey Keitel in Paris.

907. *Exquisite Corpses* (1989, Upfront Films, 96m, c). P Temistocles

Lopez & Ken Schwenker, D&W Lopez, PH Stephen McNutt, M Gary Knox, ED John Murray.

LP Zoe Tamerlaine Lund (Belinda Maloney), Gary Knox (Tim Lee), Frank Roccio (Lou), Ruth Collins (Sue), Daniel Chapman (Joe), Chuck Perley (Pat Maloney).

In this sometimes on-target black comedy, Gary Knox is a buckskin-wearing trombone player from Oklahoma, looking for fame and fortune in the Big Apple. Transformed from a down-home hick into a cynical, bisexual sophisticate who performs in decadent East Village cabarets, he gets mixed-up with mysterious femme fatale Zoe Tamerlaine Lund and murder.

908. *The Exterminator* (1980, Avco Embassy, 101m, c). P Mark Buntzman, D&W James Glickenhaus, PH Robert M. Baldwin, M Joe Renzetti, ED Corky O'Hare.

LP Christopher George (Det. James Dalton), Samantha Eggar (Dr. Megan Stewart), Robert Ginty (John Eastland), Steve James (Michael Jefferson), Tony Di Benedetto (Chicken Pimp), Dick Boccelli (Gino).

Demented Vietnam vet Robert Ginty does his impression of Charles Bronson in *Death Wish,* by arranging gruesome deaths for the members of a gang who mugged and paralyzed Ginty's friend. Christopher George is the cop out to put an end to Ginty's vigilante work.

909. *Exterminator 2* (1984, Cannon, 89m, c). P,D&W Mark Buntzman & William Sachs, PH Bob Baldwin & Joseph Mangine, M David Spear, ED George Norris & Marcus Manton.

LP Robert Ginty (Johnny Eastland), Mario Van Peebles ("X"), Deborah Geffner (Caroline), Frankie Faison (Be Gee), Scott Randolf (Eyes), Reggie Rock Bythewood (Spider), Bruce Smolanoff (Red Rat), David Buntzman (Head Mafioso).

Ex-Vietnam vet Robert Ginty is back on the revenge trail in New York City. If there were as many of these guys in real life as there are in the movies, the Big Apple would be free of criminal scum, and then the vigilantes would have to go after each other.

910. *Extreme Prejudice* (1987, Tri-Star, 104m, c). P Buzz Feitshans, D Walter Hill, W Deric Washburn & Harry Kleiner (based on a story by John Milius & Fred Rexer), PH Matthew F. Leonetti, M Jerry Goldsmith, ED Freeman Davies, PD Albert Heschong.

LP Nick Nolte (Jack Benteen), Powers Boothe (Cash Bailey), Michael Ironside (Maj. Paul Hackett), Maria Conchita Alonso (Sarita Cisneros), Rip Torn (Sheriff Hank Pearson), Clancy Brown (Sgt. Larry McRose), William Forsythe (Sgt. Buck Atwater), Matt Mulhern (Sgt. Declan Patrick Coker).

Texas Ranger Nick Nolte battles his childhood friend, drug trafficker Powers Boothe, in a violent but satisfying contemporary western. The two also compete for the affections of sultry Maria Conchita Alonso. Both men run up against a CIA-backed paramilitary group headed by Michael Ironside, who has his own ideas about making money from Boothe's drug rackets.

911. *Extremities* (1986, Atlantic, 91m, c). P Burt Sugarman, D Robert M. Young, PH William Mastrosimone, W Curtis Clark, Edwin Cook, Wendy Cotler, Andy Goldberg, Roger Steffens (based on the play by Mastrosimone), M J.A.C. Redford, ED Arthur Coburn, PD Chester Kaczenski.

LP Farrah Fawcett (Marjorie), James Russo (Joe), Diana Scarwid (Terry), Alfre Woodard (Patricia), Sandy Martin (Officer Sudow).

Farah Fawcett is admittedly an eyeful, but she needs a lot of work before she can be called an actress. She portrays a woman victimized in her own home by a taunting rapist and homicidal maniac, James Russo. When she manages to turn the tables on him, making him her captive, she is torn between taking bloody revenge and not stooping to his animal level.

912. *An Eye for an Eye* (1981, Avco Embassy, 106m, c). P Frank Capra, Jr., D Steve Carver, W William Gray & James Bruner (story by Bruner), PH Roger Shearman, M William Goldstein, ED Anthony Redman, PD Sandy Veneziano.

LP Chuck Norris (Sean Kane), Christopher Lee (Morgan Canfield), Richard Roundtree (Capt. Stevens), Matt Clark

(Tom McCoy), Mako (James Chan), Maggie Cooper (Heather Sullivan), Rosalind Chao (Linda Chan).

When his partner is killed by drug dealers, San Francisco cop and martial arts expert Chuck Norris quits the force to become a one man avenging force. It's been done before, and before, and before....

913. *Eye of the Needle* (1981, United Artists, GB, 111m, c). P Stephen Friedman, D Richard Marquand, W Stanley Mann (based on the novel by Ken Follett), PH Alan Hume, M Miklos Rozsa, ED Sean Barton, PD Wilfred Shingleton.

LP Donald Sutherland (Faber), Stephen MacKenna (Lieutenant), Philip Martin Brown (Billy Parkin), Kate Nelligan (Lucy), Christopher Cazenove (David), George Belbin (Lucy's Father), Faith Brook (Lucy's Mother), Barbara Graley (Constable), Arthur Lovegrove (Peterson).

Ruthless Nazi spy Donald Sutherland knifes anyone who gets in his way. Stationed in Great Britain during World War II, he discovers the Allied plans to invade the continent at Normandy. Trying to rendezvous with a German submarine off the Isle of Storms, he is taken in by sexually frustrated Kate Nelligan and her paralyzed husband, former RAF commander Christopher Cazenove. Sutherland makes love to Nelligan and kills Cazenove. When she discovers who Sutherland is and what he's up to, Nelligan prevents him from sending a message to the sub, shooting him several times with an ancient gun, finally killing him.

914. *Eye of the Tiger* (1986, Scotti Bros., 90m, c). P Tony Scotti, D Richard Sarafian, W Michael Montgomery, PH Peter Collister, ED Greg Prange.

LP Gary Busey (Buck Matthews), Yaphet Kotto (J.B. Deveraux), Seymour Cassel (Sheriff), Bert Remsen (Father Healey), William Smith (Blade), Kimberlin Ann Brown (Dawn), Denise Galik (Christie).

In another ripoff of *Death Wish,* ex-con, ex-vet Gary Busey seeks revenge on the motorcycle gang that murdered his wife and left his daughter in a catatonic state.

915. *Eyes of a Stranger* (1980, Warner, 85m, c). P Ronald Zerra, D Ken

Wiederhorn, W Mark Jackson & Eric L. Bloom, PH Mini Rojas, M Richard Einhorn, ED Rick Shaine.

LP Lauren Tewes (Jane), Jennifer Jason Leigh (Tracy), John DiSanti (Stanley Herbert), Peter DuPre (David), Gwen Lewis (Debbie), Kitty Lunn (Annette), Timothy Hawkins (Jeff), Ted Richert (Roger).

TV newspaperwoman Lauren Tewes tries to protect her deaf, dumb and blind sister Jennifer Jason Leigh from overweight madman John DiSanti, a next-door neighbor, who rapes and murders women.

916. *Eyes of Fire* (1984, Aquarius/Elysian, 106m, c). P Philip J. Spinelli, D&W Avery Crounse, PH Wade Hanks, M Brad Fiedel, ED Michael Barnard.

LP Dennis Lipscomb (Will Smythe), Guy Boyd (Marion Dalton), Rebecca Stanley (Eloise Dalton), Sally Klein (Fanny Dalton), Karlene Crockett (Leah), Fran Ryan (Sister), Rob Paulsen (Jewell Buchanan).

This horror film is set in the American West of the 19th century where a band of settlers are harassed by Indian spirits.

917. *Eyewitness* (1981, 20th Century-Fox, 108m, c, aka *The Janitor*). P&D Peter Yates, W Steve Tesich, PH Matthew F. Leonetti, M Stanley Silverman, ED Cynthia Scheider, PD Philip Rosenberg.

LP William Hurt (Daryll Deever), Sigourney Weaver (Tony Sokolow), Christopher Plummer (Joseph), James Woods (Aldo), Irene Worth (Mrs. Sokolow), Kenneth McMillan (Mr. Deever), Pamela Reed (Linda), Steven Hill (Lt. Jacobs), Morgan Freeman (Lt. Black).

In a modern version of "the boy who cried wolf," to impress beautiful TV newscaster Sigourney Weaver, janitor William Hurt claims to know something about a murder which took place in his building. Not only is Weaver impressed, so are the culprits. Now Hurt's life is in jeopardy.

918. *The Fabulous Baker Boys* (1989, 20th Century-Fox, 114m, c). P Paula Weinstein, Mark Rosenberg & Bill Finnegan, D&W Steve Kloves, PH Michael Ballhaus†, M Dave Grusin†, ED William Steinkamp†, PD Jeffrey Townsend.

LP Jeff Bridges (Jack Baker), Michelle Pfeiffer† (Susie Diamond), Beau Bridges (Frank Baker), Jennifer Tilly (Monica Moran), Ellie Raab (Nina), Xander Berkeley (Lloyd), Dakin Matthews (Charlie), Ken Lerner (Ray).

Not having been called on to sing in movies since her debut in the very forgettable *Grease 2* (1982), the lovely Michelle Pfeiffer once more demonstrates that she is a multitalented performer. The Bridges brothers, Jeff and Beau, are a two-piano lounge act who decide to expand to a three person group by adding a female singer. This is where the sultry, incendiary Pfeiffer fits in. Both brothers are attracted to her, but Beau, a married man and the booster of the act, is too busy to be any real competition for Jeff. It's an interesting story of slightly tawdry glamour and smart dialogue saying next to nothing. Catch Michelle's act on top of Jeff's piano.

919. *Face of the Enemy* (1989, Tri-Culture, 92m, c). P Behrouz Gueramian, Elizabeth Lynch Brown & Catherine Rocca, D Hassan Ildari, W Philip Anderson (based on a story by Ildari), PH Peter Indergand, M Esfandiar Monfaredzadeh, ED Toby Brown, PD Marina Kieser & Pierluca DeCarlo.

LP Rosanna DeSoto (Neiloufar), George DiCenzo (James Wald), Cindy Cryer (Darya).

Former U.S. embassy hostage George DiCenzo, haunted by his ordeals during 444 days in Iran, becomes obsessed with the notion that Iranian Rosanna DeSoto was part of a team that tortured him. Tit for tat, he kidnaps her and holds her prisoner in his basement.

920. *Fade to Black* (1980, American Cinema, 100m, c). P George Braunstein & Ron Hamady, D&W Vernon Zimmerman, PH Alex Phillips, Jr., ED Howard Kunin, SE James Wayne.

LP Dennis Christopher (Eric Binford), Linda Kerridge (Marilyn), Tim Thomerson (Dr. Moriarty), Morgan Paull (Gary), Hennen Chambers (Bart), Marya Small (Doreen), Eve Brent Ashe (Aunt Stella), Mickey Rourke (Richie).

That nice boy in *Breaking Away,* Dennis Christopher, a movie fanatic, romances Marilyn Monroe lookalike Linda Kerridge and murders in the style of his screen idols.

921. *Fakebook* (1989, Vested Interests, 96m, c). P&D Ralph Toporoff, W Gilbert Girion (based on a story by Toporoff & Girion), PH Joey Forsyte, M Larry Schanker, ED Jack Haigis, PD Charles Lagola.

LP Peter MacNicol (Jack Solow), Carl Capotorto (Jerry), Tim Guinee (Bobby), Bill Christopher-Myers (Lee), Jonathan Walker (Tommy), Charlotte d'Amboise (Benita), Louis Guss (Abe Katz), Zohra Lampert (Louise).

In the 1960s, blandly good-natured Peter MacNicol and four friends try to launch a jazz group. They give themselves a year to make it big, but the only gigs they can get prove to them they don't have what it takes.

922. *The Falcon and the Snowman* (1985, Orion, 131m, c). P Gabriel Katzka & John Schlesinger, D Schlesinger, W Steven Zaillian (based on the book by Robert Lindsey), PH Allen Daviau, M Pat Metheny & Lyle Mays, ED Richard Marden, PD James D. Bissell.

LP Timothy Hutton (Christopher Boyce), Sean Penn (Daulton Lee), Pat Hingle (Mr. Boyce), Richard Dysart (Dr. Lee), Lori Singer (Lana), David Suchet (Alex), Dorian Harewood (Gene), Priscilla Pointer (Mrs. Lee), Nicholas Pryor (Eddie), Sam Ingraffia (Kenny Kahn), Mady Kaplan (Laurie).

Raised by a rigid, Catholic, CIA agent father, Timothy Hutton, a dropout from the seminary, takes a job arranged for him by his father tracking spy satellites. He is soon promoted to dealing with his company's top-secret defense files. Questioning his country's morality, Hutton decides to punish the U.S. by selling secrets to the Russians. He draws his cokehead friend Sean Penn in on the deal. It is the instability of the latter which finally gets them caught.

Falcon's Gold see Robbers of the Sacred Mountain

923. *The Fall of the House of Usher* (1980, Sunn Classic, 101m, c). P Charles E. Sellier, Jr., D James L. Conway, W Stephen Lord (based on the story by Edgar Allan Poe).

LP Martin Landau (Roderick Usher), Ray Walston (Thaddeus), Charlene Tilton (Jennifer), Dimitra Arliss (Madeline), Robert Hays (Jonathan).

Landau and Walston don't distinguish themselves in this extremely poor adaptation of the Poe classic. Fortunately for Hays and Tilton, they survived this early mistake in their careers.

924. *Falling in Love* (1984, Paramount, 107m, c). P Marvin Worth, D Ulu Grosbard, W Michael Cristofer, PH Peter Suschitzky, M Dave Grusin, ED Michael Kahn, PD Santo Loquasto.

LP Robert DeNiro (Frank Raftis), Meryl Streep (Molly Gilmore), Harvey Keitel (Ed Lesky), Jane Kaczmarek (Ann Raftis), George Martin (John Trainer), David Clennon (Brian Gilmore), Dianne Wiest (Isabelle), Victor Argo (Victor Rawlins).

Owing more to *Brief Encounter* than it admits, this film stars Robert DeNiro and Meryl Streep as two married suburbanites, but not to each other, who meet and fall in love on their daily commute to the city. DeNiro rents an apartment in Greenwich village, and Streep agrees to have an affair with him, but when it comes time to make love, she can't go through with it. Nevertheless, the guilt the two feel is translated to their spouses and causes the break-up of their marriages, but it doesn't bring DeNiro and Streep together for a final clinch.

925. *Falling in Love Again* (1980, International Picture Show of Atlanta, 103m, c). P&D Steven Paul, W Paul, Susannah York & Ted Allan, PH Michael Mileham, Dick Bush & Wolfgang Suschitzky, M Michel Legrand, ED Bud Smith, Doug Jackson & Jacqueline Cambas.

LP Elliott Gould (Harry Lewis), Susannah York (Sue Lewis), Stuart Paul (Pompadour/Young Harry), Michelle Pfeiffer (Sue Wellington), Kaye Ballard (Mrs. Lewis), Robert Hackman (Mr. Lewis), Steven Paul (Stan the Con), Todd Helper (Alan Childs).

Middle-aged New Yorker Elliott Gould recalls his youthful romances and his dreams of success as he travels to his high school reunion. What 21-year-old producer-director-screenwriter Steven Paul could possibly know about mid-life crisis is beyond us.

926. *Fame* (1980, MGM/United Artists, 134m, c). P David DeSilva & Alan Marshall, D Alan Parker, W Christopher Gore†, PH Michael Seresin, M Michael Gore*, ED Gerry Hambling†, PD Geoffrey Kirkland, SONG "Fame" by Michael Gore & Dean Pitchford*, SOUND Michael J. Kohut, Aaron Rochin, Jay M. Harding & Chris Newman†.

LP Eddie Barth (Angelo), Irene Cara (Coco), Lee Curreri (Bruno), Laura Dean (Lisa), Antonia Franceschi (Hilary), Boyd Gaines (Michael), Albert Hague (Shorofsky), Tresa Hughes (Mrs. Finsecker), Steve Inwood (Francois Lafete), Paul McCrane (Montgomery), Anne Meara (Mrs. Sherwood), Barry Miller (Ralph), Gene Anthony Ray (Leroy), Debbie Allen (Lydia).

This feel-good movie succeeds with all generations, because the performers who portray the talented and troubled teens who attend Manhattan's High School for the Performing Arts seem to handle the problems of growing up just as badly as everyone else's kids, and yet none go too bad. So many of the young people were memorable, but a special tip of the hat goes to Irene Cara, Paul McCrane, Gene Anthony Ray, Lee Curreri, and Barry Miller.

927. *Family Business* (1989, Tri-Star, 115m, c). P Lawrence Gordon, D Sidney Lumet, W Vincent Patrick (based on his novel), PH Andrzej Bartkowiak, M Cy Coleman, ED Andrew Mondshein, PD Philip Rosenberg.

LP Sean Connery (Jessie McMullen), Dustin Hoffman (Vito McMullen), Matthew Broderick (Adam McMullen), Rosana DeSoto (Elaine), Janet Carroll (Margie), Victoria Jackson (Christine), Bill McCutcheon, Deborah Rush, Marilyn Cooper.

Ivy League graduate Matthew Broderick gets his grandfather Sean Connery, a long time crook, to help him pull off a high-tech robbery. If Broderick's father, a semirespectable businessman Dustin Hoffman, is unable to stop them, he'll have to join them. Connery steals scenes as well as he steals merchandise. As the amoral family head, Connery saves the dark comedy movie from being merely routine.

928. *Family Viewing* (1988, Ontario Film, Canada, 86m, c). P,D&W Atom Egoyan, PH Robert MacDonald, Mychael Danna, ED Egoyan & Bruce MacDonald.

LP David Hemblen (Stan), Aidan Tierney (Van), Gabrielle Rose (Sandra), Arsinee Khanjian (Aline), Selma Keklikian (Armen), Jeanne Sabourin (Aline's Mother), Rose Sarkisyan (Van's Mother).

In this independent/experimental film, members of Aidan Tierney's family live only for television and video, communicating only electronically.

929. *The Fan* (1981, Paramount, 95m, c). P Robert Stigwood, D Edward Bianchi, W John Hartwell & Priscilla Chapman (based on the novel by Bob Randall), PH Dick Bush, M Pino Donaggio, ED Alan Heim, PD Santo Loquasto.

LP Lauren Bacall (Sally Ross), James Garner (Jake Berman), Maureen Stapleton (Belle Goodman), Hector Elizondo (Ralph Andrews), Michael Biehn (Douglas Breen), Anna Marie Horsford (Emily Stolz), Kurt Johnson (David Branum), Feiga Martinez (Elsa).

Fan is short for fanatic, and that's precisely what Michael Biehn is about Lauren Bacall. He considers himself the greatest admirer of the actress. He's willing to kill anyone who tries to prevent him from being with his idol, even Bacall herself. Sounds a bit like Mark David Chapman and John Lennon doesn't it?

The Fanatic* see *The Last Horror Film

930. *Fandango* (1985, Warner, 91m, c). P Barrie M. Osborne & Pat Kehoe, D&W Kevin Reynolds (based on his short film *Proof*), PH Thomas Del Ruth, M Alan Silvestri, ED Arthur Schmidt & Stephen Semel.

LP Kevin Costner (Gardner Barnes), Judd Nelson (Phil Hicks), Sam Robards (Kenneth Waggener), Chuck Bush (Dorman), Brian Cesak (Lester), Elizabeth Daily (Judy), Suzy Amis (The Girl), Marvin J. McIntyre (Truman Sparks), Glenne Headly (Trellis), Robyn Rose (Lorna).

Five college roommates—Kevin Costner, Judd Nelson, Sam Robards, Chuck Bush and Brian Cesak—blast off for a wild graduation weekend drive across the Texas Badlands. It's sort of a serious *Animal House* on the road.

931. *Fanny Hill* (1983, FH Prods., GB, 92m, c). P Harry Benn, D Gerry O'Hara, W Stephen Chesley (based on the novel by John Cleland, PH Tony Spratling, M Paul Hoffert, ED Peter Boyle.

LP Lisa Raines (Fanny Hill), Oliver Reed (Lawyer), Wilfrid Hyde-White (Barville), Shelley Winters (Mrs. Cole), Alfred Marks (Lecher), Jonathan York (Charles), Paddie O'Neil (Mrs. Brown), Maria Harper (Phoebe).

This version of John Cleland's story of an orphan girl who becomes a woman of pleasure is a bit more explicit sexually than some of the earlier versions but not as pornographic as the 1965 West German production.

932. *Fantasies* (1981, Brenner, 81m, c, aka *And Once Upon a Love*). P Kevin Casselman, D,W&PH John Derek, M Jeff Silverman, ED Bret Weston.

LP Bo Derek (Anastasia), Peter Hooten (Damir), Anna Alexiadis (Mayor), Pheacton Gheorghitais (Photographer), Constantine Beladames (Godfather), Nicos Paschalidis (Priest), Boucci Simma (Beautifuloni).

Shot in 1973, but not released until after the Dereks' *Tarzan, The Ape Man,* this first collaboration of Bo and John is the pitiful tale of brother and sister (Bo Derek and Peter Hooten), falling in love on their Greek island home. It's OK, they really aren't siblings, and so the question of incest is eliminated, allowing them to marry. The Dereks are both good-looking people, but that seems to be the extent of their talents.

933. *Fantasy Man* (1984, Centaur, Australia, 79m, c). P Basil Appleby & Darrell Lass, D&W John Meagher, PH Andrew Lesnie, M Adrian Payne, ED Rod Hibberd, PD Lass.

LP Harold Hopkins (Nick Bailey), Jeanie Drynan (Liz Bailey), Kerry Mack (Donna), Kate Fitzpatrick (Neighbor), John Howitt (Howard), Colin Croft (Art Teacher).

Australian office worker Harold Hopkins is bored with his job and his wife Jeanie Drynan. She's bored with him. Hopkins lives in a fantasy world of love involving hamburger stand owner Kerry Mack, but nothing comes of it. We assume the producers of this film intended to see how boring they could be. Give them an "A" for their success.

934. *Far from Home* (1989, Vestron, 86m, c). P Donald P. Borchers, D Meiert Avis, W Tommy Lee Wallace (based on a story by Ted Gershuny), PH Paul Elliott, M Jonathan Elias, ED Marc Grossman, PD Victoria Paul.

LP Matt Frewer (Charlie Cross), Drew Barrymore (Joleen Cross), Richard Masur (Duckett), Karen Austin (Louise), Susan Tyrrell (Agnes Reed), Anthony Rapp (Pinky Sears), Jennifer Tilly (Amy), Andras Jones (Jimmy Reed).

Cute little child-star Drew Barrymore makes the transition to more grown-up roles as a voluptuous sex-kitten, stranded with her father at a trailer park in Nevada, where some mad killer is busily at work. Looks like they want us to believe that Andras Jones is the maniac, but just because he tries to rape the 14-year-old Lolita type doesn't make him a bad guy.

935. *Far North* (1988, Alive, 90m, c). P Carolyn Pfeiffer & Malcolm Harding, D&W Sam Shepard, PH Robbie Greenberg, M Red Clay Ramblers, ED Bill Yahraus, PD Peter Jamison.

LP Jessica Lange (Kate), Charles Durning (Bertrum), Tess Harper (Rita), Donald Moffat (Uncle Dane), Ann Wedgeworth (Amy), Patricia Arquette (Jilly), Nina Draxten (Gramma).

Director-writer Sam Shepard doesn't prove he can handle the dual roles of director and writer in this offbeat comedy about a rural Minnesota family. They include father Charles Durning, hospitalized when his horse runs out of control and Jessica Lange, his strong-willed pregnant and unmarried daughter, whom he orders to shoot the damn nag. Her sister Tess Harper wishes to save the horse she rode in happier days. The remaining members are Patricia Arquette, Harper's promiscuous daughter, the prematurely senile mother Ann Wedgeworth and her soon to be 100-year-old mother Nina Draxten. The roll-call is funnier than the movie.

936. *Farewell to the King* (1989, Orion, 117m, c). P Albert S. Ruddy & Andre Morgan, D&W John Milius (based on the novel *L'Adieu Au Roi* by Pierre Schoendoerffer), PH Dean Semler, M Basil Poledouris, ED Anne V. Coates & C. Timothy O'Meara, PD Gil Parrondo.

LP Nick Nolte (Learoyd), Nigel Havers (Capt. Fairbourne, Botanist), Frank McRae (Tenga), Gerry Lopez (Gwai), Marilyn Tokuda (Yoo), Choy Chang Wing (Lian), John Bennett Perry (Gen. Douglas MacArthur).

Renegade American soldier Nick Nolte eludes the Japanese in the Philippines in 1942 by making his way to Borneo. There he forges a kingdom for himself among the innocent natives, but civilization catches up to him with the arrival of the victorious Allies at the end of World War II. It's a hum-drum comic book adventure film, a poor man's "The Man Who Would Be King," which suffers from inane dialog.

The Farm see The Curse

937. *Fast Food* (1989, Double Helix/ Fries, 92m, c). P Stan Wakefield & Michael A. Simpson, D Simpson, W Clark Brandon, Randal Patrick & Lanny Horn (based on a story by Scott B. Sowers & Jim Bastille), PH Bill Mills, M Iris Gillon, ED John David Allen, AD Shad Leach.

LP Clark Brandon (Auggie), Randal Patrick (Drew), Tracy Griffith (Samantha), Michael J. Pollard (Bud), Lanny Horn (Calvin), Jim Varney (Wrangler Bob Bundy), Blake Clark (E.G. McCormick).

This straight to video release is the not-funny comedy of a war between competing fast food establishments. This film like many others of its type makes one wonder if teens should be allowed to exist.

938. *Fast Forward* (1985, Columbia, 110m, c). P John Patrick Veitch, D Sidney Poitier, W Richard Wesley (based on a story by Timothy March), PH Matthew F. Leonetti, M Tom Scott & Jack Hayes, ED Harry Keller, David Blewitt & Art Seid.

LP John Scott Clough (Matt Sherman), Don Franklin (Michael Stafford), Tamara Mark (June Wolsky), Tracy Silver (Meryl Stanton), Cindy McGee (Francine Hackett), Gretchen F. Palmer (Valerie Thompson), Monique Cintron

(Rita Diaz), Debra Varnado (Debbie Hughes).

We'd rather see Sidney Poitier *on* the screen than directing this boring "Let's put on a show" chestnut. The kids are in New York street gangs that choose break dancing rather than breaking heads.

939.   *Fast Talking* (1985, Filmtrex, Australia, 93m, c). P Ross Matthews, D&W Ken Cameron, PH David Gribble, M Sharon Calcraft, ED David Huggett, PD Neil Angwin.

LP Rod Zuanic, Toni Allaylis, Chris Truswell, Gail Sweeny, Steve Bisley, Peter Hehir, Tracey Mann, Dennis Moore.

Fourteen-year-old Sydney, Australia, petty thief Rod Zuanic runs away from home because he can no longer live with his father's drunkenness and his brother's drug dealing.

940.   *Fast Times at Ridgemont High* (1982, Universal, 92m, c). P Art Linson & Irving Azoff, D Amy Heckerling, W Cameron Crowe (adapted from his book), PH Matthew R. Leonetti, M Joe Walsh, ED Eric Jenkins.

LP Sean Penn (Jeff Spicoli), Jennifer Jason Leigh (Stacy Hamilton), Judge Reinhold (Brad Hamilton), Robert Romanus (Mike Damone), Brian Backer (Mark "Rat" Ratner), Phoebe Cates (Linda Barrett), Ray Walston (Mr. Hand), Scott Thomson (Arnold), Vincent Schiavelli (Mr. Vargas), Amanda Wyss (Lisa), D.W. Brown (Ron Johnson), Forest Whitaker (Charles Jefferson).

A lot of young talent gets a leg up in this movie, which is heavy on the sexual concerns of teenagers, but light on anything else which might give audiences any insight into the other tribulations of adolescents. Still, the film is more amusingly presented than most of the teenage exploitation films. Sean Penn, whose antics have grown a bit old since, is appealing as a hip, stoned, nonstudent. Freshman Jennifer Jason Leigh is fed a lot of misinformation about sex by senior Phoebe Cates, while Leigh's fantasizing brother Judge Reinhold's popularity seems a function of his fast-food job. Look for Eric Stoltz and Anthony Edwards is small roles.

941.   *Fast-Walking* (1982, Lorimar, 115m, c). P&D James B. Harris, W Harris (based on the novel *The Rap* by Ernest Brawley), PH King Baggot, M Lalo Schifrin, ED Douglas Stewart.

LP James Woods (Fast-Walking Miniver), Tim McIntire (Wasco), Kay Lenz (Moke), Robert Hooks (William Galliot), M. Emmet Walsh (Sgt. Sanger), Timothy Agoglia Carey (Bullet), Susan Tyrrell (Evie).

In a black comedy, pot-smoking prison guard James Woods steers johns to Susan Tyrrell's whore house. His yearning for the good life gets him involved in a prison break by black militant Hooks.

942.   *Fat Angels* (1980, Impala-Mambru, US/Spain, 92m, c). D Manuel Summers, W Summers, Chumey Chumez, Leon Tchaso & Joe Gonzalez (based on a story by Summers), PH Manuel Rojas, M Bob Dorough, ED Gloria Pineyro.

LP Farnham Scott (Mike), January Stevens (Mary), Jack Aaron (Frank), Amy Steel (Alison), Robert Reynolds (Jackie).

Obese piano-player Farnham Scott is lonely. He corresponds with January Stevens, an overweight woman living in Florida, but when she travels to New York, neither wants the other to see just how hefty they really are.

943.   *Fat Guy Goes Nutzoid* (1986, Troma Team, 85m, c). P Emily Dillon, D John Golden, W John & Roger Golden, PH John Drake, M Leo Kottke, ED Jeffrey Wolf, Krissy Boden & Kathie Weaver, PD Martin De Maat.

LP Tibor Feldman (Roger), Douglas Stone (Doogle), Max Alexander (Harold), John McEvily (Oscar), John MacKay (Ronald), Lynne Marie Brown (Hooker), Mark Alfred (Milton), Joan Allen (Lala).

Fugitive from a funny farm Max Alexander teams up with kids Tibor Feldman and Douglas Stone. He's big, fat and lovable with a Mohawk hair cut. The three misfits become good friends and have adventures of a lifetime for a few days.

944.   *Fat Man and Little Boy* (1989, Paramount, 126m, c). P Tony Garnett, D Roland Joffe, W Bruce Robinson & Joffe (based on a story by Robinson), PH

Vilmos Zsigmond, M Ennio Morricone, ED Francoise Bonnot, PD Gregg Fonseca.

LP Paul Newman (Gen. Leslie R. Groves), Dwight Schultz (J. Robert Oppenheimer), Bonnie Bedelia (Kitty Oppenheimer), John Cusack (Michael Merriman), Laura Dern (Kathleen Robinson), Ron Frazier (Peer de Silva), Natasha Richardson (Jean Tatlock), Ron Vawter (Jamie Latrobe).

In an uninspiring drama about the creation of the first atomic bombs, Paul Newman is the general responsible for the development of the bomb and Dwight Schultz is the mercurial scientist who's not so sure that he wishes to be associated with something that he suspects will have horrible consequences. The two men argue constantly, but of course we all know who won the argument. Audiences have seen the arguments between the two men before in ABC-TV's "Day One" and the 1980 documentary "The Day After Trinity" and apparently that was enough, because the movie has been a box-office bomb.

945. *Fatal Attraction*† (1987, Paramount, 119m, c). P Stanley R. Jaffe & Sherry Lansing, D Adrian Lyne†, W James Dearden†, PH Howard Atherton, M Maurice Jarre, ED Michael Kahn & Peter E. Berger†, PD Mel Bourne, AD Jack Blackman, SD George DeTitta.

LP Michael Douglas (Dan Gallagher), Glenn Close† (Alex Forrest), Anne Archer† (Beth Gallagher), Ellen Hamilton Latzen (Ellen Gallagher), Stuart Pankin (Jimmy), Ellen Foley (Hildy), Fred Gwynne (Arthur), Meg Mundy (Joan Rogerson), Tom Brennan (Howard Rogerson).

Many wives use this picture as an object lesson for their husbands. "Look what can happen if you sleep around." Lawyer Michael Douglas believes he's having a torrid one-night stand with wildly-passionate book editor Glenn Close, but the rather nutzy lady has other plans. Confronting Douglas with the news she is pregnant, she alternately insists she wants him forever and then just as quickly insults his manliness and tries to blow up his car. Finally turning on his family, Close parboils his daughter's pet

rabbit, and kidnaps the child. This last escapade causes Douglas' wife Anne Archer to have an automobile accident, Douglas comes close to killing Close in her apartment, but the coup de grâce is left to Archer, when Close invades their country home and threatens Archer with a knife. There are plenty of loose ends left dangling in this movie and many critics objected to the *Carrie*-like ending, but one must admit it keeps everyone on the edge of their seats.

946. *Fatal Beauty* (1987, MGM/United Artists, 103m, c). P Leonard Kroll, D Tom Holland, W Hilary Henkin & Dean Riesner (based on a story by Bill Svanoe), PH David M. Walsh, M Harold Faltermeyer, ED Don Zimmerman, PD James William Newport.

LP Whoopi Goldberg (Det. Rita Rizzoli), Sam Elliott (Mike Marshak), Ruben Blades (Carl Jimenez), Harris Yulin (Conrad Kroll), John P. Ryan (Lt. Kellerman), Jennifer Warren (Cecile Jaeger), Brad Dourif (Leo Nova).

In what seems another in an unending series of poor film choices for comedian Whoopi Goldberg, she portrays an unorthodox (read Eddie Murphy–like) police woman out to put away drug-pusher Harris Yulin. Where Murphy is sexist in his comments on women, Goldberg takes the obverse position, and her versions of gender insults aren't very funny either.

947. *Fatal Pulse* (1988, Great Entertainment, 86m, c). P&D Anthony J. Christopher, W James Hundhausen, PH David Lewis, M Martin Mayo.

LP Michelle McCormick, Ken Roberts, Joe Phelan, Alex Courtney, Kitty, Cindra Hodgdon, Maureen O'Hanlon, Steven Henry.

Joe Phelan (Martin Sheen's little-known brother) owns a fraternity house in which bodies are beginning to pile up. Michelle McCormick is used as bait to flush out the killer.

948. *Fatso* (1980, 20th Century-Fox, 94m, c). P Stuart Cornfield, D&W Anne Bancroft, PH Brianne Murphy, M Joe Renzetti, ED Glenn Farr, PD Peter Wooley.

LP Dom DeLuise (Dominick DiNapoli), Anne Bancroft (Antoinette),

Ron Carey (Frankie), Candice Azzara (Lydia), Michael Lombard (Charlie), Sal Viscuso (Vito), Delia Salvi (Ida Rendino), Robert Costanzo (Johnny).

In her first writer-director role, Anne Bancroft can't make up her mind whether to play the story of obese Dom DeLuise's half-hearted attempts to lose weight after the death of his fat cousin, for comedy or pathos. Audiences don't know whether to laugh or cry.

949. *Fatty Finn* (1980, Children's Films/Hoyts, Australia, 91m, c). P Brian Rosen, D Maurice Murphy, W Bob Ellis & Chris McGill (based on an idea by Ellis), PH John Seale, M Graham Bond & Rory O'Donohue, ED Bob Gibson.

LP Ben Oxenbould (Fatty Finn), Bert Newton (Mr. Finn), Noni Hazelhurst (Mrs. Finn), Gerard Kennedy (Tiger Murphy), Greg Kelly (Bruiser Murphy), Lorraine Bayly (Maggie McGrath), Henri Szeps (Mr. Zilch).

You need to be familiar with the Australian comic strip for this film to have much appeal. Ben Oxenbould, a boy-and-a-half in size, is caught in the middle of a street gang war in Depression-era Sydney.

950. *Fear* (1988, Cinetel, 95m, c). P Lisa M. Hansen, D Robert A. Ferretti, W Rick Scarry & Kathryn Connell (based on a story by Ferretti), PH Dana Christiaansen, M Alfie Kabiljo, ED Michael Eliot.

LP Cliff DeYoung (Don Haden), Kay Lenz (Sharon Haden), Robert Factor (Jack Gracie), Scott Schwartz (Brian Haden), Geri Betzler (Jennifer Haden), Frank Stallone (Robert Armitage), Charles Meshack (Cy Canelle).

Cliff DeYoung and his family aren't getting along very well. When they take a vacation together at a remote California mountain cabin, they are attacked by four escaped cons, led by a deranged Vietnam vet. DeYoung is also a Vietnam vet and this is the opportunity for the family to rally around Dad.

951. *Fear, Anxiety and Depression* (1989, Samuel Goldwyn, 85m, c). P Stanley Wlodowski, Steve Golin & Joni Sighvatsson, D&W Todd Solondz, PH Stefan Czapsky, M Karyn Rachtman, Joe Romano & Moogy Klingman, ED Peter Austin, Emily Paine & Barry Rubinow, PD Marek Dobrowolski.

LP Todd Solondz (Ira), Max Cantor (Jack), Alexandra Gersten (Janice), Jane Hamper (Junk), Jill Wisloff (Sharon), Stanley Tucci (Donny).

In a tribute to Woody Allen, director-writer Todd Solondz presents actor Solondz as a would-be intellectural hero looking for love and artistic recognition in scenes and situations which are pale copies of similar ones in Allen's movies.

952. *Fear City* (1984, Chevy Chase Distribution, 96m, c). P Bruce Cohn Curtis & Jerry Tokofsky, D Abel Ferrara, W Nicholas St. John, PH James Lemmo, M Dick Halligan, ED Jack Holmes & Anthony Redman.

LP Tom Berenger (Matt Rossi), Billy Dee Williams (Al Wheeler), Jack Scalia (Nicky Piacenza), Melanie Griffith (Loretta), Rossano Brazzi (Carmine), Rae Dawn Chong (Liela), Michael V. Gazzo (Mike), Joe Santos (Frank), Jan Murray (Goldstein), Ola Ray (Honey).

This sleazy film examines the seedy world of New York sex clubs and the perverts who visit them. Melanie Griffith is a lesbian stripper. Her lover Rae Dawn Chong is one of the many victims of a demented slasher and karate expert who hates "dirty girls." Tom Berenger, Griffith's former male lover, finally stops the killer.

953. *Fear No Evil* (1981, Avco Embassy, 99m, c). P Frank & Charles M. La Loggia, D&W Frank La Loggia, PH Fred Goodich, M F. La Laggia & David Spear, ED Edna Ruth Paul.

LP Stefan Arngrim (Andrew), Elizabeth Hoffman (Mikhail/Margaret Buchanan), Kathleen Rowe McAllen (Gabrielle/Hulie), Frank Birney (Father Daly), Daniel Eden (Tony), Jack Holland (Rafael/Father Damon), Richard Jay Silverthorn (Lucifer).

Quiet high school student Stefan Arngrim is the Antichrist. Elizabeth Hoffman and Kathleen Rowe McAllen are angels sent to defeat him, but initially they don't know their mission. When they figure it out, Arngrim swings into action, unleashing a horde of zombies at a Passion Play.

954. *Feds* (1989, Warner, 91m, c). P Ilona Herzberg & Len Blum, D Dan

Goldberg, W Goldberg & Blum, PH Timothy Suhrstedt, M Randy Edelman, ED Donn Cambern, PD Randy Ser.

LP Rebecca DeMornay (Ellie DeWitt), Mary Gross (Janis Zuckerman), Ken Marshall (Brent Sheppard), Fred Dalton Thompson (Belecki), Larry Cedar (Butz), Raymond Singer (Hupperman), James Luisi (Sperry), Rex Ryon (Parker).

Rebecca DeMornay and Mary Gross are FBI academy trainees with little in common. Naturally they become best friends as they pursue lawbreakers.

Feel the Heat see Catch the Heat

955. *Ferris Bueller's Day Off* (1986, Orion, 103m, c). P John Hughes & Tom Jacobson, D&W Hughes, PH Tak Fujimoto, M Ira Newborn, ED Paul Hirsch, PD John W. Corso.

LP Matthew Broderick (Ferris Bueller), Alan Ruck (Cameron Frye), Mia Sara (Sloane Peterson), Jeffrey Jones (Ed Rooney), Jennifer Grey (Jeanie Bueller), Cindy Pickett (Katie Bueller), Lyman Ward (Tom Bueller), Edie McClurg (School Secretary), Charlie Sheen (Boy in Police Station).

While many found this film amusing, others were turned off by the antics of title character Matthew Broderick, who takes a senior skip day with his girl Mia Sara and best friend Alan Ruck. Broderick's a know-it-all, smart-aleck, made out to be cleverer than anyone else in the movie. A possible exception is his sister Jennifer Grey, who would like bodily harm to befall her brother, a wish which is not hard to second. Broderick's parents are hopeless twerps who have lived with their gold-bricking son for nearly 18 years, and haven't seen through him yet. His teachers are just as easily fooled. Only Jeffrey Jones as a counselor-cum-truant officer realizes that Broderick is a phony, but it does him no good, since *he's* a blustering idiot.

956. *Feud* (1989, Feud Co. Production, 96m, c). P Bill D'Elia & Carole Kivett, D D'Elia, W D'Elia & Robert Uricola (based on the novel by Thomas Berger), PH John Beymer, M Brian Eddolis, ED Bill Johnson, PD Charles Lagola.

LP Rene Auberjonois (Reverton), Ron McLarty (Dolf Beeler), Joe Grifasi (Bud Bullard), Scott Allegnucci (Tony Beeler), Gayle Mayron (Bernice Beeler), David Strathairn (The Stranger), Stanley Tucci (Harvey Yelton), Lynne Killmeyer (Eva Bullard), Kathleen Doyle (Freida Bullard).

In his directorial debut Bill D'Elia's film focuses on the Beeler family of Hornbeck and the Bullards of Millville and the all-encompassing feud which runs their lives. The story is told with affection and amusement, despite the serious subject.

957. *Fever Pitch* (1985, MGM/United Artists, 95m, c). P Freddie Fields, D&W Richard Brooks, PH William A. Fraker, M Thomas Dolby & Quincy Jones, ED Jeff Jones, PD Raymond G. Storey.

LP Ryan O'Neal (Taggart), Catherine Hicks (Flo), Giancarlo Giannini (Charley), Bridgette Andersen (Amy), Chad Everett (Dutchman), John Saxon (Sports Editor), Hank Greenspun (Las Vegas Sun Publisher), William Smith (Panama Hat), Rafael Campos (Rafael), Patrick Cassidy (Soldier).

Sports writer Ryan O'Neal gets hooked while writing a series on big stakes gambling and gamblers. His wife is killed in an automobile accident while bringing him more money for his gambling sickness. O'Neal takes up with cocktail waitress Catherine Hicks, who likes gambling, but knows when to quit. Supposedly this film is antigambling and pro–Gamblers Anonymous but it's so poorly done, seven to five most members of the audience will miss the message.

958. *ffolkes* (1980, Universal, GB, 99m, c, aka *North Sea Hijack; Assault Force*). P Elliott Kastner, D Andrew V. McLaglen, W Jack Davies (based on his novel *Esther, Ruth and Jennifer*), PH Tony Imi, M Michael J. Lewis, ED Alan Strachan, SE John Richardson.

LP Roger Moore (ffolkes), James Mason (Admiral Brinsden), Anthony Perkins (Kramer), Michael Parks (Shulman), David Hedison (King), Jack Watson (Olafsen), George Baker (Fletcher), Jeremy Clyde (Tipping), David Wood (Herring), Faith Brook (Prime Minister), Lea Brodie (Sanna).

Deranged villain Anthony Perkins and

his gang hijack the ship *Esther* and demand a huge ransom or they will blow-up an oil rig named "Ruth" and a production platform, "Jennifer," in the North Sea. The Admirality calls for fussy woman-hating, cat-loving mercenary Roger Moore to lead an assault team to rout the bad guys.

959. *Field of Dreams†* (1989, Universal, 106m, c). P Lawrence & Charles Gordon, D Phil Alden Robinson, W Robinson† (based on the book *Shoeless Joe* by W.P. Kinsella), PH John Lindley, M James Horner†, ED Ian Crafford, PD Dennis Gassner.

LP Kevin Costner (Ray Kinsella), Amy Madigan (Annie Kinsella), Gaby Hoffman (Karin Kinsella), Ray Liotta (Shoeless Joe Jackson), Timothy Busfield (Mark), James Earl Jones (Terence Mann), Burt Lancaster (Dr. "Moonlight" Graham), Frank Whaley (Archie Graham), Dwier Brown (John Kinsella).

This wonderful movie fantasy is a fable about redemption, second chances at lost opportunities, and true faith. Kevin Costner, imbued with baseball lore by his deceased and distant father, builds a life for his wife Amy Madigan and child Gaby Hoffman on a marginal Iowa farm. One day in the fields, he hears a voice which says: "If you build it, he will come." No, this is not the second coming of Christ, but when Costner uses all his savings to convert his cornfield into a baseball diamond, it is visited by the spirit of Shoeless Joe Jackson (Ray Liotta). The latter was the star hitter of the disgraced 1919 Chicago White Sox, some of whom were paid by gamblers to throw the series, resulting in Jackson's and seven others' being banned from the game for life. Besides Costner and Liotta, fine performances are given by James Earl Jones as a bitter, hermit-like 60s writer and Burt Lancaster as another spirit who shows up to try his dream.

960. *Fiend* (1980, Cinema Enterprises, 93m, c). D&W Don Dohler, PH Dohler & Richard Geiwitz, M Paul Woznicki, ED Dohler, SE David W. Renwick.

LP Don Leifert (Eric), Richard Nelson (Gary), Elaine White (Marsha), George Stover (Dennis), Greg Dohler (Scotty),

Del Winans (Jimmy), Kim Dohler (Kristy), Pam Merenda (Jane), Anne Frith (Katie).

A small-town music teacher, who at times is transformed into a bug-like monster, feeds parasitically on his students to satisfy his supernatural hunger.

961. *52 Pick-Up* (1986, Cannon, 114m, c). P Menahem Golan & Yoram Globus, D John Frankenheimer, W Elmore Leonard & John Steppling (based on the novel by Leonard), PH Jost Vacano, M Gary Chang, ED Robert F. Shugrue, PD Philip Harrison.

LP Roy Scheider (Harry Mitchell), Ann-Margret (Barbara Mitchell), Vanity (Doreen), John Glover (Alan Raimy), Robert Trebor (Leo Franks), Lonny Chapman (Jim O'Boyle), Kelly Preston (Cini), Clarence Williams III (Bobby Shy).

After an affair with stunning young model Kelly Preston, wealthy businessman Roy Scheider is blackmailed by John Glover and associates. When Scheider confesses his indiscretions to wife Ann-Margret rather than be under Glover's control, the latter kills Preston with Scheider's gun and blackmails him with a murder charge. Scheider has to fight back in kind without any help from authorities.

962. *Fighting Back* (1983, Enterprise, Australia, 101m, c). P Sue Milliken & Tom Jeffrey, D Michael Caulfield, W Michael Cove & Jeffrey (based on the book *Tom* by John Embling), PH John Seale, M Colin Stead, ED Ron Williams.

LP Lewis Fitz-Gerald, Paul Smith, Kris McQuade, Robyn Nevin, Caroline Gillmer, Wyn Roberts, Ben Gabriel, Rob Steele, Ray Bennett.

Idealistic teacher Lewis Fitz-Gerald tries to tame disturbed, angry, illiterate 13-year-old Paul Smith. The latter is quite good in his acting debut in this grim and not totally successful picture.

963. *Final Assignment* (1980, Inter Ocean, Canada, 101m, c). P Lawrence Hertzog & Gail Thomson, D Paul Almond, W Marc Rosen, PH John Coquillon, M Peter Germyn, ED Debbie Karen.

LP Genevieve Bujold (Nicole Thomson), Michael York (Lyosha Petrov), Burgess Meredith (Zak), Colleen Dewhurst (Dr. Valentine Ulanova), Alexandra Stewart (Sam O'Donnell), Richard Gabourie (Bowen).

Canadian TV journalist Genevieve Bujold agrees to smuggle the daughter of scientist Colleen Dewhurst and a videotape of horrible Russian steroid experiments on children out of the U.S.S.R. She is assisted by Burgess Meredith, a Jewish fur merchant.

964. *The Final Countdown* (1980, United Artists, 104m, c). P Peter Vincent Douglas, D Don Taylor, W David Ambrose, Gerry Davis, Thomas Hunter & Peter Powell, PH Victor J. Kemper, M John Scott, ED Robert K. Lambert, PD Fernando Carrere.

LP Kirk Douglas (Capt. Matthew Yelland), Martin Sheen (Warren Lasky), Katharine Ross (Laurel Scott), James Farentino (Cmdr. Richard Owens), Ron O'Neal (Cmdr. Dan Thurman), Charles Durning (Senator Samuel Chapman).

America's finest nuclear warship *U.S.S. Nimitz* passes through a time warp and arrives at Pearl Harbor just hours before the bombing by the Japanese on December 7, 1941. It seems like a made-for TV movie.

965. *The Final Cut* (1980, GUO/Wilgar, Australia, 82m, c). P Mike Williams, D Ross Dimsey, W Jonathan Dawson & Dimsey (based on an original idea by Dawson), PH Ron Johanson, M Howard Davidson, ED Tony Patterson.

LP Louis Brown (Chris), David Clendenning (Dominic), Jennifer Cluff (Sarah), Narelle Johnson (Yvette), Carmen J. McCall (Julie/Lyn), Thaddeus Smith (Mick).

Reporter Louis Brown and his girlfriend Jennifer Cluff get the dirt on actor and entrepreneur David Clendenning, when the latter returns to Queensland after a show-business career abroad. Seems that he was involved with pornography and snuff films.

966. *Final Exam* (1981, Avco Embassy, 90m, c). P John L. Chambliss & Myron Meisel, D&W Jimmy Huston, PH Darrell Cathcart, M Gary Scott, ED John O'Connor.

LP Cecile Bagdadi (Courtney), Joel S. Rice (Radish), Ralph Brown (Wildman), Deanna Robbins (Lisa), Sherry Willis-Burch (Janet), John Fallon (Mark), Don Hepner (Dr. Reynolds), Timothy L. Raynor (Killer).

Psychological killer Timothy L. Raynor stalks college students during exam weeks. As if finals weren't enough to worry about.

967. *Final Justice* (1985, Mediterranean-Arista, 90m, c). P,D&W Greydon Clark, PH Nicholas von Sternberg, M David Bell, ED Larry Bock.

LP Joe Don Baker (Thomas Jefferson Geronimo III), Venantino Venantini (Palermo), Rossano Brazzi (Don La Manna), Bill McKinney (Chief Wilson), Patrizia Pellegrino (Gina), Helena Abella (Maria).

Macho cop Joe Don Baker's habit of bending the law gets him sacked from the Dallas police force. He's reduced to patroling the Mexican border where he kills one Mafia hitman and captures a second. While escorting the latter back to Italy for trial, his plane is forced down on Malta. Baker's captive escapes and he has just 24 hours to get him back.

968. *The Final Option* (1983, MGM, GB, 125m, c, aka *Who Dares Wins*). P Euan Lloyd, D Ian Sharp, W Reginald Rose (based on the novel *The Tiptoe Boys* by George Markstein), PH Philip Meheux, M Roy Budd, Jerry Donahue & Marc Donahue, ED John Grover, PD Syd Cain.

LP Lewis Collins (Capt. Skellen), Judy Davis (Frankie), Richard Widmark (Secretary of State), Robert Webber (Gen. Potter), Edward Woodward (Cmdr. Powell), Tony Doyle (Col. Hadley), John Duttine (Rod), Kenneth Griffith (Bishop Crick), Rosalind Lloyd (Jenny), Ingrid Pitt (Helga).

In this ludicrous story, Lewis Collins, a member of Britain's Special Air Services, infiltrates a terrorist gang that is planning to seize the American embassy.

969. *The Final Terror* (1983, Comworld/Watershed/Roth, 84m, c, aka *Campsite Massacre; Bump in the Night; The Forest Primeval*). P Joe Roth, D Andrew Davis, W Jon George, Neill Hicks &

Ronald Shusett, PH A. Davidescu, M Susan Justin, ED Paul Rubell, Erica Flaum & Hannah Washonig.

LP John Friedrich (Zorich), Rachel Ward (Margaret), Adrian Zmed (Cerone), Darryl Hannah (Windy), Joe Pantoliano (Eggar), Ernest Harden, Jr. (Hines), Mark Metcalf (Mike), Lewis Smith (Boone), Cindy Harrell (Melanie).

A group of campers are stalked by a mad killer, raging through the forest, looking for innocent victims.

970. *Finders Keepers* (1984, Warner, 96m, c). P Sandra & Terence Marsh, D Richard Lester, W Ronny Graham, Terence Marsh & Charles Dennis (based on the novel *The Next to Last Train Ride* by Dennis), PH Brian West, M Ken Thorne, ED John Victor Smith, PD Terence Marsh.

LP Michael O'Keefe (Michael Rangeloff), Beverly D'Angelo (Standish Logan), Louis Gossett, Jr. (Century), Pamela Stephenson (Georgiana Latimer), Ed Lauter (Josef Sirola), David Wayne (Stapleton), Brian Dennehy (Mayor Frizzoli).

Richard Lester's crazy, quirky comedy, set in 1973, has Michael O'Keefe, the exmanager of an all-girl roller derby team, Beverly D'angelo, a foulmouthed Las Vegas showgirl with acting aspirations, David Wayne, the world's oldest living train conductor and a couple of thieves, Pamela Stephenson and Ed Lauter, all on a wild train ride with a coffin filled with a stolen $5 million.

971. *A Fine Mess* (1986, Columbia, 86m, c). P Tony Adams, D&W Blake Edwards, PH Harry Stradling, M Henry Mancini, ED John F. Burnett & Robert Pergament, PD Rodger Maus.

LP Ted Danson (Spence Holden), Howie Mandel (Dennis Powell), Richard Mulligan (Wayne "Turnip" Farragalla), Stuart Margolin (Maurice "Binky" Dzundza), Maria Conchita Alonso (Claudia Pazzo), Jennifer Edwards (Ellen Frankenthaler), Paul Sorvino (Tony Pazzo).

Try to imagine Ted Danson and Howie Mandel as Oliver Hardy and Stan Laurel. You can't? Well you won't care for this knockabout comedy, inspired by Stan and Ollie's 1932 Oscar winning short, *The Music Box,* in which the boys try to deliver a piano. It fails on just about all levels.

972. *Fire and Ice* (1983, 20th Century–Fox, animated, 81m, c). P Ralph Bakshi & Frank Frazetta, D Bakshi, W Roy Thomas & Gerry Conway (based on a story and characters by Bakshi & Frazetta, PH Francis Grumman, M William Kraft, ED A. David Marshall.

MODELS & VOICES Randy Norton/ William Ostrander (Larn), Cynthia Leake/Maggie Roswell (Teegra), Steve Sandor (Darkwolf), Sean Hannon/Stephen Mendel (Nekron), Leo Gordon (Jarol), William Ostrander (Taro), Ellen O'Neill/Susan Tyrrell (Juliana).

Using live models as the armatures for his animated characters, director Ralph Bakshi relates the adventure tale of a battle between good and evil in a mystical prehistoric time.

973. *Fire and Ice* (1987, Concorde, 95m, c/b&w). P,D,W&PH Willy Bogner, M Harold Faltermeyer, Gary Wright, Panarama, Alan Parsons & John Denver, ED Petra Von Oelffen.

LP John Eaves (John), Suzy Chaffee (Suzy), John Denver (Narrator), John Cooper (John's Voice), Tom Sims, Steve Link, Kelby Anno, Matt Schweitzer.

French-Canadian skier John Eaves trails after Suzy Chapstick (sorry, that's Chaffee), a fellow skier, he's accidentally met and fallen in love with. Well that's it for the plot. The rest of the film is just a lot of skiing shots, often done in most imaginative ways. But if you don't care for the slopes this movie will give your frostbite.

974. *The Fire in the Stone* (1983, South Australian Film Corp., Australia, 96m, c). P Pamela Vanneck, D Gary Conway, W Graeme Koetsveld (based on the novel by Colin Thiele), PH Ross Berryman, ED Philip Reid.

LP Paul Smith (Ernie), Linda Hartley (Sophie), Theo Pertsinidis (Nick), Andrew Gaston (Willie), Alan Cassell (Robbie), Ray Meagher (Dosh).

Two white and one black Australian teens learn a great deal about each other and themselves as they attempt to recover some opals stolen by a miner in their small town.

975. *Fire with Fire* (1986, Paramount, 104m, c). P Gary Nardino, D Duncan Gibbins, W Bill Phillips, Warren Skaaren, Paul & Sharon Boorstin, PH Hiro Narita, M Howard Shore, ED Peter Berger, PD Norman Newberry.

LP Craig Sheffer (Joe Fisk), Virginia Madsen (Lisa), Jon Polito (Boss), Jeffrey Jay Cohen (Mapmaker), Kate Reid (Sister Victoria), Jean Smart (Sister Marie), Tim Russ (Jerry), D.B. Sweeney (Baxter).

Street smart kid Craig Sheffer has learned to fight for the things he wants. He finds a whole new set of things to fight for when he is sentenced to hard labor in a state youth reformatory.

976. *Firebird 2015 AD* (1981, Mara, 97m, c). P Merritt White, D David Robertson, W Barry Pearson, Biff McGuire & Maurice Hurley, PH Robert Fresco, M Paul Hoffert, Lawrence Shragge & Brenda Hoffert.

LP Darren McGavin, Doug McClure, George Touliatos, Mary Beth Rubens, Alex Diakun, R.C. Wisden.

In this tongue-in-cheek adventure film, automobile use is banned in a 21st century society because of an extreme oil shortage.

977. *Firecracker* (1981, New World, 83m, c). P Syed Kechico, D Cirio Santiago, W Ken Metcalfe, PH Don Jones.

LP Jillian Kesner (Susanne Carter), Darby Hinton (Chuck Donner), Ken Metcalfe (Erik), Chanda Romero (Malow), Tony Ferrar (Tony), Reymond King (Rey), Vic Diaz (Grip), Pete Cooper (Pete).

Female martial arts expert Jillian Kesner retaliates against the crooks who murdered her sister.

978. *Firefox* (1982, Warner, 137m, c). P&D Clint Eastwood, W Alex Lasker & Wendell Wellman (based on the novel by Craig Thomas), PH Bruce Surtees, M Maurice Jarre, ED Ferris Webster & Ron Spang.

LP Clint Eastwood (Mitchell Gant), Freddie Jones (Kenneth Aubrey), David Huffman (Buckholz), Warren Clarke (Pavel Upenskoy), Ronald Lacey (Semelovsky), Kenneth Colley (Col. Kontarsky), Klaus Lowitsch (Gen. Vladimirov), Nigel Hawthorne (Pyote Baranovich), Dimitra Arliss (Natalia).

Brought out of retirement, top pilot and special agent Clint Eastwood sneaks into the U.S.S.R. to steal a top-secret Russian warplane and fly it out of the country.

979. *Firehouse* (1987, Academy Home Entertainment, 91m, c). P J. Christian Ingvordsen & Steven Kaman, D Ingvordsen, W Ingvordsen & Kaman (based on a story by Rick Marx, Ingvordsen & Kaman, PH Kaman, M Michael Montes & David Biglin, ED Kaman, PD Debbie Devilla.

LP Gianna Rains (Barrett Hopkins), Martha Peterson (Shannon Murphy), Renee Raiford (Violet Brown), Gideon Fountain (John Anderson), Peter MacKenzie (Dickson Willoughby III), Joe Viviani (Lt. Wally), Jonathan Mandel (Timmy Ryan).

Released straight to video, this moronic film is the tale of three sexy women who join the ranks of firefighters and are continuously warming up their male co-workers. Oh, yes, the ladies thwart the attempts of a real estate developer to have buildings torched by arsonists to serve his redevelopment plans.

980. *Firestarter* (1984, Universal, 116m, c). P Frank Capra, Jr., D Mark Lester, W Stanley Mann (based on the novel by Stephen King), PH Giuseppe Ruzzolini, M Tangerine Dream, ED David Rawlins & Ron Sanders.

LP David Keith (Andrew McGee), Drew Barrymore (Charlie McGee), Freddie Jones (Dr. Joseph Wanless), Heather Locklear (Vicky McGee), Martin Sheen (Capt. Hollister), George C. Scott (John Rainbird), Louise Fletcher (Norma Manders), Moses Gunn (Dr. Pynchot), Art Carney (Irv Manders).

Stephen King's works of horror have many faithful readers; but they seldom make good movies. *Firestarter,* the story of little Drew Barrymore, a girl with psychokinetic powers, and the various villains, including the CIA who wish to exploit her talents, is no exception.

981. *Firewalker* (1986, Cannon, 104m, c). P Menahem Golan & Yoram Globus, D J. Lee Thompson, W Robert Gosnell (based on a story by Gosnell,

Jeffrey M. Rosenbaum & Norman Aladjem), PH Alex Phillips, M Gary Chang, ED Richard Marx, PD Jose Rodriguez Granada.

LP Chuck Norris (Max Donigan), Lou Gossett (Leo Porter), Melody Anderson (Patricia Goodwyn), Will Sampson (Tall Eagle), Sonny Landham (Ed Coyote), John Rhys-Davies (Corky Taylor), Ian Abercrombie (Boggs), Richard Lee-Sung (The Chinaman), Zaide S. Gutierrez (The Indian Girl).

After ten years of dangerous money-losing expeditions, fortune hunters Chuck Norris and Lou Gossett are ready to call it quits, when beautiful Melody Anderson shows up with a long-lost Aztec treasure map. Once again they get the fever, and the trio head for Guatemala and a series of adventures.

Fireworks see Three Kinds of Heat

982. *First Blood* (1982, Orion, 97m, c). P Buzz Feitshans, D Ted Kotcheff, W Michael Kozoll, William Sackheim & Q. Moonblood (based on the novel by David Morrell), PH Andrew Laszlo, M Jerry Goldsmith, ED Tom Noble & Joan Chapman, PD Wolf Kroeger.

LP Sylvester Stallone (John Rambo), Richard Crenna (Trautman), Brian Dennehy (Teasle), David Caruso (Mitch), Jack Starrett (Galt), Michael Talbott (Balford), David Crowley (Shingleton), Chris Mulkey (Ward), Don Mackay (Preston), Alf Humphreys (Lester).

In this mindless, ultraviolent film, ex–Green Beret Sylvester Stallone, taught to kill for his country in Vietnam, is wrongfully arrested by bullying sheriff Brian Dennehy in a Northwest American community. As revenge, killing-machine Stallone blows the town to pieces and most of the so-called officers of law and order. He's finally stopped on his rampage by his former commander, Richard Crenna.

983. *The First Deadly Sin* (1980, Filmways, 112m, c). P George Pappas & Mark Shanker, D Brian G. Hutton, W Mann Rubin (based on the novel by Lawrence Sanders), PH Jack Priestley, M Gordon Jenkins, ED Eric Albertson.

LP Frank Sinatra (Edward Delaney), Faye Dunaway (Barbara Delaney), David Dukes (Daniel Blank), George Coe (Dr. Bernardi), Brenda Vaccaro (Monica Gilbert), Martin Gabel (Christopher Langley), Joe Spinell (Doorman), Anthony Zerbe (Capt. Broughton), James Whitmore (Dr. Sanford Ferguson).

Police lieutenant Frank Sinatra tracks down a homicidal killer in spite of his concern for the serious illness of his wife Faye Dunaway which intrudes on his work.

984. *First Family* (1980, Warner, 104m, c). P Daniel Melnick, D&W Buck Henry, PH Fred J. Koenekamp, M John Philip Sousa, ED Stu Linder.

LP Bob Newhart (President Manfred Link), Gilda Radner (Gloria Link), Fred Willard (Presidential Assistant Feebleman), Richard Benjamin (Press Secretary Bunthorne), Bob Dishy (Vice President Shockley), Madeline Kahn (Mrs. Link), Julius Harris (Ambassador Longo), Harvey Korman (Ambassador Spender).

Periodically, there is an attempt to find a movie vehicle for the very talented comedian Bob Newhart. All attempts thus far have failed. It's just not his medium. He should have known this effort was doomed. All comical looks at the President of the United States fall on their face, because nothing about that office is funny. Even with the late Gilda Radner struggling to lose her virginity, the chuckles are few and far between.

The First Hello see The High Country

985. *First Monday in October* (1981, Paramount, 98m, c). P Paul Heller & Martha Scott, D Ronald Neame, W Jerome Lawrence & Robert E. Lee (based on their play), PH Fred J. Koenekamp, M Ian Fraser, ED Peter E. Berger, PD Philip M. Jefferies.

LP Walter Matthau (Dan Snow), Jill Clayburgh (Ruth Loomis), Barnard Hughes (Chief Justice Crawford), Jan Sterling (Christine Snow), James Stephens (Mason Woods), Joshua Bryant (Bill Russell), Wiley Harker (Justice Harold Webb), F.J. O'Neil (Justice Waldo Thompson).

Come to think of it, the Supreme Court isn't much funnier than the Presidency. Only Congress is a real joke. Grumpy, old, liberal Supreme Court Justice Walter Matthau resists the appointment of the first female justice, Jill Clayburgh. You just know that respect will grow between them, after a series of salty exchanges which could have used a bit of pepper to make them more appetizing.

986. *The First Season* (1989, Orange, Canada, 92m, c). P Robert Frederick, D Ralph L. Thomas, W Brian Ross & Victor Nicolle (based on a story by Nicolle), PH Richard Leiterman, M Graeme Coleman, ED Frank Irvine, PD David Fisher.

LP R.H. Thompson (Eric), Kate Trotter (Alex Cauldwell), Christianne Hirt (Jodie Cauldwell), Dwight Ross (Frank Cauldwell).

When a British Columbia fisherman Dwight Ross finds himself in desperate financial straits, he commits suicide, leaving his feisty wife Kate Trotter and teenage daughter Christianne Hirt to carry on.

987. *The First Time* (1983, New Line Cinema, 95m, c). P Sam Irvin, D Charlie Loventhal, W Loventhal, Susan Weiser-Finley & W. Franklin Finley, PH Steve Fierberg, M Lanny Meyers, ED Stanley Vogel.

LP Tim Choate (Charlie), Krista Errickson (Dana), Marshall Efron (Prof. Rand), Wendy Fulton (Wendy), Raymond Patterson (Ron), Wallace Shawn (Prof. Goldfarb), Wendie Jo Sperber (Eileen), Cathryn Daman (Gloria), Jane Badler (Karen), Bradley Bliss (Melanie), Eva Charney (Polly).

Tim Choate stars in this comedy about an aspiring filmmaker and college student who can't seem to score with women. What, no casting couch?

988. *The First Turn-On!* (1984, Troma, 90m, c). P Lloyd Kaufman & Michael Herz, D Herz & Samuel Weil, W Stuart Strutin, Mark Torgl, Georgia Harrell, Kaufman & Herz, PH Kaufman, ED Richard Haines, Adam Fredericks & Richard King.

LP Georgia Harrell (Michelle Farmer), Michael Sanville (Mitch), Googy Gress (Henry), John Flood (Danny Anderson), Heidi Miller (Annie Goldberg), Al Pia (Alfred), Betty Pia (Mrs. Anderson), Gilda Gumbo (Mme. Gumbo).

Troma makes movies to be shown in Drive-Ins where what's on the screen doesn't matter very much. This one has four boys at summer camp, after becoming trapped in a cave, passing the time telling how they lost their virginity.

989. *Firstborn* (1984, Paramount, 103m, c). P Paul Junger Witt, Tony Thomas & Ron Koslow, D Michael Apted, W Koslow, PH Ralf D. Bode, M Michael Small, ED Arthur Schmidt & Angelo Corrao, PD Paul Sylbert.

LP Teri Garr (Wendy), Peter Weller (Sam), Christopher Collet (Jake), Corey Haim (Brian), Sarah Jessica Parker (Lisa), Robert Downey (Lee), Christopher Gartin (Adam), James Harper (Mr. Rader), Richard Brandon (Dad), Gayle Harbor (Joanne).

Divorcée Teri Garr has a good relationship with her two sons, Christopher Collet and Corey Haim. When Garr learns her ex-husband is remarrying, almost as revenge she brings Peter Weller into her home as her lover. At firstWeller tries to be a buddy to the boys, but this is all an act. By the time Collet discovers cocaine in his mother's bedroom it's too late. She's already become a cokehead. She can't do anything when Weller becomes abusive, after discovering that Collet has hidden the cocaine Weller planned to deal. This leads to a typical movie chase sequence ending in a violent confrontation.

990. *A Fish Called Wanda* (1988, MGM, GB, 107m, c). P Michael Shamberg, D Charles Crichton†, W John Cleese† (based on a story by Cleese and Crichton), PH Alan Hume, M John Du Prez, ED John Jympson, PD Roger Murray-Leach.

LP John Cleese (Archie Leach), Jamie Lee Curtis (Wanda Gerschwitz), Kevin Kline* (Otto West), Michael Palin (Ken Pile), Maria Aitken (Wendy Leach), Tom Georgeson (George), Patricia Hayes (Mrs. Coady), Cynthia Caylor (Portia Leach).

In one of the funniest comedies in years, Kevin Kline wins a much deserved Oscar for being a dummy who can't stand anyone calling him dumb. He and multi-talented beauty Jamie Lee Curtis are out to double-cross their partners Michael Palin and Tom Georgeson after the four rob a London jeweler. The only thing is, Georgeson has hidden the loot just before being arrested and isn't telling his erstwhile friends its whereabouts. Curtis decides she may be able to use her feminine wiles on Georgeson's barrister John Cleese to get the information she seeks. The latter goes bonkers over her in only the way a Monty Python veteran could. It's a riot.

991.　*Fish Hawk* (1981, Avco Embassy, Canada, 95m, c). P Jon Slan, D Donald Shebib, W Blanche Hanalis (based on a novel by Mitchell Jayne), PH Rene Verzier, M Samuel Matlofsky, ED Ron Wisman.

LP Will Sampson (Fish Hawk), Charlie Fields (Corby), Geoffrey Bowes (Towsack), Mary Pirie (Sarah), Don Francks (Deut), Chris Wiggins (Marcus), Kay Hawtrey (Mary), Mavor Moore (Joke).

The late Will Sampson, best known for his giant silent Indian in *One Flew Over a Cuckoo's Nest,* portrays an alcoholic Redman who strikes up a friendship with young Charlie Fields when the two meet in a forest.

992.　*Fist Fighter* (1989, Izaro-Eagle-Esme/Taurus, 100m, c). P Carlos Vasallo, D Frank Zuniga, W Max Bloom (based on a story by Vasallo), PH Hans Burman, M Emilio Kauderer, ED Drake Silliman.

LP George Rivero (C.J. Thunderbird), Edward Albert (Harry "Punchy" Moses), Mike Connors (Billy Vance), Brenda Bakke (Ellen), Matthias Hues (Rhino Reinhart), Simon Andreu (Moreno).

George Rivero stars in a film which takes a look at the corrupt and dangerous world of bare-knuckle boxing in Mexico.

993.　*Fist of Fear, Touch of Death* (1980, Aquarius Releasing Inc., 90m, c). P Terry Levene, D Matthew Mallinson, W Ron Harvey (based on a story by Harvey and Mallison), PH John Hazard, M Keith Mansfield, ED Mallinson & Jeffrey Brown.

LP Bruce Lee, Fred Williamson, Ron Van Clief, Adolph Caesar, Aaron Banks, Bill Louis, Teruyuki Higa, Gail Turner, Richard Barathy, Hollywood Browde.

Yes, we know, Bruce Lee's been dead since 1973, but ghouls will be ghouls. Old film clips of Lee are pieced together which supposedly represent his childhood.

A Fistful of Chopsticks see They Call Me Bruce

994.　*Fists of Blood* (1989, TVM Studios, Australia, 84m, c). P Damien Parer, D Brian Trenchard-Smith, W Peter West, PH Simon Akkerman, M Garry Hardman & Brian Beamish, ED Kerry Regan & David Jaeger.

LP Edward John Stazak (Jason Blade), John Stanton (William Anderson), Rowena Wallace (Lucy Andrews), Jim Richards (Jim Baxter), Paris Jefferson (Gemma Anderson), Zale Daniel (Colin).

Edward John Stazak acts like a piece of stiff cardboard in this uninteresting sequel to the equally bad *Day of the Panther* (1987). Martial arts hero Stazak must rescue his redhead girlfriend Paris Jefferson from evil Jim Richards who has broken out of jail and taken her as a hostage.

995.　*Fitzcarraldo* (1982, New World, 157m, c). P Werner Herzog & Lucki Stipetic, D&W Herzog, PH Thomas Mauch, M Popol Vuh, ED Beate Mainka-Jellinghaus.

LP Klaus Kinski (Brian Sweeney Fitzgerald/Fitzcarraldo), Claudia Cardinale (Molly), Jose Lewgoy (Don Aquilino), Miguel Angel Fuentes (Cholo the Mechanic), Paul Hittscher (Capt. Orinoco Paul), Huerequeque Enrique Bohorquez (Huerequeque the Cook), Grande Othelo (Station Master), Peter Berling (Opera Manager), David Perez Espinosa (Indian Chief).

This masterful movie details the impossible quest of a charismatic Irishman, Klaus Kinski, to build an opera house in the middle of the Amazon jungle. There he will be able to present his avatar Enrico Caruso. Making the epic became almost an impossible dream for writer-director Werner Herzog, as he, his crew and the performers had to overcome major difficulties in the Amazon.

996.　*Five Corners* (1988, Cineplex Odeon, US/GB, 92m, c). P Forrest Murray & Tony Bill, D Bill, W John Patrick Shanley, PH Fred Murphy, M James Newton Howard, ED Andy Blumenthal, PD Adrianne Lobel.

LP Jodie Foster (Linda), Tim Robbins (Harry Fitzgerald), Todd Graff (James), John Turturro (Heinz Sabantino), Elizabeth Berridge (Melanie), Rose Gregorio (Mrs. Sabantino), Gregory Rozakis (Mazola).

Scripted by the author of *Moonstruck,* this film has some of the same qualities of that movie, notably slick dialogue and well-drawn characters – but there the comparison ends. Jodie Foster is saved from rape at the hands of an unhinged admirer John Turturro by pacifist Tim Robbins. This was Foster's year for suffering at the hands of men with strange notions of love.

997. *Five Days One Summer* (1982, Warner, GB, 108m, c). P&D Fred Zinnemann, W Michael Austin (based on Kay Boyle's short story "Maiden Maiden"), PH Giuseppe Rotunno, M Elmer Bernstein, ED Stuart Baird.

LP Sean Connery (Douglas), Betsy Brantley (Kate), Lambert Wilson (Johann), Jennifer Hilary (Sarah), Isabel Dean (Kate's Mother), Gerard Buhr (Brendel), Anna Massey (Jennifer Pierce), Sheila Reid (Gillian Pierce).

While on vacation in the Swiss Alps in 1932, married Scottish doctor Sean Connery has a haunting and obsessive affair with his much younger niece Betsy Brantley.

998. *The Fix* (1985, Reverie, 95m, c). P Ervin T. Melton, D Will Zens, E Zens, Esty F. Davis, Jr. & Lance Smith, Jr., PH William VanDerKloot, ED Frank Johnson.

LP Vince Edwards (Frank Lane), Richard Jaeckel (Charles Dale), Tony Dale (Doug Davis), Julie Hill (Kelly), Byron Cherry (Esty), Charles Dierkop (Hawkeye), Robert Tessier (Spook), Don Dubbins (Sheriff Bower).

Country-and-Western entertainers Vince Edwards and Tony Dale get caught up in drug smuggling. It ain't worth a plug of tobacco.

999. *The Flamingo Kid* (1984, 20th Century–Fox, 100m, c). P Michael Phillips, D Garry Marshall, W Garry & Neal Marshall (based on a story by Neal Marshall), PH James A. Contner, ED Priscilla Nedd, PD Lawrence Miller.

LP Matt Dillon (Jeffrey Willis), Hector Elizondo (Arthur Willis), Molly McCarthy (Ruth Willis), Martha Gehman (Nikki Willis), Richard Crenna (Phil Brody), Jessica Walter (Phyllis Brody), Carole R. Davis (Joyce Brody), Janet Jones (Carla Samson), Brian McNamara (Steve Dawkins).

Eighteen-year-old Matt Dillon, son of Brooklyn plumber Hector Elizondo, gets a job at a fancy Long Island beachside club, where he sees automobile dealer and club champion gin player Richard Crenna as some kind of hero. He also has a nice summer romance with Crenna's niece Janet Jones. Dillon fights with his father, insisting he no longer wants to go to college. He'd rather become an automobile salesman working for his idol. Dillon learns a lesson about which of the men in his life really care for him. He discovers his hero has feet of clay and is a card cheat as well. It's a fine movie with excellent performances all around, but particularly from Dillon and Elizondo.

1000. *Flanagan* (1985, United Film Distributors, 97m, c). P Mark Slater & Scott Goldstein, D Goldstein, W Edmond Collins & Goldstein, PH Ivan Strasburg, M Goldstein, ED Harry Peck Bolles.

LP Philip Bosco (James Flanagan), Geraldine Page (Mama), Linda Thorson (Andrea), William Hickey (Papa), Olympia Dukakis (Mary), Brian Bloom (Danny), Steven Weber (Sean), Louis Zorich (Lerner), Gwylum Evans (Church), Pierre Epstein (Morry), James Tolkan (Turner).

A fine cast is wasted in this directionless film about aspiring Shakespearean actor and New York cab driver Philip Bosco. His ex-wife Olympia Dukakis is a compulsive gambler, raising their son to be the same. His current girlfriend Linda Thorson (remember her from TV's "The Avengers"?) is cheating on him. When he angrily rejects the advances of a homosexual passenger, he discovers the man is the producer for whom he's to audition. Bosco takes revenge on everyone.

1001. *Flash Gordon* (1980, Universal, GB, 110m, c). P Dino DeLaurentiis, D Mike Hodges, W Lorenzo Semple, Jr. & Michael Allin (based on characters created by Alex Raymond), PH Gil Taylor, M Howard Blake, ED Malcolm Cooke, PD Danilo Donati, SE George Gibbs, Richard Conway & Derek Botel.

LP Sam J. Jones (Flash Gordon), Melody Anderson (Dale Arden), Topol (Dr. Hans Zarkov), Max von Sydow (Emperor Ming), Ornella Muti (Princess Aura), Timothy Dalton (Prince Barin), Brian Blessed (Prince Vultan), Peter Wyngarde (Klytus), Mariangela Melato (Kala).

Call us old fogies, but with due respect for the technical advances in production design and special effects in 45 years of movie making, and the possibilities a big budget offer, we still see Buster Crabbe as Flash, Jean Rogers as Dale Arden, Charles Middleton as Ming, Priscilla Lawson as Princess Aura and Frank Shannon as Dr. Zarkov.

1002. *A Flash of Green* (1984, Spectrafilm, 113m, c). P Richard Jordan, D&W Victor Nunez (based on the novel by John D. MacDonald), PH Nunez, M Charles Engstrom, ED Nunez.

LP Ed Harris (Jimmy Wing), Blair Brown (Kate Hubble), Richard Jordan (Elmo Bliss), George Coe (Brian Haas), Joan Goodfellow (Mitchie), Jean De Baer (Jackie Halley), Helen Stenborg (Aunt Middie), William Mooney (Leroy Shannard), Isa Thomas (Doris Rohl), John Glover (Ross Halley).

Small town Florida reporter Ed Harris' investigative job enmeshes him in a plot by amoral county official and boyhood friend Richard Jordan to blackmail ecology-minded opponents of a land-development scheme. Out of boredom, lust and curiosity Harris helps Jordan by dredging up information which will discredit the conservationists, but Jordan's tactics of deceit and coercion get out of control.

1003. *Flashdance* (1983, Paramount, 96m, c). P Don Simpson & Jerry Bruckheimer, D Adrian Lyne, W Tom Hedley & Joe Esterhas (based on a story by Hedley), PH Don Peterman†, M Giorgio Moroder, ED Bud Smith & Walt Mulconery†, PD Charles Rosen, CH Jeffrey Hornaday, SONG "Flashdance ...What a Feeling" by Giorgio Moroder, Keith Forsey & Irene Cara* & "Maniac" by Michael Sembello & Dennis Matkovsky†.

LP Jennifer Beals (Alex Owens), Michael Nouri (Nick Hurley), Lilia Skala (Hanna Long), Sunny Johnson (Jeanie Szabo), Kyle T. Heffner (Richie), Lee Ving (John C), Ron Karabatsos (Jake Mawby), Belinda Bauer (Katie Hurley), Malcolm Danare (Cecil), Phil Bruns (Frank Szabo).

The success of this nothing story of young female welder Jennifer Beals who dreams of becoming a professional ballet dancer is mainly due to the work of stand-in dancer Marine Jahan, who thrills audiences with her dance routines and the Academy Award–winning "Flashdance — What a Feeling" sung by Irene Cara.

1004. *Flashpoint* (1984, Tri-Star, 94m, c). P Skip Short, D William Tannen, W Dennis Shryack & Michael Butler (based on a book by George La Fountaine), PH Peter Moss, M Tangerine Dream, ED David Garfield, PD Paul Greimann.

LP Kris Kristofferson (Bob Logan), Treat Williams (Ernie Wiatt), Rip Torn (Sheriff), Kevin Conway (Brook), Kurtwood Smith (Carson), Miguel Ferrer (Roget), Jean Smart (Doris), Guy Boyd (Lambasmino), Mark Slade (Hawthorne), Roberts Blossom (Amarillo), Tess Harper (Ellen).

Texas border officers Kris Kristofferson and Treat Williams accidentally uncover an abandoned jeep containing $800,000 in cash. They differ on how they should handle their discovery. Williams suggests they had better find out to whom it belongs. Kristofferson feels it belongs to them. Others have different dangerous ideas.

1005. *Flesh and Blood* (1985, Orion, 126m, c). P Gys Versluys, D Paul Verhoeven, W Gerard Soeteman & Verhoeven (based on a story by Soeteman), PH Jan De Bont, M Basil Poledouris, ED Ine Schenkkan.

LP Rutger Hauer (Martin), Jennifer Jason Leigh (Agnes), Tom Burlinson (Steven), Susan Tyrrell (Celine), Ronald Lacey (Cardinal), Jack Thompson (Hawkwood), Fernando Hillbeck (Arnolfini), Brion James (Karthans).

In this gory medieval trash, Rutger Hauer is a renegade swordsman intent on overthrowing local lord Fernando Hillbeck who has betrayed Hauer and his fellow mercenaries. The film goes on and on and on with pillaging, ravaging, plundering and dying of plague among the more obvious amusements of the various combatants.

1006. *Fletch* (1984, Universal, 98m, c). P Alan Greisman & Peter Douglas, D Michael Ritchie, W Andrew Bergman (based on the novel by Gregory McDonald), PH Fred Schuler, M Harold Faltermeyer, ED Richard A. Harris, PD Boris Leven.

LP Chevy Chase (Fletch), Joe Don Baker (Chief Karlin), Dana Wheeler-Nicholson (Gail Stanwyck), Richard Libertini (Walker), Tim Matheson (Alan Stanwyck), M. Emmet Walsh (Dr. Dolan), George Wendt (Fat Sam), Kenneth Mars (Stanton Boyd), Geena Davis (Larry).

Chevy Chase is able to play a hip Walter Mitty–like character, by assuming various absurd personalities with far-out names, each of whom is taken seriously by everyone he encounters. Chase must figure out why wealthy Tim Matheson is willing to pay him $50,000 to commit murder; the victim-to-be is none other than Matheson. Chevy does some of his best work as he darts from here to there with quips for all occasions, even when romancing Matheson's lovely wife Dana Wheeler-Nicholson.

1007. *Fletch Lives* (1989, Universal, 95m, c). P Alan Greisman & Peter Douglas, D Michael Ritchie, W Leon Capetanos (based on characters created by Gregory McDonald), PH John McPherson, M Harold Faltermeyer, ED Richard A. Harris.

LP Chevy Chase (Fletch), Hal Holbrook (Ham Johnson), Julianne Phillips (Becky Culpepper), R. Lee Ermey (Jimmy Lee Farnsworth), Richard Libertini (Frank), Randall "Tex" Cobb (Ben Dover), Cleavon Little (Calculus).

Chevy Chase invades the Deep South with his bag of far-out characters. He has inherited a rundown plantation. While the first film was moderately amusing, the present edition is just a running gag, which isn't too hilarious the first time we hear it. There is no point to the movie and Chase can't make anything out of this material, even though he's still appealing.

1008. *Flicks* (1987, United, 78m, c, aka *Hollyweird; Loose Joints*). P Bert Kamerman & David Axelrod, D Peter Winograd, W Larry Arnstein, David Hurwitz, Lane Sarasohn & Winograd, PH Scott Miller, M John Morgan, ED Barbara Pokras, PD Jack McAnelly.

LP Pamela Sue Martin (Liz), Joan Hackett (Capt. Grace), Martin Mull (Arthur/Tang), Betty Kennedy (Beth Lyle), Richard Belzer, Barry Pearl, Lincoln Kilpatrick, Paula Victor, Danny Dayton, George "Buck" Flower.

Made in 1981, this film never made it to the theaters and probably would have stayed on the shelves were it not for the fact that videocassette audiences seemingly will rent anything. It's a series of blackout sketches spoofing all aspects of the motion picture world, with none done very well.

1009. *Flight of the Navigator* (1986, Buena Vista, 90m, c). P Robby Wald & Dimitri Villard, D Rindal Kleiser, W Michael Burton & Matt MacManus (based on a story by Mark H. Baker), PH James Glennon, ED Jeff Gourson, PD William J. Creber.

LP Joey Cramer (David Freeman), Veronica Cartwright (Helen Freeman), Cliff DeYoung (Bill Freeman), Sarah Jessica Parker (Carolyn McAdams), Matt Adler (Jeff at 16), Howard Hesseman (Dr. Faraday), Paul Mall (Max).

Suburban American youngster Joey Cramer helps some friendly aliens, falls and wakes up eight years later. Unaged, he possesses vast navigational powers that enable him to take a spectacular spaceship anywhere he wants to go.

1010. *Flight of the Spruce Goose* (1986, Filmhaus, 97m, c). P Michael Hausman, D Lech Majewski, W Majewski & Chris Burdza, PH Jerzy Zielinski, M Henri Seroka, ED Corky O'Hara.

LP Dan O'Shea (Adam), Jennifer Runyon (Terry), Karen Black (Mother), Dennis Christopher (Friend), George A. Romero.

Apparently this modest action-adventure romp didn't even make it to home video despite the presence of Karen Black and Dennis Christopher.

1011. *Flight to Berlin* (1984, Road Movies/BFI, GB, 90m, c). P Chris Sievernich, D Christopher Petit, W Petit & Hugo Williams (based on the novel *Strange Days* by Jennifer Potter), PH Martin Schafer, M Irmin Schmidt, ED Peter Przygodda.

LP Tusse Silberg (Susannah Lawrence), Paul Freeman (Nicholas), Lisa Kreuzer (Julie Lawrence), Jean-Francois Stevenin (Edouard), Ewan Stewart (Jack), Eddie Constantine (Himself), Tatjana Blacher (Carlotta).

Fugitive Tusse Silberg hides out with her photographer sister Lisa Kreuzer in Berlin.

1012. *Flowers in the Attic* (1987, New World, 95m, c). P Sy Levin & Thomas Fries, D&W Jeffrey Bloom (based on the novel by V.C.Andrews), PH Frank Byers & Gil Hubbs, M Christopher Young, ED Gregory F. Plotts, PD John Muto.

LP Louise Fletcher (Grandmother), Victoria Tennant (Corinne), Kristy Swanson (Cathy), Jeb Stuart Adams (Chris), Ben Ganger (Cory), Lindsay Parker (Carrie), Marshall Colt (Father), Nathan Davis (Grandfather), Alex Koba (John Hall).

This disappointing but still compelling adaptation of V.C. Andrews' horror story, popular with adolescent girls in 1979, is the tale of four kids, Kristy Swanson, Jeb Stuart Adams, Ben Ganger and Lindsay Parker. They are locked up by their evil grandmother, Louise Fletcher, while their fortune-hunting mother, Victoria Tennant, tends rich and dying Nathan Davis, adding a bit of poison to everyone's cookies.

1013. *The Fly* (1986, 20th Century-Fox, 100m, c). P Stuart Cornfeld, D David Cronenberg, W Charles Edward Pogue & David Cronenberg (based on the story by George Langelaan), PH Mark Irwin, M Howard Shore, ED Ronald Sanders, PD Carol Spier, MK Chris Walas & Stephen Dupuis*.

LP Jeff Goldblum (Seth Brundle), Geena Davis (Veronica Quaife), John Getz (Stathis Borans), Joy Boushel (Tawny), Les Carlson (Dr. Cheevers), George Chuvalo (Marky), Michael Copeman (2nd Man in Bar), David Cronenberg (Gynecologist), Carol Lazare (Nurse).

Jeff Goldblum is excellent as the unfortunate inventor who tests himself in a genetic transporting machine, which also contains a fly. The metamorphic result is that Goldblum is transformed into a half-human insect. The film is superior to the 1958 production starring Al [David] Hedison.

1014. *The Fly II* (1989, 20th Century-Fox, 104m, c). P Steven-Charles Jaffe, D Chris Walas, W Mick Garris, Jim & Ken Wheat, & Frank Darabont, PH Robin Vidgeon, M Christopher Young, ED Sean Barton, PD Michael S. Bolton.

LP Eric Stoltz (Martin Brundle), Daphne Zuniga (Beth), Lee Richardson (Anton Bartok), John Getz (Stathis), Frank Turner (Shepard), Ann Marie Lee (Jainway), Gary Chalk (Scorby).

This film is different from the sequel to the 1958 *The Fly,* namely *The Return of the Fly* (1959). Eric Stoltz, the son of Jeff Goldblum who unfortunately went to pieces in the 1986 film, is born already part human, part fly, but looks like an ordinary kid. He isn't however, much to the dismay of Daphne Zuniga, who looks a bit ill when she learns she's been to bed with an insect.

1015. *The Fog* (1980, Avco Embassy, 91m, c). P Debra Hill, D John Carpenter, W Carpenter & Hill, PH Dean Cundey, M Carpenter, ED Tommy Wallace & Charles Bornstein, PD Wallace, SE Dick Albain, Jr.

LP Adrienne Barbeau (Stevie Wayne), Hal Holbrook (Fr. Malone), Janet Leigh (Kathy Williams), Jamie Lee Curtis (Elizabeth Solley), John Houseman (Machen), Tommy Atkins (Nick Castle), Nancy Loomis (Sandy Fadel).

In John Carpenter's horror film, a ghostly fog reappears to fulfill a 100-year-old curse. The film will mainly be remembered as the answer to the trivia question, "In which movie did Janet Leigh and her daughter Jamie Lee Curtis appear together?"

1016. *Food of the Gods II* (1989, Concorde, 91m, c, aka *Gnaw*). P David Mitchell & Damian Lee, D Lee, W Richard Bennett & E. Kim Brewster (based on a story by Bennett), PH Curtis Petersen, M Parsons/Haines, ED Mitchell.

LP Paul Coufos (Neil Hamilton), Lisa Schrage (Alex Reed), Colin Fox (Edmund Delhurst), Frank Moore (Jacques), Real Andrews (Mark), Jackie Burroughs (Dr. Treger), Stuart Hughes (Al).

Food of the Gods II continues the tradition of putrid productions as a sequel to the 1976 nauseating garbage *Food of the Gods*, which was itself a remake of a 1967 disgusting abomination, *Village of the Giants*. Rats used for scientific experiments on a college campus grow to the size of large dogs and gnaw on anything in sight.

1017. Fool for Love (1985, Cannon, 106m, c). P Menahem Golan & Yoram Globus, D Robert Altman, W Sam Shepard, PH Pierre Mignot, M George Burt, ED Luce Grunenwaldt & Steve Dunn, PD Stephen Altman.

LP Sam Shepard (Eddie), Kim Basinger (May), Harry Dean Stanton (Old Man), Randy Quaid (Martin), Martha Crawford (May's Mother), Louise Egolf (Eddie's Mother), Sura Cox (Teenage May), Jonathan Skinner (Teenage Eddie), April Russell (Young May), Deborah McNaughton (The Countess).

Playwright Sam Shepard convinced Robert Altman to direct his play and Altman convinced Shepard to star in the movie version, but no one has convinced movie audiences that his photographed play is worth the price of admission. In flashbacks we learn that Shepard and Kim Basinger fell in love before they discovered that they shared a common father, who had been keeping two families. Incest isn't a firm foundation for a relationship.

1018. Foolin' Around (1980, Columbia, 111m, c). P Arnold Kopelson, D Richard T. Heffron, W Mike Kane & David Swift (based on the story by Swift), PH Philip Lathrop, M Charles Bernstein, ED Peter Zinner, PD Fernando Carrere.

LP Gary Busey (Wes), Annette O'Toole (Susan), John Calvin (Whitley), Eddie Albert (Daggert), Cloris Leachman (Samantha), Tony Randall (Peddicord), Michael Talbott (Clay), Shirley Kane (Aunt Eunice), W.H. Macy (Bronski).

Innocent Oklahoma country bumpkin Gary Busey will do just about anything to win beautiful heiress Annette O'Toole,

including crashing her lavish wedding to the chap her mother had chosen to be O'Toole's husband.

1019. Footloose (1984, Paramount, 107m, c). P Lewis J. Rachmil & Craig Zadan, D Herbert Ross, W Dean Pitchford, PH Ric Waite, M Miles Goodman & Becky Shargo, ED Paul Hirsch, PD Ron Hobbs, SONG "Footloose" by Kenny Loggins & Dean Pitchford† & "Let's Hear It for the Boy" by Tom Snow & Dean Pitchford†.

LP Kevin Bacon (Ren McCormick), Lori Singer (Ariel Moore), John Lithgow (Rev. Shaw Moore), Dianne Wiest (Vi Moore), Christopher Penn (Willard), Sarah Jessica Parker (Rusty), John Laughlin (Woody), Elizabeth Gorcey (Wendy Jo), Frances Lee McCain (Ethel McCormick), Jim Youngs (Chuck).

City kid Kevin Bacon moves to a small town where dancing has been outlawed, mainly through the efforts of fundamentalist preacher John Lithgow. But if he's prevented a whole lot of shakin' goin' on, his daughter Lori Singer isn't missing much else as she does her own bit for rebellion. After numerous false starts, Bacon is able to win over the reverend and others in town to the notion that dancing is healthy fun, not the first step to hell.

1020. For Keeps (1988, Tri-Star, 96m, c). P Jerry Belson & Walter Coblenz, D John G. Avildsen, W Tim Kazurinsky & Denise DeClue, PH James Crabe, M Bill Conti, ED Conchata Ferrell, Avildsen, PD William J. Cassidy.

LP Molly Ringwald (Darcy Elliott), Randall Batinkoff (Stan Bobrucz), Kenneth Mars (Mr. Bobrucz), Miriam Flynn (Mrs. Elliott), Conchita Ferrell (Mrs. Bobrucz), Sharon Brown (Lila), Jack Ong (Reverend Kim), Sean Frye (Wee Willy).

Even though the story of Molly Ringwald's teenage pregnancy and her subsequent marriage to her sweetheart Randall Batinkoff is just a bit too pat, making their problems and sacrifices seem little more than inconveniences, Ringwald's acting is all anyone could hope for. She has grown into a lovely, talented young woman and actress.

1021.   *For Queen and Country* (1989, Atlantic, GB, 105m, c). P Tim Bevan, D Martin Stellman, W Stellman & Trix Worrell, PH Richard Greatrex, M Michael Kamen & Geoff MacCormack, ED Stephen Singleton, PD Andrew McAlpine.

LP Denzel Washington (Reuben), Dorian Healey (Fish), Amanda Redman (Stacey), Sean Chapman (Bob), Bruce Payne (Colin), Geff Francis (Lynford), George Baker (Kilcoyne), Craig Fairbrass (Challoner).

After eight years in the British army, black man Denzel Washington returns to his working class neighborhood in London, where he finds racism, drugs, and despair. He tries to avoid the violence he finds all around him, but he cannot elude it. A wealthy white friend attempts to get Washington to enter into drug dealing. It's not a pretty picture, but it's a powerful one.

1022.   *For Your Eyes Only* (1981, United Artists, GB, 127m, c). P Albert R. Broccoli, D John Glen, W Richard Maibaum & Michael G. Wilson (based on the short stories "For Your Eyes Only" and "Risico" by Ian Fleming), PH Alan Hume, M Bill Conti, ED John Grover, PD Peter Lamont, SE Derek Meddings, M/L "For Your Eyes Only" by Conti & Michael Leeson† (sung by Sheena Easton).

LP Roger Moore (James Bond), Carole Bouquet (Melina), Topol (Columbo), Lynn-Holly Johnson (Bibi), Julian Glover (Kristatos), Cassandra Harris (Lisl), Jill Bennett (Brink), Michael Gothard (Locque), John Wyman (Kriegler), Jack Hedley (Havelock), Lois Maxwell (Moncypcnny), Desmond Llewelyn (Q), Geoffrey Keen (Minister of Defense), John Wells (Denis).

Roger Moore is called upon to prevent the Russians from acquiring a cypher box which was aboard a British spy ship deliberately sunk by international criminals led by Julian Glover. Moore's main squeeze this time around is Carole Bouquet, who wishes to avenge the murder of her parents by the same dirty scoundrels.

1023.   *Forbidden* (1984, Enterprize, GB/Ger., 114m, c). P Mark Forstater & Hans Brockmann, D Anthony Page, W Leonard Gross (based on his novel *The Last Jews in Berlin*), PH Wolfgang Treu, M Tangerine Dream, ED Thomas Schwalm.

LP Jacqueline Bisset (Nina von Halder), Jürgen Prochnow (Fritz Friedlander), Irene Worth (Ruth Friedlander), Peter Vaughan (Maj. Stauffel), Robert Dietl (Nils Arvidsson), Avis Bunnage (Frau Schmidt), Malcolm Kaye (Max Baum).

In 1939 Berlin, countess Jacqueline Bisset joins the underground while her Jewish lover Jürgen Prochnow is hidden by his mother.

Forbidden Subjects *see* ***Kinjite***

1024.   *Forbidden Sun* (1989, Filmscreen/Marlborough, GB, 88m, c, aka *Bulldance*). P Peter Watson-Wood, D Zelda Barron, W Robin Hardy, Jesse Lasky, Jr. & Pat Silver (based on a story by Hardy), PH Richard Greatrex, M Hard Rain, ED George Akers & Dennis McTaggart, PD Miljan Kljakovic.

LP Lauren Hutton (Francine Lake), Cliff DeYoung (Charles Lake), Robert Beltran (Jack), Viveka Davis (Jane), Renee Estevez (Elaine), Christine Harnos (Steph), Samantha Mathis (Paula), Renee Props (Betsey).

Headed directly to video, this silly movie has American beauties Viveka Davis and Samantha Mathis training as Olympic gymnasts at Lauren Hutton's and Cliff DeYoung's school on the island of Crete. Davis becomes obsessed with the ancient ritual of the bulldance—a gymnast vaulting over a live bull's horns, landing on its back and flipping over in a dismount. A lot of bull, you say—well, maybe.

1025.   *Forbidden World* (1982, New World, 86m, c, aka *Mutant*). P Roger Corman & Mary Ann Fisher, D Allan Holzman, W Tim Curnen (based on a story by Jim Wynorski & R.J. Robertson), PH Tim Suhrstedt, M Susan Justin, ED Holzman, PD Chris Horner & Robert Skotak.

LP Jesse Vint (Mike Colby), June Chadwick (Dr. Barbara Glasser), Dawn Dunlap (Tracy Baxter), Linden Chiles (Dr. Gordon Hauser), Fox Harris (Dr. Cal Tinburgen), Raymond Oliver (Brian Beale).

The lives of a genetic research team are threatened by the bloodsucking, maneating organism they have unleashed. This one is only for those who are aficionados of gore and poor acting.

1026. *Forbidden Zone* (1980, Borack, 76m, b&w). P&D Richard Elfman, W Matthew Bright, Martin W. Nicholson & Nick Jones, PH Gregory Sandor, M Danny Elfman, ED Nicholson, PD Marie-Pascale Elfman.

LP Herve Villechaize (King Fausto), Susan Tyrrell (Queen), Marie-Pascale Elfman (Frenchy Hercules), Viva (Ex-Queen).

Marie-Pascale Elfman is flung into a sixth-dimension kingdom ruled by crazed midget king Herve Villechaize. His domain abounds with monsters and assorted, degraded, bikini-clad females and human-like robots with whom he and his queen Susan Tyrrell perform deviate sex acts. The cast members whose names we have not revealed need not thank us — it is our pleasure.

1027. *Force: Five* (1981, American Cinema, 95m, c). P Fred Weintraub, D&W Robert Clouse (based on a screenplay by Emil Farkas & George Goldsmith), PH Gill Hubbs, M William Goldstein, ED Bob Bring, PD Joel David Lawrence.

LP Joe Lewis (Jerry Martin), Pam Huntington (Laurie), Bong Soo Han (Rev. Rhee), Richard Norton (Ezekiel), Benny "The Jet" Urquidez (Billy Ortega), Sonny Barnes (Lockjaw), Ron Hayden (Willard), Peter MacLean (Sen. Forrester), Mandy Wyss (Cindy Lester), Bob Schott (Carl).

Pam Huntington, the daughter of a very powerful man, has been taken to Bong Soo Han's island retreat to be used by members of his cult. A team of five mercenaries, led by Joe Lewis, is recruited to rescue her and destroy the island. Looks like some film careers will be aborted as well.

1028. *Forced March* (1989, Shapiro Glickenhaus, 104m, c). P Dick Atkins, D Rick King, W Atkins & Charles K. Bardosh, PH Ivan Mark, ED Evan Lottman, PD Laszlo Rajk.

LP Chris Sarandon (Kline/Miklos Radnoti), Renee Soutendijk (Myra), John Seitz (Hardy), Josef Sommer (Father).

In this movie-within-a-movie, TV star Chris Sarandon travels to Hungary to appear in a film about Hungarian poet Miklos Radnoti who was killed during a forced march from a Nazi labor camp. The role has a profound effect on him.

1029. *Forced Vengeance* (1982, MGM/United Artists, 90m, c). P John B. Bennett, D James Fargo, W Franklin Thompson, PH Rexford Metz, M William Goldstein, ED Irving C. Rosenblum, PD George B. Chan.

LP Chuck Norris (Josh Randall), Mary Louise Weller (Claire Bonner), David Opatoshu (Sam Paschal), Seiji Sakaguchi (Cam), Frank Michael Liu (David Paschal), Bob Minor (LeRoy Nicely), Lloyd Kino (Inspector Chen).

Vietnam veteran Norris is pitted against the Far East's underworld.

1030. *Foreign Body* (1986, Orion, GB, 108m, c). P Colin M. Brewer, D Ronald Neame, W Celine La Freniere (based on the novel by Roderick Mann), PH Ronnie Taylor, M/SONG Ken Howard, LYRICS Lynda Hayes, ED Andrew Nelson, PD Roy Stannard.

LP Victor Banerjee (Ram Das), Warren Mitchell (I.Q.), Geraldine McEwan (Lady Ammanford), Denis Quilley (Prime Minister), Amanda Donohoe (Susan), Eve Ferret (Norah), Anna Massey (Miss Furze), Stratford Johns (Mr. Plumb), Trevor Howard (Dr. Stirrup), Jane Laurie (Jo Masters).

Through a series of mistakes Indian immigrant Victor Banerjee (in his first role since starring in *A Passage to India*) becomes a leading Harley Street physician, even though he never attended medical school. All his female patients are anxious to get him into bed. Everyone knows that a doctor's bedside manner is important to a patient's recovery.

1031. *Foreign Nights* (1989, Norstar, Canada, 91m, c). P Justine Estee, Alan Doluboff & Izidore K. Musallam, D Musallam, W Alan Zweig & Musallam, PH Paul Mitchnick, ED Robert Benson.

LP Terri Hawkes (Leila), Youssef Abed-Alnour (Youssef), Bushra Karaman (Basma), Mohammed Bacri (Morad), Paul Morasutti (Karim), Gillian Doria (Jamie), Stephen Foster (Paul).

Canadian-born Palestinian Terri Hawkes wishes to dance but is prevented from doing so by her strict, traditional father Youssef Abed-Alnour.

1032. *The Forest* (1983, Wide World of Entertainment, 85m, c, aka *Terror in the Forest*). P&D Don Jones, W Evan Jones, PH Stuart Asbjorsen, M Richard Hieronymus & Alan Oldfield.

LP Dean Russell (Steve), Michael Brody (John), Elaine Warner (Sharon), John Batis (Charley), Ann Wilkinson (Teddi), Jeanette Kelly (Mother), Corky Pigeon (John, Jr.), Becki Burke (Jennifer).

The haunting spirits of a dead family and a cannibalistic killer terrorize a group of campers in this routine, low-budget horror film.

Forest of Fear see Bloodeaters

The Forest Primeval see The Final Terror

1033. *Forever Lulu* (1987, Tri-Star, 85m, c). P,D&W Amos Kollek, PH Lisa Rinzler, ED Jay Freund, PD Stephen McCabe.

LP Hanna Schygulla (Elaine Hines), Deborah Harry (Lulu), Alec Baldwin (Buck), Annie Golden (Diana), Paul Gleason (Robert), Dr. Ruth Westheimer (Herself), Raymond Serra (Alphonse), George Kyle (Pepe).

Despite her title billing, Deborah Harry, the former lead singer of the punk/new wave group Blondie, has little more than a cameo role. The star is Hanna Schygulla, a struggling writer who becomes embroiled in a real-life mystery involving drugs and murderers. Just as Rosanna Arquette sought Madonna in *Desperately Seeking Susan,* which this film resembles (badly), Schygulla is trying to find Harry throughout the picture.

1034. *Forever Young* (1984, 20th Century–Fox, GB, 84m, c/b&w). P Chris Griffin, D David Drury, W Ray Connolly, PH Norman Langley, M Peter Maxwell-Davies, ED Max Lemon.

LP James Aubrey (James), Nicholas

Gecks (Father Michael), Alec McCowen (Father Vincent), Karen Archer (Mary), Joseph Wright (John), Liam Holt (Paul), Jane Forster (Cathy), Jason Carter (Young Michael).

Priest Nicholas Gecks and lecturer James Aubrey, both former rock musicians, are in conflict over the mother of a boy Gecks has taken a special shine to. Aubrey wishes to get even for an earlier betrayal by Gecks.

1035. *The Formula* (1980, MGM, 117m, c). P Steve Shagan, D John G. Avildsen, W Shagan (based on his novel), PH James Crabe†, M Bill Conti, ED Avildsen & David Bretherton, PD Herman Blumenthal.

LP George C. Scott (Barney Caine), Marlon Brando (Adam Steiffel), Marthe Keller (Lisa), John Gielgud (Dr. Esau), G.D. Spradlin (Clements), Beatrice Straight (Kay Neeley), Richard Lynch (Kladen/Tedesco), John Van Dreelen (Hans Lehman), Robin Clarke (Maj. Neeley), Ike Eisenmann (Tony), Marshall Thompson (Geologist), Dieter Schidor (Assassin).

Despite many attempts on his life, hard-nosed L.A. policeman George C. Scott continues his investigation of the murder of his friend Robin Clarke. He also tracks down a formula for synthetic fuel, which would free the United States from dependency on oil. Marlon Brando was paid $3 million for three scenes in this disappointing production of Steve Shagan's fascinating novel.

1036. *Fort Apache, The Bronx* (1981, 20th Century–Fox, 125m, c). P Martin Richards & Tom Fiorello, D Daniel Petrie, W Heywood Gould (based on the experiences of Thomas Mulhearn & Pete Tessitore), PH John Alcott, M Jonathan Tunick, ED Rita Roland, PD Ben Edwards.

LP Paul Newman (Murphy), Edward Asner (Connolly), Ken Wahl (Corelli), Danny Aiello (Morgan), Rachel Ticotin (Isabella), Pam Grier (Charlotte), Kathleen Beller (Theresa), Tito Goya (Jumper/Detective), Miguel Pinero (Hernando), Jaime Tirelli (Jose), Lance William Guecia (Track Star).

Based on the real-life experiences of two New York cops who served in the beleaguered South Bronx of New York City, this decent film stars Paul Newman as a good cop trying to do his duty in a hellhole in which arson, murder, rape, prostitution, thefts, assault, gang wars, etc. are commonplace every day events. There is no central theme, just episodic adventure stories of an urban disaster area, which never gets any better.

1037. *Fortress of Amerikkka* (1989, Troma, 97m, c, aka *The Mercenaries*). P Lloyd Kaufman & Michael Herz, D&W Eric Louzil, PH Ron Chapman, M David Ouimet, ED Diane Robinson.

LP Gene LeBrok (John Whitecloud), Kellee Bradley (Jennifer), David Crane (Sheriff), Kascha Le Priol (Elizabeth), William J. Kulzer (Cmdr. Karl Denton), Karen Michaels (Leslie).

In a weak sexploitation film, Indian halfbreed Gene LeBrok is just out of jail and hot on the trail of sheriff David Crane who cold-bloodedly killed LeBrok's brother. His crusade is complicated by a band of mercenary soldiers, the "Fortress of Amerikkka" led by William J. Kulzer, whose game is killing. The acting is horrible and even all the topless busty actresses don't help matters.

1038. *Forty Deuce* (1982, Island, 89m, c). P Jean Jacques Fourgeaud, D Paul Morrissey, W Alan Browne (based on his stage play), PH Francois Reichenbach, Stefan Stapasik & Steven Fierberg, M Manu Dibango, ED Ken Aleuto.

LP Orson Bean (Mr. Roper), Kevin Bacon (Rickey), Mark Keyloun (Blow), Harris Laskaway (Augie), Tommy Citera (Crank), John Anthony (John Noonan), Carol Jean Lewis (Black Woman).

Trying to fund a drug deal, male prostitute Kevin Bacon attempts to sell a runaway boy to Orson Bean, but the kid overdoses on heroin. Viewers might feel like doing the same.

1039. *48 Hours* (1982, Paramount, 96m, c). P Lawrence Gordon & Joel Silver, D Walter Hill, W Roger Spottiswoode, Hill, Larry Gross & Steven E. de Souza, PH Ric Waite, M James Horner, ED Freeman Davies, Mark Warner & Billy Weber, PD John Vallone.

LP Nick Nolte (Jack Cates), Eddie Murphy (Reggie Hammond), Annette O'Toole (Elaine), Frank McRae (Haden), James Remar (Ganz), David Patrick Kelly (Luther), Sonny Landham (Billy Bear), Brion Jones (Kehoe), Kerry Sherman (Rosalie), Jonathan Banks (Algren), Tara King (Frizzy), Greta Blackburn (Lisa), Margot Rose (Casey), Denise Crosby (Sally).

Nick Nolte and Eddie Murphy make a good team in this comedy crime drama. Tough as nails police detective Nolte checks streetwise convict Murphy out of prison for 48 hours to help track down a pair of maniacal cop-killers. The two abuse each other with racial slurs, four-letter language and punches, but come to respect each other as they succeed in their mission. Don't go expecting any *The Defiant Ones*-like ending, however.

1040. *Four Friends* (1981, Filmways, 114m, c, aka *Georgia's Friends*). P Arthur Penn & Gene Lasko, D Penn, W Steven Tesich, PH Ghislain Cloquet, M Elizabeth Swados, ED Barry Malkin & Marc Laub, PD David Chapman.

LP Craig Wasson (Danilo Prozor), Jodi Thelen (Georgia Miles), Jim Metzler (Tom Donaldson), Michael Huddleston (David Levine), Reed Birney (Louie Carnahan), Julia Murray (Adrienne Carnahan), David Graff (Gergley).

In a charming, sentimental story, idealistic Yugoslavian immigrant Craig Wasson comes of age in the turbulent 60s with the help and love of his friends.

1041. *The Four Seasons* (1981, Universal, 107m, c). P Martin Bregman, D&W Alan Alda, PH Victor J. Kemper, M Antonio Vivaldi, ED Michael Economou, PD Jack Collis.

LP Alan Alda (Jack Burroughs), Carol Burnett (Kate Burroughs), Len Cariou (Nick Callan), Sandy Dennis (Anne Callan), Rita Moreno (Claudia Zimmer), Jack Weston (Danny Zimmer), Bess Armstrong (Ginny Newley).

Three upper-middle-class New York couples take vacations together in each of the four seasons. Their times together are a bit blunted when one couple's marriage ends and the husband marries a much younger woman. The picture is enjoyable because of the work of the charming cast, but it doesn't really have much to say about marriage or friendship.

1042. *4D Special Agents* (1981, Eyeline, GB, 60m, c). P Harold Orton & Caroline Neame, D Orton, W Orton & Peter Frances-Browne, PH Ray Orton, M Harry Robinson, ED Gordon Grimward.

LP Lisa East (Jane Bowman), Dexter Fletcher (Steve Fraser), Sarah Jenkins (Tricia), Paul Medford (Danny), Philip Cook (Olly), Bryan Marshall (Ray), James Coyle (Spider), Ken Shorter (Eddie), Neil Hallett (Insp. Porter).

A group of London's East End kids catch a gang of jewel thieves.

1043. *The Fourth Protocol* (1987, Lorimar, 119m, c). P Timothy Burrill, D John Mackenzie, W Frederick Forsyth & Richard Burridge (based on the novel by Forsyth), PH Phil Meheux, M Lalo Schifrin & Francis Shaw, ED Graham Walker, PD Allan Cameron.

LP Michael Caine (John Preston), Pierce Brosnan (Maj. Valeri Petrofsky), Joanna Cassidy (Col. Irina Vassilieva), Ned Beatty (Gen. Borisov), Betsy Brantley (Eileen MacWhirter), Peter Cartwright (Jan Marais), Sean Chapman (Capt. Lyndhurst), Rosy Clayton (Susie Adrian).

In 1987 hardly a month went by without the release of a movie starring Michael Caine. In this one he's a British agent who suspects something big is being smuggled into England. Sure enough it's the parts for an atomic bomb which at the right time will be assembled by Russian agent Pierce Brosnan. The latter is to trigger the device to make it appear that the Americans are responsible for a terrible nuclear accident and thus weaken NATO.

1044. *The Fox and the Hound* (1981, Disney, animated, 83m, c). P Wolfgang Reitherman & Art Stevens, D Stevens, Ted Berman & Richard Rich, W Various (based on the novel by Daniel P. Mannix), M Buddy Baker.

VOICES Mickey Rooney (Tod), Kurt Russell (Copper), Pearl Bailey (Big Mamma), Jack Albertson (Amos Slade), Sandy Duncan (Vixey), Jeanette Nolan (Widow Tweed), Dick Bakalyan (Dinky), Paul Winchell (Boomer), Keith Mitchell (Young Tod), Corey Feldman (Young Copper).

Begun in 1977, *The Fox and the Hound* was the first feature of a new generation of animators for Disney. A baby fox whose mother has been shot by a hunter is taken in by a widow lady. Played at this point by Keith Mitchell, the fox becomes best of friends with a natural enemy, young hound pup Corey Feldman. They pledge eternal friendship, but it's a promise hard to keep when they grow up to be Mickey Rooney and Kurt Russell.

1045. *Fox Style Killer* (1982, Aquarius, 88m, c). P Paul R. Picard, D Clyde Houston, W Houston & Michael Fox.

LP Chuck Daniel, Juanita Moore, Denise Denise, Hank Rolike, Jovita Bush, Richard Lawson, Newell Alexander, Reuben Collins.

Chuck Daniel is torn between his big city cool and his small-town roots. When the local factory back home goes on the auction block, threatening to destroy the town, he searches for the truth behind the sale.

1046. *Foxes* (1980, United Artists, 106m, c). P David Puttnam & Gerald Ayres, D Adrian Lyne, W Ayres, PH Leon Bijou, M Giorgio Moroder, ED Jim Coblentz.

LP Jodie Foster (Jeanie), Scott Baio (Brad), Sally Kellerman (Mary), Randy Quaid (Jay), Lois Smith (Mrs. Axman), Adam Faith (Bryan), Cherie Currie (Annie), Marilyn Kagan (Madge), Kandice Stroh (Deirdre).

Four trampy Los Angeles Valley teenage girls, Jodie Foster, Cherie Currie, Marilyn Kagan and Kandice Stroh struggle with growing up and dealing with their impossible parents.

1047. *Foxtrap* (1986, Snizzlefritz, US/Ital., 88m, c). P&D Fred Williamson, W Aubrey K. Rattan (based on a story by Williamson), PH John Stephens & Steve Shaw, M Patrizio Fariselli, ED Giorgio Venturoli.

LP Fred Williamson (Thomas Fox), Chris Connelly (John Thomas), Arlene Golonka (Emily), Donna Owen (Susan), Beatrice Palme (Mariana), Cleo Sebastian (Josie), Lela Rochon (Lindy).

Private detective Fred Williamson is in Europe seeking runaway Donna Owen. Her family has hired him to bring her back to her home. It's a ho-hum star feature.

Framed see *An Innocent Man*

1048. *Fran* (1985, Harron, Australia, 94m, c). P David Rapsey, D&W Glenda Hambly, PH Jan Kenny & Yuri Sokol, M Greg Schultz, ED Tai Tana.

LP Noni Hazelhurst (Fran), Annie Byron (Marge), Alan Fletcher (Jeff), Narelle Simpson (Lisa), Travis Ward (Tom), Rosie Logie (Cynthia), Danny Adcock (Ray), Rosemary Harrison (Carol), Colin McEwan (Graham).

Noni Hazelhurst's husband leaves her and their three children when he learns she's been having an affair. She takes up with Alan Fletcher, but he molests one of the kids. The authorities place the youngsters in a foster home, Fletcher leaves, and Hazelhurst is alone with no idea what to do next.

1049. *Frances* (1982, Universal, 140m, c). P Jonathan Sanger & Marie Yates, D Graeme Clifford, W Eric Bergren, Christopher DeVore & Nicholas Kazan (Frances Farmer's autobiography *Will There Really Be a Morning?* is not given credit), PH Laszlo Kovacs, M John Barry, ED John Wright, PD Richard Sylbert.

LP Jessica Lange† (Frances Farmer), Sam Shepard (Harry York), Kim Stanley† (Lillian Farmer), Bart Burns (Ernest Farmer), Jeffrey DeMunn (Clifford Odets), Jordan Chaney (Harold Clurman), Lane Smith (Dr. Symington), Donald Craig (Ralph Edwards), Sarah Cunningham (Alma Styles).

Jessica Lange gives a sterling performance as the temperamental Hollywood star Frances Farmer, who is done in by the movie powers of the late 30s and early 40s. The latter are aided and abetted by her hateful mother, appropriately played by Kim Stanley. It's pitiful and depressing to watch the treatment of this outspoken woman in mental institutions. There she is gang raped, and has all the spirit cut out of her by a brain operation. It's, tragically, a true story.

1050. *Frankenstein General Hospital* (1988, New Star, 92m, c/b&w). P Dimitri Villard, D Deborah Roberts, W Michael Kelly & Robert Deel (based on the novel *Frankenstein* by Mary Wollstonecraft Shelley), PH Tom Fraser, M John Ross, ED Ed Cotter, PD Don Day.

LP Mark Blankfield (Dr. Bob Frankenstein), Leslie Jordan (Iggy), Jonathan Farwell (Dr. Frank Reutger), Kathy Shower (Dr. Alice Singleton), Irwin Keyes (Monster), Hamilton Mitchell (Dr. Andrew Dixon), Lou Cutell (Dr. Saperstein), Katie Caple (Nurse Verna).

Mark Blankfield, the great-great-grandson of legendary Baron von Frankenstein, and his assistant Leslie Jordan, are stitching together what they hope will be a perfect human being. Well, you know that's not going to happen. What does unfold is a series of stupid, crude puns and gags, and action which unfolds at a slow pace, until the dumb picture limps to a welcome end.

1051. *Frantic* (1988, Warner, 120m, c). P Thom Mount & Tim Hampton, D Roman Polanski, W Polanski & Gerard Brach, PH Witold Sobocinski, M Ennio Morricone, ED Sam O'Steen, PD Pierre Guffroy.

LP Harrison Ford (Dr. Richard Walker), Betty Buckley (Sondra Walker), Emmanuelle Seigner (Michelle), John Mahoney (Williams), Jimmie Ray Weeks (Shaap), Yorgo Voyagis (The Kidnapper), David Huddleston (Peter), Gerard Klein (Galliard).

Returning to Paris where they spent their honeymoon 20 years earlier, Harrison Ford and wife Betty Buckley plan a romantic vacation while he's attending a medical convention. Soon after they arrive at their luxury hotel, Ford steps out of the shower to discover that Buckley has disappeared. While making a frantic search for her through the terrifying underbelly of the City of Lights, he encounters beautiful Emmanuelle Seigner who helps him solve the mystery.

1052. *Fraternity Vacation* (1985, New World, 95m, c). P Robert C. Peters, D James Frawley, W Lindsay Harrison, PH Paul Ryan, M Brad Fiedel, ED Chris Nelson, PD Roberta Neiman.

LP Stephen Geoffreys (Wendell Tvedt), Sheree J. Wilson (Ashley Taylor), Cameron Dye (Joe Gillespie), Leigh McCloskey (Charles "Chas" Lawlor III), Tim Robbins (Larry "Mother" Tucker), Matt McCoy, Jr. (J.C. Springer), Amanda Bearse (Nicole Ferret), John Vernon (Chief Ferret).

It's just one more of a score of films featuring horny male college students on the loose in a resort area, where beautiful babes wear very small bikinis, and take off their tops at the least provocation. It's customary to feature one beauty, in this case Sheree J. Wilson, who's a little harder to get. There's a bet as to whom will bed her first. And the winner, not surprisingly, is nerdish Stephen Geoffreys.

The Freak from Suckweasel Mountain see Geek Maggot Bingo

1053. *Freakshow* (1989, Brightstar Films, Canada, 92m, c). P Anthony Kramreither, D Constantino Magnatta, W Bob Farmer, PH Gilles Corbeil, M Steve Shelski & Dan Le Blanc, ED Claudio De Grano.

LP Audrey Landers (Shannon Nichols), Peter Read (Dr. Borges), Dean Richards (Fidge), Micheline Scattolon, Will Korbut.

This silly ripoff of "Alfred Hitchcock Presents" strings together four badly acted horror stories. These are linked by segments involving unpleasant TV newscaster Audrey Landers trapped in a collection of curiosity exhibits by crazy curator Peter Read.

1054. *Free Ride* (1986, Galaxy, 82m, c). P Tom Boutross & Bassem Abdallah, D Tom Trbovich, W Ronald Z. Wang, Lee Fulkerson & Robert Bell (based on a story by Wang), PH Paul Lohmann, ED Ron Honthaner, AD Daniel Webster.

LP Gary Hershberger (Dan Garton), Reed Rudy (Greg), Dawn Schneider (Jill Monroe), Peter De Luise (Carl), Brian MacGregor (Elmer), Warren Berlinger (Dean Stockwell), Mamie Van Doren (Debbie Stockwell), Babette Props (Kathy), Chick Vennera (Edgar Ness).

In another shameless clone of *Animal House,* professional student Gary Hershberger and his buddy Rudy borrow a car, finding $250,000 belonging to the mob under the seat. The boys with the wing-tip shoes want it back.

1055. *Freedom* (1985, Satori, Australia, 100m, c). P Matt Carrol, D Scott Hicks, W John Emery, PH Ron Johanson, M Cold Chisel, ED Graeme Koetsveld, PD Herbert Pinter.

LP Jon Blake (Ron), Candy Raymond (Annie), Jad Capelja (Sally), Charles "Bud" Tingwell (Cassidy), Chris Haywood (Phil), Reg Lye (Old Farmer).

Sullen, angry and unemployed, young Australian Jon Blake equates a Porsche, a white suit and a sexy blonde at his side with his idea of freedom. He acquires all three by stealing. The three, Blake, the girl Jad Capelja and the car, are off on a crime spree adventure until the expected conclusion, which results in a totaled Porsche and a few other holes in his freedom.

1056. *Freeway* (1988, New World, 91m, c). P Peter S. Davis & William Panzer, D Francis Delia, W Darrell Fetty & Delia (based on a novel by Deanne Barkley), PH Frank Byers, M Joe Delia, ED Byers, PD Douglas Metrov.

LP Darlanne Fluegel (Sunny Harper), James Russo (Frank Quinn), Billy Drago (Edward Heller), Richard Belzer (Dr. David Lazarus), Michael Callan (Lt. Boyle), Joey Palese (Gomez), Clint Howard (Ronnie).

Darlanne Fluegel's husband is killed by a freeway psycho, who cruises Los Angeles freeways, chatting with call-in radio personality Richard Belzer. Now and then the nut kills randomly. Fluegel plans her own treatment for the sickie.

1057. *The Freeway Maniac* (1989, Cannon, 93m, c, aka *Breakdown*). P Paul & Loren Winters, D P. Winters, W P. Winters & Gahan Wilson, PH Ronald Vidor, M Greg Stewart, ED David Marsh.

LP Loren Winters (Linda), James Courtney (Arthur), Shepard Sanders (Burt Overman), Donald Hotton (Steven Day), Jeff Morris (Ray), Robert Bruce (Terry), Frank Jasper (Mannie).

This horror film within a horror film is apparently meant to be a spoof of the genre, but it's hard to be certain because of the low quality of the film. Model Loren Winters is starring in a low-budget sci-fi flick. She's stalked by a slasher, who works the freeway.

1058. *The French Lieutenant's Woman* (1981, United Artists, GB, 127m, c). P Leon Clore, D Karel Reisz, W Harold Pinter† (based on the novel by John Fowles), PH Freddie Francis, M Carl Davis, ED John Bloom†, PD Assheton Gorton,

AD/SD Gordon & Ann Mollo†, COS Tom Rand†.

LP Meryl Streep† (Sarah/Anna), Jeremy Irons (Charles/Mike), Hilton McRae (Sam), Emily Morgan (Mary), Leo McKern (Dr. Grogan), Charlotte Mitchell (Mrs. Tranter), Lynsey Baxter (Ernestina), Patience Collier (Mrs. Poulteney), Peter Vaughan (Mr. Freeman), Liz Smith (Mrs. Fairley).

Those who read the Fowles novel could have predicted it would be difficult if not impossible to successfully translate to the screen. The decision to tell parallel stories hasn't made the task any easier. The film jumps back and forth from the Lyme Regis–set story of 1867 gentleman Jeremy Irons' forsaking his fiancée for Meryl Streep, the abandoned mistress of a French seaman, and the contemporary story of Irons and Streep as actors filming the story. The former is charming, the latter is an annoying intrusion.

1059. *Fresh Horses* (1988, Weintraub, Columbia, 105m, c). P Dick Berg, D David Anspaugh, W Larry Ketron (based on his play), PH Fred Murphy, M David Foster & Patrick Williams, ED David Rosenbloom, PD Paul Sylbert.

LP Molly Ringwald (Jewel), Andrew McCarthy (Matt Larkin), Patti D'Arbanville (Jean), Ben Stiller (Tipton), Leon Russom (Larkin's Dad), Molly Hagan (Ellen), Viggo Mortensen (Green), Doug Hutchison (Sproles), Chiara Peacock (Alice), Marita Geraghty (Maureen).

College engineering student Andrew McCarthy is engaged to a wealthy Cincinnati girl, when he encounters Molly Ringwald, an uneducated Kentucky country teenage drop-out. By the third time they meet, McCarthy is head-over-heels in love. But is Ringwald 20 or 16? A pathological liar? A married prostitute?

1060. *Friday the 13th* (1980, Paramount, 95m, c). P&D Sean S. Cunningham, W Victor Miller, PH Barry Abrams, M Harry Manfredini, ED Bill Freda.

LP Betsy Palmer (Mrs. Voorhees), Adrienne King (Alice), Harry Crosby (Bill), Laurie Bartram (Brenda), Mark Nelson (Ned), Jeannine Taylor (Marcie), Robbi Morgan (Annie), Kevin Bacon (Jack), Ari Lehman (Jason), Peter Brouwer (Steve).

Paramount discovered it had the Midas touch with the production of this horror film and the others in what appears to be a never-ending series. When a summer camp is reopened after many years, the grisly and gory murders which closed it down begin again. Teens loved the movie and those that followed. No wonder they don't have time for science, mathematics, history, foreign languages, art, etc. in schools, they'd rather study murder and mayhem, served up with enough gore to make adults throw up.

[Note: for convenience, the eight films in this series are here presented chronologically]

1061. *Friday the 13th, Part II* (1981, Paramount, 87m, c). P Steve Miner & Dennis Murphy, D Miner, W Ron Kurz (based on characters created by Victor Miller), PH Peter Stein, M Harry Manfredini, ED Susan E. Cunningham, PD Virginia Field.

LP Amy Steel (Ginny), John Furey (Paul), Adrienne King (Alice), Kirsten Baker (Terry), Stu Charno (Ted), Warrington Gillette (Jason), Walt Gorney (Crazy Ralph), Marta Kober (Sandra), Tom McBride (Mark), Bill Randolph (Jeff), Lauren-Marie Taylor (Vickie), Betsy Palmer (Mrs. Voorhees).

The talentless moviemakers responsible for this and others in the series of tedious, mindless bloodletting trash can't point to anything with pride. There is nothing redeeming or skillful about this essential ghastly repeat of the previous film, except that five years have passed and the murdererer is now the son of the woman responsible for all the killings in the original.

1062. *Friday the 13th, Part III* (1982, Paramount, 3-D, 95m, c). P Frank Mancuso, Jr. & Tony Bishop, D Steve Miner, W Martin Kitrosser & Carol Watson (based on characters created by Victor Miller & Ron Kurz), PH Gerald Feil, M Harry Manfredini, ED George Hively.

LP Dana Kimmel (Chris Higgins), Richard Brooker (Jason), Catherine Parks (Vera), Paul Kratka (Rick), Jeffrey Rogers (Andy), Larry Zerner (Shelly), Tracie Savage (Debbie), Rachel Howard (Chili), David Katims (Chuck).

In this edition audiences get their usual ration of senseless, ghastly murders served up in 3-D, but the film is just as stupid and gross as the others.

1063. *Friday the 13th: The Final Chapter [i.e., Part IV]* (1984, Paramount, 91m, c). P Frank Mancuso, Jr. & Tony Bishop, D Joseph Zito, W Barney Cohen (based on a story by Bruce Hidemi Sakow, and characters created by Victor Miller, Ron Kurz, Martin Kitrosser & Carol Watson), PH Joao Fernandes, Henry Manfredini, ED Joel Goodman & Daniel Loewenthal, PD Shelton H. Bishop, Jr., SE Martin Becker.

LP E. Erich Anderson (Rob), Judie Aronson (Samantha), Peter Barton (Doug), Kimberly Beck (Trish), Tom Everett (Flashlight Man), Corey Feldman (Tommy), Joan Freeman (Mrs. Jarvis), Lisa Freeman (Nurse Morgan), Thad Geer (Running Man), Richard Brooker (Jason), Crispin Glover (Jimmy).

Well, we know the title doesn't tell the truth, although Jason, after killing his usual dozen or more nubile camp counselors at Crystal Lake, gets his. But with the money this sleazy series makes, the studio will run out of Roman numerals *and* "finals" before he's finally put to rest.

1064. *Friday the 13th: A New Beginning [i.e. Part V]* (1985, Paramount, 91m, c). P Timothy Silver, D Danny Steinmann, W Martin Kitrosser, David Cohen & Steinmann, PH Stephen L. Posey, M Harry Manfredini, ED Bruce Green, PD Robert Howland.

LP John Shepard (Tommy Jarvis), Melanie Kinnaman (Pam), Shavar Ross (Reggie), Richard Young (Matt), Marco St. John (Sheriff Tucker), Juliette Cummins (Robin), Carol Lacatell (Ethel), Corey Feldman (Tommy at 12), Tiffany Helm (Violet).

As everyone knows Corey Feldman slew Jason in the previous chapter of this long running series, and that's the end of the gravy and gory train for Paramount right? Wrong! Killing Jason has a traumatic effect on Feldman, who grows up to be John Shepard. It seems he has taken up Jason's hockey mask and killing ways—or has he?

1065. *Friday the 13th, Part VI: Jason Lives* (1986, Paramount, 85m, c). P Don Behrns, D&W Tom McLoughlin, PH Jon Kranhouse, M Harry Manfredini, ED Bruce Green, PD Joseph T. Garrity, SE Martin Becker.

LP Thom Mathews (Tommy), Jennifer Cooke (Megan), David Kagen (Sheriff Garris), Kerry Noonan (Paula), Renee Jones (Sissy), Tom Fridley (Cort), C.J. Graham (Jason), Darcy DeMoss (Nikki), Tony Goldwyn (Darren).

Bet you believed Jason expired in Part IV, but he's been revived by a bolt of lightning and the body count grows and grows at a summer camp. We think there are 18 corpses, but when you're having so much fun, who's counting?

1066. *Friday the 13th, Part VII: The New Blood* (1988, Paramount, 90m, c). P Iain Paterson, D John Carl Buechler, W Daryl Haney & Manuel Fidello, PH Paul Elliott, M Harry Manfredini, ED Barry Zetlin, Maureen O'Connell & Martin Jay Sadoff, PD Richard Lawrence, SE Lou Carlucci.

LP Jennifer Banko (Young Tina), John Otrin (Mr. Shepard), Susan Blu (Mrs. Shepard), Lar Park Lincoln (Tina Shepard), Terry Kiser (Dr. Crews), Kevin Blair (Nick), Jennifer Sullivan (Melissa), Heidi Kozak (Sandra), Kane Hodder (Jason Voorhees), Staci Greason (Jane).

After killing assorted teenagers and adults with different sharp instruments, it seems that Jason is finally done in for good by a girl with psychokinetic powers. See below!

1067. *Friday the 13th, Part VIII—Jason Takes Manhattan* (1989, Paramount, 100m, c). P Randolph Cheveldave, D&W Rob Hedden, PH Bryan England, M Fred Mollin, ED Steve Mirkovich, PD David Fischer.

LP Jensen Daggett (Rennie Wickham), Scott Reeves (Sean Robertson), Peter Mark Richman (Charles McCulloch), Barbara Bingham (Colleen Van Deusen), V.C. Dupree (Julius Gaw), Kane Hodder (Jason), Sharlene Martin (Tamara Mason), Timothy Burr Mirkovich (Young Jason), Amber Pawlick (Young Rennie).

We will be happy when this subgenre of slasher movies is effectively retired. We have grown weary of watching sadistic violence visited on nubile women and any of their male friends who happen to get in the way of the madman's weird way of expressing his fixations and sexual interests. Too many people already associate violence and sex; films like these can't help. We don't propose censorship, merely better taste in movie audiences. Meanwhile back at the picture show, our Jason is still dispatching teens from Crystal Lake, only this time most of the action takes place on a cruise ship taking the dopey youngsters to Manhattan.

1068. *Friend or Foe* (1982, Children's Film Foundation, GB, 70m, c). P Gordon Scott, D&W John Krish (based on the novel by Michael Morpurgo), PH Ray Orton, M Robert Farnon, ED Peter Tanner.

LP Mark Luxford (Tucky), John Holmes (David), Stacey Tendetter (Annie Reynolds), John Bardon (Jerry Reynolds), Jennifer Piercey (Miss Evers), Valerie Lush (Miss Roberts), Jasper Jacobs (Pilot), Robin Hayter (German).

In 1940 London children evacuated to the country come across downed German pilots.

1069. *Friends, Lovers and Lunatics* (1989, SC/Fries, Canada, 87m, c. aka *Crazy Horse*). P Nicolas Stiliadis, D Stephen Withrow, W Michael Taav, PH Douglas Koch, ED Michael McMahon, PD Alan Fellows.

LP Daniel Stern, Sheila McCarthy, Damir Andrei, Deborah Foreman, Page Fletcher, Elias Koteas.

Call it Young Yuppies in Love. Call it Modern Alienation, Call it Quits.

1070. *Friendship's Death* (1988, British Film Institute, GB, 78m, c). P Rebecca O'Brien, D&W Peter Wollen (based on his short story), PH Witold Stok, M Barrington Pheloung, ED Robert Hargreaves, PD Gemma Jackson.

LP Bill Paterson (Sullivan), Tilda Swinton (Friendship), Patrick Bauchau (Kubler), Ruby Baker (Catherine), Joumana Gill (Palestinian).

Alien Tilda Swinton arrives in Amman, Jordan, sometime in the 1970s just as the city is being reduced to rubble by the civil war involving the various factions. She is not really a woman, but a new prototype computer, dubbed "Friendship," sent to earth on a peacekeeping mission. After a while she becomes sympathetic to the cause of the Palestinians and ultimately joins the PLO.

The Fright see Visiting Hours

1071. *Fright Night* (1985, Columbia, 106m, c). P Herb Jaffe, D&W Tom Holland, PH Jan Keisser, M Brad Fiedel, ED Kent Beyda, PD John De Cuir, Jr.

LP Chris Sarandon (Jerry Dandridge), William Ragsdale (Charley Brewster), Amanda Bearse (Amy Peterson), Roddy McDowall (Peter Vincent), Stephen Geoffreys (Evil Ed), Jonathan Stark (Billy Cole), Dorothy Fielding (Judy Brewster), Art J. Evans (Det. Lennox).

Don't lump this film with the usual teenage/slasher movies. It's much better than that. Teenager William Ragsdale becomes convinced that his handsome new next-door neighbor Chris Sarandon is a vampire, but no one will believe him. He enlists a reluctant and skeptical washed-up horror movie actor Roddy McDowall to combat the murderous monster. Before the two are able to expose Sarandon to dawn's early light and his doom, Ragsdale's best friend, Stephen Geoffreys, and his girlfriend Amanda Bearse are turned into vampires. Geoffreys is killed while being transformed into a wolf. McDowall is very good. He thought so, too. He advertised his performance as Oscar-worthy. He wasn't that good.

1072. *Fright Night—Part 2* (1989, New Century/Vista, 101m, c). P Herb Jaffe & Mort Engelberg, D Tommy Lee Wallace, W Tim Metcalfe, Miguel Tejada-Flores & Wallace (based on characters created by Tom Holland), PH Mark Irwin, M Brad Fiedel, ED Jay Lash Cassidy, PD Dean Tschetter, SE Rich Josephson.

LP Roddy McDowall (Peter Vincent), William Ragsdale (Charley Brewster), Traci Lin (Alex), Julie Carmen (Regine), Russell Clark (Belle), Brian Thompson (Bozworth), Jonathan Gries (Louie), Ernie Sabella (Dr. Harrison), Merritt Butrick (Ritchie).

William Ragsdale, assisted in battling vampire Chris Sarandon in the original by ex-horror screen star Roddy McDowall, is back in business. His adversaries include slinky female vampire Julie Carmen, an androgynous black, a leather-jacketed hood and a musclebound idiot.

1073. *Frightmare* (1983, Saturn, 86m, c, aka *The Horror Star*). P Patrick & Tallie Wright, D&W Norman Thaddeus Vane, PH Joel King, M Jerry Moseley, ED Robert Jackson, AD Anne Welch, SE Knott Ltd. & Chuck Stewart.

LP Ferdinand "Ferdy" Mayne (Conrad), Luca Bercovici (Saint), Nita Talbot (Mrs. Rohmer), Leon Askin (Wolfgang), Jennifer Starrett (Meg), Barbara Pilavin (Etta), Carlene Olson (Eve), Scott Thomson (Bobo).

When devotées of a deceased horror film star steal his body from its grave, the regenerated corpse goes on a mass killing spree.

1074. *The Fringe Dwellers* (1987, Atlantic, Australia, 98m, c). P Sue Milliken, D Bruce Beresford, W Bruce Beresford & Rhoisin Beresford (based on the novel by Nene Gare), PH Don McAlpine, M George Dreyfus, ED Tim Wellburn, PD Herbert Pinter.

LP Kristina Nehm (Trilby), Justine Saunders (Mollie), Bob Maza (Joe), Kyle Belling (Noonah), Denis Walker (Bartie), Ernie Dingo (Phil), Malcolm Silva (Charlie), Marlene Bell (Hannah), Michelle Torres (Audrena).

Director Bruce Beresford presents an intriguing and touching, if rambling, story of the domestic problems of a family of Aborigines. They move from a shantytown to a clean and proper suburban white neighborhood, where assimilation proves to be difficult.

1075. *The Frog Prince* (1985, Warner, GB, 93m, c). P Iain Smith, D Brian Gilbert, W Posy Simmonds & Gilbert (based on a story by Simmonds), PH Clive Tickner, M Enya Ni Bhraonain, ED Jim Clark, PD Anton Furst.

LP Jane Snowden (Jenny), Alexandre Sterling (Jean-Philippe), Jacqueline Doyen (Mme. Peroche), Raoul Delfosse (Mons. Peroche), Jeanne Herviale (Mme. Declos), Diana Blackburn (Ros), Oystein Wilk (Niels).

In 1961 Paris, English student Jane Snowden has an affair with French architect Alexandre Sterling, who wins her over by reciting verses from *Romeo and Juliet* for her on a subway platform.

From a Whisper to a Scream see The Offspring

1076. *From Beyond* (1986, Empire Pictures, 85m, c). P Brian Yuzna, D Stuart Gordon, W Dennis Paoli (based on a story by H.P. Lovecraft, adapted by Yuzna, Paoli & Gordon), PH Mac Ahlberg, M Richard Band, ED Lee Percy, PD Giovanni Natalucci.

LP Jeffrey Combs (Crawford Tillinghast), Barbara Crampton (Dr. Katherine McMichaels), Ted Sorel (Dr. Edward Pretorious), Ken Foree (Bubba Brownlee), Carolyn Purdy-Gordon (Dr. Roberta Bloch), Bunny Summers (Hester Gilman), Bruce McGuire (Jordan Fields).

This fine shocker is based on H.P. Lovecraft's classic tale of suspense about the Resonator, a gruesome machine that activates a special sixth sense in the pineal gland, a sense that makes its possessors crave human brains.

1077. *From Hollywood to Deadwood* (1989, Nightfilm, 102m, c). P Jo Peterson, D&W Rex Pickett, PH Peter Deming, M Alex Gibson & Gregory Kuehn, ED Steven Adrianson & Robert Erickson.

LP Scott Paulin (Raymond Savage), Jim Haynie (Jack Haines), Barbara Shock (Lana Dark), Jurgen Doeres (Steve Reese), Chris Mulkey (Nick Detroit), Mike Genovese (Ernie November), Norbert Weisser (Peter Mueller).

In this tongue-in-cheek comedy, private-eyes Scott Paulin and Jim Haynie are hired by a movie studio to track down actress Barbara Shock, whose disappearance has halted the production of her latest movie.

1078. *From the Hip* (1987, De Laurentiis, 111m, c). P Rene Dupont & Bob Clark, D Clark, W David E. Kelley & Clark (based on a story by David E. Kelley), PH Dante Spinotti, M Paul Zaza, ED Stan Cole, PD Michael Stringer.

LP Judd Nelson (Robin Weathers), Elizabeth Perkins (Jo Ann), John Hurt (Douglas Benoit), Darren McGavin (Craig Duncan), Dan Monahan (Larry),

David Alan Grier (Steve Hadley), Nancy Marchand (Roberta Winnaker), Allan Arbus (Phil Amos), Edward Winter (Raymond Torkenson).

The first half of this moronic insult to the legal profession (wait, is that possible?) is played as a comedy while the second half purports to be a serious courtroom film. Judd Nelson is a newly minted attorney who uses every questionable tactic he can think of to get one client off. This results in his reluctantly being made a junior partner and handed a case it's believed he can't win. He uses his usual bag of tricks to get superior-feeling professor John Hurt acquitted of molesting and murdering a young woman, that is, until Nelson decides that Hurt really is guilty.

Fugitives see Three Fugitives

Full Circle see The Haunting of Julia

1079. *Full Metal Jacket* (1987, Warner, 116m, c). P&D Stanley Kubrick, W Kubrick, Michael Herr & Gustav Hasford† (based on the novel *The Short-Timers* by Gustav Hasford), PH Douglas Milsome, M Abigail Mead, ED Martin Hunter, PD Anton Furst, AD Rod Stratford, Les Tomkins & Keith Pain, SD Stephen Simmonds.

LP Matthew Modine (Pvt. Joker), Adam Baldwin (Animal Mother), Vincent D'Onofrio (Leonard Lawrence, Pvt. Gomer Pyle), Lee Ermey (Gunnery Sgt. Hartman), Dorian Harewood (Eightball), Arliss Howard (Pvt. Cowboy), Kevyn Major Howard (Rafterman), Ed O'Ross (Walter J. Schinoski, Lt. Touchdown), John Stafford (Doc Jay), John Terry (Lt. Lockhart), Kirk Taylor (Payback).

Superior in many ways to Picture of the Year *Platoon* (1986), *Full Metal Jacket* (directed by Stanley Kubrick in his first film since *The Shining* in 1980) is a masterful film filled with humor, tension and brutality to go along with the violence. The first 44 minutes take place at a marine training camp in which gung-ho, merciless drill instructor Lee Ermey gives each of his recruits a new, usually derogatory name. In the case of overweight Vincent D'Onofrio, Ermey goes too far; the former becomes a dehuman-

ized killing machine with his first target being Ermey and his second, himself. From there the film moves to Vietnam, where Matthew Modine, the nominal star of the film or at least its Greek Chorus, is a sarcastic reporter for *Stars and Stripes* assigned to a battle-hardened platoon at the front lines. These men have had all the humanity driven from them as they move from one blazing firefight to the next, each time with more casualties in their own ranks as well as numerous dead Vietnamese soldiers. Kubrick's battle scenes are awesomely realistic as in the sequence in which the platoon is almost wiped out by a single sniper. When the sniper is discovered, she turns out to be a young girl. She takes a burst of fire and begs to be put out of her misery. Finally, Modine, the last member of the unit who has not become a killing machine, succumbs and shoots the girl. The camera pans his face, showing the change he's undergoing.

1080. *Full Moon High* (1982, Orion, 93m, c). P,D&W Larry Cohen, PH Daniel Pearl, M Gary W. Friedman.

LP Adam Arkin (Tony Walker), Elizabeth Hartman (Miss Montgomery), Ed McMahon (Mr. Walker), Roz Kelly, Kenneth Mars, Joanne Nail, Pat Morita, Alan Arkin, Louis Nye, John Blythe Barrymore.

Young Adam Arkin, a high school football star, is taken to Transylvania by his weird, right-wing father Ed McMahon and as quickly as you can say "children of the night," we have a silly but funny teenage werewolf story.

1081. *Full Moon in Blue Water* (1988, TransWorld, 94m, c). P Lawrence Turman, David Foster & John Turman, D Peter Masterson, W Bill Bozzone, PH Fred Murphy, M Phil Marshall, ED Jill Savitt.

LP Gene Hackman (Floyd), Teri Garr (Louise), Burgess Meredith (The General), Elias Koteas (Jimmy), Kevin Cooney (Charlie), David Doty (Virgil), Gil Glasgow (Baytch), Becky Gelke (Dorothy), Marietta Marich (Lois), Lexie Masterson (Annie).

Gene Hackman, the owner of a failing bar in a small town on the Texas Gulf Coast, still expects his wife, who disappeared in a boating accident a year earlier, will one day show up. Even finding her remains barely changes his mind. Despite his professed love for his wife, he has been sleeping with bus driver Teri Garr. The latter intervenes when she discovers that a real estate man is trying to force Hackman to sell his bar without Gene knowing that in a short time it will become a valuable piece of property. The film is a nice slice of life from helmer Peter Masterson, the maker of *A Trip to Bountiful*.

1082. *Funeral Home* (1982, MPM/Wescom, Canada, 93m, c, aka *Cries in the Night*). P&D William Fruet, W Ida Nelson, PH Mark Irwin, M Jerry Fielding, ED Ralph Brunjes, PD Roy Forge Smith & Susan Longmire, SE Dennis Pike.

LP Lesleh Donaldson (Heather), Kay Hawtrey (Maude), Barry Morse (Davis), Dean Garbett (Rick), Stephen Miller (Billy), Harvey Atkin (Harry), Alf Humphries (Joe), Peggy Mahon (Florie), Doris Petrik (Ruby).

Teenage Lesleh Donaldson investigates the frightening noises coming from the cellar. They seem related to the disappearance of guests from her grandmother's small motel, formerly a funeral home.

1083. *The Funhouse* (1981, Universal, 96m, c). P Derek Powers & Steven Bernhardt, D Tobe Hooper, W Larry Block, PH Andrew Laszlo, M John Beal, ED Jack Hofstra, PD Morton Rabinowitz.

LP Elizabeth Berridge (Amy), Cooper Huckabee (Buzz), Miles Chapin (Richie), Largo Woodruff (Liz), Sylvia Miles (Mme. Zena), Kevin Conway (The Barker), William Finley (Marco the Magnificent), Wayne Doba (The Monster), Shawn Carson (Joey Harper), Jack McDermott (Harper).

Four frightened teenagers spend a night in a carnival funhouse where they are brutally hacked and maimed by a crazed father and son.

1084. *Funland* (1987, Double Helix, 87m, c). P William Vanderkloot & Michael A. Simpson, D Simpson, W Simpson, Bonnie Turner & Terry Turner, PH Vanderkloot, M James Oliverio, ED Vanderkloot, Wade Watkins & Teresa Garcia.

LP William Windom (Angus Perry), David L. Lander (Bruce Burger), Bruce Mahler (Spencer), Robert Sacchi (DiMaurio/Bogie), Clark Brandon (Doug Sutterfield), Jill Carroll (Denise Wilson), Mike McManus (T.G. Hurley).

There's not much fun in this sloppy story of the weird goings-on at an amusement park.

1085. *The Funny Farm* (1982, New World/Mutual, Canada, 96m, c). P Claude Heroux, D&W Ron Clark, PH Rene Verzier, M Pierre Brousseau, ED Marcus Manton.

LP Miles Chapin (Mark), Tracy Bregman (Amy), Jack Carter (Philly), Eileen Brennan (Gail), Peter Aykroyd (Stephen), Mike MacDonald (Bruce), Howie Mandel (Larry), Jack Blum (Peter).

A group of ambitious stand-up comedians try to make it big in the crazy world of comedy at L.A.'s comedy club, The Funny Farm. It's no *Punchline*.

1086. *Funny Farm* (1988, Warner, 101m, c). P Robert L. Crawford, D George Roy Hill, W Jeffrey Boam (based on the book by Jay Cronley), PH Miroslav Ondricek, M Elmer Bernstein, ED Alan Heim, PD Henry Bumstead.

LP Chevy Chase (Andy Farmer), Madolyn Smith (Elizabeth Farmer), Joseph Maher (Michael Sinclair), Jack Gilpin (Bud Culbertson), Brad Sullivan (Brock), MacIntyre Dixon (Mayor Barclay), Caris Corfman (Betsy Culbertson), William Severs (Newspaper Editor), Mike Starr (Crocker).

Someone forgot to tell the screenwriter and the cast that this film was meant to be a comedy. Jeffrey Boam doesn't supply many laughs or funny situations and from all appearances Chevy Chase and others may have thought they were in a drama. Chase and his wife leave the big city for the quiet, contemplative life in Vermont but find they can't stand it. They offer a reward to the local residents if they will help them unload the farm they foolishly bought.

1087. *Funny Money* (1983, Cannon, GB, 97m, c). P Greg Smith, D&W James Kenelm Clarke, PH John Wyatt, M Ed

Welch, ED Bill Lennie, PD Harry Pottle.

LP Gregg Henry (Ben Turtle), Elizabeth Daily (Cass), Gareth Hunt (Keith Banks), Derren Nesbitt (Jake Sanderson), Annie Ross (Diana Sharman), Joe Prami (Limping Man), Rose Alba (Mrs. De Salle), Stephen Yardley (Ridley).

An American girl and a pianist are partners in sex and credit card crimes.

The Further Adventures of Heidi see Courage Mountain

1088. *The Further Adventures of Tennessee Buck* (1988, TransWorld, 90m, c). P Gideon Amir & Peter Shepard, D David Keith, W Barry Jacobs & Stuart Jacobs (based on a story by Paul Mason), PH Avraham Karpick, M John Debney, ED Anthony Redman, PD Erroll Kelly.

LP David Keith (Buck Malone), Kathy Shower (Barbara Manchester), Brant Van Hoffman (Ken Manchester), Sillaiyoor Selvarajan (Sinaga), Tiziana Stella (Che), Patrizia Zanetti (Monique), Sumith Mudanayaka (Chief).

Try to imagine an Indiana Jones movie with lots of profanity and busty women who can barely keep their breasts and fannies inside their clothes. Now imagine the Indy story with only modest adventure and action sequences and you have this film. David Keith is hired by nerdish Brant Van Hoffman to fly him and his beauty queen wife Kathy Shower into cannibal country where they can hunt the white tiger. Van Hoffman gets killed, Shower gets raped and Keith has his hands full getting her back to civilization.

Fury of the Succubus see Satan's Mistress

1089. *Future Cop* (1985, Empire, 85m, c, aka *Trancers*). P&D Charles Band, W Paul De Meo & Danny Bilson, PH Mac Ahlberg, M Mark Ryder, ED Ted Nicolaou, SE John Carl Buechler.

LP Tim Thomerson (Jack Deth), Helen Hunt (Leena), Michael Stefani (Whistler), Art La Fleur (McNulty), Biff Manard (Hap Ashby).

Twenty-second-century lawman Tim Thomerson journeys back in time to present-day L.A. to prevent a zombie master from changing the future. Now, won't that change the future?

1090. *Future Force* (1989, Action Intl., 84m, c). P Kimberley Casey, D David A. Prior, W Prior (based on characters created by Thomas Baldwin), PH Andrew Parke, M Tim James, Steve McClintock & Mark Mancina, ED Paul O'Bryan.

LP David Carradine (John Tucker), Robert Tessier (Becker), Anna Rapagna (Marion), William Zipp (Adams), Patrick Culliton (Grimes), D.C. Douglas (Billy), Dawn Wildsmith (Roxanne), Kimberley Casey (Alicia).

In a straight to video release, David Carradine headlines as a 1991 bounty hunter working for COPS (Civilian Operated Police Systems), an organization formed when law enforcement is turned over to the private sector. Things go badly for our hero when the head of COPS, William Zipp, puts out a bounty on Carradine because the latter sides with reporter Anna Rapagna, who believes the civilian agency is out of control.

1091. *Future Hunters* (1989, Maharaj/Santiago, 100m, c). P Anthony Maharaj, D Cirio H. Santiago, W J.L. Thompson (based on a story by Maharaj), PH Ricardo Remias, M Ron Jones, ED Bas Santos, PD Joe Mari Avellana.

LP Robert Patrick (Slade), Linda Carol (Michelle), Ed Crick (Fielding), Bob Schott (Bauer), Richard Norton (Matthew), Ursula Marquez (Amazon Queen).

Prolific director Cirio H. Santiago borrows heavily from *Mad Max, Indiana Jones* and *Romancing the Stone* to bring out an enjoyable action film which moves from the present to the year 2025.

1092. *Future-Kill* (1985, International Film Marketing, 93m, c). P Gregg Unterberger & John H. Best, D&W Ronald W. Moore, PH Jon Lewis, M Robert Renfrow.

LP Edwin Neal (Splatter), Marilyn Burns (Dorothy Grim), Gabriel Folse, Wade Reese, Barton Faulks, Rob Rowley, Craig Kanne, Jeffrey Scott.

It's a grim view of a world in which antinuclear activists have taken over the major cities, reducing them to battlefields. The metropolitan areas are unfit for anyone but the followers of the violently wicked Edwin Neal, who kills with a claw he keeps hidden under the armor he wears to cover his radiation burns.

1093. *Future Schlock* (1984, Ultimate Show, Australia, 75m, c). P,D&W Barry Peak & Chris Kiely, PH Malcolm Richards, M John McCubbery & Doug Sanders, ED Robert Martin & Ray Pond, AD Ian McWha.

LP Maryanne Fahey (Sarah), Michael Bishop (Bear), Tracey Callander (Ronnie), Tiriel Mora (Alvin), Simon Thorpe (Sammy), Peter Cox (Cap'n Fruitcake), Keith Walker (Sgt. Tatts), Evan Zachariah (Skunk).

This punk comical assault on the middle class is set in a post–civil war society of the 21st century. Conservative suburbanites have defeated the nonconformists and walled them all in a huge ghetto.

1094. *F/X* (1986, Orion, 107m, c). P Dodi Fayed & Jack Wiener, D Robert Mandel, W Robert T. Megginson & Gregory Fleeman, PH Mirislav Ondricek, M Bill Conti, ED Terry Rawlings, PD Mel Bourne.

LP Bryan Brown (Rollie Tyler), Brian Dennehy (Leo McCarthy), Diane Venora (Ellen), Cliff DeYoung (Lipton), Mason Adams (Col. Mason), Jerry Orbach (Nicholas DeFranco), Joe Grifasi (Mickey), Martha Gehman (Andy).

Bryan Brown is the movies' best special effects man (F/X is film shorthand for special effects). He specializes in gory deaths and dismemberments. The Justice Department hires him to fake the assassination of a mobster turned government witness. But he's made a stooge in a complex plot which results in his holding the proverbial bag in a murder conspiracy. He has to use all his special talents to save his own life.

1095. *Gaby—A True Story* (1987, Tri-Star, 114m, c). P Pinchas Perry & Luis Mandoki, D Luis Mandoki, W Martin Salinas & Michael James Love (based on the story developed by Mandoki from events told to him by Gabriela Brimmer), PH Lajos Koltai, M Maurice Jarre, ED Garth Craven.

LP Liv Ullmann (Sari Brimmer), Norma Aleandro† (Florencia Morales), Robert Loggia (Michel Brimmer), Rachel Levin (Gabriela "Gaby" Brimmer), Lawrence Monoson (Fernando), Robert Beltran (Luis), Beatriz Sheridan (Fernando's Mother), Tony Goldwyn (David), Danny De La Paz (Carlos), Paulina Gomez (Gaby at Age 3), Enrique Lucero (Minister of Education).

The film tells the remarkable story of Gabriela Brimmer, afflicted with severe cerebral palsy from birth and nearly immobile and deaf. With the help of devoted nurse Norma Aleandro, she overcame her handicaps to become one of Mexico's most popular and celebrated authors. Rachel Levin, who played Gaby, had herself been paralyzed by a neurological ailment but after two years of rehabilitation regained almost all of her mobility.

1096. *Galactic Gigolo* (1988, Urban Classics, 82m, c). P Gorman Bechard & Kris Covello, D Bechard, W Carmine Capobiano & Bechard, PH Bechard, M Bob Esty & Michael Bernard, ED Joe Keiser.

LP Carmine Capobianco (Eoj), Debi Thibeault (Hildy Johnson), Ruth Collins (Dr. Ruth Pepper), Angela Nicholas (Peggy Sue Peggy), Frank Stewart (Waldo Crabbo), Michael Citriniti (Sonny Corleone), Tony Kruk (Carmine).

Carmine Capobianco, a piece of broccoli from Crowak, a planet completely inhabited by vegetables, has won a two-week trip to Prospect, Connecticut, on the planet earth, the home of the horniest humans in all the galaxy (this is true, we live only 20 minutes from Prospect, located at Rte. 69, and have observed the phenomenon firsthand). He arrives in Prospect in the guise of Elvis Presley (according to the movie, a little known fact is that Elvis himself was from the planet Crowak, and overstayed his two-week visit to earth and had to be forcibly taken home). Because of his hypnotic powers, he gets all the women he can handle with smooth lines like "Hi, I'm Eoj from the planet Crowak, and I'm here to partake in sexual relations with earth women." Believe us, the description of the movie makes it sound better than it really is.

1097. *Galaxina* (1980, Crown International, 95m, c). P Marilyn J. Tenser, D&W William Sachs, PH Dean Cundey, ED Larry Bock, PD Tom Turlley.

LP Stephen Macht (Thor), Dorothy R.

LP Stephen Macht (Thor), Dorothy R. Stratten (Galaxina), James David Hinton (Buzz), Avery Schreiber (Capt. Butt), Ronald Knight (Ordric), Lionel Smith (Maurice), Tad Horino (Sam Wo).

In a *Star Wars* spoof, *Playboy* Playmate of the Year Dorothy R. Stratten makes her final appearance before being murdered by her husband. Stratten is a voluptuous (what else?) robot navigator whose space ship hurtles towards the planet Altar I in search of a mystical gem, the "Blue Star."

1098. *The Galaxy Invader* (1985, Moviecraft, 80m, c). D,W&ED Don Dohler, PH Paul E. Loeschke, M Norman Naplock, Led & Silver, SE David Donoho.

LP Richard Ruxton (Joe), Faye Tilles (Carol), George Stevens (J.J.), Greg Dohler (David), Anne Frith (Ethel), Richard Dyszel (Dr. William Tracy), Kim Dohler (Annie), Theresa Harold (Vickie), Glenn Barnes (Alien).

Glenn Barnes, a visitor from another galaxy, crashlands on Earth and proves to be an alien killing machine. The creature is stalked by a band of rednecks. Their battle pits the alien and its laser against human weapons.

1099. *Galaxy of Terror* (1981, New World, 80m, c, aka *Mindwarp; An Infinity of Terrors; Planet of Horrors*). P Roger Corman & Marc Siegler, D B.D. Clark, W Siegler & Clark, PH Jacques Haitkin, M Barry Schrader, ED Robert J. Kizer, Larry Boch & Barry Zetlin, SE Tom Campbell.

LP Edward Albert (Cabren), Erin Moran (Alluma), Ray Walston (Kore), Bernard Behrens (Ilvar), Zalman King (Baelon), Robert Englund (Ranger), Taaffe O'Connell (Damelia), Sid Haig (Quuhod), Grace Zabriskie (Capt. Trantor).

Difficulty coming up with a title is not the only problem with this extremely gross science-fiction/horror movie. Just as a sample, Erin Moran, late of TV's "Happy Days," is disemboweled and then explodes.

1100. *Gallipoli* (1981, Paramount, Australia, 110m, c). P Robert Stigwood & Patricia Lovell, D Peter Weir, W David Williamson (based on a story by Weir),

PH Russell Boyd, M Brian May, ED William Anderson, PD Wendy Weir.

LP Mark Lee (Archy), Bill Kerr (Jack), Mel Gibson (Frank Dunne), Ron Graham (Wallace Hamilton), Harold Hopkins (Les McCann), Charles Yunupingu (Zac), Heath Harris (Stockman), Gerda Nicolson (Rose Hamilton), Robert Grubb (Billy).

History blends with the story of Australian youths Mark Lee and Mel Gibson, who, lured by notions of adventure and national pride, join the army during World War I. They are sent to die in the legendary battle of Gallipoli between Aussies and Austrians, and the latter's allies the Turks. It's an extraordinary moving and realistic film.

1101. *The Game* (1989, Visual Perspectives, 116m, c). P&D Curtis Brown, W Julia Wilson & Brown (based on Brown's story), PH Paul Gibson, M Julia Wilson, ED Gloria Whittemore & Daniel Barrientos, PD Walter Jorgenson.

LP Curtis Brown (Leon Hunter), Richard Lee Ross (Jason McNair), Vanessa Shaw (Silvia Yearwood), Billy Williams (Vail Yearwood), Charles Timm (Ben Egan), Michael P. Murphy (George Paturzo), Dick Biel (Carl Rydell).

Curtis Brown, who studied filmmaking at NYU, makes his feature debut as actor and director with a timely story of a New York City mayoral election. P.R. man Brown is assigned the job of directing the campaign of mayoral candidate Dick Biel. Brown will pay any price to get his man elected.

1102. *Game for Vultures* (1980, New Line Cinema, GB, 90m, c). P Hazel Adair, D James Fargo, W Phillip Baird (based on the novel by Michael Hartmann), PH Alex Thomson, M John Field, ED Peter Tanner, AD Herbert Smith.

LP Richard Harris (David Swansey), Richard Roundtree (Gideon Marunga), Joan Collins (Nicolle), Ray Milland (Col. Brettle), Sven-Bertil Taube (Larry Prescott), Denholm Elliott (Raglan Thistle), Ken Gampu (Sixpence), Tony Osoba (Danny Batten), Neil Hallett (Tony Knight).

In a film just dripping with stereotypes and violence, Rhodesian black man Richard Roundtree, tired of the senseless sanctions, becomes a revolutionary.

Gamma 693 see Night of the Zombies

1103. *Gandhi** (1982, Columbia, GB, 188m, c). P&D Richard Attenborough* (for directing), W John Briley*, PH Billy Williams & Ronnie Taylor*, M Ravi Shankar & George Fenton†, ED John Bloom*, PD Stuart Craig, AD Bob Laing, Ram Yedekar & Norman Dorme*, SD Michael Seirton*, COS John Mollo & Bhanu Athaiya*, SOUND Gerry Humphreys, Robin O'Donoghue, Jonathan Bates & Simon Kaye†, MK Tom Smith†.

LP Ben Kingsley* (Mahatma Gandhi), Candice Bergen (Margaret Bourke-White), Edward Fox (Gen Dyer), John Gielgud (Lord Irwin), Trevor Howard (Judge Broomfield), John Mills (The Viceroy), Martin Sheen (Walker), Rohini Hattangady (Kasturba Gandhi), Ian Charleson (Charlie Andrews), Athol Fugard (Gen. Smuts), Gunter Maria Halmer (Herman Kallenbach), Saeed Jaffrey (Sardar Patel), Roshan Seth (Pandit Nehru), Harsh Nayyar (Nathuram Godse).

Richard Attenborough spent 20 years bringing this epic to the screen. In his film debut, Ben Kingsley is a most credible Gandhi, displaying much of the charisma of the man of peace and revolutionary whose weapons were passive resistance. The sainted martyr's life is shown from the time he discovered his mission in life as a young attorney in South Africa until his assassination by Godse (Harsh Nayyar). As with most epic movies, too much ground is covered by too many people to make for good drama.

1104. *The Garbage Pail Kids Movie* (1987, Topps/Atlantic, 100m, c). P&D Rod Amateau, W Melinda Palmer & Amateau, PH Harvey Genkins, M Michael Lloyd, ED Leon Carrere, PD Robert I. Jillson.

LP Anthony Newley (Capt. Manzini), Mackenzie Astin (Dodger), Katie Barberi (Tangerine), Ron MacLachlan (Juice), Kevin Thompson (Ali Gator), Phil Fondacaro (Greaser Greg), Robert Bell (Foul Phil), Larry Green (Nat Nerd), Arturo Gil (Windy Winston), Sue Rossitto (Messy Tessie), Debbie Lee Carrington (Valerie Vomit), J.P. Amateau (Wally), Marjory Graue (Blythe).

Want to bet that the geniuses behind this affront to the sensitivities of little kids spent their younger lives sitting around having belching and farting contests, enjoying the noises they could make with their hand and armpits, and other equally disgusting activities? Topps Chewing Gum Co. deserves to be boycotted for creating the disgusting Garbage Pail kids, whose names describe their gross specialties. They should never have been allowed out of their garbage pail home and neither should their movie.

1105. *Garbo Talks* (1984, MGM/United Artists, 103m, c). P Burtt Harris & Elliott Kastner, D Sidney Lumet, W Larry Grusin, PH Andrzej Bartkowiak, M Cy Coleman, ED Andrew Mondshein, PD Philip Rosenberg.

LP Anne Bancroft (Estelle Rolfe), Ron Silver (Gilbert Rolfe), Carrie Fisher (Lisa Rolfe), Catherine Hicks (Jane Mortimer), Steven Hill (Walter Rolfe), Howard da Silva (Angelo Dokakis), Dorothy Loudon (Sonya Apollinar), Hermione Gingold (Mr. Morganelli), Betty Comden (Elizabeth Rennick), Nina Zoe (Garbo).

Dying eccentric Anne Bancroft's last wish is to meet reclusive screen legend Greta Garbo. Her son Ron Silver goes to great lengths to fulfill his mother's dream.

1106. *Gardens of Stone* (1987, Tri-Star, 111m, c). P Michael I. Levy & Francis Coppola, D Coppola, W Ronald Bass (based on the novel by Nicholas Proffitt), PH Jordan Cronenweth, M Carmine Coppola, ED Barry Malkin, PD Dean Tavoularis.

LP James Caan (Sgt. Clell Hazard), Anjelica Huston (Samantha Davis), James Earl Jones (Sgt. Major "Goody" Nelson), D.B. Sweeney (Pvt. Jackie Willow), Dean Stockwell (Capt. Homer Thomas), Mary Stuart Masterson (Rachel Feld), Dick Anthony Williams (First Sgt. "Slasher" Williams), Lonette McKee (Betty Rae), Sam Bottoms (Lt. Webber).

Strong performances almost overcome the empty dialogue and funeral music in this poignant story of members of the Arlington National Cemetery's home guard at the height of the Vietnam war. James Caan, veteran of two wars in which he was proud to serve, considers the Vietnam conflict unwinnable. He and another grizzled vet, James Earl Jones, act as Dutch uncles to gung-ho D.B. Sweeney, who wants out of serving at funerals of slain soldiers and to get to the front.

1107. *Gas* (1981, Paramount, Canada, 94m, c). P Claude Heroux, D Les Rose, W Richard Wolf (based on a story by Wolf & Susan Scranton, PH Rene Verzier, M Paul Zaza, ED Patrick Dodd, PD Carol Spier.

LP Donald Sutherland (Nick the Noz), Susan Anspach (Jane Beardsley), Howie Mandel (Matt Lloyd), Sterling Hayden (Duke Stuyvesant), Sandee Curie (Sarah Marshall), Peter Aykroyd (Ed Marshall), Keith Knight (Ira), Helen Shaver (Rhonda).

Unscrupulous oil baron Sterling Hayden causes an oil shortage in a small Midwestern town, rousing the locals to fight tooth and nail to regain their precious supply of gasoline.

1108. *The Gate* (1987, New Century/Vista, Canada, 92m, c). P John Kemeny &Andras Hamori, D Tibor Takacs, W Michael Nankin, PH Thomas Vamos, M Michael Hoenig & J. Peter Robinson, ED Rit Wallis, PD William Beeton, SE Frank Carere & Randall William Cook.

LP Stephen Dorff (Glen), Christa Denton (Alexandra "Al"), Louis Tripp (Terry), Kelly Rowan (Lori Lee), Jennifer Irwin (Linda Lee), Deborah Grover (Mom), Scot Denton (Dad), Ingrid Veninger (Paula), Sean Fagin (Eric).

One weekend while he and his teenage sister Christa Denton are left alone while their parents are away, young Stephen Dorff and his friend Louis Tripp find the Gate to Hell in the former's backyard. By a bizarre twist of fate, the gate is opened. Assorted demons erupt, kidnapping Tripp and Denton, leaving Dorff to encounter the Demon Lord himself. Love conquers evil and the gate is sealed again.

1109. *Gator Bait II: Cajun Justice* (1989, Paramount, 94m, c). P,D&W Ferd & Beverly Sebastian, PH F. Sebastian, M F. Sebastian, Julius Adams & Vernon Rodrique, PD Beverly Sebastian, SE B. Sebastian.

LP Jan MacKenzie (Angelique), Tray Loren (Big T), Paul Muzzcat (Leroy), Brad Kepnick (Luke), Jerry Armstrong (Joe Boy), Ben Sebastian (Elick), Reyn Hubbard (Geke).

Gator Bait, a poorly produced 1973 film starring the late Playmate of the Year Claudia Jennings, became successful in the home-video market. The Sebastians concluded there was an audience for a sequel. City bride Jan MacKenzie needs more gumption if she's going to be able to handle the beer-slurping redneck louts who terrorize her and her Cajun neighbors.

1110. *Geek Maggot Bingo* (1983, Weirdo Films, 73m, c, aka *The Freak from Suckweasel Mountain*). P,D&W Nick Zedd (based on a story by Robert Kirkpatrick & Zedd), PH, ED & PD Zedd.

LP Robert Andrews (Dr. Frankenberry), Brenda Bergman (Buffy), Richard Hell (The Rawhide Kid), Donna Death (Scumbalina), Zacherle (Host), Bruno Zeus (Geeko), Gumby Sangler (Flavian), Jim Giacama (Dean Quagmire), Robert Martin (Street Hawker), Bob Elkin (Victim).

We appreciate it when producers go to the trouble of choosing a name that advises us to pass on their film. Apparently some of the cast were unwilling to give their real names to this spoof of horror films. It lacks any new directions and is mighty short on gags.

1111. *George and Mildred* (1980, Cinema Arts/ITC, GB, 93m, c). P Roy Skeggs, D Peter Frazer Jones, W Dick Sharples (based on the TV series of Johnnie Mortimer & Brian Cooke), M Les Reed, ED Peter Weatherley.

LP Yootha Joyce (Mildred Roper), Brian Murphy (George Roper), Stratford Johns (Harry Pinto), Norman Eshley (Jerry Fourmile), Sheila Fearn (Ann Fourmile), Kenneth Cope (Harvey), David Barry (Elvis), Sue Bond (Marlene).

While celebrating their anniversary at a hotel, Yootha Joyce and Brian Murphy become involved with gangsters. It's a meagre spin-off of a popular British TV comedy.

1112. *George's Island* (1989, Astral, Canada, 89m, c). P Maura O'Connell, D Paul Donovan, W Donovan & O'Connell, PH Les Krizsan, M Marty Simon, ED Stephan Fanfara.

LP Ian Bannen (Capt. Waters), Sheila McCarthy (Miss Birdwood), Maury

Chaykin (Mr. Droonfield), Nathaniel Moreau (George Waters), Vicki Ridler (Bonie), Brian Downey (Mr. Beane), Irene Hogan (Mrs. Beane), Gary Reineke (Capt. Kidd).

Young Nathaniel Moreau is taken from the cluttered shack near Halifax, Nova Scotia, that he shares with his cantankerous, crippled grandfather Ian Bannen. He is sent to live with foster parents Brian Downey and Irene Hogan. They keep their foster charges locked up in windowless rooms behind bars. On Halloween, Bannen rescues his grandson and takes him to an island where reportedly Captain Kidd hid a great treasure. While there, they encounter the pirate captain and his men.

Georgia's Friends *see* ***Four Friends***

1113. *Get Crazy* (1983, Embassy, 92m, c). P Hunt Lowry, D Allen Arkush, W Danny Opatoshu, Henry Rosenblum & David Taylor, PH Thomas Del Ruth, M Michael Boddicker, ED Mark Goldblatt, Kent Beyda & Michael Jablow.

LP Malcolm McDowell (Reggie), Allen [Garfield] Goorwitz (Max), Daniel Stern (Neil), Gail Edwards (Willy), Miles Chapin (Sammy), Ed Begley, Jr. (Colin), Stacey Nelkin (Susie), Bill Henderson (King Blues), Lou Reed (Auden), Howard Kaylan (Capt. Cloud).

It's New Year's Eve, 1983. Allen Goorwitz, the manager of the Saturn Theater, is planning the biggest rock 'n' roll concert of all time, but things don't run smoothly.

Get Well Soon *see* ***Visiting Hours***

Getting Even *see* ***Utilities***

1114. *Getting It On!* (1983, ComWorld, 96m, c, aka *American Voyeur*). P Jan Thompson & William Olsen, D&W William Olsen, PH Austin McKinney, M Rickey Keller, AD James Eric.

LP Martin Yost (Alex), Heather Kennedy (Sally), Jeff Edmond (Nicholas), Kathy Brickmeier (Marilyn), Mark Alan Ferri (Richard), Charles King Bibby (White), Sue Satoris (Mrs. White), Terry Loughlin (Carson).

High school student Martin Yost uses his new video equipment for voyeuristic activities. It's about what you'd expect.

1115. *Getting It Right* (1989, MCEG, 102m, c). P Jonathan D. Krane & Randal Kleiser, D Kleiser, W Elizabeth Jane Howard (based on her novel), PH Clive Tickner, M Colin Towns, ED Chris Kelly.

LP Jesse Birdsall (Gavin Lamb), Helena Bonham Carter (Minerva Munday), Peter Cook (Mr. Adrian), John Gielgud (Sir Gordon Munday), Jane Horrocks (Jenny), Lynn Redgrave (Joan), Shirley Anne Field (Anne), Judy Parfitt (Lady Stella Munday), Richard Huw (Harry), Kevin Drinkwater (Winthrop).

Jesse Birdsall, a 31-year-old West End hairdresser and virgin, lives with his Mum and Dad in a lower-middle-class suburb. He daydreams about girls but is scared to make any moves on them until he's dragged to a party and meets Lynn Redgrave, a woman dressed like a man in drag. Before long, shy sensitive Birdsall becomes quite the ladies' man. It's an enjoyable sex romp.

1116. *Getting Over* (1981, Continental, 108m, c). P John R. Daniels & Cassius V. Weathersby, Jr., D&W Bernie Rollins (based on a story by Rollins & Daniels from an original idea by Daniels), PH & ED Stephen B. Kim, M Johnny Rodgers.

LP John R. Daniels (Mike Barnett), Gwen Brisco (Gwen), Mary Hopkins (Mary), Bernice Givens (Bernice), Sheila Dean (Sheila), Renee Gentry (Renee), Sandra Sully (Sandy), Paulette Gibson (Paulette).

Promoter John R. Daniels forms an all-girl musical group, "The Love Machine." His efforts to promote the group to stardom is the essence of this unexceptional film.

1117. *Ghettoblaster* (1989, Prism, 86m, c). P David De Coteau & John Schouweiler, D Alan L. Stewart, W Clay McBride, PH Thomas Callaway, M Reg Powell & Sam Winans, ED Tony Malanowski, PD Royce Mathew.

LP Richard Hatch (Travis), R.G. Armstrong (Curtis), Courtney Gebhart (Lisa), Del Zamora (Jesus), Diane Moser (Gina), Keymar Reyes (Chato), Marco Hernandez (Hector), Harry Caesar (Mr. Dobson), Rick Telles (Luis), Richard Jaeckel (Mike Henry).

After his grocer father is killed,

Richard Hatch becomes a one-man vigilante to rout African-American and Chicano thugs who are killing each other and assorted innocent bystanders in the inner city.

1118. *Ghost Dance* (1984, Looseyard/Other, GB, 100m, c). P,D&W Ken McMullen, PH Peter Harvey, M David Cunningham, Michael Giles & Janie Muir, ED Robert Hargreaves.

LP Pascale Ogier (Pascale), Leonie Mellinger (Marianne), Jacques Derrida (Himself), Stuart Brisley, Robbie Coltrane, Dominique Pinon.

In this pretentious film, Pascale Ogier and Leonie Mellinger seek the ghosts of the past that haunt the present dream-like world in which they live.

1119. *Ghost Fever* (1987, Mirimax, 86m, c). P Edward Coe & Ron Rich, D Alan Smithee [Lee Madden], W Oscar Brodney, Ron Rich & Richard Egan, PH Zavier Cruz Ruvalcaba, M James Hart, ED James Ruxin, PD Dora Corona.

LP Sherman Hemsley (Buford/Jethro), Luis Avalos (Benny), Jennifer Rhodes (Mme. St. Espirit), Deborah Benson (Linda), Diana Brookes (Lisa), Pepper Martin (Beauregard Lee/Sheriff Clay), Myron Healey (Andrew Lee), Joe Frazier (Terrible Tucker).

This slapstick comedy stars Black Sherman Hemsley and Latino Luis Avalos as Southern cops who get mixed up with Pepper Martin, the ghost of a former slave owner. The latter resents their efforts to get the current owners of his old mansion to make way for a planned freeway through the property. The film suffers from a lot of racial stereotyping.

1120. *Ghost Story* (1981, Universal, 110m, c). P Burt Weissbourd, D John Irvin, W Lawrence D. Cohen (based on the novel by Peter Straub), PH Jack Cardiff, M Philippe Sarde, ED Tom Rolf.

LP Fred Astaire (Ricky Hawthorne), Melvyn Douglas (John Jaffrey), Douglas Fairbanks, Jr. (Edward Wanderley), John Houseman (Sears James), Craig Wasson (Don/David), Alice Krige (Alma Mobley/Eva Galley), Jacqueline Brookes (Milly), Patricia Neal (Stella), Miguel Fernandes (Gregory Bate).

For years, Fred Astaire, Melvyn Douglas, Douglas Fairbanks, Jr., and John Houseman, members of the Chowder Society, have gathered to tell ghost stories. One night a nameless fear invades the group and they all return to their homes where they experience the same nightmare.

1121. *Ghost Town* (1988, TransWorld, 85m, c). P Timothy D. Tennant, D Richard Governor, W Duke Sandefur (based on a story by David Schmoeller), PH Mac Ahlberg, M Harvey R. Cohen, ED Peter Teschner & King Wilder, PD Don De Fina.

LP Franc Luz (Langley), Catherine Hickland (Kate), Jimmie F. Skaggs (Devlin), Penelope Windust (Grace), Bruce Glover (Dealer), Zitto Kazann (Blacksmith), Blake Conway (Harper), Laura Schaefer (Etta).

Trying to locate missing socialite, Catherine Hickland, modern-day sheriff Franc Luz finds a ghost town. It is the home of the undead, cursed and unable to rest in peace. Even in death they are intimidated by Jimmie F. Skaggs, a ruffian who has kidnapped Hickland. Luz will just have to have a showdown with the varmit.

1122. *Ghost Warrior* (1986, Empire, 80m, c, aka *Swordkill*). P Charles Band, D J. Larry Carroll, W Tim Curren, PH Mac Ahlberg, M Richard Band, ED Brad Arensman, PD Pamela B. Warner & Robert Howland.

LP Hiroshi Fujioka (Yoshimitsa), John Calvin (Dr. Richards), Janet Julian (Chris), Charles Lampkin (Willie), Frank Schuller (Det. Berger), Bill Morey (Dr. Anderson), Andy Wood (Dr. Denza), Robert Kino (Prof. Tagachi).

In a violent film, 400-year-old samurai warrior Hiroshi Fujioka is found entombed in ice in a Japanese cave. He is taken to the United States where he is revived. Circumstances set him off on a killing spree in an alien environment.

1123. *Ghost Writer* (1989, Rumar, 94m, c). P David De Coteau & John Schouweiler, D&W Kenneth J. Hall, PH Nicholas von Sternberg, M Reg Powell & Sam Winans, ED Tony Malanowski, PD Royce Mathew.

LP Audrey Landers (Angela Reid), Judy Landers (Billie Blaine), Jeff Conaway (Tom Farrell), Anthony Franciosa (Vincent Carbone), David Doyle, Joey Travolta, John Matuszak, Peter Paul, David Paul, Dick Miller.

Looking more like a TV movie than something made for a theater, this low-key romantic comedy will no doubt make any receipts it has coming only via the home video market. Magazine writer Audrey Landers is looking for some R & R in a Malibu beach house. She discovers it is haunted by the ghost of her aunt's half-sister, played by Audrey's sister Judy, who does her usual dizzy blond bit.

1124. *Ghostbusters* (1984, Columbia, 107m, c). P&D Ivan Reitman, W Dan Aykroyd & Harold Ramis, PH Laszlo Kovacs & Herb Wagreitch, M Elmer Bernstein, ED Sheldon Kahn & David Blewitt, PD John De Cuir, VE Richard Edlund, John Bruno, Mark Vargo & Chuck Gaspar†, SONG "Ghostbusters" by Ray Parker, Jr.†.

LP Bill Murray (Dr. Peter Venkman), Dan Aykroyd (Dr. Raymond Stantz), Sigourney Weaver (Dana Barrett), Harold Ramis (Dr. Egon Spengler), Rick Moranis (Louis Tully), Annie Potts (Janine Melnitz), William Atherton (Walter Peck), Ernie Hudson (Winston Zeddemore), David Margulies (Mayor).

Ghostbusters Bill Murray, Dan Aykroyd, Harold Ramis and Ernie Hudson are a team of comical parapsychologists who rush around New York City capturing annoying spooks. Their biggest problem comes from a giant Pillsbury Doughboy–Michelin Tire man-like apparition who resides in the old apartment building where Sigourney Weaver and Rick Moranis live. These two become possessed by ancient Babylonian spirits, which turns shy, retiring Weaver into an aggressive sex-crazed creature and transforms Moranis from a nerdy accountant to a nerdy nut. The Marx Brothers with Margaret Dumont could have done it better.

1125. *Ghostbusters II* (1989, Columbia, 102m, c). P&D Ivan Reitman, W Harold Ramis & Dan Aykroyd, PH Michael Chapman, M Randy Edelman, ED Sheldon Kahn & Donn Cambern, PD Bo Welch.

LP Bill Murray (Dr. Peter Venkman), Dan Aykroyd (Dr. Raymond Stantz), Sigourney Weaver (Dana Barrett), Harold Ramis (Dr. Egon Spengler), Rick Moranis (Louis Tully), Ernie Hudson (Winston Zeddemore), Annie Potts (Janine Melnitz), Peter MacNicol (Janosz Poha).

Those who didn't get enough of the Ghostbusters team in the original will be thrilled by this sequel which pretty much repeats things that happened in the first film. It seems all the rudeness and hostility of New Yorkers is being fed into a reservoir of negative energy just about to explode. For those who didn't go crazy over the first film, this one is definitely a ho-hum.

1126. *Ghoulies* (1985, Empire, 84m, c). P Jefery Levy, D Luca Bercovici, W Bercovici & Levy, PH Mac Ahlberg, M Richard Band & Shirley Walker, ED Ted Nicolaou, SE John Carl Buechler.

LP Peter Liapis (Jonathan Graves), Lisa Pelikan (Rebecca), Michael Des Barres (Malcolm Graves), Jack Nance (Wolfgang), Peter Risch (Grizzel), Tamara De Treaux (Greedigut), Scott Thomson (Mike), Ralph Seymour (Mark, Toad Boy), Mariska Hargitay (Donna), Keith Joe Dick (Dick).

In this tasteless production, young Peter Liapis gets more than he expects when he inherits his father's house and discovers it crawling with evil little creatures, the ghoulies.

1127. *Ghoulies II* (1988, Empire, 90m, c). P&D Albert Band, W Dennis Paoli (based on a story by Charlie Dolan), PH Sergio Salvati, M Fuzzbee Morse, ED Barry Zetlin, PD Giovanni Natalucci, SE John Carl Buechler.

LP Damon Martin (Larry), Royal Dano (Uncle Ned), Phil Fondacaro (Sir Nigel), J. Downing (P. Hardin), Kerry Remsen (Nicole), Dale Wyatt (Dixie), Jon Maynard Pennell (Bobby), Sasha Jenson (Teddy), Starr Andreeff (Alice).

Here's more of the same dull stuff with special effects which look like they were done by a novice. The ghoulie puppets are kidnapped from a group of satanists by a priest who's unsuccessful in destroying them. The creatures take up residence in a haunted house which is part of a travelling carnival and become quite a hit with the patrons and vice versa—the ghoulies think the customers are delicious.

1128. The G.I. Executioner (1985, Troma, 82m, c, aka *Wits End; Dragon Lady*). P Marvin Farkas, D&W Joel M. Reed (based on a story by Keith Lorenz & Ian Ward), PH Farkas, M Elliot Chiprut & Jason Garfield, ED Victor Kanefsky.

LP Tom Keena (Dave Dearborn), Victoria Racimo (Foon Mai Lee), Angelique Pettyjohn (Bonnie), Janet Wood, Brian Walden, Peter Gernert, Walter Hill.

Set in Singapore, Vietnam veteran and soldier of fortune Tom Keena becomes an executioner as he tracks down a defecting scientist from China. The film was originally shot in 1971 and sat on the shelf until Troma got the nerve to release it.

1129. The Gig (1985, Gig Company, 92m, c). P Norman I. Cohen, D&W Frank D. Gilroy, PH Jeri Sopanen, ED Rick Shaine.

LP Wayne Rogers (Marty Flynn), Cleavon Little (Marshall Wilson), Andrew Duncan (Jack Larmon), Daniel Nalbach (Arthur Winslow), Jerry Matz (Aaron Wohl), Warren Vache (Gil Macrae), Joe Silver (Abe Mitgang), Celia Bressack (Lucy), Susan Egbert (Laura Macrae), Karen Ashley (Janet Larmon).

In this typical buddy film, a group of men get together once a week to play Dixieland. It turns out to be a mixed blessing for them when they are offered a two week gig, playing in the Catskill resort area of New York state.

1130. Gimme an "F" (1984, 20th Century–Fox, 100m, c). P Martin Poll, D Paul Justman, W Jim Hart, PH Mario Di Leo, M Jan Hammer, ED Tom Walls, PD Kim Colefax.

LP Stephen Shellen (Tom Hamilton), Mark Keyloun (Roscoe), Jennifer C. Cooke (Pam), Beth Miller (Mary Ann), Daphne Ashbrook (Phoebe), Karen Kelly (Lead Demon), Sarah M. Miles (Eileen), John Karlen (Bucky Berkshire/"Dr. Spirit.")

In a disgustingly silly teenage sex film, Stephen Shellen is a handsome cheerleading instructor at "Camp Beaver View" run by unscrupulous John Karlen. Shellen does a dance while taking a shower, not realizing that a group of cheerleaders are spying on him—or maybe he does, since he's taking a shower wearing shorts.

Not only does this film earn an "F," it deserves to be expelled.

1131. The Girl (1987, Shapiro Ent., GB, 104m, c). P&D Arne Mattson, W Ernest Hotch, PH Tomislav Pinter, M Alfie Kabiljo & Ilan Kabiljo, ED Derek Trigg, PD Anders Barreus.

LP Franco Nero (John Berg), Bernice Stegers (Eva Berg), Clare Powney (Pat Carlsson, the Girl), Frank Brennan (Bill Lindberg), Mark Robinson (Hans), Clifford Rose (Gen. Carlsson), Rosie Jaucken (Mrs. Carlsson).

Fourteen-year-old Clare Powney seduces attorney Franco Nero. The two are followed to an island retreat by Frank Brennan, who hopes to blackmail Nero. Powney seduces him and then coldly plunges two knives into his back. Nero sets the corpse ablaze and the two return home to his apartment. One day Powncy awakens early and kills Nero, shifting the blame to Nero's wife Bernice Stegers' lover.

1132. The Girl in a Swing (1989, Panorama Film Intl., US/GB, 117m, c). P Just Betzer & Benni Korzen, D Gordon Hessler, W Hessler (based on the novel by Richard Adams), PH Claus Loof, M Carl Davis, ED Robert Gordon, PD Rob Schilling.

LP Meg Tilly (Karin Foster), Rupert Frazer (Alan Foster), Nicholas Le Prevost (The Vicar), Elspet Gray (Mrs. Dresland), Lorna Heilbron (Flick), Claire Shepherd (Angela), Jean Both (Mrs. Taswell), Sophie Thursfield (Deidre), Lynsey Baxter (Barbara).

Ultimately, audiences learn why German-born secretary Meg Tilly has a death wish and can't find happiness with shy British ceramics dealer Rupert Frazer, even after she buys a rare ceramic treasure "The Girl in a Swing." It seems at some earlier point she had killed her baby (perhaps in *Agnes of God*?). The lovemaking scenes are graphic, but not particularly sexy. The suspense, compared to an Alfred Hitchcock movie by those touting it, is only so-so.

1133. The Girl in the Picture (1985, Rank, GB, 91m, c). P Paddy Higson, D&W Cary Parker, PH Dick Pope, M Ron Geesin, ED Bert Eeles, PD Alan J. Wands.

LP John Gordon-Sinclair (Alan), Irina Brook (Mary), David McKay (Ken), Gregor Fisher (Bill), Caroline Guthrie (Annie), Paul Young (Smiley), Rikki Fulton (The Minister), Joyce Deans, Valerie Holloway, Wendy Holloway.

Glasgow photographer John Gordon-Sinclair feels his relationship with his live-in girlfriend Irina Brook is going stale. He wants to end it, but doesn't have the nerve to tell her. Meanwhile, Gordon-Sinclair's assistant David McKay has fallen in love with an unknown girl in a picture. The film ultimately sorts out these romantic problems.

1134. *Girls' School Screamers* (1986, Troma Team, 85m, c). P John P. Finegan, Pierce J. Keating & James W. Finegan, D John P. Finegan, W John P. Finegan (based on a story by John P. Finegan, Katie Keating & Pierce Keating), PH Albert R. Jordan, M John Hodian, ED Thomas R. Rondinella, PD John P. Finegan.

LP Mollie O'Mara (Jackie/Jennifer), Sharon Christopher (Elizabeth), Mari Butler (Kate), Beth O'Malley (Karen), Karen Krevitz (Susan), Marcia Hinton (Adelle), Monica Antonucci (Rosemary).

Chalk this up as just another of the many films in which pretty young things' lives and limbs are in jeopardy from a madman.

1135. *Girls Just Want to Have Fun* (1985, New World, 87m, c). P Chuck Russell, D Alan Metter, W Amy Spies, PH Thomas Ackerman, M Thomas Newman, ED Lorenzo DeStefano, PD Jeffrey Staggs.

LP Sarah Jessica Parker (Janey Glenn), Lee Montgomery (Jeff Malene), Morgan Woodward (J.P. Sands), Jonathan Silverman (Drew), Helen Hunt (Lynne Stone), Holly Gagnier (Natalie Sands), Ed Lauter (Col. Glenn).

Trying to cash-in on Cyndi Lauper's hit record of the same name, the film finds Army brat Sarah Jessica Parker and her friends going to great lengths to win the chance to dance on a national TV show.

1136. *Girls Night Out* (1984, Aries, 96m, c, aka *The Scaremaker*). P Anthony N. Gurvis, D Robert Deubel, W Gil Spencer, Jr., Joe Bolster, Kevin Kurgis &

Gurvis, PH Joe Rivers, ED Arthur Ginsberg, PD Howard Cummings.

LP Julie Montgomery, James Carroll, Suzanne Barnes, Rutanya Alda, Hal Holbrook, David Holbrook, Lauren-Marie Taylor, Al McGuire, Matthew Dunn.

Hal Holbrook, head of campus security, sets out to stop a slasher who is murdering sorority girls participating in a scavenger hunt.

1137. *Giro City* (1982, Cinegate, GB, 102m, c, aka *And Nothing But the Truth*). P Sophi Balhetchet & David Payne, D&W Karl Francis, PH Curtis Clark, M Alun Francis, ED Neil Thomson.

LP Glenda Jackson (Sophie), Jon Finch (O'Mally), Kenneth Colley (Martin), James Donnelly (James), Emrys James (Williams), Karen Archer (Brigitte), Simon Jones (Henderson), Huw Ceredig (Elwyn Davies).

Glenda Jackson and Jon Finch, a TV director and a reporter, respectively, cause trouble when they film a fugitive IRA leader.

1138. *Give My Regards to Broad Street* (1984, 20th Century–Fox, GB, 108m, c). P Andros Epaminondas, D Peter Webb, W Paul McCartney, PH Ian McMillan, M McCartney, ED Peter Beston, M/L McCartney.

LP Paul McCartney (Paul), Bryan Brown (Steve), Ringo Starr (Ringo), Barbara Bach (Journalist), Linda McCartney (Linda), Tracey Ullman (Sandra), Ralph Richardson (Jim), John Burgess (Chauffeur).

Audiences are treated to several fine songs by Paul McCartney in an otherwise unexceptional story of a rock star searching for his stolen master recordings.

1139. *Glass* (1989, Oilrag Prod., Australia, 93m, c). P Patrick Fitzgerald & Chris Kennedy, D&W Kennedy, PH Pieter de Vries, M Mario Gregory, ED James Bradley, PD Kerry Ainsworth.

LP Lisa Peers (Julie Vickery), Allan Lovell (Richard Vickery), Adam Stone (Peter Breen), Natalie McCurry (Alison Baumer), Bernard Clisby (Inspector Ambrosoll), Rowan Jackson (Charlie), Lucinda Walker-Powell (Dianne).

Set in Sydney, this small-scale thriller revolves around yuppie business executive Allan Lovell, who has been fleeced by his lawyer Adam Stone. The latter is also having an affair with Lovell's wife Lisa Peers. Death is the reflection awaiting someone.

1140. *The Glass Menagerie* (1987, Cineplex Odeon, 134m, c). P Burtt Harris, D Paul Newman, W Tennessee Williams (based on his play), PH Michael Ballhaus, M Henry Mancini, ED David Ray, PD Tony Walton.

LP Joanne Woodward (Amanda Wingfield), John Malkovich (Tom Wingfield), Karen Allen (Laura Wingfield), James Naughton (Gentleman Caller).

At the intermission of a 1986 performance of this Tennessee Williams play starring Joanne Woodward, Karen Allen, Treat Williams and James Naughton at Long Wharf Theater in New Haven, Connecticut, we overheard two well-dressed matrons, apparently in their early 40s, discussing the play. They expressed disappointment with Woodward's interpretation of the role of a one-time belle, anxious to give her shy, crippled daughter Allen a taste of the good life, and pestering her son to bring home a gentleman caller for his sister. The ladies claimed Woodward didn't stack up to Laurette Taylor who originated the role of Amanda on Broadway. We had to resist the temptation of accusing them of being phony theater snobs. Taylor played the role in 1945, before these ladies were much out of diapers. Whether Taylor's work is superior to that of Woodward, we can't say. But it compares favorably to that of Gertrude Lawrence, who essayed the role in the 1950 film production, and to that of Katharine Hepburn in a 1973 made-for-TV movie.

1141. *Gleaming the Cube* (1989, 20th Century–Fox, 104m, c). P Lawrence Turman & David Foster, D Graeme Clifford, W Michael Tolkin, PH Reed Smoot, M Jay Ferguson, ED John Wright, PD John Muto.

LP Christian Slater (Brian Kelly), Steven Bauer (Al Lucero), Richard Herd (Ed Lawndale), Le Tuan (Colonel Trac), Min Luong (Tina Trac), Art Chudabala (Vinh Kelly), Ed Lauter (Mr. Kelly).

"Gleaming the cube" refers to achieving skateboarding cosmic bliss. Christian Slater looks like the kind of kid you don't want your kids associating with. Besides skateboarding, a movie subject whose time apparently has come, the film also details the death of young Vietnamese Chudabala, the adopted brother of Slater.

1142. *Glitch* (1988, Omega, 90m, c). P,D&W Nico Mastorakis, PH Peter Jensen, M Tom Marolda, ED Mastorakis & George Rosenberg, PD Gary New.

LP Will Egan (Todd), Steve Donmyer (Bo), Julia Nickson (Michelle), Dick Gautier (Julius Lazar), Ted Lange (DuBois), Teri Weigel (Lydia), Dan Speaker (Brucie).

Released straight to video, this raunchy comedy has Will Egan and Steve Donmyer figure that being associated with Dick Gautier's new movie *Sex and Violence* will be a good way to meet and get pretty girls into their beds.

1143. *Gloria* (1980, Columbia, 123m, c). P Sam Shaw, D&W John Cassavetes, PH Fred Schuler, M Bill Conti, ED George Villasenor, PD Rene D'Auriac & Fred Schuler.

LP Gena Rowlands† (Gloria Swenson), Juan Adames (Phil Dawn), Buck Henry (Jack Dawn), Julie Carmen (Jeri Dawn), Lupe Garnica (Margarita Vargas), Jessica Castillo (Joan Dawn), Tony Knesich (1st Man/Gangster), Tom Noonan (2nd Man/Gangster).

Gena Rowlands gives a gutsy performance as a former mobster's moll who finds she must meet violence with violence when she takes on the job of protecting Juan Adames, the son of a slain neighbor, from the mob.

1144. *Glory* (1989, Tri-Star, 122m, c). P Freddie Fields, D Edward Zwick, W Kevin Jarre (based on books *Lay This Laurel* by Lincoln Kirstein and *One Gallant Rush: Robert Gould Shaw and His Brave Black Regiment* by Peter Burchard, and letters of Col. Robert Gould Shaw), PH Freddie Francis*, M James Horner, ED Steven Rosenblum†, PD Norman Garwood*, SOUND Russell Williams*.

LP Matthew Broderick (Col. Robert Gould Shaw), Denzel Washington* (Pvt. Trip), Cary Elwes (Maj. Cabot Forbes), Morgan Freeman (Sgt. Maj. John Rawlins), Jihmi Kennedy (Pvt. Jupiter Sharts), Andre Braugher (Pvt. Thomas

Searles), John Finn (Sgt. Maj. Mulcahy), Alan North (Gov. John A. Andrew), Bob Gunton (Gen. Harker), Cliff DeYoung (Col. James Montgomery), Raymond St. Jacques (Frederick Douglass).

In a letter to his mother just prior to the Battle of Antietam on September 17, 1862, young white abolitionist Robert Gould Shaw wrote, "We fight for men and women whose poetry is not yet written." This stirring tribute to the black soldiers who fought for the Union cause in the Civil War is the story of the 54th Regiment of Massachusetts Volunteer Infantry, the first black fighting unit. Before the war was over, 186,107 blacks had fought for the Union and 37,300 of them had died. Performances by Matthew Broderick as the young Union commander of the black regiment and Oscar winners Denzel Washington and Morgan Freeman as two of the black fighting men, will endow viewers with memories that will last a lifetime. The photography is spectacular, making Freddie Francis' Oscar richly deserved. It's amazing that the film wasn't nominated as one of the five best pictures of the year.

1145. *The Glove* (1980, Pro International, 90m, c, aka *Blood Mad*). P Julian Roffman, D Ross Hagen, W Roffman & Hubert Smith, PH Gary Graver, M Robert O. Ragland, ED Bob Fitzgerald.

LP John Saxon (Sam Kellough), Roosevelt Grier (Victor Hale), Joanna Cassidy (Sheila Michaels), Joan Blondell (Mrs. Fitzgerald), Jack Carter (Walter Stratton), Keenan Wynn (Bill Schwartz), Aldo Ray (Prison Guard).

Ex-cop, ex-ballplayer John Saxon, now a bounty hunter, is offered a $20,000 fee if he brings in Roosevelt Grier. The latter is a psychotic with redeeming qualities, except when he puts on his steel gloves.

Gnaw see Food of the Gods II

1146. *Go Tell It on the Mountain* (1984, Learning in Focus, 96m, c). P Calvin Skaggs, D Stan Lathan, W Gus Edwards & Leslie Lee (based on the novel by James Baldwin), PH Hiro Narita, M Webster Lewis, ED Jay Freund, PD Charles Bennett.

LP Paul Winfield (Gabriel Grimes), Rosalind Cash (Aunt Florence), James Bond III (John Grimes), Roderick Wimberly (Roy Grimes), Olivia Cole (Elizabeth Grimes), Ving Rhames (Young Gabriel), Alfre Woodard (Esther).

James Bond III impersonates author James Baldwin in this semiautobiographical story of a young black boy who struggles to win the approval and understanding of his stern, unbending, white-hating father, Paul Winfield.

1147. *Gobots: Battle of the Rocklords* (1986, Atlantic, animated, 75m, c). P Kay Wright, D Ray Patterson, W Jeff Segal, MD Hoyt Curtin, PD Davis Doi.

VOICES Margot Kidder (Solitaire), Roddy McDowall (Nuggit), Michael Nouri (Boulder), Telly Savalas (Magmar), Arthur Bughardt (Turbo), Ike Eisenmann (Nick), Bernard Erhard (Cy-Kill), Marilyn Lightstone (Crasher).

This Hanna and Barbera feature traces the history of the Gobots from Gobotron who have been entrusted with protecting Earth from the evil Renegades.

1148. *The Gods Must Be Crazy* (1984, 20th Century–Fox, Botswana, 109m, c). P,D&W Jamie Uys, PH Buster Reynolds, Robert Lewis & Uys, M John Boshoff, ED Uys.

LP Marius Weyers (Andrew Steyn), Sandra Prinsloo (Kate Thompson), Louw Verwey (Sam Boga), N!xau (Xi), James Uys (The Reverend), Michael Thys (Mpudi), Nic De Jager (Jack Hind), Paddy O'Byrne (Narrator).

Made in 1981, in 1984 the film became the biggest foreign-film box-office smash in the world when released in the United States. The story features Bushman N!xau and his first encounter with civilization, pretty young schoolteacher Sandra Prinsloo, seeking and finding adventure, and bungling, painfully shy scientist Marius Weyers who attempts to woo her. The innocent charm of N!xau seems to be the biggest reason for the film's success.

1149. *The Gods Must Be Crazy 2* (1989, 20th Century–Fox, Botswana, 99m, c). P Boet Troskie, D&W Jamie Uys, PH Buster Reynolds, M Charles Fox, ED Renee Engelbrecht & Ivan Hall, NARRATOR Paddy O'Byrne.

LP N!xau (Xixo), Lena Farugia (Dr.

Ann Taylor), Hans Strydom (Dr. Stephen Marshall), Eiros (Xiri), Nadies (Xisa), Erick Bowen (Mateo), Treasure Tshabalala (Timi), Pierre Van Pletzen (George), Lourens Swanepoel (Brenner).

In this desert farce sequel to the surprising 1984 hit, tongue-clicking Kalahari tribesman N!xau is back dealing with the lunacies of modern civilization. When his children are innocently borne away on the trailer truck of unsuspecting ivory poachers, he has to leave his peaceful home and tribe to find them. Some critics claim that both films treat the blacks like amusing, simple children.

1150. *God's Will* (1989, Power & Light Prod., 100m, c). P,D&W Julia Cameron, PH William Nusbaum, M Christopher [Hambone] Cameron.

LP Marge Kotlisky (God), Daniel Region (Peter Potter), Laura Margolis (Gillian Potter), Domenica Cameron-Scorsese (Victoria Potter), Linda Edmond (Gwyneth), Mitchell Canoff (Mitchell), Holly Fulger (Hedy).

After shooting had wrapped on this 16mm picture for the "On Screen" women's film festival in San Francisco, the production soundtrack was stolen. What's left hardly gives audiences an opportunity to fairly judge the story of a recently deceased divorced couple who squabble in heaven over what is to become of the daughter they have left behind.

1151. *Goin' All the Way* (1982, Saturn Intl., 85m, c). P Frank Rubin & Gary Gibbs, D Robert Freedman, W Roger Stone & Jack Cooper, M Richard Hieronymus.

LP Dan Waldman, Deborah Van Rhyn, Joshua Cadman, Sherie Miller, Joe Cooligan, Sylvia Summers, Eileen Davidson.

Seventeen-year-old Deborah Van Rhyn decides she must prove her love for boyfriend Dan Waldman by going "all the way." Are girls still buying that line?

1152. *Going Ape!* (1981, Paramount, 87m, c). P Robert L. Rosen, D&W Jeremy Joe Kronsberg, PH Frank V. Phillips, M Elmer Bernstein, ED John W. Wheeler.

LP Tony Danza (Foster), Jessica Walter (Fiona), Stacey Nelkin (Cynthia), Danny De Vito (Lazlo), Art Metrano (Joey), Frank Sivero (Bad Habit), Rick

Hurst (Brandon), Howard Mann (Jules Cohen), Joseph Maher (Gridley).

Tony Danza, late of TV's "Taxi" and before his success with "Who's the Boss," co-starred with three scene-stealing orangutans. He inherited them from a circus owner, along with $5 million that he may keep if he takes care of the primates for five years. Otherwise, the beasts and the money go to a zoo. Never work with actors more appealing than you are, Tony. Ask Ronald Reagan about Bonzo.

1153. *Going Bananas* (1988, Cannon, 93m, c). P Menahem Golan & Yoram Globus, D Boaz Davidson, W Golan (based on the *Kofiko* books by Tamar Borenstein), PH Joseph Wain, M Pino Donaggio, ED Natan Zahavi & Bruria Davidson.

LP Dom DeLuise (Big Bad Joe), Jimmie Walker (Mozambo), David Mendenhall (Ben), Deep Roy (Bonzo), Warren Berlinger (Palermo), Herbert Lom (Mackintosh), Leo Sparrowhawk (Ship's captain).

It's hard to believe that anyone would even contemplate making this movie. Dom DeLuise is an African big game hunter who escorts spoiled brat David Mendenhall through the jungle with the help of wacky guide Jimmie Walker.

1154. *Going Berserk* (1983, Universal, 85m, c). P Claude Heroux, D David Steinberg, W Steinberg & Dana Olsen, PH Bobby Byrne, M Tom Scott, ED Donn Cambern, PD Peter Lansdown Smith.

LP John Candy (John Bourgignon), Joe Flaherty (Chick Leff), Eugene Levy (Sal di Pasquale), Alley Mills (Nancy Reese), Pat Hingle (Ed Reese), Ann Bronston (Patti), Eve Brent Ashe (Mrs. Reese), Elizabeth Kerr (Grandmother Reese), Paul Dooley (Dr. Ted), Richard Libertini (Sun Yi).

John Candy is funny, so the failure of this unfunny movie more than likely deserves to be laid at the feet of director-writer David Steinberg. Candy, a doltish limousine driver, is engaged to the daughter of a pompous congressman. Candy is kidnapped by a religious sect and hypnotized into making an assassination attempt on his future father-in-law.

1155. *Going Undercover* (1988, Miramax, GB, 88m, c, aka *Yellow Pages*). P

John D. Schofield & Jefferson Colegate-Stone, D&W James Kenelm Clarke, PH John Coquillon, M Alan Hawkshaw, ED Eric Boyd-Perkins & Danny Retz.

LP Chris Lemmon (Henry Brilliant), Jean Simmons (Maxine De La Hunt), Lea Thompson (Marigold De La Hunt), Mills Watson (Billy O'Shea), Viveca Lindfors (Mrs. Bellinger), Nancy Cartwright (Stephanie).

Brilliant's his name, bungling's his game. Bubble-headed Chris Lemmon is hired by Jean Simmons to protect her stepdaughter Lea Thompson in this poor lame-brained sex comedy.

1156. *The Gold Diggers* (1984, BFI, GB, 89m, c). P Nita Amy & Donna Grey, D Sally Potter, W Lindsay Cooper, Rose English & Potter, PH Babette Mangolte, M Cooper, ED Potter.

LP Julie Christie (Ruby), Colette Laffont (Celeste), Hilary Westlake (Mother), David Gale (Expert), Tom Osborn (Assistant), Jacky Lansley (Tapdancer), George Yiasoumi (Stage Manager), Trevor Stuart (Man).

In a fantasy film, black Frenchwoman and computer operator Colette Laffont and blonde dancer Julie Christie both are digging for "gold."

1157. *The Golden Child* (1986, Paramount, 96m, c). P Edward S. Feldman & Robert D. Wachs, D Michael Ritchie, W Dennis Feldman, PH Donald E. Thorin, M Michel Colombier, ED Richard A. Harris, PD J. Michael Riva.

LP Eddie Murphy (Chandler Jarrell), Charles Dance (Sardo Numspa), Charlotte Lewis (Kee Nang), Victor Wong (The Old Man), Randall "Tex" Cobb (Til), James Hong (Dr. Hong), J.L. Reate (The Golden Child).

Eddie Murphy's presence in this turkey guaranteed that it was a box-office hit. It's an illogical mixing of genres. J.L. Reate, a perfect child with magical powers, is kidnapped by Charles Dance. An ancient prediction foresaw this and also that only Murphy could rescue the holy child. Nothing can rescue this poor excuse for "Indiana Jones meets Saturday Night Live."

1158. *The Golden Seal* (1983, Goldwyn/New Realm, 94m, c). P Samuel Goldwyn, Jr., D Frank Zuniga, W John

Groves (based on the novel *A River Ran Out of Eden* by James Vance Marshall, PH Eric Saarinen, M Dana Kaproff, ED Robert Q. Lovett, PD Douglas Higgins.

LP Steve Railsback (Jim Lee), Penelope Milford (Tania Lee), Michael Beck (Crawford), Torquil Campbell (Eric), Sandra Seacat (Gladys), Seth Sakai (Semeyon), Richard Narita (Alexei), Peter Anderson (Tom).

Set on an isolated island in British Columbia, this appealing family adventure stars 10-year-old Torquil Campbell. He makes friends with a golden seal whom he must protect from adult greed.

1159. *The Gong Show Movie* (1980, Universal, 89m, c). P Budd Granoff, D Chuck Barris, W Barris & Robert Downey, PH Richard C. Glouner, M Milton De Lugg, ED James Mitchell.

LP Chuck Barris (Himself), Robin Altman (Red), Mabel King (Mabel), Lillie Shelton (Mama), Jaye P. Morgan (Herself), James B. Douglas (Buddy Didio), Rip Taylor (Maitre D').

This film provides further evidence that no matter how bad an idea for a movie is, some idiots will throw money at it and see that it's produced. The idiotic and obnoxious TV program which exploited the dreams of untalented people to appear on the tube is just as idiotic and obnoxious on the big screen, probably more so.

1160. *The Good Father* (1987, Skouras, GB, 90m, c). P Ann Scott, D Mike Newell, W Christopher Hampton (based on the novel by Peter Prince), PH Michael Coulter, M Richard Hartley, ED Peter Hollywood, PD Adrian Smith.

LP Anthony Hopkins (Bill Hooper), Jim Broadbent (Roger Miles), Harriet Walter (Emmy Hooper), Fanny Viner (Cheryl Miles), Simon Callow (Mark Varner), Joanne Whalley (Mary Hall), Miriam Margolyes (Jane Powell).

After having lost custody of his own son in a court case, bitter Anthony Hopkins rallies to the support of his buddy Jim Broadbent in the latter's struggle to win custody of his son. Broadbent's wife Fanny Viner plans to take the boy with her when she moves to Australia with her lesbian lover.

Good Morning Babilonia see ***Good Morning Babylon***

1161. *Good Morning Babylon* (1987, Vestron, Italy/Fr./US, 116m, c, aka *Good Morning Babilonia*). P Giuliani G. De Negri, D Paolo Taviani & Vittorio Taviani, W P&V Taviani & Tonino Guerra (based on an idea by Lloyd Fonvielle), PH Giuseppe Lanci, M Nicola Piovani, ED Roberto Perpignani.

LP Vincent Spano (Nicola Bonnano), Joaquim de Almeida (Andrea Bonnano), Greta Scacchi (Edna), Desiree Becker (Mabel), Omero Antonutti (Bonnano), Charles Dance (D.W. Griffith), Berangere Bonvoisin (Mrs. Moglie Griffith).

Vincent Spano and Joaquim de Almeida are two Italian brothers who come to America and find a niche as artists working on the Babylon set in D.W. Griffith's masterpiece *Intolerance*. The style of the movie is operatic, and the characters have about as much substance as those appearing in grand opera.

1162. *Good Morning, Vietnam* (1987, Touchstone, 120m, c). P Mark Johnson, Larry Brezner, Ben Moses & Harry Benn, D Barry Levinson, W Mitch Markowitz, PH Peter Sova, M Alex North, ED Stu Linder, PD Roy Walker.

LP Robin Williams† (Adrian Cronauer), Forest Whitaker (Edward Garlick), Tung Thanh Tran (Tuan), Chintara Sukapatana (Trinh), Bruno Kirby (Lt. Steven Hauk), Robert Wuhl (Marty Lee Dreiwitz), J.T. Walsh (Sgt. Major Dickerson), Noble Willingham (Gen. Taylor), Richard Edson (Pvt. Abersold), Juney Smith (Phil McPherson), Richard Portnow (Dan "The Man" Levitan), Floyd Vivino (Eddie Kirk), Cu Ba Nguyen (Jimmy Wah).

Robin Williams finally finds a movie role which fits his unique talents. In Saigon in 1956, he is an outrageous morning disc jockey on the local Armed Forces Radio network. He has been brought in by Noble Willingham to boost the morale of the troops. His far-out humor, his new playlist of blasting rock 'n' roll songs, and his irreverent political commentary does exactly that — but it upsets Bruno Kirby and J.T. Walsh, who run the station. Williams tries to get to know the Vietnamese people, particularly beautiful young Chintara Sukapatana, and her younger brother Tung Thanh Tran. The latter turns out to be in the employ of the Viet Cong. It's an entertaining, funny and occasionally moving film.

1163. *The Good Mother* (1988, Buena Vista, 103m, c). P Arnold Glimcher, D Leonard Nimoy, W Michael Bortman (based on the novel by Sue Miller), PH David Watkin, M Elmer Bernstein, ED Peter E. Berger, PD Stan Jolley.

LP Diane Keaton (Anna Dunlap), Liam Neeson (Leo Cutter), Jason Robards (Muth), Ralph Bellamy (Grandfather), Teresa Wright (Grandmother), James Naughton (Brian Dunlap), Joe Morton (Frank Williams), Asia Vieira (Molly), Katey Sagal (Ursula), Tracy Griffith (Babe).

This is a dishonest movie. Everything is set up to produce phony dramatic situations which might have been avoided with a little common sense. Diane Keaton is the divorced mother of six-year-old Asia Vieira. Her relationship with her ex-husband James Naughton seems amicable. Keaton meets Irish sculptor Liam Neeson, who moves in with mother and daughter. One night when they are making love, Vieira, frightened by a nightmare moves into bed with the couple. On another occasion while Keaton is away, Vieira walks in on Neeson as he is showering. She notes his penis and asks if she may touch it. Thinking Keaton would approve (why, we're not sure), he allows the inspection. Soon after Vieira casually reports these goings on to Daddy. He takes Keaton to court as an unfit mother and wins custody of the child. Neeson gets the boot and Keaton seems strangely serene, despite losing her child. Everything about the movie feels contrived to arrive at the strange unhappy ending. A different outcome could have easily been reached had only the adult participants acted more maturely.

1164. *Good to Go* (1986, Island, 87m, c). P Doug Dilge & Sean Ferrer, D&W Blaine Novak, PH Peter Sinclair, M Various Artists, ED Gib Jaffe, Kimberly Logan & D.C. Stringer.

LP Art Garfunkel (S.D.), Robert DoQui (Max), Harris Yulin (Harrigan), Reginald Daughtry (Little Beats), Richard Brooks (Chemist), Paula Davis

(Evette), Richard Bauer (Editor), Michael White (Gil).

This film features go-go music from the ghettoes of Washington, D.C., which did not quite catch on nationwide. Art Garfunkel is a journalist framed for murder and rape.

1165. *The Good Wife* (1987, Atlantic, Australia, 97m, c, aka *The Umbrella Woman*). P Jan Sharp, D Ken Cameron, W Peter Kenna, PH James Bartle, M Cameron Allan, ED John Scott, PD Sally Campbell.

LP Rachel Ward (Marge Hills), Bryan Brown (Sonny Hills), Steven Vidler (Sugar Hills), Sam Neill (Neville Gifford), Jennifer Claire (Daisy), Bruce Barry (Archie), Peter Cummins (Ned Hooper), Carole Skinner (Mrs. Gibson), Clarissa Kaye-Mason (Mrs. Jackson), Barry Hill (Mr. Fielding).

While Rachel Ward's husband Bryan Brown is a good provider, he's a dud in the sack. So is his brother Steven Vidler, who has a go at Ward with Brown's blessing. Ward develops an obsessive yearning for handsome stranger Sam Neill, who has bedded every woman in town, except Ward. She begs him to take her with him when he's forced to flee the town after his latest Don Juan escapade. Instead Neill merely throws her off his train. Ward returns to her dull marriage with Brown.

1166. *Goodbye Cruel World* (1983, Sharp Features, 90m, c). P Louis Sardonis & Leopold Zahn, D David Irving, W Nicholas Niciphor & Dick Shawn, PH Jerry Hartleben.

LP Dick Shawn, Cynthia Sikes, Chuck Mitchell.

Distraught television anchorman Dick Shawn has plans to commit suicide, but first he intends to spend one final day visiting and filming the relatives that have driven him to the brink.

1167. *The Goodbye People* (1984, Embassy, 104m, c). P David V. Picker, D&W Herb Gardner (based on his stage play), PH John Lindley, ED Rick Shaine, PD Tony Walton.

LP Judd Hirsch (Arthur Korman), Martin Balsam (Max Silverman), Pamela Reed (Nancie Scot), Ron Silver (Eddie Bergson), Michael Tucker (Michael Silverman), Gene Saks (Marcus Soloway), Sammy Smith (George Mooney).

Frustrated sculptor Judd Hirsch and about-to-be-single-again Pamela Reed help her 70-year-old father Martin Balsam realize his dream of once again opening his hot-dog stand at Coney Island.

1168. *Goodbye Pork Pie* (1981, Brent Walker, New Zealand, 105m, c). P Nigel Hutchinson & Geoff Murphy, D Murphy, W Murphy & Ian Mune, PH Alun Bollinger, M John Charles, ED Mike Horton.

LP Tony Barry, Kelly Johnson, Claire Oberman, Shirley Gruar, Jackie Lowitt, Don Selwyn, Shirley Dunn, Paki Cherrington, Christine Lloyd.

With the police hot on their trail, three fun-loving New Zealanders speed along on a 1,000 mile journey in a new, small, yellow, stolen car.

1169. *Goodnight, Sweet Marilyn* (1989, Studio Ent., 94m, c). P,D&W Larry Buchanan, PH Miles Anderson, M Uncredited, ED Jeff D. Buchanan & L. Buchanan.

LP Misty Rowe (Norma Jean Baker), Paula Lane (Marilyn Monroe), Jeremy Slate (Mesquite), Terrance Locke (Ralph Johnson), Patch MacKenzie (Ruth Latimer), Preston Hanson (Hal James), Marty Zagon (Irving).

Concentrating on the last day of the life of Marilyn Monroe, a fictional friend Jeremy Slate confesses that he took her life to save it. Flashbacks include almost an hour's worth of Larry Buchanan's 1975 feature *Goodbye, Norma Jean.*

1170. *Goofballs* (1987, Shapiro, 87m, c). P Dale Falconer, D Brad Turner, W Skip West, M Robert Rettberg.

LP Ben Gordon, Ron James, John Kozak, Wayne Robson, Cynthia Belliveau, Laura Johnson, Ilana Linden, Wayne Flemming, John Hemphill.

Everything about this movie has been tried before and done better. It takes place at a golf resort in the Bahamas, featuring Mafia-types, Arabs, lots of girls in bikinis and the PGA.

1171. *The Goonies* (1985, Warner, 111m, c). P Richard Donner & Harvey Bernhard, D Donner, W Chris Columbus (based on a story by Steven Spielberg), PH Nick McLean, M Dave Grusin, ED

Michael Kahn, PD J. Michael Riva, AD Rick Carter, SD Linda DeScenna, SE Matt Sweeney.

LP Sean Astin (Mikey), Josh Brolin (Brand), Jeff Cohen (Chunk), Corey Feldman (Mouth), Kerri Green (Andy), Martha Plimpton (Stef), Ke Huy Quan (Data), John Matuszak (Sloth), Robert Davi (Jake), Joe Pantoliano (Francis), Anne Ramsey (Mama Fratelli), Lupe Ontiveros (Rosalita).

This Steven Spielberg production is good fun if one doesn't think about it too much. Just enjoy the adventures of a group of kids who discover a treasure map and must flee from a gang led by Ma Barker–like Anne Ramsey, auditioning her role in *Throw Momma from the Train*. They find a hidden pirate ship filled with jewels and pieces-of-eight.

1172. Gor (1988, Cannon, 94m, c). P Harry Alan Towers & Avi Lerner, D Fritz Kiersch, W Rick Marx & Peter Welbeck (Harry Alan Towers) (based on the novel *Tarnsman of Gor* by John Norman), PH Hans Khule, ED Max Lemon & Ken Bornstein, PD Hans Nol.

LP Urbano Barberini (Tarl Cabot), Rebecca Ferratti (Talena), Jack Palance (Xenos), Paul L. Smith (Surbus), Oliver Reed (Sarm), Larry Taylor (King Marlenus), Graham Clarke (Drusus), Janine Denison (Brandy), Donna Denton (Queen Lara).

In this routine sword and sorcery flick, ordinary American Urbano Barberini is whisked off to Gor, "counter-earth," where he must contend with tyrannical villain Oliver Reed.

1173. Gorillas in the Mist (1988, Universal, 129m, c). P Arnold Glimcher, Terence Clegg, Robert Nixon & Judy Kessler, W Anna Hamilton Phelan† (based on the story by Harold T.P. Hayes), PH Seale & Alan Root, M Maurice Jarre†, ED Stuart Baird†, PD John Graysmark, AD Ken Court, SD Simon Wakefield, SOUND Andy Nelson, Brian Saunders & Peter Handford†.

LP Sigourney Weaver† (Dian Fossey), Bryan Brown (Bob Campbell), Julie Harris (Roz Carr), John Omirah Miluwi (Sembagare), Iain Cuthbertson (Dr. Louis Leakey), Constantin Alexandrov (Van Vecten), Waigwa Wachira (Mu-

kara), Iain Glenn (Brendan), David Lansbury (Larry), Maggie O'Neill (Kim), Konga Mbandu (Rushemba), Michael J. Reynolds (Howard Dowd).

Sigourney Weaver gives a laudable performance as the dedicated scientist Dian Fossey. The latter lived with and for the mountain gorilla, and when it came time, she died for them. Weaver sets up camp on the Rwanda side of the Congo border and patiently studies the gorillas. She is eventually able to overcome their natural fear of humans, but she is outraged by the local Batwa pygmy poachers and government bureaucrats who wish to exploit "her" gorillas as a tourist attraction. Weaver falls in love with married *National Geographic* photographer Bryan Brown, whose stories create worldwide interest in her work. When her favorite gorilla is slaughtered by poachers, she becomes more militant in her struggle to protect the endangered species, even resorting to black magic rituals to terrify the natives. She organizes her own militia to fight the poachers. One night while sleeping she is assassinated by an unknown assailant. She is buried near her beloved gorillas, whom she had studied for 18 years.

1174. Gorky Park (1983, Orion/ Rank, 103m, c). P Gene Kirkwood & Howard W. Koch, Jr., D Michael Apted, W Dennis Potter (based on the novel by Martin Cruz Smith), PH Ralf D. Bode, M James Horner, ED Dennis Virkler, PD Paul Sylbert.

LP William Hurt (Arkady Renko), Lee Marvin (Jack Osborne), Brian Dennehy (William Kirwill), Ian Bannen (Iamskoy), Joanna Pacula (Irina), Michael Elphick (Pasha), Richard Griffiths (Anton), Rikki Fulton (Pribluda), Alexander Knox (General).

When three strange corpses are found in Moscow's Gorky Park, police inspector William Hurt is assigned to the case. The mystery leads him to uncover a network of conspiracy. His suspects include American trader Lee Marvin, New York cop Brian Dennehy and beautiful dissident Joanna Pacula. Hurt sure isn't Mr. Excitement.

1175. Gorp (1980, AIP/Filmways, 90m, c). P Jeffrey Konvitz & Louis S. Arkoff, D Joseph Ruben, W Konvitz (based on a story by Konvitz & Martin Zweiback), PH Michel Hugo, ED Bill Butler.

LP Michael Lembeck (Kavell), Dennis Quaid (Mad Grossman), Philip Casnoff (Bergman), Franc Drescher (Evie), David Huddleston (Walrus Wallman), Robert Trebor (Rabbi Blowitz), Lou Wagner (Federman), Richard Beauchamp (Ramirez).

Anytime a movie, say *Meatballs,* becomes a box-office hit, you can bet the ranch that poor quality imitations will immediately appear. Such is the case with this tasteless and unfunny "summer-camp" film which treats audiences to obnoxious jokes about drugs, sex and racism. Keep your kids in the city, cooling themselves at fire hydrants; it will be better for their mental health.

1176. *The Gospel According to Vic* (1985, Skouras, GB, 92m, c). P Michael Relph, D&W Charles Gormley, PH Michael Coulter, M B.A. Robertson, ED John Gow, PD Rita McGurn.

LP Tom Conti (Vic Mathews), Helen Mirren (Ruth Chancellor), David Hayman (Jeff Jeffries), Brian Pettifer (Father Cobb), Jennifer Black (Nurse), Dave Anderson (Headmaster), Tom Busby (Brusse), Sam Graham (Doctor).

In Glasgow, skeptical Catholic schoolteacher Tom Conti achieves notoriety when he finds he can perform miracles.

1177. *Gotcha!* (1985, Universal, 94m, c). P Paul G. Hensler, D Jeff Kanew, W Dan Gordon (based on a story by Hensler & Gordon), PH King Baggot, M Bill Conti, ED Michael A. Stevenson.

LP Anthony Edwards (Jonathan Moore), Linda Fiorentino (Sasha), Nick Corri (Manolo), Alex Rocco (Al, Jonathan's Father), Marla Adams (Maria, Jonathan's Mother), Klaus Loewitsch (Vlad), Christopher Rydell (Bob Jensen), Brad Cowgill (Reilly), Kari Lizer (Muffy).

Shy UCLA sophomore Anthony Edwards has little luck with girls until he meets Linda Fiorentino, an apparent Czech spy. After bedding him, she uses him as an unwitting courier. She disappears and he barely makes it back home, not knowing that he's carrying secret microfilm that both the CIA and the East want very badly.

1178. *Gothic* (1987, Virgin Films, GB, 90m, c). P Penny Corke, D Ken Russell, W Stephen Volk, PH Mike Southon, M Thomas Dolby, ED Michael Bradsell, PD Christopher Hobbs.

LP Gabriel Byrne (Lord Byron), Julian Sands (Percy Bysshe Shelley), Natasha Richardson (Mary Godwin), Myriam Cyr (Claire Clairmont), Timothy Spall (Dr. John Polidori), Andreas Wisniewski (Fletcher), Alec Mango (Murray), Dexter Fletcher (Rushton), Pascal King (Justice).

Britain's bad boy director Ken Russell still is controversial at 60. He is accused of getting everything wrong, being coarse, vulgar and pretentious with his notion of the events that took place one spooky evening in 1816. Lord Byron, poet Percy Shelley, Shelley's fiancée Mary Godwin, her stepsister Claire Clairmont and Byron's former lover Dr. Polidori spent time together drinking laudanum (liquid opium and alcohol), hallucinating and fornicating.

Grace Quigley *see* ***The Ultimate Solution of Grace Quigley***

1179. *Graduation Day* (1981, IFI/Scope III, 85m, c). P David Baughn & Herb Freed, D Freed, W Anne Marisse & Freed, PH Daniel Yarussi, M Arthur Kempel, ED Martin Jay Sadoff, SE Jill Rockow.

LP Christopher George (Coach Michaels), Patch MacKenzie (Anne Ramstead), E. Danny Murphy (Kevin), E.J. Peaker (Blondie), Michael Pataki (Principal Guglione).

Who's been killing the team members of coach Christopher George's high school track team? It's just another mediocre "let's kill teens" movies.

1180. *Grandmother's House* (1989, Omega, 89m, c). P Nico Mastorakis, D Peter Rader, W Peter Jensen (based on a story by Gayle Jensen & Peter Jensen), PH Peter Jensen, M Nigel Holton & Clive Wright, ED Barry Zetlin.

LP Eric Foster (David), Kim Valentine (Lynn), Brinke Stevens (Woman), Ida Lee (Grandmother), Len Lesser (Grandfather).

When her father dies, teenager Kim Valentine and her little brother Eric Foster move in with their grandparents. A mysterious woman, Brinke Stevens, watches them from afar. Later it appears that the grandparents have killed Stevens, but nothing is quite as it seems in this illogical story.

1181. *Grandview, U.S.A.* (1984, Warner, 97m, c). P William Warren Blaylock & Peter W. Rea, D Randal Kleiser, W Ken Hixon, PH Reynaldo Villalobos, M Thomas Newman, ED Robert Gordon, PD Jan Scott.

LP Jamie Lee Curtis (Michelle "Mike" Cody), C. Thomas Howell (Tim Pearson), Patrick Swayze (Ernie "Slam" Webster), Troy Donahue (Donny Vinton), Jennifer Jason Leigh (Candy Webster), William Windom (Bob Cody), Carole Cook (Betty Welles), M. Emmet Walsh (Mr. Clark), Ramon Bieri (Mr. Pearson), Elizabeth Gorcey (Bonnie Clark).

Talented actress Jamie Lee Curtis is wasted in a raunchy slice-of-life production. Jamie struggles to keep the demolition derby she's inherited from her father. She has an affair with teenager C. Thomas Howell, whose father wants her property for a new country club, although Patrick Swayze is more her speed.

The Grass Is Singing see Killing Heat

1182. *Graveyard Shift* (1987, Shapiro, 88m, c). P Michael Bochner, D&W Gerard Ciccoritti, PH Robert Bergman, M Nicholas Pike, ED Bergman, PD Lester Berman.

LP Silvio Oliviero (Stephen Tsepes), Helen Papas (Michelle), Cliff Stoker (Eric Hayden), Dorin Ferber (Gilda).

In this low-budget shocker, Silvio Oliviero, a 350-year-old vampire cab driver, puts the bite on his late-night passengers, particularly sweet young things, virgins preferred. The film abounds with gore and nudity.

1183. *Grease 2* (1982, Paramount, 114m, c). P Robert Stigwood & Allan Carr, D&CH Patricia Birch, W Ken Finkelman, PH Frank Stanley, M Louis St. Louis, ED John F. Burnett, PD Gene Callahan.

LP Maxwell Caulfield (Michael Carrington), Michelle Pfeiffer (Stephanie Zinone), Pamela Segall (Dolores Rebchuck), Didi Conn (Frenchy), Eve Arden (Ms. McGee), Sid Caesar (Coach Calhoun), Dody Goodman (Blanche), Tab Hunter (Mr. Stuart), Dick Patterson (Mr. Spears), Connie Stevens (Miss Mason), Adrian Zmed (Johnny Nogerilli).

The second team is brought on as a sort of sequel-repeat to the huge musical success of 1978, *Grease,* with John Travolta, Olivia Newton-John, Stockard Channing and Jeff Conaway. As before music backs up the saga of the T-Birds, the Pink Ladies and the problems of young love at Rydell High. In the future this movie will be of interest because it featured Michelle Pfeiffer before she became a major star.

1184. *Great Balls of Fire* (1989, Orion, 102m, c). P Adam Fields, D Jim McBride, W Jack Baran & McBride (based on the book by Myra Lewis with Murray Silver, Jr.), PH Affonso Beato, M Various Artists, ED Lisa Day, Pembroke Herring & Bert Lovitt, PD David Nichols.

LP Dennis Quaid (Jerry Lee Lewis), Winona Ryder (Myra Gale Lewis), John Doe (J.W. Brown), Stephen Tobolowsky (John Phillips), Trey Wilson (Sam Phillips), Alec Baldwin (Jimmy Swaggart), Steve Allen (Himself), Lisa Blount (Lois Brown), Joe Bob Briggs (Dewey [Daddy-O] Phillips).

This film suggests the sexually charged excitement of Jerry Lee Lewis in person. It concentrates on one of his (to this point) six marriages. When he married his 13-year-old cousin, many of his fans turned against him. His lagging career did revive, but since the film ends in 1958, this part of his life is not shown. Dennis Quaid is everything anyone could want in the role and Winona Ryder, as his child bride, is a very appealing youngster, although with that build, no one will believe she's only 13.

1185. *The Great Mouse Detective* (1986, Buena Vista, animated, 80m, c). P Burny Mattinson, D John Musker, Ron Clements, Dave Michener & Burny Mattinson, W Pete Young, Vance Gerry, Steve Hulett, Ron Clements, John Musker, Bruce M. Morris, Matthew O'Callaghan, Mattinson, Michener & Melvin Shaw (based on the book *Basil of Baker Street* by Eve Titus).

VOICES Vincent Price (Prof. Ratigan), Barrie Ingham (Basil), Val Bet-tin (Dawson), Susanne Pollatschek (Olivia), Candy Candido (Fidget), Diana Chesney (Mrs. Judson), Eve Brenner (The Mouse Queen), Alan Young (Flaversham), Basil Rathbone (Sherlock Holmes), Laurie Main (Watson), Shani Wallis (Lady Mouse).

Barrie Ingham is the voice of a mouse, living in the home of Sherlock Holmes. He matches wits with rat villain Vincent Price. It's a pleasant enough diversion, although a far cry from the good old days of Disney animated features.

1186. *The Great Muppet Caper* (1981, Universal, GB, 95m, c). P David Lazer & Frank Oz, D Jim Henson, W Tom Patchett, Jay Tarses, Jerry Juhl, Jack Rose, PH Oswald Morris, M/L Joe Raposo, ED Ralph Kemplen, PD Harry Lange, SONG "The First Time It Happens" by Joe Raposo†.

VOICES Jim Henson (Kermit, Rowlf, Dr. Teeth, Waldorf, Swedish Chef), Frank Oz (Miss Piggy, Fozzie Bear, Animal, Sam the Eagle), Dave Goelz (The Great Gonzo, Dr. Bunsen, Honeydew), Jerry Nelson (Floyd, Pops, Lew Zealand), Richard Hunt (Scooter, Statler, Sweetums, Janice, Beaker), Charles Grodin, Diana Rigg, John Cleese, Robert Morley, Peter Ustinov, Jack Warden.

Hapless reporters Kermit, Fozzie Bear and Gonzo travel to London to follow up leads on a major jewel robbery. Miss Piggy stars in a Busby Berkley–like staged extravaganza and an Esther Williams–inspired water ballet.

1187. *The Great Outdoors* (1988, Universal, 92m, c). P Arne L. Schmidt, D Howard Deutch, W John Hughes, PH Ric Waite, M Thomas Newman, ED Tom Rolf, William Gordean & Seth Flaum, PD John W. Corso.

LP Dan Aykroyd (Roman Craig), John Candy (Chet Ripley), Stephanie Faracy (Connie Ripley), Annette Bening (Kate Craig), Chris Young (Buck Ripley), Ian Giatti (Ben Ripley), Hilary Gordon (Cara Craig), Rebecca Gordon (Maria Craig), Robert Prosky (Wally), Zoaunne LeRoy (Juanita), Lucy Deakins (Cammie).

Know-it-all Dan Aykroyd and his klutzy brother-in-law John Candy vie to take control of a shared family vacation at a Wisconsin cabin retreat. The gags are predictable and in Candy's case have been done to death. Still, because of Aykroyd's insensitive personality, one's sympathy is all with the large alumnus of Second City. Lucy Deakins, as the romantic interest of Candy's son Chris Young, is a real cutie, who may be heard from in better vehicles.

1188. *The Great Santini* (1980, Orion/Warner, 115m, c). P Charles A. Pratt, D&W Lewis John Carlino (based on the novel by Pat Conroy), PH Ralph Woolsey, M Elmer Bernstein, ED Housely Stevenson, PD Jack Poplin.

LP Robert Duvall† (Bull Meechum), Blythe Danner (Lillian Meechum), Michael O'Keefe† (Ben Meechum), Lisa Jane Persky (Mary Anne Meechum), Julie Anne Haddock (Karen Meechum), Brian Andrews (Matthew Meechum), Stan Shaw (Toomer Smalls), Theresa Merritt (Arrabelle Smalls), David Keith (Red Pettus), Paul Mantee (Col. Hedgepath).

Robert Duvall is "The Great Santini," a Marine pilot who treats his family as if they were a company of recruits in a boot camp (he affectionately calls his kids "Hogs"). He abuses them in the name of discipline, as they struggle to show him their love.

1189. *Green Ice* (1981, ITC Entertainment, GB, 115m, c). P Jack Wiener, D Ernest Day, W Edward Anhalt, Ray Hassett, Anthony Simmons & Robert de Laurentiis (based on the book by Gerald Browne), PH Gilbert Taylor, M Bill Wyman, ED John Jympson.

LP Ryan O'Neal (Joseph Wiley), Anne Archer (Holbrook), Omar Sharif (Meno Argenti), Domingo Ambriz (Miguel), John Larroquette (Claude), Philip Stone (Kellerman), Michael Sheard (Jaap), Enrique Lucero (Lucho), Manuel Ojeda (Lt. Costas).

In Mexico, naïve electronics expert Ryan O'Neal and Anne Archer, the daughter of a diamond dealer, team up with a left-wing terrorist to loot a fortune in emeralds from Colombian tycoon Omar Sharif.

Green Monkey see *Blue Monkey*

1190. *Gregory's Girl* (1982, Goldwyn, GB, 91m, c). P Clive Parsons & Davina

Belling, D&W Bill Forsyth, PH Michael Coulter, M Colin Tully, ED John Gow.

LP Gordon John Sinclair (Gregory), Dee Hepburn (Dorothy), Jake D'Arcy (Phil Menzies), Clare Grogan (Susan), Robert Buchanan (Andy), William Greenlees (Steve), Alan Love (Eric), Caroline Guthrie (Carol), Carol Macartney (Margo), Douglas Sannachan (Billy), Allison Forster (Madeline).

Clumsy Scottish daydreamer Gordon John Sinclair falls in love with new girl Dee Hepburn, the star of the school's soccer team on which Sinclair plays goalie. It's refreshing to see an adolescent confused about his feelings and suffering from painful shyness — surely this is how most people remember themselves to have been when love first bit. There's been more than enough teen-exploitation films in which sex is as natural as ordering a hamburger, fries and a shake.

1191. *Gremlins* (1984, Warner, 111m, c). P Michael Finnell, D Joe Dante, W Chris Columbus, PH John Hora, M Jerry Goldsmith, ED Tina Hirsch, PD James H. Spencer.

LP Zach Galligan (Billy), Phoebe Cates (Kate), Hoyt Axton (Rand Peltzer), Frances Lee McCain (Lynn Peltzer), Polly Holiday (Mrs. Deagle), Keye Luke (Grandfather), Scott Brady (Sheriff Frank), Harry Carey, Jr. (Mr. Anderson), Don Steele (Rockin' Ricky Rialto), Corey Feldman (Pete), Judge Reinhold (Gerald).

In this comic nightmare, Zach Galligan's strange new pet mogwai runs amok in a small town on Christmas Eve, spawning an army of vicious, violent monsters. Aimed at young children, this Steven Spielberg production is much too scary for them.

1192. *Grendel, Grendel, Grendel* (1981, Victorian Film Corp., Australia, animated, 90m, c). P Philip Adams & Alexander Stitt, D&W Stitt (based on the novel *Grendel* by John Gardner), M Bruce Smeaton, PD Stitt, ANIM D Frank Hellard.

VOICES Peter Ustinov, Keith Michell, Arthur Dignam, Ed Rosser, Bobby Bright, Ric Stone, Julie McKenna, Ernie Bourne, Allison Bird, Barry Hill.

Urbane dragon Grendel just wants to make friends, but for some reason people are afraid of him. It's an interesting retelling of Beowulf, but it drags after a while.

1193. *The Grey Fox* (1983, United Artists, Canada, 92m, c). P Peter O'Brian, D Phillip Borsos, W John Hunter, PH Frank Tidy, M Michael Conway Baker & The Chieftains, ED Frank Irvine.

LP Richard Farnsworth (Bill Miner), Jackie Burroughs (Kate Flynn), Wayne Robson (Shorty), Ken Pogue (Jack Budd), Timothy Webber (Fernie), Gary Reineke (Det. Seavey), David Peterson (Louis Colquhoun), Don MacKay (Al Sims), Samantha Langevin (Jenny), Tom Heaton (Tom).

Richard Farnsworth stars in this more-or-less true story about a turn-of-the-century stagecoach bandit released from a long prison term in 1901. When he finds there's nothing much he can do, he pulls a few more robberies and disappears. Farnsworth is excellent as the genial holdup man.

1194. *Greystoke: The Legend of Tarzan* (1984, Warner, GB, 129m, c). P Hugh Hudson & Stanley S. Canter, D Hudson, W P.H. Vazak "Robert Towne" & Michael Austin† (based on the novel *Tarzan of the Apes* by Edgar Rice Burroughs), PH John Alcott, M John Scott, ED Anne V. Coates, PD Stuart Craig, MK Rick Baker & Paul Engelen†.

LP Ralph Richardson† (The 6th Lord of Greystoke), Ian Holm (Capt. Phillippe D'Arnot), Christopher Lambert (John Clayton/Tarzan), Andie MacDowell (Jane Porter), James Fox (Lord Esker), Ian Charleson (Jefferson Brown), Nigel Davenport (Maj. Jack Downing), Paul Geoffrey (Lord Jack Clayton), Cheryl Campbell (Lady Alice Clayton), Nicholas Farrell (Sir Hugh Belcher), Elliot W. Cane (Silverbeard, Primate Father), Ailsa Berk (Kala, Primate Mother).

Perhaps the most faithful production of the most famous of Edgar Rice Burroughs' works, this film also treats the subject the most seriously. However, the treatment doesn't make it the best version. The film traces the 7th Earl of Greystoke from his birth in Africa, the slaughter of his parents, his adoption by a band of apes, his jungle unbringing, his eventual discovery and his return to his rightful place in England. In her film debut Andie MacDowell's Southern voice was dubbed by Glenn Close.

1195. *Gross Anatomy* (1989, Touchstone, 107m, c). P Howard Rosenman & Debra Hill, D Thom Eberhardt, W Ron Nyswaner & Mark Spragg, PH Steve Yaconelli, ED Bud Smith & Scott Smith, PD William F. Matthews.

LP Matthew Modine (Joe Slovak), Daphne Zuniga (Laurie Rorbach), Christine Lahti (Dr. Rachel Woodruff), Todd Field (David Schreiner), John Scott Clough (Miles Reed), Alice Carter (Kim McCauley), Zakes Mokae (Dr. Banumbra), Robert Desiderio (Dr. Banks).

Matthew Modine plays an annoying, unpredictable medical student, bright but undisciplined and unwilling to conform. Still he is able to make audiences care about him, more than he seems to care about himself or anyone else or anything else. We've all seen this kind of story many times before. We know he'll straighten out before the finale, make his mentor proud of him and win the beautiful girl — in this case Daphne Zuniga.

1196. *Grotesque* (1988, Concorde, 79m, c). P Mike Lane & Chris Morrell, D Joe Tornatore, W Mikel Angel (based on characters and concept by Tornatore), PH Bill Dickson, M Bill Loose & Jack Cookerly, SE John Naulin.

LP Linda Blair (Lisa), Tab Hunter (Rod), Donna Wilkes (Kathy), Brad Wilson (Scratch), Nels Van Patten (Gibbs), Guy Stockwell (Orville Kruger), Sharon Hughes, Michelle Bensoussan, Charles Dierkop, Chuck Morrill.

When a gang of punk rockers invade the home of a special effects makeup man and begin killing off his family, Linda Blair is the only one to escape. With her uncle, Tab Hunter, a plastic surgeon, she tracks down the killers and deforms their faces.

1197. *Ground Zero* (1987, Avenue Ent., Australia, 100m, c). P Michael Pattinson, D Pattinson & Bruce Myles, W Mac Gudgeon & Jan Sardi, PH Steve Dobson, M Tom Bahler, ED David Pulbrook, PD Brian Thomson.

LP Colin Friels (Harvey), Jack Thompson (Trebilcock), Donald Pleas-

ence (Prosper), Natalie Bate (Pat), Burnham Burnham (Charlie), Simon Chilvers (Commission President), Neil Fitzpatrick (Hocking).

Cameraman Colin Friels learns that his father may have died because of what he saw and for photographing too much during the British A-bomb tests in Australia in the 70s.

1198. *Grunt! The Wrestling Movie* (1985, New World, 90m, c). P Don Normann & Anthony Randel, D Allan Holzman, W Roger D. Manning (based on a story by Holzman, Randel, Lisa Tomei & Barry Zetlin), PH Eddie van der Enden, M Susan Justin, ED Holzman & Zetlin.

LP Greg "Magic" Schwarz (Mad Dog Joe De Curso), Marilyn Dodds Frank (Lola), Steven Cepello (The Mask), Robert Glaudini (Dr. Tweed), Jeff Dial (Lesley Uggams), Lydie Denier (Angel Face), Dick Murdoch & Dick Beyer (The Grunt Brothers).

We won't dignify this story of life-behind-the-scenes in professional wrestling by criticizing it.

1199. *The Guest* (1984, RM Productions, GB, 114m, c). P Gerald Berman, D Ross Devenish, W Athol Fugard, PH Rod Stewart, ED Lionel Selwyn, PD Jeni Halliday.

LP Athol Fugard (Eugene Marais), Marius Weyers (Dr. A.G. Visser), Gordon Vorster (Oom Doors), Wilma Stockenstrom (Tante Corrie), James Borthwick (Doorsie), Emile Aucamp (Louis), Susan MacLennan (Little Corrie), Trix Plenaar (Brenda), Dan Poho (Stuurie).

This powerful film stars Athol Fugard as South Africa's well known poet during one of the times in his life when he tries to overcome his morphine addiction.

1200. *Gulag* (1985, Lorimar/MFI, GB, 119m, c). P Barry Steinberg & Andrew Adelson, D Roger Young, W Dan Gordon (based on a story by Gordon, Raphael Shauli & Yehoshua Ben-Porat), PH Kelvin Pike, M Elmer Bernstein, ED John Jympson.

LP David Keith (Mickey Almon), Malcolm McDowell (Englishman), David Suchet (Matvei), Warren Clarke (Hooker), John McEnery (Deczek),

Nancy Paul (Susan Almon), Brian Pettifer (Vlasov), Shane Rimmer (Jay).

American sports commentator David Keith is framed and sentenced to a Russian prison camp, but after a period of hardship he escapes.

1201. Gung Ho (1986, Paramount, 120m, c). P Tony Ganz & Deborah Blum, D Ron Howard, W Lowell Ganz & Babaloo Mandel (based on a story by Edwin Blum, L. Ganz & Mandel), PH Don Peterman, ED Daniel Hanley & Michael Hill, PD James Schoppe.

LP Michael Keaton (Hunt Stevenson), George Watanabe (Kazihiro), George Wendt (Buster), Mimi Rogers (Audrey), John Turturro (Willie), Soh Yamamura (Mr. Sakamoto), Sab Shimono (Saito), Rick Overton (Googie).

Cocky Michael Keaton convinces the Japanese to reopen a car plant in his home town, not quite expecting the cultural differences that arise.

1202. Gunpowder (1987, Lazer, GB, 85m, c). P Maxine Julius, D Norman J. Warren, W Rory H. MacLean, PH Alistair Cameron, M Jeffrey Wood, ED Julius, PD Hayden Pearce, SE Ben Trumble.

LP David Gilliam (Gunn), Martin Potter (Powder), Gordon Jackson (Sir Anthony Phelps), Anthony Schaeffer (Lovell), David Miller (Dr. Vache), Debra Burton (Coffee Carradine), Susan Rutherford (Penny Keynes), Rachel Laurence (Miss Belt).

Rugged secret agent David Gilliam and his slightly effeminate sidekick Martin Potter are the only ones who can put an end to mad scientist David Miller. The crackpot is attempting to destroy the world's economy. It's Bond done badly.

1203. The Gunrunner (1989, New World, Canada, 84m, c). P Richard Sadler & Robert J. Langevin, D Nardo Castillo, W Arnie Gelbart, PH Alain Dostie, M Rex Taylor Smith, ED Diane Fingado & Andre Corriveau.

LP Kevin Costner (Ted Beaubien), Sara Botsford (Maude), Paul Soles (Lochman), Gerard Parkes (Wilson), Ron Lea (George), Mitch Martin (Rosalyn), Larry Lewis (Robert), Daniel Nalbach (Max).

Kevin Costner made this unreleased Canadian film before he became a star with *The Untouchables*. Returning to Montreal from China is 1926, Costner stars as a good-guy gangster who is gunrunning in order to support a revolution in China. Costner may be a star, but he can't pull this dog sled with him to his new heights.

Guyana, Crime of the Century see ***Guyana, Cult of the Damned***

1204. Guyana, Cult of the Damned (1980, Universal, Mex./Span./Panama, 90m, c aka *Guyana, Crime of the Century*). P&D Rene Cardona, Jr., W Cardona & Carlos Valdemar, PH Leopoldo Villasenor, M Nelson Riddle, Bob Summers & George S. Price, ED Earl Watson.

LP Stuart Whitman (Rev. James Johnson), Gene Barry (Congressman Lee O'Brien), John Ireland (David Cole), Joseph Cotten (Richard Gable), Bradford Dillman (Dr. Gary Shaw), Jennifer Ashley (Anna Kazan), Yvonne De Carlo (Susan Ames), Nadiuska (Leslie), Tony Young (Ron).

Rushed into production, this sleazy Mexican production portrays the tragic events leading up to and including the Rev. Jim Jones' ordering his cult followers to commit mass suicide by drinking cyanide-laced Kool-Aid after some of his thugs had killed a U.S. congressman who had come to Guyana to investigate the cult. It offers no insights into the causes of the tragedy.

1205. Gymkata (1985, MGM/United Artists, 90m, c). P Fred Weintraub, D Robert Clouse, W Charles Robert Carner (based on the novel *The Terrible Game* by Dan Tyler Moore). PH Godfrey Godar, ED Robert A. Ferretti, PD Veljko Despotovic.

LP Kurk Thomas (Jonathan Cabot), Tetchie Agbayani (Princess Rubali), Richard Norton (Zamir), Edward Bell (Paley), John Barrett (Gomez), Conan Lee (Hao), Bob Schott (Thorg), Buck Kartalian (The Kahn).

Olympic gynmastics star Kurt Thomas tries his hand at acting in this inferior martial arts film. He must use his skills to conquer and secure a military state in a hostile European country. He should never have let go of the rings.

1206. *Hadley's Rebellion* (1984, The East Indian Trading Co./ADI, 96m, c). P Steve Feke, D&W Fred Walton, PH David Golia, M Mike Post, ED Sam Vitale, PD Diane Campbell.

LP Griffin O'Neal (Hadley Hickman), William Devane (Coach Ball), Charles Durning (Sam Crawford), Adam Baldwin (Bobo McKenzie), Lisa Lucas (Linda Johnson), Eric Boles (Mr. Stevens), Dennis Hauge (Joe Forster).

High school wrestler Griffin O'Neal transfers from a school in the Deep South to a ritzy and snooty prep school in Southern California. Anyone over the age of 12 could write the script from this point on.

1207. *Hairspray* (1988, New Line Cinema, 87m, c). P Rachel Talalay, D&W John Waters, PH David Insley, M Various Artists, ED Janice Hampton.

LP Divine (Edna Turnblad/Arvin Hodgepile), Sonny Bono (Franklin Von Tussle), Ruth Brown (Motormouth Maybell), Debbie Harry (Velma Von Tussle), Ricki Lake (Tracy Turnblad), Jerry Stiller (Wilbur Trunblad), Mink Stole (Tammy), Pia Zadora (Beatnik Girl), Ric Ocasek (Beatnik Cat), Shawn Thompson (Corny Collins), Leslie Ann Powers (Penny Pingleton), Clayton Prince (Seaweed), Michael St. Gerard (Link Larkin), Colleen Fitzpatrick (Amber Von Tussle).

Director-writer John Waters, better known for films many consider to be in outrageously bad taste, such as *Pink Flamingos, Female Trouble and Polyester,* has come up with a delightfully charming and wacky 60s musical. It's 1962 Baltimore, when beehive hairdos are all the rage. Chubby but cute teen Ricki Lake wins a spot on the local TV dance show with her spectacular dancing. She becomes a sensation and wins the love of heart-throb Michael St. Gerard and the hatred of Colleen Fitzpatrick and her bigoted parents, Sonny Bono and Debbie Harry. Divine makes "her" last screen appearance as Lake's mother and the TV station master. He died soon after the film was completed.

1208. *Half Moon Street* (1986, 20th Century-Fox, 90m, c). P Geoffrey Reeve, D Bob Swaim, W Swaim & Edward Behr (based on the novel *Doctor Slaughter* by Paul Theroux), PH Peter Hannan, M Richard Harvey, ED Richard Marden, PD Anthony Curtis.

LP Sigourney Weaver (Lauren Slaughter), Michael Caine (Lord Bulbeck), Patrick Kavanagh (General Sir George Newhouse), Faith Kent (Lady Newhouse), Ram John Holder (Lindsay Walker), Keith Buckley (Hugo Van Arkady), Annie Hanson (Mrs. Van Arkady), Patrick Newman (Julian Shuttle).

To make ends meet, poorly paid Ph.D. Sigourney Weaver accepts an offer to become a paid "escort" for wealthy men in London. One of her clients is Michael Caine, in the midst of negotiating a volatile Arab peace settlement. The two have a stormy relationship. Generally, so-called intelligent women are not treated with much respect in films. This movie goes to the trouble to make certain the audience knows that Weaver is highly intelligent, quite able to take care of herself, and has chosen to enter the oldest profession fully aware of what she is doing and why. But by the end of the film, it presents her as a typical helpless female in need of a man to solve things. Baloney!

1209. *Halloween II* (1981, Universal, 92m, c). P Debra Hill & John Carpenter, D Rick Rosenthal, W Carpenter & Hill, PH Dean Cundey, M Carpenter & Alan Howarth, ED Mark Goldblatt & Skip Schoolnik, PD J. Michael Riva.

LP Jamie Lee Curtis (Laurie), Donald Pleasence (Sam Loomis), Charles Cyphers (Leigh), Jeffrey Kramer (Graham), Lance Guest (Jimmy), Pamela Susan Shoop (Karen), Hunter Von Leer (Gary), Dick Warlock (The Shape), Leo Rossi (Budd), Gloria Gifford (Mrs. Alves), Tawny Moyer (Jill).

Picking up at the point that the original movie ended, this inferior piece is more an imitation than a sequel. Director Rick Rosenthal doesn't have John Carpenter's cinematic style. Michael, the killer Jamie Lee Curtis thought she had dispatched several times in the original is killing again. Curtis discovers that he's her brother and sets him on fire.

1210. *Halloween III: Season of the Witch* (1982, Universal, 96m, c). P John Carpenter & Debra Hill, D&W

Tommy Lee Wallace, PH Dean Cundey, M Carpenter & Alan Howarth, ED Millie Moore, PD Peter Jamison, SE Jon G. Belyeu.

LP Tom Atkins (Dr. Challis), Stacey Nelkin (Ellie), Dan O'Herlihy (Conal), Ralph Strait (Buddy), Michael Currie (Rafferty), Jadeen Barbor (Betty), Bradley Schachter (Little Buddy), Garn Stephens (Marge), Nancy Kyes (Linda), John Terry (Starker).

This film is unrelated to the two previous *Halloween* pictures. Dan O'Herlihy is a Druid descendent with a diabolical plan to destroy all the world's children. He manufactures masks containing microchips from Stonehenge. When worn these masks will give the kiddies a Halloween they'll never forget—that is if they survive. Would W.C. Fields feel that O'Herlihy can't be all bad?

1211. *Halloween IV: The Return of Michael Myers* (1988, Galaxy, 88m, c). P Paul Freeman, D Dwight H. Little, W Alan B. McElroy (based on a story by Dhani Lipsius, Larry Rattner, Benjamin Ruffner & McElroy), PH Peter Lyons Collister, M Alan Howarth, ED Curtiss Clayton, SE Larry Fioritto.

LP Donald Pleasence (Dr. Loomis), Ellie Cornell (Rachel Carruthers), Danielle Harris (Jamie Lloyd), George P. Wilbur (Michael Myers), Michael Pataki (Dr. Hoffman), Beau Starr (Sheriff Meeker), Kathleen Kinmont (Kelly), Sasha Jenson (Brady), Gene Ross (Earl).

On the 10th anniversary of the events of *Halloween II,* it becomes clear that both the infamous "Shape" Michael Myers (George P. Wilbur) and his slightly loony pursuer Dr. Loomis (Donald Pleasence) have survived. Myers has been in a coma all the time, but when he comes to, he's as murderous as before. When Pleasence learns of this, he hightails it for Haddonfield, Illinois, the site of Myers' earlier rampages. Sure enough that's Myers destination as well, intent on finishing the work he started ten years earlier.

1212. *Halloween 5: The Revenge of Michael Myers* (1989, Galaxy Intl., 96m, c). P Ramsey Thomas, D Dominique Othenin-Girard, W Michael Jacobs, Shem Bitterman & Othenin-Girard, PH Robert Draper, M Alan Howarth, John Carpenter, ED Jerry Brady.

LP Donald Pleasence (Dr. Loomis), Danielle Harris (Jamie), Wendy Kaplan (Tina), Ellie Cornell (Rachel), Donald L. Shanks (Michael Myers), Jeffrey Landman (Billy), Beau Starr (Meeker), Betty Carvalho (Nurse Patsey).

Here's yet another dreary chapter in a series whose substance is limited to sex and gore. It is all but indistinguishable from several other series in which some mad killer keeps reappearing to inexplicably kill in the grossest ways possible. Only those who are in need of professional help can possibly keep sitting through the same old garbage.

1213. *Hambone and Hillie* (1984, New World, 89m, c). P Gary Gillingham & Sandy Howard, D Roy Watts, W Sandra K. Bailey, Michael Murphey & Joel Soisson (based on a story by Ken Barnett), PH Jon Kranhouse, M George Garavarentz, ED Robert J. Kizer, PD Helena Reif.

LP Lillian Gish (Hillie), Timothy Bottoms (Michael), Candy Clark (Nancy), O.J. Simpson (Tucker), Robert Walker (Wanderer), Jack Carter (Lester), Alan Hale (McVicker), Anne Lockhart (Roberta), William Jordan (Bert).

As Lillian Gish is preparing to board a flight in New York to return to her home in Los Angeles, her dog Hambone escapes from his travel cage and is left behind. Then begins a 3000 mile trip across the country from different shores for Gish and the pooch as they look for each other.

1214. *Hamburger: The Motion Picture* (1986, FM Entertainment, 90m, c). P Edward S. Feldman & Charles R. Meeker, D Mike Marvin, W Donald Ross, PH Karen Grossman, M Peter Bernstein, ED Steven Schoenberg & Ann E. Mills, PD George Costello.

LP Leigh McCloskey (Russell Procope), Dick Butkus (Drootin), Randi Brooks (Mrs. Vunk), Chuck McCann (Dr. Mole), Jack Blessing (Nacio Herb Zipser), Charles Tyner (Lyman Vunk), Debra Blee (Mia Vunk).

In order for Leigh McCloskey to collect on a big trust fund, he must earn a college degree. But with all the trouble he's causing at Buster Burger University, he's more likely to be kicked out on his buns before you can say two-quarter pounders, special sauce . . . on a sesame roll.

1215. *Hamburger Hill* (1987, RKO/ Paramount, 110m, c). P Marcia Nasatir & Jim Carabatsos, D John Irvin, W Jim Carabatsos, PH Peter MacDonald, M Philip Glass, ED Peter Tanner, PD Austen Spriggs.

LP Anthony Barrile (Languilli), Michael Patrick Boatman (Motown), Don Cheadle (Washburn), Michael Dolan (Murphy), Don James (McDaniel), Dylan McDermott (Sgt. Frantz), M.A. Nickles (Galvin), Harry O'Reilly (Duffy).

In 1969, the 101st Airborne Division engages in carnage with Viet Cong over control of the title piece of real estate. The battle scenes are frighteningly authentic.

1216. *Hammett* (1982, Orion/Warner, 100m, c). P Fred Roos, Ronald Colby & Don Guest, D Wim Wenders, W Ross Thomas, Dennis O'Flaherty & Thomas Pope (based on the book by Joe Gores), PH Philip Lathrop & Joseph Biroc, M John Barry, ED Barry Malkin, Marc Laub, Robert Q. Lovett & Randy Roberts.

LP Frederic Forrest (Dashiell Hammett), Peter Boyle (Jimmy Ryan), Marilu Henner (Kit Conger/Sue Alabama), Roy Kinnear (English Eddie Hagedorn), Elisha Cook (Eli the Taxi Driver), Lydia Lei (Crystal Ling), R.G. Armstrong (Lt. O'Mara), Richard Bradford (Det. Bradford), Michael Chow (Fong), David Patrick Kelly (Punk), Sylvia Sidney (Donaldina Cameron).

Frederic Forrest is believable as detective-writer Dashiell Hammett in this so-so moody period piece. He has some real-life adventures with characters he will later write about. These include Peter Boyle, his old Pinkerton boss and model for his hard-boiled detectives, Lydia Lei, a beautiful Chinese prostitute Boyle wants Forrest to find, and Marilu Henner, a cutie with a yen for Forrest. She helps him solve the mystery of who is blackmailing the city's most influential men.

1217. *The Hand* (1981, Orion/Warner, 104m, c). P Edward R. Pressman, D&W Oliver Stone (based on the book *The Lizard's Tail* by Marc Brandel), PH King Baggott, M James Horner, ED Richard Marks, PD John Michael Riva.

LP Michael Caine (Jon Lansdale), Andrea Marcovicci (Anne Lansdale), Annie McEnroe (Stella Roche), Bruce McGill (Brian Ferguson), Viveca Lindfors (Doctress), Rosemary Murphy (Karen Wagner), Mara Hobel (Lizzie Lansdale).

Gifted cartoonist Michael Caine's hand is severed in an accident. It ruins his career and his marriage. Soon a hand is on the loose ready to help Caine satisfy his obsessive need for revenge.

1218. *A Handful of Dust* (1988, New Line, GB, 118m, c). P Derek Granger, D Charles Sturridge, W Tim Sullivan, Granger & Sturridge (based on the novel by Evelyn Waugh), PH Peter Hannan, M George Fenton, ED Peter Coulson, PD Eileen Diss, COS Jane Robinson†.

LP James Wilby (Tony Last), Kristin Scott Thomas (Brenda Last), Jeanne Watts (Nanny), Angelica Huston (Mrs. Rattery), Rupert Graves (John Beaver), Judi Dench (Mrs. Beaver), Alec Guiness (Mr. Todd), Pip Torens (Jock Grant-Menzies), Cathryn Harrison (Milly).

James Wilby and Kristin Scott Thomas are excellent as a smart 30s British married couple. Their marriage is doomed due to his stifling tradition-bound ways and her selfishness. It's a rich adaptation of Evelyn Waugh's ironic story.

A Handful of Trouble see Action U.S.A.

Handgun see Deep in My Heart

1219. *The Handmaid's Tale* (1989, Cinecom, 97m, c). P Daniel Wilson, D Volker Schlondorff, W. Harold Pinter (based on the novel by Margaret Atwood).

LP Natasha Richardson (Kate/Offred), Robert Duvall (Fred), Faye Dunaway (Serena Joy), Victoria Tennant (Aunt Lydia), Elizabeth McGovern, Aidan Quinn.

This suspense drama is set in the near future in the Republic of Gilead, formerly the United States. Because of disease, only designated women are allowed to procreate. Barren Faye Dunaway conspires with Natasha Richardson, handmaiden to Robert Duvall, an aging commander, to have her bear his child.

1220. *Hangar 18* (1980, Sunn Classics, 97m, c, aka *Invasion Force*). P Charles E. Sellier, Jr., D James L. Conway, W Steven Thornley, Tom Chapman & Conway (based on a novel by Robert Weverka & Sellier), PH Paul Hipp, M John Cacavas, Ed Michael Spence, PD Paul Staheli.

LP Darren McGavin (Forbes), Robert Vaughn (Gordon), Gary Collins (Steve), James Hampton (Lew), Philip Abbott (Frank), Pamela Bellwood (Sarah), Tom Hallick (Phil), Steven Keats (Paul), William Schallert (Mills).

Darren McGavin heads a group of scientists studying a flying saucer the government has hidden in a warehouse. They decode alien plans to invade Earth. The White House is so paranoid about keeping the secret at any cost that it orders the hangar bombed. Very dull. Very stupid.

1221. *Hangmen* (1987, Shapiro, 90m, c). P J. Christian Ingvordsen, Steven W. Kaman & Richard R. Washburn, D Ingvordsen, W Ingvordsen & Kaman, PH Kaman, M Michael Montes.

LP Richard R. Washburn, Jake Lamotta, Dog Thomas, Kosmo Vinyl, Keith Bogart.

In a poorly acted, very violent film, Richard R. Washburn is an ex–CIA agent hunted by Jake Lamotta, another agent who has gone bad.

1222. *Hanky-Panky* (1982, Columbia, 105m, c). P Martin Ransohoff, D Sidney Poitier, W Henry Rosenbaum & David Taylor, PH Arthur Ornitz, M Tom Scott, ED Harry Keller, PD Ben Edwards.

LP Gene Wilder (Michael Jordan), Gilda Radner (Kate Hellman), Kathleen Quinlan (Janet Dunn), Richard Widmark (Ransom), Robert Prosky (Hiram Calder), Josef Sommer (Adrian Pruitt), Johnny Sekka (Lacey).

The producers couldn't have gotten this turkey off the ground with the aid of Michael "Air" Jordan. Gene Wilder, suspected of a murder, teams with Gilda Radner to make a chase comedy and ro-

mantic thriller. The film owes more to Hanna-Barbera than Hitchcock.

1223. *Hannah and Her Sisters*† (1986, Orion, 106m, c). P Robert Greenhut, D&W Woody Allen († for directing, * for screenplay), PH Carlo Di Palma†, M Popular and Classical Selections, ED Susan E. Morse†, PD Stuart Wurtzel, AD Wurtzel†, SD Carol Joffe†

LP Woody Allen (Mickey), Michael Caine* (Elliot), Mia Farrow (Hannah), Dianne Wiest* (Holly), Barbara Hershey (Lee), Lloyd Nolan (Hannah's Father), Maureen O'Sullivan (Hannah's Mother), Max von Sydow (Frederick), Carrie Fisher (April), Daniel Stern (Dusty).

In what many consider Woody Allen's best film to this point, the brilliant writer-director provides audiences with a revealing look at the intermingled relationships of three sisters (Mia Farrow, Dianne Wiest and Barbara Hershey) and their various husbands, ex-husbands, lovers, friends, parents and children. Allen's work is comparable to the best of legendary director Ingmar Bergman, something it seems he has always striven for. The performances are all-around first-rate, and if the story has no particular destination, the cosmopolitan dialogue at least makes the journey a treat.

1224. *Hanna's War* (1988, Cannon, 148m, c). P Menahem Golan & Yoram Globus, D Golan, W Golan (based on the books *The Diaries of Hanna Senesh* by Senesh and *A Great Wind Cometh* by Yoel Palgi), PH Elemer Ragalyi, M Dov Seltzer, ED Alain Jakubowicz, PD Kuli Sander.

LP Ellen Burstyn (Katalin Senesh), Maruschka Detmers (Hanna Senesh), Anthony Andrews (Squadron Leader McCormack), Donald Pleasence (Rosza Gabor), David Warner (Capt. Julian Simon), Vincenzo Ricotta (Yoel Palgi), Christopher Fairbank (Ruven Dafne), Rob Jacks (Peretz Goldstein).

Maruschka Detmers portrays one of Israel's greatest martyrs, Hanna Senesh, the Hungarian-born poet and daughter of a prominent playwright who emigrated to Palestine in 1938. In 1944, working for the British, she was parachuted into Yugoslavia where she was to devise escape routes for downed Allied pilots.

Captured, she was taken to Budapest, tortured, tried and ultimately executed by the Germans just as the Soviet tanks were entering the city.

1225. *The Hanoi Hilton* (1987, Cannon, 123m, c). P Menahem Golan & Yoram Globus, D&W Lionel Chetwynd, PH Mark Irwin, M Jimmy Webb, ED Penelope Shaw, PD R. Clifford Searcy.

LP Michael Moriarty (Lt. Cmdr. Williamson), Jeffrey Jones (Maj. Fischer), Paul Le Mat (Hubman), Stephen Davies (Capt. Robert Miles), Lawrence Pressman (Col. Cathcart), Aki Aleong (Maj. Ngo "Cat" Doc), Gloria Carlin (Paula), John Diehl (Murphy), David Soul (Maj. Oldham).

Audiences must endure the dramatization of American servicemen being subjected to eight long years of brutal treatment at the hands of the North Vietnamese. The trouble is, it's not much of a drama, just the same thing over and over again—but maybe that's the point.

1226. *Hansel and Gretel* (1987, Cannon, 86m, c). P Menahem Golan & Yoram Globus, D Len Talan, W Nancy Weems & Talan (based on the fairy tale by the Brothers Grimm), PH Ilan Rosenberg, M Michael Cohen (based on a score by Engelbert Humperdinck), ED Irit Rax, PD Marek Dobrowolski.

LP Hugh Pollard (Hansel), Nicola Stapleton (Gretel), Emily Richard (Mother), David Warner (Father), Cloris Leachman (Witch).

Cannon entertains with the classic Grimm fairy tale of Hansel and Gretel and their encounter with a wicked witch who plans to fatten them up to be eaten, but winds up in her own stove.

1227. *Happy Birthday, Gemini* (1980, United Artists, 107m, c). P Rupert Hitzig & Bruce Calnan, D&W Richard Benner (based on the play *Gemini* by Albert Innaurato), PH James B. Kelly, M Rich Look & Cathy Chamberlain, ED Stephan Fanfara, PD Ted Watkins.

LP Madeline Kahn (Bunny Weinberger), Rita Moreno (Lucille Pompi), Robert Viharo (Nick Geminiani), Alan Rosenberg (Francis Geminiani), Sarah Holcomb (Judith Hastings), David Marshall Grant (Randy Hastings).

The film is a disappointing production of Albert Innaurato's long-running Broadway play about the concerns of 21-year-old Robert Viharo over his sexual identity.

1228. *Happy Birthday to Me* (1981, Columbia, 108m, c). P John Dunning & Andre Link, D J. Lee Thompson, W John Saxton, Peter Jobin & Timothy Bond (based on a story by Saxton), PH Miklos Lente, M Bo Harwood & Lance Rubin, ED Debra Karen, PD Earl Preston.

LP Melissa Sue Anderson (Virginia), Glenn Ford (Dr. Faraday), Tracy Bregman (Ann), Jack Blum (Alfred), Matt Craven (Steve), Lenore Zann (Maggie), David Eisner (Rudi), Lisa Langlois (Amelia).

Members of the senior class at Crawford Academy are being killed off one by one. Melissa Sue Anderson fears she may be responsible.

1229. *The Happy Hooker Goes to Hollywood* (1980, Cannon, 85m, c). P Menahem Golan & Yoram Globus, D Alan Roberts, W Devi Goldenberg, PH Stephen Gray.

LP Martine Beswicke (Xavier Hollander) Adam West, Phil Silvers, Richard Deacon, Edie Adams, Chris Lemmon.

In the worst of the dismal trio of films charting the adventures of high-class Dutch prostitute Xavier Hollander, Martine Beswicke slips on the net stockings and tight skirts. She hies herself to Hollywood where she hopes to make a movie based on her memoirs, but finds herself up to her décolletage in scheming would-be producers.

1230. *Happy Hour* (1987, The Movie Store, 88m, c). P J. Stephen Peace & John De Bello, D De Bello, W De Bello, Constantine Dillon & Peace, PH Kevin Morrisey, M Rick Patterson & Neal Fox, ED De Bello, PD Dillon.

LP Richard Gilliland (Blake Teagarden), Jamie Farr (Crummy Fred), Tawny Kitaen (Misty Roberts), Ty Henderson (Bill) Rich Little (Mr. X/Roger Fudmunger/"Scooter" Johnson), Eddie Deezen (Hancock), Kathi Diamant (Cathy Teagarden), Debbie Gates (Meredith Casey), Jim Parrott (Barbarian Leader).

This questionable comedy details the struggle of agents for two rival breweries, trying to steal vials containing an essence which makes beer the best drink ever. As a result the legal drinking age is reduced to six-years-old, producing a nation of inebriates. This beer bust is not for you.

1231. *Happy New Year* (1987, Columbia, 85m, c). P Jerry Weintraub, D John G. Avildsen, W Warren Lane [Nancy Dowd] (based on the film *La Bonne Année* by Claude Lelouch), PH James Crabe, M Bill Conti, ED Jane Kurson, PD William J. Cassidy, MK Bob Laden†.

LP Peter Falk (Nick), Charles Durning (Charlie), Wendy Hughes (Carolyn Benedict), Tom Courtenay (Edward Sanders), Joan Copeland (Sunny), Tracy Brooks Swope (Nina), Daniel Gerroll (Curator), Bruce Malmuth (Police Lieutenant), Claude Lelouch (Man on Train).

Con men Peter Falk and Charles Durning plan a West Palm Beach jewel heist. Falk dons several neat disguises in this remake of Claude Lelouch's 1973 French comedy.

1232. *Happy Together* (1989, Vidmark, 96m, c). P Jere Henshaw, D Mel Damski, W Craig J. Nevius, PH Joe Pennella, M Robert Folk, ED O. Nicholas Brown, PD Marcia Hinds.

LP Patrick Dempsey (Christopher Wooden), Helen Slater (Alexandra Page), Dan Schneider (Gooseflesh), Kevin Hardesty (Slash), Marius Weyers (Denny Dollenbacher), Barbara Babcock (Ruth Carpenter), Gloria Hayes (Luisa Dellacova).

Through a computer error, shy college student Patrick Dempsey and extroverted Helen Slater are assigned the same dorm room at a California college. Living together with a girl of such obvious sexuality is not the paradise it might seem, but there's a happy ending.

1233. *Hard Choices* (1984, Screenland-Breakout, 90m, c). P Robert Mickelson, D&W Rick King (based on a story by King & Mickelson), PH Tom Hurwitz, M Jay Chattaway, ED Dan Loewenthal, PD Ruth Ammon.

LP Margaret Klenck (Laura Stephens), Gary McCleery (Bobby Lipscomb), John Seitz (Sheriff Mavis Johnson), John Sayles (Don), John Snyder (Ben), Martin Donovan (Josh), Larry Golden (Carl), Judson Camp (Jimmy).

Dedicated social worker Margaret Klenck tries to protect frightened juvenile offender Gary McCleery. The latter has been assigned to a brutal adult prison. Klenck is doing the right thing but she goes too far. She busts the kid out and accompanies him to the Florida Keys, where she provides the youngster with more intimate social work attention.

1234. *Hard Country* (1981, Universal, 104m, c). P David Greene & Mack Bing, D David Greene, W Michael Kane (based on a story by Kane & Michael Martin Murphey, PH Dennis Dalzell, M Jimmie Haskell, ED John A. Martinelli, PD Edward Richardson.

LP Jan-Michael Vincent (Kyle Richardson), Kim Basinger (Jodie Lynn Palmer), Michael Parks (Royce Richardson), Gailard Sartain (Johnny Bob), Tanya Tucker (Caroline Peters), Sierra Pecheur (Mama Palmer), John Chappell (Daddy Palmer), Daryl Hannah (Loretta Palmer).

The shiftless and unambitious urban cowboy Jan-Michael Vincent re-evaluates his life when girlfriend Kim Basinger chooses to break away from him.

1235. *Hard Knocks* (1980, Andromeda, Australia, 85m, c). P Don McLennan & Hilton Bonner, D McLennan, W McLennan & Bonner, PH&ED Zbigniew Friedrich.

LP Tracey Mann (Sam), John Arnold (Wally), Bill Hunter (Brady), Max Cullen (Newman), Tony Barry (Barry), Hilton Bonner (Frank), Kirsty Grant (Debbie).

Tracey Mann's efforts to straighten out her life after serving a prison term as a juvenile delinquent is put in jeopardy by her old friends and some crooked cops.

Hard Rain see An Innocent Man

1236. *Hard Ticket to Hawaii* (1987, Malibu Bay, 96m, c). P Arlene Sidaris, D&W Andy Sidaris, PH Howard Wexler, M Gary Stockdale, ED Michael Haight, PD Sal Grasso.

LP Ronn Moss (Rowdy Abilene), Dona Speir (Donna), Hope Marie Carlton (Taryn), Harold Diamond (Jade),

Rodrigo Obregon (Seth Romero), Cynthia Brimhall (Edy), Patty Duffek (Pattycakes), Wolf Larson (Jimmy-John Jackson), Lory Green (Rosie), Rustam Branaman (Kimo).

Busty former *Playboy* models (in that description there's probably at least three redundancies, no?) Dona Speir and Hope Marie Carlton find themselves involved with stolen gems and a large drug shipment. Hero Ronn Moss eliminates the opposition with a bazooka. Plenty of nudity, profanity, violence and gore to satisfy aficionados of this kind of sleaze.

1237. *Hard to Hold* (1984, Universal, 93m, c). P D. Constantine Conte, D Larry Peerce, W Tom Hedley (based on a story by Hedley & Richard Rothstein), PH Richard H. Kline, M Tom Scott & Rick Springfield, ED Bob Wyman, PD Peter Wooley.

LP Rick Springfield (James Roberts), Janet Eilber (Diana Lawson), Patti Hansen (Nicky Nides), Albert Salmi (Johnny Lawson), Gregory Itzen (Owen), Peter Van Norden (Casserole), Tracy Brooks Swope (Toby).

Australian pop singer and American soap opera actor Rick Springfield bombs in his attempt to make it on the big screen as — what else? — a pop singer. He loves Janet Eilber, a woman with no use for his life style.

1238. *Hard Traveling* (1985, Shire, 107m, c). P Helen Garry, D&W Dan Bessie (based on the novel *Bread and a Stone* by Alvah Bessie), PH David Myers, M Ernie Sheldon, ED Susan Heick.

LP J.E. Freeman (Ed Sloan), Ellen Geer (Norah Sloan), Barry Corbin (Frank Burton), James Gammon (Sgt. Slattery), Jim Haynie (Lt. Fisher), W. Scott DeVenney (Bill Gilbert), Joe Miksak (Judge), William Paterson (Sheriff).

In California of the 1930s, widow Ellen Geer sees some special qualities in illiterate janitor J.E. Freeman. They marry, but happiness is to be denied them when he's accused of murder, tried, convicted and executed. It's a simple story with moving performances from talented character actors.

1239. *Hardbodies* (1984, Columbia, 88m, c). Jeff Begun & Ken Dalton, D

Mark Griffiths, W Steve Greene, Eric Alter & Griffiths (based on a story by Greene & Alter), PH Tom Richmond, ED Andy Blumenthal, PD Gregg Fonesca.

LP Grant Cramer (Scotty), Teal Roberts (Kristi), Gary Wood (Hunter), Michael Rapport (Rounder), Sorrels Pickard (Ashby), Roberta Collins (Lana), Cindy Silver (Kimberly), Courtney Gaines (Rag), Kristi Somers (Michelle), Crystal Shaw (Candy).

Lustful middle-aged chumps Gary Wood, Michael Rapport and Sorrels Pickard rent a house on Venice beach. The three over-the-hill lechers have no luck scoring with the "hardbodies," i.e. the beautiful unwrapped babes on the beach. They seek out the advice of pro Grant Cramer, who gives them pointers on the fine art of girl-getting. It's meant to appeal to voyeurs of all ages.

1240. *Hardbodies 2* (1986, CineTel Films, 95m, c). P Jeff Begun, Ken Solomon, Dimitri Logothetis & Joseph Medawar, D Mark Griffiths, W Griffiths & Curtis Wilmot, PH Tom Richmond, M Jay Levy & Eddie Arkin, ED Andy Blumenthal.

LP Brad Zutaut (Scott), Sam Temeles (Rags), Curtis Scott Wilmot (Sean), Brenda Bakke (Morgan), Fabiana Udenio (Cleo), Louise Baker (Cookie), James Karen (Logan), Alba Francesca (Zacherly), Sorrells Pickard (Carlton Ashby), Roberta Collins (Lana Logan).

It probably really steams those voyeurs (make that viewers) who go to this movie to get their fix of scantily clad beauties to have to put up with a minor story about a Hollywood cast on an "au naturel" Greek island to make a movie.

1241. *Hardcase and Fist* (1989, United Entertainment, 92m, c). P&D Tony Zarindast, W Bud Fleischer & Zarindast (based on a story by Zarindast), ph Robert Hayes, M Tom & Matthew Tucciarone, ED Bill Cunningham, PD Alan Scott.

LP Ted Prior (Bud McCall), Carter Wong (Eddy Lee), Christina Lunde (Sharon), Maureen Lavette (Nora), Tony Zarindast (Tony Marino), Vincent Barbi (Vincent).

L.A. cop Ted Prior goes undercover in prison to prevent a con from testifying in defense of an underworld chieftain. The latter orders Prior rubbed out by Tony Zarindast, Prior's old Vietnam vet buddy. The latter decides to help his pal escape instead.

Hardcover see I, Madman

1242. *Hardly Working* (1981, 20th Century–Fox, 91m, c). P James J. McNamara & Igo Kantor, D Jerry Lewis, W Michael Janover & Lewis (based on a story by Janover), PH James Pergola, M Morton Stevens, ED Michael Luciano.

LP Jerry Lewis (Bo Hooper), Susan Oliver (Claire Trent), Roger C. Carmel (Robert Trent), Deanna Lund (Millie), Harold J. Stone (Frank Loucazi), Steve Franken (Steve Torres), Buddy Lester (Claude Reed), Leonard Stone (Ted Mitchell), Jerry Lester (Slats), Billy Barty (Sammy).

Jerry Lewis stayed away from the screen for 10 years before appearing in this predictable adult comedy. He's a circus clown who finds it difficult to adjust to real life as he moves from one job to the next. Lewis should have stayed away longer. He brings nothing new to the screen and his particular comic routines have seen their day.

1243. *Harlem Nights* (1989, Paramount, 115m, c). P Robert D. Wachs & Mark Lipsky, D&W Eddie Murphy, PH Woody Omens, M Herbie Hancock, ED George Bowers, PD Lawrence G. Paull, COS Joe I. Tompkins.

LP Eddie Murphy (Quick), Richard Pryor (Sugar Ray), Redd Foxx (Bennie Wilson), Danny Aiello (Phil Cantone), Michael Lerner (Bugsy Calhoune), Della Reese (Vera), Lela Rochon (Sunshine), Arsenio Hall (Crying Man), Berlinda Tolbert (Annie), Stan Shaw (Jack Jenkins), Jasmine Guy (Dominique La Rue).

Thoughtful fans of Eddie Murphy and those looking for him to fall on his face will both be disappointed with this film. As an actor Murphy is restrained in his role as a Harlem hit man of the 30s. As a writer he hasn't come up with much of a story or any really big laughs. On the other hand, the film seems to capture the mood and atmosphere of the period and community. Murphy has generously given free rein to his co-stars, Richard Pryor, who plays Murphy's foster father, running a Harlem after-hours club, Redd Foxx, a near-blind croupier in the club, and Della Reese as the club's madam. The language is vulgar as might be expected, but it rolls out of the mouth of these characters so naturally that it's hard to take offense.

1244. *Harry & Son* (1984, Orion, 117m, c). P Paul Newman & Ronald L. Buck, D Newman, W Newman & Buck (based on the novel *A Lost King* by Don Capite), PH Don McAlpine, M Henry Mancini, ED Dede Allen, PD Henry Bumstead.

LP Paul Newman (Harry), Robby Benson (Howard), Ellen Barkin (Katie), Wilford Brimley (Tom), Judith Ivey (Sally), Ossie Davis (Raymond), Morgan Freeman (Siemanowski), Katherine Borowitz (Nina), Maury Chaykin (Lawrence), Joanne Woodward (Lilly), Michael Brockman (Al).

Paul Newman, a tough, widowed, aging construction worker, can't seem to reach an accommodation with his free-spirit son Robby Benson, a would-be writer. Newman is convincing as a man who has lost his self-respect and wants to be reconciled with his flesh and blood before he dies.

1245. *Harry and the Hendersons* (1987, Universal, 110m, c). P Richard Vane & William Dear, D Dear, W Dear, William E. Martin & Ezra Rappaport, PH Allen Daviau, M Bruce Broughton, ED Donn Cambern, PD James Bissell, MK Rick Baker*.

LP John Lithgow (George Henderson), Melinda Dillon (Nancy Henderson), Margaret Langrick (Sarah Henderson), Joshua Rudoy (Ernie Henderson), Kevin Peter Hall (Harry), David Suchet (Jacques Lafleur), Lainie Kazan (Irene Moffitt), Don Ameche (Dr. Wallace Wrightwood), M. Emmet Walsh (George Henderson, Sr.), Bill Ontiveros (Sgt. Mancini).

As John Lithgow and his family drive home from a vacation in the woods, they hit a Bigfoot-like creature. Thinking it dead, they bring the poor thing home. But Harry, as they call it, revives and the family grows quite fond of the big hairy fellow. The tranquility of this extended family is threatened by hunter David Suchet, who plans to get him one of them Bigfoot critters as a trophy.

Harry Tracy see Harry Tracy—Desperado

1246. *Harry Tracy—Desperado* (1982, Quartet, Canada, 111m, c, aka *Harry Tracy*). P Ronald I. Cohen, D William A. Graham, W David Lee Henry, PH Allen Daviau, M Mickey Erbe & Maribeth Solomon, ED Ron Wisman, PD Karen Bromley.

LP Bruce Dern (Harry Tracy), Helen Shaver (Catherine), Michael C. Gwynne (Dave), Gordon Lightfoot (Morrie).

Bruce Dern portrays a legendary outlaw whose exploits made him both a wanted criminal and a folk hero.

1247. *Harry's Machine* (1986, Cannon, 96m, c, aka *Hollywood Harry*). P Robert Forster & The Starquilt Co., D Forster, W Curt Allen, PH Gideon Porath, M Michael Land, ED Rich Meyer.

LP Robert Forster (Harry), Joe Spinell (Max), Shannon Wilcox (Candy), Kathrine Forster (Danielle), Pete Schrum (Clapper), Redmond Gleason (Skeeter), Reed Morgan (Farmer), Mallie Jackson (Fat Woman).

Down-on-his-luck alcoholic private detective Robert Forster is forced to take his 14-year-old niece Shannon Wilcox with him on his investigations. Well maybe she can pour him some drinks and keep his revolver loaded.

1248. *Harry's War* (1981, Taft International, 98m, c). P Jack N. Reddish & Keith Merrill, D&W Merrill, PH Reed Smoot, M Merrill B. Jenson, ED B. Lovitt & Peter L. McCrea, PD Douglas G. Johnson.

LP Edward Herrmann (Harry), Geraldine Page (Beverly), Karen Grassle (Kathy), David Ogden Stiers (Ernie), Salome Jens (Wilda), Elisha Cook (Sgt. Billy), James Ray (Commissioner), Douglas Dirkson (Draper), Jerrold Ziman (Attorney), Jim McKrell (Newsman), Noble Willingham (Maj. Andrews).

Middle-class, middle-aged Edward Herrmann declares war on the IRS, employing an antique tank from the store of his aunt, Geraldine Page, who drops dead of a heart attack due to all the aggravation the government is causing her. While every taxpayer would gladly enlist in his cause, the entertainment value of the film is not enough to rally round the flag for.

1249. *Haunted Honeymoon* (1986, Orion, 83m, c). P Susan Ruskin, D Gene Wilder, W Wilder & Terence Marsh, PH Fred Schuler, M John Morris, ED Christopher Greenbury, PD Marsh.

LP Gene Wilder (Larry Abbot), Gilda Radner (Vickie Pearle), Dom DeLuise (Aunt Kate), Jonathan Pryce (Charles), Paul L. Smith (Dr. Paul Abbot), Peter Vaughan (Francis Sr.), Bryan Pringle (Pfister), Roger Ashton Griffiths (Francis Jr.), Jin Carter (Montego), Eve Ferret (Sylvia), Julann Griffin (Nora Abbot).

Everyone plays way over the top in this remarkably unfunny romp. Someone in Gene Wilder's family may be a werewolf and that person will make his or her presence known at the wedding of Wilder to Gilda Radner. The ceremonies are to take place at Wilder's crazy aunt Dom DeLuise's strange old mansion. Wilder as director, writer and star is a multitalented failure in bringing to the screen a story and production that even Mel Brooks would consider too obvious. It may have been intended as a spoof of the 30s and 40s B horror movies, but it doesn't compare favorably with the worst of them.

1250. *Haunted Summer* (1988, Cannon, GB, 115m, c). P Martin Poll, D Ivan Passer, W Lewis John Carlino (based on the novel by Anne Edwards), PH Giuseppe Rotunno, M Christopher Young, ED Cesare D'Amico, PD Stephen Grimes.

LP Eric Stoltz (Percy Shelley), Philip Anglim (Lord Byron), Alice Krige (Mary Godwin), Laura Dern (Claire Clairmont), Alex Winter (John Polidori), Giusto Lo Pipero (Berger), Don Hodson (Rushton), Terry Richards (Fletcher).

Beautifully filmed but flawed, this production of Anne Edwards' novel about the emotional meeting of poets Lord Byron and Percy Shelley and novelist Mary Godwin and others in a summer of love and experimentation in 1816 Italy is well worth viewing.

1251. *Haunters of the Deep* (1985, Longbow Films, GB, 61m, c). P Gordon Scott, D Andrew Bogle, W Bogle, Terry Barbour & Tony Attard (based on a story by Barbour), PH Ronald Maasz, M Ed Welch, ED Jeanne Henderson.

LP Andrew Keir (Capt. Tregellis), Barbara Ewing (Mrs. Holman), Bob Sherman (Roche), Brian Osborne (Holman), Tom Watson (Frank Lacey), Sean Arnold (Shannon), Peter Lovstrom (Daniel), Patrick Murray (Jack), Barry Craine (Leader), Gary Simmons (Josh).

In Cornwall, a youngster is warned by a ghost that the reopening of a mine will cause a cave-in. It does.

The Haunting of Hamilton High see Hello Mary Lou, Prom Night II

1252. *The Haunting of Julia* (1981, Discovery, GB/Canada, 96m, c, aka *Full Circle*). P Peter Fetterman & Alfred Pariser, D Richard Loncraine, W Dave Humphries & Harry Bromley Davenport (based on the novel *Julia* by Peter Straub), PH Peter Hannan, M Colin Towns, ED Ron Wisman.

LP Mia Farrow (Julia), Keir Dullea (Magnus), Tom Conti (Mark), Jill Bennett (Lily), Robin Gammell (Swift), Cathleen Nesbitt (Mrs. Rudge), Anna Wing (Mrs. Flood), Pauline Jameson (Mrs. Branscombe), Peter Sallis (Branscombe), Sophie Ward (Kate), Samantha Gates (Olivia).

After the death of her daughter, Mia Farrow is consumed with feelings of guilt. She and her husband Keir Dullea take up residence in a London house which appears to be haunted by the spirit of the deceased child. It's really an evil spirit with malevolent designs on the couple.

1253. *Hawk the Slayer* (1980, ITC, GB, 93m, c). P Harry Robertson, D Terry Marcel, W Robertson & Marcel, PH Paul Beeson, M Robertson, ED Eric Boyd-Perkins.

LP John Terry (Hawk), Jack Palance (Voltan), Bernard Bresslaw (Gort), Ray Charleson (Crow), Peter O'Farrell (Baldin), Morgan Sheppard (Ranulf), Cheryl Campbell (Sister Monica), Annette Crosbie (Abbess).

In this comic book sword and fantasy failure, John Terry, a slain ruler's son, uses a magical flying sword to kill his evil brother, Jack Palance.

1254. *Hawks* (1989, Skouras, GB, 110m, c). P Stephen Lanning & Keith Cavele, D Robert Ellis Miller, W Roy Clarke, PH Doug Milsome, M Barry Gibb & John Cameron, ED Malcolm Cooke, PD Peter Howitt.

LP Timothy Dalton (Bancroft), Anthony Edwards (Decker), Janet McTeer (Hazel), Camile Coduri (Maureen), Robert Lang (Walter), Jill Bennett (Vivian), Bruce Boa (Byron), Pat Starr (Millie).

Timothy Dalton is a terminally ill British attorney and his roommate Anthony Edwards is a terminally ill American football player. The two make the most of death and dying by carrying off any number of rebellious escapades. The film resists being mawkish and sentimental, with the message that even the dying can live.

1255. *He Knows You're Alone* (1980, MGM/United Artists, 92m, c). P George Manasse, Robert Di Milia & Nan Pearlman, D Armand Mastroianni, W Scott Parker, PH Gerald Feil, M Alexander Peskanov & Mark Peskanov, ED George T. Norris.

LP Don Scardino (Marvin), Caitlin O'Heaney (Amy), Elizabeth Kemp (Nancy), Tom Rolfing (Killer), Lewis Arlt (Gamble), Patsy Pease (Joyce), James Rebhorn (Professor), Tom Hanks (Elliot), Dana Barron (Diana).

Tom Rolfing, a sex-starved maniac attacks teenage girls with a knife. He invades a wedding with the bride-to-be his next intended victim. Even though the film is less gory than many in the subgenre, those who enjoy seeing such movies would seem to need some help.

1256. *Head Office* (1985, Tri-Star, 86m, c). P Debra Hill, D&W Ken Finkleman, PH Gerald Hirschfeld, M James Newton Howard, ED Danford B. Greene & Bob Lederman, PD Elayne Barbara Ceder.

LP Judge Reinhold (Jack Issel), Lori-Nan Engler (Rachel Helmes), Eddie Albert (Helmes), Jane Seymour (Jane), Danny DeVito (Stedman), Merritt Butrick

(John Hudson), George Coe (Senator Issel), Wallace Shawn (Hoover), Rick Moranis (Gross), Ron Frazier (Nixon).

After graduating from college, Judge Reinhold, the son of a powerful politician, is given a high-paying job with a major corporation. He enjoys a remarkable climb up the business ladder, even though he bungles every assignment. Eddie Albert, the owner of the company, hopes to get preferential government treatment. The film starts out promising to be funny but the writers seem to have run out of ideas by its second half.

1257. *Head On* (1981, Grant, Canada, 98m, c). P Michael Grant & Alan Simmonds, D Grant, W James Sanderson & Paul Illidge, PH Anthony Richmond, M Peter Mann, ED Gary Oppenheimer, PD Antonin Dimitrov.

LP Sally Kellerman (Michelle Keys), Stephen Lack (Peter Hill), John Huston (Clarke Hill), Lawrence Dane (Frank Keys), John Peter Linton (Gad Bernstein), Mina E. Mina (Karim), Hadley Kay (Stanley).

Child psychologist Sally Kellerman and professor of psychology Stephen Lack meet because of an automobile accident. They begin a bizarre sexual relationship, taking turns fulfilling each other's fantasies by playing out children's nursery rhymes. Didn't know that Mother Goose was a kinky writer, did you?

Head Over Heels* see *Chilly Scenes of Winter

1258. *Headin' for Broadway* (1980, 20th Century–Fox, 89m, c). P&D Joseph Brooks, W Brooks, Hilary Henkin & Larry Gross, M Brooks.

LP Rex Smith, Terri Treas, Vivian Reed, Paul Carafotes, Gene Foote, Gary Glendell.

In an incompetent film, Rex Smith is one of a group of talented youngsters (it says here), who are trying to make it on Broadway. Wonder if they know the answer to the question "How do I get to Carnegie Hall?" No, probably not!

1259. *The Headless Eyes* (1983, J.E.R. Pictures, 79m, c). P Ronald Sullivan, D&W Kent Bateman.

LP Bo Brundin, Gordon Ramon, Kelley Swartz, Mary Jane Early.

An artist turned housebreaker is discovered by a female victim. In a struggle, the latter gouges out the eye of the former with a spoon. He escapes, but vows revenge on the world and the gender that has maimed him.

1260. *Health* (1980, 20th Century–Fox, 102m, c). D Robert Altman, W Frank Barhydt, Paul Dooley & Altman, PH Edmond Koons, ED Dennis M. Hill.

LP Glenda Jackson, Carol Burnett, James Garner, Lauren Bacall, Dick Cavett, Paul Dooley, Henry Gibson, Donald Moffat, Alfre Woodard.

Despite the talented cast, this satire about complications at a health foods convention held at a Florida hotel would have required several story doctors for it to have survived.

1261. *Hearing Voices* (1989, Sharon Greytak Prod., 87m, c). D&W Sharon Greytak, PH Doron Schlair, M Wes York, Ad Chere Ledwith.

LP Erika Nagy (Erika), Stephen Gatta (Lee), Tim Ahearn (Michael Krieger), Michael Davenport (Carl).

In a brave offbeat picture, top New York model Erika Nagy lives with the results of ileostomy surgery while maintaining a probably doomed love affair with a gay man, Stephen Gatta.

1262. *The Hearse* (1980, Crown, 95m, c). P Mark Tenser & Charles Russell, D George Bowers, W Bill Bleich (based on an idea by Tenser), PH Mori Kawa, M Webster Lewis, ED George Berndt.

LP Trish Van Devere (Jane Hardy), Joseph Cotten (Walter Pritchard), David Gautreaux (Tom Sullivan), Donald Hotton (Rev. Winston), Med Flory (Sheriff), Donald Petrie (Luke), Christopher McDonald (Peter), Perry Lang (Paul), Frederic Franklyn (Gordon), Olive Dunbar (Mrs. Gordon).

Schoolteacher Trish Van Devere inherits a mansion from her lookalike aunt, whom the locals believe had been in league with the devil. She finds both her sanity and her life threatened by a sinister black hearse.

1263. *Heart* (1987, New World, 90m, c). P Randy Jurgensen, D James Lemmo, W Lemmo & Jurgensen, PH Jacek Laskus, M Geoff Levin & Chris Many, ED Lorenzo Marinelli, PD Vicki Paul.

LP Brad Davis (Eddie Brennan), Frances Fisher (Jeannie), Steve Buscemi (Nicky), Robinson Frank Adu (Buddy), Jesse Doran (Diddy), Sam Gray (Leo), Bill Costello (Fighter).

Despite being way over the hill, none-too-bright boxer Brad Davis, over the objections of his girlfriend Frances Fisher, makes an ill-advised comeback in the ring. He is encouraged in this unwise venture by his sleazy ex-manager Steve Buscemi. It's a predictable entry in an overdone genre.

1264. *Heart Like a Wheel* (1983, 20th Century–Fox, 113m, c). P Charles Roven, D Jonathan Kaplan, W Ken Friedman, PH Tak Fujimoto, M Laurence Rosenthal, ED O. Nicholas Brown, PD James William Newport, M/L "Born to Win" by Tom Snow (sung by Jill Michaels), COS William Ware Theiss†.

LP Bonnie Bedelia (Shirley "ChaCha" Muldowney), Beau Bridges (Connie Kalitta), Leo Rossi (Jack Muldowney), Hoyt Axton (Tex Roque), Bill McKinney ("Big Daddy" Don Garlits), Anthony Edwards (John Muldowney, age 15–23), Dean Paul Martin (Sonny Rigotti), Paul Bartel (Chef Paul), Missy Basile (Angela).

Bonnie Bedelia, wife of a service station owner, will stop at nothing to become a racing driver and a champion, despite all the sexism she encounters in what is considered a "man's sport." The film, based on the real life experiences of "ChaCha" Muldowney, is superior to most sports bio-pics.

1265. *Heart of Dixie* (1989, Orion, 95m, c). P Steve Tisch, D Martin Davidson, W Tom McCown (based on the novel *Heartbreak Hotel* by Anne Rivers Siddons), PH Robert Elswit, M Kenny Vance, ED Bonnie Koehler, PD Glenda Ganis.

LP Ally Sheedy (Maggie), Virginia Madsen (Delia), Phoebe Cates (Aiken), Treat Williams (Hoyt), Don Michael Paul (Boots), Kyle Secour (Tuck), Francesca Roberts (Keefi), Peter Berg (Jenks), Jenny Robertson (Sister), Lisa Zane (M.A.), Ashley Gardner (Jean).

In this hokey, superficial drama, Ally Sheedy, a typical 1957 sorority girl at an Alabama college, is only interested in being pinned, going to football games and becoming homecoming queen. She attends an Elvis Presley concert in Tupelo, Mississippi, and is radicalized after witnessing a black boy being viciously beaten for daring to sit in the white section of the stadium. With the encouragement of press photographer Treat Williams, Sheedy becomes a minicrusader and helps welcome the first black student to enroll at her college.

1266. *Heart of Midnight* (1989, Goldwyn, 96m, c). P Andrew Gaty, D&W Matthew Chapman, PH Ray Rivas, ED Penelope Shaw, PD Gene Rudolf.

LP Jennifer Jason Leigh (Carol Rivers), Peter Coyote ("Lt. Sharpe"/Larry), Gale Mayron (Sonny), Sam Schacht (Fletcher), Denise Dummont (Mariana), Frank Stallone (Ledray), James Rebhorn (Richard).

The mystery about this mystery is, if screenwriter and director Matthew Chapman knows what's going on. Jennifer Jason Leigh may or may not be crazy, having been raped and molested as a child. She becomes involved in a murder and other assorted violent activities.

1267. *Heart of the Stag* (1984, New World, New Zealand, 91m, c). P Don Reynolds & Michael Firth, D Firth, W Neil Illingsworth, Firth, Martyn Sanderson & Bruno Lawrence (based on a story by Firth), PH James Bartle, M Leonard Rosenman, ED Michael Horton, PD Gary Hansen.

LP Bruno Lawrence (Peter Daly), Terence Cooper (Robert Jackson), Mary Regan (Cathy Jackson), Anne Flannery (Mary Jackson), Michael Wilson (Jack Bostwick), Susanne Cowie (Young Cathy).

Domineering sheep rancher Terence Cooper forcibly has sexual relations with his daughter Mary Regan. Drifter Bruno Lawrence is hired by Cooper, and unaware of the incestuous situation tries to make friends with Regan, but she withdraws from him. At a drunken party after sheep-shearing time, Lawrence gets the story from Regan and tries to get her away from her brutal father. The latter pursues them and is killed by the antlers of a stag which grazes on his land.

1268. *Heartaches* (1981, Rising Star, Canada, 93m, c). P Pieter Kroonenburg, David J. Patterson & Jerry Raibourn, D Donald Shebib, W Terence Heffernan, PH Vic Sarin, M Simon Michael Martin, ED Gerry Hambling & Peter Boita.

LP Margot Kidder (Rita Harris), Annie Potts (Bonnie Howard), Robert Carradine (Stanley Howard), Winston Rekert (Marcello Di Stassi), George Touliatos (Mario Di Stassi), Guy Sanvido (Aldo), Arnie Achtman (Alvin), Michael Zelniker (Andy).

Annie Potts, reluctant to confess to her drunken husband Robert Carradine that she is pregnant with another man's child, runs away. She teams up with brassy Margot Kidder. The two head for Toronto where they get jobs in a mattress factory. Kidder falls for the owner's nephew while Carradine tracks Potts down, and tries to win her back.

1269. *Heartbeeps* (1981, Universal, 88m, c). P Michael Phillips, D Allan Arkush, W John Hill, PH Charles Rosher, M John Williams, ED Tina Hirsch, PD John W. Corso, MK Stan Winston†.

LP Andy Kaufman (Val), Bernadette Peters (Aqua), Randy Quaid (Charlie), Kenneth McMillan (Max), Melanie Mayron (Susan), Christopher Guest (Calvin), Richard B. Shull (Factory Boss), Dick Miller (Watchman).

It's 1995 and Andy Kaufman and Bernadette Peters, robot domestic servants, fall in love and run off together. They assemble a child for themselves in order to build a family.

1270. *Heartbreak Hotel* (1988, Buena Vista, 93m, c). P Lynda Obst & Debra Hill, D&W Chris Columbus, PH Stephen Dobson, M Georges Delerue, ED Raja Gosnell, PD John Muto.

LP David Keith (Elvis Presley), Tuesday Weld (Marie Wolfe), Charlie Schlatter (Johnny Wolfe), Angela Goethals (Pam Wolfe), Jacque Lynn Colton (Rosie Pantangellio), Chris Mulkey (Steve Ayres), Karen Landry (Irene), Tudor Sherrard (Paul Quinine), Paul Harkins (Brian Gasternick).

This inept film badly answers the question no one cares to ask: What would happen if Elvis Presley moved into the lives of a troubled family of fans? Tuesday Weld remembers the young Presley as a rebel. Her son Charlie Schlatter believes "The King" sold out in 1972. Schlatter kidnaps Presley (David Keith) and brings him home to Momma. Presley acts just like a regular person, meets the neighbors, and mows the lawn. He even appears with Schlatter in a high school talent show the latter had been barred from because the lyrics of the song he wanted to sing were considered un-American, being anti-Vietnam war.

1271. *Heartbreak Ridge* (1986, Warner, 130m, c). P&D Clint Eastwood, W James Carabatsos, PH Jack N. Green, M Lennie Niehaus, ED Joel Cox, PD Edward Carfagno.

LP Clint Eastwood (Tom Highway), Marsha Mason (Aggie), Everett McGill (Major Powers), Moses Gunn (Sgt. Webster), Eileen Heckart (Little Mary), Bo Svenson (Roy Jennings), Boyd Gaines (Lt. Ring), Mario Van Peebles (Stitch), Arlen Dean Snyder (Choozoo), Vincent Irizarry (Fragetti).

Clint Eastwood gives audiences his interpretation of the invasion of Grenada. It's a tedious, boring film which seems to last longer than the actual battle for the Caribbean island. It certainly makes the decision to send in the Marines seem ludicrous.

1272. *Heartbreaker* (1983, Emerson/ Monorex, 90m, c). P Chris P. Nebe & Chris Anders, D Frank Zuniga, W Vincente Gutierrez, PH Michael Lonzo, M Rob Walsh, ED Larry Bock, SOUND Les Fresholtz, Dick Alexander, Vern Poore & William Nelson†.

LP Fernando Allende (Beto), Dawn Dunlap (Kim), Peter Gonzales Falcon (Hector), Miguel Ferrer (Angel), Michael D. Roberts (Hopper), Robert Dryer (Wings), Pepe Serna (Loco), Rafael Campos (Alfonso), Carmen Martinez (Minnie), Carlo Allen (Gato).

Eastern L.A. explodes with turf wars when both Fernando Allende and Peter Gonzales Falcon battle over the latest heartbreaker in town, Dawn Dunlap.

1273. *Heartbreakers* (1984, Orion, 98m, c). P Bob Weis & Bobby Roth, D&W Roth, PH Michael Ballhaus, M

Tangarine Dream, ED John Carnochan, PD David Nichols.

LP Peter Coyote (Arthur Blue), Nick Mancuso (Eli Kahn), Carole Laure (Liliane), Max Gail (King), James Laurenson (Terry Ray), Carol Wayne (Candy), Jamie Rose (Libby), Kathryn Harrold (Cyd), George Morfogen (Max).

Mid-30s buddies businessman Nick Mancuso and artist Peter Coyote are immature adolescents when it comes to females. Neither wishes to make any commitment with a partner, but enjoy the sexual competition for women they provide each other. These are the kind of guys extremely frustrated women scream about when they say all men are alike. We sincerely hope not.

1274. *Heartburn* (1986, Paramount, 108m, c). P Mike Nichols & Robert Greenhut, D Nichols, W Nora Ephron (based on her novel), PH Nestor Almendros, M Carly Simon, ED Sam O'Steen, PD Tony Walton.

LP Meryl Streep (Rachel), Jack Nicholson (Mark), Jeff Daniels (Richard), Maureen Stapleton (Vera), Stockard Channing (Julie), Richard Masur (Arthur), Catherine O'Hara (Betty), Steven Hill (Harry), Milos Forman (Dmitri), Natalie Stern (Annie), Karen Akers (Thelma Rice).

Meryl Streep and Jack Nicholson are first rate in a rather ordinary and overly-long examination of the romantic problems of a busy professional couple. The failure of their marriage is predictable from the moment they meet.

1275. *Heartland* (1980, Wilderness Women Productions, 96m, c). P Michael Hausman & Beth Ferris, D Richard Pearce, W Ferris (based on the books and papers of Elinore Randall Stewart), PH Fred Murphy, M Charles Gross, ED Bill Yahraus.

LP Rip Torn (Clyde), Conchata Ferrell (Elinore), Barry Primus (Jack), Lilia Skala (Grandma), Megan Folsom (Jerrine), Amy Wright (Clara), Jerry Hardin (Cattle Buyer), Mary Boylan (Ma Gillis).

Anyone who has fond memories of a mother seemingly capable of enduring anything for her family, will be touched by this semidocumentary. In 1910, widow Conchata Ferrell, determined to find a good life for herself and her 7-year-old daughter Megan Folsom, travels to Wyoming to become housekeeper for taciturn, stingy, hard-working Scottish farmer Rip Torn. With the help of Torn and eccentric female rancher Lilia Skala, Ferrell is able to save enough money to get some land for herself. The harsh winter almost kills both Ferrell and Folson, but she is rescued by Torn. She accepts his business-like offer of marriage, becomes pregnant, delivers the child by herself, but it dies. Still the little family struggles and bears their burdens without complaint.

1276. *Heat* (1987, New Century/ Vista, 101m, c). P Keith Rotman & George Pappas, D R.M. [Dick] Richards, W William Goldman (based on his novel), PH James Contner, M Michael Gibbs, ED Jeffrey Wolf.

LP Burt Reynolds (Nick "Mex" Escalante), Karen Young (Holly), Peter MacNicol (Cyrus Kinnick), Howard Hesseman (Pinchus Zion), Neill Barry (Danny DeMarco), Diana Scarwid (Cassie), Joe Mascolo (Baby), Alfie Wise (Felix).

Add one more nail to Burt Reynolds' career coffin. He's a Las Vegas tough guy who does "favors" for friends. He's hired by wealthy young computer whiz Peter MacNicol to chaperone him around the casinos. Another friend of Reynolds is hooker Karen Young who wants Burt to rip off the private parts of Neill Barry, the sadistic young man who brutalized her. Barry just happens to be the son of a Mafia don, so this may be considered a no-no. Reynolds handles his assignments in this movie as if he's insulted that someone wants him to act—a chore which more and more, as the decade wore on, seemed beyond him.

1277. *Heat and Dust* (1983, Universal, GB, 133m, c). P Ismail Merchant, D James Ivory, W Ruth Prawer Jhabvala (based on her novel), PH Walter Lassally, M Richard Robbins, ED Humphrey Dixon, PD Wilfred Shingleton.

LP Julie Christie (Anne), Greta Scacchi (Olivia), Christopher Cazenove (Douglas Rivers), Julian Glover (Crawford), Susan Fleetwood (Mrs. Crawford), Shashi Kapoor (The Nawab),

Madhur Jaffrey (The Begum, his Mother), Nicklas Grace (Harry), Zakir Hussain (Inder Lal), Barry Foster (Maj. Minnies), Amanda Walker (Lady Mackleworth).

Greta Scacchi travels to India in the 1920s and marries a local prince. She becomes pregnant, and scandalizes the populace when she decides to abort the child. Sixty years later, her great-niece Julie Christie is in England to learn of her notorious relative. Her life parallels Scacchi, up to the point of becoming pregnant. Although the attitudes towards abortion have changed, Christie decides to have the child.

1278. Heat and Sunlight (1988, New Front Alliance, 96m, b&w). P Hildy & Steve Burns, D&W Rob Nilsson, PH Tomas Tucker, M David Byrne, ED Henk Van Eeghen, PD H&S Burns, CH Consuelo Faust.

LP Rob Nilsson (Mel Hurley), Consuelo Faust (Carmen), Don Bajema (Mitch), Ernie Fosselius (Bobby), Bill Bailey (Barney), Russell Murphy (Adam), Lynn "Christie" Ana (Raven De La Croix).

In this rambling semiautobiographical film, photographer Rob Nilsson is at the end of a troubling love affair with sexy Consuelo Faust.

1279. Heathers (1989, New World, 102m, c). P Denise Di Novi, D Michael Lehmann, W Daniel Waters, PH Francis Kenny, M David Newman, ED Norman Hollyn, PD Jon Hutman.

LP Winona Ryder (Veronica Sawyer), Christian Slater (J.D.), Shannen Doherty (Heather Duke), Lisanne Falk (Heather McNamara), Kim Walker (Heather Chandler), Penelope Milford (Pauline Fleming), Glenn Shadix (Father Ripper), Lance Fenton (Kurt Kelly), Patrick Laborteaux (Ram), Jeremy Applegate (Peter Dawson), Jon Matthews (Rodney).

The two major teen groups featured in this very black comedy are the popular insensitive in crowd, represented by the bitchy, beautiful Heathers, contrasted with the cool, weird and sometimes deranged outsiders in the persons of petulant Winona Ryder and diabolical Christian Slater. He encourages Ryder to slip the wickedest of the Heathers, Kim Walker, a concoction containing liquid plumber. When this kills the poor girl, Ryder uses her talents as a forger to come up with a beautiful, sensitive suicide note. The two also make the murder of two lame-brained football players look like a suicide of two gay lovers. Slater plans a mass suicide for the whole student body but must settle for being his only victim, while the stunning Ryder reverts to being just a "normal" high school girl.

1280. Heatwave (1983, New Line, Australia, 92m, c). P Hilary Linstead, D Phillip Noyce, W Noyce, Marc Rosenberg, Mark Stiles & Tim Gooding, PH Vincent Monton, M Cameron Allan, ED John Scott, PD Ross Major.

LP Judy Davis (Kate), Richard Moir (Steven), Chris Haywood (Peter), Bill Hunter (Robert), John Gregg (Phillip), Anna Jemison (Victoria), John Meillon (Freddy), Dennis Miller (Mick), Peter Hehir (Bodyguard).

Local residents, led by Judy Davis, oppose the building of a multi-million dollar residential complex in their neighborhood. A budding romance with the architect Richard Moir doesn't lessen her resolve. It's an Australian version of *Chinatown*.

1281. Heaven Becomes Hell (1989, Taurus, 99m, c, aka *Jealous*). P Lotte Nivelli, D&W Mickey Nivelli, PH Larry Revene, M Jonathan Hannah & Suzie Cioffi, ED Richard Dama.

LP Michael Walker (Himself), James Davies (Nick Cooney), Regan Vann (Joanie Cooney), Myla Churchill (Gloria Johnson), Ruth Collins (Rita), John Altamura (David).

With the help of his friend Michael Walker, fake evangelist James Davies pulls off a religious con to raise money to make a film in which they both will star.

1282. Heaven Can Help (1989, United Entertainment, 111m, c). P&D Tony Zarindast, W Zarindast & Bud Fleisher, PH Robert Hayes, M Alan DerMarderosian, ED Ronald Goldstein, PD Don Scott.

LP Tony Bova (Val), Jinx Dawson (Vyra), Diane Copeland (Angel Crystal), Diane Hayden (Mrs. Ferrari),

Joe Balogh (Matthew), Ted Prior (Angel Billy), Myron Natwick (Devil).

Real estate wheeler-dealer Tony Bova sees himself as a 60s singer à la Frankie Valli or James Darren. His son's computer hooks up with an angel. What's it all mean? You got us.

1283. *Heaven Help Us* (1985, Tri-Star, 104m, c, aka *Catholic Boys*). P Dan Wigutow & Mark Carliner, D Michael Dinner, W Charles Purpura, PH Miroslav Ondricek, M James Horner, ED Stephen A. Rotter, PD Michael Molly.

LP Andrew McCarthy (Michael Dunn), Mary Stuart Masterson (Danni), Kevin Dillon (Rooney), Malcolm Danare (Caesar), Jennie Dundas (Boo), Kate Reid (Grandma), Wallace Shawn (Father Abruzzi), Jay Patterson (Brother Constance), John Heard (Brother Timothy), Donald Sutherland (Brother Thadeus), George Anders (Brother Augustus), Dana Barron (Janine).

Combine teenage sexual pranks and Catholic guilt and one has this tame comedy about the students at St. Basil's Catholic Boy's School in Brooklyn. They and the stern brothers who run the institution give each other fits.

1284. *Heavenly Bodies* (1985, MGM/United Artists, 89m, c). P Robert Lantos & Stephen J. Roth, D Lawrence Dane, W Dane & Ron Base, PH Thomas Burstyn, M Irwin Mazur & Kevin Benson, ED Robert Lambert, PD Lindsey Goddard.

LP Cynthia Dale (Samantha), Richard Rebiere (Steve), Walter George Alton (Jack), Laura Henry (Debbie), Stuart Stone (Joel), Patricia Idlette (KC), Pam Henry (Patty), Linda Sorenson (TV Producer), Reiner Schwartz (TV Director), Cec Linder (Walter), Micki Moore (TV Reporter).

Without any noticeable funds, out-of-work secretary Cynthia Dale and her friends turn a warehouse into a high-powered aerobics studio. She's well on her way to her lofty ambition of becoming an aerobics instructor on TV. It's a shame, but even those most desperate to see well put together hardbodies strut their stuff in skin-tight leotards will get bored by all the stretching and bending.

1285. *The Heavenly Kid* (1985, Orion, 89m, c). P Mort Engelberg, D Cary Medoway, W Medoway & Martin Copeland, PH Steven Poster, M Kennard Ramsey, ED Christopher Greenbury, PD Ron Hobbs.

LP Lewis Smith (Bobby Fontana), Jason Gedrick (Lenny), Jane Kaczmarek (Emily), Richard Mulligan (Rafferty), Mark Metcalf (Joe), Beau Dremann (Bill McIntyre), Stephen Gregory (Fred Gallo), Anne Sawyer (Sharon).

Leather-jacketed rebel teen Lewis Smith bought the big one 17 years earlier but is back on earth as a guardian angel sent to help adolescent Jason Gedrick. The latter's sole ambition is to get laid. This film almost goes through the bridal checklist — you know, something old, something borrowed, something blue — the only thing missing is anything new.

Heavenly Pursuits see The Gospel According to Vic

1286 *Heaven's Gate* (1980, United Artists, 205m, c). P Joann Careli, D&W Michael Cimino, PH Vilmos Zsigmond, M David Mansfield, ED Tom Rolf, William Reynolds, Lisa Fruchtman & Gerald Greenberg, AD/SD Tambi Larsen & Jim Berkey†.

LP Kris Kristofferson (Marshal James Averill), Christopher Walken (Nathan D. Champion), John Hurt (Billy Irvine), Isabelle Huppert (Ella Watson), Sam Waterston (Frank Canton), Jeff Bridges (John H. Bridges), Joseph Cotten ("The Reverend Doctor"), Roseanne Vela (Beautiful Girl), Ronnie Hawkins (Wolcott), Geoffrey Lewis (Trapper), Paul Koslo (Mayor), Richard Masur (Cully), Mary C. Wright (Nell).

Considered the most out-of-control movie maker since Erich von Stroheim, director-writer Michael Cimino is by far the greater sinner; he didn't produce anything much worth seeing for all of his extravagance. His epic Western purports to tell the story of the bloody 1892 Johnson County wars in Wyoming between cattlemen and immigrants. His expensive efforts for accuracy in staging his movie don't prevent him from juggling the facts as he sees fit. It's not true that the entire real battle took less time than this movie, but it is true that one's rear end has its own criticism of this film disaster.

1287. *Heavy Metal* (1981, Columbia, Canada, animated, 91m, c). P Ivan Reitman, D Gerald Potterton, W Dan Goldberg & Len Blum (based on work and stories by Richard Corben, Angus McKie, Dan O'Bannon, Thomas Warkentin & Berni Wrightson), M Elmer Bernstein, ED Janice Brown, PD Michael Gross, ANIMATION DESIGN Warkentin, McKie, O'Bannon, Corben, Juan Gimenez & Lee Mishkin.

VOICES Roger Bumpass, Jackie Burroughs, John Candy, Joe Flaherty, Don Francks, Martin Lavut, Eugene Levy, Marilyn Lightstone, Alice Playten, Harold Ramis, Susan Roman, Richard Romanus, John Vernon.

An international team of animators produced this complicated comic strip/science fiction story that is neither appropriate nor intended for the kiddies.

1288. *Heavy Petting* (1989, Skouras, 89m, b&w). P Obie Benz, D Benz & Josh Waletzky, W Pierce Rafferty, PH Samdi Sessel, M Hal Willner, ED Waletzky, Judith Sobel & Edith Becker.

LP David Byrne, Sandra Bernhard, Spalding Gray, Ann Magnuson, Josh Mostel, Laurie Anderson.

In this generally amusing satire on sex in the dark ages of the 50s, the filmmakers detail how painful the business of adolescent sex was in a period of sexual repression. In the 90s it's dangerous and possibly deadly.

1289. *Heidi's Song* (1982, Paramount, animated, 94m, c). P Joseph Barbera & William Hanna, D Robert Taylor, W Barbera, Taylor & Jameson Brewer (based on a novel by Johanna Spyri), M Hoyt S. Curten, ED Gregory V. Watson, Jr., ANIM Hal Ambro & Charlie Downs.

VOICES Lorne Greene (Grandfather), Sammy Davis, Jr. (Head Ratte), Margery Grey (Heidi), Peter Cullen (Gruffle), Roger DeWitt (Peter), Richard Erdman (Herr Sessmann), Fritz Feld (Sebastian), Pamelyn Ferdin (Klara).

This is an animated version of the familiar story of an orphan girl living with her grumpy but loving grandfather in the Swiss Alps. The songs by Sammy Cahn and Burton Lane are not among the pair's best.

1290. *Hell Comes to Frogtown* (1988, New World, 86m, c). P Donald G. Jackson & Randall Frakes, D Jackson & R.J. Kizer, W Randall Frakes, PH Donald G. Jackson, M David Shapiro, ED R.J. Kizer & James Matheny, PD Dins Danielson, SE Steve Wang.

LP Rowdy Roddy Piper (Sam Hell), Brian Frank (Comdr. Toty), Sandahl Bergman (Spangle), Cec Verrell (Centinella), William Smith (Capt. Devlin/Count Sodom), Rory Calhoun (Looney Tunes).

Sometime in the future after war, famine and other nasty things have wiped out most everyone, Rowdy Roddy Piper is one of the few remaining unsterile men. A lot of fertile women live in Frogtown and it's his patriotic duty to make them all pregnant.

1291. *Hell High* (1989, JGM Entertainment, 79m, c, aka *Raging Fury*). P David Steinman & Douglas Grossman, D Grossman, W Leo Evans & Grossman, PH Steven Fierberg, M Rich Macar, ED Claire Simpson-Crozier & Greg Sheldon.

LP Christopher Stryker (Dickens), Maureen Mooney (Brooke Storm), Christopher Cousins (Jon Jon), Millie Prezioso (Queenie), Jason Brill (Smiler).

As a child, pretty high school biology teacher Maureen Mooney witnessed the double murder of two teens in a swampland. One night, some of her mean-spirited students, led by Christopher Stryker, terrorize her wearing masks to make them appear as monsters from the swamp. When they try to rape her, Mooney hurtles herself through a window to her apparent death. Dead or alive, she takes a grisly revenge on her tormentors.

1292. *Hell Night* (1982, Compass International, 101m, c). P Irwin Yablans & Bruce Cohn Curtis, D Tom DeSimone, W Randolph Feldman, PH Mac Ahlberg, M Dan Wyman, ED Tony DiMarco.

LP Linda Blair (Marti), Vincent Van Patten (Seth), Peter Barton (Jeff), Kevin Brophy (Peter), Jenny Neumann (May), Suki Goodwin (Denise), Jimmy Sturtevant (Scott).

Linda Blair is one of four young people who must spend the night in a mysterious mansion as part of an initiation into a fraternity and a sorority. The killer of his family who lived in the mansion returns for some additional murders.

1293. *Hell Squad* (1987, Cannon, 87m, c). P,D&W Kenneth Hartford, PH John McCoy, M Charles P. Barnett, ED Robert Ernst.

LP Bainbridge Scott, Glen Hartford, Tina Ledderman, Maureen Kelly, Penny Prior, Kim Baucum, Delynn Gardner, Lisa Nottingham, Kathy Jinnett.

When the goal is to show a lot of nude women and gore, even a story as absurd as this one will do. Las Vegas showgirls are recruited by the CIA to rescue an American kidnapped by Arab terrorists.

1294. *Hellbound: Hellraiser II* (1988, New World, 96m, c). P Christopher Figg, D Tony Randel, W Peter Atkins (based on a story by Clive Barker), PH Robin Vidgeon, M Christopher Young, PD Mike Buchanan.

LP Ashley Laurence (Kristy Cotton), Clare Higgins (Julia), Ken Cranham (Dr. Channard), Imogen Boorman (Tiffany), William Hope (Kyle Macrae), Oliver Smith (Browning), Sean Chapman (Uncle Frank), Doug Bradley (Skinhead Cenobite), Simon Bamford (Butterball Cenobite), Barbie Wilde (Female Cenobite).

This sequel picks up the action two hours after the events which ended the 1987 production of *Hellraiser* (entry 1299). Ashley Laurence's stories of the horrific things she saw are not believed, but viewers won't be disappointed in the special effects as all are returned to Hades. However the story and the acting should burn in hell.

1295. *Hellgate* (1989, New World, 88m, c). P Arant Singh & Shan Moodley, D William A. Levey, W Michael O'Rourke, PH Peter Palmer, M Max Lemmon & Chris Barnes, ED Mark Baard.

LP Ron Palillo (Matt), Abigail Wolcott (Josie), Carel Trichardt (Lucas), Petrea Curran (Pam), Evan J. Klisser (Chuck), Joanne Ward (Bobby), Frank Notard (Buzz), Lance Vaughan (Zonk), Victor Mellaney (Jonas).

Carel Trichardt, the owner of a tourist ghost town, terrorizes a group of visiting college students. The deranged one has a crystal that enables him to bring things back to life. One such reanimated corpse is his dead daughter Abigail Wolcott, who fancies Ron Palillo. She helps him escape her old man's slaughterhouse.

1296. *Hellhole* (1985, Arkoff, 95m, c). P Billy Fine & Louis Arkoff, D Pierre de Moro, W Vincent Mongol, Lance Dickson & Mark Evan Schwartz, PH Steven Posey, M Jeff Sturges, ED Steve Butler.

LP Ray Sharkey (Silk), Judy Landers (Susan), Mary Woronov (Dr. Fletcher), Marjoe Gortner (Dr. Dane), Edy Williams (Vera), Terry Moore (Sidnee Hammond), Robert Darcy (Brad), Rick Cox (Ron), Martin Beck (Monroe), Lynn Borden (Mom), Cliff Emmich (Dr. Blum).

Mad scientist Mary Woronov and her weird assistant Marjoe Gortner experiment with lobotomy operations on unsuspecting patients at their Sanitarium. One of their prospective guinea pigs is Judy Landers, who becomes an amnesiac after Ray Sharkey kills her mother. He trails Landers to Woronov's hellhole in hopes that the former will recall where her deceased mother hid some important papers. Except for Woronov, the acting is strictly junior-high level.

1297. *Hello Again* (1987, Buena Vista, 100m, c). P Frank Perry, G. Mac Brown, Martin Mickelson, Susan Isaacs & Thomas Folino, D Perry, W Susan Isaacs, PH Jan Weincke, M William Goldstein, ED Peter C. Frank & Trudy Ship, PD Edward Pisoni.

LP Shelley Long (Lucy Chadman), Judith Ivey (Zelda), Gabriel Byrne (Dr. Kevin Scanlon), Corbin Bernsen (Dr. Jason Chadman), Sela Ward (Kim Lacey), Austin Pendleton (Junior Lacey), Carrie Nye (Regina Holt), Robert Lewis (Phineas Devereux), Madeleine Potter (Felicity), Thor Fields (Danny Chadman), John Cunningham (Bruce Holt).

Suburban housewife Shelley Long chokes to death on a Korean meatball. About a year later she is brought back to life by her wacky sister Judith Ivey. Long finds her husband has remarried and no one knows quite what to do about her reappearance. This film died and no resurrection is expected.

1298. *Hello Mary Lou, Prom Night II* (1987, Simcom/Norstar, Canada, 96m, c, aka *The Haunting of Hamilton High*). P Peter Simpson, D Bruce Pittman, W Ron Oliver, PH John Herzog, M Paul Zaza, ED Nick Rotundo, PD Sandy Kybartas, SE Jim Doyle.

LP Lisa Schrage (Mary Lou Maloney), Wendy Lyon (Vicki Carpenter), Michael Ironside (Principal Bill, Sr.), Justin Louis (Bill, Jr.), Richard Monette (Father).

Here's another story of a girl, Lisa Schrage, returning from the grave. Only this time she's out to take revenge on her killers who now run the school where she was murdered.

1299. *Hellraiser* (1987, New World, GB, 90m, c). P Christopher Figg, D&W Clive Barker, PH Robin Vidgeon, M Christopher Young, ED Richard Marden, PD Mike Buchanan, SE Bob Keen, COS Joanna Johnston.

LP Andrew Robinson (Larry), Clare Higgins (Julia), Ashley Laurence (Kirsty), Sean Chapman (Frank Cotton), Oliver Smith (Frank the Monster), Robert Hines (Steve).

We might have missed this one except our daughter praised its marvelous visuals. We agree, but the story is another thing. Sean Chapman solves the secret of a small carved puzzle-box. It invokes the Cenobites, spirits devoted to an eternity of sensual pleasure. For Chapman they prove to be a pain as he tries to escape their world. He is forced to drain the life from unwitting victims to regain his humanity and be free of the otherworldly web of evil. And see entry 1294.

1300. *Hell's Angels Forever* (1983, Marvin Films, 92m, c). P Richard Chase, Sandy Alexander & Leon Gast, D Chase, Kevin Keating & Gast, W Peterson Tooke & Chase, PH Keating.

LP Hells Angels, Willie Nelson, Jerry Garcia, Johnny Paycheck, Bo Diddley.

This quasidocumentary offers no insights into a world where honor, violence and undying passion for motorcycles defines a life.

1301. *Henry...Portrait of a Serial Killer* (1989, Maljack, 83m, c). P John McNaughton, Lisa Dedmond & Steven A. Jones, D McNaughton, W Richard Fire & McNaughton, PH Charlie Lieber-man, M McNaughton, Ken Hale & Jones, ED Elena Maganini, AD Rick Paul.

LP Michael Rooker (Henry), Tom Towles (Otis), Tracy Arnold (Becky).

Michael Rooker is a serial killer proud of his work. Realizing that police look for patterns to trap people in his profession, he always varies his modus operandi. Audiences are treated to all the gory details of his various techniques.

1302. *Henry V* (1989, Goldwyn, GB, 137m, c). P Bruce Sharman, D Kenneth Branagh†, W Branagh (based on the play by William Shakespeare), PH Kenneth MacMillan, M Patrick Boyle, ED Michael Bradsell, PD Tim Harvey, COS Phyllis Dalton.

LP Kenneth Branagh† (Henry V), Derek Jacobi (Chorus), Brian Blessed (Exeter), Ian Holm (Fluellen), Paul Scofield (French King), Michael Maloney (Dauphin), Alec McCowen (Ely), Emma Thompson (Katherine), Geraldine McEwan (Alice), Robbie Coltrane (Falstaff), Simon Shepherd (Gloucester), James Larkin (Bedford), John Sessions (MacMorris), Christian Bale (Falstaff's Boy), Michael Williams, Richard Briers, Geoffrey Hutchings, Robert Stephens, Judi Dench, Harold Innocent.

It takes a brave man or a foolish one to risk comparison to Lord Laurence Olivier and his 1944 masterpiece production of *Henry V*. That film was meant to rally the English in World War II, inspiring them by the glorious battle and patriotic verses. Kenneth Branagh is not a fool. His version, although done on a relatively more limited budget and scale than Olivier's, is a welcomed addition to the films of Shakespeare's work. Branagh is not yet the new Olivier, but the day may come in which he may rightly claim the mantle. The present production, dealing with the coming of age of a young king, who leads England to triumph against the French, happily features an outstanding cast. Whether one has seen the 1944 film or not, this one is well worth viewing.

1303. *Her Alibi* (1989, Warner, 94m, c). P Keith Barish, D Bruce Beresford, W Charlie Peters, PH Freddie Francis, M Georges Delerue, ED Anne Goursaud, PD Henry Bumstead.

LP Tom Selleck (Phil Blackwood),

Paulina Porizkova (Nina Ionescu), William Daniels (Sam), James Farentino (Frank Polito), Hurd Hatfield (Troppa), Ronald Guttman ("Lucy" Comanescu), Victor Argo (Avram), Patrick Wayne (Gary Blackwood), Tess Harper (Sally Blackwood).

Mystery writer Tom Selleck claims that he and drop-dead beauty Paulina Porizkova are lovers and were together in bed at the time she was supposed to be committing a murder. His motive is to get a new story, as his muse has deserted him. When Selleck moves the dark haired beauty into his country estate, it looks like she's trying to do away with him so he can't change his story and nix her alibi.

1304. *Herbie Goes Bananas* (1980, Buena Vista, 100m, c). P Ron Miller, D Vincent McEveety, W Don Tait (based on characters created by Gordon Buford), PH Frank Phillips, M Frank De Vol, ED Gordon D. Brenner.

LP Cloris Leachman (Aunt Louise), Charles Martin Smith (D.J.), John Vernon (Prindle), Steven W. Burns (Pete), Elyssa Davalos (Melissa), Joaquin Garay III (Paco), Harvey Korman (Captain Blythe), Richard Jaeckel (Shepard), Alex Rocco (Quinn), Fritz Feld (Chief Steward).

Charles Martin Smith and Steven W. Burns take their magical Volkswagen Bug on a South American holiday. Don't we have enough problems with our South of the Border policies than to invade the region with "The Love Bug" in the 80s?

1305. *Hercules* (1983, MGM/United Artists/Cannon, 98m, c). P Menahem Golan & Yoram Globus, D&W Lewis Coates [Luigi Cozzi], PH Alberto Spagnoli, M Pino Donaggio, ED Sergio Montanari, PD & AD Antonello Geleng.

LP Lou Ferrigno (Hercules), Mirella D'Angelo (Circe), Sybil Danning (Arianna), Ingrid Anderson (Cassiopea), William Berger (King Minos), Brad Harris (King Augeius), Claudio Cassinelli (Zeus), Rossana Podesta (Hera).

Muscleman Lou Ferrigno provides the body but not the voice of the legendary strongman who fights evil William Berger, for his own survival and the love of Ingrid Anderson.

1306. *Hercules II* (1985, Cannon, 88m, c, aka *Adventures of Hercules*). P

Alfred Pecoriello, D&W Lewis Coates [Luigi Cozzi], PH Alberto Spagnoli, M Pino Donaggio, ED Sergio Montanari, PD Tony Gelleng [Massimo Antonello Geleng].

LP Lou Ferrigno (Hercules), Milly Carlucci (Urania), Sonia Viviani (Glaucia), William Berger (King Minos), Carlotta Green (Athena), Claudio Cassinelli (Zeus), Nando Poggi (Poseidon), Maria Rosaria Omaggio (Hera).

Made at the same time as the previous film, this film assigns Lou Ferrigno the task of preventing the moon from crashing into the earth. He's able to put the heavens back into harmony through his strength and his in with the Greek gods. Ferrigno's acting makes it seem that in developing his physique his brains became solid muscle.

1307. *Here Comes Santa Claus* (1984, New World, 78m, c). P&D Christian Gion, W Gion & Didier Kaminka, PH Jacques Assuerus, M Francis Lai, ED Pauline Leroy.

LP Emeric Chapuis (Simon), Armand Meffre (Santa Claus), Karen Cheryl (Teacher/Magic Fairy), Alexia (Elodic), Dominique Hulin (The Ogre), Jeanne Herviale (Simon's Grandmother), Helene Zidi (Simon's Mother).

This children's film features courageous elves, live reindeer, a beautiful fairy, an ugly Ogre, and, naturally, Santa Claus. All are awaiting 7-year-old Emeric Chapuis when he visits Santa's magical kingdom to personally deliver a very special Christmas wish.

1308. *Here Comes the Littles* (1985, Atlantic, 75m, c). P Jean Chalopin, Andy Heyward & Tetsuo Katayama, D Bernard Deyries, W Woody Kling (based on the novels of Jon Peterson), PH Hajime Hasegawa & Kenichi Kobayashi, M Haim Saban & Shuki Levy, ED Masatoshi Tsurubuchi.

VOICES Jimmy E. Keegan (Henry Bigg), Bettina Bush (Lucy Little), Donavan Freberg (Tom Little), Hal Smith (Uncle Augustus), Gregg Berger (William Little), Patricia Parris (Helen Little), Alvy Moore (Grandpa Little).

If you've passed your eighth birthday, you'll want to pass on this cartoon merchandizing gimmick. It's the deadly dull story of happy little mouse-like creatures who help Jimmy E. Keegan deal with his evil uncle.

1309. *Hero and the Terror* (1988, Cannon, 96m, c). P Raymond Wagner, D William Tannen, W Dennis Shryack & Michael Blodgett (based on the novel by Blodgett), PH Eric van Haren Noman, M David Frank, ED Christian Adam Wagner, PD Holger Gross.

LP Chuck Norris (Herrara "Hero" O'Brien), Brynn Thayer (Kay Griffith), Steve James (Bill Robinson), Jack O'Halloran (Simon Moon), Jeffrey Kramer (Dwight Hopkins), Ron O'Neal (Mayor), Murphy Dunne (Theatre Manager), Heather Blodgett (Betsy), Tony DiBenedetto (Doheny), Billy Drago (Dr. Highwater).

Police detective Chuck Norris is declared a hero by the media when he accidentally captures psycho Jack O'Halloran. The latter's specialty is snapping the necks of women whose bodies he keeps in a deserted seaside restaurant. Norris is terrified that the killer will escape and come after him, and indeed he does.

1310. *Hero at Large* (1989, MGM, 98m, c). P Stephen Friedman, D Martin Davidson, W A.J. Carothers, PH David M. Walsh, M Patrick Williams, ED Sidney Levin & David Garfield, PD Albert Brenner.

LP John Ritter (Steve Nichols), Anne Archer (J. Marsh), Bert Convy (Walter Reeves), Kevin McCarthy (Calvin Donnelly), Harry Bellaver (Eddie), Anita Dangler (Mrs. Havacheck), Jane Hallaren (Gloria Preston), Leonard Harris (Mayor), Rick Podell (Milo), Allan Rich (Marty Fields).

Idealistic young actor John Ritter, who makes public appearances as comic book hero "Captain Avenger," gets the chance to play the role for real.

1311. *Heroes Stand Alone* (1989, Concorde, 83m, c). P Luis Llosa, D Mark Griffiths, W Thomas McKelvey Cleaver, PH Cusi Barrio, M Eddie Arkin, ED Michael Thibault, AD Esteban Mejia.

LP Chad Everett (Zack Duncan), Bradford Dillman (Walt Simmons), Wayne Grace (Major Grigori), Rick Dean (Willie), Michel Chieffo (Killer),

Timothy Wead (Johnson), Elsa Olivero (Rosa).

When a U.S.-backed flyover mission violates a ceasefire in fictional Central American country San Pedro, the plane is shot down. CIA agent Chad Everett and his men are sent in to rescue the survivors and the black box of the plane before the Russians and the Cubans can get a hold of it. The villain of the piece is former CIA agent turned gunrunner Bradford Dillman.

1312. *He's My Girl* (1987, Scotti Bros., 104m, c). P Lawrence Taylor Mortorff & Angela Schapiro, D Gabrielle Beaumont, W Taylor Ames & Charles F. Bohl, PH Peter Lyons Collister, ED Roy Watts.

LP T.K. Carter (Reggie/Regina), David Hallyday (Bryan Peters), Misha McK (Tasha), Jennifer Tilly (Lisa), Warwick Sims (Simon Sledge), David Clennon (Mason Morgan), Monica Parker (Sally).

Aspiring rock-singer and song writer David Hallyday wins a trip to L.A. and a chance to meet big star Sims. The catch is he must be accompanied by a girlfriend. He chooses to have his best friend and manager T.K. Carter to dress in drag and accompany him. Oh yes, Carter is black. Laugh? We thought we'd never start.

1313. *Hey Babe!* (1984, Rafal, Canada, 105m, c). P Rafal Zielinski & Arthur Voronka, D Zielinski, W Edith Rey (based on a story by Zielinski & Rey), PH Peter Czerski, M Gino Soccio, Roger Pilon & Mature Adults, ED Scott Conrad & Afte Chiriaeff.

LP Buddy Hackett (Sammy Cohen), Yasmine Bleeth (Theresa), Marushka Stankova (Miss Wolf), Vlasta Vrana (Roy), Denise Proulx (Miss Dolores).

Twelve-year-old Yasmine Bleeth, an aspiring Shirley Temple, will do just about anything to make it in show business. She is eventually helped in more ways than one by former entertainer Buddy Hackett, whose career was ruined by booze. It's probably a bit too saccharine for 80s tastes.

1314. *Hey Good Lookin'* (1982, Warner, animated, 76m, c). P,D&W Ralph Bakshi, PH Ted C. Bemiller, M John

Madara & Ric Sandler, ED Donald W. Ernst.

VOICES Richard Romanus (Vinnie), David Proval (Crazy Shapiro), Tina Bowman (Roz), Jesse Welles (Eva), Angelo Grisanti (Solly), Juno Dawson (Waitress), Shirley Jo Finney (Chaplin), Martin Garner (Yonkel).

Ralph Bakshi takes an irreverent look backwards at growing up in the 50s in Brooklyn, which is filled with vulgar street gangs.

1315. *The Hidden* (1987, New Line Cinema, 97m, c). P Robert Shaye, Gerald T. Olson & Michael Meltzer, D Jack Sholder, W Bob Hunt, PH Jacques Haitkin, M Michael Convertino, ED Michael Knue, PD C.J. Strawn & Mick Strawn.

LP Michael Nouri (Tom Beck), Kyle MacLachlan (Lloyd Gallagher), Ed O'Ross (Cliff Willis), Clu Gulager (Ed Flynn), Claudia Christian (Brenda Lee), Clarence Felder (John Masterson), William Boyett (Jonathan Miller).

When a rash of murders and other violent crimes are committed by otherwise ordinary people. L.A. cop Michael Nouri and FBI agent Kyle MacLachlan join forces. Their investigation reveals an alien is responsible.

1316. *Hide and Go Shriek* (1988, New Star, 90m, c). P Dimitri Villard, D Skip Schoolnik, W Michael Kelly, PH Eugene Shlugleit, M John Ross.

LP Brittain Frye, Donna Baltron, George Thomas, Annette Sinclair, Scott Fults, Ria Pavia, Sean Kanan, Rebunkah Jones, Jeff Levine, Scott Kubay.

A game of hide-and-seek turns into a grisly nightmare when eight teenagers sneak into a furniture store for an all-night graduation party.

1317. *Hide in Plain Sight* (1980, MGM/United Artists, 92m, c). P Robert Christiansen & Rick Rosenberg, D James Caan, W Spencer Eastman (based on a book by Leslie Waller), PH Paul Lohmann, M Leonard Rosenman, ED Fredric Steinkamp & William Steinkamp, PD Pato Guzman.

LP James Caan (Thomas Hacklin, Jr.), Jill Eikenberry (Alisa), Robert Viharo (Jack Scolese), Joe Grifasi (Matty Stanke), Barbara Rae (Ruthie Hacklin), Kenneth McMillan (Sam), Danny Aiello (Sal), Thomas Hill (Bobby).

Factory worker James Caan becomes an innocent victim of the federal witness protection program. His ex-wife and his children disappear with her new husband, a two-bit crook, who has informed on the mob.

1318. *Hider in the House* (1989, Vestron, 105m, c). P Edward Teets & Michael Taylor, D Matthew Patrick, W Lem Dobbs, PH Jeff Jur, ED Debra Smith, PD Vicki Paul.

LP Gary Busey (Tom Sykes), Mimi Rogers (Julie Dryer), Michael McKean (Phil Dryer), Kurt Christopher Kinder (Neil Dryer), Candy Hutson (Holly Dryer), Elizabeth Ruscio (Rita Hutchinson), Bruce Glover (Gary Hufford).

As a child Gary Busey killed his abusive parents by setting fire to the house. Just released from a mental institution, he breaks into a recently renovated home and builds a secret space behind a false wall in the attic. The house belongs to the Dryer family. Their unseen guest adopts the family as his own. Busey's killing days are not over. It's a gripping psychological thriller.

1319. *Hiding Out* (1987, DEG, 98m, c). P Jeff Rothberg, D Bob Giraldi, W Joe Menosky & Rothberg, PH Daniel Pearl, M Anne Dudley, ED Edward Warschilka, PD Dan Leigh.

LP Jon Cryer (Andrew Morenski/ "Maxwell Hauser"), Keith Coogan (Patrick Morenski), Annabeth Gish (Ryan Campbell), Oliver Cotton (Killer), Claude Brooks (Clinton), Tim Quill (Kevin O'Roarke), Alexandra Auder (Melissa), Tony Soper (Ahern), Ned Eisenberg (Rodriguez).

Because of some shady dealings, young-looking New York stockbroker Jon Cryer is being hunted by a professional killer. He makes his way to Delaware, shaves his beard, dyes his hair and enrolls in the local high school as a 17-year-old student. Despite his goal of maintaining a low profile, Cryer becomes very popular with the student body. As a result his cover is blown, making it necessary to face the hit man.

1320. *The High Country* (1981, Crown, Canada, 101m, c, aka *The First*

Hello). P Bruce Mallen & Ken Gord, D Harvey Hart, W Bud Townsend, PH Robert Ryan, ED Ron Wisman.

LP Timothy Bottoms (Jim), Linda Purl (Kathy), George Sims (Larry), Jim Lawrence (Casey), Bill Berry (Carter), Walter Mills (Clem), Paul Jolicoeur (Red), Dick Butler (Herbie), Elizabeth Alderton (Maude).

Take the low ground to avoid this story of escaped convict Timothy Bottoms who teams up with handicapped Linda Purl in the Canadian Rockies. Purl demonstrates she can climb quite nicely, thank you, and when it becomes necessary, shoot proficiently at the pursuing authorities.

1321. *High Hopes* (1989, Film-Four/ Skouras, GB, 112m, c). P Victor Glynn & Simon Channing-Williams, D&W Mike Leigh, PH Roger Pratt, M Andrew Dixon, ED John Gregory, PD Diana Charnley.

LP Philip Davis (Cyril), Ruth Sheen (Shirley), Edna Dore (Mrs. Bender), Philip Jackson (Martin), Heather Tobias (Valerie), Leslie Manville (Laetitia Booth-Braine), David Bamber (Rupert Booth-Braine), Jason Watkins (Wayne), Judith Scott (Suzi).

In what is meant to be a microcosm of today's London, yuppies (or is that Sloan Rangers) Leslie Manville and David Bamber and apprentice yuppy Heather Tobias are pitted against widow Edna Dore, her working class son Philip Davis and his live-in girlfriend Judith Scott. The latter good folk keep a large cactus plant they call Thatcher — because it's a pain in the ass. It's quite clear which side director and writer Mike Leigh fancies in this class struggle.

1322. *High Risk* (1981, American Cinema, 94m, c). P Joseph Raffill & Gerald Green, D&W Stewart Raffill, PH Alex Phillips, Jr., M Mark Snow, ED Tom Walls, Jr., PD Augustin Ituarte.

LP James Brolin (Stone), Lindsay Wagner (Olivia), Anthony Quinn (Mariano), Cleavon Little (Rockney), Bruce Davison (Dan), Chick Vennera (Tony), James Coburn (Serrano), Ernest Borgnine (Clint), David Young (Bradley).

Documentary moviemaker James Brolin enlists three antiviolence buddies to steal a million dollars from South American drug dealer James Coburn. It's a violent and occasionally funny caper movie.

1323. *High Road to China* (1983, Warner, 120m, c). P Fred Weintraub, D Brian G. Hutton, W Sandra Weintraub Roland & S. Lee Pogostin (based on the novel by Jon Cleary), PH Ronnie Taylor, M John Barry, ED John Jympson, PD Robert Laing.

LP Tom Selleck (O'Malley), Bess Armstrong (Eve), Jack Weston (Struts), Wilford Brimley (Bradley Tozer), Robert Morley (Bentik), Brian Blessed (Suleiman Khan), Cassandra Gava (Alessa), Michael Sheard (Charlie).

In the twenties, heiress Bess Armstrong hires drunken pilot Tom Selleck to fly her to Afghanistan to find her father Wilford Brimley before he's declared legally dead, causing her to lose her inheritance. Selleck is a good-looking man with considerable charm, but there is no wit in the dialogue of this slim comedy-adventure film.

1324. *High Season* (1988, Hemdale, GB, 104m, c). P Clare Downs, D Clare Peploe, W Mark Peploe & Clare Peploe, PH Chris Menges, M Jason Osborn, ED Gabriella Cristiani & Peter Dansie, PD Andrew McAlpine.

LP Jacqueline Bisset (Katherine), James Fox (Patrick), Irene Papas (Penelope), Sebastian Shaw (Basil "Sharpie" Sharp), Kenneth Branagh (Rick Lamb), Lesley Manville (Carol Lamb), Robert Stephens (Konstantinis), Geoffrey Rose (Thompson), Paris Tselois (Yanni), Ruby Baker (Chloe).

Jacqueline Bisset and James Fox demonstrate what they can do when given decent material. They portray a celebrated photographer and sculptor, respectively. The estranged couple live on a beautiful Greek island, where many deplore the commercialism being pushed by enterprising young Paris Tselois. Even if not captivated by the comedy-mystery fare, the breathtaking scenery should hold your interest.

1325. *High Spirits* (1988, Tri-Star, 96m, c). P Stephen Woolley & David Saunders, D&W Neil Jordan, PH Alex

Thomson, M George Fenton, ED Michael Bradsell, PD Anton Furst.

LP Daryl Hannah (Mary), Peter O'Toole (Peter Plunkett), Steve Guttenberg (Jack), Beverly D'Angelo (Sharon), Jennifer Tilly (Miranda), Peter Gallagher (Brother Tony), Liam Neeson (Martin), Ray McAnally (Plunkett, Sr.), Liz Smith (Mrs. Plunkett).

When Irish nobleman Peter O'Toole advertises his ancestral castle to be haunted in order to attract tourists and pay his bills, he does not reckon with the fact that it actually is haunted. Two hundred years earlier Daryl Hannah and Liam Neeson died on their wedding night in a lover's quarrel without consummating the union. Hannah takes a liking to tourist Steve Guttenberg which only confirms what Neeson thought about his bride when he stabbed her to death. It's not as funny as it sounds.

1326. *High Stakes* (1989, Vidmark, 97m, c). P,D&W Amos Kollek, PH Marc Hirschfeld, M Mira J. Spektor, ED Robert Reitano.

LP Sally Kirkland (Prostitute), Robert LuPone (Wall Street Broker), Richard Lynch (Pimp).

It used to be that an Oscar nomination opened up opportunities for better roles. Don't tell that to Sally Kirkland, nominated for *Anna* in 1987. Here she's stuck being a cheap whore, caught in a struggle with her pimp and a stockbroker who seems to see her in a better light.

1327. *High Tide* (1987, Tri-Star, Australia, 103m, c). P Sandra Levy, D Gillian Armstrong, W Laura Jones, PH Russell Boyd, M Mark Moffiatt & Ricky Fataar, ED Nicholas Beauman, PD Sally Campbell.

LP Judy Davis (Lilli), Jan Adele (Bet), Claudia Karvan (Ally), Colin Friels (Mick), John Clayton (Col), Monica Trapaga (Tracey), Frankie J. Holden (Lester), Toni Scanlon (Mary), Marc Gray (Jason), Emily Stocker (Michelle).

Judy Davis, a back-up singer for an Australian Elvis impersonator, is fired. When her car breaks down at a trailer park on the shore of a beautiful beach, Davis is reunited with her daughter Claudia Karvan, whom she abandoned years earlier when her husband died.

From here on it's a three-person soap opera, involving Davis, daughter Karvan, and mother-in-law Jan Adele, who has raised the girl over the years.

1328. *Higher Education* (1988, Palisades, Canada, 92m, c). P Peter Simpson, D John Sheppard, W Sheppard & Dan Nathanson, PH Brenton Spencer, M Paul Zaza, ED Stephan Fanfara & Nick Rotundo.

LP Kevin Hicks (Andy Cooper), Isabelle Mejias (Carrie Hanson), Richard Monette (Robert Bley), Jennifer Inch (Gladys/Glitter), Emmanuel Mark (Droid), Sharolyn Sparrow (Helen Dobish), Alan Rose (Old Man/Doctor).

Usual stuff; horny guys, cute girls, just enough story to keep things rolling.

1329. *Highlander* (1986, 20th Century–Fox, 111m, c). P Peter S. Davis & William N. Panzer, D Russell Mulcahy, W Gregory Widen, Peter Bellwood & Larry Ferguson (based on a story by Widen), PH Gerry Fisher, M Michael Kamen, ED Peter Honess, PD Allan Cameron.

LP Christopher Lambert (Connor MacLeod), Roxanne Hart (Brenda Wyatt), Clancy Brown (Kurgen), Sean Connery (Ramirez), Beatie Edney (Heather), Alan North (Lt. Moran), Sheila Gish (Rachel), Jon Polito (Det. Bedsoe).

Apparently killed in battle, 14th century Scotsman Christopher Lambert becomes one of a handful of immortals who will fight each other over the centuries, right up to the present day. Its appearance is better than the story or the execution.

1330. *Highpoint* (1984, New World, Canada, 88m, c). P Daniel Fine, D Peter Carter, W Richard A. Guttman, PH Bert Dunk, M John Addison, ED Eric Wrate, PD Seamus Flannery.

LP Richard Harris (Louis Kinney), Christopher Plummer (James Hatcher), Beverly D'Angelo (Lise Hatcher), Kate Reid (Mrs. Rachel Hatcher), Peter Donat (Don Maranzella), Robin Gammell (Banner), Maury Chaykin (Falco), Saul Rubinek (Centino), George Buza (Alex), Louis Negin (Molotov).

When unemployed accountant Richard

Harris takes a job as chauffeur for wealthy Christopher Plummer's family, he finds himself in the middle of a mysterious murder. The title refers to the climatic scene which takes place atop the CN tower in Toronto. It's a fair-to-middling thriller comedy.

1331. *Highway to Hell* (1984, Anglo-American, 95m, c). P David Calloway, D&W Mark Griffiths, PH Tom Richmond, M Al Capps, ED Andy Blumenthal, PD Katherine Vallin.

LP Monica Carrico, Eric Stoltz, Stuart Margolin, Richard Bradford, Joe George, Virgil Frye, Louise Baker, Laurel Patrick, Sorrells Pickard.

Teenager Eric Stoltz, an escaped con wrongly accused of murder, teams up with hooker Monica Carrico in this road picture. There's a high body count as the result of some imaginative ways of sending victims to their final rest.

1332. *The Hills Have Eyes II* (1985, New Realm/VTC, US/GB, 86m, c). P Barry Cahn & Peter Locke, D&W Wes Craven, PH David Lewis, M Harry Manfredini, ED Richard Bracken, PD Dominick Bruno.

LP Michael Berryman (Pluto), Kevin Blair (Roy), John Bloom (The Reaper), Janus Blythe (Rachel/Ruby), Peter Frechette (Harry), Robert Houston (Bobby), Tamara Stafford (Cass), David Nichols (The Psychiatrist).

Ignoring the warnings of a survivor of a gruesome ordeal, a group of youngsters travel down a desert road. When their bus runs out of gas, they're out of luck, finding themselves at the mercy of crazed mutants.

1333. *History of the World, Part 1* (1981, 20th Century-Fox, 92m, c). P,D&W Mel Brooks, PH Woody Omens, M John Morris, ED John Howard, PD Harold Michelson.

LP Mel Brooks (Moses/Comicus/Toquemanda/Jacques/King Louis XVI), Dom DeLuise (Emperor Nero), Madeline Kahn (Empress Nympho), Harvey Korman (Count de Monet), Cloris Leachman (Madame de Farge), Ron Carey (Swiftus), Gregory Hines (Josephus), Shecky Greene (Marcus Vindictus), Sid Caesar (Chief Caveman), Howard Morris (Court Spokesman), Orson Welles (Narrator).

Someone has to take on the dirty job of making sophomoric films to appeal to those who are just crazy for sexual, sexist and bathroom humor, horrible puns, and miserable sight gags. Mel Brooks springs into the breach in this tasteless and witless account of famous episodes in history. Thank God, the film wasn't made later in the decade, because by 1989, Brooks might have carried through with his threat to produce a sequel.

1334. *The Hit* (1985, Island Alive, GB, 100m, c). P Jeremy Thomas, D Stephen Frears, W Peter Prince, PH Mike Molloy, M Paco de Lucia & Eric Clapton, ED Mick Audsley, PD Andrew Sanders.

LP Terence Stamp (Willie Parker), John Hurt (Braddock), Tim Roth (Myron), Laura del Sol (Maggie), Bill Hunter (Harry), Fernando Rey (Chief Inspector), Lennie Peters (Mr. Corrigan), Bernie Searl (Hopwood).

Ten years earlier, exiled Terence Stamp testified against some powerful gangsters, who promised him "we'll meet again." Killers John Hurt and Tim Roth abduct Stamp from Spain under orders to bring him to Paris fso he may be executed properly. Stamp doesn't seem frightened, merely expressing the hope that his execution will go off without any hitches. The intriguing interplay between professional hitman Hurt, his nervous partner Roth, Stamp and Laura del Sol, a crook's girlfriend taken as a hostage, makes the film worth seeing.

Hit and Run see Revenge Squad

1335. *Hit List* (1989, New Linc Cinema, 87m, c). P Paul Hertzberg, D William Lustig, W John Goff & Peter Brosnan, PH James Lemmo, M Garry Schyman, ED David Kern.

LP Jan-Michael Vincent (Jack Collins), Leo Rossi (Frank DeSalvo), Lance Henriksen (Chris Caleek), Charles Napier (Tom Mitchum), Rip Torn (Vic Luca), Jere Burns (Jared Riley), Ken Lerner (Gravenstein), Harriet Hall (Sandri Collins), Junior Richard (Kenny Collins).

Mafia boss Rip Torn assigns ninja-like assassin Lance Henriksen to kill witnesses who can testify against him. Unfortunately, none-too-swift Henriksen hits Jan-Michael Vincent's house which is across the street from his intended victims. When Henriksen abducts Vincent's child, old Jan-boy becomes riled and teams up with one of the original planned "hittees" to rescue the youngster.

1336. *The Hitcher* (1986, Tri-Star, 97m, c). P David Bombyk & Kip Ohman, D Robert Harmon, W Eric Red, PH John Seale, M Mark Isham, ED Frank J. Urioste, PD Dennis Gassner.

LP Rutger Hauer (John Ryder), C. Thomas Howell (Jim Halsey), Jennifer Jason Leigh (Nash), Jeffrey DeMunn (Capt. Esteridge), John Jackson (Sgt. Starr), Billy Greenbush (Trooper Donner), Jack Thibeau (Trooper Prestone).

In a grisly, violent movie, hitchhiker Rutger Hauer keeps reappearing in C. Thomas Howell's life. Is he real or a hallucination? It's been done before and generally with better results.

1337. *Hitler's S.S. Portrait in Evil* (1985, Cannon, GB, 147m, c). P Aida Young, D Jim Goddard, W Lukas Heller, PH Ernest Vincze, M Richard Hartley, ED John Shirley.

LP John Shea (Karl Hoffmann), Bill Nighy (Helmut Hoffmann), Lucy Gutteridge (Mitzi), David Warner (Reinhard Heydrich), Jose Ferrer (Prof. Rosenberg), Tony Randall (Putzi), Carroll Baker (Gerda Hoffmann), Warren Clarke (Becker), Michael Elphick (Roehm), Robert Urquhart (Albrecht Hoffmann), John Normington (Heinrich Himmler), Colin Jeavons (Adolf Hitler).

The atrocities of the Nazi S.S. are detailed by following the careers of two brothers John Shea and Bill Nighy from 1931 to 1945.

1338. *Hog Wild* (1980, Avco Embassy, Canada, 97m, c). P Claude Heroux, D Les Rose, W Andrew Peter Marin (based on an original concept by Victor Solnicki & Stephen Miller), PH Rene Verzier, ED Dominique Boisvert.

LP Michael Biehn (Tim), Patti D'Arbanville (Angie), Tony Rosato (Bull), Angelo Rizacos (Bean), Martin Doyle (Shadow), Matt Craven (Chrome), Matt Birman-Feldman (Lead), Claude Philippe (Indian), Thomas C. Kovacs (Veel).

A group of Hell's Angels are no match for a group of nerds who are seeking revenge for mistreatment. The two groups also fight over Patti D'Arbanville who can't quite decide which faction to honor with her charms. Comedy trash!

1339. *The Holcroft Covenant* (1985, EMI/Universal, GB, 112m, c). P Edie Landau & Ely Landau, D John Frankenheimer, W George Axelrod, Edward Anhalt & John Hopkins (based on the novel by Robert Ludlum), PH Gerry Fisher, M Stanislas, ED Ralph Sheldon, PD Peter Mullins.

LP Michael Caine (Noel Holcroft), Anthony Andrews (Johann Tennyson von Tiebolt), Victoria Tennant (Helden Tennyson von Tiebolt), Lilli Palmer (Althene Holcroft), Mario Adorf (Jurgen Maas/Erich Kessler), Michael Lonsdale (Manfredi), Bernard Hepton (Leighton), Richard Munch (Oberst).

American architect Michael Caine learns that he is the son of one of three Nazi generals who left $4 billion to their offspring to finance a new Reich. It's hard to keep the complicated story in focus. Best concentrate on the good-looking Victoria Tennant, who's Caine's lady, but also a co-conspirator with her brother and lover Anthony Andrews.

Hollywood see Flicks

1340. *Hollywood Chainsaw Hookers* (1988, American Independent, 74m, c). P&D Fred Olen Ray, W Ray & T.L. Lankford, PH Scott Ressler, M Michael Perilstein, ED William Shaffer, PD Corey Kaplan.

LP Gunnar Hansen (Cult Leader), Linnea Quigley (Samantha Kelso), Jay Richardson (Jack Chandler), Michelle Bauer (Mercedes), Dawn Wildsmith (Laurie).

Detective Jay Richardson is hired to locate teenage runaway Linnea Quigley. He finds her working in a strip joint, mixed up with cultists who worship chainsaws. There's plenty here for the bloodthirsty.

1341. *Hollywood Cop* (1988, Peacock, 100m, c). P Moshe Bibiyan & Simon Bibiyan, D&W Amir Shervan, PH Peter Palian, M Elton Farokh Ahi, ED Ruben Zadurian & Bob Ernst, SE Bill Kulzer.

LP Jim Mitchum (Feliciano), Cameron Mitchell (Capt. Bonano), David Goss (Turkey), Julie Schoenhofer (Rebecca), Lincoln Kilpatrick (Jaguar), Troy Donahue (Lt. Maxwell), Aldo Ray (Fong), Larry Lawrence (Joe Fresno).

The mob holds a youngster for $6 million ransom, but Jim Mitchum is on the case and he'll break all the rules to get the boy back.

Hollywood Harry see Harry's Machine

1342. Hollywood High Part II (1984, Lone Star, 85m, c). P Cotton Whittington & Colleen Meeker, D Lee Thornburg & Caruth C. Byrd, W Whittington, Meeker, Thornburg & Byrd, PH Gary Graver, M Doug Goodwin, ED Warren Chadwick.

LP April May (Bunny), Brad Cowgill (Rocky), Donna Lynn (Kiki), Drew Davis (Jock), Bruce Dobos (Skip), Camille Warner (Ginger), Alisa Ann Hull (Chessie).

This stupid movie is not really a sequel to *Hollywood High* (1977). It is the vapid story of teenage beach bums, who cheat on their ready-and-willing, sexually active girlfriends, with their equally ready-and-willing, sexually active teachers.

1343. Hollywood Hot Tubs (1984, Seymour Borde, 102m, c). P Mark Borde, D Chuck Vincent, W Borde & Craig McDonnell, PH Larry Revene, M Joel Goldsmith, ED Michael Hoggan.

LP Donna McDaniel (Leslie Maynard), Michael Andrew (Jeff), Paul Gunning (Eddie), Katt Shea (Dee Dee), Edy Williams (Desire), Jewal Shepard (Crystal).

Hollywood juvenile delinquent Michael Andrew gets a job repairing hot tubs. This offers him ample opportunity for sexual romps with the eager underdressed female owners of baths built for twosomes, threesomes and moresomes.

1344. The Hollywood Knights (1980, Columbia, 91m, c). P Richard Lederer, D Floyd Mutrux, W Mutrux (based on a story by Mutrux, Lederer & William Tennant), PH William A. Fraker, ED Danford B. Greene, Stan Allen & Scott Conrad.

LP Tony Danza (Duke), Fran Drescher (Sally), Leigh French (Jacqueline Freed-

man), Randy Gornel (Wheatly), Gary Graham (Jimmy Shine), Sandy Helberg (Officer Clark), Michelle Pfeiffer (Suzy Q), James Jeter (Smitty), Stuart Pankin (Dudley Laywicker), P.R. Paul (Simpson).

In a highly derivative youth picture, a punk ripoff of *American Grafitti,* and other like movies, 1965 teens take revenge on adults for closing down their Hollywood cruising strip. They gross out the older generation with every imaginable obscenity.

1345. Hollywood Shuffle (1987, Goldwyn, 82m, c). P&D Robert Townsend, W Townsend & Keenen Ivory Wayans, PH Peter Deming, M Patrice Rushen & Udi Harpaz, ED W.O. Garrett.

LP Robert Townsend (Bobby Taylor), Anne-Marie Johnson (Lydia), Starletta Dupois (Bobby's Mother), Helen Martin (Bobby's Grandmother), Craigus R. Johnson (Stevie Taylor), Paul Mooney (NAACP President), Lisa Mende (Casting Director), Robert Shafer (Commercial Director), John Witherspoon (Mr. Jones), Ludie Washington (Tiny), Keenen Ivory Wayans (Donald/Jerry Curl).

Robert Townsend lampoons Hollywood's treatment of blacks as he becomes the stereotype star of exploitation films such as *Attack of the Killer Pimps, Rambro,* and *There's a Bat in Our House.* It's not always funny, but when it is, it's hilarious. Watch it on video and consider the slow spots commercials.

The Hollywood Strangler see Don't Answer the Phone

1346. Hollywood Vice Squad (1986, Cinema Group, 100m, c). P Arnold Orgolini & Sandy Howard, D Penelope Spheeris, W James J. Docherty, PH John Hendricks, ED John Bowey.

LP Ronny Cox (Capt. Mike Jensen), Carrie Fisher (Officer Betty Melton), Ben Frank (Daley), Frank Gorshin (Jim Walsh), H.B. Haggerty (Det. Romero), Julius Harris (Jesse), Leon Isaac Kennedy (Det. Jerry Hawkins).

The dull undercover cops in this ripoff of TV police action shows like "Miami Vice" and "Hill Street Blues" have no style.

1347. *Hollywood Zap* (1986, Troma, 93m, c). P Bobbi Frank & Ben Frank, D&W David Cohen, PH Tom Frisby Fraser, M Art Podell, James Ackley & Paul Hertzog, ED Rick Westover.

LP Ben Frank (Nash), Ivan E. Roth (Tucker), De Waldron (Tee Tee), Annie Gaybis (Debbie), Millie Moss, Shirley Prestia, Addington Wise, Sandy Rose.

The film presents the misadventures of an unlikely pair, a naive young Southerner searching for his long lost father and a crazed ex–Wall Street broker who gave it all up for his quest to find the ultimate video game.

1348. *Home Free All* (1984, Almi, 93m, c). P Stewart Bird & Peter Belsito, D&W Bird, PH Robert Levi, M Jay Chattaway, ED Daniel Loewenthal, PD Mischa Petrow.

LP Allan Nicholls (Barry), Roland Caccavo (Roland), Maura Ellyn (Cathy), Shelley Wyant (Rita), Lucille Rivin (Lynn), Lorry Goldman (Marvin), Janet Burnham (Chastity), Jose Ramon Rosario (Carlos).

Ex-hippie Allan Nicholls, a 50s-60s radical finds himself lost in the 80s. No one in this empty picture in anyway near likeable.

1349. *Home Is Where the Hart Is* (1987, Atlantic, Canada, 94m, c). P John M. Eckert, D&W Rex Bromfield, PH Robert Ennis, M Eric N. Robertson, ED Michael Todd.

LP Valri Bromfield (Belle Haimes), Stephen E. Miller (Rex Haimes), Deanne Henry (Selma Dodge), Martin Mull (Carson Boundy), Eric Christmas (Martin Hart), Ted Stidder (Art Hart), Leslie Nielsen (Sheriff Nashville Schwartz), Joe Austin (Slim "Pappy" Hart), Enid Saunders (Minnie Hart).

Golddigging roller derby queen turned nurse Valri Bromfield eliminates the new bride of wealthy 103-year-old Joe Austin so she can get him and his money for herself. She's tracked down by the old man's 73-year-old twin sons Eric Christmas and Ted Stidder, with questionable help from bungling sheriff Leslie Nielsen. You have to be very hard up for a laugh to watch this geriatric romp.

1350. *Home of the Brave* (1986, Cinecom, 90m, c). P Paula Mazur, D&W Laurie Anderson, PH John Lindley, ED Lisa Day, AD Perry Hoberman.

LP Laurie Anderson, Joy Askew, Adrian Belew, Richard Landry, Dolette McDonald, Janice Pendarvis, Sang Won Park, David Van Tieghem.

Singer Laurie Anderson gives her fans a mix of music and provocative visuals in her concert film.

1351. *Home Remedy* (1988, Xero/Kino, 100m, c). P Kathis Hersch, D Maggie Greenwald, PH Thomas H. Jewett, M Steve Katz, ED Pamela Scott Arnold, PD Robert P. Kracik.

LP Seth Barrish (Richie Rosenbaum), Maxine Albert (Nancy Smith), Richard Kidney (P.J. Smith), David Feinman (Moshe), John Tsakonas (Donnie), Alexa (Mary), Cynde Kahn (Bambi).

The subject of this movie, released only in New York and L.A., is boredom. The cast and the production staff do a fine job of illustrating the idea.

1352. *Homeboy* (1989, J&M/20th Century-Fox, 116m, c). P Alan Marshall & Elliott Kastner, D Michael Seresin, W Eddie Cook (based on a story by Mickey Rourke), PH Gail Tattersall, M Eric Clapton & Michael Kamen, ED Ray Lovejoy, PD Brian Morris.

LP Mickey Rourke (Johnny Walker), Christopher Walken (Wesley Pendergrass), Debra Feuer (Ruby), Thomas Quinn (Lou), Kevin Conway (Grazziano), Antony Alda (Ray), Jon Polito (Moe Fingers), Bill Slayton (Bill).

Mickey Rourke is excellent in the role of a down-and-out club boxer, so he can't really be blamed for this cliché-filled and heavy-handed boxing and heist movie.

Homecoming Night see Night of the Creeps

1353. *Homer and Eddie* (1989, Kings Road, 99m, c). P Moritz Borman & James Cady, D Andrei Konchalovsky, W Patrick Cirillo, PH Lajos Koltai, M Eduard Artemyev, ED Henry Richardson, PD Michel Levesque.

LP James Belushi (Homer Lanza), Whoopi Goldberg (Eddie Cervi), Karen Black (Belle), John Waters (Robber), Robert Glaudini, Jim Mapp, James Thiel, Jeffrey Thiel.

Mentally retarded dishwasher James

Belushi hitchhikes from Arizona to Oregon to visit his father, dying of cancer. He teams up with homicidal escaped cancer patient Whoopi Goldberg. She attempts to wise Belushi up to life, even going so far as to rob a store to get money to pay for Belushi to get laid in a brothel. Whoopi's playing Bonnie-and-Clyde to Belushi's "Rain Man" doesn't work.

1354. *Homework* (1982, Jensen Farley, 90m, c). P&D James Beshears, W Maurice Peterson & Don Safran, PH Paul Goldsmith, M Tony Jones & Jim Wetzel, ED Allen Persselin.

LP Joan Collins (Diana), Michael Morgan (Tommy), Shell Kepler (Lisa), Lanny Horn (Ralph), Erin Donovan (Sheila), Lee Purcell (Ms. Jackson), Renee Harris (Cookie), Mark Brown (Mix), Steve Gustafson (John).

Sex-starved teen Michael Morgan looks good to his buddy's mother Joan Collins, who figures a 16-year-old is just what she needs for her run-down feeling. The fantasy of an older sexy woman initiating a young man is almost pornographically handled in this stinker.

1355. *Honest, Decent and True* (1985, BBC-TV, GB, 97m, c). P Graham Benson, D&W Les Blair, PH John McGlashan, M Simon Brint, ED Sue Wyatt, PD Jim Clay.

LP Derrick O'Connor (Mike), Adrian Edmondson (Alun), Juliette Mole (Davina), Gary Oldman (Derek), Richard E. Grant (Moonee), Arabella Weir (Prish), Yvonne French (Patsy), Thomas Wheatley (James Fletcher).

Originally aired on British "telly," this comedy about a London advertising agency working on a campaign for a brewery had a limited theater release.

1356. *Honey, I Shrunk the Kids* (1989, Buena Vista, 93m, c). P Penney Finkelman Cox, D Joe Johnston, W Ed Naha & Tom Schulman (based on a story by Stuart Gordon, Brian Yuzna & Naha), PH Hiro Narita, M James Horner, ED Michael A. Stevenson, PD Gregg Fonseca.

LP Rick Moranis (Wayne Szalinski), Matt Frewer (Big Russ Thompson), Marcia Strassman (Diane Szalinski), Kristine

Sutherland (Mae Thompson), Thomas Brown (Little Russ Thompson), Amy O'Neill (Amy Szalinski), Robert Oliveri (Nick Szalinski), Carl Steven (Tommy Pervis), Mark L. Taylor (Don Forrester).

This PG movie from the Disney folks is a simple, but enjoyable children's adventure film. Brilliant, distracted scientist Rick Moranis' goofy experiment with shrinking results in his son Robert Oliveri and daughter Amy O'Neill, as well as the neighbor's two kids, becoming so minuscule that a blade of grass is a giant growth. Getting through the yard and back to their house is a dangerous and frightening experience for the kids — but they know if they get back to dear old dad, he'll be able to reverse the process — won't he?

1357. *Honeymoon* (1987, Intl. Film Marketing, 100m, c). P Xavier Gelin & Rene Malo, D Patrick Jamain, W Jamain, Philippe Setbon & Robert Geoffrion (based on a story by Jamain & Setbon), PH Daniel Diot, M Robert Charlebois.

LP Nathalie Baye (Cecille), John Shea (Zack), Richard Berry (Michel), Maria Lukofsky (Sally), Peter Donat (Novak), Greg Ellwand (Bill), Cec Linder (Barnes), Alf Humphreys (Sonny), Michel Beaune (Garnier).

When Frenchwoman Nathalie Baye takes a vacation with her boyfriend in New York, he's arrested for smuggling cocaine into the country and she is targeted for deportation. She answers an ad for an agency which supplies American "husbands" for aliens for a fee. The promise is that she'll never even see him — but he shows up and won't leave her alone.

1358. *Honeysuckle Rose* (1980, Warner, 119m, c, aka *On the Road Again*). P Gene Taft, D Jerry Schatzberg, W Carol Sobieski, William D. Wittliff & John Binder (based on the story "Intermezzo" by Gosta Steven & Gustav Molander), PH Robby Muller, M Willie Nelson & Richard Baskin, ED Aram Avakian, Norman Gay, Marc Laub & Evan Lottman, PD Joel Schiller, SONG "On the Road Again" by Willie Nelson†.

LP Willie Nelson (Buck), Dyan Cannon (Viv), Amy Irving (Lily), Slim

Pickens (Garland), Joey Floyd (Jamie), Charles Levin (Sid), Priscilla Pointer (Rosella), Mickey Rooney, Jr. (Cotton), Pepe Serna (Rooster), Lane Smith (Brag), Diana Scarwid (Jeanne), Emmylou Harris (Emmylou), Rex Ludwick (Tex), Mickey Raphael (Kelly).

It just goes to show that the movie business never gives up on a good story. In this country-western remake of *Intermezzo,* Willie Nelson loves his wife Dyan Cannon and son Joey Floyd, but loves performing and liquor just as much. Amy Irving, the daughter of Nelson's long-time performing partner Slim Pickens, having always mooned over Nelson, sets her cap for him. He's flattered, but the affair ends with Nelson returning to a forgiving Cannon.

1359. *Honky Tonk Freeway* (1981, EMI/Universal, 107m, c). P Don Boyd & Howard Koch, Jr., D John Schlesinger, W Edward Clinton, PH John Bailey, M George Martin & Elmer Bernstein, ED Jim Clark.

LP Beau Bridges (Duane Hansen), Hume Cronyn (Sherm), Beverly D'Angelo (Carmen Shelby), William Devane (Mayor Calo), George Dzundza (Eugene), Teri Garr (Ericka), Joe Grifasi (Osvaldo), Howard Hesseman (Snapper), Geraldine Page (Sister Mary Clarise), Jessica Tandy (Carol), Deborah Rush (Sister Mary Magdalen), Alice Beardsley (Betty Boo Radley).

An odd assortment of characters become involved in the crazy schemes of William Devane, the mayor of a small Florida town. He wants to have an exit ramp built, leading into their town from the expressway, hoping it will save the economy of his dying community.

1360. *Honkytonk Man* (1982, Warner, 122m, c). P&D Clint Eastwood, W Clancy Carlile (based on his novel), PH Bruce Surtees, M Steve Dorff, ED Ferris Webster, Michael Kelly & Joey Cox, PD Edward Carfagno.

LP Clint Eastwood (Red Stovall), Kyle Eastwood (Whit), John McIntire (Grandpa), Alexa Kenin (Marlene), Verna Bloom (Emmy), Matt Clark (Virgil), Barry Corbin (Arnspriger), Jerry Hardin (Snuffy).

During the Depression, Clint East-

wood, a drunken aspiring country musician, is dying of tuberculosis. Still he helps his nephew, played by Eastwood's son Kyle, through the rites of passage into manhood. Perhaps it's easier to put the boy in a movie than tell him about the facts of life.

The Honorary Consul see Beyond the Limit

1361. *Hoodwink* (1981, New South Wales, Australia, 99m, c). P Pam Oliver & Erroll Sullivan, D Claude Whatham, W Ken Quinnell, PH Dean Semler, ED Nick Beauman, PD Ross Major.

LP John Hargreaves (Martin), Judy Davis (Sarah), Dennis Miller (Ralph), Les Foxcroft (Baldy), Wendy Strehlow (Martin's Sister), Wendy Hughes (Lucy), Kim Deacon (Marian), Max Cullen (Buster), Paul Sonkilla (Lancaster).

Based on an actual case, the film dramatizes the story of the decline and fall of likeable rascal, con-man, and criminal John Hargreaves.

1362. *Hoosiers* (1986, Orion, 114m, c). P Carter DeHaven & Angelo Pizzo, D David Anspaugh, W Angelo Pizzo, PH Fred Murphy, M Jerry Goldsmith†, ED C. Timothy O'Meara, PD David Nichols.

LP Gene Hackman (Coach Norman Dale), Barbara Hershey (Myra Fleener), Dennis Hopper† (Shooter), Sheb Wooley (Cletus), Fern Persons (Opal Fleener), Chelcie Ross (George), Robert Swan (Rollin), Brad Boyle (Whit), Steve Hollar (Rade), Brad Long (Buddy), David Neidorf (Everett), Kent Poole (Merle), Wade Schenck (Ollie), Scott Summers (Strap), Maris Valainis (Jimmy).

The film beautifully captures small-town Indiana in the 50s and its Hoosier-madness love-affair, just as strong 30 years later, with boys' high school basketball. Gene Hackman, the new coach in town, has radical ideas, which initially loses him some players and support, but with the help of drunken Dennis Hopper, a former local basketball star, he leads his team to the state championship. In Indiana they'll forgive a lot of strange behavior if you can do that.

1363. *Hope and Glory†* (1987, Columbia, GB, 113m, c). P John Boorman &

Michael Dryhurst, D&W Boorman† for directing & screenplay, PH Philipe Rousselot†, M Peter Martin, ED Ian Crafford, PD Anthony Pratt, AD Pratt†, SD Joan Woollard†.

LP Sarah Miles (Grace Rohan), David Hayman (Clive Rohan), Derrick O'Connor (Mac), Susan Wooldridge (Molly), Ian Bannen (Grandfather), Sebastian Rice-Edwards (Bill Rohan), Geraldine Muir (Sue Rohan), Sammi Davis (Dawn Rohan), Jean-Marc Barr (Cpl. Bruce Carey), Annie Leon (Grandmother).

Despite air raids and other harsh wartime realities, life goes on for a fictional British family living in suburban London during World War II. There is childhood innocence and adolescent romance that prove that not even the Blitz can put aside the usual growth pains of children and their parents. This isn't Mrs. Miniver and her brood—they're more real than that. Ian Bannen is a delight as the dotty old man, who each year at Christmas fondly remembers and toasts all the women he's ever had, much to the consternation of his wife and four daughters.

1364.   *Hopscotch* (1980, Avco Embassy, 104m, c). P Edie Landau & Ely Landau, D Ronald Neame, W Brian Garfield & Bryan Forbes (based on Garfield's novel), PH Arthur Ibbetson, M Ian Fraser & Wolfgang Amadeus Mozart, ED Carl Kress, PD William Creber.

LP Walter Matthau (Miles Kendig), Glenda Jackson (Isobel von Schmidt), Sam Waterston (Cutter), Ned Beatty (Myerson), Herbert Lom (Mikhail Yaskov), David Matthau (Ross), George Baker (Westlake), Ivor Roberts (Ludlum).

When top CIA agent Walter Matthau is demoted to a desk job, he writes his memoirs, designed to expose all the dirty laundry of the espionage business. Ned Beatty, his former boss, and Herbert Lom, a KGB official and old friend, are both led on a merry chase by Matthau and his lover, ex-spy Glenda Jackson.

Horror on Snape Island see Beyond the Fog

1365.   *Horror Planet* (1982, Jupiter/Almi, GB, 86m, c, aka *Inseminoid*). P Richard Gordon & David Speechley, D Norman J. Warren, W Nick Maley & Gloria Maley, PH John Metcalfe, M John Scott, ED Peter Boyle, PD Hayden Pearce.

LP Judy Geeson (Sandy), Robin Clarke (Mark), Jennifer Ashley (Capt. Holly Mackey), Stephanie Beacham (Kate), Steven Grives (Gary), Barry Houghton (Karl), Rosalind Lloyd (Gail), Victoria Tennant (Barbara), Trevor Thomas (Mitch), Heather Wright (Sharon), David Baxt (Ricky).

While investigating the caves of a distant planet with other space explorers, Judy Geeson is attacked by an alien monster that impregnates her. This causes her to go mad and kill the members of her crew. She ultimately gives birth to a monster.

1366.   *The Horror Show* (1989, MGM/United Artists, 95m, c). P Sean Cunningham, D James Isaac, W Alan Smithee [Allyn Warner] & Leslie Boehm, PH Mac Ahlberg, M Harry Manfredini, ED Edward Anton, PD Stewart Campbell, SE Peter Kuran.

LP Lance Henriksen (Lucas McCarthy), Rita Taggart (Donna McCarthy), Brion James (Max Jenke), Dedee Pfeiffer (Bonnie McCarthy), Aron Eisenberg (Scott McCarthy), Thom Bray (Peter Campbell), Matt Clark (Dr. Tower).

After mass murderer Brion James is executed, he finds a way to return from the grave to seek revenge against Lance Henriksen, the cop who arrested him. Sounds a lot like Wes Craven's *Shocker* doesn't it?

The Horror Star see Frightmare

1367.   *Hospital Massacre* (1984, Cannon, 88m, c). P Menahem Golan & Yoram Globus, D Boaz Davidson, W Marc Behm, PH Nicholas von Sternberg, M Arlon Ober, ED Jon Koslowsky.

LP Barbi Benton (Susan Jeremy), Chip Lucia (Harry), Jon Van Ness (Jack), John Warner Williams (Dr. Saxon), Den Surles (Dr. Beam), Gay Austin (Dr. Jacobs), Gloria Morrison (Nurse Dora), Karyn Smith (Nurse Kitty).

Barbi Benton gave up her country-and-western music career to appear in this film. Her role apparently is to alternate between being menaced by evil hospital orderlies and taking her clothes off.

1368. *Hostage* (1987, Blue Flower/ Alpine, 95m, c). P Thys Heyns & Paul Raleigh, D Hanro Mohr, W Norman Winski & Michael Leighton, PH Johan van der Vyver, ED Simon Grimley.

LP Wings Hauser (Sam Striker), Karen Black (Laura Lawrence), Kevin McCarthy (Col. Tim Shaw), Nancy Locke (Nicole), Robert Whitehead (Harry), Billy Second (Rona), Ian Steadman (Yamani), Robert K. Brown (Himself).

When a train full of passengers is taken over by Arab terrorists in Uganda, Wings Hauser and Kevin McCarthy recruit former soldiers to attempt a rescue mission.

1369. *Hot and Deadly* (1984, Arista, 90m, c, aka *The Retrievers*). P Elliot Hong & Larry Stamper, D Hong, PH Stephen Kim, M Ted Ashford & Paul Fontana, ED Rob "Smitty" Smith.

LP Max Thayer (Tom), Shawn Hoskins (Janice), Randy Anderson (Trigger), Lenard Miller (Danny), Bud Cramer (Philip).

Max Thayer, a new recruit of a CIA-like government agency, is given the assignment of preventing ex-agent Lenard Miller from publishing an exposé of the "company." Instead Thayer falls for Miller's sister Shawn Hoskins and does all he can to get the work printed.

1370. *Hot Child in the City* (1987, MVA-1/Prism, 85m, c). P Giovanna Nigro-Chacon, D John Florea, W George Goldsmith, PH Richard C. Glouner, M W. Michael Lewis, ED Marcy Hamilton, PD Anthony Sabatino & William H. Harris.

LP Leah Ayres Hendrix (Rachel Wagner), Shari Shattuck (Abby Wagner), Geof Prysirr (Detective Ray Osborne), Antony Alda (Charon), Will Bledsoe (Tim Bradford), Ronn Moss (Tony), Sally Kay Brown (Finelli).

It's a lame whodunit about the murder of record company executive Shari Shattuck. After the killing, her sister Leah Ayres Hendrix begins to assume Shattuck's glitzy personality. The Hollywood setting allows the producers to feature a lot of half-dressed, buxom young women who are used and abused by brutish men.

1371. *Hot Dallas Nights* (1981, Miracle Films, 83m, c). P Julian Orynski & Vivian O'Dell, D Tony Kenrick, W Robert Oakwood & Tony Kenrick, PH D.B. Cooper, M Leonard Conjurski, ED James Armin.

LP Alexander Kingsford (Duke), R.J. Reynolds (T.J.), Raven Turner (Pat), Tara Flynn (Mary Ellen), Turk Lyon (Robbie), Hillary Summers (Lyndie), Slim Grady (Rock), Greer Shapiro (Miss Millie).

Apparently the atmosphere in this independent production isn't sultry enough as it hasn't even made video shelves. Don't confuse it with *Debbie Does Dallas*—it's not that good.

1372. *Hot Dog...The Movie* (1984, MGM/United Artists, 96m, c). P Edward S. Feldman & Mike Marvin, D Peter Markle, W Marvin, PH Paul G. Ryan, M Peter Bernstein, ED Stephen Rivkin.

LP David Naughton (Dan), Patrick Houser (Harkin), Tracy N. Smith (Sunny), John Patrick Reger (Rudi), Frank Koppola (Squirrel), James Saito (Kendo), Shannon Tweed (Sylvia Fonda), George Theobold (Slasher), Lynn Wieland (Michelle), Sandy Hackett (Lester the Molester).

Manhattan punk David Naughton heads for the World Freestyle Skiing Championship. He specializes in a highly choreographed skiing technique called "hotdogging." During the days he's on the slopes and in the evenings, he's...uh... getting teasing girls into his bed.

1373. *Hot Moves* (1984, Spectrum/ Cardinal, 86m, c). P&D Jim Sotos, W Larry Anderson & Peter Foldy, PH Eugene Shugleit, M Louis Forestiari, ED Drake P. Silliman.

LP Michael Zorek (Barry), Adam Silbar (Mike), Jill Schoelen (Julie Ann), Jeff Fishman, Johnny Timko, Debi Richter, Virgil Frye, Tami Holbrook, Monique Gabrielle, David Christopher.

Overweight virgin Michael Zorek dreams of having a girlfriend all of his own. He uses a telescope to watch the beach, filled with fantasy girls for a horny teen. These hardbodies get down to the barest of bathing strings, oil their bodies, sunbath and take an occasional splash in the water.

1374. *Hot Pursuit* (1987, RKO/Paramount, 93m, c). P Pierre David &

Theodore R. Parvin, D Steven Lisberger, W Lisberger & Steven Carabatsos (based on a story by Lisberger), PH Frank Tidy, M Rareview, ED Mitchell Sinoway, PD William J. Creber.

LP John Cusack (Dan Bartlett), Wendy Gazelle (Lori Cronenberg), Robert Loggia (Mac MacLaren), Jerry Stiller (Victor Honeywell), Monte Markham (Bill Cronenberg), Shelley Fabares (Buffy Cronenberg), Dah-Ve Chodan (Ginger Cronenberg), Ben Stiller (Chris Honeywell).

Even talented, appealing, young John Cusack can't make a silk purse out of this sow's ear of a screenplay. He's a college student who misses the plane carrying his girlfriend Wendy Gazelle and her parents to a vacation cruise. The laughs are supposed to come from his frantic attempts to catch up with them. You keep hoping that something amusing will happen, but it's too much to ask.

1375. *Hot Resort* (1985, Cannon, 93m, c). P Menahem Golan & Yoram Globus, D John Robins, W Robins, Boaz Davidson & Norman Hudis (based on a story by Paul Max Rubenstein), PH Frank Flynn, M Dave Powell & Ken Brown, ED Brent Schoenfeld & Dory Lubliner.

LP Tom Parsekian (Marty), Debra Kelly (Liza), Bronson Pinchot, Mickey Berz, Daniel Schneider, Samm-Art Williams, Marcy Walker, Frank Gorshin.

Several young guys on the make spend their summer vacation working at a plush resort hotel on the Caribbean island of St. Kitts. Besides getting all the girls they want, these working class jerks show up some snobbish rich jerks. It's a nerd's fantasy.

1376. *Hot Shot* (1987, Intl. Film Marketing/Arista, 101m, c). P Steve Pappas, D Rick King, W Joe Sauter, King, Ray Errol Fox & Bill Guttentag, PH Greg Andracke & Edgar Moura, M William Orbit, ED Stan Salfas, PD Ruth Ammon & Berta Segall.

LP Jim Youngs (Jimmy Kristidis), Pele (Santos), Billy Warlock (Vinnie Fortino), Leon Russom (Coach), David Groh (Jerry Norton), Rutanya Alda (Georgia Kristidis), Peter Henry Schroeder (Nick Kristidis).

This *Karate Kid*-like story stars Jim Youngs as a hot-dogging soccer player who finally learns something about the game and life from the great Brazilian star Pele (who not surprisingly portrays a great retired Brazilian star). The film is a modest diversion for those with modest expectations.

1377. *Hot Target* (1985, Crown International, New Zealand, 93m, c). P John Barnett & Brian Cook, D Denis Lewiston, W Lewiston (based on a story by Gerry O'Hara), PH Alec Mills, M Gil Melle, ED Michael Horton, PD Josephine Ford.

LP Simone Griffeth (Christine Webber), Steve Marachuk (Greg Sandford), Brian Marshall (Clive Webber), Peter McCauley (Det. Insp. Nolan), Elizabeth Hawthorne (Suzanne Maxwell), Ray Henwood (Douglas Maxwell).

Slim, cool, witty, wealthy, intelligent, blonde Simone Griffeth, bored with her luxurious life, seduces Steve Marachuk, who has plans of robbing her home. From there on in it's a steamy Down Under *Double Indemnity* or *Body Heat*.

1378. *Hot to Trot* (1988, Warner, 83m, c). P Steve Tisch & Wendy Finerman, D Michael Dinner, W Stephen Neigher, Hugh Gilbert & Charles Peters (based on a story by Neigher & Gilbert), PH Victor J. Kemper, M Danny Elfman, ED Frank Morris, PD William Matthews.

LP Bob Goldthwait (Fred P. Chaney), Dabney Coleman (Walter Sawyer), John Candy (Voice of Don), Virginia Madsen (Allison Rowe), Jim Metzler (Boyd Osborne), Cindy Pickett (Victoria Peyton), Tim Kazurinsky (Leonard).

Stockbroker Bob Goldthwait is fed tips by a talking horse he's inherited from his mother. The voice of the horse is John Candy, who is fortunate in that he doesn't have to be seen in this unimpressive comedy.

1379. *Hotel Colonial* (1987, Orion, US/Italy, 104m, c). P Ira R. Barmak, D Cinzia Th Torrini, W Enzo Monteleone, Torrini, Robert Katz & Ira R. Barmak (based on a story by Monteleone), PH Giuseppe Rotunno, M Pino Donaggio, ED Nino Baragli.

LP John Savage (Marco Venieri), Robert Duvall (Roberto Carrasco), Rachel Ward (Irene Costa), Massimo Troisi (Werner), Claudio Baez (Mario Anderson).

John Savage's efforts to investigate the death of his brother in Colombia are aided by beautiful Rachel Ward and hampered by evil Robert Duvall. It would seem that the Americans and Italians who worked on this fiasco didn't speak a common language.

1380. *The Hotel New Hampshire* (1984, Orion, 110m, c). P Neil Hartley & James Beach, D&W Tony Richardson (based on the novel by John Irving), PH David Watkin, M Jacques Offenbach, ED Robert K. Lambert, PD Jocelyn Herbert.

LP Rob Lowe (John), Jodie Foster (Franny), Nastassja Kinski (Susie the Bear), Amanda Plummer (Miss Miscarriage), Paul McCrane (Frank), Beau Bridges (Father), Lisa Banes (Mother), Jennie Dundas (Lilly), Seth Green (Egg), Wally Aspell (Hotel Manager), Joely Richardson (Waitress), Wallace Shawn (Freud), Matthew Modine (Chip Dove/Ernst), Wilford Brimley (Iowa Bob), Anita Morris (Ronda Ray).

In this adaptation of John Irvin's convoluted and lunatic novel, Beau Bridges and Lisa Banes are the parents of an unconventional family. It includes high school student Rob Lowe, who maintains an incestuous relation with his sister Jodie Foster. Since being gang-raped, she will sleep with anyone. The rest of the family consists of their gay brother Paul McCrane and little sister Jennie Dundas, little because she has stopped growing. Their adventures and the strange people they encounter take them from New Hampshire to Vienna and to New York in pre–World War II times.

1381. *The Hound of the Baskervilles* (1980, Hemdale/Atlantic, GB, 84m, c). P John Goldstone, D Paul Morrissey, W Peter Cook, Dudley Moore & Morrissey (based on the novel by Arthur Conan Doyle), PH Dick Busch & John Wilcox, M Moore, ED Richard Marden & Glenn Hyde, PD Roy Smith.

LP Peter Cook (Sherlock Holmes), Dudley Moore (Dr. Watson/Mrs. Holmes/Mrs. Spiggott), Denholm Elliott (Stapleton), Joan Greenwood (Beryl Stapleton), Terry-Thomas (Dr. Mortimer), Max Wall (Mr. Barrymore), Irene Handl (Mrs. Barrymore), Kenneth Williams (Sir Henry Baskerville), Hugh Griffith (Frankland).

This tasteless spoof of the famous Sherlock Holmes classic is without a clue as to what constitutes humor. The game is definitely not afoot.

1382. *The Hound of the Baskervilles* (1983, Mapleton/Weintraub, GB, 100m, c). P Otto Plaschkes, D Douglas Hickox, W Charles Pogue (based on the novel by Arthur Conan Doyle), PH Ronnie Taylor, M Michael J. Lewis, ED Malcolm Cooke, PD Michael Stringer.

LP Ian Richardson (Sherlock Holmes), Donald Churchill (Dr. Watson), Martin Shaw (Sir Henry Baskerville), Nicholas Clay (Jack Stapleton), Denholm Elliott (Dr. Mortimer), Brian Blessed (Geoffrey Lyons), Ronald Lacy (Inspector Lestrade).

This remake doesn't add any new wrinkles to the familiar mystery story of a supernatural hound brought to heel by the great detective Sherlock Holmes.

1383. *The Hounds of...Notre Dame* (1980, Pan-Canadian, Canada, 95m, c). P Fil Fraser, D Zale Dalen, W Ken Mitchell, PH Ron Orieux, M Maurice Marshall, ED Tony Lower.

LP Thomas Peacocke (Father Athol Murray), Frances Hyland (Mother Therese), Barry Morse (Archbishop Williams), David Ferry (Ron Fryer), Lawrence Reese (Tom Howard), Lenore Zahn (Lila Petri).

Thomas Peacocke portrays the controversial Canadian priest who founded the College of Notre Dame in Saskatchewan, where boys are given a rugged education augmented by athletics.

1384. *Hour of the Assassin* (1987, Concorde, 93m, c). P Luis Llosa & Mary Ann Fisher, D Llosa, W Matt Leipzig, PH Cusi Barrio, M Fred Myrow & Richard Emmett, ED William Flicker.

LP Erik Estrada (Martin Fierro), Robert Vaughn (Sam Merrick), Alfred [Alfredo Alvarez] Calderon (Ortiz), Roland [Orlando] Sacha (Folco), Reynaldo Arenas (Paladora), Laura Burton [Lourdes Berninzon] (Adriana).

Former American Green Beret Erik

Estrada is hired by the military to assassinate the president of San Pedro, a fictional South America country. Robert Vaughn is the CIA agent out to stop him. Estrada finally sees the light.

1385. *House* (1986, New World, 93m, c). P Sean S. Cunningham, D Steve Miner, W Ethan Wiley (based on a story by Fred Dekker), PH Mac Ahlberg, M Harry Manfredini, ED Michael N. Knue, PD Gregg Fonseca.

LP William Katt (Roger Cobb), George Wendt (Harold Gorton), Richard Moll (Big Ben), Kay Lenz (Sandy), Mary Stavin (Tanya), Michael Ensign (Chet Parker), Erik Silver/Mark Silver (Jimmy), Susan French (Aunt Elizabeth).

Vietnam vet and horror writer William Katt, separated from his actress wife, has writer's block since the mysterious disappearance of his son. Katt inherits the very house in which the youngster disappeared.

1386. *House II: The Second Story* (1987, New World, 85m, c). P Sean S. Cunningham, D&W Ethan Wiley, PH Mac Ahlberg, M Henry Manfredini, ED Marty Nicholson, PD Gregg Fonseca.

LP Arye Gross (Jesse McLaughlin), Jonathan Stark (Charlie), Royal Dano (Gramps), Bill Maher (John), John Ratzenberger (Bill Towner), Lar Park Lincoln (Kate), Amy Yasbeck (Lana), Gregory Walcott (Sheriff).

The double-meaning title is about the cleverest thing about this sequel of a not very good original movie. Arye Gross and his girlfriend Lar Park Lincoln move into a mansion which once belonged to his great-great-grandpa Royal Dano. They discover the old boy alive in his tomb. He has pulled off this feat because he possesses an ancient crystal skull which can make people stay young. Unfortunately someone steals it and Gross must get it back.

House of Evil see The House of Sorority Row

1387. *House of Games* (1987, Orion, 102m, c). P Michael Hausman, D&W David Mamet (based on a story by Mamet & Jonathan Katz), PH Juan Ruiz Anchia, M Alaric Jans, ED Trudy Ship, PD Michael Merritt.

LP Lindsay Crouse (Dr. Margaret Ford), Joe Mantegna (Mike), Mike Nussbaum (Joey), Lilia Skala (Dr. Littauer), J.T. Walsh (Businessman), Willo Hausman (Girl with Book), Karen Kohlhaas (Prison Ward Patient), Steve Goldstein (Billy Hahn).

Pulitzer-prize winning playwright David Mamet makes an impressive debut as a director. His wife Lindsay Crouse portrays a psychologist who, in trying to help one of her patients with a gambling problem, finds herself drawn into the world of gambler, con-man and crook Joe Mantegna. Intrigued with the con, Crouse has Mantegna teach her the art. When she finds she's the victim of a con, she plays her trump card and kills her mentor.

1388. *The House of God* (1984, United Artists, 108m, c). P Charles H. Joffe & Harold Schneider, D&W Donald Wrye (based on a novel by Samuel Shem), PH Gerald Hirschfeld, M Basil Poledouris, ED Bob Wyman & Billy Weber, PD Bill Malley.

LP Tim Matheson (Dr. Basch), Charles Haid (Fats), Michael Sacks (Dr. Potts), Lisa Pelikan (Jo), Bess Armstrong (Dr. Worthington), George Coe (Dr. Leggo), James Cromwell (Officer Quick), Ossie Davis (Dr. Sanders), Howard Rollins, Jr. (Chuck).

Meant to be a black comedy, this film, made in 1979, wasted the then unknown talents of Tim Matheson, Charles Haid, Lisa Pelikan, Bess Armstrong and Howard Rollins, Jr., in the story of a group of young interns coming to terms with the daily problems they face in their high-pressure hospital work.

1389. *House of the Long Shadows* (1983, Cannon, GB, 96m, c). P Menahem Golan & Yoram Globus, D Pete Walker, M Michael Armstrong (based on the novel *Seven Keys to Baldpate* by Earl Derr Biggers), PH Norman Langley, M Richard Harvey, ED Robert Dearberg.

LP Vincent Price (Lionel Grisbane), Christopher Lee (Corrigan), Peter Cushing (Sebastian Rand), Desi Arnaz, Jr. (Kenneth Magee), John Carradine (Lord Grisbane), Sheila Keith (Victoria Quimby), Julie Peasgood (Mary Norton), Richard Todd (Sam Allison), Louise English (Diana Caulder).

This tongue-in-cheek, old-fashioned, haunted-house mystery stars four wonderful oldtimers in the horror business, Vincent Price, Christopher Lee, Peter Cushing and John Carradine. See it, smile and shriek.

1390. The House on Carroll Street (1988, Orion, 100m, c). P Peter Yates & Robert F. Colesberry, D Yates, W Walter Bernstein, PH Michael Ballhaus, M Georges Delerue, ED Ray Lovejoy, PD Stuart Wurtzel.

LP Kelly McGillis (Emily Crane), Jeff Daniels (Cochran), Mandy Patinkin (Ray Salwen), Jessica Tandy (Miss Venable), Jonathan Hogan (Alan), Remak Ramsay (Senator Byington), Christopher Rhode (Stefan), Trey Wilson (Lt. Sloan).

In 1951, idealistic photo editor Kelly McGillis loses her job, is branded a security risk and is placed under surveillance when she refuses to cooperate with a Joe McCarthy–like Senate committee. She happens on a plot to smuggle Nazi war criminals into the United States. Jeff Daniels, the FBI agent assigned to her case, becomes romantically involved with her. Together they trace the conspiracy to the highest levels of the federal government. Mandy Patinkin, portraying a key aide to the Senator investigating subversive activities, is a frightening fanatic.

1391. The House on Sorority Row (1983, Film Ventures, 91m, c, aka *House of Evil; Seven Sisters*). P Mark Rosman & John G. Clark, D Rosman, W Rosman & Bobby Fine, PH Timothy Suhrstedt, M Richard H. Band, AD Vincent Peranio, ED Jean-Marc Vasseur & Paul Trejo.

LP Kathryn McNeil (Katherine), Eileen Davidson (Vicki), Janis Zido (Liz), Robin Meloy (Jeanie), Harley Kozak (Diane), Jodi Draigie (Morgan), Ellen Dorsher (Stevie), Lois Kelso Hunt (Mrs. Slater), Christopher Lawrence (Dr. Beck).

Sorority sisters kill their housemother, but game lady that she is, she doesn't take death lying down. She gets up and has her revenge.

1392. The House Where Death Lives (1984, New American, 92m, c, aka *Delusion*). LP Alan Beattie & Peter Shana-

berg, D Beattie, W Jack Viertel (based on a story by Beattie & Viertel), PH Stephen Posey, M Don Peake, ED Robert Leighton.

LP Patricia Pearcy (Meredith Stone), David Hayward (Jeffrey Fraser), John Dukakis (Gabriel), Joseph Cotten (Ivar Langrock), Leon Charles (Phillip), Alice Nunn (Duffy), Patrick Pankhurst (Wilfred), Simone Griffeth (Pamela).

Invalid Joseph Cotten is cared for by new nurse Patricia Pearcy. Some mysterious killer eliminates members of the cast one by one, pounding in their crania with a table leg. The house isn't responsible for the mayhem.

1393. The House Where Evil Dwells (1982, MGM/United Artists, 88m, c). P Martin B. Cohen, D Kevin Connor, W Robert Suhosky (based on the novel by James Hardiman), PF Jacques Haitkin, M Ken Thorne, ED Barry Peters.

LP Edward Albert (Ted), Susan George (Laura), Doug McClure (Alex), Amy Barrett (Amy), Mako Hattori (Otami), Toshiyuki Sasaki (Shugoro), Toshiya Maruyama (Masanori), Tsuyako Okajima (Witch), Henry Mitowa (Zen Monk).

In the Japan of 1840, a double murder results when a samurai discovers his wife with another man. He then takes his own life. The three are doomed to haunt the house forever. More than a century later Eddie Albert, Susan George and their daughter Amy Barrett move into the house. Their bodies are taken over by the three ghosts.

1394. Houseboat Horror (1989, PM Terror Prods., Australia, 85m, c). P Ollie Martin, D Kendal Flanagan & Martin, W Martin, PH Bill Parnell, M Brian Mannix, Steve Harrison & Ross McLennan, ED Clayton Jacobson, PD Brian Gunst.

LP Alan Dale (Grant Evans), Christine Jeston (Tracy), Craig Alexander (Sam), Des "Animal" McKenna (Ziggie), Gavin Wood (Costello), John Michael Howson ("J"), Louise Silversen (Zelia), Peppie D'Or (Teresa).

This straight-to-video slasher picture modeled on *Friday the 13th* offers nothing new. The killer, not seen until the end of the film, is a scarred, bald psycho, taking revenge on film people at a video shoot near remote Lake Infinity. Earlier he had been badly burned on a film set, and to a schizoid all movie locations look the same.

1395. *The Housekeeper* (1987, Castle-hill-Kodiak, Canada, 106m, c, aka *A Judgement in Stone*). P Harve Sherman, D Ousama Rawi, W Elaine Waisglass (based on the novel by Ruth Rendell), PH David Herrington, M Patrick Coleman & Robert Murphy, ED Stan Cole.

LP Rita Tushingham (Eunice Parchman), Ross Petty (George Coverdale), Shelley Peterson (Jackie Coverdale), Jonathan Crombie (Bobby Coverdale), Jessica Steen (Melinda Coverdale), Jackie Burroughs (Joan Smith), Tom Kneebone (Norman Smith), Peter MacNeill (William), Donald Ewer (Mr. Parchman).

Repressed, illiterate and psychotic Englishwoman Rita Tushingham takes a position as housekeeper in the United States after murdering her domineering father. She is hired by wealthy New England couple Ross Petty and Shelley Peterson, who live with their two adolescent children. Things are all right for awhile but as Tushingham is unable to read, she fails to perform her assignments. Religious fanatic Jackie Burroughs, believing that the housekeeper is God's messenger and that her employers are sinners, convinces Rita to murder the four Coverdales with a double barreled shotgun. When the police arrive, Tushingham lets the police think that Burroughs is the murderer.

1396. *Housekeeping* (1987, Columbia, 116m, c). P Robert F. Colesberry, D&W Bill Forsyth (based on the novel by Marilynne Robinson), PH Michael Coulter, M Michael Gibbs, ED Michael Ellis, PD Adrienne Atkinson.

LP Christine Lahti (Sylvie), Sara Walker (Ruth), Andrea Burchill (Lucille), Anne Pitoniak (Aunt Lily), Barbara Reese (Aunt Nona), Margot Pinvidic (Helen), Bill Smillie (Sheriff), Wayne Robson (Mr. French).

During the early 50s, young orphans Sara Walker and Andrea Burchill are taken care of by a succession of relatives in the lakeside town of Fingerbone in the mountainous interior of the Pacific Northwest. Finally their mother's sister Christine Lahti arrives to care for them. She is young, eccentric, charming and has a history of being quite a traveller. She fascinates her nieces, and the girls learn to relate to their strange aunt in different ways.

1397. *How I Got Into College* (1989, 20th Century–Fox, 89m, c). P Michael Shamberg, D Savage Steve Holland, W Terrel Seltzer, PH Robert Elswit, M Joseph Vitarelli, ED Sonya Sones Tramer & Kaja Fehr, COS Taryn DeChellis, PD Ida Random.

LP Anthony Edwards (Kip), Corey Parker (Marlon), Lara Flynn Boyle (Jessica), Finn Carter (Nina), Charles Rocket (Leo), Christopher Rydell (Oliver), Brian Doyle-Murray (Coach), Tichina Arnold (Vera Cook), Bill Raymond (Flutter), Philip Baker Hall (Dean Patterson).

The yearly college sweepstakes are a traumatic experience for many high school students and their parents — especially if they wrongly believe that Junior or Sister must get into their number one choice or be a failure for life. This film, no doubt meant to be a comedy, is about as much fun as a session with a guidance counselor. At least Corey Parker has a good reason for wanting to get into the college of his choice — it's the college of choice of lovely Lara Flynn Boyle.

1398. *How to Beat the High Cost of Living* (1980, American International, 110m, c). P Jerome M. Zeitman & Robert Kaufman, D Robert Scheerer, W Kaufman (based on a story by Leonora Thuna), PH James Crabe, M Patrick Williams, ED Bill Butler, PD Lawrence G. Paull.

LP Susan Saint James (Jane), Jane Curtin (Elaine), Jessica Lange (Louise), Richard Benjamin (Albert), Fred Willard (Robert), Eddie Albert (Max), Dabney Coleman (Jack Heintzel), Art Metrano (Gas Station Attendant), Ronnie Schell (Bill Pike), Garrett Morris (Power & Light Man), Cathryn Damon (Natalie), Sybil Danning (Charlotte).

Susan Saint James, Jane Curtin and Jessica Lange, each in need of money, plan and carry out a goofy, blundering, shopping-mall heist. Lange has the best line: "I was always taught that a woman should fall in love with the best provider she can stomach."

1399. *How to Get Ahead in Advertising* (1989, Warner, GB, 95m, c). P David Wimbury, D&W Bruce Robinson, PH Peter Hannan, M David Dundas & Rick Wentworth, ED Alan Strachan, PD Michael Pickwoad.

LP Richard E. Grant (Dennis), Rachel Ward (Julia), Richard Wilson (Bristol), Jacqueline Tong (Penny), John Shrapnel (Psychiatrist), Susan Wooldridge (Monica), Mick Ford (Richard), Jacqueline Pearce (Maud), Roddy Maude-Roxby (Dr. Gatty).

British advertising hot-shot Richard E. Grant is having no luck coming up with an original campaign for a pimple cream. The pressure from everyone's expecting him to be brilliant causes a small boil to break out on his neck. The boil grows and grows. It starts to talk and finally takes on all of Grant's features. When at a hospital to have the boil removed, it convinces the physicians to lance the original, but they don't get all of him and now *he's* the wart on his newly-headed body. It's lunacy, but the dark humor is consistently good.

1400. *How to Score with Girls* (1980, NMD, 82m, c). P,D&W Ogden Lowell, M Earl Rose & Robert N. Langworthy.

LP Ron Osborne (Steve), Larry Jacobs (Harry), Richard Young (Frank), Sandra McKnight (Joanna), Arlana Blue (Joy), Janice Fuller (Granola), Michelle Matthau (Sue), Grace Davies (Jean), Barbara Derecktor (Robin).

The instructions in this film won't help anyone "score" with girls unless the females are remarkably dumb.

1401. *Howard the Duck* (1986, Universal, 111m, c). P Gloria Katz, D Willard Huyck, W Huyck & Katz (based on the Marvel Comics character "Howard the Duck" created by Steve Gerber), PH Richard H. Kline, M John Barry, ED Michael Chandler & Sidney Wolinsky, PD Peter Jamison.

LP Lea Thompson (Beverly Switzler), Jeffrey Jones (Dr. Jenning), Tim Robbins (Phil Blumburtt), Ed Gale/Chip Zien/Tim Rose/Steve Sleap/Peter Baird/Mary Wells/Lisa Sturz/Jordan Prentice (Howard T. Duck), Paul Guilfoyle (Lt.

Welker), Liz Sagal (Ronette), Dominique Davalos (Cal), Holly Robinson (K.C.).

Movie whiz George Lucas came up with this fantasy-comedy about a fast-talking duck from another dimension who finds himself transported to Cleveland. He has run-ins with punk rockers, motorcycle gangs and Lea Thompson with whom he almost has an unnatural love affair.

1402. *The Howling* (1981, Avco Embassy, 91m, c). P Michael Finnell & Jack Conrad, D Joe Dante, W John Sayles & Terence H. Winkless (based on the novel by Gary Brandner), PH John Hora, M Pino Donaggio, ED Mark Goldblatt & Joe Dante, SE Roger George.

LP Dee Wallace (Karen White), Patrick Macnee (Dr. George Waggner), Dennis Dugan (Chris), Christopher Stone (R. William "Bill" Neill), Belinda Balaski (Terry Fisher), Kevin McCarthy (Fred Francis), John Carradine (Erle Kenton), Slim Pickens (Sam Newfield), Elisabeth Brooks (Marsha).

TV anchorwoman Dee Wallace takes a rest at a clinic inhabited by a wide assortment of loonies. The sanitarium is surrounded by a woods where werewolves dwell. This horror and comedy movie was a box-office hit.

1403. *Howling II...Your Sister Is a Werewolf* (1985, EMI, 90m, c). P Steven Lane, D Philippe Mora, W Robert Sarno & Gary Brandner (based on the novel by Brandner), PH Geoffrey Stephenson, M Steve Parsons, PD Karel Vacek.

LP Christopher Lee (Stefan Crosscoe), Annie McEnroe (Jenny Templeton), Reb Brown (Ben White), Sybil Danning (Stirba), Marsha A. Hunt (Mariana), Judd Omen (Vlad), Ferdinand [Ferdy] Mayne (Erle), Babel (Punk Group).

Convinced that his sister has been the victim of a brutal murderer, out-of-town law officer Reb Brown is determined to bring her killer to justice.

1404. *The Howling III* (1987, Square Pictures, Australia, 94m, c, aka *The Marsupials: The Howling III*). P Charles Waterstreet & Philippe Mora, D&W Mora (based on the book *Howling III* by Gary Brandner, PH Louis Irving, M Alan Zavod, ED Lee Smith, PD Ross Major.

LP Barry Otto (Prof. Harry Beck-meyer), Imogen Annesley (Jerboa), Dasha Blahova (Olga Gorki), Max Fairchild (Thylo, Werewolf Leader), Ralph Cotterill (Prof. Sharp), Leigh Biolos (Donny Martin), Frank Thring (Jack Citron), Michael Pate (U.S. President), Barry Humphries (Dame Edna Everage), Carole Skinner (Yara).

This third movie in the series features marsupial werewolf beauty Imogen Annesley, defecting Russian ballerina Dasha Blahova, herself a werewolf, and Barry Otto, a hard-working, civil-libertarian professor whose goal in life is to study Australia's werewolf tribe.

1405. *Howling IV: The Original Nightmare* (1988, Allied, GB, 92m, c). P Harry Alan Towers, D John Hough, W Clive Turner & Freddie Rowe (based on a story by Turner from novels by Gary Brandner), PH Godfrey Godar, M David George & Barrie Guard, ED Claudia Finkle, Malcolm Burns-Errington, SE Steve Johnson.

LP Romy Windsor (Marie), Michael T. Weiss (Richard), Antony Hamilton (Tom), Suzanne Severeid (Janice), Lamya Derval (Eleanor), Norman Anstey (Sheriff), Kate Edwards (Mrs. Orstead), Clive Turner (Tow Truck Driver).

Best-selling author Romy Windsor and her husband Michael T. Weiss, believe her visions of a young nun and a demonic wolf-like creature are caused by stress and exhaustion. When they repair to a quaint cottage in a remote small town, they find they are mistaken.

1406. *Human Experiments* (1980, Crown International, 82m, c, aka *Beyond the Gate*). P Summer Brown & Gregory Goodell, D Goodell, W Richard Rothstein, PH Joao Fernandes, M Marc Bucci, ED Barbara Pokras.

LP Linda Haynes (Rachel Foster), Geoffrey Lewis (Dr. Kline), Ellen Travolta, Aldo Ray, Jackie Coogan, Darlene Carviotto.

Prison psychologist Geoffrey Lewis conducts a series of experiments in a woman's prison in which he destroys the "criminal instinct" of inmates through brute fear.

1407. *The Human Factor* (1980, MGM-UA, US/GB, 114m, c). P&D Otto Preminger, W Tom Stoppard (based on the novel by Graham Greene), PH Mike Molloy, M Richard Logan, ED Richard Trevor.

LP Nicol Williamson (Maurice Castle), Richard Attenborough (Col. John Daintry), Joop Doderer (Cornelius Muller), John Gielgud (Brig Tomlinson), Robert Morley (Dr. Percival), Ann Todd (Mrs. Castle), Richard Vernon (Sir John Hargreaves), Iman (Sarah Castle), Keith Marsh (Porter).

A Foreign Office security official suspects the wrong man of leaking information to a Soviet agent. It's an unexciting production featuring British double-agent Nicol Williamson, who is forced to defect to Russia.

1408. *Human Highway* (1982, Shakey, 90m, c). P L.A. Johnson, D Bernard Shakey [Neil Young] & Dean Stockwell, W Shakey, Jeanne Fields, Stockwell, Tamblyn & James Beshears, PH David Myers, M Neil Young & Devo.

LP Neil Young (Lionel Switch), Russ Tamblyn (Fred Kelly), Dean Stockwell (Otto Quartz), Dennis Hopper (Cracker), Charlotte Stewart (Charlotte Goodnight), Sally Kirkland (Katherine), Geraldine Baron (Irene).

Neil Young and Russ Tamblyn portray dimwitted, redneck gas station attendants in this crazy antinuke comedy.

1409. *Humanoids from the Deep* (1980, New World, 80m, c, aka *Monster*). P Martin B. Cohen & A. Hunt Lowry, D Barbara Peeters, W Frederick James (based on a story by Frank Arnold & Cohen), PH Daniel Lacambre, M James Horner, ED Mark Goldblatt.

LP Doug McClure (Jim), Ann Turkel (Dr. Susan Drake), Vic Morrow (Hank Slattery), Cindy Weintraub (Carol Hill), Anthony Penya (Johnny), Denise Galik (Linda), Lynn Theel (Peggy), Meegan King (Jerry).

Strange creatures rise from the ocean floor to attack mankind. These mutated salmons seem to have a preference for bikini-clad lovelies.

1410. *Humongous* (1982, Embassy, Canada, 91m, c). P Anthony Kramreither, D Paul Lynch, W William Gray, PH Brian Hebb, M John Mills Cockwell, ED Nick Rotundo.

LP Janet Julian (Sandy Rawlston), David Wallace (Eric Simmonds), Janet Baldwin (Donna Blake), John Wildman (Nick Simmonds), Joy Boushel (Carla Simmonds), Layne Coleman (Burt De-Foe), Shay Garner (Ida Parsons).

When a group of teenagers arrive on an island, the half-human, half-monster who lives there is not a gracious host.

1411. *The Hunger* (1983, MGM/United Artists, 99m, c). P Richard A. Shepard, D Tony Scott, W Ivan Davis & Michael Thomas (based on the novel by Whitley Strieber), PH Stephen Goldblatt, M Michel Rubini & Denny Jaeger, ED Pamela Power, PD Brian Morris.

LP David Bowie (John), Catherine Deneuve (Miriam), Susan Sarandon (Sarah Roberts), Cliff De Young (Tom Haver), Beth Ehlers (Alice Cavender), Dan Hedaya (Lt. Allegrezza), Rufus Collins (Charlie Humphries).

Ageless vampires David Bowie and Catherine Deneuve suddenly fall fatally ill after 300 years of blood-sucking. Susan Sarandon is the scientist they hope can help them. Nothing can help this sucker.

1412. *Hungry Heart* (1989, Chancom Ltd., Australia, 95m, c). P Rosa Colosimo, D&W Luigi Acquisto, PH James Grant, M Various Artists, ED Courtney Page, PD Michael Kourri.

LP Nick Carrafa (Sal Bono), Kimberley Davenport (Katie Maloney), Lisa Schouw (Jane), Norman Kaye (Mr. O'Ryan), Dasha Blahova (Mrs. Bono), Osvaldo Maione (Vito), Mark Rogers (Charlie), Gaetano Scollo (Tony).

Italian-American Nick Carrafa has completed medical school but is in no hurry to start practice. He drifts around aimlessly, becomes involved in some almost dishonest schemes, and meets and falls passionately in love with Kimberley Davenport. The affair ends about as quickly as it began when she grows tired of his criticism. Maybe it would sound better in Italian.

1413. *Hunk* (1987, Crown International, 102m, c). P Marilyn J. Tenser, D&W Lawrence Bassoff, PH Bryan England, M David Kurtz, ED Richard E. Westover.

LP John Allen Nelson (Hunk Golden), Steve Levitt (Bradley Brinkman), Deborah Shelton (O'Brien), Rebeccah Bush (Sunny), James Coco (Dr. D), Robert Morse (Garrison Gaylord), Avery Schreiber (Constantine Constapopolis).

In this version of the Faustian legend, Devil James Coco (in his last film appearance) offers nerdish weakling Steve Levitt a new spectacular body for a 30-day trial period. If he likes it he keeps it and forfeits his soul, after a certain time. If not he gets his old skinny, weakling's body back, no questions asked. Levitt feels it's worth a shot, just to enjoy the 30 days. He is transformed into John Allen Nelson, a real hunk. Of course dealing with the devil is fraught with twists and turns.

1414. *The Hunter* (1980, Paramount, 107m, c). P Mort Engelberg, D Buzz Kulik, W Ted Leighton & Peter Hyams (based on the book by Christopher Keane and the life of Ralph Thorson), PH Fred J. Koenekamp, M Michel Legrand, ED Robert Wolfe, PD Ron Hobbs.

LP Steve McQueen (Papa Thorson), Eli Wallach (Ritchie Blumenthal), Kathryn Harrold (Dotty), LeVar Burton (Tommy Price), Ben Johnson (Sheriff Strong), Richard Venture (Spota), Tracey Walter (Rocco Mason).

In his last film, Steve McQueen portrays real-life modern bounty hunter Ralph "Papa" Thorson. McQueen made worse movies, but their names escape us at the moment.

Hunter of the Apocalypse see The Last Hunter

1415. *Hunter's Blood* (1987, Concorde, 102m, c). Myrl A. Schrelbman, D Robert C. Hughes, W Emmett Alston (based on a novel by Jere Cunningham), PH Tom De Nove, M John D'Andrea, ED Barry Zetlin.

LP Sam Bottoms (David Rand), Kim Delaney (Melanie Rand), Clu Gulager (Mason Rand), Ken Swofford (Al Coleman), Joey Travolta (Marty Adler), Mayf Nutter (Ralph Coleman), Lee De-Broux (Red Beard), Bruce Glover (One

Eye), Billy Drago (Snake), Mickey Jones (Wash Pot), Charles Cyphers (Woody).

In a poor excuse for a *Deliverance* clone, five city boys from Oklahoma go deer hunting in the wilds of Arkansas. They have nothing but trouble with some dangerous redneck hillbilly poachers, who don't cotton to smart-ass louts from the outside.

1416. *Hussy* (1980, Watchgrove, GB, 95m, c). P Jeremy Watt, D&W Matthew Chapman, PH Keith Goddard, M George Fenton, ED Bill Blunden.

LP Helen Mirren (Beaty Simons), John Shea (Emory Cole), Daniel Chasen (Billy Simons), Murray Salem (Max), Paul Angelis (Alex), Jenny Runacre (Vere), Patti Boulaye (Tama), Marika Rivera (Nadine).

Club electrician John Shea worms his way into the affection of prostitute Helen Mirren via her ten-year-old son Daniel Chasen.

1417. *Hyper Sapien* (1986, Tri-Star, 92m, c). P Jack Schwartzman, D Peter Hunt, W Christopher Adcock, Christopher Blue & Marnie Paige, PH John Coquillon, M Arthur B. Rubinstein, ED Rick Benwick.

LP Dennis Holahan (Uncle Aric), Sydney Penny (Robyn), Rosie Marcel (Tavy), Ricky Paull Goldin (Dirt McAlpin), Hersha Parady (Mrs. McAlpin), Patricia Brookson (Cee Gee), Peter Jason (Mr. McAlpin), Jeremy Wilkins (Hyper Sapien Leader), Marilyn Schreffler (Voice of Kirbi, the Tri-Lat), Keenan Wynn (Grandpa McAlpin).

At the end of his career, Keenyn Wynn bows out of the movies in this country family film of only modest appeal.

1418. *Hysterical* (1983, Embassy, 86m, c). P Gene Levy, D Chris Bearde, W W., M. & B. Hudson & Trace Johnston, PH Donald Morgan, M Robert Alcivar & Robert O. Ragland, ED Stanley Frazer, PD J. Dennis Washington, SE Henry Millar.

LP William Hudson (Frederick), Mark Hudson (Paul), Brett Hudson (Fritz), Cindy Pickett (Kate), Richard Kiel (Capt. Howdy), Julie Newmar (Venetia), Bud Cort (Dr. John), Robert Donner (Ralph), Murray Hamilton (Mayor), Clint Walker (Sheriff), Charlie Callas (Dracula).

A haunted lighthouse is occupied by the vengeful spirit of a spurned woman. The Hudson Brothers prove they're not ready for the big screen. It's an unsuccessful parody of films like *The Amityville Horror.*

1419. *I Am the Cheese* (1983, Almi, 100m, c). P David Lange, D Robert Jiras, W Lange & Jiras (based on the novel by Robert Cormier), PH David Quaid, M Jonathan Tunick, ED Nicholas Smith.

LP Robert MacNaughton (Adam), Hope Lange (Betty), Don Murray (David), Robert Wagner (Dr. Brint), Cynthia Nixon (Amy), Frank McGurran (Young Adam), Russell Goslant (Gardener), Robert Cormier (Hertz).

Alienated youngster Robert MacNaughton witnesses the murder of his parents. He undergoes psychiatric treatment in an institution, where he learns the reason for their deaths.

1420. *I Love N.Y.* (1987, Manhattan/Manley, 110m, c). P Andrew Garroni & Gianni Bozzacchi, D&W Bozzacchi, PH Armando Nannuzzi, M Bill Conti.

LP Scott Baio (Mario Cotone), Christopher Plummer (John R. Yeats), Kelly Van Der Velden (Nicole Yeats), Jennifer O'Neill (Irene), Jerry Orbach (Leo), Virna Lisi (Anna Cotone).

Italian-American photograher Scott Baio, from the poor side of Manhattan, falls in love with Kelly Van Der Velden. She's the debutante daughter of Stage personality Christopher Plummer. Can two young people prove that class and money mean nothing when they're in love? "Can a girl from a mining town in the West find happiness as the wife of a wealthy and titled Englishman?" (The burning question of Radio's "Our Gal Sunday.")

1421. *I, Madman* (1989, TransWorld Ent., 89m, c, aka *Hardcover*). P Rafael Eisenman, D Tibor Takacs, W David Chaskin, PH Bryan England, M Michael Hoenig, ED Marcus Manton, PD Ron Wilson & Matthew Jacobs.

LP Jenny Wright (Virginia/Anna), Clayton Rohner (Richard), Randall William Cook (Malcolm Brand), Steven Memel (Lenny), Stephanie Hodge (Mona).

Meaning to pay homage to various horror film giants such as Tod Browning and James Whale, helmer Tibor Takacs and writer David Chaskin apparently learned nothing about making interesting movies from those worthy directors. Jenny Wright has a vivid imagination; so vivid that the horrible things she imagines come to life.

1422. *I Married a Vampire* (1988, Troma, 93m, c). P Vicky Prodromidov & Jay Raskin, D&W Raskin, PH Oren Rudavsky, M Steve Monahan, ED Raskin.

LP Rachel Golden (Viola), Brendan Hickey (Robespierre), Ted Zalewski (Gluttonshire), Deborah Carroll (Olivia), Temple Aaron (Portia).

Made in 1983, this low-budget comedy-horror film had a brief theater run in 1986 and was released to video in 1988. Rachel Golden meets a 100-year-old vampire and finds he's no worse than any of the other creeps and parasites she's encountered since striking out on her own.

1423. *I Ought to Be in Pictures* (1982, 20th Century–Fox, 108m, c). P Herbert Ross & Neil Simon, D Ross, W Simon (based on his play), PH David M. Walsh, M Marvin Hamlisch, ED Sidney Levin, PD Albert Brenner.

LP Walter Matthau (Herbert Tucker), Ann-Margret (Stephanie), Dinah Manoff (Libby), Lance Guest (Gordon), Lewis Smith (Soldier), Martin Ferrero (Monte Del Rey), Eugene Butler (Marty), Samantha Harper (Larane), Santos Morales (Mexican Truck Driver), David Faustino (Martin).

Nineteen-year-old Dinah Manoff hitchhikes from Brooklyn to L.A. Her motive is supposedly to break into the movies, but her real objective is to come to terms with her estranged father Walter Matthau, a screenwriter who deserted her, her mother and her brother 16 years earlier.

1424. *I Spit on Your Grave* (1983, Cinemagic Pictures, 100m, c, aka *Day of the Woman*). P Joseph Zbeda, D&W Meir Zarchi, PH Yuri Haviv, ED Zarchi.

LP Camille Keaton (Jennifer), Eron Tabor (Johnny), Richard Pace (Matthew), Gunter Kleeman (Andy), Alexis Magnotti (Attendant's wife), Tammy &

Terry Zarchi (Children), Traci Ferrante (Waitress), Bill Tasgal (Porter).

In this violent and poorly produced porno film, Camille Keaton takes a vacation in a woods where she is harassed by two men who beat and rape her. She crawls to her cabin, but they meet her there with two buddies. She is beaten and raped again. When she recovers she lures the men back to the cabin one by one. The first she hangs, the next is castrated, the third is killed with an axe and the fourth is disemboweled with an outboard motor.

1425. *I, the Jury* (1982, 20th Century–Fox, 109m, c). P Robert Solo, D Richard T. Heffron, W Larry Cohen (based on the novel by Mickey Spillane), PH Andrew Laszlo, M Bill Conti, ED Garth Craven, PD Robert Gundlach.

LP Armand Assante (Mike Hammer), Barbara Carrera (Charlotte Bennett), Laurene Landon (Velda), Alan King (Charles Kalecki), Geoffrey Lewis (Joe Butler), Paul Sorvino (Pat Chambers), Judson Scott (Kendricks).

Tough private eye Mike Hammer investigates the murder of his best friend. This remake of the 1953 production is able to show more graphic violence and nudity—but, as far as which is the better, it's like arguing about a beer being less filling or tasting good—who cares?

1426. *I Was a Teenage TV Terrorist* (1987, Troma, 85m, c). P Susan Kaufman, D Stanford Singer, W Singer & Kevin McDonough, PH Lisa Rinzler, M Cengiz Yaltkaya, ED Richard King.

LP Adam Nathan (Paul Pierce), Julie Hanlon (Donna Rose), John Mackay (John Reid), Walt Willey (Bill Johnson), Saul Alpiner (Frank Romance), Mikhail Druhan (Miss Murphy), Michael Griffith (Marcel Pederewsky), Guillermo Gonzalez (Rico).

This dull comedy went directly to video without having the chance to stink up any theaters. After being kicked out by his mother, teen Adam Nathan and his girlfriend Julie Hanlon move to Jersey City where his father gives them a job at his cable station. Nathan stages a mock terrorist attack, hoping to get even with his father for allowing him to go to jail for stealing station equipment.

1427. *I Was a Teenage Zombie* (1987, Horizon, 92m, c). P Richard Hirsh & John Elias Michalakias, D Michalakias, W James Martin, George Seminara & Steve McCoy, PH Peter Lewnes, M Jonathan Roberts & Craig Seeman, ED Michalakias.

LP Michael Rubin (Dan Wake), George Seminara (Gordy), Steve McCoy (Mussolini), Peter Bush (Rosencrantz), Cassie Madden (Cindy Faithful), Cindy Keiter (Miss Lugae), Gwyn Drischell (Margo), Allen L. Rickman (Lieberman).

When drug dealer Steve McCoy is murdered, he is thrown into a river contaminated by nuclear waste. He revives as a green zombie and avenges himself on his teenage killers, transforming them into flesh eating maniacs.

1428. *Ice House* (1989, Upfront Films, 86m, c). P Bo Brinkman, D Eagle Pennell, W Brinkman (based on his play), PH Brown Cooper, M Carmen Yates & Tony Fortuna, ED John Murray, PD Lynn Ruth Appel.

LP Melissa Gilbert (Kay/Mother), Bo Brinkman (Pake), Andreas Manolikakis (Vassil), Lynn Miller (Father), Buddy Quaid (Little Pake), Nikki Letts (Little Kay).

Sweet little Melissa Gilbert has left the little house on the prairie for a sleazy L.A. hotel room. She and her long-time lover and sparring partner Bo Brinkman are both a long way from their Texas homes. The dialogue consists mostly of accusations and verbal abuse.

1429. *The Ice Pirates* (1984, MGM/ United Artists, 96m, c). P John Foreman, D Stewart Raffill, W Raffill & Stanford Sherman, PH Matthew F. Leonetti, M Bruce Broughton, ED Tom Walls.

LP Robert Urich (Jason), Mary Crosby (Princess Karina), Michael D. Roberts (Roscoe), Anjelica Huston (Maida), John Matuszak (Killjoy), Ron Perlman (Zeno), John Carradine (Supreme Commander), Natalie Core (Nanny).

A group of pirates steal frozen blocks of ice to satisfy the needs of a galaxy with a diminishing water supply.

1430. *Iced* (1988, Mikon, 85m, c). P Robert Seibert, D Jeff Kwitny, W Joseph Alan Johnson, PH Eugene Shlugleit, M Dan Milner, ED Carol Oblath, PD Tim Boxell.

LP Debra Deliso (Tina), Doug Stevenson (Cory), Ron Kologie (Carl), Elizabeth Gorcey (Diane), John C. Cooke (John), Joseph Alan Johnson (Alex), Dan Smith (Jeff), Michael Picardi (Eddie), Lisa Loring (Jeanette).

Released straight to video, this is the story of a maniac who invites those he considers responsible for a fatal skiing accident at his winter resort, and picks them off one by one.

1431. *Iceman* (1984, Universal, 101m, c). P Patrick Palmer & Norman Jewison, D Fred Schepisi, W Chip Proser & John Drimmer (based on a story by Drimmer), PH Ian Baker, M Bruce Smeaton, ED Billy Weber.

LP Timothy Hutton (Dr. Stanley Shephard), Lindsay Crouse (Dr. Diane Brady), John Lone (Charlie), Josef Sommer (Whitman), David Strathairn (Dr. Singe), Philip Akin (Dr. Vermeil), Danny Glover (Loomis), Amelia Hall (Mabel), Richard Monette (Hogan), James Tolkan (Maynard).

A team of Arctic scientists discovers John Lone, a 40,000-year-old Neanderthal man encased in ice. When he revives, scientists Timothy Hutton and Lindsay Crouse establish a relationship with him. Unbelievably, some scientists want to learn from Lone's body rather than his primitive mind, which of course means first taking his life.

1432. *Identity Crisis* (1989, Block & Chip, 90m, c). P&D Melvin Van Peebles, W Mario Van Peebles, PH Jim Hinton, M E. Pearson, ED Victor Kanefsky & Melvin Van Peebles.

LP Mario Van Peebles (Chilly D.), Ilan Mitchell-Smith (Sebastian), Shelly Burch (Roxy), Richard Fancy (Yves Malmaison), Nicholas Kepros, Richard Clarke, Rick Aviles, Tab Thacker.

When French fashion designer Richard Fancy is poisoned he is reincarnated in the youthful body of black New York rapper Mario Van Peebles. The latter fell off the ledge of a building at precisely the same time. Now the fun begins—sorta.

1433. *The Idolmaker* (1980, United Artists, 107m, c). P Gene Kirkwood &

Howard W. Koch, Jr., D Taylor Hackford, W Edward Di Lorenzo, PH Adam Holender, M Jeff Barry, ED Neil Travis.

LP Ray Sharkey (Vincent Vacarri), Tovah Feldshuh (Brenda Roberts), Peter Gallagher (Caesare), Paul Land (Tommy Dee), Joe Pantoliano (Gino Pilato), Maureen McCormick (Ellen Fields), John Aprea (Paul Vacarri), Richard Bright (Uncle Tony), Olympia Dukakis (Mrs. Vacarri), Steven Apostlee Peck (Mr. Vacarri).

The story is probably based on the life and career of Bob Marcucci. He has been credited with making rock stars of Frankie Avalon and Fabian, as well as many others of the 50s "Philadelphia Sound" performers. Ray Sharkey is the promoter who catapults two talentless lads Peter Gallagher and Paul Land into rock-star phenomenons.

1434. *If Looks Could Kill* (1987, Distant Horizons, 89m, c). P&D Chuck Vincent, W Vincent & Craig Horrall, PH Larry Revene, M Susan Jopson & Jonathan Hannah, ED James Davalos & Marc Ubell [Vincent].

LP Kim Lambert [Sheri St. Claire] (Laura Williamson), Tim Gail (George Ringer), Alan Fisler (Bob Crown), Jamie Gillis (Jack Devonoff), Jeanne Marie (Jeannie Burns), James Davies (Carson), Jane Hamilton (Mary Beth).

Former porno king Chuck Vincent, still trying to break into the main stream of movie-making, comes up with a *Rear Window/Body Double* clone. Photographer Tim Gail sets up surveillance of Kim Lambert's apartment. He records her active and kinky sex life before discovering he's been nominated as the fall guy in a murder scheme.

1435. *If You Could See What I Hear* (1982, Jensen Farley, 102m, c). P Eric Till & Stuart Gillard, D Till, W Gillard (based on the book by Tom Sullivan & Derek Gill, PH Harry Makin, ED Eric Wrate.

LP Marc Singer (Tom Sullivan), R.H. Thompson (Will Sly), Sarah Torgov (Patty Steffen), Shari Belafonte Harper (Heather Johnson), Douglas Campbell (Porky Sullivan), Helen Burns (Mrs. Ruxton), Harvey Atkin (Bert), Barbara Gordon (Molly), Sharon Lewis (Helga), Lynda Mason Greene (Sharon).

While not worth a trip to a movie theater, this true-life story of blind singer-musician Tom Sullivan covering the period from his college days to his marriage is moderately amusing and worth a peck on TV. At any rate Shari Belafonte Harper is worth several peeks.

1436. *Igor and the Lunatics* (1985, Troma Team, 84m, c). P&W Jocelyn Beard & Billy Parolini (based on a story by Beard), D Parolini, Tom Doran & Brendan Faulkner, PH John Raugalis, M Sonia Rutstein, ED Parolini, SE Simon Deitch.

LP Joseph Eero, Joe Niola, T.J. Michaels, Mary Ann Schacht.

After being released from a long prison term for raising hell in a small town, a murderous cult leader picks up where he left off.

1437. *Illegally Yours* (1988, MGM/United Artists, 102m, c). P&D Peter Bogdanovich, W M.A. Stewart & Max Dickens, PH Dante Spinotti, M Phil Marshall, ED Richard Fields & Ronald Krehel, PD Jane Musky.

LP Rob Lowe (Richard Dice), Colleen Camp (Molly Gilbert), Kenneth Mars (Hal B. Keeler), Harry Carey, Jr. (Wally Finnegan), Kim Myers (Suzanne Keeler), Marshall Colt (Donald Cleary), Linda MacEwen (Ruth Harrison).

Peter Bogdanovich attempts to make a 30s screwball comedy but only succeeds in screwing up an 80s movie. Rob Lowe is a bungling jury member who falls for murder defendant Colleen Camp. Our black Labrador, Annabel, could write the rest of the script.

1438. *I'm Dancing as Fast as I Can* (1982, Paramount, 106m, c). P Edgar J. Scherick & Scott Rudin, D Jack Hofsiss, W David Rabe (based on the novel by Barbara Gordon), PH Jan De Bont, M Stanley Silverman, ED Michael Bradsell, PD David Jenkins.

LP Jill Clayburgh (Barbara Gordon), Nicol Williamson (Derek Bauer), Dianne Wiest (Julie Addison), Joe Pesci (Roger), Geraldine Page (Jean Martin), James Sutorius (Sam Mulligan), Ellen Greene (Karen Mulligan), Cordis Heard (Fran), Richard Masur (Alan Newman).

Successful documentary maker Jill Clayburgh depends on Valium to keep her going. Her live-in lover Nicol Williamson's crutch is alcohol. Theirs is not a stable relationship. Better put on a minuet.

1439.   *I'm Gonna Get You Sucka* (1988, United Artists, 87m, c). P Peter McCarthy & Carl Craig, D&W Keenan Ivory Wayans, PH Tom Richmond, M David Michael Frank, ED Michael R. Miller, PD Melba Farquhar & Catherine Hardwicke.

LP Keenen Ivory Wayans (Jack Spade), Bernie Casey (John Slade), Antonio Fargas (Flyguy), Steve James (Kung Fu Joe), Isaac Hayes (Hammer), Jim Brown (Slammer), Ja'net DuBois (Ma Bell), Dawn Lewis (Cheryl), John Vernon (Mr. Big), Clarence Williams 3d (Kalinga).

A silly but enjoyable parody, this film is a nostalgic look at the blaxploitation films of the 70s. A lot of aging former black heroes gag it up for all they're worth.

1440.   *The Imagemaker* (1986, Castle Hill, 93m, c). P Marilyn Weiner & Hal Weiner, D Hal Weiner, W Dick Goldberg & Hal Weiner, M Fred Karns, ED Terry Halle.

LP Michael Nouri (Roger Blackwell), Jerry Orbach (Byron Caine), Anne Twomey (Molly Grainger), Jessica Harper (Cynthia), Farley Granger (The Ambassador).

Michael Nouri, former media advisor to the president, has an audio tape that could incriminate his former boss. Various people are literally dying to get their hands on the tape.

1441.   *Immediate Family* (1989, Columbia, 95m, c). P Sarah Pillsbury & Midge Sanford, D Jonathan Kaplan, W Barbara Benedek, PH John W. Lindley, M Brad Fiedel, ED Jane Kurson, PD Mark Freeborn.

LP Glenn Close (Linda Spector), James Woods (Michael Spector), Mary Stuart Masterson (Lucy Moore), Kevin Dillon (Sam), Linda Darlow (Susan Drew), Jane Greer (Michael's Mother), Jessica James (Bessie), Mimi Kennedy (Eli's Mom), Charles Levin (Eli's Dad), Harrison Mohr (Eli).

James Woods and Glenn Close have been married 11 years and have not been able to have a baby. Through the efforts of lawyer Linda Darlow, they make arrangements with unwed mother-to-be Mary Stuart Masterson to adopt her baby. Together with the father of the child, Kevin Dillon, the foursome get to know and like each other. Once the baby is born, things aren't as simple anymore.

The Imp see Sorority Babes in the Slimeball Bowl-a-Rama

1442.   *The Imported Bridegroom* (1989, Lara Classics, 90m, c). P&D Pamela Berger, W Berger (based on a story by Abraham Cahan), PH Brian Heffron, M Bevan Manson & Rosalie Gerut, ED Amy Summer, PD Martha Seely.

LP Gene Troobnick (Asriel Stroon), Avi Hoffman (Shaya), Greta Cowan (Flora), Annette Miller (Mrs. Birnbaum), Miriam Varon, Andreas Teuber, Ted Jacobs, Ira Solet, Ira Goldenberg, Barry Karas, Helene Lantry.

Set in turn-of-the-century Boston, this comedy-drama tells the story of Polish Jew Gene Troobnick. He returns to the old country to renew spiritual ties. He brings home a scholar as a bridegroom for his daughter. However, she has her own marital plans.

1443.   *Improper   Channels* (1981, Rank-Crown International, Canada, 92m, c). P Alfred Pariser & Morrie Ruvinsky, D Eric Till, W Ruvinsky, Ian Sutherland & Adam Arkin (based on a story by Ruvinsky), PH Anthony Richmond, M Micky Erbe & Maribeth Solomon, ED Thom Noble.

LP Alan Arkin (Jeffrey), Mariette Hartley (Diana), Monica Parker (Gloria), Harry Ditson (Harold), Sarah Stevens (Nancy), Danny Higham (Jack), Leslie Yeo (Fred), Richard Farrell (Fraser), Ruth Springford (Mrs. Wharton).

Alan Arkin takes on the world of computers when he can't get anyone to correct the data on file which lists him as a child beater. Many people are familiar with the kind of frustration that Arkin suffers but it's not the machine messing up his life. When errors of this nature occur, you can bet there's a human behind the SNAFU.

1444.   *Impulse* (1984, ABC/20th Century–Fox, 91m, c). P Tim Zinnemann, D

Graham Baker, W Bart Davis & Don Carlos Dunaway, PH Thomas Del Ruth, M Paul Chihara, ED David Holden, PD Jack T. Collis.

LP Tim Matheson (Stuart), Meg Tilly (Jennifer), Hume Cronyn (Dr. Carr), John Karlen (Bob Russell), Bill Paxton (Eddie Russell), Amy Stryker (Margo), Claude Earl Jones (Sheriff), Robert Wightman (Howard), Lorinne Vozoff (Mrs. Russell).

The residents of a small town begin to act strangely after a mild earthquake. The quake caused the ground to shift and allow toxic chemicals to drip into the water supply of dairy cattle which in turn contaminated the milk, which made the residents mean and murderous. See what happens if you mind your Mommy and drink your milk like a good child each and every day.

1445. *Impure Thoughts* (1986, ASA Communications, 83m, c). P William VanDerKloot & Michael A. Simpson & Michael J. Malloy, D Simpson, PH/ED VanDerKloot, M James Oliverio, PD Guy Tuttle.

LP John Putch (Danny Stubbs), Terry Beaver (William Miller), Brad Dourif (Kevin Harrington), Lane Davies (Steve Barrett), Benji Wilhoite (Young Bill), J.J. Sacha (Young Danny), Sam McPhaul (Young Kevin), Jason Jones (Young Steve), Mary McDonough (Sister Juliet), Joe Conley (Father Minnelli), Judith Anderson (Narrator).

Four friends die, meet in Purgatory and reminisce about the good old days in Catholic schools. The film is occasionally on target and occasionally funny, but it's no "Growing Up Catholic."

1446. *In a Pig's Eye* (1989, Elsinore, 86m, c). P David Brownstein & John Saffron, D&W Saffron, PH Jim Hayman, ED Peter Friedman, AD Bonnie Saltzman.

LP Marian Seldes, David Canary, Tudor Sherrard, Alexa Lambert, Bobbi Jo Lathan, David Bailey.

It's a zany (it says here) comical spoof of *Grand Hotel* with confused patrons and a weird staff.

1447. *In a Shallow Grave* (1988, Skouras, 92m, c). P Kenneth Bowser &

Barry Jossen, D&W Bowser (based on the novel by James Purdy), PH Jerzy Zielinski, M Jonathan Sheffer, ED Nicholas C. Smith, PD David Wasco.

LP Michael Biehn (Garnet Montrose), Maureen Mueller (Georgina Rance), Michael Beach (Quintas Pearch), Patrick Dempsey (Potter Daventry), Thomas Boyd Mason (Edgar Doust).

Disfigured at Guadalcanal, World War II veteran Michael Biehn becomes a recluse on his family's desolate Virginia farm. Good-natured drifter Patrick Dempsey moseys along and befriends Biehn. Dempsey agrees to deliver messages to Biehn's prewar love, Maureen Mueller. The mental disfiguration of Biehn causes him to suspect Dempsey and Mueller of having an affair and the thought is too much for him.

1448. *In Country* (1989, Warner, 120m, c). P Norman Jewison & Richard Roth, D Jewison, W Frank Pierson & Cynthia Cidre (based on the novel by Bobbie Ann Mason), PH Russell Boyd, M James Horner, ED Antony Gibbs & Lou Lombardo, PD Jackson DeGovia.

LP Bruce Willis (Emmett Smith), Emily Lloyd (Samantha Hughes), Joan Allen (Irene), Kevin Anderson (Lonnie), John Terry (Tom), Peggy Rea (Mamaw), Judith Ivey (Anita), Dan Jenkins (Dwayne), Stephen Tobolowsky (Pete), Jim Beaver (Earl), Richard Hamilton (Grandpaw).

Bruce Willis gives a welcome restrained performance as a troubled Vietnam vet unwilling to explain to the folks back home what happened in Nam. He's forced to bend his rule for his 17-year-old niece Emily Lloyd, who wants to know the details of her father's death in the war (which occurred before she was born). Together, the two victims of the war try to come to terms with its effect on them.

1449. *The In Crowd* (1988, Orion, 96m, c). P Keith Rubinstein & Lawrence Konner, D Mark Rosenthal, W Rosenthal & Konner, PH Anthony Richmond, M Mark Snow, ED Jeffrey Wolf, PD Joseph T. Garrity.

LP Donovan Leitch (Del Green), Joe Pantoliano (Perry Parker), Jennifer Runyon (Vicky), Wendy Gazelle (Gail Goren), Sean Gregory Sullivan (Popeye),

Charlotte D'Amboise (Ina), Bruce Kirby (Norris).

This enjoyable film spends some time with the kids who danced on those daily TV dance shows in the 60s.

1450.   *In Dangerous Company* (1988, Sandstar, 96m, c). P Ruben Preuss & Robert Newell, D Preuss, W Mitch Brown, PH James Carter, M Berington Van Campen, ED W.O. Garrett, PD Mark Simon.

LP Cliff DeYoung (Blake), Tracy Scoggins (Evelyn), Steven Keats (Ryerson), Chris Mulkey (Chris), Henry Darrow (Alex Aguilar), Catherine Ai (Peggy), Dana Lee (Troung), Michael Shaner (Richie).

In a piece of cinema trash, beautiful Tracy Scoggins uses her body to turn two men on and against each other.

1451.   *In God We Trust* (1980, Universal, 97m, c). P Howard West & George Shapiro, D Marty Feldman, W Feldman & Chris Allen, PH Charles Correll, M John Morris, ED David Blewitt, PD Lawrence G. Paull.

LP Marty Feldman (Brother Ambrose), Peter Boyle (Dr. Melmoth), Louise Lasser (Mary), Richard Pryor (God), Andy Kaufman (Armageddon T. Thunderbird), Wilfrid Hyde-White (Abbott Thelonius), Severn Darden (Priest).

Marty Feldman portrays a naive monk sent away from the protection of the monastery to raise money for its mortgage. He encounters every kind of religious charlatan that exists in Hollywood, but nothing that happens can be described as funny.

1452.   *In Love* (1983, Platinum, 100m, c). P&D Chuck Vincent, W Rick Marx & Vincent (based on a story by Henri Pachard), PH Larry Revene, M Ian Shaw, ED James Macreading.

LP Kelly Nichols (Jill), Jerry Butler (Andy), Tish Ambrose (Janet), Joanna Storm (April), Samantha Fox (Elaine), Jack Wrangler (Dick), Michael Knight (Kip), Susan Nero (Hooker), Beth Alison Broderick (Ella), Veronica Hart (Belinda).

Chuck Vincent, who started in movies making XXX hardcore porno films, and some of his "stars," attempt to break into the straight world of cinema with soft-core porn movies like this. Except for the absence of explicit sex, there's not much difference.

1453.   *In 'n' Out* (1986, New World, US/Mex., 106m, c). P Michael James Egan, D Ricardo Franco, W Eleen Kesend & Franco, PH Juan Ruiz Anchia, M T-Bone Burnett.

LP Sam Bottoms (Murray Lewis, Jr.), Rafael Inclan (Nieves Blanco), Rebecca Jones (Lupita Blanco), Isela Vega (Mona Mur).

After his bass guitar is repossessed, his wife refuses to drop divorce proceedings and he bungles a suicide attempt, musician Sam Bottoms travels to Mexico in search of an inheritance.

1454.   *In Search of Historic Jesus* (1980, Sunn Classics, 91m, c). P Charles E. Sellier, Jr. & James L. Conway, D Henning Schellerup, W Malvin Wald & Jack Jacobs (based on the book by Lee Roddy and Sellier, Jr.), PH Paul Hipp, M Bob Summers, ED Kendall S. Rase, PD Paul Staheli.

LP John Rubinstein (Jesus), John Anderson (Caiaphas), Nehemiah Persoff (Herod Antipas), Brad Crandall (Narrator), Andrew Bloch (John), Morgan Brittany (Mary), Walter Brooke (Joseph), Annette Charles (Mary Magdalene), Royal Dano (Prophet), Anthony DeLongis (Peter), Lawrence Dobkin (Pontius Pilate), David Opatoshu (Herod).

Sunn Classics, makers of pseudodocumentary dramatizations, examines the life of Jesus Christ, based on whatever historical documentation can be found. That there isn't much is not surprising, nor significant.

1455.   *In the Mood* (1987, Lorimar, 96m, c). P Gary Adelson & Karen Mack, D&W Phil Alden Robinson (based on a story by Bob Kosberg, David Simon & Robinson), PH John Lindley, M Ralph Burns, ED Patrick Kennedy, PD Dennis Gassner.

LP Patrick Dempsey (Ellsworth "Sonny" Wisecarver), Talia Balsam (Judy Cusimano), Beverly D'Angelo (Francine Glatt), Michael Constantine (Mr. Wisecarver), Betty Jinnette (Mrs. Wisecarver), Kathleen Freeman (Mrs.

Marver), Peter Hobbs (The Judge), Tony Longo (Carlo Cusimano), Douglas Rowe (Uncle Clete), Ernie Brown (Chief "Papa Bear" Kelsey).

The movie presents the true story of "The Woo Woo Kid." In 1944 he made headlines and was sent to a reformatory for marrying older women (21 and 25) when he was only 15. The women seem taken by the boy's sweet naïveté, shyness and sincerity. It was a kinder, gentler time, so unlike most movie romances of today between older women and young boys. Patrick Dempsey, as the kid, is no Greek-god stud, and the women, Martin Balsam's daughter Talia and Beverly D'Angelo, are more than mere bored, sex-starved housewives.

1456. *In the Shadow of Kilimanjaro* (1986, Scotti Bros., 97m, c). P Gautam Das, Jeffrey M. Sneller, D Raju Patel, W Sneller & T. Michael Harry, PH Jesus Elizondo, M Arlon Ober, ED Paul Rubell & Pradip Roy Shah.

LP John Rhys-Davies (Chris Tucker), Timothy Bottoms (Jack Ringtree), Irene Miracle (Lee Ringtree), Michele Carey (Ginny), Leonard Trolley (Maitland), Patty Foley (Lucille Gagnon), Calvin Jung (Mitushi), Don Blakely (Julius).

A drought in the African bush drives baboons to become maneaters. It's a boring, gory movie.

1457. *Inchon* (1981, MGM/United Artists, Korea/US, 140m, c). P Mitsuharu Ishii, D Terence Young, W Robin Moore & Laird Koenig (based on the story by Moore & Paul Savage), PH Bruce Surtees, M Jerry Goldsmith, ED John W. Holmes, Michael J. Sheridan.

LP Laurence Olivier (Gen. MacArthur), Jacqueline Bisset (Barbara Hallsworth), Ben Gazzara (Maj. Frank Hallsworth), Toshiro Mifune (Saito-San), Richard Roundtree (Sgt. August Henderson), David Janssen (David Feld), Nam Goon Won (Park), Gabriele Ferzetti (Turkish Brigadier), Rex Reed (Longfellow), Sabine Sun (Marguerite), Dorothy James (Jean MacArthur).

The Rev. Sun Myung Moon, head of the Unification Church, decided he'd like to produce a movie about the 1950 landing of American troops, led by General MacArthur, at Inchon, Korea. Appar-

ently this is not the only bad decision made. Also at fault for one of the worst movies ever made is Laurence Olivier who can't seem to decide whether to make himself up to be MacArthur or Sir Toby Belch. Then there's Rex Reed, in his first bust since *Myra Breckenridge*. Well, at least Reed is not a one-shot failure as a movie actor.

1458. *The Incredible Shrinking Woman* (1981, Universal, 88m, c). P Hank Moonjean, D Joel Schumacher, W Jane Wagner (based on the novel *The Shrinking Man* by Richard Matheson), PH Bruce Logan, M Suzanne Ciani, ED Jeff Gourson & Anthony Redman, PD Raymond A. Brandt.

LP Lily Tomlin (Pat Kramer/Judith Beasley), Charles Grodin (Vance Kramer), Ned Beatty (Dan Beame), Henry Gibson (Dr. Eugene Nortz), Elizabeth Wilson (Dr. Ruth Ruth), Mark Blankfield (Rob), Maria Smith (Concepcion), Pamela Bellwood (Sandra Dyson), John Glover (Tom Keller).

Model homemaker and perfect mother Lily Tomlin discovers that she is shrinking as a result of an unusual blood condition brought on by having a perfume called "Sexpot" spilled on her. We're not quite sure what pigeonhole to stuff this one in. It's not funny enough to be a comedy. It has little of the appeal of *The Incredible Shrinking Man*, the very fine 1957 science fiction piece on which it is based. A farce? Well, it is absurd. Hey, maybe, it's a feminist picture. If it is, we'd prefer a film based on the song "I Am Woman."

The Incredible Torture Show see Bloodsucking Freaks

1459. *The Incubus* (1982, Film Ventures, Canada, 92m, c). P Marc Boyman & John M. Eckert, D John Hough, W George Franklin (based on the novel by Ray Russell), PH Albert J. Dunk, M Stanley Myers, ED George Appleby, PD Ted Watkins.

LP John Cassavetes (Dr. Sam Cordell), Kerrie Keane (Laura Kincaid), Helen Hughes (Agatha Galen), Erin Flannery (Jenny Cordell), Duncan McIntosh (Tim), John Ireland (Hank), Harvey Atkin (Joe), Dirk McLean (Incubus).

John Cassavetes and his teenage

daughter Erin Flannery move into a quiet New England town. There they encounter a terrifying, supernatural demon.

1460. *An Indecent Obsession* (1985, PBL, Australia, 100m, c). P Ian Bradley, D Lex Marinos, W Denise Morgan, PH Ernest Clark, M Dave Skinner, ED Philip Howe, PD Michael Relph.

LP Wendy Hughes (Honour Langtry), Gary Sweet (Michael Wilson), Richard Moir (Luce Daggett), Jonathan Hyde (Neil Parkinson), Bruno Lawrence (Matt Sawyer), Mark Little (Benedict Maynard), Tony Sheldon (Nuggett Jones), Bill Hunter (Col. Chinstrap), Julia Blake (Matron).

Compassionate nurse Wendy Hughes is assigned to the Wacko ward of a World War II hospital, inhabited by shell-shocked soldiers. She is sexually drawn to new patient Gary Sweet and ultimately takes him to her bed just as the war ends. This is too much to bear for patient Richard Moir, who loves Hughes, so he commits suicide.

1461. *Independence Day* (1983, Warner, 110m, c). P Daniel H. Blatt & Robert Singer, D Robert Mandel, W Alice Hoffman, PH Charles Rosher, M Charles Bernstein, ED Dennis Virkler, PD Stewart Campbell.

LP Kathleen Quinlan (Mary Ann Tyler), David Keith (Jack Parker), Frances Sternhagen (Carla Taylor), Cliff DeYoung (Les Morgan), Dianne Wiest (Nancy Morgan), Josef Sommer (Sam Taylor), Bert Remsen (Red Malone), Richard Farnsworth (Evan), Brooke Alderson (Shelly).

Small town photographer Kathleen Quinlan chooses not to move on to bigger and better things because of her love for racing car enthusiast David Keith.

1462. *Indiana Jones and the Last Crusade* (1989, Paramount, 127m, c). P Robert Watts, D Steven Spielberg, W Jeffrey Boam (based on a story by George Lucas & Menno Meyjes), PH Douglas Slocombe, M John Williams†, ED Michael Kahn, PD Elliot Scott, SOUND Ben Burtt†.

LP Harrison Ford (Indiana Jones), Sean Connery (Prof. Henry Jones), Denholm Elliott (Marcus Brody), Alison Doody (Elsa), John Rhys-Davies (Sallah), Julian Glover (Walter Donovan), River Phoenix (Young Indy), Michael Byrne (Vogel).

Sequels are seldom as good as the original film, particularly when the first is a blockbuster of the size and popularity of *Raiders of the Lost Ark*. The third film in a series usually has a tremendous fall-off in quality. Such, we are delighted to report, is not the case of this film. It is considerably better than the sequel and compares favorably with the original for action, excitement, chills, and nasty villains. Best of all it has Sean Connery as Harrison Ford's dad. Connery is a marvelous plus, working very well with Ford. Jones père and fils both bed beautiful Alison Doody — or to be more precise, she beds them both. Father and son seek the Holy Grail, before it falls into the hands of some really nasty Nazis. Two more plusses are the fine work of good guys, the marvelous actor Denholm Elliott as a helpless but willing colleague of both Joneses (his appearance was little more than a cameo in the first film), and the superb John Rhys-Davies, the best heavyweight actor since Sidney Greenstreet and Laird Cregar. This is a film well worth seeing several times, and for years into the future. Let's hope for one more Indy picture of such wit and action. Come on Ford, never say never.

1463. *Indiana Jones and the Temple of Doom* (1984, Paramount, 118m, c). P Robert Watts, D Steven Spielberg, W Willard Huyck & Gloria Katz (based on a story by George Lucas and characters from the movie *Raiders of the Lost Ark* by Lawrence Kasdan), PH Douglas Slocombe, M John Williams†, ED Michael Kahn, PD Elliot Scott, VE Dennis Muren, Michael McAlister, Lorne Peterson & George Gibbs*.

LP Harrison Ford (Indiana Jones), Kate Capshaw (Willie Scott), Ke Huy Quan (Short Round), Amrish Puri (Mola Ram), Roshan Seth (Chattar Lal), Philip Stone (Capt. Blumburtt), Roy Chiao (Lao Che), David Yip (Wu Han), Ric Young (Kao Kan), Chua Kah Joo (Chen), Dan Aykroyd (Weber), D.R. Nanayakkara (Shaman).

Compared to the original and the third

film in this series,, this picture is a major disappointment. The other two movies give audiences a good fright; this one tends to gross them out. The opening nightclub scene is fun, but once Harrison Ford, Kate Capshaw and Ke Huy Quan make it somewhere over the Himalayas and are convinced to rescue a village's magic stone and its children, audiences are in for numerous nauseating scenes. The trio find themselves in a hell-hole of an underground Hades where hearts are plucked from the bodies of unlucky victims. Ford, who never smiles in any of his pictures anyway, doesn't look too thrilled by the whole thing, while little Quan is more an annoying brat with a big mouth than an appealing orphan. Capshaw is pretty, but she seems just excess baggage.

1464. *Inferno* (1986, 20th Century–Fox, 83m, c). P Claudio Argento, D&W Dario Argento, PH Romano Albani, M Keith Emerson, ED Franco Francelli.

LP Leigh McCloskey (Mark), Irene Miracle (Rose), Eleonora Giorgi (Sara), Daria Nicolodi (Elise), Sacha Pitoeff (Kazanian), Alida Valli (Carol), Veronica Lazar (Nurse), Gabriele Lavia (Carlo).

All the voices in this Italian horror film are dubbed including that of American Leigh McClosky. He comes to the aid of his sister when she discovers that her apartment is the home of an ancient evil spirit.

An Infinity of Terrors see Galaxy of Terror

1465. *The Initiation* (1984, New World, 97m, c). P Scott Winant, D Larry Stewart, W Charles Pratt, Jr., PH George Tirl, M Gabriel Black & Lance Ong, ED Ronald LaVine.

LP Vera Miles (Frances Fairchild), Clu Gulager (Dwight Fairchild), Daphne Zuniga (Kelly Terry), James Read (Peter), Marilyn Kagan (Marcia), Patti Heider (Nurse), Robert Dowdell (Jason Randall), Frances Peterson (Megan).

In still another dumb slasher film, with a very limited theater run, Daphne Zuniga portrays a pledge at the Delta Rho Chi sorority. She is having disturbing dreams involving her parents Vera Miles and Clu Gulager. Some nut is running amok in the sorority house with a knife.

1466. *Innerspace* (1987, Warner, 120m, c). P Michael Finnell & Chip Proser, D Joe Dante, W Jeffrey Boam & Proser (based on a story by Proser), PH Andrew Laszlo, M Jerry Goldsmith, ED Kent Beyda, PD James H. Spencer, VE Dennis Muren, William George, Harley Jessup & Kenneth Smith*.

LP Dennis Quaid (Lt. Tuck Pendelton), Martin Short (Jack Putter), Meg Ryan (Lydia Maxwell), Kevin McCarthy (Victor Scrimshaw), Fiona Lewis (Dr. Margaret Canker), Vernon Wells (Mr. Igoe), Robert Picardo (The Cowboy), Wendy Schaal (Wendy), Harold Sylvester (Pete Blanchard).

Daring test pilot Dennis Quaid is assigned a bizarre mission. He is placed in a capsule which is then reduced in size until it is smaller than a molecule. The capsule is first to be injected in a rabbit. If successful, future surgeons will be able to operate from within a patient's diseased organs. By accident the capsule and Quaid are accidentally injected into Martin Short. The two are able to communicate as they desperately seek a way to get Quaid back to his normal size.

1467. *The Innocent* (1985, TVS/Curzon, GB, 96m, c). P Jackie Stoller, D John MacKenzie, W Ray Jenkins (based on the novel *The Aura and the Kingfisher* by Tom Hart), PH Roger Deakins, M Francis Monkman, ED Tony Woollard, PD Andrew Mollo.

LP Andrew Hawley (Tim Dobson), Kika Markham (Mrs. Dobson), Kate Foster (Win), Liam Neeson (John Carns), Patrick Daley (Eddie King), Paul Askew (Stanley), Lorraine Peters (Grandmother), Tom Bell (Frank Dobson), Miranda Richardson (Mary Turner).

In Yorkshire in 1932, a sacked miner's epileptic son is used as a go-between by a poet and a married woman.

1468. *An Innocent Man* (1989, Touchstone, 113m, c, aka *Framed; Hard Rain*). P Ted Field, Robert W. Cort & Neil A. Machlis, D Peter Yates, W Larry Brothers, PH William A. Fraker, M Howard Shore, ED Stephen A. Rotter & William S. Scharf, PD Stuart Wurtzel.

LP Tom Selleck (Jimmie Rainwood), F. Murray Abraham (Virgil Cane), Laila

Robins (Kate Rainwood), David Rasche (Mike Parnell), Richard Young (Danny Scalise), Badja Djola (John Fitzgerald), Todd Graff (Robby), M.C. Gainey (Malcolm), Peter Van Norden (Peter Feldman).

In what we hope is an improbable story, happy solid citizen Tom Selleck steps into a shower and emerges into a nightmare. Two crooked cops break into his home, see him blow-drying his hair with a hair dryer which they mistake for a gun, and shoot him. When they discover their mistake, they set him up on a phony drug charge which gets him six years in the slammer. In the pen, Selleck becomes toughened with the help of mentor F. Murray Abraham. Meanwhile Selleck's wife Laila Robins is working to prove he was framed. There's a lot going on but Selleck still hasn't convinced audiences that he belongs on the big screen.

Inseminoid see Horror Planet

1469. *Inside Moves* (1980, Goodmark/Associated, 113m, c). P Mark M. Tanz & R.W. Goodwin, D Richard Donner, W Valerie Curtin & Barry Levinson (based on the novel by Todd Walton), PH Laszlo Kovacs, M John Barry, ED Frank Morriss, PD Charles Rosen.

LP John Savage (Roary), David Morse (Jerry), Diana Scarwid† (Louise), Amy Wright (Ann), Tony Burton (Lucius Porter), Bill Henderson (Blue Lewis), Steve Kahan (Burt), Jack O'Leary (Max), Bert Remsen (Stinky), Harold Russell (Wings), Pepe Serna (Herrada), Harold Sylvester (Alvin Martin), Arnold Williams (Benny).

The film tries to focus on the problems of handicapped citizens in everyday life. Failed suicide John Savage has only succeeded in partly paralyzing himself. David Morse is a volatile basketball star recovering from a crippling knee surgery. The film is well-meaning, but the characters are more clichés than complex individuals. An exception, perhaps because he really is "physically challenged," is Harold Russell, making his first film appearance since his Oscar-winning performance in *The Best Years of Our Lives.*

1470. *Inside Out* (1986, Beckerman, 87m, c). P Sidney Beckerman, D Robert Taicher, W Taicher & Kevin Bartelme, PH Jack Wallner, M Peer Raben, ED David Finfer.

LP Elliott Gould (Jimmy Morgan), Howard Hesseman, Jennifer Tilly, Beah Richards, Nicole Norman, John Bleifer, Dana Elcar.

Life is hell for Elliott Gould, a man who suffers from agoraphopia, the fear of being outside one's home. He ought to feel OK in movie theaters where this film is shown. Few are likely to show up to see it.

1471. *Insignificance* (1985, Island Alive, GB, 108m, c). P Jeremy Thomas, D Nicolas Roeg, W Terry Johnson (based on his play), PH Peter Hannan, M Will Jennings, Roy Orbison & Stanley Myers, ED Tony Lawson, PD David Brockhurst.

LP Gary Busey (The Ballplayer), Tony Curtis (The Senator), Michael Emil (The Professor), Theresa Russell (The Actress), Will Sampson (Elevator Attendant), Patrick Kilpatrick (Driver), Ian O'Connell (Assistant), George Holmes (Actor), Richard Davidson (Photographer).

In 1954 New York City, Joe DiMaggio, Senator Joseph McCarthy, Albert Einstein and Marilyn Monroe spend a night at a hotel. Although not so identified, there can be little doubt that these are the four writer Terry Johnson has in mind. Theresa Russell (Monroe), explains the theory of relativity to Michael Emil (Einstein). Interesting initially, the concept begins to drag about half way through.

1472. *The Instructor* (1983, American Eagle, 91m, c). P,D&W Don Bendell, PH Ron Hughes, M Marti Lunn, ED Shirley Bendell, AD Joyce Edwards.

LP Bob Chaney (The Instructor), Bob Saal (Bud), Lynda Scharnott (Dee), Bruce Bendell (Fender), Tony Blanchard (Ben), Don Bendell (Thumper), Jack Holderbaum (Shank), Hank Gordon (Grasshopper), Denise Blankenship (Choo-Choo).

The head of a karate school demonstrates his skill when he's threatened by a rival.

1473. *Into the Fire* (1988, Moviestore Ent., Canada, 92m, c, aka *The Legend of*

Wolf Lodge). P Nicolas Stiliadis, D Graeme Campbell, W Jessie Ballard, PH Rhett Morita, M Andy Thompson, ED Harvey Zlatarits.

LP Susan Anspach (Rosalind Winfield), Art Hindle (Dirk Winfield), Olivia D'Abo (Liette), Lee Montgomery (Wade Burnett), Maureen McRae (Vivian), Steve Pirnie (Policeman), John Dondertman (Jimmy).

We don't usually recommend committing a film to the fire, but this scummy story qualifies for immolation on most levels: acting, directing, screenwriting, etc. Drifter Lee Montgomery becomes the patsy for an insurance scam that leads to murder.

1474. *Into the Night* (1985, Universal, 115m, c). P George Folsey, Jr. & Ron Koslow, D John Landis, W Koslow, PH Robert Paynter, M Ira Newborn, ED Malcolm Paynter Campbell, PD John Lloyd.

LP Jeff Goldblum (Ed Orkin), Michelle Pfeiffer (Diana), Paul Mazursky (Bud Herman), Kathryn Harrold (Christie), Richard Farnsworth (Jack Caper), Dan Aykroyd (Herb), David Bowie (Colin Morris), Irene Papas (Shaheen Parvizi), Vera Miles (Joan Caper).

More than a dozen directors, including Roger Vadim, John Landis, Don Siegel, David Cronenberg and Jack Arnold, make guest appearances in the film. Jeff Goldblum is a nerdish aerospace engineer with insomnia and an unfaithful wife. Michelle Pfeiffer is the beautiful woman he meets late one night at an airport. She's being chased by killers, who she claims are after six perfect emeralds she has smuggled into the country from Iran. From here on the story becomes a trifle convoluted.

1475. *Intruder* (1989, Phantom, 83m, c). P Lawrence Bender, D Scott Spiegel, W Spiegel (based on a story by Bender & Spiegel), PH Fernando Arguelles, M APM, ED King Wilder.

LP Elizabeth Cox (Jennifer), Renée Estevez (Linda), Danny Hicks (Bill), David Byrnes (Craig), Sam Raimi (Randy), Eugene Glazer (Danny).

In another direct to video horror film, David Byrnes is wrongly suspected of being the murderer of most of the cast. The film keeps the identity of the real killer well hidden until the very nasty ending.

1476. *Invaders from Mars* (1986, Cannon, 94m, c). P Menahem Golan & Yoram Globus, D Tobe Hooper, W Dan O'Bannon & Don Jakoby (based on a screenplay by Richard Blake), PH Daniel Pearl, M Christopher Young, ED Alain Jakubowicz, PD Leslie Dilley, SE John Dykstra.

LP Karen Black (Linda), Hunter Carson (David), Timothy Bottoms (George), Laraine Newman (Ellen), James Karen (Gen. Wilson), Bud Cort (NASA Scientist), Louise Fletcher (Mrs. McKeltch), Eric Pierpoint (Sgt. Rinaldi), Christopher Allport (Capt. Curtis).

This is a decent remake of a fine 50s sci-fi film about a little boy who is the only witness of the landing of an alien space ship. The Martians capture and brainwash residents of a small town. Jimmy Hunt, who played the boy in the 1953 film, appears as a police chief in the remake. Hunter Carson, the real-life son of Karen Black, is the youngster this time around.

1477. *Invasion Earth: The Aliens Are Here* (1988, New World, 83m, c). P Max J. Rosenberg, D George Maitland, W Miller Drake, PH Austin McKinney, M Anthony R. Jones, ED Drake & William B. Black, PD Michael Novotny, SE Dennis Skotak & Michael McCracken.

LP Janice Fabian (Joanie), Christian Lee (Billy), Larry Bagby III (Tim), Dana Young (Mike), Mel Welles (Mr. Davar), Corey Burton & Tony Pope (Voices).

Released straight to video, this film depicts an alien invasion of a small-town movie theater. The space creatures take over the bodies of members of the audience after first putting them into catatonic states by subjecting them to constant showings of 50s horror and sci-fi films.

Invasion Force see Hangar 18

1478. *Invasion U.S.A.* (1985, Cannon, 108m, c). P Menahem Golan & Yoram Globus, D Joseph Zito, W James Bruner & Chuck Norris (based on a story by Aaron Norris & Bruner), PH Joao Fernandes, M Jay Chattaway, ED Daniel Loewenthal & Scott Vickery, PD Ladislav Wilheim.

LP Chuck Norris (Matt Hunter), Richard Lynch (Rostov), Melissa Prophet (McGuire), Alexander Zale (Nikko), Alex Colon (Tomas), Eddie Jones (Cassidy), Jon DeVries (Johnston), James O'Sullivan (Harper), Billy Drago (Mickey), Jaime Sanchez (Castillo), Dehl Berti (John Eagle).

In this idiotic thriller, the United States is invaded by boatloads of vicious killers. They pile into rented trucks and spread out across Florida, using grenades, machine guns and bazookas to destroy anything that represents a wholesome American image. Chuck Norris is brought in to round 'em up and move 'em out.

1479.   The Invisible Kid (1988, Columbia, 96m, c). P Philip J. Spinelli, D&W Avery Crounse, PH Michael Barnard, M Steve Hunter & Jan King, ED Gabrielle Gilbert.

LP Jay Underwood (Grover Dunn), Wally Ward (Milton McClane), Chynna Phillips (Cindy Moore), Mike Genovese (Officer Chuck Malone), Nicolas de Toth (Donny Zanders), Thomas Cross (Officer Terell), John Madden Towey (Principal Baxter), Brother Theodore (Dr. Theodore), Karen Black (Mom).

Teenage nerd Jay Underwood stumbles onto a formula which makes him invisible. Naturally he uses his powers to make his way into the girl's locker room. It's a dumb movie, perhaps only noteworthy for Chynna Phillips, who has inherited her mother Michelle's striking good looks.

1480.   Invisible Strangler (1984, New Century, 85m, c). P Earle Lyon, D John Florea, W Arthur C. Pierce (based on a story by Lyon & Pierce), PH Alan Stensvold, M Richard Hieronymous & Alan Oldfield, ED Bud S. Isaacs, SE Roger George.

LP Robert Foxworth (Lt. Charles Barrett), Stefanie Powers (Candy Barrett), Elke Sommer (Chris), Sue Lyon (Miss DeLong), Leslie Parrish (Coleen Hudson), Marianna Hill (Bambi), Mark Slade (Sgt. Holt), Frank Ashmore (Rodger Sands), Alex Dreier.

A young nutcake is locked away in an asylum after having killed his mother. She had cruelly informed him she should have aborted him rather than given him life. When he learns an ancient Buddhist technique for making himself invisible, he escapes and goes on a murder spree, invisibly killing off his mother's friends.

1481.   Invitation to the Wedding (1985, Avatar/Chancery Lane, GB, 90m, c). P&D Joseph Brooks, W William Fairchild, PH Freddie Young, M Brooks, ED Gerry Hambling, PD Andrew Mollo.

LP Ralph Richardson (Bishop Willie), John Gielgud (Clyde Ormiston), Paul Nicholas (David Anderson), Elizabeth Shepherd (Lady Caroline), John Standing (Earl Braunceston), Edward Duke (Nigel), Susan Brooks (Lady Anne), Ronald Lacey (Charles/Clara Eatwell), Janet Burnell (Annabel).

In this modest comedy, Paul Nicholas, an American standing in for the groom, is accidentally married to an impoverished earl's daughter.

1482.   Iron Eagle (1986, Tri-Star, 119m, c). P Ron Samuels & Joe Wizan, D Sidney J. Furie, W Kevin Elders & Furie, PH Adam Greenberg, M Basil Poledouris, ED George Grenville, PD Robb Wilson King.

LP Louis Gossett, Jr. (Chappy), Jason Gedrick (Doug Masters), David Suchet (Minister of Defense), Tim Thomerson (Ted), Larry B. Scott (Reggie), Caroline Lagerfelt (Elizabeth), Jerry Levine (Tony), Robbie Rist (Milo).

Eighteen-year-old Jason Gedrick commandeers an F-16 fighter jet and flies it to the Middle East to rescue his father, who has been taken prisoner. He's helped by renegade Colonel Louis Gossett, Jr. A lot of jingoistic nonsense.

1483.   Iron Eagle II (1988, Tri-Star, Canada/Israel, 105m, c). P Jacob Kotzky, Sharon Herel & John Kemeny, D Sidney J. Furie, W Kevin Elders & Furie, PH Alain Dostie, M Amin Bhatia, ED Rit Wallis.

LP Louis Gossett, Jr. (Chappy), Mark Humphrey (Cooper), Stuart Margolin (Stillmore), Alan Scarfe (Varkovsky), Sharon H. Brandon (Valeri), Maury Chaykin (Downs), Colm Feore (Yuri), Clark Johnson (Graves).

Louis Gossett, Jr., has won a general's star since the original film. He's leading a joint mission of U.S. and Soviet pilots with the assignment of destroying a nuclear weapons base in some unnamed country in the Middle East.

1484. *The Iron Triangle* (1989, Scotti Bros., 91m, c). P Tony Scotti & Angela P. Schapiro, D Eric Weston, W Weston, John Bushelman, Larry Hilbrand & Marshall Drazen, PH Irv Goodnoff, M Michael Lloyd, John D'Andrea & Nick Strimple, ED Roy Watts, PD Errol Kelly.

LP Beau Bridges (Capt. Keene), Haing S. Ngor (Capt. Tuong), Johnny Hallyday (Jacques), Liem Whatley (Ho), James Ishida (Khoi), Ping Wu (Pham), Iilana B'Tiste (Khan Ly).

Here's a switch: The film presents the Vietnamese enemy as at least occasionally sensitive and idealistic. Seventeen-year-old Viet Cong guerrilla Liem Whatley captures Beau Bridges and protects him from cruel James Ishida. Whatley's character is treated sympathetically. *The Killing Fields'* Oscar winner Haing S. Ngor has a small role as a communist officer.

1485. *Ironweed* (1987, Tri-Star, 144m, c). P Keith Barish, Marcia Nasatir, Gene Kirkwood & C.O. Erickson, D Hector Babenco, W William Kennedy (based on his novel), PH Lauro Escorel, M John Morris, ED Anne Goursaud, PD Jeannine C. Oppewall, AD Robert Guerra, SD Leslie Pope, SE Steve Kirshoff.

LP Jack Nicholson† (Francis Phelan), Meryl Streep† (Helen Archer), Carroll Baker (Annie Phelan), Michael O'Keefe (Billy Phelan), Diane Venora (Peg Phelan), Fred Gwynne (Oscar Reo), Margaret Whitton (Katrina), Tom Waits (Rudy), Jake Dengel (Pee Wee), Nathan Lane (Harold Allen), James Gammon (Rev. Chester), Will Zahrn (Rowdy Dick), Laura Esterman (Nora), Joe Grifasi (Jack).

If it weren't for the superb acting by a brilliant cast, this relentlessly depressing film might be more than most people could stomach. Set in Albany in 1938, at various points it flashes back to 1916 and 1901 to show how one-time major league baseball player and family man Jack Nicholson came to be a wandering bum, who drinks to ward off the cold and sleeps wherever he can. He's accompanied in his travels to nowhere by Meryl Streep, who has also resigned from life, giving up belongings and belonging. The picture

only hints at what sent Streep on her downward spiral, but is very specific about Nicholson. Some 22 years earlier he deserted his family after dropping his infant son, cracking the child's head and killing him. Nicholson visits his family who haven't seen him in all the intervening years. Wife Carroll Baker, a most understanding woman, is willing to take him back, no questions asked. His son is also amicable, but his daughter initially demonstrates her resentment. Streep wears out and dies. Their friend Tom Waits (in a memorable performance), who gleefully announces that he's got cancer, observing that he's never had anything in his whole life, is killed by a club swinging mob. Nicholson doesn't go home; he just moves on. There is no conclusion to the movie; for some life is over, for others it continues, a struggle which almost makes the fate of the deceased seem preferable.

1486. *Irreconcilable Differences* (1984, Warner, 114m, c). P Arlene Sellers & Alex Winitsky, D Charles Shyer, W Nancy Meyers & Shyer, PH William A. Fraker, M Paul de Senneville & Olivier Toussaint, ED John F. Burnett, PD Ida Random.

LP Ryan O'Neal (Albert Brodsky), Shelley Long (Lucy Van Patten Brodsky), Drew Barrymore (Casey Brodsky), Sam Wanamaker (David Kessler), Allen Garfield [Goorwitz] (Phil Hanner), Sharon Stone (Blake Chandler), Hortensia Colorado (Maria Hernandez).

In this frequently amusing comedy, little Drew Barrymore files suit for divorce from her parents when their individual career successes leave no time for her or each other.

1487. *Island* (1989, Atlantis, Australia, 93m, c). P,D&W Paul Cox, PH Mike Edols, M Anil Acharya, ED John Scott, PD Neil Angwin.

LP Eva Sitta (Eva), Irene Papas (Marquise), Anoja Weerasinghe (Sahana), Chris Haywood (Janis), Norman Kaye (Henry), Francois Bernard (Frenchman).

The island of the title is Astypales, in the Dodecanese chain of Greek islands in the Aegean. The story deals with three women, each refugees from something. Irene Pappas lives alone with tragic memories, Eva Sitta is an Australian drug addict. Anoja Weerasinghe, from Sri Lanka, waits on the island for her political refugee husband.

1488. *The Island* (1980, Universal, 114m, c). P Richard D. Zanuck & David Brown, D Michael Ritchie, W Peter Benchley (based on his novel), PH Henri Decae, M Ennio Morricone, ED Richard A. Harris, PD Dale Hennesy.

LP Michael Caine (Maynard), David Warner (Nau), Angela Punch-McGregor (Beth), Frank Middlemass (Windsor), Don Henderson (Rollo), Dudley Sutton (Dr. Brazil), Colin Jeavons (Hizzoner), Zakes Mokae (Wescott), Brad Sullivan (Stark), Jeffrey Frank (Justin).

While investigating the disappearance of a ship in the Bermuda Triangle, British journalist Michael Caine encounters the murderous descendents of 17th century pirates on a deserted island.

1489. *Island Claws* (1981, CBS, 82m, c, aka *The Night of the Claw*). D Hernan Cardenas, W Jack Cowden & Ricou Browning (based on a story by Hernan & Colby Cardenas), PH James Pergola, M Bill Justis, SE Glen Robinson, Ray Scott & Don Chandler.

LP Robert Lansing, Steve Hanks, Nita Talbot, Jo McDonnell, Barry Nelson, Luke Halpin.

A group of marine biologists working on a tropical isle discover the "island claw," which has evolved as a result of toxic waste seeping into the ocean.

1490. *Isaac Littlefeathers* (1984, Cinema Concepts/Lauron, Canada, 94m, c). P Barry Pearson & Bill Johnston, D Les Rose, W Rose & Pearson, PH Ed Higginson, M Paul Zaza.

LP Lou Jacobi (Abe Kapp), William Korbut (Isaac Littlefeathers), Scott Hylands (Jesse Armstrong), Lorrain Behnan (Golda Hersh), George Clutesi (Moses Ankewat), Thomas Heaton (Mike Varco).

Jewish shopkeeper Lou Jacobi takes in William Korbut, the half-breed son of a ne'er-do-well hockey player and a Canadian Indian woman. The boy grows up with much confusion because of all of the different cultures to which he has been exposed.

1491. *Ishtar* (1987, Columbia, 107m, c). P Warren Beatty, D&W Elaine May, PH Vittorio Storaro, M Bahjawa, ED Stephen A. Rotter, William Reynolds & Richard Cirincione, PD Paul Sylbert.

LP Warren Beatty (Lyle Rogers), Dustin Hoffman (Chuck Clarke), Isabelle Adjani (Shirra Assel), Charles Grodin (Jim Harrison), Jack Weston (Marty Freed), Tess Harper (Willa), Carol Kane (Carol), Aharon Ipale (Emir Yousef), Fijad Hageb (Abdul), David Margulies (Mr. Clarke), Rose Arrick (Mrs. Clarke), Julie Garfield (Dorothy), Christine Rose (Siri Darma).

Those who gleefully enjoy seeing a big hitter on a golf course top a ball, a handsome, charming stud strike out with a beauty, or some arrogant rich bastard refused a seat in an expensive restaurant, may enjoy this movie. It's made by extremely talented people who, at least in this instance, are as much losers as the rest of us. Warren Beatty and Dustin Hoffman portray the worst song composer and lyricist east or west of Tin Pan Alley. But they're too dumb to realize it. An agent finally gets them a gig in Morocco, where they become involved with CIA agent Charles Grodin and beautiful Isabelle Adjani. A member of the underground, she must bare her breasts to let dumb Beatty realize that she's a girl and not a homosexual trying to pick him up as he fears. Hoffman has already survived this disaster, winning an Oscar for his work in *Rain Man,* but in that film he portrays an autistic man, an individual brighter and more worldly than his character in *Ishtar.* It appears that Beatty's career has also been salvaged after this $57 million zero with 1990's *Dick Tracy.*

1492. *It Came from Hollywood* (1982, Paramount, 80m, c). P Susan Strausberg & Jeff Stein, D Andrew Solt & Malcolm Leo, W Dana Olsen, PH Fred J. Koenekamp, ED Bert Lovitt.

PRESENTORS Dan Aykroyd, John Candy, Cheech and Chong, Gilda Radner.

This compilation of "classic" bad moments from scores of bad films is a mixed bag, not abetted by the intrusions of the presenters. It's not bad enough to be featured in *It Came from Hollywood II* if one is ever made.

It Came... Without Warning see Without Warning

1493. *It Couldn't Happen Here* (1988, Liberty, GB, 90m, c). P,D&W Jack Bond (based on a story by Bond & James Dillon), PH Simon Archer, M/L Neil Tennant & Chris Lowe, ED Rodney Holland.

LP Neil Tennant, Chris Lowe, Joss Ackland, Dominique Barnes, Neil Dickson, Carmen Du Sautoy, Gareth Hunt, Barbara Windsor, Nicholas Haley, Jonathan Haley, Wyn McLeod.

The Pet Shop Beach Boys (Neil Tennant & Chris Lowe) embark on a cross-country journey. They encounter an odd assortment of people, including naughty nuns, a blind priest, a deranged pilot, a businessman who doesn't notice he's on fire and a ventriloquist with a chatty dummy. Throughout, the sound track is filled with the music of Tennant & Lowe.

1494. *It Don't Pay to Be an Honest Citizen* (1985, Object, 85m, c). D Jacob Burckhardt, W Burckhardt, Rochelle Kraut & Reed Bye, PH Burckhardt, M Hugh Levick, ED Burckhardt.

LP Reed Bye (Warren), Allen Ginsberg (Sidney the Lawyer), William S. Burroughs (Mafia Don), Mary Tepper (Anita), Rudy Burckhardt (Bum).

Reed Bye portrays an independent moviemaker whose film for his latest project has been stolen. He searches throughout Brooklyn for the missing can of film, running into Beat-era writers Allen Ginsberg and William Burroughs along the way. Whatever independent film director Jacob Burckhardt intended to say with this work he's kept to himself.

1495. *It Fell from the Sky* (1980, Firebird, 87m, c, aka *Alien Dead*). P&D Fred Olen Ray, W Ray & Allan Nicholas.

LP Mike Bonavia (Miller Haze), John Leirier (Paisley), Rich Vogan (Krelboin), Buster Crabbe (Sheriff Kowalski), Raymond Roberts, Linda Lewis.

People on a houseboat turn into ghouls. Seventyish Buster Crabbe doesn't quite seem to know what it's all about. The make-up of the ghouls looks like it came from the five and ten.

1496. *It Had to Be You* (1989, Limelite Studios, 105m, c). P Richard Abramson & Tom Yanez, D&W Renee Taylor & Joseph Bologna, PH Bart Lau, M Charles Fox, LY Hal David, ED Tom Finan, PD Stephen Wolf.

LP Renee Taylor (Theda Blau), Joseph Bologna (Vito Pignoli), William Hickey (Schornberg), Eileen Brennan (Judith), Donna Dixon (Dede), Tony Randall (Milton), Gabriel Bologna (Alfred).

The limited release of this filming of Renee Taylor and Joseph Bologna's stage production is not very surprising. The off-beat sexual comedy featuring Taylor as a broken-down bit player, convinced that she can make it as a playwright if she can only get Bologna, a director to read her play, is old hat and not an Easter bonnet at that.

It Hurts Only When I Laugh see Only When I Laugh

1497. *It Takes Two* (1988, MGM/United Artists, 81m, c). P Robert Lawrence, D David Beaird, W Richard Christian Matheson & Thomas Szollosi, PH Peter Deming, M Carter Burwell, ED David Garfield, PD Richard Hoover.

LP George Newbern (Travis Rogers), Leslie Hope (Stephi Lawrence), Kimberly Foster (Jonni Tigersmith), Barry Corbin (George Lawrence), Anthony Geary (Wheel), Frances Lee McCain (Joyce Rogers), Patrika Darbo (Dee Dee).

Ten days before his marriage to his childhood sweetheart, 20-year-old Texan George Newbern takes $5,000 of his savings and heads to Dallas for a final prenuptial fling. Yippee-ki-yi-yay!

1498. *It's Alive III: Island of the Alive* (1988, Warner, 91m, c). P Paul Stader, D&W Larry Cohen, PH Daniel Pearl, M Laurie Johnson, ED David Kern, SE Steve Neill, Rick Baker & William Hedge.

LP Michael Moriarty (Steve Jarvis), Karen Black (Ellen Jarvis), Laurene Landon (Sally), James Dixon (Dr. Perkins), Neal Israel (Dr. Brewster), Art Lund (Swenson), Ann Dane (Miss Morrell), Macdonald Carey (Judge Watson), Gerrit Graham (Ralston), William Watson (Cabot), C.L. Sussex (Hunter).

The previous films in this series were released in 1974 *(It's Alive)* and 1978 *(It Lives Again)*. The American government forced pregnant mothers suspected of carrying mutants to have abortions, and the monsters already born were executed. Michael Moriarty, the father of one, successfully convinces the government to allow his child to survive. He's placed on a desert island with other mutant kids. Years later Moriarty and some scientists go to the island to see what's happened to the mutants. They have grown to adulthood and Moriarty is a grandfather. The mutants kill all but Moriarty and escape the island, but are done in by a simple case of the measles.

1499. *It's My Turn* (1980, Columbia, 91m, c). P Martin Elfand, D Claudia Weill, W Eleanor Bergstein, PH Bill Butler, M Patrick Williams, ED Byron "Buzz" Brandt, Marjorie Fowler & James Coblentz, PD Jack DeGovia.

LP Jill Clayburgh (Kate Gunzinger), Michael Douglas (Ben Lewin), Charles Grodin (Homer), Beverly Garland (Emma), Steven Hill (Jacob), Teresa Baxter (Maryanne), Joan Copeland (Rita), John Gabriel (Hunter), Charles Kimbrough (Jerome), Roger Robinson (Flicker), Jennifer Salt (Maisie).

The mathematician half of your authorial team is pleased that in one of the very few movies to feature a Ph.D. mathematician, namely Jill Clayburgh, she is not seen doing trivial arithmetic passed off to those with math-phobia as something difficult. Clayburgh, a University of Chicago professor, has a perfectly good relationship with business developer Charles Grodin, until she attends the wedding of her father Steven Hill to Beverly Garland. Then she falls for Garland's son Michael Douglas, a former major league baseball player. He's not your stereotyped jock. He's intelligent, sensitive and informed.

1500. *I've Heard the Mermaids Singing* (1987, Miramax, Canada, 81m, c/b&w). P Patricia Rozema & Alexandra Raffe, D&W Rozema, PH Douglas Koch, M Mark Korven, ED Rozema.

LP Sheila McCarthy (Polly Vandersma), Paule Baillargeon (Gabrielle St. Peres), Ann-Marie McDonald (Mary Joseph), John Evans (Warren), Brenda Kamino (Japanese Waitress), Richard Monette (Critic).

The title of the movie is from the line, "I have heard the mermaids singing, each to each. I do not think that they will sing to me" from T.S. Eliot's "The Love Song of J. Alfred Prufrock." Naïve 31-year-old Toronto photographer Sheila McCarthy longs for a place in the elitist art world. She is hired at an upscale gallery and falls helplessly for the female curator Paule Baillargeon. Still she is shocked when she discovers the latter is engaged in a lesbian affair with Ann-Marie McDonald. McCarthy dreams of flying through the air and walking on water, while listening to the mermaids sing.

Jack London's Klondike Fever see Klondike Fever

1501. *Jacknife* (1989, Cineplex Odeon, 102m, c). P Robert Schaffel & Carol Baum, D David Jones, W Stephen Metcalfe (based on his play *Strange Snow*), PH Brian West, M Bruce Broughton, ED John Bloom, PD Edward Pisoni.

LP Robert DeNiro (Joseph "Megs" Megessey), Kathy Baker (Martha), Ed Harris (Dave), Tom Isbell (Bobby Buckman), Charles Dutton (Jake), Loudon Wainwright 3d (Ferretti), Elizabeth Franz (Pru Buckman).

In a somber film Vietnam good-old-boy vet Robert DeNiro, also known as Jacknife, shows up unexpectedly at the Connecticut home of his wartime buddy Ed Harris to go fishing — or so he says. DeNiro has a romance with Harris' high school teacher sister Kathy Baker, but his real purpose seems to be to bring Harris back into reality, something the latter's avoided since coming home from the war.

1502. *Jack's Back* (1988, Palisades, 97m, c). P Tim Moore & Cassian Elwes, D&W Rowdy Herrington, PH Shelly Johnson, M Danny Di Paolo, ED Harry B. Miller III, PD Piers Plowden.

LP James Spader (John & Rick Wesford), Cynthia Gibb (Christine Moscari), Rod Loomis (Dr. Sidney Tannerson), Rex Ryon (Jack Pendler), Robert Picardo (Dr. Carlos Battera), Jim Haynie (Sgt. Gabriel), Wendell Wright (Capt. Walter Prentis).

James Spader projects just the right degree of strange in dual roles in this thriller about a Jack the Ripper type plying his deadly trade in modern day L.A.

1503. *Jaded* (1989, Olpal, 93m, c). P Gary Graver & Oja Kodar, D Kodar, W Kodar, PH Graver, M Alexander Welles, ED Maria Foss, PD Julia Riva.

LP Randall Brady (Joe), Elizabeth Brooks (Rita), Scott Kaske (Angel), Jillian Kesner (Sara), Oja Kodar (Rossanda), Kelli Maroney (Jennifer), Todd Starks (George).

The film takes a repetitive, violent look at a group of low-lifes living at Venice Beach, California. When they aren't fornicating with people of all sexes, they are beating up on each other or being beaten. It's difficult to feel anything but disgust for any of them.

1504. *Jagged Edge* (1985, Columbia, 108m, c). P Martin Ransohoff, D Richard Marquand, W Joe Estzerhas, PH Matthew F. Leonetti, M John Barry, ED Sean Barton, Conrad Buff, PD Gene Callahan.

LP Jeff Bridges (Jack Forrester), Glenn Close (Teddy Barnes), Peter Coyote (Thomas Krasny), Robert Loggia† (Sam Ransom), Leigh Taylor-Young (Virginia Howell), John Dehner (Judge Carrigan), Karen Austin (Julie Jensen), Lance Henriksen (Frank Martin), James Karen (Andrew Hardesty).

We first saw *Jagged Edge* on a flight from New York to the Caribbean's Ste. Martin one New Year's day a few years ago. The plane landed before the film had finished and many passengers were so hooked by the suspense that they refused to disembark until they had seen the conclusion. Although curious to learn if Jeff Bridges had murdered his wife and would make his new love, lawyer Glenn Close, his next victim, the sun and water beckoned. We waited until returning north to discover the answers.

1505. *Jailbird Rock* (1988, Trans-World/Continental, 92m, c). P J.C. Crespo, D Philip Schuman, W Carole Stanley & Edward Kovach (based on a story by Eduard Sarlui), PH Leonardo Solis, M Rick Nowecs, ED Peter Teschner & Raja Gosnell.

LP Robin Antin (Jessie Harris), Valerie Gene Richards (Peggy), Robin Cleaver (Echo), Rhonda Aldrich (Max), Jacqueline Houston (Samantha), Debra Laws (Lisa), Erica Jordan (Judy), Perry Lang (Denny).

Talented dancer Robin Antin shoots her stepfather when she discovers him giving her mother another one of many beatings. She is sent to prison on a manslaughter rap for two years. She runs afoul of big-shot prisoner Rhonda Aldrich, who uses the in-house show that Antin is putting on for the inmates to cover her attempted escape from the pen.

1506. *Jake Speed* (1986, New World, 104m, c). P Andrew Lane, Wayne Crawford & William Fay, D Lane, W Crawford & Lane, PH Bryan Loftus, M Mark Snow, ED Fred Stafford & Michael Ripps, PD Norm Baron.

LP Wayne Crawford (Jake Speed), Dennis Christopher (Desmond Floyd), Karen Kopins (Margaret Winston), John Hurt (Sid), Leon Ames (Pop), Roy London (Maurice), Donna Pescow (Wendy), Barry Primus (Lawrence).

Paperback pulp hero Wayne Crawford comes to life for a real adventure in this action-thriller spoof. John Hurt makes a fine comedic villain.

1507. *James Clavell's Tai-Pan* (1986, De Laurentiis, 127m, c, aka *Tai-Pan*). P Raffaella De Laurentiis, D Daryl Duke, W John Briley & Stanley Mann (based upon the novel by James Clavell), PH Jack Cardiff, M Maurice Jarre, ED Antony Gibbs, PD Tony Masters.

LP Bryan Brown (Tai-Pan), Joan Chen (May-May), John Stanton (Brock), Tim Guinee (Culum), Bill Leadbitter (Gorth), Russell Wong (Gordon), Katy Behean (Mary), Kyra Sedgwick (Tess), Janine Turner (Shevaun).

In a campy stew of a truncated TV miniseries, boiling with plenty of seamy sex, exotic locations and poor acting, Bryan Brown is a mid-19th century trader, longing to establish a colony of commerce at a place to be called Hong Kong. He and his lovely concubine Joan Chen experienced a series of predictable difficulties along the way.

1508. *James Joyce's Women* (1985, Universal, 91m, c). P Fionnula Flanagan, D Michel Pearce, W Flanagan (based on the life and works of James

Joyce and the play directed by Burgess Meredith), PH John Metcalfe, M Noel Kelehan, Arthur Keating, Vincent Kilduff & Garrett O'Connor, ED Arthur Keating & Dan Perry.

LP Fionnula Flanagan (Nora Barnacle Joyce/Sylvia Beach/Harriet Shaw Weaver/Gerty McDowell/The Washerwoman/Molly Bloom), Timothy E. O'Grady (The Interviewer), Chris O'Neill (James Joyce), Tony Lyons (Leopold Bloom), Paddy Dawson (Stannie Joyce), Martin Dempsey (The Father).

Essentially a one-woman show, Fionnula Flanagan portrays seven different characters from the life and works of James Joyce. The humor and the sensuality of the author's work are well presented.

1509. *Jane and the Lost City* (1987, New World, GB, 93m, c). P Harry Robertson, D Terry Marcel, W Mervyn Haisman (based on the comic strip by Norman Pett), PH Paul Beeson, M Robertson, ED Alan Jones, PD Mick Pickwoad.

LP Sam Jones (Jungle Jack Buck), Maud Adams (Lola Pagola), Kirsten Hughes (Jane), Jasper Carrott (Heinrich), Robin Bailey (Colonel), Ian Roberts (Carl), Elsa O'Toole (Leopard Queen).

Based on a popular British comic strip, Kirsten Hughes and Sam Jones take on a band of nasty Nazis led by Maud Adams. Both groups are trying to find a legendary "lost city" and its fabulous diamonds.

1510. *Jane Austen in Manhattan* (1980, Contemporary, 108m, c). P Ismail Merchant, D James Ivory, W Ruth Prawer Jhabvala (based on the libretto of "Sir Charles Grandison" by Jane Austen and Samuel Richardson), PH Ernst Vincze, M Richard Robbins, ED David McKenna.

LP Anne Baxter (Lilianna), Robert Powell (Pierre), Michael Wager (George Midash), Tim Choate (Jamie), John Guerrasio (Gregory), Katrina Hodiak (Katya), Kurt Johnson (Victor), Nancy New (Jenny), Sean Young (Ariadne).

In her last film appearance, Anne Baxter is a teacher who argues with her colleague Robert Powell about bringing to the stage a play written by Jane Austen when she was 12 years old. Baxter wants

it performed as an operetta, Powell as an avant-garde piece.

The Janitor see Eyewitness

1511. *The January Man* (1989, MGM, 97m, c). P Norman Jewison & Ezra Swerdlow, D Pat O'Connor, W John Patrick Shanley, PH Jerzy Zielinski, M Marvin Hamlisch, ED Lou Lombardo, PD Philip Rosenberg.

LP Kevin Kline (Nick Starkey), Susan Sarandon (Christine Starkey), Mary Elizabeth Mastrantonio (Bernadette Flynn), Harvey Keitel (Frank Starkey), Danny Aiello (Vincent Alcoa), Rod Steiger (Eamon Flynn).

Ex-police detective and now fireman Kevin Kline must track down a serial killer in Manhattan to help out his police commissioner brother Harvey Keitel. The latter, now married to Kline's ex-girlfriend Susan Sarandon, is taking a lot of heat from mayor Rod Steiger, whose daughter Mary Elizabeth Mastrantonio falls in love with Kline. A bit confusing you say? Compared to the movie our explanation is blessed with perfect clarity.

1512. *Jaws: The Revenge* (1987, Universal, 89m, c). P&D Joseph Sargent, W Michael de Guzman (based on characters created by Peter Benchley), PH John McPherson, M Michael Small & John Williams, PD John J. Lloyd, SE Henry Millar.

LP Lorraine Gary (Ellen Brody), Lance Guest (Michael Brody), Mario Van Peebles (Jake), Karen Young (Carla Brody), Michael Caine (Hoagie), Judith Barsi (Thea Brody), Lynn Whitfield (Louisa), Mitchell Anderson (Sean Brody), Jay Mello (Young Sean), Cedric Scott (Clarence).

Apparently fine British actors such as Michael Caine are not concerned that terrible pictures will adversely affect their careers, as long as the money is right. Caine must have taken comfort from the experience of his co-star in *Sleuth,* Laurence Olivier, whose title as the world's greatest actor was not challenged when he took the money and ran after appearing in some miserable flicks. In this unseaworthy film, the action once again takes place in the waters off the New England town of Amity. Roy Scheider wisely has absented himself from the scene but his wife and brood of children, as well as Caine, are front-and-center. There is a new visitation by a terrorizing shark, with the apparent mission of killing the various Brodys, no doubt as revenge for all of the shark's relatives killed in earlier films in the series.

1513. *Jaws of Satan* (1980, United Artists, 92m, c, aka *King Cobra*). P Bill Wilson, D Bob Claver, W Gerry Holland (based on the story by James Callaway), PH Dean Cundey, M Roger Kellaway, ED Len Miller.

LP Fritz Weaver (Father Farrow), Gretchen Corbett (Dr. Sheridan), Jon Korkes (Paul), Norman Lloyd (Monsignore), Diana Douglas (Evelyn), Bob Hannah (Matt), Nancy Priddy (Elizabeth), Christina Applegate (Kim).

Satan, disguised as a snake, causes Fritz Weaver no end of trouble. If slimy crawly creatures make you ill, avoid this film.

1514. *Jaws 3-D* (1983, Universal, 97m, c, 3-D). P Rupert Hitzig, D Joe Alves, W Richard Matheson & Carl Gottlieb (based on a story by Guerdon Trueblood suggested by the novel *Jaws* by Peter Benchley), PH James A. Contner, M Alan Parker (shark theme, John Williams), ED Randy Roberts, PD Woods Mackintosh.

LP Dennis Quaid (Mike Brody), Bess Armstrong (Kathryn Morgan), Simon MacCorkindale (Philip FitzRoyce), Louis Gossett, Jr. (Calvin Bouchard), John Putch (Sean Brody), Lea Thompson (Kelly Ann Bukowski), P.H. Moriarty (Jack Tate), Dan Blasko (Dan), Liz Maurer (Ethel).

Gossett owns Florida's Sea World, where two of Amity Island's sheriff Roy Scheider's now fully grown sons, Dennis Quaid and John Putch, work. A fisherman brings in a baby great white shark, that Gossett sets up as a feature attraction. Momma comes looking for baby and she's very snappish.

1515. *The Jazz Singer* (1980, Associated Film, 115m, c). P Jerry Leider, D Richard Fleischer, W Herbert Baker & Stephen H. Foreman (based on the play by Samuel Raphaelson), PH Isidore Mankofsky, M Neil Diamond, ED Frank J. Urioste & Maury Weintrobe, PD Harry Horner.

LP Neil Diamond (Jess Robin), Laurence Olivier (Cantor Rabinovitch), Lucie Arnaz (Molly Bell), Catlin Adams (Rivka Rabinovitch), Franklyn Ajaye (Bubba), Paul Nicholas (Keith Lennox), Sully Boyar (Eddie Gibbs), Mike Bellin (Leo), James Booth (Paul Rossini), Luther Waters (Teddy).

If this version of the sentimental story of a young Jewish man who alienates himself from his cantor father by choosing singing popular tunes over working in a synagogue had been the first talky, we'd all be watching silent films today. Perhaps to compensate for Neil Diamond's complete lack of emotion in his performance, Laurence Olivier embarrasses himself by overacting. He portrays the cantor as an ailing, effeminate cross between Shylock and Fagin, screeching his lines in a most obnoxious manner. The film bombed, even though Diamond came through with a hit song, "America."

Jealous see Heaven Becomes Hell

1516. *Jekyll and Hyde...Together Again* (1982, Paramount, 87m, c). P Lawrence Gordon, D Jerry Belson, W Monica Johnson, Harvey Miller, Belson & Michael Lesson (based on the novel *The Strange Case of Dr. Jekyll and Mr. Hyde* by Robert Louis Stevenson), PH Philip Lathrop, M Barry DeVorzon, ED Billy Weber, PD Peter Wooley.

LP Mark Blankfield (Jekyll/Hyde), Bess Armstrong (Mary), Krista Errickson (Ivy), Tim Thomerson (Dr. Lanyon), Michael McGuire (Dr. Carew), Neil Hunt (Queen), Cassandra Peterson (Busty Nurse), Jessica Nelson (Barbara), Peter Brocco (Hubert).

In this updated version of the classical psychological horror, research scientist Mark Blankfield snorts cocaine and is transformed from something of a nerd to a very hip Mr. Hyde. The latter immediately dumps his alter ego's mousy fiancée Bess Armstrong for more with-it Krista Errickson. It's watchable, but barely.

1517. *Jenny Kissed Me* (1985, Nilsen Premiere, Australia, 98m, c). P Tom

Broadbridge, D Brian Trenchard-Smith, W Judith Colquhoun, Warwick Hind & Alan Lake, PH Bob Kohler, M Trevor Incas & Ian Mason.

LP Tamsin West (Jenny West), Ivar Kants (Lindsay Fenton), Deborra-Lee Furness (Carol Grey), Paula Duncan (Gaynor Roberts), Mary Ward (Grace), Steven Grives (Neighbor).

"Say that fame and fortune missed me, but say also that Jenny kissed me" is the last line of Leigh Hunt's poem "Jenny Kissed Me." It may in part be responsible for so many girls being named Jenny and Jennifer. The kisses of the Jenny of the movie don't seem as valuable as those of the girl of the poem. Australian lass Tamsin West, her live-in boyfriend, and her parents have about as many problems as the fictitious Tyrone family in Eugene O'Neill's *Long Day's Journey Into Night,* but the film has nowhere near the power of that masterpiece.

1518. *The Jewel of the Nile* (1985, 20th Century–Fox, 105m, c). P Michael Douglas, D Lewis Teague, W Mark Rosenthal & Lawrence Konner (based on characters created by Diane Thomas), PH Jan DeBont, M Jack Nitzsche, ED Michael Ellis & Peter Boita, PD Richard Dawking & Terry Knight.

LP Michael Douglas (Jack), Kathleen Turner (Joan), Danny DeVito (Ralph), Spiros Focas (Omar), Avner Eisenberg (Holy Man), Paul David Magid (Tarak), Howard Jay Patterson (Barak), Randall Edwin Nelson (Karak), Samuel Ross Williams (Arak), Timothy Daniel Furst (Sarak).

This rather disappointing sequel to the surprise hit *Romancing the Stone* has traded humor, romance and crazy excitement for spectacle but it's not an even trade. After a period of domesticity on his ship, Michael Douglas and Kathleen Turner split. She's been offered the opportunity to write the story of Mideast super-strongman Spiros Focas. It's not long until everyone recognizes him for the despotic villain he really is, and even nasty Danny DeVito rallies to the rebel cause.

1519. *The Jigsaw Man* (1984, United Film Dist., GB, 91m, c). P S. Benjamin Fisz, D Terence Young, W Jo Eisinger (based on the novel by Dorothea Bennett), PH Freddie Francis, M John Cameron, ED Derek Trigg, PD Michael Stringer.

LP Michael Caine (Sir Philip Kimberly), Laurence Olivier (Adm. Sir Gerald Scaith), Susan George (Penny), Robert Powell (Jamie), Charles Gray (Sir James Charley), Michael Medwin (Milroy), Anthony Shaw (Matthews), Maureen Bennett (Susan), Patrick Dawson (Ginger).

Michael Caine, a Kim Philby–like British spy for the Soviets, long ago defected and is living in Moscow. He is given plastic surgery and a new assignment in Britain to undercover a microfilmed list of Soviet spies. He is to bring home those whose cover has been blown. He is opposed in his mission by longtime rival Laurence Olivier and by agent Robert Powell, who just happens to live with Caine's daughter.

1520. *Jimmy the Kid* (1982, New World, 85m, c). P Ronald Jacobs, D Gary Nelson, W Sam Bobrick (based on the novel by Donald E. Westlake), PH Dennis Dalzell, M John Cameron, ED Richard C. Meyer.

LP Gary Coleman (Jimmy), Paul LeMat (John), Dee Wallace (May), Don Adams (Harry), Walter Olkewicz (Andrew), Ruth Gordon (Bernice), Cleavon Little (Herb), Fay Hauser (Nina), Avery Schreiber (Dr. Stevens), Pat Morita (Maurice).

So many TV situation comedy stars have bombed when they tried to take their act to the big screen that it can't just be a coincidence. Apparently the couch potatoes who made them a hit on the telly don't go to movies in great numbers. Little big-talking Gary Coleman is kidnapped from his upper-class home by two totally incompetent crooks. Switch channels, will you?

1521. *Jinxed!* (1982, MGM/United Artists, 103m, c). P Herb Jaffe, D Don Siegel, W David Newman & Bert Blessing (based on a story by Blessing), PH Vilmos Zsigmond, M Bruce Roberts & Miles Goodman, ED Doug Stewart, PD Ted Haworth.

LP Bette Midler (Bonita), Ken Wahl (Willie), Rip Torn (Harold), Val Avery (Milt), Jack Elam (Otto), Benson Fong (Dr. Wing).

Bette Midler and casino dealer Ken Wahl hatch a plan to kill her lover Rip Torn and collect his insurance in this not-quite-ready-for-prime-time movie comedy.

1522. The Jitters (1989, Gaga Communications, US/Japan, 79m, c). P&D John M. Fasano, W Jeff McKay & Sonoko Kondo, PH Paul Mitchnick, M Dann Linck & Tom Borton, ED Ray Van Doorn.

LP Sal Viviano (Michael), Marilyn Yokuda (Alice Lee), James Hong (Tony Yang, Sr.), Frank Dietz (Rat), Handy Atmadja (Frank Lee).

In a tongue-in-cheek fantasy, Japanese girl Marilyn Yokuda and her Caucasian boyfriend Sal Viviano avenge the death of her father. The latter has become one of the Gyonsii, a group of vampire-like beings trapped in limbo between heaven and hell—i.e. earth.

1523. Jo Jo Dancer, Your Life Is Calling (1986, Columbia, 97m, c). P&D Richard Pryor, W Rocco Urbisci, Paul Mooney & Pryor, PH John Alonzo, M Herbie Hancock, ED Donn Cambern, PD John De Cuir.

LP Richard Pryor (Jo Jo Dancer/Alter Ego), Debbie Allen (Michelle), Art Evans (Arturo), Fay Hauser (Grace), Barbara Williams (Dawn), Carmen McRae (Grandmother), Paula Kelly (Satin Doll), Diahnne Abbott (Mother), Scoey Mitchill (Father), Billy Eckstine (Johnny Barnett).

In an autobiographical film, Richard Pryor takes credits for his successes as a performer, but blames society for his problems, cocaine addiction and his little accident with free-basing which almost took his life. It's a little too neat, lacking in any real dramatic quality. Pryor's attempt to produce a classical tragedy falls flat.

1524. Jocks (1987, Crown, 90m, c, aka *Road Trip*). P Ahmet Yasa, D Steve Carver, W Michael Lanahan & David Oas, PH Adam Greenberg, M David McHugh, ED Richard Halsey & Tom Siiter.

LP Scott Strader (The Kid), Perry Lang (Jeff), Mariska Hargitay (Nicole), Richard Roundtree (Chip Williams), R.G. Armstrong (Coach Beetlebom), Christopher Lee (President White), Stoney Jackson (Andy), Adam Mills (Tex), Trinidad Silva (Chico), Don Gibb (Ripper).

The president of a college in L.A. instructs the athletic director to produce a winning men's tennis team or abolish the sport. That's fine with the AD, but tennis coach Richard Roundtree doesn't wish to lose his job. He must turn a motley crew of beer-drinking idlers, whose minds are only on casual sex, into a championship team. Lots of luck, coach!

1525. Joe and Maxi (1980, Cohen & Gold, 80m, c). P Maxi Gold, D Joel Gold & Maxi Cohen, PH Joel Gold, ED Pat Powell, Marion Kraft & Maxi Cohen.

LP Joe Cohen (Father), Maxi Cohen (Daughter), Barry Cohen (Brother), Danny Cohen (Brother), Bea Metzman (Aunt), Dan Metzman (Uncle), Ronnie Kestenbaum (Barry's Friend).

This comedy is a family affair, but the ethnic humor is definitely not for everyone.

1526. Joe's Bed-Stuy Barbershop: We Cut Heads (1983, First Run, 60m, c). P Zimmie Shelton & Spike Lee, D,W&ED Spike Lee, PH Ernest Dickerson, M Bill Lee, AD Felix DeRooy.

LP Monty Ross (Zachariah Homer), Donna Bailey (Ruth Homer), Stuart Smith (Teapot), Tommie Hicks (Nicholas Lovejoy), Horace Long (Joe Ballard).

First released in 1983, the film introduced multitalented Spike Lee to movie audiences. It was re-released in 1989, sharing billing with a documentary, *Making "Do the Right Thing."* The movie is Lee's New York University thesis film. It's about a barber who finds himself in a no-win situation with black mobsters.

1527. Joey (1985, Satori, 99m, c). P,D&W Joseph Ellison (based on a story by Ellen Hammill), PH Oliver Wood, M Jim Roberge, ED Christopher Andrews.

LP Neill Barry (Joey), James Quinn (Joey's Father), Elisa Heinsohn (Janie), Linda Thorson (Principal O'Neill), Ellen Hammill (Bobbie), Rickey Ellis (John), Dee Hourican (Bonnie), Dan Grimaldi (Ted).

James Quinn, a former doo-wopper, looks back on his life as a musician as a waste of time. He isn't pleased when his son Neill Barry takes up a rock guitar to follow his own musical career.

1528. *John and the Missus* (1987, Cinema Group, Canada, 100m, c). P Peter O'Brian & John Hunter, D&W Gordon Pinsent (based on his novel), PH Frank Tidy, M Michael Conway Baker, ED Bruce Nyznik, AD Earl Preston.

LP Gordon Pinsent (John Munn), Jackie Burroughs (Missus), Randy Follet (Matt), Jessica Steen (Faith), Roland Hewgill (Fred Budgell), Timothy Webber (Denny Boland), Neil Munro (Tom Noble), Michael Wade (Sid Peddigrew).

The photography of the coast of Newfoundland is exquisite. The story about the closing of a local mine and the effect on the inhabitants is depressing without any discernible focus or point.

1529. *Johnny Be Good* (1988, Orion, 84m, c). P Adam Fields, D Bud Smith, W Steve Zacharias, Jeff Buhai & David Obst, PH Robert D. Yeoman, M Jay Ferguson, ED Scott Smith, PD Gregg Fonseca.

LP Anthony Michael Hall (Johnny Walker), Robert Downey, Jr. (Leo Wiggins), Paul Gleason (Wayne Hisler), Uma Thurman (Georgia Elkans), Steve W. James (Coach Sanders), Seymour Cassel (Wallace Gibson), Michael Greene (Tex Wade), Deborah May (Mrs. Walker), Jennifer Tilly (Connie Hisler).

Anthony Michael Hall, the know-it-all geek of *Sixteen Candles* and the delightful nerd in *The Breakfast Club,* has grown up to be the most sought after high school football quarterback in the country. In addition to having trouble seeing Hall as a super athlete, viewers are cheated out of what might have been an intriguing story—the buying of jocks by colleges with offers of money, cars, apartments, and all the sex an adolescent could dream of. Instead, the film chooses to play things for cheap laughs and sexual exploitation, and even this is done poorly.

1530. *Johnny Dangerously* (1984, 20th Century-Fox, 89m, c). P Michael Hertzberg, D Amy Heckerling, W Norman Steinberg, Bernie Kukoff, Harry Colomby & Jeff Harris, PH David M. Walsh, M John Morris, ED Pembroke J. Herring, PD Joseph R. Jennings.

LP Michael Keaton (Johnny Dangerously), Joe Piscopo (Vermin), Marilu Henner (Lil), Maureen Stapleton (Mom), Peter Boyle (Dundee), Griffin Dunne (Tommy), Glynnis O'Connor (Sally), Dom DeLuise (The Pope), Richard Dimitri (Maroni), Danny DeVito (Burr), Ron Carey (Pat).

This 30s and 40s gangster-movie spoof doesn't have enough funny bits to become a box office hit. Gangster films are not good sources for satire, and the public didn't buy the result.

1531. *Johnny Handsome* (1989, Tri-Star, 95m, c). P Charles Roven, D Walter Hill, W Ken Friedman (based on the novel *The Three Worlds of Johnny Handsome* by John Godey), PH Matthew F. Leonetti, M Ry Cooder, ED Freeman Davies, PD Gene Rudolf.

LP Mickey Rourke (John Sedley), Ellen Barkin (Sunny Boyd), Elizabeth McGovern (Donna McCarty), Morgan Freeman (Drones), Forest Whitaker (Dr. Resher), Lance Henriksen (Rafe Garrett), Scott Wilson (Mikey Chalmette).

Born with a badly disfigured face, Mickey Rourke grows up to be a petty criminal. During a robbery, he and Scott Wilson are double-crossed by Ellen Barkin and Lance Henriksen, the other two members of the gang. Wilson is killed and Rourke is sentenced to prison, where kindly plastic surgeon Forrest Whitaker soon has him looking like Rourke. The latter is allowed out of prison each day to work, meets and falls in love with Elizabeth McGovern, but his aching for revenge results in a very downbeat ending.

1532. *Joni* (1980, World Wide Pictures, 108m, c). P Frank R. Jacobson, D&W James F. Collier (based on the book by Joni Eareckson), PH Frank Raymond, M Ralph Carmichael, ED Duane Hartzell.

LP Joni Eareckson (Herself), Bert Remsen (Mr. Eareckson), Katherine De Hetre (Jay), Cooper Huckabee (Dick), John Milford (Doctor), Michael Mancini (Don), Richard Lineback (Steve).

Joni Eareckson effectively recreates her life as a woman who becomes a quadriplegic after breaking her spine in a diving accident. She learns to paint using just her mouth to hold the brush and finds comfort and peace in religion.

1533. *Joshua Then and Now* (1985, 20th Century–Fox, Canada, 127m, c). P Robert Lantos & Stephen J. Roth, D Ted Kotcheff, W Mordecai Richler (based on his novel), PH Francois Protat, M Philippe Sarde, ED Ron Wisman, PD Anne Pritchard.

LP James Woods (Joshua Shapiro), Gabrielle Lazure (Pauline Shapiro), Alan Arkin (Reuben Shapiro), Michael Sarrazin (Kevin Hornby), Linda Sorensen (Esther Shapiro), Alan Scarfe (Jack Trimble), Kate Trotter (Jane Trimble), Alexander Knox (Senator Hornby), Eric Kimmel (Young Joshua Shapiro).

This uneven ethnic comedy stars James Woods as a successful Canadian Jewish writer, now involved in a domestic scandal. He recalls his childhood in the Montreal Jewish underworld, his beginnings as a writer in London, and his romance, marriage and break-up with WASP Gabrielle Lazure, a prominent senator's daughter.

1534. *The Journey of Natty Gann* (1985, Buena Vista, 101m, c). P Mike Lobell, D Jeremy Kagan, W Jeanne Rosenberg, PH Dick Bush, M James Horner, ED David Holden, PD Paul Sylbert, COS Albert Wolsky†.

LP Meredith Salenger (Natty Gann), John Cusack (Harry), Ray Wise (Sol Gann), Lainie Kazan (Connie), Scatman Crothers (Sherman), Barry Miller (Parker), Verna Bloom (Farm Woman), Bruce M. Fischer (Charles Linfield), John Finnegan (Logging Boss).

Set during the Depression, gutsy youngster Meredith Salenger hits the road in search of her missing father Wise. She adopts the hobo life in order to survive. Audiences are treated to the growing up of a delightful tomboy.

1535. *Journey to Spirit Island* (1988, Pal-Seven Wonders, 93m, c). P Bruce Clark, D Laszlo Pal, W Crane Webster, PH Vilmos Zsigmond, M Fred Myrow, ED Bonnie Koehler, PD Bruce Jackman.

LP Bettina (Maria), Marie Antoinette Rodgers (Jimmy Jim), Brandon Douglas (Michael), Gabriel Damon (Willie), Tarek McCarthy (Klim), Tony Acierto (Hawk), Nick Ramus (Tom), Atilla Gombacsi (Phil).

Ambitious young Indian Tony Acierto wishes to turn his tribe's sacred burial ground on Spirit Island into a multimillion-dollar resort. He is opposed by Bettina, whose great-great-grandfather once sent his only son to the white man to get them to leave the island alone. Both disappeared, never to be seen again. The novelty of this film is that Indian Acierto is the bad guy and the white contractor, who refuses to violate the sacred Indian land, is a good guy.

1536. *Journey to the Center of the Earth* (1989, Cannon, 79m, c). P&D Rusty Lemorande, W Debra Ricci, Regina Davis, Kitty Chalmers & Lemorande (based on the novel by Jules Verne), PH David Watkin & Tom Fraser, ED Roxanne Zingale & Victor Livingston, PD Geoffrey Kirkland.

LP Nicola Cowper (Chrystina), Ilan Mitchell-Smith (Bryan), Paul Carafotes (Richard), Janie du Plessis (Gen. Rykov/ Shank), Jeff Weston (Tola), Jaclyn Bernstein (Sara), Kathy Ireland (Wanda), Lochner de Kock (Professor).

This jumbled film keeps little of the Jules Verne story. Four young people, exploring a cave in Hawaii, fall into a world below. It's hard to say who deserves the most blame for this busted balloon, but if we are to assume that the editors tried their best to bring some continuity to the story, they were given an almost impossible task.

1537. *Joy of Sex* (1984, Paramount, 93m, c). P Frank Konigsberg, D Martha Coolidge, W Kathleen Rowell & J.J. Salter (based on the book by Alex Comfort), PH Charles Correll, M Bishop Holiday, Scott Lipsker & Harold Payne, ED Alan Jacobs, William Elias, Ned Humphreys & Eva Gardos.

LP Cameron Dye (Alan Holt), Michelle Meyrink (Leslie Hindenberg), Colleen Camp (Liz Sampson), Ernie Hudson (Mr. Porter), Lisa Langlois (Melanie), Charles Van Eman (Max Holt), Joanne Baron (Miss Post), Darren Dalton (Ed Ingalls), Christopher Lloyd (Coach Hindenberg).

In an embarrassingly poor high school sex comedy, Michelle Meyrink, mistakenly believing she has only nine weeks to live, wishes to lose her virgin rating before biting the dust. Cameron Dye is equally anxious to lose his amateur status and he'd be more than willing to accommodate Meyrink, but his fear of emasculation at the hands of her father Christopher Lloyd is stronger than his desire. The film, which has nothing to do with Alex Comfort's book, is neither funny nor sexy.

1538.   *Joysticks* (1983, Jensen Farley, 88m, c, aka *Video Madness*). P&D Greydon Clark, W Al Gomez, Mickey Epps & Curtis Burch, PH Nicholas von Sternberg, M John Caper, Jr., ED Larry Bock.

LP Joe Don Baker (Mr. Rutter), Leif Green (Eugene Groebe), Jim Greenleaf (Jonathan Andrew McDorfus), Scott McGinnis (Jefferson Bailey), Jonathan Gries (King Vidoit), Corinne Bohrer (Patsy Rutter).

The kids of River City fight Joe Don Baker's campaign to shut down the town's video game parlor. You couldn't even get denizens of video parlors to watch this cheap piece of junk.

1539.   *Judgement Day* (1989, Rockport/Ferde Grofe Film, 93m, c). P Ferde Gorfe, Jr. & Keith Lawrence, D&W Grofe, PH Pete Warrilow, M Lucas Richman, ED Joe Zucchero & William Schleuter.

LP Kenneth McLeod (Pete Johnson), David Anthony Smith (Charlie Manners), Monte Markham (Priest), Cesar Romero (Octavio), Gloria Hayes (Maria), Peter Mark Richman (Sam).

Backpacking youths Kenneth McLeod and David Anthony Smith arrive in a small village in some unnamed Latin American country, where they learn of a strange custom. Once a year, all the villagers move out of their homes for a day—the day that Satan takes up residence. Naturally the two ugly and dumb Americans stay and must work like the devil to keep from going to hell.

1540.   *Judgment in Berlin* (1988, New Line, 92m, c). P Joshua Sinclair & Ingrid Windisch, D Leo Penn, W Sinclair & Penn (based on the book by Herbert J. Stern), PH Gabor Pogany, M Peter Goldfoot, ED Teddy Darvas.

LP Martin Sheen (Herbert J. Stern), Sam Wanamaker (Bernard Hellring), Max Gail (Judah Best), Jurgen Heinrich (Uri Andreyev), Heinz Hoenig (Helmut Thiele), Harris Yulin (Bruno Ristau), Sean Penn (Gunther X), Carl Lumbly (Edwin Palmer), Max Volkert Martens (Hans Schuster).

In a true story, Martin Sheen portrays the judge in the trial of two East Germans accused of violently hijacking a Polish airplane in order to escape from behind the Iron Curtain to safety in West Berlin. Sean Penn, son of the director, has a small but important role as a key defense witness.

Judgement in Stone see The House-keeper

1541.   *Julia and Julia* (1988, Cinecom, Italy, 96m, c). D Peter Del Monte, W Silvia Napolitano, Sandro Petraglia & Del Monte, PH Giuseppe Rotunno, M Maurice Jarre, ED Michael Chandler.

LP Kathleen Turner (Julia), Gabriel Byrne (Paolo), Sting (Daniel), Gabriele Ferzetti (Paolo's Father), Angela Goodwin (Paolo's Mother), Lidia Broccolino (Carla), Alexander Van Wyk (Marco), Renato Scarpa (Commissioner).

Widow Kathleen Turner encounters her dead husband Gabriel Byrne in another dimension, where he has survived, and they live together with their children. Meanwhile back in the real world—or is *it* the fantasy world—she's making time with Sting; creating a most unusual romantic triangle. Too bad, the writers and directors weren't able to make the intriguing idea work.

1542.   *Jumpin' Jack Flash* (1986, 20th Century–Fox, 100m, c). P Lawrence Gordon & Joel Silver, D Penny Marshall, W David H. Foanzoni, J.W. Melville, Patricia Irving & Christopher Thompson (based on a story by Fanzoni), PH Matthew F. Leonetti, M Thomas Newman, ED Mark Goldblatt, PD Robert Boyle.

LP Whoopi Goldberg (Terry Doolittle), Stephen Collins (Marty Phillips), John Wood (Jeremy Talbot), Carol Kane (Cynthia), Annie Potts (Liz Carlson), Peter Michael Goetz (Mr. Page), Roscoe Lee Browne (Archer Lincoln), Jeroen Krabbe (Mark Van Meter), Jonathan Pryce (Jack).

Whoopi Goldberg is a clever stand-up comedienne, brilliant in brief skits. She has proven her acting ability in *The Color Purple,* but thus far she has been unable to make a feature length comedy work. Part of the problem is the weakness of the plots she's given to work with. In this case, she's a computer operator drawn into the spy business when she begins to receive mysterious transmissions on her terminal from a British spy. Another part of the problem is that Goldberg tends to ham up her parts, making them burlesque routines, not comedy. Let's hope she's given more promising material to work with and she learns to handle it more appropriately.

1543. *Jungle Assault* (1989, Action Intl., 85m, c). P Fritz Matthews, D&W David A. Prior, PH Stephen Ashley Blake, M Brian Bennett, ED Paul O'Bryan, AD Ted Prior.

LP William Smith (Gen. Mitchell), William Zipp (Kelly), Ted Prior (Becker), Maria Rosado (Rosa), David Marriott (McClusky), Darwin Swalve (Crusher), Jeannie Moore (Elaine Mitchell).

Retired U.S. army general William Smith organizes a small force to go to Latin America to rescue his daughter Jeannie Moore who has been duped into helping anti–American forces.

1544. *Jungle Warriors* (1984, Aquarius, US/Ger./Mexico, 93m, c). P&D Ernst R. von Theumer, W von Theumer & Robert Collector, PH Nicholas von Sternberg, M Roland Baumgartner, ED Juan Jose Marino & Warren Chadwick.

LP Nina Van Pallandt (Joanna), Paul L. Smith (Cesar), John Vernon (Vito), Alex Cord (Nicky), Sybil Danning (Angel), Woody Strode (Luther), Kai Wulff (Ben), Dana Elcar (Michael), Suzi Horne (Pam), Mindy Iden (Marci), Marjoe Gortner (Larry).

Considering what it is, this exploitation film about a group of models falling into the hands of a brutal South American cocaine producer, Paul L. Smith, and his perverted sister, Sybil Danning, isn't half bad. There's just enough violence, gore, profanity and nudity to please aficionados of this sub-subgenre.

1545. *The Junkman* (1982, Halicki, 96m, c). P,D&W H.B. Halicki, PH Tony Syslo, ED Warner E. Leighton, PD Halicki.

LP H.B. Halicki, Christopher Stone, Hoyt Axton, Susan Shaw, Lang Jeffries, George Barris, Lynda Day George, Freddy Cannon, The Belmonts.

There's not much story, but for those who like such things, the film abounds with car crashes, racing autos, screeching wheels and exploding vehicles.

1546. *Just Before Dawn* (1980, Juniper-Picturemedia, 90m, c). P David Sheldon & Doro Vlado Hreljanovic, D Jeff Lieberman, W Mark L. Arywitz & Gregg Irving (based on a story by Joseph Middleton), PH J. King & D. King, M Brad Fiedel.

LP Chris Lemmon, Gregg Henry, Deborah Benson, George Kennedy, Mike Kellin, Ralph Seymour, John Hunsacker, Jamie Rose.

Teenagers just don't listen any more (did they ever?). Forest ranger George Kennedy warns them to stay out of the woods after dark — but they pay him no heed, meeting up with two machete-wielding mutant twins.

1547. *Just Between Friends* (1986, Orion, 110m, c). P Edward Teets & Allan Burns, D&W Burns, PH Jordan Cronenweth, M Patrick Williams & Earl Klugh, ED Ann Goursaud, PD Sydney Z. Litwack.

LP Mary Tyler Moore (Holly Davis), Christine Lahti (Sandy Dunlap), Ted Danson (Chip Davis), Sam Waterston (Harry Crandall), Salome Jens (Helga), Susan Rinell (Kim Davis), Timothy Gibbs (Jeff Davis), Jane Greer (Ruth Chadwick), Mark Blum (George Margolin).

This modest tearjerker explores the relationship of new friends Christine Lahti and Mary Tyler Moore. After Moore's husband Ted Danson dies of a heart attack, she learns that Lahti was having an affair with Danson long before she met Moore. Lahti is excellent in this all-too-neat package and Moore does yeowoman's work, but that high-pitched voice of hers hurts her in dramatic films.

1548. *Just One of the Guys* (1985, Columbia, 100m, c). P Andrew Fogelson, D Lisa Gottlieb, W Dennis Feldman & Jeff Franklin, PH John McPherson, M Tom

Scott, ed Lou Lombardo, PD Paul Peters.

LP Joyce Hyser (Terry), Clayton Rohner (Rick), Billy Jacoby (Buddy), Toni Hudson (Denise), William Zabka (Greg), Leigh McCloskey (Kevin), Sherilyn Fenn (Sandy), Deborah Goodrich (Deborah), Arye Gross (Willie).

When Joyce Hyser doesn't win a journalism prize in her high school, she's convinced it's because of her sex. She puts on male clothes and enrolls in a high school across town, with hopes of winning a like journalism prize, this time as a male. She falls head over heels for hunk Clayton Rohner, who should have suspected his/her sex, as Hyser, unlike other horny males, doesn't seem to want to jump on the bones of every girl who passes by.

1549.   *Just Tell Me What You Want* (1980, Warner, 112m, c). P Jay Presson Allen & Sidney Lumet, D Lumet, W Allen (based on her novel), M Charles Strouse, ED John J. Fitzstephens, PD Tony Walton.

LP Ali McGraw (Bones Burton), Alan King (Max Herschel), Myrna Loy (Stella Liberti), Keenan Wynn (Seymour Berger), Tony Roberts (Mike Berger), Peter Weller (Steven Routledge), Sara Truslow (Cathy), Judy Kaye (Baby), Dina Merrill (Connie Herschel).

Ali McGraw, mistress of wealthy businessman Alan King, considers leaving him for Peter Weller, but King, not wanting to lose her, regularly offers her whatever she wants to stay. It's an enjoyable old-fashioned comedy-drama.

1550.   *Just the Way You Are* (1984, MGM/United Artists, 94m, c). P Leo L. Fuchs, D Edouard Molinaro, W Allan Burns, PH Claude Lecomte, M Vladimir Cosma, ED Claudio Ventura & Georges Klotz.

LP Kristy McNichol (Susan Berlanger), Michael Ontkean (Peter Nichols), Kaki Hunter (Lisa), Andre Dussollier (Francois), Catherine Salviat (Nicole), Robert Carradine (Sam Carpenter), Alexandra Paul (Bobbie).

Talented flautist Kristy McNichol, not exactly beautiful, sexy or fascinating, seems all these things to the men she encounters in this dumb movie. Maybe it's her game leg which attracts all the guys.

It's such a problem constantly having men falling all over you.

1551.   *Justice Denied* (1989, CBC Production, Canada, 98m, c). P Adam Symansky, D&W Paul Cowan, PH David de Volpi, M Jean Corriveau, ED Rita Roy & Cowan, PD Emmanuel Janasch.

LP Billy Merasty (Donald Marshall, Jr.), Thomas Peacocke (John MacIntyre), Wayne Robson (Roy Ebsary), Peter MacNeill (Harry Wheaton), J. Winston Carroll (Jim Carroll), Daniel McIver (Jimmy MacNeill).

One night in 1971 in Sydney, Nova Scotia, Micmac Indian Billy Merasty and a black friend go to a park, planning to mug someone. Instead they encounter Robson, a deeply disturbed man who stabs the black man to death. Instead of arresting Robson, the police accused Merasty of the crime and he served 11 years in prison for a crime he didn't commit. The film is based on an actual incident.

1552.   *K-9* (1989, Universal, 102m, c). P Lawrence Gordon & Charles Gordon, D Rod Daniel, W Steven Siegel & Scott Myers, PH Dean Semler, M Miles Goodman, ED Lois Freeman-Fox, PD George Costello.

LP James Belushi (Dooley), Mel Harris (Tracy), Kevin Tighe (Lyman), Ed O'Neill (Brannigan), Jerry Lee (K-9), James Handy (Byers), Cotter Smith (Gilliam), Daniel Davis (Halstead).

In a variation on the many male-bonding movies, San Diego narcotics cop James Belushi is teamed with drug sniffing German Shepherd Jerry Lee (named after rock singer Jerry Lee Lewis). The latter upstages his partner throughout the movie. It's long on cutesy and predictable twists on the buddy theme, but short on any real plot. Get it on video!

1553.   *Kandyland* (1988, New World, 93m, c). P Rich Blumenthal, D Robert Schnitzer, W Schnitzer & Toni Serritello, PH Robert Brinkman, M George Michalski, ED Jeffrey Reiner, PD Paul Sussman.

LP Kim Evenson (Joni Sekorsy), Charles Laulette (Frank), Sandahl Bergman (Harlow Divine), Cole Stevens (Roy), Bruce Baum (Mad Dog), Alan Toy

(Eppy), Irwin Keyes (Biff), Steve Kravitz (Bruce Belnap).

The plot of this story of a novice stripper learning the ropes from a more experienced peeler is about as transparent as the costumes.

1554. *Kangaroo* (1987, Cineplex Odeon, Australia, 105m, c). P Ross Dimsey, D Tim Burstall, W Evan Jones (based on the novel by D.H. Lawrence), PH Dan Burstall, M Nathan Waks, ED Edward McQueen-Mason.

LP Colin Friels (Richard Somers), Judy Davis (Harriet Somers), John Walton (Jack Calcott), Julie Nihill (Vicki Calcott), Hugh Keays-Byrne (Kangaroo), Peter Hehir (Jaz), Peter Cummins (Struthers), Tim Robertson (O'Neill).

In a thinly disguised autobiographical story, Colin Friels appears as a D.H. Lawrence–like character who together with his wife, Judy Davis, travels to Australia to find a better life after being vilified in England for writing sexually explicit novels.

1555. *Kansas* (1988, TransWorld, 106m, c). P George Litto, D David Stevens, W Spencer Eastman, PH David Eggby, M Pino Donaggio, ED Robert Barrere, PD Matthew Jacobs.

LP Matt Dillon (Doyle Kennedy), Andrew McCarthy (Wade Corey), Leslie Hope (Lori Bayles), Alan Toy (Nordquist), Andy Romano (Fleener), Brent Jennings (Buckshot), Brynn Thayer (Connie), Kyra Sedgwick (Prostitute Drifter), Harry Northrup (Governor), Clint Allen (Ted).

Drifter Andrew McCarthy unwisely teams up with psychopath Matt Dillon and finds himself involved in a bank robbery. He later becomes a hero by saving the governor's daughter from drowning and wins stuck-up rich girl Leslie Hope from her country club boyfriend. The film should have spent more time with Dillon.

1556. *The Karate Kid* (1984, Columbia, 126m, c). P Jerry Weintraub, D John G. Avildsen, W Robert Mark Kamen, PH James Crabe, M Bill Conti, ED Bud Smith, Walt Mulconery & Avildsen, PD William J. Cassidy.

LP Ralph Macchio (Daniel), Noriyuki

"Pat" Morita† (Mr. Miyagi), Elisabeth Shue (Ali), Martin Kove (Kreese), Randee Heller (Lucille), William Zabka (Johnny), Ron Thomas (Bobby), Rob Garrison (Tommy), Chad McQueen (Dutch), Tony O'Dell (Jimmy).

Those who enjoyed having their emotions manipulated by the producers of *Rocky* will get the same thrill in this film. Ralph Macchio, with his mother, moves across country from New Jersey to California. For how out of place the youngster feels, the relocation might as well have been to the moon. He runs afoul of karate fighter William Zabka and his motorcycle-riding pals. Fortunately for Macchio he meets Noriyuki Morita, who teaches the boy about life and karate in a manner reminiscent of Alec Guinness instructing Mark Hamill about the "force." Macchio defeats the bigger Zabka in a tournament, proving he's learned the lessons of the way of life better than has his opponent.

1557. *The Karate Kid Part II* (1986, Columbia, 113m, c). P Jerry Weintraub, D John G. Avildsen, W Robert Mark Kamen, PH James Crabe, M Bill Conti, ED David Garfield, Jane Kurson & John G. Avildsen, PD William J. Cassidy, SONG "Glory of Love" by Peter Cetera, David Foster & Diane Nini†.

LP Noriyuki "Pat" Morita (Mr. Miyagi), Ralph Macchio (Daniel), Martin Kove (Kreese), William Zabka (Johnny), Chad McQueen (Dutch), Danny Kamekona (Sato), Nobu McCarthy (Yukie), Yuji Okumoto (Chozen), Tamlyn Tomita (Kumiko), Charlie Tanimoto (Miyagi's Father).

Supposedly picking up the story just at the point of the end of the previous picture, Noriyuki Morita gets a call to return to Okinawa to visit his ailing father. He invites Ralph Macchio along for the trip. Both find romance and encounter menacing villains.

1558. *The Karate Kid Part III* (1989, Columbia, 111m, c). P Jerry Weintraub, D John G. Avildsen, W Robert Mark Kamen (based on characters created by Kamen), PH Steve Yaconelli, M Bill Conti, ED John Carter & Avildsen, PD William F. Matthews.

LP Ralph Macchio (Daniel), Noriyuki

"Pat" Morita (Mr. Miyagi), Robyn Lively (Jessica), Thomas Ian Griffith (Terry), Martin L. Kove (Kreese), Sean Kanan (Mike Barnes), Jonathan Avildsen (Snake), Christopher Paul Ford (Dennis).

Ralph Macchio (who has celebrated his 27th birthday) is back competing in the under-18 category of a California Karate Tournament. Perhaps he's not too old for these things, but all but the most uncritical fans surely must have grown weary of essentially the same old story. Noriyuki Morita teaches Macchio about peace and tranquility, but before the film is out, one or both must resort to tremendous violent kicking and grunting to put away villains whose consciousness requires raising.

1559. *The Keep* (1983, Paramount, 96m, c). P Gene Kirkwood & Howard W. Koch, Jr., D&W Michael Mann (based on a novel by F. Paul Wilson), PH Alex Thomson, M Tangerine Dream, ED Dov Hoenig, PD John Box.

LP Scott Glenn (Glaeken Trismegestus), Alberta Watson (Eva), Jurgen Prochnow (Woermann), Robert Prosky (Father Fonescu), Gabriel Byrne (Kempffer), Ian McKellen (Dr. Cuza), Morgan Sheppard (Alexandru), Royston Tickner (Tomescu), Michael Carter (Radu).

It wasn't planned for audiences to laugh during this metaphysical horror thriller, but they did. Set in a Carpathian castle, a group of Nazi officers and a dying Jewish scientist confront an evil force. Mysterious traveler Scott Glenn, brought by psychic impulses to battle the force, acts like he wasn't given any instructions as to the nature of his mission.

1560. *Keep My Grave Open* (1980, Jefferson & Century, 78m, c). P&D S.F. Brownrigg, W F. Amos Powell, PH John Valtenburgs, M Robert Farrar.

LP Camilla Carr (Lesley Fontaine), Gene Ross, Stephen Tobolowsky, Ann Stafford, Annabelle Weenick, Chelcie Ross, Sharon Bunn, Bill Thurman.

Camilla Carr confuses herself with her long-missing brother, imagining the two are having an incestuous affair. Now and then she kills a man or so who makes a pass at her, imagining it is her brother

protecting her. Talk about split personalities!

1561. *Key Exchange* (1985, 20th Century–Fox, 90m, c). P Mitchell Maxwell & Paul Kurta, D Barnet Kellman, W Kevin Scott & Kurta (based on the play by Kevin Wade), PH Fred Murphy, M Mason Daring, Michael Jay & Kenny White, ED Jill Savitt, PD David Gropman.

LP Brooke Adams (Lisa), Danny Aiello (Carabello), Daniel Stern (Michael), Tony Roberts (Slattery), Ben Masters (Philip), Nancy Mette (April), Seth Allen (Frank), Sandra Beall (Marcy).

Mystery writer Ben Masters exchanges apartment keys with talk show producer Brooke Adams, but he can't bring himself to make an exclusive commitment to her as she wishes.

1562. *KGB: The Secret War* (1986, Cinema Group, 89m, c, aka *Lethal*). P Sandy Howard & Keith Rubinstein, D Dwight Little, W Sandra K. Bailey (based on a story by Dwight Little & Bailey), PH Peter Lyons Collister, M Misha Segal. ED Stanley Sheff, John Peterson.

LP Michael Billington (Peter Hubbard), Denise DuBarry (Adele Martin), Michael Ansara (Lyman Taylor), Walter Gotell (Nicholai), Sally Kellerman (Fran Simpson), Christopher Cary (Alex Stefanac).

The film is standard Cold War stuff, as bloody and deadly as any shooting war, but nothing to get too excited about.

1563. *Kickboxer* (1989, Pathe, GB, 105m, c). P Mark DiSalle, D DiSalle & David Worth, W Glenn Bruce (based on a story by DiSalle & Jean-Claude Van Damme), PH Jon Kranhouse, M Paul Hertzog, ED Wayne Wahrman.

LP Jean-Claude Van Damme (Kurt Sloane), Denis Alexio (Eric Sloane), Dennis Chan (Xian Chow), Tong Po (Himself), Haskell Anderson (Winston Taylor), Rochelle Ashana (Mylee).

When World Kickboxing champion Denis Alexio is crippled by top Thai fighter Tong Po, his younger brother Jean-Claude Van Damme swears revenge. It's a cross between *Rocky* and *The Karate Kid*.

1564. *Kidco* (1984, 20th Century–Fox, 104m, c). P Frank Yablans & David

Niven, Jr., D Ronald F. Maxwell, W Bennett Trainer, PH Paul Lohmann, M Michael Small, ED David McKenna, PD Fred Price.

LP Scott Schwartz (Dickie Cessna), Cinnamon Idles (Nene Cessna), Tristine Skyler (Bette Cessna), Elizabeth Gorcey (June Cessna), Charles Hallahan (Richard Cessna), Maggie Blye (Joan Cessna).

It's kids like those featured in this picture that made America world leaders in business and industry. Too bad more like them aren't being developed so the country might maintain that leadership. It's the true story of some preteens who go into the fertilizer business, their product the result of cleaning out the stables of area horses. The government steps in and ruins their business.

1565. *The Kidnapping of the President* (1980, Crown International, Canada, 113m, c). P George Mendeluk & John Ryan, D Mendeluk, W Richard Murphy (based on the novel by Charles Templeton), PH Michael Molloy, M Paul J. Zaza, ED Michael MacLaverty.

LP Michael Shatner (Jerry O'Connor), Hal Holbrook (President Adam Scott), Van Johnson (Vice President Ethan Richards), Ava Gardner (Beth Richards), Miguel Fernandes (Roberto Assanti), Cindy Girling (Linda Steiner), Michael J. Reynolds (MacKenzie), Elizabeth Shepherd (Joan Scott), Gary Reineke (Dietrich).

Third-world terrorist Miguel Fernandes handcuffs himself to President Hal Holbrook, claiming to be wired with explosives, which he will set off unless his demands are met. William Shatner is the Secret Service officer in charge of saving Holbrook. Dull stuff!

1566. *Kill and Kill Again* (1981, Film Ventures, 100m, c). P Igo Kantor, D Ivan Hall, W John Crowther, PH Tai Krige, ED Peter Thornton & Robert Leighton.

LP James Ryan (Steve Chase), Anneline Kriel (Kandy Kane), Ken Gampu (Gorilla), Norman Robinson (Gypsy Billy), Stan Schmidt (The Fly), Bill Flynn (Hotdog), Michael Mayer (Marduk), Marloe Scott-Wilson (Minerva).

Evil scientist Michael Mayer wishes to use the mind-controlling drug a scientist has inadvertently created, for his own

dastardly ambitions. James Ryan must rescue the kidnapped scientist from his mad captor.

Kill Castro see Sweet Dirty Tony

1567. *Kill Me Again* (1989, MGM/ United Artists, 94m, c). P David W. Warfield, Sigurjon Sighvatsson & Steve Golin, D John Dahl, W Dahl & Warfield, PH Jacques Steyn, M William Olvis, ED Frank Jimenez & Jonathan Shaw, PD Michelle Minch.

LP Joanne Whalley-Kilmer (Fay Forrester), Val Kilmer (Jack Andrews), Michael Madsen (Vince Miller), Pat Mulligan (Sammy), Nick Dimitri (Marty), Bibi Besch (Jack's Secretary), Jonathan Gries (Alan Swayzie), Michael Sharrett (Tim).

Set in modern day Nevada, the story has small-time con team Joanne Whalley-Kilmer and Michael Madsen scoring big when they come across a bag of Mafia money. Whalley-Kilmer decides she wants the loot for herself, knocks out her partner and hires seedy detective Val Kilmer to fake her murder. He's glad to oblige.

1568. *The Kill-Off* (1989, Filmworld Intl., 95m, c). P Lydia Dean Pilcher, D Maggie Greenwald, W Greenwald (based on a novel by Jim Thompson), PH Declan Quinn, M Evan Lurie, ED James Y. Kwei, PD Pamela Woodbridge.

LP Loretta Gross (Luane DeVore), Andrew Lee Barrett (Bobby), Jackson Sims (Pete), Steve Monroe (Ralph), Cathy Haase (Danny Lee), William Russell (Rags), Jorjan Fox (Myra).

Gossip-monger Loretta Gross is despised by everyone in her little community. She feigns a bedridden, feeble condition to get her dim-witted, 20-years-younger husband Steve Monroe to cater to her every whim. Finally the locals, including Monroe and his new girlfriend Cathy Haase, decide to get rid of her.

1569. *Kill or Be Killed* (1980, Film Ventures, 90m, c). P Ben Volk, D Ivan Hall, W C.F. Beyers-Boshoff, PH Mane Eotha, ED Brian Varaday.

LP James Ryan, Charlotte Michelle, Norman Combes, Daniel DuPlessis.

Look for a lot of karate fighting in this grudge match between an ex–Nazi general and karate coach, and his Japanese counterpart, whose team defeated the Germans during World War II.

1570. ***Kill Squad*** (1982, Summa Vista, 83m, c). P Michael D. Lee & Patrick G. Donahue, D&W Donahue, PH Christopher W. Strattan, M Joseph Conlan, ED Rick Yacco.

LP Cameron Mitchell (Dutch), Jean Glaude, Jeff Risk, Jerry Johnson, Bill Cambra, Francisco Ramirez, Marc Sabin, Gary Fung, Alan Marcus.

Six martial arts experts are rounded up to save their former Vietnam squad commander from the dastardly plans of Cameron Mitchell, who intends to take over the man's electronics business.

Killbots see Chopping Mall

The Killer Behind the Mask see Savage Weekends

1571. ***Killer Klowns from Outer Space*** (1988, TransWorld, 88m, c). P Edward Chiodo, Stephen Chiodo & Charles Chiodo, D S. Chiodo, W C. & S. Chiodo, PH Alfred Taylor, M John Massari, ED Chris Roth, PD C. Chiodo.

LP Grant Cramer (Mike), Suzanne Snyder (Debbie), John Allen Nelson (Officer Dave Hanson), Royal Dano (Farmer Green), John Vernon (Officer Mooney), Michael Siegel (Rich), Peter Licassi (Paul).

A circus-tent space ship lands on earth, releasing evil, clown-like aliens who shoot their victims with cotton candy which wraps bodies in giant pink cocoons. These nasty Emmett Kellys are eventually dispatched when it is discovered that they can be killed if hit in their big red noses. It's a straight horror film—not a spoof.

1572. ***Killer Party*** (1986, United Artists/MGM, 91m, c). P Michael Lepiner, D William Fruet, W Barney Cohen, PH John Lindley, M John Beal, ED Eric Albertson, PD Reuben Freed.

LP Martin Hewitt (Blake), Ralph Seymour (Martin), Elaine Wilkes (Phoebe), Paul Bartel (Prof. Zito), Sherry Willis-Burch (Vivia), Alicia Fleer (Veronica), Woody Brown (Harrison), Joanna Johnson (Jennifer).

In this stupid picture about fraternity brothers and sorority sisters holding their April Fool's party in an abandoned house, the slasher wears a deep sea diver's outfit but still is fast enough of foot to end a lot of lives.

1573. ***Killer Workout*** (1987, Winters Group, 86m, c, aka *Aerobicide*). P Peter Yuval & David A. Prior, D&W Prior, PH Peter Bonilla & Stephen Ashley-Blake, W Todd Hayen, ED Prior.

LP Marcia Karr (Rhonda Johnson/ Valerie Johnson), David James Campbell (Lt. Morgan), Fritz Matthews (Jimmy Hallick), Ted Prior (Chuck Dawson), Teresa Vander Woude (Jaimy), Richard Bravo (Tom), Dianne Copeland (Debbie), Laurel Mock (Diane Matthews), Lynn Meighan (Cathy).

As most of the scenes in this combination whodunit and slasher film are held in a health club, there's ample opportunity to leer at a bunch of scantily dressed women, one of the essentials of this subgenre. The message seems to be that a juicy-looking woman arouses the murdering beast in some men and they must draw blood to get relief. It's sick, but unfortunately it sells.

1574. ***The Killers*** (1984, Roth Film, 60m, c). P,D&W Patrick Roth (based on "Short Story" by Charles Bukowski), PH Patrick Prince, M Doug Lynner & Bill Boydstun, ED Daniel Gross.

LP Jack Kehoe (Harry), Raymond Mayo (Bill), Allan Magicovsky (Husband), Susanne Reed (Wife), Anne Ramsey (1st Ragpicker), Susan Tyrrell (Susu, 2nd Ragpicker), Charles Bukowski (The Author).

Former insurance man Jack Kehoe meets small-time thief Raymond Mayo in an all night cafe. The latter convinces Kehoe to help him burglarize a mansion. In doing so they awaken the owners, Allan Magicovsky and Susanne Reed. After taunting the husband, Mayo cuts the man's throat. Aroused, Kehoe rapes Reed, after which he kills her. The two leave, taking nothing.

1575. ***A Killing Affair*** (1988, Hemdale, 100m, c). P Michael Rauch & Peter R. McIntosh, D&W David Saperstein (based on the novel *Monday, Tuesday, Wednesday* by Robert Houston), PH Dominique Chapuis, M John Barry, ED Patrick McMahon, PD John J. Moore.

LP Peter Weller (Baston Morris), Kathy Baker (Maggie Gresham), Bill Smitrovich (Pink Gresham), John Glover.

Filmed in 1985, this World War II–era Gothic story takes place in the backwoods of West Virginia. Peter Weller holds Kathy Baker captive in her isolated cabin for three days after killing her husband in the outhouse. He claims the deceased had tried to run away with Weller's wife and children.

1576. *Killing Dad* (1989, Applecross, GB, 93m, c). P Iain Smith, D&W Michael Austin (based on the novel *Berg* by Ann Quinn), PH Gabriel Beristain, ED Edward Marnier, PD Adrienne Atkinson.

LP Denholm Elliott (Nathy Berg), Julie Walters (Judith), Richard E. Grant (Alistair Berg), Anna Massey (Edith Berg), Laura del Sol (Luisa), Ann Way, Jonathan Phillips, Kevin Williams.

Anna Massey receives a letter from her long absent husband Denholm Elliott, claiming he wishes to return to her and start life anew. Their son, Richard E. Grant, not pleased, sets out to kill his father, whom he encounters at a faded Scottish hotel. Elliott is a drunk and a liar who lives with Julie Walters. Grant mistakenly strangles Elliott's ventriloquist's dummy. Walters is convinced that Grant killed Elliott because of his love for her. Grant takes Walters home to mother, whom he finds in bed with Elliott. Disgusted, Grant sets off to find exotic dancer Laura del Sol, who took a shine to him back at the hotel. It's a black comedy, we suppose.

1577. *The Killing Fields*† (1984, Warner, GB, 141m, c). P David Puttnam, D Roland Joffe†, W Bruce Robinson† (based on the magazine article "The Death and Life of Dith Pran" by Sidney Schanberg), PH Chris menges*, M Mike Oldfield, ED Jim Clark*, PD Roy Walker, AD Roger Murray Leach & Steve Spence, SD Tessa Davies.

LP Sam Waterston† (Sidney Schanberg), Haing S. Ngor* (Dith Pran), John Malkovich (Al Rockoff), Julian Sands (Jon Swain), Craig T. Nelson (Military Attache), Spalding Gray (U.S. Consul), Bill Paterson (Dr. Macentire), Athol Fugard (Dr. Sundesval), Graham Kennedy (Dougal), Katherine Krapum Chey (Ser Moeun), Oliver Pierpaoli (Titonel), Edward Entero Chey (Sarun), Monirak Sisowath (Phat).

This highly charged drama is based on the experiences of Pulitzer Prize–winning, *New York Times* writer Sidney Schanberg and his Cambodian friend and translator Dith Pran. The two cover the war together in Southeast Asia, until the writer (Sam Waterston) is forced to leave Cambodia just as the country is taken over by the brutal Khmer Rouge. Pran, brilliantly portrayed by Dr. Haing S. Ngor (who himself had to escape from his country), is left behind. He survives by convincing the Khmer Rouge leaders that he's merely a simple, uneducated laborer. With a lot of luck he is able to make it out of Cambodia and is reunited with his family in the United States, whom the writer had gotten out before the fall of the country. The total lack of respect for human life of the Khmer Rouge, many of whom are mere children, is appalling, but the heart-rending treatment of the story is one that should be seen and endured by those who lived safely in the world as genocide was taking place in Cambodia.

1578. *The Killing Game* (1988, City Lights Home Video, 83m, c). P Richard Pepin & Joseph Merhi, D&W Merhi, PH Pepin, M John Gonzalez.

LP Chard Hayward, Cynthia Killion, Geoffrey Sadwith, Robert Zdar, Bette Rae, Julie Noble, Monique Monet, Brigitte Burdine.

Made especially for home video, this film is the story of hit man and gambler Chard Hayward who finds himself a blackmail victim after killing a man and his mistress.

1579. *Killing Heat* (1984, Satori, 104m, c, aka *The Grass Is Singing*). P Mark Forstater, D&W Michael Raeburn (based on the novel *The Grass Is Singing* by Doris Lessing), PH Billie August & Fritz Schroder, M Bjorn Isfalt & Temba Tana, ED Thomas Schwalm, PD Disley Jones.

LP Karen Black (Mary Turner), John Thaw (Dick Turner), John Kani (Moses), John Moulder-Brown (Tony Marston), Patrick Mynhardt (Charlie), Bjorn Gedda (Sgt. Denham), Ian Nygren (Doctor).

City career woman Karen Black falls in love with a South African farmer John Thaw. After their marriage she has a struggle adjusting to life in a primitive region.

1580. *The Killing of Angel Street* (1983, Satori, Australia, 101m, c). P Anthony Buckley, D Donald Crombie, W Evan Jones, Michael Craig & Cecil Holmes (based on a story by Craig), PH Peter James, M Brian May, ED Tim Wellburn.

LP Liz Alexander (Jessica), John Hargreaves (Elliot), Alexander Archdale (B.C.), Reg Lye (Riley), Gordon McDougall (Sir Arthur), David Downer (Alan), Ric Herbert (Ben), Brendon Lunney (Scott).

Communist John Hargreaves and geologist Liz Alexander battle corrupt real estate manipulators who are trying to drive homesteaders off their land.

1581. *The Killing Time* (1987, New World, 95m, c). P Peter Abrams & Robert L. Levy, D Rick King, W Don Bohlinger, James Nathan & Bruce Franklin Singer, PH Paul H. Goldsmith, M Paul Chihara, ED Lorenzo de Stefano, PD Bernt Amadeus Capra.

LP Beau Bridges (Sheriff Sam Wayburn), Kiefer Sutherland (Brian Mars), Wayne Rogers (Jake Winslow), Joe Don Baker (Sheriff Carl Cunningham), Camelia Kath (Laura Winslow), Janet Carroll (Lila Dagget), Michael Madsen (Stu).

Everybody seems involved in killing in a small California town. But mainly the film deals with deputy sheriff Beau Bridges' plot to take out his mistress' monstrous husband Wayne Rogers.

1582. *Killpoint* (1984, Crown, 89m, c). P Frank Harris & Diane Stevenett, D,W&PH Harris, M Herman Jeffreys & Daryl Stevenett, ED Harris.

LP Leo Fong (Lt. James Long), Richard Roundtree (Bill Bryant), Cameron Mitchell (Joe Marks), Stack Pierce (Nighthawk), Hope Holiday (Anita), Diana Leigh (Candy), Bernie Nelson (Pawnbroker).

Martial arts expert and police officer Leo Fong is out to avenge the rape-murder of his wife. The trail leads to a gang of gunrunners headed by sadistic Cameron Mitchell.

1583. *Killzone* (1985, Shapiro, 87m, c). P Jack Marino, D David A. Prior, W Prior & Marino, PH Victor Alexander, M Robert A. Higgins, ED Alexander.

LP Fritz Matthews (The Vet), Ted Prior (Mitchell), David James Campbell (Crawford), David Kong (Ling), Richard Massery (Lucas), William Joseph Zipp (Manley), Lawrence Udy (Matthews), Richard Brailford (Johnson).

Here's still another look at a deranged Vietnam vet whose mind snaps, making him believe he's back in the jungles of 'Nam. He does what he was taught to do, kill and kill again.

1584. *The Kindred* (1987, F-M Entertainment, 91m, c). P Jeffrey Obrow, D Obrow & Stephen Carpenter, W Obrow, Carpenter, John Penney Joseph Stefano & Earl Ghaffari, PH Carpenter, M David Newman, ED Penney & Earl Ghaffari, PD Chris Hopkins.

LP David Allen Brooks (John Hollins), Rod Steiger (Dr. Phillip Lloyd), Amanda Pays (Melissa Leftridge), Talia Balsam (Sharon Raymond), Kim Hunter (Amanda Hollins), Timothy Gibbs (Hart Phillips), Peter Frechette (Brad Baxter), Julie Montgomery (Cindy Russell).

Whether the worst thing about this movie is the script or the cast could be argued endlessly. Just let it go that both are dreadful. The story has something or other to do with genetic experimentation. Quality actors such as Rod Steiger and Kim Hunter must be at the lowest points in their careers. Hunter is fortunate enough to die early in the film.

1585. *King Blank* (1983, Metafilms, 71m, b&w). P&D Michael Oblowitz, W Oblowitz & Rosemary Hochschild, PH Oblowitz, M Anton Fig, ED Susanne Rostack.

LP Rosemary Hochschild (Queenie Blank), Ron Vawter (King Blank), Will Patton (Bar Customer), Pete Richardson (Bouncer).

The setting for the break-up of the marriage of Vietnam veteran Ron Vawter and his wife Rosemary Hochschild takes place in their room at a cheap motel near the airport and the motel's bar.

King Cobra see Jaws of Satan

1586. *King David* (1985, Paramount, 114m, c). P Martin Elfand, D Bruce Beresford, W Andrew Birkin & James Costigan (based on a story by Costigan and "The Books of Samuel I and II," "Chronicles I" and "The Psalms of David"), PH Donald McAlpine, M Carl Davis, ED William Anderson, PD Ken Adam.

LP Richard Gere (David), Ian Sears (Young David), Alice Krige (Bathsheba), Edward Woodward (Saul), Cherie Lunghi (Michal), Jack Klaff (Jonathan), Aiche Nana (Ahinoab), Gina Bellman (Tamar), James Coombes (Amnon), Jean-Marc Barr (Absalom), Jason Carter (Solomon), Denis Quilley (Samuel), Niall Buggy (Nathan), Hurd Hatfield (Ahimelech).

How dare Paramount attempt a biblical epic now that Cecil B. De Mille is dead? This story of the decline of King Saul and the emergence of David is not too bad, particularly in the first half, despite the presence of Richard Gere in the title role, who is overrated by those who think he's merely a mediocre actor.

1587. *King Kong Lives* (1986, De Laurentiis, 105m, c). P Martha Schumacher, D John Guillermin, W Ronald Shusett & Steven Pressfield (based on the character King Kong created by Merian C. Cooper & Edgar Wallace), PH Alec Mills, M John Scott, ED Malcolm Cooke, PD Peter Murton.

LP Peter Elliot (King Kong), George Yiasoimi (Lady Kong), Brian Kerwin (Hank Mitchell), Linda Hamilton (Amy Franklin), John Ashton (Col. Nevitt), Peter Michael Goetz (Dr. Ingersoll), Frank Maraden (Dr. Benson Hughes).

When Kong toppled from the World Trade Center in the 1976 picture, bet you thought he was dead. No way, he was just in a coma and in need of one hell of a big heart transplant. Lady Kong shows up to help him convalesce, after which she'll have some questions about the bleached-out little blonde tramps he's been messing around with.

1588. *King Lear* (1988, Cannon, US/Switz. 91m, c). P Menahem Golan & Yoram Globus, D&W Jean-Luc Godard (based on the play by William Shakespeare), PH Sophie Maintigneux.

LP Peter Sellars (William Shakespeare, the Fifth), Burgess Meredith (Don Learo), Molly Ringwald (Cordelia), Norman Mailer (Himself), Kate Mailer (Herself), Jean-Luc Godard (The Professor), Woody Allen (Mr. Alien).

This film has no real structure and appears to be just an excuse for Jean-Luc Godard to experiment with film as the mood moves him. Peter Sellars, a descendent of Shakespeare, in attendance at a post–Apocalypse Swiss hotel, is trying to locate the works of his ancestor which have been lost. He encounters modern-day Mafia leader Burgess Meredith, a Lear-like figure, and his daughter, Molly Ringwald, who mouth lines from Shakespeare's play.

1589. *The King of Comedy* (1983, 20th Century–Fox, 108m, c). P Arnon Milchan, D Martin Scorsese, W Paul D. Zimmerman, PH Fred Schuler, M Robbie Robertson, ED Thelma Schoonmaker, PD Boris Leven.

LP Robert De Niro (Rupert Pupkin), Jerry Lewis (Jerry Langford), Diahnne Abbott (Rita), Sandra Bernhard (Masha), Ed Herlihy (Himself), Lou Brown (Band Leader), Whitey Ryan (Stage Door Guard), Doc Lawless (Chauffeur), Marta Heflin (Young Girl), Liza Minnelli (Herself), Catherine Scorsese (Rupert's Mother), Cathy Scorsese (Dolores).

Aspiring comedian Robert De Niro is driven to kidnap Jerry Lewis in order to be given a TV appearance where he can be "King of Comedy" if only for one night. In what is not a comedy in the usual sense, De Niro gives a brilliant performance as a man whose ambition and narcissism has made his need for recognition an obsession.

1590. *King of the Mountain* (1981, Universal, 90m, c). P Jack Frost Sanders, D Noel Nosseck, W H.R. Christian (based on the magazine article by David Barry called "Thunder Road"), PH Donald Peterman, M Michael Melvion, ED William Steinkamp, PD James H. Spencer.

LP Harry Hamlin (Steve), Joseph Bottoms (Buddy), Deborah Van Valkenburgh (Tina), Richard Cox (Roger), Dennis Hopper (Cal), Dan Haggerty (Rick), Seymour Cassel (Barry Tanner), Jon Sloan (Billy T.).

In this pretentious melodrama, garage mechanic Harry Hamlin and his beer drinking buddies race their cars along L.A.'s treacherous Mulholland Drive. Hamlin is the best at this sport, with Dennis Hopper appearing as a burnt-out former "king."

1591. *King Solomon's Mines* (1985, Cannon, 100m, c). P Menahem Golan & Yoram Globus, D J. Lee Thompson, W Gene Quintano & James R. Silke (based on the novel by H. Rider Haggard), PH Alex Phillips, M Jerry Goldsmith, ED John Shirley, PD Luciano Spadoni.

LP Richard Chamberlain (Quatermain), Sharon Stone (Jessie), Herbert Lom (Colonel Bockner), John Rhys-Davies (Dogati), Ken Gampu (Umbopo), June Buthelezi (Gagoola), Sam Williams (Scragga), Shai K. Ophir (Kassam), Fidelis Che A (Mapaki Chief), Mick Lesley (Dorfman).

There was no good reason to refilm H. Rider Haggard's novel even in 1950, even to see the story in Technicolor. Ted Turner would have eventually gotten around to colorizing the 1937 version which had Cedric Hardwicke and Paul Robeson searching for Solomon's lost diamond mine in Africa. The 1985 version's merely an excuse for some well-known hams to parade their questionable talents in a tongue-in-cheek version of a story suffering from jungle rot.

1592. *Kings and Desperate Men* (1984, Blue Dolphin, GB, 118m, c). P&D Alexis Kanner, W Kanner & Edmund Ward, PH Henry Lucas [Kanner] & Paul van der Linden, M Michael Robidoux & Pierre F. Brault, ED Lucas [Kanner], PD & COS Will McGow.

LP Patrick McGoohan (John Kingsley), Alexis Kanner (Lucas Miller), Andrea Marcovicci (The Girl), Margaret Trudeau (Elizabeth Kingsley), John-Pierre Brown (Kingsley Child), Robin Spry (Harry Gibson), Frank Moore (Herrera), Budd Knapp (Judge McManus).

When political extremist Alexis Kanner forcibly takes over a radio station, a talk show host encourages telephone callers to express their opinions as he stages a phone-in "trial."

1593. *Kingsgate* (1989, Howe/One Prods. Ltd., Canada, 110m, c). P,D&W Jack Darcus, PH Doug McKay, M Michael Conway Baker, ED Doris Dyck, PD Michael Nemirsky.

LP Elizabeth Dancoes (Fee), Duncan Fraser (Ellis), Barbara March (Brenda Kingsgate), Roberta Maxwell (Marlene), Alan Scarfe (Daniel Kingsgate), Christopher Plummer (Tom).

A long yelling and drinking match involving three couples takes up the entire 110 minutes of this nothing-to-see film.

1594. *Kinjite: Forbidden Subjects* (1989, Cannon, 97m, c, aka *Forbidden Subjects*). P Pancho Kohner, D J. Lee-Thompson, W Harold Nebenzal, PH Gideon Porath, M Greg DeBelles, ED Peter Lee-Thompson & Mary E. Jochem.

LP Charles Bronson (Lt. Crowe), Perry Lopez (Eddie Rios), Juan Fernandez (Duke), Peggy Lipton (Kathleen Crowe), James Pax (Hiroshi Hada), Sy Richardson (Lavonne), Marion Kodama Yue (Kazuko Hada).

The title refers to taboo subjects that the Japanese suppress. It should have been applied to this very lackluster Charles Bronson film. He portrays a mean L.A. police detective who is down on teenage prostitution and anything Japanese. The two hatreds are brought together to give Bronson a chance to display his usual spitefulness against whomever he deems to be the bad guys. One must admit that Juan Fernandez is a despicable creep.

1595. *Kipperbang* (1984, MGM/United Artist Classics, GB, 85m, c, aka *P'Tang, Yang, Kipperbang*). P Chris Griffin, D Michael Apted, W Jack Rosenthal, PH Tony Pierce-Roberts, M David Earl, ED John Shirley.

LP John Albasiny (Alan "Quack Quack" Duckworth), Abigail Cruttenden (Ann), Maurice Dee (Geoffrey), Alison Steadman (Miss Land), Garry Cooper (Tommy), Robert Urquhart (Headmaster), Mark Brailsford (Abbo).

It's a nostalgic look at the romantic fantasies and predicaments that young British teens and their teachers shared in the year 1948. The main story line deals with young John Albasiny's plan to get his first kiss from classmate Abigail Cruttenden. Seems a modest sexual ambition by the standards of most teenage sex comedies of the decade.

1596. *The Kiss* (1988, Tri-Star, 101m, c). P Pen Densham & John Watson, D Densham, W Stephen Volk & Tom Ropelewski (based on a story by Volk), PH Francois Protat, M J. Peter Robinson, ED Stan Cole, PD Roy Forge Smith.

LP Pamela Collyer (Hilary Halloran), Peter Dvorsky (Father Joe), Joanna Pacula (Felice), Meredith Salenger (Amy Halloran), Mimi Kuzyk (Brenda Carson), Nicholas Kilbertus (Jack Halloran), Sabrina Boudot (Heather).

Meredith Salenger correctly surmises that her recently arrived aunt, Joanna Pacula, is a witch. It's a hokey horror show.

1597. *Kiss Daddy Good Night* (1987, Beast of Eden, 80m, c). P Maureen O'Brien & William Ripka, D Peter Ily Huemer, W Huemer & Michael Gabrieli (based on a story by Huemer), PH Bobby Bukowski, M Don King & Duncan Lindsay, ED Ila von Hasperg.

LP Uma Thurman (Laura), Paul Dillon (Sid), Paul Richards (William B. Tilden), Steve Buscemi (Johnny), Annabelle Gurwitch (Sue), David Brisbin (Nelson Blitz).

Beautiful 16-year-old ex-fashion model Uma Thurman portrays a crazed blonde who dons sexy clothes and wigs to lure men back to her apartment. Once there she drugs them and steals their money. Her neighbor Paul Richards becomes obsessed with the girl, who resembles his daughter.

1598. *Kiss Me Goodbye* (1982, 20th Century-Fox, 101m, c). P&D Robert Mulligan, W Charlie Peters (based on material by Jorge Amado & Bruno Barreto), PH Donald Peterman, M Ralph Burns, ED Sheldon Kahn, PD Philip M. Jefferies.

LP Sally Field (Kay Villano), James Caan (Jolly Villano), Jeff Bridges (Rupert Baines), Paul Dooley (Kendall), Claire Trevor (Charlotte Banning), Mildred Natwick (Mrs. Reilly), Dorothy Fielding (Emily), William Prince (Rev. Hollis), Maryedith Burrell (Mrs. Newman).

This film's romantic triangle consists of young widow Sally Field, her new hus-band Jeff Bridges and the ghost of her deceased husband, James Caan. In the end Caan dematerializes because he realizes he's just in the way. If he had never shown up in the first place there would have been no reason for this humorless comedy.

1599. *Kiss of the Spider Woman†* (1985, Island Alive, US/Brazil, 119m, b&w/c). P David Weisman, D Hector Babenco†, W Leonard Schrader† (based on a novel by Manuel Puig), PH Rodolfo Sanchez, M John Neschling & Nando Carnerio & Wally Badarou, ED Mauro Alice, SD Felipe Crescenti, AD Clovis Bueno.

LP William Hurt* (Luis Molina), Raul Julia (Valentin Arregui), Sonia Braga (Leni Lamaison/Marta/Spider Woman), Jose Lewgoy (Warden), Milton Goncalves (Pedro), Herson Capri (Werner), Miriam Pires (Mother).

Essentially a two-man show, brilliantly created by director Hector Babenco, William Hurt is a homosexual window dresser jailed on a morals charge. He is thrown into a bleak cell with political prisoner Raul Julia in some unnamed South American police state. Their initial distrust turns to friendship and love as Hurt whiles away the time by recalling film plots involving beautiful Sonia Braga, for his cellmate Julia. Hurt is also supposed to be getting information from Julia, but Hurt uses this assignment to get better food and conditions for the two. When Hurt is released, his attempt to become involved in Julia's cause leads to his assassination.

1600. *Kitty and the Bagman* (1983, Quartet, Australia, 95m, c). P Anthony Buckley, D Donald Crombie, W John Burney & Phillip Comford, PH Dean Semler.

LP Liddy Clark (Kitty O'Rourke), Val Lehman (Lil), John Stanton (Bagman), Gerard McGuire (Cyril), Collette Mann (Doris), Reg Evans (Chicka), Kylie Foster (Sarah), Ted Hepple (Sam).

With the help of a crooked cop, Liddy Clark works her way up to become Queen of the Sydney Underworld during the 20s.

1601. *Klondike Fever* (1980, CFI Investments, 106m, c, aka *Jack London's Klondike Fever*). P Gilbert W. Taylor, D

Peter Carter, W Charles E. Israel & Martin Lager, PH Bert Dunk, M Hagood Hardy, ED Stan Cole, PD Seamus Flannery.

LP Jeff East (Jack London), Rod Steiger (Soapy Smith), Angie Dickinson (Belinda McNair), Lorne Greene (Sam Steele), Barry Morse (John Thornton), Michael Hogan (Will Ryan), Merritt Sloper (Robin Gammell).

In a poorly made adventure yarn, Jeff East portrays the young Jack London. He has several misadventures in the Klondike which will eventually be the basis for some of his stories.

1602. *Knightriders* (1981, United Film Distribution, 145m, c). P Richard P. Rubinstein, D&W George A. Romero, PH Michael Gornick, M Donald Rubinstein, ED Romero & Pasquale Buba, PD Cletus Anderson.

LP Ed Harris (Billy), Gary Lahti (Alan), Tom Savini (Morgan), Amy Ingersoll (Linet), Patricia Tallman (Julie), Christine Forrest (Angie), Warner Shook (Pippin), Brother Blue (Merlin), Cynthia Adler (Rocky), John Amplas (Whiteface), Ken Hixon (Steve), John Hostetter (Tuck).

Ed Harris envisions himself as a latter day King Arthur and his motorcycle followers as knights of a modern round table, living by a code similar to that of Camelot. They joust on "hogs" and try to live by an old-fashioned notion of honor. Of course there is an evil adversary, Tom Savini, out to ruin everything.

1603. *Knights and Emeralds* (1986, Warner, GB, 94m, c). P Susan Richards & Raymond Day, D&W Ian Emes, PH Richard Greatrex, M Colin Towns, ED John Victor Smith.

LP Christopher Wild (Kevin), Beverly Hills (Melissa), Warren Mitchell (Kirkpatrick), Bill Leadbitter (Enoch), Rachel Davies (Mrs. Fontain), Tracie Bennett (Tina), Nadim Sawalha (Bindu), Tony Milner (Ted).

Audiences are treated to a pleasant story of a white drummer in a marching band switching to an all-black band just before a big competition.

1604. *Knights of the City* (1986, New World, 87m, c). P Leon Isaac Kennedy &

John C. Strong, III, D Dominic Orlando, W Kennedy (based on a story by Kennedy & David Wilder), PH Rolf Kesterman, M Misha Segal, ED John O'Connor, Nicholas Smith & Paul LaMori.

LP Leon Isaac Kennedy (Troy), Nicholas Campbell (Joey), John Mengatti (Mookie), Stoney Jackson (Eddie), Dino Henderson (Dino), Curtis Lema (Ramrod), Marc Lemberger (Mr. Freeze), Jeff Moldovan (Carlos).

The Royals, one of Miami's tough street gangs, hope to get out of turf warfare games by making a name for themselves as a rock group.

1605. *Kokoda Crescent* (1989, Phillip Emanuel, Australia, 83m, c). P Phillip Emanuel, D Ted Robinson, W Patrick Cook, PH Dan Burstall, M Peter Best, ED Rob Gibson, PD Les Binns.

LP Warren Mitchell (Stan), Bill Kerr (Russ), Ruth Cracknell (Alice), Madge Ryan (Margaret), Martin Vaughan (Eric), Patrick Thompson (Brett), Steve Jacobs (Policeman).

Three World War II vets set out to avenge the death of one's grandson by an overdose of heroin supplied by a corrupt policeman.

1606. *Krull* (1983, Columbia, GB, 117m, c). P Ron Silverman, D Peter Yates, W Stanford Sherman, PH Peter Suschitzky, M James Horner, ED Ray Lovejoy, PD Stephen Grimes, SE Derek Meddings, John Evans & Mark Meddings.

LP Ken Marshall (Colwyn), Lysette Anthony (Lyssa), Freddie Jones (Ynyr), Francesca Annis (Widow of the Web), Alun Armstrong (Torquil), David Battley (Ergo), Bernard Bresslaw (Cyclops), Liam Neeson (Kegan), John Welsh (Seer), Graham McGrath (Titch), Tony Church (Turold).

This sword and sorcery story has borrowed widely from an assortment of adventure films, coming up with the familiar and nonc-too-cxciting story of Ken Marshall's quest to retrieve his fiancée from the Beast who has abducted her.

1607. *Krush Grove* (1985, Warner, 97m, c, aka *Rap Attack*). P Michael Schultz & Doug McHenry, D Schultz, W Ralph Farquhar, PH Ernest Dickerson, M Various Composers, ED Alan J. Koslowski, Jerry Bixman & Conrad M. Gonzalez.

LP Sheila E., Run-D.M.C., The Fat Boys, Kurtis Blow, Blair Underwood, New Edition.

Sometime in the future, this film's name will be the answer in a pop music category of the game show Jeopardy, whose correct question is: "What was the first film to feature rapping?"

1608. *Kung Fu Master* (1989, Expanded Entertainment, 80m, c). P,W&D Agnes Varda (based on a short story by Jane Birkin), PH Pierre-Laurent Chenieux, M Joanna Bruzdowicz, ED Marie-Josee Audiard.

LP Jane Birkin (Mary-Jane), Mathieu Demy (Julien), Charlotte Gainsbourg (Lucy), Lou Doillon (Lou), Eva Simonet (The Friend), Judy Campbell (The Mother), David Birkin (The Father), Andrew Birkin (The Brother).

Forty-year-old Jane Birkin, mother of two daughters, for no apparent reasons fall in love with 15-year-old Mathieu Demy, a schoolmate of her daughter. His greatest ambition is to win a video game called Kung Fu Master. It's the pits.

1609. *L.A. Bounty* (1989, Alpine Releasing Group, 81m, c). P Sybil Danning & Michael W. Leighton, D Worth Keeter, W Leighton (based on a story by Danning), PH Gary Graver, M Howard Leese, ED Stewart Schill.

LP Sybil Danning (Ruger), Wings Hauser (Cavanaugh), Henry Darrow (Lt. Chandler), Lenore Kasdorf (Kelly Rhodes), Robert Hanley (Mike Rhodes), Van Quattro (Michaels), Bob Minor (Martin), Frank Doubleday (Rand), Maxine Wasa (Model), Robert Quarry (Jimmy).

Sybil Danning portrays a macha Clint Eastwood-like bounty hunter on the trail of artist and drug bigwig Wings Hauser, who has kidnapped the mayor.

1610. *L.A. Crackdown* (1988, City Lights, 84m, c). P Joseph Merhi & Richard Pepin, D&W Merhi, PH Pepin, M John Gonzalez, ED Pepin.

LP Pamela Dixon (Karen Shore), Tricia Parks, Kita Harrison, Jeffrey Olsen, Robert D'Lorrio, Michael Coon, Tyron Van Haynes, Achmed Rubell.

City Lights makes movies exclusively for video. Police psychologist Pamela Dixon gives a home to two troubled teenage girls, a black prostitute and a member of a crack-dealing gang who wants to quit. When the last two become victims of the L.A. streets, Dixon vows vengeance.

1611. *L.A. Crackdown II* (1988, City Lights, 87m, c). P Joseph Merhi & Richard Pepin, D&W Merhi, PH Pepin, M John Gonzalez, ED Paul Volk.

LP Pamela Dixon (Karen Shore), Anthony Gates, Joe Vance, Cynthia Miguel, Lisa Anderson, Cheri Reardon, Donna Erickson, Bo Sabato.

In this sequel, dedicated cop Pamela Dixon is seeking a serial killer who has been brutally mutilating taxi dancers.

1612. *L.A. Heat* (1989, PM Entertainment Group, 85m, c). P Joseph Merhi & Richard Pepin, D Merhi, W Charles T. Kanganis, PH Pepin, M John Gonzalez, ED Paul Volk.

LP Lawrence-Hilton Jacobs (Jon Chance), Jim Brown (Captain), Kevin Benton (Clarence), Myles Thoroughgood (Spyder), Pat Johnson (Jane), Jay Richardson (Boris).

Cop Lawrence-Hilton Jacobs dreams of being a Western gunfighter but his L.A. police captain Jim Brown is on his ass to clean up a drug case.

1613. *L.A. Vice* (1989, Raedon, 83m, c). P Richard Pepin & Joseph Merhi, D Merhi, W Charles T. Kanganis, PH F. Smith Martin, M John Gonzalez, ED Steve Waller, AD Matt Manis.

LP Lawrence-Hilton Jacobs (Jon Chance), William Smith (Capt. Joe Wilks), Jean Levine (Evelyn), Jastereo Coviare (Bear), Bonnie Paine (Victoria).

In this sequel to L.A. Heat, Lawrence-Hilton Jacobs is assigned to a big kidnapping case. He calls his former Captain, William Smith, out of retirement to act as backup. Unfortunately Smith is killed and Jacobs quits the police force, but not the case.

1614. *La Bamba* (1987, Columbia, 108m, c). P Taylor Hackford & Bill Borden, D&W Luis Valdez, PH Adam Greenberg, M Carlos Santana & Miles Goodman, ED Sheldon Kahn & Don Bruchu, PD Vince Cresciman.

LP Lou Diamond Phillips (Ritchie Valens), Esai Morales (Bob Morales), Rosana De Soto (Connie Valenzuela),

Elizabeth Pena (Rosie Morales), Danielle von Zerneck (Donna Ludwig), Joe Pantoliano (Bob Keene), Rick Dees (Ted Quillin), Marshall Crenshaw (Buddy Holly), Howard Huntsberry (Jackie Wilson).

The film is a poignant, sensitive detailing of the short life of Ricardo Valenzuela, who as Ritchie Valens would produce two smash rock 'n' roll hits "Donna" and "La Bamba" in the late 50s. Lou Diamond Phillips is excellent as the talented Mexican-American who came out of barrio poverty in the San Fernando Valley to be a rock shooting star. He died when the plane carrying him, Buddy Holly and J.P. Richardson, The Big Bopper, crashed in a snow storm in 1959, killing all aboard. Also excellent in the film is Esai Morales as Phillips' half-brother, torn by his pride for his brother and his jealousy.

1615. *La Traviata* (1982, Universal, 105m, c). P Tarak Ben Ammar, D&W Franco Zeffirelli (based on the libretto of Francesco Maria Piave from the novel by Alexandre Dumas entitled *The Lady of the Camelias*), PH Ennio Guarnieri, M Giuseppe Verdi, ED Peter Taylor & Franca Sylvi, MD James Levine, PD Zeffirelli, AD/SD Zeffirelli & Gianni Quaranta*, COS Piero Tosi†.

LP Teresa Stratas (Violetta Valery), Placido Domingo (Alfredo Germont), Cornell MacNeil (Giorgio Germont), Alan Monk (Baron), Axelle Gall (Flora Betvoix), Pina Cei (Annina), Maurizio Barbacini (Gastone), Robert Sommer (Doctor Grenvil), Ricardo Oneto (Marquis d'Obigny).

Teresa Stratas and Placido Domingo are outstanding as the doomed lovers in this emotionally charged production of the Verdi opera. The arias are sung in Italian with English subtitles. The camera work by Ennio Guarnieri is ideal.

1616. *Labyrinth* (1986, Tri-Star, 101m, c). P Eric Rattray, D Jim Henson, W Terry Jones (based on a story by Dennis Lee & Jim Henson), PH Alex Thomson, M Trevor Jones, ED John Grover, PD Elliot Scott, SE George Gibbs, SONGS David Bowie, COS Brian Froud.

LP David Bowie (Jareth), Jennifer Connelly (Sarah), Toby Froud (Toby), Shelley Thompson (Stepmother), Christopher Malcolm (Father), Natalie Finland (Fairy), Shari Weiser & Brian Henson (Hoggle), Ron Mueck & Rob Mills (Ludo).

Jennifer Connelly wishes that her baby brother be taken away by goblins, and she gets her wish. To rescue him, she must enter the Castle and face David Bowie, but before she gets to the castle, she must get through the Labyrinth.

1617. *Ladder of Swords* (1989, Film Four International, GB, 98m, c). P Jennifer Howarth, D Norman Hull, W Neil Clarke (based on a story by Clarke & Hull), PH Thaddeus O'Sullivan, M Stanley Myers, ED Scott Thomas, PD Caroline Hananis.

LP Martin Shaw (Don Demarco), Eleanor David (Denise Demarco), Bob Peck (Det. Insp. Atherton), Juliet Stevenson (Alice Howard), Simon Molloy (Sgt. Bilby), Pearce Quigley (Constable Lowe), Anthony Benson (Grumpy Gun).

When his wife leaves him and his performing bear dies, circus performer Martin Shaw takes comfort with widow Juliet Stevenson. He comes up with a new act in which he ascends a ladder of upturned Samurai swords.

1618. *Ladies and Gentlemen, the Fabulous Stains* (1982, Paramount, 87m, c). P Joe Roth, D Lou Adler, W Rob Morton, PH Bruce Surtees, ED Tom Benko, PD Leon Erickson.

LP Diane Lane (Corinne Burns), Ray Winstone (Billy), Peter Donat (Harley Dennis), David Clennon (Dave Robell), John Lehne (Stu McGrath), Cynthia Sikes (Alicia Meeker), Laura Dern (Jessica McNeil), Marin Kanter (Tracy Burns).

Diane Lane heads up an all-girl, no-talent punk rock group, whose trademark is skunkish died hair and the motto "We don't put out." By accident they become an overnight sensation, receive a gold record, appear on the cover of People magazine and make a music video. Ah, fame!

1619. *The Ladies Club* (1986, New Line Cinema, 90m, c). P Nick J. Mileti & Paul Mason, D A.K. Allen, W Mason & Fran Lewis Ebeling (based on the novel *Sisterhood* by Betty Black & Casey

Bishop), PH Adam Greenberg, M Lalo
Schifrin, ED Marion Segal & Randall
Torno, PD Stephen Myles Berger.

LP Karen Austin (Joan Taylor), Diana
Scarwid (Lucy Bricker), Christine Bel-
ford (Dr. Constance Lewis), Bruce Davi-
son (Richard Harrison), Shera Danese
(Eva), Beverly Todd (Georgiane), Mari-
lyn Kagan (Rosalie), Kit McDonough
(Carol), Arliss Howard (Ed Bricker),
Randee Heller (Harriet).

Victimized by brutal rapes, a determined group of women take matters in
their own hands when the courts set their
attackers free. The members of the
Ladies Club decide that castration is the
proper justice for the men who made
them suffer. While the outrage of rape
victims is understandable, the dramatic
quality of the movie and the acting leaves
much to be desired.

1620. *Ladies of the Lotus* (1987,
North American Pictures, Canada, 88m,
c). P John A. Curtis & Lloyd A. Simandl,
D Simandl & Douglas C. Nicolle, W Jane
Mengering Hausen, PH Victor Nicolle,
M Greg Ray, ED Simandl & D. Nicolle,
PD Lynn J. Grantham.

LP Richard Dale (Phillip), Angela
Read (Dominique), Patrick Bermel
(Sean), Darcia Carnie (Tara), Martin
Evans, Nathan Andrews, Lisanne Burk,
April Alkins.

Girls from the New Horizons modeling
agency are in great demand—so much so
that someone is kidnapping them and
selling them into white slavery. They are
forced to work at Lotus, Inc., a modeling
studio which is a front for drug distribution and prostitution. The film offers
voyeurs, that is viewers, ample opportunity to see pretty girls in various stages
of undress. There's not much in the way
of cinematic value.

1621. *Lady and the Tramp* (1988 Re-
release, Disney, animated, 75m, c). D
Hamilton Luske & Clyde Geronimi, W
Ward Greene, M Oliver Wallace, SONGS
Peggy Lee & Oliver Wallace.

VOICES Peggy Lee (Darling, Peg, Si,
Am), Barbara Luddy (Lady), Larry
Roberts (Tramp), Bill Thompson (Jock,
Bull, Daschie), Bill Baucon (Trusty),
Stan Freberg (Beaver).

Continuing their long-standing policy,
the Disney studio re-released the 1955
favorite featuring a cocker spaniel named
Lady and a handsome mongrel called
Tramp who fall in love in circa 1910. As
with most human romances, the canine
affair's road is not without its bumps and
pains. Miss Peggy Lee is outstanding
singing three of the five songs she wrote
for the feature, including "He's a Tramp."

1622. *Lady Avenger* (1989, Marco
Colombo, 82m, c). P John Schouweiler &
David De Coteau, D De Coteau, W Will
Schmitz & Keith Kaczorek, PH Thomas
Callaway, M Jay Levy, ED Miriam L.
Preissel & Mary Schmitz, PD Royce
Mathew.

LP Peggie Sanders (Maggie Blair),
Tony Josephs (Jack), Jacolyn Leeman
(Mary), Michelle Bauer (Annaline),
Daniel Hirsch (Ray), Bill Butler (Kevin).

This direct to video release has Peggie
Sanders starring as a marauding female
avenging force. She has just escaped from
prison and is on the trail of the gang that
murdered her brother.

1623. *Lady Beware* (1987, Interna-
tional Video Entertainment, 108m, c). P
Tony Scotti & Lawrence Taylor Mortorff,
D Karen Arthur, W Susan Miller &
Charles Zev Cohen, PH Tom Neuwirth,
M Craig Safan, ED Roy Watts.

LP Diane Lane (Katya Yarno), Michael Woods (Jack Price), Cotter Smith
(Mac Odell), Peter Nevargic (Lionel), Edward Penn (Thayer), Tyra Ferrell (Nan).

Diane Lane sets tongues a-wagging
with her erotic, provocative window dis-
plays for a stodgy old downtown Pittsburgh department store. Her work also
attracts a psychopathic admirer.

1624. *Lady Grey* (1980, Maverick,
100m, c). P Earl Owensby, D Worth
Keeter, W Tom McIntyre, PH Darrell
Cathcart, M Arthur Smith & Clay Smith,
ED Jim Laudenslager.

LP Ginger Alden (Lady Grey), David
Allen Coe (Black Jack Donovan), Paul
Ott (Don Sands), Herman Bloodsworth
(Johnny Nyland), Ed Grady (Hubbard
Jackson), Paula Baldwin (Pru).

Apparently Ginger Alden got this film
opportunity on the basis of being Elvis
Presley's last love. As a country femme
fatale singer, Alden makes Elvis, by comparison, look like John Gielgud.

1625. *Lady in White* (1988, New Century/Vista, 112m, c). P Andrew G. La Marca & Frank LaLoggia, D&W LaLoggia, PH Russell Carpenter, M LaLoggia, ED Steve Mann, PD Richard K. Hummel.

LP Lukas Haas (Frankie Scarlatti), Len Cariou (Phil), Alex Rocco (Angelo Scarlatti), Katherine Helmond (Amanda), Jason Presson (Geno Scarlatti), Renata Vanni (Mama Assunta), Angelo Bertolini (Papa Charlie), Jared Rushton (Donald).

Young Lukas Haas encounters the ghost of a murdered girl when he's locked into a classroom cloakroom as a prank. He is determined to solve the crime. Despite a strong atmosphere for the supernatural, the film is just too long.

1626. *Lady Jane* (1986, Paramount, GB, 144m, c). P Peter Snell, D Trevor Nunn, W David Edgar (based on a story by Chris Bryant), PH Douglas Slocombe, M Stephen Oliver, ED Anne V. Coates, PD Allan Cameron, COS Sue Blane & David Perry, AD Fred Carter, Martyn Hebert & Mark Raggett, SD Harry Cordwell.

LP Helena Bonham Carter (Lady Jane Grey), Cary Elwes (Guilford Dudley), John Wood (John Dudley, Duke of Northumberland), Michael Hordern (Dr. Feckenham), Jill Bennett (Mrs. Ellen), Jane Lapotaire (Princess Mary), Sara Kestelman (Frances Grey, Duchess of Suffolk), Patrick Stewart (Henry Grey, Duke of Suffolk), Warren Saire (King Edward VI), Joss Ackland (Sir John Bridges), Ian Hogg (Sir John Gates).

The film is based on the true story of the 16-year-old girl who reluctantly found herself married and made Queen of England after the death of young King Edward VI. Her reign was but nine days, after which both she and her young husband were sent to the chopping clock by Princess Mary. It's a well-produced film, with likeable performances from Helena Bonham Carter and Cary Elwes as the doomed young lovers.

1627. *Lady, Stay Dead* (1982, Ryntare, Australia, 95m, c). P,D&W Terry Rourke, PH Ray Henman, M Bob Young.

LP Chard Hayward (Gordon), Louise Howitt, Deborah Coulls, Roger Ward.

Gardener Chard Hayward murders a woman, hoping that will solve his problems, but he's called in to use this means of dealing with his difficulties again and again.

1628. *The Lady Vanishes* (1980, Rank, GB, 99m, c). P Tom Sachs, D Anthony Page, W George Axelrod (based on the novel by Ethel Lina White), PH Douglas Slocombe, M Richard Hartley, ED Russell Lloyd, PD Wilfred Shingleton.

LP Elliott Gould (Robert Condon), Cybill Shepherd (Amanda Kelly), Angela Lansbury (Miss Froy), Herbert Lom (Dr. Hartz), Arthur Lowe (Charters), Ian Carmichael (Caldicott), Gerald Harper (Mr. Todhunter), Jean Anderson (Baroness Kisling), Jenny Runacre (Mrs. Todhunter).

For those who loved Hitchcock's 1938 thriller, this remake should be avoided at all costs. Angela Lansbury portrays the British spy who mysteriously disappears on an European passenger train. She is missed only by Cybill Shepherd; all others have their own reasons for denying ever having seen Lansbury. As it is in color, we assume the film must have been made for those younger types who subscribe to Ted Turner's adage that black and white movies are not worth viewing.

1629. *Ladyhawke* (1985, Warner/20th Century–Fox, 121m, c). P Richard Donner & Lauren Shuler, D Donner, W Edward Khmara, Michael Thomas & Tom Mankiewicz (based on a story by Khmara), PH Vittorio Storaro, M Andrew Powell, ED Stuart Baird, PD Wolf Kroeger, SOUND Les Fresholtz, Dick Alexander, Vern Poore & Bud Alper†, SOUND EFFECTS ED Bob Henderson & Alan Murray†.

LP Matthew Broderick (Phillipe Gaston), Rutger Hauer (Navarre), Michelle Pfeiffer (Isabeau), Leo McKern (Imperius), John Wood (Bishop), Ken Hutchison (Marquet), Alfred Molina (Cezar), Giancarlo Prete (Fornac), Loris Loddi (Jehan), Alessandro Serra (Mr. Pitou).

Looking more unearthly beautiful than any woman has a right to, Michelle Pfeiffer and her lover, mysterious knight Rutger Hauer, have been enchanted by evil 13th century bishop John Wood.

Having lost his mistress Pfeiffer to Hauer's love, Wood calls down a curse on the two. By day Hauer is a man, by night he is a wolf, while Pfeiffer is a woman at night and a hawk during the day. Thus they are always together, but never together. With the help of young pickpocket Matthew Broderick and Leo Mc-Kern, a remorseful priest who had betrayed the pair to the bishop, and the help of an ellipse, a way is found to break the curse.

1630. *The Lair of the White Worm* (1988, Vestron, GB, 94m, c). P,D&W Ken Russell (based on the novel by Bram Stoker), PH Dick Bush, M Stanislas Syrewicz, ED Peter Davies, SE Geoff Portass.

LP Amanda Donohoe (Lady Sylvia Marsh), Hugh Grant (Lord James D'Ampton), Catherine Oxenberg (Eve Trent), Sammi Davis (Mary Trent), Peter Capaldi (Angus Flint), Stratford Johns (Peters), Paul Brooke (P.C. Erny), Imogen Claire (Dorothy Trent), Chris Pitt (Kevin), Christopher Gable (Joe Grant), Lloyd Peters (Jesus Christ).

This offbeat horror film deals with the worship of an ancient worm/snake kept by a vampire-like creature Amanda Donohoe. She is seeking a nice virgin for the worm and believes that Catherine Oxenberg will fit the bill, but the latter is rescued just in the nick of time by Scottish archaeologist Peter Capaldi, the local lord, Christopher Gable, and Oxenberg's sister Sammi Davis.

1631. *Lamb* (1985, Films Four, GB, 109m, c). D Colin Gregg, W Bernard MacLaverty (based on his novel), PH Mike Garfath, M Van Morrison, ED Peter Delfgou.

LP Liam Neeson (Michael Lamb), Ian Bannen (Owen Kane), Frances Tomelty, Dudley Sutton, Hugh O'Conor.

Hugh O'Conor, an epileptic youngster, and understanding Christian brother Liam Neeson develop a friendship at the reform school where the lad is sent when he gets into trouble. Neeson attempts to fill the void in the boy's life caused by the death of his father.

Lamp see The Outing

1632. *The Land Before Time* (1988, Universal, animated, 70m, c). P Don Bluth, Gary Goldman & John Pomeroy, D Bluth, W Stu Krieger (based on a story by Judy Freudberg & Tony Geiss), M James Horner, ED Dan Molina & John K. Carr, PD Bluth.

VOICES Pat Hingle (Narrator/Rooter), Helen Shaver (Littlefoot's Mother), Gabriel Damon (Littlefoot), Candice Houston (Cera), Burker Barnes (Daddy Topps), Judith Barsi (Ducky), Will Ryan (Petrie).

This delightful animated tale is the story of a fatherless baby Brontosaurus named Littlefoot who must depend on his mother and ancient grandparents for support. Soon thereafter his mother is killed fighting off a vicious Tyrannosaurus Rex, and Littlefoot is separated from his grandparents. He will eventually lead other baby dinosaurs to the fabled Great Valley to be reunited with their families.

1633. *The Land of No Return* (1981, International Picture Show, 84m, c, aka *Challenge to Survive; Snowman*). P&D Kent Bateman, W Bateman & Frank Ray Perilli, PH Joao Fernandes, M Ralph Geddes, ED Dick Alweis.

LP Mel Torme (Zak O'Brien), William Shatner (Curt Benell), Donald Moffat (Air Traffic Controller), "Caesar" (The Eagle), "Romulus" (The Wolf).

What is "The Velvet Fog" Mel Torme doing in a film about a TV animal trainer whose private airplane crashes in the rugged peaks of Utah? Looking terribly out of place, that's what. Where's the lounge show?

1634. *Landlord Blues* (1988, Double Helix Films, 96m, c). P&D Jacob Burckhardt, W Burckhardt & William Gordy (based on a story by George Schneeman), PH Carl Teitelbaum, M Roy Nathanson & Marc Ribot, ED Burckhardt & Gordy, PD Wendy Walker.

LP Mark Boone, Jr. (George), Raye Dowell (Viv), Richard Litt (Albert Streck), Bill Rice (Roth), Rosemary Moore (Mrs. Streck), Susan Lydia Williams (Rose), George Schneeman (Walter), Mary Schultz (Drug Queen).

Mark Boone, Jr., is the proud owner of a bike shop located on Manhattan's Lower East Side. His greedy yuppie landlord Richard Litt, who sells cocaine on the side to support his wife's expensive lifestyle, is trying to break Boone's lease so he can rent the space to an art gallery at highly inflated prices. Things go from bad to worse, leading to murder.

1635. *Las Vegas Weekend* (1985, Shapiro, 82m, c). P,D&W Dale Trevillion, PH Christopher Tufty, M Scarlet Rivera & Alan St. Johns, ED David Kern.

LP Barry Hickey (Percy Doolittle), Jace Damon, Macka Foley, Vickie Benson, Kimberlee Kaiser, Dyanne DiRosario, Ray Dennis Steckler.

In a thoroughly dumb movie, Barry Hickey is a chubby computer expert who tries the gambling tables of Las Vegas. He jumps into the world of high stakes with both feet, but no brains.

1636. *Lassiter* (1984, Warner, GB, 100m, c). P Albert S. Ruddy, D Roger Young, W David Taylor, PH Gil Taylor, M Ken Thorne, ED Benjamin A. Weissman & Richard Hiscott, PD Peter Mullins.

LP Tom Selleck (Lassiter), Jane Seymour (Sara), Lauren Hutton (Kari), Bob Hoskins (Becker), Joe Regalbuto (Breeze), Ed Lauter (Smoke), Warren Clarke (Max Hofer), Edward Peel (Allyce), Paul Antrim (Askew).

Set in London in 1934, popular TV star Tom Selleck portrays a suave jewel thief. He is forced by the British and American governments to accept an assignment of pilfering some $10 million in diamonds from the German embassy meant to help the Nazi plans of aggression in Europe.

1637. *The Last American Virgin* (1982, Cannon, 90m, c). P Menahem Golan & Yoram Globus, D&W Boaz Davidson, PH Adam Greenberg, ED Bruria Davidson.

LP Lawrence Monoson (Gary), Diane Franklin (Karen), Steve Antin (Rick), Joe Rubbo (David), Louisa Moritz (Carmela), Brian Peck (Victor), Kimmy Robertson (Rose), Tessa Richarde (Brenda), Winifred Freedman (Millie), Gerri Idol (Roxanne).

In yet another teen sexploitation film, three high school friends, a hunk, the class clown and a sensitive type have little on their minds other than sex. Why do so many directors and screenwriters feel obligated to celebrate their coming of age through such dreary and smutty films?

1638. *The Last Chase* (1981, Crown International, 101m, c). P&D Martyn Burke, W C.R. O'Christopher, Taylor Sutherland & Burke, PH Paul Van Der Linden, M Gil Melle, ED Steve Weslake.

LP Lee Majors (Frank Hart), Burgess Meredith (Capt. Williams), Chris Makepeace (Ring), Alexandra Stewart (Eudora), George Touliatos (Hawkings), Ben Gordon (Morely), Diane D'Aquila (Santana).

Late in the 80s, oil shortages cause the abandonment of automobile travel. Twenty years later ex-race car driver Lee Majors rebuilds his old Porsche and becomes a symbol of freedom as he races all over the country.

1639. *The Last Dragon* (1985, Tri-Star, 109m, c, aka *Berry Gordon's The Last Dragon*). P Rupert Hitzig, D Michael Schultz, W Louis Venosta, PH James A. Contner, M Misha Segal, ED Christopher Holmes, PD Peter Larkin.

LP Taimak (Leroy), Vanity (Laura), Christopher Murney (Eddie Arkadian), Julius J. Carry III (Sho' Nuff), Faith Prince (Angela), Leo O'Brien (Richie), Mike Starr (Rock), Jim Moody (Daddy Green).

Would-be kung-fu master Taimak gets mixed up with glamorous video deejay Vanity and some mean gangsters. He kicks the hell out of the baddies. It's silly but as things go in martial arts pictures, it's not too bad.

1640. *The Last Emperor** (1987, Columbia, 160m, c). P Jeremy Thomas, D Bernardo Bertolucci*, W Mark Peploe & Bertolucci*, PH Vittorio Storaro*, M Ryuichi Sakamoto, David Byrne & Cong Su*, ED Gabriella Cristiani*, PD Ferdinando Scarfiotti*, AD/SD Scarfiotti, Bruno Cesari & Osvaldo Desideri*, COS James Acheson*, SOUND Bill Rowe & Ivan Sharrock*.

LP John Lone (Aisin-Gioro "Henry" Pu Yi as an adult), Joan Chen (Wan Jung, "Elizabeth"), Peter O'Toole (Reginald Johnston, "R.J."), Ying Ruocheng (The Governor), Victor Wong (Chen Pao Shen), Dennis Dun (Big Li), Ryuichi Sakamoto (Masahiko Amakasu), Maggie Han (Eastern Jewel), Ric Young (Interrogator), Wu Jun Mei (Wen Hsiu), Cary Hiroyuki Tagawa (Chang), Jade Go (Ar

Mo), Richard Vuu (Pu Yi, age 3), Tijger Tsou (Pu Yi, age 8), Wu Tao (Pu Yi, age 15), Lisa Lu (Tzu Hsui, The Empress Dowager).

We've disagreed with the Academy of Motion Picture Arts and Sciences before. While we admired many things about this movie, we wouldn't vote for it as best picture of the year. Any film that gets us to wondering when it will end, no matter how well made and no matter how intriguing the subject matter, just isn't our notion of best. Having said that we are happy to add our voices of praise for this most interesting telling of the life of China's last emperor. At the age of three, he was brought by the Empress Dowager to the Forbidden City to become the new emperor. He essentially becomes a captive of the thieving eunuchs who run the place, until with the help of his tutor, Englishman Peter O'Toole, his wife Joan Chen and concubine Wu Jen Mei, he kicks them out. Later in the person of John Lone he is expelled from the Forbidden City by an invading warlord. He is given safe conduct to Tientsin by the Japanese, where he lives the life of a playboy. He allows the Japanese to install him as a puppet emperor, a crime which earns him a prison sentence and re-education by the Communists after World War II. He is finally released, a meek, aging man who works as a gardener until his death in 1967.

1641. *The Last Fight* (1983, Movie and Pictures International, 86m, c). P Jerry Masucci, D&W Fred Williamson (based on a story by Masucci), PH James Limmo, M Jay Chattaway, ED Daniel Loewenthal.

LP Willie Colon (Joaquin Vargas), Ruben Blades (Andy "Kid" Clave), Fred Williamson (Jesse Crowder), Joe Spinell (Boss), Darlanne Fluegel (Sally), Nereida Mercado (Nancy), Anthony Sirico (Frankie).

Nightclub singer Ruben Blades takes to the boxing ring when his debts pile up. He gets a shot at the champ but loses. Too bad!

1642. *The Last Flight of Noah's Ark* (1980, Buena Vista, 97m, c). P Ron Miller, D Charles Jarrott, W Steven W. Carabatsos, Sandy Glass & George Ar-

thur Bloom (based on the story by Ernest K. Gann), PH Charles F. Wheeler, M Maurice Jarre, ED Gordon D. Brenner.

LP Elliott Gould (Noah Dugan), Genevieve Bujold (Bernadette Lafleur), Ricky Schroder (Bobby), Tammy Lauren (Julie), Vincent Gardenia (Stoney), John Fujioka (Cleveland), Yuki Shimoda (Hiro), Dana Elcar (Benchley), Ruth Manning (Charlotte Braithwaite).

In another sweetness and light Disney movie, crabby pilot Elliott Gould is talked into flying some animals to an island. Unbeknownst to him, Ricky Schroder and Tammy Lauren stow away. The plane crashes on a small island inhabited by two Japanese soldiers who haven't been informed that World War II has come to an end.

The Last Great Treasure* see *Mother Lode

1643. *The Last Horror Film* (1984, Twin Continental Films, 87m, c, aka *The Fanatic*). P Judd Hamilton & David Winters, D Winters, W Hamilton, Winters & Tom Chasen, PH Tom De Nove, M Jesse Frederick & Jeff Koz, ED Chris Barnes & Edward Salier, PD Geoff Sharpe.

LP Caroline Munro (Jana Bates), Joe Spinell (Vinny Durand), Judd Hamilton (Alan Cunningham), Devin Goldenberg (Marty Bernstein), David Winters (Stanley Kline), Stanley Susanne Benton (Susan Archer).

This nonsensical slasher film (is there any other kind?), has taxidriver Joe Spinell following actress Caroline Munro to Cannes, because he believes under his direction she can become a great star. She thinks he's nuts when he details his plan to her after breaking into her bathroom while she's taking a bath. It's something of an understatement to say he's not pleased with her reaction.

1644. *The Last Hunter* (1984, World Northal, Italy, 95m, c, aka *Hunter of the Apocalypse*). P Gianfranco Couyoumdjian, D Anthony M. Dawson (Antonio Margheriti), W Dardano Sacchetti, PH Riccardo Pallottini, M Franco Micalizzi, ED Alberto Moriani.

LP David Warbeck (Capt. Harry Morris), Tisa Farrow (Jane), Tony King (Sgt.

Washington), Bobby Rhodes (Carlos), Margit Evelyn Newton (Carol), John Steiner (Maj. Cash).

In a very forgettable flick, soldier David Warbeck fights for his life behind enemy lines during the Vietnam War.

1645. *The Last Married Couple in America* (1980, Universal, 103m, c). P Edward S. Feldman & John Herman Shaner, D Gilbert Cates, W Shaner, PH Ralph Woolsey, M Charles Fox, ED Peter E. Berger.

LP George Segal (Jeff Thomson), Natalie Wood (Mari Thomson), Richard Benjamin (Marv Cooper), Arlene Golonka (Sally Cooper), Alan Arbus (Al), Marilyn Sokol (Alice Squib), Oliver Clark (Max Dryden), Priscilla Barnes (Helena Dryden), Dom DeLuise (Walter Holmes), Valerie Harper (Barbara), Bob Dishy (Howard).

George Segal and Natalie Wood are concerned that so many of their married friends are getting divorces. Their marriage seems safe until Valerie Harper, a friend of Wood, makes Segal an offer he can't refuse. As a result he picks up a social disease from Harper which he passes on to Wood. It looks like the end for another marriage, but after Segal and Wood experiment with some new young partners, they discover they still love each other. The film ends with them in reconciliation — but for how long?

1646. *Last Night at the Alamo* (1984, Cinecom, 80m, c). P Kim Henkel & Eagle Pennell, D Pennell, W Henkel, PH Brian Huberman & Eric Edwards, M Chuck Pennell & Wayne Bell, ED Eagle Pennell.

LP Sonny Carl Davis (Cowboy), Louis Perryman (Claude), Steven Matilla (Ichabod), Tina-Bess Hubbard (Mary), Amanda LaMar (Lisa), Peggy Pinnell (Ginger), Doris Hargrave (Janice), J. Michael Hammond (Steve).

A lot of good ole boys gather in a soon to be torn down Houston watering-hole for one final blowout. They drink, swear and lie a lot as they see part of their life passing them by, without knowing what to do about it.

1647. *The Last of the Knucklemen* (1981, Hexagon, Australia, 93m, c). P,D&W Tim Burstall (based on the play by John Powers), PH Dan Burstall, M Bruce Smeaton, ED Edward McQueen-Mason.

LP Gerard Kennedy (Tarzan), Michael Preston (Pansy), Peter Hehir (Tom), Michael Duffield (Methuselah), Dennis Miller (Horse), Stephen Bisley (Mad Dog), Michael Caton (Monk), Stewart Faichney (Tassie).

Gerard Kennedy is in charge of a group of disgruntled mining town workers. Perpetual braggart Michael Preston gets on Kennedy's nerves and finally he must give Preston a well-deserved beating.

1648. *Last Plane Out* (1983, New World, 92m, c). P Jack Cox & David Nelson, D Nelson, W Ernest Tidyman, PH Jacques Haitkin.

LP Jan-Michael Vincent (Jack), Julie Carmen (Maria), Mary Crosby (Liz), David Huffman (Jim), William Windom (James), Lloyd Battista (Anastasio Somoza), Yeg Wilson (Harry), Anthony Feijo (Ramon).

Texas journalist Jan-Michael Vincent, sent on assignment to Nicaragua, falls in love with Julie Carmen, a Sandinista rebel.

1649. *Last Resort* (1986, Concorde, 84m, c, aka *Club Sandwich*). P Julie Corman, D Zane Buzby, W Steve Zacharias & Jeff Buhai, PH Stephen Katz & Alex Nepomniaschy, M Steve Nelson & Thom Sharp, ED Gregory Scherick, PD Curtis A. Schnell.

LP Charles Grodin (George Lollar), Robin Pearson Rose (Sheila Lollar), John Ashton (Phil Cocoran), Ellen Blake (Dorothy Cocoran), Megan Mullally (Jessica Lollar), Christopher Ames (Brad Lollar), Scott Nemes (Bobby Lollar).

In a tasteless and witless comedy, recently unemployed Charles Grodin impulsively takes his oversexed family to a Club-Med like vacation resort. The results are predictable and the laughs almost nonexistent.

1650. *Last Rites* (1980, Cannon, 88m, c, aka *Dracula's Last Rites*). P Kelly Van Horn, D Domonic Paris, W Ben Donnelly & Paris, PH Paris, M Paul Jost & George Small, ED Elizabeth Lombardo.

LP Patricia Lee Hammond, Gerald Fielding, Victor Jorge, Michael Lally, Mimi Weddell.

A vampire mortician in cahoots with the local sheriff and doctor harasses a family whose surname is Fonda. It's a horrible horror picture.

1651. *Last Rites* (1988, MGM/United Artists, 103m, c). P Donald P. Bellisario & Patrick McCormick, D&W Bellisario, PH David Watkin, M Bruce Broughton, ED Pembroke J. Herring, PD Peter Larkin.

LP Tom Berenger (Father Michael Pace), Daphne Zuniga (Angela), Chick Vennera (Nuzo), Anne Twomey (Zena Pace), Dane Clark (Carlo Pace), Paul Dooley (Father Freddie), Vassili Lambrinos (Tio).

Tom Berenger must struggle with his conscience over questions of responsibility, loyalty, abstinence and the sanctity of the confessional as he portrays a Catholic priest who is the son of a Mafia chief.

1652. *The Last Starfighter* (1984, Universal, 101m, c). P Gary Adelson & Edward O. DeNault, D Nick Castle, W Jonathan Betuel, PH King Baggot, M Craig Safan, ED C. Timothy O'Meara, PD Ron Cobb.

LP Lance Guest (Alex Rogan), Dan O'Herlihy (Grig), Catherine Mary Stewart (Maggie Gordon), Barbara Bosson (Jane Rogan), Norman Snow (Xur), Robert Preston (Centauri), Kay E. Kuter (Enduran), Chris Hebert (Louis Rogan), Dan Mason (Lord Kril), John O'Leary (Rylan Bursar).

Young Lance Guest, a whiz at a video game called "Starfighter," finds himself whisked off to another galaxy to become a real starfighter and help save this universe from the evil Kodan forces which are attacking the Star League.

1653. *The Last Temptation of Christ* (1988, Universal, 164m, c). P Barbara De Fina, D Martin Scorsese†, W Paul Schrader (based on the novel by Nikos Kazantzakis), PH Michael Ballhaus, M Peter Gabriel, ED Thelma Schoonmaker, PD John Beard.

LP Willem Dafoe (Jesus Christ), Harvey Keitel (Judas), Barbara Hershey (Mary Magdalene), Harry Dean Stanton (Saul/Paul), David Bowie (Pontius Pilate), Verna Bloom (Mary, Mother of Jesus), Andre Gregory (John the Baptist), Juliette Caton (Girl Angel), Roberts Blossom (Aged Master), Irvin Kershner (Zebedee), Tomas Arana (Lazarus).

Martin Scorsese and his movie have been lambasted by fundamentalists who haven't seen the film, because as in Nikos Kazantzakis's novel he has chosen to concentrate on Jesus Christ's human nature, rather than portray him as a thoroughly confident divinity at all times, as has been the case in most films about Christ. For those who have been taught that Christ was both God and man, this shouldn't be so shocking. Even his natural sexual instincts, aroused by Mary Magdalene, seem natural and appropriate for a man who was tempted in the desert by Satan but withstood it. It shouldn't be any trick for God to renounce the devil's temptations, but for a man it takes considerable strength of character. With all the hullabaloo about the picture, judging it as a drama seems to be lost. While Willem Dafoe is quite good in the title role, others, especially Harry Dean Stanton and David Bowie, are miscast and the dialogue includes the usual boring pithy clichés which producers often mistake for reverence.

1654. *The Last Unicorn* (1982, ITC, animated, 84m, c). P&D Arthur Rankin, Jr. & Jules Bass, W Peter S. Beagle (based on the novel by Beagle), PH Hiroyasu Omoto, M Jimmy Webb, ED Tomoko Kida, PD Rankin.

VOICES Alan Arkin (Schmendrick the Magician), Jeff Bridges (Prince Lir), Mia Farrow (The Last Unicorn/Lady Amalthea), Tammy Grimes (Molly Grue), Robert Klein (The Butterfly), Angela Lansbury (Mommy Fortuna), Christopher Lee (King Haggard), Keenan Wynn (Capt. Cully), Paul Frees (The Talking Cat), Rene Auberjonois (The Speaking Skull).

Mia Farrow is the voice of a unicorn whose mission is to free others of her kind from an evil king. It's a lovely piece of animation.

1655. *The Last Warrior* (1989, SVS/ITC, GB, 94m, c, aka *Coastwatcher*). P Keith Watkins, D&W Martin Wragge, PH Fred Tammes, M Adrian Strijdom, ED Jacqueline Le Cordeur.

LP Gary Graham (Jim Kemp), Maria Holvoe (Katherine), Cary-Hiroyuki Tagawa (Imperial Marine), John Carson (Priest).

Gary Graham, a man of the 80s, is transported back in time to a Japanese controlled World War II island. He shares the danger with beautiful novice nun Maria Holvoe. Didn't we see this with Robert Mitchum and Deborah Kerr in *Heaven Knows, Mr. Allison?*

1656. *Latino* (1985, Cinecom International, 105m, c). P Benjamin Berg, D&W Haskell Wexler, PH Tom Sigel, M Diane Louie, ED Robert Dalva.

LP Robert Beltran (Eddie Guerrero), Annette Cardona (Marlena), Tony Plana (Ruben), Julio Medina (Edgar Salasar), Gavin McFadden (Metcalf), Luis Torrentes (Luis), Juan Carlos Ortiz (Juan Carlos), Marta Tenorio (Rosa-Madre).

Chicano Vietnam Green Beret vet Robert Beltran is in Honduras, advising the U.S.-backed Nicaraguan Contras. He falls for Annette Cardona, a supporter of the Sandinistas, causing him to undergo a moral re-evaluation of his position. For some this will be considered left-wing propaganda, for others it is the gospel truth. Let the viewer decide.

1657. *Laughter House* (1984, Film Four, GB, 93m, c, aka *Singleton's Pluck*). P Ann Scott, D Richard Eyre, W Brian Glover, PH Clive Tickner, M Dominic Meldowney, ED David Martin.

LP Ian Holm (Ben Singleton), Penelope Wilton (Alice Singleton), Stephanie Tague (Emma Singleton), Bill Owen (Amos Lintott), Richard Hope (Hubert), Aran Bell (Tristram), Rosemary Martin (Sylvia).

Ian Holm becomes a folk hero when he is forced to drive his geese a hundred miles to the slaughterhouse because a strike has ruined his goose farm.

1658. *The Lawless Land* (1989, Concorde, 80m, c). P Tony Cinciripini & Larry Leahy, D Jon Hess, W Cinciripini & Leahy (based on a story by Cinciripini), PH Makoto Watanabe, M Lucia Hwong, ED Bernard Caputo & Steven Kane, PD Rafael Sanudo.

LP Nick Corri (Falco), Leon (Road Kill), Xander Berkeley (EZ Andy), Amanda Peterson (Diana), Patricio Bunetta (Don Enrique), Walter Kliche (Chairman), Alejandro Heinisch (Billy), Ann-Marie Peterson (Venus).

Mad Max–like survivor Nick Corri runs afoul of industrial magnate Walter Kliche when he elopes with the latter's daughter Amanda Peterson. The couple is pursued by a gang of goons led by Leon.

1659. *Lawrence of Arabia (Re-release)** (1989, Columbia, 216m, c). P Sam Spiegel & David Lean, D Lean*, W Robert Bolt† & Michael Wilson (based on *The Seven Pillars of Wisdom* by T.E. Lawrence), PH Freddie Young*, M Maurice Jarre*, ED Anne V. Coates*, PD John Box.

LP Peter O'Toole† (T.E. Lawrence), Alec Guinness (Prince Feisal), Anthony Quinn (Auba Abu Tayi), Jack Hawkins (Gen. Allenby), Jose Ferrer (Turkish Bey), Anthony Quayle (Col. Harry Brighton), Claude Rains (Mr. Dryden), Arthur Kennedy (Jackson Bentley), Donald Wolfit (Gen. Murray), Omar Sharif† (Sherif Ali Ibn El Kharish), I.S. Johar (Gasim), Gamil Ratib (Majid).

The 1962 epic about the life of adventurer T.E. Lawrence, who made the Arab cause his, was cut from 222 minutes to 202 minutes five weeks after the film premiered. Film restorers Robert A. Harris and Jim Painten took almost 20 years to locate the missing 20 minutes of film, which had made for truncated sequences in David Lean's masterpiece. Restoration of the missing minutes is not the only improvement in the film. The re-released version is on a new 70mm print (from a large-format 65mm negative), that creates sharper images with a resolution that is 125 percent greater than possible in today's films.

1660. *Lean on Me* (1989, Warner, 104m, c). P Norman Twain, D John G. Avildsen, W Michael Schiffer, PH Victor Hammer, M Bill Conti, ED John Carter & Avildsen, PD Doug Kraner.

LP Morgan Freeman (Joe Clark), Robert Guillaume (Dr. Frank Napier), Beverly Todd (Ms. Levias), Lynne Thigpen (Leona Barrett), Jermaine Hopkins (Thomas Sams), Karen Malina White (Kaneesha Carter).

Morgan Freeman is outstanding in his

portrayal of the man who uses controversial means to bring discipline back to the out-of-control, mainly black Eastside High in Paterson, New Jersey. While applauding his efforts to rid the school of drug dealers, and other elements which have no business in a place of education, one is forced to question what lessons he's teaching and if in fact his methods have done anything to improve the quality of education in his school. One can understand the man's anger and frustration, but his is not the solution to the problems in our schools.

1661. Legal Eagles (1986, Universal, 116m, c). P&D Ivan Reitman, W Jim Cash & Jack Epps, Jr. (based on a story by Reitman, Cash & Epps), PH Laszlo Kovacs, M Elmer Bernstein, ED Sheldon Kahn, Pembroke Herring, Jr. & William Gordean, PD John De Cuir.

LP Robert Redford (Tom Logan), Debra Winger (Laura Kelly), Daryl Hannah (Chelsea Deardon), Brian Dennehy (Cavanaugh), Terence Stamp (Victor Taft), Steven Hill (Bower), David Clennon (Blanchard), John McMartin (Forrester), Jennie Dundas (Jennifer Logan), Roscoe Lee Browne (Judge Dawkins).

In merely a so-so production, Robert Redford shines as an assistant D.A. who finds himself involved with flaky lawyer Debra Winger and her even flakier client Daryl Hannah. The latter finds herself constantly being accused of murder. The chemistry between Redford and Winger is all wrong, while Hannah plays her usual role of an ever available golden girl from some other plane of life.

1662. Legend (1986, 20th Century-Fox/Universal, 89m, c). P Arnon Milchan & Tim Hampton, D Ridley Scott, W William Hjortsberg, PH Alex Thomson, M Jerry Goldsmith (U.S. score by Tangerine Dream), ED Terry Rawlings, PD Assheton Gorton, MK Rob Bottin & Peter Robb-King†.

LP Tom Cruise (Jack), Mia Sara (Lili), Tim Curry (Darkness), David Bennent (Gump), Alice Playten (Blix), Billy Barty (Screwball), Cork Hubbert (Brown Tom), Peter O'Farrell (Pox), Kiran Shah (Blunder).

The 89 minute version for American release of this fairy story is definitely not for the little kiddies. Tom Cruise portrays a Tarzan/Puck–like character and looks foolish doing so. There is a longer but not better European version of the story about unicorns, elves, a princess and Tim Curry as a nasty villain.

Legend in Leotards see The Return of Captain Invincible

1663. The Legend of Billie Jean (1985, Tri-Star, 96m, c). P Rob Cohen, Lawrence Konner & Mark Rosenthal, D Matthew Robbins, W Rosenthal & Konner, PH Jeffrey L. Kimball, M Craig Safan, ED Cynthia Scheider, PD Ted Haworth.

LP Helen Slater (Billie Jean), Keith Gordon (Lloyd), Christian Slater (Binx), Richard Bradford (Pyatt), Martha Gehman (Ophelia), Yeardley Smith (Putter), Dean Stockwell (Muldaur), Peter Coyote (Ringwald), Mona Fultz (Donna Davey).

Helen Slater is made out to be a folk hero when she goes on the run with her little brother who has accidentally shot a nasty man. She's willing to surrender, but not before someone coughs up $608 to pay for her brother's vandalized bike. Slater likes her champion role so much she cuts her hair like Joan of Arc. Some may be offended by an inept attempt to manipulate them into seeing Slater as a Frank Capra-like heroine.

1664. The Legend of the Lone Ranger (1981, Universal, 98m, c). P Walter Coblenz, D William A. Fraker, W Ivan Goff, Ben Roberts, Michael Kane, William Roberts & Jerry Berloshan (based on the stories and characters created by George W. Trendle), PH Laszlo Kovacs, M John Barry, ED Thomas Stanford, PD Albert Brenner.

LP Klinton Spilsbury (John Reid, The Lone Ranger), Michael Horse (Tonto), Christopher Lloyd (Butch Cavendish), Matt Clark (Sheriff Wiatt), Juanin Clay (Amy Striker), Jason Robards (President Grant), John Bennett Perry (Dan Reid), David Hayward (Collins), John Hart (Lucas Striker), Richard Farnsworth (Wild Bill Hickok), Lincoln Tate (General Custer), Ted Flicker (Buffalo Bill Cody).

Some may ask whatever happened to Klinton Spilsbury (if they can remember his name), but it's unfair to place all the blame on him alone for this miserable attempt to film the Lone Ranger legend. There's enough shame to go around. All the writers deserve some of the discredit. The director seems to have had no control over the movie. It seems as if actors were allowed to arrange themselves in front of the cameras and do pretty much as they pleased. No, Klinton, wherever you are, come out of hiding. It isn't all your fault.

1665.   *The Lemon Sisters* (1989, Miramax/J&M, 89m, c). P Diane Keaton & Joe Kelly, D Joyce Chopra, W Jeremy Pikser, PH Bobby Byrne, M Howard Shore, ED Michael R. Miller, PD Patrizia von Brandenstein.

LP Diane Keaton (Eloise Hamer), Carol Kane (Franki DeAngelo), Kathryn Grody (Nola Frank), Elliott Gould (Fred), Aidan Quinn (Frankie), Ruben Blades (C.W.), Richard Libertini (Nicholas Panas).

Set in Atlantic City, friends Diane Keaton, Carol Kane and Kathryn Grody maintain their close relationship even after their nightclub act breaks up. Each is a trifle eccentric, but if one expects this to produce many amusing situations, one would be wrong.

1666.   *Leo and Loree* (1980, United Artists, 97m, c). P Jim Begg, D Jerry Paris, W James Ritz, PH Costa Petals, M Lance Rubin, ED Ed Cotter.

LP Donny Most (Leo), Linda Purl (Loree), David Huffman, Jerry Paris, Shannon Farnon, Allan Rich, Susan Lawrence.

Ron Howard is the executive producer of this nothing little comedy featuring Donny Most as an aspiring actor who has a romance with Linda Purl. She's the daughter of an Academy Award winner and is also trying to break into the movies.

1667.   *Leonard Part 6* (1987, Columbia, 85m, c). P Bill Cosby, D Paul Weiland, W Jonathan Reynolds (based on a story by Cosby), PH Jan De Bont, M Elmer Bernstein, ED Gerry Hambling & Peter Boita, PD Geoffrey Kirkland.

LP Bill Cosby (Leonard), Tom Courtenay (Frayn, Leonard's Butler), Joe Don Baker (Snyderburn), Moses Gunn (Gior-

gio), Pat Colbert (Allison), Gloria Foster (Medusa), Victor Rowell (Joan), Anna Levine (Nurse Carvalho), David Maier (Man Ray), Grace Zabriskie (Jefferson).

This unfunny film proves that not everything Bill Cosby touches turns to gold. His commercials for Jello pudding are funnier. He's a high tech spy who sets out to stop an evil genius working on turning animals into killers. The "six" in the title refers to the fact that this is Cosby's sixth assignment, the first five cannot be revealed because of national security considerations. It's not only a zero, it deserves a negative number rating.

1668.   *Less Than Zero* (1987, 20th Century–Fox, 96m, c). P Jon Avnet, Jordan Kerner & Marvin Worth, D Marek Kanievska, W Harley Peyton (based on the novel by Bret Easton Ellis), PH Edward Lachman, M Thomas Newman & Rick Rubin, ED Peter E. Berger & Michael Tronick, PD Barbara Ling.

LP Andrew McCarthy (Clay Easton), Jami Gertz (Blair), Robert Downey, Jr. (Julian Wells), James Spader (Rip), Tony Bill (Bradford Easton), Nicholas Pryor (Benjamin Wells), Donna Mitchell (Elaine Easton).

Fast friends Andrew McCarthy, Jami Gertz and Robert Downey, Jr., are rich kids with everything anyone might want, and something they can do without, a drug problem for Downey which may cost him his life. Gertz wants McCarthy to save Downey.

1669.   *Let It Ride* (1989, Paramount, 86m, c). P David Giler, D Joe Pytka, W "Ernest Morton" (Nancy Dowd), (based on Jay Cronley's novel *Good Vibes*), PH Curtis J. Wehr, M Giorgio Moroder, ED Dede Allen & Jim Miller, PD Wolf Kroeger.

LP Richard Dreyfuss (Jay Trotter), David Johansen (Looney), Teri Garr (Pam Trotter), Jennifer Tilly (Vicki), Allen Garfield (Greenberg), Ed Walsh (Marty), Michelle Phillips, Mary Woronov, Robbie Coltrane.

Don't bet on this hackneyed film about cab driver Richard Dreyfuss who gets a tip on a sure thing in a horse race. Starting with $50, he parlays his win into a streak which makes him thousands of dollars and allows him to mingle with hoi polloi. His success almost prevents a reconciliation with wife Teri Garr. It's not a great movie, but if you're in a silly mood, it's not a bad way to spend an hour and a half.

Lethal see KGB: The Secret War

1670. *Lethal Weapon* (1987, Warner, 110m, c). P Richard Donner & Joel Silver, D Donner, W Shane Black, PH Stephen Goldblatt, M Michael Kamen & Eric Clapton, ED Stuart Baird, PD J, Michael Riva, SOUND Les Fresholtz, Dick Alexander, Vern Poore & Bill Nelson†.

LP Mel Gibson (Martin Riggs), Danny Glover (Roger Murtaugh), Gary Busey (Joshua), Mitchell Ryan (The General), Tom Atkins (Michael Hunsaker), Darlene Love (Trish Murtaugh), Traci Wolfe (Rianne Murtaugh), Jackie Swanson (Amanda Hunsaker), Damon Hines (Nick Murtaugh), Ebonie Smith (Carrie Murtaugh), Lycia Naff (Dixie).

With villains like Gary Busey and Mitchell Ryan, one can't help but cheer when Mel Gibson and Danny Glover take them out at the climax of this film. Of course, lethal weapon Gibson, a suicidal cop since his wife was killed, blows away many others before he gets around to the real baddies. Glover is a family man who would prefer to keep his gun in his holster, but when his daughter is taken captive by Ryan and Busey, he's ready to adopt partner Gibson's effective tactics. Although it's a very violent film, it's hard not to like the teaming of Gibson and Glover. Busey deserves a lot of credit for making audiences absolutely despise him. He and other Vietnam vets run a very successful drug smuggling ring, employing military-like strategy and severe brutality.

1671. *Lethal Weapon 2* (1989, Warner, 113m, c). P Richard Donner & Joel Silver, D Donner, W Jeffrey Boam (based on a story by Shane Black & Warren Murphy), PH Stephen Goldblatt, M Michael Kamen, Eric Clapton & David Sanborn, ED Stuart Baird, PD J. Michael Riva, SE Robert Henderson & Alan Robert Murray†.

LP Mel Gibson (Martin Riggs), Danny Glover (Roger Murtaugh), Joe Pesci (Leo Getz), Joss Ackland (Arjen Rudd), Derrick O'Connor (Pieter Vorstedt), Patsy Kensit (Rika van den Haas), Darlene Love (Trish Murtaugh), Traci Wolfe (Rianne Murtaugh), Steve Kahan (Capt. Murphy).

A lot of bad guys get on Mel Gibson and Daniel Glover's case and a lot of bad guys (at least two dozen) die, in this excellent sequel to the 1987 hit. Once again wild man cop Gibson and family man Glover make a wonderful team as they combine humor with mayhem in fighting the prevalent baddies of the 80s, big-league drug dealers from South Africa, sporting diplomatic passports. Rounding out the fun team of Gibson and Glover is a superb comical portrayal by Joe Pesci as an accountant who helped the drug lords launder their profits and needs witness protection now that he's telling all. Gibson gets in a little loving with the very pretty Patsy Kensit, but he just has no luck with lasting relationships. Glover finds himself stuck on a toilet, rigged to blow his you-know-what-off if he gets up. Once again the bad guys are so nasty, one cheers when they get theirs in various horrible ways.

1672. *Lethal Woman* (1989, Pure Gold Film Ventures, 95m, c, aka *The Most Dangerous Woman Alive*). P John Karie, S.D. Nethersole & Josh Spencer, D Christian Marnham, W Michael Olson & Gabriel Elias, PH Vincent G. Cox, M Meir Eshel, ED Ettie Feldman & Wayne Lines.

LP Merete Van Kamp (Christine/Diana), Robert Lipton (Major Derek Johnson), Shannon Tweed (Tory), James Luisi (Col. Maxim), Deep Roy (Grizabella), Graeme Clarke (Major Burlington), Prudence Solomon, Nita, Linda Warren, Phillipa Vernon.

Army Brat Merete Van Kamp is raped by commanding officer James Luisi. His fellow officers and even her fiancé cover up his deed. Embittered Vam Kamp plans her own revenge, gathering other rape victims. They settle on an island, lure the rapists to the island and then hunt them down one by one, killing their prey in various ghastly ways.

1673. *Let's Get Harry* (1986, Tri-Star, 100m, c). P Daniel H. Blatt & Robert Singer, D Alan Smithee [Stuart Rosenberg], W Charles Robert Carner (based on a story by Mark Feldberg & Samuel Fuller), PH James A. Contner, M Brad Fiedel, ED Ralph E. Winters, Rick R. Sparr & Robert Hyams.

LP Gary Busey (Jack "Smilin' Jack" Abernathy), Cecile Callan (Theresa), Elpidia Carrillo (Veronica), Michael Schoeffling (Corey Burke), Tom Wilson (Pachowski), Glenn Frey (Spence), Robert Duvall (Norman Shrike), Rick Rossovich (Curt Klein), Ben Johnson (Harry Burke, Sr.), Matt Clark (Walt Clayton), Gregory Sierra (Alphonso), Mark Harmon (Harry Burke, Jr.).

Five ordinary men hire mercenary Robert Duvall to lead them on a mission to Colombia to rescue their friend Mark Harmon, a pipeline worker, who along with the ambassador has been kidnapped by an underground group of drug dealers. It lacks excitement and suspense.

1674. *Letter to Brezhnev* (1986, Circle Releasing Corp., GB, 94m, c). P Janet Goddard, D Chris Bernard, W Frank Clarke, M Alan Gill, ED Lesley Walker, PD Lez Brotherston, Nick Englefield & Jonathan Swain.

LP Alfred Molina (Sergei), Peter Firth (Peter), Margi Clarke (Teresa), Tracy Lea (Tracy), Alexandra Pigg (Elaine), Susan Dempsey (Girl in yellow pedal pushers), Ted Wood (Mick), Carl Chase (Taxi Driver).

Two high-spirited and bored Liverpool girls, Margi Clarke and Alexandra Pigg, meet two Russian sailors Alfred Molina and Peter Firth. After a brief romance the girls want to pack up their bags and move to Russia with their new loves.

1675. *Leviathan* (1989, MGM, 98m, c). P Luigi & Aurelio De Laurentiis, D George P. Cosmatos, W David Peoples & Jeb Stuart, PH Alex Thomson, M Jerry Goldsmith, ED Roberto Silvi & John F. Burnett, PD Ron Cobb.

LP Peter Weller (Beck), Richard Crenna (Doc), Amanda Pays (Willie), Daniel Stern (Sixpack), Ernie Hudson (Jones), Michael Carmine (DeJesus), Lisa Eilbacher (Bowman), Hector Elizondo (Cobb).

The film attempts to be *Alien* of the deep. An American commercial mining crew comes across a sunken Soviet freighter. It contains some strange serpent-like beasts which infect and kill members of the crew as they feed on their victims.

1676. *Lianna* (1983, United Artists, 110m, c). P Jeffrey Nelson & Maggie Renzi, D&W John Sayles, PH Austin de Besche, M Mason Daring, ED Sayles.

LP Linda Griffiths (Lianna), Jane Hallaren (Ruth), Jon DeVries (Dick), Jo Henderson (Sandy), Jessica Wright MacDonald (Theda), Jesse Solomon (Spencer), John Sayles (Jerry), Stephen Mendillo (Bob).

The film is a sensitive treatment of a lesbian love affair. Married housewife Linda Griffiths decides to have an affair and eventually moves in with Jane Hallaren.

1677. *Liar's Dice* (1980, Makdissy-Eubanks, 95m, c). P Butros Makdissy & Ed Eubanks, D Issam B. Makdissy, W Terry Eubanks-Makdissy, PH Douglas Murray, M Coleman Burke & Gary Yamani, ED Issam B. Makdissy.

LP Robert Ede (Joe), Terry Eubanks-Makdissy (Anne), Issam B. Makdissy (Samir), Frank Triest (Jack), D.G. Buckles (Pete), Norma Small (Dottie), Phran Gauci (Janice), Rafik Assad (Jamil).

Lonely artist Terry Eubanks-Makdissy works as a cocktail waitress. She becomes involved with two men, a married foreigner, Issam B. Makdissy and an older man, Robert Ede. It's about as exciting as the description.

1678. *Liar's Moon* (1982, Crown International, 106m, c). P Don P. Behrns, D David Fisher, W Fisher (based on a story by Janice Thompson & Billy Hanna), PH John Hora, ED Christopher Greenbury.

LP Matt Dillon, Cindy Fisher, Christopher Connelly, Hoyt Axton, Yvonne DeCarlo, Maggie Blye, Susan Tyrrell, Broderick Crawford.

Sensitive poor boy Matt Dillon elopes with Cindy Fisher, daughter of a wealthy banker. Their parents are against the move and audiences are mostly against the movie, which was released with two different endings. In one Fisher dies after a botched abortion. In the other she survives.

1679. *License to Drive* (1988, 20th Century–Fox, 88m, c). P Jeffrey A. Mueller & Andrew Licht, D Greg Beeman, W Neil Tolkin, PH Bruce Surtees, M Jay Ferguson, ED Wendy Greene Bricmont, PD Lawrence G. Paull.

LP Corey Haim (Les), Corey Feldman (Dean), Carol Kane (Les' Mom), Richard Masur (Les' Dad), Heather Graham (Mercedes), Michael Manasseri (Charles), Harvey Miller (Professor), M.A. Nickles (Paolo), Helen Hanft (Miss Heilberg).

Sixteen-year-old Corey Haim fails his driver's test, but he easily fools his parents into believing he has passed. He "borrows" his grandfather's classic car when he gets a date with hot-stuff Heather Graham, for whom he will do anything. For those who are not taken with teen exploitation films, this one will be expecially distasteful.

1680. *Licence to Kill* (1989, MGM/United Artists, GB, 133m, c). P Albert R. Broccoli & Michael G. Wilson, D John Glen, W Richard Maibaum & Wilson, PH Alec Mills, M Michael Kamen, ED John Grover, PD Peter Lamont, AD Michael Lamont, SE John Richardson.

LP Timothy Dalton (James Bond), Carey Lowell (Pam Bouvier), Robert Davi (Franz Sanchez), Talisa Soto (Lupe Lamora), Anthony Zerbe (Milton Krest), Frank McRae (Sharkey), Everett McGill (Killifer), Wayne Newton (Joe Butcher), Benicio del Toro (Dario), Desmond Llewelyn (Q), David Hedison (Felix Leiter), Priscilla Barnes (Della Churchill), Robert Brown (M), Caroline Bliss (Miss Moneypenny).

Critics differ on whether to recommend this latest Bond issue, depending upon how they see Timothy Dalton in the part of 007. Those who applauded Sean Connery's charm and Roger Moore's humor are not as impressed with Dalton's dark reserved looks and actions. Others describe him as just what Ian Fleming had in mind for Bond. At any rate this pic is set in exotic locales which support the thrills and chills one always anticipates in a Bond movie. Bond has temporarily been relieved of his license to kill as he goes after the drug big shot Robert Davi who has badly mauled our boy's Ameri-

can CIA agent friend David Hedison and murdered the latter's new wife. The beauties in the film, Talisa Soto and Carey Lowell, are the usual minimally talented but attractive scenery. There are a few spectacular scenes in the climactic chase.

1681. *Lies* (1984, New Empire/Westcom, GB, 102m, c). P Ken Wheat, Jim Wheat & Shelley Hermann, D&W K. Wheat & J. Wheat, PH Robert Ebinger, M Marc Donahue, ED Michael Ornstein & Dennis Hill, PD Christopher Henry.

LP Ann Dusenberry, Gail Strickland, Bruce Davison, Clu Gulager, Terence Knox, Bert Remsen, Stacy Keach, Sr., Douglas Leonard, Patience Cleveland, Julie Philips.

Actress Ann Dusenberry is duped into helping con artists cheat an heiress out of her fortune.

1682. *Life Is Cheap* (1989, Far East Stars, 90m, c). P Winnie Fredriksz, D Wayne Wang & Spencer Nakasako, W Nakasako, PH Amir M. Mokri, M Mark Adler, ED Chris Sanderson, AD Colette Koo.

LP Spencer Nakasako (Man with No Namee), Cora Miao (Money), Victor Wong (Blind Man), John K. Chan (The Anthropologist), Chan Kim Wan (The Duck Killer), Cheng Kwan Min (Uncle Cheng), Allen Fong (Taxi Driver), Cinda Hui (Kitty), Lam Chung (The Red Guard), Lo Wai (The Big Boss).

Spencer Nakasako is half–Chinese, half–Japanese and All-American. He agrees to act as a courier for a San Francisco Triad (Chinese Mafia) to the Big Boss in Hong Kong. Nakasako encounters many funny and flawed characters as he tries to unlock the enigma of "5,000 years of Chinese culture."

1683. *Lifeforce* (1985, Tri-Star/Cannon, 101m, c). P Menahem Golan & Yoram Globus, D Tobe Hooper, W Dan O'Bannon & Don Jakoby (based on the novel *The Space Vampires* by Colin Wilson), PH Alan Hume, M Henry Mancini & Michael Kamen, ED John Grover, PD John Graysmark.

LP Steve Railsback (Carlsen), Peter Firth (Caine), Frank Finlay (Fallada), Patrick Stewart (Dr. Armstrong), Michael Gothard (Bukovsky), Nicholas Ball (Derebridge), Aubrey Morris (Sir Percy), Nancy Paul (Ellen), John Hallam (Lamson).

A space shuttle discovers a giant space ship inside Halley's Comet. Inside the ship they discover three human-looking aliens who, when brought back to earth, prove to be blood-sucking vampires.

1684. *Light of Day* (1987, Tri-Star, 107m, c). P Rob Cohen & Keith Barish, D&W Paul Schrader, PH John Bailey, M Thomas Newman, ED Jacqueline Cambas, PD Jeannine Claudia Oppewall.

LP Michael J. Fox (Joe Rasnick), Gena Rowlands (Jeanette Rasnick), Joan Jett (Patti Rasnick), Michael McKean (Bu Montgomery), Thomas G. Waites (Smittie), Cherry Jones (Cindy Montgomery), Michael Dolan (Gene Bodine), Paul J. Harkins (Billy Tettore).

Raunchy rocker and single mother Joan Jett is constantly at odds with her religious mother Gena Rowlands, who can never forgive her daughter for having a child out of wedlock. Brother Michael J. Fox, also a soft-rock musician, is caught in the middle. Just goes to show that not everyone's problems make for a good dramatic story.

1685. *The Lighthorsemen* (1988, Cinecom, Australia, 115m, c). P Ian Jones & Simon Wincer, D Wincer, W Jones, PH Dean Semler, M Mario Millo, ED Adrian Carr, PD Bernard Hides.

LP Jon Blake (Scotty), Peter Phelps (Dave Mitchell), Tony Bonner (Lt. Col. [Swagman Bill] Bourchier), Bill Kerr (Lt. Gen. Sir Harry Chauvel), John Walton (Tas), Gary Sweet (Frank), Tim McKenzie (Chiller), Sigrid Thornton (Anne).

This cliché-laden war epic deals with the campaign of Australian horsemen against the Turks and Germans in Beersheba, Palestine, during World War I.

1686. *Lightning — The White Stallion* (1986, Cannon, 95m, c). P Harry Alan Towers, D William A. Levey, W Peter Welbeck (Towers), PH Steven Shaw, ED Ken Bornstein.

LP Mickey Rooney (Barney Ingram), Isabel Lorca (Steff), Susan George (Madame Rene), Billy Wesley (Lucas).

Even Mickey Rooney can't save this weak family story. He's a wealthy man whose racehorse is stolen.

1687. *The Lightship* (1985, CBS/Warner, 89m, c). P Bill Benenson & Moritz Borman, D Jerzy Skolimowski, W William Mai & David Taylor (based on the novel *Das Feuerschiff* by Siegfried Lenz), PH Charly Steinberger, M Stanley Myers, ED Barrie Vince & Scott Hancock.

LP Robert Duvall (Caspary), Klaus Maria Brandauer (Capt. Miller), Tom Bower (Coop), Robert Costanzo (Stump), Badja Djola (Nate), William Forsythe (Gene), Arliss Howard (Eddie), Michael Lyndon (Alex), Tim Phillips (Thorne).

Klaus Maria Brandauer is a captain of a retired ship moored off the mid–Atlantic coast. His vessel is boarded by psychotic Robert Duvall and his band of fugitives just as a hurricane bears down on the area.

1688. *Like Father, Like Son* (1987, Tri-Star, 98m, c). P Brian Grazer & David Valdes, D Rod Daniel, W Lorne Cameron & Steven L. Bloom (based on a story by Lorne Cameron), PH Jack N. Green, M Miles Goodman, ED Lois Freeman-Fox, PD Dennis Gassner.

LP Dudley Moore (Dr. Jack Hammond), Kirk Cameron (Chris Hammond), Margaret Colin (Ginnie Armbruster), Catherine Hicks (Dr. Amy Larkin), Patrick O'Neal (Dr. Armbruster), Sean Astin (Trigger), Cami Cooper (Lori Beaumont), Micah Grant (Rick Anderson), Bill Morrison (Uncle Earl), Skeeter Vaughan (Medicine Man).

This film is one reason to ship Dudley Moore off to the island of ex-movie stars. As for Kirk Cameron, he's an unappealing TV teen, too glib for his own good. The story is one of several dealing with mind transformations and probably the weakest of the bunch. Physician Moore and teen son Cameron's brains and personalities are switched as a result of an old Navajo mind-switching drug. The two make predictable asses of themselves as they try to adjust to each other's routines and environments.

1689. *Lily in Love* (1985, New Line, US/Hungary, 108m, c, aka *Playing for Keeps*). P Robert Halmi, D Karoly

Makk, W Frank Cucci, PH John Lindley, M Szabolcs Fenyes & Irwin Fisch, ED Norman Gay.

LP Christopher Plummer (Fitzroy Wynn/Roberto Terranova), Maggie Smith (Lily Wynn), Elke Sommer (Alicia Braun), Adolph Green (Jerry Silber), Szabo Sander (Teodor), Janos Kende (Gabor), Rosetta Lenoire (Rosanna).

In an uncredited remake of Ferenc Molnar's *The Guardsman,* Christopher Plummer and Maggie Smith portray a vain actor and his playwright wife. She no longer sees her husband as the man to play the romantic lead in her new play. To prove he's not washed up, Plummer disguises himself as a Don Juan–like devil who tries to sweep Smith off her feet. His seduction of Smith goes all too well.

1690. *Limit Up* (1989, Sterling/MCEG, 89m, c). P Jonathan D. Krane, D Richard Martini, W Martini & Lu Anders (based on a story by Martini), PH Peter Lyons Collister, M John Tesh, ED Sonny Baskin, PD R. Clifford Searcy.

LP Nancy Allen (Casey Falls), Dean Stockwell (Peter Oak), Brad Hall (Marty Callahan), Danitra Vance (Nike), Ray Charles (Julius), Rance Howard (Chuck Feeney), Sandra Bogan (Andy Lincoln).

In a switch on the Faust story, Chicago Board of Trade "runner" Nancy Allen gets her chance to be a trader with the help of devil Danitra Vance who offers fame and riches for the usual price.

1691. *The Line* (1982, Enterprise, 95m, c). P&D Robert J. Siegel, W Reginald Shelborne & Patricia Maxwell, PH Sol Negrin, M Rod McBrien, ED Dennis Golub & Shelborne.

LP Russ Thacker, Lewis J. Stadlen, Brad Sullivan, Kathleen Tolan, Jacqueline Brookes, David Doyle, Andrew Duncan, Russell Horton.

Robert J. Siegel borrowed part of his 1972 picture *Parades* to make this film about a Vietnam deserter who is sent to a military stockade during a sitdown strike by the prisoners.

1692. *Link* (1986, Cannon, GB, 103m, c). P&D Richard Franklin, W Everett De Roche (based on a story by Leo Zlotoff and Tom Ackerman), PH Mike Molloy, M Jerry Goldsmith, ED Andrew London, PD Norman Garwood.

LP Terence Stamp (Dr. Steven Philip), Elisabeth Shue (Jane Chase), Steven Pinner (David), Richard Garnett (Dennis), David O'Hara (Tom), Kevin Lloyd (Bailey), Joe Belcher (Taxi Driver).

In this lackluster horror film, scientist Terence Stamp's experiments with apes make a monkey out of him.

1693. *Lion of the Desert* (1981, United Film, Libya/GB, 162m, c). P&D Moustapha Akkad, W H.A.L. Craig, PH Jack Hildyard, M Maurice Jarre, ED John Shirley, PD Mario Garbuglia & Syd Cain.

LP Anthony Quinn (Omar Mukhtar), Oliver Reed (Gen. Rodolfo Graziani), Rod Steiger (Benito Mussolini), John Gielgud (Sharif El Gariani), Irene Papas (Mabrouka), Raf Vallone (Diodiece), Gastone Moschin (Major Tomelli).

In a much too long desert epic, Anthony Quinn is the charismatic elderly leader of the rebels who stand in the way of Mussolini's conquest of Libya. The Italians brutally slaughter the natives and ultimately hang Quinn.

1694. *Lionheart* (1987, Orion, 104m, c). P Stanley O'Toole & Talia Shire, D Franklin J. Schaffner, W Menno Meyjes & Richard Outten (based on a story by Meyjes), PH Alec Mills, M Jerry Goldsmith, ED David Bretherton, PD Gil Parrondo.

LP Eric Stoltz (Robert Nerra), Gabriel Byrne (The Black Prince), Nicola Cowper (Blanche), Dexter Fletcher (Michael), Deborah Barrymore (Mathilda), Nicholas Clay (Charles de Montfort), Bruce Purchase (Simon Nerra), Neil Dickson (King Richard), Chris Pitt (Odo).

Intended for gullible youngsters, this turkey has 12th century kids searching for King Richard the Lionheart.

1695. *Liquid Sky* (1982, Z Films, 118m, c). P&D Slava Tsukerman, W Tsukerman, Anne Carlisle & Nina V. Kerova, PH Yuri Neyman, M Tsukerman, Brenda I. Hutchinson & Clive Smith, ED Sharyn Leslie Ross, PD Marina Levikova.

LP Anne Carlisle (Margaret/Jimmy), Paula E. Sheppard (Adrian), Susan Doukas (Sylvia), Otto von Wernherr (Johann), Bob Brady (Owen), Elaine C.

Grove (Katherine), Stanley Knap (Paul), Jack Adalist (Vincent).

In this outrageous film from Russian émigré Slava Tsukerman, aliens seek a heroin-like substance produced by the human brain during sex. One feeds off the lovers of new-wave punk fashion model Anne Carlisle, who not only portrays a lesbian, but also a homosexual male model.

1696.   *Listen to Me* (1989, Columbia, 107m, c). P Marykay Powell, D&W Douglas Day Stewart, PH Fred Koenekamp, M David Foster, ED Anne V. Coates, PD Gregory Pickrell.

LP Kirk Cameron (Tucker Muldowney), Jami Gertz (Monica Tomanski), Roy Scheider (Charlie Nichols), Amanda Peterson (Donna Lumis), Tim Quill (Garson McKellar), George Wyner (Dean Schwimmer), Anthony Zerbe (Sen. McKellar), Christopher Atkins (Bruce Arlington), Quinn Cummings (Susan Hooper).

Even with abortion the issue, this comedy-drama about a college debate team isn't much. The producers don't even have the good sense to show how debaters use wit, intelligence and telling comments to make their points. These forensic morons rely on sophomoric rejoinders and lewd antics.

1697.   *Listen to the City* (1984, International Spectra Film, Canada, 87m, c). P&D Ron Mann, W Mann & Bill Schroeder (based on a story by Schroeder), PH Rene Ohashi, M Gordon Deppe, ED Elaine Foreman.

LP P.J. Soles (Sophia), Michael Glassbourg (Goodman), Sandy Horne (Arete), Jim Carroll (Hupar), Barry Callaghan (Arete's Father), Sky Gilbert (Shadow), Mary Hawkins (White), Real Andrews (Green).

TV journalist P.J. Soles investigates a large corporation threatening a shutdown. The film is loaded with pretentious symbolism.

1698.   *The Little Convict* (1980, Roadshow, Australia, animated, 90m, c). P&D Yoram Gross, W John Palmer, ANIM Paul McAdam.

LP Rolf Harris (Grandpa).

Rolf Harris narrates, acts and sings along with the animated characters in this tale of an English boy sentenced to deportation to Australia for innocently helping a highwayman.

1699.   *Little Darlings* (1980, Paramount, 92m, c). P Stephen J. Friedman, D Ronald F. Maxwell, W Kimi Peck & Dalene Young, PH Fred Batka, M Charles Fox, ED Pembroke J. Herring, PD William Hiney.

LP Tatum O'Neal (Ferris Whitney), Kristy McNichol (Angel), Armand Assante (Gary), Matt Dillon (Randy), Maggie Blye (Ms. Bright), Nicolas Coster (Whitney), Krista Errickson (Cinder), Alexa Kenin (Dana).

During summer camp, adolescents Tatum O'Neal and Kristy McNichol make a bet on who will be the first to lose her unwanted virginity. The film does a decent job of relating how scary initial sexual experiences can be.

1700.   *Little Dorrit* (1988, Cannon, GB, 360m, c, Part 1: *Nobody's Fault* and Part 2: *Little Dorrit's Story*). P John Brabourne & Richard Goodwin, D&W Christine Edzard† (for screenplay) (based on the novel by Charles Dickens), PH Bruno de Keyzer, M Giuseppe Verdi, ED Olivier Stockman & Fraser Maclean.

LP Alec Guinness† (William Dorrit), Derek Jacobi (Arthur Clennam), Cyril Cusack (Frederick Dorrit), Sarah Pickering (Little Dorrit), Joan Greenwood (Mrs. Clennam), Max Wall (Flintwinch), Amelda Brown (Fanny Dorrit), Daniel Chatto (Tip Dorrit), Miriam Margolyes (Flora Finching), Bill Fraser (Mr. Casby), Roshan Seth (Mr. Pancks), Roger Hammond (Mr. Mcagles), Sophie Ward (Minnie Meagles), Michael Elphick (Mr. Merdle), Robert Morley (Lord Decimus Barnacle).

Christine Edzard has brought to the screen one of Dickens' best works, but one which has not been as widely read as his more sentimental earlier works. The exceptionally well-done film is shown in two three-hour parts. The first part is told from the point of view of middle-aged bachelor Derek Jacobi, who returns to England after spending 20 years in China. He takes an interest in Sarah Pickering and her debilitated father Alec Guinness. By the end of part one, Guinness has reclaimed a lost fortune. Part two is told from Pickering's point of view. It runs from her birth in debtor's prison, to her attempts to play mother for her irresponsible family, her falling in love with Jacobi, her shunning of society once Guinness gets his fortune, through his death and her going to debtor's prison once again to care for the newly destitute and gravely ill Jacobi. It ends when they finally are able to leave the prison once and for all to marry.

1701. *The Little Dragons* (1980, Eastwind/Aurora, 90m, c). P Hannah Hempstead & Curtis Hanson, D Hanson, W Harvey Applebaum, Louis G. Attlee, Rudolph Borchert & Alan Ormsby, PH Stephen Katz, M Ken Lauber.

LP Charles Lane (J.J.), Ann Sothern (Angel), Chris Petersen (Zack), Pat Petersen (Woody), Sally Boyden (Carol), Rick Lenz (Dick Forbinger), Sharon Weber (Ruth Forbinger), Joe Spinell (Yancey), John Chandler (Carl).

Karate experts Chris and Pat Petersen are forced to rescue Sally Boyden, kidnapped by Joe Spinell and John Chandler, who live with their mother Ann Sothern in an abandoned car. The police are too dumb to solve the case.

1702. *The Little Drummer Girl* (1984, Warner, 130m, c). P Robert L. Crawford, D George Roy Hill, W Loring Mandel (based on the novel by John Le Carré), PH Wolfgang Treu, M Dave Grusin, ED William Reynolds, PD Henry Bumstead.

LP Diane Keaton (Charlie), Yorgo Voyagis (Joseph), Klaus Kinski (Kurtz), Sami Frey (Khalil), David Suchet (Mesterbein), Eli Danker (Litvak), Ben Levine (Dimitri), Jonathan Sagalle (Teddy), Shlomit Hagoel (Rose), Juliano Mer (Julio), Danni Roth (Oded).

This adaptation of John Le Carré's best-selling spy thriller is poorly put together and not in the least believable. Still Diane Keaton is very good as a Palestinian actress recruited by counterintelligence officer Klaus Kinski to become an Israeli agent. She gets caught up in international terrorism and a romance with Yorgo Voyagis. Watch out for the Commander; he's played by author John Le Carré using his real name David Cornwell.

1703. *Little Lord Fauntleroy* (1980, Rosemont, GB, 103m, c). P Norman Rosemont, D Jack Gold, W Blanche Hanalis (based on the novel by Frances Hodgson Burnett), PH Arthur Ibbetson, M Allyn Ferguson, ED Keith Palmer.

LP Ricky Schroder (Ceddie Errol), Alec Guinness (Earl of Dorincourt), Eric Porter (Havisham), Colin Blakely (Hobbs), Connie Booth (Mrs. Errol), Rachel Kempson (Lady Lorradaile), Carmel McSharry (Mary).

This chestnut was unappetizing when Freddie Bartholomew played the son of a disinherited father. The lad treats his mother like a lover and wins over his grandfather, an earl. Despite a good cast and an earnest performance by Ricky Schroder it hasn't improved with age.

1704. *The Little Mermaid* (1989, Buena Vista, animated, 82m, c). P Howard Ashman & John Musker, D&W Musker & Ron Clements (based on the fairy tale by Hans Christian Andersen), ANIM D Mark Henn, Glen Keane, Duncan Marjoribanks, Ruben Aquino, Andreas Deja & Matthew O'Callaghan, M Alan Menken*, SONGS "Under the Sea"* & "Kiss the Girl" by Menken & Howard Ashman, AD Michael A. Peraza, Jr. & Donald A. Towns.

VOICES Jodi Benson (Ariel), Pat Carroll (Ursula), Samuel E. Wright (Sebastian), Kenneth Mars (Triton), Buddy Hackett (Scuttle), Jason Marin (Flounder), Christopher Daniel Barnes (Eric), Rene Auberjonois (Louis), Ben Wright (Grimsby).

In this delightful Walt Disney animation, mermaid princess Ariel lives in the undersea world of her sea-lord father Triton, but yearns to live a life about the waves. She rescues a handsome young prince from the sea. She disobeys her father and puts up her beautiful voice as collateral in order to get help from the seawitch to make the prince fall in love with her.

1705. *Little Miss Marker* (1980, Universal, 103m, c). P Jennings Lang, D&W Walter Bernstein (based on a story by Damon Runyon), PH Philip Lathrop, M Henry Mancini, ED Eve Newman, PD Edward C. Carfagno.

LP Walter Matthau (Sorrowful Jones),

Julie Andrews (Amanda), Tony Curtis (Blackie), Bob Newhart (Regret), Lee Grant (The Judge), Sara Stimson (The Kid), Brian Dennehy (Herbie), Kenneth McMillan (Brannigan), Andrew Rubin (Carter), Joshua Shelley (Benny).

It's not that Walter Matthau is not believable as the Damon Runyon character previously played by Adolphe Menjou and Bob Hope, it's just that contemporary Damon Runyan characters are not believable. In the all-too-familiar story, bookie Matthau is left holding the bag when the father of Sara Stimson, left behind as a marker for a bet, is killed. Walter is not pleased, but with a little boost from Julie Andrews he comes to love the little tyke. It's enough to make one ill.

1706. *Little Monsters* (1989, MGM/United Artists, 100m, c). P Jeffrey Mueller, Andrew Licht & John A. Davis, D Richard Alan Greenberg, W Terry Rossio & Ted Elliott, PH Dick Bush, M David Newman, ED Patrick McMahon, PD Paul Peters.

LP Fred Savage (Brian), Howie Mandel (Maurice), Daniel Stern (Glen), Margaret Whitton (Holly), Rick Ducommun (Snik), Frank Whaley (Boy), Ben Savage (Eric), William Murray Weiss (Todd), Deven Rattray (Ronnie).

Howie Mandel portrays a hyperactive monster with a bad complexion who pops out from underneath a bed at night to wreak havoc in an old house, with the blame placed on the kids.

1707. *Little Nikita* (1988, Columbia, 98m, c). P Harry Gittes, D Richard Benjamin, W John Hill & Bo Goldman (based on a story by Tom Musca & Terry Schwartz), PH Laszlo Kovacs, M Marvin Hamlisch, ED Jacqueline Cambas, PD Gene Callahan.

LP Sidney Poitier (Roy Parmenter), River Phoenix (Jeff Grant), Richard Jenkins (Richard Grant), Caroline Kava (Elizabeth Grant), Richard Bradford (Konstantin Karpov), Richard Lynch (Scuba), Loretta Devine (Verna McLaughlin), Lucy Deakins (Barbara Kerry).

Little makes any sense in this movie which features Sidney Poitier as an FBI agent who befriends young River Phoenix after the latter learns that his parents are Communist spies. The talents of both Poitier and Phoenix are wasted.

1708. *A Little Sex* (1982, Universal, 94m, c). P Robert de Laurentiis & Bruce Paltrow, D Paltrow, W de Laurentiis, PH Ralf D. Bode, M Georges Delerue, ED Bill Butler, PD Stephen Hendrickson.

LP Tim Matheson (Michael Donovan), Kate Capshaw (Katherine), Edward Herrmann (Tommy), John Glover (Walter), Joan Copeland (Mrs. Harrison), Susanna Dalton (Nancy Barwood), Wendie Malick (Philomena), Wallace Shawn (Oliver), Sharon Bamber (Theresa Donovan), Tanya Berezin (Joyce).

Whatever made Tim Matheson believe he could settle down to a monogamous marriage with Kate Capshaw, when the sight of any beautiful girl kicks his glands into high gear? This unbelievable pic might have made it as a made-for-TV-movie. Beautiful desirable girls literally throw themselves at Matheson at all times, in just about every conceivable place and he's more than just sorely tempted.

1709. *Little Shop of Horrors* (1986, Warner, 88m, c). P David Geffen, D Frank Oz, W/L Howard Ashman, M Alan Menken (based on the musical stage play by Ashman & Menken), PH Robert Paynter, ED John Jympson, PD Roy Walker, VE Lyle Conway, Bran Ferren & Martin Gutteridge†, SONG "Mean Green Mother from Outer Space" by Alan Menken & Howard Ashman†.

LP Rick Moranis (Seymour Krelborn), Ellen Greene (Audrey), Vincent Gardenia (Mushnik), Steve Martin (Orin Scrivello, D.D.S.), James Belushi (Patrick Martin), John Candy (Wink Wilkinson), Bill Murray (Arthur Denton), Levi Stubbs (The Voice of "Audrey II").

In this entertaining black comedy musical, nebbish Rick Moranis, in love with Ellen Greene, she of the big heart (among other big things), is losing out to sadistic dentist Steve Martin. Moranis develops an unusual new plant which craves meat and blood — human meat and blood, that is. Levi Stubbs, leader of the Four Tops, is the marvelous voice of the plant which solves Moranis' problem with his love life. The film is based on Roger Corman's low-budget 1960 film.

1710. *The Little Sister* (1985, American Playhouse, 103m, c). P Steve Wax, D&W Jan Egleson, PH Ed Lachman, M Pat Metheny, ED Sonya Polonsky.

LP John Savage (Tim Donovan), Tracy Pollan (Nicki Davis), Roxanne Hart (Sarah), Jack Kehoe, Henry Tomaszewski, Richard Jenkins.

Probation officer John Savage attempts to save Tracy Pollan from her bad habits and bad friends in Boston's notorious "Combat Zone" where she works.

1711. *Little Treasure* (1985, Tri-Star, 95m, c). P Herb Jaffe, D&W Alan Sharp, PH Alex Phillips, M Leo Kottke, ED Garth Craven, PD Jose Rodriguez, Granada Estevez & Enrique Estevez.

LP Margot Kidder (Margo), Ted Danson (Eugene), Burt Lancaster (Teschemacher), Joseph Hacker (Norman Kane), Malena Doria (Evangelina), John Pearce (Joseph), Gladys Holland (Sadie), Bill Zuckert (Charlie).

In a most forgettable movie, stripper Margot Kidder visits her dying father Burt Lancaster in Mexico. While there, she teams up with traveling projectionist Ted Danson to find money Lancaster had supposedly hidden in a ghost town years earlier. They encounter a number of unsavory characters during their quest.

1712. *The Living Daylights* (1987, United Artists, GB, 130m, c). P Albert R. Broccoli & Michael G. Wilson, D John Glen, W Richard Maibaum & Wilson (based on a story by Ian Fleming), PH Alec Mills, M John Barry, ED John Grover & Peter Davies, PD Peter Lamont, SE John Richardson.

LP Timothy Dalton (James Bond), Maryam d'Abo (Kara), Joe Don Baker (Whitaker), Art Malik (Kamran Shah), Jeroen Krabbe (Gen. Georgi Koskov), John Rhys-Davies (Gen. Leonid Pushkin), Andreas Wisniewski (Necros), Thomas Wheatley (Saunders), Desmond Llewelyn (Q), Robert Brown (M), Geoffrey Keen (Minister of Defence), Walter Gotell (Gen. Anatol Gogol), Caroline Bliss (Miss Moneypenny).

Agent 007 foils the Soviet KGB and money-grubbing arms dealers by parachuting from a helicopter onto the Rock of Gibraltar, where he successfully takes on armies of notorious drug dealers and terrorists. Timothy Dalton gives a new interpretation to Ian Fleming's hero. The former Shakespearean actor portrays Bond as a suave man who enjoys danger and is totally confident of his ability to handle any situation with a little help from the gadgets provided by Q.

1713. *Living Legend* (1980, Maverick, 92m, c). P Earl Owensby, D Worth Keeter, W Tom McIntyre, PH Darrell Cathcart, ED Richard Aldridge.

LP Earl Owensby (Eli Canfield), William T. Hicks (Jim Cannon), Ginger Alden (Jeannie Loring), Jerry Rushing (Chad), Greg Carswell (Teddy), Toby Wallace (Dean), Kristine Reynolds (Susan).

Roy Orbison sings the songs lip-synched by Earl Owensby, a hard-living country boy who becomes a singing legend and is not Elvis Presley, according to the movie's disclaimer. It must be mere coincidence that Ginger Alden was Presley's main squeeze at the time of his death.

1714. *Living on Tokyo Time* (1987, Skouras, 83m, c). P Lynn O'Donnell & Dennis Hayashi, D Steven Okazaki, W John McCormick & Okazaki, PH Okazaki & Zand Gee, ED Okazaki.

LP Minako Ohashi (Kyoko), Ken Nakagawa (Ken), Mitzie Abe (Mimi), Bill Bonham (Carl), Brenda Aoki (Michelle), Kate Connell (Lana), John McCormick (Richie), Sue Matthews (Nina), Jim Cranna (Jimbo).

Minako Ohashi, a 19-year-old Japanese girl from Tokyo, arrives in San Francisco, determined to make it on her own despite objections from her very traditional family. Eventually she marries Japanese-American dullard Ken Nakagawa, whose only ambition is to become a heavy-metal rock star. The two can't communicate very well, as her English is limited and he knows no Japanese. Eventually Ohashi gets up the nerve to leave Nakagawa and return to Tokyo, happy for her American experience, but happy to be home where she belongs.

1715. *Living the Blues* (1989, Gwyn & Alan Görg, 78m, c). P&W Gwyn & Alan Görg, D Alan Görg, PH Philip Holahan, M Sam Taylor, Andrew Albright. Louis

Stone, Clay Mitchell & the Görgs, ED Clay Mitchell.

LP Galyn Görg (Mana Brown), Sam Taylor (Sam Brown), Michael Kerr (Abel Wilson), Martin Raymond (Zanzibar Brown), Gwyn Görg (Effie Brown), Karlene Bradley (Mary Wilson), Fred Nelson (George Wilson).

Dancer Galyn Görg falls in love with aspiring blues guitarist Michael Kerr, but they find both their families objecting to the match.

1716. *Lobster Man from Mars* (1989, Electric Pictures, 93m, c). P Eyal Rimmon & Steven S. Greene, D Stanley Sheff, W Bob Greenberg, PH Gerry Lively, M Sasha Matson, ED Sheff & Joan Peterson, PD Daniel White.

LP Tony Curtis (J.P. Sheildrake), Deborah Foreman (Mary), Patrick Macnee (Professor Piccostomos), Billy Barty (Throckmorton), Anthony Hickox (John), Dean Jacobsen (Stevie Horowitz), Fred Holiday (Col. Ankrum), Bobby Pickett (King of Mars/The Astrologer), S.D. Nemeth (The Dreaded Lobster Man), Dr. Demento (Narrator).

Told that he needs a flop for tax purposes, movie mogul Tony Curtis previews the title film written and produced by a real loser. The film within a film takes up most of the 93-minute running time. It's a poor ripoff of sci-fi films of the 50s in which monsters from outer space showed up and threatened to destroy earth only to be thwarted by the efforts of a valiant band of scientists who find the one logical solution to stop the intruder. The movie sure looks bad enough but as in *The Producers* it becomes a hit and Curtis is ruined.

1717. *Local Hero* (1983, Warner, GB, 111m, c). P David Puttnam, D&W Bill Forsyth, PH Chris Menges, M Mark Knopfler, ED Michael Bradsell, PD Roger Murray-Leach.

LP Burt Lancaster (Happer), Peter Riegert (Mac), Fulton MacKay (Ben), Denis Lawson (Urquhart), Norman Chancer (Moritz), Peter Capaldi (Oldsen), Rikki Fulton (Geddes), Alex Norton (Watt), Jenny Seagrove (Marina), Jennifer Black (Stella), Christopher Rozycki (Victor), Christopher Asante (Rev. MacPherson).

Utterly charming, this whimsy by Bill Forsyth is the story of the inhabitants of a small village on the west coast of Scotland. Peter Reigert is sent by Houston oil baron Burt Lancaster, obviously mad as a hatter, to negotiate with the locals for the purchase of the entire village so his company can drill for North Sea oil reserves. It's a delightful comedy in which the amateurs out-fox the professionals. The characters, particularly Fulton MacKay, a beachcomber who owns the beach, and solicitor Denis Lawson, are unforgettable and the humor is sparkling and heart-warming. It's a real gem.

1718. *Lock Up* (1989, Tri-Star, 106m, c). P Lawrence Gordon & Charles Gordon, D John Flynn, W Richard Smith, Jeb Stuart & Henry Rosenbaum, PH Donald E. Thorin, M Bill Conti, ED Michael N. Knue & Donald Brochu, PD Bill Kenney.

LP Sylvester Stallone (Frank Leone), Donald Sutherland (Warden Drumgoole), John Amos (Meissner), Sonny Landham (Chink), Tom Sizemore (Dallas), Frank McRae (Eclipse), Darlanne Fluegel (Melissa), William Allen Young (Braden), Larry Romano (First Base).

Sylvester Stallone appears as another of his comic strip heroes. This time he's an easygoing, peaceful con who is transferred from a minimum-security institution to Donald Sutherland's savage prison. The only reason seems to be that Donald doesn't like Sly and he wants to brutalize him. Nothing about the movie is credible.

1719. *The Lone Runner* (1988, Trans-World, 85m, c). P Maurizio Maggi, D Ruggero Deodato, W Chris Trainor & Steven Luotto, PH Roberto Forges Davanzati, M Carlo Maria Cordio, ED Eugenio Alabiso.

LP Miles O'Keeffe (Garrett, the Lone Runner), Savina Gersak (Analisa Summerking), Michael J. Aronin (Emerik), John Steiner (Skorm), Hal Yamanouchi (Nimbus), Donald Hodson (Mr. Summerking), Ronald Lacey (Misha).

Rugged loner Miles O'Keeffe, equipped with a cross-bow and explosive arrows, comes to the rescue of beautiful European heiress Savina Gersak, kidnapped and held for ransom by Moroccan desert bandits.

1720. *Lone Wolf* (1989, Flash Features, 96m, c). P Sarah Liles & Doug Olson, D John Callas, W Michael Krueger, PH David Lewis, M Jon Kull, ED Kurt Tiegs.

LP Dyann Brown (Julie Martin), Kevin Hart (Joel), Jamie Newcomb (Eddie), Ann Douglas (Deirdre), Siren (Colleen), Jeff Harris (Joseph Simmons), Tom Henry (The Wolf).

When a rash of killings occur in a small town, police are slow to pick up on the clues that suggest a werewolf is responsible, but as the gory attacks increase, they begin to get the message.

1721. *Lone Wolf McQuade* (1983, Orion, 107m, c). P Yoram Bel-Ami & Steve Carver, D Carver, W B.J. Nelson (based on a story by H. Kaye Dyal & Nelson), PH Roger Shearman, M Francesco De Masi, ED Anthony Redman, PD Norm Baron.

LP Chuck Norris (J.J. McQuade), David Carradine (Rawley Wilkes), Barbara Carrera (Lola Richardson), Leon Isaac Kennedy (Jackson), Robert Beltran (Kayo), L.Q. Jones (Dakota), Dana Kimmell (Sally).

Chuck Norris, a contemporary Texas Ranger and one man army, is after gunrunner David Carradine who steals U.S. Army shipments and sells them to Central American terrorists. The two antagonists share Barbara Carrera as a love interest, but there's no love lost between these two in their climactic martial arts battle.

1722. *The Lonely Guy* (1984, Universal, 90m, c). P&D Arthur Hiller, W Ed Weinberger, Stan Daniels & Neil Simon (based on the novle *The Lonely Guy's Book of Life* by Bruce Jay Friedman), PH Victor J. Kemper, M Jerry Goldsmith, ED William Reynolds & Raja Gosnell, PD James D. Vance.

LP Steve Martin (Larry Hubbard), Charles Grodin (Warren Evans), Judith Ivey (Iris), Steve Lawrence (Jack Fenwick), Robyn Douglass (Danielle), Merv Griffin (Himself), Dr. Joyce Brothers (Herself), Candi & Randi Brough (Anita & Chelsea, the Schneider Twins).

When nerdish Steve Martin is thrown over by his girlfriend, he finds he's not alone. Soulmate Charles Grodin introduces Martin to New York City's society of Lonely Guys.

1723. *Lonely Hearts* (1983, Samuel Goldwyn, Australia, 95m, c). P John B. Murray, D Paul Cox, W Cox & John Clarke, PH Yuri Sokol, M Norman Kaye, ED Tim Lewis.

LP Wendy Hughes (Patricia Curnov), Norman Kaye (Peter Thompson), Jon Finlayson (George), Julia Blake (Pamela), Jonathan Hardy (Bruce), Irene Inescort (Patricia's Mother), Vic Gordon (Patricia's Father), Ted Grove-Rogers (Peter's Father).

In this pleasant comedy, office worker Wendy Hughes has missed most of life's experiences until she meets Norman Kaye, an outgoing middle-aged piano tuner. Their romance includes many charming light-hearted moments.

1724. *The Lonely Lady* (1983, Universal, 92m, c). P Robert R. Weston, D Peter Sasdy, W John Kershaw & Shawn Randall (based on the adaptation by Ellen Shepard of the novel by Harold Robbins), PH Brian West, M Charles Calello, ED Keith Palmer, PD Enzo Bulgarelli.

LP Pia Zadora (Jerilee), Lloyd Bochner (Walter), Bibi Besch (Veronica), Joseph Cali (Vincent), Anthony Holland (Guy), Jared Martin (George), Ray Liotta (Joe), Carla Romanelli (Carla), Olivier Pierre (George).

Few actresses so roundly roasted for their first film as was Pia Zadora ever were given the opportunity to make a second one. On the other hand few actresses have the backing of a man as wealthy and doting as Zadora's (real-life) multimillionaire husband. Here she portrays an aspiring screenwriter who sleeps with all comers of both sexes to make it to the top. Unfortunately, she does it without any style and makes even hot tub orgies look terribly boring.

1725. *The Lonely Passion of Judith Hearne* (1987, Island, GB, 110m, c). P Peter Nelson & Richard Johnson, D Jack Clayton, W Nelson, PH Peter Hannan, M Georges Delerue, ED Terry Rawlings, PD Michael Pickwoad.

LP Maggie Smith (Judith Hearne), Bob Hoskins (James Madden), Wendy

Hiller (Aunt D'Arcy), Marie Kean (Mrs. Rice), Ian McNeice (Bernard), Alan Devlin (Father Quigley), Rudi Davies (Mary), Prunella Scales (Moira O'Neill), Aine Ni Mhuri (Edie Marinan), Sheila Reid (Miss Friel).

Set in Dublin in the 1950s, Maggie Smith is a pious old maid piano teacher who is desperate to catch a husband. She is courted by Bob Hoskins, another tenant in the rooming house where she lives. He's just back in Ireland after 30 years in the United States. He's not interested in Smith romantically, but figuring she has money to invest in his entrepreneurial plans, courts her anyway. When she discovers his true motives, it brings on a crisis of faith for her. Smith and Hoskins are just tremendous. One of these days Hoskins will walk off with a much deserved Oscar for one of his triumphant performances. Unfortunately for this fine outing he wasn't even nominated. Smith is equally impressive.

The Loner see ***Ruckus***

1726. *The Long Good Friday* (1982, Embassy, GB, 105m, c). P Barry Hanson, D John Mackenzie, W Barrie Keefe, PH Phil Meheux, M Francis Monkman, ED Mike Taylor.

LP Bob Hoskins (Harold), Helen Mirren (Victoria), Eddie Constantine (Charlie), Dave King (Parky), Bryan Marshall (Harris), George Coulouris (Gus), Derek Thompson (Jeff), Bruce Alexander (Mac), Paul Barber (Errol), Pierce Brosnan (1st Irishman).

Bob Hoskins is brilliant as a London underworld boss who finds himself in a battle with the IRA during an Easter weekend.

1727. *The Long Riders* (1980, United Artists, 99m, c). P Tim Zinneman, D Walter Hill, W Bill Bryden, Steven Phillip Smith & Stacy Keach, PH Ric Waite, M Ry Cooder, ED David Holden, PD Jack T. Collis.

LP David Carradine (Cole Younger), Keith Carradine (Jim Younger), Robert Carradine (Bob Younger), James Keach (Jesse James), Stacy Keach (Frank James), Dennis Quaid (Ed Miller), Randy Quaid (Clell Miller), Kevin Brophy (John Younger), Harry Carey, Jr. (George Arthur), Christopher Guest (Charlie Ford), Nicholas Guest (Bob Ford), Shelby Leverington (Annie Ralston), Pamela Reed (Belle Starr).

Probably the last great western made, the film details the famous James-Younger gang, their disastrous raid on Northfield, Minnesota, and the familiar tale of the murder of Jesse James by the "dirty little coward" Bob Ford. In an unusual casting decision, the various brothers are for the most part played by real-life brothers. It's a gritty, realistic filming of the exploits of legendary badmen.

1728. *The Long Road Home* (1989, Lauron, Canada, 95m, c). P Ronald Lillie & William Johnston, D Johnston, W Dan Datree, PH Vic Sarin, ED Judy Krupanszky & Johnston.

LP Denis Forest (Michael Posen), Kelly Rowan (Cynthia), Gareth Bennett (Ronald Schubert).

This story about an American draft dodger in Ontario in 1969 is short on drama but tall on scenery.

1729. *Long Shot* (1981, Mithras, GB, 85m, b&w/c). P&D Maurice Hatton, W Hatton, Eoin McCann & the Cast, PH Michael Davis, Michael Dodds, Ivan Strasburg, Hatton & Teo Davis, M Terry Dougherty & Antonio Vivaldi, ED Howard Sharp.

LP Charles Gormley (Charlie), Neville Smith (Neville), Ann Zelda (Anne), David Stone (A Distributor), Suzanne Danielle (Sue), Ron Taylor (American Director), Stephen Frears (Biscuit Man), Jim Haines (Professor of Sexual Politics).

The performers in this film about the difficulties of making a movie are for the most part not actors. If you think you'd like to make a movie, it might be a good idea to see this one before beginning.

1730. *The Long Weekend (O'Despair)* (1989, Desperate Pictures, 87m, c). P,D,W&ED Gregg Araki, PH Araki, M Various Artists.

LP Bretton Vail (Michael), Maureen Bondanvile (Rachel), Andrea Beane (Leah), Nicole Dillenberg (Sara), Marcus D'Amico (Greg), Lance Woods (Alex).

Gregg Araki attempts to present a new

"Lost Generation" of mostly homosexuals and bisexuals and fails.

1731. *The Longshot* (1986, Orion, 89m, c). P Lang Elliott, D Paul Bartel, W Tim Conway, PH Robby Muller, M Charles Fox, ED Alan Toomayan.

LP Tim Conway (Dooley), Jack Weston (Elton), Harvey Korman (Lou), Ted Wass (Stump), Pat Li (Ono), Garry Goodrow (Josh), Brad Tumbull (Track Cop), Anne Meara (Madge), Benny Baker (Mr. Hooper), Yvonne Del Walker (Mrs. Hooper).

Carol Burnett's veteran second bananas Tim Conway and Harvey Korman team up with Jack Weston and Ted Wass as four simps who borrow $5,000 from the mob to bet on a horse. Naturally they lose. Naturally they have no means to pay their debt. Naturally the boys in three-piece suits and wingtips want the money or the chumps' lives. Hardly enough material here for a 15-minute sketch on Carol's TV show.

Look Down and Die see Steel

1732. *Look Who's Talking* (1989, Tri-Star, 93m, c). P Jonathan D. Krane, D&W Amy Heckerling, PH Thomas Del Ruth, M David Kitay, ED Debra Chiate.

LP John Travolta (James), Kirstie Alley (Mollie), Olympia Dukakis (Rosie), George Segal (Albert), Abe Vigoda (Grandpa), Bruce Willis (Voice of Mikey), Twink Caplan (Rona), Jason Schaller, Jaryd Waterhouse, Jacob Haines & Christopher Aydon (Mikey).

In this cute but not very appealing movie, Bruce Willis is the voice of a baby named Mikey who tries to find Mr. Right for his unwed mother Kirstie Alley. She was stupid enough to get pregnant by a man she doesn't care for. Mikey's prime candidate is John Travolta in his best role in years. One-joke movies drag after a while. This one is no exception. The plot is basically Danielle Steele material. It's the kind of movie you see once, laugh at Willis' remarks and soon forget.

1733. *Looker* (1981, Warner, 94m, c). P Howard Jeffrey, D&W Michael Crichton, PH Paul Lohmann, M Barry DeVorzon, ED Carl Kress, PD Dean Edward Mitzner.

LP Albert Finney (Dr. Larry Roberts),

James Coburn (John Reston), Susan Dey (Cindy), Leigh Taylor-Young (Jennifer Long), Dorian Harewood (Lt. Masters), Tim Rossovich (Moustache Man), Darryl Hickman (Dr. Jim Belfield), Kathryn Witt (Tina), Terri Welles (Lisa).

Plastic surgeon Albert Finney becomes a murder suspect when two models upon whom he has operated are found murdered.

1734. *Lookin' to Get Out* (1982, Paramount, 104m, c). P Robert Schaffel, D Hal Ashby, W Al Schwartz, PH Haskell Wexler, M Johnny Mandel, ED Robert C. Jones, PD Robert Boyle.

LP Jon Voight (Alex Kovac), Ann-Margret (Patti Warner), Burt Young (Jerry Feldman), Bert Remsen (Smitty), Jude Farese (Harry), Allen Keller (Joey), Richard Bradford (Bernie Gold).

After losing $10,000 belonging to thugs, losers Jon Voight and Burt Young leave New York for Las Vegas. There they team up with former callgirl Ann-Margret and break the bank of the casino at the MGM Grand Hotel.

1735. *Looks and Smiles* (1982, Black Lion-Kestrel, GB, 104m, c). P Irving Teitelbaum, D Kenneth Loach, W Barry Hines, PH Chris Menges, M Marc Wilkinson, Richard & The Taxmen, ED Steve Singleton.

LP Phil Askham, Pam Darrell, Graham Green, Tracey Goodlad, Stuart Golland, Patti Nicholls, Tony Pitts, Arthur Davies, Cilla Mason.

The cast of this film are all amateurs. It is the story of two high-school dropouts: one enlists in the military and is sent to Belfast where he terrorizes Catholics, while the other remains home and becomes more and more destitute.

1736. *The Looney Looney Looney Bugs Bunny Movie* (1981, Warner, 80m, c). P&D Friz Freleng, W John Dunn, David Detiege & Freleng, VOICE CHARACTERIZATIONS Mel Blanc, June Foray, Frank Nelson, Frank Welker, Stan Freberg & Ralph James, ED Jim Champin, ANIM D Warren Batchelder, Charles Downs, Marcia Fertig, Bob Matz, Manuel Perez, Virgil Ross & Lloyd Vaughan.

LP Bugs Bunny, Porky Pig, Elmer

Fudd, Foghorn Leghorn, Yosemite Sam, Tweety Pie, Daffy Duck, etc.

This feature length compilation of classic Warner Bros. cartoons is tied together with new animation.

1737. *Loophole* (1981, Brent Walker, GB, 105m, c). P David Korda & Julian Holloway, D John Quested, W Jonathan Hales (based on the novel by Robert Pollock), PH Michael Reed, M Lalo Schifrin, ED Ralph Sheldon, PD Syd Cain.

LP Albert Finney (Mike Daniels), Martin Sheen (Stephen Booker), Susannah York (Dinah Booker), Colin Blakely (Gardner), Jonathan Pryce (Taylor), Alfred Lynch (David), Christopher Guard (Cliff), Robert Morley (Godfrey), Terence Hardiman (David), Bridget Brice (Emily).

Albert Finney and Martin Sheen star in a lackluster heist film. Architect Sheen, deeply in debt, is recruited by Finney to help his gang of thieves rob a large London bank.

1738. *Loose Connections* (1984, 20th Century–Fox, GB, 96m, c). P Simon Perry, D Richard Eyre, W Maggie Brooks, PH Clive Tickner, M Dominic Muldowney.

LP Lindsay Duncan (Sally), Stephen Rea (Harry), Carole Harrison (Kay), Frances Low (Laurie), Andrew De La Tour (Journalist), David Purcell (Photographer), Keith Allen (Keith), Robbie Coltrane (Drunk).

In a routine road comedy, dedicated feminist Lindsay Duncan travels from London to Munich with Stephen Rea, who pretends to be gay.

Loose Joints see Flicks

1739. *Loose Screws* (1985, Concorde, 76m, c). P Maurice Smith, D Rafal Zielinski, W Michael Cory & Phil Keuber, PH Brian Foley, M Fred Mollin, ED Stephan Fanfara, PD Ken Gord.

LP Brian Genesse (Brad Lovett), Lance Van Der Kolk (Steve Hardman), Alan Deveau (Hugh G. Rection), Jason Warren (Marvin Eatmore), Cyd Belliveau (Mona Lott), Karen Wood (Gail Poulet), Annie Mcauley (Nikki Mystroke), Mike McDonald (Principal Arsenault), Liz Green (Tracy Gratehead), Debora Lobbin (Miss Van Blow).

Don't you just hate movies in which the characters are given puns for names? You don't? Well then this sleazy teen sex comedy might just knock your socks off, because the naming of the characters is the cleverest thing in it. The film has the usual ingredients, horny males, sexy, teasing females, and idiotic adults.

1740. *Loose Shoes* (1980, Atlantic, 74m, c, aka *Coming Attractions*). P Joel Chernoff, D Ira Miller, W Varley Smith, Ian Paiser, Royce D. Applegate & Miller, PH John P. Beckett, M Murphy Dunne, ED Alan Balsam.

LP Lewis Arquette (Warden), Danny Dayton (Bartender), Buddy Hackett (Himself), Ed Lauter (Sheriff), Jaye P. Morgan (Stop-It Nurse), Bill Murray (Lefty), Avery Schreiber (Theater Manager), Susan Tyrrell (Boobies), Murphy Dunne (Tough G.I.), Howard Hesseman (Ernie Piles).

A cast of comedians, who occasionally have proven to be individually funny, working together on a failed spoof of B movies in the vein of *Kentucky Fried Movie,* are unable to raise more than an occasional chuckle.

1741. *The Lords of Discipline* (1983, Paramount, 102m, c). P Herb Jaffe & Gabriel Katzka, D Franc Roddam, W Thomas Pope & Lloyd Fonvielle (based on the novel by Pat Conroy), PH Brian Tufano, M Howard Blake, ED Michael Ellis, PD John Graysmark.

LP David Keith (Will), Robert Prosky (Bear), G.D. Spradlin (Gen. Durrell), Barbara Babcock (Abigail), Michael Biehn (Alexander), Rick Rossovich (Pig), John Lavachielli (Mark), Mitchell Lichtenstein (Trado), Mark Breland (Pearce), Malcolm Danare (Poteete), Judge Reinhold (Macabbee).

In an emotionally charged film, David Keith stars as a military academy student who risks his life to help the school's first black cadet, Mark Breland. A Hitler Youth–like secret cadre of cadets, who call themselves The Ten, wish to at least castrate the unwelcome newcomer, and almost kill him.

1742. *Lords of the Deep* (1989, Concorde, 82m, c). P Roger Corman, D Mary Ann Fisher, W Howard Cohen & Daryl

Haney, PH Austin McKinney, M Jim Berenholtz, ED Nina Gilberti.

LP Bradford Dillman (Dobler), Priscilla Barnes (Claire), Melody Ryane (Barbara), Daryl Haney (O'Neill), Eb Lottimer (Seaver), Greg Sobeck (Engel), Richard Young (Chadwick), Stephen Davies (Fernandez).

In a too familiar story, a crew of scientists are all at sea when they pick up some evil-looking foaming goop which kills whatever it comes in contact with. If this wasn't enough of a life threat, the commander of the submarine, Bradford Dillman, is a psychopath who does some of his own killing.

1743. *Losin' It* (1983, Embassy, 104m, c). P Bryan Gindoff & Hannah Hempstead, D Curtis Hanson, W B.W.L. Norton (based on a story by Norton), PH Gil Taylor, M Ken Wannberg, ED Richard Halsey, PD Robb Wilson King.

LP Tom Cruise (Woody), Jackie Earle Haley (Dave), John Stockwell (Spider), Shelley Long (Kathy), John P. Navin, Jr. (Wendell), Henry Darrow (El Jefe), James Victor (Lawyer), Hector Elias (Chuey).

Four high school seniors head for Tijuana to lose their virginity with some local señoritas for hire. They get mixed up with waitress Shelley Long, who has come along for the ride to get a quickie divorce. The film is filled with stereotypes and the boys are not the kind to make parents proud.

1744. *Lost Angels* (1989, Orion, 116m, c). P Howard Rosenman & Thomas Baer, D Hugh Hudson, W Michael Weller, PH Juan Ruiz Anchia, M Philippe Sarde, ED David Gladwell, PD Assheton Gorton.

LP Donald Sutherland (Dr. Charles Loftis), Adam Horovitz (Tim Doolan), Amy Locane (Cheryl Anderson), Don Bloomfield (Andy Doolan), Celia Weston (Felicia Marks), Graham Beckel (Richard Doolan), Patricia Richardson (Mrs. Anderson), Ron Frazier (Barton Marks).

This film, none too subtly or effectively, explores the meaningless existence of teens in sun-drenched Southern California. Adam Horovitz, a member of the Beastie Boys rap band, gives a sympathetic but not altogether believable performance as a youngster in whom violence lies just below the surface. He can't understand why his life seems so empty, despite having so much. It's a new-wave look at *Rebel Without a Cause.*

1745. *The Lost Boys* (1987, Warner, 97m, c). P Harvey Bernhard, D Joel Schumacher, W Janice Fischer, James Jeremias & Jeffrey Boam (based on a story by Fischer & Jeremias), PH Michael Chapman, M Thomas Newman, ED Robert Brown, PD Bo Welch.

LP Jason Patric (Michael), Corey Haim (Sam), Dianne Wiest (Lucy), Barnard Hughes (Grandpa), Edward Herrmann (Max), Kiefer Sutherland (David), Jami Gertz (Star), Corey Feldman (Edgar Frog), Jamison Newlander (Alan Frog), Brooke McCarter (Paul), Billy Wirth (Dwayne).

Kiefer Sutherland leads a gang of teenage biker vampires. They recruit Jason Patric into their blood-crazed brand of fun, but with the help of his brother Corey Haim, he is able to save himself and ensure that good triumphs over evil. The horror show has a number of comical angles.

1746. *The Lost Empire* (1985, JGM Enterprises, 83m, c). P,D&W Jim Wynorski, PH Jacques Haitkin, M Alan Howarth, ED Larry Bock, PD Wayne Springfield.

LP Melanie Vincz (Angel Wolfe), Raven de la Croix (Whitestar), Angela Aames (Heather), Paul Coufos (Rick), Bob Tessier (Koro), Angus Scrimm (Dr. Sin Do), Blackie Dammett (Krager), Linda Shayne (Cindy), Angelique Pettyjohn (Whiplash).

In this pitifully poor spoof of adventure films, Angus Scrimm is an evil-cult leader, living on an atoll in the Pacific Ocean. Having made a pact with the devil he is able to cause earthquakes, hurricanes and other seemingly natural disasters. Concerned that this might not be enough to keep the interest of people who mistakenly wandered into a theater showing this pap, the producers make certain that the girls wear as little as possible throughout the film.

1747. *Lost in America* (1985, Warner, 91m, c). P Marty Katz, D Albert Brooks,

W Brooks & Monica Johnson, PH Eric Saarinen, M Arthur B. Rubinstein, ED David Finfer, PD Richard Sawyer.

LP Albert Brooks (David Howard), Julie Hagerty (Linda Howard), Michael Greene (Paul Dunn), Tom Tarpey (Brad Tooley), Garry K. Marshall (Casino Manager), Maggie Roswell (Patty), Ernie Brown (Pharmacist), Art Frankel (Employment Agent), Joey Coleman (Skippy).

Did you ever have the dream to give up everything you have and are in order to move to another part of the country to start over in God's country? The message of this movie seems to be, roll over and go back to sleep. Albert Brooks and Julie Hagerty quit their well-paid jobs, sell everything, buy a large motor home and set out to discover America. Instead they discover that problems are functions of people not locations. In the end they hurry back to Manhattan to resume their former lifes, perhaps now a little wiser.

1748. *Love* (1982, Levinson-Velvet, Canada, 105m, c). P Renee Perlmutter, D Mai Zetterling (Episodes 1,2,5), Liv Ullmann (Episode 6), Nancy Dowd (Episode 3), Annette Cohen (Episode 4), W Zetterling, Joni Mitchell, Dowd, Gael Greene, Edna O'Brien, Ullmann, PH Reginald Morris & Norman Leigh, M Tim McCauley, ED Donald Ginsberg, Wayne Griffin & Stephan Fanfara, PD Claude Bonniere.

LP Maureen Fitzgerald (Mum), Gordon Thomson (Tony), Joni Mitchell (Paula), Winston Rekert (John), Nicholas Campbell (Danny), Toni Kalem (The Girl), Marilyn Lightstone (Marilyn), Moses Znaimer (Marvin), Linda Rennhofer (Shirley), Janet-Laine Green (Julia), Charlie Jolliffe (Old Man), Rita Tuckett (Wife).

Four female directors examine love in six different episodes, entitled: "Love from the Marketplace," "The Black Cat in the Black Mouse Socks," "Por Vida/For Life," "Love on Your Birthday," "Julia," and "Parting."

1749. *Love and Money* (1982, Paramount, 90m, c). P,D&W James Toback, PH Fred Schuler, M Aaron Copland, ED Dennis Hill.

LP Ray Sharkey (Byron Levin), Ornella Muti (Catherine Stockheinz), Klaus Kinski (Frederick Stockheinz), Armand Assante (Lorenzo Prado), King Vidor (Walter Klein), Susan Heldfond (Vicky), William Prince (Ambassador Paultz), Tony Sirico (Raoul).

The great American director King Vidor makes an appearance in this clumsy thriller as the 87-year-old senile grandfather of Ray Sharkey. The latter is a nobody from L.A. who is drawn into the violence and intrigue of a silver-rich Latin American country, through his affair with Ornella Muti, the wife of business magnate Klaus Kinski.

1750. *Love at Stake* (1987, Tri-Star/Hemdale, 83m, c). P Michael Gruskoff, D John Moffitt, W Terry Sweeney & Lanier Laney, PH Mark Irwin, M Charles Fox, ED Danford B. Greene.

LP Patrick Cassidy (Miles Campbell), Kelly Preston (Sara Lee), Georgia Brown (Widow Chastity), Barbara Carrera (Faith Stewart), Bud Cort (Parson Babcock), Annie Golden (Abigail), David Graff (Nathaniel), Anne Ramsey (Old Witch), Dr. Joyce Brothers (Herself), Audrie J. Neenan (Mrs. Babcock), Stuart Pankin (Judge John), Dave Thomas (Mayor Upton).

The film is a spoof of the Salem witch trials in the tradition of Mel Brooks. That means it's a success or failure depending upon your tolerance for obvious and broad humor. Barbara Carrera is a very sexy, very wicked witch. Stuart Pankin and Dave Thomas shine as corrupt officials.

1751. *The Love Butcher* (1982, Mirror Releasing, 83m, c). P Gary Williams & Micki Belski, D Mikel Angel & Don Jones, W Jones & James Evergreen, PH Jones & Austin McKinney, M Richard Hieronymous, ED Robert Freeman.

LP Erik Stern (Caleb/Lester), Kay Near (Florence), Jeremiah Beecher (Russell), Edward Roehm (Capt. Stark), Robin Sherwood (Sheila).

Gardener Erik Stern gets his revenge on his female employers who constantly mistreat him, when his alter-ego rapes and murders them.

1752. *Love Child* (1982, Warner, 97m, c). P Paul Maslansky, D Larry

Peerce, W Anne Gerard & Katherine Specktor (based on a story by Gerard), PH James Pergola, M Charles Fox, ED Bob Wyman.

LP Amy Madigan (Terry Jean Moore), Beau Bridges (Jack Hansen), Mackenzie Phillips (J.J.), Albert Salmi (Capt. Ellis), Joanna Merlin (Supt. Sturgis), Margaret Whitton (Jacki Steinberg), Lewis Smith (Jesse Chaney), Dennis Lipscomb (Arthur Brady), Anna Maria Horsford (Mara).

Based on a true story, Amy Madigan is sent to prison for a crime committed by her cousin. She is befriended by guard Beau Bridges. This leads to an affair and her becoming pregnant. Instead of agreeing to give up the child she fights to be allowed to keep it while in prison.

1753. *Love in a Taxi* (1980, Davey, 90m, c). P&D Robert Sickinger, W Michael Kortchmar, PH Joseph Mangine, M Susan Minsky, ED Bill Freda.

LP Diane Sommerfield (Carine), James H. Jacobs (Sam), Earl Monroe (Gary), Malik Murray (Davey), Lisa Jane Persky (Marian), Lyle Kessler (Jimmy), Karen Grannum (Norman), Phil Rubinstein (Monk).

This warm-hearted little delight is the story of a romance between a New York Jewish cab driver, James H. Jacobs, and a black bank clerk, Diane Sommerfield.

1754. *Love Letters* (1983, New World, 98m, c, aka *My Love Letters*). P Roger Corman, D&W Amy Jones, PH Alec Hirschfeld, M Ralph Jones, ED Wendy Green.

LP Jamie Lee Curtis (Anna), James Keach (Oliver), Amy Madigan (Wendy), Bud Cort (Danny), Matt Clark (Winter), Bonnie Bartlett (Mrs. Winter), Phil Coccioletti (Ralph), Shelby Leverington (Edith), Rance Howard (Chelsey), Betsy Toll (Marcia), Sally Kirkland (Sally).

Jamie Lee Curtis gives a sensitive performance as a young woman who after discovering her dead mother's correspondence with a lover, has an affair with older married man James Keach.

1755. *Love Streams* (1984, MGM/United Artists, 141m, c). P Menahem Golan & Yoram Globus, D John Cassavetes, W Ted Allan & Cassavetes (based

on the play by Allan), PH Al Ruban, M Bo Harwood, ED George C. Villasenor.

LP Gena Rowlands (Sarah Lawson), John Cassavetes (Robert Harmon), Diahnne Abbott (Susan), Seymour Cassel (Jack Lawson), Margaret Abbott (Margarita), Jakob Shaw (Albie Swanson), Michele Conway (Agnes Swanson), Eddy Donno (Stepfather Swanson), Joan Foley (Judge Dunbar).

Successful writer John Cassavetes is troubled by conflicts between the demands of his career and the needs of his young son. He also is troubled by his relationship with his divorced sister Gena Rowlands.

1756. *The Loveless* (1982, Atlantic, 84m, c). P Grafton Nunes & A.K. Ho, D&W Kathryn Bigelow & Monty Montgomery, PH Doyle Smith, M Robert Gordon, ED Nancy Kanter, PD Lilly Kivert.

LP J. Don Ferguson (Tarver), Willem Dafoe (Vance), Marin Kanter (Telena), Robert Gordon (Davis), Tina L'Hotsky (Debbie), Lawrence Matarese (LaVille), Daniel Rosen (Ricky), Phillip Mont Kimbrough (Hurley), Ken Call (Buck).

Nothing much happens in this tribute to *The Wild One* and Edward Hopper's paintings. It was made by two recently graduated high school students.

1757. *Lovelines* (1984, Tri-Star, 93m, c). P Hal Taines & Michael Lloyd, D Rod Amateau, W Chip Hand & William Hillman (based on a story by Hand, Hillman & Lloyd), PH Duke Callaghan, ED David Bretherton & Fred A. Chulack.

LP Greg Bradford (Rick Johnson), Mary Beth Evans (Piper), Michael Winslow (J.D.), Don Michael Paul (Jeff), Tammy Taylor (Priscilla), Stacey Toten (Cynthia), Robert Delapp & Frank Zagarino (Godzilla).

In this boring teen sex-comedy, two competing high schools have a battle of the bands. The title refers to a teenage phone service.

1758. *Lovely But Deadly* (1983, Juniper, 93m, c). P Doro Vlado Hreljanovic & David Sheldon, D Sheldon, W Sheldon & Patricia Joyce (based on a story by Lawrence D. Foldes), PH Robert Roth, M Robert O. Ragland, ED Richard Brummer.

LP Lucinda Dooling (Lovely), John Randolph (Franklin), Richard Herd (Honest Charley), Susan Mechsner (Martial Arts Teacher), Mel Novak, Marie Windsor, Mark Holden, Rick Moser.

After her brother dies of an overdose of drugs, young Lucinda Dooling wages a war against the drug dealers in her school.

1759. *Lover Boy* (1989, Seon Films, Australia, 60m, c). P Daniel Scharf, D&W Geoffrey Wright, PH Michael Williams, M John Clifford, ED Grant Fenn, PD Jody Borland.

LP Noah Taylor (Mick), Gillian Jones (Sally), Ben Mendelsohn (Gaz), Daniel Pollock (Duck), Alice Garner (Rhonda), Peter Hosking (Lex).

Sixteen-year-old Noah Taylor enters into a passionate affair with lonely 43-year-old Gillian Jones. She rejects him when a former lover shows up. Taylor comes to her defense when he finds the interloper beating her and is fatally stabbed for his trouble.

1760. *Loverboy* (1989, Tri-Star, 98m, c). P Gary Foster & Willie Hunt, D Joan Micklin Silver, W Robin Schiff, Tom Ropelewski & Leslie Dixon (based on a story by Schiff), PH John Hora, M Michel Colombier, ED Rick Shaine, PD Dan Leigh.

LP Patrick Dempsey (Randy Bodek), Kate Jackson (Diane Bodek), Robert Ginty (Joe Bodek), Nancy Valen (Jenny), Barbara Carrera (Alex), Charles Hunter Walsh (Jory), Kirstie Alley (Joyce), Carrie Fisher (Monica), Kim Miyori (Kyoko).

Pizza delivery boy Patrick Dempsey lives a wet dream. He's constantly encountering scantily clad, sexy women who just adore his bean-pole physique, clumsy ways and teenage enthusiasm in bed.

1761. *Lovesick* (1983, Warner, 95m, c). P Charles Okun, D&W Marshall Brickman, PH Gerry Fisher, M Philippe Sarde, ED Nina Feinberg, PD Philip Rosenberg.

LP Dudley Moore (Saul Benjamin), Elizabeth McGovern (Chloe Allen), Alec Guinness (Sigmund Freud), Christine Baranski (Nymphomaniac), Gene Saks (Frantic Patient), Renee Taylor (Mrs. Mondragon), Kent Broadhurst (Gay), Lester Rawlins (Silent Patient), Wallace Shawn (Otto Jaffe).

Dudley Moore portrays a psychiatrist who falls in love with patient Elizabeth McGovern. He consults with the ghost of Freud, Alec Guinness, about his dilemma.

1762. *Loving Couples* (1980, 20th Century–Fox, 97m, c). P Renee Valente, D Jack Smight, W Martin Donovan, PH Philip Lathrop, M Fred Karlin, ED Grey Fox & Frank Urioste.

LP Shirley MacLaine (Evelyn), James Coburn (Walter), Susan Sarandon (Stephanie), Stephen Collins (Gregg), Sally Kellerman (Mrs. Liggett), Nan Martin (Walter's Nurse), Shelly Batt (Dulcy), Bernard Behrens (Elegant Doctor), Anne Bloom (Nurse).

Physicians Shirley MacLaine and James Coburn are too busy to have much time for each other any more. Real estate salesman Stephen Collins lives with TV weatherwoman Susan Sarandon. MacLaine meets Collins and starts an affair. Sarandon blows the whistle on the cheating couple to Coburn. They find revenge and solace in each other's arms. After awhile the generations get sorted out the way they should, but not before Collins has to show Sally Kellerman the special virtues of the bedroom of a house she's considering buying. The demonstration ends just as the owner arrives home. Collins finds everything except his shoes and socks as he desperately tries to get out before he's discovered.

Loving Walter see Walter and June

1763. *Low Blow* (1986, Crown International, 90m, c, aka *Savage Sunday*). P&W Leo Fong, D&PH Frank Harris, M Steve Amundsen & Samuel S. Cardon, ED Harris.

LP Leo Fong (Joe Wong), Cameron Mitchell (Yarakunda), Troy Donahue (John Templeton), Diane Stevenett (Diane), Akosua Busia (Karma), Patti Bowling (Karen Templeton), Stack Pierce (Corky), Woody Farmer (Fuzzy).

Millionaire Troy Donahue hires commandos to break into a religious cult's hideaway and rescue his daughter Patti Bowling. Dull! Dull! Dull!

1764. *Loyalties* (1987, Cinema Group, Canada, 98m, c). P William Johnston & Ronald Lillie, D Anne Wheeler, W Sharon Riis (based on a story by Riis & Wheeler), PH Vic Sarin, ED Judy Krupanszky, AD Richard Hudolin.

LP Kenneth Welsh (David Sutton), Tantoo Cardinal (Rosanne Ladouceur), Susan Wooldridge (Lily Sutton), Vera Martin (Beatrice), Diane Debassige (Leona), Tom Jackson (Eddy), Jeffrey Smith (Nicholas).

In this predictable psychological drama, Kenneth Welsh and Susan Wooldridge are a very proper British couple who settle in a remote Canadian village. Things get interesting when they take hell-raising, half-Indian Tantoo Cardinal as a housekeeper.

1765. *Lucas* (1986, 20th Century–Fox, 100m, c). P David Nicksay, D&W David Seltzer, PH Reynaldo Villalobos, M Dave Grusin, ED Priscilla Nedd.

LP Corey Haim (Lucas), Kerri Green (Maggie), Charlie Sheen (Cappie), Courtney Thorne-Smith (Alise), Winona Ryder (Rina), Thomas E. Hodges (Bruno), Ciro Poppiti (Ben), Guy Boyd (Coach), Jeremy Piven (Spike), Kevin Gerard Wixted (Tonto), Emily Seltzer (Marie).

Corey Haim is very appealing as an underweight but not underspirited 14 year old who longs for an "older woman," 16-year-old Kerri Green. He's willing to climb any mountain, swim any ocean to win her approval, even go out for the football team and wear a uniform which fits him like a tent. Surprise, he doesn't get the girl. And perhaps that's why this youth film is superior to the others. These kids seem real, and all those who were oh, so shy, and athletically inferior can identify with a lad for whom things work out, but not exactly as he had hoped for.

1766. *The Luckiest Man in the World* (1989, Second Effort Co., 82m, c). P Norman I. Cohen, D&W Frank D. Gilroy, PH Jeri Sopanen, M Warren Vache & Jack Gale, ED John Gilroy, PD Nick Romanec.

LP Philip Bosco (Sam Posner), Doris Belack (Mrs. Posner), Joanne Camp (Laura), Matthew Gottlieb (Sheldon), Arthur French (Cleveland), Stan Lachow (Schwartz), Yamil Borges (Mrs. Gonzalez), J.D. Clarke (Robert Whitley), Moses Gunn (Voice).

When mean-spirited New York garment district businessman Philip Bosco narrowly misses death in a plane crash, he resolves to mend his ways. But his new kinder, gentler behavior only upsets and irritates everyone around him.

1767. *The Lucky Star* (1980, Tele Metropole Internationale, Canada, 110m, c). P Claude Leger, D Max Fischer, W Fischer & Jack Rosenthal (based on an original idea by Roland Topor), PH Frank Tidy, M Art Phillips, ED Yves Langlois.

LP Rod Steiger (Col. Gluck), Louise Fletcher (Loes Bakker), Lou Jacobi (Elia Goldberg), Brett Marx (David Goldberg), Helen Hughes (Rose Goldberg), Yvon Dufour (Burgomaster), Jean Gascon (Priest).

After his parents are taken away by the Nazis, young Jewish boy Brett Marx is given shelter on a Rotterdam farm run by Louise Fletcher. The boy, a lover of Hollywood B westerns, single-handedly takes on German officer Rod Steiger.

1768. *Lucky Stiff* (1989, New Line Cinema, 82m, c, aka *Mr. Christmas Dinner*). P Gerald T. Olson, D Anthony Perkins, W Pat Proft, PH Jacques Haitkin, M Tom Jenkins, ED Michael N. Knue & Tom Walls, PD C.J. Strawn.

LP Donna Dixon (Cynthia Mitchell), Joe Alaskey (Ron Douglas), Jeff Kober (Ike Mitchell), Barbara Howard (Frances), Fran Ryan (Ma Mitchell), Morgan Sheppard (Pa Mitchell), Leigh McCloskey (Eric West).

When overweight Joe Alaskey's bride-to-be fails to show up for their wedding, sister and brother team Donna Dixon and Jeff Kober latch on to him as a meal ticket for their family of inbred cannibals. You probably missed this black comedy in the theaters, but it's worth a trip to your favorite video store.

Lucky 13 see Running Hot

1769. *Luggage of the Gods* (1983, General, 74m, c). P Jeff Folmsbee, D&W David Kendall, PH Steven Ross, M Cengiz Yaltkaya, ED Jack Haigis.

LP Mark Stolzenberg (Yuk), Gabriel Barre (Tull), Gwen Ellison (Hubba),

Martin Haber (Zoot), Rochelle Robins (Kono), Lou Leccese (Flon), Dog Thomas (Gum), John Tarrant (Whittaker), Conrad Bergschneider (Lionel).

Reminiscent of *The Gods Must Be Crazy,* the lives of a group of cavemen and cavewomen are drastically changed when a set of luggage mysteriously falls among them from a passing jet liner.

1770. *Luigi's Ladies* (1989, Tra La La Films, Australia, 95m, c). P Patric Juillet, D Judy Morris, W Jennifer Claire, Ronald Allan, Wendy Hughes & Morris, PH Steve Mason, M Sharon Calcraft, ED Pamela Barnetta.

LP Wendy Hughes (Sara), Sandy Gore (Cee), Anne Tenney (Jane), David Rappaport (Luigi), John Walton (Steve), Serge Lazaroff (Trev), Ray Meagher (Lance).

David Rappaport is the glue which holds together the story of three female friends whose lives are drastically changed by the stock market crash of 1987. He's the maitre d' at a ritzy restaurant who provides a sympathetic ear for all their problems.

1771. *Lunch Wagon* (1981, Seymour Borde, 88m, c, aka *Lunch Wagon Girls; Come 'n Get It*). P Mark Borde, D Ernest Pintoff, W Leon Phillips, Marshall Harvey & Terrie Frankle, PH Fred Lemler, M Richard Band, ED Edward Salier.

LP Pamela Bryant (Marcy), Rosanne Katon (Shannon), Candy Moore (Diedra), Rick Podell (Al Schmeckler), Rose Marie (Mrs. Schmeckler), Chuck McCann (The Turtle), Jimmie Van Patten (Biff), Nels Van Patten (Scotty), Michael Tucci (Arnie).

Three young out-of-work lovelies inherit a lunch wagon and set up business at construction sites where they become very successful, due more because of their looks than their food. They have trouble with a rival lunch wagon which in reality is a front for a gang of jewel thieves.

Lunch Wagon Girls see Lunch Wagon

1772. *Lurkers* (1988, Reeltime/Crown, 90m, c). P Walter E. Sear, D Roberta Findlay, W Ed Kelleher & Hariette Vidal, PH Findlay, M Sear, ED Sear & Findlay.

LP Christine Moore (Cathy), Gary Warner (Bob), Marina Taylor (Monica), Carissa Channing (Sally), Tom Billett (Leo "The Hammer"), Dana Nardelli (Cathy as a Girl).

Ever since childhood Christine Moore has been women by Satanists, seeking her soul. Even her boyfriend Gary Warner serves the hoofed one.

1773. *Lust for Freedom* (1987, Troma, 90m, c). P,D&W Eric Louzil, PH Ron Chapman, M John Massari, ED Steve Mann, Thomas R. Rondinella & David Khachatorian.

LP Melanie Coll (Gillian Kaites), William J. Kulzer (Sheriff Coale), Judi Trevor (Ms. Pusker), Howard Knight (Warden Maxwell), Elizabeth Carlisle (Vicky), Dee Booher (Big Eddie).

Undercover detective Melanie Coll loses her cool when her partner and fiancé is killed during a drug bust. She later finds herself in a women's prison. The movie is just a feeble excuse for showing a lot of brutality and perversion in the pen.

1774. *Lust in the Dust* (1985, New World, 87m, c). P Allan Glaser & Tab Hunter, D Paul Bartel, W Philip John Taylor, PH Paul Lohmann, M Peter Matz, ED Alan Toomayan, PD Walter Pickette.

LP Tab Hunter (Abel Wood), Divine (Rosie Velez), Lainie Kazan (Marguerita Ventura), Geoffrey Lewis (Hard Case Williams), Henry Silva (Bernardo), Cesar Romero (Father Garcia), Gina Gallego (Ninfa), Nedra Volz (Big Ed), Courtney Gains (Red Dick Barker), Woody Strode (Blackman).

The stars of John Waters' *Polyester,* Tab Hunter and 300-pound female impersonator Divine, are transported from Baltimore to the wild west in a campy spoof of western clichés. It falls on its face more often than it stands up on its hindlegs and howls.

1775. *Mac and Me* (1988, Orion, 91m, c). P R.J. Louis, D Stewart Raffill, W Raffill & Steve Feke, PH Nick McLean, M Alan Silvestri, ED Tom Walls, PD W. Stewart Campbell.

LP Christine Ebersole (Janet Cruise), Jonathan Ward (Michael Cruise), Katrina Caspary (Courtney), Lauren Stanley (Debbie), Jade Calegory (Eric Cruise), Vinnie Torrente (Mitford), Martin West (Wickett), Ivan Jorge Rado (Zimmerman), Danny Cooksey (Jack, Jr.), Laura Waterbury (Linda).

In this unabashed ripoff of *E.T. The Extra-Terrestrial,* young Jade Calegory, a boy from a fatherless family, is confined to a wheelchair and ribbed by his schoolmates. Nevertheless he is able to reunite MAC — Mysterious Alien Creature — with his family, but not before the film gives out with dozens of commercials, the greatest number being for McDonald's hamburgers.

1776. *Mack the Knife* (1989, 21st Century–Fox, 120m, c). P Stanley Chase, D&W Menahem Golan (based on the musical play "The Threepenny Opera" by Bertolt Brecht & Kurt Weill), PH Elemer Ragalyi, MD Dov Seltzer, ED Alain Jakubowicz, CH David Toguri, PD Tivadar Bertalan.

LP Raul Julia (MacHeath), Richard Harris (Mr. Peachum), Julia Migenes (Jenny), Roger Daltrey (Street Singer), Julie Walters (Mrs. Peachum), Rachel Robertson (Polly Peachum), Clive Revill (Money Matthew), Bill Nighy (Tiger Brown), Erin Donovan (Lucy), Julie T. Wallace (Coaxer).

Unfortunately for those involved in this production, the material no longer has much shock value. In the story of thieves, beggars and murderers, actors prove to be terrible hams. The songs of Kurt Weill, while still the best thing in the film, won't appeal to many these days.

1777. *McVicar* (1982, Crown International, GB, 111m, c). P Bill Curbishley, Roy Baird & Roger Daltrey, D Tom Clegg, W John McVicar (based on his book *McVicar by Himself*), PH Vernon Layton, M Jeff Wayne, ED Peter Boyle, AD Brian Ackland-Snow.

LP Roger Daltrey (McVicar), Adam Faith (Probyn), Cheryl Campbell (Sheila), Steven Berkoff (Harrison), Brian Hall (Stokes), Jeremy Blake (Johnson), Leonard Gregory (Collins), Peter Jonfield (Harris), Anthony Trent (Tate).

Roger Daltrey portrays a real-life British convict who escapes from prison, pulls a few jobs and finds himself back behind bars. It's a realistic depiction of crime and punishment.

Mad Magazine's Up the Academy see Up the Academy

1778. *Mad Max Beyond Thunderdome* (1985, Warner, Australia, 106m, c). P George Miller, Doug Mitchell & Terry Hayes, D Miller & George Ogilvie, W Hayes & Miller, PH Dean Semler, M Maurice Jarre, ED Richard Francis-Bruce, PD Graham "Grace" Walker.

LP Mel Gibson (Mad Max), Bruce Spence (Jedediah), Adam Cockburn (Jedediah, Jr.), Tina Turner (Aunty Entity), Frank Thring (The Collector), Angelo Rossitto (The Master), Paul Larsson (The Blaster), Angry Anderson (Ironbar), Robert Grubb (Pigkiller), George Spartels (Blackfinger), Edwin Hodgeman (Dr. Dealgood), Helen Buday (Savannah Nix).

Mel Gibson is back as the Road Warrior. He tangles with power-mad dominatrix Tina Turner, the would-be ruler of Bartertown. She induces Gibson to take on Masterblaster in Thunderdome, where two men enter but only one leaves and the rules are, there are no rules. Gibson survives, but is banished. He teams up with some kids who believe he's the "Captain Walker" whose coming to lead them has been foretold.

Mad Max II see The Road Warrior

1779. *Madame Sousatzka* (1988, Universal, 122m, c). P Robin Dalton, D John Schlesinger, W Ruth Prawer Jhabvala & Schlesinger (based on the novel by Bernice Rubens), PH Nat Crosby, M Gerald Gouriet, ED Peter Honess, PD Luciana Arrighi.

LP Shirley MacLaine† (Madame Irina Sousatzka), Dame Peggy Ashcroft (Lady Emily), Twiggy (Jenny), Shabana Azmi (Sushila), Navin Chowdhry (Manek Sen), Leigh Lawson (Ronnie Blum), Geoffrey Bayldon (Cordle), Lee Montague (Vincent Pick).

Great piano teacher Shirley MacLaine takes little notice of the real world, only living for her music and her students. At the time of the movie, she is almost obsessed with her brilliant new protégé Navin Chowdhry. In order to develop his talent she dominates the lad against his wishes and those of his mother. Although generally harsh with him, she eventually develops genuine affection for the teen. MacLaine is remarkable in a tour de force performance.

1780. *Maddalena Z* (1989, Teacup Films, 88m, c). P&D Marc Schwartz, W Geoffrey Francis Dunn, PH Gene Evans, M Randy Masters, ED Mona Lynch, PD George Arthur & Edith Hutton.

LP Bill Ackridge (Dominic), Dunja Djordjevic (Zandy), Geoffrey Dunn (Tony), Liz Rolfe (Stella), Gene Matisoff (Mario), Ken Hill (Dirk), Lorna Ho (Julia), Deborah Gray (Sally).

Aging fisherman Bill Ackridge's skills in a small boat are no match for the big boats and regulatory bureaucracy. A May and December romance develops when college student Dunja Djordjevic, doing a paper on the fishing industry, interviews Ackridge.

1781. *Made in Heaven* (1987, Lorimar, 102m, c). P Raynold Gideon, Bruce A. Evans & David Blocker, D Alan Rudolph, W Evans & Gideon, PH Jan Kiesser, M Mark Isham, ED Tom Walls, PD Paul Peters.

LP Timothy Hutton (Mike Shea/Elmo Barnett), Kelly McGillis (Annie Packert/Ally Chandler), Maureen Stapleton (Aunt Lisa), Ann Wedgeworth (Annette Shea), James Gammon (Steve Shea), Mare Winningham (Brenda Carlucci), Don Murray (Ben Chandler), Debra Winger [uncredited] (Emmett Humbird), Ellen Barkin [uncredited] (Lucille), Amanda Plummer (Wiley Foxx).

In the late 40s, Timothy Hutton drowns as he saves two children and their mother. In heaven, he meets Kelly McGillis, an unborn soul, and they fall in love. When Kelly is sent to earth to be born, Hutton, determined not to lose her, makes a deal with heaven's manager. He can return to earth as a new person, but have only 30 years to find McGillis. To add to the difficulty of the task, they will have almost no memory of the lover they shared.

1782. *Made in U.S.A.* (1988, Hemdale/DEG, 87m, c). P Charles Roven, D&W Ken Friedman (based on a story by Friedman & Nick Wexler), PH Curtis Clark, M Sonic Youth, ED Curtiss Clayton, PD James Newport.

LP Adrian Pasdar (Dar), Christopher Penn (Tuck), Lori Singer (Annie), Jackie Murphy (Cora), Judy Baldwin (Dorie), Dean Paul Martin (Cowboy).

Traveling in stolen cars, three young people travel across America from Centralia, Pennsylvania, to Los Angeles.

1783. *Madman* (1982, Farley, 88m, c). P Gary Sales, D&W Joe Giannone, PH James Momel, M Sales & Stephen Horelick, ED Dan Lowenthal, SE Jo Hansen.

LP Alexis Dubin (Betsy), Tony Fish (T.P.), Harriet Bass (Stacey), Seth Jones (Dave), Jan Claire (Ellie), Alex Murphy (Bill), Paul Ehlers (Madman Marz), Carl Fredericks (Max).

In another film trying hard to win the distinction of being the most godawful slasher film, a crazed killer is terrorizing a summer camp filled with nubile counselors.

1784. *The Mahabharata* (1989, Reiner Mortiz, GB/France/US, 171m, c). P Michel Propper, D Peter Brook, W Jean-Claude Carrière, PH William Lubtchansky, M Toshi Tsuchitori, ED Nicolas Gaster, PD Chloe Obolensky.

LP Robert Langton-Lloyd (Vyasa), Antonin Stahly-Vishwanadan (Boy), Bruce Myers (Ganesha/Krishna), Vittorio Mezzogiorno (Arjuna), Andrzej Seweryn (Yudhishthira), Jean-Paul Denzion (Nakula), Mahmoud Tabrizi-Zadeh (Sahadeva), Mallika Sarabhai (Droupadi), Miriam Goldschmidt (Kunti).

Jean-Claude Carrière worked 11 years, reducing the enormous Indian manuscript (15 times longer than the Bible) to manageable length. It is built around Vyasa, the storyteller who unfolds for a young boy an allegory of the entire history of the human race from creation through destruction to eventual redemption. Although the film is an intellectual and literary feast, as with most epics, it isn't good cinema. How could it be?

1785. *Maid to Order* (1987, New Century/Vista, 96m, c). P Herb Jaffe & Mort Engelberg, D Amy Jones, W Amy Jones, Perry Howze & Randy Howze, PH Shelly Johnson, M Georges Delerue, ED Sidney Wolinsky, PD Jeffrey Townsend.

LP Ally Sheedy (Jessie Montgomery), Beverly D'Angelo (Stella), Michael Ontkean (Nick McGuire), Valerie Perrine (Georgette Starkey), Dick Shawn (Stan Starkey), Tom Skerritt (Charles Montgomery), Merry Clayton (Audrey James), Begona Plaza (Maria), Rainbow Phoenix (Brie Starkey).

In an updated mix of Cinderella with *It's a Wonderful Life,* bored, spoiled-rich Ally Sheedy is turned into a nonentity by her hip fairy godmother, Beverly D'Angelo. Ally is forced to take a job as a maid in a Malibu mansion owned by Dick Shawn and Valerie Perrine, whose taste is all in their mouths. Sheedy is constantly upstaged by the supporting cast.

1786. *Major League* (1989, Paramount, 107m, c). P Chris Chesser & Irby Smith, D&W David S. Ward, PH Reynaldo Villalobos, M James Newton Howard, ED Dennis M. Hill, PD Jeffrey Howard.

LP Tom Berenger (Jake Taylor), Charlie Sheen (Rickie Vaughn), Corbin Bernsen (Roger Dorn), Margaret Whitton (Rachel Phelps), James Gammon (Lou Brown), Rene Russo (Lynn Wells), Bob Uecker (Harry Doyle), Dennis Haysbert (Pedro Cerrano), Charles Cyphers (Charlie Donovan), Chelcie Ross (Eddie Harris), Wesley Snipes (Willie Mays Hayes).

A number of baseball announcers have recommended this movie to fans. Well, what do they know? The film fails both as a movie and a baseball story. It stars a team of misfits whose season goes down to the usual crucial last inning. Tom Berenger, an over-the-hill catcher from the Mexican League, is pressed into service to give the team some leadership. Charlie Sheen portrays the punk kid pitcher ("a juvenile delinquent in the off-season," as one sportscaster puts it) who personifies the guy who's in the game for himself alone, personal records meaning more than those of the team. These two are just a few of the many human sports clichés found in the movie. It wouldn't be so bad, if it didn't have to be compared to the really good movie and baseball story, *Bull Durham.*

1787. *The Majorettes* (1988, Major Films, 92m, c). P John Russo, D Bill Hinzman, W Russo (based on his novel), PH Paul McCollough, M McCollough, ED Hinzman & McCollough, SE Gerald Gergely.

LP Kevin Kindlin (Jeff), Terrie Godfrey (Vicky), Mark V. Jevicky (Sheriff Braden), Sueanne Seamens (Judy), Denise Huot (Helga), Carl Hetrick (Roland).

In this straight to video piece, a hooded killer is murdering high school cheerleaders. A ruthless nurse tries to use the serial killer to beat her granddaughter out of a large inheritance.

1788. *Making Love* (1982, 20th Century-Fox, 113m, c). P Allen Adler & Daniel Melnick, D Arthur Hiller, W Barry Sandler (based on a story by A. Scott Berg), PH David M. Walsh, M Leonard Rosenman, ED William H. Reynolds, PD James D. Vance.

LP Michael Ontkean (Zack), Kate Jackson (Claire), Harry Hamlin (Bart), Wendy Hiller (Winnie), Arthur Hill (Henry), Nancy Olson (Christine), John Dukakis (Tim), Terry Kiser (Harrington), Dennis Howard (Larry).

Kate Jackson's seemingly perfect marriage to Michael Ontkean is shattered when he falls in love with homosexual novelist Harry Hamlin.

1789. *Making Mr. Right* (1987, Orion, 95m, c). P Mike Wise & Joel Tuber, D Susan Seidelman, W Floyd Byars & Laurie Frank, PH Edward Lachman, M Chaz Jankel, ED Andrew Mondshein, PD Barbara Ling.

LP John Malkovich (Dr. Jeff Peters/ Ulysses), Ann Magnuson (Frankie Stone), Glenne Headly (Trish), Ben Masters (Congressman Steve Marcus), Laurie Metcalf (Sandy), Polly Bergen (Estelle Stone), Harsh Nayyar (Dr. Ravi Ramdas), Susan Berman (Ivy Stone), Polly Draper (Suzy Duncan).

If very fine actor John Malkovich's career continues in the direction it seems to be going the last few years, the day may come when he would just as soon forget that he appeared in dual roles in this lame comedy. He plays a scientist who has created an affable android, and the android himself. Ann Magnuson portrays a high-powered publicist, hired to work some magical transformation on the mischievous robot. For what end is not clear. For that matter, very little is clear about the film, except it's a waste of Malkovich's talent.

1790. *Making the Grade* (1984, MGM/Cannon/United Artists, 105m, c, aka *Preppies*). P Gene Quintano, D Dorian Walker, W Quintano (based on a story by Quintano & Charles Gale), PH Jacques Haitkin, M Basil Poledouris, ED Dan Wetherbee.

LP Judd Nelson (Eddie Kenton), Jonna Lee (Tracey Hoover), Gordon Jump (Mr. Harriman), Walter Olkewicz (Coach Wordman), Ronald Lacey (Nicky), Dana Olsen (Palmer Woodrow), Carey Scott (Rand), Scott McGinnis (Bif).

Tough New Jersey street kid Judd Nelson poses as a preppie to settle some debts owed to the mob.

1791. *Mala Noche [Bad Night]* (1989, Northern/Frameline, 78m, b&w/c). P,D,W&ED Gus Van Sant, Jr. (based on the novella by Walt Curtis), PH John Campbell, M Creighton Lindsay, Karen Kitchen & Peter Daamaan.

LP Tim Strecter (Walt Curtis), Doug Cooeyate (Johnny), Ray Monge (Roberto Pepper), Nyla McCarthy (Betty).

This film made in 1985 on a shoestring budget was released when Van Sant's film *Drugstore Cowboy* received critical acclaim. Skid-row liquor store owner Tim Strecter falls in love with 18-year-old illegal Mexican immigrant Doug Cooeyate. The latter is willing to take Strecter's money, but prefers the latter's sister, Nyla McCarthy, as a bed-partner.

1792. *Malcolm* (1986, Vestron, Australia, 90m, c). P Nadia Tass & David Parker, D Tass, W Parker, PH Parker, M Simon Jeffes, ED Ken Sallows.

LP Colin Friels (Malcolm), John Hargreaves (Frank), Lindy Davies (Judith), Chris Haywood (Willy), Charles Tingwell (Tramways Supervisor), Beverly Phillips (Mrs. T.), Judith Stratford (Jenny), Heather Mitchell (Barmaid), Katerina Tassopoulos (Jenny's Mother).

Colin Friels is a charmer as an innocent who is fired from his job with a local rapid-transit company for building his own tram with company parts. He falls in with thieves and loves it.

1793. *The Malibu Bikini Shop* (1987, Wescom-Romax, 99m, c). P Gary Mehlman, J. Kenneth Rotcop & Leo Leichter, D&W David Wechter, PH Tom Richmond, ED Jean-Marc Vasseur, MD Don Perry.

LP Michael David Wright (Alan), Bruce Greenwood (Todd), Barbra Horan (Ronnie), Debra Blee (Jane), Jay Robinson (Ben), Galyn Gorg (Cindy), Ami Julius (Kathy), Kathleen Freeman (Loraine Bender), Jon Rashad Kamal (Eric Greene), Beverly Sanders (Berta Hilgard), Rita Jenrette (Aunt Ida).

Look for some nudity and profanity in this sexploitation comedy about two brothers, college business school graduate Michael David Wright and his beach bum brother Bruce Greenwood. They inherit a bikini shop from their aunt, Rita Jenrette.

1794. *Malone* (1987, Orion, 93m, c). P Leo L. Fuchs, D Harley Cokliss, W Christopher Frank (based on the novel *Shotgun* by William Wingate), PH Gerald Hirschfeld, M David Newman, ED Todd Ramsay, PD Graeme Murray.

LP Burt Reynolds (Richard Malone), Cliff Robertson (Charles Delaney), Kenneth McMillan (Sheriff Hawkins), Cynthia Gibb (Jo Barlow), Scott Wilson (Paul Barlow), Lauren Hutton (Jamie), Philip Anglim (Harvey), Tracey Walter (Calvin Bollard), Dennis Burkley (Dan Bollard).

Take any one of a hundred old B westerns about a gunfighter forced to strap on his guns once more to defend the people he has come to care about and you have this story about ex–CIA agent Burt Reynolds. He has to stand-up to·assassins hired by Cliff Robertson, the leader of a fanatical right-wing group, as well as the dangerous Lauren Hutton, sent by the CIA to off Reynolds, because no one is just allowed to walk away from the "company."

1795. *Malou* (1983, Quartet, 93m, c). P Regina Ziegler, D&W Jeanine Meerapfel, PH Michael Ballhaus, M Peer Raben, ED Dagmar Hirtz.

LP Ingrid Caven (Malou), Grischa

Huber (Hannah), Helmut Griem (Martin), Ivan Desny (Paul), Marie Colbin (Lotte), Peter Chatel (Albert), Margarita Calahorra (Lucia), Lo Van Hensbergen (Paul's Father), Liane Saalborn (Paul's Mother).

While traveling through Germany, France and South America, Ingrid Craven learns that her mother's life was completely controlled by men. She decides that she will not allow herself to be trapped in a traditional marriage.

1796. *Malpractice* (1989, Film Australia, Australia, 91m, c). P Tristam Miall, D Bill Bennett, W Jenny Ainge and the cast, PH Steve Arnold, M Michael Atkinson, ED Denise Hunter.

LP Caz Lederman (Coral Davis), Bob Baines (Doug Davis), Ian Gilmour (Dr. Frank Harrison), Pat Thomson (Sr. Margaret Beattie), Charles Little (Dr. Tom Cotterslow), Janet Stanley (Sr. Diane Shaw), Dorothy Alison (Maureen Davis).

Caz Lederman, mother of two, enters the hospital to give birth to her third child. Her regular gynecologist is away and his replacement, Ian Gilmour, makes some bad decisions which even frighten the nurses. A boy is born, but loss of oxygen during a caesarian birth after Gilmour has bungled a forceps delivery may cause the child to be retarded and crippled. When she recovers, Lederman insists on finding out what went wrong, despite her husband's willingness to accept things as they are. The doctors initially try to protect Gilmour, but he is ultimately brought before a medical tribunal.

1797. *The Man from Snowy River* (1983, 20th Century–Fox, Australia, 102m, c). P Geoff Burrowes, D George Miller, W John Dixon & Fred Cullen (based on the poem by A.B. "Banjo" Paterson), PH Keith Wagstaff, M Bruce Rowland, ED Adrian Carr.

LP Kirk Douglas (Harrison/Spur), Jack Thompson (Clancy), Tom Burlinson (Jim Craig), Terence Donovan (Henry Craig), Tommy Dysart (Mountain Man).

Kirk Douglas plays the dual roles of two brothers, one a wealthy landowner and the other a one-legged prospector. These characterizations are based on an age-old Australian legend about the heroic adventures of a young man, Tom Burlinson, accepting the challenge of taming wild horses.

1798. *A Man in Love* (1987, Cinecom, US/France/Italy, 117m, c). P Marjorie Israel, Armand Barbault & Roberto Guissani, D Diane Kurys, W Kurys & Israel Horovitz, PH Bernard Zitermann, M Georges Delerue, ED Joele Van Effenterre, AD Dean Tavoularis.

LP Peter Coyote (Steve), Greta Scacchi (Jane), Peter Riegert (Michael), John Berry (Harry), Vincent Lindon (Bruno), Jean Pigozzi (Pizani), Elia Katz (Sam), Constantin Alexandrov (De Vitta), Michele Melega (Paolo).

In this sensual romance, married American actor Peter Coyote falls in love with his leading lady Greta Scacchi while making a movie in Rome.

The Man in the Skull Mask see Who?

1799. *Man of Flowers* (1984, Spectrafilm, Australia, 91m, c). P Jane Ballantyne & Paul Cox, D Cox, W Cox & Bob Ellis, PH Yuri Sokol, M Gaetano Donizetti, ED Tim Lewis.

LP Norman Kaye (Charles Bremer), Alyson Best (Lisa), Chris Haywood (David), Sarah Walker (Jane), Julia Blake (Art Teacher), Bob Ellis (Psychiatrist), Barry Dickins (Postman).

Sexually repressed middle-aged artist Norman Kaye has a mercurial affair with young model Alyson Best.

1800. *Man Outside* (1988, Virgin Vision, 109m, c). P Mark Stouffer & Robert E. Yoss, D Stouffer, W Ira Steven Levine & Pat Duncan (based on a story by Stouffer), PH William Wages, M John McEuen, ED Tony Lombardo, PD Deborah Stouffer.

LP Robert Logan (Jack Avery), Kathleen Quinlan (Grace Freemont), Bradford Dillman (Frank Simmons), Levon Helm (Sheriff Leland Laughlin), Andrew Barach (Leo Greenfield), Alex Liggett (Toby Riggs), Rick Danko (Jim Riggs), Patricia Ralph (Velma Riggs), Mary Ingalls (Momma).

Lawyer Robert Logan drives his Porsche into the Arkansas backwoods and stays there. He lives off the land, choosing a hermit's existence. Anthropology professor Kathleen Quinlan becomes intrigued with discovering why a man would cut himself off from all society. So naturally she feels free to invade his privacy.

1801.   *The Man Who Envied Women* (1985, First Run Features, 125m, b&w/c). D&W Yvonne Rainer, PH Mark Daniels, ED Rainer & Christine LeGoff.

LP William Raymond (Jack Deller No. 1), Larry Loonin (Jack Deller No. 2), Trisha Brown (Trisha), Jackie Raynal (Jackie).

Middle-aged William Raymond attempting to cope with his failed marriage, is forced to examine his smug conceptions of social order and sexual roles.

1802.   *The Man Who Loved Women* (1983, Columbia, 118m, c). P Blake Edwards & Tony Adams, D Edwards, W Edwards, Milton Wexler & Geoffrey Edwards (based on a comedy by François Truffaut), PH Haskell Wexler, M Henry Mancini, ED Ralph E. Winters, PD Rodger Maus.

LP Burt Reynolds (David), Julie Andrews (Marianna), Kim Basinger (Louise), Marilu Henner (Agnes), Cynthia Sikes (Courtney), Jennifer Edwards (Nancy), Sela Ward (Janet), Ellen Bauer (Svetlana), Denise Crosby (Enid), Tracy Vaccaro (Legs), Barry Corbin (Roy).

This production fails to match the charm and innocence of the 1977 French film by François Truffaut. Burt Reynolds is so crazy for women that he will drop anything and everything to pursue and bed even those with whom he has had but a chance meeting. Reynolds is not quite subtle or sensitive enough for the role.

1803.   *The Man Who Wasn't There* (1983, Paramount, 111m, c). P Frank Mancuso, Jr., D Bruce Malmuth, W Stanford Sherman, PH Frederick Moore, M Miles Goodman, ED Harry Keller.

LP Steve Guttenberg (Sam), Lisa Langlois (Cindy), Jeffrey Tambor (Boris), Art Hindle (Ted), Morgan Hart, Bill Forsythe, Bruce Malmuth, Ivan Naranjo.

In this 3-D comedy, Steve Guttenberg receives a formula from a dying spy that will turn him invisible. He's pursued by both Russian and American agents, but since he can become invisible, it's a bit difficult for them to find him.

1804.   *The Man with Bogart's Face* (1980, 20th Century–Fox, 106m, c, aka *Sam Marlow, Private Eye*). P Andrew J. Fenady, D Robert Day, W Fenady (based on his novel), PH Richard C. Glouner, M George Duning, ED Eddie Saeta, PD Robert Kinoshita.

LP Robert Sacchi (Sam Marlow), Franco Nero (Hakim), Michelle Phillips (Gena Anastas), Olivia Hussey (Elsa Borsht), Misty Rowe (Duchess), Victor Buono (Commodore Anastas), Herbert Lom (Mr. Zebra), Sybil Danning (Cynthia).

Actor Robert Sacchi has undergone facial surgery so he will more closely resemble Humphrey Bogart. He opens up his own detective agency in this rollicking sendup of mystery movies.

1805.   *The Man with One Red Shoe* (1985, 20th Century–Fox, 93m, c). P Victor Drai, D Stan Dragoti, W Robert Klane (based on the motion picture *Le Grand Blond Avec Une Chaussure Noire* by Francis Veber & Yves Robert), PH Richard H. Kline, M Thomas Newman, ED Bud Molin & O. Nicholas Brown, PD Dean E. Mitzner.

LP Tom Hanks (Richard), Dabney Coleman (Cooper), Lori Singer (Maddy), Charles Durning (Ross), Carrie Fisher (Paula), Edward Herrmann (Brown), Jim Belushi (Morris), Irving Metzman (Virdon), Tom Noonan (Reese).

In another of the many CIA bashing movies, clodish violinist Tom Hanks is accidentally ensnared in a web of intrigue. Warring CIA agents mistake him for a contact because he arrives on an airplane in Washington wearing just one red shoe. There are not enough laughs to make it all worth while.

The Man with the Deadly Lens* see *Wrong Is Right

1806.   *The Man with Two Brains* (1983, Warner, 93m, c). P David V. Picker & William E. McEuen, D Carl Reiner, W Reiner, Steve Martin & George Gipe, PH Michael Chapman, M Joel Goldsmith, ED Bud Molin, PD Polly Platt.

LP Steve Martin (Dr. Michael Hfuhruhurr), Kathleen Turner (Dolores Benedict), David Warner (Dr. Necessiter), Paul Benedict (Butler), Richard Brestoff

(Dr. Pasteur), Sissy Spacek (Voice of the Brain), George Furth (Timon), Peter Hobbs (Dr. Brandon), Merv Griffin (Elevator Killer).

Wacko brain surgeon Steve Martin marries beautiful, sexy, coldhearted nymphomaniac Kathleen Turner. He later falls in love with the brain of a woman who is just perfect for him — if she only had a body.

A Man Without a Face see Who?

1807. *Man, Woman and Child* (1983, Paramount, 99m, c). P Elmo Williams & Elliot Kastner, D Dick Richards, W Erich Segal & David Z. Goodman (based on the novel by Segal), PH Richard H. Kline & Jean Tournier, M Georges Delerue, ED David Bretherton, PD Dean Edward Mitzner.

LP Martin Sheen (Bob Beckwith), Blythe Danner (Sheila Beckwith), Craig T. Nelson (Bernie Ackerman), David Hemmings (Gavin Wilson), Nathalie Nell (Nicole Guerin), Maureen Anderman (Margo), Sebastian Dungan (Jean-Claude Guerin), Arlene McIntyre (Jessica Beckwith).

It's quite a shock to Martin Sheen and his wife Blythe Danner, when Sebastian Dungan shows up, announcing he's Sheen's son by his former lover Nathalie Nell.

1808. *Manchurian Avenger* (1985, Facet Film, 81m, c). P Robyn Bensinger, D Ed Warnick, W Pat Hamilton & Timothy Stephenson (based on a story by Richard Kim), PH Rich Lerner, M Paul Conly, ED Hal Freeman.

LP Bobby Kim (Joe), Bill [Superfoot] Wallace (Kamikaze), Michael Stuart (Diego), Leila Hee (Booyong), Jose Payo (Kilo), Bob Coulson (Harry), Barbara Minardi (Maria).

In this martial-arts western, desperadoes have wrested control of a Colorado gold rush town from Bobby Kim's parents, but he soon puts that right.

1809. *Manganinnie* (1982, Tasmanian/Contemporary, Australia, 91m, c). P Gilda Baracchi, D John Honey, W Ken Kelso (based on the novel by Beth Roberts), PH Gary Hansen, M Peter Sculthorpe, ED Mike Woolveridge.

LP Mawuyul Yathalawuy (Manganin-nie), Anna Ralph (Joanna Waterman), Phillip Hinton (Edward Waterman), Elaine Mangan (Margaret Waterman), Buruminy Dhamarrandji (Meenopeeka-meena), Reg Evans (Quinn).

Lost in the desert, Anna Ralph runs across Aborigine woman Mawuyul Yathalawuy searching for her lost tribe. Despite not knowing each other's language, they manage to communicate.

1810. *The Mango Tree* (1981, Pisces/Sator, Australia, 93m, c). P Michael Pate, D Kevin Dobson, W Pate (based on the novel by Ronald McKie), PH Brian Probyn, M Marc Wilkinson, ED John Scott.

LP Geraldine Fitzgerald (Grandma Carr), Robert Helpmann (The Professor), Christopher Pate (Jamie Carr), Gerard Kennedy (Preacher Jones), Gloria Dawn (Pearl), Carol Burns (Maudie Plover), Barry Pierce (Angus McDonald).

Set in Queensland during World War I, the film is the story of the coming of age of young Christopher Pate. He's the producer's son and seems overmatched by the role.

1811. *The Manhattan Project* (1986, 20th Century–Fox, 120m, c). P Jennifer Ogden & Marshall Brickman, D Brickman, W Brickman & Thomas Baum, PH Billy Williams, M Philippe Sarde, ED Nina Feinberg, PD Philip Rosenberg.

LP John Lithgow (John Mathewson), Christopher Collet (Paul Stephens), Jill Eikenberry (Elizabeth Stephens), John Mahoney (Lt. Col. Conroy), Cynthia Nixon (Jenny Anderman), John David Cullum (Eccles), Charlie Fields (Price), Manny Jacobs (Moore).

Precocious youngster Christopher Collet breaks into a top-secret plant, steals some plutonium and builds his own nuclear reactor. He almost blows up the world with his showing off.

1812. *Manhunter* (1986, De Laurentiis, 118m, c). P Richard Roth, D&W Michael Mann (based on the book *Red Dragon* by Thomas Harris), PH Dante Spinotti, M Various Artists, ED Dov Hoenig, PD Mel Bourne.

LP William Petersen (Will Graham), Kim Greist (Molly Graham), Joan Allen (Reba), Brian Cox (Dr. Lektor), Dennis Farina (Jack), Stephen Lang (Freddie),

Tom Noonan (Francis), David Seaman (Kevin Graham).

When former FBI agent William Petersen is called back into service to stop a serial killer, he succeeds by thinking just like the maniac.

1813. *Maniac* (1980, Magnum/Analysis, 87m, c). P Andrew Garroni & William Lustig, D Lustig, W C.A. Rosenberg & Joe Spinell (based on a story by Spinell), PH Robert Lindsay, M Jay Chattaway, ED Lorenzo Marinelli.

LP Joe Spinell (Frank Zito), Caroline Munro (Ann D'Antoni), Gail Lawrence (Rita), Kelly Piper (Nurse), Rita Montone (Hooker), Tom Savini (Disco Boy), Hyla Marrow (Disco Girl), James Brewster (Beach Boy), Linda Lee Walter (Beach Girl).

Having been mistreated by his mother as a child, Joe Spinell gets even by scalping beautiful young women and hanging their hair on mannequins he keeps in his apartment.

1814. *Maniac Cop* (1988, Shapiro Glickenhaus, 85m, c). P Larry Cohen, D William Lustig, W Cohen, PH Vincent J. Rabe, M Jay Chattaway, ED David Kern.

LP Tom Atkins (Lt. McCrae), Bruce Campbell (Jack Forrest), Laurene Landon (Theresa Mallory), Richard Roundtree (Commissioner Pike), William Smith (Capt. Ripley), Sheree North (Sally Noland), Rober Z'ar (Matt Cordell).

New York City is terrorized by a homicidal killer, dressed in a police uniform. He's dubbed the "Maniac Cop" by the press. The department denies that the killer is a cop. Tom Atkins who is assigned to the case finds that the killer is somehow getting information from inside the department.

1815. *Manifesto* (1988, Cannon, 96m, c). P Menahem Golan & Yoram Globus, D&W Dusan Makavejev (based on a story by Emile Zola), PH Tomislav Pinter, M Nicola Piovani, ED Tony Lawson, PD Veljko Despotovic.

LP Camilla Soeberg (Svetlana Vargas), Alfred Molina (Avanti), Simon Callow (Police Chief Hunt), Eric Stoltz (Christopher), Lindsay Duncan (Lily Sacher), Rade Serbedzija (Emile), Svetozar Cvet-kovic (Rudi Kugelhopf), Chris Haywood (Wango), Patrick Godfrey (Dr. Lombrosow).

This political comedy is set in the 1930s in a fictional Eastern European country. Camilla Soeberg arrives in a small town, prepared to take part in a plot to assassinate a visiting king. Also new to the town is Alfred Molina, who has secret agent written all over him. Revolutionaries abound in the village, but everyone seems as interested in bedding one another as involving themselves in the various political schemes.

1816. *Mankillers* (1987, Action International, 90m, c). P Peter Yuval, D&W David A. Prior, PH Keith Holland, M Tim James, Steve McClintock & Tim Heintz, ED Alan Carrier, SE Phoeniz.

LP Edd Byrnes (Jack Marra), Gail Fisher (Joan Hanson), Edy Williams (Sgt. Roberts), Lynda Aldon (Rachael McKenna), William Zipp (John Mickland), Christine Lunde (Maria Rosetti), Susanne Tegman (Terry Davis), Marilyn Stafford (Roxanne Taylor), Paul Bruno (Bruno), Byron Clark (Williams).

In an up-dated female version of *The Dirty Dozen,* Lynda Aldon recruits 12 of the toughest and sexiest females she can find in a prison. They are to be trained as a team that will go South of the Border to eliminate a CIA agent gone bad. Their reward will be a full pardon if they are successful. The film is terrible, doing nothing for the moribund careers of former television headliners Edd Byrnes and Gail Fisher.

1817. *Mannequin* (1987, 20th Century–Fox, 89m, c). P Art Levinson, D Michael Gottlieb, W Edward Rugoff & Michael Gottlieb, PH Tim Suhrstedt, M Sylvester Levay, ED Richard Halsey & Frank Jimenez, PD Josan Russo, SONG "Nothing's Gonna Stop Us Now" by Albert Hammond & Diane Warren†.

LP Andrew McCarthy (Jonathan Switcher), Kim Cattrall (Emmy, Mannequin), Estelle Getty (Clare Timkin), James Spader (Richards), G.W. Bailey (Felix), Carole Davis (Roxie), Stephen Vinovich (B.J. Wert), Christopher Maher (Armand), Meshach Taylor (Hollywood Montrose).

Department store window designer

Andrew McCarthy falls in love with mannequin Kim Cattrall who now and then comes to life. With her help, McCarthy becomes a big success, even though there are those who want him to fail. McCarthy and Cattrall's roles are not what serious performers want in their résumés. However, they are outdone in bad taste by James Spader, a sleazy vice president, Stephen Vinovich, the owner of a competing department store, G.W. Bailey, doing a variation on his role in the never ending *Police Academy* films, and Meshach Taylor as a flamboyant gay black man, whose performance insults both minority groups.

1818. *Mapantsula* (1989, Max Montocchio, South Africa/GB/Australia, 105m, c). P Max Montocchio, D Oliver Schmitz, W Schmitz & Thomas Mogotlane, PH Rod Stewart, M The Ouens, ED Mark Baard.

LP Thomas Mogotlane (Panic), Marcel Van Heerden (Stander), Thembi Mtshali (Pat), Dolly Rathebe (Ma Mobise), Peter Sephuma (Duma), Eugene Majola (Sam).

"Mapantsula" is Zulu for small-time crook. It refers to black South African thief Thomas Mogotlane in this story of apartheid from the point of view of a black man.

Marianne see Mirrors

1819. *Maria's Lovers* (1985, Cannon, 103m, c). P Bosko Djordjevic & Lawrence Taylor Mortorff, D Andrei Konchalovsky, W Gerard Brach, Konchalovsky, Paul Zindel & Marjorie David, PH Juan Ruiz Anchia, M Gary S. Remal, ED Humphrey Dixon, PD Jeannine Oppewall.

LP Nastassja Kinski (Maria Bosic), John Savage (Ivan Bibic), Robert Mitchum (Ivan's Father), Keith Carradine (Clarence Butts), Anita Morris (Mrs. Wynic), Bud Cort (Harvey), Karen Young (Rosie), Tracy Nelson (Joanie), John Goodman (Frank), Danton Stone (Joe), Vincent Spano (Al Griselli).

In Russian director Andrei Konchalovsky's first American film, World War II veteran John Savage has seen a lot of bloodshed and is happy to be home in his small Pennsylvanian steel town. Throughout his service Savage idealized his girlfriend Nastassja Kinski as virginal womanhood. On his return he finds she's been lusted after by most of the men in the region, including his father Robert Mitchum. At present she's dating Vincent Spano, another returned serviceman. Savage seeks solace with older woman Anita Morris, but the love of the two young people is strong enough to get them back together.

1820. *Marie* (1985, MGM/United Artists, 112m, c). P Frank Capra, Jr., D Roger Donaldson, W John Briley (based on the book *Marie: A True Story* by Peter Maas), PH Chris Menges, M Francis Lai, ED Neil Travis.

LP Sissy Spacek (Marie Ragghianti), Jeff Daniels (Eddie Sisk), Keith Szarabajka (Kevin McCormack), Morgan Freeman (Charles Traughber), Lisa Banes (Toni Greer), Fred Thompson (Himself), Trey Wilson (FBI Agent).

In a true story, idealistic mother-of-three Sissy Spacek becomes the first woman to head the Tennessee State Board of Paroles and Pardons. When she uncovers a nest of corruption she is railroaded out of her job. Spacek fights back, sees some of the worst offenders ousted from their positions of power and wins back her job.

1821. *A Marriage* (1983, Cinecom, 90m, c). P David Greene, D&W Sandy Tung, PH Benjamin Davis, M Jack Waldman, ED Michael R. Miller, AD Farrel Levy Duffy.

LP Ric Gitlin (Ted), Isabel Glasser (Nancy), Jane Darby (Jane), Jack Rose (Mark).

The film traces the love affair of high school sweethearts, their marriage and the disintegration of the union, leading to their divorce.

1822. *Married to the Mob* (1988, Orion, 103m, c). P Kenneth Utt & Edward Saxon, D Jonathan Demme, W Barry Strugatz & Mark R. Burns, PH Tak Fujimoto, M David Byrne, ED Craig McKay, PD Kristi Zea.

LP Michelle Pfeiffer (Angela De Marco), Matthew Modine (Mike Downey), Dean Stockwell† (Tony [The Tiger] Russo), Mercedes Ruehl (Connie Russo), Alec Baldwin (Frank [Cucumber] De

Marco), Joan Cusack (Rose), Ellen Foley (Theresa), O-Lan Jones (Phyllis), Anthony J. Nici (Joey De Marco).

When hitman Alec Baldwin beds mob boss Dean Stockwell's latest mistress, the offended Mafioso eliminates both. Stockwell, quite a lady's man in his own mind, has eyes for Baldwin's widow Michelle Pfeiffer. The latter tries to make a break from the mob life, but Stockwell is on her scent. So is Matthew Modine as a government man trying to get something on Stockwell and believing that Pfeiffer is his latest mistress. Stockwell's wife Mercedes Ruehl suspects the same and she's in a killing and maiming mood. It's a likeable black comedy with Stockwell and Ruehl walking off with acting honors.

The Marsupials: The Howling III see The Howling III

1823. *Martin's Day* (1985, MGM/United Artists, Canada, 98m, c). P Richard F. Dalton & Roy Krost, D Alan Gibson, W Allan Scott & Chris Bryant, PH Frank Watts, M Wilfred Josephs, ED David de Wilde, PD Trevor Williams.

LP Richard Harris (Martin Steckert), Lindsay Wagner (Dr. Mennen), James Coburn (Lt. Lardner), Justin Henry (Martin), Karen Black (Karen), John Ireland (Brewer).

An unusual friendship develops between escaped convict Richard Harris and Justin Henry, the little boy whom he kidnaps.

1824. *Marvin and Tige* (1983, Major, 104m, c). P Wanda Dell, D Eric Weston, W Weston & Dell (based on a novel by Frankcina Glass), PH Brian West, M Patrick Williams, ED Fabien Dahlen Tordjmann.

LP John Cassevetes (Marvin Stewart), Billy Dee Williams (Richard Davis), Denise Nicholas-Hill (Vanessa Jackson), Gibran Brown (Tige Jackson), Fay Hauser (Brenda Davis), Georgia Allen (Carrie Carter).

When alcoholic ad executive John Cassavetes meets street-wise 11-year-old Gibran Brown, a would-be suicide, they become fast friends.

1825. *Mask* (1985, Universal, 120m, c). P Martin Starger & Howard Alston, D Peter Bogdanovich, W Anna Hamilton

Phelan (based on the true story of Rocky Dennis), PH Laszlo Kovacs, ED Barbara Ford, MK Michael Westmore & Zoltan Elek*.

LP Cher (Rusty Dennis), Sam Elliott (Gar), Eric Stoltz (Rocky Dennis), Estelle Getty (Evelyn), Richard Dysart (Abe), Laura Dern (Diana), Micole Mercurio (Babe), Harry Carey, Jr. (Red), Dennis Burkley (Dozer), Lawrence Monoson (Ben), Ben Piazza (Mr. Simms), Alexandra Powers (Lisa).

Young Californian Eric Stoltz is afflicted with craniodiaphyseal dysplasia, which gives him a grotesque appearance. He overcomes this handicap and revels in the joys of short life with his mother Cher and his extended adoptive family of bikers. Many critics and fans believed that Cher — essaying the role of a woman of loose morals and dependency on controlled substances, but a fighter for her son — had given an Oscar-worthy performance.

Masque of the Red Death see Edgar Allan Poe's Masque of the Red Death

1826. *Masquerade* (1988, MGM/United Artists, 91m, c). P Michael I. Levy, D Bob Swaim, W Dick Wolf, PH David Watkin, M John Barry, ED Scott Conrad, PD John Kasarda.

LP Rob Lowe (Tim Whalan), Meg Tilly (Olivia Lawrence), Kim Cattrall (Brooke Morrison), Doug Savant (Mike McGill), John Glover (Tony Gateworth), Dana Delany (Anne Briscoe), Erik Holland (Chief of Police), Brian Davies (Granger Morrison), Barton Heyman (Tommy McGill).

In a flawed attempt to restage Alfred Hitchcock's *Suspicion,* Rob Lowe is the charming young man who may or may not be after heiress Meg Tilly's money and life. It's very difficult to see Lowe in any role remotely associated with Cary Grant, and Tilly is not exactly on a par with Joan Fontaine.

1827. *Mass Appeal* (1984, Universal, 100m, c). P Lawrence Turman & David Foster, D Glenn Jordan, W Bill C. Davis (based on his stage play), PH Don Peterman, M Bill Conti, ED John Wright, PD Philip Jefferies.

LP Jack Lemmon (Father Farley),

Zeljko Ivanek (Mark Dolson), Charles Durning (Msgr. Burke), Louise Latham (Margaret), Alice Hirson (Mrs. Hart), Helene Heigh (Mrs. Hart's Mother), Sharee Gregory (Marion Hart), James Ray (Father De Nicola), Lois De Banzie (Mrs. Dolson), Talia Balsam (Liz Dolson).

This adaptation by Bill C. Davis' presents an ideological debate between a devout and dedicated young seminarian, Zeljko Ivanek, and Jack Lemmon, an immensely popular pastor of an affluent L.A. parish. Ivanek accuses Lemmon of practicing "song-and-dance theology."

1828. *Massive Retaliation* (1984, One Pass-Hammermark, 90m, c). P&D Thomas A. Cohen, W Larry Wittnebert & Richard Beban, PH Richard Lerner, M Harn Soper & Paul Potyen, ED B.J. Sears.

LP Tom Bower (Kirk Fredericks), Karlene Crockett (Marianne Briscoe), Peter Donat (Lee Briscoe), Marilyn Hassett (Lois Fredericks), Susan O'Connell (Jackie Tolliver), Michael Pritchard (Harry Tolliver).

When word comes of a nuclear war in the Middle East, three families leave their city homes and head for a survivalist retreat which they had prepared for just such an eventuality.

1829. *Masterblaster* (1987, Radiance-First American Entertainment, 84, c). P Randy Grinter, D Glenn R. Wilder, W Grinter, Wilder & Moldovan (based on a story by Grinter), PH Frank Pershing Flynn, M Alain Salvati, ED Angelo Ross.

LP Jeff Moldovan (Jeremy Hawk), Donna Rosae (Samantha), Joe Hess (DeAngelo), Peter Lundblad (Lewis), Robert Goodman (Mike), Richard St. George, George Gill, Earleen Carey, Jim Reynolds.

In an assassination game in which victims are supposed to be "killed" by guns which shoot only paint, someone is using real bullets.

1830. *Masters of the Universe* (1987, Cannon, 106m, c). P Menahem Golan & Yoram Globus, D Gary Goddard, W David Odell, PH Hanania Baer, M Bill Conti, ED Anne V. Coates, PD William Stout.

LP Dolph Lundgren (He-Man), Frank Langella (Skeletor), Meg Foster (Evil-Lyn), Billy Barty (Gwildor), Courteney Cox (Julie Winston), James Tolkan (Det. Lubic), Christina Pickles (Sorceress of Castle Greyskull).

He-Man, a doll and Saturday morning cartoon hero, is brought to life in this violent film. It's probably not appropriate for viewing by the audience for which it was made, kids.

1831. *Mata Hari* (1985, Cannon, 108m, c). P Rony Yacov, D Curtis Harrington, W Joel Ziskin, PH David Gurfinkel, M Wilfred Josephs & Sri Hastanto, ED Henry Richardson.

LP Sylvia Kristel (Mata Hari), Christopher Cazenove (Capt. Karl Von Byerling), Oliver Tobias (Capt. Ladoux), Gaye Brown (Fraulein Doktor), Gottfried John (Herr Wolff), William Fox (Maitre Clunet), Michael Anthony (Duke of Montmorency), Vernon Dobtcheff (Prosecutor).

Sylvia Kristel uses her seductive charms to win secrets from the leaders of Europe during World War I, but in the end she is executed as a spy by the French.

1832. *Matewan* (1987, Cinecom, 132m, c). P Peggy Rajski & Maggie Renzi, D&W John Sayles, PH Haskell Wexler†, M Mason Daring, ED Sonya Polonsky, PD Nora Chavooshian.

LP Chris Cooper (Joe Kenehan), James Earl Jones (Few Clothes Johnson), Mary McDonnell (Elma Radnor), Will Oldham (Danny Radnor), Jace Alexander (Hillard), Ken Jenkins (Sephus Purcell), Bob Gunton (C.E. Lively), Kevin Tighe (Hickey), Gordon Clapp (Griggs), Josh Mostel (Mayor Cabell Testerman), James Kizer (Tolbert), Michael Preston (Ellix).

Set in Matewan, West Virginia, in 1920, the film is a dramatization of the massacre which led to the West Virginia Coal Mine War. When the Stone Mountain Coal Company proposes a wage cut, the immigrants and blacks brought into to work the mines go out on strike. The company brings in scabs, but these are ultimately induced to join the strike. Sabotage, deceptions and murders lead to a bloody battle.

1833. *Matinee* (1989, Summit, Canada, 90m, c). P Kim Steer & Cal Schumiatcher, D&W Richard Martin, PH Cyrus Block, M Graeme Coleman, ED Bruce Lange & Debra Rurak.

LP Gillian Barber (Marilyn), Ron White (Al Jason), Tim Webber (Oslam), Jeff Schultz (Lawrence), Beatrice Boepple (Sherri), R. Nelson Brown (Warren).

This tongue-in-cheek suspense thriller is set in a small town, filled with murdering eccentrics. It's a must for horror film junkies.

Matt Riker: Mutant Hunter see Mutant Hunter

1834. *Maurice* (1987, Cinecom, GB, 140m, c). P Ismail Merchant, D James Ivory, W Kit Hesketh-Harvey & James Ivory (based on the novel by E.M. Forster), PH Pierre Lhomme, M Richard Robbins, ED Katherine Wenning, PD Brian Ackland-Snow, AD Peter James, COS Jenny Beavan & John Bright†.

LP James Wilby (Maurice Hall), Hugh Grant (Clive Durham), Rupert Graves (Alec Scudder), Denholm Elliott (Dr. Barry), Simon Callow (Mr. Ducie), Billie Whitelaw (Mrs. Hall), Ben Kingsley (Lasker-Jones), Judy Parfitt (Mrs. Durham), Phoebe Nicholls (Anne Durham), Mark Tandy (Risley), Helena Michell (Ada Hall), Kitty Aldridge (Kitty Hall).

While a student at Cambridge, James Wilby is stunned when his friend Hugh Grant tells him that he loves him. Wilby soon confesses that he loves Grant as well. Wilby's attempts to physically consummate the love is rejected by Grant, who believes that to do "the unspeakable" would sully their love. Their passionate but platonic relationship lasts for years, until Grant announces that he plans to marry. Wilby is forced to confront his homosexuality when Grant's servant Rupert Graves comes to Wilby's bedroom one night, ravishes him and finally gives Wilby the physical love he had wanted all along.

1835. *Mausoleum* (1983, Motion Picture Marketing, 96m, c). P Robert Barich & Robert Madero, D Michael Dugan, W Barich & Madero (based on the screenplay and story by Katherine Rosenwink), PH Barich, M Jaime Mendoza-Nava, ED Richard C. Bock, AD Robert Burns, SE Roger George.

LP Marjoe Gortner (Oliver), Bobbie Bresee (Susan), Norman Burton (Dr. Andrews), Maurice Sherbanee (Ben), Laura Hippe (Aunt Cora), LaWanda Page (Elsie), Sheri Mann (Dr. Logan), Julie Christy Murray (Susan at 10), Bill Vail (Final Demon).

Only Marjoe Gortner can save Bobbie Bresee from an ancient curse which damns her to a living hell of a life, filled with terrible telekinectic behavior.

1836. *Max Dugan Returns* (1983, 20th Century–Fox, 98m, c). P Neil Simon & Herbert Ross, D Ross, W Simon, PH David M. Walsh, M David Shire, ED Richard Marks, PD Albert Brenner.

LP Marsha Mason (Nora), Jason Robards, Jr. (Max Dugan), Donald Sutherland (Brian), Matthew Broderick (Michael), Dody Goodman (Mrs. Litke), Sal Viscuso (Coach), Panchito Gomez (Luis), Charley Lau (Himself), Mari Gorman (Pat).

Ex-con man Jason Robards, fresh from prison, comes visiting his daughter Marsha Mason and grandson Matthew Broderick. He brings a suitcase filled with stolen money that he spends lavishly, giving Mason and Broderick everything he thinks they will need or want. You can't buy love—but you can try.

1837. *Maxie* (1985, Orion, 98m, c). P Carter DeHaven, D Paul Aaron, W Patricia Resnick (based on the novel *Marion's Wall* by Jack Finney), PH Fred Schuler, M Georges Delerue, ED Lynzee Klingman, PD John Lloyd.

LP Glenn Close (Jan/Maxie), Mandy Patinkin (Nick), Ruth Gordon (Mrs. Lavin), Barnard Hughes (Bishop Campbell), Valerie Curtin (Miss Sheffer), Googy Gress (Father Jerome), Michael Ensign ("Cleopatra" Director).

Glenn Close, the precocious ghost of a fun-loving flapper, invades the body of librarian Mandy Patinkin's wife (also Close) so she can get the chance she missed when she was alive to appear in movies. It's not Close at her best, but it's moderately entertaining.

1838. *Maximum Overdrive* (1986, De Laurentiis, 97m, c). P Martha Schumacher, D&W Stephen King, PH Armando Nannuzzi, M AC/DC, ED Evan Lottman, PD Giorgio Postiglione.

LP Emilio Estevez (Bill Robinson), Pat Hingle (Hendershot), Laura Harrington (Brett), Yeardley Smith (Connie), John Short (Curt), Ellen McElduff (Wanda June), J.C. Quinn (Duncan), Holter Graham (Deke).

Making his directorial debut, Stephen King films his story of trucks terrorizing employees at an interstate truck stop. The twelve-wheelers come to life and are mad as hell at humans.

1839. *Maya* (1982, Claridge, 114m, c). P Antiqua Domsa, D Agust Agustsson & Ruth Schell, W Berta Dominguez D & Joseph D. Rosevich, PH Oliver Wood, M Bika Reed & Don Salmon Guacaran, ED Ruth Schell.

LP Berta Dominguez D (Maya Murillo), Joseph D. Rosevich (Martin Kingman), Luis Manuel (Juan Dominguez), Valeria Riccardo (Valeria), Mario Rabaglia (Hollywood).

This amateurish effort to film a *Fame*-like story, featuring a school for kids training to become fashion designers and models, is nauseatingly sweet and sticky with cornpone performances.

1840. *The Mean Season* (1985, Orion, 106m, c). P David Foster & Lawrence Turman, D Phillip Borsos, W Leon Piedmont (based on the novel *In the Heat of the Summer* by John Katzenbach), PH Frank Tidy, M Lalo Schifrin, ED Duwayne Dunham, PD Philip Jefferies.

LP Kurt Russell (Malcolm Anderson), Mariel Hemingway (Christine Connelly), Richard Jordan (Alan Delour), Richard Masur (Bill Nolan), Joe Pantoliano (Andy Porter), Richard Bradford (Phil Wilson), Andy Garcia (Ray Martinez).

Miami reporter Kurt Russell gets the scoop of his life when serial killer Richard Jordan agrees to give Russell the grisly details of his murder spree.

1841. *Meantime* (1986, Film Forum, GB, 100m, c). P Graham Benson, D&W Mike Leigh, PH Roger Pratt, M Andrew Dickson, ED Lesley Walker.

LP Marion Bailey (Barbara), Tim Roth (Colin), Jeff Robert (Frank), Gary Oldman (Coxy), Phil Daniels (Mark), Pam Ferris (Mavis), Alfred Molina (John), Tilly Vosburgh (Hayley).

The film traces the bleak life of a working-class London family. It's well done but not absorbing.

1842. *Meatballs Part II* (1984, Tri-Star, 95m, c). P Tony Bishop & Stephen Poe, D Ken Wiederhorn, W Bruce Singer (based on a story by Martin Kitrosser & Carol Watson), PH Donald M. Morgan, M Ken Harrison, ED George Berndt, PD James William Newport.

LP Archie Hahn (Jamie), John Mengatti (Flash), Tammy Taylor (Nancy), Kim Richards (Cheryl), Ralph Seymour (Eddie), Richard Mulligan (Giddy), Hamilton Camp (Hershey), John Larroquette (Meathead), Paul Reubens (Albert).

It seems that sequels should have something to do with the original film (*Meatballs*, 1979), but such is not the case with this tacky film. Camp counselor John Mengatti, a tough city street kid, falls for sweet young thing Kim Richards. He puts on the gloves to defend his camp's honor against a rival recreation spot.

1843. *Meatballs III* (1987, The Movie Store, 88m, c). P Don Carmody & John Dunning, D George Mendeluk, W Michael Paseornek & Bradley Kesden (based on a story by Chuck Workman), PH Peter Benison, M Paul Zaza, ED Debra Karen, PD Charles Dunlop.

LP Sally Kellerman (Roxy Du Jour), Patrick Dempsey (Rudy), Al Waxman (Saint Peter), Isabelle Mejias (Wendy), Shannon Tweed (The Love Goddess), Jan Taylor (Rita), George Buza (Mean Gene).

Sally Kellerman, the ghost of a porno star, must do one good deed to be allowed admittance to heaven. Does getting 14-year-old nerd Patrick Dempsey laid qualify as a good deed? Lots of T & A in this tasteless comedy, which bears no resemblance to the original Bill Murray–Chris Makepeace film.

1844. *Medium Straight* (1989, Overseas Filmgroup, 85m, c). P I.M. Ecks, D Adam Friedman, W Robert Litz, PH Douglas E. Carnevale, M Rick Borgia & Lisa G. Bond, ED Michael Blocher & Susan Brookman.

LP Jerome Lepage (Nick Harding), Richard Schiff (Pat Harding), Anne Lilly (Grandee), Ron Sanborn (Joey Mannucci), Brian Straub (Mel Burns), Patrick Minietta (Hilton).

While smalltime thug Jerome Lepage is making a drug deal with Ron Sanborn, son of the New Jersey mob leader, they struggle with a gun which goes off. Lepage believes that he's killed Sanborn and is in deep trouble. He hides out, but his level-headed cousin Richard Schiff works everything out and no one gets killed.

1845. *Meet the Hollowheads* (1989, Moviestore, 86m, c). P Joseph Grace & John Chavez, D Tom Burman, W Burman & Lisa Morton, PH Marvin Rush, M Glenn Jordan, ED Carl Kress, PD Ed Eyth.

LP John Glover (Henry Hollowhead), Nancy Mette (Miriam Hollowhead), Richard Portnow (Mr. Crabneck), Matt Shakman (Billy Hollowhead), Juliette Lewis (Cindy Hollowhead), Lightfield Lewis (Bud Hollowhead), Joshua Miller (Joey), Anne Ramsey (Babbleaxe), Logan Ramsey (Top Drone).

In a futuristic situation comedy of a post-nuclear age, the Hollowheads, like their neighbors, live in tunnels. They spend most of their time preparing unappetizing and unrecognizable food for their meals, while making terrible puns and vulgar bathroom humor comments. It isn't funny and shouldn't even make a failed pilot for a TV series—but we've underestimated TV before.

1846. *Megaforce* (1982, 20th Century–Fox, 99m, c). P Albert S. Ruddy, D Hal Needham, W James Whittaker, Ruddy, Needham & Andre Morgan (based on a story by Robert Kachler), PH Michael Butler, M Jerrold Immel, ED Patrick Roark & S. Skip Schoolnik, PD Joel Schiller.

LP Barry Bostwick (Ace Hunter), Persis Khambatta (Zara), Michael Beck (Dallas), Edward Mulhare (Byrne-White), George Furth (Professor Eggstrum), Henry Silva (Guerera), Michael Kulcsar (Ivan), Ralph Wilcox (Zac).

In a futuristic thriller, Megaforce, a military task force, is sent to save a small democratic nation from invasion by a technologically advanced superpower.

1847. *Melancholia* (1988, British Film Institute, GB/Germany, 88m, c). P Colin MacCabe, D Andi Engel, W Engel & Lewis Rodia, PH Denis Crossan, M Simon Fisher Turner, ED Christopher Roth, PD Jock Scott.

LP Jeroen Krabbe (David Keller), Susannah York (Catherine), Ulrich Wildgruber (Manfred), Jane Gurnett (Sarah Yelin), Kate Hardie (Rachel).

Jeroen Krabbe, a 60s political activist, now works as an art critic in London. He receives a call from his former associates who wish to kill a South American potentate and torturer. He agrees to do so, but discovers that the "assassination" plan has been superseded by a more pragmatic alternative. Krabbe chooses to take things into his own hands.

1848. *Melanie* (1982, Embassy, Canada, 109m, c). P Peter Simpson, D Rex Bromfield, W Robert Guza, Jr. & Richard Paluck (based on the story by Michael Green), PH Richard Ciupka, M Paul Zaza, ED Brian Rovak, PD Roy Forge Smith.

LP Glynnis O'Connor (Melanie Daniel), Burton Cummings (Rick Manning), Paul Sorvino (Walter Greer), Trudy Young (Rondo Colton), Don Johnson (Carl Daniel), James Dick (Tyler Daniel), Donann Caven (Ginny).

Refusing to see herself labeled an unfit mother, illiterate Arkansas woman Glynnis O'Connor strives to regain custody of her son, whom the courts have given to her husband Don Johnson. She also enters into a relationship with has-been rock star Burton Cummings and helps him get back on the top.

1849. *Melvin and Howard* (1980, Universal, 93m, c). P Art Linson & Don Phillips, D Jonathan Demme, W Bo Goldman*, PH Tak Fujimoto, M Bruce Langhorne, ED Craig McKay, PD Toby Rafelson.

LP Jason Robards† (Howard Hughes), Paul LeMat (Melvin Dummar), Elizabeth Cheshire (Darcy Dummar), Mary Steenburgen* (Lynda Dummar), Chip Taylor (Clark Taylor), Michael J. Pollard (Little Red), Denise Galik (Lucy), Gloria Grahame (Mrs. Sisk), Melvin E. Dummar (Bus Depot Counterman), Dabney

Coleman (Judge Keith Hayes), Pamela Reed (Bonnie Dummar).

According to Melvin Dummar, one night in the desert he picked up an old bum who claimed to be Howard Hughes. For this kindness, the billionaire leaves his money to Dummar. Unfortunately for Dummar, the courts don't uphold his claim, based on the so-called Mormon will. At least Dummar had his moment in the sun as a celebrity, much in the way Andy Warhol defined the term.

1850. *Melvin, Son of Alvin* (1984, Roadshow, Australia, 85m, c). P James McElroy, D John Eastway, W Morris Gleitzman, PH Ross Berryman, M Colin Stead, ED John Hollands, PD Jon Dowding.

LP Gerry Sont (Melvin Simpson), Lenita Psillakis (Gloria Giannis), Graeme Blundell (Alvin Purple), Jon Finlayson (Burnbaum), Tina Bursill (Dee Tanner), Colin McEwan (Mr. Simpson), Abigail (Mrs. Simpson).

This sequel to *Alvin Purple* (1973), the largest grossing Australian film of the time, stars Gerry Sont as the 18-year-old son of Alvin. He has the same animal magnetism as his father, but he fears women. There's nothing happening here that would explain the great success of the earlier film.

1851. *Memed My Hawk* (1984, Jadran/Focus, GB/Yugo., 110m, c). P Fuad Kavur, D&W Peter Ustinov (based on the novel by Yashar Kemal), PH Freddie Francis, M Manos Hadjidakis, ED Peter Honess, AD Veljko Despotovic.

LP Peter Ustinov (Abdi Aga), Herbert Lom (Ali Safa Bey), Denis Quilley (Rejeb), Michael Elphick (Jabbar), Simon Dutton (Memed), Leonie Mellinger (Hatche), Relja Basic (Mad Durdu), Edward Burnham (Naked Man), Ernest Clark (Father).

A tyrant's involvement in the feudal life of Turkey in the 1950s leads to his own destruction.

1852. *Memoirs of a Survivor* (1981, EMI, GB, 115m, c). P Michael Medwin & Penny Clark, D David Gladwell, W Gladwell & Kerry Crabbe (based on the novel by Doris Lessing), PH Walter Lassally, M Mike Thorn, ED William Shapter, PD Keith Wilson, SE Effects Associates.

LP Julie Christie ("D"), Christopher Guard (Gerald), Leonie Mellinger (Emily Mary Cartwright), Debbie Hutchings (June), Nigel Hawthorne (Victorian Father), Pat Keen (Victorian Mother), Georgina Griffiths (Victorian Emily), Christopher Tsangarides (Victorian Son).

Decaying in a post–nuclear holocaust society, Julie Christie crosses over into the Victorian past of her memory.

1853. *Memories of Me* (1988, MGM, 104m, c). P Alan King, Billy Crystal & Michael Hertzberg, D Henry Winkler, W Eric Roth & Crystal, PH Andrew Dintenfass, M Georges Delerue, ED Peter F. Berger, PD William J. Cassidy.

LP Billy Crystal (Abbie Polin), Alan King (Abe Polin), JoBeth Williams (Lisa), Janet Carroll (Dorothy Davis), Sean Connery (Himself), Janet Carroll (Dorothy Davis), David Ackroyd (First Assn't Director).

When heart surgeon Billy Crystal suffers a heart attack, he admits to mortality, but is still not keen on reconciling with his father, movie extra Alan King. Crystal considers the older man an embarrassment. Somehow these two clichés of soft-heartedness find they really do care for each other.

Men of Steel see Steel

1854. *The Men's Club* (1986, Atlantic, 100m, c). P Howard Gottfried, D Peter Medak, W Leonard Michaels, PH John Fleckenstein, M Lee Holdridge, ED Cynthia Scheider, David Dresher & Bill Butler, PD Ken Davis.

LP David Dukes (Phillip), Richard Jordan (Kramer), Harvey Keitel (Solly Berlinger), Frank Langella (Harold Canterbury), Roy Scheider (Cavanaugh), Craig Wasson (Paul), Treat Williams (Terry), Stockard Channing (Nancy), Gina Gallego (Felicia), Cindy Pickett (Hannah), Gwen Welles (Redhead), Penny Baker (Lake), Rebeccah Bush (Stella), Jennifer Jason Leigh (Teensy).

It's the boy's night out. Plenty of drinking, bragging about sex, love, marriage and careers. The friendly taunts lead to bitter brawls and the last stop of the night at "The House of Affections."

1855. *Mercenary Fighters* (1988, Cannon, 91m, c). P Menahem Golan & Yoram Globus, D Riki Shelach, W Bud

Schaetzle, Dean Tschetter & Andrew Deutsch (based on a story by Schaetzle & Tschetter), PH Daniel Schneor, M Harold Morgan, ED Michael Campbell & Dean Goodhill, PD Leonard Coen Cagli.

LP Peter Fonda (Virelli), Reb Brown (T.J. Christian), Ron O'Neal (Cliff), James Mitchum (Wilson Jeffords), Robert Doqui (Kyemba), Jerry Biggs (Mac Jeffords), Joanna Weinberg (Ruth), Henry Cele (Jaunde).

The ruler of an African nation hires mercenaries Peter Fonda and others to get rid of tribesmen who are blocking the building of a new dam. When they discover that the dam will force the tribesmen from their ancestral homeland, fighting breaks out among the mercenaries who don't all believe they are doing the right thing. When did mercenaries think of the consequences of their work?

The Mercenaries see Fortress of Amerikka

1856. *Merry Christmas, Mr. Lawrence* (1983, Universal, GB/Japan, 124m, c). P Jeremy Thomas, D Nagisa Oshima, W Oshima & Paul Mayersberg (based on the novel *The Seed and The Sower* by Laurens Van Der Post), PH Toichiro Narushima, M Ryuichi Sakamoto, ED Tomoyo Oshima, PD Shigemasa Toda.

LP David Bowie (Celliers), Tom Conti (Col. John Lawrence), Ryuichi Sakamoto (Capt. Yoni), Takeshi (Sgt. Hara), Jack Thompson (Hicksley-Ellis), Johnny Okura (Kanemoto), Alistair Browning (DeJong).

Cultures clash in a Japanese POW camp in Java during World War II. The ranking English officer, Tom Conti, is in constant conflict with the arrogant samurai-inspired Japanese commander, Ryuichi Sakamoto.

1857. *Messenger of Death* (1988, Cannon, 90m, c). P Pancho Kohner, D J. Lee Thompson, W Paul Jarrico (based on the novel *The Avenging Angel* by Rex Burns), PH Gideon Porath, M Robert O. Ragland, ED Peter Lee Thompson.

LP Charles Bronson (Garret Smith), Trish Van Devere (Jastra Watson), Laurence Luckenbill (Homer Foxx), Daniel Benzali (Chief Barney Doyle), Marilyn Hassett (Josephine Fabrizio), Jeff Corey

(Willis Beecham), John Ireland (Zenas Beecham), Penny Peyser (Trudy Pike).

Reporter Charles Bronson finds himself in the middle of a deadly religious war involving two extremist factions of Mormons.

1858. *Metalstorm: The Destruction of Jared-Syn* (1983, Universal, 84m, c). P Charles Band & Alan J. Adler, D Band, W Adler, PH Mac Ahlberg, M Richard Band, ED Brad Arensman, SE Joe Quinlan & Gregory Van Der Veer.

LP Jeffrey Byron (Dogen), Mike Preston (Jared-Syn), Tim Thomerson (Rhodes), Kelly Preston (Dhyana), Richard Moll (Hurok), R. David Smith (Baal), Larry Pennell (Alex), Marty Zagon (Zax), Mickey Fox (Poker Annie).

This low-budget 3-D movie doesn't deliver on the destruction promised in the title. Space ranger Jeffrey Byron saves the planet Lemuria from mad intergalactic magician Mike Preston.

1859. *The Method* (1989, Pacific Star, 105m, c). P&D Joseph Despins, W Rob Nilsson, Joel Adelman & Destein, PH Stephen Lighthill, M Ray Obiedo, ED Jay Boekelheide & Victoria Lewis, AD Gary Frutkoff.

LP Melanie Dreisbach (Anna Beringer), Richard Arnold (Nick), Deborah Swisher (Monique), Anthony Cistaro (Tony), Robert Elross (Vincenzio), Jack Rikess (Greg).

Melanie Dreisbach, a 40-year-old housewife from Oregon, is studying to become a "method" actor. Audiences see her learning to become a method actor, being a method actor and going on to stardom as a method actor.

1860. *Micki and Maude* (1984, Columbia, 118m, c). P Tony Adams, D Blake Edwards, W Jonathan Reynolds, PH Harry Stradling, Jr., M Lee Holdridge, ED Ralph E. Winters, PD Rodger Maus, M/L "Something New in My Life" by Michel Legrand, Alan and Marilyn Bergman.

LP Dudley Moore (Rob Salinger), Amy Irving (Maude Salinger), Ann Reinking (Micki Salinger), Richard Mulligan (Leo Brody), George Gaynes (Dr. Eugene Glztszki), Wallace Shawn (Dr. Elliot Fibel), John Pleshette (Hap Ludlow),

H.B. Haggerty (Barkhas Guillory), Lu Leonard (Nurse Verbeck).

TV reporter Dudley Moore so wants a family that when it appears that lawyer wife Ann Reinking is too involved with her career to have a baby, he meets and marries cellist Amy Irving. Bigamist Moore soon discovers that both wives are pregnant. Wouldn't you just know that they are prepared to deliver at the same time, in the same hospital and are suffering loudly in adjoining labor rooms. It has its moments, but it's much too much contrived.

1861. *Microwave Massacre* (1983, Reel Life, 76m, c). P Thomas Singer & Craig Muckler, D Wayne Berwick, W Singer (based on a story by Muckler), PH Karen Grossman, M Leif Horvath, ED Steven Nielson, AD Robert Burns.

LP Jackie Vernon (Donald), Loren Schein (Roosevelt), Al Troupe (Philip), Claire Ginsberg (May), Lou Ann Webber (Dee Dee Dee), Anna Marlow (Chick), Sarah Alt (Evelyn), Cindy Grant (Susan).

How low is low? Moviemakers Thomas Singer and Craig Muckler work very hard to set a new record for grotesque horror films. Construction worker Jackie Vernon brings women home for sex and then cooks them in his microwave. He acquired this taste accidentally when he started his culinary expertise with his wife Claire Ginsberg.

1862. *The Midday Sun* (1989, Missing Piece, Canada, 95m, c). P Christopher Zimmer, D&W Lulu Keating, PH Manfred Guthe, M Sandy Moore, ED Miume Jan, PD Mary Steckle.

LP Isabelle Mejias (Maggie Cameron), George Seremba (Julian), Robert Bockstael (Bruno), Jackie Burroughs (Lillian), Roland Hewgill (Watson), Dominic Kanaventi (Anthony), Kathy Kuleya (Elizabeth).

Pretty, naive, 20-year-old redhead Isabelle Mejias arrives in Africa to help hardworking missionary George Seremba. She makes mistake after mistake, mostly in trying to impose her Western values on the people. She makes another mistake by having an affair with racist German Robert Bockstael. It's not until her houseboy is arrested (after her home is robbed), immediately tried, and on little evidence found guilty and sentenced to ten years in prison, that she begins to develop some insight into the struggles of the African people.

1863. *Middle Age Crazy* (1980, 20th Century–Fox, Canada, 89m, c). P Robert Cooper & Ronald Cohen, D John Trent, W Carl Kleinschmitt (based on a song by Jerry Lee Lewis), PH Reginald Morris, M Matthew McCauley, ED John Kelly, AD Karen Bromley.

LP Bruce Dern (Bobby Lee), Ann-Margret (Sue Ann), Graham Jarvis (J.D.), Eric Christmas (Tommy), Helen Hughes (Ruth), Geoffrey Bowes (Greg), Michael Kane (Abe Titus), Diane Dewey (Wanda Jean), Vivian Reis (Becky), Deborah Wakeham (Nancy), Patricia Hamilton (Barbara Pickett).

When Houston building contractor Bruce Dern turns 40, he has a mid-life crisis. To deal with it, he buys a Porsche and some new younger-looking clothes, dumps long-time wife Ann-Margret and takes up with Dallas Cowboy cheerleader Deborah Wakeham. He comes to his senses.

1864. *Midnight* (1983, Independent International, 91m, c). P Donald Redinger, D&W John A. Russo (based on his novel), PH Paul McCollough, M The Sand Castle, ED McCollough.

LP Lawrence Tierney (Bert Johnson), Melanie Verlin (Nancy Johnson), John Hall (Tom), Charles Jackson (Hank), Doris Hackney (Harriet Johnson), John Amplos (Abraham), Robin Walsh (Cynthia), David Marchick (Cyrus).

Teenager Melanie Verlin is forced out of her home by her lecherous policeman stepfather. Unfortunately, she meets two thieves, members of a cult family who sacrifice young girls to their master, the devil.

1865. *Midnight* (1989, SVS Film, 84m, c). P Norman Thaddeus Vane & Gloria J. Morrison, D&W Vane, PH David Golia, M Michael Wetherwax, ED Sam Adelman, AD Mark Simon.

LP Lynn Redgrave (Midnight [Vera]), Tony Curtis (Mr. B), Steve Parrish (Mickey Modine), Rita Gam (Heidi), Gustav Vintas (Siegfried), Karen Witter (Missy), Frank Gorshin (Ron), Robert Miano (Arnold).

Lynn Redgrave, an Elvira-like TV

horror show hostess, sounds like she's attempting a terrible impersonation of Tallulah Bankhead. She might as well have imitated Gloria Swanson as the film tries to imitate *Sunset Boulevard*. Young gigolo Steve Parrish moves into her mansion, which she shares with a doting Von Stroheim–like butler, Gustav Vintas. It's all pretty bad, with the acting uniformly atrocious.

1866. *Midnight Crossing* (1988, Vestron, 96m, c). P Mathew Hayden & Doug Weiser, D Roger Holzberg, W Holzberg & Weiser (based on a story by Holzberg), PH Henry Vargas, M Paul Buckmaster & Al Gorgoni, ED Earl Watson, PD Jose Duarte.

LP Faye Dunaway (Helen Barton), Daniel J. Travanti (Morely Barton), Kim Cattrall (Alexa Schubb), John Laughlin (Jeffrey Schubb), Ned Beatty (Ellis), Pedro De Pool (Captain Mendoza), Doug Weiser (Miller).

Insurance agent Daniel J. Travanti and his blind wife Faye Dunaway are intent on recovering some loot that he buried years earlier. It's a soapy adventure story.

1867. *Midnight Madness* (1980, Buena Vista, 110m, c). P Ron Miller, D&W David Wechter & Michael Nankin, PH Frank Phillips, M Julius Wechter, ED Norman R. Palmer & Jack Sekely, SE Danny Lee.

LP David Naughton (Adam), Debra Clinger (Laura), Eddie Deezen (Wesley), Brad Wilkin (Lavitas), Maggie Roswell (Donna), Stephen Furst (Harold), Irene Tedrow (Mrs. Grimhaus), Michael J. Fox (Scott).

This is the first Disney PG-rated film. It's a dumb comedy in which college students search all over the city of Los Angeles for clues to a scavenger hunt which will lead them to thousands of dollars in buried treasure. Michael J. Fox makes his film debut in this bomb.

1868. *Midnight Run* (1988, Universal, 122m, c). P&D Martin Brest, W George Gallo, PH Donald Thorin, M Danny Elfman, ED Billy Weber, Chris Lebenzon & Michael Tronick, PD Angelo Graham, SE Roy Arbogast.

LP Robert De Niro (Jack Walsh), Charles Grodin (Jonathan Mardukas),

Yaphet Kotto (Alonzo Mosely), John Ashton (Marvin Dorfler), Dennis Farina (Jimmy Serrano), Joe Pantoliano (Eddie Moscone), Richard Foronjy (Tony Darvo), Robert Miranda (Joey), Jack Kehoe (Jerry Geisler), Wendy Phillips (Gail), Danielle DuClos (Denise).

One wonders what might have happened if this excellent action film had been released during the Oscar sweeps in December, rather than in July. The Academy overlooked two marvelous performances by Robert De Niro and Charles Grodin as a bounty hunter and his prey, respectively. Both actors are so uniformly good, it is easy to overlook their work. The two work almost seamlessly together. De Niro is hired to bring Mafia accountant Grodin, who has jumped bail, back across the country from New York to California. The mob, the FBI and other bounty hunters are desperate to snatch Grodin from De Niro by any means. The two make use of every mode of transportation available on their trip. De Niro doesn't want to know anything about his captive, but idealist Grodin takes a very personal interest in De Niro and his problems.

1869. *Midnight Warrior* (1989, P/M Entertainment Group, 86m, c). P Richard Pepin & Joseph Merhi, D Merhi, W Charles T. Kanganis, PH Pepin, M John Gonzalez, ED Paul Volk.

LP Kevin Bernhardt (Nick Branca), Lilly Melgar (Angelina), Bernie Angel (Buddy), Heidi Paine (Liz Brown), Marty Brinton (Sam), Michelle Berger, Rita Rogers, David Parry, Jeanette Mateus.

In this direct to video movie principled TV news cameraman Kevin Bernhardt succumbs to the lure of the fast buck.

1870. *A Midsummer Night's Sex Comedy* (1982, Orion/Warner, 88m, c). P Robert Greenhut, D&W Woody Allen, PH Gordon Willis, M Felix Mendelssohn, ED Susan E. Morse, PD Mel Bourne.

LP Woody Allen (Andrew), Mia Farrow (Ariel), Jose Ferrer (Leopold), Julie Hagerty (Dulcy), Tony Roberts (Maxwell), Mary Steenburgen (Adrian), Adam Redfield (Student Foxx), Moishe Rosenfeld (Mr. Hayes), Timothy Jenkins (Mr. Thompson), Michael Higgins (Reynolds).

In Woody Allen's tribute to Ingmar Bergman's *Smiles of a Summer Night,* audiences may enjoy a modest comedy about three couples who spend an idyllic and farciful weekend in upstate New York at the turn of the century.

1871. *A Midsummer's Night Dream* (1985, Mainline, GB/Spain, 78m, c). P Miguel Campos, D Celestino Coronado, W Coronado & Lindsay Kemp (based on the play by William Shakespeare), PH Peter Middleton, M Carlos Miranda.

LP Lindsay Kemp (Puck), Manuela Vargas (Hippolyta), Incredible Orlando (Titania), Michael Matou (Oberon), Francois Testory (Snout/Tree/Changeling), David Meyer (Lysander), Neil Caplan (Theseus/Beast), David Haughton (Demetrius), Cheryl Hazelwood (Helena), Atilio Lopez (Bottom/Romeo), Christian Michaelson (Flute/Juliet), Kevin L'Anglaise (Snug/Lion).

In Shakespeare's fantasy, the fairy king's mischievous sprite Puck, enjoyably played by Lindsay Kemp, mixes up the affections of two couples in the woods of Athens.

1872. *Mighty Mouse in the Great Space Chase* (1983, Filmation-Viacom/Miracle, animated, 87m, c). P Lou Scheimer, Norma Prescott & Don Christensen, D Ed Friedman & Lou Kachivas, Marsh Lamore, Gwen Wetzler, Kay Wright & Lou Zukor, PH R.W. Pope, M Yvette Blais & Jeff Michael, ED James Blodgett, Ann Hagerman & Earl Biddle.

VOICES None given.

The superman of the mouse world gets his first feature length animated film.

1873. *The Mighty Quinn* (1989, MGM, 99m, c). P Sandy Lieberson, D Carl Schenkel, W Hampton Fancher (based on the novel *Finding Maubee* by A.H.Z. Carr), PH Jacques Steyn, M Anne Dudley, ED John Jympson, PD Roger Murray-Leach.

LP Denzel Washington (Xavier Quinn), James Fox (Elgin), Mimi Rogers (Hadley), M. Emmet Walsh (Miller), Sheryl Lee Ralph (Lola), Art Evans (Jump), Esther Rolle (Ube Pearl), Norman Beaton (Governor Chalk), Alex Colon (Patina), Robert Townsend (Maubee), Keye Luke (Dr. Raj).

Denzel Washington is well on his way to becoming the first black matinee idol since Sidney Poitier. Here he portrays a Caribbean-born, FBI-trained official whose job is to maintain the peace in a small island country. Things get hairy when a rich American tourist and businessman is found decapitated in a Jacuzzi at his hotel. The prime suspect is Washington's childhood friend Robert Townsend. This is a thoroughly enjoyable film.

1874. *Mike's Murder* (1984, Warner, 97m, c). P Kim Kurumada & Jack Larson, D&W James Bridges, PH Reynaldo Villalobos, M John Barry & Joe Jackson, ED Jeff Gourson & Dede Allen, PD Peter Jamison.

LP Debra Winger (Betty Parrish), Mark Keyloun (Mike), Paul Winfield (Phillip), Darrell Larson (Pete), Brooke Alderson (Patty), Robert Crosson (Sam), Daniel Shor (Richard), William Ostrander (Randy).

Bank teller Debra Winger seeks the truth about the murder of her lover Mark Keyloun, a tennis teacher and drugpusher, who called her only when he wanted sex.

1875. *The Milagro Beanfield War* (1988, Universal, 117m, c). P Robert Redford & Moctesuma Esparza, D Redford, W David Ward & John Nichols (based on the novel by Nichols), PH Robbie Greenberg, M Dave Grusin*, ED Dede Allen & Jim Miller.

LP Ruben Blades (Sheriff Bernabe Montoya), Richard Bradford (Ladd Devine), Sonia Braga (Rudy Archuleta), Julie Carmen (Nancy Mondragon), James Gammon (Horsethief Shorty), Melanie Griffith (Flossie Devine), John Heard (Charlie Bloom), Carlos Riquelme (Armarante Cordova), Daniel Stern (Herbie Platt), Christopher Walken (Kyril Montana), Chick Vennera (Joe Mondragon).

Chicano handyman Chick Vennera irrigates his northern New Mexico beanfield with water reserved for a major real estate development. The repercussions of this act cause the locals to band together like Capra people to fight to maintain their way of life. It's an enjoyable comedy-drama with some very fine performances.

1876. *Miles from Home* (1988, Cinecom, 112m, c). P Frederick Zollo & Paul Kurta, D Gary Sinise, W Chris Gerolmo, PH Elliot Davis, M Robert Folk, ED Jane Schwartz Jaffe, PD David Gropman.

LP Richard Gere (Frank Roberts, Jr.), Kevin Anderson (Terry Roberts), Brian Dennehy (Frank Roberts, Sr.), John Malkovich (Barry Maxwell), Judith Ivey (Frances), Jason Campbell (Young Frank), Austin Bamgarner (Young Terry), Larry Poling (Nikita Khrushchev), Terry Kinney (Mark), Laurie Metcalf (Ellen), Penelope Ann Miller (Sally), Helen Hunt (Jennifer).

Richard Gere and Kevin Anderson burn their farm rather than see it taken over by a bank. As a result they become genuine folk heroes in the rural areas. Gere is more and more drawn to revolutionary acts, while Anderson would like some domestic stability. The struggle between the two becomes intense and almost ruins their close relationship.

1877. *Milk and Honey* (1989, Castle Hill, Canada, 94m, c). P Peter O'Brian, D Rebecca Yates & Glen Salzman, W Salzman & Trevor Rhone, PH Guy Dufaux, M Mickey Erbe & Maribeth Solomon, ED Bruce Nyznik.

LP Josette Simon (Joanna Bell), Lyman Ward (Adam Bernardi), Richard Mills (David), Djanet Forbes (Del), Leonie Forbes (Miss Emma), Jane Dingle (Maureen), Errol Slue (Gordon).

Josette Simon leaves her Jamaican home for a better life in Toronto. She finds her new life isn't really much of an improvement. She discovers she's not valued in her new environment and she has trouble getting her son to move to her new home.

1878. *Millennium* (1989, 20th Century–Fox, 108m, c). P Douglas Leiterman, D Michael Anderson, W John Varley (based on his short story "Air Raid"), PH Rene Ohashi, M Eric N. Robertson, ED Ron Wisman, PD Gene Rudolf, SE Light and Motion.

LP Kris Kristofferson (Bill Smith), Cheryl Ladd (Louise Baltimore), Daniel J. Travanti (Arnold Mayer), Robert Joy (Sherman), Lloyd Bochner (Walters).

Kris Kristofferson leads a group investigating the mid-air crash of a 747 and a DC-10. He encounters Cheryl Ladd, a commando leader of a group of women from 1,000 years in the future. The future civilization is incapable of reproducing and Ladd is looking for some stud service from the good old 20th century.

1879. *Million Dollar Mystery* (1987, DEG, 95m, c). P Stephen F. Kesten, D Richard Fleischer, W Tim Metcalfe, Miguel Tejada-Flores & Rudy De Luca, PH Jack Cardiff, M Al Gorgoni, ED John W. Wheeler, PD Jack G. Taylor, Jr.

LP Eddie Deezen (Rollie), Wendy Sherman (Lollie), Rick Overton (Stuart Briggs), Mona Lyden (Barbara Briggs), Douglas Emerson (Howie Briggs), Royce D. Applegate (Tugger), Pam Matteson (Dotty), Penny Baker (Charity), Tawny Fere (Faith), LaGena Hart (Hope), Tom Bosley (Sidney Preston).

The last words of double-dealing government agent Tom Bosley send 22 hapless fortune hunters on a race across the country seeking a prize of $4 million.

1880. *Mind Games* (1989, MGM/United Artists/MIA/Persik, 93m, c). P Mary Apick, D Bob Yari, W Kenneth Dorward, PH Arnie Sirlin, M David Richard Campbell, ED Robert Gordon.

LP Maxwell Caulfield (Eric Garrison), Edward Albert (Dana Lund), Sharon Weatherly (Rita Lund), Matt Norero (Kevin Lund).

This psychological thriller for four actors sees mysterious stranger Maxwell Caulfield being picked up by Edward Albert, Shawn Weatherly and their 10-year-old son Matt Norero, as they travel through the Southwest. Caulfield commands the film as he manipulates the three in an interesting pot-boiler.

1881. *Mind Killer* (1987, Prism-Flash, 86m, c). P Sarah H. Liles, D Michael Krueger, W Krueger, Dave Sipos & Curtis Hannum (based on a story by Krueger & Doug Olson), PH Jim Kelley, M Jeffrey Wood, ED Jonathan Moser, SE Ted A. Bohus & Vincent J. Guastini.

LP Joe McDonald (Warren), Christopher Wade (Larry), Shirley Ross (Sandy), Kevin Hart (Brad), Tom Henry (Vivac Chandra), Diana Calhoun (Mrs. Chandra), George Flynn (Townsend).

Librarian Joe McDonald, a loser where women are concerned, comes across a collection of books which explain how to utilize the potential of one's brain.

Mindways see Galaxy of Terror

1882. *Ministry of Vengeance* (1989, Concorde, 93m, c). P Brad Krevoy & Steven Stabler, D Peter Maris, W Brian D. Jeffries, Mervyn Emryys & Ann Narus (based on a story by Randal Patrick), PH Mark Harris, M Scott Roewe, ED Michael Haight, PD Stephen Greenberg.

LP John Schneider (David Miller), Ned Beatty (Reverend Bloor), James Tolkan (Colonel Freeman), Yaphet Kotto (Mr. Whiteside), George Kennedy (Reverend Hughes), Apollonia Kotero (Zarah), Robert Miano (Ali Aboud).

There is to be no turn-the-other-cheek for minister John Schneider when his wife and daughter are killed at a Rome airport by terrorists. He trails the killers to Lebanon where he engages in a bloodbath of vengeance, without the least pang of conscience.

1883. *Miracle Mile* (1989, Hemdale Pictures, 87m, c). P John Daly & Derek Gibson, D&W Steve DeJarnatt, PH Theo Van de Sande, M Tangerine Dream, ED Stephen Semel & Kathie Weaver, PD Christopher Horner.

LP Anthony Edwards (Harry Washello), Mare Winningham (Julie Peters), John Agar (Ivan Peters), Lou Hancock (Lucy Peters), Mykel T. Williamson (Wilson), Kelly Minter (Charlotta), Kurt Fuller (Gerstead), Denise Crosby (Landa).

Late at night Anthony Edwards picks up a ringing phone in an empty Los Angeles booth. He believes the voice on the other end which announces that the United States is beginning a nuclear strike within the hour. Strange no one else believes him, and audiences aren't certain whether they are supposed to or not.

1884. *Miracles* (1987, Orion, 87m, c). P Steve Roth & Bernard Williams, D&W Jim Kouf, PH John Alcott, M Peter Bernstein, ED Susan E. Morse & Dennis Virkler, PD Terence Marsh.

LP Tom Conti (Dr. Roger Briggs), Teri Garr (Jean Briggs), Paul Rodriguez (Juan), Christopher Lloyd (Harry),

Adalberto Martinez "Resortes" (Witch Doctor), Jorge Russek (Judge), Jorge Reynoso (K'ln), Charles Rocket (Michael), Barbara Whinnery (Hooker), Ken Hixon (Missionary).

Tom Conti and Teri Garr, a recently divorced couple, are whisked away to a South American hellhole by jewel thief Paul Rodriguez. They try vainly to put some humor in this knockoff of *Romancing the Stone.*

1885. *The Mirror Crack'd* (1980, EMI, GB, 105m, c). P John Brabourne & Richard Goodwin, D Guy Hamilton, W Jonathan Hales & Barry Sandler (based on the novel *The Mirror Crack'd from Side to Side* by Agatha Christie), PH Christopher Challis, M John Cameron, ED Richard Marden, PD Michael Stringer.

LP Angela Lansbury (Miss Marple), Geraldine Chaplin (Ella Zielinsky), Tony Curtis (Marty N. Fenn), Edward Fox (Inspector Craddock), Rock Hudson (Jason Rudd), Kim Novak (Lola Brewster), Elizabeth Taylor (Marina Rudd), Anthony Steel (Sir Derek Ridgeley), Dinah Sheridan (Lady Amanda Ridgeley).

While filming *Mary, Queen of Scots* in the English countryside, a disagreeable American actress is murdered. Miss Marple, played effectively by Angela Lansbury, will identify the killer.

1886. *Mirrors* (1984, First American, 88m, c, aka *Marianne*). P John T. Parker & Stirling W. Smith, D Noel Black, W Sidney L. Stebel, PH Michael D. Murphy, M Stephen Lawrence, ED Robert Estrin, PD Ronald Weinberg.

LP Kitty Winn (Marianne), Peter Donat (Dr. Godard), William Swetland (Charbonnet), Mary-Robin Redd (Helene), William Burns (Gary), Lou Wagner (Chet), Don Keefer (Peter), Vanessa Hutchinson (Marie).

Kitty Winn's nightmares lead to horror and murder in New Orleans.

1887. *Mischief* (1985, 20th Century–Fox, 97m, c). P Sam Manners & Michael Nolin, D Mel Damski, W Noel Black, PH Donald E. Thorin & Jan De Bont, ED O. Nicholas Brown, PD Paul Peters.

LP Doug McKeon (Jonathan), Catherine Mary Stewart (Bunny), Kelly

Preston (Marilyn), Chris Nash (Gene), D.W. Brown (Kenny), Jami Gertz (Rosalie), Maggie Blye (Claire Miller), Graham P. Jarvis (Mr. Travis).

Nerd Doug McKeon gets help from town newcomer, cyclist Chris Nash, in winning the lovely Kelly Preston from rich kid D.W. Brown. It's a youth-oriented comedy of the 50s.

1888. *The Misfit Brigade* (1988, TransWorld, 101m, c). P Just Betzer & Benni Korzen, D Gordon Hessler, W Nelson Gidding (based on the novel *Wheels of Terror* by Sven Hassel), PH George Nikolic, M Ole Hoyer, ED Bob Gordon, PD Vladislav Lasic.

LP Bruce Davison (Porta), David Patrick Kelly (The Legionnaire), Don W. Moffett (Capt. von Barring), Jay O. Sanders (Tiny), Keith Szarabajka ("Old Man"), Oliver Reed (The General), David Carradine (Col. Von Weisshagen).

In this tongue-in-cheek knockoff of *The Dirty Dozen,* assorted criminals from a Nazi penal brigade are offered their freedom if they survive a dangerous mission.

1889. *Misplaced* (1989, Subway Films, 95m, c). P Lisa Zwerling, D Louis Yansen, W Yansen & Thomas DeWolfe, PH Igor Sunara, M Michael Urbaniak, ED Michael Berenbaum, PD Beth Kukn, COS Cocuzzo.

LP John Cameron Mitchell (Jacek Nowak), Viveca Lindfors (Zofia), Elzbieta Czyzewska (Halina Nowak), Drew Snyder (Bill), Deirdre O'Connell (Ella).

Writer-director Louis Yansen presents a largely autobiographical story of the trials of a Polish mother and her son as they seek to become assimilated into American culture.

1890. *Miss Firecracker* (1989, Corsair Pictures, 102m, c). P Fred Berner, D Thomas Schlamme, W Beth Henley (based on her play *The Miss Firecracker Contest*), PH Arthur Albert, M David Mansfield, ED Peter C. Frank, PD Kristi Zea.

LP Holly Hunter (Carnelle Scott), Mary Steenburgen (Elain Rutledge), Tim Robbins (Delmount Williams), Scott Glenn (Mac Sam), Veanne Cox (Tessy Mahoney), Ann Wedgeworth (Miss Blue), Trey Wilson (Benjamin Drapper), Amy Wright (Missy Mahoney).

Even talented and appealing Miss Holly Hunter, repeating her stage role, can't save this superficial tale of an easy lay in Yazoo City, Mississippi. To change her dubious image, she dyes her hair Raggedy Ann red and enters the annual Fourth of July Miss Firecracker Contest. Oddball characters abound in the film, but none force more than an occasional smile at their supposedly outlandish behavior.

1891. *Missing†* (1982, Universal, 122m, c). P Edward & Mildred Lewis, D Costa-Gavras, W Donald Stewart & Costa-Gavras* (based on *The Execution of Charles Horman* by Thomas Hauser), PH Ricardo Aronovich, M Vangelis, ED Francoise Bonnot, PD Peter Jamison, AD Augustin Ytuarte & Luceoro Isaac, SD Linda Spheeris.

LP Jack Lemmon† (Ed Horman), Sissy Spacek† (Beth Horman), Melanie Mayron (Terry Simon), John Shea (Charles Horman), Charles Cioffi (Capt. Ray Tower), David Clennon (Consul Phil Putnam), Richard Venture (U.S. Ambassador), Jerry Hardin (Col. Sean Patrick), Richard Bradford (Carter Babcock), Joe Regalbuto (Frank Teruggi).

American businesesman Jack Lemmon seeks his son who has disappeared in Chile. At first he believes his son, John Shea, and his leftist wife Sissy Spacek, have been putting their noses where they don't belong, but by the time he learns that his son is among the thousands who have been murdered by the Chilean government, with the tacit approval of the American government, he has become radicalized. It's chilling fiction based on fact.

1892. *Missing in Action* (1984, Cannon, 101m, c). P Menahem Golan & Yoram Globus, D Joseph Zito, W James Bruner (based on a story by John Crowther & Lance Hool, from characters created by Arthur Silver, Larry Levinson & Steve Bing), PH Joao Fernandes, M Jay Chattaway, ED Joel Goodman & Daniel Loewenthal.

LP Chuck Norris (Col. James Braddock), M. Emmet Walsh (Tuck), David Tress (Sen. Porter), Lenore Kasdorf

(Ann), James Hong (Gen. Tran), Ernie Ortega (Vinh), Pierrino Mascarino (Jacques), E. Erich Anderson (Masucci).

Former karate star Chuck Norris just barely escapes looking ridiculous in this Vietnam action thriller. He's a former POW who attempts to free MIAs still being held by the Viet Cong.

1893. *Missing in Action 2: The Beginning* (1985, Cannon, 96m, c). P Menahem Golan & Yoran Globus, D Lance Hool, W Arthur Silver, Larry Levinson & Steve Bing, PH Jorge Stahl, M Brian May, ED Mark Conte & Marcus Manton, PD Michael Baugh.

LP Chuck Norris (Col. James Braddock), Soon-Teck Oh (Col. Yin), Steven Williams (Nester), Bennett Ohta (Col. Ho), Cosie Costa (Mazilli), Joe Michael Terry (Opeika), John Wesley (Franklin), David Chung (Dou Chou).

Army Colonel Chuck Norris and his men are subjected to insidious torture by Soon-Teck Oh. The latter is a sadistic North Vietnamese colonel who captures them during a mid-air rescue operation. This film is a prequel to Norris's successful *Missing in Action*.

1894. *The Missing Link* (1989, Universal, 91m, c). P Dennis D. Kane, D,W&PH David & Carol Hughes, M Mike Trim & Sammy Hurden, ED David Dickie.

LP Peter Elliott (Ape-man), Michael Gambon (narrator).

In a film with no dialogue, Peter Elliott appears as the last apeman, doomed to extinction by the violent race of man.

1895. *The Mission*† (1986, Warner, GB, 125m, c). P Fernando Ghia & David Puttnam, D Roland Joffe†, W Robert Bolt, PH Chris Menges*, M Ennio Morricone†, ED Jim Clark†, PD Stuart Craig, AD Craig†, SD Jack Stephens†, COS Enrico Sabbatini†.

LP Robert De Niro (Mendoza), Jeremy Irons (Gabriel), Ray McAnally (Altamirano), Aidan Quinn (Felipe), Cherie Lunghi (Carlotta), Ronald Pickup (Hontar), Chuck Low (Cabeza), Liam Neeson (Fielding), Bercelio Moya (Indian Boy), Sigifredo Ismare (Witch Doctor), Asuncion Ontiveros (Indian Chief).

Spanish Jesuit Jeremy Irons has come to the South American wilderness to build a mission so he may convert the Indians to Christianity. Robert De Niro is a slave hunter who undergoes a personal redemption and joins forces with Irons. When the Spanish sell the colony to Portugal, the two are forced to defend what they have built from the Portuguese aggressors. Irons is excellent as a man of God, but De Niro is not credible as a born-again Christian.

1896. *Mission Kill* (1987, Goldfarb Dist., 97m, c). P&D David Winters, W Maria Dante, PH Tom De Nove, M Jesse Frederick & Jeff Koz, ED Ned Humphreys, SE Wayne Beauchamp.

LP Robert Ginty (J.F. Cooper), Cameron Mitchell (Harry), Merete Van Kamp (Sydney), Olivia D'Abo (Rebel Girl), Henry Darrow (Borghini), Sandy Baron (Bingo), Clement St. George (Kennedy), Eduardo Lopez Rojas (Ariban).

When demolition expert Robert Ginty's friend is brutally murdered delivering illegal arms to besieged Latin American freedom fighters, he vows revenge.

1897. *The Missionary* (1982, Columbia, GB, 90m, c). P Neville C. Thompson & Michael Palin, D Richard Loncraine, W Palin, PH Peter Hannan, M Mike Moran, ED Paul Green, AD Norman Garwood.

LP Michael Palin (Rev. Charles Fortesque), Maggie Smith (Lady Ames), Trevor Howard (Lord Ames), Denholm Elliott (The Bishop), Michael Hordern (Slatterthwaite), Graham Crowden (Rev. Fitzbanks), Phoebe Nicholls (Deborah), Tricia George (Ada), Valerie Whittington (Emmeline).

Former Monty Python comedian Michael Palin appears as a missionary given the assignment of saving fallen women in London. But he finds himself not only sharing his bed with his charges, but being pursued as well by Maggie Smith, a wealthy married aristocrat looking for a little romance in her life. And then of course there's Palin's childhood sweetheart who wishes to get married.

1898. *Mississippi Burning*† (1988, Orion, 125m, c). P Frederick Zollo & Robert F. Colesberry, D Alan Parker†,

W Chris Gerolmo, PH Peter Biziou*, M Trevor Jones, ED Gerry Hambling†, PD Philip Harrison & Geoffrey Kirkland, AD John Willett, SD Jim Erickson, SOUND Robert Litt, Elliot Tyson, Richard C. Kline & Danny Michael†.

LP Gene Hackman† (Anderson), Willem Dafoe (Ward), Frances McDormand† (Mrs. Pell), Brad Dourif (Deputy Pell), R. Lee Ermey (Mayor Tillman), Gailard Sartain (Sheriff Stuckey), Stephen Tobolowsky (Townley), Michael Rooker (Frank Bailey), Pruitt Taylor Vince (Lester Cowens), Badja Djola (Agent Monk), Kevin Dunn (Agent Bird).

Although a fictional story, the plot truthfully follows the FBI probe into the 1964 murders of three civil rights workers in Mississippi. The investigation is handled by humorless Harvard graduate Willem Dafoe and ex-Southern sheriff Gene Hackman, who is able to joke his way into the confidence of people. The two run into resistance from both the guilty whites and the terrified blacks. Hackman and Dafoe are each in their own way superbly right for their characters. Frances McDormand as a deputy's wife gives a riveting performance as a decent woman married to an insensitive brute. The pace is almost frantic. The chases, violence, lynchings and burnings should generate moral indignation in most sensitive people.

Mr. Christmas Dinner see Lucky Stiff

1899. Mr. Love (1986, Warner, GB, 92m, c). P Susan Richards & Robert Douet, D Roy Battersby, W Kenneth Eastaugh, PH Clive Tickner, M Willy Russell, ED Alan J. Cumner-Price, PD Adrienne Atkinson.

LP Barry Jackson (Donald Lovelace), Maurice Denham (Theo), Margaret Tyzack (Pink Lady), Linda Marlowe (Barbara), Christina Collier (Ester), Helen Cotterill (Lucy Nuttall), Julia Deakin (Melanie), Donal McCann (Leo), Marcia Warren (Doris Lovelace).

Barry Jackson stars in this sly, racy British comedy. He's a man stuck for thirty years in a loveless marriage, but who discovers the extraordinary power of love. Despite the fact that everyone considers him a joke, when he dies all sorts of grieving women show up for his funeral.

1900. Mr. Mom (1983, 20th Century-Fox, 91m, c). P Lynn Loring & Lauren Shuler, D Stan Dragoti, W John Hughes, PH Victor J. Kemper, M Lee Holdridge, ED Patrick Kennedy, PD Alfred Sweeney.

LP Michael Keaton (Jack), Teri Garr (Caroline), Frederick Koehler (Alex), Taliesin Jaffe (Kenny), Courtney & Brittany White (Megan), Martin Mull (Ron), Ann Jillian (Joan), Jeffrey Tambor (Jinx), Christopher Lloyd (Larry), Tom Leopold (Stan).

Michael Keaton is appealing as an automobile engineer who loses his job. He stays home to take care of the house and three kids while his wife Teri Garr becomes the breadwinner. She works for an ad agency run by lecherous Martin Mull. Although most of the bits in the film are predictable, Keaton makes them fun.

1901. Mr. North (1988, Samuel Goldwyn, 92m, c). P Steven Haft & Skip Steloff, D Danny Huston, W Janet Roach, John Huston & James Costigan (based on the novel *Theophilus North* by Thornton Wilder), PH Robin Vidgeon, M David McHugh, ED Roberto Silvi, PD Eugene Lee.

LP Anthony Edwards (Theophilus North), Robert Mitchum (James McHenry Bosworth), Lauren Bacall (Mrs. Amelia Cranston), Harry Dean Stanton (Henry Simmons), Anjelica Huston (Persis Bosworth-Tennyson), Mary Stuart Masterson (Elspeth Skeel), Virginia Madsen (Sally Boffin), Tammy Grimes (Sarah Baily-Lewis), David Warner (Dr. Angus McPherson).

An impressive cast and production crew come together on this last film involving John Huston. He co-scripted the piece and acted as executive producer. Still the Thornton Wilder fable suffers from an uneven production in Danny Huston's first directorial assignment. Anthony Edwards portrays an "electrical" young charmer who makes a major impact on Newport society during the 20s.

1902. Mr. Patman (1980, Film Consortium, Canada, 105m, c). P Bill Marshall & Alexander MacDonald, D John Guillermin, W Thomas Hedley, PH John Coquillon, M Paul Hoffert, ED Max Benedict & Vince Hatherly, PD Trevor Williams.

LP James Coburn (Mr. Patman), Kate Nelligan (Peabody), Fionnula Flanagan (Abadaba), Les Carlson (Abernathy), Candy Kane (Mrs. Beckman), Michael Kirby (Dr. Turley), Alan McRae (Dr. Bloom), Jan Rubes (Vrakatas).

Charming and caring orderly James Coburn is slowly revealed to be as wacko as the patients he tends in the psychiatric ward of a Canadian hospital.

1903. *Mr. Wrong* (1985, Preston Laing, New Zealand, 88m, c, aka *Dark of Night*). P Robin Laing & Gaylene Preston, D Preston, W Preston, Geoff Murphy & Graeme Tetley (based on the story by Elizabeth Jane Howard), PH Thom Burstyn, M Jonathan Crayford, ED Simon Reece.

LP Heather Bolton (Meg), David Letch (Mr. Wrong), Margaret Umbers (Samantha), Suzanne Lee (Val), Gary Stalker (Bruce), Danny Mulheron (Wayne), Perry Piercy (Mary Carmichael), Philip Gordon (Clive).

Heather Bolton buys a used Jaguar to be her symbol of independence but instead she discovers it is haunted. The ghost of Perry Piercy, killed by an unknown hitchhiker, is looking for his murderer.

1904. *Mrs. Soffel* (1984, MGM/United Artists, 110m, c). P Edgar J. Scherick, Scott Rudin & David A. Nicksay, D Gillian Armstrong, W Ron Nyswaner, PH Russell Boyd, M Mark Isham, ED Nicholas Beauman, PD Luciana Arrighi.

LP Diane Keaton (Kate Soffel), Mel Gibson (Ed Biddle), Matthew Modine (Jack Biddle), Edward Herrmann (Peter Soffel), Trini Alvarado (Irene Soffel), Jennie Dundas (Margaret Soffel), Danny Corkill (Eddie Soffel), Harley Cross (Clarence Soffel), Terry O'Quinn (Buck McGovern).

The film is based on the true story of a warden's wife, Diane Keaton, who helped two brothers, Mel Gibson and Matthew Modine, escape from a Pittsburgh prison in 1901. Keaton is completely taken in by Gibson's charm and apparent sincerity when he claims he wishes he had a chance to live his life differently. The two men are killed in a shoot-out, but Keaton survives a suicide attempt.

1905. *Misunderstood* (1984, MGM/United Artists, 91m, c). P Tarak Ben Ammar, D Jerry Schatzberg, W Barra Grant (based on the novel by Florence Montgomery and the screenplay for *Incompreso* by Leo Benvenuti & Piero De Bernardi), M Luci Drudi Demby & Guiseppe Mangione, PH Pasqualino DeSantis, M Michael Hoppe, ED Marc Laub, PD Joel Schiller.

LP Gene Hackman (Ned), Henry Thomas (Andrew), Rip Torn (Will), Huckleberry Fox (Miles), Maureen Kerwin (Kate), Susan Anspach (Lilly), June Brown (Mrs. Paley), Helen Ryan (Lucy), Nadim Sawalha (Ahmed).

Only after their mother, Susan Anspach, dies of a mysterious malady, does the relationship between two brothers, Henry Thomas and Huckleberry Fox, and their father, Gene Hackman, become close.

1906. *Mixed Blood* (1984, Sara-Cinevista, 98m, c). P Antoine Gannage & Steven Fierberg, D Paul Morrissey, W Morrissey & Alan Browne, PH Stefan Zapasnik, M Andy "Sugarcoated" Hernandez, ED Scott Vickrey, AD Stephen McCabe.

LP Marilia Pera (Rita La Punta), Richard Ulacia (Thiago), Linda Kerridge (Carol), Geraldine Smith (Toni), Angel David (Juan the Bullet), Ulrich Berr (The German), Marcelino Rivera (Hector).

Renowned underground film director Paul Morrissey presents an acclaimed comedy drama detailing a drug war between the New York City gang run by Marilia Pera and her rival Angel David.

1907. *Mob Story* (1989, O'Meara Production, Canada, 103m, c). P Anthony Kramreither, D Jancarlo Markliw & Gabriel Markliw, W J. & G. Markliw & David Flaherty, PH Gilles Corbeil, ED Michael Todd.

LP John Vernon (Luce), Kate Vernon (Mindy), Al Waxman (Sam), Margot Kidder (Dolores), Diana Barrington (Maria), Robert Morelli (Gianni), Angelo Pedari (Tom), Brian Paul (Heinrich), Eric Zivot (Lance).

Mafia boss John Vernon flies to freezing Winnipeg to track down his ex-lover and his long-lost son. His second in command Al Waxman sees this as an opportunity to rub out the boss and move into the number one position. The film often becomes slapstick. The script is poorly written and very few people will ever see the film in theaters.

1908. *Mob War* (1989, Cinema Sciences/Shapiro Glickenhaus, 96m, c). P J. Christian Ingvordsen, Steven Kaman & John Weiner, D Ingvordsen, W Ingvordsen & Weiner, PH & ED Kamen, PD Chris Johnson.

LP Johnny Stumper (Todd Barrett), David Henry Keller (John Falcone), Jake La Motta (Don Ricci), Sven Nuvo (Martin Spustein), John Rano (Hectort), Oliver Daniels (Juan), Adrianna Maxwell (Whitney Barrett).

Public relations expert Johnny Stumper finds himself becoming married to the mob when he takes on a Mafia client.

1909. *Modern Girls* (1986, Atlantic, 82m, c). P Gary Goetzman, D Jerry Kramer, W Laurie Craig, PH Karen Grossman, M Jay Levy & Ed Arkin, ED Mitchell Sinoway, PD Laurence Bennett.

LP Daphne Zuniga (Margo), Virginia Madsen (Kelly), Cynthia Gibb (Cece), Clayton Rohner (Clifford/Bruno X), Chris Nash (Ray), Steve Shellen (Brad), Rick Overton (Marsalis), Quin Kessler (Retro Vamp), Pamela Springsteen (Tanya).

Daphne Zuniga, Virginia Madsen and Cynthia Gibb spend a night in L.A. rock clubs. It's for younger audiences who may appreciate the music.

1910. *Modern Problems* (1981, 20th Century–Fox, 91m, c). P Alan Greisman & Michael Shamberg, D Ken Shapiro, W Shapiro, Tom Sherohman & Arthur Sellers, PH Edmond Koons, M Dominic Frontiere, ED Michael Jablow, PD Jack Senter.

LP Chevy Chase (Max), Patti D'Arbanville (Darcy), Mary Kay Place (Lorraine), Nell Carter (Dorita), Brian Doyle-Murray (Brian), Mitch Kreindel (Barry), Dabney Coleman (Mark), Sandy Helberg (Pete).

After being exposed to nuclear waste, overworked air traffic controller Chevy Chase develops telekinetic powers. He uses them to get back at his professional and romantic rivals.

1911. *Modern Romance* (1981, Columbia, 93m, c). P Andrew Scheinman & Martin Shafer, D Albert Brooks, W Brooks & Monica Johnson, PH Eric Saarinen, M Lance Rubin, ED David Finfer, PD Edward Richardson.

LP Albert Brooks (Robert Cole), Kathryn Harrold (Mary Harvard), Tyann Means (Waitress), Bruno Kirby (Jay), Jane Hallaren (Ellen), Karen Chandler (Neighbor), Dennis Kort (Health Food Salesman), Thelma Leeds (Mother).

Albert Brooks is extremely funny as a neurotic film editor who continuously breaks up with his girlfriend Kathryn Harrold and then tries to win her back.

1912. *The Moderns* (1988, Alive Film, 128m, c). P Carolyn Pfeiffer & David Blocker, D Alan Rudolph, W Rudolph & Jon Bradshaw, PH Toyomichi Kurita, M Mark Isham, ED Debra T. Smith & Scott Brock, PD Steven Legler.

LP Keith Carradine (Nick Hart), Linda Fiorentino (Rachel Stone), John Lone (Bertram Stone), Wallace Shawn (Oiseau), Genevieve Bujold (Libby Valentin), Geraldine Chaplin (Nathalie de Ville), Kevin J. O'Connor (Hemingway), Elsa Raven (Gertrude Stein), Ali Giron (Alice B. Toklas).

This interesting but flawed film examines the lives of a group of Bohemians in Paris during the 20s. Geraldine Chaplin hires art forger Keith Carradine to copy three works owned by her soon-to-be ex-husband. Carradine seems miscast, but John Lone is very good as a U.S. condom manufacturing baron. So also is Linda Fiorentino, as his wife and one time lover of Carradine's.

1913. *Mommie Dearest* (1981, Paramount, 129m, c). P Frank Yablans, D Frank Perry, W Yablans, Perry, Tracy Hotchner & Robert Getchell (based on the book by Christina Crawford), PH Paul Lohmann, M Henry Mancini, ED Peter E. Berger, PD Bill Malley.

LP Faye Dunaway (Joan Crawford), Diana Scarwid (Christina Crawford as an adult), Steve Forrest (Greg Savitt), Howard da Silva (Louis B. Mayer), Mara Hobel (Christina as a child), Rutanya Alda (Carol Ann), Harry Goz (Al Steele), Michael Edwards (Ted Gelber), Jocelyn Brando (Barbara Bennett).

This hatchet job on the life and career of movie actress Joan Crawford, based on the "tell-all" story by her adopted daughter Christina, didn't do Joan's reputation much good. But this is nothing compared to the harm the work has done to Faye Dunaway's fading career. Although Dunaway in some exaggerated way looks like Crawford in the film, she demonstrates that she's nowhere near the actress the long time star was.

1914. *Mona Lisa* (1986, Island Pictures, GB, 104m, c). P Stephen Woolley & Patrick Cassavetti, D Neil Jordan, W Jordan & David Leland, PH Roger Pratt, M Michael Kamen, ED Lesley Walker, PD Jamie Leonard.

LP Bob Hoskins† (George), Cathy Tyson (Simone), Michael Caine (Mortwell), Clarke Peters (Anderson), Kate Hardie (Cathy), Robbie Coltrane (Thomas), Zoe Nathenson (Jeannie), Sammi Davis (May), Rod Bedall (Terry), Joe Brown (Dudley), Pauline Melville (Dawn), David Halliwell (Devlin).

Bob Hoskins is a wonder as a small-time British hood given the assignment of driver-bodyguard high-priced black callgirl Cathie Tyson. Their appreciation for each other grows as they find themselves caught in a web of intrigue, while journeying through London's dark, sleazy underworld.

1915. *The Money Pit* (1986, Universal, 91m, c). P Frank Marshall, Kathleen Kennedy & Art Levinson, D Richard Benjamin, W David Giler, PH Gordon Willis, M Michel Colombier, ED Jacqueline Cambas, PD Patrizia Von Brandenstein.

LP Tom Hanks (Walter Fielding), Shelley Long (Anna Crowley), Alexander Godunov (Max Beissart), Maureen Stapleton (Estelle), Joe Mantegna (Art Shirk), Philip Bosco (Curly), Josh Mostel (Jack Schnittman), Yakov Smirnoff (Shatov), Carmine Caridi (Brad Shirk).

It's sort of a cross between *Mr. Blandings Builds His Dream House* and a visit from the Three Stooges. Live-in lovers Tom Hanks and Shelley Long buy a stately looking house, only to find that everything possible is wrong with it. Somehow it should have been funnier.

1916. *Mongrel* (1982, Rondo-Sutherland & Jenkins, 91m, c). D&W Robert A. Burns, PH Richard Kooris, M Ed Guinn.

LP Terry Evans (Jerry), Aldo Ray, Catherine Molloy, Mitch Pileggi, J.M. Ingraffia.

Terry Evans is plagued by nightmares that may or may not be real. At any rate he becomes a canine-like creature that rips out the throats of anyone it can get near to.

1917. *Monkey Grip* (1983, Pavilion-Cinecom-Mainline, Australia, 102m, c). P Patricia Lovell, D Ken Cameron, W Cameron & Helen Garner (based on the novel by Garner), PH David Gribble, M Bruce Smeaton & Stephen McIntyre, ED David Huggett, PD Clark Munro.

LP Noni Hazelhurst (Nora), Colin Friels (Javo), Alice Garner (Gracie), Harold Hopkins (Willie), Candy Raymond (Lillian), Michael Caton (Clive), Tim Burns (Martin), Christina Amphlett (Angela).

Single mother Noni Hazelhurst becomes involved with disagreeable drug addict Colin Friels.

Monkey Shines: An Experiment in Fear see Ella

1918. *Monsignor* (1982, 20th Century-Fox, 122m, c). P Frank Yablans & David Niven, Jr., D Frank Perry, W Abraham Polonsky & Wendell Mayes (based on the novel by Jack Alain Leger), PH Billy Williams, M John Williams, ED Peter E. Berger, PD John De Cuir.

LP Christopher Reeve (Flaherty), Genevieve Bujold (Clara), Fernando Rey (Santoni), Jason Miller (Appolini), Joe Cortese (Varese), Adolfo Celi (Vinci), Leonardo Cimino (Pope), Tomas Milian (Francisco), Robert J. Prosky (Bishop Walkman), Joe Pantoliano (Musso).

Watching this movie, one must question Christopher Reeve's calling to the priesthood. As a World War II chaplain, he mans a machine gun. While in Rome he seduces a young nun, Genevieve Bujold. According to the script this supervenal, capeless cleric helps the Vatican get back on its feet after the war through his clever dealings with the Mafia. Sounds interesting, but it isn't.

Monster see Humanoids from the Deep

1919. *The Monster Club* (1981, ITC, GB, 97m, c). P Milton Subotsky, D Roy Ward Baker, W Edward & Valerie Abraham (based on the novel by Ronald Chetwynd-Hayes), ED Peter Tanner.

LP Vincent Price (Erasmus), John Carradine (Ronald Chetwynd-Hayes), Roger Sloman (Club Secretary), Fran Fullenwider (Buxom Beauty), Anthony Steel (Lintom Busotsky), Suzanna Willis (The Stripper).

Vampire Vincent Price brings horror story writer John Carradine to a Transylvanian disco where the entertainment includes The Pretty Things and The Viewers.

1920. *Monster in the Closet* (1987, Troma, 87m, c). P David Levy & Peter L. Bergquist, D&W Bob Dahlin (based on a story by Dahlin & Bergquist), PH Ronald W. McLeish, M Barrie Guard, ED Raja Gosnell & Stephanie Palewski, PD Lynda Cohen.

LP Donald Grant (Richard Clark), Denise DuBarry (Diane Bennett), Henry Gibson (Dr. Pennyworth), Howard Duff (Father Finnegan), Donald Moffat (Gen. Turnbull), Claude Akins (Sheriff Ketchum), Paul Walker (The Professor), John Carradine (Old Joe), Paul Dooley (Roy Crane), Stella Stevens (Margo Crane), Jesse White (Ben Bernstein), Kevin Peter Hall (The Monster).

The producers of *Toxic Avenger* made this spoof of 50s creature features in the tradition of *Creep Show.* The title character, played by Kevin Peter Hall, is a better than the average man-in-a-latex-suit.

1921. *Monster Island* (1981, Fort Films-Almena, US/Spain, 100m, c, aka *Mystery on Monster Island*). P&D Juan Piquer Simon, W Jorge Grau, Piquer Simon & R. Gantman (based on the story by Jules Verne), PH Andres Beranguer, M Alfonso Agullo, AD Gumer Andres, SE Emilio Ruiz.

LP Terence Stamp (Taskinar), Peter Cushing (Kolderup), Gerard Tichy (Capt. Turkott), Paul Naschy (Flynt), Ian Serra (Jeff Morgan), David Hutton (Mr. Arttelet), Gasphar Ipua (Carefinatu), Blanca Estrada (Dominique).

Boaters are shipwrecked on an island ruled by Terence Stamp and inhabited by prehistoric monsters — among other things.

1922. *The Monster Squad* (1987, Tri-Star, 82m, c). P Jonathan A. Zimbert & Neil A. Machlis, D Fred Dekker, W Shane Black & Dekker, PH Bradford May, M Bruce Broughton, ED James Mitchell, PD Albert Brenner.

LP Andre Gower (Sean), Robby Kiger (Patrick), Stephen Macht (Del, Sean's Father), Duncan Regehr (Count Dracula), Tom Noonan (Frankenstein), Brent Chalem (Horace), Ryan Lambert (Rudy), Ashley Bank (Phoebe).

In the tradition of *Ghostbusters,* if you're plagued by monsters just dial 1-800-MONSTER and a monster squad will be right out to deal with your problem.

1923. *A Month in the Country* (1988, Orion Classic, GB, 96m, c). P Kenith Trodd, D Pat O'Connor, W Simon Gray (based on the novel by J.L. Carr), PH Ken Macmillan, M Howard Blake, ED John Victor Smith, PD Leo Austin.

LP Colin Firth (Birkin), Kenneth Branagh (Moon), Miranda Richardson (Mrs. Keach), Patrick Malahide (Reverend Keach), Tony Haygarth (Douthwaite), Jim Carter (Ellerbeck), Richard Vernon (Colonel Hebron).

Shell shocked World War I veteran Colin Firth arrives at a small Yorkshire village where he is to uncover a medieval painting on a wall of a church. It's a slow moving but lovely and rewarding drama.

1924. *Monty Python's the Meaning of Life* (1983, Universal, GB, 107m, c). P John Goldstone, D Terry Jones, W Graham Chapman, John Cleese, Terry Gilliam, Eric Idle, Jones & Michael Palin, PH Peter Hannan, M Idle & John du Prez, ED Julian Doyle, PD Harry Lange.

LP Graham Chapman, John Cleese, Terry Gilliam, Eric Idle, Terry Jones, Michael Palin, Carol Cleveland, Judy Loe, Simon Jones, Andrew MacLachlan.

In a wildly uneven film, the Monty Python crew probe religion, birth control, food, the military, education, sex, life and death.

1925. *Moon in Scorpio* (1987, Trans-World, 90m, c). P Alan Amiel, D Gary

Graver, W Robert S. Aiken, PH Graver, M Robert O. Ragland, ED Omer Tal.

LP Britt Ekland (Linda), John Phillip Law (Allen), William Smith (Burt), Lewis Van Bergen (Mark), April Wayne (Isabel), Robert Quarry (Dr. Khokda), Jillian Kesner (Claire), Bruno Marcotulli (The Driver).

When three Vietnam vets and their girlfriends go on a sailing trip, the flashbacks of the war experienced by one of the ex-soldiers turns the trip to one of horror.

1926. *Moon Over Parador* (1988, Universal, 105m, c). P Paul Mazursky, Pato Guzman & Geoffrey Taylor, D Mazursky, W Leon Capetanos & Mazursky (based on a story by Charles G. Booth), PH Donald McAlpine, M Maurice Jarre, ED Stuart Pappe, PD Guzman.

LP Richard Dreyfuss (Jack Noah), Raul Julia (Roberto Strausmann), Sonia Braga (Madonna), Jonathan Winters (Ralph), Fernando Rey (Alejandro), Sammy Davis, Jr. (Himself), Michael Greene (Clint), Polly Holliday (Midge), Milton Goncalves (Carlo), Charo (Madame Loop), Marianne Sagebrecht (Magda), Richard Russell Ramos (Dieter Lopez).

The 1939 film, *The Magnificent Fraud,* in which French actor Akim Tamiroff is forced to impersonate an assassinated South American dictator, is the inspiration for this film. American actor Richard Dreyfuss, making a movie in the fictional South American country Parador, is recruited by Raul Julia, the head of the secret police, to portray the country's dictator, when the latter dies of a heart attack. It takes a fake assassination before Dreyfuss finally can get away about a year later.

1927. *Moon Over the Alley* (1980, British Film Institute, GB, 107m, c). D Joseph Despins, W William Dumaresq, PH Peter Hannan, M Galt MacDermot, ED Despins.

LP Doris Fishwick, Peter Farrell, Erna May, John Gay, Sean Caffrey, Sharon Forester, Patrick Murray, Lesley Roach, Basil Clarke.

This amateur film takes a look at the hippie residents of London's Portobello Road.

1928. *Moonlighting* (1982, Universal, GB, 97m, c). P Mark Shivas & Jerzy Skolimowski, D Skolimowski, W Skolimowski, Boleslaw Sulik, Barrie Vince & Danuta Witold Stok, PH Tony Pierce-Roberts, M Stanley Myers & Hans Zimmer, ED Vince, PD Tony Woollard.

LP Jeremy Irons (Nowak), Eugene Lipinski (Banaszak), Jiri Stanislav (Wolski), Eugeniusz Hackiewicz (Kudaj), Dorothy Zienciowska (Lot Airline Girl), Edward Arthur (Immigration Officer), Denis Holmes (Neighbor), Renu Setna (Junk Shop Owner).

Four Polish workers travel to London to renovate a London mansion. Only their boss, Jeremy Irons, speaks English. When martial law is declared in Poland and Solidarity is outlawed, Irons decides not to tell his comrades what's happening on the home front.

1929. *Moonstruck*† (1987, MGM/United Artists, 102m, c). P Patrick Palmer & Norman Jewison, D Norman Jewison†, W John Patrick Shanley*, PH David Watkin, M Dick Hyman, ED Lou Lombardo, PD Philip Rosenberg.

LP Cher* (Loretta Castorini), Nicolas Cage (Ronny Cammareri), Vincent Gardenia† (Cosmo Castorini), Olympia Dukakis* (Rose Castorini), Danny Aiello (Johnny Cammareri), Julie Bovasso (Rita Cappomaggi), John Mahoney (Perry), Louis Guss (Raymond Cappomaggi), Feodor Chaliapin, Jr. (Loretta's Grandfather), Anita Gillette (Mona), Nada Despotovitch (Chrissy).

The "feel-good" movie of the year, *Moonstruck* is the story of young widow Cher. The night before he travels to Italy to be with his ailing old mother Cher accepts a proposal of marriage from Danny Aiello, a good but not very exciting man. He requests that she invite his alienated brother Nicolas Cage to their wedding. When Cher and Cage meet, sparks fly and before you can say "big pasta pie" they are in bed making passionate love. Apparently a particularly large moon which years earlier had a similar romantic effect on Cher's father Vincent Gardenia, caused their love at first sight. Despite ambivalent feelings, Cher wishes to put the episode with Cage behind her, but agrees to meet him one last time at the opera. She goes to a beauty parlor for a complete makeover and buys all new clothes for the occasion. At the opera, she runs across her pop who is escorting his little tootsie Anita Gillette. Mother Olympia Dukakis knows her husband is having an affair; she just doesn't understand why. A Lothario professor, John Mahoney, whom Dukakis meets at a restaurant, helps her find an answer. By the next morning Aiello is back from Italy, and is told that Cher is marrying his brother instead of him. He's not too broken up, because his mother who has recovered, doesn't want him to marry. Dukakis tells Gardenia she wants his affair with Gillette to end and he accedes in a way to make one believe he really will end it. The performances are marvelous, with only Cage's sounding a sour note. He seems too hammy in comparison with the others and also much too young and ordinary to generate so much passion in a woman like Cher.

1930. *Moontrap* (1989, Shapiro Glickenhaus Ent., 90m, c). P&D Robert Dyke, W Tex Ragsdale, PH Peter Klein, M Joseph LoDuca, ED Steven C. Craig & Kevin Trent, PD B.K. Taylor.

LP Walter Koenig (Col. Jason Grant), Bruce Campbell (Ray Tanner), Leigh Lombardi (Mera), Robert Kurcz (Koreman), John J. Saunders (Barnes), Reavis Graham (Haskell).

Star Trek's Walter Koenig is promoted to a William Shatner–like role. He's an astronaut who jumps at the opportunity to head up the first manned U.S. moon mission in decades. He and his followers run into mechanical monsters.

1931. *Moonwalker* (1989, Warner, 93m, c). P Dennis Jones & Jerry Kramer, D Colin Chivers & Kramer, W David Newman (based on a story by Michael Jackson), PH John Hora, M Bruce Broughton, ED David E. Blewitt, PD Michael Ploog, Bryan Jones & John Walker.

LP Michael Jackson (Michael), Sean Lennon (Sean), Kellie Parker (Katie), Brandon Ames (Zeke [Baby Bad] Michael), Joe Pesci (Mr. Big).

This straight to video piece is a hodgepodge of Michael Jackson's music video and his musings on various subjects. It will be precious to Jackson fans; but others will walk away from it, scratching their heads, wondering what's it all supposed to mean.

1932. *Morgan Stewart's Coming Home* (1987, New Century/Vista, 96m, c). P Stephen Friedman, D Alan Smithee [Terry Winsor & Paul Aaron], W Ken Hixon & David Titcher, PH Richard Brooks, M Peter Bernstein, ED Bob Letterman, PD Charles Bennett.

LP Jon Cryer (Morgan Stewart), Lynn Redgrave (Nancy Stewart), Nicholas Pryor (Senator Tom Stewart), Viveka Davis (Emily), Paul Gleason (Jay Springsteen), Andrew Duncan (Gen. Fenton), Savely Kramarov (Ivan).

After being kept in prep schools for seven years, Jon Cryer suddenly finds his parents want him home—to serve their own political ambitions. Cryer is determined to turn his father and mother into the caring parents he always hoped to have.

1933. *Morgan's Cake* (1988, L.L. Production, 83m, b&w/c). P,D,W&ED Rick Schmidt, PH Kathleen Beeler, M Gary Thorp.

LP Morgan Schmidt-Feng (Morgan), Willie Boy Walker (Morgan's Dad), M. Louise Stanley (Morgan's Mother), Rachel Pond (Rachel), Aaron Leon Kenin (Leon), Eliot Kenin (Leon's Dad), John Claudio (John).

The total cost of this film is reportedly $15,000. The 19-year-old title character was named for the David Warner character in the wild 1966 British comedy, directed by Karel Reisz. Morgan Schmidt-Feng lives in a cramped San Francisco apartment with his impoverished, divorced father. He remains cheerful, despite his impending draft registration, his being fired from a job as a delivery boy, and the pregnancy of his girlfriend.

1934. *The Morning After* (1986, 20th Century–Fox, 103m, c). P Bruce Gilbert, D Sidney Lumet, W James Hicks, PH Andrzej Bartkowiak, M Paul Chihara, ED Joel Goodman, PD Albert Brenner.

LP Jane Fonda† (Alex Sternbergen), Jeff Bridges (Turner Kendall), Raul Julia (Joaquin Manero), Diane Salinger (Isabel Harding), Richard Foronjy (Sgt. Greenbaum), Geoffrey Scott (Bobby Kor-shack), James "Gypsy" Haake (Frankie), Kathleen Wilhoite (Red).

It's a fair bet that this is among Jane Fonda's worst pictures (what does the Oscar nominating committee know?). She wakes up in a strange bed next to a murdered man. She flees in panic that eventually turns to terror. Jeff Bridges portrays a redneck ex-cop who tries to help her.

1935. *Morons from Outer Space* (1985, EMI/Universal, GB, 87m, c). P Barry Hanson, D Mike Hodges, W Griff Rhys Jones, Mel Smith & Bob Mercer, PH Phil Meheux, M Peter Brewis, ED Peter Boyle, PD Brian Eatwell.

LP Mel Smith (Bernard), Griff Rhys Jones (Graham Sweetley), James B. Sikking (Col. Laribee), Dinsdale Landen (Comdr. Matteson), Jimmy Nail (Desmond), Joanne Pearce (Sandra), Paul Brown (Julian).

Usually explorers from other planets are depicted as aliens with superior intellects who have something to teach the inhabitants of earth. This movie looks at the other side of the coin. This time the space visitors are moronic. It doesn't take long before the novelty wears off and the film runs out of yuks.

1936. *Mortal Passions* (1989, Gibraltar, 98m, c). P Gwen Field, D Andrew Lane, W Alan Moskowitz, PH Christian Sebaldt, M Parmer Fuller, ED Kimberly Ray, AD Tucker Johnston.

LP Zach Galligan (Todd), Michael Bowen (Berke), Krista Errickson (Emily), Sheila Kelly (Adele), David Warner (Dr. Powers), Luca Bercovici (Darcy), Cassandra Gava (Cinda).

In a better than average independent production, lovely Krista Errickson is turned on to sex and murder.

1937. *Mortuary* (1983, Film Ventures, 91m, c). P Howard Avedis & Marlene Schmidt, D Avedis, W Avedis & Schmidt, PH Gary Graver, M John Cacavas, ED Stanford C. Allen.

LP Mary McDonough (Christie Parsons), David Wallace (Greg Stevens), Lynda Day George (Eve Parsons), Christopher George (Dr. Hank Andrews), Bill Paxton (Paul Andrews).

Mary McDonough has been having horrible nightmares ever since her father drowned in the family swimming pool. Her nightmares begin coming startlingly close to reality.

1938. *Mortuary Academy* (1988, Taurus Ent., 85m, c). P Dennis Winfrey & Chip Miller, D Michael Schroeder, W William Kelman, PH Roy H. Wagner, M David Spear, ED Ellen Keneshea, PD Jon Rothschild.

LP Paul Bartel (Dr. Paul Truscott), Mary Woronov (Mary Purcell), Perry Lang (Sam Grimm), Tracey Walter (Dickson), Christopher Atkins (Max Grimm), Lynn Danielson (Valerie), Stoney Jackson (James Dandridge).

Aspects of failed black humor, horror spoof, a juvenile story and uninspired acting make this a film to miss.

1939. *Moscow on the Hudson* (1984, Columbia, 115m, c). P&D Paul Mazursky, W Mazursky & Leon Capetanos, PH Don McAlpine, M David McHugh, ED Richard Halsey, PD Pato Guzman.

LP Robin Williams (Vladimir Ivanoff), Maria Conchita Alonso (Lucia Lombardo), Cleavant Derricks (Lionel Witherspoon), Alejandro Rey (Orlando Ramirez), Savely Kramarov (Boris), Elya Baskin (Anatoly), Oleg Rudnik (Yury).

While on tour in the United States with a Russian circus, saxophonist Robin Williams defects in New York City's Bloomingdale's department store. Audiences are treated to a new look at America as Williams happily adjusts to his new home.

1940. *The Mosquito Coast* (1986, Warner, 117m, c). P Jerome Hellman, D Peter Weir, W Paul Schrader (based on the novel by Paul Theroux), PH John Seale, M Maurice Jarre, ED Thom Noble, PD John Stoddart.

LP Harrison Ford (Allie Fox), Helen Mirren (Mother), River Phoenix (Charlie), Jadrien Steele (Jerry), Hilary Gordon (April), Rebecca Gordon (Clover), Martha Plimpton (Emily Spellgood), Andre Gregory (Rev. Spellgood), Melanie Boland (Mrs. Spellgood), Conrad Roberts (Mr. Haddy).

Brilliant inventor Harrison Ford, fed up with what he considers the rape of America, takes his wife and four children to the untamed wilderness of the Mosquito Coast. He hopes to build his Paradise on earth. His wife Helen Mirren is initially in awe of her husband's zeal, but this gives way to the recognition that he's mad.

The Most Dangerous Woman Alive see Lethal Woman

Motel see Pink Motel

1941. *Motel Hell* (1980, United Artists, 106m, c). P Steven-Charles Jaffe & Robert Jaffe, D Kevin Connor, W Jaffe & Jaffe, PH Thomas Del Ruth, M Lance Rubin, ED Bernard Gribble, SE Adams R. Calvert.

LP Rory Calhoun (Vincent Smith), Paul Linke (Bruce Smith), Nancy Parsons (Ida Smith), Nina Axelrod (Terry), Wolfman Jack (Rev. Billy), Elaine Joyce (Edith Olsen), Dick Curtis (Guy Robaire), Monique St. Pierre (Debbie).

Is the tantalizing flavor of Farmer Rory Calhoun's popular smoked meats, which he serves at his mysterious motel, related to the disappearance of passers-by?

Motel Vacancy see Talking Walls

1942. *Mother Lode* (1982, Agamemnon, 101m, c, aka *Search for the Mother Lode; The Last Great Treasure*). P Fraser Clarke Heston, D Charlton Heston & Joe Canutt, W Fraser Clarke Heston, PH Richard Leiterman, M Ken Wannberg, ED Eric Boyd-Perkins, PD Douglas Higgins.

LP Charlton Heston (Silas McGee/Ian McGee), Nick Mancuso (Jean Dupre), Kim Basinger (Andrea Spalding), John Marley (Elijah), Dale Wilson (Gerard Elliot), Ricky Zantolas (George Patterson), Marie George (Elijah's Wife).

After the disastrous *The Mountain Men* (See below), Charlton Heston, by agreeing to team with his son in making this mediocre adventure film, shows that he is more a father caring for a talentless son than a judge of film stories. Heston plays twin Scottish brothers who run a gold mine in British Columbia. At least the scenery is worth looking at.

1943. *Mother's Day* (1980, United Film Distribution, 98m, c). P Michael Kravitz & Charles Kaufman, D Kaufman, W Kaufman & Warren D. Leight,

PH Joe Mangine, M Phil Gallo & Clem Vicari.

LP Nancy Hendrickson (Abbey), Deborah Luce (Jackie), Tiana Pierce (Trina), Holden McGuire (Ike), Billy Rae McQuade (Addley), Rose Ross (Mother).

Three former college roommates find their reunion ruined when they are dragged to a isolated house by a mother and her brutal sons. Watch out for that electric carving knife, girls!

1944. *The Mountain Men* (1980, Columbia, 102m, c). P Martin Shafer & Andrew Scheinman, D Richard Lang, W Fraser Clarke Heston, PH Michel Hugo, M Michel Legrand, ED Eva Ruggiero, PD Bill Kenney.

LP Charlton Heston (Bill Tyler), Brian Keith (Henry), Victoria Racimo (Running Moon), Stephen Macht (Heavy Eagle), John Glover (Nathan), Seymour Cassel (LaBont), David Ackroyd (Medicine Wolf), Cal Bellini (Cross Otter).

This yarn about mountain men in the American West of the 1880s stinks up the great outdoors like a frightened skunk in a house with all the windows and doors closed. Apparently talent for movie making has not been passed along to Charlton Heston's son Fraser.

1945. *Mountaintop Motel Massacre* (1986, New World, 96m, c). P&D Jim McCullough, Sr., W Jim McCullough, Jr., PH Joe Wilcots, M Ron DiIulio, ED Mindy Daucus.

LP Bill Thurman (Rev. Bill McWilley), Anna Chappell (Evelyn), Will Mitchel (Al), Virginia Loridans (Tanya), Major Brock (Crenshaw), James Bradford (Sheriff), Amy Hill (Prissy), Marian Jones (Mary).

Guests at a remote mountaintop motel don't know it's run by a deeply disturbed middle-aged woman, slowly going berserk.

1946. *The Mouse and the Woman* (1981, Alvicar/Facelift, 105m, c). P Hayden Pearce & Karl Francis, D Francis, W Vincent Kane & Francis (based on the story by Dylan Thomas), PH Nick Gifford, M Alun Francis, ED Neil Thomson, AD Hayden Pearce.

LP Dafydd Hywel (Morgan), Karen Archer (Gilda), Alan Devlin (Edward),

Peter Sproule (Miles), Patricia Napier (Bran), Howard Lewis (Doctor), Ionette Lloyd Davies (Emily), Beti Jones (Mother), Basil Painting (Capt. Furse).

In 1920 Wales, shell-shocked miner Dafydd Hywel is driven mad when his mistress Karen Archer has their baby aborted.

1947. *Movers and Shakers* (1985, MGM/United Artists, 80m, c). P Charles Grodin, William Asher, Richard Carrothers & Dennis D. Hennessey, D Asher, W Grodin, PH Robbie Greenberg, Michael Gershman & Michael A. Jones, M Ken Welch & Mitzi Welch, ED Tom Benko.

LP Walter Matthau (Joe Mulholland), Charles Grodin (Herb Derman), Vincent Gardenia (Saul Gritz), Tyne Daly (Nancy Derman), Bill Macy (Sid Spokane), Gilda Radner (Livia Machado), Earl Boen (Marshall), Michael Lerner (Arnie).

Hollywood producer Walter Matthau agrees to make a movie with a title *Love Is Sex,* yet to be written by screenwriter Charles Grodin. Grodin's marriage break-up makes him the wrong man for the job. Nobody moves, nobody shakes in this lousy movie.

1948. *Moving* (1988, Warner, 89m, c). P Stuart Cornfield & Kim Kurumada, D Alan Metter, W Andy Breckman, PH Donald McAlpine, M Howard Shore, ED Alan Balsam, PD David L. Snyder.

LP Richard Pryor (Arlo Pear), Beverly Todd (Monica Pear), Dave Thomas (Gary Marcus), Dana Carvey (Brad Williams), Randy Quaid (Frank/Cornell Crawford), Stacey Dash (Casey Pear), Raphael Harris (Marshall Pear), Ishmael Harris (Randy Pear), Robert LaSardo (Perry).

Out-of-work, mass-transit engineer Richard Pryor makes a near hopeless search for work in New Jersey. He finally finds a job, but he and his family must relocate to Idaho. Isn't that a riot?

1949. *Moving Targets* (1987, South Australian Academy, Australia, 95m, c). P Harley Manners, D Chris Langman, W Graham Hartley (based on the novel *When We Ran* by Keith Leopold), PH Ernest Clark, M Robert Kretschmer, ED Andrew Prowse, PD Alistair Livingstone.

LP Carmen Duncan (Eve), Michael Aitkens (Riley), Shane Briant (Terrier), Redmond Symons (Pitt), Nicholas Eadie (Toe), Annie Jones (Chrissie), David Clencie (Paul), Peter Stratford (Meyerdahl), Simone Buchanan (Cathy).

Now living quietly in Sydney with her 15-year-old daughter, Annie Jones, ex-German terrorist Carmen Duncan is not pleased to see her ex-lover, IRA killer Michael Aitkens, show up. He's looking for part of her hidden ill-gotten gains, so that he may escape his former colleagues who have targeted him for refusing to kill one of his victim's innocent family. The movie becomes a chase across Australia for all concerned.

1950. *Moving Violations* (1985, 20th Century–Fox, 90m, c). P Joe Roth, Harry Ufland & Robert Israel, D Neal Israel, W N. Israel & Pat Proft (based on a story by Paul Boorstin & Sharon Boorstin), PH Robert Elswit, M Ralph Burns, ED Tom Walls.

LP John Murray (Dana Cannon), Jennifer Tilly (Amy Hopkins), James Keach (Deputy Halik), Brian Backer (Scott Greeber), Ned Eisenberg (Wink Barnes), Clara Peller (Emma Jean), Wendie Jo Sperber (Joan Pudillo), Nedra Volz (Mrs. Loretta Houk), Lisa Hart Carroll (Deputy Virginia Morris).

Bill Murray's little brother John looks like his more famous sibling and mouths off like him, but that's where the similarity ends. The film is a meager story of tree planter Murray who has accumulated so many traffic tickets issued by James Keach and his partner, Lisa Hart Carroll, that he is sent to traffic school.

1951. *Ms. 45* (1981, Navaron/Rochelle, 84m, c, aka *Angel of Vengeance*). D Abel Ferrara, W Nicholas St. John, PH James Momel, M Joe Delia, ED Christopher Andrews.

LP Zoe Tamerlis (Thana), Steve Singer (Photographer), Jack Thibeau (Man in Bar), Peter Yellen (2nd Rapist), Darlene Stuto (Laurie), Editta Sherman (Landlady), Albert Sinkys (Boss), Jimmy Laine [Abel Ferrara] (1st Rapist).

Mute garment district worker Zoe Tamerlis goes on a killing spree after being raped twice in the same day. Seventeen-year-old Tamerlis wears black leather and a .45 strapped to her shapely thigh. She uses the gun to kill her attackers and every other man she encounters. Finally a female co-worker ends her reign of terror by stabbing Tamerlis with a knife.

Mugsy's Girls see Delta Pi

1952. *Munchies* (1987, MGM/United Artists, 85m, c). P Roger Corman & Ginny Nugent, D Bettina Hirsch, W Lance Smith, PH Jonathan West, SE Roger George.

LP Harvey Korman (Cecil/Simon), Charles Stratton (Paul), Nadine Van Der Velde (Cindy), Alix Elias (Melvis), Charlie Phillips (Eddie), Hardy Rawls (Big Ed), Jon Stafford (Dude), Robert Picardo (Bob Marvelle), Wendy Schaal (Marge Marvelle), Scott Sherk (Buddy Holly).

Junk food junkies from outer space menace the residents of a small town. All the humans in this dull picture give witless performances. Harvey Korman demonstrates that he should have been content to be second banana to Carol Burnett on her TV show.

1953. *The Muppets Take Manhattan* (1984, Tri-Star, 94m, c). P David Lazer, D Frank Oz, W Oz, Tom Patchett & Jay Tarses (based on a story by Patchett & Tarses), PH Robert Paynter, M Jeff Moss†, ED Evan Lottman, PD Stephen Hendrickson.

LP Jim Henson (Kermit/Rowlf/Dr. Teeth/Swedish Chef, Waldorf), Frank Oz (Miss Piggy/Fozzie/Animal), Dave Goelz (Gonzo/Chester/Rat/Bill/Zoot), Art Carney, James Coco, Dabney Coleman, Gregory Hines, Linda Lavin, Joan Rivers, Elliott Gould, Liza Minnelli, Brooke Shields.

The Muppets attempt to transfer a successful college musical to Broadway. This one doesn't work as well as the other Muppet films, probably because the idea is so ancient, associated with the Mickey Rooney and Judy Garland movies of the late 30s and early 40s.

1954. *Murder by Decree* (1980, Columbia-EMI-Warner, GB/Canada, 121m, c). P Rene Dupont & Bob Clark, D Clark, W John Hopkins (based on characters created by Sir Arthur Conan Doyle and the book *The Ripper File* by John Lloyd & Elwyn Jones), PH Reginald Morris, M Carl Zittrer, ED Stan Cole.

LP Christopher Plummer (Sherlock Holmes), James Mason (Dr. Watson), David Hemmings (Insp. Foxborough), Susan Clark (Mary Kelly), Anthony Quayle (Sir Charles Warren), John Gielgud (Prime Minister), Frank Finlay (Insp. Lestrade), Donald Sutherland (Robert Lees), Genevieve Bujold (Annie Crook), Chris Wiggins (Dr. Harding), Teddi Moore (Mrs. Lees).

Nineteenth-century Sherlock Holmes and Dr. Watson, well played by Christopher Plummer and James Mason, respectively, expose the masonic cover-up of the Jack the Ripper murders. It's a violent, gory film, with a rather murky story.

Murder by Mail see Schizoid

1955. *Murder by Phone* (1983, New World, Canada, 79m, c, aka *Bells; The Calling*). P Robert Cooper, D Michael Anderson, W Michael Butler, Dennis Shryack & John Kent Harrison, PH Reginald Morris, M John Barry, ED Martin Pepier, PD Seamus Flannery.

LP Richard Chamberlain (Nat Bridger), John Houseman (Dr. Stanley Markowitz), Sara Botsford (Ridley Taylor), Robin Gammell (Noah Clayton), Gary Reineke (Det. Meara), Barry Morse (Fred Watts).

A crazed killer has the police baffled because he kills his victims long distance—that is via the victims' phone receivers.

1956. *Murder Lust* (1987, Easy Street Filmworks, 90m, c). P James Lane, D Donald Jones, W Lane, PH James Mattison, M Lane, ED Jones.

LP Eli Rich (Steve), Rochelle Taylor (Cheryl), Dennis Gannon (Neil), Bonnie Schneider (Marene), Lisa Nichols (Debbie), H. Burton Leary (Joe), Bill Walsh (Lyman).

Sexually impotent security guard Eli Rich picks up prostitutes and strangles them. He fakes credentials, allowing him to get a job as a counselor at an adolescent crisis center, which puts him into contact with loads of unstable young girls.

1957. *Murder One* (1988, Miramax, Canada, 95m, c). P Nicolas Stiliadis, D Graeme Campbell, W Tex Fuller, PH Ludek Bogner, M Mychael Danna, ED

Michael McMahon, PD John Dondertman & Bora Bulajic.

LP Henry Thomas (Billy Issacs), James Wilder (Carl Issacs), Stephen Shellen (Wayne Coleman), Errol Slue (George Dungee).

The film is based on a real killing spree which took place in Georgia in 1973. The slaughter of a family of six by escaped convicts is seen through the eyes of Henry Thomas, the 15-year-old brother of the leader of the gang of killers.

1958. *Murder Rap* (1988, Image/Resolution, 107m, c). P Kliff Kuehl & Joe M. South, D&W Kuehl, PH Michael Delahoussaye, M Robert Renfrow.

LP John Hawkes, S. Kathleen Feighny, Coquina Dunn, Tim Mateer, Sara Roucloux, Kerry Awn, David Frizzell, James Michael Costello, Julius Tennon.

John Hawkes must fake his own death to escape the web of murder and violence in which S. Kathleen Feighny has entrapped him. This one went straight to video release.

1959. *Murphy's Fault* (1988, Triax, GB, 96m, c). P Chris Davies & Lionel A. Ephraim, D&W Robert J. Smawley, PH Rod Stewart, ED Simon Grimley.

LP Patrick Dollaghan (David Wayne), Stack Pierce (Spider), Anne Curry (Samantha), Matthew Stewardson.

"Whatever can go wrong, will go wrong" is Murphy's Law and it applies to nightwatchman Patrick Dollaghan, desperate to quit his menial job and become a writer.

1960. *Murphy's Law* (1986, Cannon, 100m, c). P Pancho Kohner, D J. Lee Thompson, W Gail Morgan Hickman, PH Alex Phillips, M Marc Donahue & Valentine McCallum, ED Peter Lee Thompson, PD William Cruise.

LP Charles Bronson (Jack Murphy), Kathleen Wilhoite (Arabella McGee), Carrie Snodgress (Joan Freeman), Robert F. Lyons (Art Penney), Richard Romanus (Frank Vincenzo), Angel Tompkins (Jan), Bill Henderson (Ben Wilcove), James Luisi (Ed Reineke).

After homicide cop Charles Bronson is framed for murder and sentenced to prison, he breaks out of jail, handcuffed

to Kathleen Wilhoite, a foul-mouthed female car thief. They battle each other as they attempt to unmask the real killer. The idea worked better with Robert Donat and Madeleine Carroll in *The 39 Steps.*

1961. *Murphy's Romance* (1985, Columbia, 107m, c). P Laura Ziskin, D Martin Ritt, W Harriet Frank, Jr. & Irving Ravetch (based on the novella by Max Schott), PH William A. Fraker†, M Carole King, ED Sidney Levin, PD Joel Schiller.

LP Sally Field (Emma Moriarity), James Garner† (Murphy Jones), Brian Kerwin (Bobby Jack Moriarity), Corey Haim (Jake Moriarity), Dennis Burkley (Freeman Coverly), Georgann Johnson (Margaret), Dortha Duckworth (Bessie).

In a small Arizona town, aging pharmacist James Garner and young mother Sally Field share a romance until her rotten, no-good, ex-husband shows up.

1962. *Music Box* (1989, Tri-Star, 124m, c). P Irwin Winkler, D Costas-Gavras, W Joe Eszterhas, PH Patrick Blossier, M Philippe Sarde, ED Joele Van Effenterre, PD Jeannine Claudia Oppewall.

LP Jessica Lange† (Ann Talbot), Armin Mueller-Stahl (Mike Laszlo), Frederic Forrest (Jack Burke), Donald Moffat (Harry Talbot), Lukas Haas (Mikey Talbot), Cheryl Lynn Bruce (Georgine Wheeler), Mari Torocsik (Magda Zoldan), Michael Rooker (Karchy).

Divorced Chicago lawyer Jessica Lange must interrupt her work to contest federal charges that her father Armin Mueller-Stahl is a Nazi war criminal. The testimony against him tests Lange's belief that the monster of the concentration camp couldn't be the stern but kindly mill worker who raised her and her brother. The performances of Lange as the zealous daughter and lawyer and Mueller-Stahl are powerful.

1963. *The Music of the Spheres* (1984, Lightscape, Canada, 82m, c). P&D G. Philip Jackson, W Jackson & Gabrielle de Montmollin, PH Nadine Humenick, ED Fred P. Gauthier, AD James Stuart Allan.

LP Anne Dansereau (Melody), Peter Brikmanis (Andrew), Jacques Couture (Paul), Ken Lemaire (The Bureaucrat), Kenneth Gordon (Einstein), Grant Roll (Security Officer), Sandy Kaiser (Dr. Moriarte).

Strictly for science fiction freaks, this low-budget film is set in the 21st century. The world, no longer made up of nations, is run by a web of supercomputers headed by computer central—"The Beast."

Mutant see Forbidden Worlds

Mutant see Night Shadows

1964. *Mutant Hunt* (1987, Wizard Video-Infinity, 77m, c, aka *Matt Riker: Mutant Hunter*). P Cynthia DePaula, D&W Tim Kincaid, PH Thomas Murphy, ED Barry Zetlin, MD Tom Milano, PD Ruth Lounsbury.

LP Rick Gianasi (Matt Riker), Mary Fahey (Darla Haynes), Ron Reynaldi (Johnny Felix), Taunie Vrenon (Elaine Eliot), Bill Peterson (Z), Mark Umile (Dr. Paul Haynes), Stormy Spill (Domina), Doug De Vos (Hydro).

New York is besieged by mutant cyborgs with an insatiable lust for ripping humans apart. Rick Gianasi is called upon to save the city.

1965. *Mutant on the Bounty* (1989, Skouras, 94m, c). P Robert Torrance & Martin Lopez, D Torrance, W Lopez (based on a story by Lopez & Torrance), PH Randolph Sellars, M Tim Torrance, ED Craig A. Colton, PD Clark Hunter.

LP John Roarke (Carlson), Deborah Benson (Justine), John Furey (Dag), Victoria Catlin (Babette), John Fleck (Lizardo), Kyle T. Heffner (Max), Scott Williamson (Rick O'Shay), John Durbin (Manny the Weasel), Pepper Martin (Captain Lloydes).

We wouldn't be surprised to learn that Robert Torrence and Martin Lopez wrote the story for this movie *after* coming up with the title. Despite the catchy name, it's a witless sci-fi parody. Saxophone player Kyle T. Heffner is brought back to life after 23 years to roam the *USS Bounty* in 2048. But there's nothing to fear from him even though his face has the worst case of eczema you'd ever not want to see.

1966. *Mutants in Paradise* (1989, Caridi Ent., 77m, c). P William Moses, Jr., D&W Scott Apostolou, PH G. Neal Means, M Jep Epstein, ED Apostolou & Thomas Lucas, PD Frank Harris.

LP Brad Greenquist (Steve Awesome), Anna Nicholas (Alice Durchfall), Robert Ingham (Oscar Tinman), Skipp Suddeth (Boris/Bob), Edith Massey (Dr. Durchfall), Ray "Boom Boom" Mancini (Trainer).

The sci-fi spoof was shot about five years earlier as a University of Virginia student film. Brad Greenquist is a nerdish guinea pig for scientist Robert Ingham's efforts to come up with a nuclear-proof man to survive an impending war.

1967. *The Mutilator* (1985, Ocean King, 86m, c). P Buddy Cooper, D Cooper & John S. Douglass, W Cooper, PH Peter Schnall, M Michael Minard, ED Stephen Mack.

LP Matt Mitler (Ed, Jr.), Jack Chatham (Jack, Sr.), Trace Cooper (Younger Ed, Jr.), Ruth Martinez (Junior's Girl Friend), Frances Raines, Bill Hitchcock, Morey Lampley, Connie Rogers (Junior's Friends).

A deranged maniac stalks his son and his friends, killing them in a number of gory and exotic ways.

1968. *My American Cousin* (1986, Spectrafilm, Canada, 95m, c). P Peter O'Brian, D&W Sandy Wilson, PH Richard Leiterman, ED Haida Paul.

LP Margaret Langrick (Sandy), John Wildman (Butch Walker), Richard Donat (Maj. Wilcox), Jane Mortifee (Kitty Wilcox), T.J. Scott (Lenny McPhee), Camille Henderson (Shirley Darling), Babs Chula (Mr. Walker), Terry Moore (Mrs. Walker).

This delightful comedy details the changes in the life of 12-year-old Canadian girl Margaret Langrick when her hunkish 17-year-old male cousin, John Wildman, arrives from California for an extended visit.

1969. *My Beautiful Laundrette* (1986, Orion Classics, GB, 93m, c). P Sarah Radclyffe & Tim Bevan, D Stephen Frears, W Hanif Kureishi†, PH Oliver Stapleton, M Ludus Tonalis, ED Mick Audsley, PD Hugo Luczyc Whyhowski.

LP Daniel Day-Lewis (Johnny), Saeed Jaffrey (Nasser), Roshan Seth (Papa), Gordon Warnecke (Omar), Shirley Anne Field (Rachel), Rita Wolf (Tania), Richard Graham (Genghis), Charu Bala Choksi (Bilquis), Souad Faress (Cherry), Derrick Branche (Salim).

Set in the Pakistani community of South London, the movie focuses on Daniel Day-Lewis and Gordon Warnecke, friends and lovers from schooldays. Warnecke is given a menial job by his wealthy uncle Saeed Jaffrey. The latter turns over a rundown laundrette to Warnecke which the young man sees as starting him on the road to riches.

1970. *My Best Friend Is a Vampire* (1988, Kings Road, 90m, c). P Dennis Murphy, D Jimmy Huston, W Tab Murphy, PH James Bartle, M Steve Dorff, ED Janice Hampton & Gail Yasunaga, PD Michael Molly.

LP Robert Sean Leonard (Jeremy Capello), Evan Mirand (Ralph), Cheryl Pollak (Darla Blake), Rene Auberjonois (Modoo), Cecilia Peck (Nora), Fannie Flagg (Mrs. Capello), David Warner (Prof. McCarthy), Paul Wilson (Grimsdyke).

Teenage delivery boy Robert Sean Leonard, dropping off some groceries at a spooky old mansion, is seduced by a sexy vampire. Her kisses and love bites turn him into a vampire, which is a real bummer for his family and friends.

1971. *My Bloody Valentine* (1981, Paramount, Canada, 91m, c). P John Dunning, Andre Link & Stephen Miller, D George Mihalka, W John Beaird (based on a story concept by Miller), PH Rodney Gibbons, M Paul Zaza, ED Jean La Fleur, Rit Wallis & Gerald Vansier.

LP Paul Kelman (T.J.), Lori Hallier (Sarah), Neil Affleck (Axel), Keith Knight (Hollis), Alf Humphreys (Howard), Cynthia Dale (Patty), Helene Udy (Sylvia), Rob Stein (John), Tom Kovacs (Mike), Terry Waterland (Harriet).

In another *Halloween* clone, a crazed miner shows up at a Valentine's Day party and cuts out the hearts of the guests with a pickaxe. He then delivers them to the cops in candy boxes. Wonder what they can do with *Easter?*

1972. *My Bodyguard* (1980, 20th Century–Fox, 96m, c). P Don Devlin, D Tony Bill, W Alan Ormsby, PH Michael D. Margulies, M Dave Grusin, ED Stu Linder, PD Jackson DeGovia.

LP Chris Makepeace (Clifford), Adam Baldwin (Linderman), Matt Dillon (Moody), Paul Quandt (Carson), Joan Cusack (Shelley), Dean R. Miller (Hightower), Tim Reyna (Koontz), Richard Bradley (Dubrow), Denise Baske (Leilani), Hank Salas (Mike), Ruth Gordon (Gramma), Martin Mull (Mr. Peache), John Houseman (Dobbs).

In a sensitively produced film, undersized high school student Chris Makepeace's life is made miserable by school bully Matt Dillon and his cronies. Chris hires large moody loner Adam Baldwin (who has the reputation of having supposedly killed someone) to act as his bodyguard. Ultimately Makepeace must stand up to Dillon himself. The film is well worth seeing.

1973. *My Breakfast with Blassie* (1983, Artist Endeavours, 60m, c). P&D Johnny Legend & Linda Lautrec, W (based on an idea by Legend and Lautrec), M Linda Mitchel, ED Legend, Lautrec & Lynne Marguilies.

LP Andy Kaufman, Freddie Blassie, Lynne Elaine, Laura Burdick, Linda Burdick, Linda Hirsch, Bob Zmuda.

In this strange take-off of *My Dinner with Andre,* comedian Andy Kaufman and pro wrestler Freddie Blassie try to outdue each other with ego stories.

1974. *My Brilliant Career* (1980, New South Wales/GUO/Analysis, Australia, 98m, c). P Margaret Fink, D Gillian Armstrong, W Eleanor Witcombe (based on the novel by Miles Franklin), PH Don McAlpine, M Nathan Waks, ED Nick Beauman, PD Luciana Arrighi, COS Anna Senior†.

LP Judy Davis (Sybylla Melvyn), Sam Neill (Harry Beecham), Wendy Hughes (Aunt Helen), Robert Grubb (Frank Hawdon), Max Cullen (Mr. McSwat), Pat Kennedy (Aunt Gussie), Aileen Brittain (Grandma Bossier), Peter Whitford (Uncle Julius), Carole Skinner (Mrs. McSwat).

In the Australian outback of the late 19th century, Judy Davis' parents despair at her refusal to resign herself to a life of convention and drudgery. Her refusal of marriage proposals shocks her family and friends. The headstrong young woman wants a career. She's determined to be independent. The film doesn't deal with her lesbianism, which is pivotal in the book.

1975. *My Brother's Wedding* (1983, Charles Burnett, 116m, c). P Charles Burnett & Gaye Shannon-Burnett, D,W&PH Charles Burnett, ED Tom Pennick.

LP Everett Silas (Pierce Monday), Jessie Holmes (Mrs. Monday), Gaye Shannon-Burnett (Sonia), Ronnie Bell (Soldier Richards), Dennis Kemper (Wendell Monday), Sy Richardson (Sonia's Father), Frances Nealy (Sonia's Mother).

Everett Silas, a black resident of the Watts area of L.A. has a love-hate relationship with his community. His feelings are put to the test when he must choose between attending the funeral of a dear friend or the wedding of his upwardly mobile brother whom he resents.

1976. *My Chauffeur* (1986, Crown International, 97m, c). P Marilyn J. Tenser, D&W David Beaird, PH Harry Mathias, M Paul Hertzog, ED Richard E. Westover, PD C.J. Strawn.

LP Deborah Foreman (Casey Meadows), Sam J. Jones (Battle Witherspoon), Sean McClory (O'Brien), Howard Hesseman (McBride), E.G. Marshall (Witherspoon), Penn Jillette (Bone), John O'Leary (Giles).

Deborah Foreman becomes the first female chauffeur to work for the Brentwood Limousine Company, the most prestigious driving service in Los Angeles. It's moderately amusing.

1977. *My Dark Lady* (1987, Film Gallery, 104m, c). P Carole Terranova & Stratton Rawson, D Frederick King Keller, W Fred W. Keller, Gene Brook & F.K. Keller (based on an original story by F.A. Keller), PH Thom Marini, M Ken Kaufman, ED Darren Kloomok, PD Rawson.

LP Fred A. Keller (Sam Booth), Lorna Hill (Lorna Dahomey), Raymond Holder (Malcolm Dahomey), John Buscaglia (Jonathan Park), Evan Perry (Samuel T. MacMillan), Barbara Cady (Sarah Teasdale), Stuart Roth (Horace Babinski), Tess Spangler (Minnie O'Hara), Steven Cooper (Terry Terranova).

Failed Shakespearean actor Fred A. Keller is caught shoplifting while wearing a Santa Claus suit. He escapes and holes up in a boarding house run by black woman Lorna Hill. Keller becomes friendly with his landlady's son Raymond Holder, who shows acting talent. Keller helps Hill make a success of her boarding house and arranges for Holder to be sent to an elite boarding school. They have some trouble with bigoted headmaster John Buscaglia.

1978. *My Demon Lover* (1987, New Line Cinema, 86m, c). P Robert Shaye, D Charles Loventhal, W Leslie Ray, PH Jacques Haitkin, M David Newman, ED Ronald Roose, PD Brent Swift.

LP Scott Valentine (Kaz), Michelle Little (Denny), Arnold Johnson (Fixer), Robert Trebor (Charles), Alan Fudge (Capt. Phil Janus), Gina Gallego (Sonia).

Every time Scott Valentine is turned on by his dream girl Michelle Little, he is literally turned into a beast. It wears thin fairly quickly.

1979. *My Dinner with Andre* (1981, New Yorker, 110m, c). P George W. George & Beverly Karp, D Louis Malle, W Wallace Shawn & Andre Gregory, PH Jeri Sopanen, M Allen Shawn, ED Suzanne Baron, PD David Mitchell.

LP Wallace Shawn (Wally), Andre Gregory (Andre), Jean Lenauer (Waiter), Roy Butler (Bartender).

Two friends, Wallace Shawn and Andre Gregory, haven't seen each other in a long time. They catch up on each other's lives over a leisurely dinner. The talk is good, but whether this is a good film, will depend on one's willingness to sit through nearly two hours of a conversation dominated by Gregory.

1980. *My Favorite Year* (1982, MGM/United Artists, 92m, c). P Michael Gruskoff, D Richard Benjamin, W Norman Steinberg & Dennis Palumbo (based on a story by Palumbo), PH Gerald Hirschfeld, M Ralph Burns, ED Richard Chew, PD Charles Rosen.

LP Peter O'Toole† (Alan Swann), Mark Linn-Baker (Benjy Stone), Jessica

Harper (K.C. Downing), Joseph Bologna (King Kaiser), Bill Macy (Sy Benson), Lainie Kazan (Belle Carroca), Anne DeSalvo (Alice Miller), Basil Hoffman (Herb Lee), Lou Jacobi (Uncle Morty), Adolph Green (Leo Silver), Tony DiBenedetto (Alfie Bumbacelli), Cameron Mitchell (Karl Rojeck).

Peter O'Toole is perfection as an Errol Flynn–like drunken, womanizing, but ever-charming adventure-film star. He is to guest-star on a 1954 Sid Caesar–like TV comedy show. Mark Linn-Baker, the least important member of the writing staff and one of the guest's biggest fans, is placed in charge of the irresponsible and unreliable O'Toole. Linn-Baker is to see that O'Toole shows up for the live show and doesn't cause too much of a scandal beforehand. It's a lovely nostalgic production with enjoyable performances all around. Especially good are O'Toole, Joseph Bologna and Lainie Kazan.

1981. *My First Wife* (1985, Spectrafilm, Australia, 96m, c). P Paul Cox & Jane Ballentyne, D Cox, W Cox & Bob Ellis, PH Yuri Sokol, ED Tim Lewis, PD Santhana Naidu.

LP John Hargreaves (John), Wendy Hughes (Helen), Lucy Angwin (Lucy), David Cameron (Tom), Julia Blake (Kirstin), Anna Jemison (Hilary), Charles Tingwell (Helen's Mother), Robin Lovejoy (John's Father), Lucy Uralov (John's Mother).

Classical music programmer John Hargreaves discovers that his wife Wendy Hughes doesn't love him anymore. This breakup of a marriage story is uneven, but ends on a positive note.

1982. *My Kind of Town* (1984, Milltown/Petra, Canada, 76m, c). D&W Charles Wilkinson, PH David Geddes, M Wilkinson, ED Frank Irvine.

LP Peter Smith (Peter Hall), John Cooper (Sam the Mayor), Martina Schleisser (Astrid Heim), Michael Paul (Michael Hall), Michael Marks (Brad), Roy Evarts (Uncle Roy), Frank Irvine (Frank Hall), Haida Paul (Margaret Hall).

It's a pleasant little tale about life in a small Vancouver Island town suffering a severe unemployment problem because of an economic recession.

1983. *My Left Foot†* (1989, Miramax, GB, 98m, c). P Noel Pearson, D Jim Sheridan†, W Shane Connaughton & Sheridan†, PH Jack Conroy, M Elmer Bernstein, ED J. Patrick Duffner, AD Austen Spriggs.

LP Daniel Day-Lewis* (Christy Brown), Ray McAnally (Mr. Brown), Brenda Fricker* (Mrs. Brown), Ruth McCabe (Mary), Fiona Shaw (Dr. Eileen Cole), Eanna MacLiam (Older Benny), Alison Whelan (Older Sheila), Declan Croghan (Older Tom), Hugh O'Conor (Younger Christy), Cyril Cusack (Lord Castlewelland).

Inventive actor Daniel Day-Lewis gives an inspiring and nearly unbelievably brilliant performance as the Irish writer and painter Christy Brown. Born with cerebral palsy into a poor family, he shatters the prediction at his birth that he will be little more than a vegetable all his life. He learns to write and paint, using only his left foot. His foot is the instrument of his remarkable will, intelligence and talent. Day-Lewis' performance is both a physical and intellectual tour-de-force. Also brilliant in this sentimental film which resists sentimentality is Oscar winner Brenda Fricker as the loving mother who gives her son the love, strength and encouragement he needs, the late Ray McAnally as Christy's brutish hardworking father, and Hugh O'Conor, who superbly portrays Christy as a boy. If you feel like cheering at the end of the movie—go ahead—it's deserved and it'll make you feel good. That Day-Lewis was given the Academy Award seems to indicate the maturing of Oscar voters, giving up their jingoistic and box-office justifications for their picks, and voting instead for talent and achievement.

1984. *My Little Girl* (1987, Hemdale, 119m, c). P&D Connie Kaiserman, W Kaiserman & Nan Mason, PH Pierre Lhomme, M Richard Robbins, ED Katherine Wenning, PD Dan Leigh.

LP Mary Stuart Masterson (Franny Bettinger), James Earl Jones (Ike Bailey), Geraldine Page (Grandmother Molly), Pamela Payton-Wright (Mrs. Bettinger), Peter Michael Goetz (Mr. Bettinger), Traci Lin (Alice), Erika Alexander (Joan), Anne Meara (Mrs. Chopper),

Peter Gallagher (Kai), Naeemah Wilmore (Camille).

Filmed in 1985, the picture had a brief theater release in 1987. Wealthy Mary Stuart Masterson takes a job in a home for wayward girls. She is assigned three hard cases, silent black 10-year-old Naeemah Wilmore, her 24-year-old sister Erika Alexander, and 17-year-old hooker Traci Lin. Masterson slowly wins their trust and respect.

1985. *My Little Pony* (1986, De Laurentiis, animated, 87m, c). P Joe Bacal, Tom Griffin & Michael Joens, D Joens, W George Arthur Bloom, M/L Tommy Goodman, Rob Walsh & Barry Harman.

VOICES Danny DeVito (Grundle King), Madeline Kahn (Draggle), Cloris Leachman (Hydia), Rhea Perlman (Reeka), Tony Randall (Moochick), Tammy Amerson (Megan), Jon Bauman (Smooze), Alice Playten (Baby Lickety Split/Bushwoolie 1).

Geared to the under-seven age group, the picture is the story of little ponies threatened by the witch family of Madeline Kahn, Cloris Leachman and Rhea Perlman.

My Love Letters see Love Letters

1986. *My Mom's a Werewolf* (1989, Crown International, 84m, c). P Steven J. Wolfe, D Michael Fischa, W Mark Pirro, PH Bryan England, M Barry Fasman & Dana Walden, ED Claudia Finkle.

LP Susan Blakely, John Saxon, Katrina Caspary, John Schuck, Ruth Buzzi, Marcia Wallace, Marilyn McCoo.

When pet-store owner and werewolf John Saxon puts the bite on housewife Susan Blakely's toe she becomes a werewife. It's mildly amusing, but will only be found in your local video store.

1987. *My New Car* (1988, New Century/Vista, 96m, c). P Robert Lawrence, D David Beaird, W Richard Matheson & Thomas Solloszi.

LP Craig Sheffer, Jennifer Beals, Jeff Fahey, Gene Hackman.

This tongue-in-cheek comedy features a young rural man, who on the eve of his wedding, goes to town to buy his first car. Anything that can go wrong does.

1988. *My Science Project* (1985, Buena Vista, 95m, c). P Jonathan Taplin, D&W Jonathan Betuel, PH David M. Walsh, M Peter Bernstein, ED C. Timothy O'Meara, PD David L. Snyder, SE John Scheele.

LP John Stockwell (Michael Harlan), Danielle Von Zerneck (Ellie Sawyer), Fisher Stevens (Vince Latello), Raphael Sbarge (Sherman), Richard Masur (Detective Isadore Nulty), Barry Corbin (Lew Harlan), Ann Wedgeworth (Dolores), Dennis Hopper (Bob Roberts).

In this tasteless and unfunny sci-fi spoof, obnoxious high school students unearth a device which creates time and space warps. Dennis Hopper, as a science teacher, gives the only interesting performance.

1989. *My Stepmother Is an Alien* (1988, Columbia, 108m, c). P Franklin R. Levy & Ronald Parker, D Richard Benjamin, W Jerico & Herschel Weingrod, Timothy Harris & Jonathan Reynolds, PH Richard H. Kline, M Alan Silvestri, ED Jacqueline Cambas, PD Charles Rosen.

LP Dan Aykroyd (Dr. Steve Mills), Kim Basinger (Celeste), Jon Lovitz (Ron Mills), Alyson Hannigan (Jessie Mills), Joseph Maher (Dr. Lucas Budlong), Seth Green (Fred Grass), Wesley Mann (Grady), Ann Prentiss (The Voice of Purse), Harry Shearer (The Voice of Carl Sagan).

Those who feel that Kim Basinger's awesome beauty and sexy looks are otherwordly will not be surprised to find that in this comedy she comes from another galaxy. Unfortunately, her comical talents aren't on a par with her looks in this silly film. Dan Aykroyd doesn't seem the type that such an alien would seek out, let alone do the earthly thing of marrying. Once they tie the knot, the new family unit, which also includes teen Alyson Hannigan, engages in your usual situation comedy stuff.

1990. *My Tutor* (1983, Crown International, 97m, c). P Marilyn J. Tenser, D George Bowers, W Joe Roberts (based on the story by Mark Tenser), PH Mac Ahlberg, M Webster Lewis, ED Sidney Wolinsky.

LP Caren Kaye (Terry), Matt Lattanzi (Bobby Chrystal), Kevin McCarthy (Mr.

Chrystal), Clark Brandon (Billy), Bruce Bauer (Don), Arlene Golonka (Mrs. Chrystal), Crispin Glover (Jack), Amber Denyse Austin (Bonnie), John Vargas (Manuel), Maria Melendez (Maria).

Some kids have all the luck. It's not enough that teenager Matt Lattanzi lives in a mansion, wears the best threads, drives a hot car, and has all the money he wants. When it appears he may fail French, dear old Dad, Kevin McCarthy, hires Caren Kaye, who looks like she walked out of a *Sports Illustrated* swimsuit issue, to tutor the boy. McCarthy may have been thinking that he was renting a toy for himself, but Kaye's not interested in the older man, preferring the sensitive teen instead. Just so Lattanzi gets her message, each midnight she swims in the nude in the Olympic-sized pool which is located just outside Matt's bedroom. All things considered, the film is not the usual teenage sexploitation film, concentrating instead on the helplessness Lattanzi feels as sexual awareness overtakes him.

1991. *Mystery Mansion* (1984, Pacific International, 95m, c). P Arthur R. Dubs, D David E. Jackson, W Jack Duggan, Arn Wihtol & Jackson, PH Milas C. Hinshaw, M William Loose, Jack K. Tillar & Marty Wereski, ED Stephen Johnson.

LP Dallas McKennon (Sam), Greg Wynne (Gene), Jane Ferguson (Mary), Randi Brown (Susan), Lindsay Bishop (Billy), David Wagner (Johnny), Barry Hostetler (Fred), Joseph D. Savery (Willy).

A hundred-year-old mystery leads three kids to search for a fortune in gold hidden in an old mansion.

Mystery of Monster Island see Monster Island

1992. *Mystery Train* (1989, Orion Classics, 110m, c). P Jim Stark, D&W Jim Jarmusch, PH Robby Muller, M John Lurie, ED Melody London, PD Dan Bishop.

LP Masatoshi Nagase (Jun), Youki Kudoh (Mitzuko), Screamin' Jay Hawkins (Night Clerk), Cinque Lee (Bellboy), Nicoletta Braschi (Luisa), Elizabeth Bracco (DeeDee), Joe Strummer (Johnny), Rick Aviles (Will Robinson), Steve Buscemi (Charlie).

The film consists of three vignettes about different sets of people who find themselves staying in one of the seedy rooms of the run-down Memphis hotel, the Arcade. Every room is equipped with a portrait of Elvis Presley. Some have suggested that Jim Jarmusch's stories are of the shaggy-dog variety. Perhaps so, but his dialogue is clever and the characters interesting. Who can resist Masatoshi Nagase and Youki Kudoh?

1993. *Mystic Pizza* (1988, Goldwyn, 104m, c). P Mark Levinson & Scott Rosenfelt, D Donald Petrie, W Amy Jones, Perry Howze, Randy Howze & Alfred Uhry (based on a story by Amy Jones), PH Timothy Suhrstedt, M David McHugh, ED Marion Rothman & Don Brochu.

LP Julia Roberts (Daisy Araujo), Annabeth Gish (Kat Araujo), Lili Taylor (Jojo Barboza), Phillip D'Onofrio (Bill Montijo), William R. Moses (Tim Travers), Adam Storke (Charles Gordon Winsor), Conchata Ferrell (Leona Valsouano), Porscha Radcliffe (Phoebe Travers), Joanna Merlin (Margaret), Arthur Walsh (Manny), John Fiore (Jake), Gene Amoroso (Ed Barboza).

Set in the Connecticut seaside town of Mystic, the film is the story of the romances and heartbreaks of three Portuguese-American waitresses, Julia Roberts, Annabeth Gish and Lili Taylor, who work in the title establishment. It's an enjoyable romantic comedy, even though most Connecticut residents know the best pizza is found in Wooster Square in New Haven.

Mystique see Circle of Power

1994. *Nadine* (1987, Tri-Star, 83m, c). P Arlene Donovan, D&W Robert Benton, PH Nestor Almendros, M Howard Shore, ED Sam O'Steen, PD Paul Sylbert.

LP Jeff Bridges (Vernon Hightower), Kim Basinger (Nadine Hightower), Rip Torn (Buford Pope), Gwen Verdon (Vera), Glenne Headly (Renee Lomax), Jerry Stiller (Raymond Escobar), Jay Patterson (Dwight Estes), William Youmans (Boyd), Mickey Jones (Floyd), Gary Grubbs (Cecil).

Jeff Bridges and Kim Basinger, a loving, warring couple on the way to a divorce court in Texas of the 50s, get sidetracked by murder, mistaken identity and the opportunity to strike it rich. It's an innocuous romantic comedy from the director of *The Late Show* and *Kramer vs. Kramer*. As usual Rip Torn makes an excellent villain. He looks right sad when he tells Basinger that he's never killed a woman before. She'll be his first.

1995. *Nail Gun Massacre* (1987, Futuristic Films/Reel Movies, 84m, c). P Terry Lofton, D Lofton & Bill Leslie, W Lofton, PH Leslie, M Whitey Thomas, ED Lynn Leneau Calmes, SE Lofton.

LP Rocky Patterson (Doc), Michelle Meyer (Linda), Ron Queen (Sheriff), Beau Leland (Bubba), Sebrina Lawless, Monica Lawless, Mike Coady.

After a Texas girl is gang raped by construction workers, a mysterious figure in army fatigues and motorcycle helmet goes around killing the rapists with a nail gun. Suppose this is where the makers of *Lethal Weapon 2* got the idea?

1996. *The Naked Cage* (1986, Cannon, 97m, c). P Chris D. Nebe, D&W Paul Nicholas, PH Hal Trussell, M Various Artists, ED Anthony Di Marco, SE A&A Special Effects.

LP Shari Shattuck (Michelle), Angel Tompkins (Diane), Lucinda Crosby (Rhonda), Christina Whitaker (Rita), Faith Minton (Sheila), Stacey Shaffer (Amy), Nick Benedict (Smiley), John Terlesky (Willy).

Shari Shattuck, an innocent young girl, very fond of horseback riding, is forced into a different type of exercise when she is unjustly sent to prison. It's an excessively brutal film.

1997. *The Naked Face* (1984, Cannon, 103m, c). P Menahem Golan & Yoram Globus, D Bryan Forbes, W Forbes (based on the novel by Sidney Sheldon), PH David Gurfinkel, M Michael J. Lewis, ED Philip Shaw, PD William Fosser.

LP Roger Moore (Dr. Judd Stevens), Rod Steiger (Lt. McGreavy), Elliott Gould (Angeli), Art Carney (Morgens), Anne Archer (Ann Blake), David Hedison (Dr. Hadley), Deanna Dunagan (Mrs. Hadley), Ron Parady (Cortini).

Psychiatrist Roger Moore is the number one suspect in a murder case. While the police are investigating him, the real killer is tracking down Moore.

1998. *The Naked Gun* (1988, Paramount, 85m, c). P Robert K. Weiss, D David Zucker, W Jerry Zucker, Jim Abrahams, David Zucker & Pat Proft, PH Robert Stevens, M Ira Newborn, ED Michael Jablow, PD John J. Lloyd.

LP Leslie Nielsen (Frank Drebin), George Kennedy (Ed Hocken), Priscilla Presley (Jane Spencer), Ricardo Montalban (Vincent Ludwig), O.J. Simpson (Nordberg), Nancy Marchand (Mayor), Jeannette Charles (Queen).

From the team that brought you *Airplane!* comes an irreverent, hilarious, wacky, not-for-everyone movie, starring Leslie Nielsen as a clumsy detective (the same role he played on TV's "Police Squad," which proved too hip for couch potatoes) with George Kennedy as his equally inept sidekick. The two wreak havoc on the streets of L.A. trying to protect a visiting Queen Elizabeth lookalike from an assassination while at the same time hoping to tie shipping magnate Ricardo Montalban to drug smuggling.

1999. *Naked Vengeance* (1985, Westbrook/M.P. Films, 97m, c). P Anthony Maharaj & Cirio Santiago, D Santiago, W Reilly Askew (based on a story by Maharaj), PH Ricardo Remias, ED Pacifico Sanchez & Noah Blough, M Ron Jones.

LP Deborah Tranelli (Carla), Kaz Garas (Fletch), Bill McLaughlin (Sheriff Cates), Ed Crick (Burke).

After her husband is murdered, Deborah Tranelli is beaten and raped. She becomes a raging killing machine seeking revenge.

Naked Weekend see *Circle of Power*

Nam see *Platoon Leader*

2000. *Nam Angels* (1989, Concorde, 93m, c). P Christopher R. Santiago, D Cirio H. Santiago, W Dan Gagliasso, PH Rick Remias & Chris Squires, M Jaime Fabregas, ED Edgar Viner.

LP Brad Johnson (Calhoun), Vernon Wells, Kevin Duffs, Rick Dean, Mark Venturini, Jeff Griffith, Romy Diaz, Ken Metcalfe.

Filipino director Cirio Santiago has

made several films about the Vietnam War, but this one featuring Hell's Angels motorcyclists in Nam may be the strangest.

2001. *The Name of the Rose* (1986, 20th Century–Fox, 130m, c). P Bernd Eichinger, D Jean-Jacques Annaud, W Andrew Birkin, Gerard Brach, Howard Franklin & Alain Godard (a Palimpsest of the novel by Umberto Eco), PH Tonino Delli Colli, M James Horner, ED Jane Seitz, PD Dante Ferretti.

LP Sean Connery (William of Baskerville), F. Murray Abraham (Bernardo Gui), Christian Slater (Adso of Melk), Elya Baskin (Severinus), Feodor Chaliapin, Jr. (Jorge de Burgos), William Hickey (Ubertino de Casale), Michael Lonsdale (The Abbot), Ron Perlman (Salvatore), Volker Prechtel (Malachia), Helmut Qualtinger (Remigio de Varagine), Valentina Vargas (The Girl).

Arriving at a 14th century Benedictine abbey is Franciscan Sean Connery and his companion, novice Christian Slater. Connery, who has a reputation as an investigator, is called on to use his talents when a series of deaths of monks take place. All who have died have come in contact with a secret volume of Aristotle's lost second book of Poetics — about comedy. Seems laughter can be deadly. Arriving about the time that Connery solves the mystery is his long-time adversary, F. Murray Abraham, a ruthless persecutor of heretics. The latter wishes to increase the body count at the monastery. The production is spectacular, but the film didn't go over well with American audiences, who it would seem prefer contemporary slasher movies to suspenseful murder mysteries of a time long gone.

2002. *Nanou* (1986, Umbrella Films, GB/France, 110m, c). P Simon Perry & Patrick Sandrin, D&W Conny Templeman, PH Martin Fuhrer, M John Kean, ED Tom Priestley, PD Andrew Mollo.

LP Imogen Stubbs (Nanou), Jean-Philippe Ecoffey (Luc), Christophe Lidon (Jacques), Daniel Day-Lewis (Max), Valentine Pelca, Roger Ibanez.

Imogen Stubbs gives a stellar performance as a young British woman who carries on an uneven affair with a French architect.

2003. *Nate and Hayes* (1983, Paramount, US/New Zealand, 100m, c, aka *Savage Islands*). P Lloyd Phillips & Rob Whitehouse, D Ferdinand Fairfax, W John Hughes & David Odell (based on a screen story by Odell and a story by Phillips), PH Tony Imi, M Trevor Jones, ED John Shirley, PD Maurice Cain.

LP Tommy Lee Jones (Capt. Bully Hayes), Michael O'Keefe (Nate Williamson), Max Phipps (Ben Pease), Jenny Seagrove (Sophie), Grant Tilly (Count von Rittenberg), Peter Rowley (Louis Beck), Bill Johnson (Rev. Williamson), Kate Harcourt (Mrs. Williamson).

This swashbuckler set in 19th century South Pacific has missionaries, imperalists, slavers and bootleggers carving up paradise. Pirate Tommy Lee Jones and missionary Michael O'Keefe share lovely Jenny Seagrove.

2004. *National Lampoon's Christmas Vacation* (1989, Warner, 97m, c). P John Hughes & Tom Jacobson, D Jeremiah S. Chechik, W Hughes, PH Thomas Ackerman, M Angelo Badalamenti, ED Jerry Greenberg, PD Stephen Marsh.

LP Chevy Chase (Clark Griswold, Jr.), Beverly D'Angelo (Ellen Griswold), Randy Quaid (Eddie), Diane Ladd (Nora), Mae Questel (Aunt Bethany), William Hickey (Uncle Lewis), John Randolph (Clark Griswold, Sr.), E.G. Marshall (Art), Doris Roberts (Frances), Julia Louis-Dreyfus (Margo Chester).

If your idea of humor is Chevy Chase taking a series of pratfalls, destruction of property, and double-entendres for the kindergarten set, then this third film about the middle–American Griswold family, will light your fire. As ever, Dad is a clumsy ass, Mom is a sexy patient soul, and the children are quarrelsome brats. The ho-hum collection of disjointed gags, which were funny in the first film, a bit drab in the second, are by now punchless. The saving grace of the film is Randy Quaid, who as Cousin Eddie, steals the movie.

2005. *National Lampoon's Class Reunion* (1982, 20th Century–Fox, 84m, c). P Matty Simmons, D Michael Miller, W John Hughes, PH Phil Lathrop, ED Richard C. Meyer & Ann Mills, PD Dean

Edward Mitzner, M/L Peter Bernstein & Mark Goldenberg.

LP Gerrit Graham (Bob Spinnaker), Michael Lerner (Dr. Young), Fred McCarren (Gary Nash), Miriam Flynn (Bunny Packard), Stephen Furst (Hubert Downs), Marya Small (Iris Augen), Shelley Smith (Meredith Modess), Zane Buzby (Delores Salk).

The producers of this stupid, unfunny movie attempt to combine a comical class reunion with a slasher-like horror story. It's gross and totally inept.

2006. *National Lampoon's European Vacation* (1985, Warner, 95m, c). P Matty Simmons & Stuart Cornfield, D Amy Heckerling, W John Hughes & Robert Klane (based on a story by Hughes), PH Robert Paynter, M Charles Fox, ED Pembroke Herring, PD Robert Cartwright.

LP Chevy Chase (Clark W. Griswold), Beverly D'Angelo (Ellen Griswold), Dana Hill (Audrey Griswold), Jason Lively (Rusty Griswold), John Astin (Kent), Eric Idle (Bike Rider), Elizabeth Arlen (Mrs. Garland), David Gersh (Mr. Garland), Sylvie Badalati (Cherie), William Zabka (Jack), Claudia Neidig (Claudia), Victor Lanoux (The Thief).

This sequel to *National Lampoon's Vacation* falls far short of its predecessor for giggly adolescent humor and the shock effect of strong language. The Griswolds win an all-expenses-paid European vacation, and then play ugly Americans in England, France, Germany and Italy. Let's hope they don't follow this one up with a vacation trip to the Orient, or Africa, or anyplace.

2007. *National Lampoon's Vacation* (1983, Warner, 98m, c). P Matty Simmons, D Harold Ramis, W John Hughes, PH Victor J. Kemper, M Ralph Burns, ED Pembroke Herring, PD Jack Collis.

LP Chevy Chase (Clark Griswold), Beverly D'Angelo (Ellen Griswold), Imogene Coca (Aunt Edna), Randy Quaid (Cousin Eddie), Anthony Michael Hall (Rusty Griswold), Dana Barron (Audrey Griswold), Eddie Bracken (Roy Walley), Christie Brinkley (Girl in Red Ferrari), John Candy (Lasky).

This is a funny movie. It's not adult humor but it's the kind that just breaks up youngsters who like seeing a supposedly responsible adult like Chevy Chase screw up time after time, while his two teenage kids Anthony Michael Hall and Dana Barron are so much more with it than their accident prone Dad. Chase insists on driving his wife and two kids from Chicago to California for a trip to a Disney-like amusement park. Along the way, he ruins his new station wagon, loses his credit cards, picks up his wife's aunt, Imogene Coca, who expires during the trip, kills a mean dog he forgot was tied to the bumper of his car, has a running flirtation with Christie Brinkley, and gets his family into the closed-for-repairs amusement park by brandishing a gun.

2008. *Native Son* (1986, Cinecom, 112m, c). P Diane Silver, D Jerrold Freedman, W Richard Wesley (based on the novel by Richard Wright), PH Thomas Burstyn, M James Mtume, ED Aaron Stell, PD Stephen Marsh.

LP Carroll Baker (Mrs. Dalton), Akosua Busia (Bessie), Matt Dillon (Jan), Art Evans (Doc), John Karlen (Max), Victor Love (Bigger Thomas), Elizabeth McGovern (Mary Dalton), John McMartin (Mr. Dalton), Geraldine Page (Peggy), Willard E. Pugh (Gus), Oprah Winfrey (Mrs. Thomas).

This is the second filming of Richard Wright's acclaimed novel of an unfortunate black man who is sentenced to death after accidentally murdering a white girl. This version provides considerable nudity, violence and gore.

2009. *The Natural* (1984, Tri-Star, 134m, c). P Mark Johnson, D Barry Levinson, W Roger Towne & Phil Dusenberry (based on the novel by Bernard Malamud), PH Caleb Deschanel†, M Randy Newman†, ED Stu Linder, PD Angelo Graham & Mel Bourne, AD/SD Graham, Bourne, James J. Murakami, Speed Hopkins, Bruce Weintraub†.

LP Robert Redford (Roy Hobbs), Robert Duvall (Max Mercy), Glenn Close† (Iris), Kim Basinger (Memo Paris), Wilford Brimley (Pop Fisher), Barbara Hershey (Harriet Bird), Robert Prosky (The Judge), Darren McGavin (Gambler), Richard Farnsworth (Red Blow), Joe Don Baker (The Whammer), John Finnegan (Sam Simpson).

Robert Redford stars in a baseball story which captures the special importance the game holds for fans while also presenting it as something mystical and bigger than life. At the beginning he's a 19-year-old on the way to the big leagues. Unfortunately he gets waylaid by mysterious Barbara Hershey who associates sex with the death of those who are the best at something. She shoots Redford and that puts his baseball career on hold for 15 years. He joins the New York Knights, a team with a terrible record. Soon he shows signs of being the team's savior with his herculean home runs and leadership. The team's owner Robert Prosky can make more money if his team doesn't win the pennant. He sicks sexy Kim Basinger onto Redford and she takes her toll on the man. Fortunately for Redford and the Knights, his long lost girlfriend Glenn Close shows up and inspires him to win the pennant with what almost proves to be his last ounce of strength.

2010. *The Navigator* (1989, Arena-film–Film Investment Group of New Zealand, Australia, 92m, c). P John Maynard & Gary Hannam, D Vincent Ward, W Ward, Kelly Lyons & Geoff Chapple, PH Geoffrey Simpson, M Davood A. Tabrizi, ED John Scott, PD Sally Campbell.

LP Bruce Lyons (Connor), Chris Haywood (Arno), Hamish McFarlane (Griffin), Marshall Napier (Searle), Noel Appleby (Ulf), Paul Livingston (Martin), Sarah Pierse (Linnet).

This strange film begins in 1348 in Cumbria, New England. Young psychic Hamish McFarlane dreams of a way to save his village from the advancing black plague. Somehow, he and four others get transported to the present time in New Zealand with a mission which will save their people.

2011. *Near Dark* (1987, DeLaurentiis Entertainment Group, 95m, c). P Steven-Charles Jaffe & Eric Red, D Kathryn Bigelow, W Red & Bigelow, PH Adam Greenberg, M Tangerine Dream, ED Howard Smith, PD Stephen Altman.

LP Adrian Pasdar (Caleb), Jenny Wright (Mae), Lance Henriksen (Jesse), Bill Paxton (Severen), Jenette Goldstein (Diamondback), Tim Thomerson (Loy), Joshua Miller (Homer), Marcie Leeds (Sarah).

In this stylish horror movie, farmhand Adrian Pasdar finds himself drawn to a band of nomadic vampires led by a Civil War veteran.

2012. *Necromancer* (1989, Bonnaire Films/Spectrum, 88m, c). P Roy Mc-Aree, D Dusty Nelson, W Bill Naud, PH Richard Clabaugh, Eric Cayla, M Gary Stockdale, Kevin Klinger & Bob Mamet, ED Carole A. Kenneally.

LP Elizabeth Kaitan (Julie), Russ Tamblyn (Prof. Charles DeLonge), John Tyler (Eric), Rhonda Durton (Freda), Stan Hurwitz (Paul), Edward Wright (Carl), Shawn Eisner (Allan), Waide A. Riddle (Ernest), Lois Masten (Lisa, a Necromancer).

Acting student Elizabeth Kaitan, gang raped by her classmates, is blackmailed into not reporting the attack. Her roommate talks Kaitan into answering a "revenge" ad in the newspaper. Kaitan makes contact with necromancer Lois Masten who has contacts with the devil. Masten uses her client's desire for revenge to assume Kaitan's form, seduce her attackers and kill them.

2013. *Necropolis* (1987, Empire, 76m, c). P Cynthia DePaula & Tim Kincaid, D&W Bruce Hickey, PH Arthur D. Marks, M Don Great & Tom Milano, ED Barry Zetlin & Tom Meshelski, SE Ed French.

LP Leanne Baker (Eva), Jacquie Fitz (Dawn), Michael Conte (Billy), William K. Reed (Rev. Henry James), Paul Ruben (Benny), Andrew Bausili (Tony/Preacher), Gy Mirano (Rosa), Letnam Yekim (Rudy).

Three-hundred-year-old witch Leanne Baker (looking very good for her age) is in Manhattan trying to complete a ceremonial virgin sacrifice which was interrupted in 1685.

2014. *Neighbors* (1981, Columbia, 95m, c). P Richard D. Zanuck & David Brown, D John G. Avildsen, W Larry Gelbart (based on the novel by Thomas Berger), PH Gerald Hirschfeld, M Bill Conti, ED Jane Kurson, PD Peter Larkin.

LP John Belushi (Earl Keese), Kathryn Walker (Enid Keese), Cathy Moriarty (Ramona), Dan Aykroyd (Vic), Igors Gavon (Chic), Dru-Ann Chukron (His

Wife), Tim Kazurinsky (Pa Greavy), Tino Insana (Perry).

John Belushi and wife Kathryn Walker are a sedate suburban couple whose lives are turned upside down when Dan Aykroyd and wife Cathy Moriarty move next door. The latter couple is completely wacko. It's not a laugh-a-minute but one is always curious as to what the next outrageous stunt might be.

2015.   *Neon Maniacs* (1986, Bedford, 91m, c). P Steven Mackler & Chris Arnold, D Joseph Mangine, W Mark Patrick Carducci, PH Mangine & Oliver Wood, M Kendall Schmidt, ED Timothy Snell.

LP Allan Hayes (Steven), Leilani Sarelle (Nathalie), Donna Locke (Paula), Victor Elliot Brandt (Devin).

An unstoppable hideous incarnation of evil zombies terrorizes San Francisco, killing at will. They are called neon maniacs because they can only be seen in the dark.

2016.   *The Nest* (1988, Concorde, 88m, c). P Julie Corman, D Terence H. Winkless, W Robert King (based on a novel by Eli Cantor [Gregory A. Douglas]), PH Ricardo Jacques Gale, M Rick Conrad, ED James A. Stewart & Stephen Mark, SE Cary Howe.

LP Robert Lansing (Mayor Elias Johnson), Lisa Langlois (Elizabeth Johnson), Franc Luz (Sheriff Richard Tarbell), Terri Treas (Dr. Morgan Hubbard), Stephen Davies (Homer), Diana Bellamy (Mrs. Pennington).

Trouble comes to a sleepy California port town when the scientists of a powerful corporation develop a super breed of cockroaches that wants meat—cats, dogs, cattle, humans. To make matters worse the bugs become what they eat, hideous half-roachs, half-dinner. Gross!

2017.   *The Nesting* (1981, Feature Films, 104m, c, aka *Phobia*). P&D Armand Weston, W Weston & Daria Price, PH Joao Fernandes, M Jack Malken & Kim Scholes, ED Jack Foster, SE Matt Vogel.

LP Robin Groves (Lauren Cochran), Christopher Loomis (Mark Felton), Michael David Lally (Daniel Griffiths), John Carradine (Col. LeBrun), Gloria Grahame (Florinda Costello), Bill Rowley (Frank Beasley).

Robin Groves, a writer of gothic thriller novels, attempts to overcome her writer's block by moving into a secluded Victorian mansion. It has a gruesome-gory past and in the present turns Groves' life into a living hall.

Never Cry Devil see Night Visitor

2018.   *Never Cry Wolf* (1983, Buena Vista, 91m, c). P Lewis Allen, Jack Couffer & Joseph Strick, D Carroll Ballard, W Curtis Hanson, Sam Hamm, Richard Kletter, C.M. Smith, Eugene Corr & Christina Luescher (based on the book by Farley Mowat), PH Hiro Narita, M Mark Isham, ED Peter Parasheles & Michael Chandler, SOUND Alan R. Splet, Todd Boekelheide, Randy Thom & David Parker†.

LP Charles Martin Smith (Tyler), Brian Dennehy (Rosie), Zachary Ittimangnaq (Ootek), Samson Jorah (Mike), Hugh Webster (Drunk), Martha Ittimangnaq (Woman).

Scientist Charles Martin Smith is chosen to study Alaskan wolves to determine if they are responsible for the disappearing caribou herds. It's a top-notch, gripping animal adventure film.

2019.   *Never Never Land* (1982, Sharp, GB, 86m, c). P Diane Baker, D Paul Annett, W Marjorie L. Sigley, PH Brian West, M Ron Grainer, ED Teddy Darvas.

LP Petula Clark (Bee Melvin), Cathleen Nesbitt (Edith Forbes), Anne Seymour (Zena), Michael J. Shannon (Peter), John Castle (Jim), Evelyn Laye (Millie), Roland Culver (Old Man on Park Bench), Heather Miller (Jennie Harris).

Heather Miller, a lonely child, resorts to manufacturing playmates from her imagination and fairy tales. She develops a friendship with Cathleen Nesbitt, who is suffering from loneliness because of her advanced age.

2020.   *Never on Tuesday* (1989, Palisades, 90m, c). P Brad Wyman & Lionel Wigram, D&W Adam Rifkin, PH Alan Jones, M Richard Stone, ED Ed Rothkowitz, PD Bobby Bernhardt.

LP Claudia Christian (Tuesday), Andrew Lauer (Matt), Pete Berg (Eddie), Gilbert Gottfried (Larry Lupin), Charlie

Sheen (Thief), Judd Nelson (Motorcycle Cop), Emilio Estevez (Tow-truck man).

Made in 1987, this piece showcases the beauty of Claudia Christian. Her car is involved in a crash with the car of Andrew Lauer and Pete Berg, leaving all three stranded. No one stops to pick them up. Christian deflates the lecherous boys by announcing she's a lesbian. The cameo appearances of young stars Charlie Sheen, Judd Nelson and Emilio Estevez gives the film a chance in the video market.

2021. *Never Say Die* (1989, Everard Films, New Zealand, 103m, c). P Geoff Murphy & Murray Newey, D&W Murphy, PH Rory O'Shea, M Billy Kristian, ED Scott Conrad, PD Bill Gruar.

LP Temuera Morrison (Alf), Lisa Eilbacher (Melissa), Tony Barry (Insp. Evans), George Wendt (Witten), John Clarke, Martyn Sanderson, Phillip Gordon, Judith Fyfe.

Temuera Morrison, back in New Zealand with his American girlfriend Lisa Eilbacher, is convinced that someone is out to kill one or both of them. While hiding out on an island, they kill an intruder who may or may not have been following them, and now they also have the police on their trail. It's a skimpy plot, but the cast and director Geoff Murphy make it work.

2022. *Never Say Never Again* (1983, Warner, 137m, c). P Jack Schwartzman, D Irvin Kershner, W Lorenzo Semple, Jr. (based on a story by Kevin McClory, Jack Whittingham & Ian Fleming), PH Douglas Slocombe, M Michel Legrand, ED Robert Lawrence & Ian Crafford, PD Philip Harrison & Stephen Grimes, AD Leslie Dilley, Michael White & Roy Stannard, SD Peter Howitt, SE David Dryer & Ian Wingrove.

LP Sean Connery (James Bond), Klaus Maria Brandauer (Largo), Max von Sydow (Ernst Stavro Blofeld), Barbara Carrera (Fatima Blush), Kim Basinger (Domino), Bernie Casey (Felix Leiter), Alec McCowen (Q/Algy), Edward Fox (M), Pamela Salem (Miss Moneypenny), Rowan Atkinson (Small-Fawcett).

After a 12 year absence, Sean Connery once again takes up the role of 007, with even more charm than before, but unfortunately in an inferior story. *Spectre* is still looking for world domination, with Klaus Maria Brandauer a nice grinning villain. His mistress Kim Basinger is the good girl of the piece, but Barbara Carrera makes a nasty and deadly lover.

2023. *Never Too Young to Die* (1986, Paul Entertainment, 92m, c). P Steven Paul, D Gil Bettman, W Lorenzo Semple, Steven Paul, Anton Fritz & Bettman (based on a story by Stuart Paul & Steven Paul), PH David Worth, M Various Artists, ED Bill Anderson, Paul Seydor & Ned Humphreys, PD Dale Allen Pelton.

LP John Stamos (Lance Stargrove), Vanity (Danja Deering), Gene Simmons (Velvet Von Ragner/Carruthers), George Lazenby (Drew Stargrove), Peter Kwong (Cliff), Ed Brock (Pyramid), John Anderson (Arliss), Robert Englund (Riley).

Gene Simmons, a vicious hermaphrodite, wants control of the city. Only heroic John Stamos and beautiful Vanity stand in the way of the perverse villain. George Lazenby, who had a brief career as James Bond in *On Her Majesty's Secret Service* in 1969 has a supporting role. Robert Englund went on to bigger things in the *Nightmare on Elm Street* series.

2024. *The New Adventures of Pippi Longstocking* (1988, Columbia, 100m, c). P Gary Mehlman, Walter Moshay & Ken Annakin, D&W Annakin (based on the books by Astrid Lindgren), PH Roland "Ozzie" Smith, M Misha Segal, ED Ken Zemke, PD Jack Senter.

LP Tami Erin (Pippi), David Seaman, Jr. (Tommy), Cory Crow (Annika), Eileen Brennan (Miss Bannister), Dennis Dugan (Mr. Settigren), Dianne Hull (Mrs. Settigren), George Di Cenzo (Mr. Blackhart), J.D. Dickinson (Rype), Chub Bailly (Rancid), Dick Van Patten (Glue Man).

If you're a kid, you're bound to admire Pippi's notions of irresponsibility, anarchy, and doing precisely what she likes. Fortunately for Pippi and her friends such attitudes and behavior don't require them to do anything really bad. All Astrid Lindgren's little tomboy with the wired pigtails and permanent smile wants is for everyone to have fun.

2025. *The New Kids* (1985, Columbia, 90m, c). P Sean S. Cunningham & Andrew Fogelson, D Cunningham, W

Stephen Gyllenhaal (based on a story by Gyllenhaal & Brian Taggert), PH Steven Poster, M Lalo Schifrin, ED Rita Roland.

LP Shannon Presby (Loren), Lori Loughlin (Abby), James Spader (Dutra), John Philbin (Gideon), David H. MacDonald (Moonie), Vincent Grant (Joe Bob), Theron Montgomery (Gordo), Eric Stoltz (Mark).

Shannon Presby and Lori Loughlin try to make friends at their new high school but get in bad with town bully, James Spader, when they refuse to accept his superiority. Things get violent in this trashy horror film from gore expert Sean S. Cunningham.

2026. *A New Life* (1988, Paramount, 104m, c). P Martin Bregman, D&W Alan Alda, PH Kelvin Pike, M Joseph Turrin, ED William Reynolds, PD Barbara Dunphy.

LP Alan Alda (Steve Giardino), Ann-Margret (Jackie Giardino), Hal Linden (Mel Arons), Veronica Hamel (Dr. Kay Hutton), John Shea (Doc), Mary Kay Place (Donna), Beatrice Alda (Judy), David Eisner (Billy), Victoria Snow (Audrey).

Ann-Margret leaves husband Alan Alda because he neglects her. After dating some of the usual creeps waiting for newly divorced women, she discovers John Shea, a young sculptor, who caters to her every whim. Meanwhile Alda discovers that the bar scene and dating has changed a great deal since he last sought female company. He suffers a mild heart attack and falls in love with his physician Veronica Hamel. They marry and despite reservations, he agrees to her desire to have a child. Things don't look too good for his new marriage, but writer-director Alda comes up with a pat solution to all problems. He even has Ann-Margret grow weary of the constant attention, dump Shea and find happiness in a career as a teacher.

2027. *New Year's Day* (1989, International Rainbow Picture, 89m, c). P Judith Wolinsky, D&W Henry Jaglom, PH Hanania Baer & Nesya Blue.

LP Maggie Jakobson (Lucy), Gwen Welles (Annie), Melanie Winter (Winona), Henry Jaglom (Drew), David Duchovny (Billy), Milos Forman (Lazlo),

Michael Emil (Dr. Stadthagen), Tracy Reiner (Marjorie).

In the midst of a midlife crisis, Henry Jaglom returns to his New York apartment from L.A. There he finds three young women who thought they had until the end of the day to get out. Jaglom immediately takes an interest in their personal problems as well as sharing his own with them. Throughout the day, several people stop by for a drink and to expose their souls to perfect strangers. Newcomer Maggie Jakobson appears to be a real find, a raven-haired beauty beloved by the camera.

2028. *New Year's Evil* (1980, Cannon, 90m, c). P Menahem Golan & Yoram Globus, D Emmett Alston, W Leonard Neubauer (based on a story by Alston, Neubauer), M Laurin Rinder & W. Michael Lewis.

LP Roz Kelly (Diane Sullivan), Kip Niven (Richard Sullivan), Louisa Moritz (Sally), Chris Wallace (Lt. Clayton), Jed Mills (Ernie), Grant Cramer (Derek Sullivan), Taaffe O'Connell (Jane).

In this horrid horror film, psychopath Kip Niven plans to execute one person an hour on New Year's Eve. He calls Roz Kelly, a disk jockey hosting a punk rock party, and keeps her informed of his killings. Then he invades the party and tries to kill off Kelly.

2029. *New York Nights* (1984, Bedford, 102m, c). P Romano Vanderbes, D Simon Nuchtern, W Vanderbes (based on the play *Reigen* by Arthur Schnitzler), PH Alan Doberman, M Linda Schreyer, ED Victor Zimet.

LP Corinne Alphen (Brooke), George Ayer (Jesse), Bobbi Burns (Leonora Woolf), Peter Matthey (Werner Richards), Missy O'Shea (Christina), Nicholas Cortland (Harris), Marcia McBroom (Nicki), Cynthia Lee (Margo), William Dysart (Owen).

In this "La Ronde"-like tale, nine rich and glamorous New Yorkers have a set of overlapping affairs. It's pretty tame and trite stuff.

2030. *New York Stories* (1989, Touchstone Pictures, 130m, c). P Robert Greenhut, Fred Roos and Fred Fuchs & Barbara DeFina, D Woody Allen, Francis Coppola & Martin Scorsese, W Allen, Francis and Sofia Coppola & Richard Price, PH Sven Nykvist, Vittorio Storaro & Nestor Almendros, M Various Artists & Composers, ED Susan E. Morse, Barry Malkin & Thelma Schoonmaker, PD Santo Loquasto, Dean Tavoularis & Kristi Zea.

LP *Oedipus Wrecks:* Woody Allen (Sheldon Mills), Marvin Chatinover (Psychiatrist), Mae Questel (Mother), Mia Farrow (Lisa), Julie Kavner (Treva); *Life Without Zoe:* Heather McComb (Zoe), Talia Shire (Charlotte), Giancarlo Giannini (Claudio), Don Novello (Hector), Carole Bouquet (Princess Soroya); *Life Lessons:* Nick Nolte (Lionel Dobie), Patrick O'Neal (Phillip Fowler), Rosanna Arquette (Paulette), Jesse Borrego (Reuben Toro).

This film is the work of three major directors and cinematographers. In Woody Allen's piece, he's a lawyer whose mother, Mae Questel, without meaning to be cruel, embarrasses him at every opportunity. She's marvelous. Just be happy she's someone else's mother. Francis Coppola's contribution features Heather McComb as a latter-day little Eloise who lives in a large luxury hotel and loves to shop. Martin Scorsese gets his oar in with renowned painter Nick Nolte, obsessively in love with his assistant Rosanna Arquette who has grown weary of her role as his inspiration.

2031. *New York's Finest* (1988, Platinum, 86m, c). P&D Chuck Vincent, W Craig Horrall, PH Larry Revene, M Joey Mennonna, ED James Davalos & Marc Ubell.

LP Jennifer Delora (Loretta Michaels), Ruth Collins (Joy Sugarman), Heidi Paine (Carley Pointer), Scott Baker (Dougie), Jane Hamilton [Veronica Hart] (Bunny), Alan Naggar (Fillmore), John Altamura (Brian Morrison), Alan Fisler (Tennison Alderman), Josey Duval (Papillion).

In a take-off on *How to Marry a Millionaire,* three low-class hookers, Jennifer Delora, Ruth Collins and Heidi Paine, take lessons on being "ladies" from a transvestite, rent a luxury apartment and set out to catch rich husbands. They are forced to live double lives when a blackmailing madame forces them to alternate turning tricks with out-of-town johns and dating socialites. Things don't work out quite as they hoped but they do find three guys who want to marry them despite their pasts.

2032. *The Newlydeads* (1988, City Lights, 77m, c). P Richard Pepin & Joseph Merhi, D Merhi, W Sean Dash & Merhi, PH Pepin, M John Gonzalez, SE Judy Yonemoto.

LP Jim Williams, Jean Levine, Jay Richardson, Roxanna Michaels, Scott Kaske, Rebecca Barrington, Michael Springer, Michelle Smith.

Jim Williams takes his new bride to a honeymoon hotel, where 15 years earlier he killed a transvestite when he discovered that she was a he. The decaying body of his victim seeks revenge.

2033. *Next of Kin* (1989, Warner, 108m, c). P Les Alexander & Don Enright, D John Irvin, W Michael Jenning (based, uncredited, on screenplay by Jenning & Jeb Stuart), PH Steven Poster, M Jack Nitzsche, ED Peter Honess, PD Jack T. Collis.

LP Patrick Swayze (Truman Gates), Liam Neeson (Briar Gates), Adam Baldwin (Joey Rosselini), Helen Hunt (Jessie Gates), Andreas Katsulas (John Isabella), Bill Paxton (Gerald Gates), Ben Stiller (Lawrence Isabella), Michael J. Pollard (Harold).

When Kentucky hills boy Bill Paxton is ruthlessly killed by mafia enforcer Adam Baldwin, Paxton's brother, Chicago cop Patrick Swayze, is determined to find the killer. Swayze's older brother Liam Neeson wants an eye-for-an-eye vengeance. The climatic scene is an elaborate battle in a Chicago cemetery between Baldwin's mobsters and Neeson's Kentucky kin.

2034. *The Next One* (1982, Allstar, US/Greece, 105m, c). D&W Nico Mastorakis, PH Ari Stavrou, M Stanley Myers, PD Paul Acciari.

LP Keir Dullea (Glenn), Adrienne Barbeau (Andrea Johnson), Jeremy Licht (Tim Johnson), Peter Hobbs (Dr. Barnaby Caldwell).

In a mediocre fantasy film, Keir Dullea, a Christ-like visitor from the future, washes up on a Greek island where Adrienne Barbeau is living with her son. She falls in love with Dullea.

2035. *Ngati* (1987, Pacific Films, New Zealand, 88m, c). P John O'Shea, D Barry Barclay, W Tama Poata, PH Rory O'Shea, M Dalvanius, ED Dell King.

LP Tuta Ngarimu Tamati (Uncle Eru), Ngawai Harrison (Hine), Wi Kuki Kaa (Iwi), Oliver Jones (Ropata), Ross Girven (Greg Shaw), Johnny Coleman (Drover), Judy McIntosh (Jenny Bennett), Barry Allen (Headmaster).

In the first film written and directed by Maoris, a young Australian, fresh from medical school, is to be sent on a world tour by his father on the condition that he visit a tiny New Zealand village where he was born. While there he feels right at home and learns that his mother had been a Maori. Eventually, he decides to stay and serve his people's medical needs, just as his father hoped he would.

2036. *Nice Girls Don't Explode* (1987, New World, 92m, c). P Doug Curtis & John Wells, D Chuck Martinez, W Paul Harris, PH Stephen Katz, M Brian Banks & Anthony Marinelli, ED Wende Phifer Mate, PD Sarina Rotstein.

LP Barbara Harris (Mom), Michelle Meyrink (April), William O'Leary (Andy), Wallace Shawn (Ellen), James Nardini (Ken), Margot Gray (Little April), Jonas Baugham (Little Andy), William Kuhlke (Dr. Stewart).

Most girls raise the temperatures of their boyfriends, but Michelle Meyrink all but lights them up. She has a tendency to start fires telekinetically when confronted with members of the opposite sex to whom she is attracted, such as William O'Leary. But her mom, Barbara Harris, knows more about the problem than she's telling.

2037. *Nickel Mountain* (1985, Ziv International, 88m, c). P Jacob Magnusson, D&W Drew Denbaum (based on the novel by John Gardner), PH David Bridges, M Lincoln Mayorga, ED Robert Jenkis.

LP Michael Cole (Henry Soames), Heather Langenkamp (Callie Wells), Patrick Cassidy (Willard Freund), Brian Kerwin (George), Grace Zabriskie (Ellie Wells), Don Beddoe (Doc Cathey), Ed Lauter (W.D. Freund), Harry Northrup (Frank).

When 16-year-old waitress Heather Langenkamp becomes pregnant, she is offered money for an abortion by the father's father. Instead she accepts the marriage proposal of overweight Michael Cole, a one-time suitor of her mother's, now suffering from a heart condition.

2038. *The Night Before* (1988, Kings Road, 85m, c). P Martin Hornstein, D Thom Eberhardt, W Gregory Scherick & Eberhardt (based on a story by Scherick), PH Ron Garcia, PD Michel Levesque.

LP Keanu Reeves (Winston Connelly), Lori Loughlin (Tara Mitchell), Theresa Saldana (Rhonda), Trinidad Silva (Tito), Suzanne Snyder (Lisa), Morgan Lofting (Mom), Gwil Richards (Dad), Michael Greene (Capt. Mitchell).

Filmed in 1986, this movie was minimally released. Keanu Reeves' prom date Lori Loughlin, daughter of a mean police captain, has only accepted his invitation after losing a bet. Reeves accidentally sells her to a pimp, loses his virginity with a whore and is just able to rescue Loughlin and get her home before midnight as he promised her dad.

2039. *Night Crossing* (1982, Buena Vista, 106m, c). P Tom Leetch, D Delbert Mann, W John McGreevey, PH Tony Imi, M Jerry Goldsmith, ED Gordon D. Brenner, PD Rolf Zehetbauer.

LP John Hurt (Peter Strelzyks), Jane Alexander (Doris Strelzyks), Doug McKeon (Frank Strelzyks), Keith McKeon (Fitscher Strelzyks), Beau Bridges (Gunter Wetzel), Glynnis O'Connor (Petra Wetzel), Geoffrey Liesik (Little Peter Wetzel), Michael Liesik (Andreas Wetzel).

In a true story, two families escape from East to West Germany via a hot-air balloon. Unfortunately, the adventure is dully presented.

2040. *Night Game* (1989, Trans-World, 95m, c). P George Litto, D Peter Masterson, W Spencer Eastman & Anthony Palmer (based on a story by Eastman), PH Fred Murphy, M Pino Donaggio, ED Robert Barrere.

LP Roy Scheider (Seaver), Karen

Young (Roxy), Richard Bradford (Nelson), Paul Gleason (Broussard), Carlin Glynn (Alma), Lane Smith (Witty), Anthony Palmer (Mendoza), Alex Morris (Gries).

In Galveston, Texas, veteran police officer Roy Scheider is tracking down a serial killer who has been using a grappling hook to slash the throats of young women along the city's beach front. There's a relationship between the killings, the strikeout victories of a star pitcher with the Houston Astros and the fact that Scheider was a former minor league baseball player.

2041. *Night Games* (1980, Avco Embassy, 100m, c). P Andre Morgan & Robert Lewis, D Roger Vadim, W Anton Diether & Clarke Reynolds (based on a story by Diether & Barth Jules Sussman), PH Denis Lewiston, M John Barry, ED Peter Hunt, PD Robert Laing.

LP Cindy Pickett (Valerie), Joanna Cassidy (Julie), Barry Primus (Jason), Paul Jenkins (Sion), Gene Davis (Timothy), Juliet Fabriga (Alicia), Clem Parsons (Jun), Carla Reynolds (Valerie at 13).

Due to a childhood rape, beautiful Cindy Pickett has horrible nightmares and a fear of sex which threatens to ruin her marriage. Her choice of a sex therapist is not prudent.

2042. *A Night in Heaven* (1983, 20th Century–Fox, 83m, c). P Gene Kirkwood & Howard W. Koch, Jr., D John G. Avildsen, W Joan Tewkesbury, PH David Quaid, M Jan Hammer, ED Avildsen, PD William Cassidy.

LP Christopher Atkins (Rick), Lesley Ann Warren (Faye), Robert Logan (Whitney), Deborah Rush (Patsy), Deney Terrio (Tony), Sandra Beall (Slick), Alix Elias (Shirley), Carrie Snodgress (Mrs. Johnson).

Married college professor Lesley Ann Warren attends a male striptease club, where she discovers Christopher Atkins, a student flunking her course, is the star attraction. Somehow the unlikely twosome get together for a brief affair, which means next to nothing to Atkins, and seems to be as much pain as pleasure for Warren.

2043. *A Night in the Life of Jimmy Reardon* (1988, 20th Century–Fox, 92m, c). P Russell Schwartz, D&W William Richert (based on his novel *Aren't You Even Gonna Kiss Me Goodbye?*), PH John Connor, M Bill Conti, ED Suzanne Fenn, PD Norman Newberry.

LP River Phoenix (Jimmy Reardon), Ann Magnuson (Joyce Fickett), Meredith Salenger (Lisa Bentwright), Ione Skye (Denise Hunter), Louanne (Suzie Middleberg), Matthew L. Perry (Fred Roberts), Paul Koslo (Al Reardon), Jane Hallaren (Faye Rearden), Jason Court (Mathew Hollander).

Teenage lothario River Phoenix plans to duck his parents' plans for him to attend college by running off to Hawaii with rich Meredith Salenger. Not just another teen sexploitation film, it is highly personal, which isn't too surprising, since it is based on director William Richert's novel written when he was 19. Phoenix has no trouble finding female bed companions—they seem to materialize without even a fantasy thought on his part. When Salenger decides she's ready to sacrifice her virginity to Phoenix, she's too late—he's just had a fling with a friend of his mom, and he's not quite up to accommodating Salenger.

2044. *Night Life* (1989, Wild Night/ Creative Movie Marketing, 89m, c). P Charles Lippincott, D David Acomba, W Keith Critchlow, PH Roger Tonry, M Roger Bouland, ED Michael Bateman, PD Philip Thomas.

LP Scott Grimes (Archie Melville), Cheryl Pollak (Charly), John Astin (Verlin Flanders), Anthony Geary, Alan Blumenfeld, Kenneth Ian Davis, Darcy DeMoss, Lisa Fuller.

Scott Grimes works in his uncle's mortuary. He takes a lot of kidding from two football jocks and their cheerleading girlfriends. When the latter four are killed in a car accident, they end up in Grimes' care, but a lightning storm brings back to life to torment Grimes some more.

2045. *'Night, Mother* (1986, Universal, 96m, c). P Aaron Spelling & Alan Greisman, D Tom Moore, W Marsha Norman (based on her play), PH Stephen M. Katz,

M David Shire, ED Suzanne Pettit, PD Jack De Govia.

LP Sissy Spacek (Jessie Cates), Anne Bancroft† (Thelma Cates), Ed Berke (Dawson Cates), Carol Robbins (Loretta Cates), Jennifer Roosendahl (Melodie Cates), Michael Kenworthy (Kenny Cates).

Anne Bancroft chews up the scenery as the mother of unhappy Sissy Spacek. The latter plans to commit suicide in her mother's house, but not before the two almost talk each other to death. It's a depressing subject, depressingly presented and depressingly acted.

Night of the Claw see Island Claws

2046. *Night of the Comet* (1984, Atlantic, 95m, c). P Andrew Lane & Wayne Crawford, D&W Thom Eberhardt, PH Arthur Albert, M David Richard Campbell, ED Fred Stafford, PD John Muto, SE Court Wizard.

LP Robert Beltran (Hector), Catherine Mary Stewart (Regina), Kelli Maroney (Samantha), Sharon Farrell (Doris), Mary Woronov (Audrey), Geoffrey Lewis (Carter), John Achorn (Oscar), Michael Bowen (Larry).

In this smart comedy the world almost comes to an end, leaving only a few California Valley girls left to fight over Robert Beltran, a surviving man. Armed to the teeth they enter the city for an ultimate shopping spree and encounter degenerate zombies who were only partially exposed to a destructive comet's rays.

2047. *Night of the Creeps* (1986, Tri-Star, 85m, c, aka *Homecoming Night*). P Charles Gordon, D&W Fred Dekker, PH Robert C. New, M Barry DeVorzon, ED Michael N. Knue, PD George Costello.

LP Jason Lively (Chris), Steve Marshall (J.C.), Jill Whitlow (Cynthia), Tom Atkins (Ray), Wally Taylor (Det. Landis), Bruce Solomon (Sgt. Raimi), Vic Polizos (Coroner), Allan J. Kayser (Brad).

In this humorous horror film, which pays homage to the genre, a college campus is ravaged by gruesome creatures that turn their victims into zombies.

2048. *Night of the Demons* (1988, International Film Marketing, 89m, c). P Joe Augustyn, D Kevin S. Tenney, W Augustyn, PH David Lewis, M Dennis Michael Tenney, ED Daniel Duncan.

LP Lance Fenton (Jay), Cathy Podewell (Judy), Alvin Alexis (Roger), Hal Havins (Stooge), Mimi Kinkade (Angela), Linnea Quigley (Suzanne), Phillip Tanzini (Max), Jill Terashita (Fran), Allison Barron (Helen), William Gallo (Sal), Donnie Jeffcoat (Billy).

Teens hold a seance on Halloween in a funeral home. They conjure up more than they bargained for and find themselves sent into the pit of hell.

2049. *Night of the Juggler* (1980, Columbia, 100m, c). P Jay Weston, D Robert Butler, W Bill Norton, Sr. & Rick Natkin (based on the novel by William P. McGivern), PH Victor J. Kemper, M Artie Kane, ED Argyle Nelson, PD Stuart Wurtzel.

LP James Brolin (Sean Boyd), Cliff Gorman (Gus Soltic), Richard Castellano (Lt. Tonelli), Linda G. Miller (Barbara), Barton Heyman (Preacher), Sully Boyar (Larry), Julie Carmen (Marie).

Tough ex-cop James Brolin searches all the boroughs of New York for psychopath Cliff Gorman who has kidnapped his daughter.

Night of the Wehrmacht Zombies see Night of the Zombies

2050. *Night of the Zombies* (1981, NMD, 85m, c, aka *Gamma 693; Night of the Wehrmacht Zombies*). P Lorin E. Price, D&W Joel M. Reed, PH Ron Dorfman, M Onomatopoeia Inc., Matt Kaplowitz & Maggie Nolin, ED Samuel Pollard & Victor Kanefsky, SE Peter Kunz.

LP James Gillis (Nick Monroe), Ryan Hilliard (Dr. Proud), Samantha Grey (Susan), Ron Armstrong (Capt. Fleck), Richard de Faut (Sgt. Freedman), Juni Kulis (GRO Officer Schuller), Alphonse de Noble (CIA Agent), Joel M. Reed (Neo-Nazi).

Porno star James Gillis portrays a CIA agent on the trail of a gang of cannibalistic World War II zombie soldiers. They continue fighting the war even though it's over and they are dead.

2051. *Night Patrol* (1984, New World, 82m, c). P Bill Osco & Jackie

Kong, D Kong, W Osco, Kong, Murray Langston & Bill Levey, PH Jurg Walthers & Hanania Baer, ED Kong.

LP Linda Blair (Sue), Pat Paulsen (Kent), Jaye P. Morgan (Kate), Jack Riley (Dr. Ziegler), Billy Barty (Capt. Lewis), Murray Langston (Melvin/Unknown Comic), Pat Morita (Rape Victim), Sidney Lassick (Peeping Tom), Kent Perkins (Tex).

Some Gong Show alumni get together in a totally tasteless comedy and bore the hell out of audiences. Instead of stopping their act by hitting a gong, one should turn off the VCR. For those who might care, the story has cop Murray Langston wishing to be a comic. To keep his identity secret he performs with a paper bag over his head.

2052. *Night School* (1981, Paramount, 88m, c, aka *Terror Eyes*). P Larry Babb & Ruth Avergon, D Kenneth Hughes, W Avergon, PH Mark Irwin, M Brad Fiedel, ED Robert Reitano.

LP Leonard Mann (Lt. Judd Austin), Rachel Ward (Eleanor Adjai), Drew Snyder (Prof. Millett), Joseph R. Sicari (Taj), Nicholas Cairis (Gus).

Women who attend a local night school are being found decapitated. Police investigator Leonard Mann discovers the murders are part of a demonic ritual.

2053. *Night Shadows* (1984, Film Ventures, 99m, c, aka *Mutant*). P Igo Kantor, D John "Bud" Cardos, W Peter Z. Orton, Michael Jones & John C. Kruize (based on a story by Jones & Kruize), PH Al Taylor, M Richard Band, ED Michael J. Duthie, SE Paul Stewart.

LP Wings Hauser (Josh), Bo Hopkins (Sheriff Will Stewart), Lee [Harcourt] Montgomery (Mike), Jennifer Warren (Dr. Myra Tate), Jody Medford (Holly), Marc Clement (Albert), Cary Guffey (Billy).

When brothers Wings Hauser and Lee Montgomery take a trip to rural Georgia, they catch hell from both rednecks and zombies.

2054. *Night Shift* (1982, Warner, 105m, c). P Brian Grazer, D Ron Howard, W Lowell Ganz & Babaloo Mandel, PH James Crabe, M Burt Bacharach, ED Robert J. Kern, Jr., Daniel P. Hanley & Mike Hill, PD Jack Collis.

LP Henry Winkler (Chuck Lumley), Michael Keaton (Bill Blazejowski), Shelley Long (Belinda Keaton), Gina Hecht (Charlotte Koogle), Pat Corley (Edward Koogle), Bobby DiCicco (Leonard), Nita Talbot (Vivian), Basil Hoffman (Drollhauser), Tim Rossovich (Luke).

Night shift morgue attendants Henry Winkler and Michael Keaton pick up hooker Shelley Long, who has lost her pimp. They offer her and other working girls the use of the morgue as a nighttime brothel. Winkler, falling in love with Long, and mobsters wanting to muscle in on the action, cause complications.

2055. *The Night Stalker* (1987, Almi, 89m, c). P Don Edmonds, D Max Kleven, W John Goff & Edmonds, PH Don Burgess, M David Kitay, ED Stanford C. Allen, PD Allen Terry.

LP Charles Napier (Sgt. J.J. Striker), Michelle Reese (Rene), Katherine Kelly Lang (Denise), Robert Viharo (Charlie Garrett), Joey Gian (Buddy Brown), Robert Zdar (Sommers), Leila Carlin (Terry), Gary Crosby (Vic Gallegher).

Charles Napier is seeking a killer, impervious to bullets, who murders prostitutes and paints their bodies with Chinese characters.

2056. *The Night the Lights Went Out in Georgia* (1981, Avco Embassy, 110m, c). P Elliot Geisinger, Howard Kuperman, Ronald Saland & Howard Smith, D Ronald F. Maxwell, W Bob Bonney (based on a song by Bobby Russell), PH Bill Butler & Fred Batka, M David Shire, ED Anne Goursaud, PD Gene Rudolf.

LP Kristy McNichol (Amanda Child), Dennis Quaid (Travis Child), Mark Hamill (Conrad), Sunny Johnson (Melody), Don Stroud (Seth), Arlen Dean Snyder (Andy), Barry Corbin (Wimbish), Lulu McNichol (Boogie Woogie).

Despite crediting Bobby Russell's song, this cornpone story has nothing to do with the story of the song. Country singer Dennis Quaid is being pushed to stardom in Nashville by his sister-manager Kristy McNichol.

2057. *Night Train to Terror* (1985, Visto International, 93m, c). P Jay

Schlossberg-Cohen, D John Carr, Schlossberg-Cohen, Philip Marshak, Tom McGowan & Gregg Tallas, W Philip Yordan, PH Susan Haljan, ED Evan Stoliar & Steve Nielsen, SE William Stromberg.

LP John Phillip Law (Harry Billings), Cameron Mitchell (Detective Stern), Marc Lawrence (Weiss/Dieter), Charles Moll (James Hansen/Orderly), Meredith Haze (Gretta Connors), Ferdy Mayne (God), Lu Sickler (Devil).

The destination is hell for the unfortunate trapped in a horrifying journey into the darkest regions of the human soul — and that's only the fate of the audience who stumbled into this turkey by mistake.

2058. *Night Vision* (1988, Prism-Flash, 100m, c). P Sarah Liles-Olson & Douglas Olson, D Michael Krueger, W Nancy Gallanis, Leigh Pomeroy & Krueger, PH Jim Kelley, M Bob Drake, Ron Miles & Eric Jacobson, ED Jonathan Moser.

LP Stacy Carson, Shirley Ross, Tony Carpenter, Ellie Martins, Stacy Shane, Tom Henry, Glenn Reed.

Working in a video store, would-be writer Stacy Carson is possessed by a VCR made by a satanic cult.

2059. *Night Visitor* (1989, MGM/ United Artists, 93m, c, aka *Never Cry Devil*). P Alain Silver, D Rupert Hitzig, W Randal Visovich, PH Peter Jansen, M Parmer Fuller, ED Glenn Erickson, PD Jon Rothschild.

LP Elliott Gould (Ron Devereaux), Richard Roundtree (Captain Crane), Allen Garfield (Zachary Willard), Michael J. Pollard (Stanley Willard), Derek Rydall (Billy Colton), Teresa Van Der Woude (Kelly Fremont), Shannon Tweed (Lisa Grace), Brooke Bundy (Mrs. Coulton), Kathleen Bailey (Det. Dolan), Henry Gibson (Dr. Lawrence).

Familiar faces abound in this dull movie. A high school student sees his history teacher slaughter a call girl in a satanic rite and can't get anyone to believe what he saw.

Night Warning see Butcher Baker (Nightmare Maker)

2060. *Nightbeast* (1982, Amazing Films, 80m, c). P,D&W Don Dohler, PH Richard Geiwitz, M Rob Walsh, Jeffrey Abrams, Arlon Ober & Leonard Rogowski, ED Dohler, SE John Dods, Ernest D. Farino & Kinetic Image.

LP Tom Griffith (Sheriff Cinder), Jamie Zemarel (Jamie), Karin Kardian (Lisa), George Stover (Steven), Don Leifert (Drago), Anne Frith (Ruth), Eleanor Herman (Mary Jane).

In a throwback to the sci-fi flicks of the 50s, the earth is threatened with total destruction when a space ship crashlands and lets loose a giant people-eating monster.

2061. *Nightfall* (1988, Concorde, 80m, c). P Julie Corman, D&W Paul Mayersberg (based on a story by Isaac Asimov), PH Darlusz Wolski, M Frank Serafine, ED Brent Schoenfeld.

LP David Birney (Aton), Sarah Douglas (Roa), Alexis Kanner (Sar), Andra Millian (Ana), Starr Andreeff (Bet).

Set on a distant three-sun planet, blind seer Alexis Kanner predicts that night will come to the planet. Never having experienced sunset before, the population divides into two camps as to how to deal with what they believe will bring massive death and destruction.

2062. *Nightflyers* (1987, Vista/New Century, 89m, c). P Robert Jaffe, D "T.C. Blake" Robert Collector, W Jaffe (based on the novella by George R.R. Martin), PH Shelly Johnson, M Doug Timm, ED Tom Siiter, PD John Muto.

LP Catherine Mary Stewart (Miranda), Michael Praed (Royd), John Standing (D'Branin), Lisa Blount (Audrey), Glenn Withrow (Keelor), James Avery (Darryl), Helene Udy (Lilly), Annabel Brooks (Eliza), Michael Des Barres (Jon Winderman).

Scientists rent a decrepit old space ship which they launch in a search for evidence of a fabled race of aliens known as the Voleryn. They discover they have some unpleasant company on their trip.

2063. *Nightforce* (1987, Vestron, 82m, c). P Victoria Paige Meyerink, Lawrence D. Foldes, Russell W. Colgin & William S. Weiner, D Foldes, W Foldes, Colgin, Michael Engel & Don O'Melveny (based on a story by Foldes), PH Roy H. Wagner & Billy Dickson, M Nigel Harrison & Bob Rose, ED Ed Hansen, PD Curtis A. Schnell.

LP Linda Blair (Carla), James Van Patten (Steve Worthington), Richard Lynch (Bishop), Chad McQueen (Henry), Dean R. Miller (Eddie), James Marcel (Mack), Claudia Udy (Christy Hanson), Bruce Fisher (Estoban), Cameron Mitchell (Senator Hanson), Cork Hubbert (Raoul).

When Claudia Udy, the daughter of outspoken antiterrorist Senator Cameron Mitchell, is kidnapped by South American terrorists, the politician can do nothing to save his daughter. But her friends James Van Patten, Chad McQueen, Dean R. Miller and James Marcel, together with tough broad Linda Blair and former CIA agent Richard Lynch, go south of the border to get her back.

2064. Nighthawks (1981, Universal, 99m, c). P Martin Poll, D Bruce Malmuth, W David Shaber (based on a story by Shaber & Paul Sylbert), PH James A. Contner, M Keith Emerson, ED Christopher Holmes, PD Peter Larkin.

LP Sylvester Stallone (Deke DaSilva), Billy Dee Williams (Matthew Fox), Lindsay Wagner (Irene), Persis Khambatta (Shakka), Nigel Davenport (Peter Hartman), Rutger Hauer (Wulfgar), Hilarie Thompson (Pam), Joe Spinell (Lt. Munafo).

Tough New York cop Sylvester Stallone must outsmart terrorist Rutger Hauer who holds several hostages and has killed a number of people. Outsmart?

2065. Nightmare (1981, 21st Century, 97m, c). P John L. Watkins, D&W Romano Scavolini, PH Gianni Fiore, M Jack Eric Williams, ED Robert T. Megginson.

LP Baird Stafford (George Tatum), Sharon Smith (Susan Temper), C.J. Cooke (C.J. Temper), Mik Cribben (Bob Rosen), Kathleen Ferguson (Barbara), Danny Ronan (Kathy).

In a revolting film, Baird Stafford is a psychopathic killer. He got that way when as a child he observed his father and his mistress in some violent sex scenes.

The boy hacked the two to death with an axe and hasn't been himself since.

2066. Nightmare at Shadow Woods (1987, FCG, 84m, c). P Marianne Kanter, D John W. Grissmer, W Richard Lamden, PH Richard E. Brooks, M Richard Einhorn, ED Michael R. Miller, PD Jim Rule, SE Ed French.

LP Louise Lasser (Maddy), Mark Soper (Todd/Terry), Marianne Kanter (Dr. Berman), Julie Gordon (Karen), Jayne Bentzen (Julie), William Fuller (Brad).

Mark Soper plays two brothers, one good, one evil. One night at a drive-in movie, the evil brother slashes a patron's throat, splashes blood on his good brother, hands him the knife and poses as a perfect little gentleman while his sibling is dragged off to an institution for the criminally insane. Ten years later, the good brother escapes, delighting the evil one who can now go on a new slashing spree.

Nightmare Island see The Slayers

Nightmare Maker see Butcher Baker (Nightmare Maker)

2067. A Nightmare on Elm Street (1984, New Line, 91m, c). P Robert Shaye & Sara Risher, D&W Wes Craven, PH Jacques Haitkin, M Charles Bernstein, ED Rick Shaine, PD Greg Fonseca, SE Jim Doyle, MK David Miller.

LP John Saxon (Lt. Thompson), Ronee Blakley (Marge Thompson), Heather Langenkamp (Nancy Thompson), Amanda Wyss (Tina Gray), Nick Corri (Rod Lane), Johnny Depp (Glen Lantz), Charles Fleischer (Dr. King), Joseph Whipp (Sgt. Parker), Robert Englund (Freddy Krueger).

Probably the best of the horror films of the decade. Several teenagers each have the same nightmare of being tracked by a horribly scarred man wearing a slouch hat and dirty red and green gloves fitted with knives at the fingers. But this horror leaves their dreams and kills them. The teens learn from one of their mothers that years earlier Freddy Krueger (Robert Englund) had killed nearly 20 neighborhood children in a boiler room. He was freed on a technicality and a group of angry parents tracked him to his boiler room, setting it ablaze, killing Freddy. But now it seems Freddy has returned to take revenge on his killers by killing their children. "One, two, Freddy's comin' for you; three, four, better lock your door; five, six, grab your crucifix; seven, eight, gonna stay up late; nine, ten, never sleep again."

2068.   *A Nightmare on Elm Street Part 2: Freddy's Revenge* (1985, New Line, 85m, c). P Robert Shaye & Sara Risher, D Jack Sholder, W David Chaskin, PH Jacques Haitkin, M Christopher Young, ED Arline Garson & Bob Brady, SE A&A Special Effects, MK Kevin Yagher.

LP Mark Patton (Jesse Walsh), Kim Myers (Lisa Poletti), Robert Rusler (Grady), Clu Gulager (Mr. Walsh), Hope Lange (Mrs. Walsh), Marshall Bell (Coach Schneider), Melinda O. Fee (Mrs. Poletti), Thom McFadden (Mr. Poletti), Sydney Walsh (Kerry), Robert Englund (Freddy Krueger).

Five years have passed since dream killer Freddy Krueger was bested by a clever woman, and a new family has moved into the cursed house on Elm Street. Their teenage son Mark Patton begins having horrible nightmares about Freddy, who ultimately takes control of Patton's body so he can return from the dead and kill again.

2069.   *A Nightmare on Elm Street 3: Dream Warriors* (1987, New Line, 97m, c). P Robert Shaye & Sara Risher, D Chuck Russell, W Wes Craven, Bruce Wagner, Russell & Frank Darabont (based on a story by Craven, Wagner and characters created by Craven), PH Roy Wagner, M Angelo Badalamenti, ED Terry Stokes & Chuck Weiss, MK Kevin Yagher, Mark Shostrum, Chris Biggs, Greg Cannon & Matthew Mungle, SE Hoyt Yeatman & Peter Chesney.

LP Heather Langenkamp (Nancy Thompson), Patricia Arquette (Kristen Parker), Larry Fishburne (Max), Priscilla Pointer (Dr. Elizabeth Simms), Craig Wasson (Dr. Neil Goldman), Brooke Bundy (Elaine Parker), Rodney Eastman (Joey), Robert Englund (Freddy Krueger).

Heather Langenkamp, the heroine of the first film in the series turns up as a nurse assigned to look after seven nightmare-plagued teens. Razor-fingered

Freddy is back haunting the corridors of the psychiatric ward. The Dream Warriors band together in defense — but who can escape Freddy's grisly game of terror?

2070.   *A Nightmare on Elm Street 4: The Dream Master* (1988, New Line, 93m, c). P Robert Shaye & Rachel Talalay, D Renny Harlin, W Scott Pierce & Brian Helgeland (based on a story by William Kotzwinkle & Helgeland), PH Steven Fierberg, M Craig Safan, ED Michael N. Knue & Chuck Weiss, PD Mick Strawn & C.J. Strawn, SE Jim Doyle.

LP Robert Englund (Freddy Krueger), Rodney Eastman (Joey), Danny Hassel (Danny), Andras Jones (Rick), Tuesday Knight (Kristen), Toy Newkirk (Sheila), Ken Sagoes (Kincaid), Brooke Theiss (Debbie), Lisa Wilcox (Alice), Brooke Bundy (Kristen's Mother).

Dream murderer Robert Englund kills off the Dream Warrior survivors from Part 3. Finally having killed all the children of the parents who murdered him years earlier, he next goes after mousy Lisa Wilcox and is able to kill off her brother and friends in her dreams. But Wilcox takes on the strongest characteristics of her friends and becomes a Dream Warrior who is a worthy adversary for Englund.

2071.   *A Nightmare on Elm Street 5: The Dream Child* (1989, New Line, 90m, c). P Robert Shaye & Rupert Harvey, D Stephen Hopkins, W Leslie Bohem (based on a story by John Skip, Craig Spector, Leslie Bohem), PH Peter Levy, M Various Artists, ED Chuck Weiss & Brent Schoenfield, PD C.J. Strawn.

LP Robert Englund (Freddy Krueger), Lisa Wilcox (Alice), Joe Seely (Mark), Whitby Hertford (Jacob), Beatrice Boepple (Amanda Krueger), Danny Hassel (Dan), Kelly Jo Minter (Yvonne).

Freddy's mother was a nursing nun trapped in a ward for the criminally insane one terrible weekend. The result of her hundred rapes is Freddy, the child murderer who appears in dreams of teens and kills them for real. In this film his mother's spirit warns Lisa Wilcox who survived *Elm Street 4* that Freddy must be stopped. Wilcox is pregnant and Freddy is trying to be born again as a new soul.

2072. *Nightmare Sisters* (1989, Cinema Home Video, 81m, c, aka *Sorority Sisters*). P&D Dave DeCoteau, W Kenneth J. Hall, PH Voya Mikulic, M Del Casher, ED Tony Malanowski, PD Royce Mathew.

LP Linnea Quigley (Melody), Brinke Stevens (Marci), Michelle Bauer (Mickey), Richard Gabai (Kevin), Marcus Vaughter (Freddy), Timothy Kaufman (Phil), Sandy Brooke (Amanda), Michael D. Sonye (Omar).

Linnea Quigley, Brinke Stevens and Michelle Bauer appear as plain-to-ugly sorority sisters who become knockouts thanks to a magic crystal ball. Unfortunately, it also gives them some unpleasant side effects which their boyfriends aren't happy with.

2073. *Nightmares* (1983, Universal, 99m, c). P Christopher Crowe, D Joseph Sargent, W Crowe & Jeffrey Bloom, PH Mario DiLeo & Gerald Perry Finnerman, M Craig Safan, ED Rod Stephens & Michael Brown, PD Dean Edward Mitzner.

LP Cristina Raines (Wife), Joe Lambie (Husband), Emilio Estevez (J.J.), Mariclare Costello (Mrs. Cooney), Moon Zappa (Pamela), Lance Henriksen (MacLeod), Tony Plana (Del Amo), Richard Masur (Steven), Veronica Cartwright (Claire).

A pack of cigarettes, a video game, a pick-up truck and a stately home all figure prominently in the four horror stories which are incorporated in this rather scary movie.

2074. *Nightstick* (1987, Production Dist. Co., Canada, 94m, c, aka *Calhoun*). P Martin Walters, D Joseph L. Scanlan, W James L. Docherty, PH Robert Fresco, M Robert O. Ragland, ED Richard Wells & Daniel Radford.

LP Bruce Fairbairn (Jack Calhoun), Kerrie Keane (Robin Malone), Robert Vaughn (Ray Melton), John Vernon (Adam Beardsley), Leslie Nielsen (Evans), Walker Boone (Roger Bantam), Tony De Santis (Jerry Bantam).

Trigger-happy New York cop Bruce Fairbairn puts his life on the line to capture three bloodthirsty extortionists.

2075. *Nightwars* (1988, Action International, 88m, c). P Fritz Matthews, D&W David A. Prior, PH Stephen Ashley Blake, M Tim James, Steve McClintick & Mark Mancina, ED Reinhard Schreiner.

LP Brian O'Connor (Trent Matthews), Dan Haggerty, Cameron Smith, Steve Horton, Chet Hood, Jill Foor, Mike Hickam.

Having left a buddy behind in the jungles of Vietnam, Brian O'Connor and Cameron Smith experience the same horrifying nightmare night after night. Ultimately the two must arm themselves and deal with the terrors in their dreams.

2076. *Nijinsky* (1980, Paramount, GB, 129m, c). P Nora Kaye & Stanley O'Toole, D Herbert Ross, W Hugh Wheeler (based on the book *Nijinsky* by Romola Nijinsky and *The Diary of Vaslav Nijinsky*), PH Douglas Slocombe, M John Lanchbery, ED William Reynolds, PD John Blezard, AD Tony Roman & George Richardson, COS Alan Barrett.

LP Alan Bates (Sergei Diaghilev), George De La Pena (Vaslac Nijinsky), Leslie Browne (Romola De Pulsky), Alan Badel (Baron De Gunzburg), Carla Fracci (Tamara Karsavina), Colin Blakely (Vassili), Ronald Pickup (Igor Stravinsky), Ronald Lacey (Leon Bakst), Vernon Dobtcheff (Sergei Grigoriev), Jeremy Irons (Mikhail Fokine).

The production of this biopic of the great Russian ballet star is handsomely mounted, but the story is the usual "and then I danced" type of plot. Alan Bates as Sergei Diaghilev is excellent.

2077. *9½ Weeks* (1986, MGM/United Artists, 113m, c). P Antony Rufus Isaacs & Zalman King, D Adrian Lyne, W Patricia Knop, King & Sarah Kernochan (based on the novel by Elizabeth McNeill), PH Peter Biziou, ED Tom Rolf, PD Ken Davis.

LP Mickey Rourke (John), Kim Basinger (Elizabeth), Margaret Whitton (Molly), David Margulies (Harvey), Christine Baranski (Thea), Karen Young (Sue), William De Acutis (Ted), Dwight Weist (Farnsworth).

Rich commodities broker Mickey Rourke and sultry art gallery entrepreneur Kim Basinger have a sadomasochistic affair in this disappointing film which promises more than it delivers. It's hard to feel sorry for victim Basinger who so willingly becomes psychologically dominated by Rourke. Mickey doesn't even bother to act.

2078. *9 Deaths of the Ninja* (1985, Crown International, 94m, c). P Ashok Amritraj, D&W Emmett Alston, PH Roy H. Wagner, M Cecile Colayco, ED Alston, Victor Ordonez & Robert Waters, PD Rodell Cruz, SE Danilo Dominquez, STUNTS Alan Amiel.

LP Sho Kosugi (Spike Shinobi), Brent Huff (Steve Gordon), Emilia Lesniak (Jennifer Barnes), Blackie Dammett (Alby the Cruel), Regina Richardson (Honey Hump), Vijay Amritraj (Rankin).

Sho Kosugi leads a squad of Ninja rescuers, kicking and screaming, after an American tour bus hijacked in the Philippines by a gang of political terrorists.

2079. *976-Evil* (1989, New Line Cinema, 93m, c). P Lisa M, Hansen, D Robert Englund, W Rhet Topham & Brian Helgeland, PH Paul Elliot, M Thomas Chase & Steve Rucker, ED Stephen Myers.

LP Stephen Geoffreys (Hoax), Sandy Dennis (Aunt Lucy), Patrick O'Bryan (Spike), Jim Metzler (Marty), Maria Rubell (Angella), Lezlie Deane (Suzie), Jim Thiebaud (Rags), Gunther Jensen (Airhead).

Robert Englund who portrays Freddy Krueger in the *Elm Street* movie series, tries his hand at directing in this forgettable horror story. Stephen Geoffreys, an undersized teen, lives with his religious zealot mother, Sandy Dennis. He slowly is transformed into the devil and proceeds to claw to death everyone who's ever given him a bad time.

2080. *Nine to Five* (1980, 20th Century–Fox, 110m, c). P Bruce Gilbert, D Colin Higgins, W Higgins & Patricia Resnick (based on a story by Resnick), PH Reynaldo Villalobos, M Charles Fox, ED Pembroke J. Herring, PD Dean Mitzner, M/L "Nine to Five" by Dolly Parton† (sung by Parton).

LP Jane Fonda (Judy Bernly), Lily Tomlin (Violet Newstead), Dolly Parton (Doralee Rhodes), Dabney Coleman (Franklin Hart, Jr.), Sterling Hayden (Tinsworthy), Elizabeth Wilson (Roz), Henry Jones (Hinkle), Lawrence Pressman (Dick), Marian Mercer (Missy Hart).

In an enjoyable comedy, three L.A. office workers, Jane Fonda, Lily Tomlin and Dolly Parton, conspire to get rid of their cruel sexist boss Dabney Coleman. With him out of the way, they make the office run much more smoothly and productively, winning the praise of the company's owner, Sterling Hayden.

2081. *1918* (1985, Cinecom, 91m, c). P Lillian Foote & Ross Milloy, D Ken Harrison, W Horton Foote (based on his play), PH George Tirl, ED Leon Seith.

LP William Converse-Roberts (Horace Robedaux), Hallie Foote (Elizabeth Robedaux), Rochelle Oliver (Mrs. Vaughn), Michael Higgins (Mr. Vaughn), Matthew Broderick (Brother), Jeannie McCarthy (Bessie).

In a thoughtful character study, the lives of the residents of a small Texas town are irrevocably changed in 1918 by World War I and the flu epidemic.

2082. *1984* (1984, Atlantic, GB, 117m, c). P Simon Perry, D Michael Radford, W Radford & Jonathan Gems (based on the novel by George Orwell), PH Roger Deakins, M The Eurythmics & Dominic Muldowney, ED Tom Priestley, PD Allan Cameron.

LP John Hurt (Winston Smith), Richard Burton (O'Brien), Suzanna Hamilton (Julia), Cyril Cusack (Charrington), Gregor Fisher (Parsons), James Walker (Syme), Andrew Wilde (Tillotson).

It figured that someone in 1984 would come up with a new film version of George Orwell's classic novel. It also figured that it would be less than successful at the box office. It's an appropriately grim story starring John Hurt as a citizen of Oceania. His job is rewriting history for Big Brother in a world in which there is constant war and all freedoms have been banned, including thinking uncontrolled thoughts. Sex is also outlawed, but Hurt experiments with Suzanna Hamilton, until he is betrayed by his friend and superior Richard Burton, who must then reprogram him.

2083. *Nineteen Nineteen* (1986, Spectrafilm, GB, 99m, c). P Nita Amy, D

Hugh Brody, W Brody & Michael Ignatieff (based on an idea by Ignatieff), PH Ivan Strasburg, M Brian Gascoigne, ED David Gladwell.

LP Paul Scofield (Alexander), Maria Schell (Sophie), Frank Finlay (The Voice of Dr. Sigmund Freud), Diana Quick (Anna), Clare Higgins (Young Sophie), Colin Firth (Young Alexander), Sandra Berkin (Nina).

In a boring production, Paul Scofield and Maria Schell are former patients of Sigmund Freud who come together years later to reminisce.

2084. *1969* (1989, Atlantic, 90m, c). P Daniel Grodnik & Bill Badalato, D&W Ernest Thompson, PH Jules Brenner, M Michael Small, ED William Anderson, PD Marcia Hinds.

LP Robert Downey, Jr. (Ralph), Kiefer Sutherland (Scott), Bruce Dern (Cliff), Mariette Hartley (Jessie), Winona Ryder (Beth), Joanna Cassidy (Ev), Christopher Wynne (Alden), Keller Kuhn (Marsha).

In a less than gripping story, Robert Downey, Jr., and Kiefer Sutherland are two college students and long-time friends. They have adopted a radical stance which doesn't fit well in 1969 with their families in a small Maryland town. They don't seem to be for anything, just wishing to avoid the draft.

2085. *90 Days* (1986, Cinecom, Canada, 99m, c). P&W David Wilson & Giles Walker, D Walker, PH Andrew Kitzanuk, M Richard Gresko, ED Wilson.

LP Stefan Wodoslawsky (Blue), Christine Pak (Hyang-Sook), Sam Grana (Alex), Fernanda Tavares (Laura), Daisy De Bellefeuille (Mother).

The movie has two parallel plots. In one story Stefan Wodoslawsky and his Korean mail-order bride-to-be, Christine Pak, try to get to know each other before the wedding. In the second story, Wodoslawsky's friend adjusts to the prospects of becoming a sperm donor.

2086. *Ninja III—The Domination* (1984, Cannon, 95m, c). P Menahem Golan & Yoram Globus, D Sam Firstenberg, W James R. Silke, PH Hanania Baer, M Udi Harpaz, Misha Segal & Arthur Kempel, ED Michael J. Duthie.

LP Sho Kosugi (Yamada), Lucinda Dickey (Christie), Jordan Bennett (Secord), David Chung (Black Ninja), Dale Ishimoto (Okuda), James Hong (Miyashima), Bob Craig (Netherland), Pamela Ness (Alana).

An evil Ninja, killed by the police, forces his spirit on innocent Lucinda Dickey.

2087. *Ninja Turf* (1986, Ascot, 86m, c, aka *L.A. Streetfighters*). P Phillip Rhee, D Richard Park, W Simon Blake Hong, PH David D. Kim & Maximo Munzi, M Charles Pavlosky, Gary Falcone & Chris Stone, ED Alex Chang, PD David Moon Park.

LP Jun Chong (Young), Phillip Rhee (Tony), James Lew (Chan), Rosanna King (Lily), Bill "Sugerfoot" Wallace (Kruger), Dorin Mukama (Dorin), Arlene Montano (Chan's Girlfriend).

Just another of the many chop-chop movies; it's no better and no worse than the others.

The Ninth Configuration see Twinkle, Twinkle "Killer" Kane

2088. *No Dead Heroes* (1987, Cineventures, 86m, c). P&D J.C. Miller, W Miller & Arthur N. Gelfield, PH Freddie C. Grant, M Marita M. Wellman, ED Edgar Viner.

LP Max Thayer (Ric Sanders), John Dresden (Harry Cotter), Toni Nero (Barbara Perez), Nick Nicholson (Ivan Dimanovitch), Mike Monty (Frank Baylor), Dave Anderson (Gen. Craig).

Green Beret Captain John Dresden is captured by insane KGB agent Nick Nicholson in the jungles of Vietnam. A microchip is implanted in Dresden's brain which makes him a killing machine. Now he roams the world to kill on command.

2089. *No Holds Barred* (1989, New Line Cinema, 91m, c). P Michael Rachmil, D Thomas J. Wright, W Dennis Hackin, PH Frank Beascoechea, M Jim Johnston, ED Tom Pryor, PD James Shanahan.

LP Hulk Hogan (Rip), Kurt Fuller (Brell), Joan Severance (Samantha Moore), Tom [Tiny] Lister (Zeus), Mark Pellegrino (Randy), Bill Henderson (Charlie), Charles Levin (Ordway), David Palmer (Unger).

In this unusually poor picture, Hulk Hogan plays the World Wrestling Federation champ (a title Hogan actually holds). A tyrannical TV network boss Kurt Fuller is trying to lure away Hogan and almost causes him to throw a match—horrors!

2090. *No Justice* (1989, Richfield, 91m, c). P,D&W Richard Wayne Martin, PH Karen Edmundsen Bean, M Mike Headrick, ED Barbara J. Boguski, AD Gretchen Oehler.

LP Bob Orwig (Virgel Johnson), Cameron Mitchell (Mayor Johnson), Steve Murphy (Sheriff Smith), Phillip Newman (Bo Johnson), Susan Ashley Pohlman (Susie Willis), Liza Case (Sissy Taylor).

In this good old boy—red neck—drive-in movie, sadistic Bob Orwig is appointed sheriff by his uncle Cameron Mitchell when Steve Murphy skips town with pretty young Susan Ashley Pohlman. This dimwitted monster rapes his girlfriend, imprisons and tortures her brother and generally raises hell. When state officials refuse to interfere in Orwig's fun, Murphy returns to "do what a man has to do."

2091. *No Man's Land* (1987, Orion, 107m, c). P Joseph Stern & Dick Wolf, D Peter Werner, W Wolf, Jack Behr & Sandy Kroopf, PH Hiro Narita, M Basil Poledouris, ED Steve Cohen, PD Paul Peters.

LP D.B. Sweeney (Benjy Taylor), Charlie Sheen (Ted Varrick), Lara Harris (Ann Varrick), Randy Quaid (Lt. Vincent Bracey), Bill Duke (Malcolm), R.D. Call (Frank Martin), Arlen Dean Snyder (Lt. Loos), M. Emmet Walsh (Capt. Haun).

Rookie cop D.B. Sweeney is chosen by Randy Quaid to go undercover inside a Porsche-stealing ring headed by suspected cop-killer Charlie Sheen.

2092. *No Mercy* (1986, Tri-Star, 107m, c). P D. Constantine Conte, D Richard Pearce, W Jim Carabatsos, PH Michel Brault, M Alan Silvestri, ED Jerry Greenberg & Bill Yahraus, PD Patrizia Von Brandenstein.

LP Richard Gere (Eddie Jillette), Kim Basinger (Michel Duval), Jeroen Krabbe (Losado), George Dzundza (Captain Stemkowski), Gary Basaraba (Joe Collins), William Atherton (Allan Deveneux), Terry Kinney (Paul Deveneux), Bruce McGill (Lt. Hall), Ray Sharkey (Angles Ryan).

In this predictable cop thriller, Bayou bimbo Kim Basinger, almost mute throughout the film, always looks dripping-wet-and-sweaty-hot. Richard Gere, as always a man of unchanging expression, is a Chicago cop roaming the grungy environs of the Big Easy, New Orleans, to avenge the death of his partner. The main villain is Dutch actor Jeroen Krabbe, impressively brutal, evil and almost indestructible. There's a lot of sexual tension in the air, but the chemistry between pouty Basinger and stolid Gere is minimal.

2093. *No Retreat, No Surrender* (1986, New World, 90m, c). P Ng See Yuen, D Corey Yuen, W Keith W. Strandberg (based on a story by Ng See Yuen & Corey Yuen), PH John Huneck & David Golia, ED Alan Poon, Mark Pierce, James Melkonian & Dane Davis.

LP Kurt McKinney (Jason Stillwell), Jean-Claude Van Damme (Ivan), J.W. Fails (R.J. Madison), Kathie Sileno (Kelly Reilly), Kim Tai Chong (Sensei Lee), Kent Lipham (Scott), Ron Pohnel (Ian Reilly).

In what must be one of the lowest points in the history of martial arts films, the cast and crew of this film are mostly amateur and look it. The story has something to do with a young fighter who idolizes Bruce Lee. The latter's ghost trains him for a big match with nasty Commie monster Jean-Claude Van Damme.

2094. *No Safe Haven* (1989, Overseas Filmgroup, 91m, c). P Gary Paul, D Ronnie Rondell, W Wings Hauser & Nancy Locke, PH Steven McWilliams, M Joel Goldsmith, ED Drake Sullivan.

LP Wings Hauser (Clete Harris), Robert Tessier (Randy), Robert Ahola (Carlos), Marina Rice (Carol), Branscombe Richmond (Manuel), Tom Campitelli (Buddy Harris), Harvey Martin (Harvey Latham).

Wings Hauser, a U.S. spy in Honduras, hurries home to take revenge when his mother and younger brother are killed by mobsters, then rushes back south of the border to clean up a gang of drug dealers.

2095. *No Small Affair* (1984, Columbia, 102m, c). P William Sackheim, D Jerry Schatzberg, W Charles Bolt & Terence Mulcahy (based on a story by Bolt), PH Vilmos Zsigmond, M Rupert Holmes, ED Priscilla Nedd, Eve Newman & Melvin Shapiro, PD Robert Boyle.

LP Jon Cryer (Charles Cummings), Demi Moore (Laura Victor), George Wendt (Jake), Peter Frechette (Leonard), Elizabeth Daily (Susan), Anne Wedgeworth (Joan Cummings), Jeffrey Tambor (Ken), Judy Baldwin (Stephanie), Jennifer Tilly (Mona), Scott Getlin (Scott).

Smartass 16-year-old photographer Jon Cryer has quite a crush on 23-year-old rock singer Demi Moore. He'll do anything to get her to care for him and his passion eventually paves the way for her big career break. It's a disappointing comedy, with some very good spots, but many more stupid ones.

2096. *No Surrender* (1986, Circle, GB, 100m, c). P Mamoun Hassan, D Peter Smith, W Alan Bleasdale, PH Mick Coulter, M Daryl Runswick, ED Rodney Holland & Kevin Brownlow, PD Andrew Mollo.

LP Michael Angelis (Mike), Avis Bunnage (Martha Gorman), James Ellis (Paddy Burke), Tom Georgeson (Mr. Ross), Bernard Hill (Bernard), Ray McAnally (Billy McRacken), Mark Mulholland (Norman), Joanne Whalley (Cheryl), J.G. Devlin (George Gorman).

Opposing political types are accidentally gathered at the same dingy Irish nightclub one New Year's Eve.

2097. *No Way Out* (1987, Orion, 114m, c). P Laura Ziskin & Robert Garland, D Roger Donaldson, W Garland (based on the novel *The Big Clock* by Kenneth Fearing), PH John Alcott, M Maurice Jarre, ED Neil Travis, PD Dennis Washington & Kai Hawkins.

LP Kevin Costner (Lt. Cmdr. Tom Farrell), Gene Hackman (David Brice), Sean Young (Susan Atwell), Will Patton (Scott Pritchard), Howard Duff (Senator Willy Duvall), George Dzundza (Dr. Sam Hesselman), Jason Bernard (Maj. Dono-

van), Iman (Nina Beka), Fred Dalton Thompson (Marshall).

The setting of this remake of *The Big Clock,* first filmed in 1948 with Ray Milland and Charles Laughton, is transferred from a magazine empire to the Pentagon. Decorated U.S. Navy Lieutenant Kevin Costner finds himself in the unlikely and unappealing position of hunting himself down in a murder case involving sexy callgirl Sean Young and Secretary of Defense Gene Hackman. The heat from the love making of Costner and Young in a limousine is enough to make the vehicle throw a rod.

2098. *Nobody's Fool* (1986, Island Pictures, 107m, c). P James C. Katz & Jon S. Denny, D Evelyn Purcell, W Beth Henley, PH Mikhail Suslov, M James Newton Howard, ED Dennis Virkler, PD Jackson DeGovia.

LP Rosanna Arquette (Cassie), Eric Roberts (Riley), Mare Winningham (Pat), Jim Youngs (Billy), Louise Fletcher (Pearl), Gwen Welles (Shirley), Stephen Tobolowsky (Kirk), Charlie Barnett (Nick), J.J. Hardy (Ralphy), William Steis (Frank).

Writer Beth Henley, so good for her Pulitzer Prize–winning *Crimes of the Heart,* disappoints in this memoir of her own youthful desire to become an actress. Her alter ego, played by Rosanna Arquette, is a flaky country girl who falls for the acting profession and handsome Eric Roberts, a technician with a visiting Shakespearean troupe. Henley isn't successful in making audiences care about the outcast unwed mother and her acting ambitions.

2099. *Nobody's Perfect* (1989, August Entertainment, 91m, c). P Benni Korzen, D Robert Kaylor, W Annie Korzen & Joel Block (based on a story by Steven Ader), PH Claus Loof, M Robert Randles, ED Robert Gordon, PD Gilbert Wong.

LP Chad Lowe (Stephen/Stephanie), Gail O'Grady (Shelly), Patrick Breen (Andy), Kim Flowers (Jackie), Vitas Geruliatis (Tennis Coach), Robert Vaughn (Doctor), Annie Korzen (Professor Lucci).

In a sort of big screen Bosom Buddies, Chad Lowe, too shy to put a move on beautiful classmate Gail O'Grady, dons a wig and female clothes to get near her. His ruse has the desired romantic results. Are you surprised?

2100. *Nobody's Perfekt* (1981, Columbia, 96m, c). P Mort Engelberg, D Peter Bonerz, W Tony Kenrick (based on the novel *Two for the Price of One* by Kenrick), PH James Pergola, M David McHugh, ED Neil Travis.

LP Gabe Kaplan (Dibley), Alex Karras (Swaboda), Robert Klein (Walter), Susan Clark (Carol), Paul Stewart (Dr. Segal), Alex Rocco (Boss), Arthur Rosenberg (Mayor), James Cromwell (Dr. Carson).

Three losers, Gabe Kaplan, Alex Karras and Robert Klein, take on the city when they don't get the payment they believe they are entitled to after wrecking their car in a cavernous pothole. Potholes aren't funny, neither is this picture.

2101. *Nomads* (1986, Atlantic, 95m, c). P George Pappas & Cassian Elwes, D&W John McTiernan, PH Stephen Ramsey, M Bill Conti, ED Michael John Bateman, PD Marcia Hinds.

LP Pierce Brosnan (Pommier), Lesley-Anne Down (Flax), Anna-Maria Montecelli (Niki), Adam Ant (Number One), Hector Mercado (Ponytail), Josie Cotton (Silver Ring), Mary Woronov (Dirty Blond), Frank Doubleday (Razor).

French anthropologist Pierce Brosnan is brutally and mortally wounded by the "Nomads." Before he dies he passes the memories of his last days on to a beautiful emergency room doctor Lesley-Anne Down who had tried to save his life. She finds herself the next target of these malevolent spirits, posing as punks, junkies and whores.

2102. *Norman Loves Rose* (1982, Atlantic, Australia, 98m, c). P Henri Safran & Basil Appleby, D&W Safran, PH Vince Monton, M Mike Perjanik, PD Darrell Lass.

LP Carol Kane, Tony Owen, Warren Mitchell, Myra De Groot, David Downer, Barry Otto, Sandy Gore, Virginia Hey, Louise Pajo.

In a charmless comedy, a 13-year-old boy is initiated into sex by his sister-in-law who then has his baby.

2103. *Norman's Awesome Experience* (1989, Norstar, Canada, 90m, c). P Paul

Donovan & Peter Simpson, D&W Donovan, PH Vic Sarin, M Paul Zaza, ED Stephen Fanfara, PD Emmanuel Jannasch & Bruce McKenna.

LP Tom McCamus (Norman), Laurie Paton (Erika), Jacques Lussier (Umberto), Lee Broker (Titanus), David Hemblen (Fabius), Marcos Woinsky (Serpicus), Gabriela Salas (Felix), Armando Capo (Blacksmith), Brian Downey (Dr. Nobbelmeyer).

In this direct to video movie, lab assistant Tom McCamus and pretty model Laurie Paton are whisked back to the days of ancient Rome where they fight barbarians.

North Sea Highjack see ffolkes

2104. *North Shore* (1987, Universal, 96m, c). P William Finnegan, D William Phelps, W Tim McCanlies & Phelps (based on a story by Phelps & Randal Kleiser), PH Peter Smokler, M Richard Stone, ED Robert Gordon, PD Mark Balet.

LP Matt Adler (Rick), Gregory Harrison (Chandler), Nia Peeples (Kiani), John Philbin (Turtle), Gerry Lopez (Vince), Laird Hamilton (Lance Burkhart), Robbie Page (Alex Rogers), Mark Occhilupo (Occy).

After winning a competition in his native Arizona, naive surfer Matt Adler goes to Hawaii where the waves are larger and the competition greater.

2105. *Not for Publication* (1984, Goldwyn/EMI, 88m, c). P Anne Kimmel, D Paul Bartel, W John Meyer & Bartel, PH George Tirl, M Meyer, ED Alan Toomayan, PD Robert Schulenberg.

LP Nancy Allen (Lois Thorndyke), David Naughton (Barry), Laurence Luckenbill (Mayor Claude Franklyn), Alice Ghostley (Doris), Richard Paul (Troppogrosso), Barry Dennen (Senor Woparico), Cork Hubbert (Odo).

By day Nancy Allen works for the reelection of Mayor Lawrence Luckenbill. By night she is a reporter for a smutty newspaper. One night while covering an orgy, her two worlds come together.

2106. *Not of This Earth* (1988, Concorde, 80m, c). P Jim Wynorski & Murray Miller, D Wynorski, W R.J. Robertson & Wynorski (based on the original script by Charles B. Griffith & Mark

Hanna), PH Zoran Hochstatter, ED Kevin Trent.

LP Traci Lords (Nadine Story), Arthur Roberts (The Alien), Lenny Juliano (Jeremy), Ace Mask (Dr. Rochelle), Roger Lodge (Harry), Michael Delano (Vacuum Cleaner Salesman), Rebecca Perle (Alien Woman).

Arthur Roberts is a blood-thirsty alien who investigates earth as a possible source of his favorite liquid. It's a remake of the 1957 science-fiction comedy film.

2107. *Not Quite Jerusalem* (1985, Rank, GB, 117m, c, aka *Not Quite Paradise*). P Lewis Gilbert & William P. Cartlidge, D Gilbert, W Paul Kember (based on his play), PH Tony Imi, M Rondo Veniziano & Gian Reverberi, ED Alan Strachan, PD John Stoll.

LP Joanna Pacula (Gila), Sam Robards (Mike), Kevin McNally (Pete), Todd Graff (Rothwell T. Schwartz), Selina Cadell (Carrie), Bernard Strother (Dave), Ewan Stewart (Angus), Kate Ingram (Grace), Gary Cady (Steve).

When American Jewish boy Sam Robards joins a kibbutz in Israel, he falls for native Israeli Joanna Pacula. She initially treats him like an Arab enemy.

Not Quite Paradise see Not Quite Jerusalem

2108. *Not Since Casanova* (1988, Owen-Thompson Prod., 80m, c). P Bradford Owen & Brett Thompson, D&W Thompson, PH Andreas Kossak, M John Debney, ED Arthur Farkus & Thompson, PD Robyn Reichek.

LP Charles Solomon (Prepski Morris), Diana Frank (Gina), Tomi Griffin (Tommi), Leslie Mitts (Laurie), Lucy Winn (Denise Harrington), Karen Smith (Serina Skelly), Kare N. Marcus (Hilary).

Young Charles Solomon, the product of a broken home, refuses to grow up and accept adult responsibilities, especially romantic commitments. He suffers from the "Peter Pan Syndrome," also known as the "Casanova Complex" in which he searches for a perfect, no-catches relationship.

2109. *Nothing in Common* (1986, Tri-Star, 118m, c). P Alexandra Rose, D Garry Marshall, W Rick Podell & Michael Preminger, PH John A. Alonzo, M Patrick Leonard, ED Glenn Farr, PD Charles Rosen.

LP Tom Hanks (David Basner), Jackie Gleason (Max Basner), Eva Marie Saint (Lorraine Basner), Hector Elizondo (Charlie Gargas), Barry Corbin (Andrew Woolridge), Bess Armstrong (Donna Mildred Martin), Sela Ward (Cheryl Ann Wayne), Cindy Harrell (Shelley), John Kapelos (Roger).

Obnoxious, wisecracking, self-centered successful ad man Tom Hanks is annoyed that he must care for his irascible, ill father, Jackie Gleason, when the latter and Hank's mother, Eva Marie Saint, break up. Hanks and Gleason have nothing in common and in this honorable failure—that's enough.

2110. *Nothing Lasts Forever* (1984, MGM/United Artists, 82m, c). P Lorne Michaels & John Head, D&W Tom Schiller, PH Fred Schuler, ED Kathleen Dougherty & Margot Francis.

LP Zach Galligan (Adam Beckett), Apollonia van Ravenstein (Mara Hofmeier), Lauren Tom (Ely), Dan Aykroyd (Buck Heller), Imogene Coca (Daisy Schackman), Anita Ellis (Aunt Anita), Sam Jaffe (Father Knickerbocker), Paul Rogers (Hugo), Mort Sahl (Uncle Mort).

In a strange comedy set sometime in the future, Zach Galligan is an aspiring New York City artist. He has some funny experiences when he takes a trip to the moon.

2111. *Nothing Personal* (1980, AIP/Filmways, Canada, 97m, c). P David M. Perlmutter, D George Bloomfield, W Robert Kaufman, PH Laszlo George & Arthur Ibbetson, ED George Appleby.

LP Donald Sutherland (Prof. Roger Keller), Suzanne Somers (Abigail Adams), Lawrence Dane (Robert Ralston), Roscoe Lee Browne (Mr. Paxton), Dabney Coleman (Tom Dickerson), Saul Rubinek (Peter Braden), Catherine O'Hara (Janet Samson).

Constitutional law professor Donald Sutherland and top Washington attorney Suzanne Somers team up to prevent the government from killing baby seals. The teaming of Sutherland and Somers is not inspired.

2112. *Now and Forever* (1983, Inter Planetary, Australia, 93m, c). P Treisha Ghent & Carnegie Fieldhouse, D Adrian Carr, W Richard Cassidy (based on the novel by Danielle Steel), PH Don McAlpine, M Graham Russell.

LP Cheryl Ladd (Jessie Clark), Robert Coleby (Ian Clark), Carmen Duncan (Astrid Bonner), Christine Amor (Margaret Burton).

Cheryl Ladd suffers nobly as her husband Robert Coleby first cheats on her and then is jailed on a phony rape charge.

2113. *Nowhere to Hide* (1987, New Century/Vista, Canada, 90m, c). P Andras Hamori, D Mario Azzopardi, W Alex Rebar & George Goldsmith (based on a story by Rebar), PH Vic Sarin, M Brad Fiedel, ED Rit Wallis.

LP Amy Madigan (Barbara Cutter), Daniel Hugh Kelly (Rob Cutter), Robin MacEachern (Johnny Cutter), Michael Ironside (Ben), John Colicos (Gen. Howard).

Amy Madigan is wasted in this stupid action film. She's a Marine widow pursued by bad guys trying to recover a faulty helicopter part that her young son is hiding in one of his toys.

2114. *Nowhere to Run* (1980, MTM Productions, 103m, c). P Jim Byrnes, D Richard Lang, W Byrnes (based on Charles Einstein's novel), PH Charles G. Arnold, M Jerrold Immel, ED Gary Griffin.

LP David Janssen (Harry Adams), Stefanie Powers (Marian Adams), Allen Garfield (Herbie Stoltz), Linda Evans (Amy Kessler), Neva Patterson (Marian's Mother), John Randolph (Marian's Father).

Disgruntled David Janssen has devised a winning blackjack system as part of an elaborate scheme to love his unfaithful wife Stefanie Powers.

2115. *Nowhere to Run* (1989, Concorde, 85m, c, aka *Temptation Blues*). P Julie Corman, D Carl Franklin, W Jack Canson & Nancy Barr (based on a story by Canson), PH Phedon Papamichael, M Barry Goldberg, ED Carol Oblath, PD Sherman Williams.

LP David Carradine (Harman), Jason Priestley (Howard), Jillian McWhirter (Cynthia), Kieran Mulroney (Jerry Lee), Henry Jones (Judge Culbert), Kelly Ashmore (Saralynn), Brenda Bakke (Joanie), Andy Wood (Sheriff Tooley).

This film set in a small Texas town in 1960 is crammed with characters, plots and subplots. Escaped killer David Carradine seems to figure in all of the convoluted strings of stories.

2116. *The Nude Bomb* (1980, Universal, 94m, c, aka *The Return of Maxwell Smart*). P Jennings Lang, D Clive Donner, W Arne Sultan, Bill Dana & Leonard B. Stern (based on characters created by Mel Brooks & Buck Henry), PH Harry L. Wolf, M Lalo Schifrin, ED Walter Hannemann & Phil Ticker, PD William Tuntke.

LP Don Adams (Maxwell Smart), Sylvia Kristel (Agent 34), Rhonda Fleming (Edith Von Secondberg), Dana Elcar (Chief), Pamela Hensley (Agent 36), Andrea Howard (Agent 22), Norman Lloyd (Carruthers), Bill Dana (Jonathan Levinson Seigle), Gary Imhoff (Jerry Krovney), Vittorio Gassman (Nino Salvatore Sebastiani).

Where did anyone get the idea that people were anxiously awaiting the return of Maxwell Smart? The film is certainly a bomb, filled with repetitive humor for which only the brain-damaged could be nostalgic.

2117. *Number One* (1984, Videoform/Stageform, GB, 105m, c). P Mark Forstater & Raymond Day, D Les Blair, W G.F. Newman, PH Bahram Manocheri, M David Mackay, ED John Gregory, PD Martin Johnson.

LP Bob Geldof (Harry [Flash] Gordon), Mel Smith (Billy Evans), Alison Steadman (Doreen), P.H. Moriarty (Mike the Throat), Phil Daniels (Terry the Boxer), Alfred Molina (D-C Rogers), James Marcus (D-C Fleming).

Bob Geldof, lead singer of The Boomtown Rats, best known for his fundraising efforts on behalf of starving people of the world, is a snooker (pool) hustler, convinced to compete in a big professional match. He's pressured to throw the match, but of course he doesn't.

2118. *Number One with a Bullet* (1987, Cannon, 101m, c). P Menahem Golan &

Yoram Globus, D Jack Smight, W Gail Morgan Hickman, Andrew Kurtzman, Rob Riley & James Belushi (based on a story by Hickman), PH Alex Phillips, M Alf Clausen, ED Michael J. Duthie, PD Norm Baron.

LP Robert Carradine (Nicholas "Nick" Berzak), Billy Dee Williams (Frank Hazeltine), Valerie Bertinelli (Teresa Berzak), Peter Graves (Capt. P. Ferris), Doris Roberts (Mrs. Berzak), Bobby Di Cicco (Malcolm), Ray Girardin (Lt. Larry Kaminski), Barry Sattels (Harry Da Costa).

Robert Carradine and Billy Dee Williams will bend or break any rule to bring down seemingly respectable Barry Sattels. The latter just happens to be Mr. Big of local drug activities.

2119. *Nutcracker, The Motion Picture* (1986, Atlantic, 89m, c). P Willard Carroll, Donald Kushner, Peter Locke & Thomas L. Wilhite, D Carroll Ballard, W Kent Stowell & Maurice Sendak (based on the story by E.T.A. Hoffman), PH Stephen H. Burum, M Peter Ilyich Tchaikovsky, ED John Nutt & Michael Silvers, PD/COS Sendak, CH Stowell, MP London Symphony Orchestra, CONDUCTOR Sir Charles MacKerras.

LP Hugh Bigney (Herr Drosselmeier), Vanessa Sharp (Young Clara), Patricia Barker (Dream Clara/Ballerina Doll), Wade Walthall (Nutcracker), Maia Rosal (Frau Stahlbaum), Carey Homme (Dr. Stahlbaum), Gregory Draper (Uncle), Courtland Weaver (Sword Dancer), Russell Burnett (Fritz), Jacob Rice (Nutcracker in Fight Scene).

Viewers will be disappointed with this production of Tchaikovsky's Nutcracker, performed by the Pacific Northwest Ballet. The camera doesn't seem able to pick out what the eyes of members of an audience of a live performance would. Of course the music is magnificent.

2120. *Nuts* (1987, Warner, 116m, c). P Barbra Streisand, D Martin Ritt, W Tom Topor, Darryl Ponicsan & Alvin Sargent (based on the play by Topor), PH Andrzej Bartkowiak, M Streisand, ED Sidney Levin, PD Joel Schiller.

LP Barbra Streisand (Claudia Draper), Richard Dreyfuss (Aaron Levinsky), Maureen Stapleton (Rose Kirk), Karl Malden (Arthur Kirk), Eli Wallach (Dr. Herbert A. Morrison), Robert Webber (Francis MacMillan), James Whitmore (Judge Stanley Murdoch), Leslie Nielsen (Allen Green), William Prince (Clarence Middleton).

Barbra Streisand is in top form as a callgirl who has killed one of her clients in self-defense. She is diagnosed as being mentally ill. She's certainly not easy to like but she insists she's sane enough to stand trial. Her stepfather Karl Malden, hiding a guilty secret, wants to put her away forever. With the help of public defender Richard Dreyfuss, she is able to prove in a sanity hearing that just because one is cantankerous, irreverent, loud and disrespectful, it doesn't mean one is nuts.

2121. *The Oasis* (1984, Titan, 92m, c). P Myron Meisel & Sparky Greene, D Greene, W Tom Klassen (based on a story by Meisel & Greene), PH Alexander Gruszynski, M Chris Young, ED Mary Bauer, PD Woodward Romine.

LP Chris Makepeace (Matt), Scott Hylands (Jake), Richard Cox (Paul), Dori Brenner (Jill), Rick Podell (Alex), Mark Metcalf (Eric), Ben Slack (Louis), Anne Lockhart (Anna), Suzanne Snyder (Jennifer).

Chris Makepeace stars in a grim, unpleasant, and bloody tale of survivors of a plane crash in a Mexican desert.

2122. *Obsessed* (1988, New Star, Canada, 103m, c). P Robin Spry & Jamie Brown, D Spry, W Douglas Bowie (based on a story by Bowie & Spry, suggested by the book *Hit and Run* by Tom Alderman), PH Ron Stannett, M Jean-Alain Roussel, ED Diann Ilnicki, PD Claude Pare.

LP Kerrie Keane (Dinah Middleton), Daniel Pilon (Max Middleton), Saul Rubinek (Owen Hughes), Lynne Griffin (Karen Hughes), Mireille Deyglun (Francoise Boyer), Ken Pogue (Det. Sgt. Sullivan), Colleen Dewhurst (The Judge), Alan Thicke (Conrad Vaughan), Leif Anderson (Alex Middleton).

In Montreal, a car driven by New York businessman Saul Rubinek hits and kills 12-year-old skateboarder Leif Anderson, the son of divorced couple Kerrie Keane and Daniel Pilon. Rubinek runs away but is tracked down. Because of a U.S.-

Canada treaty, he can't be extradited. Still Rubinek returns to Canada to face trial, but a manslaughter charge is thrown out on a technicality. Keane still wants justice, law or no law.

2123.   *O.C. and Stiggs* (1987, MGM/ United Artists, 109m, c). P Robert Altman & Peter Newman, D Altman, W Donald Cantrell & Ted Mann (based on the story by Tod Carroll & Mann from a story in "National Lampoon" magazine), PH Pierre Mignot, M King Sunny Ade and his African Beats, ED Elizabeth Kling, PD Scott Bushnell.

LP Daniel H. Jenkins (Oliver Cromwell "O.C." Ogilvie), Neill Barry (Mark Stiggs), Paul Dooley (Randall Schwab), Jane Curtin (Elinore Schwab), Jon Cryer (Randall Schwab, Jr.), Ray Walston (Gramps), Louis Nye (Garth Sloan), Tina Louise (Florence Beaugereaux), Martin Mull (Pat Coletti), Dennis Hopper (Sponson).

Two rambunctious teens, Daniel H. Jenkins and Neill Barry, dedicate their summer to making life miserable for insurance kingpin Paul Dooley, who has cancelled Jenkin's grandfather's old age insurance. This poorly paced comedy has few laughs and will probably result in unknowns Jenkins and Barry staying that way.

2124.   *The Occultist* (1989, Urban Classics, 80m, c). P Cynthia DePaula, D&W Tim Kincaid, PH Arthur D. Marks, M Guy Moon & Carlo Dante, ED Joe Keiser & Bari Wheaten, PD Kim Meinelt & John Paino.

LP Rick Gianasi (Waldo Warren), Joe Derrig (Barney Sanford), Jennifer Kanter (Anjanette Davalos), Mizan Nunes (Marianna Davalos), Richard Mooney (Harold), Matt Mitler (Col. Esteve), Betty Vaughn (Mama Dora).

Originally called *Maximum Thrust,* the film is a voodoo picture. Rick Gianasi is a private detective hired by authorities of the island of San Caribe to protect their president during a New York visit. The president's daughter, Jennifer Kanter, supports the revolutionaries out to assassinate her father.

2125.   *Ocean Drive Weekend* (1985, Troma, 77m, c). P Marvin Almeas, D&W Bryan Jones, M Alan Kaufman, ED John Godwin.

LP Charles Redmond (Miller), Robert Peacock (Chuck), P.J. Grethe (Jeannie), Sharon Brewer (Patty), Tony Freeman (Allen), Jon Kohler (Kirk).

It's one of the cheaper knockdowns of *Animal House* and *American Graffiti.*

2126.   *The Octagon* (1980, American Cinema, 103m, c). P Joel Freeman, D Eric Karson, W Leigh Chapman (based on a story by Paul Aaron & Chapman), PH Michel Hugo, M Dick Halligan, ED Dann Cahn, PD James Schoppe.

LP Chuck Norris (Scott James), Karen Carlson (Justice), Lee Van Cleef (McCarn), Art Hindle (A.J.), Carol Bagdasarian (Aura), Kim Lankford (Nancy), Tadashi Yamashita (Seikura), Kurt Grayson (Doggo), Yuki Shimoda (Katsumoto).

Retired martial arts expert Chuck Norris is brought back to deal with a secret citadel of ninja warriors. Plenty of body-slamming for those who enjoy that kind of thing.

2127.   *Octopussy* (1983, MGM/United Artists, GB, 130m, c). P Albert R. Broccoli, D John Glen, W George MacDonald Fraser, Richard Maibaum & Michael G. Wilson (based on the stories "Octopussy" and "The Property of a Lady" by Ian Fleming), PH Alan Hume, M John Barry, ED John Grover, Peter Davies & Henry Richardson, PD Peter Lamont, AD John Fenner, SD Jack Stephens, SE John Richardson, M/L "All Time High" by Barry & Tim Rice (sung by Rita Coolidge).

LP Roger Moore (James Bond), Maud Adams (Octopussy), Louis Jourdan (Kamal), Kristina Wayborn (Magda), Kabir Bedi (Gobinda), Steven Berkoff (Gen. Orlov), David Meyer & Tony Meyer (Twin Assassins), Vijay Amritraj (Vijay), Desmond Llewelyn (Q), Robert Brown (M), Walter Gotell (Gogol), Suzanne Jerome (Gwendoline), Cherry Gillespie (Midge).

In a disappointing Bond movie, Roger Moore looks too old for the job — and of course he is. Louis Jourdan as the Afghan villain who is stealing Russian art treasures with the help of a Soviet military officer isn't very menacing. The lovely ladies who lure Moore in and out of bed, headed by Maud Adams, appear more bored than passionate.

2128. *Odd Birds* (1985, Pomeranian, 90m, c). P Jeanne Collachia & Charles A. Domokos, D&W Collachia, PH John Morrill, M Dick Hamilton, ED Collachia & Domokos.

LP Michael Moriarty (Brother T.S. Murphy), Donna Lai Ming Lew (Joy Chan), Nancy Lee (Mrs. Chan), Bruce Gray (Gower Champion), Scott Crawford (Eric).

Chinese-American Donna Lai Ming Lew wants a career as a singing star. Her more practical mother wants her to become a nurse. Her teacher Michael Moriarty encourages her singing ambitions. When Lew gets a chance to audition for director Bruce Gray, her future in show business looks bright.

2129. *Odd Jobs* (1986, Tri-Star, 88m, c). P Keith Fox Rubinstein, D Mark Story, W Robert Conte & Peter Martin Wortmann, PH Arthur Albert & Peter Lyons Collister, M Robert Folk, ED Dennis M. Hill, PD Robert R. Benton.

LP Paul Reiser (Max), Robert Townsend (Dwight), Scott McGinnis (Woody), Rick Overton (Roy), Paul Provenza (Byron), Leo Burmester (Wylie), Thomas Quinn (Frankie), Savannah Smith Boucher (Loretta/Lynette).

When five college buddies are fired from their summer jobs, they go into the moving business. They have problems with loan sharks and some sleazy competition. The humor is childish but harmless.

2130. *Of Men and Angels* (1989, Farley Film Group, 91m, c). P Simon Edery & William Farley, D Farley, W Deborah Rogin, Farley & Marjorie Berger, PH Kathleen Beeler, M Eric Muhler, ED Ian Turner, Farley, PD Jack Wright.

LP Jack Byrne (Mike O'Donahue), John Molloy (Padric Reilly), Theresa Saldana (Maria Montoya), Paul Finocchiaro (Danny), Nicky C. O'Brien (Roy), Regina Waldon (Dolly), Larallee Westaway (Dorothy), James McCann (Moriarty).

Would-be writer and San Francisco cabbie Jack Byrne picks up his drunken literary hero, aging Irish writer John Molloy, and brings him home to stay with Byrne and his live-in lady, Theresa Sal-

dana. The old man settles in for the duration, becomes a hero at the local Irish pub and belittles Byrne's writing efforts.

2131. *Of Unknown Origin* (1983, Warner, Canada, 88m, c). P Claude Heroux, D George Pan Cosmatos, W Brian Taggert (based on the novel *The Visitor* by Chauncey G. Parker, III), PH Rene Verzier, M Ken Wannberg, ED Robert Silvi, PD Anne Pritchard.

LP Peter Weller (Bart), Jennifer Dale (Lorrie), Lawrence Dane (Eliot), Kenneth Welsh (James), Louis Del Grande (Clete), Shannon Tweed (Meg), Keith Knight (Salesman), Maury Chaykin (Dan).

When his family goes away on vacation, Peter Weller is beset by a horde of rats which have invaded the townhouse he has just renovated. It's not for those with a weak stomach or a fear of rats.

2132. *Off Beat* (1986, Buena Vista, 93m, c). P Joe Roth & Harry Ufland, D Michael Dinner, W Mark Medoff (based on a story by Dezso Magyar), PH Carlo DiPalma, M James Horner, ED Dede Allen & Angelo Corrao, PD Woods MacKintosh.

LP Judge Reinhold (Joe Gower), Meg Tilly (Rachel Wareham), Cleavant Derricks (Abe Washington), Joe Mantegna (Pete Peterson), Jacques d'Amboise (August), Amy Wright (Mary Ellen Gruenwald), Anthony Zerbe (Mr. Wareham), Fred Gwynne (Commissioner), Harvey Keitel (Mickey).

Timid librarian Judge Reinhold is conned into impersonating a cop at a policeman's variety show. When Meg Tilly falls for him, uniform and all, he finds it difficult to revert to his former life.

2133. *Off Limits* (1988, 20th Century-Fox, 102m, c). P Alan Barnette, D Christopher Crowe, W Crowe & Jack Thibeau, PH David Gribble, M James Newton Howard, ED Douglas Ibold, PD Dennis Washington.

LP Willem Dafoe (Buck McGriff), Gregory Hines (Albaby Perkins), Fred Ward (Sgt. Benjamin Dix), Amanda Pays (Nicole), Kay Tong Lim (Lime Green), Scott Glenn (Col. Dexter Armstrong), David Alan Grier (Rogers).

Vietnam MPs Willem Dafoe and Gregory Hines are on the trail of an unknown U.S. army officer who kills prostitutes. This behind the scenes thriller is a traditional whodunit filled with one-dimensional stereotyped characters.

2134. *Off the Mark* (1987, Fries Entertainment, 90m, c, aka *Crazy Legs*). P Temple Matthews & Ira Trattner, D Bill Berry, W Matthews & Berry, PH Arledge Armenaki, M David Frank.

LP Mark Neely, Terry Farrell, Clarence Gilyard, Jr., Norman Alden, Virginia Capers, Jon Cypher, Barry Corbin, Billy Barty.

College triathlon star Mark Neely trains for a meet in which he will compete with ambitious Terry Farrell and a Russian exchange student. Neely suffers from an unusual disorder manifested by convulsions which make his legs act as if they had a mind of their own.

2135. *Off the Wall* (1983, Hot Dog/Farley, 85m, c). P Frank Mancuso, D Rick Friedberg, W Ron Kurz, Dick Chudnow & Friedberg, PH Donald M. Morgan, M Dennis McCarthy, ED George Hively, PD Richard Sawyer.

LP Paul Sorvino (Warden), Rosanna Arquette (Governor's Daughter), Patrick Cassidy (Randy), Billy Hufsey (Rico), Ralph Wilcox (Johnny), Dick Chudnow (Miskewicz), Monte Markham (Governor), Brianne Leary (Jennifer).

Two Northern boys hitchhiking in the South get thrown into jail on a trumped-up charge, escape and are picked up by a sexy speed demon. Everyone associated with this bomb should be arrested.

2136. *The Offenders* (1980, B Movies, 100m, c). D,W&PH Scott B & Beth B, M Bob Mason, Adele Bertei, Lydia Lunch, John Lurie, Scott B, Beth B, Terry Burns, Ed Steinberg & Alley.

LP Adele Bertel (Laura), Bill Rice (Dr. Moore), John Lurie (The Lizard), Johnny O'Kane, Robin Winters, Pat Place, Laura Kennedy.

The film is a cheaply made, off-beat, "punk melodrama" featuring New Wave music and a quirky kidnapping.

2137. *Offerings* (1989, Arista, 92m, c). P,D&W Christopher Reynolds, PH R.E. Braddock, M Russell D. Allen, ED Reynolds.

LP Loretta Leigh Bowman (Gretchen), Elizabeth Greene (Kacy), G. Michael Smith (Sheriff Chism), Jerry Brewer (Jim Paxton), Richard A. Buswell (John Radley).

If cannibalism turns you off, this film about a mute who goes on a murderous rampage ten years after killing and eating his nasty mom, may ruin your appetite.

2138. *An Officer and a Gentleman* (1982, Paramount, 126m, c). P Martin Elfand, D Taylor Hackford, W Douglas Day Stewart†, PH Donald Thorin, M Jack Nitzsche†, ED Peter Zinner†, PD Philip M. Jefferies, M/L "Up Where We Belong" by Nitzsche, Buffy St. Marie & Will Jennings* (performed by Joe Cocker and Jennifer Warnes).

LP Richard Gere (Zack Mayo), Debra Winger† (Paula Pokrifki), David Keith (Sid Worley), Robert Loggia (Byron Mayo), Lisa Blount (Lynette Pomeroy), Lisa Eilbacher (Casey Seeger), Louis Gossett, Jr.* (Sgt. Emil Foley), Tony Plana (Emiliano Della Serra), Harold Sylvester (Perryman), David Caruso (Tooper Daniels).

Poor-boy loser Richard Gere deserts his alcoholic father to enlist in a gruelling training course to become a navy pilot. He is put through hell by sadistic sergeant Lou Gossett, Jr. Gere falls in love with local bimbo Debra Winger, who is hoping to hook an officer and gentleman and escape her fate in a nothing community. Gere gives one of his best performances in a film that received higher praise than it probably deserves.

2139. *The Offspring* (1987, TMS, 96m, c, aka *From a Whisper to a Scream*). P Darin Scott & William Burr, D Jeff Burr, W Courtney Joyner, Scott & J. Burr, PH Craig Greene, M Jim Manzie & Pat Regan, ED W.O. Garrett.

LP Vincent Price (Julian White), Clu Gulager (Stanley Burnside), Terry Kiser (Jesse Hardwicke), Harry Caesar (Felder Evans), Rosalind Cash (The Snake Woman), Cameron Mitchell (Sgt. Gallen), Susan Tyrrell (Bess Chandler), Martine Beswicke (Katherine White).

Vincent Price, the historian of the small town of Oldfield and the only thing of class in this abomination, relates four tales of evil that took place in the town's past. The stories are at best disgusting.

2140. *Oh, God! Book II* (1980, Warner, 94m, c). P&D Gilbert Cates, W Josh Greenfeld, Hal Goldman, Fred S. Fox, Seaman Jacobs & Melissa Miller (based on a story by Greenfeld), PH Ralph Woolsey, M Charles Fox, ED Peter E. Berger, PD Preston Ames.

LP George Burns (God), Suzanne Pleshette (Paula), David Birney (Don), Louanne (Tracy), John Louie (Shingo), Conrad Janis (Mr. Benson), Anthony Holland (Dr. Jerome Newell), Hugh Downs (Newscaster), Dr. Joyce Brothers (Herself), Hans Conried (Dr. Barnes), Wilfred Hyde-White (Judge Miller).

George Burns was such a hit in the 1977 film, that he is brought back for this weak sequel. He enlists children to remind people that he is still around. Rather than keeping it funny, the producers are attempting to become reverent — a sure way for movies to make God look bad.

2141. *Oh, God! You Devil* (1984, Warner, 96m, c). P Robert M. Sherman, D Paul Bogart, W Andrew Bergman, PH King Baggot, M David Shire, ED Randy Roberts, Andy Zall, PD Peter Wooley.

LP John Doolittle (Arthur Shelton), Julie Lloyd (Bea Shelton), Ian Giatti (Young Bobby), George Burns (God/The Devil), Ted Wass (Bobby Shelton), Janet Brandt (Mrs. K), Roxanne Hart (Wendy Shelton), Belita Moreno (Mrs. Vega), Danny Ponce (Joey Vega).

In another working of the Faust legend, Ted Wass, married to Roxanne Hart with a little one on the way, is having a tough time making ends meet. He exclaims the usual statement of "selling his soul to the devil" and George Burns shows up to exchange Wass' life for that of a fabulously wealthy rock star. After awhile, Wass wants out, and wins back his soul from Burns in a poker game.

2142. *Oh, Heavenly Dog!* (1980, 20th Century–Fox, 103m, c). P&D Joe Camp, W Rod Browning & Camp, PH Don Reddy, M Evel Box, ED Leon Seith, PD Garrett Lewis.

LP Chevy Chase/Benji (Benjamin Browning), Jane Seymour (Jackie Howard), Omar Sharif (Malcolm Bart),

Robert Morley (Bernie), Alan Sues (Freddie), Donnelly Rhodes (Montanero), John Stride (Alistair Becket).

Private eye Chevy Chase is reincarnated as a dog to solve his own murder. This is the other side of the coin of the 1951 movie, *You Never Can Tell,* in which a murdered dog comes back to earth as Dick Powell to solve his murder. Skip this film and wait for the earlier one to show up at a video store.

2143. *Old Enough* (1984, Orion Classics, 91m, c). P Dina Silver, D&W Marisa Silver, PH Michael Ballhaus, M Julian Marshall, ED Mark Burns, PD Jeffrey Townsend.

LP Sarah Boyd (Lonnie Sloan), Rainbow Harvest (Karen Bruckner), Neill Barry (Johnny Bruckner), Danny Aiello (Mr. Bruckner), Susan Kingsley (Mrs. Bruckner), Roxanne Hart (Carla), Fran Brill (Mrs. Sloan), Gerry Bamman (Mr. Sloan).

This is a charming, but sometimes forced story of 12-year-old rich kid Sarah Boyd and her tenuous friendship with slightly older Rainbow Harvest, a girl from a different socioeconomic class.

2144. *Old Gringo* (1989, Columbia, 119m, c). P Lois Bonfiglio, D Luis Puenzo, W Aida Bortnik & Puenzo (based on the novel *Gringo Viejo* by Carlos Fuentes, PH Felix Monti, M Lee Holdridge, ED Juan Carlos Macias, William Anderson & Glenn Farr, PD Stuart Wurtzel & Bruno Rubeo.

LP Jane Fonda (Harriet Winslow), Gregory Peck (Ambrose Bierce), Jimmy Smits (Arroyo), Patricio Contreras (Col. Frutos Garcia), Jenny Gago (La Garduna), Jim Metzler (Ron), Gabriela Roel (La Luna), Anne Pitoniak (Mrs. Winslow), Pedro Armendariz, Jr. (Pancho Villa), Sergio Calderon (Zacarias).

Gregory Peck is embittered, sardonic journalist Ambrose Bierce, Jane Fonda is a widow on the run in the middle of the Mexican Revolution and Jimmy Smits is a charismatic general in Pancho Villa's Popular Front. The acting of the three is first rate, but the story and the semiromantic triangle involving them might have been better served in a less epic film. Some folks may be taken by the smoldering looks of Smits.

2145. *Oliver & Company* (1988, Buena Vista, animated, 72m, c). P Silver Screen Partners, D George Scribner, W Jim Cox, Timothy J. Disney & James Mangold (based on the novel *Oliver Twist* by Charles Dickens), PH Various Artists, M J.A.C. Redford, ED Jim Melton & Mark Hester, SUPERVISING ANIMATORS Mike Gabriel, Hendel Butoy, Glen Keane, Mark Henn, Ruben A. Aquino & Doug Krohn, AD Dan Hansen.

VOICES Joey Lawrence (Oliver), Billy Joel (Dodger), Richard [Cheech] Marin (Tito), Bette Midler (Georgette), Dom DeLuise (Fagin), Roscoe Lee Browne (Francis), Richard Mulligan (Einstein), Sheryl Lee Ralph (Rita), Natalie Gregory (Jenny), Robert Loggia (Sykes), Taurean Blacque (Roscoe).

This animated Walt Disney story is very loosely based on the Charles Dickens tale, *Oliver Twist*. Oliver is a cute orange kitten and Dodger is one of a gang of dogs cared for by a human named Fagin. When the latter is given three days to come up with the money he owes another human, Sykes, or else, the animals rally round, helping out. Kids will love it.

2146. *Omega Syndrome* (1987, New World, 88m, c). P Luigi G. Cingolani, D Joseph Manduke, W John Sharkey, PH Harvey Genkins, M Nicholas Carras & Jack Cookerly, ED Stephen A. Isaacs.

LP Ken Wahl (Jack Corbett), George DiCenzo (Philadelphia "Phil" Horton), Nicole Eggert (Jessie Corbett), Doug McClure (Detective Milnor), Patti Tippo (Sally), Robert Kim (Detective Lo), Perla Walter (Spanish Lady).

The Omega Syndrome is a secret army of urban rightwing terrorists in Los Angeles. Ken Wahl and George DiCenzo penetrate the organization and implement a plan to push the group to the brink of destruction.

On Dangerous Ground see *Choke Canyon*

2147. *On Golden Pond*† (1981, ITC-IPC-Universal-AFD, 109m, c). P Bruce Gilbert, D Mark Rydell†, W Ernest Thompson* (based on his play), PH Billy Williams†, M Dave Grusin†, ED Robert L. Wolfe†, PD Stephen Grimes, SD Emad Helmy, SOUND Richard Portman & David Ronne†.

LP Katharine Hepburn* (Ethel Thayer), Henry Fonda* (Norman Thayer, Jr.), Jane Fonda† (Chelsea Thayer Wayne), Doug McKeon (Billy Ray), Dabney Coleman (Bill Ray), William Lanteau (Charlie Martin), Chris Rydell (Sumner Todd).

It's an amazing tribute to the careers of Katharine Hepburn and Henry Fonda that so many people attended this well-acted, decent presentation, making it a box-office hit. It's the rather sentimental story of a cantankerous 80-year-old retired professor, his wise and understanding wife, and his daughter, Jane Fonda, from whom he is alienated, spending what may be a last holiday together at their lakeside New England cottage. Henry Fonda's Oscar was a long time coming. His performances in other films were more deserving, but it's fortunate that this very, very fine actor was able to get the ultimate accolade of his profession while he was still alive.

2148. *On the Edge* (1986, Skouras, 91m, c). P Jeffrey Hayes & Rob Nilsson, D&W Nilsson (based on a story by Nilsson & Roy Kissin), PH Stefan Czapsky, M Herb Pilhofer, ED Rich Harkness & Bert Lovitt.

LP Bruce Dern (Wes Holman), John Marley (Elmo Glidden), Bill Bailey (Flash), Jim Haynie (Owen Riley), Jean Shelton (Ellie), Frank Triest (Tomaso), John Tidwell (Johnny), Walt Stack (Walt).

Middle-aged runner Bruce Dern attempts to regain the glory denied him 20 years earlier when he was disqualified from the 1964 Olympic trials. He competes in the gruelling 14.2 mile annual Cielo Sea Race over California's Mount Tamalpais.

2149. *On the Line* (1987, Miramax, US/Spain, 103m, c). P Steven Kovacs & Jose Luis Borau, D Borau, W Borau & Barbara P. Solomon, PH Teo Escamilla, M Joel Goldsmith, ED Curtiss Clayton & Cari Coughlin, AD Philip Thomas.

LP David Carradine (Bryant), Scott Wilson (Mitch), Victoria Abril (Engracia), Jeff Delger (Chuck), Paul Richardson (Jonathan), Jesse Vint (Chief), Sam Jaffe (El Gabacho), David Estuardo (Pimp).

David Carradine smuggles aliens

across the Mexican border. Scott Wilson is an official intent on putting an end to Carradine's business.

2150. *On the Make* (1989, Taurus, 77m, c). P Fred Carpenter, D Samuel Hurwitz, W Carpenter & James McTernan (based on a story by Carpenter), PH Gerard Hughes, M Phil Cardonna, Don Kehr, Michael Stein & Kirk Fisher, ED Ross Gelosi.

LP Steve Irlen (Bobby), Mark McKelvey (Kurt), Teresina (Lori), Kirk Baltz (Richard), Tara Leigh (Jane), Jennifer Dempster (Vivian), Laura Grady (Tina), Michael Ross (Danny), Don Alexander (Paul).

Starting at a funeral of an AIDS victim, this somewhat preachy film advocates safe sex. It is told in flashbacks of the life of the callous victim Mark McKelvey. He proudly announces that he has had 100 female partners, one of whom apparently infected him with the deadly disease.

2151. *On the Nickel* (1980, Rose's Park, 96m, c). P,D&W Ralph Waite, PH Ric Waite, M Fredric Myrow, ED Wendy Greene Bricmont.

LP Donald Moffat (Sam), Ralph Waite (C.G.), Hal Williams (Paul), Penelope Allen (Rose), Jack Kehoe (Bad Mood), Danny Ades (God Bless), Paul Weaver (Hill), Ina Gould (Estelle), Jack O'Leary (Big William).

This slow-moving, overly sentimental film looks at the lives of the denizens of an L.A. "Skid Row."

2152. *On the Right Track* (1981, 20th Century-Fox, 97m, c). P Ronald Jacobs, D Lee Philips, W Tina Pine, Avery Buddy & Richard Moses, PH Jack Richards, M Arthur B. Rubinstein, ED Bill Butler.

LP Gary Coleman (Lester), Maureen Stapleton (Mary/Big Lady), Norman Fell (Mayor), Michael Lembeck (Frank), Lisa Eilbacher (Jill), Bill Russell (Robert), Herb Edelman (Sam), David Selburg (Felix).

You got to be a Gary Coleman fan to enjoy this sentimental piece. He's a boy who lives by his wits in a railway station and is unofficially adopted by the people who frequent the terminal.

On the Road Again see Honeysuckle Rose

2153. *On the Run* (1983, Cineworld, Australia, 101m, c). P&D Mende Brown, W Michael Fisher, PH Paul Onorato, M Laurie Lewis, ED Richard Hindley.

LP Paul Winfield (Harry), Rod Taylor (Payette), Beau Cox (Paul), Shirley Cameron, Ray Meagher, Danny Adcock.

Paul Winfield, an American convict in Australia, befriends young Beau Cox. The boy's life is in danger after he witnesses a murder. He's targeted for death by Winfield's boss, Rod Taylor.

2154. *On Valentine's Day* (1986, Angelika Films, 105m, c). P Lillian V. Foote & Calvin Skaggs, D Ken Harrison, W Horton Foote (based on his play *Valentine's Day*), PH George Tirl, M Jonathan Sheffer, ED Nancy Baker, AD Howard Cummings.

LP Hallie Foote (Elizabeth Robedaux), William Converse-Roberts (Horace Robedaux), Michael Higgins (Mr. Vaughn), Steven Hill (George Tyler), Rochelle Oliver (Mrs. Vaughn), Richard Jenkins (Bobby Pate).

The film takes place in 1917 Harrison, Texas, where Hallie Foote and William Converse-Roberts are moving up in the world just as her wastrel brother, town eccentric Steven Hill, is losing his social standing.

2155. *Once Bitten* (1985, Samuel Goldwyn, 97m, c). P Dimitri Villard, Robby Wald & Frank E. Hildebrand, D Howard Storm, W David Hines, Jeffrey Hause & Jonathan Roberts (based on a story by Villard), PH Adam Greenberg, M John Du Prez, ED Marc Grossman, PD Gene Rudolf.

LP Lauren Hutton (Countess), Jim Carrey (Mark Kendall), Karen Kopins (Robin Pierce), Cleavon Little (Sebastian), Thomas Ballatore (Jamie), Skip Lackey (Russ), Jeb Adams (WWI Ace Vampire), Joseph Brutsman (Confederate Vampire), Stuart Charno (Cabin Boy Vampire), Robin Klein (Flowerchild Vampire).

Now living in the L.A. of the 80s, centuries-old vampire Lauren Hutton requires a triple feeding of virgin blood before every Halloween to maintain her youthful appearance and beauty. Unfortunately L.A. virgins of either sex are as scarce as hen's teeth. Hutton pins her hopes on teenage virgin Jim Carrey, but with a little help from his girlfriend Karen Kopins, the innocent becomes useless to the fetching vampire.

2156.   *One More Saturday Night* (1986, Columbia, 95m, c). P Tova Laiter, Robert Kosberg & Jonathan Bernstein, D Dennis Klein, W Al Franken & Tom Davis, PH James Glennon, M David McHugh, ED Gregory Prange, AD Maher Ahmad.

LP Tom Davis (Larry), Al Franken (Paul), Moira Harris (Peggy), Frank Howard (Eddie), Bess Meyer (Tobi), Dave Reynolds (Russ Caldwell), Chelcie Ross (Dad Lundahl), Eric Saiet (Doug).

The laughs are few and far between in this nowhere film about locals kicking up their heels once a week in St. Cloud, Minnesota.

2157.   *Once Upon a Time in America* (1984, Warner, 227m, c). P Arnon Milchan, D Sergio Leone, W Leonardo Benvenuti, Piero De Bernardi, Enrico Medioli, Franco Arcalli, Franco Ferrini, Leone & Stuart Kaminsky (based on the novel *The Hoods* by Harry Grey), PH Tonio Delli Colli, M Ennio Morricone, ED Nino Baragli, AD Carlo Simi & James Singelis.

LP Robert DeNiro (Noodles), James Woods (Max), Elizabeth McGovern (Deborah), Treat Williams (Jimmy O'Donnell), Tuesday Weld (Carol), Burt Young (Joe), Joe Pesci (Frankie), Danny Aiello (Police Chief), Bill Forsythe (Cockeye), James Hayden (Patsy), Darlanne Fleugel (Eve), Larry Rapp (Fat Moe), Dutch Miller (Van Linden), Robert Harper (Sharkey), Dick "Richard" Bright (Chicken Joe), Scott Tiler (Young Noodles), Rusty Jacobs (Young Max), Brian Bloom (Young Patsy), Jennifer Donnelly (Young Deborah).

Italian director Sergio Leone presents an insightful but frustrating film of the roots of organized crime. He follows the careers of a group of Jewish boys who team up with some Italian gangsters in 1923. They run into trouble with Irish toughs who resent the competition. By 1933, one of the boys, grown to be Robert

DeNiro, bows out only to return in 1968. He is still trying to sort out the events of his life and is still pursuing Elizabeth McGovern, a girl who has eluded him from the time of his youth. James Woods is the ambitious second-in-command to the DeNiro character of the 1923 to 1933 period. In trying to save his friends, DeNiro informs on Woods' plans to rob a Federal Reserve bank, but most of the gang are killed, with Woods burned beyond recognition. In 1968, DeNiro discovers that Woods survived, has taken a new identity and is now a respected and rich politician, married to none other than McGovern. Scandal erupts in Woods' life and he begs DeNiro to kill him. DeNiro refuses and Woods is forced to handle the assignment himself. The structure of the film will upset some, but if one can sit through the nearly 4 hour movie, the experience is well worth it. (The film has in some cases been shown in a 143 minute version—avoid it.)

2158.   *One Crazy Summer* (1986, Warner, 95m, c). P Michael Jaffe, D&W Savage Steve Holland, PH Isidore Mankofsky, M Cory Lerios & James Di Pasquale, ED Alan Balsam, PD Herman Zimmerman.

LP John Cusack (Hoops McCann), Linda Warren (Mrs. McCann), Joel Murray (George Calamari), Kristen Goelz (Squid Calimari), Demi Moore (Cassandra), John Matuszak (Stain), Bobcat Goldthwait (Egg Stork), Tom Villard (Clay Stork), Kimberly Foster (Cookie Campbell).

Some wild and crazy kids have a swell summer preventing money-hungry contractors from ruining a large portion of Nantucket Island with fast-food joints and condos.

2159.   *One Dark Night* (1983, ComWorld, 89m, c). P Michael Schroeder, D Tom McLoughlin, W McLoughlin & Michael Hawes, PH Hal Trussel, M Bob Summers, ED Charles Tetoni & Michael Spence.

LP Meg Tilly (Julie), Melissa Newman (Olivia), Robin Evans (Carol), Leslie Speights (Kitty), Donald Hotton (Dockstader), Elizabeth Daily (Leslie), David Mason Daniels (Steve), Adam West (Allan), Leo Gorcey, Jr. (Barlow).

A dead man with telekinetic powers drains the bioenergy of teenage girls, who are spending a night in his mausoleum as initiation into a teenage club.

2160. *One Down, Two to Go* (1982, Almi, 84m, c). P&D Fred Williamson, W Jeff Williamson, PH James Lemmo, M Joe Trunzo & Herb Hetzer, ED Daniel Loewenthal.

LP Fred Williamson (Cal), Jim Brown (J), Jim Kelly (Chuck), Richard Roundtree (Ralph), Paula Sills (Teri), Laura Loftus (Sally), Tom Signorelli (Mario), Joe Spinell (Joe Spangler), Louis Neglia (Armando).

When Richard Roundtree is cheated out of the receipts of a martial arts tournament he promoted, his friends Fred Williamson, Jim Brown and Jim Kelly come to his rescue. It's kung-fu/blaxploitation trash.

2161. *One from the Heart* (1982, Columbia, 107m, c). P Gray Frederickson, Armyan Bernstein & Fred Roos, D Francis Coppola, W Bernstein & Coppola (based on the story by Bernstein), PH Vittorio Storaro & Ronald V. Garcia, M Tom Waits†, ED Anne Goursaud, Rudi Fehr & Randy Roberts, PD Dean Tavoularis.

LP Frederic Forrest (Hank), Teri Garr (Frannie), Raul Julia (Ray), Nastassia Kinski (Leila), Lainie Kazan (Maggie), Harry Dean Stanton (Moe), Allen Goorwitz [Garfield] (Restaurant Owner).

This $27 million dollar sleeping tablet is the story of Las Vegas married couple Frederic Forrest and Teri Garr, who love each other but are curious as to how it would be with other lovers. One Independence Day, they go their separate ways. He picks up Nastassia Kinski, she finds Raul Julia—but they get back together by the end, probably no wiser than before.

2162. *One Magic Christmas* (1985, Buena Vista, 88m, c). P Peter O'Brian, D Phillip Borsos, W Thomas Meehan (based on a story by Meehan, Borsos & Barry Healey), PH Frank Tidy, M Michael Conway Baker, ED Sidney Wolinsky, PD Bill Brodie.

LP Mary Steenburgen (Ginny Grainger), Gary Basaraba (Jack Grainger), Elisabeth Harnois (Abbie Grainger), Arthur Hill (Caleb Grainger), Wayne Robson (Harry Dickens), Harry Dean Stanton (Gideon), Jan Rubes (Santa Claus), Elias Koteas (Eddie).

This attempt to bring the message of Christmas to despondent wife and mother Mary Steenburgen, who is contemplating ending it all, is almost enough to drive members of the audience to do likewise.

2163. *One Man Force* (1989, Academy, 89m, c). P,D&W Dale Trevillion, PH Constantine Makris, M David Michael Frank, ED Lori Kornspun, PD Stephen Rice.

LP John Matuszak (Jake Swan), Ronny Cox (Lt. McCoy), Charles Napier (Dante), Sharon Farrell (Shirley), Sam Jones (Pete), Chance Boyer (Ronnie), Richard Lynch (Adams), Stacey Q (Lea Jennings).

Tough guy John Matuszak gets a rare starring role in his last film. He plays a tough, sensitive L.A. police detective, fired from the force after going on a rampage when his partner Sam Jones is killed. He's hired to find the murderer of a rock star. The two murders are linked to a money-laundering ring.

2164. *One Minute to Midnight* (1988, Curtin, 103m, c). P Dara Murphy, D Robert Michael Ingria, W Lawrence Curtin, PH Ingria, ED Curtin & Murphy.

LP Lawrence Curtin (David Lawrence), Diane Coyne (Bo), Rob Fuller (Brock), Nelson Brungart (Mike), Sydney Messett (First Wife).

Lawrence Curtin relives his own personal problems, including two failed marriages, a trip to a mental hospital and his toying with the idea of suicide. It's a vanity piece that others need not endure.

2165. *One Night Stand* (1984, Hoyts/Astra, Australia, 94m, c). P Richard Mason, D&W John Duigan, PH Tom Cowan, M William Motzing, ED John Scott, PD Ross Major.

LP Tyler Coppin (Sam), Cassandra Delaney (Sharon), Jay Hackett (Brendan), Saskia Post (Eva).

It's New Year's Eve on a hot summer night in Sydney. The news comes that a nuclear war has broken out in Europe and North America and that U.S. facilities in Australia have been bombed. It's a long night for two teenage girls Cassandra Delaney and Saskia Post and the two young men, Tyler Coppin and Jay Hackett, with whom they team up.

2166. *One-Trick Pony* (1980, Warner, 98m, c). P Michael Tannern & Michael Hausman, D Robert M. Young, W Paul Simon, PH Dick Bush, M Simon, ED Edward Beyer, Barry Malkin & David Ray, PD David Mitchell.

LP Paul Simon (Jonah), Blair Brown (Marion), Rip Torn (Walter Fox), Joan Hackett (Lonnie Fox), Allen Goorwitz [Garfield] (Cal Van Damp), Mare Winningham (Modeena Dandridge), Michael Pearlman (Matty Levin).

Paul Simon plays a singer, once on top of the charts, now reduced to opening for punk bands. He's separated from his wife, Blair Brown, who still loves him, hoping that someday he'll grow up.

2167. *Only When I Laugh* (1981, Columbia, 120m, c, aka *It Hurts Only When I Laugh*). P Roger M. Rothstein & Neil Simon, D Glenn Jordan, W Simon (based on his play *The Gingerbread Lady*), PH David M. Walsh, M David Shire, ED John Wright, PD Albert Brenner.

LP Marsha Mason† (Georgia), Kristy McNichol (Polly), James Coco† (Jimmy), Joan Hackett† (Toby), David Dukes (David), John Bennett Perry (Lou), Guy Boyd (Man), Ed Moore (Dr. Komack).

Just home from a 90-day drying out period in a sanitorium, divorced, alcoholic actress Marsha Mason tries to reestablish a relationship with her teenage daughter Kristy McNichol. Her former lover David Dukes has written a play in which he expects her to make her Broadway comeback. There are more tears than laughs in this dreary piece.

2168. *Open House* (1987, Intercontinental, 95m, c). P Sandy Cobe, D Jag Mundhra, W David Mickey Evans (based on a story by Mundhra), PH Robert Hayes & Gary Louzon, M Jim Studer, ED Dan Selakovich, PD Naomi Shohan.

LP Joseph Bottoms (Dr. David Kelley), Adrienne Barbeau (Lisa Grant), Rudy Ramos (Rudy Estevez), Mary Stavin (Katie Thatcher), Scott Thompson Baker (Joe Pearcy), Darwyn Swalve (Harry), Robert Miano (Shapiro).

Beverly Hills realtors and their clients are being killed. The only person with a lead to the murders is Joseph Bottoms, a talk show psychologist.

2169. *Options* (1989, Vestron, 92m, c). P Lance Hool, D Camilo Vila, W Edward Decter & John J. Strauss (based on a story by Decter, Strauss, Stephen Doran & Paul Schneider), PH Tony Imi, James Robb & Leo Napolitano, M Roger Bellon, ED Christopher Greenbury, PD Hans Van Den Zanden.

LP Matt Salinger (Donald Anderson), Joanna Pacula (Princess Nicole), John Kani (Jonas), Danny Keough (Philippe), Tobie Cronje (Rajid), James Keach (Ed Sloan), Alan Pierce (Raff), Siobhan Taylor (Priscilla).

Matt Salinger, a Stanford MBA, and Joanna Pacula, a disinherited Belgian princess, have a "Romancing the Stone"–like series of adventures in Zambia. She's sort of a female "Crocodile Dundee." Don't waste your time.

2170. *The Oracle* (1987, Laurel/Reeltime, 94m, c). P Walter E. Sear, D Roberta Findlay, W R. Allen Leider, PH Findlay, M Sear & Michael Litovsky, ED Findlay, SE Horrorefx.

LP Caroline Capers Powers (Jennifer), Roger Neil (Ray), Pam LaTesta (Farkas), Victoria Dryden (Dorothy Graham), Chris Maria DeKoron (Pappas), Dan Lutzky (Tom Varney), Stacey Graves (Cindy).

In this low budget gore film, a murdered businessman reaches from beyond the grave for a sadistic bloodbath of vengeance using Caroline Capers Powers as his medium of horror and hatred.

2171. *Ordeal by Innocence* (1984, MGM/United Artists, GB, 88m, c). P Jenny Craven, D Desmond Davis, W Alexander Stuart (based on the novel by Agatha Christie), PH Billy Williams, M Dave Brubeck, ED Timothy Gee, PD Ken Bridgeman.

LP Donald Sutherland (Dr. Arthur Calgary), Faye Dunaway (Rachel Calgary), Christopher Plummer (Leo Argyle), Sarah Miles (Mary Durrant), Ian McShane (Philip Durrant), Diana Quick (Gwenda Vaughan).

In a film sans Miss Marple or Hercule Poirot, Agatha Christie has written a talky and tangled mystery involving the death of Faye Dunaway that ordinary detective Donald Sutherland must solve.

Order of Death see Corrupt

2172. *Order of the Black Eagle* (1988, International Film Marketing, 93m, c). P Betty J. Stephens & Robert P. Eaton, D Worth Keeter, W Phil Behrens, PH Irl Dixon, M Dee Barton, ED Matthew Mallinson.

LP Ian Hunter (Duncan Jax), Charles K. Bibby (Star), William Hicks (Baron von Tepish), Anna Rapagna (Maxie Ryder), Jill Donnellan (Tiffany Youngblood), Flo Hyman (Spike), Shan Tai Tuan (Sato).

This is the sequel to *Unmasking the Idol,* another straight to video movie. Ian Hunter is a secret agent with a tuxedo-wearing baboon as his sidekick. His assignment is to prevent William Hicks from using stolen laser technology to rule the world. We liked the baboon.

2173. *Order of the Eagle* (1989, Action International, 82m, c). P William Zipp, D Thomas Baldwin, W Zipp, PH Stephen Ashley Blake, M William Stromberg, ED Rick Brown, PD Thom Atcheson.

LP Frank Stallone (Quill), William Zipp (Billings), Jill Foor (Monica), Perry Hill (Freddie), Casey Hirsch (Greg), David Roger Harris (Leo), David Marriott (Jack LaRouse).

Eagle Scout Casey Hirsch discovers secret computer disks at a plane crash site. They contain secret Star Wars defense information which crooked businessman Frank Stallone wants no matter what the cost. If you think Sylvester Stallone is a not-very-gifted actor, wait until you see brother Frank.

2174. *Ordinary People** (1980, Paramount, 124m, c). P Ronald L. Schwary, D Robert Redford*, W Alvin Sargent* (based on the novel by Judith Guest), PH John Bailey, M Marvin Hamlisch, ED Jeff Kanew, AD Phillip Bennett & J. Michael Riva, SD Jerry Wunderlich.

LP Donald Sutherland (Calvin), Mary Tyler Moore† (Beth), Judd Hirsch† (Berger), Timothy Hutton* (Conrad), M.

Emmet Walsh (Swim Coach), Elizabeth McGovern (Jeannine), Dinah Manoff (Karen), Fredric Lehne (Lazenby), James B. Sikking (Ray).

When the eldest son of a family is killed in a swimming accident, the adjustment period is most noticeably hard on the deceased's brother Timothy Hutton. The drowning has all but ruined the marriage between Donald Sutherland and Mary Tyler Moore, and has left the parents with no understanding of the needs of their surviving son. The acting is excellent.

2175. *Orphans* (1987, Lorimar, 115m, c). P Alan J. Pakula & Susan Solt, D Pakula, W Lyle Kessler (based on his play), PH Donald McAlpine, M Michael Small, ED Evan Lottman, PD George Jenkins.

LP Albert Finney (Harold), Matthew Modine (Treat), Kevin Anderson (Phillip), John Kellogg (Barney), Anthony Heald (Man in Park), Novella Nelson (Mattie), Elizabeth Parrish (Rich Woman).

Maladjusted young Matthew Modine supports himself and his seemingly retarded brother Kevin Anderson by petty thievery. He brings drunken, street-smart crook Albert Finney to their squalid home. Modine plans to hold Finney for ransom, but the latter talks himself out of his bonds and ends up acting as a father figure for the two young men.

2176. *Osa* (1985, Alexandrov, 94m, c). P Constantin Alexandrov, D&W Oleg Egorov, PH John Drake, M Mason Daring, ED Suzanne Fenn.

LP Kelly Lynch (Osa), Daniel Grimm (Mr. Big), Phillip Vincent (Speedway), Etienne Chicot (Allan), John Forristal (Crooner), Peter Walker (Trooper), David Hausman (Weasel), Bill Moseley (Quilt Face), Len Stanger (Mr. Hammond), Brenda King (Mrs. Hammond).

After a nuclear war, radiation-free water is going for $200 a gallon. Len Stanger holds the franchise but spunky Kelly Lynch plans to end the former's monopoly. Lynch bests Stanger's homosexual security head in a deadly futuristic game.

2177. *The Osterman Weekend* (1983, 20th Century–Fox, 102m, c). P Peter S. Davis & William N. Panzer, D Sam Peckinpah, W Alan Sharp & Ian Masters (based on the book by Robert Ludlum), PH John Coquillon, M Lalo Schifrin, ED Edward Abroms & David Rawlins.

LP Rutger Hauer (John Tanner), John Hurt (Lawrence Fassett), Craig T. Nelson (Bernard Osterman), Dennis Hopper (Richard Tremayne), Chris Sarandon (Joseph Cardone), Burt Lancaster (Maxwell Danforth), Meg Foster (Ali Tanner), Helen Shaver (Virginia Tremayne), Cassie Yates (Betty Cardone).

Ruthless CIA operative John Hurt convinces Rutger Hauer, the news director of a TV station, that his friends are Soviet agents. The convoluted plot has a lot of killing, but doesn't add much to the subgenre of spy thrillers.

2178. *Otello* (1986, Cannon, 122m, c). P Menahem Golan & Yoram Globus, D Franco Zeffirelli, W Zeffirelli, Masolino D'Amico, PH Ennio Guarnieri, M Giuseppe Verdi, LIBRETTO Arrigo Boito, ED Peter Taylor & Franca Sylvi, PD Gianni Quaranta, SD Bruno Carlino & Stefano Paltrinieri, COND Lorin Maazel, COS Anna Anni & Maurizio Millenotti†.

LP Placido Domingo (Otello), Katia Ricciarelli (Desdemona), Justino Diaz (Iago), Petra Malakova (Emilia), Urbano Barberini (Cassio), Massimo Foschi (Lodovico), Edwin Francis (Montano), Sergio Nicolai (Roderigo), Remo Remotti (Brabanzio), Antonio Pierfederici (Doge).

Franco Zeffirelli provides a lush adaptation of Giuseppe Verdi's greatest opera. Placido Domingo as the jealous Moor, Justino Diaz as the malevolent Iago and Katia Ricciarelli as the tragic and innocent Desdemona are all superb, both as actors and opera singers.

2179. *Othello* (1989, Uptown, 123m, c). P Katherine A. Kaspar, D Ted Lange, W Lange (based on the play by William Shakespeare), PH James M. Swain, M Domenick Allen, ED Tim Tobin, PD Christine Remsen.

LP Ted Lange (Othello), Hawthorne James (Iago), Mary Otis (Desdemona), Domenick Allen (Cassio), Dawn Comer (Emilia), Marina Palmier (Bianca), Stuart Rogers (Roderigo).

This low-budget filming of the classic play has black actor Ted Lange playing the title role. He and black actor Hawthorne James as Iago are laudable in their roles.

2180. *Other Halves* (1985, Oringham, New Zealand, 102m, c). P Tom Finlayson & Dean Hill, D John Laing, W Sue McCanley (based on her novel), PH Leon Narbey, M Don McGlashan, ED Harley Oliver, PD Robert Gillies.

LP Lisa Harrow (Liz), Mark Pilsi (Tug), Fraser Stephen-Smith (Michael), Paul Gittins (Ken), Emma Piper (Audrey), Bruce Purchase (Irwin), John Bach (Jim), Clare Clifford (Aileen), Temuera Morrison (Tony).

Middle-class housewife Lisa Harrow, recently separated from her husband and young son, meets streetwise Polynesian Mark Pilsi in contemporary Auckland. Their relationship helps each other.

2181. *Out* (1988, Cinema Group Home Video, 88m, c). P&D Eli Hollander, W Hollander & Ronald Sukenick (based on Sukenick's novel), PH Robert Ball, M David Cope, ED Hollander.

LP Peter Coyote, O-Lan, Jim Haynie, Grandfather Semu Haute, Scott Beach, Danny Glover, Michael Grodenchik, Gail Dartez.

Structured like a novel, this road picture sees Peter Coyote leaving Greenwich Village for Venice, California. As he travels cross country, he keeps running into the same people in various towns but with new identities.

2182. *Out Cold* (1989, Hemdale, 87m, c). P George G. Braunstein & Ron Hamady, D Malcolm Mowbray, W Leonard Glasser & George Malko (based on a story by Glasser), PH Tony Pierce-Roberts, M Michel Colombier, ED Dennis M. Hill, PD Linda Pearl.

LP John Lithgow (Dave), Teri Garr (Sunny Cannald), Randy Quaid (Lester Atlas), Bruce McGill (Ernie Cannald), Lisa Blount (Phyllis), Alan Blumenfeld (Lew).

This black comedy is the story of pragmatic, calculating Teri Garr, a villain you got-to-love. She diapatches her blowhard husband Bruce McGill, when the opportunity presents itself. But McGill's partner in the butcher business, John Lithgow, who is in love with Garr, draws the line at carving up the frozen body of his deceased friend.

2183. *Out of Africa** (1985, Universal, 150m, c). P&D Sydney Pollack* (for directing), W Kurt Luedtke* (based on *Out of Africa* and other writings by Isak Dinesen, *Isak Dinesen: The Life of a Storyteller* by Judith Thurman and *Silence Will Speak* by Errol Trzebinski), PH David Watkin*, M John Barry*, ED Fredric Steinkamp, William Steinkamp, Pembroke Herring & Sheldon Kahn†, AD Stephen Grimes & Josie MacAvin*, COS Milena Canonero†, SOUND Chris Jenkins, Gary Alexander, Larry Stensvold & Peter Handford*.

LP Meryl Streep† (Karen Blixen-Finecke), Robert Redford (Denys Finch Hatton), Klaus Maria Brandauer† (Baron Bror Blixen-Finecke), Michael Kitchen (Berkeley), Malick Bowens (Farah), Joseph Thiaka (Kamante), Stephen Kinyanjui (Kinanjui), Michael Gough (Delamere), Suzanne Hamilton (Felicity), Rachel Kempson (Lady Belfield), Graham Crowden (Lord Belfield), Leslie Phillips (Sir Joseph), Shane Rimmer (Belknap).

Set in 1914, a strong-willed woman, Meryl Streep, and her ne'er-do-well husband Klaus Maria Brandauer run a coffee plantation in Kenya. Somewhat to her surprise she begins to fall in love with the country, the people and most especially mysterious white hunter Robert Redford. The film is justifiably praised, being a top-notch production with an excellent cast.

2184. *Out of Bounds* (1986, Columbia, 93m, c). P Charles Fries & Mike Rosenfeld, D Richard Tuggle, W Tony Kayden, PH Bruce Surtees, M Stewart Copeland, ED Kent Beyda & Larry Bock, PD Norman Newberry.

LP Anthony Michael Hall (Daryl Cage), Jenny Wright (Dizz), Jeff Kober (Roy Gaddis), Glynn Turman (Lt. Delgado), Raymond J. Barry (Hurley), Pepe Serna (Murano), Jerry Levine (Marshall).

Young Iowa farm boy Anthony Michael Hall visits his brother in L.A. He mistakes a bag containing heroin for his

at the airport. Murderous psychopaths are determined to regain their belongings and don't much care what happens to Master Hall.

2185. *Out of Control* (1985, New World, 78m, c). P Fred Weintraub & Daniel Grodnik, D Allan Holzman, W Sandra Weintraub Roland & Vicangelo Bulluck, PH John A. Alonzo, M Hawk, ED Robert Ferretti & Allan Holzman.

LP Martin Hewitt (Keith), Betsy Russell (Chrissie), Claudia Udy (Tina), Andrew J. Lederer (Elliot), Cindi Dietrich (Robin), Richard Kantor (Gary), Sherilyn Fenn (Katie), Jim Youngs (Cowboy).

Wealthy high school senior Martin Hewitt promises to take girlfriend Betsy Russell and their friends to an island his parents own. On the way, their plane crashes into the sea. The pilot is killed but the kids make it to the island where they find a cache of liquor. This leads to an orgy. In the morning, they find they are not on a deserted island and must contend with a gang of vicious smugglers.

2186. *Out of the Blue* (1982, Discovery, 94m, c). P Leonard Yakir, D Dennis Hopper, W Yakir, Brenda Nielson & Gary Jules Jouvenat, PH Marc Champion, M Tom Lavin, ED Doris Dyck.

LP Linda Manz (CeBe), Sharon Farrell (Kathy), Dennis Hopper (Don), Raymond Burr (Brean), Don Gordon (Charlie).

Dennis Hopper is just out of prison where he served five years for manslaughter, having drunkenly driven into a school bus filled with children, killing several. He's trying to make something out of his life, but it's not easy. While he's been away, his wife Sharon Farrell has developed quite a reputation for being a tramp, alcoholic and druggie, and his daughter Linda Manz is a confused and fatalistic teen.

2187. *Out of the Dark* (1988, Cinetel, 90m, c). P Zane W. Levitt, D Michael Schroeder, W J. Greg De Felice & Levitt, PH Julio Macat, M Paul F. Antonelli & David Wheatley, ED Mark Manos, PD Robert Schulenberg.

LP Cameron Dye (Kevin), Karen Black (Ruth), Bud Cort (Stringer), Lynn Danielson (Kristi), Divine (Det. Langella),

Lainie Kazan (Hooker Nancy), Paul Bartel (Clerk), Geoffrey Lewis (Dennis), Tracey Walter (Lt. Meyers), Tab Hunter (Driver).

In a kinky but inept thriller, a murderer wearing a clown mask carves up women working for Suite Nothings, a telephone sex service. Divine, the "male actress," makes his last film appearance in an almost cameo role.

2188. *Out of the Darkness* (1985, Rank, GB, 68m, c). P Gordon L.T. Scott, D&W John Krish (based on the novel *The Ivy Garland* by John Hoyland), PH Ray Orton, M Ed Welch, ED Krish.

LP Gary Halliday (Tom), Michael Flowers (Mike), Emma Ingham (Penny), Anthony Winder (Ghost Boy), Michael Carter (Julian Reid), Jenny Tarren (Mrs. Neil), Eric Mason (Mr. Barrow), Charlotte Mitchell (Mrs. Barrow).

Three Derbyshire children see the ghost of a dead boy. With the help of the town's museum keeper, they discover that the ghost is that of a 17th century boy who had been smuggled from a nearby plague-stricken village for his safety. He was lynched by the townsfolk, fearing he might be contagious.

2189. *Out of Time* (1989, ATP/Tamido, GB/Egypt, 94m, c). P&D Anwar Kawadri, W Jesse Graham, PH Fred Tammes, M Alan Parker, ED John Shirley.

LP Jeff Fahey (Jake), Camilla More (Rene), Spiros Focas (Stavros Eliomotis), Michael Gothard (Haros), Michael Russo (Nikos), Tuck Milligan (Donald), Gamil Rateb (Omar).

Archeologist Jeff Fahey and seeming air-head Camilla More compete with villain Focas to find an Egyptian treasure once belonging to Alexander the Great.

2190. *Out on Bail* (1989, TransWorld, 102m, c). P Alan Amiel, D Gordon Hessler, W Michael D. Sonye, Jason Booth & Tom Badal, PH Johan van der Vyer, M John David Hiler & Briani, ED Brian Varaday, PD Gavin Bitter.

LP Robert Ginty (John Dee), Kathy Shower (Sally Anne Lewis), Tom Badal (Sheriff Taggert), Sidney Lassick (Smiley), Leo Sparrowhawk (Mayor Farley).

Robert Ginty, a stranger to Fairfield,

Tennessee, is thrown into jail for fighting with thugs involved in a drug deal. The corrupt sheriff and a shady lawyer offer Ginty the chance to escape if he will assassinate the reform candidate for mayor.

2191. *Outback* (1989, Samuel Goldwyn, Australia, 91m, c). P John Sexton, D Ian Barry, W Sexton, PH Ross Berryman, M Mario Millo, ED Henry Dangar, PD Owen Paterson.

LP Jeff Fahey (Creed), Tushka Bergen (Alice Richards), Steve Vidler (Jack Donaghue), Richard Moir (Thompson), Shane Briant (Allenby), Drew Forsythe (Henry Iverson), Sandy Gore (Aunt Maude), Fred Parslow (Richards), Cornelia Frances (Caroline Richards).

In this turn-of-the-century Australian Western, Tushka Bergen's father Fred Parslow's mismanagement has driven him to the edge of bankruptcy. He is in danger of losing his lavish property to villainous neighbor Shane Briant. Bergen is spared the loss of her home by the intercession of American businessman Jeff Fahey and her drover boyfriend, Steve Vidler.

2192. *Outcasts* (1982, Cinegate, GB, 104m, c). P Tony Dollard, D&W Robert Wynne-Simmons, PH Seamus Corcoran, M Stephen Cooney, ED Arthur Keating.

LP Mary Ryan (Maura O'Donnell), Mick Lally (Scarf Michael), Don Foley (Hugh O'Donnell), Tom Jordan (Conor Farrell), Cyril Cusack (Myles Kennan), Brenda Scallon (Breda O'Donnell).

In 1810 Ireland, a widower's daughter accused of witchcraft is saved by a magical fiddler.

Outer Heat* see *Alien Nation

Outer Touch* see *Spaced Out

The Outing* see *Scream

2193. *The Outing* (1987, HIT/TMS, 85m, c, aka *The Lamp*). P Warren Chaney, D Tom Daley, W Chaney, PH Herbert Raditschnig, M Joel Rosenbaum, ED Claudio Cutry, PD Robert Burns, SE Frank Inez, Martin Becker & Reel EFX Inc.

LP Deborah Winters (Eve Farrell), James Huston (Dr. Al Wallace), Andra St. Ivanyi (Alex Wallace), Scott Bankston (Ted Pinson), Mark Mitchell (Mike Daley), Andre Chimene (Tony Greco), Damon Merrill (Babe).

A group of teenagers invade a museum with plans to spend the night and mess around a bit. What they don't know is that one of them has released an evil genie from an ancient lamp. Their ignorance will prove horribly fatal.

2194. *Outland* (1981, Warner, GB, 109m, c). P Richard A. Roth, D&W Peter Hyams, PH Stephen Goldblatt, M Jerry Goldsmith, ED Stuart Baird, PD Philip Harrison, AD Malcolm Middleton, SOUND John K. Wilkinson, Robert W. Glass, Jr., Robert M. Thirwell & Robin Gregory†.

LP Sean Connery (O'Neil), Peter Boyle (Sheppard), Frances Sternhagen (Lazarus), James B. Sikking (Montone), Kika Markham (Carol), Clarke Peters (Ballard), Steven Berkoff (Sagan), John Ratzenberger (Tarlow), Nicholas Barnes (Paul O'Neil).

In this sci-fi remake of *High Noon,* Sean Connery is the marshal of a mining base on the third moon of Jupiter, waiting for hired killers to arrive from Earth to assassinate him.

2195. *Outlaw Force* (1988, Trans-World, 95m, c). P David Heavener & Ronnie Hadar, D&W Heavener, PH David Huey & James Mathers, M Donald Hulette, ED Peter Miller.

LP David Heavener (Billy Ray Dalton), Paul Smith (Inspector Wainwright), Frank Stallone (Grady), Robert Bjorklund (Washington), Devin Dunsworth (Jesse), Stephanie Cicero (Holly Dalton), Warren Berlinger (Capt. Morgan), Cecilea Xavier (Billy's Wife).

David Heavener, a decent family man, gets into troubles with rednecks when he comes to the aid of a black gas station attendant they are attacking. The meanies track down Heavener's wife, rape and kill her, and kidnap his daughter, planning to sell her into kiddie porn. Heavener turns to the police for help, but when they can't do anything, he becomes Charles Bronson.

2196. *Outrageous Fortune* (1987, Buena Vista, 100m, c). P Ted Field, Robert W. Cort, Peter V. Herald, Scott Kroopf & Martin Mickelson, D Arthur Hiller, W Leslie Dixon, PH David M. Walsh, M Alan Silvestri, ED Tom Rolf, PD James D. Vance.

LP Shelley Long (Lauren Ames), Bette Midler (Sandy Brozinsky), Peter Coyote (Michael), Robert Prosky (Stanislov Korzenowski), John Schuck (Atkins), George Carlin (Frank), Anthony Heald (Weldon), Ji-Tu Cumbuka (Cab Driver).

The fun of this familiar plot is the interplay of Shelley Long's maddeningly superior "Cheers" character and Bette Midler as a loud-mouth tramp. The two team together to chase after disappeared Peter Coyote, who had been bedding both. They want to find out which one he prefers, but discover he was only using both in his plot to sell a vial of deadly serum to the highest bidder.

2197. *The Outsider* (1980, Paramount, 128m, c). P Philippe Modave, D&W Tony Luraschi (based on the novel *The Heritage of Michael Flaherty* by Colin Leinster), PH Ricardo Aronovich, M Ken Thorne, ED Catherine Kelber.

LP Craig Wasson (Michael Flaherty), Patricia Quinn (Siobhan), Sterling Hayden (Seamus Flaherty), Niall Toibin (Farmer), Elizabeth Begley (Mrs. Cochran), T.P. McKenna (John Russell), Frank Grimes (Tony Coyle).

American Vietnam veteran Craig Wasson joins the IRA in Belfast. He ultimately learns that he's to be a sacrificial lamb in a plot to have it appear that he was killed by the British, thereby gaining the sympathy of Irish-Americans to the revolutionary cause.

2198. *The Outsiders* (1983, Warner, 91m, c). P Fred Roos & Gray Frederickson, D Francis Ford Coppola, W Kathleen Knutsen Rowell (based on the novel by S.E. Hinton), PH Stephen H. Burum, M Carmine Coppola, ED Anne Goursaud, PD Dean Tavoularis.

LP Matt Dillon (Dallas Winston), Ralph Macchio (Johnny Cade), C. Thomas Howell (Ponyboy Curtis), Patrick Swayze (Darrel Curtis), Rob Lowe (Sodapop Curtis), Emilio Estevez (Two-Bit Matthews), Tom Cruise (Steve Randle), Glenn Withrow (Tim Shephard), Diane Lane (Cherry Valance), Leif Garrett (Bob Sheldon).

Remarkable for all the young talent, the story of the battle between rich kids and poor thugs in 1966 Tulsa is unremarkable. The fault lies with director Frances Ford Coppola, who hasn't let his actors in on the fact that he was planning an epic.

2199.   *Outtakes* (1987, Sell Pictures, 71m, c). P Jack M. Sell & Adrianne Richmond, D Sell, W Sell, Richmond & Jim Fay, PH Ron Bell & Sell, M Sell, Rich Daniels & Chris Lay, ED Sell.

LP Forrest Tucker, Bobbi Wexler, Joleen Lutz, Curt Colbert, Marilyn Abrams, Warren Davis, Coleen Downey, Jim Fay, Jack M. Sell.

This totally offensive film, consisting of bawdy, sexy and sexist comedy skits, is hosted by Forrest Tucker. It was started in 1983, finished in 1985 and had a brief theatrical release in 1987 before ending up in video stores in 1988.

2200.   *Over the Brooklyn Bridge* (1984, MGM/United Artists, 106m, c). P Menahem Golan & Yoram Globus, D Golan, W Arnold Somkin, PH Adam Greenberg, M Pino Donaggio, ED Mark Goldblatt, AD John Lawless.

LP Elliott Gould (Alby Sherman), Margaux Hemingway (Elizabeth Anderson), Sid Caesar (Uncle Benjamin), Burt Young (Phil Romano), Shelley Winters (Becky Sherman), Carol Kane (Cheryl Goodman), Robert Gosset (Eddie), Karen Shallo (Mariena).

If you find stereotyped Jews and WASPs amusing, you may howl at this romantic comedy starring Elliott Gould as a Brooklyn luncheonette owner struggling to get the down payment for his dream restaurant in Manhattan. His relatives will come up with the dough if he dumps gentile Margaux Hemingway and settles down with the nice Jewish girl they have in mind for him.

2201.   *Over the Top* (1987, Warner/Cannon, 93m, c). P Menahem Golan & Yoram Globus, D Golan, W Stirling Silliphant & Sylvester Stallone (based on a story by Gary Conway & David C. Engelbach), PH David Gurfinkel, M Giorgio Moroder, ED Don Zimmerman & James Symons, PD James Schoppe.

LP Sylvester Stallone (Lincoln Hawk),

Robert Loggia (Jason Cutler), Susan Blakely (Christina Hawk), Rick Zumwalt (Bob "Bull" Hurley), David Mendenhall (Michael Cutler), Chris McCarty (Tim Salanger), Terry Funk (Ruker).

In one of the biggest turkeys of the year, truck driver Sylvester Stallone struggles to win the love and respect of his son David Mendenhall. He hasn't seen much of the boy since his wife divorced him and remarried. Father and son travel cross country on a three day trip, participating in arm wrestling contests (surely, one of the least interesting sports events ever devised). The film could be called "Rocky and Rambo visit the Champ."

2202.   *Overboard* (1987, MGM/United Artists, 112m, c). P Alexandra Rose & Anthea Sylbert, D Garry Marshall, W Leslie Dixon, PH John A. Alonzo, M Alan Silvestri, ED Dov Hoenig & Sonny Baskin, AD James Shanahan & Jim Dultz.

LP Goldie Hawn (Joanna Stayton/ "Annie Proffitt"), Kurt Russell (Dean Proffitt), Edward Herrmann (Grant Stayton, III), Roddy McDowall (Andrew), Michael Hagerty (Billy Pratt), Katherine Helmond (Edith Mintz), Jared Rushton (Charlie Proffitt), Jeffrey Wiseman (Joey Proffitt), Brian Price (Travis Proffitt), Jamie Wild (Greg Proffitt).

Pampered rich bitch Goldie Hawn falls overboard from her yacht near Elk Cove, Oregon. She loses her memory of who she is. Kurt Russell, a carpenter whom she stiffed for the cost of some work he did to her stateroom, sees an opportunity to get even. He claims her as his wife, sealing the identificaton by describing a birthmark on her bottom, which he noticed when she wore a very revealing bikini aboard her yacht. Russell takes Hawn to his squalid home to meet his four unruly and undisciplined boys. Predictably, everyone comes to love each other and when Hawn regains her memory, audiences just know that leaving her "family" won't be permanent.

2203.   *Overkill* (1987, Movie Factory-Manson, 81m, c). P&D Ulli Lommel, W Lommel & David Scott Kroes, PH James Takashi, M Bill Roebuck, ED Ron Norman, PD Manuel Riva.

LP Steve Rally (Mickey Delano), John Nishio (Akashi), Laura Burkett (Jamie), Allen Wisch (Collins), Antonio Caprio (Chief of Police), Roy Summersett (Steiner), Shiro Tomita (Naguma, Sr.). Maverick L.A. detective Steve Rally and John Nishio, the brother of a Yakuza executioner victim, join forces to fight the Japanese mobsters.

2204. *Oxford Blues* (1984, MGM/ United Artists, 93m, c). P Cassian Elwes & Elliott Kastner, D&W Robert Boris, PH John Stanier, M John DuPrez, ED Patrick Moore & James Symons, PD Terry Pritchard.

LP Rob Lowe (Nick Di Angelo), Ally Sheedy (Rona), Amanda Pays (Lady Victoria), Julian Sands (Colin), Julian Firth (Geordie), Alan Howard (Simon), Gail Strickland (Las Vegas Lady), Michael Gough (Dr. Ambrose).

In a lightweight attempt to remake *A Yank at Oxford,* Rob Lowe portrays an obnoxious know-it-all American at Oxford. He puts the rush on Amanda Pays and offends just about everyone—but he finally proves his mettle in a rowing scull.

2205. *Pacific Inferno* (1985, VCL, US/Philippines, 89m, c). P Spencer Jourdain & Cassius V. Weathersby, D Rolf Bayer, W Bayer, Roland S. Jefferson & Eric P. Jones, PH Mars [Nonong] Rasca, ED Richard C. Meyer & Ann Mills.

LP Jim Brown (Clyde Preston), Richard Jaeckel (Dealer), Tim Brown (Dawson), Tad Horino (Yamada), Dino Fernando (Totoy), Wilma Reading (Tita), Rik von Nutter (Dennis), Jimmy Shaw (Leroy).

In 1942 General Douglas MacArthur ordered the dumping of $16 million worth of silver pesos into Manila Bay to prevent its use by the invading Japanese. Captured U.S. Navy divers are forced to recover it. Jim Brown organizes an escape to recruit local guerrillas to whom he plans to turn over the silver. This action movie was filmed in 1977, but not released until eight years later.

2206. *The Package* (1989, Orion, 108m, c). P Beverly J. Camhe, D Andrew Davis, W John Bishop, PH Frank Tidy, M James Newton Howard, ED Don Zimmerman & Billy Weber, PD Michel Levesque.

LP Gene Hackman (Johnny Gallagher), Joanna Cassidy (Eileen Gallagher), Tommy Lee Jones (Thomas Boyette), John Heard (Col. Glen Whitacre), Dennis Franz (Milan Delich), Pam Grier (Ruth Butler), Kevin Crowley (Walter Henke), Reni Santoni (Police Lt.), Ron Dean (Karl Richards), Thalmus Rasulala (Secret Service).

Career army officer Gene Hackman is given the assignment of escorting troublesome soldier Tommy Lee Jones—the package—from East Berlin to the States to stand trial. Jones gets away and Hackman must recapture him. The series of coincidences in this not very fresh political thriller are enough to make one believe in Kismet. It's not very interesting, and Hackman has been better, but it may be worth a peek when it hits cable.

2207. *Palais Royale* (1988, Spectrafilm, Canada, 100m, c). P David Daniels & Lawrence Zack, D Martin Lavut, W Hugh Graham, Daniels, Zack & Jo Ann Mcintyre, PH Brenton Spencer, M Jonathan Goldsmith, ED Susan Martin, AD Ruben Freed.

LP Kim Cattrall (Odessa), Matt Craven (Gerald), Kim Coates (Tony), Dean Stockwell (Dattalico), Brian George (Gus), Michael Hogan (Sgt. Leonard).

In a Toronto-based film noir, shy Matt Craven has ambitions of becoming an ace advertising man. He fantasizes about a beautiful model on a billboard outside his window. He meets the girl of his dreams, Kim Cattrall, and follows her to the Palais Royale, a sinister nightclub. He gets mixed up with the mobsters who run her life. Sounds sort of like Edward G. Robinson, Joan Bennett and *The Woman in the Window.*

2208. *Pale Rider* (1985, Warner, 115m, c). P&D Clint Eastwood, W Michael Butler & Dennis Shryack, PH Bruce Surtees, M Lennie Niehaus, ED Joel Cox, PD Edward Carfagno.

LP Clint Eastwood (Preacher), Michael Moriarty (Hull Barret), Carrie Snodgress (Sarah Wheeler), Christopher Penn (Josh LaHood), Richard Dysart (Coy LaHood), Sydney Penny (Megan Wheeler), Richard Kiel (Club), Doug McGrath (Spider Conway), John Russell (Stockburn), Charles Hallahan (McGill).

Nameless stranger Clint Eastwood rides into a small California gold rush town and finds himself in the middle of a bloody war between independent prospectors and a mining syndicate. Lots of lead flies in this violent but interesting Western. John Russell is very good being very bad as the head of the killers brought in by the mine owners to intimidate the competition.

2209. *Pallet on the Floor* (1984, Mirage, New Zealand, 90m, c). P Larry Parr, D Lynton Butler, W Martyn Sanderson, Robert Rising & Butler (based on the novel by Ronald Hugh Morrieson), PH Kevin Hayward, M Bruno Lawrence & Jonathan Crayford, ED Patrick Monaghan, PD Lyn Bergquist.

LP Bruce Spence (Basil Beaumont-Foster), Peter McCauley (Sam Jamieson), Jillian O'Brien (Sue Jamieson), Shirley Gruar (Miriam Breen), Alistair Douglas (Stanley Breen), Tony Barry (Larkman), John Bach (Jack Voot).

One has to wonder what message if any is intended in this strange tale of murder and lust set in a small New Zealand coastal town.

2210. *Pandemonium* (1982, MGM/United Artists, 82m, c, aka *Thursday the 12th*). P Doug Chapin, D Alfred Sole, W Richard Whitley & Jaime Klein, PH Michel Hugo, M Dana Kaproff, ED Eric Jenkins, PD Jack DeShields.

LP Tom Smothers (Cooper), Debralee Scott (Sandy), Candy Azzara (Bambi), Suzanne Kent, Phil Hartmann, Michael Kless, David L. Lander, Paul Reubens, Eve Arden, Kaye Ballard, Tab Hunter, Donald O'Connor, Carol Kane, Judge Reinhold.

You'd have to consider an entire cheerleading squad's being skewered by one javelin to be funny, to enjoy this spoof of slasher movies. Someone is murdering the students of "It Had to Be U." It's a big nothing.

2211. *Paperhouse* (1989, Vestron, GB, 94m, c). P Tim Bevan & Sarah Radclyffe, D Bernard Rose, W Mathew Jacobs (based on the novel *Marianne Dreams* by Catherine Storr), PH Mike Southon, M Hans Zimmer & Stanley Myers, ED Dan Rae, PD Gemma Jackson.

LP Charlotte Burke (Anna), Elliott Spiers (Marc), Glenne Headly (Kate), Ben Cross (Dad), Gemma Jones (Dr. Sarah Nichols), Sarah Newbold (Karen), Samantha Cahill (Sharon).

The film explores the fantasy world of little sick girl Charlotte Burke. As her illness becomes more serious, she spends more and more time in a dream world of her own invention. When her physician tells Burke about another sick youngster, Elliott Spiers, she incorporates him into her fantasies and they become friends. It's part psychological thriller, part ghost story.

2212. *Paradise* (1982, Embassy, 100m, c). P Robert Lantos & Stephen J. Roth, D&W Stuart Gillard, PH Adam Greenberg, M Paul Hoffert, ED Howard Terrill, PD Claude Bonniere.

LP Willie Aames (David), Phoebe Cates (Sarah), Richard Curnock (Geoffrey), Tuvia Tavi (The Jackal), Neil Vipond (Reverend), Aviva Marks (Rachel), Joseph Shiloach (Ahmed).

When Willie Aames and Phoebe Cates find themselves abandoned at a desert oasis, their hormones heat up, and they do what comes naturally. An old blue movie at the local American Legion Hall would be more interesting.

2213. *Paradise Motel* (1985, Saturn International, 92m, c). P Gary Gibbs & Frank Rubin, D Cary Medoway, W Roger Stone & Medoway, PH James L. Carter, M Rick White & Mark Governor, ED Doug Jackson.

LP Gary Hershberger (Daniel Kehoe), Robert Krantz, Joanna Leigh Stack, Bob Basso.

Centered around a seedy motel where rooms are rented by the hour, high school boys battle for the attentions of aptly named classmate Joanna Leigh Stack.

2214. *Paramedics* (1988, Vestron, 91m, c). P Leslie Greif, D Stuart Margolin, W Barry Bardo & Richard Kriegsman, PH Michael Watkins, ED Allan A. Moore, M Murray MacLeod, PD Jack Marty.

LP George Newbern (Uptown), Christopher McDonald (Mad Mike), Javier Grejeda (Bennie), Lawrence-Hilton Jacobs (Blade Runner), Elaine Wilkes (Savannah), Lydie Denier (Lisette), John P. Ryan (Capt. Prescott).

Male paramedics are given the mission of breaking up a ring selling internal organs which have been acquired in unconventional ways. The boys have time for plenty of sexual adventures along the way.

2215. *Parasite* (1982, Embassy, 3-D, 85m, c). P&D Charles Band, W Alan Adler, Michael Shoob & Frank Levering, PH Mac Ahlberg, M Richard Band, ED Brad Arensman, AD Pamela B. Warner, SE Stan Winston, James Kagel, Doug White & Lance Anderson.

LP Robert Glaudini (Dr. Paul Dean), Demi Moore (Patricia), Luca Bercovici (Ricus), James Davidson (Merchant), Al Fann (Collins), Vivian Blaine (Miss Daley), Tom Villard (Zeke), Cherie Currie (Dana), James Cavan (Buddy).

In 1992, scientist Robert Glaudini infects victims with little creatures who eat themselves out of their hosts' bodies. Disgusting and gross.

2216. *Parenthood* (1989, Universal, 124m, c). P Brian Grazer, D Ron Howard, W Lowell Ganz & Babaloo Mandel (based on a story by Ganz, Mandel, Howard), PH Donald McAlpine, M Randy Newman, ED Michael Hill & Daniel Hanley, PD Todd Hallowell, SONG "I Love to See You Smile" by Randy Newman*.

LP Steve Martin (Gil), Mary Steenburgen (Karen), Dianne Wiest† (Helen), Jason Robards (Frank), Rick Moranis (Nathan), Tom Hulce (Larry), Martha Plimpton (Julie), Keanu Reeves (Tod), Dennis Dugan (David Brodsky), Leaf Phoenix (Garry), Eileen Ryan (Marilyn), Helen Shaw (Grandma), Jasen Fisher (Kevin), Paul Linke (George Bowman).

Director Ron Howard gives audiences a sometimes too sentimental, but generally excellent ensemble comedy. It focuses on one extended and wildly diverse middle class American family. Jason Robards, the patriarch of the family, neglected his children when they were young, but can't totally escape his responsibilites now that they are grown. Steve Martin will do just about anything to deal with his 8-year-old son's emotional problems. Rick Moranis is a weird nerd, trying to force-feed learning and culture on his

3-year-old daughter. Tom Hulce is a ne'er-do-well who has moved back in with Robards, bringing with him a half-black son and bad debts to some angry mobsters. Diane Wiest is a single parent, trying to cope with her rebellious teens, Martha Plimpton and Leaf Phoenix, and Plimpton's ardent boyfriend Keanu Reeves. It's a funny, touching look at yuppies who once might have been part of the Big Chill generation.

2217. *Parents* (1988, Vestron, 83m, c). P Bonnie Palef, D Bob Balaban, W Christopher Hawthorne, PH Ernest Day & Robin Vidgeon, M Jonathan Elias, ED Bill Pankow, AD Andris Hausmanis.

LP Randy Quaid (Nick Laemle), Marybeth Hurt (Lily Laemle), Sandy Dennis (Millie Dew), Bryan Madorsky (Michael Laemle), Juno Mills-Cockell (Sheila Zellner), Kathryn Grody (Miss Baxter).

The Laemle family seems to be typical 50s folks, but there's something about their eating habits. They always seem to have leftovers — but leftovers from what? Newcomer Bryan Madorsky is quite effective as the son who suffers from violent nightmares, hearing strange sounds coming from the cellar. Is his problem bad dreams and too vivid an imagination? Don't be silly. Some may find the ending of the film a bit too gruesome, but as these films go, it's a fairly intelligent effort.

2218. *Paris by Night* (1989, Cineplex Odeon, GB, 101m, c). P Patrick Cassavetti, D&W David Hare, PH Roger Pratt, M Georges Delerue, ED George Akers, PD Anthony Pratt.

LP Charlotte Rampling (Clara Paige), Michael Gambon (Gerald Paige), Robert Hardy (Adam Gillvray), Iain Glenn (Wallace Sharp), Andrew Ray (Michael Swanton), Jane Asher (Pauline), Linda Bassett (Janet Swanton), Niamh Cusack (Jenny Swanton).

To put an end to her Paris affair, high-profile Tory politician and Member of Parliament Charlotte Rampling pushes Andrew Ray into the Seine to drown. The rest of the film deals with her efforts to cover up her crime.

2219. *Paris, Texas* (1984, 20th Century–Fox, 150m, c). P Don Guest, D Wim

Wenders, W Sam Shepard (based on a story adapted by L.M. Kit Carson), PH Robby Muller, M Ry Cooder, ED Peter Pryzgodda.

LP Harry Dean Stanton (Travis Clay Henderson), Nastassja Kinski (Jane), Dean Stockwell (Walt Henderson), Aurore Clement (Anne), Hunter Carson (Hunter), Bernhard Wicki (Dr. Ulmer), Socorro Valdez (Carmelita), John Lurie (Slater).

This strange, slow-moving, but interesting film stars Harry Dean Stanton, taken home by brother Dean Stockwell after he is found wandering in a Texas desert. Stockwell has been raising Stanton's son Hunter Carson for several years and thinks of the boy as his own. After Stanton recovers somewhat and once again begins talking, father and son set out to find their missing wife and mother Nastassja Kinski, who now works in a Texas "lonely hearts" parlor.

2220. *Parker* (1985, Virgin, GB, 97m, c). P Nigel Stafford Clark, D Jim Goddard, W Trevor Preston, PH Peter Jessop, M Richard Hartley, Hector Berlioz, ED Ralph Sheldon, AD Andrew McAlpine.

LP Bryan Brown (Parker), Cherie Lunghi (Jenny), Kurt Raab (Inspector Haag), Bob Peck (Rohl), Beate Finkh (Sister), Gwyneth Strong (Andrea), Simon Rouse (Richard), Uwe Ochsenknecht (Boots), Dana Gillespie (Monika).

Australian businessman Bryan Brown is kidnapped by a Munich gang and held for a heroin ransom. When released he investigates the circumstances of his abduction. It leads to the murder of his mistress and all those involved in the kidnapping.

2221. *Parting Glances* (1986, Cinecom, 90m, c). P Yoram Mandel & Arthur Silverman, D&W Bill Sherwood, PH Jacek Laskus, M Sherwood, ED Sherwood, PD John Loggia.

LP Richard Ganoung (Michael), John Bolger (Robert), Steve Buscemi (Nick), Adam Nathan (Peter), Kathy Kinney (Joan), Patrick Tull (Cecil), Yolande Bavan (Betty), Richard Wall (Douglas).

The film concentrates on the final stages of the life of a man dying of AIDS and his relationship with his gay lover.

2222. *Partners* (1982, Paramount, 93m, c). P Aaron Russo, D James Burrows, W Francis Veber, PH Victor J. Kemper, M Georges Delerue, ED Danford B. Greene, PD Richard Sylbert.

LP Ryan O'Neal (Benson), John Hurt (Kerwin), Kenneth McMillan (Chief Wilkens), Robyn Douglass (Jill), Jay Robinson (Halderstam), Denise Galik (Clara), Joseph R. Sicari (Walter), Michael McGuire (Monroe), Rick Jason (Douglas), James Remar (Edward K. Petersen).

Ryan O'Neal is a ladies' man, John Hurt is a homosexual. They're cops. Their assignment: pose as a gay couple so they can solve the murder of a prominent homosexual. It's an embarrassing comedy with sophomoric homophobic jokes.

Partners see Duet for Four

2223. *Party Camp* (1987, Lightning, 96m, c). P Mark Borde, D Gary Graver, W Paul L. Brown, PH Graver, M Dennis Dreith, ED Michael B. Hoggan & Joyce L. Hoggan.

LP Andrew Ross (Jerry Riviera), Kerry Brennan (Heather), Billy Jacoby (D.A.), Jewal Shepard (Dyanne), Peter Jason (Sarge), Kirk Cribb (Tad), Dean R. Miller (Cody), Corky Pigeon (Winslow), Stacy Baptist (Kelly).

Andrew Ross takes a job as a camp counselor when he sees a picture of the girl of his dreams Kerry Brennan in the camp's brochure. He's assigned the "Squirrels," the cabin of least respect. It's always shown up by the elite cabin, the "Falcons," until a climactic race. Teenybopper junk.

Party Girls see Party Incorporated

2224. *Party Incorporated* (1989, Platinum Pictures, 79m, c, aka *Party Girls*). P&D Chuck Vincent, W Craig Horrall & Edd Rockis, PH Larry Revene, M Joey Mennonna, ED James Davalos, AD Todd Rutt.

LP Marilyn Chambers (Marilyn), Kurt Woodruff (Peter), Christina Veronica (Christina), Kimberly Taylor (Felicia), Kurt Schwoebel (Ronald Weston), Frank Stewart (Griswald), Ruth Collins (Betty).

In this typical softcore sex comedy, Marilyn Chambers, playing herself, invites a film crew into her mansion to shoot a TV documentary about her life as a porn queen. At least here she doesn't have to pretend she is an actress.

2225. *Party Line* (1988, Westwood/ SVS, 91m, c). P Tom Byrnes, Kurt Anderson, William Webb & Monica Webb, D William Webb, W Richard Brandes (based on a story by Byrnes), PH John Huneck, M Sam Winans, ED Paul Koval. LP Richard Hatch (Lt. Dan Bridges), Shawn Weatherly (Stacy Sloane), Leif Garrett (Seth), Greta Blackburn (Angelina), Richard Roundtree (Capt. Barnes), James O'Sullivan (Henry), Terrence McGovern (Simmons).

A brother and sister slasher team prey on teens who call into the 976 party lines. For those unfamiliar with the service, the number puts horny youngsters into contact with others having the same kind of sleaze on their minds. Sis lures victims into her bedroom and Bro cuts their throats with a razor.

2226. *Party Party* (1983, A&M Sound Pictures, GB, 98m, c). P Davina Belling & Clive Parsons, D Terry Winsor, W Daniel Peacock & Winsor, PH Sydney Macartney, M Richard Hartley, ED Eddy Joseph.

LP Daniel Peacock (Toby), Karl Howman (Johnny Reeves), Perry Fenwick (Larry Ascot), Sean Champman (Sam Diggins), Phoebe Nicholls (Rebecca), Gary Olsen (Terry), Clive Mantle (Bobby), Caroline Quentin (Shirley), Kate Williams (Mrs. Ascot), Kenneth Farrington (Mr. Ascot).

While his parents are away at a New Year's dance, teenager Daniel Peacock throws a wild bash at his house. Aren't there any teens like in *Our Town* anymore? Were there ever?

2227. *Pascali's Island* (1988, Avenue-Initial-Film Four, GB, 104m, c). P Eric Fellner, D James Dearden, W Dearden (based on the novel by Barry Unsworth), PH Roger Deakins, M Lock Dikker & Franz Schubert, ED Edward Marnier, PD Andrew Mollo.

LP Ben Kingsley (Basil Pascali), Charles Dance (Anthony Bowles), Helen Mirren (Lydia Neuman), George Murcell (Herr Gesing), Sheila Allen (Mrs. Marchant), Nadim Sawalha (Pasha), Stefan Gryff (Izzet Effendi).

The time is 1908. For twenty years half-Turkish, half-European Ben Kingsley has lived on the sun-drenched island of Nisi. He has spied on its visitors and the Greek natives, sending his reports to the sultan of the Ottoman Empire in Constantinople. He has no idea if his long, carefully prepared reports have ever been read, because no one has ever replied to them. His passive service to Turkey comes to an end in a violent climax when he helps a pseudo-archaeologist find a treasure, a centuries-old statue.

2228. *Pass the Ammo* (1988, New Century-Vista, 97m, c). P Herb Jaffe & Mort Engelberg, D David Beaird, W Neil Cohen & Joel Cohen, PH Mark Irwin, M Carter Burwell, ED Bill Yahraus, PD Dean Tschetter.

LP Bill Paxton (Jesse), Linda Kozlowski (Claire), Tim Curry (Rev. Ray Porter), Annie Potts (Darla Porter), Dennis Burkley (Big Joe Becker), Glenn Withrow (Arnold Limpet), Anthony Geary (Stonewall), Brian Thompson (Kenny Hamilton), Logan Ramsey (Jim Bob Collins).

The timing of this film about TV evangelists couldn't have been more opportune. Good ole folks Linda Kozlowski and her husband Bill Paxton take religious TV pitchman Tim Curry and his daffy wife, Annie Potts, hostage in an attempt to get back money Curry had squeezed out of her family.

2229. *The Passage* (1988, Spectrum-Carrera/Manson Intl., 105m, c). P Raul Carrera, D Harry Thompson, PH Peter Stein, M Paul Loomis, ED Peter Appleton.

LP Alexandra Paul (Annie May Bonner), Ned Beatty (Matthew Bonner), Barbara Barrie (Rachel Bonner), Brian Keith (Byron Monroe), Dee Law (Jesse Monroe).

During the Depression, Southern landowner Ned Beatty disinherits his daughter Alexandra Paul when she becomes pregnant by one of his employees. Years later after his wife dies, Beatty seeks a reconciliation with his daughter, now married to her lover, and his four grandchildren.

2230. *A Passage to India*† (1984, Columbia, GB, 163m, c). P John Brabourne

& Richard Goodwin, D&W David Lean† (for both direction and screenplay) (based on the play by Santha Rama Rau and the novel by E.M. Forster), PH Ernest Day†, M Maurice Jarre*, ED Lean†, PD John Box, AD Box, Leslie Tomkins†, SD Hugh Scaife†, COS Judy Moorcroft†, SOUND Graham V. Hartstone, Nicholas Le Messurier, Michael A. Carter & John Mitchell†.

LP Judy Davis† (Adela Quested), Victor Banerjee (Dr. Aziz), Peggy Ashcroft* (Mrs. Moore), James Fox (Richard Fielding), Alex Guinness (Godbole), Nigel Havers (Ronny Heaslop), Richard Wilson (Turton), Antonia Pemberton (Mrs. Turton), Michael Culver (McBryde), Art Malik (Mahmoud Ali), Saeed Jaffrey (Hamidullah), Clive Swift (Maj. Callendar).

Highly praised, this visually appealing film about India under the Raj is like most epics, less than the sum of its parts. It's overlong with some decent acting from various members of the cast, most notably Peggy Ashcroft and Judy Davis. The latter accuses native doctor Victor Banerjee of raping her.

2231. *Paternity* (1981, Paramount, 94m, c). P Lawrence Gordon & Hank Moonjean, D David Steinberg, W Charlie Peters, PH Bobby Byrne, M David Shire, ED Donn Cambern, PD Jack Collis.

LP Burt Reynolds (Buddy Evans), Beverly D'Angelo (Maggie Harden), Norman Fell (Larry), Paul Dooley (Kurt), Elizabeth Ashley (Sophia Thatcher), Lauren Hutton (Jenny Lofton), Juanita Moore (Celia), Peter Billingsley (Tad), Jacqueline Brookes (Aunt Ethel), Linda Gillin (Cathy).

At 44, having lived the life of a swinging bachelor, Burt Reynolds wants someone to carry on his name. He wants a child but not a wife. Beverly D'Angelo is willing to carry his baby without commitment in order to get the money to go to school in Paris. The two fall in love just before the blessed event.

2232. *The Patriot* (1986, Crown International, 88m, c). P Michael Bennett, D&PH Frank Harris, W Andy Ruben & Katt Shea Ruben, M Jay Ferguson, ED Richard E. Westover, AD Brad Einhorn.

LP Gregg Henry (Ryder), Simone Griffeth (Sean), Michael J. Pollard (Howard), Jeff Conaway (Mitchell), Stack Pierce (Atkins), Leslie Nielsen (Adm. Frazer), Glenn Withrow (Pink), Larry Mintz (Bite).

Gregg Henry must foil a group of terrorists who have discovered a way to intercept nuclear weapons on their way to a government installation.

2233. *Patti Rocks* (1988, Filmdallas, 86m, c). P Gwen Field & Gregory M. Cummins, D David Burton Morris, W Morris, Chris Mulkey, John Jenkins & Karen Landry (based on characters created by Victoria Wozniak in the film *Loose Ends*), PH&ED Cummins, M Doug Maynard, PD Charlotte Whitaker.

LP Chris Mulkey (Billy), John Jenkins (Eddie), Karen Landry (Patti), Buffy Sedlachek (Steambeast), Joy Langer (Steambeast's Daughter), Brian Lambert (Gas Station Attendant), Joe Minjares (Chicano Mechanic), David L. Turk (Barge Worker), Stephen Yoakam (Bartender).

Chris Mulkey and John Jenkins drive halfway across Minnesota so Mulkey can tell his girlfriend Karen Landry that he's married. On the way they talk and talk about what men do to women because of what women do to men. When they arrive at pregnant Landry's apartment, although annoyed with Mulkey's announcement, she doesn't really care. A free spirit, she wants the baby, not Mulkey and marriage.

2234. *Patty Hearst* (1988, Atlantic-Zenich, 108m, c). P Marvin Worth, D Paul Schrader, W Nicholas Kazan (based on the autobiography *Every Secret Thing* by Patricia Campbell Hearst with Alvin Moscow), PH Bojan Bazelli, M Scott Johnson, ED Michael R. Miller, PD Jane Musky.

LP Natasha Richardson (Patricia Hearst), William Forsythe (Teko), Ving Rhames (Cinque), Frances Fisher (Yolanda), Jodi Long (Wendy Yoshimura), Olivia Barash (Fahizah), Dana Delany (Celina), Marek Johnson (Zoya), Kitty Swink (Gabi), Pete Kowanko (Cujo), Tom O'Rourke (Jim Browning), Scott Kraft (Steven Weed), Ermal Williamson (Randolph A. Hearst).

Natasha Richardson portrays California heiress Patty Hearst, who in real-life in 1974 was kidnapped by a self-styled revolutionary group calling itself The Symbionese Liberation Army. For 57 days she is brainwashed with their confused political rhetoric. Seduced and raped by the males, and taught by the females that she must be sexually receptive to everyone in the movement, Hearst takes part in the robbery of the Hibernia bank. When she is later captured by the FBI, she is brought to trial on charges of armed robbery and sentenced to prison. The prisoner of war and victim is thus punished by a society which has changed from concern for her to anger that she was politically seduced by her captors.

2235. *Pavlova: A Woman for All Times* (1985, Poseidon/Mosfilm, GB/U.S.S.R., 133m, c). P Frixos Constantine, D Emil Lotianou, W Lotianou & Nicolas Locke (based on a story by Lotianou), PH Evgeni Guslinsky, M Evgeny Dogas, ED I. Kalatikova.

LP Galina Beliaeva (Anna Pavlova), James Fox (Victor D'Andre), Sergei Shakourov (Mikhail Fokine), Vsevolod Larionov (Diaghilev), Martin Scorsese (Gatti-Cassaza), Bruce Forsyth (Alfred Batt), Roy Kinnear (Gardener), Lina Boultakova (Pavlova as a child).

The film is the biography of Anna Pavlova, a Russian dressmaker's daughter who becomes one of the world's most renowned ballerinas.

Peacemaker see The Ambassador

2236. *The Peanut Butter Solution* (1985, Cineplex Odeon, Canada, 90m, c). P Rock Demers & Nicole Robert, D&W Michael Rubbo, PH Thomas Vamos, M Lewis Furey, ED Jean-Guy Montpetit, AD Vianney Gauthier.

LP Mathew Mackay (Michael), Siluck Saysanasy (Connie), Alison Podbrey (Suzie), Michael Hogan (Billy), Michel Maillot (The Signor), Helen Hughes (Mary), Griffith Brewer (Tom).

Eleven-year-old Mathew Mackay has a vivid imagination, but nothing he can dream up can match his experiences when he visits a burned down haunted mansion. What he sees causes him to lose all his hair. Two ghosts visit him and spread a concoction on his head which includes dead flies, kitty litter and peanut butter. His hair grows all the way to the floor. Mackay is kidnapped by Michel Maillot who has set up a magic paint brush factory and uses Mackay's never ending supply of hair for the brushes.

2237. *Pee-Wee's Big Adventure* (1985, Warner, 90m, c). P Robert Shapiro & Richard Gilbert Abramson, D Tim Burton, W Phil Hartman, Paul Reubens & Michael Varhol, PH Victor J. Kemper, M Danny Elfman, ED Billy Weber, PD David L. Snyder.

LP Paul Reubens (Pee-Wee Herman), Elizabeth Daily (Dottie), Mark Holton (Francis), Diane Salinger (Simone), Judd Omen (Mickey), Irving Hellman (Neighbor), Monte Landis (Mario), Damon Martin (Chip), Daryl Roach (Chuck), Starletta DuPois (Sgt. Hunter).

Paul Reubens has come up with a unique comedy personality, moronic Pee-Wee Herman. In this imaginative comedy, Herman with his strained little-boy voice in an adult body makes an almost surreal search across the country for his prize possession, a brightly painted and accessory-filled bicycle. Different, to say the least, but the star, his character and his antics may take some getting used to.

2238. *Peggy Sue Got Married* (1986, Tri-Star, 104m, c). P Paul R. Gurian, Francis Ford Coppola, W Jerry Leichtling & Arlene Sarner, PH Jordan Cronenweth†, M John Barry, ED Barry Malkin, PD Dean Tavoularis, COS Theadora Van Runkle†.

LP Kathleen Turner† (Peggy Sue Kelcher Bodell), Nicolas Cage (Charlie Bodell), Barry Miller (Richard Norvik), Catherine Hicks (Carol Heath), Kevin J. O'Connor (Michael Fitzsimmons), Barbara Harris (Evelyn Kelcher), Don Murray (Jack Kelcher), Maureen O'Sullivan (Elizabeth Alvorg), Leon Ames (Barney Alvorg), Helen Hunt (Beth Bodell), Joan Allen (Maddy Nagle).

The mother of two, Kathleen Turner is considering divorcing her husband Nicolas Cage. As she is being crowned queen of her 25th class reunion, she passes out and wakes up back in the time of her high school years. She has the opportunity to relive, rethink and possibly alter the events that shaped her life. It's much ado about nothing.

2239.   *The Penitent* (1988, New Century-Vista, 94m, c). P Michael Fitzgerald, D&W Cliff Osmond, PH Robin Vidgeon, M Alex North, ED Peter Taylor.

LP Raul Julia (Ramon Guerola), Armand Assante (Juan Marco), Rona Freed (Celia Guerola), Julie Carmen (Corina), Lucy Reina (Margarita), Eduardo Lopez Rojas (Major), Jose Gonzales Rodriguez (Rezador), Paco Mauri (Pitero), Justo Martinez (Enfermero), Enrique Novi (Jose).

Mexican farmer Raul Julia belongs to a Penitent religious cult that believes in self-flagellation. The cult recreates the suffering of Christ each Good Friday by affixing one of their members to a cross and leaving him in the desert sun for an entire day—to die, if that is God's will. Julia is having trouble with his wife Rona Freed, who is afraid to consummate their marriage. When Julia's old friend Armand Assante arrives after spending five years in prison, it's no big trick for him to seduce Freed. Julia realizes what is happening, but hopes that Freed will be a loving wife when Assante leaves. Instead, Assante falls in love with Freed, and convinces Julia that as the stronger of the two he should take Julia's place on the cross. They will fight over Freed after he has endured the penitence. Instead, Freed sees Assante as the "Christo" and wants nothing further to do with him.

2240.   *Penitentiary II* (1982, MGM/United Artists, 103m, c). P,D&W Jamaa Fanaka, PH Steve Posey, M Jack W. Wheaton, ED James F. Nownes.

LP Leon Isaac Kennedy (Too Sweet Gordon), Ernie Hudson (Half Dead), Mr. T (Himself), Glynn Turman (Charles), Peggy Blow (Ellen), Cepheus Jaxon (Do Dirty), Marvin Jones (Simp), Donovan Womack (Jesse "The Bull"), Ebony Wright (Sugar).

After boxing his way to freedom in the 1979 film *Penitentiary,* Leon Isaac Kennedy decides to start a new and honest life. His old buddies have other ideas and kill his girlfriend. As a result Kennedy is returned to prison to fight the champ.

2241.   *Penitentiary III* (1987, Cannon, 91m, c). P Jamaa Fanaka & Leon Isaac Kennedy, D&W Fanaka, PH Marty Ollstein, M Garry Schyman, ED Ed Harker, PD Marshall Toomey.

LP Leon Isaac Kennedy (Too Sweet Gordon), Anthony Geary (Serenghetti), Steve Antin (Roscoe), Ric Mancini (Warden), Kessler Raymond (Midnight Thud Jessup), Jim Bailey (Cleopatra), Magic Schwarz (Hugo), Windsor Taylor Randolph (Sugar).

When his manager slips a drug into his water, making him a madman, boxer Leon Isaac Kennedy beats his opponent and friend to death. For this he is given a three-year manslaughter stretch in a prison. The pen is equally divided into two dangerous camps, the warden's and that controlled by convicted mobster Anthony Geary. Both want to get Kennedy back in the ring.

2242.   *Penn and Teller Get Killed* (1989, Warner, 89m, c). P&D Arthur Penn, W Penn Jillette & Teller, PH Jan Weincke, M Paul Chihara, ED Jeffrey Wolf, PD John Arnone.

LP Penn Jillette (Penn), Teller (Himself), Caitlin Clarke (Carlotta), David Patrick Kelly (Fan), Leonardo Cimino (Ernesto), Christopher Durang (Jesus Freak), Alan North (Old Cop), Jon Cryer (bit).

Penn & Teller play themselves, opening with their self-proclaimed "bad boys of magic act" on a TV program. Penn cracks a joke about how funny it would be if a killer actually was stalking him. Well, maybe there is a killer out to do them in, but since the boys' practical jokes are included in the film, audiences can't be sure what's part of their act and what's part of the sick story. You're either going to love or hate the movie, depending on how you feel about the bizarre antics of Penn & Teller.

2243.   *Pennies from Heaven* (1981, MGM, 109m, c). P Herbert Ross & Nora Kaye, D Ross, W Dennis Potter† (based on his TV series), PH Gordon Willis, M Marvin Hamlisch & Billy May, ED Richard Marks, AD Fred Tuch & Bernie Cutler, COS Bob Mackie†, SOUND Michael J. Kohut, Jay M. Harding, Richard Tyler & Al Overton†.

LP Steve Martin (Arthur), Bernadette Peters (Eileen), Christopher Walken

(Tom), Jessica Harper (Joan), Vernel Bagneris (Accordion Man), John Mc-Martin (Mr. Warner), John Karlen (Detective), Jay Garner (Banker), Robert Fitch (Al), Tommy Rall (Ed).

Dennis Potter's TV series staring Bob Hoskins was a big hit in Britain. This musical adaptation stars Steve Martin as a 30's sheet music salesman accused of murder. It cost $20 million and made $4 million. That's a lot of wasted pennies.

2244. *Perfect* (1985, Columbia, 115m, c). P&D James Bridges, W Aaron Latham & Bridges (based on articles in *Rolling Stone* by Latham), PH Gordon Willis, M Ralph Burns, ED Jeff Gourson, PD Michael Haller.

LP John Travolta (Adam), Jamie Lee Curtis (Jessie), Stefan Gierasch (Charlie), Jann Wenner (Mark Roth), Anne De Salvo (Frankie), Marilu Henner (Sally), Laraine Newman (Linda), Chelsea Field (Randy), Kenneth Welsh (Joe McKenzie).

Jamie Lee Curtis is a fine advertisement for physical fitness. However, this film with John Travolta as a *Rolling Stone* reporter writing an article on the exercise fad is all pain and no gain. Travolta's article exploits Curtis, a cute, curvy, former Olympic swimmer, now aerobics instructor at Los Angeles' "The Sports Connection." It's the all too familiar story of a reporter writing an exposé and becoming a convert because of love.

2245. *The Perfect Match* (1987, Airtight, 93m, c). P Mark Deimel & Bob Torrance, D Deimel, W Nick Duretta, David Burr & Deimel, PH Bob Torrance, M Tim Torrance, ED Craig Colton, PD Maxine Shepard.

LP Marc McClure (Tim Wainright), Jennifer Edwards (Nancy Bryant), Diane Stilwell (Vicki), Rob Paulsen (John Wainright).

Jennifer Edwards, a thirtyish college student, answers an ad placed by loner Marc McClure. At their first meeting both put on airs and pretend they are what they are not. Their first dates go badly, but they don't give up. When they become truthful about who they are, it appears as if there may be a future for them as a couple.

2246. *The Perfect Model* (1989, Chicago Cinema, 89m, c). P&D Darryl Rob-

erts, W Roberts, Theresa McDade & Ivory Ocean, PH Sheldon Lane, M Joe Thomas & Steve Grissette, ED Tom Miller, PD Phillipe & Darryl Roberts.

LP Stoney Jackson (Stedman Austin), Anthony Norman McKay (Mario Sims), Liza Cruzat (Linda Johnson), Tatiana Tumbtzen (Crystal Jennings), Catero Colbert (David Johnson), Reggie Theus (Dexter Sims).

Black Hollywood star Anthony Norman McKay hasn't forgotten his Chicago ghetto roots. He agrees to host a beauty contest run by his childhood chum Stoney Jackson. McKay falls in love with Liza Cruzat, an aerobics instructor struggling to make ends meet for her and her young brother. Despite his feelings for her, McKay is embarrassed by her ghetto ways, when they are around his high classed friends.

2247. *Perfect Strangers* (1984, Hemdale/New Line, 94m, c). P Paul Kurta, D&W Larry Cohen, PH Paul Glickman, M Dwight Dixon, ED Armond Lebowitz.

LP Anne Carlisle (Sally), Brad Rijn (Johnny), John Woehrle (Fred), Matthew Stockley (Matthew), Stephen Lack (Lt. Burns), Ann Magnuson (Maida), Zachary Hains (Maletti), Otto Von Wernherr (Pvt. Det.), Kitty Summerall (Joanne).

After three-year-old Matthew Stockley witnesses a murder, the killer Brad Riln plans to kidnap the boy to keep him quiet. But his plans are complicated when he falls in love with the lad's mother, Anne Carlisle.

2248. *Perfect Victim* (1988, Vertigo, 100m, c). P Jonathon Braun, D Shuki Levy, W Levy, Joe Hailey & Bob Barron, PH Frank Byers & Michael Mathews, M Levy, ED Braun.

LP Deborah Shelton (Liz Winters), Lyman Ward (Steven Hack), Tom Dugan (Brandon Poole), Clarence Williams, III (Lt. Kevin White), Nikolette Scorsese (Melissa Cody), Jackie Swanson (Carrie Marks).

An AIDS-infected killer rapes a pair of fashion models and has modeling agency head Deborah Shelton targeted as his next victim.

2249. *The Perils of P.K.* (1986, Green Pictures, 90m, c). P Sheila MacRae, D

Joseph Green, W,ED&M Naura Hayden, PH Paul Glickman.

LP Naura Hayden, Kaye Ballard, Sheila MacRae, Heather MacRae, Larry Storch, Norma Storch, Dick Shawn, Sammy Davis, Jr., Louise Lasser, Irwin Corey, Virginia Graham, Jackie Mason, Joey Heatherton, Anne Meara.

Plenty of guest stars show up in corny bits in this film featuring Naura Hayden. She's an actress on psychiatrist Dick Shawn's couch relating her fall from star to stripper.

2250. *Permanent Record* (1988, Paramount, 92m, c). P Frank Mancuso, Jr., D Marisa Silver, W Jarre Fees, Alice Liddle & Larry Ketron, PH Frederick Elmes, M Joe Strummer, ED Robert Brown, PD Michel Levesque.

LP Alan Boyce (David Sinclair), Keanu Reeves (Chris Townsend), Michelle Meyrink (M.G.), Jennifer Rubin (Lauren), Pamela Gidley (Kim), Michael Elgart (Jake), Richard Bradford (Leo Verdell), Dakin Matthews (Mr. McBain).

The film examines the effect of the suicide of a popular, well-adjusted high school senior on his closest friends.

2251. *Permanent Vacation* (1981, Cinesthesia/Gray City, 75m, c). P,D&W Jim Jarmusch, PH James A. Lebovitz, Thomas DiCillo, M Jarmusch, ED Jarmusch.

LP Chris Parker (Aloysious Parker), Leila Gastil (Leila), Maria Duval (Latin Girl), Ruth Bolton (Mother), Richard Boes (War Veteran), John Lurie (Saxophone player), Eric Mitchell (Car Fence).

Jim Jarmusch made this promising film on a shoestring budget. Chris Parker, an alienated youth, wanders the streets of New York City, meeting an assortment of unusual people.

2252. *Personal Best* (1982, Warner, 124m, c). P,D&W Robert Towne, PH Michael Chapman & Allan Gornick, Jr., M Jack Nitzsche & Jill Fraser, ED Ned Humphreys, Jere Huggins, Jacqueline Cambas, Walt Mulconery, Bud Smith.

LP Mariel Hemingway (Chris Cahill), Scott Glenn (Terry Tingloff), Patrice Donnelly (Tory Skinner), Kenny Moore (Denny Stites), Jim Moody (Roscoe Travis), Kari Gosswiller (Penny Brill), Jodi Anderson (Nadia "Pooch" Anderson), Maren Seidler (Tanya), Martha Watson (Sheila).

While training for the Olympics, runner Mariel Hemingway discovers that she is bisexual. She participates in rather explicit sex scenes with both fellow runner Patrice Donnelly and one-time Olympian Kenny Moore. Overall, it's a rather boring film, with too many slow motion frames used to catch female athletes' straining and sweating bodies in motion.

2253. *Personal Choice* (1989, Moviestore/Five Star, 88m, c). P Joseph Perez, D&W David Saperstein, PH John Bartley, M Geoff Levin & Chris Smart, ED Pat McMahon, PD John Jay Moore.

LP Martin Sheen (Paul Andrews), Christian Slater (Eric), Robert Foxworth (Richard Michaels), Sharon Stone (Laurie McCall), Olivia d'Abo (Mara Simon), F. Murray Abraham (Harry), Don Davis (Phil).

Astronaut Martin Sheen is stricken with fatal radiation poisoning, received during his moonwalk on a mid-70's Apollo mission. It's a talky message film, and the message is murky. It was falsely advertised as a space adventure.

2254. *Personal Foul* (1987, Personal Foul Ltd., 92m, c). P Ted Lichtenheld & Kathleen Long, D&W Lichtenheld, PH J. Leblanc, M Greg Brown, ED Steve Mullenix, PD Bill Jones.

LP Adam Arkin (Jeremy), David Morse (Ben), Susan Wheeler Duff (Lisa), F. William Parker (Principal).

Lonely grade school teacher Adam Arkin loves teaching but abhors bureaucracy. He makes friends with drifter David Morse, who lives in a van and earns a little money selling paper flowers. A third party in this independent production is Susan Wheeler Duff, a personable young woman to whom Arkin is attracted. Nothing much happens as Arkin learns how to live with these friendships.

2255. *Personal Services* (1987, Vestron, GB, 105m, c). P Tim Bevan, D Terry Jones, W David Leland, PH Roger Deakins, M John Duprez, ED George Akers, PD Hugo Luczyc-Wyhowski.

LP Julie Walters (Christine Painter), Alec McCowen (Wing Cmdr. Morton), Shirley Stelfox (Shirley), Danny Schiller (Dolly), Victoria Hardcastle (Rose), Tim Woodward (Timms), Dave Atkins (Sydney), Leon Lissek (Mr. Popozogolou), Benjamin Whitrow (Mr. Marsden).

Julie Walters, so charming in *Educating Rita,* portrays a working girl who moves up the sex-for-hire ladder from callgirl to the most beloved madam in all of Great Britain. The kinky adult film is based on the career of English madam Cynthia Payne.

2256. *The Personals* (1982, New World, 90m, c). P Patrick Wells, D&W Peter Markle, PH Markle & Greg Cummins, M Will Sumner, ED Stephen E. Rivkin.

LP Bill Schoppert (Bill), Karen Landry (Adrienne), Paul Eiding (Paul), Michael Laskin (David), Vicki Dakil (Shelly), Chris Forth (Jennifer), Patrick O'Brien (Jay).

Nerdy young Bill Schoppert places an ad in a newspaper personal column after his wife leaves him. Most of the dates he makes with respondents end disastrously. At last he falls in love with literate psychologist Karen Landry — only to discover she's already married. Sort of "the shoe's on the other foot" plot, we suppose.

2257. *Pet Sematary* (1989, Paramount, 102m, c). P Richard P. Rubinstein, D Mary Lambert, W Stephen King (based on his novel), PH Peter Stein, M Elliot Goldenthal, ED Michael Hill & Daniel Hanley, PD Michael Z. Hanan.

LP Dale Midkiff (Louis Creed), Fred Gwynne (Jud Crandall), Denise Crosby (Rachel Creed), Brad Greenquist (Victor Pascow), Michael Lombard (Irwin Goldman), Blaze Berdahl (Ellie Creed), Miko Hughes (Gage Creed), Susan Blommaert (Missy Dandridge), Stephen King (Minister).

In a contemporary thriller, the Creed family moves from Chicago to Ludlow, Maine. Adjacent to their property is an ancient Indian burial ground, customarily used by children as a graveyard for their pets. When the family's cat is killed, they bury it but the animal comes back to life and then the unspeakable occurs — everyone in the film overacts.

2258. *Peter Pan [Re-issue]* (1989, Disney/RKO, animated, 76m, c). P Walt Disney, D Hamilton Luske, Clyde Geronimi & Wilfred Jackson, W Ted Sears, Bill Peet, Joe Rinaldi, Erdman Penner, Winston Hibler, Milt Banta & Ralph Wright (based on the play by Sir James Barrie), M Oliver Wallace & Edward H. Plumb, ANIM D Milt Kahl, Franklin Thomas, Marc Davis, John Lounsbery, Wolfgang Reitherman, Ward Kimball, Eric Larson, Oliver Johnston, Jr., Les Clark & Norman Ferguson.

VOICES Bobby Driscoll (Peter Pan), Kathryn Beaumont (Wendy), Hans Conried (Capt. Hook/Mr. Darling), Bill Thompson (Mr. Smee), Heather Angel (Mrs. Darling), Paul Collins (Michael Darling), Tommy Luske (John), Candy Candido (Indian Chief), Tom Conway (Narrator).

First released in 1953, Disney's animation feature is almost as delightful as the Mary Martin television special. It's the story of a boy, Peter Pan, who never grows up. He takes the three Darling children with him to Never-Never Land, because he and the Lost Boys need a mother. Wendy Darling is to fill that roll, but shapely little fairy Tinker Bell objects seriously to any female competition where Peter is concerned. Hans Conried is a suitably nasty Captain Hook. The Sammy Cahn and Sammy Fain songs include "You Can Fly, You Can Fly," "Your Mother and Mine" and "Never Smile at a Crocodile."

2259. *Phantasm II* (1988, Universal, 93m, c). P Roberto A. Quezada, D&W Don Coscarelli, PH Daryn Okada, M Fred Myrow & Christopher L. Stone, ED Peter Teschner, PD Philip Duffin.

LP James Le Gros (Mike Pearson), Reggie Bannister (Reggie), Angus Scrimm (The Tall Man), Paula Irvine (Liz), Samantha Phillips (Alchemy), Kenneth Tigar (Father Meyers), Ruth C. Engel (Grandma), Mark Anthony Major (Mortician), Rubin Kushner (Grandpa), Stacey Travis (Jeri).

The 1979 film *Phantasm* was a fascinating horror story whose hero is a 15-year-old named Mike. It includes a cemetery sex scene, a ghostly mortician with yellow embalming fluid in his veins, and flying spheres which imbed themselves into victims' faces, drilling a hole through the head, so the blood may gush out the other side. This sequel picks up the gore where the earlier film left off, but can't top the original.

2260. *The Phantom Empire* (1989, American Independent, 83m, c). P&D Fred Olen Ray, W T.L. Lankford & Ray, PH Gary Graver, M Robert Garrett, ED Robert A. Ferretti & William Shaffer, PD Cory Kaplan.

LP Ross Hagen (Cort Eastman), Jeffrey Combs (Andrew Paris), Dawn Wildsmith (Eddy Colchilde), Robert Quarry (Prof. Artemis Strock), Susan Stokey (Denea Chambers), Michelle Bauer (Cave Bunny), Russ Tamblyn (Bill), Sybil Danning (Alien Queen).

This shoestring production overflows with in-jokes about old-time sci-fi movies. A mutant creature emerges from a cave and kills some picnickers. A team is put together to search the caves for the lost city of Rilah. They locate the city, inhabited by a race of mutants and a gaggle of beautiful bikini-clad girls.

2261. *Phantom of the Mall* (1989, Fries Entertainment, 88m, c). P Tom Fries, D Richard Friedman, W Scott Schneid, Robert King & Tony Michelman (based on a story by Fred Ulrich & Schneid), PH Harry Mathias, M Stacy Widelitz, ED Amy Tompkins & Gregory F. Plotts.

LP Kari Whitman (Melody), Morgan Fairchild (Mayor Karen Wilton), Derek Rydall (Eric Matthews), Jonathan Goldsmith (Harv), Rob Estes (Peter), Pauly Shore (Buzz), Kimber Sissons (Susie), Tom Fridley (Justin), Gregory Scott Cummins (Christopher), Ken Foree (Acardi).

When a new shopping mall opens, customers are killed by a masked figure who makes the airshafts his or her home. It's a poor reworking of the Phantom of the Opera tale, with waitress Kari Whitman favored by the killer.

2262. *The Phantom of the Opera* (1989, 21st Century, 95m, c). P Harry Alan Towers, D Dwight H. Little, W Duke Sandefur (based on the screenplay by Gerry O'Hara), PH Elemer Ragalyi, M Misha Segal, ED Charles Bornstein, AD Tivadar Bertalan.

LP Robert Englund (The Phantom), Jill Schoelen (Christine), Alex Hyde-White (Richard), Bill Nighy (Barton), Stephanie Lawrence (Carlotta).

It's quite a time for the Gaston Leroux novel, what with three musicals on Broadway and in tour, a new television production, and this film starring Robert Englund, Freddy of *Nightmare on Elm Street* infamy. Unfortunately, Englund hasn't been told that the Phantom is a different character. More attention is paid to his sewing scraps of human flesh to make a mask for his disfigured face than to the story of a lovesick man, haunting an opera house in order to enhance the career of his lovely protégée, here played by Jill Schoelen.

2263. *Phar Lap* (1984, 20th Century–Fox, Australia, 108m, c). P John Sexton, D Simon Wincer, W David Williamson (based on the book *The Phar Gap Story* by Michael Wilkinson), PH Russell Boyd, M Bruce Rowland, ED Tony Paterson, PD Lawrence Eastwood.

LP Tom Burlinson (Tommy Woodcock), Ron Leibman (Dave Davis), Martin Vaughan (Harry Telford), Judy Morris (Bea Davis), Celia De Burgh (Vi Telford), Richard Morgan ("Cashy" Martin), Robert Grubb (William Neilsen).

It's a so-so story of an outstanding New Zealand racehorse of the 30s which died mysteriously after winning the biggest race of its career.

2264. *The Philadelphia Experiment* (1984, New World, 102m, c). P Douglas Curtis & Joel B. Michaels, D Stewart Raffill, W William Gray & Michael Janover (based on a story by Wallace Bennett & Don Jakoby from the book by William I. Moore & Charles Berlitz), PH Dick Bush, M Ken Wannberg, ED Neil Travis, AD Chris Campbell.

LP Michael Pare (David Herdeg), Nancy Allen (Allison), Eric Christmas (Longstreet), Bobby Di Cicco (Jim Parker), Kene Holliday (Maj. Clark), Louise Latham (Pamela), Joe Dorsey (Sheriff Bates).

When a scientist aboard a 1943 battleship attempts to make it invisible to the enemy's radar, seamen Michael Pare and Bobby Di Cicco fall through a time warp.

They end-up in 1984 and have a heck of a time getting back.

Philly see Private Lessons

2265. *Phobia* (1980, Paramount, Canada, 94m, c). P Zale Magder, D John Huston, W Lew Lehman, Jimmy Sangster & Peter Bellwood (based on a story by Gary Sherman & Ronald Shusett), PH Reginald H. Morris, M Andre Gagnon, ED Stan Cole, AD David Jaquest.

LP Paul Michael Glaser (Dr. Peter Ross), John Colicos (Inspector Barnes), Susan Hogan (Jenny), Alexandra Stewart (Barbara), Robert O'Ree (Bubba), David Bolt (Henry), David Eisner (Johnny), Lisa Langlois (Laura).

All of psychiatrist Glaser's patients suffering from phobias are being killed. Their basic fear is used as the means of their destruction.

Phobia see The Nesting

2266. *Physical Evidence* (1989, Columbia, 99m, c). P Martin Ransohoff, D Michael Crichton, W Bill Phillips (based on a story by Steve Ransohoff, Phillips), PH John A. Alonzo, M Henry Mancini, ED Glenn Farr, PD Dan Yarhi.

LP Burt Reynolds (Joe Paris), Theresa Russell (Jenny Hudson), Ned Beatty (James Nicks), Kay Lenz (Deborah Quinn), Ted McGinley (Kyle), Tom O'Brien (Matt Farley), Kenneth Walsh (Harry Norton), Ray Baker (Strickler).

Suspended cop Burt Reynolds, accused of murder, is defended by yuppie public defender Theresa Russell. There's not much here to like. It's hard to care if Reynolds has been framed and by whom. It must be hell for someone like Reynolds, once a charming star, to find that contemporary audiences are no longer taken in by his boyish playfulness and sensitive toughness. They expect good acting and an exciting story. Beautiful Russell adds nothing to the film; she sounds like she's reading her lines from a teleprompter.

2267. *P.I. Private Investigations* (1987, MGM/United Artists, 91m, c). P Steven Golin & Sigurjon Sighvatsson, D Nigel Dick, W John Dahl & David Warfield (based on a story by Dick), PH David Bridges & Bryan Duggan, M Murray Munro, ED Scott Chestnut, PD Piers Plowden.

LP Clayton Rohner (Joey Bradley), Ray Sharkey (Ryan), Paul LeMat (Det. Wexler), Talia Balsam (Jenny Fox), Phil Morris (Eddie Gordon), Martin Balsam (Cliff Dowling), Anthony Zerbe (Charles Bradley), Robert Ito (Kim).

The plot of this movie has been done to death. Clayton Rohner is an architect who becomes mixed up with police corruption and some nasty mobsters. Crusading newspaper reporter Anthony Zerbe believes that Rohner knows something that may expose their schemes. So do the bad guys. The camerawork and the hard-driving rock soundtrack are the movie's best features. Rohner is charmless.

2268. *Picasso Trigger* (1989, Malibu Bay Films, 99m, c). P Arlene Sidaris, D&W Andy Sidaris, PH Howard Wexler, M Gary Stockdale, ED Michael Haight, PD Peter Munneke.

LP Steve Bond (Travis Abilene), Dona Speir (Donna), Hope Marie Carlton (Taryn), Harold Diamond (Jade), John Aprea (Picasso Trigger), Roberta Vasquez (Agent Pantera), Guich Koock (L.G. Abilene).

In this James Bond–like thriller, T & A are served up with the action as U.S. agent Steve Bond tracks down assassin John Aprea. The latter uses a fish from a painting he admires as his trademark.

2269. *The Pick-Up Artist* (1987, 20th Century-Fox, 81m, c). P David L. Macleod [Warren Beatty], D&W James Toback, PH Gordon Willis, M Georges Delerue, ED David Bretherton & Angelo Corrao, PD Paul Sylbert.

LP Molly Ringwald (Randy Jensen), Robert Downey (Jack Jericho), Dennis Hopper (Flash Jensen), Danny Aiello (Phil), Mildred Dunnock (Nellie), Harvey Keitel (Alonzo), Brian Hamill (Mike), Tamara Bruno (Karen), Vanessa Williams (Rae).

Robert Downey won't take no for an answer from any women, even if it costs him his job or some hard times from a girl's boyfriend. Molly Ringwald is more than a match for the fast-talking Downey in this modestly enjoyable romantic comedy.

2270. *Pick-Up Summer* (1981, Film Ventures, 92m, c, aka *Pinball Summer; Pinball Pick-Up*). P Jack F. Murphy, D George Mihalka, W Richard Zelniker, M Jay Bolvin & Germain Gauthier.

LP Michael Zelniker, Carl Marotte, Karen Stephen, Helene Udy.

Suburban boys Michael Zelniker and Carl Marotte cruise their town chasing after voluptuous Karen Stephen and Helene Udy.

2271. *The Picture Show Man* (1980, Limelight, Australia, 99m, c). P Joan Long, D John Power, W Long, PH Geoff Burton, M Peter Best, ED Nick Beauman, AD David Copping.

LP Rod Taylor (Palmer), John Meillon (Pop), John Ewart (Freddie), Harold Hopkins (Larry), Patrick Cargill (Fitzwilliam), Yelena Zagon (Mme. Cavalli), Garry McDonald (Lou), Sally Conabere (Lucy), Judy Morris (Miss Lockhart), Jeannie Drynan (Mrs. Duncan).

In a nostalgic and charming look at the early days of movies in Australia, would-be movie mogul John Meillon goes into the outback, taking the world of film to the amazed population. His major competition comes from villain Rod Taylor, who gets his hands on more modern equipment.

2272. *Pieces* (1983, FVI/Artists Releasing, Span./Puerto Rico, 85m, c). P Dick Randall & Steve Manasian, D Juan Piquer Simon, W Randall & John Shadow, PH Juan Marino, M Cam.

LP Christopher George (Lt. Bracken), Lynda Day George (Mary), Edmund Purdom (Dean), Paul Smith (Willard), Frank Brana (Sgt. Hoden), Ian Sera (Kendall), Jack Taylor (Prof. Brown), Gerard Tichy (Dr. Jennings).

Some nut at a Boston University uses a chainsaw to get parts for the human jigsaw puzzle he's assembling at home.

Pigs see Daddy's Deadly Darling

2273. *The Pilot* (1981, New Line/Summit, 99m, c). P C. Gregory Earls, D Cliff Robertson, W Robertson & Robert P. Davis (based on the novel by Davis), PH Walter Lassally, M John Addison, ED Evan Lottman & Fima Noveck, AD William DeSeta, SD Bonnie Derham.

LP Cliff Robertson (Mike Hagan), Diane Baker (Pat Simpson), Frank Converse (Jim Cochran), Milo O'Shea (Dr. O'Brien), Dana Andrews (Randolph Evers), Gordon MacRae (Joe Barnes), Ed Binns (Larry Zanoff), Jennifer Holton (Cricket), Kitty Sullivan (Nancy), Leigh Court (Jean Hagan), Bob Willis (Ken Howland).

Cliff Robertson is regarded as the best pilot in the sky for North American Airlines—be he drunk or be he sober.

2274. *Pin* (1989, Lance/New World, Canada, 102m, c). P Rene Malo, D&W Sandor Stern, PH Guy Dufaux, M Peter Manning Robinson, ED Patrick Dodd.

LP David Hewlett (Leon Linden), Cyndy Preston (Ursula Linden), John Ferguson (Sam Fraker), Terrance O'Quinn (Dr. Linden), Bronwen Nantel (Mrs. Linden).

Conservative physician Terrance O'Quinn uses a plastic see-through medical teaching dummy to throw his voice into, when he communicates with his children. As a result they feel closer to the dummy, called Pin, than to their rigid parents.

Pinball Pick-Up see Pick-Up Summer

Pinball Summer see Pick-Up Summer

2275. *Pink Cadillac* (1989, Warner, 122m, c). P David Valdes, D Buddy Van Horn, W John Eskow, PH Jack N. Green, M Steve Dorff, ED Joel Cox, PD Edward C. Carfagno.

LP Clint Eastwood (Tommy Nowak), Bernadette Peters (Lou Ann McGuinn), Timothy Carhart (Roy McGuinn), John Dennis Johnston (Waycross), Michael Des Barres (Alex), Geoffrey Lewis (Ricky Z.), William Hickey (Mr. Barton), Bill McKinney (Bartender), Paul Benjamin (Judge), Frances Fisher (Dinah), Jim Carrey (Lounge Entertainer), Mara Corday (Stick Lady).

In this mediocre Clint Eastwood film, the aging star is a skip tracer. Bernadette Peters is a tiny cute felon on the lam in her husband's pink Cadillac. Unbeknownst to her the Caddy is the hiding place of a quarter-million dollars in counterfeit bills. Sometimes Eastwood plays his usual laconic loner and sometimes he's a poor imitation of a Chevy Chase–like Fletch.

2276. *Pink Floyd—The Wall* (1982, MGM/United Artists, GB, 99m, c). P Alan Marshall, D Alan Parker, W Roger Waters (based on the album "The Wall" by Pink Floyd), PH Peter Biziou, ED Gerry Hambling, PD Brian Morris.

LP Bob Geldof (Pink), Christine Hargreaves (Pink's Mother), James Laurenson (Pink's Father), Eleanor David (Pink's Wife), Kevin McKeon (Young Pink), Bob Hoskins (Rock & Roll Manager), David Bingham (Little Pink), Jenny Wright (American Groupie), Alex McAvoy (Teacher).

In a surreal, impressionistic movie, Kevin McKeon grows up with the horrors of World War II. As a man he becomes Bob Geldof, a rock star who discovers the power he has to manipulate crowds for his own pleasure. His insensitivity and desensitivity allow him to build a wall around himself to deflect the pain and suffering of life, which he chooses to deny.

2277. *Pink Motel* (1983, New Image, 88m, c, aka *Motel*). P M, James Kouf, Jr. & Ed Elbert, D Mike McFarland, W Kouf, Jr., PH Nicholas J. von Sternberg, M Larry K. Smith, ED Earl Watson.

LP Slim Pickens (Roy), Phyllis Diller (Margaret), John Macchia (Skip), Cathryn Hartt (Charlene), Christopher Nelson (Max), Terri Berland (Marlene), Tony Longo (Mark), Cathy Sawyer-Young (Lola).

In this dreadful sex comedy, Slim Pickens and Phyllis Diller own a pink stucco no-tell motel with rooms for rent by the hour to couples in need of a place to make whoopee.

2278. *Pink Nights* (1985, Koch/Marschall, 84m, c). P Philip Koch & Sally Marschall, D&W Koch, PH Charlie Lieberman, M Jim Tullio & Jeffrey Vanston, ED Koch & Marschall, SD Gail Specht.

LP Kevin Anderson (Danny), Shaun Allen (Terry), Peri Kaczmarek (Esme), Jessica Vitkus (Marcy), Larry King (Jeff), Jonathan Jancovic Michaels (Zero), Mike Bacarella (Bruno), Ron Dean (Pop), Tom Towles (Ralph).

Kevin Anderson doesn't have much luck with the opposite sex. Still he finds a way to live with three pretty girls.

2279. *Pinocchio and the Emperor of the Night* (1987, New World, animated, 88m, c). P Lou Scheimer, D Hal Sutherland, W Robby London, Barry O'Brien & Dennis O'Flaherty (based on a story by O'Flaherty from "The Adventures of Pinnochio" by Carlo Collodi), PH Ervin L. Kaplan, M Anthony Marinelli & Brian Banks, ED Jeffrey Patrick Gehr.

VOICES Edward Asner (Scalawag), Tom Bosley (Geppetto), Lana Beeson (Twinkle), James Earl Jones (Emperor of the Night), Rickie Lee Jones (Fairy Godmother), Don Knotts (Gee Willikers), Scott Grimes (Pinocchio), Linda Gary (Bee-atrice), Jonathan Harris (Lt. Grumblebee), William Windom (Puppetino), Frank Welker (Igor).

It's a wholesome but rather too-sweet attempt to rival the great Disney animated story. Pinocchio is lured towards the self-indulgent pleasures of life, but comes down on the side of selflessness in the end.

Piranha II: The Spawning see The Spawning

2280. *The Pirate Movie* (1982, 20th Century–Fox, Australia, 98m, c). P David Joseph, D Ken Annakin, W Trevor Farrant (based on *The Pirates of Penzance* by Sir William Gilbert and Sir Arthur Sullivan), PH Robin Copping, ED Kenneth W. Zemke, PD Tony Woollard.

LP Kristy McNichol (Mabel), Christopher Atkins (Frederic), Ted Hamilton (Pirate King), Bill Kerr (Maj. General), Maggie Kirkpatrick (Ruth), Garry McDonald (Sgt./Inspector), Linda Nagle (Aphrodite), Kate Ferguson (Edith), Rhonda Burchmore (Kate), Catherine Lynch (Isabel).

Savoyards will be aghast at the blending of the work of Gilbert and Sullivan with modern pop music in this amateurish production. A modern girl, Kristy McNichol, daydreams herself into the story of "The Pirates of Penzance." Movie lovers will be equally upset.

2281. *Pirates* (1986, Cannon, France/Tunisian, 124m, c). P Tarak Ben Ammar, D Roman Polanski, W Gerard Brach & Polanski, PH Witold Sobocinski, M Philippe Sarde, ED Herve De Luze & William Reynolds, PD Pierre Guffroy, COS Anthony Powell†.

LP Walter Matthau (Capt. Red), Cris Campion (The Frog), Damien Thomas (Don Alfonso), Olu Jacobs (Boomako),

Ferdy Mayne (Capt. Linares), David Kelly (Surgeon), Anthony Peck, Anthony Dawson (Spanish Officers), Emilio Fernandez (Angelito), Charlotte Lewis (Dolores), Roy Kinnear (Dutch), Michael Elphick (Senery), Bill Fraser (Governor).

Walter Matthau is loads of fun in this robust pirate-comedy. He's the roughest-toughest buccaneer ever to sail the seven seas. With his protégé Cris Campion, he takes on a Spanish galleon filled with Aztec gold. It's a rouser on a grand scale.

2282.   *The Pirates of Penzance* (1983, Universal, 112m, c). P Joseph Papp, D&W Wilford Leach (based on the operetta by Sir William Gilbert and Sir Arthur Sullivan), PH Douglas Slocombe, M Sullivan, ED Anne V. Coates, PD Elliot Scott.

LP Kevin Kline (Pirate King), Angela Lansbury (Ruth), Linda Ronstadt (Mabel), George Rose (Major-General), Rex Smith (Frederic), Tony Azito (Sergeant), David Hatton (Samuel, sung by Stephen Hanan), Louise Gold (Edith, sung by Alexandra Korey), Teresa Codling (Kate, sung by Marcia Shaw).

This screening of Joseph Papp's successful stage version of the Gilbert and Sullivan classic is lively and fun. Kevin Kline shows some of the glorious goofiness that would win him an Oscar for *A Fish Named Wanda*. George Rose is marvelously cast as the Major-General; Rex Smith makes a quite adequate Frederic and Linda Ronstadt is a brilliant, beautiful, charming Mabel.

2283.   *The Pit* (1984, New World, 96m, c). P Bennet Fode, D Lew Lehman, W Ian A. Stuart, PH Fred Guthe, M Victor Davies, ED Riko Morden, AD Peter E. Stone.

LP Sammy Snyders (Jamie), Jeannie Elias (Sandra), Laura Hollingsworth (Marg), Sonja Smits (Mrs. Lynde), Laura Press (Mrs. Benjamin), Andrea Swartz (Abergail).

Sammy Snyders, a 12-year-old autistic boy, gets the opportunity to take revenge against all those in his town who humiliated him. He comes across a huge hole in the forest, at the bottom of which are strange and deadly creatures, willing to do his bidding.

2284.   *P.K. & The Kid* (1987, Sunn Classics/Lorimar, 90m, c). P Joe Roth, D Lou Lombardo, W Neal Barbera, PH Ed Koons, M James Horner, ED Tony Lombardo, PD Chet Allen.

LP Paul LeMat (William "Kid" Kane), Molly Ringwald (Paula Kathleen "P.K." Bayette), Alex Rocco (Les), Charles Hallahan (Bazooka), John Disanti (Benny), Fionnula Flanagan (Flo), Bert Remsen (Al), Leigh Hamilton (Louise).

If Molly Ringwald had not become a star this film would have stayed on the shelves where it was placed after being made in 1982. Molly portrays a likeable 15-year-old who runs away from home because of her sadistic father Alex Rocco. She teams up with Paul LeMat, who dreams of winning a national arm wrestling title. They travel together and meet a series of strange characters along the way. Rocco shows up and must be dealt with by LeMat.

2285.   *Places in the Heart*† (1984, Tri-Star, 112m, c). P Arlene Donovan, D&W Robert Benton† (for both direction and screenplay), PH Nestor Almendros, M John Kander & Howard Shore, ED Carol Littleton, PD Gene Callahan, AD Sydney Z. Litwack, SD Lee Poll & Derek Hill.

LP Sally Field* (Edna Spalding), Lindsay Crouse† (Margaret Lomax), Ed Harris (Wayne Lomax), Amy Madigan (Viola Kelsey), John Malkovich† (Mr. Will), Danny Glover (Moze), Yankton Hatten (Frank), Gennie James (Possum), Lane Smith (Albert Denby), Terry O'Quinn (Buddy Kelsey).

Sally Field won her second Best Actress Oscar for her portrayal of the widow of a small town Texas sheriff. After his murder in 1935 she struggles to keep and run the family farm, despite tornadoes, falling cotton prices and the Ku Klux Klan. She is aided by itinerant laborer Danny Glover. The film is overly sentimental and makes the dubious point that hard work will overcome adversity every time. Still it's good to look at and John Malkovich, as Field's blind tenant, makes an impressive film debut.

2286.   *The Plague Dogs* (1984, United International, GB/US, animated, 103m, c). P,D&W Martin Rosen (based on a novel by Richard Adams), PH James

Farrell, Marilyn O'Connor, Ron Jackson, Ted Bemiller, Jr., Bill Bemiller, Robert Velguth & Thane Berti, M Patrick Gleeson & Alan Price, PD Gordon Harrison.

VOICES John Hurt, Christopher Benjamin, James Bolam, Nigel Hawthorne, Warren Mitchell, Bernard Hepton, Brian Stirner, Penelope Lee, Geoffrey Mathews, Barbara Leigh-Hunt.

The film's message gets a bit lost via the animation route. A pair of dogs escape from a scientific research center and race around England scrounging for food. Unfortunately, they are in danger of infecting the nation with a deadly virus with which they have been injected.

2287. *Plain Clothes* (1988, Paramount, 98m, c). P Richard Wechsler & Michael Manheim, D Martha Coolidge, W A. Scott Frank (based on a story by Frank & Dan Vining), PH Daniel Hainey, M Scott Wilk, ED Patrick Kennedy & Edward Abroms, PD Michel Levesque.

LP Arliss Howard (Nick Dunbar/ "Nick Springsteen"), Suzy Amis (Robin Torrence), George Wendt (Chet Butler), Diane Ladd (Jane Melway), Seymour Cassel (Ed Malmburg), Larry Pine (Dave Hechtor), Jackie Gayle (Coach Zeffer), Abe Vigoda (Mr. Wiseman), Robert Stack (Mr. Gardner).

Young-looking cop Arliss Howard goes undercover in a high school to find a teacher's killer. His younger brother is the prime suspect. While tracking down the real killer, Howard must fight off the advances of his homeroom teacher and falls in love with the daughter of the gym teacher.

2288. *Planes, Trains & Automobiles* (1987, Paramount, 93m, c). P,D&W John Hughes, PH Don Peterman, M Ira Newborn, ED Paul Hirsch, PD John W. Corso, AD Harold Michelson.

LP Steve Martin (Neal Page), John Candy (Del Griffith), Laila Robins (Susan Page), Michael McKean (State Trooper), Kevin Bacon (Taxi Racer), Dylan Baker (Owen), Carol Bruce (Joy Page), Olivia Burnette (Marti), Diana Douglas (Peg), William Windom (Boss).

For fastidious businessman Steve Martin, trying to get home to Thanksgiving dinner with his family in Chicago after a business trip to New York, is an almost Kafkaesque experience. He spends two days traveling across country, employing various modes of transportation, with loud, obnoxious, overbearing, talkative, shower-curtain salesman John Candy. This may not be exactly hell, but it's certainly purgatory. As is usually the case in road pictures, the two develop an appreciation for each other before reaching their destination — and so does the audience.

Planet of Horrors see *Galaxy of Terror*

2289. *Platoon** (1986, Orion, 120m, c). P Arnold Kopelson, D&W Oliver Stone* (for directing), PH Robert Richardson†, M Georges Delerue & Budd Carr, ED Claire Simpson*, PD Bruno Rubeo, SOUND John K. Wilkinson, Richard Rogers, Charles "Bud" Grenzbach & Simon Kaye*, AD Rodel Cruz & Doris Sherman Williams.

LP Tom Berenger† (Sgt. Barnes), Willem Dafoe† (Sgt. Elias), Charlie Sheen (Chris), Forest Whitaker (Big Harold), Francesco Quinn (Rhah), John C. McGinley (Sgt. O'Neill), Richard Edson (Sal), Kevin Dillon (Bunny), Reggie Johnson (Junior), Keith David (King), Johnny Depp (Lerner), David Neidorf (Tex), Mark Moses (Lt. Wolfe).

The film is the moving, terrifying account of a group of U.S. infantryman fighting in Vietnam. It is seen mostly through the eyes of young recruit Charlie Sheen, who struggles to retain his humanity in the midst of all the brutality. One sergeant, Tom Berenger, commits an atrocity which another sergeant, Willem Dafoe, intends to report, but Dafoe isn't allowed to live long enough to do so. Many Vietnam vets reported that the film caught the real feeling of the psychological and physical hell of the war.

2290. *Platoon Leader* (1988, Cannon, 100m, c, aka *Nam*). P Harry Alan Towers, D Aaron Norris, W Rick Marx, Andrew Deutsch, David Walker & Peter Welbeck [Towers] (based on the book by James R. McDonough), PH Arthur Wooster, M George S. Clinton, ED Michael J. Duthie.

LP Michael Dudikoff (Lt. Jeff Knight), Robert F. Lyons (Sgt. Michael McNamara), Michael De Lorenzo (Pvt. Raymond Bacera), Rich Fitts (Robert

Hayes), Jesse Dabson (Joshua Parker), Brian Libby (Roach).

Green First Lieutenant Michael Dudikoff must prove his mettle to battle-weary veterans in the jungles of Vietnam.

2291. *Play Dead* (1981, Troma, 89m, c). P Francine C. Rudine, D Peter Wittman, W Lothrop W. Jordan, PH Robert E. Bethard, AD Robert Burns, M Bob Farrar, ED Eugenie Nicoloff.

LP Yvonne De Carlo (Hester), Stephanie Dunnam (Audrey), David Cullinane (Jeff), Glenn Kezer (Otis), Ron Jackson (Richard).

Strangely twisted Yvonne De Carlo trains her dog to be a vicious killer. Atta boy, be a nice bad doggie.

2292. *Play Me Something* (1989, BFI, GB, 80m, b&w/c). P Kate Swan, D Timothy Neat, W Neat & John Berger (based on Berger's short story), PH Chris Cox, M Jim Sutherland, ED Russell Fenton, PD Annette Gillies.

LP John Berger (The Stranger), Hamish Henderson (TV repairman), Tilda Swinton (Hairdresser), Stewart Ennis (Motorcyclist), Margaret Bennett (Schoolteacher), Lucia Lanzarini (Marietta), Charlie Barron (Bruno).

As he and other passengers wait for their plane at a small Scottish Outer Hebrides airport, stranger John Berger relates the tale of a short love affair between a musical Italian peasant and a pretty secretary.

2293. *Playing Away* (1987, Alive Films, GB, 100m, c). P Brian Skilton & Vijay Amarnani, D Horace Ove, W Caryl Phillips, M Junior Giscombe, ED Graham Whitlock.

LP Norman Beaton (Willie-Boy), Robert Urquhart (Godfrey), Helen Lindsay (Marjorie), Nicholas Farrell (Derek), Brian Bovell (Stuart), Gary Beadle (Errol), Suzette Llewellyn (Yvette), Trevor Thomas (Jeff).

In a modest comedy, the lives of the stuffy residents of an English village are disrupted by the arrival of a cricket team from the West Indies.

Playing for Keeps see Lily in the Lake

2294. *Plenty* (1985, 20th Century–Fox, GB, 125m, c). P Edward R. Pressman & Joseph Papp, D Fred Schepisi, W David Hare (based on his play), PH Ian Baker, M Bruce Smeaton, ED Peter Honess, PD Richard Macdonald, AD Tony Reading & Adrian Smith, SD Peter James.

LP Meryl Streep (Susan Traherne), Charles Dance (Raymond Brock), Tracey Ullman (Alice Park), John Gielgud (Sir Leonard Darwin), Sting (Mick), Ian McKellen (Sir Andrew Charleson), Sam Neill (Lazar), Burt Kwouk (Mr. Aung), Pik Sen Lim (Mme. Aung), Andre Maranne (Villon), Ian Wallace (Medlicott).

As a teenager Meryl Streep fought in the French Resistance. She pines for the emotional charges and purity of purpose that she found in war. When she can't recapture the heroic feelings in herself or others, she drifts into cruelty, irrationality and finally madness.

2295. *The Ploughman's Lunch* (1984, Goldwyn, GB, 107m, c). P Simon Relph & Ann Scott, D Richard Eyre, W Ian McEwan, PH Clive Tickner, M Dominic Muldowney, ED David Martin, PD Luciana Arrighi.

LP Jonathan Pryce (James Penfield), Tim Curry (Jeremy Hancock), Rosemary Harris (Ann Barrington), Frank Finlay (Matthew Fox), Charlie Dore (Susan Barrington), David De Keyser (Gold), Nat Jackley (Mr. Penfield).

Burnt-out BBC radio journalist Jonathan Pryce plans to write a book on the British role in the 1956 Suez crisis in light of the events of the Falklands War. His research leads to his becoming enamored of TV researcher Charlie Dore, and making love with her mother, Rosemary Harris, an eminent leftwing historian and expert on Suez.

2296. *The Plumber* (1981, Cinema Ventures, Australia, 76m, c). P Matt Carroll, D&W Peter Weir, PH David Sanderson, M Gerry Tolland, ED G. Tunney-Smith, AD Ken James & Herbert Pinter.

LP Judy Morris (Jill Cowper), Robert Coleby (Brian Cowper), Ivar Kants (Max the Plumber), Candy Raymond (Meg), Henri Szeps (Department Head).

Plumber Ivar Kants invades the home of Judy Morris and Robert Coleby. His few-days' stay almost drives Morris mad. Strangely she gets no sympathy from her husband.

2297. *Police Academy* (1984, Warner, 95m, c). P Paul Maslansky, D Hugh Wilson, W Neal Israel, Pat Proft & Wilson (based on a story by Israel & Proft), PH Michael D. Margulies, M Robert Folk, ED Robert Brown & Zach Staenberg, PD Trevor Williams.

LP Steve Guttenberg (Carey Mahoney), G.W. Bailey (Lt. Harris), George Gaynes (Commandant Lassard), Michael Winslow (Larvell Jones), Kim Cattrall (Karen Thompson), Bubba Smith (Moses Hightower), Andrew Rubin (George Martin), Donovan Scott (Leslie Barbara), Leslie Easterbrook (Sgt. Callahan), David Graff (Eugene Tackleberry), Marion Ramsey (Laverne Hooks).

When the mayor of an American city eliminates all standards for jobs with the police force, an assortment of misfits show up for training at the Police Academy. Steve Guttenberg has been given the choice of attending the academy or having a police record all his own. He tries everything to get out of it, until he falls for fellow recruit Kim Cattrall. The film is basically a series of grade school dirty jokes, stereotypes, and sniggering scenes of ineptitude, until sure enough the recruits put down a riot.

2298. *Police Academy 2: Their First Assignment* (1985, Warner, 87m, c). P Paul Maslansky & Leonard Kroll, D Jerry Paris, W Barry Blaustein & David Sheffield (based on characters created by Neal Israel & Pat Proft), PH James Crabe, M Robert Folk, ED Robert Wyman, PD Trevor Williams.

LP Steve Guttenberg (Carey Mahoney), Bubba Smith (Moses Hightower), David Graff (Eugene Tackleberry), Michael Winslow (Larvell Jones), Bruce Mahler (Doug Fackler), Marion Ramsey (Laverne Hooks), Colleen Camp (Kirkland), Howard Hesseman (Pete Lassard), Art Metrano (Lt. Mauser), George Gaynes (Commandant Lassard), Bob Goldthwait (Zed), Julie Brown (Chloe).

In a moronic, scatological follow-up to the enormously successful *Police Academy,* the nitwits in blue are given their first assignment in the toughest precinct in the city. Art Metrano intends to make hay of their expected failure, but instead, led by Steve Guttenberg, they

foil a gang of ruthless street punks headed by Bob Goldthwait.

2299. *Police Academy 3: Back in Training* (1986, Warner, 82m, c). P Paul Maslansky, D Jerry Paris, W Gene Quintano (based on characters created by Neal Israel & Pat Proft), PH Robert Saad, M Robert Folk, ED Bud Molin, PD Trevor Williams.

LP Steve Guttenberg (Sgt. Mahoney), Bubba Smith (Sgt. Hightower), David Graff (Sgt. Tackleberry), Michael Winslow (Sgt. Jones), Marion Ramsey (Sgt. Hooks), Leslie Easterbrook (Lt. Callahan), Art Metrano (Commandant Masur), Tim Kazurinsky (Cadet Sweetchuck), Bobcat Goldthwait (Cadet Zed), George Gaynes (Commandant Lassard), Shawn Weatherly (Cadet Adams).

Having learned very little the first time through, the hapless boys and girls in blue are back at the Police Academy for additional training and hijinks. It's the same old menu, but there were plenty of paying customers, happy to howl at the childish, scatological, sexist jokes.

2300. *Police Academy 4: Citizens on Patrol* (1987, Warner, 87m, c). P Paul Maslansky, D Jim Drake, W Gene Quintano (based on characters created by Neal Israel & Pat Proft), PH Robert Saad, M Robert Folk, ED David Rawlins, PD Trevor Williams.

LP Steve Guttenberg (Carey Mahoney), Bubba Smith (Moses Hightower), Michael Winslow (Larvelle (Jones), David Graff (Eugene Tackleberry), Tim Kazurinsky (Sweetchuck), Sharon Stone (Claire Mattson), Leslie Easterbrook (Debbie Callahan), Marion Ramsey (Laverne Hooks), Lance Kinsey (Proctor), G.W. Bailey (Capt. Harris), Bobcat Goldthwait (Zed), George Gaynes (Commandant Lassard).

Near retirement, Commandant Lassard implements a master plan, consisting of supplementing his knucklebrained men and women in blue with John Q. Public. He asks members of the general public to step forward and take training from his cops so they may become active in crime prevention. Naturally Capt. Harris opposes the plan and will stop at nothing to see it fail. The film is filled with tasteless jokes which seem to have audiences both foreign and domestic rolling in the aisles.

2301. *Police Academy 5: Assignment Miami Beach* (1988, Warner, 90m, c). P Paul Maslansky & Donald West, D Alan Myerson, W Stephen J. Curwick (based on the characters created by Neal Israel & Pat Proft), PH James Pergola, M Robert Folk, ED Hubert C. de La Bouillerie, PD Trevor Williams.

LP Matt McCoy (Nick), Janet Jones (Kate Stratton), George Gaynes (Commandant Lassard), G.W. Bailey (Capt. Harris), Rene Auberjonois (Tony Stark), Bubba Smith (Moses Hightower), David Graff (Eugene Tackleberry), Michael Winslow (Larvelle Jones), Leslie Easterbrook (Debbie Callahan), Marion Ramsey (Laverne Hooks).

Commandant Lassard (George Gaynes) is in Miami to accept an award before his retirement. Long time adversary Capt. Harris (G.W. Bailey) is along hoping to gum up the proceedings. The picture that started this series barely had enough laughs to amuse horny boys with subaverage IQs. This fifth film in the series is even less funny than all that have gone before, as impossible as it may seem.

2302. *Police Academy 6: City Under Siege* (1989, Warner, 83m, c). P Paul Maslansky, D Peter Bonerz, W Stephen J. Curwick (based on characters created by Neal Israel & Pat Proft), PH Charles Rosher, Jr., M Robert Folk, ED Hubert de la Bouillerie, PD Tho E. Azzari.

LP Bubba Smith (Moses Hightower), David Graff (Eugene Tackleberry), Michael Winslow (Larvelle Jones), Leslie Easterbrook (Debbie Callahan), Marion Ramsey (Laverne Hooks), Lance Kinsey (Proctor), Matt McCoy (Nick), Bruce Mahler (Fackler), G.W. Bailey (Capt. Harris), George Gaynes (Commandant Lassard), Kenneth Mars (Mayor), Gerrit Graham (Ace), George R. Robertson (Police Commissioner Hurst).

This series of modern day Keystone Kops may continue forever. Explaining what attracts audiences to these films is a service we are unable to provide. It's apparent that a lack of new jokes or a meaningful story line doesn't discourage fans of the series from plopping down their cash for tickets. If the content was as en-joyable as an old Abbott & Costello routine, such as "Who's on First?," we might understand the applauding acceptance of the same old stuff time after time. Commander Lassard and his team of numbskulls are assigned to put an end to a series of robberies and discover the identity of Mr. Big.

2303. *Poltergeist* (1982, MGM/United Artists, 114m, c). P Steven Spielberg & Frank Marshall, D Tobe Hooper, W Spielberg, Michael Grais & Mark Victor, PH Matthew F. Leonetti, M Jerry Goldsmith†, ED Michael Kahn, PD James H. Spencer, VE Richard Edlund, Michael Wood & Bruce Nicholson†.

LP Craig T. Nelson (Steve Freeling), JoBeth Williams (Diane Freeling), Beatrice Straight (Dr. Lesh), Dominique Dunne (Dana), Oliver Robins (Robbie Freeling), Heather O'Rourke (Carol Anne Freeling), Zelda Rubinstein (Tangina), Martin Casella (Marty), Richard Lawson (Ryan).

Menacing spirits terrorize a middle-class family in their perfect new house in the suburbs. The ghosts transport the youngest Freeling, Heather O'Rourke, into a world beyond. Apparently the subdivision was built on a sacred Indian burial ground and the spirits are not pleased.

2304. *Poltergeist II: The Other Side* (1986, MGM, 92m, c). P&W Mark Victor & Michael Grais, D Brian Gibson, PH Andrew Laszlo, M Jerry Goldsmith, ED Thom Noble, PD Ted Haworth, SE Richard Edlund.

LP JoBeth Williams (Diane Freeling), Craig T. Nelson (Steve Freeling), Heather O'Rourke (Carol Ann Freeling), Oliver Robins (Robbie Freeling), Zelda Rubinstein (Tangina Barrons), Will Sampson (Taylor), Julian Beck (Kane), Geraldine Fitzgerald (Grandma Jess), John P. Whitecloud (Old Indian).

Just a few months' screen time after the conclusion of *Poltergeist,* the Freelings are once again at the mercy of ghosts who make their life a living hell.

2305. *Poltergeist III* (1988, MGM/United Artists, 97m, c). P Barry Bernardi, D Gary Sherman, W Sherman & Brian Taggert, PH Alex Nepomniaschy, M Joe Renzetti, ED Ross Albert, PD

Paul Eads, VE Richard Edlund, John Bruno, Garry Waller & William Neil†.

LP Tom Skerritt (Bruce Gardner), Nancy Allen (Patricia Gardner), Heather O'Rourke (Carol Anne Freeling), Zelda Rubinstein (Tangina Barrons), Lara Flynn Boyle (Donna Gardner), Kip Wentz (Scott), Richard Fire (Dr. Seaton), Nathan Davis (Rev. Kane), Paul Graham (Martin), Meg Weldon (Sandy).

"They're back . . ." again, or so it would appear. Heather O'Rourke, who has moved to Chicago to live with her aunt Nancy Allen and uncle Tom Skerritt, is not believed by skeptical psychologist Richard Fire, investigating the child's past experiences. He claims the poltergeists that have haunted O'Rourke were caused by mass hypnosis brought about by the child's suggestions. But the evil Rev. Kane has followed her to Chicago, appearing to her in mirrors and reflections, beckoning her "into the light." Twelve-year-old O'Rourke died of a bowel obstruction six months after this film was completed.

2306. *Polyester* (1980, New Line Cinema, 86m, c). P,D&W John Waters, PH David Insley, M Chris Stein & Michael Kamen, ED Charles Roggero, PD Vincent Pernaio.

LP Divine (Francine Fishpaw), Tab Hunter (Todd Tomorrow), Edith Massey (Cuddles), Mink Stole (Sandra), David Samson (Elmer Fishpaw), Joni Ruth White (LaRue, Mother), Mary Garlington (Lulu Fishpaw), Ken King (Dexter Fishpaw), Hans Kramm (Chauffeur), Stiv Bators (Bo-Bo).

In a family of misfits, forlorn housewife Divine pines away for Tab Hunter, the man of her dreams, while the rest of her life is falling apart. Members of the audience were given scratch and sniff cards upon entering the movie with instructions as to when to take a whiff of the unpleasant smells. The picture is probably only for the cult followers of John Waters.

2307. *The Pope of Greenwich Village* (1984, MGM/United Artists, 120m, c). P Gene Kirkwood, D Stuart Rosenberg, W Vincent Patrick (based on his novel), PH John Bailey, M Dave Grusin, ED Robert Brown, PD Paul Sylbert.

LP Eric Roberts (Paulie), Mickey Rourke (Charlie), Daryl Hannah (Diane), Geraldine Page† (Mrs. Ritter), Kenneth McMillan (Barney), Tony Musante (Pete), M. Emmet Walsh (Burns), Burt Young (Bed Bug Eddie), Jack Kehoe (Bunky), Philip Bosco (Paulie's Father), Val Avery (Nunzi).

On the mean streets of New York City, Eric Roberts and his cousin Mickey Rourke commit what seems to be an uncomplicated robbery. But they accidentally kill a corrupt cop and find both the police and the Mafia on their trail.

2308. *Popeye* (1980, Paramount, 114m, c). P Robert Evans, D Robert Altman, W Jules Feiffer (based on the comic strip character created by E.C. Segar), PH Giuseppe Rotunno, M Harry Nilsson, ED Tony Lombardo, PD Wolf Kroeger.

LP Robin Williams (Popeye), Shelley Duvall (Olive Oyl), Ray Walston (Poopdeck Pappy), Paul L. Smith (Bluto), Paul Dooley (Wimpy), Richard Libertini (Geezil), Roberta Maxwell (Nana Oyl), Donald Moffat (Taxman), Wesley Ivan Hurt (Swee' Pea).

Robin Williams is credible as the cartoon sailor who searches for his long-lost father Ray Walston. Along the way he meets Shelley Duvall, adopts little Wesley Ivan Hurt and has plenty of trouble with Paul L. Smith. Director Robert Altman fails to make this dud interesting, amusing or appealing.

2309. *Porky's* (1982, 20th Century–Fox, 94m, c). P Don Carmody & Bob Clark, D&W Clark, PH Reginald H. Morris, M Carl Zittrer & Paul Zaza, ED Stan Cole, PD Reuben Freed.

LP Dan Monahan (Pee Wee), Mark Herrier (Billy), Wyatt Knight (Tommy), Roger Wilson (Mickey), Cyril O'Reilly (Tim), Tony Ganios (Meat), Kaki Hunter (Wendy), Kim Cattrall (Honeywell), Nancy Parsons (Balbricker), Scott Colomby (Brian Schwartz), Boyd Gaines (Coach Brackett), Susan Clark (Cherry Forever), Wayne Maunder (Cavanaugh), Alex Karras (Sheriff Wallace), Chuck Mitchell (Porky).

There's a lot of talking about sex in this teenage sexploitation film, which features a group of unappealing horny Florida high school students of the early 50s.

Dreaming only of how they can get laid, they invade the next county, where Chuck Mitchell runs a raunchy gambling den and whorehouse called Porky's. When they are not treated with the respect they believe they deserve as potential customers, they take revenge by destroying Mitchell's business.

2310. *Porky's II: The Next Day* (1983, 20th Century-Fox, 95m, c). P Don Carmody & Bob Clark, D Clark, W Clark, Roger E. Swaybill & Alan Ormsby, PH Reginald H. Morris, M Carl Zittrer, ED Stan Cole.

LP Dan Monahan (Pee Wee), Wyatt Knight (Tommy), Mark Herrier (Billy), Roger Wilson (Mickey), Cyril O'Reilly (Tim), Tony Ganios (Meat), Kaki Hunter (Wendy), Scott Colomby (Brian), Nancy Parsons (Balbricker), Joseph Running Fox (John Henry), Bill Wiley (Rev. Bubba Flavel).

Set the next day after the action of the surprising 1982 hit, this putrid piece doesn't even feature Porky (Chuck Mitchell). Instead it serves up a bigoted fundamentalist minister Bill Wiley and corrupt politicians. There's still plenty of giggling about sex, nudity and to top it all off a vomiting scene in a restaurant. Gross!

2311. *Porky's Revenge* (1985, 20th Century-Fox, 92m, c). P Robert L. Rosen, D James Komack, W Ziggy Steinberg (based on characters created by Bob Clark), PH Robert Jessup, M Dave Edmunds, ED John W. Wheeler, PD Peter Wooley.

LP Dan Monahan (Pee Wee), Wyatt Knight (Tommy), Tony Ganios (Meat), Mark Herrier (Billy), Kaki Hunter (Wendy), Scott Colomby (Brian), Nancy Parsons (Ms. Balbricker), Chuck Mitchell (Porky Wallace), Rose McVeigh (Miss Webster), Fred Buch (Mr. Dobbish), Wendy Feign (Blossom), Kimberley Evenson (Inga).

In the second sequel to the surprisingly successful idiotic, tasteless teenage sexploitation film *Porky,* the group of horny high school students (definitely not led by Dan Callahan) once again makes contact with obese title character Chuck Mitchell. He's put together his combination gambling casino–whorehouse on a paddlewheel riverboat and is pressuring the

high school coach to have his boys throw the state championship basketball game. Our heroes snicker all the way as they deal with this threat.

2312. *Posed for Murder* (1989, Double Helix, 85m, c). P Carl Fury & Jack Fox, D Brian Thomas Jones, W John A. Gallagher & Chuck Dickenson (based on Fox's story), PH Bob Paone, M Tom Marolda, ED Brian O'Hara, PD Claudia Mohr.

LP Charlotte J. Helmkamp (Laura Shea), Carl Fury (Rick Thompson), Rick Gianasi (Det. Steve Barnes), Michael Merrings (Danny), William Beckwith (Clifford Devereux), Roy MacArthur (Serge LaRue), Terri Brennan (Terri).

Former real-life *Playboy* pinup Charlotte Helmkamp (appearing therein as Charlotte Kemp), here a buxom model for *Thrill* magazine, is trying to break into movies with a role in the horror film *Meat Cleavers from Mars.* Some maniac is stalking our gal, killing off her friends and acquaintances one by one.

2313. *Positive I.D.* (1987, Universal, 102m, c). P,D&W Andy Anderson, PH Paul Barton, ED Anderson & Robert J. Castaldo.

LP Stephanie Rascoe (Julie Kenner), John Davies (Don Kenner), Steve Fromholz (Roy/Lt. Mercer), Laura Lane (Dana), Gail Cronauer (Melissa), Audeen Casey (Dr. Sterling), Matthew Sacks (Mr. Tony).

Rape victim Stephanie Rascoe assumes a new identity. She hangs out at a seedy downtown bar playing the role of a seductress. The ending of this low-budget thriller makes the film almost worth watching.

2314. *The Postman Always Rings Twice* (1981, Paramount, 125m, c). P Charles Mulvehill & Bob Rafelson, D Rafelson, W David Mamet (based on the novel by James M. Cain), PH Sven Nykvist, M Michael Small, ED Graeme Clifford, PD George Jenkins.

LP Jack Nicholson (Frank Chambers), Jessica Lange (Cora Papadakis), John Colicos (Nick Papadakis), Christopher Lloyd (Salesman), Michael Lerner (Katz), John P. Ryan (Kennedy), Angelica Huston (Madge), William Traylor (Sackett), Tom Hill (Barlow).

This production of James M. Cain's story of infidelity and murder is able to present more explicit love-making scenes, but it doesn't improve on the presentation of the sexual tension shown so effectively in the 1946 movie with John Garfield and Lana Turner. Drifter Jack Nicholson is befriended and given a job by roadhouse owner John Colicos. The latter is repaid when Nicholson and the man's young wife Jessica Lange have an affair and kill him for his insurance money.

2315. Pound Puppies and the Legend of Big Paw (1988, Tri-Star, animated, 76m, c). P Donald Kushner & Peter Locke, D Pierre DeCelles, W Jim Carlson & Terrence McDonnell, M Richard Kosinski, Sam Winans & Bill Reichenbach, ED John Blizek.

VOICES George Rose (McNasty), B.J. Ward (Whopper), Ruth Buzzi (Nose Marie), Brennan Howard (Cooler), Cathy Cadavini (Collette), Nancy Cartwright (Bright Eyes).

Whether tots will fall for these TV type cartoon characters is debatable. Kids nowadays are more sophisticated. The Pound Puppies try to retrieve the fabled "Bone of Scone," which legend has it enables kids and dogs to communicate.

2316. P.O.W. The Escape (1986, Cannon, 89m, c). P Menahem Golan & Yoram Globus, D Gideon Amir, W Jeremy Lipp, James Bruner, Malcolm Barbour & John Langley (based on a story by Avi Kleinberger & Amir), PH Yechiel Ne'eman, M Michael Linn, ED Marcus Manton, PD Marcia Hinds.

LP David Carradine (Col. Cooper), Charles R. Floyd (Sparks), Mako (Capt. Vinh), Steve James (Jonston), Phil Brock (Adams), Daniel Demorest (Thomas), Tony Pierce (Waite), Steve Freedman (Scott), James Acheson (McCoy).

In a Rambo-like imitation, American POWs, led by David Carradine, make their escape to freedom as Saigon falls to the Communists.

2317. Power (1986, 20th Century–Fox, 111m, c). P Reene Schisgal & Mark Tarlov, D Sidney Lumet, W David Himmelstein, PH Andrzej Bartkowiak, M Cy Coleman, ED Andrew Mondshein, PD Peter Larkin.

LP Richard Gere (Pete St. John), Julie Christie (Ellen Freeman), Gene Hackman (Wilfred Buckley), Kate Capshaw (Syd-

ney Betterman), Denzel Washington (Arnold Billings), E.G. Marshall (Senator Sam Hastings), Beatrice Straight (Claire Hastings), Fritz Weaver (Wallace Furman), Michael Learned (Governor Andrea Stannard).

Sidney Lumet, who brought audiences *Network,* once again examines the corruption of a major institution—this time he shows how dehumanized the political process has become. Ruthless hustler Richard Gere helps package candidates, but even he is disappointed when he discovers the only politician he respected, E.G. Marshall, has become a pawn of the political power trade.

2318. The Power (1984, Film Ventures, 84m, c). P Jeffrey Obrow, D&W Obrow & Stephen Carpenter (based on a story by Obrow, Carpenter, John Penny & John Hopkins), PH Carpenter, M Chris Young, ED Obrow & Carpenter, PD Chris Hopkins.

LP Susan Stokey (Sandy), Warren Lincoln (Jerry), Lisa Erickson (Julie), Chad Christian (Tommy), Ben Gilbert (Matt), Chris Morrill (Ron Prince), Rod Mays (Lee McKennah), J. Dinan Mytretus (Francis Lott), Jay Fisher (Raphael).

As a small Aztec idol is passed down from one generation to the next, it becomes more powerful. Three high school students come into possession of the idol when it is stolen by Warren Lincoln. He becomes possessed by a demon and is transformed into a monster.

2319. Powerforce (1983, Bedford Entertainment, 98m, c). P George Mason, D Michael King, W Terry Chalmers & Dennis Thompsett, PH Bob Huke & Robert Hope, M Chris Babida.

LP Bruce Baron, Mandy Moore, James Barnett, Jovy Couldry, Frances Fong, Olivia Jeng, Randy Channel, Seon Blake, Sam Sorono, Bruce Li.

In yet another routine martial-arts film, CIA agent Bruce Baron kicks and chops his way through a bunch of baddies.

2320. Powwow Highway (1989, Handmade Films, GB/US, 91m, c). P Jan Wieringa, D Jonathan Wacks, W Janet Heany & Jean Stawarz (based on the novel by David Seals), PH Toyomichi Kurita, M Barry Goldberg, ED James Austin Stewart, PD Cynthia Sowder.

LP A. Martinez (Buddy Red Bow), Gary Farmer (Philbert Bono), Amanda Wyss (Rabbit Layton), Joanelle Nadine Romero (Bonnie Red Bow), Sam Vlahos (Chief Joseph), Wayne Waterman (Wolf Tooth), Margo Kane (Imogene), Geoff Rivas (Sandy Youngblood), Roscoe Born (Agent Jack Novall).

Based on an underground novel by actor/activist David Seals, this film tells of the comic adventures of two desperate Indians, A. Martinez and Gary Farmer. They rediscover their heritage while on a weekend journey along a scenic interstate, near Lame Deer, Montana, known as the Powwow Highway. Martinez is an angry Vietnam vet and Indian activist, while Farmer is a gentle, generous soul, guided by visions, always looking for links with his people's past.

2321. *Prancer* (1989, Orion, 103m, c). P Raffaella De Laurentiis, D John Hancock, W Greg Taylor (based on his story), PH Misha Suslov, M Maurice Jarre, ED Dennis O'Connor, PD Chester Kaczenski.

LP Sam Elliott (John Riggs), Rebecca Harrell (Jessica Riggs), Cloris Leachman (Mrs. McFarland), Rutanya Alda (Aunt Sarah), John Joseph Duda (Steve Riggs), Abe Vigoda (Dr. Orel Benton), Michael Constantine (Mr. Stewart/Santa), Ariana Richards (Carol Wetherby), Boo (Prancer), Frank Welker (Prancer's Voice).

This one's for the kiddies. A little girl nurses a reindeer back to health, believing the animal to be Santa Claus's Prancer. Writer Greg Taylor admits that he modeled his story on E.T. in that he's taken a child from a troubled household and put her with an alien creature lost in the woods. Nice try. It's sweet, and not too sugary. The reindeer behaves as if he doesn't want to be an actor.

2322. *Pray for Death* (1986, American Distribution Group, 92m, c). P Don Van Atta, D Gordon Hessler, W James Booth, PH Roy Wagner, M Thomas Chase, Steve Rucker, ED Bill Butler, Steve Butler, AD Adrian Gorton.

LP Sho Kosugi (Akira), James Booth (Limehouse), Robert Ito (Koga), Michael Constantine (Newman), Donna Kei Benz (Aiko Saito), Kane Kosugi (Takeshi), Shane Kosugi (Tomoya), Norman Burton (Lt. Anderson), Parley Baer (Sam Green).

A Japanese immigrant and his family are victimized by American mobsters, only to have a Ninja appear to further complicate things.

2323. *A Prayer for the Dying* (1987, Goldwyn, GB, 104m, c). P Peter Snell, D Mike Hodges, W Edmund Ward & Martin Lynch, PH Mike Garfath, M Bill Conti, ED Peter Boyle, PD Evan Hercules.

LP Mickey Rourke (Martin Fallon), Alan Bates (Jack Meehan), Bob Hoskins (Father Da Costa), Sammi Davis (Anna), Christopher Fulford (Billy), Liam Neeson (Liam Docherty), Alison Doody (Siobhan Donovan), Camille Coduri (Jenny).

An IRA detachment to which Mickey Rourke belongs accidentally blows up a school bus in Northern Ireland, instead of the intended troop transport. This causes Rourke to desert the cause and head to London, hoping to make it to America. The IRA doesn't allow desertions or resignations and they are after Rourke, using their London underworld contacts to chase him.

2324. *Predator* (1987, 20th Century–Fox, 107m, c). P Lawrence Gordon, Joel Silver & John Davis, D John McTiernan, W Jim Thomas & John Thomas, PH Donald McAlpine, M Alan Silvestri, ED John F. Link & Mark Helfrich, PD John Vallone, VE Joel Hynek, Robert M. Greenberg, Richard Greenberg & Stan Winston†.

LP Arnold Schwarzenegger (Major Alan "Dutch" Schaefer), Carl Weathers (Dillon), Elpidia Carrillo (Anna), Bill Duke (Mac), Jesse Ventura (Sgt. Blain), Sonny Landham (Billy), Richard Chaves (Pancho), R.G. Armstrong (Gen. Phillips), Shane Black (Hawkins), Kevin Peter Hall (Predator).

Arnold Schwarzennegger leads his troops into a Latin American jungle to rescue some hostages. Arnie must go up against giant, alien, chameleon-like meateater Kevin Peter Hall.

Preppies see *Making the Grade*

2325. *The President's Women* (1981, Krona, 76m, c). P Cael Gurevich, D&ED John Avildsen, W David Odell, Jack

Richardson & Don Greenberg, PH Ralf D. Bode, M Stan Vincent & Gary William Friedman.

LP Zero Mostel (President/Godfather), Estelle Parsons (First Lady/Barmaid), Pat Paulsen (Norman), Paul Dooley (Salesman), Jerry Orbach (Lorsey), George S. Irving (Roberto/Reverend), Irwin Corey (Professor).

Despite a name cast, this feeble political comedy disappeared before many even knew it had been released.

2326. *The Presidio* (1988, Paramount, 97m, c). P D. Constantine Conte, D Peter Hyams, W Larry Ferguson, PH Hyams, M Bruce Broughton, ED James Mitchell, PD Albert Brenner.

LP Sean Connery (Lt. Col. Alan Caldwell), Mark Harmon (Jay Austin), Meg Ryan (Donna Caldwell), Jack Warden (Sgt. Maj. Ross "Top" Maclure), Mark Blum (Arthur Peale), Dana Gladstone (Lt. Col. Paul Lawrence), Jenette Goldstein (Patti Jean Lynch).

There's a triangle here, Presidio Military Compound Provost Marshal Sean Connery, San Francisco cop Mark Harmon, and Connery's daughter Meg Ryan. There's a lot of chasing around, but not much of a plot. The two law enforcers reluctantly join forces in a case of murder, corruption and smuggled diamonds. Forget the story, enjoy flinty Connery and sexy Ryan.

2327. *Pretty in Pink* (1986, Paramount, 96m, c). P Lauren Shuler, D Howard Deutch, W John Hughes, PH Tak Fujimoto, M Michael Gore, ED Richard Marks, PD John W. Corso.

LP Molly Ringwald (Andie), Harry Dean Stanton (Jack), Jon Cryer (Duckie), Annie Potts (Iona), James Spader (Steff), Andrew McCarthy (Blane), Jim Haynie (Donnelly), Alexa Kenin (Jena), Kate Vernon (Benny).

Even though high school girl Molly Ringwald comes from the wrong side of the tracks, wealthy heartthrob Andrew McCarthy asks her to the prom. His friends don't approve and almost ruin the budding romance. It's a bittersweet story, with a none too credible happy ending.

2328. *Pretty Smart* (1987, New World, 84m, c). P Ken Solomon, Jeff Begun & Melanie J. Alschuler, D Dimitri

Logothetis, W Dan Hoskins (based on an original story by Begun & Alschuler), PH Dimitri Papacostantis, M Jay Levy & Eddie Arkin, ED Daniel Gross, PD Beau Peterson.

LP Tricia Leigh Fisher (Daphne "Zigs" Ziegler), Lisa Lorient (Jennifer Ziegler), Dennis Cole (Richard Crawley), Patricia Arquette (Zero), Paris Vaughn (Torch), Kimberly B. Delfin (Yuko), Brad Zutaut (Alexis), Kim Waltrip (Sara Gernhy).

Tricia Leigh Fisher and Lisa Lorient are two extremely different sisters. Sent to the same finishing school, they become enemies, until they discover that the headmaster has been using them in a drug-dealing, pornographic sideline to running the school.

2329. *Prettykill* (1987, Spectrafilm, 95m, c). P John R. Bowey & Martin Walters, D George Kaczender, W Sandra K. Bailey, PH Joao Fernandes, M Robert O. Ragland, ED Tom Merchant.

LP David Birney (Sgt. Larry Turner), Season Hubley (Heather Todd), Susannah York (Toni), Yaphet Kotto (Lt. Harris), Suzanne Snyder (Francie/Stella/Paul), Germaine Houde (Jacques Mercier), Lenore Zann (Carrie).

Murder and madness menace honest cop David Birney and his callgirl girlfriend Season Hubley. Hubley's seemingly innocent Southern belle protégée Suzanne Snyder is actually a dangerous schizoid.

2330. *The Prey* (1984, New World, 80m, c). P Summer Brown & Randy Rovins, D Edwin Scott Brown, W Summer Brown & E.S. Brown, PH Teru Hayashi, M Don Peake, ED Michael Barnard.

LP Debbie Thureson (Nancy), Steve Bond (Joel), Lori Lethin (Bobbie), Robert Wald (Skip), Gayle Gannes (Gail), Philip Wenckus (Greg), Carel Struycken (The Giant), Jackson Bostwick (Mark), Jackie Coogan (Lester).

Looking for a mate in the Colorado Rockies, a predator kills five campers in the process.

2331. *Prick Up Your Ears* (1987, Goldwyn, GB, 111m, c). P Andrew Brown, D Stephen Frears, W Alan Bennett (based on the biography of John Lahr), PH Oliver Stapleton, M Stanley

Myers, ED Mick Audsley, PD Hugo Luczyc-Wyhowski.

LP Gary Oldman (Joe Orton), Alfred Molina (Kenneth Halliwell), Vanessa Redgrave (Peggy Ramsay), Wallace Shawn (John Lahr), Lindsay Duncan (Anthea Lahr), Julie Walters (Elsie Orton), James Grant (William Orton), Janet Dale (Mrs. Sugden), Dave Atkins (Mr. Sugden).

This unflinching look at homosexuality in the British theatre is the story of the relationship between playwright Joe Orton and his longtime lover Kenneth Halliwell. The latter's jealousy of Orton's success leads him to murder the 60s author of black comedies.

2332. *Priest of Love* (1981, Filmways, GB, 125m, c). P Christopher Miles & Andrew Donally, D Miles, W Alan Plater (based on a novel by Harry T. Moore and the writings of D.H. Lawrence), PH Ted Moore, M Joseph James, ED Paul Davies, PD Ted Tester & David Brockhurst.

LP Ian McKellen (D.H. Lawrence), Janet Suzman (Frieda Lawrence), Ava Gardner (Mabel Dodge Luhan), Penelope Keith (The Honorable Dorothy Brett), Jorge Rivero (Tony Luhan), Maurizio Merli (Angelo Ravagli), John Gielgud (Herbert G. Muskett), James Faulkner (Aldous Huxley).

This disappointing, aimless picture explores the last years in the life of D.H. Lawrence. After his books are banned, he seeks a warmer climate to combat his tuberculosis.

2333. *Primal Scream* (1988, Unistar, 92m, c). P Howard Foulkrod, D&W William Murray, PH Dennis Peters, M Mark Knox, ED Keith L. Reamer, SE David Di Pietro.

LP Kenneth J. McGregor (Corby McHale), Sharon Mason (Samantha Keller), Julie Miller (Caitlin Foster), Jon Maurice (Capt. Frank Gitto), Joseph White (Nicky Fingeas), Mickey Shaughnessy (Charlie Waxman), Stephan Caldwell (Olan Robert Foster).

This film combines elements of science fiction and detective thrillers, but not the best parts of either. There's a tenuous relationship between Hellfire, an energy catalyst in the 21st century, and private eye Kenneth J. McGregor's investigation of a series of murders which leave the victims smoldering embers.

2334. *Prime Risk* (1985, Mikas I/Almi, 100m, c). P Herman Grigsby, D&W Michael Farkas, PH Mac Ahlberg, M Phil Marshall, ED Bruce Green, AD Christopher Henry.

LP Toni Hudson (Julie Collins), Lee Montgomery (Michael Fox), Samuel Bottoms (Bill Yeoman), Clu Gulager (Paul Minsky), Keenan Wynn (Dr. Lasser), Lois Hall (Dr. Holt), Rick Rakowski (John), John Lykes (Vance), James O'Connell (Terry Franklin), Randy Pearlman (Ed Harrington).

Not having any luck getting a job, recent college graduate and computer whiz Toni Hudson comes up with a way to electronically break into automatic teller machines. She's doing all right withdrawing all the cash she wants until she comes across a group of secret agents doing the same thing, hoping to destroy the American financial system. Well, it's one thing to be a crook—but at least she's an American crook. Hudson devises a way to foil the foreign competition and wins the gratitude of the FBI, saving the Federal Reserve in the nick of time.

2335. *Prince Jack* (1985, LMF/Castle Hill, 100m, c). P Jim Milio, D&W Bert Lovitt, PH Hiro Narita, M Elmer Bernstein, ED Janice Hampton, PD Michael Corenblith.

LP Robert Hogan (Jack Kennedy), James F. Kelly (Bobby Kennedy), Kenneth Mars (Lyndon B. Johnson), Lloyd Nolan (Joseph Kennedy), Cameron Mitchell (General Walker), Robert Guillaume (Martin Luther King), Theodore Bikel (Russian Ambassador), Dana Andrews (The Cardinal), Jim Backus (Dealy), William Windom (Ferguson).

It's an inconsequential presentation of episodes in the presidential career of John F. Kennedy.

2336. *Prince of Darkness* (1987, Universal, 101m, c). P Larry Franco, D John Carpenter, W Martin Quatermass [Carpenter], PH Gary B. Kibbe, M Carpenter & Alan Howarth, ED Steve Mirkovich, PD Daniel Lomino.

LP Donald Pleasence (Priest), Jameson Parker (Brian), Victor Wong (Professor Birack), Lisa Blount (Catherine), Dennis Dun (Walter), Susan Blanchard (Kelly), Anne Howard (Susan), Ann Yen (Lisa).

Priest Donald Pleasence calls together a group of scientists to stave off the threat from the contents of a 7,000,000-year-old cannister said to contain the very spirit of Satan.

2337. *The Prince of Pennsylvania* (1988, New Line, 87m, c). P Joan Fishman & Kerry Orent, D&W Ron Nyswaner, PH Frank Prinzi, ED Bill Sharf, PD Toby Corbett.

LP Keanu Reeves (Rupert Marshetta), Amy Madigan (Carla Headlee), Bonnie Bedelia (Pam Marshetta), Fred Ward (Gary Marshetta), Joseph De Lisi (Roger Marshetta), Jeff Hayenga (Jack Sike), Tracy Ellis (Lois Sike).

Frustrated and troubled by his right-wing conservative nutcake of a father, Fred Ward, and his mother, Bonnie Bedelia's, affair with her father's best friend, Pennsylvania mining town teen Keanu Reeves comes under the influence of ex-hippie Amy Madigan. The latter convinces the youngster to kidnap his father and hold him for ransom. It's an unusual black comedy, with many of the parts sadly missing.

2338. *Prince of the City* (1981, Warner, 167m, c). P Burtt Harris, D Sidney Lumet, W Jay Presson Allen & Lumet† (based on the book by Robert Daley), PH Andrzej Bartkowiak, W Paul Chihara, ED John J. Fitzstephens, PD Tony Walton.

LP Treat Williams (Daniel Ciello), Jerry Orbach (Gus Levy), Richard Foronjy (Joe Marinaro), Don Billett (Bill Mayo), Kenny Marino (Dom Bando), Carmine Caridi (Gino Mascone), Tony Page (Raf Alvarez), Norman Parker (Rick Cappalino), Paul Roebling (Brooks Paige).

In a long, dragged-out film, Treat Williams, a New York cop on the drug beat, agrees to inform on his corrupt fellow officers as long as he doesn't have to turn in his immediate partners.

2339. *The Princess Academy* (1987, Empire, US/Yugo/France, 90m, c). P Sandra Weintraub, D Bruce Block, W Sandra Weintraub (based on an idea by Fred Weintraub), PH Kent Wakeford, M Roger Bellon, ED Martin Cohen.

LP Eva Gabor (Countess), Lar Park Lincoln (Cindy), Lu Leonard (Fraulein Stickenschmidt), Richard Paul (Drago), Carole Davis (Sonia), Badar Howar (Sarah), Barbara Rovsek (Izzie), Yolande Palfrey (Pamela).

Eva Gabor is the headmistress of a Swiss finishing school where the young ladies are taught how to catch rich husbands, fake an orgasm, shop, and other activities essential to useless females. The acting, story and direction are horrid.

2340. *The Princess Bride* (1987, 20th Century-Fox, 98m, c). P Andrew Scheinman & Rob Reiner, D Reiner, W William Goldman (based on his novel), PH Adrian Biddle, M Mark Knopfler, ED Robert Leighton, PD Norman Garwood, SONG "Storybook Love" by Willy DeVille†, COS Phyllis Dalton.

LP Cary Elwes (Westley), Mandy Patinkin (Inigo Montoya), Chris Sarandon (Prince Humperdinck), Christopher Guest (Count Rugen), Wallace Shawn (Vizzini), Andre the Giant (Fezzik), Fred Savage (The Grandson), Robin Wright (Buttercup), Peter Falk (The Grandfather), Peter Cook (The Impressive Clergyman), Mel Smith (The Albino), Carol Kane (Valerie), Billy Crystal (Miracle Max).

Stuck in bed with the flu, Fred Savage is entertained by his grandfather Peter Falk, who relates the fairy tale story of the true love of the beautiful princess Buttercup, played by Robin Wright, and her one-and-only Westley, bravely portrayed by Cary Elwes. The two are menaced by numerous villains, including Wallace Shawn, Andre the Giant, Mandy Patinkin and, most particularly, Chris Sarandon.

2341. *The Principal* (1987, Tri-Star, 109m, c). P Thomas H. Brodek, D Christopher Cain, W Frank Deese, PH Arthur Albert, M Jay Gruska, ED Jack Hofstra, AD Mark Billerman, SD Rick Brown.

LP James Belushi (Rick Lattimer), Louis Gossett, Jr. (Jake Phillips), Rae Dawn Chong (Hilary Orozco), Michael Wright (Victor Duncan, Jr.), J.J. Cohen ("White Zac"), Esai Morales (Raymi Rojas), Troy Winbush ("Baby" Emile), Jacob

Vargas (Arturo Diego), Thomas Ryan (Robert Darcy).

In his first starring role James Belushi, a messed-up teacher with a failed personal life, is given the ultimatum of becoming principal at the district's most trouble-filled school or being fired. He accepts and finds the high school filled with violent gangs, drug dealers and delinquents of all stripes. Life isn't easy for him, but eventually with the help of Lou Gossett, head of security (a terrible thing to need in a high school), he is able to gain some respect from the students and teachers with his "No More" policy—no more drugs, no more violence, no more arson, no more extortion, etc. He and Gossett have a climactic fight with Michael Wright, the leader of the vicious gang that runs the school.

2342. *Prison* (1988, Empire, 102m, c). P Irwin Yablans, D Renny Harlin, W C. Courtney Joyner (based on a story by Yablans), PH Mac Ahlberg, M Richard Band & Christopher Stone, ED Andy Horvitch, PD Philip Duffin.

LP Viggo Mortensen (Connie Burke), Chelsea Field (Katherine Walker), Lane Smith (Ethan Sharpe), Lincoln Kilpatrick (Cresus), Tom Everett (Rabbitt), Ivan Kane (Lasagna), Andre De Shields (Sandor), Tom Lister, Jr. (Tiny).

In 1964 an innocent man is executed for the murder of a prison inmate. The deceased was actually killed by brutal prison guard Lane Smith. Shortly thereafter the prison is shut down. Twenty years later, because of overcrowding, the old prison is reopened with Smith as its warden. The vengeful ghost of the unjustly executed man is accidentally released. He begins killing guards and prisoners alike, working his way up to Smith. It's scary!

Prisoner of the Skull see Who?

2343. *Prisoners of the Lost Universe* (1984, Premier, GB, 91m, c). P Harry Robertson, D Terry Marcel, W Marcel & Robertson, PH Derek Browne, M Robertson, ED Alan Jones.

LP Richard Hatch (Dan Roebuck), Kay Lenz (Carrie Madison), John Saxon (Kleel), Peter O'Farrell (Malachi), Ray Charleson (Greenman), Kenneth Hendel

(Dr. Hartmann), Philip Van Der Byl (Kahar), Larry Taylor (Vosk).

A TV journalist and a martial arts champ are transported to a primitive world via a matter transmitter.

2344. *Private Benjamin* (1980, Warner, 109m, c). P Nancy Meyers, Charles Shyer & Harvey Miller, D Howard Zieff, W Meyers, Shyer & Miller†, PH David M. Walsh, M Bill Conti, ED Sheldon Kahn, PD Robert Boyle.

LP Goldie Hawn† (Judy Benjamin), Eileen Brennan† (Capt. Doreen Lewis), Armand Assante (Henri Tremont), Robert Webber (Col. Clay Thornbush), Sam Wanamaker (Teddy Benjamin), Barbara Barrie (Harriet Benjamin), Mary Kay Place (Pvt. Mary Lou Glass), Harry Dean Stanton (Sgt. Jim Ballard), Albert Brooks (Yale Goodman), Sally Kirkland (Helga).

When her bridegroom Albert Brooks dies during lovemaking on their wedding day, wealthy Jewish widow Goldie Hawn, at a loss of what to do with her life, joins the army. Her spoiled ways don't sell well with tough officer Eileen Brennan—but Goldie shapes up and does herself proud.

2345. *The Private Eyes* (1980, Tri-Star/New World, 91m, c). P Lang Elliott & Wanda Dell, D Elliott, W Tim Conway & John Myhers, PH Jacques Haitkin, M Peter Matz, ED Fabien Tordjmann & Patrick M. Crawford.

LP Tim Conway (Dt. Tart), Don Knotts (Inspector Winship), Trisha Noble (Mistress Phyllis Morley), Bernard Fox (Justin), Grace Zabriskie (Nanny), John Fujioka (Mr. Uwatsum), Stan Ross (Tibet), Irwin Keyes (Jock).

Television comedians Tim Conway and Don Knotts once again prove that their humor and popularity cannot be transformed to the big screen. They portray a pair of bungling Scotland Yard detectives investigating murders in a haunted mansion. All the usual stale jokes are brought out in wheelchairs, as it were.

2346. *A Private Function* (1985, Hand Made/Island Alive, GB, 93m, c). P Mark Shivas, D Malcolm Mowbray, W Alan Bennett (based on a story by Bennett & Mowbray), PH Tony Pierce-Roberts, M John Du Prez, ED Barrie Vince, PD Stuart Walker.

LP Michael Palin (Gilbert Chilvers), Maggie Smith (Joyce Chilvers), Denholm Elliott (Dr. Swaby), Richard Griffiths (Allardyce), Tony Haygarth (Sutcliff), John Normington (Lockwood), Bill Paterson (Wormold).

In a comedy set in 1947 Yorkshire, villagers flaunt food rationing rules and secretly fatten an illicit pig for the Royal Wedding festivities.

Private Investigations see P.I. Private Investigations

2347. *Private Lessons* (1981, Jensen Farley, 87m, c, aka *Philly*). P R. Ben Efraim, D Alan Myerson, W Dan Greenburg (based on the novel *Philly* by Greenburg), PH Jan de Bont, M Various Artists, ED Fred Chulack.

LP Sylvia Kristel (Nicole), Howard Hesseman (Lester), Eric Brown (Philly), Patrick Piccininni (Sherman), Ed Begley, Jr. (Jack Travis), Pamela Bryant (Joyce), Meredith Baer (Miss Phipps), Ron Foster (Philly's Dad).

In another of the many teen sex-fantasy movies, 15-year-old Eric Brown is initiated into the rites by gorgeous maid Sylvia Kristel.

2348. *A Private Life* (1989, Totem, GB, 95m, c). P Francis Gerard & Roland Robinson, D Gerard, W Andrew Davies, PH Nat Crosby, M Trevor Jones, ED Robin Sales, PD Mark Wilby.

LP Bill Flynn (Jack), Jana Cilliers (Stella), Kevin Smith (Older Paul), Embeth Davidtz (Older Karen), Lance Maron (Older Gary), Justin John (Young Paul), Talia Leibman (Young Karen), Warren Hetz (Young Gary).

In the 1950s Cape Town policeman Bill Flynn falls in love with Jana Cilliers. When she applies for a "white" identification card, she is turned down and is classified as colored. When she finds herself pregnant, she and Flynn begin a life of lies. Every attempt to have her reclassified as "white" fails. Over the years the strain of trying to protect their three children from the consequences of colored bias leads to a son's choosing to kill himself when he is unable to marry the white woman he loves.

2349. *Private Property* (1986, Park Lane, 90m, c, aka *Young Lady Chatterley II*). P Alan Roberts & Stanton Korey, D Roberts, W Anthony Williams, PH Bob Brownell & Bryan England, M Misha Segal, ED Gregory Saunders, PD Warren Skip Wildes.

LP Harlee McBride (Cynthia Chatterley), Brett Clark (Thomas), Adam West (Arthur Bohart, Jr.), Sybil Danning (Judith), Alex Sheaf (French Count).

Based on the classic D.H. Lawrence novel, Harlee McBride as Lady Chatterley inherits the family mansion and continues her fooling around.

2350. *Private Resort* (1985, Tri-Star, 82m, c). P R. Ben Efraim & Don Enright, D George Bowers, W Gordon Mitchell (based on a story by Ken Segall, Allen Wenkus & Mitchell), PH Adam Greenberg, ED Sam Pollard, PD Michael Corenblith.

LP Rob Morrow (Ben), Johnny Depp (Jack Marshall), Emily Longstreth (Patti), Karyn O'Bryan (Dana), Hector Elizondo (The Maestro), Dody Goodman (Amanda Rawlings), Leslie Easterbrook (Bobby Sue).

Johnny Depp and Rob Morrow are girl-crazy teens hanging out at a plush Miami resort, hoping to score with the wealthy beauties who stay there. Their hijinks are interrupted by jewel-thief-in-drag Hector Elizondo.

2351. *Private School* (1983, Universal, 97m, c). P R. Ben Efraim & Don Enright, D Noel Black, W Dan Greenburg & Suzanne O'Malley, PH Walter Lassally, ED Fred Chulack, PD Ivo Cristante.

LP Phoebe Cates (Christine), Betsy Russell (Jordan), Kathleen Wilhoite (Betsy), Matthew Modine (Jim), Michael Zorek (Bubba), Fran Ryan (Miss Dutchbok), Ray Walston (Chauncey), Sylvia Kristel (Ms. Copuletta), Jonathan Prince (Roy), Kari Lizer (Rita), Julie Payne (Coach Whelan).

Filmed to appeal to prurient interests, this story of the sexual mingling of students at a boys academy and a neighboring girls school has plenty of T & A, with pouting bad-girl Betsy Russell exposing herself the most frequently.

2352. *Privates on Parade* (1984, Orion Classics, GB, 100m, c). P Simon Relph, D Michael Blakemore, W Peter Nichols (based on his play), PH Ian Wilson, M Dennis King, ED Jim Clark, PD Luciana Arrighi.

LP John Cleese (Maj. Giles Flack), Denis Quilley (Acting Capt. Terri Dennis), Michael Elphick (Sgt. Maj. Reg Drummond), Nicola Pagett (Acting Lt. Sylvia Morgan), Bruce Payne (Flight Sgt. Kevin Artwright), Joe Melia (Sgt. Len Bonny), David Bamber (Sgt. Charles Bishop).

This homosexual farce tells of the none too amusing antics of a British song and dance army unit entertaining the troops in Malaya during the late 1940s.

2353. *Privileged* (1982, Oxford, GB, 94m, c). P Richard Stevenson, D Michael Hoffman, W Hoffman, David Woolcombe & Rupert Walters, PH Fiona Cunningham Reid, M Rachel Portman, ED Derek Goldman, PD Jason Cooper.

LP Robert Woolley (Edward), Diana Katis (Anne), Hughie Grant (Lord Adrian), Victoria Studd (Lucy), James Wilby (Jamie), Simon Shackleton (Justin), Mark Williams (Wilf).

Selfish Oxford undergraduate Robert Woolley gets involved with acting, girls and a suicide.

2354. *Prizzi's Honor†* (1985, 20th Century–Fox, 129m, c). P John Foreman, D John Huston†, W Richard Condon & Janet Roach† (based on the novel by Condon), PH Andrzej Bartkowiak, M Alex North, ED Rudi Fehr & Kaja Fehr†, PD Dennis Washington, AD Michael Helmy & Tracy Bousman, SD Charles Truhan & Bruce Weintraub, COS Donfeld†.

LP Jack Nicholson† (Charley Partanna), Kathleen Turner (Irene Walker), Robert Loggia (Eduardo Prizzi), John Randolph (Angelo "Pop" Partanna), William Hickey† (Don Corrado Prizzi), Lee Richardson (Dominic Prizzi), Michael Lombard (Filargi "Finlay"), Anjelica Huston* (Maerose Prizzi), George Santiopietro (Plumber), Lawrence Tierney (Lt. Hanley), C.C.H. Pounder (Peaches Altamont).

In an entertaining black comedy gem, Jack Nicholson is superb as an aging hit man working for William Hickey, the head of one of New York's powerful Mafia families. Nicholson has been engaged to Hickey's granddaughter, Anjelica Huston, but when he sees Kathleen Turner at a gangster's wedding, he falls in love. Nicholson courts the beautiful Turner, unaware that she also is a hired killer, and her target-to-be is Nicholson. Turner and Nicholson marry, but when it comes to loyalty, marriage means much less than the honor of the Prizzi family to whom Nicholson owes everything.

2355. *The Prodigal* (1984, World Wide, 105m, c). P Ken Wales, D&W James F. Collier, PH Frank Stanley, M Bruce Broughton, ED Bill Brame, PD Bill Creber.

LP John Hammond (Greg Stuart), Hope Lange (Anne Stewart), John Cullum (Elton Stuart), Morgan Brittany (Sheila Holt-Browning), Ian Bannen (Riley Wyndham), Joey Travolta (Tony), Arliss Howard (Scott Stuart), Sarah Rush (Laura).

Pressures of today nearly cause the members of a family to lose their faith.

2356. *Programmed to Kill* (1987, TransWorld, 91m, c, aka *Retaliator*). P Don Stern, D Allan Holzman & Robert Short, W Short, PH Nitcho Lion Nissim & Ernest Holzman, M Jerry Immel & Craig Huxley, ED Michael Kelly, SE Vern Hyde & John Carter.

LP Robert Ginty (Eric Mathews), Sandahl Bergman (Samira), James Booth (Broxk), Alex Courtney (Blake), Paul W. Walker (Jason), Louise Claire Clark (Sharon), Peter Bromilow (Donovan), George Fisher (Mike).

PLO terrorist Sandahl Bergman is fatally wounded in a raid by the CIA. During radical bionic surgery a team of surgeons implant computer chips in her brain-dead body, turning her into a killing machine who obeys orders. When she malfunctions and turns on her creators, only Roberty Ginty can halt her frenzy.

2357. *Project X* (1987, 20th Century–Fox, 108m, c). P Walter F. Parkes & Lawrence Lasker, D Jonathan Kaplan, W Stanley Weiser (based on a story by

Weiser & Lasker), PH Dean Cundey, M James Horner, ED O. Nicholas Brown, PD Lawrence G. Paull.

LP Matthew Broderick (Jimmy Garrett), Helen Hunt (Teresa "Teri" McDonald), Bill Sadler (Dr. Lynnard Carroll), Johnny Ray McGhee (Isaac Robertson), Jonathan Stark (Sgt. "Kreig" Kreiger), Robin Gammell (Col. Niles).

When a young chimpanzee named Virgil is chosen for a deadly military experiment, would-be pilot Matthew Broderick and expert chimp trainer Helen Hunt fight to prevent the certain destruction of the chimps in the program.

2358. *Prom Night* (1980, Avco Embassy, 91m, c). P Peter Simpson, D Paul Lynch, W William Gray (based on a story by Robert Guza, Jr.), PH Robert New, M Carl Zittrer & Paul Zaza, ED Brian Ravok.

LP Leslie Nielsen (Hammond), Jamie Lee Curtis (Kim), Casey Stevens (Nick), Eddie Benton (Wendy), Antoinette Bower (Mrs. Hammond), Michael Tough (Alex), Robert Silverman (Sykes), Pita Oliver (Vicki), David Mucci (Lou).

Some mysterious figure is killing off all the teens involved in the death of Jamie Lee Curtis' little sister some 11 years earlier.

2359. *Promised Land* (1988, Vestron, 92m, c). P Rick Stevenson, D&W Michael Hoffman, PH Ueli Steiger, M James Newton, ED David Spiers, PD Eugenio Zanetti.

LP Jason Gedrick (Davey Hancock), Kiefer Sutherland (Danny Rivers), Meg Ryan (Bev), Tracy Pollan (Mary Daley), Googy Gress (Baines), Deborah Richter (Pammie), Oscar Rowland (Mr. Rivers), Sondra Seacat (Mrs. Rivers).

This crime story takes place in Ashville, Utah. Ex-basketball player Jason Gedrick, now a town cop whose dreams didn't pan out, confronts high school misfit Kiefer Sutherland and his wife, weirdo beauty Meg Ryan, after the latter two rob a local convenience store.

2360. *Prostitute* (1980, Kestrel/Mainline, GB, 98m, c). P,D&W Tony Garnett, PH Charles Stewart, M David Platz, ED Bill Shapter.

LP Eleanor Forsythe (Sandra), Kate Crutchley (Louise), Kim Lockett (Jean), Nancy Samuels (Rose Wilson), Richard Mangan (David Selby), Phyllis Hickson (Mother), Joseph Senior (Joseph), Ann Whitaker (Amanda).

Birmingham prostitute Eleanor Forsythe joins a group to reform the laws regulating her trade and becomes a high-priced London callgirl.

2361. *The Protector* (1985, Golden Harvest, US/Hong Kong, 95m, c). P David Chan, D&W James Glickenhaus, PH Mark Irwin, M Ken Thorne, ED Evan Lottman, AD William F. De Seta & Oliver Wong.

LP Jackie Chan (Billy Wong), Danny Aiello (Danny Garoni), Roy Chiao (Mr. Ko), Victor Arnold (Police Captain), Kim Bass (Stan Jones), Richard Clarke (Supt. Whitehead), Saun Ellis (Laura Shapiro).

In this martial arts film, a Hong Kong to New York heroin ring is broken.

2362. *Protocol* (1984, Warner, 96m, c). P Anthea Sylbert, D Herbert Ross, W Buck Henry (based on a story by Charles Shyer, Nancy Meyers & Harvey Miller), PH William A. Fraker, M Basil Poledouris, ED Paul Hirsch, PD Bill Malley.

LP Goldie Hawn (Sunny), Chris Sarandon (Michael Ransome), Richard Romanus (Emir), Andre Gregory (Nawaf Al Kabeer), Gail Strickland (Mrs. St. John), Cliff De Young (Hilley), Keith Szarabajka (Crowe), Ed Begley, Jr. (Hassler), Kenneth Mars (Lou).

When Washington waitress and dancer Goldie Hawn accidentally prevents the assassination of a visiting Arab dignitary, she is given a job with the State Department as a protocol official. All that glitters is not "Goldie" at her best.

2363. *The Prowler* (1981, Graduation/Sandhurst, 88m, c, aka *Rosemary's Killer*). P Joseph Zito & David Streit, D Zito, W Glenn Leopold & Neal F. Barbera, PH Raoul Lumas, M Richard Einhorn, ED Joel Goodman, PD Lorenzo Mans.

LP Vicki Dawson (Pam McDonald), Christopher Goutman (Mark London), Cindy Weintraub (Lisa), Farley Granger (Sheriff George Fraser), John Seitz (Kingsley).

In this clone of *Halloween,* a returning World War II soldier comes home to find his girl having an affair with another man. He dispatches both with a pitchfork. Thirty-five years later, he returns to his hometown and begins killing all the teens he can get near.

2364. *Psycho from Texas* (1982, New American, 89m, c). P,D&W Jim Feazell, PH Paul Hipp, M Jaime Mendoza-Nava, ED Arjay.

LP John King, III (Wheeler), Herschell Mays (William Phillips), Tommy Lamey (Slick), Candy Dee (Connie Phillips), Janel King (Ellen), Juanne Bruno (Bertha), Reed Johnson (Steve), Jack Collins (Sheriff), Christian Feazell (Young Wheeler).

The message of this poorly-made film is that child-abuse may lead to just about anything, including kidnapping when the kid grows up.

2365. *Psycho II* (1983, Universal, 113m, c). P Hilton A. Green, D Richard Franklin, W Tom Holland (based on characters created by Robert Bloch), PH Dean Cundey, M Jerry Goldsmith, ED Andrew London, PD John W. Corso.

LP Anthony Perkins (Norman Bates), Vera Miles (Lila Loomis), Meg Tilly (Mary), Robert Loggia (Dr. Raymond), Dennis Franz (Toomey), Hugh Gillin (Sheriff Hunt), Claudia Bryar (Mrs. Spool), Robert Alan Browne (Statler), Ben Hartigan (Judge), Lee Garlington (Myrna).

Despite protests from Vera Miles, the sister of his victim 22 years ago, Anthony Perkins is released from a mental institution and returns home to the Bates Hotel ... and then the murders begin again.

2366. *Psycho III* (1986, Universal, 93m, c). P Hilton A. Green, D Anthony Perkins, W Charles Edward Pogue (based on characters created by Robert Bloch), PH Bruce Surtees, M Carter Burwell, ED David Blewitt, PD Henry Bumstead.

LP Anthony Perkins (Norman Bates), Diana Scarwid (Maureen), Jeff Fahey (Duane), Roberta Maxwell (Tracy), Hugh Gillin (Sheriff Hunt), Lee Garlington (Myrna), Robert Alan Browne (Statler), Gary Bayer (Father Brian), Patience Cleveland (Sister Margaret).

Anthony Perkins directs and stars in this second sequel to the Hitchcock classic. Norman Bates is normal again, but mother still seems to be acting up.

2367. *Psychos in Love* (1987, ICN Bleecker-Infinity, 87m, c). P&D Gorman Bechard, W Carmine Capobianco & Bechard, PH Bechard, M Capobianco & Bechard, ED Bechard.

LP Carmine Capobianco (Joe), Debi Thibeault (Kate), Frank Stewart (Herman), Cecilia Wilde (Nikki), Donna Davidge (Heather), Patti Chambers (Girl in Bed), Carla Bragoli (Girl in Woods), Carrie Gordon (Girl in Toilet), Angela Nicholas (Dianne).

Carmine Capobianco, a lonely psycho killer, kills his dates after having sex with them. Debi Thibeault also eliminates the men in her life when she becomes annoyed by their approaches to get her into bed. It's a match made in hell when they get together.

2368. *The Psychotronic Man* (1980, International Harmony, 90m, c). P Peter Spelson, D Jack M. Sell, W Spelson & Sell (based on a story by Spelson), PH Sell, M Tommy Irons, ED Bill Reese.

LP Peter Spelson (Rocky Foscoe), Christopher Carbis (Lt. Walter O'Brien), Curt Colbert (Sgt. Chuck Jackson), Robin Newton (Kathy), Paul Marvel (Dr. Steinberg), Jeff Caliendo (Officer Maloney), Lindsey Novak (Mrs. Foscoe).

In this cheaply made production from Chicago, Peter Spelson portrays a psychic barber. Unknown forces cause people to die when he blinks at them.

P'Tang, Yang, Kipperbang* see *Kipperbang

2369. *Puberty Blues* (1983, Limelight/Universal Classics, Australia, 81m, c). P Joan Long & Margaret Kelly, D Bruce Beresford, W Kelly (based on the novel by Kathy Lette & Gabrielle Carey), PH Don McAlpine, M Les Gock, ED Jeanine Chialvo & William Anderson, PD David Copping.

LP Nell Schofield (Debbie), Jad Capelja (Sue), Geoff Rhoe (Garry), Tony Hughes (Danny), Sandy Paul (Tracy), Leander Brett (Cheryl), Jay Hackett (Bruce), Ned Lander (Strach), Joanne Olsen (Vicki), Julie Medana (Kim).

In order to be accepted as part of the in-crowd of their high school, teens Nell Schofield and Jad Capelja join the local surfing scene.

2370. *Pulse* (1988, Columbia, 91m, c). P Patricia A. Stallone, D&W Paul Golding, PH Peter Lyons Collister, M Jay Ferguson, ED Gib Jaffe, PD Holger Gross.

LP Cliff De Young (Bill), Roxanne Hart (Ellen), Joey Lawrence (David), Matthew Lawrence (Stevie), Charles Tyner (Old Man), Dennis Redfield (Pete), Robert Romanus (Paul), Myron D. Healey (Howard).

In a sci-fi version of "the boy who cried wolf," no one will believe Joey Lawrence's explanation for strange behavior in his neighborhood. He claims that an alien force is communicating destructive messages to earth via sudden pulses of electricity through appliances in several homes in the area.

2371. *Pumpkinhead* (1988, MGM/United Artists, 86m, c, aka *Vengeance: The Devil*). P Richard C. Weinman & Howard Smith, D Stan Winston, W Mark Patrick Carducci & Gary Gerani (based on a story by Carducci, Stan Winston & Weinman), PH Bojan Bazclli, M Richard Stone, ED Marcus Manton, SE Alec Gillis.

LP Lance Henriksen (Ed Harley), Matthew Hurley (Billy Harley), Jeff East (Chris), John DiAquino (Joel), Kimberly Ross (Kim), Joel Hoffman (Steve), Cynthia Bain (Tracy), Kerry Remsen (Maggie), Madeleine Taylor Holmes (Witchwoman), Tom Woodruff, Jr. (Pumpkinhead).

When bikers in a rural area run down the 10-year-old son of kindly widower farmer Lance Henriksen, he seeks help in taking revenge from a vicious demon known as Pumpkinhead. The latter, an eight foot tall alien, hunts down the bikers and dispatches them one by one. With each killing the alien begins to look more and more like Henriksen. Filled with remorse, Henriksen commits suicide, destroying Pumpkinhead in the process.

2372. *Punchline* (1988, Columbia, 128m, c). P Daniel Melnick & Michael Rachmil, D&W David Seltzer, PH Reynaldo Villalobos, M Charles Gross, ED Bruce Green, PD Jackson DeGovia.

LP Sally Field (Lilah Krytsick), Tom Hanks (Steven Gold), John Goodman (John Krytsick), Mark Rydell (Romeo), Kim Greist (Madeline Urie), Paul Mazursky (Arnold), Pam Matteson (Utica Blake), George Michael McGrath (Singing Nun), Taylor Negron (Albert Emperato), Barry Neikrug (Krug), Angel Salazar (Rico), Damon Wayans (Percy), Joycee Katz (Joycee), Mac Robbins (Billy Lane).

In a backstage look at aspiring stand-up comics, Tom Hanks is slightly more successful but no more dedicated than Sally Field to making the mark as a comedian. Her dreams are having a hell of a negative effect on her marriage and family. Hanks, who is supposed to be attending medical school like all the other men in his family, gives Field a boost and some confidence. They think they may have fallen in love, but learn better, as Field realizes that her husband John Goodman is the good and supportive man she needs and wants.

2373. *Puppet Master* (1989, Full Moon, 90m, c). P Hope Perello, D David Schmoeller, W Joseph G. Collodi (based on a story by Charles Band & Kenneth J. Hall), PH Sergio Salvati, M Richard Band, ED Tom Meshelski, PD John Myrhe, PUPPET EFFECTS David Allen Prods.

LP Paul Le Mat (Alex), Irene Miracle (Dana Hadley), Matt Roe (Frank), Kathryn O'Reilly (Clarissa), Robin Frates (Megan Gallagher), Marya Small (Theresa), Jimmie F. Scaggs (Neil), William Hickey (Andre Toulan).

This direct-to-video horror film features cute/scary little puppets, crafted by William Hickey, who committed suicide in 1939 at the Bodega Bay Hotel. Years later, they come to life to terrorize a group of psychics staying at the hotel.

2374. *Purgatory* (1989, New Star, 93m, c). P&D Ami Artzi, W Felix Kroll & Paul Aratow, PH Tom Fraser, M Julian Laxton, ED Ettie Feldman, PD Robert van der Coolwijk.

LP Tanya Roberts (Carly Arnold), Julie Pop (Melanie), Hal Orlandini (Bledsoe), Rufus Swart (Paul Cricks), Adrienne Pearce (Janine), Marie Human (Kirsten), David Sherwood (Stern), Clare Marshall (Ruth Arnold), Hugh Rouse (Rivers), John Newland (Ambassador Whitney).

Sexy Peace Corps worker Tanya Roberts and her pal Julie Pop are arrested in a fictional African country on trumped-up drug charges. They are each sentenced to 11 years in a prison known menacingly as Purgatory. The evil warden turns his prettiest inmates into prostitutes. To this end, Roberts is forced into a discreetly filmed scene of fellatio while Pop is gang-raped by the guards, causing her to commit suicide.

2375. *Purple Haze* (1983, Triumph, 97m, c). P Thomas Anthony Fucci, D David Burton Morris, W Vittoria Wozniak (based on the story by Wozniak, Morris & Tom Kelsey), PH Richard Gibb, ED Dusty Dennisson.

LP Peter Nelson (Matt Caulfield), Chuck McQuary (Jeff Maley), Bernard Baldan (Derek Savage), Susanna Lack (Kitty Armstrong), Bob Breuler (Walter Caulfield), Joanne Bauman (Margaret Caulfield), Kay Horsch (Phoebe Caulfield), Heidi Helmer (Angela).

Two friends Peter Nelson and Chuck McQuary experience the 60s — drugs, avoiding the draft, dealing with insensitive parents, and fighting the "Establishment." Anyone seeing this film who was unfamiliar with the period would surely think the decade was rather dull.

2376. *Purple Hearts* (1984, Warner, 115m, c). P&D Sidney J. Furie, W Rick Natkin & Furie, PH Jan Kiesser, M Robert Folk, ED George Grenville, AD Francisco Balangue.

LP Ken Wahl (Don Jardian), Cheryl Ladd (Deborah Solomon), Stephen Lee (Wizard), Annie McEnroe (Hallaway), Paul McCrane (Brenner), Cyril O'Reilly (Zuma), David Harris (Hanes), Hillary Bailey (Jill), Lee Ermey (Gunny).

This film is about the nothing romance of Navy doctor Ken Wahl who falls in love with nurse Cheryl Ladd in Vietnam during the war.

2377. *The Purple People Eater* (1988, Concorde, 92m, c). P Brad Krevoy &

Steve Stabler, D&W Linda Shayne (based on the song by Sheb Wooley), PH Peter Deming, M Various Artists, ED Cari Ellen Coughlin, PD Stephen Greenberg.

LP Ned Beatty (Grandpa), Neil Patrick Harris (Billy Johnson), Shelley Winters (Rita), Peggy Lipton (Mom), James Houghton (Dad), Thora Birch (Molly Johnson), John Brumfeld (Mr. Noodle), Little Richard (Mayor), Chubby Checker (Singer).

Most viewers of this film probably weren't around when Sheb Wooley had a 1958 hit song with a silly novelty number called "Purple People Eater." In the film a one-eyed, purple, people-eater alien drops in on earth when 12-year-old daydreaming Neil Patrick Harris plays a record from his parents' 50s collection. Fear not, the visitor is not hungry for human flesh — just music.

2378. *Purple Rain* (1984, Warner, 111m, c). P Robert Cavallo, Joseph Ruffalo & Steven Fargnoli, D Albert Magnoli, W Magnoli & William Blinn, PH Donald Thorin, M Michel Colombier, ED Magnoli & Ken Robinson, PD Ward Preston, M/L "When Doves Cry," "The Beautiful Ones," "Darling Nikki" & "Purple Rain" by Prince*.

LP Prince (The Kid), Apollonia Kotero (Apollonia), Morris Day (Morris), Olga Karlatos (Mother), Clarence Williams, III (Father), Jerome Benton (Jerome), Billy Sparks (Billy), Jill Jones (Jill), Charles Huntsberry (Chick), Dez Dickerson (Dez).

In this quasiautobiographical showcase for pop star Prince, audiences learn of his struggle for love, attention, admiration and recognition. What he comes away with is more money than most people could ever imagine.

2379. *The Purple Rose of Cairo* (1985, Orion, 84m, c/b&w). P Robert Greenhut, D&W Woody Allen† (for writing), PH Gordon Willis, M Dick Hyman, ED Susan E. Morse, PD Stuart Wurtzel, AD Edward Pisoni, SD Carol Joffe.

LP Mia Farrow (Cecilia), Jeff Daniels (Tom Baxter/Gil Shepherd), Danny Aiello (Monk), Dianne Wiest (Emma), Van Johnson (Larry), Zoe Caldwell (The Countess), John Wood (Jason), Milo

O'Shea (Father Donnelly), Deborah Rush (Rita).

During the Depression, mousy housewife Mia Farrow escapes the harshness of her existence and marriage to loutish womanizer Danny Aiello by attending movies. She sees *The Purple Rose of Cairo* over and over again. On one occasion, Jeff Daniels, a character on the screen, turns and begins talking directly to Farrow in the audience. Finally he leaves the screen to be with her and learn what real life is about.

2380. ***The Purple Taxi*** (1980, Quartet, Fr./Ital./Ireland, 107m, c). P Peter Rawley & Hugo Lodrini, D Yves Boisset, W Michel Deon & Boisset (based on the book by Deon), PH Tonino Delli Colli, M Philippe Sarde, ED Albert Jurgensen.

LP Charlotte Rampling (Sharon), Philippe Noiret (Philippe), Agostina Belli (Anne Taubelman), Peter Ustinov (Taubelman), Fred Astaire (Dr. Scully), Edward Albert (Jerry), Mairin O'Sullivan (Colleen), Jack Watson (Sean).

Despite its origins, this multinational effort is an English language film. A collection of expatriates come together for a brief period to share angst, love and friendship and then go their separate ways.

2381. ***The Pursuit of D.B. Cooper*** (1981, Universal, 100m, c). P Daniel Wigutow & Michael Taylor, D Roger Spottiswoode, W Jeffrey Alan Fiskin (based on the book *Free Fall* by J.D. Reed), PH Harry Stradling, M James Horner, ED Robbe Roberts & Allan Jacobs, PD Preston Ames.

LP Robert Duvall (Gruen), Treat Williams (Meade), Kathryn Harrold (Hannah), Ed Flanders (Brigadier), Paul Gleason (Remson), R.G. Armstrong (Dempsey), Dorothy Fielding (Denise), Nicolas Coster (Avery).

Skyjacker Treat Williams bails out of a plane with the $200,000 ransom he was paid not to blow it up. He's chased by various people after the reward for his capture.

2382. ***Puss in Boots*** (1989, Cannon, 96m, c). P Menahem Golan & Yoram Globus, D Eugene Marner, W Carole Lucia Satrina (based on the fairy tale by Charles Perrault), PH Avi Karpick, M Rafi Kadishson, ED Satrina & Marner, PD Marek Dobrowolski.

LP Christopher Walken (Puss), Jason Connery (Corin), Carmela Marner (Vera), Yossi Graber (King), Elki Jacobs (Lady Clara), Amnon Meskin (Ogre).

Christopher Walken portrays a song and dance cat who helps young Jason Connery make his fortune by fooling a king into awarding his daughter, Carmela Marner, to Connery. He also appropriates the vast wealth of ogre Amnon Meskin.

2383. ***Q: Quetzalcoatl*** (1982, UFD, 100m, c, aka *Winged Serpent*). P,D&W Larry Cohen, PH Fred Murphy, M Robert O. Ragland, ED Armond Lebowitz, SE David Allen, Randy Cook & Peter Kuran.

LP Michael Moriarty (Jimmy), Candy Clark (Joan), David Carradine (Shepard), Richard Roundtree (Powell), James Dixon (Lt. Murray), Malachy McCourt (Commissioner), Fred J. Scollay (Capt. Fletcher).

A prehistoric Aztec deity flies from its nest atop a Manhattan skyscraper to tear off the heads of sunbathers and other unwary victims.

2384. ***Quarantine*** (1989, Atlantis, Canada, 97m, c). P,D&W Charles Wilkinson, PH Tobias Schliessler, ED Allan Lee, AD Robert Logevall.

LP Beatrice Boepple (Ivan Joad), Garwin Sanford (Spencer Crown), Jerry Wasserman (Sen. Edgar Ford), Tom McBeath (Lt. Beck), Michele Goodger (Berlin Ford), Kaj-Erik Eriksen (The Kid), Susan Chappelle (Councilwoman Campbell), Lee Taylor (Dr. Jim).

In a confusing mishmash, dictatorial Senator Jerry Wasserman arranges to move those caring for people dying of some unnamed disease to camps where they are kept as prisoners. A super computer is working on the eradication of the disease, but few viewers will care.

2385. ***Quartet*** (1981, New World, GB/Fr., 101m, c). P Ismail Merchant & Jean Pierre Mahot de la Querantonnais, D James Ivory, W Ruth Prawer Jhabvala & Ivory (based on the novel by Jean Rhys), PH Pierre Lhomme, M Richard

Robbins, ED Humphrey Dixon, AD Jean Jacques Caziot.

LP Alan Bates (H.J. Heidler), Maggie Smith (Lois), Isabelle Adjani (Marya), Anthony Higgins (Stephen), Armelia McQueen (Nell), Daniel Chatto (Guy), Pierre Clementi (Theo), Suzanne Flon (Mme. Hautchamp).

When her husband Anthony Higgins is sent to prison, Isabelle Adjani is taken in by Alan Bates and his indulgent painter wife Maggie Smith. Bates seduces Adjani, who becomes his lover. It's a story by Jean Rhys, loosely based on her life with Ford Madox Ford in Paris in the 1920s. Adjani loses out all around by the end of the film.

2386. *Quatermass Conclusion* (1980, Euston, GB, 105m, c). P Ted Childs, D Piers Haggard, W Nigel Kneale, PH Ian Wilson, M Marc Wilkinson & Nick Rowley, ED Keith Palmer.

LP John Mills (Prof. Bernard Quatermass), Simon MacCorkindale, Barbara Kellerman, Margaret Tyzack, Brewster Mason.

John Mills gives an outstanding interpretation of the sometimes eccentric scientist in this Armageddon epic. The old gent saves mankind from a killer broadcast beam, but sacrifices his life in the effort.

2387. *Queen of Hearts* (1989, Cinecom, GB, 112m, c). P John Hardy, D Jon Amiel, W Tony Grisoni, PH Mike Southon, M Michael Convertino, ED Peter Boyle, PD Jim Clay.

LP Vittorio Duse (Nonno), Joseph Long (Danilo), Anita Zagaria (Rosa), Eileen Way (Mama Sibilla), Vittorio Amandola (Barbariccia), Ian Hawkes (Eddie), Tat Whalley (Beetle).

The story is seen through the eyes of Ian Hawkes, a young boy living in the Italian community in London. He loves his mischievous grandfather Vittorio Duse, but learns of the harshness of life when Vittorio Amandola, once a contender for his mother's hand, arrives to take his revenge, causing the family to lose their modest cafe.

2388. *Quest for Fire* (1982, 20th Century–Fox, Fr./Canada, 97m, c). P John Kemeny, Denis Heroux, Jacques Dorf-

mann & Vera Belmont, D Jean-Jacques Annaud, W Gerard Brach (based on the novel *La Guerre de Feu* by J.H. Rosny, Sr.), PH Claude Agostini, M Philippe Sarde, ED Yves Langlois, PD Brian Morris & Guy Comtois, MK Sarah Monzani & Michele Burke*.

LP Everett McGill (Naoh), Ron Perlman (Amoukar), Nameer El-Kadi (Gaw), Rae Dawn Chong (Ika), Gary Schwartz, Frank Oliver Bonnet, Jean-Michel Kindt, Kurt Schiegl, Brian Gill.

The film is an imaginative and usually exciting story of prehistoric man's (and woman's) attempt to survive the Ice Age. Three members of the Ulam tribe are sent to find fire after their only source is accidentally extinguished. They encounter the barbarous Ivakas tribe that has knowledge of creating fire, using sticks and flints.

2389. *Quest for Love* (1989, Distant Horizon, South Africa, 93m, c). P Shan Moodley, D&W Helena Noguiera (based on the novel *Q.E.D.* by Gertrude Stein and the writings of Antonio A. Goncalves), PH Roy Macgregor, M Tony Rudner, ED Noguiera, PD Beverly Lanyon.

LP Jana Cilliers (Alex), Sandra Prinsloo (Dorothy), Andrew Buckland (Michael), Joanna Weinberg (Mabel), Wayne Bowman (Zaccharia), Lynn Gaines (Isabella), S. Prince Mokhini (Cokwana), Frances Ndlazilwana (Mapule).

Tormented Jana Cilliers, recently released from prison in South Africa, must sort out her political and sexual feelings. She ultimately commits herself to building a school destroyed by the South Africans and becoming Sandra Prinsloo's full-time lover.

2390. *Quicker Than the Eye* (1989, Condor, Switzerland, 92m, c). P Peter-Christian Fueter, D Nicolas Gessner, W Joseph Morhaim & Gessner (based on the novel by Claude Cueni), PH Wolfgang Treu, M George Garvarentz, ED Daniela Roderer, PD Max Stubenrauch.

LP Ben Gazzara (Ben Norell), Mary Crosby (Mary Preston), Jean Yanne (Inspector Sutter), Catherine Jarrett (Catherine Lombard), Wolfgang Berger (Kurt), Dinah Hinz (Gertrude), Ivan

Desny (Schneider), Sophie Carle (Silke), Robert Liensol (Pres. Makabutu).

Made especially for the U.S. video market, this Swiss production stars Ben Gazzara as a magician touring Europe with his assistant Mary Crosby. Ivan Desny plans to use Gazzara in a plot to kill an African leader attending a summit conference being held in Lucerne.

2391. *Quicksilver* (1986, Columbia, 106m, c). P Michael Rachmil & Daniel Melnick, D&W Tom Donnelly, PH Thomas Del Ruth, M Tony Banks, ED Tom Rolf, PD Charles Rosen.

LP Kevin Bacon (Jack Casey), Jami Gertz (Terri), Paul Rodriguez (Hector), Rudy Ramos (Gypsy), Andrew Smith (Gabe), Gerald S. O'Loughlin (Mr. Casey), Larry Fishburne (Voodoo), Louis Anderson (Tiny).

After blowing his and his parents' savings, Wall Street wizard Kevin Bacon is reduced to being a bicycle messenger. In this guise he becomes involved with drug dealers and an independent girl Jami Gertz who gets in over her head with the villains.

2392. *Quiet Cool* (1986, New Line Cinema, 86m, c). P Robert Shaye & Gerald T. Olson, D Clay Borris, W Borris & Susan Vercellino, PH Jacques Haitkin, M Jay Ferguson, ED Bob Brady.

LP James Remar (Joe Dillon), Adam Coleman Howard (Joshua Greer), Daphne Ashbrook (Katy Greer), Jared Martin (Mike Prior), Nick Cassavetes (Valence), Fran Ryan (Ma).

In a ludicrous action film, New York cop James Remar goes to the Pacific Northwest with Adam Coleman Howard to confront the maniacal marijuana growers who have killed Howard's parents.

2393. *The Quiet Earth* (1985, Skouras, New Zealand, 91m, c). P Sam Pillsbury & Don Reynolds, D Geoffrey Murphy, W Bill Baer, Bruno Lawrence & Pillsbury (based on the novel by Craig Harrison), PH James Bartle, M John Charles, ED Michael Horton, PD Josephine Ford.

LP Bruno Lawrence (Zac Hobson), Alison Routledge (Joanne), Peter Smith (Api), Anzac Wallace (Api's Mate), Norman Fletcher (Perrin), Tom Hyde (Scientist).

In what is probably New Zealand's first science fiction movie, scientist Bruno Lawrence wakes up one morning to find himself the only person left on earth. All others having mysteriously vanished. Eventually a few other survivors show up.

2394. *Rabid Grannies* (1989, Troma, 83m, c). P James Desert & Jonathan Rambert, D&W Emmanuel Kervyn, PH Hugh Labye, M Peter Castelain & J.B. Castelain, ED Philippe Ravoet, PD Luke Bertrand, SE Steven Fernandez.

LP Catherine Aymerie (Helen), Caroline Braekman (Suzie), Danielle Daven (Elisabeth), Raymond Lescot (Rev. Father), Elliot Lison (John), Michel Lombet (Roger), Anne Marie Fox (Victoria), Paule Herreman (Miss Barnstable), Bobette Jouret (Erika).

How about that for a great title? Various members of a family gather to celebrate the birthdays of wealthy grannies Danielle Daven and Anne Marie Fox, whose money they hope to soon inherit. A gift arrives from the black sheep of the family, one into satanic activities. When the present is opened it turns the old gals into cannibalistic monsters. Special effects expert Steven Fernandez has created some effects which should gross out just about everyone.

2395. *Race for Glory* (1989, New Century/Vista, 96m, c). P Jon Gordon & Daniel A. Sherkow, D Rocky Lang, W Scott Swanton (based on a story by Lang), PH Jack N. Green, M Jay Ferguson, ED Maryann Brandon, PD Cynthia Charette.

LP Alex McArthur (Cody), Peter Berg (Chris), Pamela Ludwig (Jenny), Ray Wise (Jack), Oliver Stritzel (Klaus), Burt Kwouk (Yoshiro Tanaka), Jerome Dempsey (Ray Crowley), Lane Smith (Joe Gifford).

Alex McArthur, a daredevil motorcycle racer, is trying for the big-time in International racing. He abandons his best friend and mechanic Peter Berg and his hometown girlfriend, Pamela Ludwig, when a Japanese company offers to sponsor him. Only later does he learn that they have given him an inferior bike so he won't threaten their big star Oliver Stritzel. Will McArthur come to his senses in time for the big race? Will his former friend and girlfriend rally around when his father dies? Are there any clichés this picture doesn't use?

Race for the Yankee Zephyr see Treasure of the Yankee Zephyr

2396. *The Rachel Papers* (1989, United Artists/Virgin, GB, 95m, c). P Andrew S. Karsch, D&W Damian Harris (based on the novel by Martin Amis), PH Alex Thomson, M Chaz Jankel, ED David Martin, PD Andrew McAlpine.

LP Dexter Fletcher (Charles Highway), Ione Skye (Rachel Seth-Smith), Jonathan Pryce (Norman), James Spader (DeForrest), Bill Paterson (Charles' father), Lesley Sharp (Jenny), Michael Gambon (Oxford Don).

Nineteen-year-old Dexter Fletcher has plenty of money and all the sexual conquests he can handle. He meets and falls in love with beautiful 19-year-old American Ione Skye. She resists his charms for a short time, but comes around. They have a steamy passionate affair, but the fires burn out and it's over. Finis.

2397. *Rachel River* (1989, Taurus, 90m, c). P Timothy Marx, D Sandy Smolan, W Judith Guest (based on the stories of Carol Bly), PH Paul Elliott, M Arvo Part, ED Susan Crutcher, PD David Wasco.

LP Pamela Reed (Mary Graving), Viveca Lindfors (Harriet White), Craig T. Nelson (Marlyn), Zeljko Ivanek (Momo), James Olson (Jack Canon), Ailene Cole (Svea).

This slice-of-life film stays on the sentimental and depressing side of Rachel River, a fictional town in Northern Minnesota. It appears to have died long ago and its residents are only awaiting their time to join it in the grave.

Racing Fury see Hell High

2398. *Racing with the Moon* (1984, Paramount, 108m, c). P Alain Bernheim & John Kohn, D Richard Benjamin, W Steven Kloves, PH John Bailey, M Dave Grusin, ED Jacqueline Cambas, PD David L. Snyder.

LP Sean Penn (Henry "Hopper" Nash), Elizabeth McGovern (Caddie Winger), Nicolas Cage (Nicky), John Karlen (Mr. Nash), Rutanya Alda (Mrs. Nash), Max Showalter (Mr. Arthur),

Crispin Glover (Gatsby Boy), Barbara Howard (Gatsby Girl), Bob Maroff (Al).

In 1942 two young California men, Sean Penn and Nicolas Cage, have six months to say goodbye to their girlfriends before entering the Marine Corps. The main failure of this movie is that no one connected with the film seems to have any feeling for the period.

2399. *Rad* (1986, Tri-Star, 93m, c). P Robert L. Levy, D Hal Needham, W Sam Bernard & Geoffrey Edwards, PH Richard Leiterman, M James Di Pasquale, ED Carl Kress, AD Shirley Inget.

LP Bill Allen (Cru), Lori Laughlin (Christian), Talia Shire (Mrs. Jones), Ray Walston (Burton Timmer), Alfie Wise (Elliott Dole), Jack Weston (Duke Best), Bart Connor (Bart Taylor), Marta Kober (Becky).

In this almost unwatchable sports drama, teen Bill Allen moves from his paper route to competition in BMX bike competition against arrogant champ Bart Connor. The latter, an ex–Olympic gold-medalist gymnast, should have stuck to the rings and parallel bars.

2400. *Radio Days* (1987, Orion, 85m, c). P Robert Greenhut, D&W Woody Allen† (for screenplay), PH Carlo Di Palma, MD Dick Hyman, ED Susan E. Morse, PD Santo Loquasto†, AD/SD Santo Loquasto, Carol Joffe, Les Bloom & George DeTitta, Jr.†

LP Woody Allen (Narrator), Seth Green (Little Joe), Julie Kavner (Mother), Michael Tucker (Father), Dianne Wiest (Aunt Bea), Josh Mostel (Uncle Abe), Renee Lippin (Aunt Ceil), William Magerman (Grandpa), Leah Carrey (Grandma), Joy Newman (Ruthie), Mia Farrow (Sally White), Julie Kurnitz (Irene), Wallace Shawn (Masked Avenger), Jeff Daniels (Biff Baxter), Danny Aiello (Rocco), Gina DeAngelis (Rocco's Mother), Kenneth Mars (Rabbi Baumel), Tony Roberts ("Silver Dollar" Emcee), Diane Keaton (New Year's Singer).

Woody Allen provides a warmly nostalgic and comical look at his extended Jewish family. Living in a Brooklyn neighborhood in the 40s, the radio was everyone's contact with the big outside world. Allen presents not so much a story as a series of incidents and vignettes which take place in the family and to the various radio personalities brought into their home through the ever-playing instrument.

2401. Radio On (1980, Unifilm, GB/Ger., 101m, c). P Keith Griffiths, D Christopher Petit, W Petit & Heidi Adolph, PH Martin Schafer, M David Bowie, Sting, Kraftwerk, Eddie Cochran & Wreckless Eric, ED Anthony Sloman, AD Susannah Buxton.

LP David Beames (Robert), Lisa Kreuzer (Ingrid), Sandy Ratcliff (Kathy), Andrew Byatt (Deserter), Sue Jones-Davies (Girl), Sting (Just Like Eddie), Sabina Michael (Aunt), Katja Kersten (German Woman), Paul Hollywood (Kid).

Emotionally dead disc jockey David Beames returns to his Bristol home to investigate the mysterious circumstances of his brother's death.

2402. Radioactive Dreams (1986, De Laurentiis, 94m, c). P Thomas Karnowski & Moctesuma Esparza, D&W Albert F. Pyun, PH Charles Minsky, M Pete Robinson, ED Dennis O'Connor, PD Chester Kaczenski.

LP John Stockwell (Phillip), Michael Dudikoff (Marlowe), George Kennedy (Spade), Don Murray (Dash), Michele Little (Rusty), Norbert Weisser (Sternwood), Lisa Blount (Miles).

It's as funny as you might expect a post-apocalypse story to be. Two jerks, John Stockwell and Michael Dudikoff, raised on 1940s pulp detective novels, emerge from their hiding after the danger of radiation has worn off. They travel through a world filled with mutants, bikers and punks. Everyone including beautiful Michele Little and Lisa Blount are searching for the world's last atomic bomb.

2403. Rage of Honor (1987, TransWorld, 91m, c). P Don Van Atta, D Gordon Hessler, W Robert Short & Wallace Bennett (based on a story by Short), PH Julio Bragado, M Stelvio Cipriani, ED Robert Gordon, PD Adrian Gorton.

LP Sho Kosugi (Shiro Tanaka), Lewis Van Bergen (Drug Lord), Robin Evans (Jennifer), Richard Wiley (Ray Jones), Armando Caro (Juan), Marlee Jepson (Girl in Convertible).

Martial arts expert Sho Kosugi is a narcotics agent working out of Phoenix. His partner Richard Wiley is set up and murdered by a drug kingpin. Kosugi gets angry. It's routine stuff.

2404. Rage to Kill (1989, Action International, 92m, c). P&D David Winters, W Winters & Ian Yule, PH Vincent Cox, M Tim James, Steven McClintock & Mark Mancina, ED Bill Asher.

LP James Ryan (Blaine Striker), Oliver Reed (Gen. Turner), Cameron Mitchell (Miller), Maxine John (Trishia Baker), Henry Cele (Wally Arn), Ian Yule (Slade).

US racing driver James Ryan heads to the Caribbean island of St. Heron to check on his medical student brother now that control of the island nation has been taken over by Oliver Reed. Ryan is taken hostage, but organizes the students and with the aid of CIA man Cameron Mitchell teams up with the rebels headed by Henry Cele to kick out Reed.

2405. Raggedy Man (1981, Universal, 94m, c). P Burt Weissbourd & William D. Wittliff, D Jack Fisk, W Wittliff, PH Ralf Bode, M Jerry Goldsmith, ED Edward Warschilka, AD John Lloyd.

LP Sissy Spacek (Nita), Eric Roberts (Teddy), Sam Shepard (Bailey), William Sanderson (Calvin), Tracey Walter (Arnold), R.G. Armstrong (Rigby), Henry Thomas (Harry), Carey Hollis, Jr. (Henry), Ed Geldart (Mr. Calloway), Bill Thurman (Sheriff), Suzi McLaughlin (Jean Lester).

It's World War II in a small Texas town. Lonely divorcée Sissy Spacek, raising two sons alone, risks the anger of several determined suitors, who believe all divorcées are "hot-to-trot," when she allows sailor Eric Roberts to move in with her. The period atmosphere and naturalistic dialogue almost make up for the understated plot.

2406. The Raggedy Rawney (1988, Handmade Films, GB, 104m, c). P Bob Weis, D Bob Hoskins, W Hoskins & Nicole de Wilde, PH Frank Tidy, M Michael Kamen, ED Alan Jones, PD Jiri Matolin.

LP Bob Hoskins (Darky), Dexter Fletcher (Tom), Zoe Nathenson (Jessie), Dave Hill (Lamb), Ian Drury (Weasel), Zoe Wanamaker (Elle), J.G. Devlin (Jake).

A Rawney is a half-made creature with magical powers. So says actor Bob Hoskins who invented the creature for his debut as both screenwriter and director. The Rawney in Hoskins story is Dexter Fletcher, a young soldier, so traumatized by the horrors of war that he flees into the forests of the night and finally finds some comfort with a band of gypsies.

2407. ***Raging Bull†*** (1980, United Artists, 129m, b&w). P Irwin Winkler & Robert Chartoff, D Martin Scorsese†, W Paul Schrader & Mardik Martin (based on the book by Jake LaMotta with Joseph Carter & Peter Savage), PH Michael Chapman†, ED Thelma Schoonmaker†, PD Gene Rudolf, SOUND Donald O. Mitchell, Bill Nicholson, David J. Kimball & Les Lazarowitz†.

LP Robert De Niro* (Jack LaMotta), Cathy Moriarty† (Vickie LaMotta), Joe Pesci† (Joey), Frank Vincent (Salvy), Nicholas Colasanto (Tommy Como), Theresa Saldana (Lenore), Frank Adonis (Patsy), Mario Gallo (Mario), Frank Topham (Toppy/Handler), Lori Anne Flax (Irma), Joseph Bono (Guido).

Boxing films make the best sports movies, because the film concentrates on individual struggles, achievements and problems, rather than contributions to a team. Robert DeNiro, an actor who really gets into his parts, went so far as to gain 50 pounds so that he would be more credible as the washed up middleweight boxer Jake LaMotta. This marvelous cinematic achievement details the life and career of a talented but basically unlikeable champion. Many critics have designated the film as the best picture of the eighties. We find it hard to believe that anyone could seriously rank movies by any criteria so as to isolate one as the "best." This one would certainly make our unranked list of outstanding films of the decade.

2408. ***Ragtime*** (1981, Paramount, GB, 156m, c). P Dino De Laurentiis, D Milos Forman, W Michael Weller† (based on the novel by E.L. Doctorow), PH Miroslav Ondricek†, M Randy Newman†, ED Anne V. Coates, Antony Gibbs & Stanley Warnow, PD John Graysmark, AD/SD Graysmark, Patrizia Von Brandenstein, Anthony Reading, George de Titta, Sr., George de Titta, Jr. & Peter Howitt†, M/L "One More Hour" by Newman† (sung by Jennifer Warnes), COS Anna Hill Johnstone†.

LP James Cagney (Police Commissioner Rhinelander Waldo), Brad Dourif (Younger Brother), Moses Gunn (Booker T. Washington), Elizabeth McGovern† (Evelyn Nesbit), Kenneth McMillan (Willie Conklin), Pat O'Brien (Delmas), Donald O'Connor (Evelyn's Dance Instructor), James Olson (Father), Mandy Patinkin (Tateh), Howard E. Rollins† (Coalhouse Walker, Jr.), Mary Steenburgen (Mother), Debbie Allen (Sarah), Jeff DeMunn (Harry Houdini), Robert Joy (Harry K. Thaw), Norman Mailer (Stanford White).

Based on a patchwork novel which examined how world events just prior to World War I affected various Americans; the movie is confused and confusing. The film concentrates on a minor event in the book which the moviemakers must have felt was more relevant to modern times. The performances by Elizabeth McGovern as "The Girl in the Red Velvet Swing" and Howard Rollins as an early black activist are splendid. Of considerable interest to many fans is the final teaming (if it can be said to be a teaming, they don't appear together in any scene) of James Cagney and Pat O'Brien. This isn't the way to remember the two grand, spunky, Irish actors.

2409. ***Raiders of the Living Dead*** (1989, Cineronde-Canada, 83m, c). P Dan Q. Kennis, D Samuel M. Sherman, W Sherman & Brett Piper, PH Douglas Meltzer, M Tim Ferrante, ED John Donaldson, PD Ruth Seidman.

LP Robert Deveau (Morgan Randall), Donna Asali (Shelly), Scott Schwartz (Jonathan), Bob Allen (Dr. Carstairs), Bob Sacchetti (Man in Black), Zita Johann (Librarian), Corri Burt (Michelle).

Begun in 1983 as *Graveyard* this minor zombie picture is the tale of newspaper reporter Robert Deveau who tracks down a mad scientist at an abandoned island prison. The bad doctor is up to no good, reanimating corpses. Zita Johann appeared with Boris Karloff in Universal's classic 1932 horror film, *The Mummy*. Welcome back, Zita. Where have you been for so long?

2410. ***Raiders of the Lost Ark†*** (1981, Paramount, 115m, c). P Frank Marshall, D Steven Spielberg†, W Lawrence

Kasdan (based on a story by George Lucas & Philip Kaufman), PH Douglas Slocombe†, M John Williams†, ED Michael Kahn*, PD Norman Reynolds, AD/SD Reynolds, Leslie Dilley & Michael Ford*, SE Richard Edlund, Kit West, Bruce Nicholson & Joe Johnston*, SOUND Bill Varney, Stew Maslow, Gregg Landaker & Roy Charman*.

LP Harrison Ford (Indiana Jones), Karen Allen (Marion Ravenswood), Paul Freeman (Belloq), Ronald Lacey (Toht), John Rhys-Davies (Sallah), Denholm Elliott (Brody), Wolf Kahler (Dietrich), Anthony Higgins (Gobler), Alfred Molina (Satipo), Vic Tablian (Barranca), Don Fellows (Col. Musgrove), William Hootkins (Maj. Eaton).

Some critics dismiss this action-adventure film as merely a piece of exciting fluff, meant to entertain children of all ages. But perhaps they forget that one of the several functions of movies is to entertain and provide harmless escape from the everyday cares of the world. And that's precisely what this enjoyable spoof of every adventure film ever made does with great vigor and fun. American archaeologist Harrison Ford struggles with 30s Nazis for possession of the priceless treasure and holy relic, the Ark of the Covenant. The film is a never ending series of visual shocks, like a roller coaster, constantly diving from a very high drop. The acting is adequate for what it needs to be and the story, incredible but absorbing.

2411. *Rain Man** (1988, MGM/United Artists, 140m, c). P Mark Johnson, D Barry Levinson*, W Ronald Bass & Barry Morrow* (based on a story by Morrow), PH John Seale†, M Hans Zimmer†, ED Stu Linder†, PD Ida Random, AD/SD Random & Linda DeScenna†.

LP Dustin Hoffman* (Raymond Babbitt), Tom Cruise (Charlie Babbitt), Valeria Golino (Susanna), Jerry Molen (Dr. Bruner), Jack Murdock (John Mooney), Michael D. Roberts (Vern), Ralph Seymour (Lenny).

In one of the finest movies to come down the pike in many a year, Tom Cruise portrays a selfish young hustler who returns home for the reading of his estranged father's will. He learns that he has an older brother who has been left the bulk of the $3 million estate. The brother, brilliantly interpreted by Dustin Hoffman, is an autistic savant, a person extremely limited in most mental areas but supremely gifted in others. Cruise effectively kidnaps Hoffman from the safety of the institution where he has lived for many years. He hopes to be named Hoffman's guardian and get his hands on the money. Driving cross country gives the two a chance to know each other, not that Hoffman changes much. But Cruise, so lacking in kindness and understanding, undergoes a slow and believable transformation, as he learns to care for the brother he called "Rainman" as a child, being unable to pronounce "Raymond." Director Barry Levinson took risks with the movie. If he had played it for more humor, it might have seemed that he was having a laugh at Hoffman's plight; any less humor and the film would be unbearably depressing; any more spirit-raising and it would be pure sentimentality; any offered hope that Hoffman's condition would change and it wouldn't be credible. Hoffman, who almost acted himself out of movies with *Ishtar,* is back at the top of his form. Cruise, oddly cast in the part of Hoffman's younger, almost cruelly uncaring brother, nevertheless does a credible job. Italian actress Valeria Golino is most effective as Cruise's sensitive, long-suffering girlfriend who is touched by and touches Hoffman.

2412. *The Rainbow* (1989, Vestron, GB, 112m, c). P&D Ken Russell, W Ken Russell & Vivian Russell (based on the novel by D.H. Lawrence), PH Billy Williams, M Carl Davis, ED Peter Davies, PD Luciana Arrighi, AD Ian Whittaker.

LP Sammi Davis (Ursula Brangwen), Paul McGann (Anton Skrebensky), Amanda Donohoe (Winifred), Christopher Gable (Will Brangwen), David Hemmings (Uncle Henry), Glenda Jackson (Anna Brangwen), Dudley Sutton (MacAllister), Jim Carter (Mr. Harby), Judith Paris (Miss Harby), Ken Colley (Mr. Brunt), Glenda McKay (Gudrun).

Director Ken Russell returns to the works of D.H. Lawrence, filming a sort of prequel to *Women in Love,* which Russell brought brilliantly to the screen in

1970. It's the story of the sexual awakening of Ursula Brangwen, played this time by Sammi Davis, and by Jennie Linden in the earlier film. Glenda Jackson who portrayed Ursula's sister Gudrun in the 1970 picture, appears here as the girls' mother. Davis' initiation to sex comes from her swimming instructor, beautiful Amanda Donohoe. Davis later finds herself attracted to a man, career soldier Paul McGann, whose lovemaking is not as gentle as that of Donohoe. The film is a fine companion piece to *Women in Love*.

2413. ***Rainbow Brite and the Star Stealer*** (1985, Warner, 97m, animated, c). P John Chalopin, Andy Heyward & Tetsuo Katayama, D Bernard Deyries & Kimio Tabuki, W Howard R. Cohen (based on characters developed by Hallmark Properties), M Haim Saban & Shuki Levy, ED Yutaka Chikura.

VOICES Bettina (Rainbow Brite), Patrick Fraley (Lurky, On-X, Buddy Blue, Dog, Spectran, Slurthie, Glitterbot), Peter Cullen (Murky, Castle Monster, Glitterbot, Guard, Skydancer, Slurthie), Robbie Lee (Twink, Shy Violet, Indigo, La La Orange, Spectran, Sprites), Andre Stojka (Starlite, Wizard, Spectran), David Mendenhall (Krys), Rhonda Aldrich (The Princess, The Creature).

Rainbow Brite (Bettina) saves the world's color from an evil princess who has stolen the planet Spectra, the universe's source of all light.

2414. ***Raise the Titanic*** (1980, Associated Film Distribution, GB, 112m, c). P William Frye, D Jerry Jameson, W Adam Kennedy & Eric Hughes (based on the novel by Clive Cussler), PH Matthew F. Leonetti, M John Barry, ED J. Terry Williams & Robert F. Shugrue, PD John F. De Cuir.

LP Jason Robards (Adm. James Sandecker), Richard Jordan (Dirk Pitt), David Selby (Dr. Gene Seagram), Anne Archer (Dana Archibald), Alec Guinness (John Bigalow), J.D. Cannon (Capt. Joe Burke), Bo Brundin (Capt. Andre Prelov), M. Emmet Walsh (MCPO Vinnie Giordino), Robert Broyles (Willis).

In a film with surprisingly little action, suspense or plot, a group of Americans led by Jason Robards and Richard Jordan attempt to recover rare minerals

from the wreck of the *Titanic* that sunk on its maiden voyage in 1912 when it hit an iceberg in the North Atlantic. The Russians are also interested.

2415. ***Raising Arizona*** (1987, 20th Century-Fox, 94m, c). P Ethan Coen & Mark Silverman, D Joel Coen, W Ethan Coen & Joel Coen, PH Barry Sonnenfeld, M Carter Burwell, ED Michael R. Miller, PD Jane Musky.

LP Nicolas Cage (H.I. McDonnough), Holly Hunter (Edwina), Trey Wilson (Nathan Arizona, Sr.), John Goodman (Gale), William Forsythe (Evelle), Sam McMurray (Glen), Frances McDormand (Dot), Randall "Tex" Cobb (Leonard Smalls), T.J. Kuhn (Nathan Arizona, Jr.).

Nicolas Cage makes a living robbing convenience stores. Each time he's arrested, his mug shot is taken by pretty officer Holly Hunter. As a result the two fall in love and marry. Their happiness is almost ruined when they discover they can't have children. Because of his record, they are unable to adopt a child. When a local wealthy family is blessed with quints, Cage and Hunter decide that one won't be missed. They kidnap Nathan Arizona, Jr., whom they hope to raise as their own. Their problems are far from over in this quirky comedy.

2416. ***Rambo: First Blood Part II*** (1985, Tri-Star, 92m, c). P Buzz Feitshans, D George P. Cosmatos, W Sylvester Stallone & James Cameron (based on a story by Kevin Jarre & characters by David Morrell), PH Jack Cardiff, M Jerry Goldsmith, ED Mark Goldblatt & Mark Helfrich, PD Bill Kenney, SE ED Frederick J. Brown†.

LP Sylvester Stallone (John Rambo), Richard Crenna (Trautman), Charles Napier (Murdock), Steven Berkoff (Podovsky), Julia Nickson (Co Bao), George Kee Cheung (Tay), Andy Wood (Banks), Martin Kove (Ericson), William Ghent (Vinh), Vojo Goric (Yushin).

The message of this violent film is that neither the United States' former enemies in Southeast Asia nor the U.S. government can be trusted to deal with the problem of the MIAs. Direct action by killing moron Sylvester Stallone is the answer.

2417. *Rambo III* (1988, Tri-Star, 101m, c). P Buzz Feitshans, D Peter Mac-Donald, W Sylvester Stallone & Sheldon Lettich (based on characters created by David Morrell), PH John Stanier, M Jerry Goldsmith, ED James Symons, Andrew London, O. Nicholas Brown & Edward Warschilka, PD Bill Kenney.

LP Sylvester Stallone (John Rambo), Richard Crenna (Colonel Trautman), Marc de Jonge (Colonel Zaysen), Kurt-wood Smith (Griggs), Spiros Focas (Masoud), Sasson Gabai (Mousa), Doudi Shoua (Hamid), Randy Raney (Gen. Kourov), Marcus Gilbert (Tomask).

Having "cleaned-up" Southeast Asia, Sylvester Stallone turns his attention to other commies; this time those in Afghanistan. He's there to rescue his buddy Richard Crenna. For those who enjoy jingoistic films, this one ought to prove a treat.

2418. *Rampage* (1987, DEG, 97m, c). P David Salven, D&W William Friedkin (based on the novel by William P. Wood), PH Robert D. Yeoman, M Ennio Morricone, ED Jere Higgins, PD Buddy Cone.

LP Michael Biehn (Anthony Fraser), Alex McArthur (Charles Reece), Nicholas Campbell (Albert Morse), Deborah Van Valkenburgh (Kate Fraser), John Harkins (Dr. Keddie), Art Lafleur (Mel Sanderson), Billy Green Bush (Judge McKinsey), Royce D. Applegate (Gene Tippetts), Grace Zabriskie (Namoi Reece).

Although personally opposed to capital punishment, prosecutor Michael Biehn is forced to ask for the death penalty for serial killer Alex McArthur. The latter's lawyer is trying to get his client off on an insanity plea.

Rap Attack see Krush Grove

2419. *Rappin'* (1985, Cannon, 92m, c). P Menahem Golan & Yoram Globus, D Joel Silberg, W Robert Litz & Adam Friedman, PH David Gurfinkel, M Michael Linn, ED Andy Horvitch & Bert Glatstein, PD Steve Miller.

LP Mario Van Peebles (John Hood), Tasia Valenza (Dixie), Charles Flohe (Duane), Leo O'Brien (Allan), Eriq La Salle (Ice), Richie Albanes (Richie), Kadeem Hardison (Moon), Melvin Plowden (Fats), Harry Goz (Thorndike), Rony Clanton (Cedric).

Ex-con Mario Van Peebles wants to go straight but finds that his girlfriend Tasia Valenza has taken up with the leader of a street gang. The latter works for an evil contractor who is trying to evict his tenants so he can tear down the whole neighborhood. Van Peebles rallies the tenants and legally defeats the contractor. He also wins a record contract for his rap songs.

2420. *A Rare Breed* (1981, New World, 94m, c). P Jack Cox, D David Nelson, W Gardner Simmons, PH Darryl Cathcart.

LP George Kennedy (Nathan Hill), Forrest Tucker (Jess Cutler), Tom Hallick (Lou Nelson), Don Defore (Frank Nelson), Tracy Vaccaro (Anne Cutler).

While en route to Europe for training, young Tracy Vaccaro and her filly Carnauba are kidnapped, setting off a race against time to rescue them before the big race.

2421. *Ratboy* (1986, Warner, 104m, c). P Fritz Manes, D Sondra Locke, W Rob Thompson, PH Bruce Surtees, M Lennie Niehaus, ED Joel Cox, PD Edward Carfagno.

LP Sondra Locke (Nikki Morrison), Robert Townsend (Manny), Christopher Hewett (Acting Coach), Larry Hankin (Jewell), Gerrit Graham (Billy Morrison), Louie Anderson (Omer Morrison), S.L. Baird (Ratboy).

Sondra Locke's directorial debut sees actress Locke as a journalist who discovers and exploits S.L. Baird, part boy, part rodent. We don't like rats, even partial rats. Very few people, except for some French critics, bothered to watch it.

The Rats see Deadly Eyes

2422. *Raw Courage* (1984, New World, 90m, c, aka *Courage*). P Ronny Cox & Robert L. Rosen, D Rosen, W Ronny & Mary Cox, PH F. Pershing Flynn, M Johnny Harris, ED Steven Polivka, PD Don Nunley.

LP Ronny Cox (Pete Canfield), Lois Chiles (Ruth), Art Hindle (Roger Bower), M. Emmet Walsh (Colonel Crouse), Tim Maier (Craig Jensen), William Russ (Sonny), Lisa Sutton (Stephanie), Noel Conlon (Clay Matthews).

While participating in a 72-mile supermarathon race, three runners pass through a New Mexico desert, where they get more than they bargained for from a group of survivalists, training for war.

2423. *Raw Deal* (1986, De Laurentiis, 97m, c). P Martha Schumacher, D John Irvin, W Gary M. DeVore & Norman Wexler (based on a story by Luciano Vincenzoni & Sergio Donati), PH Lucio Trentini, M Clifford Capone, ED Anne V. Coates, PD Giorgio Postiglione.

LP Arnold Schwarzenegger (Kaminski), Kathryn Harrold (Monique), Sam Wanamaker (Patrovita), Paul Shenar (Rocca), Robert Davi (Max), Ed Lauter (Baker), Darren McGavin (Shannon), Joe Regalbuto (Baxter), Mordecai Lawner (Marcellino), Steven Hill (Lamanski), Blanche Baker (Amy Kaminski).

Kicked out of the FBI because of his unconventional means of conducting investigations, Arnold Schwarzenegger gets another chance when the bureau needs someone to infiltrate the Chicago mob machine and tear it apart. The mass-destruction finale is awesome, but we're forced to inform the makers of this movie that Arnie must have let some of the baddies get away, because the mob is alive and well in the Windy City.

2424. *Raw Force* (1982, American Panorama, 86m, c, aka *Shogun Island*). P Frank Johnson, D&W Edward Murphy, PH Johnson, M Walter Murphy, ED Eric Lindemann.

LP Cameron Mitchell (Captain), Geoff Binney (Mike), Jillian Kesner (Cookie), John Dresden (John), Jennifer Holmes (Ann), Hope Holiday (Hazel), Rey King (Chin), Vic Diaz (Monk).

Three karate experts travel to an island inhabited by a tribe of cannibalistic monks with the power to raise the dead.

2425. *Rawheard Rex* (1987, Empire, GB, 89m, c). P Kevin Attew & Don Hawkins, D George Pavlou, W Clive Barker (based on his short story), PH John Metcalfe, M Colin Towns, ED Andy Horvitch, AD Len Huntingford.

LP David Dukes (Howard Hallenbeck), Kelly Piper (Elaine Hallenbeck), Ronan Wilmot (Declan O'Brien), Niall Toibin (Rev. Coot), Niall O'Brien (Det. Insp. Isaac Gissing), Heinrich Von Schellendorf (Rawhead Rex).

A satanic demon terrorizes a small Ireland village when it is accidentally unearthed.

2426. *Razorback* (1984, UAA/Warner, Australia, 95m, c). P Hal McElroy, D Russell Mulcahy, W Everett DeRoche (based on the novel by Peter Brennan), PH Dean Semler, M Ira Davies, ED William Anderson, PD Bryce Walmsley.

LP Gregory Harrison (Carl Winters), Arkie Whiteley (Sarah Cameron), Bill Kerr (Jake Cullen), Chris Haywood (Benny Baker), Judy Morris (Beth Winters), John Howard (Danny), John Ewart (Turner), Don Smith (Wallace).

In a small Australian outback community, a man is tried for the murder of his grandson. The child actually has been carried off by a giant wild boar. Shades of *A Cry in the Dark.*

2427. *The Razor's Edge* (1984, Columbia, 128m, c). P Robert P. Marcucci, Harry Benn, D John Byrum, W Byrum & Bill Murray (based on the novel by W. Somerset Maugham), PH Peter Hannan, M Jack Nitzsche, ED Peter Boyle, PD Philip Harrison.

LP Bill Murray (Larry Darrell), Theresa Russell (Sophie), Catherine Hicks (Isabel), Denholm Elliott (Elliott Templeton), James Keach (Gray Maturin), Peter Vaughan (MacKenzie), Brian Doyle-Murray (Piedmont), Stephen Davies (Malcolm), Saeed Jaffrey (Raaz), Faith Brook (Louisa Bradley).

Audiences found it difficult to take Bill Murray seriously in a dramatic role. But its not all their fault. Murray failed to deliver a dramatic performance in the Somerset Maugham story of a well-to do young man who spends the years between the world wars looking for essential truth. Murray is a charming performer but he doesn't convey the necessary spirituality of the part. But for that matter Tyrone Power also had difficulty with that chore in 1946. Denholm Elliott as Murray's uncle is his usual fine form.

2428. *Reaching Out* (1983, Par Films, 87m, c). P,D&W Pat Russell, PH David Sperling, M Elizabeth Mazel, ED Russell, Sperling & Jim McCreading.

LP Pat Russell (Pat Stuart), Tony Craig (John Stevens), Frank McCarthy

(Frank Mesina), Betty Andrews (Mrs. Stuart), Douglas Stark (Mr. Stuart), Tyre Alls (Florence), Ralph Carlson (Agent), Marketa Kimbrel (Acting Teacher).

Originally shot in 1973, this film's initial release was ten years later. Considering the thinness of the story about actress Pat Russell trying to make it on Broadway, one is surprised it was ever released.

Reactor see Deadly Reactor

2429. *Real Genius* (1985, Tri-Star, 105m, c). P Brian Grazer, D Martha Coolidge, W Neal Israel, Pat Proft & Peter Torokvei (based on a story by Israel & Proft), PH Vilmos Zsigmond, M Thomas Newman, ED Richard Chew, PD Josan F. Russo.

LP Val Kilmer (Chris Knight), Gabe Jarret (Mitch Taylor), Michelle Meyrink (Jordan), William Atherton (Prof. Hathaway), Patti D'Arbanville (Sherry Nugil), Robert Prescott (Kent), Louis Giambalvo (Maj. Carnagle), Ed Lauter (Decker).

When the brilliant students at a California technical institute discover that their class projects are being used for offensive military purposes, they come up with a strategic defensive initiative of their own. It's a disappointing comedy from director Martha Coolidge.

2430. *Real Life* (1984, Bedford, GB, 92m, c). P Mike Dineen, D Francis Megahy, W Megahy & Bernie Cooper, PH Peter Jessop, M David Mindel, ED Peter Delfgou, PD John White.

LP Rupert Everett (Tim), Cristina Raines (Laurel), Catherine Rabett (Kate), James Faulkner (Robin), Isla Blair (Anna), Norman Beaton (Leon), Warren Clarke (Gerry), Lynsey Baxter (Jackie), Annabel Leventon (Carla), Michael Cochrane (Lipton).

Mischievous lad Rupert Everett spices up his life by telling tall tales. He creates a story about the theft of a Rembrandt painting, taken by a gang working for a big-shot boss, who in turn is operating in behalf of South African guerrillas. Everett's in trouble when his story comes true.

2431. *Real Men* (1987, MGM/United Artists, 96m, c). P Martin Bregman, D&W Dennis Feldman, PH John A. Alonzo, AD William J. Cassidy & James Allen.

LP James Belushi (Nick Pirandello), John Ritter (Bob Wilson), Barbara Barrie (Mom), Bill Morey (Cunard), Iva Andersen (Dolly), Gail Berle (Sherry), Mark Herrier (Bradshaw), Matthew Brooks (Bob, Jr.).

Bond-like CIA agent James Belushi attempts to build up the confidence of a wimpy partner who is reluctantly posing as a dead spy. It's a candidate for a short shelf life in a video store.

2432. *Re-Animator* (1985, Empire, 86m, c). P Brian Yuzna, D Stuart Gordon, W Dennis Paoli, William J. Norris & Gordon (based on the story "Herbert West: The Re-Animator" by H.P. Lovecraft), PH Mac Ahlberg, M Richard Band, ED Lee Percy, AD Robert A. Burns, SE Anthony Doublin & John Naulin.

LP Jeffrey Combs (Herbert West), Bruce Abbott (Dan Cain), Barbara Crampton (Megan Halsey), David Gale (Dr. Carl Hill), Robert Sampson (Dean Halsey), Gerry Black (Mace), Peter Kent (Melvin the Re-animated).

This black-humor horror film, based on the work of H.P. Lovecraft, in which medical student Jeffrey Combs is able to reanimate the dead, has become a cult favorite.

2433. *Rebel* (1985, Vestron, Australia, 91m, c). P Phillip Emanuel, D Michael Jenkins, W Jenkins & Bob Herbert (based on the play *No Names...No Packdrill* by Herbert), PH Peter James, M Chris Neal, ED Michael Honey, PD Brian Thompson.

LP Matt Dillon (Rebel), Debbie Byrne (Kathy McLeod), Bryan Brown (Tiger Kelly), Bill Hunter (Browning), Ray Barrett (Bubbles), Julie Nihill (Joycie), John O'May (Bernie), Kim Deacon (Hazel).

In Sydney during World War II, young U.S. Marine Matt Dillon goes AWOL and falls in love with a married nightclub singer, Debbie Byrne. He's torn between wanting to escape the war and staying with her in Australia. There are too many suds in this soap opera.

2434. *Rebel Love* (1985, Troma, 90m, c). P John Quenelle, D&W Milton

Bagby, Jr., PH Joseph A. Whigham, M Bobby Horton, ED Melinda Bridges, PD Bill Teague.

LP Jamie Rose (Columbine Cromwell), Terence Knox (McHugh/Hightower), Fran Ryan (Granny Plug), Carl Spurlock (Sergeant), Rick Wain (Corporal), Larry Larson (Aaron Cromwell), Charles Hill (The Captain).

In a cheaply-made Civil War drama, Yankee widow Jamie Rose finds escape from her loneliness on a solitary Indiana farm in the arms of rebel spy Terence Knox.

Rebel Waves see Rising Storm

2435. *Reckless* (1984, MGM/United Artists, 90m, c). P Edgar J. Scherick & Scott Rudin, D James Foley, W Chris Columbus, PH Michael Ballhaus, M Thomas Newman, ED Albert Magnoli, PD Jeffrey Townsend.

LP Aidan Quinn (Johnny Rourke), Daryl Hannah (Tracey Prescott), Kenneth McMillan (John Rourke, Sr.), Cliff De Young (Phil Barton), Lois Smith (Mrs. Prescott), Adam Baldwin (Randy Daniels), Dan Hedaya (Peter Daniels).

Aidan Quinn, the son of the town drunk, has a bad reputation. He falls in love with straitlaced cheerleader Daryl Hannah, a girl from a good family. Their passion and rebellion upset their little West Virginia town.

2436. *Recruits* (1986, Concorde, 82m, c). P Maurice Smith, D Rafal Zielinski, W Charles Wiener, B.K. Roderick, PH Peter Czerski, M Steve Parsons, ED Stephan Fanfara & Christie Wilson, AD Craig Richards.

LP Steve Osmond (Steve), Doug Annear (Mike), Alan Deveau (Howie), John Terrell (Winston), Lolita Davidoff (Susan), Tracey Tanner (Brazil), Annie McAuley (Tanya), Tony Travis (Stonewall), Mike McDonald (Magruder).

In a cheap rip-off of *Police Academy* (how is that possible, you ask?), a sheriff hires hookers, thieves, winos and bums as deputies.

2437. *Red Dawn* (1984, MGM/United Artists, 100m, c). P Buzz Feitshans & Barry Beckerman, D John Milius, W Kevin Reynolds & Milius (based on the novel by Reynolds), PH Ric Waite, M Basil Poledouris, ED Thom Noble, PD Jackson de Govia.

LP Patrick Swayze (Jed), C. Thomas Howell (Robert), Lea Thompson (Erica), Charlie Sheen (Matt), Darren Dalton (Daryl), Jennifer Grey (Toni), Brad Savage (Danny), Doug Toby (Aardvark), Ben Johnson (Mason), Harry Dean Stanton (Mr. Eckert), Ron O'Neal (Bella), William Smith (Strelnikov), Vladek Sheybal (Bratchenko), Powers Boothe (Andy).

In this commie-bashing movie which makes the NRA's point about the need for keeping guns, Russian invaders overrun the United States heartland, taking over the country. Eight small-town teenagers hide out in the rugged countryside and harrass the Russkies with guerrilla warfare. It's not a very believable story, but the youngsters work hard to make it exciting.

2438. *Red-Headed Stranger* (1986, Alive Films, 105m, c). P Willie Nelson & William Wittliff, D&W Wittliff, PH Neil Roach, M Willie Nelson, ED Eric Austin Williams & Stephen H. Purvis, PD Cary White.

LP Willie Nelson (Julian), Morgan Fairchild (Raysha), Katharine Ross (Laurie), R.G. Armstrong (Scoby), Royal Dano (Larn Claver), Sonny Carl Davis (Odie Claver), Marinell Madden (Cindy), Ted J. Crum (Cauley Felps).

Montana preacher Willie Nelson is troubled by his wayward wife Morgan Fairchild, good woman Katharine Ross and some bad guys headed by Royal Dano who rule the roost in his town. He'll just have to do something about all of this other than sing.

2439. *Red Heat* (1988, Tri-Star, 106m, c). P Walter Hill & Gordon Carroll, D Hill, W Harry Kleiner, Hill & Troy Kennedy Martin (based on a story by Hill), PH Matthew F. Leonetti, M James Horner, ED Freeman Davies, Carmel Davies & Donn Aron, PD John Vallone.

LP Arnold Schwarzenegger (Capt. Ivan Danko), James Belushi (Det. Sgt. Art Ridzik), Peter Boyle (Police Comdr. Lou Donnelly), Ed O'Ross (Viktor Rostavili), Larry Fishburne (Lt. Stobbs), Gina Gershon (Cat Manzetti), Richard Bright (Sgt. Gallagher), J.W. Smith (Salim).

No nonsense Soviet police officer Arnold Schwarzenegger follows Georgian drug dealer Ed O'Ross to Chicago. He's forced to team up with slovenly wise-cracking cop James Belushi to catch his man. It's close enough to director Walter Hill's *48 Hours* to be considered a re-working of the plot, but it's fast moving and fun.

2440. *Red Heat* (1988, Vestron, US/Ger., 104m, c). P Ernst R. Theumer, D Robert Collector & Gary Drucker, PH Wolfgang Dickmann, M Tangerine Dream, ED Anthony Redman.

LP Linda Blair (Chris Carlson), Sylvia Kristel (Sofia), Sue Kiel (Hedda), William Ostrander (Michael), Elisabeth Volkmann (Einbeck), Albert Fortell (Ernst), Herb Andress (Werner), Barbara Spitz (Meg), Kati Marothy (Barbara), Dagmar Michal-Schwarz (Lillian).

Although completed 1984 this dumb women-in-prison film wasn't released in the US until 1988. In Berlin to be with her soldier fiancé, American Linda Blair witnesses the abduction of an East German woman who has just defected. The kidnappers throw Blair into the van as well. Blair is convicted of espionage and sent to an East German prison. Pens for women are the same the world over, ruthless guards, rampant lesbianism, nudity, violence, etc.

2441. *Red Nights* (1988, TransWorld, 89m, c). P Ron Wolotzky, D Izhak Hanooka, W Hanooka, PH Jacob Eleasari, M Tangerine Dream, ED David Lloyd, PD Rina Binyamini.

LP Christopher Parker (Randy), Brian Matthews (David), Tom Badal (Bruce), Patti Bauer (Betty), Jack Carter (Uncle Solly), James Mayberry (Jeff), William Smith (Phillip), Ivan E. Roth (Peter), Tawny Capriccio (Helen), Anna Louise (Stripper).

New Hampshire lad Christopher Parker goes to Hollywood to pursue a career as an actor. He puts his career plans on hold long enough to go after the killers of a friend. Not too surprisingly the film went direct to video.

Red on Red see *Scarred*

2442. *Red Riding Hood* (1987, Cannon, 80m, c). P Menahem Golan & Yoram Globus, D Adam Brooks, W Carole Lucia Satrina (based on the fairytale by the Brothers Grimm), PH Danny Shnegur & Ye'ehi Neyman, M Stephen Lawrence, ED David Tour.

LP Craig T. Nelson (Godfrey/Percival), Isabella Rossellini (Lady Jeanne), Amelia Shankley (Red Riding Hood), Rocco Sisto (Dagger/The Wolf), Linda Kaye (Badger Kate), Helen Glazary (Nancy Bess), Julian Joy-Chagrin (Allen Owen).

Here's another of Cannon's fairytale films having a brief theater release before heading for home video. The familiar tale has been replaced with a new storyline and several songs. Craig T. Nelson plays twin princes, one good, one evil. Amelia Shankley as Red Riding Hood possesses a magic coat which protects her from Rocco Sisto, the evil prince's lackey. He has been changed into a wolf by a magic spell.

2443. *Red Scorpion* (1989, Shapiro Glickenhaus, 102m, c). P Jack Abramoff, D Joseph Zito, W Arne Olsen (based on a story by Robert and Jack Abramoff & Olsen, PH Joao Fernandes, M Jay Chattaway, ED Daniel Loewenthal, PD Ladislav Wilheim.

LP Dolph Lundgren (Lt. Nikolai), M. Emmet Walsh (Dewey Ferguson), Al White (Kallunda), T.P. McKenna (Gen. Vortek), Carmen Argenziano (Zayas), Alex Colon (Mendez), Brion James (Krasnov), Regopstaan (Gao, bushman).

Dull! Dull! Dull! Unless you are taken by musclebound men with nothing between their ears, this grade Z story has stone-faced Dolph Lundgren playing a Russian special services officer. It would seem that he carries a can of Crisco with him so he can get that all-over glistening look. Besides flexing his muscles, the Soviet killing machine is assigned to assassinate a rebel leader fighting the Communist regime in some faraway country.

2444. *Red Sonja* (1985, MGM/United Artists, 89m, c). P Christian Ferry, D Richard Fleischer, W Clive Exton & George MacDonald Fraser (based on characters created Robert E. Howard), PH Giuseppe Rotunno, M Ennio Morricone, ED Frank J. Urioste, PD Danilo Donati.

LP Arnold Schwarzenegger (Kalidor), Brigitte Nielsen (Red Sonja), Sandahl Bergman (Queen Gedren), Paul Smith (Falkon), Ernie Reyes, Jr. (Tarn), Ronald Lacey (Ikol), Pat Roach (Brytag), Terry Richards (Djart), Janet Agren (Varna), Donna Osterbuhr (Kendra, the High Priestess).

It says here that Arnold Schwarzenegger is not portraying Conan in this sword-and-sorcery fantasy, but it's hard to tell the difference. At least he has a costar, Brigitte Nielsen, whose lack of talent makes him look like quite a thespian. The statuesque Nielsen joins forces with Arnie to fight an evil queen who has killed her family.

The Red Tide see Blood Tide

2445. Reds† (1981, Paramount, 200m, c). P&D Warren Beatty* (for direction), W Beatty & Trevor Griffiths†, PH Vittorio Storaro*, M Stephen Sondheim & Dave Grusin, ED Dede Allen & Craig McKay†, PD Richard Sylbert, AD/SD Sylbert & Michael Seirton†, COS Shirley Russell†, SOUND Dick Vorisek, Tom Fleischman & Simon Kaye†.

LP Warren Beatty† (John Reed), Diane Keaton† (Louise Bryant), Edward Herrmann (Max Eastman), Jerzy Kosinski (Grigory Zinoviev), Jack Nicholson† (Eugene O'Neill), Paul Sorvino (Louis Fraina), Maureen Stapleton* (Emma Goldman), Nicolas Coster (Paul Trullinger), M. Emmet Walsh (Speaker at the Liberal Club), Ian Wolfe (Mr. Partlow), Bessie Love (Mrs. Partlow), MacIntyre Dixon (Carl Walters), Pat Starr (Helen Walters), Eleanor D. Wilson (Mrs. Reed), Max Wright (Floyd Dell), George Plimpton (Horace Whigham), Henry Miller, Adela Rogers St. John, Hamilton Fish, Rebecca West, Will Durant, Adele Nathan, George Jessel, Harry Carlisle (Witnesses).

The film is long but well worth the time. It is the story of the last years of American writer John Reed, inspiringly played by Warren Beatty. After a stormy romance with free-lover feminist Louise Bryant, impersonated by Diane Keaton, he helped found the American Communist Party. Reed travels to Russia in time for the Bolshevik Revolution, which he documented in his book *Ten Days That Shook the World*. Reed became the only American to be buried within the walls of the Kremlin. It's rather amazing that this project succeeded in 1981, but it was widely praised and even broke even at the box-office.

2446. Reflections (1984, Film Four, GB, 103m, c). P David Deutsch & Kevin Billington, D Billington, W John Banville, PH Mike Malloy, M Rachel Portman, ED Chris Risdale, AD Martin Johnson.

LP Gabriel Byrne (William Masters), Donal McCann (Edward Lawless), Harriet Walter (Ottilie Granger), Fionnula Flanagan (Charlotte Lawless), Gerard Cummins (Michael Lawless), Niall Toibin (Prunty), Paedar Lamb (Doctor), Des Nealon (Tom Mittler), Margaret Wade (Bunny Mittler).

Made for British TV, this film was shown theatrically. Researcher Gabriel Byrne, preparing a study of the life of Sir Isaac Newton, rents a cottage in Ireland in which to do his writing. Instead he falls in love with Harriet Walter and her married aunt Fionnula Flanagan.

2447. Reform School Girls (1986, New World, 94m, c). P Jack Cummings, D&W Tom DeSimone, PH Howard Wexler, M Various Artists, ED Michael Spence, PD Becky Block.

LP Linda Carol (Jenny), Wendy O. Williams (Charlie), Pat Ast (Edna), Sybil Danning (Sutter), Charlotte McGinnis (Dr. Norton), Sherri Stoner (Lisa), Denise Gordy (Claudia), Laurie Schwartz (Nicky), Tiffany Helm (Fish).

Knowledgeable drive-in movie fans will hear the title of this film and know they are in for some female nudity, stereotyped prisoners, cruel guards, one understanding authority figure, suggested lesbianism, etc. — and this spoof of the subgenre won't disappoint them.

2448. The Rejuvenator (1988, SVS, 86m, c). P Steven Mackler, D Brian Thomas Jones, W Simon Nuchtern & Jones, PH James McCalmont, M Larry Juris, ED Brian O'Hara, PD Susan Bolles.

LP Vivian Lanko (Elizabeth Warren/Monster), John MacKay (Dr. Gregory Ashton), James Hogue (Wilhelm), Katell

Pleven (Dr. Stella Stone), Marcus Powell (Dr. Germaine), Jessica Dublin (Ruth Warren), Roy MacArthur (Hunter), Louis F. Homyak (Tony).

Wealthy old Jessica Dublin funds mad scientist John MacKay's experiment with a serum, made from human gray matter, which reverses the aging process. When Dublin tries the formula, it works and she becomes young, beautiful Vivian Lanko. The catch is the serum periodically turns Lanko into a monster, and greater amounts of the serum is needed to bring her back to normal.

2449. *Relentless* (1989, New Line Cinema, 92m, c). P Howard Smith, D William Lustig, W "Jack T.D. Robinson" (Phil Alden Robinson), PH James Lemmo, M Jay Chattaway, ED David Kern, PD Gene Abel.

LP Judd Nelson (Buck Taylor), Robert Loggia (Bill Malloy), Leo Rossi (Sam Dietz), Meg Foster (Carol Dietz), Patrick O'Bryan (Todd Arthur), Mindy Seger (Francine), Ron Taylor (Capt. Blakely), Beau Starr (Ike Taylor).

Judd Nelson appears as a maniacal serial murderer, known as the "Sunset Killer." The character is kept under control by the actor, making him all the more frightening in this taunt suspense thriller. Through flashbacks audiences learn the reason for Nelson's psychotic behavior. He is pursued by Leo Rossi and Robert Loggia, both giving excellent performances.

2450. *Religion, Inc.* (1989, Chronicle, 87m, c). P Michael Mailer, D Daniel Adams, W Adams & Mailer (based on a story by Adams), PH John Drake, M Kip Martin, ED Thomas R. Rondinella, PD Paola Ridolfi.

LP Jonathan Penner (Morris Codman), Gerald Orange (Dr. Ian Clarity), Sandra Bullock (Debby), George Plimpton (God), Wendy Adams (Peggy).

God, in the person of preppie-like George Plimpton, appears on the TV screen of failing and executive Jonathan Penner. The Almighty suggests that Penner start a new religion—and so he does. Its tenets are selfishness, greed, cruelty and adultery, because this is what market research says religious consumers want. A bit cynical, would you say?

2451. *Rembrandt Laughing* (1989, Jost, 100m, c). P Jon Jost & Henry Rosenthal, D Jost, W Jost & Den Darstellern, PH Jost, M Jon A. English.

LP Jon A. English, Barbara Hammes, Jennifer Johanson, Ed Green, Nathaniel Dorsky, Jerry Barrish.

In cinéma verité fashion independent producer-director Jon Jost follows the daily encounters of ex-lovers Jon A. English and Barbara Hammes five years after their break-up. As a cameraman Jost is too artsy for the good of the movie.

2452. *Remo Williams: The Adventure Begins* (1985, Orion, 121m, c). P Larry Spiegel, D Guy Hamilton, W Christopher Wood (based on characters created by Warren Murphy & Richard Sapir in "The Destroyer" series), PH Andrew Laszlo, M Craig Safan, ED Mark Melnick, PD Jackson de Govia, MK Carl Fullerton†.

LP Fred Ward (Remo Williams), Joel Gray (Chiun), Wilford Brimley (Harold Smith), J.A. Preston (Conn MacCleary), George Coe (Gen. Scott Watson), Charles Cioffi (George Grove), Kate Mulgrew (Maj. Rayner Fleming).

Remo Williams, the hero of "The Destroyer" adventure novel series, a James Bond-like good guy, can walk on water and dodge bullets after being instructed by a Korean martial arts master.

2453. *Remote Control* (1988, Vista, 88m, c). P Scott Rosenfelt & Mark Levinson, D&W Jeff Lieberman, PH Timothy Suhrstedt, M Peter Bernstein, ED Scott Wallace, PD Curtis Schnell.

LP Kevin Dillon (Cosmo), Deborah Goodrich (Belinda), Christopher Wynne (Georgie), Frank Beddor (Victor), Jennifer Tilly (Allegra), Kaaren Lee (Patricia), Bert Remsen (Bill Denver).

When the manager of a video store discovers that several of his customers have been brutally murdered after viewing a particular cassette, he figures he'd better investigate.

2454. *Renegades* (1989, Universal, 107m, c). P David Madden, D Jack Sholder, W David Rich, PH Phil Meheux, M Michael Kamen, ED Caroline Biggerstaff, PD Carol Spier.

LP Kiefer Sutherland (Buster), Lou

Diamond Phillips (Hank), Jami Gertz (Barbara), Rob Knepper (Marino), Bill Smitrovich (Finch), Floyd Westerman (Red Crow), Joe Griffin (Matt), Clark Johnson (J.J.).

In a fast-moving, violent, implausible film, Philadelphia cop Kiefer Sutherland infiltrates a gang in order to expose a rogue cop. As the gang escapes they kill Lou Diamond Phillips' brother and steal a lance sacred to the Lakota Sioux Indian tribe. Phillips teams with Sutherland, going after the killer and retrieving the lance.

2455. *Reno and the Doc* (1984, New World, Canada, 88m, c). P David Mitchell & Sean Ryerson, D&W Charles Dennis (based on a story by Damien Lee), PH Ludek Bogner, M Betty Lazebnik & Brian Bell, ED Jim Lahti & Mairin Wilkison, PD Stephen Surjik.

LP Ken Walsh (Reginald "Reno" Coltchinsky), Henry Ramer (Hugo "Doc" Billings), Linda Griffiths (Savannah Gates), Gene Mack (Stan Kukamunga), Cliff Welsh (Cliff), Laura Dickson (Agnes), Sean Ryerson (Long Jack).

Middleaged Ken Walsh and Henry Ramer, both battling mid-life crises, team up to test themselves in the world of professional skiing.

2456. *Rent-a-Cop* (1988, Kings Road, 96m, c). P Raymond Wagner, D Jerry London, W Dennis Shryack & Michael Blodgett, PH Giuseppe Rotunno, M Jerry Goldsmith, ED Robert Lawrence, PD Tony Masters.

LP Burt Reynolds (Church), Liza Minnelli (Della), James Remar (Dancer), Richard Masur (Roger), Dionne Warwick (Beth), Bernie Casey (Lemar), Robby Benson (Pitts), John Stanton (Alexander), John P. Ryan (Wieser).

Busted cop Burt Reynolds is reduced to taking a job as a security guard after a blown drug arrest. Liza Minnelli is a kooky but affectionate lady-of-the-evening. Their performances makes one nostalgic for earlier films of these two talented performers when they seemed to try harder to please. Reynolds does his usual number, but with not much enthusiasm. Liza shows spunk, but it's a shame the day of the musicals, where her singing and dancing could turn on an audience, is past.

2457. *Rent Control* (1981, Group S, 95m, c). P Benni Korzen, D Gian L. Polidoro, W John Menegold & Sherill Tippins, PH Benito Frattari, M Oscar De Mejo & Ian North, ED Ed Orshan & Jim Cookman.

LP Brent Spiner (Leonard), Elizabeth Stack (Anne), Leonard Melfi (Milton), Jeanne Ruskin (Margaret), Annie Korzen (Nancy), Leslie Cifarelli (Barbara), Charles Laiken (Jim), Roy Brocksmith (Stan).

Aspiring writer Brent Spiner makes the near-impossible quest to find a rent-controlled apartment in Manhattan. He believes that's what it will take to get his wife, who has run away with a cosmetician, to return to him.

2458. *Rented Lips* (1988, Vista, 80m, c). P Mort Engelberg, D Robert Downey, W Martin Mull, PH Robert D. Yeoman, M Van Dyke Parks, ED Christopher Greenbury, Brian Berdan & Jay Ignaszewski, PD George Costello.

LP Martin Mull (Archie Powell), Dick Shawn (Charlie Slater), Jennifer Tilly (Mona Lisa), Edy Williams (Heather Darling), Robert Downey, Jr. (Wolf Dangler), Kenneth Mars (Rev. Farrell), Shelley Berman (Bill Slotnik).

Documentary filmmakers Martin Mull and Dick Shawn (in his last screen appearance), are induced by public TV station manager Shelley Berman to complete a porno movie, left unfinished when the director died. This silly movie dies long before that.

2459. *Repo Man* (1984, Universal, 92m, c). P Jonathan Wacks & Peter McCarthy, D&W Alex Cox, PH Robby Muller, M Tito Larriva & Steven Hufsteter, ED Dennis Dolan.

LP Harry Dean Stanton (Bud), Emilio Estevez (Otto), Tracey Walter (Miller), Olivia Barash (Leila), Sy Richardson (Lite), Susan Barnes (Agent Rogers), Fox Harris (J. Frank Parnell), Tom Finnegan (Oly).

Spaced out L.A. teen Emilio Estevez is recruited by Harry Dean Stanton to become a repossession man for an auto loan company. The youngster finds himself in a nightmarish world, constantly on the run from all kinds of dangers.

2460. *The Rescue* (1988, Buena Vista, 98m, c). P Laura Ziskin, D Ferdinand Fairfax, W Jim Thomas & John Thomas, PH Russell Boyd, M Bruce Broughton, ED David Holden & Carroll Timothy O'Meara, PD Maurice Cain.

LP Kevin Dillon (J.J. Merrill), Christina Harnos (Adrian Phillips), Marc Price (Max Rothman), Ned Vaughn (Shawn Howard), Ian Giatti (Bobby Howard), Charles Haid (Cmdr. Howard), Edward Albert (Cmdr. Merrill), Timothy Carhart (Lt. Phillips), Michael Gates Phenicie (Wicks).

A team of Americans are captured by North Koreans as they attempt to locate and destroy a United States nuclear submarine sunk in North Korean waters. Their children, Kevin Dillon, Christina Harnos, Ned Vaughn and Ian Giatti, are outraged that the government is doing nothing to rescue their fathers from the godless commies. The kids take things in their own hands and make the rescue.

2461. *The Rescuers [Re-issue]* (1989, Disney, animated, 76m, c). P Wolfgang Reitherman, D Reitherman, John Lounsbery & Art Stevens, W Ken Anderson, Vance Gerry, Larry Clemmons, David Michener, Burny Mattinson, Frank Thomas, Fred Lucky, Ted Berman & Dick Sebast (based on the stories "The Rescuers" and "Miss Bianca" by Margery Sharp), M Artie Butler, ED James Melton & Jim Koford, ANIM D Ollie Johnston, Milt Kahl & Don Bluth, AD Don Griffith.

VOICES Bob Newhart (Bernard), Eva Gabor (Miss Bianca), Geraldine Page (Mme. Medusa), Joe Flynn (Mr. Snoops), Jeanette Nolan (Ellie Mae), Pat Buttram (Luke), Jim Jordan (Orville), John McIntire (Rufus), Michelle Stacy (Penny).

Initially released in 1977, the film demonstrated that the Disney studio still had it when it came to producing a first-rate animated feature. In the story two mice (voices of Bob Newhart and Eva Gabor) set out to rescue a girl (Michelle Stacy) from the evil Mme. Medusa (Geraldine Page). It gets a bit scary in parts and may be too much for real little tykes.

2462. *Restless Natives* (1985, EMI, GB, 89m, c). P Rick Stevenson, D Michael Hoffman, W Ninian Dunet, PH Oliver Stapleton, M Stuart Adamson, ED Sean Barton, PD Adrienne Atkinson.

LP Vincent Friell (Will Bryce), Joe Mullaney (Ronnie Wotherspoon), Teri Lally (Margot), Ned Beatty (Fritz Bender), Robert Urquhart (Detective Inspector Baird), Anne Scott-James (Mother).

In Edinburgh, two bored lads, Vincent Friell and Joe Mullaney, decide to become latter-day highwaymen. They don disguises and comical masks to rob tourists.

2463. *Resurrected* (1989, St. Pancras/ Hobo, GB, 94m, c). P Tara Prem & Adrian Hughes, D Paul Greengrass, W Martin Allen, PH Ivan Strasburg, ED Dan Rae, PD Christopher Burke.

LP David Thewlis (Kevin Deakin), Tom Bell (Mr. Deakin), Rita Tushingham (Mrs. Deakin), Michael Pollitt (Gregory Deakin), Rudi Davies (Julie), William Hoyland (Capt. Sinclair).

Eighteen-year-old David Thewlis is reported missing, presumed dead, during fighting in the Falklands. Several weeks later he appears at a nearby farmhouse. When he returns to England, the press alleges that he was a deserter.

2464. *Resurrection* (1980, Universal, 103m, c). P Renee Missel & Howard Rosenman, D Daniel Petrie, W Lewis John Carlino, PH Mario Tosi, M Maurice Jarre, ED Rita Roland, PD Paul Sylbert.

LP Ellen Burstyn† (Edna McCauley), Sam Shepard (Cal Carpenter), Richard Farnsworth (Esco), Roberts Blossom (John Harper), Clifford David (George), Pamela Payton-Wright (Margaret), Jeffrey DeMunn (Joe McCauley), Eva Le-Gallienne† (Grandma Pearl), Lois Smith (Kathy).

Ellen Burstyn has an out-of-body experience and "comes back from the dead" following an automobile accident in L.A. that killed her husband. She returns to her rural Kansas home where she discovers she has the power of healing. She also attracts Sam Shepard, the troubled young son of a preacher, with whom she has an affair. He comes to believe that Burstyn is the second coming of Jesus and to prove her godness he shoots her.

Retaliator see Programmed to Kill

2465. *Retribution* (1988, Renegade/
United, 107m, c). P&D Guy Magar, W
Guy Magar & Lee Wasserman, PH Gary
Thieltges, M Alan Howarth, ED Magar
& Alan Shefland, PD Robb Wilson King.
LP Dennis Lipscomb (George Miller),
Leslie Wing (Dr. Jennifer Curtis),
Suzanne Snyder (Angel), Jeff Pomerantz
(Dr. Alan Falconer), George Murdock
(Dr. John Talbot), Pamela Dunlap (Sally
Benson), Susan Peretz (Mrs. Stoller),
Clare Peck (Carla Minelli).
On Halloween night, destitute, wimpy
artist Dennis Lipscomb attempts to take
his life by jumping from the roof of the
seedy hotel where he lives. When he hits
the pavement he has an out-of-body-
experience and survives. Three months
later upon being released from a sanitarium he returns home. He has horrible
dreams of visiting places he's never been
before and killing people he's never seen
before. When he wakes the papers are
filled with stories of his dream murders.

The Retrievers see Hot and Deadly

2466. *Return* (1986, A Silver Prod.,
82m, c). P Philip Spinelli, D&W Andrew
Silver, PH Janos Zsombolyai, M Ragnar
Grippe & Michael Shrieve, ED Gabrielle
Gilbert.
LP Karlene Crockett (Diane Stoving),
John Walcutt (Day Whittaker), Lisa
Richards (Ann Stoving), Frederic Forrest
(Brian Stoving), Anne Lloyd Francis
(Eileen Sedgely), Lenore Zann (Susan),
Thomas Rolopp (Lucky).
Her investigation of the mysterious
death of her grandfather leads Karlene
Crockett to make several bizarre dis-
coveries at her birthplace.

2467. *The Return of Captain Invincible*
(1983, Keys, Australia/US, 90m, c, aka
Legend in Leotards). P Andrew Gaty, D
Philippe Mora, W Steve de Souza &
Gaty, PH Mike Molloy, M William Mot-
zing, ED John Scott, PD David Copping.
LP Alan Arkin (Capt. Invincible),
Christopher Lee (Mr. Midnight), Kate
Fitzpatrick (Patty), Bill Hunter (Tupper),
Graham Kennedy (Prime Minister), Mi-
chael Pate (President), Hayes Gordon
(Kirby), Max Phipps (Admiral), Noel
Ferrier (General).

In an unsuccessful parody, retired
superhero Alan Arkin is called back
to deal with super-villain Christopher
Lee.

2468. *The Return of Josey Wales* (1987,
Reel Movies Intl., 90m, c). P Mickey
Grant, D Michael Parks & R.O. Taylor,
W Forrest Carter & Taylor (based on the
novel *Vengeance Trail of Josey Wales* by
Carter), PH Brant A. Hughes, M Rusty
Thornhill, ED Ivan L. Bigley, AD Larry
Melton.
LP Michael Parks (Josey Wales),
Rafael Campos (Chato), Charlie McCoy
(Charlie), Everett Sifuentes (Capt. Jesus
Escobedo), Suzie Humphreys (Rose),
John Galt (Kelly), Joe Kurtzo (Nacole),
Paco Vela (Paco).
While reminiscing about gunman
Josey Wales, two friends are gunned
down by maurading Rurales. When the
Rurales take Wales' last remaining ex-
comrade as a hostage, Wales (Michael
Parks) comes out of hiding and sets off on
a trail of bloody vengeance.

*The Return of Maxwell Smart see The
Nude Bomb*

2469. *Return of the Jedi* (1983, 20th
Century-Fox, 133m, c). P Howard
Kazanjian, Robert Watts & Jim Bloom,
D Richard Marquand, W Lawrence Kas-
dan & George Lucas (based on a story by
Lucas), PH Alan Hume, Jack Lowin &
Jim Glennon, M John Williams†, ED
Sean Barton, Marcia Lucas, Duwayne
Dunham & Arthur Repola, PD Norman
Reynolds, AD/SD Reynolds, Fred Hole,
James Schoppe & Michael Ford, SE Roy
Arbogast, Kit West, Richard Edlund,
Dennis Muren & Ken Ralston, SOUND
Ben Burtt, Gary Summers, Randy Thom
& Tony Dawe†, SE ED Burtt†.
LP Mark Hamill (Luke Skywalker),
Harrison Ford (Han Solo), Carrie Fisher
(Princess Leia), Billy Dee Williams
(Lando Calrissian), Anthony Daniels
(See Threepio [C-3PO]), Peter Mayhew
(Chewbacca), Sebastian Shaw (Anakin
Skywalker), Ian McDiarmid (Emperor
Palpatine), Frank Oz (Yoda), David
Prowse (Darth Vader), James Earl Jones
(voice of Darth Vader), Alec Guinness
(Ben Obi-Wan Kenobi), Kenny Baker (Ar-
too-Detoo [R2-D2]), Michael Penning-

ton (Moff Jerjerrod), Ken Colley (Adm. Piett).

George Lucas presents "Episode Six" on the *Star Wars* serial in which Luke Skywalker (Mark Hamill) and his friends combat Darth Vader and Jabba the Hutt. Luke learns how to become a Jedi warrior from Yoda (Frank Oz) and that Vader is actually his father. In the end Vader sacrifices his own life for Luke. These entertaining movies with all of their spectacular special effects and impressive sets are, after all, only huge video games, but they manage to capture the attention of millions of fans.

2470. *Return of the Killer Tomatoes* (1988, New World, 98m, c). P J. Stephen Peace & Lowell D. Blank, D John De-Bello, W DeBello, Stephen F. Andrich & Constantine Dillon, M Rick Patterson & Neal Fox, ED DeBello & Andrich, PD Dillon.

LP Anthony Starke (Chad), George Clooney (Matt), Karen Mistal (Tara), Steve Lundquist (Igor), John Astin (Prof. Gangrene), Charlie Jones, Rock Peace, Frank Davis, C.J. Dillon, Teri Weigel.

This sequel to *Attack of the Killer Tomatoes* (1977), picks up where the latter left off. Earth has made ketchup of the killer tomatoes, but are they all really gone? Surround them with pasta!

2471. *The Return of the Living Dead* (1985, Orion, 91m, c). P Tom Fox & Graham Henderson, D&W Dan O'Bannon (based on a story by Rudy Ricci, John Russo & Russell Streiner), M Matt Clifford, ED Robert Gordon, PD William Stout, SE MK Bill Munns.

LP Clu Gulager (Burt), James Karen (Frank), Don Calfa (Ernie), Thom Mathews (Freddy), Beverly Randolph (Tina), John Philbin (Chuck), Jewal Shepard (Casey), Miguel A. Nunez, Jr. (Spider), Brian Peck (Scuz).

In a fast-moving spoof of the living dead subgenre, the army is called in to repel an attack of zombies.

2472. *Return of the Living Dead Part II* (1988, Lorimar, 89m, c). P Tom Fox, D&W Ken Wiederhorn, PH Robert Elswit, M J. Peter Robinson, ED Charles Bornstein.

LP Michael Kenworthy (Jesse Wilson), Thor Van Lingen (Billy), Jason Hogan (Johnny), James Karen (Ed), Marsha Dietlein (Lucy Wilson), Thom Mathews (Joey), Suzanne Snyder (Brenda), Dana Ashbrook (Tom Essex), Philip Bruns (Doc Mandel).

This sequel to *The Return of the Living Dead* has nothing to do with the 1968 cult favorite *Night of the Living Dead.* It does have sloppy creatures oozing out of their graves at night to terrorize the local townsfolks. Seems for the dead, live human brains are a delicacy.

2473. *The Return of the Musketeers* (1989, Universal, GB/Fr./Span., 94m, c). P Pierre Spengler, D Richard Lester, W George MacDonald Fraser (based on *Twenty Years After* by Alexander Dumas), PH Bernard Lutic, M Jean-Claude Petit, ED John Victor Smith, PD Gil Arrondo.

LP Michael York (D'Artagnan), Oliver Reed (Athos), Frank Finlay (Porthos), C. Thomas Howell (Raoul), Kim Cattrall (Justine De Winter), Richard Chamberlain (Aramis), Philippe Noiret (Cardinal Mazarin), Roy Kinnear (Planchet), Geraldine Chaplin (The Queen), Christopher Lee (Rochefort), Euscbio Lazaro (Beaufort), Jean-Pierre Cassel (Cyrano De Bergerac), David Birkin (King Louis), Alan Howard (Oliver Cromwell).

Set 20 years after director Richard Lester's hits *The Three Musketeers* and *The Four Musketeers,* this film finds everyone older and looking very tired. Its a convoluted story of the reunited musketeers serving the widowed Queen (Geraldine Chaplin), her 10-year-old son (David Birkin), now king, and the Queen's lover and prime minister (Philippe Noiret). Somehow they must foil the plot to execute England's king by Madame de Winter's daughter (Kim Cattrall), working in league with Oliver Cromwell (Alan Howard).

2474. *The Return of the Secaucus Seven* (1980, Salsipuedes/Libra, 110m, c). P William Aydelott & Jeffrey Nelson, D&W John Sayles, PH Austin de Besche, M K. Mason Daring, ED Sayles.

LP Matt Arnold (Jeff), Gordon Clapp (Chip), Maggie Cousineau (Frances), Brian Johnston (Norman Gaddis), Adam

LeFevre (J.T.), Bruce MacDonald (Mike), Jean Passanante (Irene), Maggie Renzi (Kate), John Sayles (Howie).

In sort of a precursor to the more polished *The Big Chill,* seven friends who were activists during the 60s gather years later for a weekend reunion. It's earnest and intelligent.

2475. *The Return of the Soldier* (1983, 20th Century–Fox, GB, 102m, c). P Ann Skinner & Simon Relph, D Alan Bridges, W Hugh Whitemore (based on the novel by Rebecca West), PH Stephen Goldblatt, M Richard Rodney Bennett, ED Laurence Clark, PD Luciana Arrighi.

LP Alan Bates (Capt. Chris Baldry), Ann-Margret (Jenny), Glenda Jackson (Margaret Gray), Julie Christie (Kitty Baldry), Jeremy Kemp (Frank), Edward D. De Souza (Edward), Frank Finlay (William Grey), Jack May (Brigadier), Ian Holm (Dr. Gilbert Anderson), Emily Irvin (Jenny as a child), William Booker (Chris as a child).

In 1919, shell-shocked World War I officer Alan Bates forgets his wife Julie Christie but remembers his love for his childhood sweetheart Ann-Margret.

2476. *The Return of Swamp Thing* (1989, Millimeter Films, 86m, c). P Ben Melniker & Michael Uslan, D Jim Wynorski, W Derek Spencer & Grant Morris (based on the characters appearing in magazines published by DC Comics, Inc.), PH Zoran Hochstatter, M Chuck Cirino, ED Leslie Rosenthal, PD Robb Wilson King.

LP Louis Jourdan (Dr. Anton Arcane), Heather Locklear (Abby Arcane), Sarah Douglas (Dr. Lana Zurrell), Dick Durock (Swamp Thing), Joey Sagal (Gunn), Ace Mask (Dr. Rochelle), Chris Doyle (Leechman).

This horror is meant to be comical and on occasion succeeds. Louis Jourdan, a mad doctor who lives in a mansion on the edge of the bayou, performs unspeakable experiments in his quest to maintain his youth. Swamp Thing is all that remains of one of his former colleagues. This more-vegetable-than-man does his best to save the beautiful women fleeing Jourdan's unholy experiments. If the film sounds much like the 1982 original *Swamp Thing,* that's only because it is.

2477. *Return to Horror High* (1987, New World, 95m, c). P Mark Lisson, D Bill Froehlich, W Froehlich, Lisson, Dana Escalante & Greg H. Sims, PH Roy Wagner, M Stacy Widelitz, ED Nancy Forner, PD Greta Grigorian.

LP Lori Lethin (Callie Cassidy/Sarah/Susan), Brendan Hughes (Steven Blake), Alex Rocco (Harry Sleerik), Scott Jacoby (Josh Forbes), Andy Romano (Principal Kastleman), Richard Brestoff (Arthur Lyman [Kastleman]), Vince Edwards (Richard Birnbaum).

The murderer of several students at Crippen High was never found and now he's back. The finale is a disappointing cop-out.

2478. *Return to Oz* (1985, Buena Vista, 110m, c). P Paul Maslansky, D Walter Murch, W Murch & Gill Dennis (based on the novels *The Land of Oz* and *Ozma of Oz* by L. Frank Baum), PH David Watkin, M David Shire, ED Leslie Hodgson, PD Norman Reynolds, VE Will Vinton, Ian Wingrove, Zoran Perisic & Michael Lloyd†.

LP Fairuza Balk (Dorothy), Nicol Williamson (Dr. Worley/Nome King), Jean Marsh (Nurse Wilson/Princess Mombi), Piper Laurie (Aunt Em), Matt Clark (Uncle Henry), Michael Sundin & Tim Rose (Tik Tok), Sean Barrett (Tik Tok's voice), Mak Wilson (Billina), Denise Bryer (Billina's voice), Brian Henson (Jack Pumpkinhead's voice), Stewart Larange (Jack Pumpkinhead), Emma Ridley (Ozma), Justin Case (Scarecrow), Deep Roy (Tin Man), John Alexander (Cowardly Lion).

After returning from Oz, Dorothy is placed by Auntie Em and Uncle Henry in the care of an electroshock therapist who promises to cure her delusions about the land over the rainbow. But another natural disaster transports Dorothy back to Oz where she must confront the evil Nome King and Princess Mombi. Kids of all ages will hate it.

2479. *A Return to Salem's Lot* (1988, Warner, 95m, c). P Paul Kurta, D Larry Cohen, W Cohen & James Dixon, PH Daniel Pearl, M Michael Minard, ED Armond Lebowitz, SE Steve Neill.

LP Michael Moriarty (Joe Weber), Ricky Addison Reed (Jeremy), Samuel

Fuller (Van Meer), Andrew Duggan (Judge Axel), Evelyn Keyes (Mrs. Axel), Jill Gatsby (Sherry), June Havoc (Aunt Clara), Ronee Blakley (Sally).

Anthropologist Michael Moriarty and his estranged teenage son Ricky Addison Reed travel to Salem's Lot, Maine, to refurbish a house left to him by his aunt. To their surprise the community is the home to 300-year-old vampires who crossed the Atlantic at the same time as did the Pilgrims. Having grown rich through shrewd real estate investments they have become conservative Republicans. They drink cattle blood for substance, because human blood has become contaminated with things like AIDS. They want Moriarty to write their history and clear up all the myths about how horrible they are.

2480. *Return to Snowy River, Part II* (1988, Buena Vista, Australia, 100m, c). P&D Geoff Burrowes, W John Dixon & Burrowes, PH Keith Wagstaff, M Bruce Rowland, ED Gary Woodyard, PD Leslie Binns.

LP Tom Burlinson (Jim Craig), Sigrid Thornton (Jessica Harrison), Brian Dennehy (Harrison), Nicholas Eadie (Alistair Patton), Mark Hembrow (Seb), Bryan Marshall (Hawker), Rhys McConnochie (Patton, Sr.), Peter Cummins (Jake), Cornelia Frances (Mrs. Darcy).

While still quite a treat for the eyes, this sequel to *The Man from Snowy River* (1982) is not as good. Tom Burlinson is back, taking on villain Nicholas Eadie who has his sights set on Burlinson's beloved Sigrid Thornton.

2481. *Return to the River Kwai* (1989, Rank, GB, 98m, c). P Kurt Unger, D Andrew V. McLaglen, W Sargon Tamimi & Paul Mayersberg (based on the book by Joan and Clay Blair, Jr.), PH Arthur Wooster, M Lalo Schifrin, ED Alan Strachan, PD Michael Stringer.

LP Nick Tate (Hunt), Timothy Bottoms (Miller), George Takei (Tanaka), Edward Fox (Benford), Christopher Penn (Crawford), Richard Graham (Perry), Tatsuya Nakadai (Harada), Denholm Elliott (Grayson), Masato Nagamori (Yamashita), Etsushi Takahashi (Ozawa), Michael Dante (Davidson).

This artless action film, filled with war movie stereotypes, picks up where the classic 1957 *Bridge on the River Kwai* left off, that is with the blowing up of the bridge in enemy-occupied Thailand. The remaining prisoners, now mostly Australian, are herded by rail and sea to Japan to serve as slave labor. In the climax the POWs have taken over the Japanese ship, but it is sunk by a U.S. submarine in the South China Sea.

2482. *Reuben, Reuben* (1983, 20th Century–Fox, 101m, c). P Walter Shenson, D Robert Ellis Miller, W Julius J. Epstein† (based on the novel by Peter DeVries and the play *Spofford* by Herman Shumlin), PH Peter Stein, M Billy Goldenberg, ED Skip Lusk, PD Peter Larkin.

LP Tom Conti† (Gowan McGland), Kelly McGillis (Geneva Spofford), Roberts Blossom (Frank Spofford), Cynthia Harris (Bobby Springer), E. Katherine Kerr (Lucille Haxby), Joel Fabiani (Dr. Haxby), Kara Wilson (Edith McGland), Lois Smith (Mare Spofford), Ed Grady (Dr. Ormsby).

Tom Conti is charming as a drunken Irish poet who sponges off women. He's on a speaking tour in New England when he meets Kelly McGillis in a small community. She decides that Conti is worth saving. Her love makes him wish to turn his life around, but her dog Reuben is his undoing.

2483. *Reunion* (1989, Les Films Ariane-Fr3/Nef/CLG, Fr./West Ger./GB, 110m, c). P Anne Francois, D Jerry Schatzberg, W Harold Pinter (based on the novel by Fred Uhlman), PH Bruno de Keyzer, M Philippe Sarde, ED Martine Barraque, PD Alexandre Trauner.

LP Jason Robards (Henry Strauss), Christian Anholt (Hans Strauss), Samuel West (Konrad von Lohenburg), Francoise Fabian (Countess von Lohenburg), Maureen Kerwin (Lisa), Barbara Jefford (Mme. Strauss), Bert Parnaby (Dr. Jakob Strauss), Dorothea Alexander (Old Countess Gertrud).

This interesting English-language film is the story of two German boys, Jewish Christian Anholt and his aristocratic friend Samuel West. In 1933 Stuttgart, they witness the rise of the Nazis and the increase in anti-Semitism. The long central part of the film is framed by a contemporary narrative in which Anholt, grown to become Jason Robards, returns to Stuttgart, which he hasn't visited since 1933, to find out what has happened to his boyhood friend.

Revenge of the Innocents see South Bronx Heroes

2484. *Revenge of the Living Zombies* (1989, H&G Films, 84m, c). P&D Bill Hinzman, W Bill Randolph & Hinzman (based on a story by Hinzman), PH Simon Manses, M Erica Portnoy, ED Paul McCullough & Hinzman, SE Gerald Gergely.

LP Bill Hinzman (Flesh Eater), John Morwood (Bob), Leslie Ann Wick (Sally), Kevin Kindlin (Ralph), James J. Rutan (Eddie), Denise Morrone, Charles Kirkpatrick Acuff, Lisa Smith, Mark Strycula.

In a tribute to George Romero's *Night of the Living Dead* (1968), Bill Hinzman rises from the ground to reprise his role as "Flesh Eater." He attacks teens on Halloween, turning them into cannibalistic ghouls.

2485. *Revenge of the Nerds* (1984, 20th Century–Fox, 90m, c). P Ted Field & Peter Samuelson, D Jeff Kanew, W Steve Zacharias & Jeff Buhai (based on a story by Tim Metcalfe, Miguel Tejada-Flores, Zacharias & Buhai, PH King Baggot, M Thomas Newman, ED Alan Balsam, PD James Schoppe.

LP Robert Carradine (Lewis), Anthony Edwards (Gilbert), Tim Busfield (Poindexter), Andrew Cassese (Wormser), Curtis Armstrong (Booger), Larry B. Scott (Lamar), Brian Tochi (Takashi), Julie Montgomery (Betty), Michelle Meyrink (Judy), Ted McGinley (Stan), Donald Gibb (Ogre), Bernie Casey (U.N. Jefferson).

A group of nerdish college freshmen led by Robert Carradine get even with a fraternity of jocks which had them evicted from their dorm. For the subgenre to which this belongs, teenage college capers, it's quite a funny movie. That is if you can get around the notion that bright people are weird looking, talk funny, have poor eyesight and coordina-tion, and lack common sense; while the college in-crowd consists of good-looking, athletic clods, who get all the great-looking women.

2486. *Revenge of the Nerds II: Nerds in Paradise* (1987, 20th Century–Fox, 92m, c). P Ted Field, Robert Cort & Peter Bart, D Joe Roth, W Dan Guntzelman & Steve Marshall (Based on characters created by Tim Metcalfe, Miguel Tejada-Flores, Steve Zacharias & Jeff Buhai), PH Charles Correll, M Mark Mothersbaugh & Gerald V. Casale, ED Richard Chew, PD Trevor Williams.

LP Robert Carradine (Lewis Skolnick), Curtis Armstrong (Dudley "Booger" Dawson), Larry B. Scott (Lamar Latrelle), Timothy Busfield (Arnold Poindexter), Courtney Thorne-Smith (Sunny Carstairs), Andrew Cassese (Harold Wormser), Donald Gibb (Ogre), Bradley Whitford (Roger), Ed Lauter (Buzz), Anthony Edwards (Gilbert).

The nerds, geeky as ever, attend the National United Fraternity Conference at Fort Lauderdale. The manager of the hotel at which they are registered tries just about any dirty trick to get them out of his hotel.

2487. *Revenge of the Ninja* (1983, MGM/United Artists/Cannon, 88m, c). P Menahem Golan & Yoram Globus, D Sam Firstenberg, W James R. Silke, PH David Gurfinkel, M Rob Walsh, W. Michael Lewis & Laurin Rinder, ED Mark Helfrich & Michael J. Duthie, SE Joe Quinlivan.

LP Sho Kosugi (Cho), Keith Vitali (Dave), Virgil Frye (Lt. Dime), Arthur Roberts (Braden), Mario Gallo (Caifano), Grace Oshita (Grandmother), Ashley Ferrare (Cathy), Kane Kosugi (Kane), John LaMotta (Joe).

Ninja Sho Kosugi is in Los Angeles, hoping to put his bloody past behind him. Unfortunately, he gets mixed up with drug trafficker Arthur Roberts, an American Ninja, who is his archenemy.

2488. *Revenge Squad* (1983, Comworld, 94m, c, aka *Hit and Run*). P&D Charles Braverman, W Don Enright (based on the novel *80 Dollars to Stamford* by Lucille Fletcher), PH Tony Mitchell, M Brad Fiedel, ED Dale Beldin, PD Paul Eads.

LP Paul Perri (David Marks), Claudia Cron (Diana Douglas), Will Lee (Joseph Kahn), Bart Braverman (Jerry Ramundi).

Manhattan cab driver Paul Perri is haunted by recurring flashbacks of the freakish hit-and-run accident that took his wife's life.

2489. *Revolution* (1985, Warner, 125m, c). P Irwin Winkler, D Hugh Hudson, W Robert Dillon, PH Bernard Lutic, M John Corigliano, ED Stuart Baird, PD Assheton Gorton.

LP Al Pacino (Tom Dobb), Donald Sutherland (Sgt. Maj. Peasy), Nastassja Kinski (Daisy McConnahay), Joan Plowright (Mrs. McConnahay), Dave King (Mr. McConnahay), Steven Berkoff (Sgt. Jones), John Wells (Corty), Annie Lennox (Liberty Woman), Dexter Fletcher (Ned Dobb), Sid Owen (Young Ned).

Living in the colonies, Scottish trapper Al Pacino is caught up in the American Revolution. This would-be epic film fails on just about every level. Somehow, films about the American Revolution don't seem to attract audiences. Maybe it's not the subject, but as in this case, the poor quality of the stories and performances.

2490. *Rhinestone* (1984, 20th Century-Fox, 111m, c). P Howard Smith, Marvin Worth, Bill Blake & Richard M. Spitalny, D Bob Clark, W Phil Alden Robinson & Sylvester Stallone (based on the song "Rhinestone Cowboy" by Larry Weiss, story by Robinson), PH Timothy Galfas, M Mike Post, ED Stan Cole & John Wheeler, PD Robert Boyle.

LP Sylvester Stallone (Nick), Dolly Parton (Jake), Richard Farnsworth (Noah), Ron Leibman (Freddie), Tim Thomerson (Barnett), Steven Apostle Pec (Father), Penny Santon (Mother), Russell Buchanan (Elgart).

Dolly Parton brags that she can turn anyone into a country and western singer. Her bluff is called and she must put up or shut up when faced with turning sow's ear cabbie Sylvester Stallone into a silk purse Conway Twitty.

2491. *Rich and Famous* (1981, MGM/ United Artists, 117m, c). P William Allyn, D George Cukor, W Gerald Ayres (based on the play *Old Acquaintance* by John Van Druten), PH Don Peterman, M Georges Delerue, ED John F. Burnett, PD Jan Scott.

LP Jacqueline Bisset (Liz Hamilton), Candice Bergen (Merry Noel Blake), David Selby (Doug Blake), Hart Bochner (Chris Adams), Steven Hill (Jules Levi), Meg Ryan (Debby at 18), Matt Lattanzi (Jim as a boy), Daniel Faraldo (Ginger Trinidad), Nicole Eggert (Debby at 8).

This film is a contemporary sexed-up remake of the bitchy production *Old Acquaintance* (1943), which starred wild cats Bette Davis and Miriam Hopkins as two novelists who interfere in each other's lives over a period of many years. In the modern version, Jacqueline Bisset and Candice Bergen meet at Smith in 1959. A decade later their paths cross once again. Bisset is an acclaimed but unsold novelist. She gives Bergen some advice which helps the latter become a Jackie Collins–like success writing trashy novels. It's talky and not very good talk.

2492. *Richard's Things* (1981, New World, GB, 104m, c). P Mark Shivas, D Anthony Harvey, W Frederic Raphael (based on his novel), PH Freddie Young, M Georges Delerue, ED Lesley Walker, AD Ian Whittaker.

LP Liv Ullmann (Kate), Amanda Redman (Josie), Tim Pigott-Smith (Peter), Elizabeth Spriggs (Mrs. Sells), David Markham (Morris), Mark Eden (Richard), Gwen Taylor (Margaret), John Vine (Dr. Mace).

After a man's death, his wife Liv Ullmann and mistress Amanda Redman (with whom he was making love when he suffered a fatal heart attack) find love and comfort in each other's arms.

2493. *Ricky* (1988, Tapeworm, 90m, c). P,D&W Bill Naud, PH David Golia, M Joel Goldsmith, ED Naud.

LP Michael Michaud (Ricky Wanero), Maggie Hughes (Angela), James Herbert, Lane Montano, Peter Zellers, Jon Chaney, Brent Beckett.

Filmed in 1983, this spoof of *Rocky* features Michael Michaud as a boxer who's given up the sport to please his girl, but still would like a shot at the champ.

2494. *Riddle of the Sands* (1984, Rank, GB, 102m, c). P Drummond

Challis, D Tony Maylam, W Maylam & John Bailey (based on the novel by Erskine Childers), PH Christopher Challis, M Howard Blake, ED Peter Hollywood, AD Terry Pritchard.

LP Michael York (Charles Carruthers), Jenny Agutter (Clara Dollman), Simon MacCorkindale (Arthur Davies), Alan Badel (Dollmann), Jurgen Andersen (Von Bruning), Olga Lowe (Frau Dollman), Hans Meyer (Grimm).

Made in 1979, the film was released in the U.S. in 1984. It's based on the novel considered the forerunner of the modern espionage novel. In 1901 yachtsman Simon MacCorkindale learns of a plot by the Kaiser to invade England. He enlists his college chum Michael York to foil the plan.

Riders of the Storm see The American Way

2495. *Riding High* (1981, Enterprise, GB, 96m, c). P Michael & Tony Klinger, D Derek Ford, W Ross Cramer (based on a story by Ford), PH Brian Tufano, M Paul Fishman, ED John Jympson.

LP Eddie Kidd (Dave Munday), Irene Handl (Gran), Marella Oppenheim (Zoro), Murray Salem (Marvin Ravensdorf), Bill Mitchell (Judas S. Charriot), Zoot Money (Dorking), Paul Humpoletz (Gelt), Lynda Bellingham (Miss Mott).

Motorcyclist Eddie Kidd becomes a stunt rider.

2496. *Riding the Edge* (1989, Trans-World, 95m, c). P Wolf Schmidt, D James Fargo, W Ronald A. Suppa, PH Bernard Salzmann, M Michael Gibbs, ED James Ruxin, PD James Shanahan.

LP Raphael Sbarge (Matt Harman), Catherine Mary Stewart (Maggie Kemp), Peter Haskell (Dean Stradling), Lyman Ward (Dr. Harman), Asher Sarfati (Moussa), Benny Bruchim (Boy), Michael Sarne (Kroll), Nili Zomer (Karima).

When terrorists in North Africa kidnap Lyman Ward, they demand that his son Raphael Sbarge act as a courier. The youth is to deliver a secret microprocessor in exchange for his father. Sbarge teams up with secret agent Catherine Mary Stewart and an Arab princeling to rescue dear old dad without giving up the hardware.

2497. *Rigged* (1985, CineStar, 94m, c). P K.A. Roberson, Jr., D C.M. Cutry, W John Goff (based on the novel *Hit and Run* by James Hadley Chase), PH Eddy Van Der Enden, M Brian Banks & Anthony Marinelli, ED John R. Bowen.

LP Ken Roberson (Mason Morgan), Pamela Bryant (Monique), George Kennedy (Benjamin Wheeler), Dene Hofteizer Anton (Cheryl), John Goff (West), Ramon Gonzales Cuevas (Lopez).

Rigger Ken Roberson learns of oil baron George Kennedy's plot to import not only petroleum from Venezuela but cocaine as well. This information and his overly friendly ways with Kennedy's girlfriend Pamela Bryant, mark Roberson for extermination.

2498. *The Right Hand Man* (1987, New World, Australia, 101m, c). P Steven Grives, Tom Oliver & Basil Appleby, D Di Drew, W Helen Hodgman (based on the novel by Kathleen Peyton), PH Peter James, M Alan Zavod, ED Don Saunders, PD Neil Angwin.

LP Rupert Everett (Harry Ironminster), Hugo Weaving (Ned Devine), Arthur Dignam (Dr. Redbridge), Jennifer Claire (Lady Ironminster), Catherine McClements (Sarah Redbridge), Ralph Cotterill (Sam), Adam Cockburn (Violet Head), Tim Eliott (Lord Ironminster).

Rupert Everett, the wealthy diabetic heir to a 1860 Australian fortune, goes into a coma while driving the family buggy. As a result his father is killed and Everett loses an arm. His domineering mother blames Everett for the death of her husband, causing the young man to become deeply depressed. Everett hires Hugo Weaving to be his righthand man, to run his estate and even to be the surrogate father of his children, as he is unwilling to risk bringing diabetic children into the world.

2499. *The Right Stuff*† (1983, Warner, 192m, c). P Irwin Winkler & Robert Chartoff, D&W Philip Kaufman (based on the book by Tom Wolfe), PH Caleb Deschanel†, M Bill Conti*, ED Glenn Farr, Lisa Fruchtman, Stephen A. Rotter, Tom Rolf & Douglas Stewart*, PD Geoffrey Kirkland, AD/SD Kirkland, Richard J. Lawrence, W. Stewart Campbell, Peter Romero, Pat Pending &

George R. Nelson†, SOUND Mark Berger, Tom Scott, Randy Thom & David MacMillan*, SE ED Jay Boekelheide*.

LP Sam Shepard† (Chuck Yeager), Scott Glenn (Alan Shepard), Ed Harris (John Glenn), Dennis Quaid (Gordon Cooper), Fred Ward (Gus Grissom), Barbara Hershey (Glennis Yeager), Kim Stanley (Bancho Barnes), Veronica Cartwright (Betty Grissom), Pamela Reed (Trudy Cooper), Scott Paulin (Deke Slayton), Charles Frank (Scott Carpenter), Lance Henriksen (Wally Schirra), Donald Moffat (Lyndon B. Johnson), Levon Helm (Jack Ridley), Mary Jo Deschanel (Annie Glenn).

The film is a reasonably gripping examination of the Mercury Space program, which consisted of the first men recruited and trained to become astronauts. It also is the story of test pilot Chuck Yeager (Sam Shepard), who took aviation to new heights within the earth's atmosphere.

2500. *Rikky and Pete* (1988, MGM/United Artists, Australia, 101m, c). P Nadia Tass & David Parker, D Tass, W Parker (based on a story by Parker), PH Parker, M Phil Judd & Eddie Raynor, ED Ken Sallows, PD Josephine Ford.

LP Stephen Kearney (Pete), Nina Landis (Rikky), Tetchie Agbayani (Flossie), Bill Hunter (Whitstead), Bruno Lawrence (Sonny), Bruce Spence (Ben), Dorothy Alison (Mrs. Menzies), Don Reid (Mr. Menzies), Lewis Fitz-gerald (Adam), Peter Cummins (Delahunty).

This quirky comedy-drama features Stephen Kearney as a Melbourne genius of Rube Goldberg–like inventions. His sister Nina Landis is trying to find herself. Together they flee in their mother's Bentley to a remote mining village. Before long, his inventions and her resourcefulness set them up in business for themselves, each finding romance in the bargain.

2501. *The Rise and Fall of Idi Amin* (1981, Intermedia, GB/Kenya, 105m, c, aka *Amin — The Rise and Fall*). P Sharad Patel & Christopher Sutton, D Patel, W Wade Huie, PH Harvey Harrison, M Christopher Gunning, ED Keith Palmer.

LP Joseph Olita (Idi Amin), Geoffrey

Keen (High Commissioner), Denis Hills (Himself), Leonard Trolley (Bob Astles), Andre Maranne (Ambassador), Diane Mercier (Wife), Tony Sibbald (Commissioner Davis), Thomas Baptiste (Dr. Michael Oloya), Louis Mahoney (Ofumbi).

This purports to be the true story of the 1971–78 reign of a soldier who proclaimed himself president of Uganda. He ruled by genocide, using most cruel and horrible ways of torturing and killing any who opposed him.

2502. *Rising Damp* (1980, Black Lion/ITC, GB, 98m, c). P Roy Skeggs, D John McGrath, W Eric Chappell (based on the TV series by Chappell), PH Frank Watts, M David Lindup, ED Peter Weatherley.

LP Leonard Rossiter (Rigsby), Frances de la Tour (Miss Jones), Denholm Elliott (Seymour), Don Warrington (Philip), Christopher Strauli (John), Carrie Jones (Sandra), Glynn Edwards (Cooper), John Cater (Bert).

In this comedy, landlord Leonard Rossiter attempts to woo stand-offish spinster Frances de la Tour.

2503. *Rising Storm* (1989, Gibraltar, 96m, c, aka *Rebel Waves*). P Jay Davidson & James Buchfuehrer, D Francis Schaeffer, W Gary Rosen & William Fay, PH Robb D. Hinds, M Julian Laxton, ED Alan Baumgarten.

LP Zach Galligan (Artie Gage), Wayne Crawford (Joe Gage), June Chadwick (Mila Hart), John Rhys-Davies (Don Waldo), Elizabeth Keifer (Blaise Hart), Graham Clark (Lt. Ulmer).

In the year 2009, what's left of the U.S. is ruled by a totalitarian theocracy headed by an oily television evangelist. Just out of jail, brothers Zach Galligan and Wayne Crawford team with blond sisters June Chadwick and Elizabeth Keifer. They are being chased by villain John Rhys-Davies who enjoys sadistically torturing his victims.

2504. *Risky Business* (1983, Warner, 98m, c). P Jon Avnet & Steve Tisch, D&W Paul Brickman, PH Reynaldo Villalobos & Bruce Surtees, M Tangerine Dream, ED Richard Chew, PD William J. Cassidy.

LP Tom Cruise (Joel), Rebecca De

Morney (Lana), Joe Pantoliano (Guido), Richard Masur (Rutherford), Bronson Pinchot (Barry), Curtis Armstrong (Miles), Nicholas Pryor (Joel's Father), Janet Carroll (Joel's Mother), Shera Danese (Vicki), Raphael Sbarge (Glenn), Bruce A. Young (Jackie).

Tom Cruise became a star after this appearance as a 17-year-old Chicago youngster left in charge of his parents' luxurious house while they are off on a vacation. As soon as they are out of sight, honor student Cruise is no longer honor-bright. Before long his home is filled with prostitutes, pimps and customers — providing our young man with a lucrative business. His dancing in his BVD's didn't hurt his career as far as female members of the audience were concerned.

2505. *Rita, Sue and Bob Too!* (1987, Orion Classics, GB, 95m, c). P Sandy Lieberson & Patsy Pollock, D Alan Clarke, W Andrea Dunbar (based on her plays *The Arbor* and *Rita, Sue and Bob Too!*), PH Ivan Strasburg, M Michael Kamen, ED Stephen Singleton, AD Len Huntingford.

LP Michelle Holmes (Sue), Siobhan Finneran (Rita), George Costigan (Bob), Lesley Sharp (Michelle), Willie Ross (Sue's Father), Patti Nicholls (Sue's Mother), Kulvinder Ghir (Aslam), Paul Oldham (Lee), Bryan Heeley (Michael).

Hefty teenagers Michelle Holmes and Siobhan Finneran babysit for George Costigan and his frigid wife Lesley Sharp. Rather than take them home at the end of the evening, Costigan drives the girls to the Moors where he rather easily convinces them to have sex with him. This cozy arrangement is continued, until Sharp grows wise, and takes the children and leaves Costigan. He's not too broken up, inviting Holmes and Finneran to move in with him, which they do.

Rituals *see* ***The Creeper***

2506. *The River* (1984, Universal, 122m, c). P Edward Lewis & Robert Cortes, D Mark Rydell, W Robert Dillon & Julian Barry (based on a story by Dillon), PH Vilmos Zsigmond†, M John Williams†, ED Sidney Levin, PD Charles Rosen, SOUND Nick Alphin, Robert Thirlwell, Richard Portman & David Ronne†.

LP Mel Gibson (Tom Garvey), Sissy Spacek† (Mae Garvey), Shane Bailey (Lewis Garvey), Becky Jo Lynch (Beth Garvey), Scott Glenn (Joe Wade), Don Hood (Sen. Neiswinder), Billy Green Bush (Harve Stanley), James Tolkan (Howard Simpson), Bob W. Douglas (Hal Richardson), Andy Stahl (Dave Birkin), Lisa Sloan (Judy Birkin).

Husband and wife team Mel Gibson and Sissy Spacek struggle to save the family farm from the bank, developers, the elements and a wide assortment of other trials and challenges. It was a banner year for films featuring hard working farmers, their families and assorted tribulations.

2507. *River of Death* (1989, Cannon, 100m, c). P Harry Alan Towers & Avi Lerner, D Steve Carver, W Andrew Deutsch & Edward Simpson (based on a novel by Alistair MacLean), PH Avi Karpick, M Sasha Matson, ED Ken Bornstein.

LP Michael Dudikoff (John Hamilton), Robert Vaughn (Dr. Mantueffel), Donald Pleasence (Heinrich Spaatz), Herbert Lom (Col. Diaz), L.Q. Jones (Hiller), Cynthia Erland (Maria), Sarah Maur Thorp (Anna), Foziah Davidson (Dahlia), Ian Yule (Long John).

When his pretty client Sarah Maur Thorp is captured in the Amazon jungle by cannibals, guide Michael Dudikoff puts together a motley crew to fetch her back. For most, the interest in the missing girl is secondary to reaching a lost city.

2508. *The River Rat* (1984, Paramount, 93m, c). P Bob Larson, D&W Tom Rickman, PH Jan Keisser, M Mike Post, ED Dennis Virkler, PD John J. Lloyd.

LP Tommy Lee Jones (Billy), Martha Plimpton (Jonsy), Brian Dennehy (Doc), Shawn Smith (Wexel), Nancy Lea Owen (Vadie), Norman Bennett (Sheriff Cal), Tony Frank (Polcy), Angie Bolling (Joyce), Roger Copeland (Young Billy).

Ex-convict Tommy Lee Jones is reunited with his young daughter Martha Plimpton along the Mississippi River after wrongly spending 13 years in prison. She teaches him the value of love.

2509. *Riverbend* (1989, Intercontinental/Vandale, 100m, c). P Sam Vance,

D Sam Firstenberg, W Vance, PH Ken Lamkin, M Paul Loomis, ED Marcus Manton.

LP Steve James (Major Quinton), Margaret Avery (Bell), Tony Frank (Sheriff Jake), Julius Tennon (Tony), Alex Morris (Butch), Vanessa Tate (Pauline), T.J. Kennedy (Capt. Monroe). The time is 1966, the place is Riverbend, Georgia. Three black soldiers, headed by Steve James, have escaped from MPs taking them to a court martial for failing to follow orders in Vietnam. The escapees help the local blacks train themselves to face the cruel white folk, led by evil sheriff Tony Frank. The new allies take over the town and focus media attention on the hotspot. Both the injustices visited on the black people of the town and the unfairness to James and his buddies are placed in the spotlight.

2510. *River's Edge* (1987, Hemdale/Island, 99m, c). P Sarah Pillsbury, Midge Sanford & David Streit, D Tim Hunter, W Neal Jimenez, PH Frederick Elmes, M Jurgen Knieper, ED Howard Smith & Sonya Sones, PD John Muto.

LP Crispin Glover (Layne), Keanu Reeves (Matt), Ione Skye Leitch (Clarissa), Daniel Roebuck (Samson "John" Tollette), Dennis Hopper (Feck), Joshua Miller (Tim), Roxana Zal (Maggie), Josh Richman (Tony), Phil Brock (Mike), Tom Bower (Bennett), Constance Forslund (Madeleine), Leo Rossi (Jim). Based on an actual incident, this is the frightening story of a closely-knit group of teenagers who do not divulge that one of their numbers has killed a girlfriend. They visit her body which lies near the river's edge, but are able to find a way to blame the poor dead girl, rather than their friend.

2511. *Roadgames* (1981, Avco Embassy, Australia, 101m, c). P Barbi Taylor & Richard Franklin, D Franklin, W Everett DeRoche, PH Vincent Monton, M Brian May, ED Edward McQueen-Mason, PD/AD Jon Dowding.

LP Stacy Keach (Pat Quid), Jamie Lee Curtis (Hitch/Pamela), Marion Edward (Frita Frugal), Grant Page (Smith or Jones), Thaddeus Smith (Abbott), Bill Stacey (Capt. Careful), Stephen Millichamp (Costello).

Long-distance truck driver Stacy Keach unwittingly picks up a murderer on the run. The killer targets truck drivers.

Road Gangs *see* ***Spacehunter: Adventures in the Forbidden Zone***

2512. *Road House* (1989, MGM/United Artists, 114m, c). P Joel Silver, D Rowdy Herrington, W David Lee Henry & Hilary Henkin (based on a story by Henry), PH Dean Cundey, M Michael Kamen, ED Frank Urioste & John Link.

LP Patrick Swayze (Dalton), Kelly Lynch (Doc), Sam Elliott (Wade Garrett), Ben Gazzara (Brad Wesley), Marshall Teague (Jimmy), Julie Michaels (Denise), Red West (Red Webster), Sunshine Parker (Emmet). Patrick Swayze, the heartthrob from *Dirty Dancing,* is stuck in a turkey. He plays a loner hired to clean up a bar, frequented by lowlifes and bikers. The film degenerates into an endless round of fistfights and a little gratuitous nudity with leggy local doctor Kelly Lynch.

Road Trip *see* ***Jacks***

2513. *The Road Warrior* (1982, Warner, Australia, 94m, c, aka *Mad Max II*). P Byron Kennedy, D George Miller, W Terry Hayes, Miller & Brian Hannat, PH Dean Semler, M Brian May, ED David Stiven, Tim Wellburn & Michael Chirgwin, AD Graham Walker.

LP Mel Gibson (Max), Bruce Spence (Gyro Captain), Vernon Wells (Wez), Emil Minty (Feral Kid), Mike Preston (Pappagallo), Kjell Nilsson (Humungus), Virginia Hey (Warrior Woman), Syd Heylen (Curmudgeon), Moira Claux (Big Rebecca), David Slingsby (Quiet Man). In this action-filled sequel to *Mad Max,* Mel Gibson is the only one who can save terrorized pilgrims, barricaded in a desert commune. They are beseiged by punk villains after their primitive oil refinery.

2514. *Roadhouse 66* (1984, Atlantic, 90m, c). P Scott M. Rosenfelt & Mark Levinson, D John Mark Robinson, W Galen Lee & George Simpson (based on a story by Lee), PH Tom Ackerman, M Gary Scott, ED Jay Lash Cassidy, PD Chester Kaczenski.

LP Willem Dafoe (Johnny Harte), Judge Reinhold (Beckman Hallsgood,

Jr.), Kaaren Lee (Jesse Duran), Kate Vernon (Melissa Duran), Stephen Elliott (Sam), Alan Autry (Hoot), Kevyn Major Howard (Dink), Peter Van Norden (Moss), Erica Yohn (Thelma).

Hitchhiker Willem Dafoe and Ivy Leaguer Judge Reinhold are stuck overnight in an Arizona town while their car is being repaired. They enter their 1955 T-bird in a drag race and fall in love with a couple of local girls. It's not as exciting as it sounds.

2515. *Roadie* (1980, United Artists, 105m, c). P Carolyn Pfeiffer, D Alan Rudolph, W Big Boy Medlin & Michael Ventura (based on a story by Medlin, Ventura, Rudolph & Zalman King), PH David Myers, M Craig Hundley, ED Carol Littleton & Tom Walls, PD Paul Peters.

LP Meatloaf (Travis W. Redfish), Kaki Hunter (Lola Bouilliabase), Art Carney (Corpus C. Redfish), Gailard Sartain (B.B. Muldoon), Don Cornelius (Mohammed Johnson), Rhonda Bates (Alice Poo), Richard Marion (George).

Roadie Meatloaf and Kaki Hunter (you remember her, she was the good-time had by all in the *Porky's* series) waste nearly two hours of audiences' time trying to meet Alice Cooper.

2516. *Roadkill* (1989, Cinephile, Canada, 80m, b&w). P Bruce McDonald & Colin Brunton, D McDonald, W Don McKellar, PH Miroslaw Baszak, M Nash the Slash, ED Mike Munn.

LP Valerie Buhagiar (Ramona), Gerry Quigley (Roy Seth), Larry Hudson (Buddie), Bruce McDonald (Bruce Shack), Shaun Bowring (Matthew), Don McKellar (Russel), Mark Tarantino (Luke).

Compliant Valerie Buhagiar, an employee of a big time rock promoter, is sent from Toronto to northern Ontario to track down a missing touring band. Unable to drive, she takes a cab. Her driver promptly strands her. Her on-the-road experiences include meeting an intinerant documentary film director, a would-be serial killer and a 15-year-old country boy who seduces her.

2517. *Robbers of the Sacred Mountain* (1982, Heller Prods., Canada, 97m, c, aka *Falcon's Gold*). P Keith Rothman, D Bob Schulz, W Olaf Pooley & Walter Bell, PH Laszlo George, M Lalo Schifrin, ED Ralph Brunjes, PD Dave Davis.

LP John Marley (Dr. Falcon), Simon MacCorkindale (Hank Richards), Louise Vallance (Tracey Falcon), Blanca Guerra (B.G. Alvarez), George Touliatos (Murdoch), Jorge Reynoso (Marques).

The late John Marley stars as an archaeologist called from an Arabian dig to Mexico. His expertise is needed to identify a fertility goddess statuette, part of a fabulous treasure lost in a 1645 earthquake. The film resembles *Raiders of the Lost Ark* in numerous ways, unfortunately not in the quality of the acting.

2518. *Robbery Under Arms* (1985, ITC, Australia, 141m, c). P Jock Blair, D Ken Hannam & Donald Crombie, W Graeme Koestveld & Tony Morphett (based on the novel by Rolf Boldrewood), PH Ernest Clark, M Garry McDonald & Laurie Stone, ED Andrew Prowse, PD George Liddle.

LP Sam Neill (Capt. Starlight), Steven Vidler (Dick Marston), Christopher Cummins (Jim Marston), Liz Newman (Gracey), Deborah Coulls (Kate), Susie Lindeman (Jeannie), Tommy Lewis (Warrigal), Ed Devereux (Ben Marston).

The story of Australian highwayman Capt. Starlight and two farming brothers who join his gang has been filmed four times before. It still isn't much to see.

2519. *Robocop* (1987, Orion, 103m, c). P Arne Schmidt, D Paul Verhoeven, W Edward Neumeier & Michael Miner, PH Jost Vacano, M Basil Poledouris, ED Frank J. Urioste†, PD William Sandell, SOUND Michael J. Kohut, Carlos de Larios, Aaron Rochin & Robert Wald†.

LP Peter Weller (Alex J. Murphy/ Robocop), Nancy Allen (Anne Lewis), Ronny Cox (Richard "Dick" Jones), Kurtwood Smith (Clarence J. Boddicker), Miguel Ferrer (Robert Morton), Robert DoQui (Sgt. Reed), Daniel O'Herlihy (The Old Man), Ray Wise (Leon Nash).

In a crime-ridden, corrupt Detroit of the future, a large corporation has assumed responsibility for policing the city. Peter Weller, a brave cop killed in the line of duty, is transformed into a cyborg (half-man, half-robot), designed to be a superinforcer of the law. In reality, Robocop is merely a pawn of the internecine struggles of executives in the corporation. The latter hadn't counted on the human part of Robocop assuming control.

2520. *Robot Holocaust* (1987, Wizard Video-Infinity, 79m, c). P Cynthia DePaula, D&W Tim Kincaid, PH Arthur D. Marks, ED Barry Zetlin, PD Medusa, SE Jeremie Frank, Ralph Cordero & Valarie McNeill.

LP Norris Culf (Neo), Nadine Hart (Deeja), Joel Von Ornsteiner (Klyton), Jennifer Delora (Myta), Andrew Howarth (Kai), Angelika Jager (Valaria), Rick Gianasi (Torque), Michael Dowend (Jorn), George Gray (Bray).

Millions of servant robots have revolted, with the result that humans are nearly extinct. Those remaining are slaves of the "Dark One" who control them by poisoning the atmosphere. But if you could keep good men and women down forever, there wouldn't be an excuse for this movie, would there? Now there's a thought.

2521. *Rock & Rule* (1983, Canada Trust Co., Canada, animated, 85m, c). D Clive A. Smith, M Lou Reed, Iggy Pop, Debbie Harry, Cheap Trick.

VOICES Don Francks, Paul Le Mat, Susan Roman, Sam Langevin, Catherine O'Hara.

This animated rock and roll fantasy is from Canada's Nelvana animation studio. The music is good, the humor is adult, and there is no story to speak of.

2522. *Rock 'n' Roll Nightmare* (1987, Shapiro, Canada, 83m, c, aka *The Edge of Hell*). P Jon-Miki Thor, D John Fasano, W Thor, PH Mark MacKay, ED Robert Williams, AD Wolfgang Siebert, M/L Various Artists.

LP Jon-Miki Thor (John Triton), Jillian Peri (Lou Anne), Frank Dietz (Roger Eburt), Dave Lane (Max), Teresa Simpson (Randy), Clara Pater (Mother), Jesse D'Angelo (Little Boy), Chris Finkel (Father), Liane Abel (Mary).

When a hot new rock 'n' roll group takes their sexy young girlfriends to an out of the way farm for a fun weekend, they didn't count on terror.

2523. *Rocket Gibralter* (1988, Columbia, 100m, c). P Jeff Weiss & Marcus Viscidi, D Daniel Petrie, W Amos Poe, PH Jost Vacano, M Andrew Powell, ED Melody London, PD Bill Groom.

LP Burt Lancaster (Levi Rockwell), Suzy Amis (Aggie Rockwell), Patricia Clarkson (Rose Black), Frances Conroy (Ruby Hanson), Sinead Cusack (Amanda "Billi" Rockwell), John Glover (Rolo Rockwell), Bill Pullman (Crow Black), Kevin Spacey (Dwayne Hanson), John Bell (Orson Rockwell).

The family of Burt Lancaster gathers for his 77th birthday at his Coastal Long Island estate. His children love but don't understand the dying old man. His grandchildren resolve to give him what they think he wants, a Viking funeral. When he dies without his children noting his passing, the youngest generation haul his corpse down to the water, and lovingly place it in an old boat, the Rocket Gibralter, which they had prepared for the event. They set the vessel adrift and shoot burning arrows into it. You may find a tear or two in your eyes at this point.

2524. *Rocky III* (1982, MGM/United Artists, 99m, c). P Irwin Winkler & Robert Chartoff, D&W Sylvester Stallone, PH Bill Butler, M Bill Conti, ED Don Zimmerman & Mark Warner, PD William J. Cassidy, M/L "Eye of the Tiger" by Jim Peterik & Frankie Sullivan, III†.

LP Sylvester Stallone (Rocky Balboa), Carl Weathers (Apollo Creed), Mr. T (Clubber Lang), Talia Shire (Adrian Balboa), Burt Young (Paulie), Burgess Meredith (Mickey), Ian Fried (Rocky, Jr.), Hulk Hogan (Thunderlips), Al Silvani (Al).

Would you believe that someone could be found to make Rocky Balboa look bright? Well just take a look at brutal loud-mouthed slugger Clubber Lang played by that fine thespian Mr. T. He beats our hero in the ring the first time, but we know that Sylvester Stallone's character has to take several shots to the head before one has his attention. Watch out for that rematch, Mr. T.

2525. *Rocky IV* (1985, MGM/United Artists, 91m, c). P Irwin Winkler &

Robert Chartoff, D&W Sylvester Stallone, PH Bill Butler, M Vince DiCola & Bill Conti, ED Don Zimmerman & John W. Wheeler, PD Bill Kenney.

LP Sylvester Stallone (Rocky Balboa), Talia Shire (Adrian Balboa), Burt Young (Paulie), Carl Weathers (Apollo Creed), Brigitte Nielsen (Ludmilla), Tony Burton (Duke), Michael Pataki (Nicoli Koloff), Dolph Lundgren (Drago).

The Russian champion, blond cold-blooded giant Dolph Lundgren, who looks like a perfect Aryan Nazi, kills Carl Weathers in an exhibition match. Sylvester Stallone wraps the flag around himself and goes through intense training so he can climb into the ring and wipe up the floor with the dirty commie killer. Statuesque Brigitte Nielsen, briefly Stallone's wife, appears as Lundgren's wife and keeper.

2526. *Roller Blade* (1986, New World, 97m, c). P,D&PH Donald G. Jackson, W Jackson & Randall Frakes (based on a story by Jackson), M Robert Garrett, ED Ron Amick.

LP Suzanne Solari (Sister Sharon Cross), Jeff Hutchinson (Marshall Goodman), Shaun Michelle (Hunter/Sister Fortune), Katina Garner (Mother Speed), Sam Mann (Waco), Robby Taylor (Deputy/Dr. Saticoy).

In a postholocaust world, a group of Amazons use martial arts and mysticism to battle the forces of evil.

2527. *Rolling Vengeance* (1988, Apollo, 90m, c). P&D Steven H. Stern, W Michael Montgomery, PH Laszlo George, M Phil Marshall, ED Ron Wisman, AD Harold Thrasher.

LP Don Michael Paul (Joey Rosso), Lawrence Dane (Big Joe), Ned Beatty (Tiny Doyle), Susan Hogan (Big Joe's Wife), Lisa Howard (Misty), Barclay Hope (Steve), Todd Duckworth (Vic Doyle), Michael J. Reynolds (Lt. Sly).

When his family is killed and his girlfriend raped, trucker Don Michael Paul builds an 8-ton killing machine with 73-inch tires and a 600 horsepower engine. Then he sets out to take revenge against nasty redneck Ned Beatty, the latter's rotten family, and all their vehicles.

2528. *Rollover* (1981, Warner, 118m, c). P Bruce Gilbert, D Alan J. Pakula, W David Shaber (based on a story by Shaber, Howard Kohn & David Weir), PH Giuseppe Rotunno & William Garroni, M Michael Small, ED Evan Lottman, PD George Jenkins & John Jay Moore.

LP Jane Fonda (Lee Winters), Kris Kristofferson (Hub Smith), Hume Cronyn (Maxwell Emery), Josef Sommer (Roy Lefcourt), Bob Gunton (Sal Naftari), Macon McCalman (Mr. Fewster), Ron Frazier (Gil Hovey), Jodi Long (Betsy Okamoto), Crocker Nevin (Warner Ackerman).

Jane Fonda, the widow of a murdered bank president, becomes involved with banker Kris Kristofferson. The two are caught up in a high-powered Arab investment plot. The plot is so complex, it's difficult to know what's going on.

2529. *Romancing the Stone* (1984, 20th Century–Fox, 105m, c). P Michael Douglas, D Robert Zemeckis, W Diane Thomas, PH Dean Cundey, M Alan Silvestri, ED Donn Cambern & Frank Morriss†, PD Lawrence G. Paull.

LP Michael Douglas (Jack Colton), Kathleen Turner (Joan Wilder), Danny DeVito (Ralph), Zack Norman (Ira), Alfonso Arau (Juan), Manuel Ojeda (Zolo), Holland Taylor (Gloria), Mary Ellen Trainor (Elaine), Eve Smith (Mrs. Irwin), Kym Herrin (Angelina), Bill Burton (Jessie), Ted White (Grogan).

When she is forced to go to Colombia to rescue her kidnapped sister, best-selling romance novelist Kathleen Turner finds herself living the exciting, dangerous and romantic life of one of her heroines. She teams up with handsome hunter Michael Douglas. Together they encounter various villains, including the hilarious Danny De Vito, who wish to get hold of a treasure map she unwittingly possesses. It's all good boisterous fun.

2530. *Romantic Comedy* (1983, MGM/United Artists, 103m, c). P Walter Mirisch & Morton Gottlieb, D Arthur Hiller, W Bernard Slade (based on his play), PH David M. Walsh, M Marvin Hamlisch, ED John C. Howard, PD Alfred Sweeney.

LP Dudley Moore (Jason), Mary Steenburgen (Phoebe), Frances Sternhagen (Blanche), Janet Eilber (Allison), Robyn Douglass (Kate), Ron Leibman

(Leo), Roziska Halmos (Maid), Alexander Lockwood (Minister).

Broadway playwright Dudley Moore takes on New England schoolteacher Mary Steenburgen as a collaborator and then falls in love with her. It's a tedious comedy that isn't very romantic.

2531. Romero (1989, Four Seasons, 105m, c). P Rev. Ellwood E. Keiser, D John Duigan, W John Sacret Young, PH Geoff Burton, M Gabriel Yared, ED Frans Vandenburg, PD Roger Ford.

LP Raul Julia (Archbishop Oscar Arnulfo Romero), Richard Jordan (The Rev. Rutilio Grande), Ana Alicia (Arista Zelada), Eddie Velez (Lt. Columa), Alejandro Bracho (The Rev. Alfonzo Osuna), Tony Plana (The Rev. Manuel Morantes), Harold Gould (Francisco Galedo), Lucy Reina (Lucia).

Raul Julia is convincing if not inspiring as the heroic liberal archbishop of San Salvador. The prelate was assassinated by right wingers while saying mass in 1980, because he refused to be a tool of the rich, speaking out against the injustices and the misery of the poor in his country.

2532. Rooftops (1989, New Visions, 95m, c). P Howard W. Koch, Jr., D Robert Wise, W Terence Brennan (based on a story by Allan Goldstein & Tony Mark), PH Theo Van de Sande, M David A. Stewart & Michael Kamen, ED William Reynolds, PD Jeannine C. Oppewall.

LP Jason Gedrick (T), Troy Beyer (Elana), Eddie Velez (Lobo), Tisha Campbell (Amber), Alexis Cruz (Squeak), Allen Payne (Kadim), Steve Love (Jackie-Sky), Rafael Baez (Raphael).

Squatter Jason Gedrick lives in an abandoned water tower atop a tenement. He's a martial arts enthusiast who decides to take a stand against Eddie Velez when the latter turns the tenement into a crack house.

2533. A Room with a View† (1986, Cinecom, GB, 115m, c). P Ismail Merchant, D James Ivory†, W Ruth Prawer Jhabvala* (based on the novel by E.M. Forster), PH Tony Pierce-Roberts†, M Richard Robbins, ED Humphrey Dixon, AD Gianni Quaranta & Brian Ackland-Snow*, SD Brian Savegar & Elio Altra-

mura*, COS Jenny Beaven & John Bright*.

LP Maggie Smith† (Charlotte Bartlett), Helena Bonham Carter (Lucy Honeychurch), Denholm Elliott† (Mr. Emerson), Julian Sands (George Emerson), Daniel Day-Lewis (Cecil Vyse), Simon Callow (Rev. Beebe), Judi Dench (Miss Lavish), Rosemary Leach (Mrs. Honeychurch), Rupert Graves (Freddy Honeychurch), Patrick Godfrey (Mr. Eager), Fabia Drake (Catherine Alan), Joan Henley (Teresa Alan).

Films seldom look or sound better than this one. The photography is magnificent, the settings are a delight, and throughout the film some of the most beautiful music ever written perfectly sets the mood. Innocent Edwardian girl Helena Bonham Carter, travelling in Italy with her aunt, Maggie Smith, has her eyes opened to real life and the excitement of romance. It's a precious, simple movie, with no great story line—but with most enjoyable performances by all of the principals.

2534. The Rosary Murders (1987, New Line, 105m, c). P Robert G. Laurel, D Fred Walton, W Elmore Leonard & Walton (based on the novel by William X. Kienzle), PH David Golia, M Bobby Laurel & Don Sebesky, ED Sam Vitale.

LP Donald Sutherland (Father Bob Koesler), Charles Durning (Father Ted Nabors), Josef Sommer (Lt. Walt Koznicki), Belinda Bauer (Pat Lennon), James Murtaugh (Javison), John Danelle (Detective Harris), Addison Powell (Father Killeen), Kathleen Tolan (Sister Ann Vania).

What is unorthodox priest Donald Sutherland to do when the serial murderer of Detroit priests and nuns confesses his crimes in the confessional? Why team with beautiful reporter Belinda Bauer and crack the case without cracking the seal of the confessional. Just remember to avoid occasions of sin, Father!

2535. The Rose Garden (1989, Pathe Intl., West Ger./US, 112m, c). P Artur Brauner, D Fons Rademakers, W Paul Hengge, PH Gernot Roll, M Egisto Macchi, ED Kees Lindhorst, PD Jan Schlubach.

LP Liv Ullmann (Gabriele Schlucter-

Freund), Maximilian Schell (Aaron Reichenbacher), Peter Fonda (Herbert Schlueter), Jan Niklas (Paessler), Katarina Lena Muller (Tina), Kurt Hubner (Arnold Krenn), Hanns Zischler (Prof. Eckert), Gila Almagor (Ruth Levi).

The title refers to a plot of flowered land next to a Hamburg street. As the British army approached the city in 1945, the Nazis hanged 20 Jewish children being used for medical experiments. Years later, Maximilian Schell, the only child to escape this fate, is determined to bring the SS officer responsible for the order to trial. Beware! The film shows the hangings in a documentary-like style.

2536.   *The Rosebud Beach Hotel* (1984, Almi, 105m, c). P Irving Schwartz & Harry Hurwitz, D Hurwitz, W Harry Narunsky, Schwartz & Thomas Rudolph, PH Joao Fernandes, M Jay Chattaway, ED Daniel Lowenthal.

LP Colleen Camp (Tracy), Peter Scolari (Elliott), Christopher Lee (King), Fran Drescher (Linda), Eddie Deezen (Sydney), Chuck McCann (Dorfman), Hank Garrett (Kramer), Hamilton Camp (Matches), Jonathan Schmock (Dennis).

In a mediocre adult comedy, Peter Scolari tries his hand at managing a run down hotel in order to please his girlfriend Colleen Camp. Bellhop Fran Drescher doubles as a call girl and Camp's father Christopher Lee plots to blow the place up for the insurance money.

Rosemary's Killer   see   The Prowler

2537.   *R.O.T.O.R.* (1988, Imperical, 90m, c). P Cullen Blaine, Budd Lewis & Richard Gesswein, D Blaine, W Lewis, PH Glenn Roland, M David Adam Newman, ED Douglas Bryan.

LP Richard Gesswein, Margaret Trigg, Jayne Smith, James Cole, Clark Moore, Carroll Brandon Baker.

The acronym R.O.T.O.R. stands for Robot Officer Tactical Operation Research, so you know you're in for a rip-off of *Terminator* and *Robocop,* and not a very good one at that.

2538.   *Rotweiler: Dogs of Hell* (1984, Owensby, 3-D, 90m, c, aka *Dogs of Hell*). P Earl Owensby, D Worth Keeter, III, W Tom McIntyre.

LP Earl Owensby, Bill Gribble, Jerry Rushing.

This boring horror film, produced to be shown in Southern drive-ins, features a pack of dogs attacking the inhabitants of a small North Carolina mountain retreat.

2539.   *Rough Cut* (1980, Paramount, GB, 112m, c). P David Merrick, D Don Siegel, W Francis Burns [Larry Gelbart] (based on the novel *Touch the Lion's Paw* by Derek Lambert), PH Freddie Young, M Nelson Riddle (adapted from the music of Duke Ellington and collaborators), ED Doug Stewart, PD Ted Haworth.

LP Burt Reynolds (Jack Rhodes), Lesley-Anne Down (Gillian Bromley), David Niven (Chief Inspector Cyril Willis), Timothy West (Nigel Lawton), Patrick Magee (Ernst Mueller), Al Matthews (Ferguson), Susan Littler (Sheila), Joss Ackland (Insp. Vanderveld), Isabel Dean (Mrs. Willis).

Retiring Scotland Yard inspector David Niven has never been able to apprehend notorious jewel thief Burt Reynolds. Desperate to remove this blotch from his record he sets up a trap, employing kleptomaniac society woman Lesley-Anne Down as bait. Instead she falls in love with Reynolds and becomes his partner in a plan to steal $30,000,000 in jewels during a flight from Antwerp to Amsterdam. Neither Niven nor Reynolds are up for this tepid comedy.

2540.   *Round Midnight* (1986, Warner, US/Fr., 133m, c). P Irwin Winkler, D Bertrand Tavernier, W David Rayfiel & Tavenier (based on incidents in the lives of Francis Paudras and Bud Powell), PH Bruno de Keyzer, M Herbie Hancock*, ED Armand Psenny, PD Alexandre Trauner.

LP Dexter Gordon† (Dale Turner), Francois Cluzet (Francis Borier), Gabrielle Haker (Berangere), Sandra Reaves-Phillips (Buttercup), Lonette McKee (Darcey Leigh), Christine Pascal (Sylvie), Herbie Hancock (Eddie Wayne), Bobby Hutcherson (Ace).

This jazz buff's tribute to Bud Powell and Lester Young features the late real-life musician Dexter Gordon in a sparkling performance as a talented but self-destructive saxophonist whose career is rescued by French fan Francois Cluzet. The Herbie Hancock score won a much deserved Oscar.

2541. *Roxanne* (1987, Columbia, 107m, c). P Michael Rachmil & Daniel Melnick, D Fred Schepisi, W Steve Martin (based on the play *Cyrano de Bergerac* by Edmond Rostand), PH Ian Baker, M Bruce Smeaton, ED John Scott, PD Jack DeGovia.

LP Steve Martin (Charlie "C.D." Bales), Daryl Hannah (Roxanne Kowalski), Rick Rossovich (Chris McDonell), Shelley Duvall (Dixie), John Kapelos (Chuck), Fred Willard (Mayor Deebs), Max Alexander (Dean), Michael J. Pollard (Andy), Shandra Beri (Sandy), Brian George (Dr. David Schepisi).

In a very appealing, romantic update of Cyrano de Bergerac, Steve Martin is the fire chief in a sleepy ski town in Washington state. Because of a rather long and distinctive nose, he's afraid of expressing his true feelings for recently arrived Daryl Hannah. Instead he fronts for dumb hunk Rick Rossovich. However since Martin is the screenwriter, he makes certain he gets the girl by the final reel.

2542. *R.S.V.P.* (1984, Platinum, 86m, c). P John Amero, D Lem Amero, W LaRuc Watts, PH Larry Revene, M Ian Shaw, ED L. Amero, AD Watts & Fabian Stuart.

LP Adam Mills (Toby), Lynda Wiesmeier (Jennifer), Veronica Hart (Ellen), Ray Colbert (Bill), Harry Reems (Grant), Katt Shea (Rhonda), Lola Mason (Polly), Allene Simmons (Patty), Dustin Stevens (Jonathan).

For some of these performers, making a soft core picture must be a nice change. Several, including Veronica Hart and Harry Reems, have usually starred in executive producer Chuck Vincent's XXX films. In this one, things go wrong at a Hollywood party being held to honor a writer when a body (dead, that is) is found in the guest of honor's pool.

2543. *Ruckus* (1981, New World, 91m, c, aka *The Loner*). P Paul Maslansky, D&W Max Kleven, M/L Willie Nelson & Hank Cochran.

LP Dirk Benedict, Linda Blair, Richard Farnsworth, Matt Clark, Jon Van Ness, Ben Johnson, Taylor Lacher.

No one gets killed in this Rambo-like story. Vietnam vet Dirk Benedict escapes from a military psychiatric ward and ends up in a little Southern town where the locals hassle him. But they are made to feel sorry for it.

2544. *Rude Awakening* (1989, Orion, 100m, c). P Aaron Russo, D David Greenwalt, Russo, W Neil Levy & Richard LaGravenese, PH Tim Sigel, M Jonathan Elias, ED Paul Fried, PD Mel Bourne.

LP Cheech Marin (Hesus), Eric Roberts (Fred), Julie Hagerty (Petra), Robert Carradine (Sammy), Buck Henry (Lloyd), Louise Lasser (Ronnie), Cindy Williams (June), Andrea Martin (April), Cliff De Young (Brubaker).

Flower children Cheech Marin and Eric Roberts emerge after 20 years of living in a jungle commune in a fictitious Latin American country. On their return to the U.S., they encounter several old friends, who have changed in attitude and outlook. It's moderately amusing; but preachy. Gurus of the 60s Timothy Leary, Jerry Rubin and Bobby Seale make cameo appearances.

2545. *Rude Boy* (1980, Atlantic, GB, 120m, c). P&D Jack Hazan & David Mingay, W Hazan, Mingay & Ray Gange, PH Hazan, M Joe Strummer & Mick Jones, ED Mingay & Peter Goddard.

LP Ray Gange (Ray), The Clash (Themselves), John Green (Road Manager), Barry Baker (Roadie), Terry McQuade (Terry), Caroline Coon (Clash Girl Friend), Elizabeth Young & Sarah Hall (Ray's Girl Friends).

Ray Gange, a London young man with no prospects, takes a job as a roadie with the rock group The Clash, but ends up back where he started from. If you're into the alienated punk generation this picture ought to pleasingly bum you out.

2546. *Rumble Fish* (1983, Universal, 105m, c). P Fred Roos & Doug Claybourne, D Francis Ford Coppola, W S.E. Hinton & Coppola (based on a novel by Hinton), PH Stephen H. Burum, M Stewart Copeland, ED Barry Malkin, PD Dean Tavoularis.

LP Matt Dillon (Rusty-James), Mickey Rourke (Motorcycle Boy), Diane Lane

(Patty), Dennis Hopper (Father), Diana Scarwid (Cassandra), Vincent Spano (Steve), Nicolas Cage (Smokey), Christopher Penn (B.J.), Larry Fishburne (Midget), William Smith (Patterson).

Tulsa teen Matt Dillon, living with his drunken father Dennis Hopper, strives to be like his biker brother Mickey Rourke. He works in a petshop and likens himself to the rumble fish, which fights even its own image in the glass. Rourke knows that his way leads nowhere and he tries to redirect his brother's hero-worship.

2547. *Rumpelstiltskin* (1987, Cannon, 92m, c). P Menahem Golan & Yoram Globus, D&W David Irving, PH David Gurfinkel, M Max Robert, ED Tova Neeman, PD Marek Dobrowolski, COS Debbie Leon.

LP Amy Irving (Katie), Clive Revill (King Mezzer), Billy Barty (Rumpelstiltskin), Priscilla Pointer (Queen Grizelda), Robert Symonds (Victor), John Moulder-Brown (The Prince).

Menahem Golan and Yoram Globus please audiences with a charming version of the familiar story of the foolish miller who claims his daughter can spin straw into gold. She does so with the help of dwarf Billy Barty who demands her baby as payment, unless she can guess his name.

2548. *Runaway* (1984, Tri-Star, 100m, c). P Michael Rachmil, D&W Michael Crichton, PH John A. Alonzo, M Jerry Goldsmith, ED Glenn Farr, PD Douglas Higgins.

LP Tom Selleck (Sgt. Jack Ramsey), Cynthia Rhodes (Sgt. Karen Thompson), Gene Simmons (Luther), Kirstie Alley (Jackie), Stan Shaw (Marvin), G.W. Bailey (Chief), Joey Cramer (Bobby), Chris Mulkey (Johnson).

Robotics expert Tom Selleck and his pretty blond policewoman partner Cynthia Rhodes are given the assignment of tracking down killer robots. The latter, termed runaways (they were household help until they were deliberately short-circuited), are wreaking havoc in a metropolitan city.

2549. *Runaway Train* (1985, Cannon, 111m, c). P Menahem Golan & Yoram Globus, D Andrei Konchalovsky, W

Djordje Milicevic, Paul Zindel & Edward Bunker (based on the screenplay by Akira Kurosawa, Ryuzo Kikushima & Hideo Oguni), PH Alan Hume, M Trevor Jones, ED Henry Richardson†, PD Stephen Marsh.

LP Jon Voight† (Manny), Eric Roberts† (Buck), Rebecca DeMornay (Sara), Kyle T. Heffner (Frank Barstow), John P. Ryan (Ranken), T.K. Carter (Dave Prince), Kenneth McMillan (Eddie MacDonald), Stacey Pickren (Ruby).

One can never accuse Jon Voight of repeating a role. Here he plays an almost samurai-like convict in an Alaskan prison. He's a hero to all the other prisoners because he stands up to sadistic warden John P. Ryan, no matter what the consequences. Voight escapes from the pen for the third time; this time taking along young Eric Roberts, by crawling through a smelly, filthy sewer. They board a passing train consisting of four engines coupled together. Unbeknownst to them the engineer suffers a fatal heart attack, his dead body moving the throttle to full speed ahead. The cons and Rebecca DeMornay, a railroad employee and the only other person on the train, are on a runaway train. In the end Voight saves Roberts and DeMornay but takes his hated enemy Ryan, who has boarded the speeding train via a helicopter, with him to their doom.

The Runaways see South Bronx Heroes

2550. *Runners* (1983, Cinegate, GB, 106m, c). P Barry Hanson, D Charles Sturridge, W Stephen Poliakoff, PH Howard Atherton, M George Fenton, ED Peter Coulson.

LP Kate Hardie (Rachel Lindsay), James Fox (Tom Lindsay), Jane Asher (Helen), Eileen O'Brien (Gillian Lindsay), Ruti Simon (Lucy Lindsay), Bridget Turner (Teacher), Robert Lang (Wilkins).

A Nottingham father and a Reading mother search all over London for their runaway children.

2551. *Running Brave* (1983, Buena Vista, Canada, 105m, c). P Ira Englander, D D.S. Everett [Donald Shebib], W Henry Bean & Shirl Hendryx, PH

Francois Protat, M Mike Post, ED Tony Lower & Earl Herdan, PD Carol Spier.

LP Robby Benson (Billy Mills), Pat Hingle (Coach Easton), Claudia Cron (Pat Mills), Jeff McCracken (Dennis), August Schellenberg (Billy's Father), Denis Lacroix (Frank), Graham Greene (Eddie), Margo Kane (Catherine).

This film wouldn't make a good made-for-TV movie. It purports to tell the true story of a young Sioux from the reservation who faces extreme pressures from the world of the white man as he becomes an Olympic runner. Looks like the movies are still in the mood to massacre the redman.

2552. *Running Hot* (1984, New Line, 95m, c, aka *Lucky 13*). P David Calloway & Zachary Feuer, D&W Mark Griffiths, PH Tom Richmond, M Al Capps, ED Andy Blumenthal, PD Katherine Vallin.

LP Monica Carrico (Charlene Andrews), Eric Stoltz (Danny Hicks), Stuart Margolin (Officer Trent), Virgil Frye (Ross the Pimp), Richard Bradford (Tom Bond), Louise Baker (Shane), Joe George (Officer Berman), Laurel Patrick (Angie).

Seventeen-year-old Eric Stoltz has been convicted of murdering his father and is sentenced to be executed. Instead he escapes and hides out with prostitute Monica Carrico, who has written to him while he was in prison. Stoltz may really be innocent, but nevertheless he's killed in the end.

2553. *The Running Man* (1987, Tri-Star, 100m, c). P Tim Zinnemann & George Linder, D Paul Michael Glaser, W Steven E. de Souza (based on the novel by Richard Bachman [Stephen King]), PH Thomas Del Ruth & Reynaldo Villa-lobos, M Harold Faltermeyer, ED Mark Roy Warner, Edward A. Warschilka & John Wright, PD Jack T. Collis.

LP Arnold Schwarzenegger (Ben "Butcher of Bakersfield" Richards), Maria Conchita Alonso (Amber Mendez), Yaphet Kotto (Laughlin), Jim Brown (Fireball), Richard Dawson (Damon Killian), Dweezil Zappa (Stevie), Mick Fleetwood (Mic), Jesse Ventura (Captain Freedom), Erland Van Lidth (Dynamo).

In the year 2019 A.D., the U.S. is a totalitarian state. Framed as a mass murderer Arnold Schwarzenegger has a Hobson's choice of appearing on "A Most Dangerous Game"–inspired TV program. Convicted felons are given the chance to run for their lives, but with the stalkers on their tails, none have ever escaped or survived—until now. You just know Arnie means it when he tells unctuous game show host Richard Dawson, "I'll be back!"

2554. *Running on Empty* (1988, Warner, 116m, c). P Amy Robinson & Griffin Dunne, D Sidney Lumet, W Naomi Foner†, PH Gerry Fisher, M Tony Mottola, ED Andrew Mondshein, PD Philip Rosenberg.

LP Christine Lahti (Annie Pope), River Phoenix† (Danny Pope), Judd Hirsch (Arthur Pope), Martha Plimpton (Lorna Phillips), Jonas Arby (Harry Pope), Ed Crowley (Mr. Phillips), L.M. Kit Carson (Gus Winant), Steven Hill (Mr. Patterson), Augusta Dabney (Mrs. Patterson).

Former 60s radicals Judd Hirsch and Christine Lahti are still sought by the FBI twenty years later. They are also parents of two children, River Phoenix and Jonas Arby, the former desperately wanting to emerge from the underground and make a life for himself. His biggest fear is that his parents may be exposed if he enters college.

2555. *Running Scared* (1986, MGM/UA, 107m, c). P David Foster & Lawrence Turman, D&PH Peter Hyams, W Gary DeVore & Jimmy Huston (based on a story by DeVore), M Rod Temperton, ED James Mitchell, PD Albert Brenner.

LP Gregory Hines (Ray Hughes), Billy Crystal (Danny Costanzo), Steven Bauer (Frank), Darlanne Fluegel (Anna Costanzo), Joe Pantoliano (Snake), Dan Hedaya (Captain Logan), Jonathan Gries (Tony), Tracy Reed (Maryann), Jimmy Smits (Julio Gonzales), John DiSanti (Vinnie).

Before retiring to the sunny south, two long-time Chicago cops, Gregory Hines and Billy Crystal, have one last murdering drug dealer to put away. It's an exciting, likeable comedy-action film, with a great car chase on the El (elevated train) tracks. The nonstop banter in this male-bonding film is often very funny.

2556. *Russkies* (1987, New Century/ Vista, 98m, c). P Mark Levinson & Scott Rosenfelt, D Rick Rosenthal, W Allan Jay Glueckman, Sheldon Lettich & Michael Nankin, PH Reed Smoot, M James Newton Howard, ED Antony Gibbs, PD Linda Pearl, SE Tom Anderson & Karl Herrmann.

LP Whip Hubley (Mischa), Leaf Phoenix (Danny), Peter Billingsley (Adam), Stefan DeSalle (Jason), Susan Walters (Diane), Patrick Kilpatrick (Raimy), Vic Polizos (Sulock), Charles Frank (Mr. Vandermeer).

In this formula teen comedy, three Florida youngsters pick up Russian sailor Whip Hubley. He has become stranded when his raft capsizes, forcing him to abort his mission to pick up a stolen American defense weapon. This reworking of *The Russians Are Coming!, The Russians Are Coming!* is well meaning, but rather corny.

2557. *Rustler's Rhapsody* (1985, Paramount, 88m, c). P David Giler, D&W Hugh Wilson, PH Jose Luis Alcaine, M Steve Doriff, ED John Victor Smith, PD Gil Parrondo.

LP Tom Berenger (Rex O'Herlihan), G.W. Bailey (Peter), Marilu Henner (Miss Tracy), Fernando Rey (Railroad Colonel), Andy Griffith (Col. Ticonderoga), Sela Ward (Colonel Ticonderoga's Daughter), Brant Van Hoffman (Jim), Christopher Malcolm (Jud), Patrick Wayne (Bob Barber).

In a satire of the 30s and 40s B Westerns, singing cowboy Tom Berenger rides into town. He picks town drunk G.W. Bailey to be his sidekick, deals with a whore with a heart of gold, a corrupt sheriff, a shy young schoolteacher, terrified sheepherders, and an evil cattle baron. Finally he faces a hired gunman dressed all in white, in the person of Patrick Wayne. All the clichés are here— even if they are a bit skewed.

2558. *Ruthless People* (1986, Buena Vista, 93m, c). P Michael Peyser, D Jim Abrahams, David Zucker & Jerry Zucker, W Dale Launer, PH Jan De Bont, M Michel Colombier, ED Arthur Schmidt & Gib Jaffe, AD Donald Woodruff.

LP Danny DeVito (Sam Stone), Bette Midler (Barbara Stone), Judge Reinhold (Ken Kessler), Helen Slater (Sandy Kessler), Anita Morris (Carol), Bill Pullman (Earl), William G. Schilling (Police Commissioner), Art Evans (Lt. Bender), Clarence Felder (Lt. Walters).

Having been cheated out of a design process that made a millionaire of rascally Danny De Vito, Judge Reinhold and his wife Helen Slater kidnap the Spandex king's wife Bette Midler, demanding a large ransom. Wishing to be free of Midler so he can be with Anita Morris (who is two-timing him with dumb Bill Pullman), DeVito refuses to pay the money. He hopes the kidnappers will go through with their threat to kill Midler. Instead, Reinhold and Slater, two of the most spiritless people you'd ever encounter, team up with Midler to give DeVito his comeuppance.

2559. *Ryder P.I.* (1986, YGB Distribution, 92m, c). P Karl Hosch, D Hosch, W Hosch, Chuck Walker, Dave Hawthorne, Bob Nelson, PH Phil Arfman, M Kevin Kelly, ED Keith Brooke, AD Kenneth Hosch.

LP Dave Hawthorne (Sky Ryder), Bob Nelson (Eppie), Frances Raines (Valerie), John Mulrooney (Gang Leader), Bob Woods (Prof. Throckmorton), Howard Stern (Ben Wah), Kim Lurie (Maria), Chuck Rader (Det. Hoolihan).

This routine private eye film made on a shoestring has little to recommend it.

2560. *Sacred Ground* (1984, Pacific International, 100m, c). P Arthur R. Dubs, D,W&PH Charles B. Pierce, M Gene Kauer & Don Bagley, ED David E. Jackson, Steven L. Johnson & Lynne Sutherland.

LP Tim McIntire (Matt), Jack Elam (Witcher), L.Q. Jones (Tolbert), Mindi Miller (Wannetta), Eloy Phil Casados (Prairie Fox), Serene Hedin (Little Doe), Vernon Foster (Wounded Leg), Lefty Wild Eagle (Medicine Man), Larry Kenoras (Brave Beaver).

Trapper Tim McIntire and his pregnant wife unwittingly build their shelter on sacred Indian burying grounds. When the wife dies in childbirth, McIntire kidnaps an Indian woman, who has just buried her deceased infant, to care for his child.

2561. *Sacred Hearts* (1984, Reality/ Film Four, GB, 89m, c). P Dee Dee Glass, D&W Barbara Rennie, PH Diane Tammes, M Dirk Higgins, ED Martin Walsh, AD Hildegard Echtler.

LP Anna Massey (Sister Thomas), Katrin Cartlidge (Doris), Oona Kirsh (Maggie), Fiona Shaw (Sister Felicity), Anne Dyson (Sister Perpetua), Annette Badland (Sister Mercy), Sadie Wearing (Mary), Ann-Marie Gwatkin (Lizzie).

Even though she's not Catholic, at the start of World War II, Katrin Cartlidge enters an English convent school run by tyrannical Anna Massey. Cartlidge, a German Jew, is attempting to avoid persecution by the Nazis in case they successfully invade Britain.

2562. *Safari 3000* (1982, MGM/United Artists, 92m, c). P Arthur Gardner & Jules V. Levy, D Harry Hurwitz, W Michael Harreschou (based on a story by Levy, Gardner & Harreschou), PH Adam Greenberg, M Ernest Gold, ED Samuel E. Beetley, AD Peter Williams.

LP David Carradine (Eddie), Stockard Channing (J.J. Dalton), Christopher Lee (Count Borgia), Hamilton Camp (Feodor), Ian Yule (Freddie), Hugh Rouse (Hawthorne), Mary Ann Berold (Victoria), Peter J. Elliott (Stewart).

Top race-car driver David Carradine is forced to take *Playboy* photographer Stockard Channing along for the ride in a trans-African auto race. Amid much adversity and antagonism, love blossoms.

2563. *Sahara* (1984, MGM/United Artists, GB, 104m, c). P Menahem Golan & Yoram Globus, D Andrew V. McLaglen, W James R. Silke (based on a story by Golan), PH David Gurfinkel & Armando Nannuzzi, M Ennio Morricone, ED Alan Strachan & Michael J. Duthie, PD Luciano Spadoni.

LP Brooke Shields (Gordon Dale), Lambert Wilson (Jaffar), John Rhys-Davies (Rasoul), Horst Buchholz (Von Glessing), Perry Lang (Andy), Cliff Potts (String), John Mills (Cambridge), Steve Forrest (R.J. Gordon).

Brooke Shields, the daughter of a deceased Detroit car designer, disguises herself as a boy in order to enter and win a 1927 Sahara car race. Her sheik Lambert Wilson is a bit of a sissy, but she carries off the masquerade because the people she's around aren't too swift.

2564. *Saigon Commandos* (1988, Concorde, 83m, c). P John Schouweiler & Isabel Sumayao, D Clark Henderson, W Thomas McKelvey Cleaver (based on the novel *Saigon Commandos — Mad Minute* by Jonathan Cain), PH Juanito Pereira & Conrado Baltazar, M Samuel Asuncion & Noli Aurillo, ED Pacifico Sanchez.

LP Richard Young (Sgt. Mark Stryker), P.J. Soles (Jean Lassiter), John Allen Nelson (Tim Bryant), Jimi B., Jr. (Will Thomas), Spanky Manikan (Jon Toi), Joonee Gamboa (Nguyen Huu Tri), Fred Bailey (Capt. Daniels).

A.P. reporter P.J. Soles finds a link between drug-related murders in South Vietnam and corrupt politicians.

2565. *St. Elmo's Fire* (1985, Columbia, 110m, c). P Lauren Shuler, D Joel Schumacher, W Schumcher & Carl Kurlander, PH Stephen H. Burum & Jim Hovey, M David Foster, ED Richard Marks, AD William Sandell.

LP Emilio Estevez (Kirbo), Rob Lowe (Billy), Andrew McCarthy (Kevin), Demi Moore (Jules), Judd Nelson (Alex), Ally Sheedy (Leslie), Mare Winningham (Wendy), Martin Balsam (Mr. Beamish), Andie MacDowell (Dale Biberman), Joyce Van Patten (Mrs. Beamish), Jenny Wright (Felicia).

Seven recent graduates from Georgetown University must confront adult problems for the first time. It's tough to have midlife crises when you're only 22. The cast almost makes their plight believable.

2566. *St. Helens* (1981, Parnell, 90m, c). P Michael Murphy, D Ernest Pintoff, W Peter Bellwood & Larry Ferguson, PH Jacques Haitkin, M Goblin and Buckboard, ED George Berndt, SE Magic Lantern.

LP Art Carney (Harry Truman), David Huffman (Geologist), Cassie Yates (His Girlfriend), Ron O'Neal (Helicopter Pilot), Bill McKinney, Albert Salmi, Tim Thomerson, Henry Darrow, Nehemiah Persoff.

On May 18, 1980, after plenty of warning, active volcano Mount St. Helen's erupted. This cheap production is Hollywood's memorial to an old man with the improbable name of Harry Truman (Art Carney) who refused to leave his home on the slope of the mountain and naturally was killed.

2567. *The Salamander* (1982, ITC, US/Ital./GB, 101m, c). P Paul Maslansky, D Peter Zinner, W Robert Katz (based on a novel by Morris West), PH Marcello Gatti, M Jerry Goldsmith, ED Claudio Cutry, AD Giantito Burchiellaro.

LP Franco Nero (Dante Matucci), Anthony Quinn (Bruno Manzini), Martin Balsam (Stefanelli), Sybil Danning (Lili Anders), Christopher Lee (Director Baldassare), Cleavon Little (Maj. Malinowsky), Eli Wallach (Leporello), Claudia Cardinale (Elena).

Despite an international cast of talented performers, this intriguing thriller about a possible coup d'état by fascists in modern-day Italy suffers from a hokey script.

2568. *Salome's Last Dance* (1988, Vestron, 89m, c). P Penny Corke & Robert Littman, D Ken Russell, W Russell (based on the play *Salome* by Oscar Wilde), PH Harvey Harrison, MD Richard Cooke & Ray Beckett, ED Timothy Gee, AD Michael Buchanan, SD Christopher Hobbs, COS Michael Arrals.

LP Glenda Jackson (Herodias/Lady Alice), Stratford Johns (Herod/Alfred Taylor), Nickolas Grace (Oscar Wilde), Douglas Hodge (John the Baptist/Lord Alfred "Bosie" Douglas), Imogen Millais-Scott (Salome/Rose), Denis Ull (Tigellenus/Chilvers), Russell Lee Nash (Pageboy), Alfred Russell (Cappadodem), Ken Russell (Kenneth).

In this play within a film, Oscar Wilde (Nickolas Grace) and his lover "Bosie" Douglas (Douglas Hodge) attend a bordello in London on a rainy November 5, 1892. As a surprise for the author a performance of his banned play *The Tragedy of Salome* is to be performed, with Douglas portraying John the Baptist and various bordello employees appearing in other roles. It's director Ken Russell's most interesting work in years.

2569. *Salsa* (1988, Cannon, 97m, c). P Menahem Golan & Yoram Globus, D Boaz Davidson, W Davidson, Tomas Benitez & Shepard Goldman (based on a story by Davidson & Eli Tabor), PH David Gurfinkel, M/L Various Artists, ED Alain Jakubowicz, PD Mark Haskins.

LP Robby Rosa (Rico), Rodney Harvey (Ken), Magali Alvarado (Rita), Miranda Garrison (Luna), Moon Orona (Lola), Angela Alvarado (Vicki), Loyda Ramos (Mother), Valente Rodriguez (Chuey), Daniel Rojo (Orlando).

In a scriptless clone of *Dirty Dancing,* automobile mechanic Robby Rosa would rather be swaying to a salsa beat.

2570. *The Salute of the Jugger* (1989, Filmpac, Australia, 102m, c). P Charles Roven, D&W David Webb Peoples, PH David Eggby, M Todd Boekelheide, ED Richard Francis-Bruce, PD John Stoddart.

LP Rutger Hauer (Sallow), Joan Chen (Kidda), Vincent Phillip D'Onofrio (Young Gar), Delroy Lindo (Mbulu), Anna Katarina (Big Cimber), Gandhi Macintyre (Gandhi), Justin Monju (Dog Boy), Max Fairchild (Gonzo), Hugh Keays-Byrne (Lord Vile).

Juggers are a band of futuristic wandering gladiators, led by Rutger Hauer, once a member of the ruling elite, called the League, but since banished over a misdemeanor. He has plans for a comeback and challenges the League's juggers to do battle.

2571. *Salvador* (1986, Hemdale, 123m, c). P Gerald Green & Oliver Stone, D Stone, W Stone & Richard Boyle†, PH Robert Richardson, M Georges Delerue, ED Claire Simpson, PD Bruno Rubeo.

LP James Woods† (Richard Boyle), James Belushi (Dr. Rock), Michael Murphy (Ambassador Thomas Kelly), John Savage (John Cassidy), Elpedia Carrillo (Maria), Tony Plana (Major Max), Colby Chester (Jack Morgan), Cindy Gibb (Cathy Moore), Will MacMillan (Col. Hyde), Valerie Wildman (Pauline Axelrod).

Based on the 1980–81 experiences of journalist Richard Boyle in strife-ridden El Salvador, this compelling drama has James Woods and James Belushi as a pair of not-completely likeable newsmen. Slowly their indifference to the people of El Salvador changes as the brutality of the regime and the right-wing death squads radicalize them.

2572. *Salvation* (1987, B Movies/Circle, 80m, c, aka *Salvation! Have You Said Your Prayers Today?*). P Beth B. & Michael H. Shamberg, D Beth B., W Beth B. & Tom Robinson, PH Francis Kenny, ED Elizabeth Kling, PD Lester Cohen.

LP Stephen McHattie (Rev. Edward Randall), Dominique Davalos (Lenore Finley), Exene Cervenka (Rhonda Stample), Viggo Mortensen (Jerome Stample), Rockets Redglare (Oliver), Billy Bastiani (Stanley).

This black comedy takes on TV evangelism. Stephen McHattie makes the fire-and-brimstone sermons, appealing for money from the unwashed and uneducated out in TV-land. He's a fake with feet of clay, set up by some of his followers for a bit of blackmail.

Salvation: Have You Said Your Prayers Today? see Salvation

Sam Marlow: Private Eye see The Man with Bogart's Face

2573. *Sammy and Rosie Get Laid* (1987, Cinecom, GB, 97m, c). P Tim Bevan & Sarah Radclyffe, D Stephen Frears, W Hanif Kureishi, PH Oliver Stapleton, M Stanley Myers, ED Mick Audsley, PD Hugo Luczyc Wyhowski.

LP Shashi Kapoor (Rafi), Frances Barber (Rosie), Claire Bloom (Alice), Ayub Khan Din (Sammy), Roland Gift (Danny), Wendy Gazelle (Anna), Suzette Llewellyn (Vivia), Meera Syal (Rani), Badi Uzzaman (Ghost).

Pakistani politician Shashi Kapoor takes up exile in England, which he remembers fondly from times spent there years before. He finds his English mistress Claire Bloom has grown tired of waiting for him. His accountant son Khan Din and the latter's social worker wife Frances Barber sleep only with others, and their neighborhood has erupted into a race riot. Nothing stays the same anymore.

2574. *Sam's Son* (1984, Worldvision/Invictus, 104m, c). P Kent McCray, D&W Michael Landon, PH Ted Voigtlander, M David Rose, ED John Loeffler, AD George Renne.

LP Eli Wallach (Sam Orowitz), Anne Jackson (Harriet Orowitz), Timothy Patrick Murphy (Gene Orowitz), Hallie Todd (Cathy Stanton), Alan Hayes (Robert Woods), Jonna Lee (Bonnie Barnes), Michael Landon (Gene Orman).

Timothy Patrick Murphy's athletic prowess at throwing the javelin opens the door for a Hollywood acting career. Orowitz is the real name of "Bonanza's" and "Little House on the Prairie's" Michael Landon.

2575. *Santa Claus: The Movie* (1985, Tri-Star, 112m, c). P Ilya Salkind & Pierre Spengler, D Jeannot Szwarc, W David Newman (based on a story by David Newman & Leslie Newman), PH Arthur Ibbetson, M Henry Mancini, ED Peter Hollywood, PD Anthony Pratt.

LP Dudley Moore (Patch), John Lithgow (B.Z.), David Huddleston (Claus), Burgess Meredith (Ancient Elf), Judy Cornwell (Anya), Jeffrey Kramer (Towzer), Christian Fitzpatrick (Joe), Carrie Kei Heim (Cornelia).

We suppose this movie featuring Dudley Moore as an elf won't harm anybody but we wouldn't want our granddaughter to see it. Moore leaves the North Pole, gets mixed up with crooked toy manufacturer John Lithgow and needs Santa to straighten things out.

2576. *Satan's Mistress* (1982, Motion Picture Marketing, 91m, c, aka *Fury of the Succubus; Demon Rage; Dark Eyes*). P James Polakof & Beverly Johnson, D Polakof, W Polakof & Johnson, PH James L. Carter, M Roger Kellaway, ED George Trirogoff, AD Fred Cutter & John Flaherty, SE Karen Kubeck, Dennis Dion & Tom Shouse.

LP Britt Ekland (Anne-Marie), Lana Wood (Lisa), Kabir Bedi (The Spirit), Don Galloway (Carl), John Carradine (Father Stratton), Sherry Scott (Michelle), Elise-Anne (Belline), Chris Polakof (Cissy), Howard Murphy (The Beast).

Neglected housewife Britt Ekland comes under the power of a demented lover.

2577. *Satisfaction* (1988, 20th Century-Fox, 92m, c). P Aaron Spelling & Alan Greisman, D Joan Freeman, W

Charles Purpura, PH Thomas Del Ruth, M Michel Colombier, ED Joel Goodman, PD Lynda Paradise.

LP Justine Bateman (Jennie Lee), Liam Neeson (Martin Falcon), Trini Alvarado (May "Mooch" Stark), Scott Coffey (Nickie Longo), Britta Phillips (Billy Swan), Julia Roberts (Daryle Shane), Debbie Harry (Tina), Chris Nash (Frankie Malloy).

In this bomb, four girls and a guy form a garage rock 'n' roll band. They get their first professional gig at a seaside resort owned by Liam Neeson, once a Grammy-winning songwriter. The five musicians crash in one small room and the film makes as much of the sleeping arrangements as it can before going on to pairing everyone in more equitable proportions.

2578. *Saturday the 14th* (1981, New World, 75m, c). P Julie Corman & Jeff Begun, D&W Howard R. Cohen (based on a story by Begun), PH Daniel Lacambre, ED Joanne D'Antonio & Kent Beyda, AD Arlene Alen.

LP Richard Benjamin (John), Paula Prentiss (Mary), Severn Darden (Van Helsing), Jeffrey Tambor (Waldemar), Kari Michaelsen (Debbie), Kevin Brando (Billy), Nancy Lee Andrews (Yolanda), Craig Coulter (Duane).

If the intent of this spoof of holiday slasher movies was to put them to rest, it failed miserably. As a comedy, it wasn't very funny either.

2579. *Saturday the 14th Strikes Back* (1988, Concorde, 78m, c). P Julie Corman, D&W Howard R. Cohen, PH Levie Isaacks, M Parmer Fuller, ED Bernard Caputo.

LP Ray Walston (Gramps), Jason Presson (Eddie Baxter), Avery Schreiber (Frank), Patty McCormack (Kate), Julianne McNamara (Linda), Rhonda Aldrich (Alice), Daniel Will-Harris (Bert), Pamela Stonebrook (Charlene).

More is less in this sequel to the 1981 turkey. This dimwitted spoof of horror movies has an assortment of monsters attacking Presson on his birthday.

2580. *Saturn 3* (1980, Associated Film Distributors, 88m, c). P&D Stanley Donen, W Martin Amis (based on the story by John Barry), PH Billy Williams, M Elmer Bernstein, ED Richard Marden, PD Stuart Craig.

LP Farrah Fawcett (Alex), Kirk Douglas (Adam), Harvey Keitel (Benson), Douglas Lambert (Capt. James), Ed Bishop (Harding), Christopher Muncke (2nd Crewman).

Research scientists Farrah Fawcett and Kirk Douglas create a futuristic Garden of Eden in an isolated part of the solar system. Their tranquility is interrupted with the arrival of crazed scientist Harvey Keitel and his eight-foot robot who lusts after Fawcett.

2581. *Savage Beach* (1989, Malibu Bay, 95m, c). P Arlene Sidaris, D&W Andy Sidaris, PH Howard Wexler, M Gary Stockdale, ED Michael Haight, PD Jimmy Hadder.

LP Dona Speir (Donna), Hope Marie Carlton (Taryn), John Aprea (Capt. Andreas), Bruce Penhall (Bruce Christian), Rodrigo Obregon (Martinez), Michael Mikasa (Japanese Warrior), Michael Shaner (Shane Abilene).

Government drug enforcement officers Dona Spier and Hope Marie Carlton's plane crashlands on a remote island where numerous opposing forces are searching for a cache of gold stolen from the Philippines by the Japanese in 1943.

2582. *Savage Dawn* (1984, Media Home Ent., 102m, c). D Simon Nuchtern, W William P. Milling, PH Gerald Feil, ED Gerald B. Greenberg.

LP George Kennedy (Tick Rand), Lance Henriksen (Ben Stryker), Karen Black, Richard Lynch, Claudia Udy.

A group of motorcycle creeps terrorize a small Southern town, until a macho hero stomps their asses.

2583. *Savage Harvest* (1981, 20th Century-Fox, 87m, c). P Ralph Helfer, Sandy Howard & Lamar Card, D Robert Collins, W Collins & Robert Blees (based on a story by Helfer & Ken Noyle), PH Ronnie Taylor, M Robert Folk, ED Patrick Kennedy & Scott Wallace, PD Brian Eatwell.

LP Tom Skerritt (Casey), Michelle Phillips (Maggie), Shawn Stevens (Jon), Anne-Marie Martin (Wendy), Derek Partridge (Derek), Arthur Malet (Dr. MacGruder), Tana Helfer (Kristie), Vincent Isaac (Jurogi).

In this scary but senseless film, lions prey on Tom Skerritt, Michelle Phillips and some children in Africa.

2584. *Savage Island* (1985, Empire, US/Ital./Span., 74m, c). P Robert Amante & Mark Alabiso, D Edward Muller & Nicholas Beardsley, W Michelle Tomski & Beardsley, M Mark Ryder, ED Tomski.

LP Linda Blair (Daly), Anthony Steffen (Laredo), Ajita Wilson (Marie), Christina Lai (Muriel), Leon Askin (Luker).

Linda Blair, a former inmate of a brutal South American labor camp, escapes and takes revenge.

Savage Islands see Nate and Hayes

2585. *Savage Streets* (1984, Motion Picture Marketing, 93m, c). P John C. Strong III, D Danny Steinmann, W Norman Yonemoto & Steinmann, PH Stephen Posey, M Michael Lloyd & John D'Andrea, ED Bruce Stubblefield & John O'Connor, AD Ninkey Dalton.

LP Linda Blair (Brenda), John Vernon (Principal Underwood), Robert Dryer (Jake), Johnny Venocur (Vince), Sal Landi (Fargo), Scott Mayer (Red), Debra Blee (Rachel), Lisa Freeman (Francine), Linnea Quigley (Heather).

Linda Blair, wearing a revealing commando outfit and a crossbow, leads a no-nonsense girl gang called the "Satins." They teach a lesson to the "Scars," a male gang, led by Robert Dryer, which gang-raped Blair's deafmute sister.

Savage Sunday see Low Blow

2586. *Savage Weekend* (1983, Cannon, 83m, c, aka *The Killer Behind the Mask; The Upstate Murders*). P John Mason Kirby & David Paulsen, D&W Paulsen, PH Zoli Vidor, M Dov Seltzer, ED Zion Avrahamian & Jonathan Day.

LP Christopher Allport (Nicky), James Doerr (Robert), Marilyn Hamlin (Marie), Kathleen Heaney (Shirley), David Gale (Mac), Devin Goldenberg (Jay), Jeffrey David Pomerantz (Greg), William Sanderson (Otis).

Originally filmed in 1976, this soft-core porno horror film was briefly released in 1981 and re-released in 1983. Two families visit upstate New York for a weekend and are picked off one-by-one.

2587. *Savannah Smiles* (1983, Gold Coast, 104m, c). P Clark L. Paylow, D Pierre DeMoro, W Mark Miller (based on his story), PH Stephen W. Gray, M Ken Sutherland, ED Eva Ruggiero, PD Charles Stewart.

LP Mark Miller (Alvie), Donovan Scott (Boots), Bridgette Andersen (Savannah Driscoll), Peter Graves (Harland Dobbs), Chris Robinson (Richard Driscoll), Michael Parks (Lt. Savage), Barbara Stanger (Joan Driscoll), Pat Morita (Father O'Hara), Philip Abbott (Chief Pruitt).

Six-year-old runaway Bridgette Andersen befriends two escaped convicts, Mark Miller and Donovan Scott. Their plans to hold her for ransom go out the window when this cute little tyke smiles at them.

2588. *Saving Grace* (1986, Embassy, 112m, c). P Herbert Solow, D Robert M. Young, W David S. Ward & Richard Kramer (based on the novel by Celia Gittelson), PH Reynaldo Villalobos, ED Peter Zinner, PD Giovanni Natalucci.

LP Tom Conti (Pope Leo XIV), Giancarlo Giannini (Abalardi), Erland Josephson (Monsignor Francesco Ghezzi), Fernando Rey (Cardinal Stefano Biondi), Patricia Mauceri (Lucia Fedelia), Edward James Olmos (Ciolino).

This man-of-the-people pope (Tom Conti) leaves the Vatican one day and ends up in a remote village which has no priest. Everyone pretends to be quarantined in order to receive relief money. The Pope's absence is kept from the world until he's able to redeem the townspeople.

2589. *Say Anything* (1989, 20th Century-Fox, 100m, c). P Polly Platt, D&W Cameron Crowe, PH Laszlo Kovacs, M Richard Gibbs & Anne Dudley, ED Richard Marks, PD Mark Mansbridge.

LP John Cusack (Lloyd Dobler), Ione Skye (Diane Court), John Mahoney (James Court), Lili Taylor (Corey Flood), Amy Brooks (D.C.), Pamela Segall (Rebecca), Jason Gould (Mike Cameron), Loren Dean (Joe), Glenn Walker Harris, Jr. (Jason).

John Cusack, an appealing young actor, usually plays appealing young men. This film is no exception. He's an aimless high school jock with no plans until he falls for beautiful Ione Skye, a cool princess type and class valedictorian. Can this relationship work? What a silly question. It's good escapism.

2590. *Say Yes* (1986, CineTel, 90m, c). P Rosemary Le Roy Layng & Larry Yust, D&W Yust, PH Isidore Mankofsky, ED Margaret Morrison.

LP Jonathan Winters (W.D. Westmoreland), Art Hindle (Luke), Lissa Layng (Annie), Logan Ramsey (George), Maryedith Burrell (Gladys), Jensen Collier (Belinda), Jacque Lynn Colton (Message Taker), Devon Ericson (Cynthia), Art La Fleur (Ernest), John Milford (Sailor), Laurie Prange (First Bride), Anne Ramsey (Major).

When multimillionaire Jonathan Winters dies, he leaves his fortune to his son Art Hindle on the condition that he marry before his 35th birthday, just one day away. He finds a bride and love with Lissa Layng just in the nick of time.

2591. *Scalps* (1983, 21st Century, 82m, c). P The Eel (T.L. Lankford), D&W Fred Olen Ray, PH Brett Webster & Larry van Loon, M Drew Neumann & Eric Rasmussen, ED John Barr.

LP Kirk Alyn (Dr. Howard Machen), Carroll Borland (Dr. Reynolds), Jo Ann Robinson (D.J.), Richard Hench (Randy), Roger Maycock (Kershaw), Barbara Magnusson (Ellen), Frank McDonald (Ben), Carol Sue Flockhart (Louise).

In this horribly amateurish film, a group of teens stir up the spirit of an Indian warrior when they mess around in a sacred burial ground.

2592. *Scandal* (1989, Miramax, GB, 106m, c). P Stephen Woolley, D Michael Caton-Jones, W Michael Thomas, PH Michael Molloy, M Carl Davis, ED Angus Newton, PD Simon Holland.

LP John Hurt (Stephen Ward), Joanne Whalley-Kilmer (Christine Keeler), Bridget Fonda (Mandy Rice-Davies), Ian McKellen (John Profumo), Leslie Phillips (Lord Astor), Britt Ekland (Mariella Novotny), Daniel Massey (Mervyn Griffith-Jones), Jeroen Krabbe (Eugene Ivanov), Deborah Grant (Valerie Hobson Profumo).

Ambitious London osteopath Dr. Stephen Ward (John Hurt) finds ways to ingratiate himself with the high born and powerful of British society. One method is to introduce the powerful and rich to the young and beautiful, such as Christine Keeler (Joanne Whalley-Kilmer). This compelling examination of the affair with Keeler of John Profumo (Ian McKellen), the Secretary of State for War under Harold Macmillan, makes Hurt out to be a victim rather than the villain of the scandal as he was painted by the real-life press in 1963. Whatever the truth, Ward took his own life. Hurt is an extraordinary actor, particularly adept at portraying flawed men such as Ward.

2593. *Scandalous* (1984, GB, Orion, 92m, c). P Arlene Sellers & Alex Winitsky, D Rob Cohen, W Cohen & John Byrum (based on a story by Byrum, Rob Cohen & Larry Cohen), PH Jack Cardiff, M Dave Grusin, ED Michael Bradsell, PD Peter Mullins.

LP Robert Hays (Frank Swedlin), Pamela Stephenson (Fiona Maxwell Sayle), Ron Travis (Porno Director), M. Emmet Walsh (Simon Reynolds), John Gielgud (Uncle Willie), Ed Dolan (Purser), Paul Reeve (Flight Coordinator).

Bungling American TV reporter Robert Hays becomes involved with a gang of British con artists led by Pamela Stephenson and John Gielgud. They see to it that he is framed for the murder of his wife.

2594. *Scanners* (1981, Avco Embassy, Canada, 102m, c). P Claude Heroux, D&W David Cronenberg, PH Mark Irwin, M Howard Shore, ED Ron Sanders, AD Carol Spier, SE Dick Smith, Gary Zeller, Henry Pierrig & Chris Walas.

LP Stephen Lack (Cameron Vale), Jennifer O'Neill (Kim), Patrick McGoohan (Dr. Paul Ruth), Lawrence Dane (Keller), Charles Shamata (Gaudi), Adam Ludwig (Crostic), Michael Ironside (Darryl Revok), Victor Desy (Dr. Gatineau).

"Scanners" are mutants born to pregnant women who had been given a thalidomide-like drug. The Scanners are able to will other people to literally explode. Some plan to use this power for evil purposes. Well, who would've have thought it?

2595. *Scarecrows* (1988, Effigy/Forum, 88m, c). P Cami Winikoff &

William Wesley, D Wesley, W Richard Jefferies & Wesley (based on a story by Wesley), PH Peter Deming, M Terry Plumeri, ED Wesley, SE J.B. Jones & Norman Cabrera.

LP Ted Vernon (Corbin), Michael Simms (Curry), Richard Vidan (Jack), Kristina Sanborn (Roxanne), Victoria Christian (Kellie), David Campbell (Al), B.J. Turner (Bert), Dax Vernon (Dax the Dog).

The film starts with a group of paramilitary types pulling off a heist at a Marine base, hijacking a plane, kidnapping the pilot and his daughter, and then being double-crossed by one of their numbers. The real meat is about mysterious scarecrows who kill their victims with scythes. When the jolly little band of mercenaries land their plane in a remote area with only one abandoned house around, the battle is joined.

2596. *Scared to Death* (1981, Lone Star, 95m, c, aka *The Terror Factor*). P Rand Marlis & Gil Shelton, D&W William Malone, PH Patrick Prince, M Tom Chase & Ardell Hake, ED Warren Chadwick, SE Malone & Robert Short.

LP John Stinson (Ted Lonergan), Diana Davidson (Jennifer Stanton), Jonathan David Moses (Lou Capell), Toni Jannotta (Sherry Carpenter), Kermit Eller (Syngenor), Walker Edmiston, Pamela Bowman.

Police inspector David Moses and ex-cop John Stinson had never seen murder victims like this before. Their bodies have been mutilated. Well, what do you expect, their killer isn't human....

The Scaremaker see *Girls Night Out*

2597. *Scarface* (1983, Universal, 170m, c). P Martin Bregman & Peter Saphier, D Brian De Palma, W Oliver Stone (based on the 1932 script by Ben Hecht), PH John A. Alonzo, M Giorgio Moroder, ED Jerry Greenberg & David Ray, AD Ed Richardson.

LP Al Pacino (Tony Montana), Steven Bauer (Manny Ray), Michelle Pfeiffer (Elvira), Mary Elizabeth Mastrantonio (Gina), Robert Loggia (Frank Lopez), Miriam Colon (Mama Montana), F. Murray Abraham (Omar), Paul Shenar (Alejandro Sosa), Harris Yulin (Bernstein), Angel Salazar (Chi Chi).

Optimists tend to have high expectations for updated reworkings of film classics, especially when the production has the cast and crew of this film. This said, we must report that this remake of the 1932 film *Scarface* starring Paul Muni is a ghastly bomb. The extra 71 minutes is not used to advantage. It only gives Cuban refugee Al Pacino, who works his way up to becoming a major Miami drug lord, a greater opportunity to exhibit his foul-mouthed vocabulary. The film's grisly scenes put the various splatter exploitation films to shame. It seems that the spilling of blood and guts in various nauseatingly cruel ways takes the place of story and acting. We don't so much object to director Brian De Palma's making a movie for sickies, but it's so poorly done.

2598. *Scarred* (1984, Seymour Borde, 85m, c, aka *Red on Red; Street Love*). P Marie Turko, Mark Borde & Dan Halperine, D&W Turko, PH Michael Miner, ED Turko, AD Cecilia Rodarte.

LP Jennifer Mayo (Ruby Star), Jackie Berryman (Carla), David Dean (Easy), Rico L. Richardson (Jojo), Debbie Dion (Sandy), Lili (Rita), Randolph Pitts & Walter Klenhard (Tricks).

In order to support her baby, unwed mother Jennifer Mayo turns to street prostitution. It's an honest look at a seedy life but budget restrictions hurt it.

2599. *Scavengers* (1988, Anglo Pacific/Triax, 94m, c). P Chris Davies & David Barrett, D&W Duncan McLachlan, PH Johan Van Der Veer, M Nick Picard & Ferdi Brendgen, ED C.J. Appel, PD Roy Rudolphe.

LP Kenneth David Gilman (Tom Reed), Brenda Bakke (Kimberly Blake), Crispin De Nys (Col. Chenko), Cocky "Two-Bull" Tihothalemaj (February), Norman Anstey (Boris), Somizi Mhlongo (Jeffrey), Patrick Mynhart (Pavloski).

Ornithologist Kenneth David Gilman, known as the "Vulture Man," is mistaken for a government agent. He soon finds himself in Africa with his former girlfriend Brenda Bakke being chased by both Russian agents and drug-runners.

2600. *Scenes from the Class Struggle in Beverly Hills* (1989, Cinecom, 102m, c).

P James C. Katz. D Paul Bartel, W Bruce Wagner (based on a story by Bartel & Wagner), PH Steven Fierberg, M Stanley Myers, ED Alan Toomayan, PD Alex Tavoularis.

LP Jacqueline Bisset (Clare), Ray Sharkey (Frank), Robert Beltran (Juan), Mary Woronov (Lisabeth), Ed Begley, Jr. (Peter), Wallace Shawn (Howard), Arnetia Walker (To-bel), Paul Mazursky (Sidney), Rebecca Schaeffer (Zandra), Edith Diaz (Rosa), Paul Bartel (Dr. Mo Van de Kamp).

This farce from the maker of *Eating Raoul,* like that black comedy, is a series of comical set pieces with a great number of funny lines, but no cohesive plot. It's really more the presentation of a group of unusual characters interacting in strange but amusing ways. It definitely isn't for every one, but if camp is your ticket, it might please.

2601. *Scenes from the Goldmine* (1988, Hemdale, 105m, c). P Danny Eisenberg, Marc Rocco & Pierre David, D Rocco, W Rocco, John Norvet & Danny Eisenberg, PH Cliff Ralke, M Steve Delacy, Rocco & Eisenberg, ED Russell Livingstone, PD Matthew Jacobs.

LP Catherine Mary Stewart (Debi Di-Angelo), Cameron Dye (Niles Dresden), Steve Railsback (Harry), Joe Pantoliano (Manny), John Ford Coley (Kenny Bond), Timothy B. Schmit (Dennis), Alex Rocco (Nathan DiAngelo).

Things are not all peaches and cream in the rock 'n' roll world. Promising female keyboardist/songwriter Catherine Mary Stewart has a hellish time when her unscrupulous manager convinces band leader Cameron Dye and Stewart's current lover to take credit for the songs she's written.

2602. *Schizoid* (1980, Cannon, 91m, c, aka *Murder by Mail*). P Menahem Golan & Yoram Globus, D&W David Paulsen, PH Norman Leigh, M Craig Hundley, ED Robert Fitzgerald & Dick Brummer, AD Kathy Curtis Cahill.

LP Klaus Kinski (Dr. Peter Fales), Marianna Hill (Julie), Craig Wasson (Doug), Donna Wilkes (Alison Fales), Richard Herd (Donahue), Joe Regalbuto (Jake), Christopher Lloyd (Gilbert), Flo Gerrish (Pat).

One-by-one, the nubile young women who make up psychiatrist Klaus Kinski's group-therapy patients are being slashed by someone wielding a pair of scissors. These same cutting instruments are being used to cut out letters for a correspondence between the killer and advice columnist Marianna Hill, who just happens to be a member of the therapy group.

2603. *School Daze* (1988, Columbia, 120m, c). P,D&W Spike Lee, PH Ernest Dickerson, M Bill Lee, ED Barry Alexander Brown, PD Wynn Thomas.

LP Larry Fishburne (Dap Dunlap), Giancarlo Esposito (Julian "Big Brother Almighty" Eaves), Tisha Campbell (Jane Toussaint), Kyme (Rachel Meadows), Joe Seneca (President McPherson), Art Evans (Cedar Cloud), Ellen Holly (Odrie McPherson), Ossie Davis (Coach Odom), Spike Lee (Half-Pint), Gregg Burge (Virgil Cloyd).

Spike Lee shows a split in the attitudes of blacks by examining the social and political divisions of two fraternities in a fictional Southern black school. The dark-skinned "Jigaboos" want total and immediate divestment of the school's South African investments, and the light-skinned "Wannabees" (wanna be white) favor a more gradual approach.

2604. *School Spirit* (1985, Concorde, 90m, c). P Ashok Amritraj & Jeff Begun, D Alan Holleb, PH Robert Ebinger, M Tom Bruner, ED Sonya Sones, PD Peter Knowlton.

LP Tom Nolan (Billy Batson), Elizabeth Foxx (Judith Hightower), Larry Linville (President Grimshaw), Daniele Arnaud (Madeleine), Nick Segal (Gregg), Marta Kober (Ursula), Robert Collins (Helen Grimshaw).

Racing his car to get back to campus for an assignation with sorority cutey Elizabeth Foxx, Tom Nolan runs into a truck and is killed. Game fellow, he gets up and portrays his ghost for the rest of the movie. He especially enjoys his ability to be seen or not at will as he roams the sorority shower room. Try and imagine a ghostly *Porky's* and you have the idea.

2605. *Scorpion* (1986, Crown Intl., 98m, c, aka *The Summons*). P,D&W William Riead, PH Bill Philbin, M Sean Murray, ED Gigi Coello.

LP Tommy Tulleners (Steve), Don Murray (Gifford), Robert Logan (Gordon), Allen Williams (Keller), Kathryn Daley (Jackie), Ross Elliott (Sam), John Anderson (Neal), Bart Braverman (Mehdi), Thom McFadden (Lt. Woodman).

Tommy Tulleners, a martial arts expert who takes on a bunch of terrorists, makes other martial arts actors look like Lord Olivier.

2606. Scream (1985, Vestron, 81m, c, aka *The Outing*). P Clara Huff, Hal Buchanan & Larry Quisenberry, D&W Byron Quisenberry, PH Rick Pepin, M Joseph Conlan, ED B.W. Kestenberg.

LP Pepper Martin (Bob), Hank Worden (John), Alvy Moore (Al), John Ethan Wayne (Stan), Julie Marine (Laura), Gregg Palmer (Ross), Woody Strode (Charlie).

Vacationers in a western ghost town are bumped off one-by-one. It's a slow-moving, lifeless squandering of film.

2607. Scream for Help (1984, Lorimar, 88m, c). P&D Michael Winner, W Tom Holland, PH Robert Paynter, M John Paul Jones, ED Arnold Ross, AD Tony Reading.

LP Rachel Kelly (Christie Cromwell), Marie Masters (Karen Cromwell Fox), David Brooks (Paul Fox), Lolita Lorre (Brenda Bohle), Rocco Sisto (Lacey Bohle), Corey Parker (John Dealey), Sandra Clark (Janey).

Rachel Kelly can't get the police to take seriously her fears that her stepfather David Brooks is plotting to kill her mother Marie Masters, even when a couple of murder traps kill two innocent parties by mistake.

2608. Screamplay (1985, Boston Movie Co., 90m, b&w). P Dennis M. Piana, D Rufus Butler Seder, W Seder & Ed Greenberg, PH Piana, M George Cordeiro & Basil J. Bova, ED Seder, AD Cheryl Hirschman.

LP Rufus Butler Seder (Edgar Allen), George Kuchar (Holly), George Cordeiro (Sgt. Joe Blatz), Basil J. Bova (Tony Cassano), M. Lynder Robinson (Mina Ray), Eugene Seder (Al Weiner).

It's just one more low-budget horror film featuring a crazy killer.

2609. Screamtime (1986, Rugged Films, GB, 89m, c). P&D Al Beresford, W Michael Armstrong, PH Don Lord, Alain Pudney & Mike Spera, M KPM, ED Uncredited.

LP Robin Bailey (Jack Grimshaw), Ann Lynn (Lena), Ian Saynor (Tony), Yvonne Nicholson (Susan), David Van Day (Gavin), Dora Bryan (Emma).

When two fiendish friends swipe some horror videos, strange things happen after they watch them.

2610. Screen Test (1986, CinTel Films, 88m, c). P&W Sam Auster & Laura Auster, D Sam Auster, PH Jeff Jur, M Don Harrow, ED Carol Eastman.

LP Michael Allan Bloom (Terry), Monique Gabrielle (Roxanne), David Simpatico (Stevie), Paul Leuken (Dan), William Dick (Dr. DeSade), Robert Bundy (Clayton).

Four horny teen boys arrange for phony porno video screen tests to attract girls. The casting call is a mixed bag — the Mafia princess causes the most trouble for our heroes.

2611. Screwball Hotel (1989, Universal, US/GB, 101m, c). P Maurice Smith, D Rafal Zielinski, W B.K. Roderick, Phil Kueber, Charles Wiener & Nick Holeris, PH Thomas F. De Nove, M Nathan Wang, ED Joseph Tornatore, PD Naomi Shohan.

LP Michael C. Bendetti (Mike), Jeff Greenman (Norman), Andrew Zeller (Herbie), Kelly Monteith (Mr. Ebbel), Corinne Alphen (Cherry Amour), Charles Ballinger (Stoner), Laurah Guillen (Miss Walsh).

Michael C. Bendetti, Jeff Greenman and Andrew Zeller are loose in a resort setting, surrounded by beautiful girls. They work for the Rochester Hotel, which they try to save from being taken over by corrupt schemer Charles Ballinger. They come up with some bizarre fundraising techniques, not all legal.

2612. Screwballs (1983, New World, 80m, c). P Maurice Smith, D Rafal Zielinski, W Linda Shayne & Jim Wynorski, PH Miklos Lente, M Tim McCauley, ED Brian Ravok, AD Sandra Kybartas.

LP Peter Keleghan (Rick McKay), Linda Speciale (Purity Busch), Alan

Daveau (Howie Bates), Kent Deuters (Brent Van Dusen, III), Jason Warren (Melvin Jerkovski), Linda Shayne (Bootsie Goodhead), Jim Coburn (Tim Stevenson).

A group of teenage boys at T&A High go *Porky's* one better. Their sport is strip bowling. They also cause a lot of trouble for the school's snooty and virginal homecoming queen, Linda Speciale.

2613. *Scrooged* (1988, Paramount, 101m, c). P Richard Donner, Art Linson & Ray Hartwick, D Donner, W Mitch Glazer & Michael O'Donoghue, PH Michael Chapman, M Danny Elfman, ED Fredric Steinkamp & William Steinkamp, PD J. Michael Riva, MK Tom Burman & Bari Dreiband-Burman†.

LP Bill Murray (Frank Cross), Karen Allen (Claire Phillips), John Forsythe (Lew Hayward), John Glover (Brice Cummings), Bobcat Goldthwait (Eliot Loudermilk), David Johansen (Ghost of Christmas Past), Carol Kane (Ghost of Christmas Present), Robert Mitchum (Preston Rhinelander), Nicholas Phillips (Calvin Cooley), Michael J. Pollard (Herman).

Bill Murray, a cynical TV network executive, has lost the meaning of Christmas. While overseeing a production of Dickens' *A Christmas Carol,* three ghostly figures from the past, present and future arrive to rekindle the spirit within him. Give us Alastair Sim if you don't mind.

2614. *Scrubbers* (1984, Orion, GB, 90m, c). P Don Boyd, D Mai Zetterling, W Zetterling, Roy Minton & Jeremy Watt, PH Ernest Vincze, M Michael Hurd & Ray Cooper, ED Rodney Holland, AD Celia Barnett.

LP Amanda York (Carol), Chrissie Cotterill (Annetta), Elizabeth Edmonds (Kathleen), Kate Ingram (Eddie), Debbie Bishop (Doreen), Dana Gillespie (Budd), Camille Davis (Sharon), Amanda Symonds (Mac), Kathy Burke (Glennis).

This is an unflinching look at British girls' reform schools. Amanda York is the naive youngster who is the target of the obligatory lesbian.

2615. *Scum* (1980, World Northal, GB, 96m, c). P Davina Belling & Clive Parsons, D Alan Clarke, W Roy Minton, PH Phil Meheux, ED Mike Bradsell, AD Mike Porter.

LP Ray Winstone (Carlin), Mick Ford (Archer), John Judd (Sands), Phil Daniels (Richards), John Blundell (Banks), Ray Burdis (Eckersley), Julian Firth (Davis), Alrick Riley (Angel), John Fowler (Woods).

Transferred to a rough and tough prison for his rebellious behavior, Ray Winstone runs afoul of John Blundell who violently attacks the newcomer. Winstone befriends Mick Ford, an older con, and eventually leads the prisoners in a riot to protest conditions.

2616. *Sea of Love* (1989, Universal, 110m, c). P Martin Bregman & Louis A. Stroller, D Harold Becker, W Richard Price, PH Ronnie Taylor, M Trevor Jones, ED David Bretherton, PD John Jay Moore.

LP Al Pacino (Frank Keller), Ellen Barkin (Helen), John Goodman (Sherman), Michael Rooker (Terry), William Hickey (Frank, Sr.), Richard Jenkins (Gruber), Paul Calderon (Serafino), Gene Canfield (Struk), Barbara Baxley (Miss Allen), Jacqueline Brookes (Helen's Mother).

Lonely cop Al Pacino drinks too much and is essentially an emotional and physical wreck. He and his partner John Goodman are working on a case of murders committed by someone who is ridding the world of womanizers who meet females by answering ads in personal columns. Each man has been found face down on a bed, nude, with fatal wounds in his back. Pacino and Goodman put their own ads in the personal columns to see what they can come up with. The chief suspect among the respondents is Ellen Barkin who also seems the most likely solution to Pacino's loneliness. Unfortunately Pacino makes very few movies and when he does, fans hope they will be better than this sluggish, long-winded puffball.

2617. *The Sea Wolves* (1981, Paramount, GB, 120m, c). P Euan Lloyd, D Andrew V. McLaglen, W Reginald Rose (based on the novel *The Boarding Party* by James Leasor), PH Tony Imi, M Roy Budd, ED John Glen, PD Syd Cain.

LP Gregory Peck (Col. Lewis Pugh), Roger Moore (Capt. Gavin Stewart), David Niven (Col. Bill Grice), Trevor Howard (Jack Cartwright), Barbara Kellerman (Mrs. Cromwell), Patrick MacNee (Maj. Yogi Crossley), Patrick Allen (Colin MacKenzie), Bernard Archard (Underhill).

Gregory Peck leads a fine cast in this wartime true-story thriller about a commando style operation undertaken in 1943 India by a group of middle-aged boozing British businessmen.

2618. *Search and Destroy* (1981, Film Ventures, 93m, c). P James Margellos, D William Fruet, W Don Enright, PH Rene Verzier, M FM, ED Donald Ginsberg.

LP Perry King (Kip Moore), Don Stroud (Buddy Grant), Tisa Farrow (Kate), Park Jong Soo (Assassin), George Kennedy (Anthony Fusqua), Tony Sheer (Frank Malone).

After the Vietnam war, a Vietnamese official left behind by the U.S. troops during the evacuation travels to the U.S. to get revenge for his abandonment.

Search for the Mother Lode see Mother Lode

Searchers of the Voodoo Mountain   see Warriors of the Apocalypse

2619. *Season of Fear* (1989, MGM/United Artists, 89m, c). P Scott J. Mulvaney, D Doug Campbell, W Campbell (based on a story by Campbell & Mulvaney), PH Chuy Elizondo, M David Wolinski, ED Dan Selakovich, PD Phillip Michael Brandes.

LP Michael Bowen (Mick Drummond), Ray Wise (Fred Drummond), Clancy Brown (Ward), Clara Wren (Sarah Drummond), Michael J. Pollard (Bob).

Even though Michael Bowen's father Ray Wise left him and his mother 20 years earlier, the bitter and resentful son responds positively when his father invites him for a visit. When Bowen arrives for the weekend, there's no sign of his father, but beautiful blond Clara Wren makes him feel right at home in her bed. She's his stepmother and has some plans for him and his father, à la *Body Heat*.

2620. *Second-Hand Hearts* (1981, Paramount, 102m, c). P James William Guercio, D Hal Ashby, W Charles Eastman, PH Haskell Wexler, M Willis Alan Ramsey, ED Amy Holden Jones, PD Peter Wooley.

LP Robert Blake (Loyal Muke), Barbara Harris (Dinette Dusty), Collin Boone (Human), Amber Rose Gold (Iota), Jessica Stansbury & Erica Stansbury (Sandra Dee), Bert Remsen (Voyd), Sondra Blake (Ermy), Shirley Stoler (Maxy).

Robert Blake and Barbara Harris are two dumb Texans, who meet, marry and decide that they can find more happiness in California, so they travel there. Along the way they see a bit of the country and a few characters. Something's missing here.

2621. *Second Sight* (1989, Warner, 83m, c). P Mark Tarlov, D Joel Zwick, W Tom Schulman & Patricia Resnick, PH Dana Christiaansen, M John Morris, ED David Ray, PD James L. Schoppe.

LP John Larroquette (Wills), Bronson Pinchot (Bobby McGee), Stuart Pankin (Dr. Preston Pickett), Bess Armstrong (Sister Elizabeth), John Schuck (Lt. Manoogian), James Tolkan (Captain Coolidge), Christine Estabrook (Priscilla).

TV comedians John Larroquette ("Night Court") and Bronson Pinchot ("Perfect Strangers") haven't altered their characters much for their roles in this not-so-funny story. Upon being hit by lightning simple-minded Pinchot becomes a psychic who is exploited by his misanthropic business partner Larroquette.

2622. *Second Thoughts* (1983, Universal, 98m, c). P Lawrence Turman & David Foster, D Turman, W Steve Brown (based on a story by Brown & Terry Louise Fisher), PH King Baggot, M Henry Mancini, ED Neil Travis, PD Paul Peters.

LP Lucie Arnaz (Amy), Craig Wasson (Will), Ken Howard (John Michael), Anne Schedeen (Janis), Arthur Rosenberg (Dr. Eastman), Peggy McCay (Dr. Martha Carpenter), Tammy Taylor (Sharon), Alan Stock (Hondo).

Frustrated attorney Lucie Arnaz divorces her husband Ken Howard to move in with one of her hippie clients Craig Wasson. She soon finds the new relationship isn't working out and leaves him. When she finds she's pregnant and opts for an abortion, Wasson kidnaps her to prevent it.

2623. *Second Time Lucky* (1984, United International, Australia/New Zealand, 98m, c). P Anthony I. Ginnane, D Michael Anderson, W Ross Dimsey, David Sigmund & Howard Grigsby (based on a story by Dimsey & Sigmund), PH John McLean, M Garry McDonald & Laurie Stone, ED Terry Paterson, PD David Copping.

LP Diane Franklin (Eve), Roger Wilson (Adam), Robert Helpmann (The Devil), Jon Gadsby (Gabriel), John-Michael Howson (The Devil's Assistant), Bill Ewens (Chuck), Robert Morley (God).

The devil makes a bet with God that if the world were to start over again, Adam and Eve would make the same mistake. Sounds like a sucker bet to us.

2624. *Secret Admirer* (1985, Orion, 98m, c). P Stephen J. Roth & Jim Kouf, D David Greenwalt, W Kouf & Greenwalt, PH Victor J. Kemper, M Jan Hammer, ED Dennis Virkler, PD William J. Cassidy.

LP C. Thomas Howell (Michael Ryan), Lori Loughlin (Toni), Kelly Preston (Debora Anne Fimple), Dee Walker Stone (Connie Ryan), Cliff De Young (George Ryan), Fred Ward (Lou Fimple), Leigh Taylor-Young (Elizabeth Fimple), Casey Siemaszko (Roger Despard).

Teen Lori Loughlin leaves love notes for C. Thomas Howell but they are misdirected. Loughlin and Howell's respective parents believe that the notes are indications of unfaithlessness of their mates. The story insults the intelligence of even the most hardened teen exploitation fans.

2625. *The Secret Diary of Sigmund Freud* (1984, 20th Century–Fox, 99m, c). P Wendy Hyland & Peer Oppenheimer, D Danford B. Greene, W Roberto Mitrotti & Linda Howard, PH George Nikolic, M V. Boris, AD Miodrag Miric.

LP Bud Cort (Sigmund Freud), Carol Kane (Martha Bernays), Klaus Kinski (Dr. Max Bauer), Marisa Berenson (Emma Herrmann), Carroll Baker (Mama Freud), Dick Shawn (The Ultimate Patient), Ferdinand Mayne (Herr Herrmann), Nikola Simic (Papa Freud), Rade Markovic (Dr. Schtupmann).

In this strange comedy, Bud Cort as Sigmund Freud learns about sex from his mother Carroll Baker, experiments with drugs, and hypnotizes his assistant Carol Kane into falling madly in love with him. The latter becomes extremely jealous of Cort's first patient Marisa Berenson.

2626. *Secret Honor* (1984, Cinecom, 90m, c, aka *Secret Honor: The Last Testament of Richard M. Nixon; Secret Honor: A Political Myth*). P&D Robert Altman, W Donald Freed & Arnold M. Stone (based on their stage play), PH Pierre Mignot, M George Burt, ED Juliet Weber, AD Stephen Altman.

LP Philip Baker Hall (President Richard M. Nixon).

In this scathing portrait of Richard M. Nixon, actor Philip Baker Hall portrays the ex-president pacing around his study, reminiscing and bitterly attacking the memories of politicians with whom he interacted over the years. Even Nixon-haters will find it difficult to enjoy this mean-spirited and malicious film.

Secret Honor: The Last Temptation of Richard M. Nixon see Secret Honor

Secret Honor: A Political Myth see Secret Honor

2627. *The Secret of My Success* (1987, Universal, 110m, c). P&D Herbert Ross, W Jim Cash & Jack Epps, Jr., A.J. Carothers (based on a story by Carothers), PH Carlo Di Palma, M David Foster, ED Paul Hirsch, PD Edward Pisoni, Peter Larkin.

LP Michael J. Fox (Brantley Foster), Helen Slater (Christy Wills), Richard Jordan (Howard Prescott), Margaret Whitton (Vera Prescott), John Pankow (Fred Melrose), Christopher Murney (Barney Rattigan), Gerry Banman (Art Thomas), Fred Gwynne (Donald Davenport).

Michael J. Fox tries to prove that one can succeed in the business world on the basis of talent, not through sleeping your way to the top. He seems defeated by the notion that advancement is made in the sack. He's bedded by Margaret Whitton, his boss' wife, while Helen Slater, the girl of his dreams, is sleeping with his boss, Richard Jordan.

2628. The Secret of N.I.M.H. (1982, MGM/United Artists, animated, 82m, c). P Don Bluth, Gary Goldman & John Pomeroy, D Bluth, W Bluth, Goldman, Pomeroy & Will Finn (based on the novel *Mrs. Frisby and the Rats of N.I.M.H.* by Robert C. O'Brien), PH Joe Jiuliano, Charles Warren & Jeff Mellquist, M Jerry Goldsmith, ED Jeffrey Patch.

VOICES Derek Jacobi (Nicodemus), Elizabeth Hartman (Mrs. Brisby), Arthur Malet (Ages), Dom DeLuise (Jeremy), Hermione Baddeley (Auntie Shrew), John Carradine (Great Owl), Peter Strauss (Justin), Paul Shenar (Jennar).

Disney-trained animators bring to the screen Robert C. O'Brien's charming tale about a newly-widowed mouse and her four little ones that need to be protected from danger. They get some help from escaped laboratory rats with superior intelligence.

2629. The Secret of the Sword (1985, Atlantic, animated, 100m, c). P Arthur H. Nadel, D Ed Friedman, Lou Kachivas, Marsh Lamore, Bill Reed & Gwen Wetzler, W Larry Ditillo & Robert Forward, M Shuki Levy, Haim Saban & Erika Lane, ED Joe Gall, Rich Gehr & Robert Crawford.

VOICES John Erwin (He-Man), Melendy Britt (She-Ra), George DiCenzo (Hordak), Linda Gary, Erika Scheimer, Erick Gunden, Alan Oppenheimer.

He-Man must rescue his sister She-Ra from the evil clutches of evil ruler Hordak. Not for anyone over 10 — or under.

2630. Secret Places (1984, 20th Century–Fox, GB, 98m, c). P Simon Relph & Ann Skinner, D Zelda Barron, W Barron (based on the novel by Janice Elliott), PH Peter MacDonald, M Michel Legrand, ED Laurence Mery-Clark, PD Eileen Diss.

LP Marie-Theres Relin (Laura Meister), Tara MacGowran (Patience), Claudine Auger (Sophy Meister), Ann-Marie Gwatkin (Rose), Pippa Hinchley (Barbara), Klaus Barner (Wolfgang Meister), Jenny Agutter (Miss Lowrie), Cassie Stuart (Nina), Sylvia Coleridge (Miss Trott), Rosemary Martin (Mrs. MacKenzie).

This drama is the story of the friendship of shy ugly-duckling Tara MacGowran and sophisticated refugee Marie-Theres Relin at a 1942 British girls school. Relin is the daughter of a German gentile couple, forced to flee Nazi Germany when they were denounced by their Hitler Youth son.

2631. Secrets (1984, Samuel Goldwyn, GB, 78m, c). P Chris Griffin, D Gavin Millar, W Noella Smith, PH Christopher Challis, M Guy Woolfenden, ED Eric Boyd-Perkins, AD Jeffrey Woolbridge.

LP Helen Lindsay (Mother), John Horsley (Dr. Jefferies), Anna Campbell-Jones (Louise), Daisy Cockburn (Sydney), Rebecca Johnson (Trottie), Lucy Goode (Jane), Richard Tolan (Paul), Carol Gillies (Miss Quick), Jane Briers (Miss Strickland).

Thirteen-year-old Anna Campbell-Jones, an innocent British school girl, is the victim of a mess of misunderstanding when a box of condoms is found in her room.

2632. The Seduction (1982, Avco Embassy, 104m, c). P Irwin Yablans & Bruce Cohn Curtis, D&W David Schmoeller, PH Mac Ahlberg, M Lalo Schifrin, ED Tony DiMarco.

LP Morgan Fairchild (Jamie), Michael Sarrazin (Brandon), Vince Edwards (Maxwell), Andrew Stevens (Derek), Colleen Camp (Robin), Kevin Brophy (Bobby), Wendy Smith Howard (Julie), Woodrow Parfrey (Salesman).

Newscaster Morgan Fairchild is stalked and tormented by psychotic photographer Andrew Stevens, obsessed with her beauty.

2633. Seduction: The Cruel Woman (1989, First Run Features, Ger., 90m, c). P,D&W Elfi Mikesch & Monika Treut, PH Mikesch, ED Renate Merck.

LP Mechthild Grossmann (Wanda), Carola Regnier (Caren), Udo Kier (Gregor), Sheila McLaughlin (Justine), Georgette Dee (Friederike), Peter Weibel (Herr Marsch).

Mechthild Grossmann runs a sex gallery where her friends and lovers perform S&M scenes for the entertainment of her audiences.

2634. *See No Evil, Hear No Evil* (1989, Tri-Star, 103m, c). P Marvin Worth, D Arthur Hiller, W Earl Barret, Arne Sultan, Eliot Wald, Andrew Kurtzman & Gene Wilder (based on a story by Barret, Sultan & Worth), PH Victor J. Kemper, M Stewart Copeland, ED Robert C. Jones, PD Robert Gundlach.

LP Richard Pryor (Wally), Gene Wilder (Dave), Joan Severance (Eve), Kevin Spacey (Kirgo), Alan North (Braddock), Anthony Zerbe (Sutherland), Louis Giambalvo (Gatlin), Kirsten Childs (Adele).

Once upon a time Gene Wilder and Richard Pryor appeared together in a movie and were moderately funny together. Ever since they have been trying to recapture that minor glory. Once again they have only partially succeeded. Their movie about deaf Wilder and blind Pryor who somehow complement each other is not this year's *Rain Man*. Somehow the two must solve a murder involving a beautiful woman, whose perfume Pryor remembers and whose legs have made a deep impression on Wilder. Most of the jokes are predictable and fall flat, just short of being offensive and insensitive to the physically challenged.

2635. *See You in the Morning* (1989, Warner, 116m, c). P,D&W Alan J. Pakula, PH Donald McAlpine, M Michael Small, ED Evan Lottman, PD George Jenkins.

LP Jeff Bridges (Larry Livingston), Alice Krige (Beth Goodwin), Farrah Fawcett (Jo), Drew Barrymore (Cathy), Lukas Haas (Petey), David Dukes (Peter), Frances Sternhagen (Neenie), Linda Lavin (Sidney).

Director Alan J. Pakula's film deals with adjustments which must be made in second marriages while everyone still feels guilty for messing up their first less-than-blissful union. Talented photographer Alice Krige can't forgive herself for her concert pianist husband's taking his own life when he became despondent due to a paralyzed left hand. Psychiatrist Jeff Bridges was married to Farrah Fawcett, America's most famous TV model, and couldn't deal with it. Almost reluctantly Krige and Bridges marry, hoping they and their respective children can suc-cessfully make the needed adjustments. This romantic comedy is advertised as "a personal family drama."

Seed of Innocence   see   Teen Mothers

2636. *Seems Like Old Times* (1980, Columbia, 102m, c). P Ray Stark, D Jay Sandrich, W Neil Simon, PH David M. Walsh, M Marvin Hamlisch, ED Michael A. Stevenson, PD Gene Callahan.

LP Goldie Hawn (Glenda), Chevy Chase (Nick), Charles Grodin (Ira), Robert Guillaume (Fred), Harold Gould (Judge), George Grizzard (Governor), Yvonne Wilder (Aurora), T.K. Carter (Chester), Judd Omen (Dex), Marc Alaimo (Bee Gee).

When Chevy Chase innocently gets involved in a bank robbery, he seeks help from his ex-wife Goldie Hawn, a very liberal lawyer. She's now married to the local district attorney, Charles Grodin. By the end of the film, the latter is out of the picture as far as Chase and Hawn are concerned.

Self Defense   see   Siege

2637. *The Sender* (1982, Paramount, GB, 91m, c). P Edward S. Feldman, D Roger Christian, W Thomas Baum, PH Roger Pratt, M Trevor Jones, ED Alan Strachan, PD Malcolm Middleton.

LP Kathryn Harrold (Gail Farmer), Zeljko Ivanek (The Sender), Shirley Knight (Jerolyn), Paul Freeman (Dr. Denman), Sean Hewitt (The Messiah), Harry Ditson (Dr. Hirsch), Olivier Pierre (Dr. Erskine).

Psychiatrist Kathryn Harrold discovers her amnesiac patient Zeljko Ivanek is a "sender" who can transmit his nightmares to others. Ivanek's mother Shirley Knight is raising him to be another Messiah.

2638. *Senior Week* (1988, Skouras, 98m, c). P Ken Schwenker & Matt Ferro, D Stuart Goldman, W Jan Kubicki, Goldman & Stacey Lynn Fravel, PH John A. Corso, M Ken Mazur & Russ Landau, ED Richard Dama, PD John Lawless.

LP Michael St. Gerard (Everett), Gary Kerr (Jody), George Klek (Jamie), Jennifer Gorey (Tracy), Leesa Bryte (Stacy), Alan Naggar (Kevin), Barbara Gruen (Miss Bagley).

A group of New Jersey teens hit the road for Daytona Beach and a final fling before graduation. It's the usual teenage sexploitation nonsense. Films like this and hardcore pornography both suffer from a lack of any real sexiness.

2639. *A Sense of Freedom* (1985, Island, GB, 85m, c). P Jeremy Isaacs, D John Mackenzie, W Peter McDougall (based on the book by Jimmy Boyle), PH Chris Menges, M Frankie Miller & Rory Gallagher, PD Geoff Nixon.

LP David Hayman (Jimmy Boyle), Alex Norton (Malkie), Jake D'Arcy (Robbie), Sean Scanlon (Jackie), Fulton Mackay (Inspector Davidson), John Murtagh (Piper), Roy Hanlon (Chief Officer), Martin Black (Bobbie).

The film is based on the real-life career of a Glaswegian gangster who was quick with his fists. He was seemingly unintimidated by anyone as he was transferred from one prison to another. Ultimately, he reformed and married a psychiatrist, with whom he established a series of halfway houses for the rehabilitation of convicts.

2640. *Separate Vacations* (1986, RSL Entertainment, Canada, 82m, c). P Robert Lantos & Stephen J. Roth, D Michael Anderson, W Robert Kaufman, PH Francois Protat, ED Ron Wisman, PD Csaba Kertesz.

LP David Naughton (Richard Moore), Jennifer Dale (Sarah Moore), Mark Keyloun (Jeff Ferguson), Laurie Holden (Karen), Blanca Guerra (Alicia), Suzie Almgren (Helen Gilbert), Lally Cadeau (Shelle).

David Naughton and Jennifer Dale decide to take separate vacations. He travels to Mexico where he constantly strikes out with beautiful women. She takes the kids skiing and is pursued by a ski instructor. They each have flashbacks of their courting days, trying to figure why the romance went out of their relationship.

2641. *Separate Ways* (1983, Crown Intl., 92m, c). P&D Howard Avedis, W Leah Appet (based on the story by Appet, Avedis & Marlene Schmidt), PH Dean Cundey, M John Cacavas, ED John Wright, AD Chuck Seaton.

LP Karen Black (Valentine Colby), Tony LoBianco (Ken Colby), Arlene Golonka (Annie), David Naughton (Jerry), Jack Carter (Barney), Sharon Farrell (Karen), William Windom (Huey), Robert Fuller (Woody).

Unhappy housewife Karen Black begins an affair with art student David Naughton. When she discovers that her bored husband Tony LoBianco is also having an affair, she moves out and takes a job as a waitress. The rest of the movie is about how the couple get back together and form a new perspective of themselves and their marriage.

2642. *September* (1987, Orion, 82m, c). P Robert Greenhut, D&W Woody Allen, PH Carlo di Palma, ED Susan E. Morse, PD Santo Loquasto.

LP Mia Farrow (Lane), Elaine Stritch (Diane), Dianne Wiest (Stephanie), Sam Waterston (Peter), Denholm Elliott (Howard), Jack Warden (Lloyd), Rosemary Murphy (Mrs. Mason), Ira Wheeler (Mr. Raines), Jane Cecil (Mrs. Raines).

A funny thing happened during the production of this Woody Allen film. When the principal photography was first completed, Maureen O'Sullivan was Diane, Sam Shepard was Peter and Charles Durning was Howard. Allen wanted to re-shoot part of the movie, but these three actors were no longer available so Allen started over. The film is not a comedy. It features Mia Farrow as the emotionally crippled daughter of celebrity Elaine Stritch. Mia confronts Elaine with their disturbing past (something akin to that of Lana Turner and daughter Cheryl Crane). The action or shall we say lack of action all takes place in a Vermont country house.

2643. *Serial* (1980, Paramount, 91m, c). P Sidney Beckerman, D Bill Persky, W Rich Eustis & Michael Elias (based on the novel by Cyra McFadden), PH Rexford Metz, M Lalo Schifrin, ED John W. Wheeler, AD Bill Sandell.

LP Martin Mull (Harvey), Tuesday Weld (Kate), Jennifer McAlister (Joan), Sam Chew, Jr. (Bill), Sally Kellerman (Martha), Anthony Battaglia (Stokeley), Bill Macy (Sam), Nita Talbot (Angela), Pamela Bellwood (Carol).

Nothing is sacred in this film, which

spoofs open marriage, health foods, exercise, psychiatry, cult religions and anything else which makes life worthwhile in California's Marin county.

2644.   *The Serpent and the Rainbow* (1988, Universal, 98m, c). P David Ladd & Doug Claybourne, D Wes Craven, W Richard Maxwell & A.R. Simoun, PH John Lindley, M Brad Fiedel, ED Glenn Farr, PD David Nichols.

LP Bill Pullman (Dennis Alan), Cathy Tyson (Marielle Celine), Zakes Mokae (Dargent Peytraud), Paul Winfield (Lucien Celine), Michael Gough (Schoonbacher), Paul Guilfoyle (Andrew Cassedy), Dey Young (Mrs. Cassedy), Theresa Merritt (Simone), Brent Jennings (Mozart).

Harvard anthropologist Bill Pullman journeys to Haiti to investigate voodoo ceremonies. He wishes to determine if the poison they use is responsible for turning participants into zombies. Pullman was the extremely stupid, but funny Earl in *Ruthless People,* and Cathy Tyson was the extremely beautiful call girl chauffeured by Bob Hoskins in *Mona Lisa.*

2645.   *Sesame Street Presents: Follow That Bird* (1985, Warner, 88m, c). P Tony Garnett, D Ken Kwapis, W Tony Geiss & Judy Freudberg, PH Curtis Clark, M Van Dyke Parks & Lennie Niehaus, ED Evan Landis, AD Carol Spier.

LP Carroll Spinney (Big Bird/Oscar), Jim Henson (Kermit the Frog/Ernie), Frank Oz (Cookie Monster/Bert/Grover), Paul Bartel (Grouch Cook), Sandra Bernhard (Grouch Waitress), John Candy (State Trooper), Chevy Chase (Newscaster), Waylon Jennings (Truck Driver), Sally Kellerman (Miss Finch).

Suffering an identity crisis, Big Bird leaves Sesame Street to live with real birds, but soon misses his home. His return journey is filled with danger.

Set-Up see Tango and Cash

2646.   *Seven Doors of Death* (1983, Aquarius, 89m, c). P Terry Levene, D Louis Fuller, W Ray Corchoran, PH Glenn Kimbell, M Mitchell Yuspeh & Ira Yuspeh.

LP Katherine MacColl, David Warbeck, Sarah Keller, Tony Saint John, Veronica Lazar.

Katherine MacColl inherits a hotel inhabited by evil zombies who came from the netherworld to invade Earth. It's pretty gruesome.

2647.   *Seven Hours to Judgement* (1988, TransWorld, 88m, c). P Mort Abrahams, D Beau Bridges, W Walter Davis & Elliot Stephens, PH Hanania Baer, M John Debney, ED Bill Butler, PD Phedon Papamichael.

LP Beau Bridges (Judge John Eden), Ron Leibman (David Reardon), Julianne Phillips (Lisa Eden), Tiny Ron (Ira), Al Freeman, Jr. (Danny Larwin), Reggie Johnson (Chino), Glen-Michael Jones (Doctor), Chris Garcia (Victor).

Judge Beau Bridges is forced to release a gang of punks charged with the brutal mugging death of Ron Leibman's wife. The latter gives Bridges seven hours to produce the evidence that will convict the street gang, or have his own wife Julianne Phillips killed.

2648.   *The Seven Magnificent Gladiators* (1984, MGM/United Artists, 86m, c). P Menahem Golan & Yoran Globus, D Bruno Mattei, W Claudio Fragasso, PH Silvano Ippoliti, M Ennio Morricone, AD Amedeo Mellone.

LP Lou Ferrigno (Gan), Sybil Danning (Julia), Brad Harris (Scipio), Dan Vadis (Nicerote), Carla Ferrigno (Pandora), Mandy Rice-Davies (Lucello), Yehuda Erfoni (Emperor).

This is sort of a *Magnificent Seven* set in mythical times. Seven gladiators do battle with a tyrant forcing a village to pay him tribute.

2649.   *Seven Minutes in Heaven* (1986, Warner, 90m, c). P Fred Roos, D Linda Feferman, W Jane Bernstein & Feferman, PH Steven Fierberg, M Robert Kraft, ED Marc Laub, PD Vaughan Edwards.

LP Jennifer Connelly (Natalie), Maddie Corman (Polly), Byron Thames (Jeff), Alan Boyce (Casey), Polly Draper (Aileen), Marshall Bell (Gerry), Michael Zaslow (Bob), Denny Dillon (Aunt Gail).

In this endearing coming-of-age story, Jennifer Connelly is an earnest student competing both in an essay contest and, with her best friend Maddie Corman, for a handsome classmate.

Seven Sisters see The House on Sorority Road

2650. *The Seventh Sign* (1988, Tri-Star, 97m, c). P Ted Field & Robert W. Cort, D Carl Schultz, W W.W. Wicket [Ellen Green] & George Kaplan [Clifford Green], PH Juan Ruiz Anchia, M Jack Nitzsche, ED Caroline Biggerstaff, PD Stephen Marsh.

LP Demi Moore (Abby Quinn), Michael Biehn (Russell Quinn), Jurgen Prochnow (David, the Boarder), Peter Friedman (Father Lucci), Manny Jacobs (Avi), John Taylor (Jimmy Zaragoza), Lee Garlington (Dr. Inness), Akosua Busia (Penny).

Demi Moore is convinced that the Apocalypse is now and that Jurgen Prochow is an avenging angel, perhaps even Christ come again. She believes he wants her baby for some end-of-the-world machinations. It's a finely crafted suspense film.

2651. *Severance* (1988, 20th Century–Fox/Lorber, 95m, c). P Ann Bohrer & David Max Steinberg, D Steinberg, W Steinberg & Cynthia Hochman, PH Steinberg, M Daniel May, ED Steinberg, Thomas R. Rodinella & Cecilia Zanuso.

LP Lou Liotta (Ray Ponti), Lisa Nicole Wolpe (Cly Ponti), Linda Christian-Jones (P.J.), Carl Pistilli (Marty), Sandra Soehngen (Sonia), Martin Haber (Lyle), Lou Bonaki (Georgie).

When Air Force officer Lou Liotta loses his wife in an automobile accident, he hits the bottle hard. Having no place else to go, he moves in with Lisa Nicole Wolpe, his go-go dancer daughter who has just purchased the house where she lived as a child.

2652. *Sex Appeal* (1986, Platinum Pictures, 84m, c). P&D Chuck Vincent, W Vincent & Craig Horrall (based on film by Jimmy James and Vincent), PH Larry Revene, M Ian Shaw & Kai Joffe, ED Marc Ubell [Vincent].

LP Louie Bonnano (Tony), Tally Brittany (Corinne), Marcia Karr (Christina), Jerome Brenner (Joseph), Marie Sawyer (Louise), Philip Campanaro (Ralph), Jeff Eagle (Donald Cromronic).

Trying to make it in the straight film world, porno-maker Chuck Vincent here shoots a softcore version of one of his XXX films. Many in his cast and production team worked with him in his more explicit features.

2653. *Sex, Lies and Videotape* (1989, Miramax, 100m, c). P Robert Newmyer & John Hardy, D&W Steven Soderbergh† (for original screenplay), PH Walt Lloyd, M Cliff Martinez, ED Soderbergh, AD Joanne Schmidt.

LP James Spader (Graham), Andie MacDowell (Ann Millaney), Peter Gallagher (John Millaney), Laura San Giacomo (Cynthia Bishop), Ron Vawter (Therapist), Steven Brill (Barfly).

Twenty-six-year-old director and writer Steven Soderbergh presents a unique look at a group of young people for whom sex is everything and nothing. Andie MacDowell can no longer stand to have her yuppie husband Peter Gallagher touch her, but she's hiding a sexuality which she doesn't understand. Meanwhile Gallagher is having an affair with Laura San Giacomo, MacDowell's sister. San Giacomo's interest in Gallagher seems more as competition with her "perfect" sister than any passion for him. Into all this walks James Spader, a one-time buddy of Gallagher, and just what Mac-Dowell seems to be missing. But he announces he's impotent and his sexual kicks comes from making videotapes of women he interviews about their sex lives. It's an intelligent, beautifully controlled film and one of the most appealing independently made movies to come along in years.

2654. *Sexbomb* (1989, Phillips & Mora Ent., 89m, c). P Rick Eye, D Jeff Broadstreet, W Robert Benson, PH Dale Larson, M Leonard Marcel, ED Todd Felker, AD Liz Simakis.

LP Robert Quarry (King Faraday), Linnea Quigley (Phoebe Love), Stuart Benton (Lou Lurrod), Delia Sheppard (Candy), Stephan Liska (Gersch/Steve), Kathryn Stanleigh (Lola), Spice Williams (Rake).

This is an ultra-low-budget dark comedy parody of ultra-low-budget filmmaking. Some will check it out of a video store for its modest humor. Others will do so to get a look at B-movie queen Linnea Quigley bare-breasted and in a black garter belt. To each his own.

2655. *Sexpot* (1988, Platinum, 93m, c). P&D Chuck Vincent, W Craig Horrall (based on the film *Mrs. Barrington* by James Vidos & Vincent), PH Larry Revene, M Joey Mennonna, ED James Davalos, AD Edmond Ramage.

LP Ruth Collins (Ivy Barrington), Joyce Lyons (Boopsie), Frank Stewart (Jackson), Gregory Patrick (Damon), Jane Hamilton (Beth), Jennifer Delora (Barbara), Christina Veronica (Betty), Troy Donahue (Phillip), Jack Carter (Cal Farnsworth), Scott Bergold (Gorilla).

This remake of Chuck Vincent's 1974 movie *Mrs. Barrington* is about a woman who marries wealthy old men and then murders them. The deaths all seem accidental, but three disinherited daughters compare notes and smell something rotten. *Black Widow* it isn't.

2656. *Shadey* (1987, Skouras, GB, 90m, c). P Otto Plaschkes, D Philip Saville, W Snoo Wilson, PH Roger Deakins, M Colin Towns, ED Chris Kelly, PD Norman Garwood.

LP Antony Sher (Oliver Shadey), Billie Whitelaw (Dr. Cloud), Patrick Macnee (Sir Cyril Landau), Leslie Ash (Carol Landau), Bernard Hepton (Capt. Amies), Larry Lamb (Dick Darnley), Katherine Helmond (Lady Constance Landau), Jon Cartwright (Shulman).

Auto mechanic Antony Sher has the ability to transmit visions of his mind to film. Secret agent Billie Whitelaw wants him to use his power to uncover strategic Russian submarine plans. But peaceloving Sher only wants to earn enough money to pay for a sex-change operation.

2657. *Shadow Play* (1986, New World, 101m, c). P Dan Biggs, Susan Shadburne & Will Vinton, D&W Susan Shadburne, PH Ron Orieux, M John Newton, ED Kenji Yamamoto.

LP Dee Wallace Stone (Morgan Hanna), Cloris Leachman (Millie Crown), Ron Kuhlman (John Crown), Barry Laws (Jeremy Crown), Delia Salvi (Bette Mertz), Susan Dixon (Zelda), Al Strobel (Byron Byron), Glen Baggerly (Archie).

After her lover takes his own life, New York playwright Dee Wallace Stone goes to his hometown where she has visions of him. Whether this is her imagination or something more sinister is the subject of the remainder of the movie. Whatever the explanation, Stone goes mad very nicely.

2658. *Shadows in the Storm* (1988, Mediacom/Vidmark, 81m, c). P Strath Hamilton & J. Daniel Dusek, D&W Terrell Tannen, PH John Connor, M Sasha Matson, ED Marcy Hamilton, AD Elizabeth Moore.

LP Ned Beatty (Thelo), Mia Sara (Melanie), Michael Madsen (Earl), Donna Mitchell, James Widdoes, Joe Dorsey, William Bumiller.

In an unusual casting decision, Ned Beatty is a John Dunne–quoting librarian and poet, fired for drunkenness. He takes to the woods to live a quiet existence, but is soon joined by exotic Mia Sara and her companion Michael Madsen. Beatty and Sara becomes lovers. He commits murder because of her and is blackmailed.

2659. *Shag* (1989, Hemdale, 98m, c). P Julia Chasman & Stephen Woolley, D Zelda Barron, W Robin Swicord, Lanier Laney & Terry Sweeney (based on a story by Laney & Sweeney), PH Peter MacDonald, ED Laurence Mery-Clark, PD Buddy Cone.

LP Phoebe Cates (Carson), Scott Coffey (Chip), Bridget Fonda (Melaina), Annabeth Gish (Pudge), Page Hannah (Luanne), Robert Rusler (Buzz), Tyrone Power, III (Harley), Jeff Yagher (Jimmy Valentine).

In the summer of 1963, three of Phoebe Cates' friends, Bridget Fonda, Annabeth Gish and Page Hannah, have mixed feeling about her imminent marriage to unliberated Tyrone Power, III. They whisk her off to Myrtle Beach for a few fun-filled days. Nothing much happens — but catch young Fonda.

2660. *Shakedown* (1988, Universal, 105m, c). P J. Boyce Harman, Jr., D&W James Glickenhaus, PH John Lindley, M Jonathan Elias, ED Paul Fried, PD Charles Bennett.

LP Peter Weller (Roland Dalton), Blanche Baker (Gail Feinberger), Patricia Charbonneau (Susan Cantrell), Sam Elliott (Richie Marks), Antonio Fargas

(Nicky Carr), Tom Waites (Officer Kelly), Kathryn Rossetter (Mrs. O'Leary).

Public defender Peter Weller teams with undercover cop Sam Elliott to fight corruption in the NYC police force. This sleazy thriller is packed with action, but the story is farfetched.

2661. Shaker Run (1985, Mirage/Aviscom/Laurelwood, New Zealand, 90m, c). P Larry Parr & Igo Kantor, D Bruce Morrison, W James Kouf, Jr., Henry Fownes & Morrison, PH Kevin Hayward, M Stephen McCurdy, ED Ken Zamke & Bob Richardson, PD Ron Highfield.

LP Cliff Robertson (Judd Pierson), Leif Garrett (Casey Lee), Lisa Harrow (Dr. Christine Rubin), Shane Briant (Paul Thoreau), Peter Hayden (Michael Connolly), Ian Mune (Barry Gordon).

Out-of-work stunt drivers Cliff Robertson and Leif Garrett help research scientist Harrow transport a vial of viral culture from New Zealand to America. Their assignment is menaced by terrorists intent on getting the culture from them.

2662. Shallow Grave (1988, E.L.F./Intl. Film, 89m, c). P Barry H. Waldman, D Richard Styles, W George E. Fernandez (based on a story by Fernandez & Carolyn J. Horton), PH Orson Ochoa, M Mason Daring, ED Horton.

LP Tony March (Sheriff Dean), Lisa Stahl (Sue Ellen), Tom Law (Deputy Scott), Carol Cadby (Patty), Donna Baltron (Rose), Just Kelly (Cindy), Vince Tumeo (Chad), Gregory Todd Davis (Owen).

On their way to Florida, four college girls stop in Medley, Georgia. Two are killed after witnessing a man murder his girlfriend. All three females are buried together in a shallow grave. The local authorities, good ol' boys, rednecks and ignoramuses, don't believe the survivors.

2663. Shame (1988, Skouras, Australia, 92m, c). P Damien Parer & Paul D. Barron, D Steve Jodrell, W Beverly Blankenship & Michael Brindley, PH Joseph Pickering, M Mario Millo, ED Kerry Regan, PD Phil Peters.

LP Deborra-Lee Furness (Asta Cadell), Tony Barry (Tim Curtis), Simone Buchanan (Lizzie Curtis), Gillian Jones (Tina Farrel), Peter Aanensen (Sgt. Wal Cuddy), Marjorie Ford (Norma Curtis), David Franklin (Danny Fiske), Bill McClusky (Ross).

In this stirring feminist film, tough, independent lawyer Deborra-Lee Furness is on a motorbiking holiday in rural Australia. She is forced to stay over in a small town when her bike needs repairs. She is put up by the owner of the service station. She discovers that the owner's daughter, Simone Buchanan, and several other young women of the town have been gang-raped. The rapists have gone unpunished because no one will bring charges. It takes the death of Buchanan to get the women and responsible men of the town to finally deal with the rapists.

2664. Shanghai Surprise (1986, MGM, 97m, c). P John Kohn, D Jim Goddard, W Kohn & Robert Bentley (based on the novel *Faraday's Flowers* by Tony Kenrick), PH Ernie Vincze, M George Harrison & Michael Kamen, ED Ralph Sheldon, PD Peter Mullins.

LP Sean Penn (Glendon Wasey), Madonna (Gloria Tatlock), Paul Freeman (Walter Faraday), Richard Griffiths (Willis Tuttle), Philip Sayer (Justin Kronk), Clyde Kusatsu (Joe Go), Kay Tong Lim (Mei Gan), Sonserai Lee (China Doll), Victor Wong (Ho Chong).

The break-up of Madonna and Sean Penn's marriage is not too high a prize to pay to guarantee that the two won't be teamed again in a stinker like this picture. The time is 1937 and the material girl is a missionary who hires roguish Penn to track down an opium shipment.

2665. Sharkey's Machine (1981, Warner, 122m, c). P Hank Moonjean, D Burt Reynolds, W Gerald Di Pego (based on the novel by William Diehl), PH William A. Fraker, M Snuff Garrett & Al Capps, ED William Gordean, PD Walter Scott Herndon.

LP Burt Reynolds (Tom Sharky), Vittorio Gassman (Victor), Brian Keith (Papa), Charles Durning (Friscoe), Earl Holliman (Hotchkins), Bernie Casey (Arch), Henry Silva (Billy Score), Richard Libertini (Nosh), Darryl Hickman (Smiley), Rachel Ward (Dominoe).

Undercover cop Burt Reynolds is on the trail of underworld Atlanta drug kingpin Vittorio Gassman. He turns a crew of vice cops into his personal avenging army, falling for Rachel Ward, a high-priced call girl whom he has under surveillance.

2666. *Sharma and Beyond* (1986, Cinecom, GB, 82m, c). P Chris Griffin, D&W Brian Gilbert, PH Ernest Vincze, ED Max Lemon, AD Maurice Cain.

LP Suzanne Burden (Natasha Gorley-Peters), Robert Urquhart (Evan Gorley-Peters), Michael Maloney (Stephen Archer), Antonia Pemberton (Myrna), Benjamin Whitrow (Anton Heron), Tom Wilkinson (Vivian).

Would-be science fiction writer Michael Maloney falls in love with Suzanne Burden whose father Robert Urquhart is a famous science fiction author.

2667. *She Dances Alone* (1982, D.H.D./CD, Austria/US, 87m, c). P Frederico DeLaurentiis & Earle Mack, D Robert Dornhelm, W Paul Davis & Jon Bradshaw (based on an idea by Dornhelm), PH Karl Kofler, M Gustavo Santolalla, ED Tina Frese.

LP Kyra Nijinsky (Herself), Bud Cort (Director), Patrick Dupond (Dancer), Sauncey LeSueur (Kyra as a child), Walter Kent (Doctor), Rosine Bena (Ballerina), Jeanette Etheridge (Girlfriend), Max von Sydow (Voice of Nijinsky).

This film within a film shows the attempt to make a documentary about famous Russian dancer Nijinsky's daughter. She tried to pursue her own career as a dancer. Sixty-year-old Kyra Nijinsky adds authority to the production.

2668. *She-Devil* (1989, Orion, 99m, c). P Jonathan Brett & Susan Seidelman, D Susan Seidelman, W Mark R. Burns & Barry Strugatz (based on the novel *The Life and Loves of a She-Devil* by Fay Weldon), PH Oliver Stapleton, M Howard Shore, ED Craig McKay, PD Santo Loquasto.

LP Meryl Streep (Mary Fisher), Roseanne Barr (Ruth Patchett), Ed Begley, Jr. (Bob Patchett), Linda Hunt (Hooper), Sylvia Miles (Mrs. Fisher), Elizabeth Peters (Nicolette), Bryan Larkin (Andy), A. Martinez (Garcia).

TV's Roseanne Barr makes her film debut as a dowdy wife who loses her husband Ed Begley, Jr., to glamorous romance novelist Meryl Streep. Having been accused of being a she-devil, Barr decides to become one for real, taking delicious revenge. That's the plot—but the execution works only in the case of Streep, who is a delight every time she is before the camera. Barr is given seedy material she can't do a thing with. Begley is a zero.

She Drives Me Crazy   see   Crazy Horse

2669. *She Must Be Seeing Things* (1987, McLaughlin, 90m, c). P,D&W Sheila McLaughlin, PH Mark Daniels & Heinz Emigholz, M John Zorn, ED Ila Von Hasperg, AD Leigh Kyle.

LP Sheila Dabney (Agatha), Lois Weaver (Jo), Kyle DeCamp (Catalina), John Erdman (Eric).

Lesbian filmmaker Lois Weaver is working on a new project. Jealous lover Sheila Dabney must learn to deal with Weaver's innocent flirtations.

2670. *She'll Be Wearing Pink Pajamas* (1985, Film Four Intl., GB, 90m, c). P Tara Prem & Adrian Hughes, D John Goldschmidt, W Eva Hardy, PH Clive Tickner, M John du Prez, ED Richard Key, PD Colin Pocock.

LP Julie Walters (Fran), Anthony Higgins (Tom), Jane Evers (Catherine), Janet Henfrey (Lucy), Paula Jacobs (Doreen), Penelope Nice (Ann), Maureen O'Brien (Joan), Alyson Spiro (Anita), Jane Wood (Judith).

Eight women volunteer to take part in an outdoor survival course in the hills of Britain's Lake District and learn more than they bargained for.

2671. *She's Back* (1989, Vestron, 90m, c, aka *Dead and Married*). P Cynthia DePaula, D Tim Kincaid, W Buddy Giovinazzo, PH Arthur D. Marks, M Jimmie Haskell, ED Mary Hickey.

LP Carrie Fisher (Beatrice), Robert Joy (Paul), Matthew Cowles (Sherman Bloom), Joel Sweto (Razorface), Sam Coppola (Det. Brophy), Donna Drake (Sally), Bobby DiCicco (Bob).

Robert Joy and his wife Carrie Fisher move to Queens. When their home is robbed by a neighborhood gang, Fisher is killed, but she's soon back as a ghost only Joy can see. She was a nag when alive, but now she's really on Joy's case to go out each night and kill another member of the gang that did her in. With a little bit of help from gung-ho Korean vet Matthew Cowles, the body count grows higher and higher.

2672. *She's Been Away* (1989, BBC Films, GB, 106m, c). P Kenith Trodd, D Peter Hall, W Stephen Poliakoff, PH Philip Bonham-Carter, M Richard Hartley, ED Ardan Fisher, PD Gary Wilkinson.

LP Peggy Ashcroft (Lillian Huckle), Geraldine James (Harriet Ambrose), James Fox (Hugh Ambrose), Jackson Kyle (Dominic Ambrose), Rebecca Pidgeon (Young Lillian), Rosalie Crutchley (Gladys), Rachel Kempson (Matilda), Hugh Lloyd (George).

Peggy Ashcroft's performance as an old woman who emerges from a mental institution after 60 years is glorious. She can't cope with the modern world and would rather be back in the now closed hospital. Her return to the home she lived in when she was first institutionalized brings back too many painful memories. She lives with her great-nephew James Fox and his wife Geraldine James. The latter's behavior is every bit as strange as was that of Ashcroft when she was put away.

2673. *She's Gotta Have It* (1986, Island Pictures, 100m, c/b&w). P Sheldon J. Lee, D,W&ED Spike Lee, PH Ernest Dickerson, M Bill Lee, PD Wynn Thomas.

LP Tracy Camila Johns (Nola Darling), Tommy Redmond Hicks (Jamie Overstreet), John Canada Terrell (Greer Childs), Spike Lee (Mars Blackmon), Raye Dowell (Opal Gilstrap), Joie Lee (Clorinda Bradford), Epatha Merkinson (Dr. Jamison), Bill Lee (Sonny Darling).

In this sexually frank film from auteur Spike Lee, beautiful black Brooklynite Tracy Camila Johns juggles three lovers, vain actor John Canada Terrell, sensitive romantic Tommy Redmond Hicks, and class clown Spike Lee. Among the many amusing scenes is a montage of male come-ons.

2674. *She's Having a Baby* (1988, Paramount, 106m, c). P,D&W John Hughes, PH Don Peterman, M Stewart Copeland, ED Alan Heim, PD John Corso.

LP Kevin Bacon (Jefferson "Jake" Briggs), Elizabeth McGovern (Kristy Briggs), Alec Baldwin (Davis McDonald), Isabel Lorca (Fantasy Girl), William Windom (Russ Bainbridge), James Ray (Jim Briggs), Holland Taylor (Sarah Briggs), James Ray (Jim Briggs).

As if his Ferris Bueller wasn't enough of a selfish drop-out, writer-director John Hughes presents audiences with Kevin Bacon. He marries a women he doesn't care for, takes a job in which he has no interest and moves to a home in a suburb that's enough to make anyone blue. Poor Elizabeth McGovern gets stuck with being an unintentional ball and chain in this dreadful look at blissless marriage.

2675. *She's Out of Control* (1989, Columbia, 97m, c, aka *Daddy's Little Girl*). P Stephen Deutsch, D Stan Dragoti, W Seth Winston & Michael J. Nathanson, PH Donald Peterman, M Alan Silvestri, ED Dov Hoenig, PD David L. Snyder.

LP Tony Danza (Doug Simpson), Catherine Hicks (Janet Pearson), Wallace Shawn (Dr. Fishbinder), Dick O'Neill (Mr. Pearson), Ami Dolenz (Katie Simpson), Laura Mooney (Bonnie Simpson), Derek McGrath (Jeff), Dana Ashbrook (Joey), Matthew L. Perry (Timothy).

Tony Danza is a single father trying to cope with teenage daughter Ami Dolenz, who goes from an ugly-duckling wallflower to an in-demand beautiful swan almost over night. Danza merely plays his TV role on "Who's the Boss." If you can get it for free, why pay to see it in the theater?

2676. *Sheena* (1984, Columbia, 117m, c). P Paul Aratow, D John Guillermin, W David Newman & Lorenzo Semple, Jr. (based on a story by Newman & Leslie Stevens from the comic strip "Sheena, Queen of the Jungle" by W. Morgan Thomas "S.M. Eiger & Will Eisner"), PH Pasqualino De Santis, M Richard Hartley, ED Ray Lovejoy, PD Peter Murton.

LP Tanya Roberts (Sheena), Ted Wass (Vic Casey), Donovan Scott (Fletcher), Elizabeth of Toro (Shaman), France Zobda (Countess Zanda), Trevor Thomas (Prince Otwani), Clifton Jones (King Jabalani), John Forgeham (Jorgenson).

Tanya Roberts, once one of TV's Charlie's Angels, is a gorgeous woman, and her undress in this film is remarkable for a PG film. But the picture is a miserable failure, filled with inconsistencies and laughable lapses. It's the story of a white child, lost in an African jungle, raised by the Zambouli tribe, who grows up to be Roberts. She champions her adopted tribe when bad guys threaten them. Strangely, Roberts speaks in a halting English, while the natives sound like they were educated at Oxford.

2677. *The Shining* (1980, Warner, 146m, c). P&D Stanley Kubrick, W Kubrick & Diane Johnson (based on the novel by Stephen King), PH John Alcott, M Bela Bartok, Wendy Carlos, Rachel Elkind, Gyorgy Ligeti & Krzysztof Penderecki, ED Ray Lovejoy, PD Roy Walker.

LP Jack Nicholson (Jack Torrance), Shelley Duvall (Wendy Torrance), Danny Lloyd (Danny Torrance), Scatman Crothers (Halloran), Barry Nelson (Ullman), Philip Stone (Grady), Joe Turkel (Lloyd), Anne Jackson (Doctor).

Terror overwhelms a family isolated and snowbound in a huge closed resort hotel with a macabre history of violence. Jack Nicholson is excellent as the father who threatens his wife and son when he cracks. Who will forget his maniacal "Heeeeeere's Johnny" as he smashes through a door with a fire axe.

2678. *Shirley Valentine* (1989, Paramount, 108m, c). P&D Lewis Gilbert, W Willy Russell (based on his play), PH Alan Hume, M George Hatzinassios, ED Lesley Walker, PD John Stoll, SONG "The Girl Who Used to Be Me" by Willy Russell†.

LP Pauline Collins† (Shirley Valentine Bradshaw), Tom Conti (Costas Caldes), Alison Steadman (Jane), Julia McKenzie (Gillian), Joanna Lumley (Marjorie), Bernard Hill (Joe Bradshaw), Sylvia Syms (Headmistress), Gillian Kearney (Young Shirley), Catherine Duncan (Young Marjorie).

Pauline Collins recreates her acclaimed stage role in this romantic comedy. She's a 42-year-old mother and housewife from Liverpool, who dreams of getting away from it all. She does when she accompanies her best friend on a two-week vacation in Greece. She encounters Tom Conti, falling in love with him and life.

2679. *Shock Treatment* (1981, 20th Century-Fox, 94m, c). P John Goldstone, D Jim Sharman, W Sharman, Richard O'Brien & Brian Thomson (based on a book by O'Brien), PH Mike Molloy, M Richard Hartley, ED Richard Bedford, PD Thomson.

LP Jessica Harper (Janet Majors), Cliff DeYoung (Brad Majors/Farley Flavors), Richard O'Brien (Cosmo McKinley), Patricia Quinn (Nation McKinley), Charles Gray (Judge Oliver Wright), Ruby Wax (Betty Hapschatt).

This turkey is meant to be a followup to the midnight cult film *The Rocky Horror Picture Show.* Jessica Harper and Cliff DeYoung, in the roles played earlier by Susan Sarandon and Barry Bostwick, are married contestants on the TV game show "Marriage Maze." Their problem is to get off the show. Audiences have the problem of finding theater exits.

2680. *Shocker* (1989, Universal, 110m, c). P Marianne Maddalena & Barin Kumar, D&W Wes Craven, PH Jacques Haitkin, M William Goldstein, ED Andy Blumenthal, PD Cynthia Kay Charette.

LP Michael Murphy (Lt. Don Parker), Peter Berg (Jonathan Parker), Mitch Pileggi (Horace Pinker), Cami Cooper (Alison), Richard Brooks (Rhino), Theodore Raimi (Pac Man), John Tesh (TV newscaster), Dr. Timothy Leary (TV evangelist), Heather Langenkamp (Victim), Bingham Ray (Bartender).

The ads read "On October 2nd, at 6:45 a.m. mass murderer Horace Pinker was put to death. Now, he's really mad." Director-writer Wes Craven provides audiences craving sick humor all they can stomach in this mayhem-filled action thriller.

Shogun Island see ***Raw Force***

2681. *Shoot the Moon* (1982, MGM, 124m, c). P Alan Marshall, D Alan Parker, W Bo Goldman, PH Michael Seresin, ED Gerry Hambling, PD Geoffrey Kirkland.

LP Albert Finney (George Dunlap), Diane Keaton (Faith Dunlap), Karen Allen (Sandy), Peter Weller (Frank

2

Henderson), Dana Hill (Sherry), Viveka Davis (Jill), Tracey Gold (Marianne), Tina Yothers (Molly), George Murdock (French DeVoe), Leora Dana (Charlotte DeVoe).

The film is the less than compelling story of the disintegration of the marriage of Albert Finney and Diane Keaton, and the effect this has on the affluent Marin county couple and their four daughters.

2682. *Shoot to Kill* (1988, Buena Vista, 106m, c). P Daniel Petrie, Jr. & Ron Silverman, D Roger Spottiswoode, W Petrie, Harv Zimmel & Michael Burton, PH Michael Chapman, M John Scott, ED Garth Craven & George Bowers, PD Richard Sylbert.

LP Sidney Poitier (Warren Stantin), Tom Berenger (Jonathan Knox), Kirstie Alley (Sarah), Clancy Brown (Steve), Richard Masur (Norman), Andrew Robinson (Harvey), Kevin Scannell (Ben), Frederick Coffin (Ralph), Michael MacRae (Fournier).

Shot in Vancouver and the mountainous regions of British Columbia, the film teams Sidney Poitier, a streetwise FBI agent, with skilled wilderness trail guide Tom Berenger. They go after Berenger's girlfriend Kirstie Alley who has been taken hostage by a savage killer who has fled with her across the border into the mountains.

2683. *The Shooting Party* (1985, European Classics, GB, 97m, c). P Geoffrey Reeve, D Alan Bridges, W Julian Bond (based on the novel by Isabel Colegate), PH Fred Tammes, M John Scott, ED Peter Davies, PD Morley Smith, COS Tom Rand.

LP James Mason (Sir Randolph Nettleby), Dorothy Tutin (Lady Minnie Nettleby), Edward Fox (Lord Gilbert Hartlip), Cheryl Campbell (Lady Aline Hartlip), John Gielgud (Cornelius Cardew Gordon Jackson (Tom Harker), Aharon Ipale (Sir Reuben Hergesheimer), Rupert Frazer (Lionel Stephens), Robert Hardy (Lord Bob Lilburn), Judi Bowker (Lady Olivia Liburn), Sarah Badel (Ida Nettleby), Rebecca Saire (Cicely Nettleby), Joris Stuyck (Count Tibor Rakassyi), Frank Windsor (Glass).

To describe this film as a nostalgic look at the English aristocracy in the period just before World War I would do it a great disservice. It is a perfectly splendid period piece, beautifully capturing a time when the classes were separate and apparently content to be so. English nobleman James Mason has a variety of guests staying at his country estate for a weekend of shooting pheasants and other game. Mason senses that the times are changing and his order is about over. He will not fight the change but is sad to see the life he knew and loved come to an end. Mason could not have wanted for a better curtain call to his long and distinguished career. He is sheer brilliance. Everyone involved in the production can forever be proud of their contribution. The acting, right down to the smallest part is thoroughly convincing and touching. The photography is superb, and the director has put his performers through their paces as if they were willing them. To one and all, bravo!

2684. *Short Circuit* (1986, Tri-Star, 99m, c). P David Foster & Lawrence Turman, D John Badham, W S.S. Wilson & Brent Maddock, PH Nick McLean, M David Shire, ED Frank Morriss, AD Dianne Wager.

LP Ally Sheedy (Stephanie Speck), Steve Guttenberg (Newton Crosby), Fisher Stevens (Ben Jabituya), Austin Pendleton (Howard Marner), G.W. Bailey (Skroeder), Brian McNamara (Frank), Tim Blaney (Voice of Number Five), Marvin McIntyre (Duke).

When lightning hits a robot made for military purposes, it acquires human qualities. Number Five, as it is called, escapes, taking refuge with animal-lover Ally Sheedy, who thinks it's some adorable alien. Its creators, Steve Guttenberg and Fisher Stevens, search for the missing robot, while insensitive military man G.W. Bailey orders its mission aborted and the charming robot destroyed.

2685. *Short Circuit 2* (1988, Tri-Star, 110m, c). P David Foster, Lawrence Turman & Gary Foster, D Kenneth Johnson, W S.S. Wilson & Brent Maddock, PH John McPherson, M Charles Fox, ED Conrad Buff, PD Bill Brodie.

LP Fisher Stevens (Ben Jahrvi), Michael McKean (Fred Ritter), Cynthia

Gibb (Sandy Banatoni), Jack Weston (Oscar Baldwin), Dee McCafferty (Saunders), David Hemblen (Jones), Tim Blaney (Voice of Johnny Five), Don Lake (Manic Mike), Damon D'Oliveira (Bones).

Inventor Fisher Stevens, whose shtik is mangling the English language, goes into the toy business with street hustler Michael McKean. Their greatest asset is Johnny Five, a most appealing, intelligent and trusting robot. Bad guys working for Jack Weston take advantage of this trio of unlikely heroes and almost kill Johnny Five, who is really alive.

2686.   Shy People (1988, Cannon, 119m, c). P Menahem Golan & Yoram Globus, D Andrei Konchalovsky, W Gerard Brach, Konchalovsky & Marjorie David (based on a story by Konchalovsky), PH Chris Menges, M Various Artists, ED Alain Jakubowicz, PD Stephen Marsh.

LP Jill Clayburgh (Diana Sullivan), Barbara Hershey (Ruth Sullivan), Martha Plimpton (Grace Sullivan), Merritt Butrick (Mike Sullivan), John Philbin (Tommy Sullivan), Don Swayze (Mark Sullivan), Pruitt Taylor Vince (Paul Sullivan), Mare Winningham (Candy), Michael Audley (Louie).

New York writer Jill Clayburgh and her troubled, troublesome daughter Martha Plimpton travel to Louisiana to visit their Cajun cousins, headed by strong-willed matriarch Barbara Hershey. It's a half-baked drama of a strange and violent family, with beliefs and behavior bordering on the maniacal. Hershey's acting almost makes up for the film's excesses.

2687.   The Sicilian (1987, 20th Century–Fox, 115m, c). P Michael Cimino & Joann Carelli, D Cimino, W Steve Shagan (based on the novel by Mario Puzo), PH Alex Thomson, M David Mansfield, ED Francoise Bonnot, PD Wolf Kroeger.

LP Christopher Lambert (Salvatore Giuliano), Terence Stamp (Prince Borsa), Joss Ackland (Don Masino Croce), John Turturro (Aspanu Pisciotta), Richard Bauer (Prof. Hector Adonis), Barbara Sukowa (Camilla), Giulia Boschi (Giovanna Ferra).

Based on a second-rate Mario Puzo novel, directed by Michael Cimino, and starring over-eager actor Christopher Lambert, this dull but violent movie is the story of a sort-of Sicilian Robin Hood who stands up to the Mafia chiefs before being betrayed by his best friend.

2688.   Sid & Nancy (1986, Samuel Goldwyn, GB, 111m, c). P Eric Fellner, D Alex Cox, W Cox & Abbe Wool, PH Roger Deakins, M The Pogues, Joe Strummer, Pray for Rain, ED David Martin, PD Andrew McAlpine.

LP Gary Oldman (Sid Vicious), Chloe Webb (Nancy Spungen), Drew Schofield (Johnny Rotten), David Hayman (Malcolm McLaren), Debby Bishop (Phoebe), Tony London (Steve), Perry Benson (Paul), Ann Lambton (Linda).

This is the true story of the sordid relationship between Sex Pistol's bassist Sid Vicious and American junkie-groupie Nancy Spungen. Gary Oldman and Chloe Webb are excellent in this depressing examination of a downward spiral into tragedy in the drug and music world of London in the 70s.

2689.   Sidewalk Stories (1989, Island, silent, 97m, b&w). P,D&W Charles Lane, PH Bill Dill, M Marc Marder, ED Anne Stein & Lane, PD Lyn Pinezich.

LP Charles Lane (Artist), Nicole Alysia (Child), Sandye Wilson (Young Woman), Darnell Williams (Father), Trula Hoosier (Mother), George Riddick (Street Partner), Tom Hoover (Portrait Artist).

In this Chaplin-inspired silent comedy, Charles Lane portrays a street artist who draws charcoal caricatures in Greenwich Village. When he witnesses the murder of a man, Lane adopts the deceased's baby daughter, providing her shelter in the abandoned building which is his "home." He hopes to reunite the child with her mother, but first there is a chase sequence, involving the murderers, Lane and the baby in a horse-drawn carriage.

2690.   Siege (1983, Summa Vista, Canada, 83m, c, aka *Self Defense*). P Michael Donovan, John Walsch, Maura O'Connell & Paul Donovan, D P. Donovan & O'Connell, W P. Donovan (based on an idea by Marc Vautour), PH Les Krizsan, M Peter Jermyn & Drew King, ED Ian McBride, PD Malachi Salter.

LP Doug Lennox (Cube), Tom Nardini (Horatio), Brenda Bazinet (Barbara), Darel Haney (Chester), Terry-David (Daniel), Jeff Pustil (Goose), Jack Blum (Patrick), Keith Knight (Steve), Brad Wadden (Ian).

The film is the story of the clash between a vigilante right-wing group and the patrons of a gay bar called the Crypt. Things get pretty violent.

2691. ***The Siege of Firebase Gloria*** (1988, Fries Entertainment, Australia, 100m, c). P Howard Grigsby & Rudolfos S.M. Confesor, D Brian Trenchard-Smith, W William Nagle & Tony Johnston, PH Kevan Lind, M Paul Shutze, ED Andrew Prowse, PD Toto Castillo.

LP Wings Hauser (DiNardo), R. Lee Ermey (Hafner), Albert Popwell (Sgt. Jones), Robert Arevalo (Cao Van), Mark Neely (Murphy), Gary Hershberger, Clyde R. Jones, Margi Gerard, Richard Kuhlman.

Wings Hauser portrays a sadistic marine who, with a few others, holds on at the forward outpost Gloria during the 1968 Tet Offensive in Vietnam.

2692. ***Siesta*** (1987, Lorimar, 97m, c). P Gary Kurfirst & Chris Brown, D Mary Lambert, W Patricia Louisiana Knop (based on the novel by Patrice Chaplin), PH Bryan Loftus & Michael Lund, M Marcus Miller, ED Glenn A. Morgan, PD John Beard.

LP Ellen Barkin (Claire), Gabriel Byrne (Augustine), Julian Sands (Kit), Isabella Rossellini (Marie), Martin Sheen (Del), Alexi Sayle (Cabbie), Grace Jones (Conchita), Jodie Foster (Nancy), Anastassia Stakis (Desdra).

This experimental, shaggy-dog film follows the romantic exploits of daredevil skydiver Ellen Barkin with various lovers and an insistent rapist.

2693. ***Signal 7*** (1984, Taylor-Myron, 92m, c). D&W Rob Nilsson, PH Geoff Schaaf & Tomas Tucker, M Andy Narrell, ED Richard Harkness, AD Hildy Burns & Steve Burns.

LP Bill Ackridge (Speed), Dan Leegant (Marty), John Tidwell (Johnny), Herb Mills (Steve), Don Bajema (Roger), Phil Polakoff (Phil), Don Defina (Setts), Frank Triest (Tommy), Jack Tucker (Hank).

This is a touching but muddled stream-of-consciousness story of two aging San Francisco cabdriver friends, Bill Ackridge and Dan Leegant. Some may find it one of the better films of the decade.

2694. ***Signs of Life*** (1989, Avenue, 91m, c). P Marcus Viscidi & Andrew Reichsman, D John David Coles, W Mark Malone, PH Elliot Davis, M Howard Shore, ED William A. Anderson & Angelo Corrao, PD Howard Cummings.

LP Beau Bridges (John Alder), Vincent Philip D'Onofrio (Daryl Monahan), Arthur Kennedy (Owen Coughlin), Kevin J. O'Connor (Eddie Johnson), Will Patton (Mr. Coughlin, Sr.), Kate Reid (Mrs. Wrangway), Michael Lewis (Joey Monahan), Kathy Bates (Mary Beth Alder), Georgia Engel (Betty).

This film is about the salt-of-the-earth folks in the small town of Easthasset, Maine. It explores the effect on the residents of the closing of the 200-year-old family boat business owned by Kennedy. It's a dreary business with enough subplots to delight any soap opera fan.

2695. ***The Silence at Bethany*** (1988, American Playhouse, 90m, c). P Tom Cherones & Fred Gerber, D Joel Oliansky, W Joyce Keener, PH Charles Minsky, M Lalo Schifrin, ED Pasquale Buba, PD Cletus Anderson.

LP Tom Dahlgren (Phares Mitgang), Richard Fancy (Elam Swope), Dakin Matthews (Sam Mitgang), Mark Moses (Ira Martin), Susan Wilder (Pauline Mitgang Martin), Megan Bellwoar (Phyllis Mitgang), Robert Billbrough (Junior Mitgang).

Set in a Mennonite Pennsylvania farm community, the film is the story of the doctrinal conflicts between two good men of faith: liberal, newly ordained minister Mark Moses, and his wife's uncle, older, orthodox bishop Tom Dahlgren.

2696. ***Silence of the North*** (1981, Universal, Canada, 94m, c). P Murray Shostak, D Allan Winton King, W Patricia Louisiana Knop (based on the book by Olive Fredrickson & Ben East), PH Richard Leiterman, M Allan MacMillan, ED Arla Saare, PD Bill Brodie.

LP Ellen Burstyn (Olive Fredrickson), Tom Skerritt (Walter Reamer), Gordon

Pinsent (John Fredrickson), Jennifer McKinney (Little Olive Reamer), Donna Dobrijevic (Vala Reamer), Jeff Banks (Lewis Reamer).

This is the true story of a widow with three children who survived rugged pioneer conditions in 1919 on the Canadian frontier.

2697.   *Silent Assassins* (1988, Action/Panache-Forum, 92m, c). P Jun Chong & Phillip Rhee, D Lee Doo-yong & Scott Thomas, W Will Gates & Ada Lin (based on a story by John Bruner), PH Son Hyun-Chae, M Paul Gilman, ED William Hoy, AD John Nakayama.

LP Sam J. Jones (Sam Kettle), Linda Blair (Sara), Jun Chong (Jun Kim), Phillip Rhee (Bernard), Bill Erwin (Dr. London), Gustav Vintas (Kendrick), Mako (Oyama), Rebecca Ferratti (Miss Amy), Peter Looney (Dr. Thomas).

LA cop Sam Jones comes out of retirement to go up against a former CIA agent gone bad. The villain, earlier responsible for the death of Jones' partners during a stakeout, now has kidnapped a research scientist to get his hands on a formula for a new biological weapon.

2698.   *Silent Madness* (1984, Almi, 3-D, 97m, c). P Simon Nuchtern & William P. Milling, D Nuchtern, W Milling, Robert Zimmerman & Nelson de Mille, PH Gerald Feil, M Barry Salmon, ED Philip Stockton, AD Brian Martin.

LP Belinda Montgomery (Dr. Joan Gilmore), Viveca Lindfors (Mrs. Collins), Solly Marx (Howard Johns), David Greenan (Mark McGowan), Sidney Lassick (Sheriff Liggett), Roderick Cook (Dr. Kruger), Stanja Lowe (Dr. Anderson).

Brilliant psychiatrist Belinda Montgomery is shocked to learn that maniacal killer Solly Marx has mistakenly been released from a mental institution. She flies to a small college where Marx committed his original murders to pose as a sorority girl in a hope to catch him before he kills again.

2699.   *Silent Night, Deadly Night* (1984, Tri-Star, 79m, c). P Ira Richard Barmak, D Charles E. Sellier, Jr., W Michael Hickey (based on a story by Paul Caimi), PH Henning Schellerup, M Perry Botkin, ED Michael Spence, PD Dian Perryman.

LP Lilyan Chauvin (Mother Superior), Gilmer McCormick (Sister Margaret), Toni Nero (Pamela), Robert Brian Wilson (Billy at 18), Britt Leach (Mr. Sims), Nancy Borgenicht (Mrs. Randall), H.E.D. Redford (Capt. Richards), Danny Wagner (Billy at 8), Linnea Quigley (Denise).

The combination of witnessing the killing of his parents killed by someone wearing a Santa Claus suit when he was only 8 and cruel treatment in an orphanage has unhinged Robert Brian Wilson. He takes a job as a department-store Santa, but is definitely not a jolly old elf. He goes off on a murder spree, wearing his red suit.

2700.   *Silent Night, Deadly Night Part II* (1987, Ascot, 88m, c). P Lawrence Applebaum, D Lee Harry, W Harry & Joseph H. Earle (based on a story by Harry, Earle, Dennis Paterson, Applebaum and a character created by Michael Hickey & Paul Caimi), PH Harvey Genkins, M Michael Armstrong.

LP Eric Freeman, James L. Newman, Elizabeth Clayton, Jean Miller, Lilyan Chauvin.

In this unnecessary follow-up to the story of a Santa Claus–dressed killer, the latter's younger brother has taken up his psychotic sibling's slaughtering ways.

2701.   *Silent Night, Deadly Night III: Better Watch Out!* (1989, Quiet Films, 91m, c). P Arthur H. Gorson, D Monte Hellman, W Carlos Laszlo (based on a story by Laszlo, Hellman & Richard N. Gladstein), PH Josep M. Civit, M Steven Soles, ED Ed Rothkowitz, PD Philip Thomas.

LP Richard Beymer (Dr. Newbury), Bill Moseley (Ricky), Samantha Scully (Laura), Eric Da Re (Chris), Laura Herring (Jerri), Elizabeth Hoffman (Granny), Robert Culp (Lt. Connelly), Isabel Cooley (Receptionist).

This third entry in the series of notorious "Santa Claus" horror series went directly to video. It's fairly standard stuff and won't disappoint the audience for whom it has been made — others will eagerly avoid it.

2702.   *The Silent One* (1984, Gibson, New Zealand, 95m, c). P Dave Gibson, D Yvonne Mackay, W Ian Mune (based on the novel by Jan Crowley), PH Ian Paul, Ron Taylor & Valerie Taylor, M Jenny McLeod, ED Jamie Selkirk, PD Tony Rabbitt.

LP Telo Malese (Jonasi), George Henare (Paul Tel Po), Pat Evison (Luisa), Anzac Wallace (Tasiri), Rongo Tupatea Kahu (Taruga), Jo Pahu (Etika), Reg Ruka (Bulai), Anthony Gilbert (Aesake).

Having arrived from the sea as an infant, strange mysterious Telo Malese, tagged the "silent one" because he neither speaks nor hears, maintains a nautical relationship with a sea turtle.

2703. *Silent Rage* (1982, Columbia, 100m, c). P Anthony B. Unger, D Michael Miller, W Joseph Fraley, PH Robert Jessup & Neil Roach, M Peter Bernstein & Mark Goldenberg, ED Richard C. Meyer, AD Jack Marty.

LP Chuck Norris (Dan Stevens), Ron Silver (Dr. Tom Halman), Steven Keats (Dr. Philip Spires), Toni Kalem (Alison Halman), William Finley (Dr. Paul Vaughn), Brian Libby (John Kirby), Stephen Furst (Charlie), Stephanie Dunnam (Nancy Halman).

Martial arts star Chuck Norris portrays a small town Texas sheriff. He must contend with a mysterious killer made almost indestructible by genetic breeding.

2704. *Silkwood* (1983, 20th Century–Fox, 131m, c). P Mike Nichols & Michael Hausman, D Nichols†, W Nora Ephron & Alice Arlen†, PH Miroslav Ondricek, M Georges Delerue, ED Sam O'Steen†, PD Patrizia Von Brandenstein.

LP Meryl Streep† (Karen Silkwood), Kurt Russell (Drew Stephens), Cher† (Dolly Pelliker), Craig T. Nelson (Winston), Diana Scarwid (Angela), Fred Ward (Morgan), Ron Silver (Paul Stone), Charles Hallahan (Earl Lapin), Josef Sommer (Max Richter), Sudie Bond (Thelma Rice).

The film is a dramatization of the life of nuclear plant worker and activist Karen Silkwood, who died in 1974 under suspicious circumstances while investigating unsafe practices at the plant where she worked. The film raises many intriguing questions, but offers few answers. The work of Meryl Streep, Kurt Russell and Cher makes the film worth seeing.

2705. *Silver City* (1985, Samuel Goldwyn, Australia, 110m, c). P Joan Long, D Sophia Turkiewicz, W Turkiewicz & Thomas Keneally, PH John Seale, M William Motzing, ED Don Saunders, AD Igor Nay.

LP Gosia Dobrowoska (Nina), Ivar Kants (Julian), Anna Jemison (Anna), Steve Bisley (Viktor), Debra Lawrance (Helena), Ewa Brok (Mrs. Bronowska), Joel Cohen (Young Daniel), Tim McKenzie (Mr. Roy), Dennis Miller (Max).

The film details the plight of Polish immigrants and their conflicts with native Australians in 1949.

2706. *Silver Dream Racer* (1983, Rank/Almi, GB, 111m, c). P Rene Dupont, D&W David Wickes, PH Paul Beeson, M David Essex, ED Peter Hollywood, AD Malcolm Middleton.

LP David Essex (Nick Freeman), Beau Bridges (Bruce McBride), Cristina Raines (Julie Prince), Clarke Peters (Cider Jones), Harry H. Corbett (Wiggins), Diane Keen (Tina), Lee Montague (Jack Freeman), Sheila White (Carol).

Garage mechanic David Essex inherits his late brother's super motorcycle which he enters in a race in which his main competition is American punk racer Beau Bridges.

2707. *Silverado* (1985, Columbia, 132m, c). P&D Lawrence Kasdan, W L. Kasdan & Mark Kasdan, PH John Bailey, M Bruce Broughton†, ED Carol Littleton & Mia Goldman, PD Ida Random, SOUND Donald O. Mitchell, Rick Kline, Kevin O'Connell & David Ronne†.

LP Kevin Kline (Paden), Scott Glenn (Emmett), Rosanna Arquette (Hannah), John Cleese (Sheriff Langston), Kevin Costner (Jake), Brian Dennehy (Cobb), Danny Glover (Mal), Jeff Goldblum (Slick), Linda Hunt (Stella), Ray Baker (McKendrick), Joe Seneca (Ezra), Lynn Whitfield (Ray), Jeff Fahey (Tyree), Patricia Gaul (Kate), Amanda Wyss (Phoebe).

This attempt to revise the Western genre had a lot going for it; a talented and enthusiastic young cast, lots of action and gunfighting, traditional western subplots, and the excitement of a lawless time. Unfortunately, the public didn't take to the movie in sufficient numbers to offer hope that the western genre, frequently described as moribund, was on its way to a healthy recovery. Maybe it was the lack of Indians.

2708. *Simon* (1980, Orion, 97m, c). P Martin Bregman, D&W Marshall Brickman, PH Adam Holender, M Stanley Silverman, ED Nina Feinberg, PD Stuart Wurtzel.

LP Alan Arkin (Simon), Austin Pendleton (Becker), Judy Graubart (Lisa), William Finley (Fichandler), Jayant (Barundi), Wallace Shawn (Von Dongen), Max Wright (Hundertwasser), Fred Gwynne (Korey), Madeline Kahn (Cynthia), Adolph Green (Commune Leader).

A group of demented think tank geniuses convince inept college professor Alan Arkin that he's an alien from outerspace. Things get out of hand when Arkin becomes a TV messiah.

2709. *Simply Irresistible* (1983, Essex, 100m, c). P Summer Brown, D Edwin Brown, W Sandra Winters & E. Brown, PH Teru Hyashi, M Geoffrey Petrofsky, ED Terrance O'Reilly.

LP Richard Pacheco (Walter), Samantha Fox (Arlene), Gayle Sterling (Juliet), Star Wood (Cleopatra), Gina Gianetti (Sunshine), Nicole Black (Mata Hari), Dorothy Lemay (Hitchhiker), Misha Garr (Miracle).

For reasons not totally apparent Richard Pacheco is "simply irresistible" to a variety of women in this soft porno piece.

2710. *A Sinful Life* (1989, New Line, 90m, c). P Daniel Raskov, D William Schreiner, W Melanie Graham, PH Jonathan West, M Todd Hayen, ED Jeffrey Reiner, PD Robert Zentis.

LP Anita Morris (Claire Vin Blanc), Rick Overton (Janitor Joe), Dennis Christopher (Nathan Flowers), Blair Tefkin (Baby), Mark Rolston (Teresa Tremaine), Cynthia Szigeti (Mrs. Crow), Kirsten Price (Sweetie).

Anita Morris, a former dancer with the Sonny and Cher show, is raising a mentally handicapped daughter named Baby. Unless Morris can find a husband who will take them away from their squalid living conditions, she may have Baby taken from her. It's meant to be a black comedy, in case you care.

2711. *Sing* (1989, Tri-Star, 97m, c). P Craig Zadan, D Richard Baskin, W Dean Pitchford, PH Peter Sova, M Jay Gruska, ED Bud Smith, Jere Huggins & Scott Smith, PD Carol Spier.

LP Lorraine Bracco (Miss Lombardo), Peter Dobson (Dominic), Jessica Steen (Hannah), Louise Lasser (Rosie), George DiCenzo (Mr. Marowitz), Patti LaBelle (Mrs. DeVere), Susan Peretz (Mrs. Tucci), Laurnea Wilkerson (Zena), Rachel Sweet (Cecelia).

Probably hoping to have another *Fame, Flashdance* or *Footloose,* instead, the genius behind this teen musical disappoints with stale music and stereotyped characters.

Singleton's Pluck   see   Laughter House

2712. *Sir Henry at Rawlinson End* (1980, Charisma, GB, 72m, b&w). P Tony Stratton Smith, D Steve Roberts, W Roberts & Vivian Stanshall, PH Martin Bell, M Stanshall, ED Chris Rose, AD Jim Acheson.

LP Trevor Howard (Sir Henry Rawlinson), Patrick Magee (Rev. Slodden), Denise Coffey (Mrs. E), J.G. Devlin (Old Scrotum), Harry Fowler (Buller Bullethead), Sheila Reed (Florrie), Vivian Stanshall (Hubert).

Eccentric gentleman Trevor Howard seeks to exorcise the ghost of his brother Vivian Stanshall during an annual dinner.

2713. *Sister, Sister* (1988, New World, 91m, c). P Walter Coblenz, D Bill Condon, W Condon, Joel Cohen & Ginny Cerrella, PH Stephen M. Katz, M Richard Einhorn, ED Marion Rothman, SE Wayne Beauchamp & Paul Hickerson.

LP Eric Stoltz (Matt Rutledge), Jennifer Jason Leigh (Lucy Bonnard), Judith Ivey (Charlotte Bonnard), Dennis Lipscomb (Sheriff Cleve Doucet), Anne Pitoniak (Mrs. Bettleheim), Benjamin Mouton (Etienne LeViolette), Natalia Nogulich (Fran Steuben).

In an unappealing Southern gothic horror story, Jennifer Jason Leigh and Judith Ivey, the siblings of the title, have transformed their parents' Louisiana bayou mansion into a dreary guest house. Released repressed sexual tensions and murder arrive at about the same time as does Congressional aide Eric Stolz.

2714. *Sisterhood* (1988, Concorde, 76m, c). P&D Cirio H. Santiago, W Thomas McKelvey Cleaver, PH Ricardo Remias, MD Jun Latonio, ED Edgar Viner, PD Joe Mari Avellana.

LP Rebecca Holden (Alee), Chuck Wagner (Mikal), Lynn-Holly Johnson (Marya), Barbara Hooper (Vera), Henry Strzalkowski (Jon), Robert Dryer (Lord Barah).

After the apocalypse, female warriors led by Rebecca Holden and Barbara Hooper have no intention of allowing surviving males ever to become dominant again. The Sisterhood makes a dangerous trek across the deadly Forbidden Zone to find a place of peace.

2715. *Sitting Ducks* (1980, International Rainbow, 90m, c). P Meira Attia Dor, D&W Henry Jaglom, PH Paul Glickman, M Richard Romanus.

LP Michael Emil (Simon), Zack Norman (Sidney), Patrice Townsend (Jenny), Irene Forrest (Leona), Richard Romanus (Moose), Henry Jaglom (Jenny's Friend).

In this rollicking comedy, friends Michael Emil and Zack Norman steal money from gangsters so they can go to Central America and live the good life.

2716. *Six Pack* (1982, 20th Century–Fox, 110m, c). P Michael Trikilis, D Daniel Petrie, W Mike Marvin & Alex Matter, PH Mario Tosi, M Charles Fox, ED Rita Roland, PD William J. Creber.

LP Kenny Rogers (Brewster Baker), Diane Lane (Breezy), Erin Gray (Lilah), Barry Corbin (Sheriff), Terry Kiser (Terk), Bob Hannah (Diddler), Tom Abernathy (Louis), Robbie Fleming (Little Harry), Anthony Michael Hall (Doc), Robby Still (Swifty), Benji Wilhoite (Steven).

Racing car driver Kenny Rogers returns to the circuit with the help of six larcenous orphans adept at mechanics.

2717. *Six Weeks* (1982, Universal, 107m, c). P Peter Guber & Jon Peters, D Tony Bill, W David Seltzer (based on a novel by Fred Mustard Stewart), PH Michael D. Margulies, M Dudley Moore, ED Stu Linder, PD Sandy Veneziano.

LP Dudley Moore (Patrick Dalton), Mary Tyler Moore (Charlotte Dreyfus), Katherine Healy (Nicole Dreyfus), Shannon Wilcox (Peg Dalton), Bill Calvert (Jeff Dalton), Joe Regalbuto (Bob Crowther), John Harkins (Arnold Stillman).

In a hollow, pretentious and unconvincing tearjerker, politician Dudley Moore meets precocious little Katherine Healy, who is dying of leukemia. Despite being married, he enters into a romance with the child's mother Mary Tyler Moore.

2718. *Sixteen Candles* (1984, Universal, 93m, c). P Hilton Green, D&W John Hughes, PH Bobby Byrne, M Ira Newborn, ED Edward Warschilka, PD John W. Corso.

LP Molly Ringwald (Samantha Baker), Justin Henry (Mike Baker), Michael Schoeffling (Jake), Haviland Morris (Caroline), Gedde Watanabe (Long Duk Dong), Anthony Michael Hall (Ted the Geek), Paul Dooley (Jim Baker), Carlin Glynn (Brenda Baker), Blanche Baker (Ginny), Edward Andrews (Howard), Billie Bird (Dorothy), John Cusack (Bryce).

It's difficult to remember a teen performer arriving on the scene in a more appealing role than Molly Ringwald. She's a sweet, normal, redheaded teen whose 16th birthday is completely forgotten by her family because of excitement over her older sister's marriage. She admires senior hunk Michael Schoeffling from afar and is in turn idolized by nerdish but marvelous Anthony Michael Hall. He promises Molly he will use his good offices to set her up with Schoeffling if she will give him a pair of her panties. She does. Hall makes a tidy sum, charging his freshmen classmates to view the undergarments. Somehow Schoeffling, who has grown tired of trampy Blanche Baker, takes notice of Ringwald on his own.

2719. *'68* (1988, New World, 98m, c). P Dale Djerassi, Isabel Maxwell & Steven Kovacs, D&W Kovacs, PH Daniel Lacambre, M Various Artists, ED Cari Coughlin.

LP Eric Larson (Peter Szabo), Robert Locke (Sandy Szabo), Sandor Tecsi (Zoltan Szabo), Anna Dukasz (Zsuzsa Szabo), Miran Kwun (Alana Chan), Terra Vandergaw (Vera Kardos), Shony

Alex Braun (Tibor Kardos), Donna Pecora (Piroska Kardos).

Hungarian immigrant Sandor Tecsi and his wife Anna Dukasz fled the old country during the 1956 revolution. They settle in San Francisco where they start a small restaurant. Years later, Tecsi is constantly at odds with his two sons, Eric Larson, a political activist of the protest era, and Robert Locke, who is gay.

2720. *Sizzle Beach U.S.A.* (1987, Troma Team, 93m, c). P Eric Louzil, D Richard Brander, W Craig Kusaba, PH John Sprung.

LP Terry Congie (Janice Johnston), Leslie Brander (Dit McCoy), Roselyn Royce (Cheryl Percy), Robert Acey (Steve), Kevin Costner (John Logan), Larry DeGraw (Brent Richardson), James Pascucci (Von Titale).

Made in 1974 and never seen in a darkened theater, this extremely low-budget bikini-beach-bimbos film was released because one of its young players, Kevin Costner, became a star.

2721. *Skeleton Coast* (1989, Sivertree Pictures, 98m, c). P Harry Alan Towers, D John (Bud) Cardos, W Nadia Calliou (based on a story by Peter Welbeck [Towers]), PH Hanro Mohr, M Colin Shapiro & Barry Bekker, ED Allan Morrison & Mac Errington.

LP Ernest Borgnine (Col. Smith), Robert Vaughn (Col. Schneider), Oliver Reed (Capt. Simpson), Herbert Lom (Elia), Daniel Greene (Rick Weston), Leon Isaac Kennedy (Chuck), Simon Sabela (Gen. Sekatri), Nancy Mulford (Sam).

Ernest Borgnine organizes a seven member rescue team to move into Angola to bring out his son. The latter is a CIA agent captured and being tortured by evil East German commandant Robert Vaughn.

2722. *Ski Country* (1984, Warren Miller, 93m, c). P,D,W Warren Miller, PH Don Brolin, Fletcher Manley, Gary Nate, Gary Capo, Lex Fletcher, Gary Bigham, Fletcher Anderson, Brian Sissleman, Karl Herrimann, Miller, ED Michael Usher, Ray Laurent, Kim Schneider, Robert Knop, Hamilton Camp.

LP Greg Smith, Hans Fahlen, Lhasa Fahlen, Gunner Moberg, Pierre Vuarnet,

John Low, Fred Noble, Otto Lang, Scott Brookshank, Mike Chew.

In this adventure film, expert skiers risk their limbs on slopes all over the world. For skiers, it's the peaks; for winter-haters, it's the pits.

2723. *Skin Deep* (1989, 20th Century-Fox, 102m, c). P Tony Adams, D&W Blake Edwards, PH Isidore Mankofsky, M Various Artists, ED Robert Pergament, PD Rodger Maus.

LP John Ritter (Zach), Vincent Gardenia (Barney), Alyson Reed (Alex), Joel Brooks (Jake), Julianne Phillips (Molly), Chelsea Field (Amy), Peter Donat (Sparky), Nina Foch (Alex's Mother).

John Ritter is a Hollywood screenwriter whose preoccupation with sex and beautiful women wreaks havoc with both his marriage and his mistresses. When one mistress finds him in bed with a new one, Ritter says, "What can I say?" The offended woman responds as she pulls out a pistol, "Try 'the Lord is my shepherd.'"

2724. *Skull: A Night of Terror* (1989, Geonib/Lightshow, Canada, 77m, c, aka *Don't Turn Out the Light*). P&D Robert Bergman, W Bergman & Gerard Ciccoritti (based on his story), PH Bergman, M Philip Strong, ED Bergman.

LP Robert Bideman (David King), Nadia Capone (Jennifer King), Robbie Rox (Skull), Erica Lancaster (Lisa King), Paul Saunders (Kiel Adams), Nial Lancaster (Gideon King), Bonnie Beck (Sarah Adams), Isabelle Merchant (Ash).

Cop Robert Bideman is haunted by the memory of killing an innocent woman being used by young toughs as a human shield. When some cons take a woman as a hostage to make their escape, they take refuge in his farmhouse home. They torment his wife Nadia Capone and kill Bonnie Beck, his secret mistress and wife of his partner Paul Saunders. Well, a man's gotta do what a man's gotta do.

2725. *Skullduggery* (1989, BBC-TV, GB, 90m, c). P Ann Scott, D&W Philip Davis (based on his play), PH Barry McCann, M Carl Davis, ED Peter Harris, PD Gerry Scott.

LP David Thewlis (Tony), Steve Sweeney (Sweeney), Paul McKenzie (Terry), Chris Pitt (Gombo), Robin Weaver (Kak), Gillian Raine (Tony's mum).

This production starts out as an amusing study of four young friends in a British public housing project. By the end it's a weird black comedy.

2726. *Sky Bandits* (1986, Galaxy Intl., GB, 93m, c). P Richard Herland, D Zoran Perisic, W Thom Keyes, PH David Watkin, M Alfie Kabiljo & Roland Shaw, ED Peter Tanner, PD Tony Woollard.

LP Scott McGinnis (Barney), Jeff Osterhage (Luke), Ronald Lacey (Fritz), Miles Anderson (Bannock), Valerie Steffen (Yvette), Ingrid Held (Mitsou), Keith Buckley (Commander von Schlussel), Terrence Harvey (Col. Canning).

Scott McGinnis and Jeff Osterhage are miscast as two Western buddies who become pilots during World War I. These latter-day Butch Cassidy and Sundance Kid characters stink up the screen. The film is reportedly the most expensive independent British production ever made.

2727. *Slamdance* (1987, Island/Zenith, US/GB, 99m, c). P Rupert Harvey & Barry Opper, D Wayne Wang, W Don Opper, PH Amir Mokri, M Mitchell Froom, ED Lee Percy, PD Eugenio Zanetti.

LP Tom Hulce (C.C. Drood), Mary Elizabeth Mastrantonio (Helen Drood), Adam Ant (Jim), Judith Barsi (Bean Drood), Rosalind Chao (Mrs. Bell), Sasha Delgado (Girl at Nursery), Joshua Caceras (Boy at Nursery), Don Opper (Buddy).

Down-on-his luck cartoonist Tom Hulce becomes the main suspect in the murders of high-priced L.A. call girls. It's a decent thriller.

2728. *Slammer Girls* (1987, Vestron, 80m, c). P&D Chuck Vincent, W Craig Horrall, Vincent, Rick Marx & Larue Watts, PH Larry Revene, M Ian Shaw & Kai Joffe, ED Marc Ubell.

LP Devon Jenkin (Melody), Jeff Eagle (Harry Wiener), Jane Hamilton [Veronica Hart] (Miss Crabapples), Ron Sullivan (Gov. Caldwell), Tally Brittany, Darcy Nychols, Stasia Micula [Samantha Fox], Sharon Cain.

Chuck Vincent and some of his hardcore porno stars present a softcore story about busty females in the Loch Ness Penitentiary for Women. It has all the predictable bawdy goings-on.

2729. *Slapstick of Another Kind* (1984, Intl. Film Marketing, 87m, c). P,D&W Steven Paul (based on the novel *Slapstick* by Kurt Vonnegut), PH Anthony Richmond, M Morty Stevens, ED Doug Jackson, PD Joel Schiller.

LP Jerry Lewis (Wilbur Swain/Caleb Swain), Madeline Kahn (Eliza Swain/Letitia Swain), Marty Feldman (Sylvester), John Abbott (Dr. Frankenstein), Jim Backus (U.S. President), Samuel Fuller (Col. Sharp), Merv Griffin (Anchorman), Virginia Graham (Gossip Specialist), "Noriyuki" Pat Morita (Ambassador Ah Fong), Orson Welles (Voice of Alien Father).

Jerry Lewis and Madeline Kahn give birth to enormous twins (also Lewis and Kahn), aliens sent to earth to solve its woes. Once their mission is discovered, a group of midget Chinese try to kidnap the pair. You'll have to be a devoted and uncritical fan of Jerry Lewis to like this dismal production of Kurt Vonnegut's intriguing novel.

2730. *Slash Dance* (1989, Glencoe, 83m, c). P Andrew Maisner, D&W James Shyman, PH Geza Sinkovics, M Emilio Kauderer, ED Lawrence Rosen.

LP Cindy Maranne (Tori Raines), James Carroll Jordan (Logan), Jay Richardson (Edison), Joel Von Ornsteiner (Amos), John Bluto (Rupert), Jackson Daniel (Jeff).

After several women auditioning for a musical show are killed by a maniac, beautiful cop Cindy Maranne goes undercover as a dancer to smoke out the murderer.

2731. *Slate, Wyn & Me* (1987, Hemdale, Australia, 90m, c). P Tom Burstall, D&W Don McLennan (based on the novel *Slate and Wyn and Blanche McBride* by Georgia Savage), PH David Connell, M Peter Sullivan, ED Peter Friedrich, PD Paddy Reardon.

LP Sigrid Thornton (Blanche McBride), Simon Burke (Wyn Jackson), Martin Sacks (Slate Jackson), Tommy Lewis (Morgan), Lesley Baker (Molly), Harold Baigent (Sammy), Michelle Torres (Daphne), Murray Fahey (Martin).

Brothers Simon Burke and Martin Sacks rob a bank, kill a cop and kidnap

Sigrid Thornton who witnessed the crime. All the good stuff happens in the first 20 minutes. From then on, it's boring!

2732. *Slaughter High* (1987, Vestron, 88m, c). P Steve Minasian & Dick Randall, D&W George Dugdale, Mark Ezra & Peter Litten, PH Alain Pudney, M Harry Manfredini, ED Jim Connock, PD Geoff Sharpe.

LP Caroline Munro (Carol), Simon Scuddamore (Marty), Carmine Iannaccone (Skip), Donna Yaeger (Stella), Gary Hartman (Joe), Billy Martin (Frank), Michael Saffran (Ted), John Segal (Carl), Kelly Baker (Nancy).

Everyone makes fun of nerd Simon Scuddamore. The jocks' and pretty girls' teasing continues until one of their jokes at his expense backfires, disfiguring him for life. Five years later, he throws a reunion party for all those he considers responsible. He's still mad, but he's going to get even. . . .

2733. *Slaughter in San Francisco* (1981, World Northal, 87m, c). P Leonard K.C. Ho, D&W William Lowe, PH David Bailes, M Joe Curtis, ED Fred Cumings.

LP Don Wong, Chuck Norris, Sylvia Channing, Robert Jones, Dan Ivan, Bob Talbert, Robert J. Herguth, James Economides, Chuck Boyde.

In this routine martial arts entry, Chinese-American cop Don Wong leads a one-man fight against corruption in the San Francisco Police Department.

2734. *Slaughterday* (1981, Intercontinental, 86m, c). D Peter Patzak, W Patzak, Walter Kindler & Ossi Bronner, PH Kindler.

LP Rita Tushingham, Michael Hausserman, Frederick Jaeger, William Berger, Gordon Mitchell, Vicki Wolf, Klaus Dahlen.

Once prominent British actress Rita Tushingham's star must have fallen quite far, for her to appear in this cheap horror film.

2735. *Slaughterhouse* (1988, American Artists, 85m, c). P Ron Matonak, D&W Rick Roessler, PH Richard Benda, M Joseph Garrison, ED Sergio Uribe, PD Michael Scaglione, SE Barney Burman & Mark Lane.

LP Sherry Bendorf (Liz Borden), Don Barrett (Lester Bacon), William Houck (Sheriff), Joe Barton (Buddy), Jane Higginson (Annie), Eric Schwartz (Skip), Jeff Grossi (Buzz).

A slasher film without dumb teens wouldn't have a chance. Don't worry, the boys and girls in this gory movie are really obtuse. The star maniac is a nut who slaughters people as if they were farm animals.

2736. *Slaughterhouse Rock* (1988, First American/Arista, 90m, c). P Louis George, D Dimitri Logothetis, W Ted Landon, PH Nicholas Von Sternberg, M/L Mark Mothersbaugh & Gerald V. Castle, ED Daniel Gross, PD Peter Paul Raubertas.

LP Nicholas Celozzi (Alex Gardner), Tom Reilly (Richard Gardner), Donna Denton (Carolyn Harding), Toni Basil (Sammy Mitchell), Hope Marie Carlton (Krista Halpern), Steven Brian Smith (Jack), Ty Miller (Marty), Al Fleming (The Commandant).

Nicholas Celozzi dreams about a prison of the dead where he's an inmate. When these nightmares begin interfering with his everyday life, Celozzi goes to an expert on the occult who identifies the prison as Alcatraz, and advises Celozzi to visit "the Rock" to confront his fears head-on. Turns out this isn't sound advice.

2737. *Slave Girls from Beyond Infinity* (1987, Titan/Urban Classics, 72m, c). P Ken Dixon, John Eng & Mark Wolf, D&W Dixon, PH Ken Wiatrak & Thomas Callaway, M Carlo Dante, ED Bruce Stubbleficld & James A. Stewart.

LP Elizabeth Cayton (Daria), Cindy Beal (Tisa), Brinke Stevens (Shela), Don Scribner (Zed), Carl Horner (Rik), Kirk Graves (Vak), Randolph Roehbling (Krel).

Years and years from now, two beautiful girls are serving life on a prison galley ship. With no hope of a future, they escape, believing anything has to be an improvement. They are incorrect.

2738. *Slaves of New York* (1989, Tri-Star, 125m, c). P Ismail Merchant & Gary Hendler, D James Ivory, W Tama Janowitz (based on her stories), PH Tony

Pierce-Roberts, M Richard Robbins, ED Katherine Wenning, PD David Gropman.

LP Bernadette Peters (Eleanor), Chris Sarandon (Victor Okrent), Marybeth Hurt (Ginger Booth), Madeleine Potter (Daria), Adam Coleman Howard (Stash), Nick Corri (Marley), Mercedes Ruehl (Samantha), Betty Comden (Mrs. Wheeler), Steve Buscemi (Wilfredo), Tama Janowitz (Abby), Bruce Peter Young (Mikell), Tammy Grimes (Georgette).

The film drifts rather aimlessly from situation to situation. Scads of talented young people try to make it in New York, but find the Big Apple almost unbearable to live in.

2739. *The Slayer* (1982, 21st Century, 80m, c, aka *Nightmare Island*). P William R. Ewing, D J.S. Cardone, W Cardone & Ewing, PH Karen Grossman, M Robert Folk, ED Edward Salier, SE Robert Babb.

LP Sarah Kendall (Kay), Frederick Flynn (Eric), Carol Kottenbrook (Brooke), Alan McRae (David), Michael Holmes (Marsh), Carl Kraines (The Slayer).

While vacationing on a small island off the coast of Georgia four friends become dinner for an unseen monster.

2740. *Slayground* (1984, Universal, GB, 89m, c). P John Dark & Gower Frost, D Terry Bedford, W Trevor Preston (based on the novel by Richard Stark), PH Stephen Smith & Herb Wagreitch, M Colin Towns, ED Nicolas Gaster, PD Keith Wilson.

LP Peter Coyote (Stone), Mel Smith (Terry Abbott), Billie Whitelaw (Madge), Philip Sayer (Costello), Bill Luhrs (Joe Sheer), Marie Masters (Joni), Clarence Felder (Orxel), Ned Eisenberg (Lonzini).

During a botched armored car robbery, Peter Coyote's little girl is killed. He sets out to revenge his daughter's death.

2741. *Sleepaway Camp* (1983, United Film, 85m, c). P Michele Tatosian & Jerry Silva, D&W Robert Hiltzik, PH Benjamin Davis, M Edward Bilous, ED Ron Kalish & Sharyn L. Rose, PD William Billowit, SE Ed Fountain.

LP Mike Kellin (Mel), Felissa Rose (Angela), Jonathan Tierston (Ricky), Karen Fields (Judy), Christopher Collet (Paul), Paul De Angelo (Ron), Robert Earl Jones (Ben), Katherine Kamhi (Meg), John E. Dunn (Kenny).

A crazed killer hacks to death unhappy campers at a once peaceful summer camp.

2742. *Sleepaway Camp 2: Unhappy Campers* (1988, Double Helix, 80m, c). P Jerry Silva & Michael A. Simpson, D Simpson, W Fritz Gordon (based on a story idea by Robert Hiltzik), PH Bill Mills, M James Oliverio, ED John David Allen, SE Bill Johnson.

LP Pamela Springsteen (Angela Baker), Brian Patrick Clarke (T.C.), Renee Estevez (Molly), Walter Gotell (Uncle John), Susan Maria Snyder (Mare), Heather Binion (Phoebe).

Bruce Springsteen's younger sister Pamela teaches a harsh lesson to the "bad kids" of Camp Rolling Hills, who smoke, drink, swear and fornicate at every opportunity. She murders them in an assortment of grisly ways, including slashing, drilling, choking, drowning and beating.

2743. *Sleepaway Camp 3: Teenage Wasteland* (1989, Double Helix, 79m, c). P Jerry Silva & Michael A. Simpson, D Simpson, W Fritz Gordon (based on an idea by Robert Hiltzik), PH Bill Mills, M James Oliverio, ED Amy Carey & John David Allen.

LP Pamela Springsteen (Angela), Tracy Griffith (Marcia), Michael J. Pollard (Herman), Mark Oliver (Tony), Kim Wall (Cindy), Kyle Holman, Daryl Wilcher, Haynes Brooke, Stacie Lambert, Kashina Kessler.

Pamela Springsteen is back killing kids attending a summer camp (catering to both rich kids and underprivileged kids). Not content with merely dispatching those whose behavior offends her in some grisly fashion, Springsteen likes to crack jokes about her victims while she's offing them.

2744. *Sleeping Beauty* (1987, Cannon, 90m, c). P Menahem Golan & Yoram Globus, D David Irving, W Michael Berz (based on a story by Charles Perrault), PH David Gurfinkel, ED Tova Neeman, PD Marek Dobrowlski.

LP Morgan Fairchild (Queen), David Holliday (King), Tahnee Welch (Rosebud), Nicholas Clay (Prince), Sylvia Miles (Red Fairy), Kenny Baker (Elf), Jane Weidlin (White Fairy), Julian Chagrin (Court Advisor).

It's the familiar story of the beautiful princess put under an evil magic spell, dooming her to sleep for 100 years unless Prince Charming comes along and awakens her with a kiss.

2745. *Sleeping Dogs* (1982, Aardvark/Satori, New Zealand, 107m, c). P&D Roger Donaldson, W Ian Mune & Arthur Baysting (based on the novel *Smith's Dream* by Karl Stead), PH Michael Seresin, M Murray Grindlay, David Calder & Mathew Brown, ED Ian John.

LP Sam Neill (Smith), Bernard Kearns (Prime Minister), Nevan Rowe (Gloria), Ian Mune (Bullen), Ian Watkin (Dudley), Don Selwyn (Taupiri), Tommy Tinirau (Old Maori Man), Bill Johnson (Cousins).

Set in the near future, New Zealand has come under the control of extreme right-wing forces, following the assassination of democratic leaders. Sam Neill joins a violent resistance movement.

2746. *Slime City* (1988, Slime City, 85m, c). P Gregory Lamberson, Peter Clark & Marc Makowski, D&W Lamberson, PH Peter Clark, M Robert Tomaro, ED Lamberson & Britton Petrucelly, PD Bonnie Brinkley.

LP Robert C. Sabin (Alex), Mary Huner (Lori/Nicole), T.J. Merrick (Jerry), Dick Biel (Irish), Jane Reibel (Lizzy), Bunny Levine (Ruby), Dennis Embry (Roman), Marilyn Oran (Selina).

A crazed cultist turns the inhabitants of an apartment building into slime monsters that ooze into humans, possessing them. Well what do you expect for a measly $50,000?

2747. *Slipping into Darkness* (1989, MCEG, 87m, c). P Jonathan D. Krane, D&W Eleanor Gaver, PH Loren Bivens, M Joey Rand, ED Barbara Pokras, PD Patricia Woodbridge.

LP Michelle Johnson (Carlyle), John DiAquino (Fritz), Neill Barry (Ebin), Anastasia Fielding (Genevieve), Cristen Kaufman (Alex), Vyto Ruginis (Otis).

River's Edge was the inspiration for this film featuring Michelle Johnson, Anastasia Fielding and Cristen Kauffman as three college coeds looking for and finding trouble in a small town filled with bikers.

2748. *Slow Burn* (1989, North American Releasing, Canada, 100m, c, aka *Brothers in Arms*). P Geoff Griffiths, D John E. Eyres, W Steven Lister, PH Nathaniel Massey, M Alan Grey.

LP Anthony James, William Smith, Ivan Rogers, Scott Andersen, Mellisa Conroy.

In the beginning of the film, a Mafia hood murders a family, sparing the youngest son. He will regret this good deed.

2749. *Slow Moves* (1984, Jon Jost, 93m, c). P,D,W,PH,M&ED Jon Jost.

LP Roxanne Rogers, Marshall Gaddis, Debbie Krant, Barbara Hammes, Geoffrey Rotwein, Bebe Bright, Roger Ruffin.

Roxanne Rogers and Marshall Gaddis meet on the Golden Gate Bridge and become lovers. They wander across the country in a beat-up car, robbing stores to finance the trip. It finally comes to an end when Gaddis is killed by a store owner unwilling to be robbed.

2750. *The Slugger's Wife* (1985, Columbia, 105m, c). P Ray Stark, D Hal Ashby, W Neil Simon, PH Caleb Deschanel, M Patrick Williams, ED George Villasenor & Don Brochu, PD J. Michael Riva.

LP Michael O'Keefe (Darryl Palmer), Rebecca De Mornay (Debby Palmer), Martin Ritt (Burley De Vito), Randy Quaid (Goose Granger), Cleavant Derricks (Manny Alvarado), Lisa Langlois (Aline Cooper), Loudon Wainwright, III (Gary), Georgann Johnson (Marie De Vito).

Michael O'Keefe is an outfielder for the Atlantic Braves. His wife Rebecca De Morney is a rock singer. The conflicts of their careers take the glue out of their marriage.

2751. *The Slumber Party Massacre* (1982, Santa Fe/PFC, 78m, c). P Amy Jones, D Jones & Aaron Lipstadt, W Rita Mae Brown, PH Steve Posey, M Ralph

Jones, ED Wendy Green, AD Francesca Bartoccini.

LP Michele Michaels (Trish), Robin Stille (Valerie), Michael Villela (Russ), Andre Honore (Jackie), Debra Deliso (Kim), Gina Mari (Diane), David Milbern (Jeff), Joe Johnson (Neil), Pamela Roylance (Coach Joan).

Mad killer Michael Villela invades a girl's slumber party wielding a power drill. The film, meant to be a spoof of the subgenre of slasher films, misses the mark.

2752. *Slumber Party Massacre II* (1987, Concorde/Embassy, 75m, c). P Deborah Brock & Don Daniel, D&W Brock, PH Thomas Callaway, ED William Flicker, AD Frank Novak, M Various Artists.

LP Crystal Bernard (Courtney), Jennifer Rhodes (Mrs. Bates), Kimberly McArthur (Amy), Patrick Lowe (Matt), Juliette Cummins (Sheila), Heidi Kozak (Sally), Cynthia Eilbacher (Valerie), Atanas Ilitch (The Driller Killer), Joel Hoffman (T.J.).

Crystal Bernard dreams of the return of the killer with a power drill. Ultimately her nightmare becomes reality.

2753. *A Small Circle of Friends* (1980, United Artists, 113m, c). P Tim Zinnemann, D Rob Cohen, W Ezra Sacks, PH Michael Butler, M Jim Steinman, ED Randy Roberts, PD Joel Schiller.

LP Brad Davis (Leo DaVinci), Karen Allen (Jessica), Jameson Parker (Nick Baxter), Shelley Long (Alice), John Friedrich (Haddox), Gary Springer (Greenblatt), Craig Richard Nelson (Harry), Harry Caesar (Jimmy the Cook).

This attempt to depict the conditions on college campuses during the turbulent 60s winds up being just an examination of the questionable mores of three inseparable friends, Brad Davis, Karen Allen and Jameson Parker, as they live and love at Harvard during the demonstrations and riots.

2754. *Smash Palace* (1982, Atlantic, New Zealand, 100m, c). P&D Roger Donaldson, W Peter Hanson, Donaldson & Bruno Lawrence, PH Graeme Cowley, M Sharon O'Neill, ED Mike Horton, AD Reston Griffiths.

LP Bruno Lawrence (Al Shaw), Anna Jemison (Jacqui Shaw), Greer Robson (Georgie Shaw), Keith Aberdein (Ray Foley), Desmond Kelly (Tiny).

Former race car champion Bruno Lawrence is torn between his love for his sport and his wife Anna Jemison.

2755. *Smithereens* (1982, New Line, 90m, c). P&D Susan Seidelman, W Ron Nyswaner & Peter Askin (based on a story by Nyswaner & Seidelman), PH Chririne El Khadem, M Glenn Mercer & Bill Million, ED Seidelman, AD Franz Harland.

LP Susan Berman (Wren), Brad Rinn (Paul), Richard Hell (Eric), Nada Despotovitch (Cecile), Roger Jett (Billy), Kitty Summerall (Blondie), Robynne White (Landlady), D.J. O'Neill (Ed), Joel Rooks (Xerox Boss).

In her directorial debut, Susan Seidelman *(Desperately Seeking Susan),* uses a tried-and-true formula to present the tribulations of Susan Berman, who comes to the Big Apple to become a star.

Smokey and the Bandit Ride Again see *Smokey and the Bandit II*

2756. *Smokey and the Bandit II* (1980, Universal, 95m, c, aka *Smokey and the Bandit Ride Again*). P Hank Moonjean, D Hal Needham, W Jerry Belson & Brock Yates (based on a story by Michael Kane and characters created by Needham & Robert L. Levy), PH Michael Butler, M Snuff Garrett, ED Donn Cambern & William Gordean, PD Henry Bumstead.

LP Burt Reynolds (Bandit), Jackie Gleason (Sheriff Buford T. Justice/Reginald Van Justice/Gaylord Van Justice), Jerry Reed (Cledus), Dom DeLuise (Doc), Sally Field (Carrie), Paul Williams (Little Enos), David Huddleston (John Conn), Mike Henry (Junior), Pat McCormick (Big Enos).

Working on the principle that nothing succeeds like excess, Burt Reynolds and Hal Needham go back to the wall for a sequel to their 1977 hit *Smokey and the Bandit.* They add little to the almost nonexistent plotline, except to make Reynolds a crushed alcoholic who has lost his cult status, his girlfriend Sally Field and just about everything else. He gets rolling again by monotonous repeats of the mindless chases of the first film.

2757. *Smokey and the Bandit—Part 3* (1983, Universal, 88m, c). P Mort Engelberg, D Dick Lowry, W Stuart Birnbaum & David Dashev (based on characters created by Hal Needham & Robert L. Levy), PH James Pergola, M Larry Cansler, ED Byron "Buzz" Brandt, David Blewitt & Christopher Greenbury, AD Ron Hobbs.

LP Jackie Gleason (Buford T. Justice), Jerry Reed (Cledus/Bandit), Paul Williams (Little Enos), Pat McCormick (Big Enos), Mike Henry (Junior), Colleen Camp (Dusty Trails), Faith Minton (Tina), Burt Reynolds (The Real Bandit).

Burt Reynolds had the good grace to take only a cameo role in this third in the series of infantile and moronic chase films. Jerry Reed moves up to the "bandit" chased by Jackie Gleason's rednecked sheriff.

2758. *Smokey and the Hotwire Gang* (1980, NMD, 85m, c). P,D&ED Anthony Cardoza, W T. Gary Cardoza (based on his story), PH Gregory Sandor, M Valerie Jeanne & Danny Bravin.

LP James Keach (Joshua), Stanley Livingston (Russ), Tony Lorea (Filbert), Alvy Moore (Sheriff), Skip Young (Junior), Carla Ziegfeld (Elena/Hotwire), George Barris (Billy), Ray Cantrell (Ron), Tanya George (Nancy).

This "comedy" features CB'ers, "hot babes," fast cars and an armored car robbery.

2759. *Smokey Bites the Dust* (1981, New World, 85m, c). P Roger Corman & Gale Hurd, D Charles B. Griffith, W Max Apple (based on a story by Brian Williams), PH Gary Graver, M Bent Myggen, ED Larry Bock.

LP Jimmy McNichol (Roscoe Wilton), Janet Julian (Peggy Sue Turner), Walter Barnes (Sheriff Turner), Patrick Campbell (Lester), Kari Lizer (Cindy), John Blythe Barrymore (Harold), Kedric Wolfe (Deputy Bentley), Bill Forsythe (Kenny).

Small town delinquent Jimmy McNichol smashes stolen car after stolen car with the town's homecoming queen Janet Julian as his passenger.

2760. *Smooth Talk* (1985, Spectrafilm, 92m, c). P Martin Rosen, D Joyce Chopra, W Tom Cole (based on the story "Where Are You Going, Where Have You Been?" by Joyce Carol Oates), PH James M. Glennon, M Bill Payne, Russell Kunkel & George Massenburg, ED Patrick Dodd, PD David Wasco.

LP Treat Williams (Arnold Friend), Laura Dern (Connie), Mary Kay Place (Katherine), Elizabeth Berridge (June), Levon Helm (Harry), Sarah Inglis (Jill), Margaret Welch (Laura), Geoff Hoyle (Ellie), William Ragsdale (Jeff), David Berridge (Eddie).

In this adaptation of Joyce Carol Oates' short story, small town teenage beauty Laura Dern plays with fire when she innocently attracts potentially dangerous stranger Treat Williams.

2761. *Smorgasbord* (1983, Warner, 83m, c, aka *Cracking Up*). P Peter Nelson & Arnold Orgolini, D Jerry Lewis, W Lewis & Bill Richmond, PH Gerald Perry Finnerman, M Morton Stevens, ED Gene Fowler, Jr., AD Terry Bousman.

LP Jerry Lewis (Warren Nefron/Dr. Perks), Herb Edelman (Dr. Jonas Pletchick), Zane Busby (Waitress), Foster Brooks (Pilot), Buddy Lester (Passenger), Milton Berle (Female Patient).

It's long past the time that Jerry Lewis should be put out to pasture. His slapstick routines had their day, but can now only be viewed as an embarrassment to the comedian. In this film he's a goofy nut who visits his psychiatrist and relates through flashbacks his failed attempts at keeping a job.

Snapshot see ***The Day After Halloween***

2762. *Sno-Line* (1986, Vandom Intl., 89m, c). P Robert Burge, D Douglas F. O'Neons, W Robert Hilliard, PH Guy Thieltges, M Richard Bellis, ED Beth Conwell, PD Chuck Stewart.

LP Vince Edwards (Steve King), Paul Smith (Duval), June Wilkinson (Audrey), Phil Foster (Ralph Salerno), Louis Guss (Gus), Carey Clark (Michael), Charity Ann Zachary (Tina).

New York gangster Vince Edwards moves to Texas where he wipes out all competition in his way to becoming a drug and gambling king.

2763. *Snow White* (1987, Cannon, 83m, c). P Menahem Golan & Yoram Globus, D&W Michael Berz, AD Etan Levy.

LP Diana Rigg (Mean Queen), Billy Barty (Iddy), Sarah Patterson (Snow White at 16), Nicola Stapleton (Snow White at 7), Mike Edmunds (Biddy), Ricardo Gil (Kiddy), Malcolm Dixon (Diddy), Gary Friedkin (Fiddy), Tony Cooper (Liddy), Douglas Sheldon (King).

Diana Rigg hams it up as the nasty queen not taken with the beauty of Snow White in this version of the fairy tale, which won't steal admirers from the Disney version.

2764. *Snow White and the Seven Dwarfs* (1987, Walt Disney, animated, 82m, c). P Walt Disney, SUPERVISING DIRECTOR David Hand, SEQUENCE DIRECTORS Perce Pearce, Larry Morey, William Cottrell, Wilfred Jackson & Ben Sharpsteen, SUPERVISING ANIM Hamilton Luske, Vladimir Tytla, Fred Moore & Norman Ferguson, M Frank Churchill, Leigh Harline & Paul Smith†.

VOICES Adriana Caselotti (Snow White), Harry Stockwell (Prince Charming), Lucille LaVerne (The Queen), Moroni Olsen (Magic Mirror), Billy Gilbert (Sneezy), Pinto Colvig (Sleepy/Grumpy), Otis Harlan (Happy), Scotty Mattraw (Bashful), Roy Atwell (Doc), Stuart Buchanan (Humbert, the Queen's Huntsman).

Originally released December 21, 1937, this Disney classic was his first feature animation, a mammoth undertaking which many called Disney's Folly. Once upon a time, there lived a princess named Snow White whose beauty enraged her vain stepmother, the Queen. The latter ordered her huntsman to take Snow White into the woods, kill her and bring back her heart as proof the deed was done. The huntsman could not bring himself to kill one so good, kind, beautiful and young, so he abandoned her in the woods and brought back the heart of an animal. Snow White was discovered by seven Dwarfs: Doc, Happy, Grumpy, Sleepy, Sneezy, Bashful and Dopey, who lived and worked in the forest. They took her in and she cared for their house. The Queen discovered she had been tricked when she asked her magic mirror the now famous line, "Who's the fairest one of all?" and the mirror once again replied, "Snow White!" Disguising herself as an old hag, the Queen tempted Snow White with a poisoned apple which put the fair one into a death-like sleep, from which she could only be awakened by the kiss of her Prince Charming. He showed up and everyone lived happily ever after. The marvelous songs of the film included "Whistle While You Work," "Heigh-Ho," "Some Day My Prince Will Come" and "One Song."

Snowman see *The Land of No Return*

2765. *S.O.B.* (1981, Paramount, 121m, c). P Blake Edwards & Tony Adams, D&W Edwards, PH Harry Stradling, Jr., M Henry Mancini, ED Ralph E. Winters, PD Rodger Maus.

LP Julie Andrews (Sally Miles), William Holden (Tim Culley), Marisa Berenson (Mavis), Larry Hagman (Dick Benson), Robert Loggia (Herb Maskowitz), Stuart Margolin (Gary Murdock), Richard Mulligan (Felix Farmer), Robert Preston (Dr. Irving Finegarten), Craig Stevens (Willard), Loretta Swit (Polly Reed), Robert Vaughn (David Blackman), Robert Webber (Ben Coogan), Shelley Winters (Eva Brown), Jennifer Edwards (Lila).

In Blake Edward's bitter farce about Hollywood and the movie business, Julie Andrews portrays an actress whose sweetness and purity in films have seen their day. Her latest multimillion-dollar film is a flop. Her husband, Richard Mulligan, gets the idea of rescripting and shooting the film as an X-rated feature. For her art Andrews exposes her breasts. No big deal, everyone knew she had 'em. There just was no clamor to see them.

2766. *Society* (1989, Wild Street Pictures, 99m, c). P Keith Walley, D Brian Yuzna, W Woody Keith & Rick Fry, PH Rick Fichter, M Mark Ryder & Phil Davies, ED Peter Teschner, PD Mathew C. Jacobs.

LP Billy Warlock (Bill Whitney), Devin Devasquez (Clarissa), Evan Richards, Ben Meyerson, Charles Lucia, Connie Danese, Patrice Jennings.

In this obnoxious horror film, everyone believes that teen Billy Warlock is paranoid when he suspects that not only is he adopted but that his "parents" are having incestuous orgies with his sister.

2767. Soggy Bottom U.S.A. (1982, Gaylord, 90m, c). P Elmo Williams, D Ted Flicker, W Eric Edson & Stephen C. Burnham & Joy N. Houck, Jr. (based on a story by Hal L. Harrison, Jr.).

LP Ben Johnson, Ann Wedgeworth, Lois Nettleton, Dub Taylor, Anthony Zerbe, Jack Elam, P.J. Soles, Lane Smith, Don Johnson.

The cast tries diligently in this story of a sheriff having difficulty keeping the peace in a small Southern community. But they don't have much to work with.

2768. Solarbabies (1986, MGM/United Artists, 94m, c). P Irene Walzer & Jack Frost Sanders, D Alan Johnson, W Walon Green & Douglas Anthony Metrov, PH Peter MacDonald, M Maurice Jarre, ED Conrad Buff, PD Anthony Pratt, VE Richard Edlund.

LP Richard Jordan (Grock), Jami Gertz (Terra), Jason Patric (Jason), Lukas Haas (Daniel), James Le Gros (Metron), Claude Brooks (Rabbit), Peter DeLuise (Tug), Pete Kowanko (Gavial), Adrian Pasdar (Darstar), Sarah Douglas (Shandray), Charles Durning (Warden), Frank Converse (Greentree).

In the distant future, a group of teens who play a version of hockey on roller skates join forces with a mystical force to wrestle the control of the world's water supply from an evil empire.

2769. The Soldier (1982, Embassy, 96m, c, aka *Codename: The Soldier*). P,D&W James Glickenhaus, PH Robert M. Baldwin, Jr., M Tangerine Dream, ED Paul Fried, PD William DeSeta.

LP Ken Wahl (The Solider), Klaus Kinski (Dracha), William Prince (U.S. President), Alberta Watson (Susan Goodman), Jeremiah Sullivan, Joaquim DeAlmeida, Peter Hooten, Steve James, Alexander Spencer.

The Russians hold the world ransom to their demands because of a pile of stolen plutonium. A single soldier, Ken Wahl, is in the position of carrying out a dangerous unauthorized plan which may preserve the world's balance of power.

2770. A Soldier's Story† (1984, Columbia, 101m, c). P Norman Jewison, Ronald L. Schwary & Patrick Palmer, D Jewison, W Charles Fuller† (based on his stage play *A Soldier's Play*), PH Russell Boyd, M Herbie Hancock, ED Mark Warner & Caroline Biggerstaff, PD Walter Scott Herndon.

LP Howard E. Rollins, Jr. (Capt. Davenport), Adolph Caesar† (Sgt. Waters), Art Evans (Pvt. Wilkie), David Alan Grier (Cpl. Cobb), David Harris (Pvt. Smalls), Dennis Lipscomb (Capt. Taylor), Larry Riley (C.J. Memphis), Robert Townsend (Cpl. Ellis), Denzel Washington (Pfc. Peterson), William Allen Young (Pvt. Henson), Patti LaBelle (Big Mary), Wings Hauser (Lt. Byrd).

Black army attorney Howard E. Rollins, Jr., is sent to a Southern military base to investigate the murder of unpopular black sergeant Adolph Caesar. A series of flashbacks reveal much about the character of the deceased and his relationship with his men. Caesar, a fine character actor, gives the performance of his career.

2771. Sole Survivor (1984, Grand National, 90m, c). P Don Barkemeyer, D&W Thom Eberhardt, PH Russ Carpenter, M David F. Anthony, ED Eberhardt.

LP Anita Skinner (Denise Watson), Caren Larae Larkey (Karla Davis), Robin Davidson (Kristy Cutler), Kurt Johnson (Brian Richardson).

A group of zombies search for beautiful advertising executive Anita Skinner, the only survivor of an airplane crash in a remote area.

2772. Some Girls (1988, MGM/United Artists, Canada, 94m, c). P Rick Stevenson, D Michael Hoffman, W Rupert Walters, PH Ueli Steiger, M James Newton Howard, ED David Spiers.

LP Patrick Dempsey (Michael), Jennifer Connelly (Gabby), Sheila Kelly (Irenka), Andre Gregory (Father), Ashley Greenfield (Simone), Florinda Bolkan (Mrs. D'Arc), Lila Kedrova (Granny).

In this mildly amusing comedy, American college student Patrick Dempsey has accepted the offer of his sleep-in girlfriend Jennifer Connelly to spend Christmas with her family in Quebec City. When Dempsey arrives, she informs him that she no longer loves him and he will be sleeping alone. That doesn't fit with Dempsey's needs and the randy youngster makes every effort to win back his bedtime privileges. Connelly's two nubile sisters seem more than willing to accommodate Dempsey's needs for sleeping companions.

2773. *Some Kind of Hero* (1982, Paramount, 97m, c). P Howard W. Koch, D Michael Pressman, W James Kirkwood & Robert Boris (based on the novel by Kirkwood), PH King Baggot, M Patrick Williams, ED Christopher Greenbury, AD James L. Schoppe.

LP Richard Pryor (Eddie Keller), Margot Kidder (Toni), Ray Sharkey (Vinnie), Ronny Cox (Col. Powers), Lynne Moody (Lisa), Olivia Cole (Jesse), Paul Benjamin (Leon), David Adams (The Kid), Martin Azarow (Tank).

When Vietnam prisoner-of-war Richard Pryor comes home, he finds his world a much changed place. His wife has left him for another man. The government is suspicious of the statements he signed while a prisoner to prevent his buddies from being tortured and he's low on cash. He meets high-priced call girl Margot Kidder with the proverbial heart-of-gold. Together, they briefly use some mob money to arrange for their future.

2774. *Some Kind of Wonderful* (1987, Paramount, 93m, c). P John Hughes, D Howard Deutch, W Hughes, PH Jan Kiesser, M Stephen Rague & John Musser, ED Bud Smith & Scott Smith, PD Josan Russo.

LP Eric Stoltz (Keith Nelson), Mary Stuart Masterson (Watts "Drummer Girl"), Lea Thompson (Amanda Jones), Craig Sheffer (Hardy Jenns), John Ashton (Cliff Nelson), Elias Koteas (Skinhead), Molly Hagan (Shayne), Maddie Corman (Laura Nelson), Jane Elliot (Carol Nelson).

Eric Stoltz is a high school student who has this thing for Lea Thompson. Not being able to get to first base with her, he turns to tomboy Mary Stuart Masterson for help. He's too dense to see that she's mad for him and it takes the whole film to realize that she's better for him than the more glamorous but shallow Thompson.

2775. *Someone to Love* (1988, Rainbow-Castle Hill, 110m, c). P M.H. Simonsons, D&W Henry Jaglom, PH Hanania Baer, M Various Artists, ED Ruth Wald.

LP Orson Welles (Danny's Friend), Henry Jaglom (Danny Sapir), Andrea Marcovicci (Helen Eugene), Michael Emil (Mickey Sapir), Sally Kellerman (Edith Helm), Oja Kodar (Yelena), Stephen Bishop (Blue), Dave Frishberg (Harry).

While filmmaker Henry Jaglom has people at a St. Valentine's Day party speak to the camera, explaining why they are lonely, Orson Welles, in his last screen appearance, sits near by and makes profound comments.

2776. *Someone to Watch Over Me* (1987, Columbia, 106m, c). P Thierry de Ganay & Harold Schneider, D Ridley Scott, W Howard Franklin, PH Stephen Poster, M Michael Kamen, ED Claire Simpson, PD Jim Bissell.

LP Tom Berenger (Mike Keegan), Mimi Rogers (Claire Gregory), Lorraine Bracco (Ellie Keegan), Jerry Orbach (Lt. Garber), John Rubinstein (Neil Steinhart), Andreas Katsulas (Joey Venza), Tony DiBenedetto (T.J.).

Detective Tom Berenger is assigned to protect Mimi Rogers, the prime witness in a murder case. He finds he doesn't quite fit into her glamorous life style, but he falls for her nevertheless and that's dangerous for both of them.

2777. *Something Special* (1987, Concorde, 90m, c, aka *Willy Milly*). P M. David Chilewich & Fred Berner, D Paul Schneider, W Walter Carbone & Carla Reuben (based on the story "Willy Milly" by Alan Friedman), PH Dominique Chapuis, M David McHugh, ED Michael R. Miller, PD Nora Chavooshian.

LP Pamela Segall (Milly/Willy Niceman), Eric Gurry (Alfie Bensdorf), Mary Tanner (Stephanie), Patty Duke (Mrs. Doris Niceman), John Glover (Mr. Fred Niceman), Seth Green (Malcolm), John David Cullum (Tom).

Teenage girl Pamela Segall wants to become a teenage boy. She succeeds with the help of some magical powder and a solar eclipse. Then "he" discovers that it's not just girls who have problems.

2778. *Something Wicked This Way Comes* (1983, Buena Vista, 94m, c). P Peter Vincent Douglas, D Jack Clayton, W Ray Bradbury (based on his novel), PH Stephen H. Burum, M James Horner, ED Argyle Nelson & Barry Mark Gordon, PD Richard MacDonald.

LP Jason Robards, Jr. (Charles Halloway), Jonathan Pryce (Mr. Dark), Diane Ladd (Mrs. Nightshade), Pam Grier (Dust Witch), Royal Dano (Tom Fury), Vidal Peterson (Will Halloway), Shawn Carson (Jim Nightshade), Angelo Rossitto (Little Person No. 1), Peter D. Risch (Little Person No. 2).

Ray Bradbury's classic fantasy novel is the basis for an excellent moody piece featuring Jonathan Pryce and his mysterious traveling carnival. When it arrives in a small Illinois town in the early part of the century, it proves to be much more than it seems. The film lost lots of money, but is well worth viewing if one gets the Disney Channel.

2779. *Something Wild* (1986, Orion, 113m, c). P Jonathan Demme & Kenneth Utt, D Demme, W E. Max Frye, PH Tak Fujimoto, M John Cale & Laurie Anderson, ED Craig McKay, PD Norma Moriceau.

LP Jeff Daniels (Charles Driggs), Melanie Griffith (Audrey Hankel), Ray Liotta (Ray Sinclair), Margaret Colin (Irene), Tracey Walter (The Country Squire), Dana Preu ("Peaches"), Jack Gilpin (Larry Dillman).

In a kooky comedy, straight-shooting businessman Jeff Daniels takes off for a few days with wild, flaky, sexy Melanie Griffith, who turns his life inside out.

2780. *Somewhere in Time* (1980, Universal, 103m, c). P Stephen Deutsch, D Jeannot Szwarc, W Richard Matheson (based on his novel *Bid Time Return*), PH Isidore Mankofsky, M John Barry (Sergei Rachmaninov), ED Jeff Gourson, PD Seymour Klate, COS Jean-Pierre Dorleac.

LP Christopher Reeve (Richard Collier), Jane Seymour (Elise McKenna), Christopher Plummer (W.F. Robinson), Teresa Wright (Laura Roberts), Bill Erwin (Arthur), George Voskovec (Dr. Gerald Finney), Susan French (Older Elise), John Alvin (Arthur's Father).

Playwright Christopher Reeve falls in love with an old portrait of Jane Seymour and through self-hypnosis transforms himself back in time to discover what their relationship might have been.

Son see Bad Blood

2781. *Songwriter* (1984, Tri-Star, 94m, c). P Sydney Pollack, D Alan Rudolph, W Bud Shrake, PH Matthew F. Leonetti, M Kris Kristofferson†, ED Stephen Lovejoy & George A. Martin, PD Joel Schiller.

LP Willie Nelson (Doc Jenkins), Kris Kristofferson (Blackie Buck), Melinda Dillon (Honey Carder), Rip Torn (Dino McLeish), Lesley Ann Warren (Gilda), Mickey Raphael (Arly and Harmonica), Rhonda Dotson (Corkie).

In yet another attempt to show the way it really is in the country and western music world, Willie Nelson and Kris Kristofferson portray one time performing partners who break away to work solo. Nelson becomes the dean of C&W, wracked with personal and tax problems, while Kristofferson maintains his stance as a rebel.

2782. *Sons* (1989, Pacific Pictures, 88m, c). P Marc Toberoff, D Alexandre Rockwell, W Rockwell & Brandon Cole, PH Stefan Czapsky, M Mader, ED Jay Freund.

LP William Forsythe (Mikey), D.B. Sweeney (Ritchie), Robert Miranda (Fred), Samuel Fuller (Father), Stephane Audran (Florence), Judith Godreche (Florence, Jr.), William Hickey (Roger), Bernard Fresson (Baker), Jennifer Beals (Transvestite), Shirley Stoler (German Housewife).

Three sons take their incapacitated father Samuel Fuller on a trip to Normandy to find his long lost love Stephane Audran.

2783. *Sophie's Choice* (1982, Universal, 157m, c). P Alan J. Pakula & Keith Barish, D Pakula, W Pakula† (based on the novel by William Styron), PH Nestor Almendros†, M Marvin Hamlisch†, ED Evan Lottman, PD George Jenkins, COS Albert Wolsky†.

LP Meryl Streep* (Sophie Zawistowska), Kevin Kline (Nathan Landau), Peter MacNicol (Stingo), Josef Sommer

(Narrator), Rita Karin (Yetta Zimmerman), Stephen D. Newman (Larry), Greta Turken (Leslie Lapidus), Josh Mostel (Morris Fink), Marcell Rosenblatt (Astrid Weinstein), Moishe Rosenfeld (Moishe Rosenblum), Gunther Maria Halmer (Rudolf Hoess), Karlheinz Hackl (SS Doctor), Ulli Fessl (Frau Hoess).

Polish Auschwitz survivor Meryl Streep settles in Brooklyn after the war and tries to forget her past. But the recollection that she was forced to choose which of her children was to be sent to the gas chamber immediately on arriving at the death camp and which would be allowed to live a bit longer, proves to be too much for her. Her stormy relationship with unstable Kevin Kline doesn't help.

2784. *Sorceress* (1983, New World, 75m, c). P Jack Hill, D Brian Stuart, W Jim Wynorski, PH Alex Phillips, Jr., ED Larry Bock & Barry Zetlin, PD Charles Grodin.

LP Leigh Harris (Mira), Lynette Harris (Mara), Bob Nelson (Erlick), David Milbern (Pando), Bruno Rey (Baldar), Ana De Sade (Dellisia), Robert Ballesteros (Traigon), Douglas Sanders (Hunnu), Tony Stevens (Khrakannon).

Despotic ruler and master of the Black Arts Robert Ballesteros plans to become master of the world. The film is just an excuse to exploit the beautiful bodies of the Harris twins, who have been disguised as males to prevent their father Ballesteros from sacrificing them to gain more power. They experience each other's feeling—you know, like, orgasms.

2785. *Sorority Babes in the Slimeball Bowl-O-Rama* (1988, Urban Classics, 78m, c, aka *The Imp*). P David DeCoteau & John Schouweiler, D David DeCoteau, W Sergei Hasenecz, PH Stephen Ashley Blake, M Guy Moon, ED Barry Zetlin & Tom Meshelski, PD Royce Mathew.

LP Linnea Quigley (Spider), Michelle Bauer (Lisa), Andras Jones (Calvin), Robin Rochelle (Babs), Brinke Stevens (Taffy), Kathi Obrecht (Rhonda), Carla Baron (Frankie), Hal Havins (Jimmie), John Stuart Wildman (Keith), George [Buck] Flower (Janitor), Michael D. Sonye (The Imp's Voice).

Sorority pledges Michelle Bauer and Linnea Quigley, along with some college nerds caught spying on the kinky initiation rites, are forced to steal a bowling trophy. They succeed, but drop it, and out pops a surly genie, who gives each of the college students a wish. When he tricks the girls, turning them into monsters, the movie gets down to business.

2786. *Sorority House Massacre* (1987, Concorde, 73m, c). P Ron Diamond, D&W Carol Frank, PH Marc Reshovsky, M Michael Wetherwax, ED Eve Gage.

LP Angela Maegan O'Neill (Laura/Beth), Wendy Martel (Linda), Pamela Ross (Sara), Nicole Rio (Tracy), John C. Russell (Killer/Bobby), Marcus Vaughter (Andy), Vinnie Bilancio (John), Joe Nassi (Craig).

While most of her snippy sisters are away on holiday, shy sorority pledge Angela Maegan O'Neill becomes the prey of a psychopath who used to live in the sorority house.

Sorority Sisters see Nightmare Sisters

2787. *Soul Man* (1986, New World, 101m, c). P Steve Tisch, D Steve Miner, W Carol Black, PH Jeffrey Jur, M Tom Scott, ED David Finfer, PD Gregg Fonseca, AD Don Diers & John Rienhart.

LP C. Thomas Howell (Mark Watson), Arye Gross (Gordon Bloomfeld), Rae Dawn Chong (Sarah Walker), James Earl Jones (Professor Banks), Melora Hardin (Whitney Dunbar), Leslie Nielsen (Mr. Dunbar), James B. Sikking (Bill Watson).

In order to earn a scholarship to Harvard, C. Thomas Howell dons an Afro wig, uses tanning pills and passes for black. Howell discovers much about racial stereotyping and falls in love with Rae Dawn Chong.

2788. *Soup for One* (1982, Warner, 87m, c). P Marvin Worth, D&W Jonathan Kaufer, PH Fred Schuler, M Nile Rodgers, Bernard Edwards & Johnny Mandel, ED David Rawlins, PD Philip Rosenberg.

LP Saul Rubinek (Allan), Marcia Strassman (Maria), Gerrit Graham (Brian), Teddy Pendergrass (Nightclub Singer), Richard Libertini (Angelo), Andrea Martin (Concord Seductress), Mordecai Lawner (Furniture Salesman).

Young conservative Jewish New

Yorker Saul Rubinek searches for his "dream girl" in this bittersweet comedy. When various dates fizzle, womanizer friend Graham takes Rubinek to the Catskills for a singles weekend.

Soup to Nuts see Waitress

2789. *South Bronx Heroes* (1985, Zebra/Continental, 85m, c, aka *The Runaways; Revenge of the Innocents*). P&D William Szarka, W Szarka & Don Schiffrin, PH Eric Schmitz, M Al Zima & Mitch Herzog, ED Jim Rivera, Eli Haviv & Szarka.

LP Brendan Ward (Paul), Mario van Peebles (Tony), Megan van Peebles (Chrissie), Melissa Esposito (Michelle), Martin Zurla (Bennett), Jordan Abeles (Scott), Barry Lynch, Dan Lauria, Bo Rucker, Sean Ward.

Mario Van Peebles stars in this obscure independent film which poignantly tells the story of victims of child abuse and pornography.

2790. *South of Reno* (1988, Open Road/Castle-Hill, 94m, c). P Robert Tinnell, D Mark Rezyka, W Rezyka & T.L. Lankford, PH Bernard Auroux, M Nigel Holton & Clive Wright, ED Marc Grossman, PD Philip Duffin.

LP Jeffrey Osterhage (Martin Clark), Lisa Blount (Anette Clark), Joe Phelan (Hector), Lewis Van Bergen (Willard), Julie Montgomery (Susan), Brandis Kemp (Brenda), Danitza Kingsley (Louise).

None-too-bright Jeffrey Osterhage and his wife Lisa Blount live in a remote desert shack in Nevada, spending most of their time watching their one channel TV. He dreams of visiting Reno, but must be content with the make-believe Reno which he creates with thousands of Christmas lights. She has a rather apparent affair with auto mechanic Joe Phelan. Ultimately Osterhage fights the latter for Blount's affection.

2791. *Southern Comfort* (1981, 20th Century–Fox, 100m, c). P David Giler, D Walter Hill, W Michael Kane, Hill & Giler, PH Andrew Laszlo, M Ry Cooder, ED Freeman Davies, PD John Vallone.

LP Keith Carradine (Spencer), Powers Boothe (Hardin), Fred Ward (Reece), Franklyn Seales (Simms), T.K. Carter (Cribbs), Lewis Smith (Stuckey), Les Lannom (Casper), Peter Coyote (Poole), Carlos Brown (Bowden).

In a frightening story, nine members of a National Guard patrol, on routine weekend maneuvers in Louisiana, are marked for death by Cajuns who have mistaken the purpose of the soldiers.

2792. *Space Avenger* (1989, Manley Prods., 88m, c). P Ray Sundlin, Robert A. Harris & Richard W. Haines, D Haines, W Haines & Lynwood Sawyer, PH Mustupha Barat, M Richard Fiocca, ED Haines.

LP Robert Prichard, Mike McClerie, Charity Staley, Gina Mastrogiacomo, Kirk Fairbanks Fogg, Angela Nicholas.

Four alien convicts escape from an outer galaxy prison, ending up in an American woods circa 1930. They possess the bodies of two couples driving by, hoping to put the agents on their trail off their scent. To repair their spaceship they realize that they'll have to wait until earth technology has advanced sufficiently. When this takes place 50 years later, the aliens are just as ornery as ever.

2793. *Space Mutiny* (1989, Action Intl., 91m, c). P&D David Winters, W Maria Dante, PH Vincent Cox, M Tim James, Steve McClintock & Mark Mancina, ED Bill Asher, Charlotte Konrad & Catherine Meyburgh.

LP Reb Brown (Dave Ryder), John Phillip Law (Kaglan), James Ryan (MacPhearson), Cameron Mitchell (Alex Jansen), Cissie Cameron (Lea Jansen), Graham Clark (Scott Dyers).

Reb Brown helps Cameron Mitchell and his daughter Cissy Cameron fight off a spaceship mutiny led by John Phillip Law and James Ryan.

2794. *Space Rage* (1987, Vestron, 77m, c). P Morton Reed & Eric Barrett, D Conrad E. Palmisano & Peter McCarthy, W Jim Lenahan (based on a story by Reed), PH Timothy Suhrstedt & Tom Richmond, M Billy Ferrick & Zander Schloss, ED W. Peter Miller & Arthur Bressan, Jr.

LP Richard Farnsworth (The Colonel), Michael Pare (Grange), John Laughlin (Walker), Lee Purcell (Maggie), William Windom (Gov. Tovah), Lewis Van Bergen (Drago), Dennis Redfield (Quinn), Hank Worden (Old Codger).

Set on a prison planet, Richard Farnsworth must strap on a six-laser and teach the baddies a lesson. The film is a disgrace to several genres.

2795. *Space Raiders* (1983, New World, 82m, c, aka *Star Child*). P Roger Corman, D&W Howard R. Cohen, PH Alec Hirschfeld, M James Horner, ED Anthony Randel & Robert J. Kizer, AD Wayne Springfield, SE Tom Campbell.

LP Vince Edwards (Hawk), David Mendenhall (Peter), Patsy Pease (Amanda), Thom Christopher (Flightplan), Luca Bercovici (Ace), Drew Snyder (Alderbarian), Ray Stewart (Zariatin), George Dickerson (Tracton).

Lucky ten-year-old David Mendenhall blasts off to a fantastic world filled with intergalactic desperadoes, alien mercenaries and star ship battles. Producer Roger Corman has put together this dud from leftovers of earlier pictures including *Battle Beyond the Stars, Sorceress* and *Screwballs.*

2796. *Spaceballs* (1987, MGM/United Artists, 96m, c). P&D Mel Brooks, W Brooks, Thomas Meehan & Ronny Graham, PH Nick McLean, M John Morris, ED Conrad Buff IV, PD Terence Marsh.

LP Mel Brooks (President Skroob/Yogurt), John Candy (Barf the Mawg), Rick Moranis (Lord Dark Helmet), Bill Pullman (Lone Starr), Daphne Zuniga (Princess Vespa), Dick Van Patten (King Roland), George Wyner (Col. Sandurz), Michael Winslow (Radar Technician), Joan Rivers (Voice of Dot Matrix), Lorene Yarnell (Dot Matrix).

Mel Brooks' spoof of *Star Wars* misses the target by light-years. The story is just about the same as Steven Spielberg's, except where Brooks takes a few liberties to show more of his childish attempts at humor. The performances of the cast match the ineptitude of producer-director-writer Brooks.

2797. *Spacecamp* (1986, 20th Century–Fox, 112m, c). P Patrick Bailey & Walter Coblenz, D Harry Winer, W W.W. Wicket & Casey T. Mitchell (based on a story by Bailey & Larry B. Williams,

PH William Fraker, M John Williams, ED John W. Wheeler & Timothy Board, PD Richard MacDonald.

LP Kate Capshaw (Andie), Lea Thompson (Kathryn), Kelly Preston (Tish), Larry B. Scott (Rudy), Leaf Phoenix (Max), Tate Donovan (Kevin), Tom Skerritt (Zach), Barry Primus (Brennan), Terry O'Quinn (Launch Director).

Astronaut Kate Capshaw, a reluctant instructor at the U.S. Space Camp in Alabama, and five of her teenage and younger charges board a real space ship and are accidentally launched on a space journey.

2798. *Spaced Out* (1981, Miramax, GB, 90m, c, aka *Outer Touch*). P David Speechley, D Norman J. Warren, W Andrew Payne, Bob Saget & Jeff de Hart, PH John Metcalfe & Peter Sinclair, M Alan Brawer & Anna Pepper, ED Edward Glass.

LP Barry Stokes (Oliver), Tony Maiden (Willy), Glory Annen (Cosia), Michael Rowlatt (Cliff), Ava Cadell (Partha), Kate Ferguson (Skipper), Lynne Ross (Prudence).

This British sex comedy is a parody of films such as *Star Wars* and *2001: A Space Odyssey.*

2799. *Spacehunter: Adventures in the Forbidden Zone* (1983, Columbia, 3-D, 90m, c, aka *Adventures in the Creep Zone; Road Gangs*). P Don Carmody, Andre Link & John Dunning, D Lamont Johnson, W David Preston, Edith Rey, Dan Goldberg & Len Blum (based on a story by Stewart Harding & Jean LaFleur), PF Frank Tidy, M Elmer Bernstein, ED Scott Conrad, PD Jackson DeGovia.

LP Peter Strauss (Wolff), Molly Ringwald (Niki), Ernie Hudson (Washington), Andrea Marcovicci (Chalmers), Michael Ironside (Overdog McNabb), Beeson Carroll (Grandma Patterson), Hrant Alianak (Chemist).

Molly Ringwald's career has withstood this stupid science fiction film featuring galactic bounty hunter Peter Strauss, who agrees to rescue three stranded girls whose space ship has crashed on the planet Terra Eleven. But in years to come she may well wish to leave it out of her filmography.

2800. *Spaceship* (1983, Creature Features, 88m, c, aka *The Creature Wasn't Nice*). P Mark Haggard, D&W Bruce Kimmel, PH Denny Lavil, M David Spear, ED David Blangsted, PD Lee Cole.

LP Cindy Williams (McHugh), Bruce Kimmel (John), Leslie Nielsen (Jameson), Gerrit Graham (Rodzinski), Patrick Macnee (Stark), Ron Kurowski (Creature).

Stopping at a small planet, the crew of a lone spaceship picks up a clump of matter which turns into a monster. When hooked up with a communication computer it does a song and dance routine called "I Want to Eat Your Face."

2801. *Spasms* (1983, Famous Players/PDC, Canada, 89m, c, aka *Death Bite*). P John G. Pozhke & Maurice Smith, D William Fruet, W Don Enright (based on the novel *Death Bite* by Mitchell Maryk & Brent Monahan), PH Mark Irwin, M Eric N. Robertson & Tangerine Dream, ED Ralph Brunjes.

LP Peter Fonda (Dr. Brasilian), Oliver Reed (Jason), Kerrie Keane (Susanne), Al Waxman (Crowley), Miguel Fernandes (Mendes), Marilyn Lightstone (Dr. Rothman), Angus MacInnes (Duncan), Laurie Brown (Allison).

In this forgettable sf/horror film a killer devil-snake resurfaces every seven years to claim the souls of the dead.

2802. *The Spawning* (1983, Saturn Intl., Italy/US, 95m, c, aka *Piranha II: The Spawning*). P Chako van Leuwen & Jeff Schechtman, D James Cameron, W H.A. Milton, PH Roberto D'Ettore Piazzoli, M Steve Powder, ED Roberto Silvi.

LP Tricia O'Neil (Anne), Steve Marachuk (Tyler), Lance Henriksen (Steve), Ricky G. Paul (Chris), Ted Richert (Raoul), Leslie Graves (Allison).

Those who are turned-off by flesh-eating fish shouldn't see this movie. That's just one of many groups of people who shouldn't see this dreadful sequel to *Piranha* (1978).

2803. *Speaking Parts* (1989, Cinephile, Canada, 92m, c). D Atom Egoyan, W Egoyan, PH Paul Sarossy, M Mychael Danna, ED Bruce McDonald.

LP Michael McManus (Lance), Arsinee Khanjian (Lisa), Gabrielle Rose (Clara), David Hemblen (Producer), Patricia Collins (Housekeeper), Gerard Parkes (The Father), Jackie Samuda (The Bride), Peter Krantz (The Groom).

Michael McManus works for a hotel, cleaning rooms and servicing female guests on orders of the housekeeper. After getting some parts as an extra, he wants to break into movies.

2804. *Special Effects* (1984, New Line, 93m, c). P Paul Kurta, D&W Larry Cohen, PH Paul Glickman, M Michael Minard, ED Armond Lebowitz.

LP Zoe Tamerlis (Andrea/Elaine), Eric Bogosian (Neville), Brad Rijn (Keefe), Kevin O'Connor (Delroy), Bill Oland, Richard Greene.

Having just finished a major special effects movie failure, film director Eric Bogosian meets aspiring actress Zoe Tamerlis. He kills her while a hidden camera records the murder, then sets about to find another actress who looks just like the deceased (again Tamerlis), and makes a movie about the killing.

2805. *Speed Zone!* (1989, Orion, US/Canada, 95m, c). P Murray Shostak, D Jim Drake, W Michael Short, PH Francois Protat & Robert Saad, M David Wheatley, ED Mike Economou, PD Richard Hudolin.

LP John Candy (Charlie), Donna Dixon (Tiffany), Matt Frewer (Alec), Joe Flaherty (Vic), Tim Matheson (Jack), Mimi Kuzyk (Heather), Melody Anderson (Lee), Shari Belafonte (Margaret), Peter Boyle (Chief Edsel).

This film about a *Cannonball Run*–like cross-country car chase stars John Candy. Guest stars in cameo roles, such as Tom & Dick Smothers, John Schneider, Jamie Farr, Lee Van Cleef, Eugene Levy, Michael Spinks, Brooke Shields and Carl Lewis, don't take it out of the boring zone.

2806. *Spellbinder* (1988, MGM/United Artists, 98m, c). P Joe Wizan & Brian Russell, D Janet Greek, W Tracey Torme, PH Adam Greenberg, M Basil Poledouris, ED Steve Mirkovich, PD Rodger Maus.

LP Timothy Daly (Jeff Mills), Kelly Preston (Miranda Reed), Rick Rossovich

(Derek Clayton), Audra Lindley (Mrs. White), Anthony Crivello (Aldys), Diana Bellamy (Grace Woods), Cary-Hiroyuki Tagawa (Lt. Lee).

In a *Fatal Attraction*–inspired film, yuppie lawyer Timothy Daly goes after woman-in-distress Kelly Preston, only to discover that she's a witch trying to escape her coven, which wants her back.

2807. *Sphinx* (1981, Warner, 117m, c). P Stanley O'Toole, D Franklin J. Schaffner, W John Byrum (based on the novel by Robin Cook), PH Ernest Day, M Michael J. Lewis, ED Robert E. Swink & Michael F. Anderson, PD Terence Marsh.

LP Lesley-Anne Down (Erica Baron), Frank Langella (Ahmed Khazzan), Maurice Ronet (Yvon), John Gielgud (Abdu Hamdi), Vic Tablian (Khalifa), Martin Benson (Muhammed), John Rhys-Davies (Stephanos Markoulis).

Tough archaeologist Lesley-Anne Down stumbles across a secret hidden for centuries in the tomb of an Egyptian king. The experience nearly costs her life as well as worse things.

2808. *Spies Like Us* (1985, Warner, 109m, c). P Brian Grazer & George Folsey, Jr., D John Landis, W Dan Aykroyd, Lowell Ganz & Babaloo Mandel (based on a story by Aykroyd & Dave Thomas), PH Robert Paynter, M Elmer Bernstein, ED Malcolm Campbell, PD Peter Murton.

LP Chevy Chase (Emmett Fitz-Hume), Dan Aykroyd (Austin Millbarge), Steve Forrest (Gen. Sline), Donna Dixon (Karen Boyer), Bruce Davison (Mr. Ruby), Bernie Casey (Col. Rhombus), William Prince (Mr. Keyes), Tom Hatten (Gen. Miegs), Frank Oz (Test Monitor).

Other than make fools of themselves, we don't know what Chevy Chase and Dan Aykroyd accomplish in this sad tale of a pair of the dumbest CIA agents ever recruited. Even dumber than Chase and Aykroyd are those they encounter as they bungle through their mission. Aykroyd deserves a double-dose of shame-shame, to be shared with director Landis, because he had a hand in writing the trash. It's Chase and Aykroyd's *Ishtar*.

2809. *Spike of Bensonhurst* (1988, Film Dallas, 101m, c). P David Weisman, Nelson Lyon & Mark Silverman, D Paul Morrissey, W Alan Bowne & Morrissey, PH Steven Fierberg, M Coati Mundi, ED Stan Salfas, PD Stephen McCabe.

LP Sasha Mitchell (Spike Fumo), Ernest Borgnine (Baldo Cacetti), Anne DeSalvo (Sylvia Cacetti), Sylvia Miles (Congresswoman), Geraldine Smith (Helen Fumo), Antonio Rey (Bandana's Mother), Rick Aviles (Bandana), Maria Pitillo (Angel), Talisa Soto (India).

Big dumb Sasha Mitchell is under the protection of Mafia boss Ernest Borgnine, because his father is doing a term in Sing Sing for Borgnine. Mitchell sees himself as a boxer. Most of the fights he wins are fixed by Borgnine. Mitchell falls in love with Borgnine's daughter, Maria Pitillo, who the mob boss has plans to marry to the son of congresswoman Sylvia Miles. Pitillo comes up for a plan to win her father's acceptance of Mitchell as a son-in-law by becoming pregnant. Unfortunately, Mitchell has also impregnated Talisa Soto. Everything is sorted out in a boxing ring.

2810. *Spiker* (1986, Seymour Borde & Associates, 104m, c). P&D Roger Tilton, W Marlene Matthews (based on a story by Tilton & Matthews), PH Robert A. Sherry, M Jeff Barry, ED Richard S. Brummer.

LP Patrick Houser, Kristi Ferrell, Jo McDonnel, Natasha Shneider, Stephan Burns, Christopher Allport, Michael Parks, Ken Michelman, Eric Matthew.

In what is probably the first film with a volleyball theme, Patrick Houser and the Olympic gold medal–winning U.S. Men's National Team star in the drama of a young man who sacrifices everything for a chance at Olympic gold in 1984.

Spinal Tap see *This Is Spinal Tap*

2811. *Spirits of the Air: Gremlins of the Clouds* (1989, Meaningful Eye Contact Prod., Australia, 93m, c). P Andrew McPhail & Alex Proyas, D&W Proyas, PH David Knaus, M Peter Miller, ED Craig Wood, PD Sean Callinan.

LP Michael Lake (Felix Crabtree), Melissa Davis (Betty Crabtree), Norman Boyd (Smith).

Manic Michael Lake and his sister Melissa Davis live in a wooden house in the middle of a desert. The two have a religious fixation, and their house is filled with crucifixes and other icons. Trapped in this primitive setting, the two are struggling to build a flying machine to escape. Along comes Norman Boyd, lost in the wilderness. He helps them build their primitive plane, but by this time Davis is completely off her rocker. Lake decides to stay with his sister and Boyd flies off alone. What does it all mean? We have no idea. We wonder if director-writer Alex Proyas has any clue.

2812. *Splash* (1984, Buena Vista, 111m, c). P Brian Grazer, D Ron Howard, W Lowell Ganz, Babaloo Mandel & Bruce Jay Friedman† (based on the story by Grazer & Friedman), PH Don Peterman, M Lee Holdridge, ED Daniel P. Hanley & Michael Hill, PD Jack T. Collis.

LP Tom Hanks (Allen Bauer), Daryl Hannah (Madison), Eugene Levy (Walter Kornbluth), John Candy (Freddie Bauer), Dody Goodman (Mrs. Stimler), Shecky Greene (Mr. Buyrite), Richard B. Shull (Dr. Ross), Bobby Di Cicco (Jerry), Howard Morris (Dr. Zidell).

Mermaid Daryl Hannah arrives buck naked in New York City looking for Tom Hanks, the man she has fallen for. She needs to avoid water or her legs turn to a tail. She's very affectionate and a quick study in everything from making love to learning English and charging things at Bloomingdale's. This surprise hit from Ron Howard is fun if it's not examined too closely.

2813. *Splatter University* (1984, Troma, 77m, c). P Richard W. Haines & John Michaels, D Haines, W Haines, Michaels & Michael Cunningham, PD Fred Cohen & Jim Grib, M Chris Burke, ED Haines.

LP Francine Forbes (Julie Parker), Dick Biel (Father Janson/Daniel Grayham), Cathy Lacommare (Cathy), Ric Randig (Mark), Joanna Mihalakis, George Seminara, Don Eaton, Sal Lumetta, Denise Texeira.

After escaping from an asylum, a deranged killer begins a reign of terror at a local college where he slaughters and mutilates pretty coeds.

2814. *Split* (1989, Starker Film, 85m, c). P Barbara Horscraft, D,W,PH&ED Chris Shaw, M Chris Shaw, Robert Shaw & Ugi Tojo.

LP Chris Shaw, Tim Dwight, Joan Bechtel, John Flynn.

In this futuristic chase-thriller, a prophet of peace, who wishes to liberate humankind from the mass media and junk ideas, is menaced by an evil genius. It doesn't seem to be a completed film and the plot is vague.

2815. *Split Decisions* (1988, New Century/Vista, 95m, c). P Joe Wizan, D David Drury, W David Fallon, PH Timothy Suhrstedt, M Basil Poledouris, ED John W. Wheeler, Jeff Freeman & Thomas Stanford.

LP Craig Sheffer (Eddie McGuinn), Jeff Fahey (Ray McGuinn), Gene Hackman (Dan McGuinn), John McLiam (Pop McGuinn), Jennifer Beals (Barbara Uribe), Eddie Velez (Julian "Snake" Pedroza), Carmine Caridi (Lou Rubia), James Tolkan (Benny Platone).

Things look up for the youngest son (Craig Sheffer) of the Fighting McGuinn family when he is offered a boxing scholarship to a major university. His hopes for the Olympics are dashed when he feels he must become a professional to enter the ring against the man responsible for his brother's (Jeff Fahey) killing by mobsters when the latter refuses to throw a fight.

2816. *Split Image* (1982, Orion, 111m, c). P&D Ted Kotcheff, W Scott Spencer, Robert Kaufman & Robert Mark Kamen (based on the story by Spencer), PH Robert Jessup, M Bill Conti, ED Jay Kamen, PD Wolf Kroeger.

LP Michael O'Keefe (Danny), Karen Allen (Rebecca), Peter Fonda (Kirklander), James Woods (Pratt), Elizabeth Ashley (Diana), Brian Dennehy (Kevin), Ronnie Scribner (Sean), Pamela Ludwig (Jane).

Possible Olympian gymnast Michael O'Keefe falls in with a religious cult, headed by Peter Fonda. His parents Brian Dennehy and Elizabeth Ashley hire James Woods, an expert in deprogramming, to get him back.

2817. *Splitz* (1984, Film Ventures, 83m, c). P Kelly Van Horn & Stephen

Low, D Domonic Paris, W Paris, Bianca Littlebaum, Harry Azorin & Van Horn, PH Ronnie Taylor, M George Small, AD Tom Allen.

LP Robin Johnson (Gina), Patti Lee (Joan), Chuck McQuary (Chuck), Barbara M. Bingham (Susie), Shirley Stoler (Dean Hunta), Raymond Serra (Vito), Martin Rosenblatt (Louie), Sal Carollo (Tony).

When a female rock band helps a sorority at Hoofer College win a strip basketball game and a lingerie wrestling conquest, it doesn't sit well with dictatorial dean Shirley Stoler. (Those deans are such party-poopers.) Don't movie colleges ever have anything higher than a dean?

2818. Spookies (1988, Safir, 84m, c). P Eugenie Joseph, Thomas Doran, Brendan Faulkner & Frank M. Farel, D Joseph, Doran & Faulkner, W Farel, Doran, Faulkner & Joseph Burgund, PH Robert Chappell & Ken Kelsch, M Kenneth Higgins & James Calabrese, ED Joseph.

LP Felix Ward (Kreon), Dan Scott (Kreon's Servant), Alec Nemser (Billy), Maria Pechukas (Isabelle).

Trying to resurrect his wife, dead for 70 years, ancient sorcerer Felix Ward is in need of some human sacrifices. A group of youngsters show up at his mansion and they'll do just fine, thank you.

2819. Spring Break (1983, Columbia, 101m, c). P&D Sean S. Cunningham, W David Smilow, PH Stephen Poster, M Harry Manfredi, ED Susan Cunningham & Angie Ross, PD Virginia Field.

LP David Knell (Nelson), Steve Bassett (O.T.), Perry Lang (Adam), Paul Land (Stu), Richard B. Shull (Eddie), Corinne Alphen (Joan), Jayne Modean (Susie), Donald Symington (Ernest Dalby), Mimi Cozzens (May Dalby).

Four college students are thrown together in a small motel room in Fort Lauderdale during Spring Break, looking for fun and to get laid. That's about the extent of the minuscule plot.

2820. Spring Fever (1983, Amulet/Comworld, Canada, 100m, c). P John F. Bassett, D Joseph L. Scanlan, W Fred Stefan & Stuart Gillard, PH Donald

Wilder, M Fred Mollin, ED Kirk Jones & Tony Lower, AD Bruno Rubeo & Carmi Gallo.

LP Susan Anton (Stevie Castle), Frank Converse (Louis Corman), Jessica Walter (Celia Berryman), Stephen Young (Neil Berryman), Carling Bassett (Karen Castle), David Mall (Beechman), Lisa Brady (Rhoda), Barbara Cook (Chris).

Young tennis star Carling Bassett finds it difficult to establish friendships at a junior tennis championship because her mother Susan Anton is just too good looking.

2821. Square Dance (1987, Island, 112m, c). P&D Daniel Petrie, W Alan Hines (based on his novel), PH Jacek Laskus, M Bruce Broughton, ED Bruce Green, PD Jan Scott.

LP Jason Robards, Jr. (Dillard), Jane Alexander (Juanelle), Winona Ryder (Gemma Dillard), Rob Lowe (Rory), Deborah Richter (Gwen), Guich Koock (Frank), Elbert Lewis (Beecham), Charlotte Stanton (Aggie), J. David Moeller (Dub Mosley), Dixie Taylor (Dolores).

Thirteen-year-old, Godfearing Winona Ryder becomes disenchanted with life on her crotchety grandfather Jason Robards' farm and runs away to live with her mother, Jane Alexander, who left her years before. Ryder falls in love with Rob Lowe, an emotionally disturbed young man. It's a poignant coming of age drama with Ryder quite good.

2822. The Squeeze (1987, Tri-Star, 101m, c). P Rupert Hitzig & Michael Tannen, D Roger Young, W Daniel Taplitz, PH Arthur Albert, M Miles Goodman, ED Harry Keramidas, PD Simon Waters.

LP Michael Keaton (Harry Berg), Rae Dawn Chong (Rachel Dobs), John Davidson (Honest Tom T. Murray), Ric Abernathy (Bouncer), Danny Aiello, III (Ralph Vigo), Bobby Bass (Poker Player), Leslie Bevis (Gem Vigo).

Down-and-out new wave artist Michael Keaton tries every scam to make it big with little success. He teams up with Rae Dawn Chong, a would-be detective, to uncover an outrageous lottery-fixing scheme worth $56 million.

2823. Squizzy Taylor (1984, Satori, Australia, 98m, c) P Roger LeMesurier,

D Kevin Dobson, W Roger Simpson, PH Dan Burstall, M Bruce Smeaton, ED David Pulbrook, PD Logan Brewer.

LP David Atkins (Squizzy Taylor), Jacki Weaver (Dolly), Kim Lewis (Ida), Michael Long (Inspector Piggot), Fred Cullen (Henry), Alan Cassell (Detective Brophy), Steve Bisley (Snowy), Peter Paulsen (Harry).

The film is the true story of the rise and fall of an Australian mob boss, Squizzy Taylor.

2824. *Stacking* (1987, Spectrafilm, 97m, c). P&D Martin Rosen, W Victoria Jenkins, PH Richard Bowen, M Patrick Gleeson, ED Patrick Dodd, PD David Wasco.

LP Christine Lahti (Kathleen Morgan), Frederic Forrest (Buster McGuire), Megan Follows (Anna Mae Morgan), Jason Gedrick (Gary Connaloe), Ray Baker (Dan Morgan), Peter Coyote (Photographer), James Gammon (Clate Connaloe).

Some of the performances in this dull account of the growing up of young Megan Follows in the rural West of the 50s, are laudable, but they are not enough to prevent audiences from becoming bored. "Stacking" refers to the operation of stacking bales of hay with the help of a large tractor-like piece of farm machinery.

2825. *Stacy's Knights* (1983, Crown, 100m, c, aka *Double Down*). P JoAnn Locktov & Freddy Sweet, D Jim Wilson, W Michael Blake, PH Raoul Lomas, M Norton Buffalo, ED Bonnie Koehler, AD Florence Fellman.

LP Andra Millian (Stacy), Kevin Costner (Will), Eve Lilith (Jean), Mike Reynolds (Shecky), Ed Semenza (Kid), Don Hackstaff (Lawyer), Gary Tilles (Rudy), Garth Howard (Mr. C.), Cheryl Ferris (Marion).

Andra Millian is an innocent young girl with amazing skills at blackjack. She teams up with a group of backers, her "knights," to set up an incredible sting operation.

2826. *Stakeout* (1987, Buena Vista, 115m, c). P Jim Kouf & Cathleen Summers, D John Badham, W Kouf, PH John Seale, M Arthur B. Rubinstein, ED Tom Rolf & Michael Ripps, PD Philip Harrison.

LP Richard Dreyfuss (Chris Lecce), Emilio Estevez (Bill Reimers), Madeleine Stowe (Maria McGuire), Aidan Quinn (Richard "Stick" Montgomery), Dan Lauria (Phil Coldshank), Forest Whitaker (Jack Pismo), Earl Billings (Capt. Gilles).

When nasty killer Aidan Quinn escapes from prison, Seattle police figure he will come for his former girlfriend Madeleine Stowe. Richard Dreyfuss and Emilio Estevez make up one of the teams staking out her apartment. Dreyfuss makes things more complex than usual by becoming romantically involved with Stowe. The film has some nice humor and decent excitement when Quinn finally shows up.

2827. *Stand Alone* (1985, New World, 94m, c). P Leon Williams, D Alan Beattie, W Roy Carlson, PH Tom Richmond & Tim Suhrstedt, M David Richard Campbell, ED Fabien Dahlen Tordjmann, AD Pam Warner.

LP Charles Durning (Louis), Pam Grier (Catherine), James Keach (Isgro), Bert Remsen (Paddie), Barbara Sammeth (Meg), Lu Leonard (Mrs. Whitehead), Luis Contreras (Look-Out), Willard Pugh (Macombers), Bob Tzudiker (Farley), Mary Ann Smith (Nurse Warren).

Decorated World War II veteran Charles Durning witnesses a street-gang killing. Despite warnings from his lawyer Pam Grier not to get involved, Durning refuses to be intimidated, even when the low-lifes responsible for the killing beat up his buddy Bert Remsen. Durning arms himself to the teeth and waits in his home for them to come for him. He doesn't have long to wait.

2828. *Stand and Deliver* (1988, Warner, 105m, c). P Tom Musca, D Ramon Menendez, W Menendez & Musca, PH Tom Richmond, M Craig Safan, ED Nancy Richardson, AD Milo.

LP Edward James Olmos† (Jamie Escalante), Lou Diamond Phillips (Angel), Rosanna De Soto (Fabiola Escalante), Andy Garcia (Ramirez), Ingrid Oliu (Lupe), Karla Montana (Claudia), Vanessa Marquez (Ana), Mark Eliot (Tito), Patrick Baca (Javier), Will Gotay

(Pancho), Daniel Villarreal (Chuco), Carmen Argenziano (Molina), Virginia Paris (Raquel Ortega), Lydia Nicole (Rafaela).

This is the inspiring, hopeful true story of someone who has made a difference. Edward James Olmos superbly portrays the electronics employee Escalante who gives up a good job so he can teach in East L.A.'s Garfield High to barrio kids. Although initially very few of his students see any advantage in learning mathematics, their dedicated and demanding teacher gets a bunch of them to study advanced placement calculus. They all pass the exam, which means they get college credit for their study, but at first there is some suspicion, probably racially motivated, that they cheated. This is cleared up in this stand-up-and-cheer film, and as we learn at the closing credits, each year more and more Garfield students take and pass AP calculus, because of the efforts of Escalante. The only complaint that we can make about this marvelous movie is that more isn't shown as to how Escalante was able to get indifferent students to overcome their suspicion that education wouldn't do much for them and become diligent pupils who would come to school early, stay late and skip vacations so they might learn. Now that's a lesson our schools and teachers need to learn.

2829. ***Stand by Me*** (1986, Columbia, 87m, c). P Andrew Scheinman, Bruce A. Evans & Raynold Gideon, D Rob Reiner, W Gideon & Evans† (based on the novella *The Body* by Stephen King), PH Thomas Del Ruth, M Jack Nitzsche, ED Robert Leighton, PD Dennis Washington.

LP Wil Wheaton (Gordie Lachance), River Phoenix (Chris Chambers), Corey Feldman (Teddy Duchamp), Jerry O'Connell (Vern Tessio), Richard Dreyfuss (The Writer), Kiefer Sutherland (Ace Merrill), Casey Siemaszko (Billy Tessio), Gary Riley (Charlie Hogan), Bradley Gregg (Eyeball Chambers).

In a spectacular film, four young boys spend the last weekend of summer searching for the body of a boy believed hit by a train. Sometimes funny, sometimes sad, this coming of age film is perfectly

enhanced by the old title song, sung by Ben E. King.

2830. ***The Stand-In*** (1985, Stand-In, 87m, c). P&D Robert N. Zagone, W Zagone & Edward Azlant, PH Rick Butler, M Don Lewis, ED Kenji Yamamoto & Norm Levy, AD Don De Fina.

LP Danny Glover, Christa Victoria, Joe Bellan, Jane Dornacker, Marc Hayashi, Bob Sarlatte.

Made in San Francisco before becoming a star, Danny Glover is featured as the independent filmmaker who accidentally kills a crude biker. To cover up the crime, he assumes the identity of his victim.

2831. ***The Star Chamber*** (1983, 20th Century-Fox, 109m, c). P Frank Yablans, D Peter Hyams, W Roderick Taylor & Hyams (based on a story by Taylor), PH Richard Hannah, M Michael Small, ED Jim Mitchell & Charles Tetoni, PD Bill Malley.

LP Michael Douglas (Steven Hardin), Hal Holbrook (Benjamin Caulfield), Yaphet Kotto (Detective Harry Lowes), Sharon Gless (Emily Hardin), James B. Sikking (Dr. Harold Lewin), Joe Regalbuto (Arthur Cooms), Don Calfa (Lawrence Monk), John DiSanti (Detective James Wickman).

A team of judges gets together to retry defendents who have escaped justice because of legal technicalities. If found guilty, the jurists have them executed by hired assassins.

2832. ***Star 80*** (1983, Warner, 102m, c). P Wolfgang Glattes & Kenneth Utt, D&W Bob Fosse (based on *Death of a Playmate* by Teresa Carpenter), PH Sven Nykvist, M Ralph Burns, ED Alan Heim, AD Jack G. Taylor, Jr.

LP Mariel Hemingway (Dorothy Stratten), Eric Roberts (Paul Snider), Cliff Robertson (Hugh Hefner), Carroll Baker (Dorothy's Mother), Roger Rees (Aram Nicholas), David Clennon (Geb), Josh Mostel (Private Detective).

This is the unappetizing account of the short life and career of Playmate of the Year Dorothy Stratten, who was murdered by her husband, after which he took his own life. Mariel Hemingway had her breasts enlarged by surgery for the role.

2833. *Star Slammer: The Escape* (1988, Vidmark, 86m, c, aka *Prison Ship*). P Jack H. Harris & Fred Olen Ray, D Ray, W Michael D. Sonye (based on a story by Sonye, Miriam Preissel & Ray), PH Paul Elliott, M Anthony Harris, ED Preissel, PD Michael Novotny.

LP Sandy Brooke (Taura), Susan Stokey (Mike), Ross Hagen (Bantor), Marya Gant (Warden Exene), Aldo Ray (The Inquisitor), Dawn Wildsmith (Muffin), Richard Alan Hench (Garth), Michael D. Sonye (Krago), Lindy Skyles (The Sovereign), Bobbie Bresee (Marai), John Carradine (The Judge).

Fred Olen Ray has made a women's prison film with a science-fiction setting and for good measure throws in some decent laughs. It went directly to the shelves of your local video store.

2834. *Star Trek II: The Wrath of Khan* (1982, Paramount, 113m, c). P Robert Sallin, D Nicholas Meyer, W Jack B. Sowards (based on a story by Harve Bennett, Sowards and the TV program "Star Trek" created by Gene Roddenberry), PH Gayne Rescher, M James Horner, ED William P. Dornisch, PD Joseph R. Jennings.

LP William Shatner (Adm. James T. Kirk), Leonard Nimoy (Mr. Spock), DeForest Kelley (Dr. Leonard "Bones" McCoy), James Doohan (Chief Engineer Montgomery "Scotty" Scott), Walter Koenig (Chekov), George Takei (Sulu), Nichelle Nichols (Cmdr. Uhura), Bibi Besch (Dr. Carol Marcus), Merritt Butrick (David), Paul Winfield (Starship Reliant Captain Terrell), Kirstie Alley (Saavik), Ricardo Montalban (Khan).

The crew of the starship *Enterprise* must counter the evil genius Ricardo Montalban, an old foe who blames William Shatner for the death of his wife.

2835. *Star Trek III: The Search for Spock* (1984, Paramount, 105m, c). P Harve Bennett, D Leonard Nimoy, W Bennett (based on the TV production "Star Trek" by Gene Roddenberry), PH Charles Correll, M James Horner, ED Robert F. Shugrue, AD John E. Chilberg, II, SD Tom Pedigo, SE Rocky Gehr.

LP William Shatner (Kirk), Leonard Nimoy (Spock), DeForest Kelley (Mc-Coy), James Doohan (Scotty), Walter Koenig (Chekov), George Takei (Sulu), Nichelle Nichols (Uhura), Robin Curtis (Saavik), Merritt Butrick (David), Phil Morris (Trainee Foster), Scott McGinnis ("Mr. Adventure"), Robert Hooks (Adm. Morrow), Christopher Lloyd (Kurge, Klingon), John Larroquette (Maltz, Klingon), James B. Sikking (Capt. Styles), Judith Anderson (High Priestess of Vulcans).

Captain Kirk (William Shatner) and the remaining crew of the starship *Enterprise* journey to the Genesis planet to discover if Spock (Leonard Nimoy) still lives.

2836. *Star Trek IV: The Voyage Home* (1986, Paramount, 119m, c). P Harve Bennett, D Leonard Nimoy, W Steve Meerson & Peter Krikes (based on a story by Nimoy & Bennett and the TV series "Star Trek" created by Gene Roddenberry), PH Don Peterman†, M Leonard Rosenman†, ED Peter E. Berger, PD Jack T. Collis, SOUND Terry Porter, Dave Hudson, Mel Metcalfe & Gene Cantamessa†, SOUND EFFECTS ED Mark Manginit†.

LP William Shatner (Kirk), Leonard Nimoy (Spock), DeForest Kelley (Mc-Coy), James Doohan (Scotty), Walter Koenig (Chekov), Nichelle Nichols (Uhura), George Takei (Sulu), Jane Wyatt (Amanda), Catherine Hicks (Gillian), Mark Lenard (Sarek), Robin Curtis (Lt. Saavik), John Schuck (Klingon Ambassador), Brock Peters (Admiral Cartwright).

In an uncharacteristic but welcomed switch, the crew of the *Enterprise* try their hands at comedy. They exit the 23rd century universe, which is on the verge of destruction by an alien probe, to seek humanity's salvation in the 20th century United States.

2837. *Star Trek V: The Final Frontier* (1989, Paramount, 106m, c). P Harve Bennett, D William Shatner, W David Loughery (based on a story by Shatner, Bennett & Loughery and the TV series "Star Trek" created by Gene Roddenberry), PH Andrew Laszlo, M Jerry Goldsmith, ED Peter Berger.

LP William Shatner (Kirk), Leonard Nimoy (Spock), DeForest Kelley

(McCoy), James Doohan (Scotty), Walter Koenig (Chekov), Nichelle Nichols (Uhura), George Takei (Sulu), David Warner (St. John Talbot), Laurence Luckinbill (Sybok), Charles Cooper (Korrd), Cynthia Gouw (Caithlin Dar), Todd Bryant (Captain Klaa), Spice Williams (Vixis).

In this disappointing entry in the Star Trek series, unimaginatively directed by William Shatner, Laurence Luckinbill, in Kabuki-like makeup, is a renegade Vulcan who kidnaps the crew of the *Enterprise* and makes them fly to a never-before explored galaxy to seek the meaning of life. They don't find it.

2838. *Starchaser: The Legend of Orin* (1985, Atlantic, animated, 3-D, 101m, c). P Steven Hahn, D Hahn & John Sparey, W Jeffrey Scott, M Andrew Belling, ED Donald W. Ernst, PD Louis Zingarelli.

VOICES Joe Colligan (Orin), Carmen Argenziano (Dagg), Noelle North (Elan/Aviana), Anthony Delongis (Zygon), Les Tremayne (Arthur), Tyke Caravelli (Silica), Ken Sansom (Magreb), John Moschitta, Jr. (Auctioneer/Z. Gork), Mickey Morton (Minemaster).

In this animated fantasy, Orin, using a magic sword, saves the world of the future from malevolent hordes.

Starchild see Space Raiders

2839. *Stardust Memories* (1980, United Artists, 90m, b&w). P Robert Greenhut, D&W Woody Allen, PH Gordon Willis, ED Susan E. Morse, PD Santo Loquasto.

LP Woody Allen (Sandy Bates), Charlotte Rampling (Dorrie), Jessica Harper (Daisy), Marie-Christine Barrault (Isobel), Tony Roberts (Tony), Daniel Stern (Actor), Amy Wright (Shelley), Helen Hanft (Vivian Orkin), John Rothman (Jack Abel).

In a painfully autobiographical film, Woody Allen as an increasingly melancholy comedian attends a retrospective of his career and is plagued by feelings of failure and inadequacy. Allen pokes fun at those who admire his films to the point of making them cult pieces.

2840. *Stark Raving Mad* (1983, Independent Artists, 88m, c). P Tiger Warren & Don Gronquist, D George F. Hood, W

Uncredited, PH J. Wilder, ED Hood, AD W.S. Warren.

LP Russell Fast (Richard), Marcie Severson (Laura), B. Joe Medley (Francis), Mike Walter (David), Janet Galen (Barbara), Don Beekman (Norman), Mildred Card (Dorothy), Marjorie Hall (Maid).

The title tells it all in this cheaply produced independent horror film.

2841. *Starlight Hotel* (1988, Republic Pictures, New Zealand, 93m, c). P Finola Dwyer & Larry Parr, D Sam Pillsbury, W Grant Hinden Miller (based on his novel *The Dream Monger*), PH Warrick Attewell, ED Mike Horton, PD Mike Becroft.

LP Peter Phelps (Patrick), Greer Robson (Kate), Marshall Napier (Detective Wallace), The Wizard (Spooner), Alice Fraser (Aunt), Patrick Smyth (Uncle), Bruce Phillips (Dave Marshall), Donogh Rees (Helen).

In 1929, 12-year-old runaway Peter Phelps, bound for Australia, travels across the New Zealand countryside. It's violent.

2842. *Starman* (1984, Columbia, 115m, c). P Larry J. Franco, D John Carpenter, W Bruce A. Evans & Raynold Gideon, PH Donald M. Morgan, M Jack Nitzsche, ED Marion Rothman, PD Daniel Lomino.

LP Jeff Bridges† (Starman), Karen Allen (Jenny Hayden), Charles Martin Smith (Mark Shermin), Richard Jaeckel (George Fox), Robert Phalen (Maj. Bell), Tony Edwards (Sgt. Lemon), John Walter Davis (Brad Heinmuller).

When an alien from an advanced civilization lands in Wisconsin, he finds a less than warm welcome from the military. To disguise himself, he clones himself into the form of Jeff Bridges, the recently deceased husband of grieving Karen Allen. With hostile authorities in hot pursuit, the alien and the widow race to his rendezvous spot in Arizona, falling in love along the way.

2843. *Stars and Bars* (1988, Columbia, 94m, c). P Sandy Lieberson, D Pat O'Connor, W William Boyd (based on his novel), PH Jerzy Zielinski, M Stanley Myers, ED Michael Bradsell, PD Leslie Dilley & Stuart Craig.

LP Daniel Day-Lewis (Henderson

Dores), Harry Dean Stanton (Loomis Gage), Kent Broadhurst (Sereno), Maury Chaykin (Freeborn Gage), Matthew Cowles (Beckman Gage), Joan Cusack (Irene Stein), Keith David (Teagarden), Spalding Gray (Rev. Cardew), Glenne Headly (Cora Gage).

In this overbaked, misfiring comedy, very proper British Daniel Day-Lewis is sent to Georgia to negotiate the purchase of a Renoir and runs afoul of boorish, combative Southerners.

2844. *Starstruck* (1982, Cinecom, Australia, 102m, c). P David Elfick & Richard Brennan, D Gillian Armstrong, W Stephen Maclean, PH Russell Boyd, ED Nicholas Beauman, PD Brian Thomson.

LP Jo Kennedy (Jackie Mullens), Ross O'Donovan (Angus Mullens), Pat Evison (Nana), Margo Lee (Pearl), Max Cullen (Reg), Melissa Jaffer (Mrs. Booth), Ned Lander (Robbie), John O'May (Terry Lambert).

In a pleasant musical 14-year-old Ross O'Donovan decides to make his new wave, punk-rock cousin Jo Kennedy into a major star, no matter what it takes.

2845. *The State of Things* (1983, Gray City/Artificial Eye, 121m, b&w). P Chris Sievernich, D Wim Wenders, W Wenders & Robert Kramer, PH Henri Alekan & Fred Murphy, M Jurgen Knieper, ED Barbara von Weitershausen.

LP Isabelle Weingarten (Anna), Rebecca Pauly (Joan), Jeffrey Kime (Mark), Geoffrey Carey (Robert), Camilla Mora (Julia), Alexandra Auder (Jane), Patrick Bauchau (Friedrich, Director), Paul Getty, III (Dennis, Writer).

The film is the saga of filmmaker Patrick Bauchau and his crew shooting a remake of a Hollywood B movie, *The Most Dangerous Man on Earth,* in the boondocks of Spain.

2846. *Static* (1985, Film Forum, 93m, c). P Amy Ness, D Mark Romanek, W Romanek & Keith Gordon, PH Jeff Jur, ED Emily Paine, SD Cynthia Sowder.

LP Keith Gordon (Ernie), Amanda Plummer (Julia), Bob Gunton (Frank), Barton Heyman (Sheriff William Orling), Lily Knight (Patty), Jane Hoffman (Emitly), Reathel Bean (Fred Savins), Kitty Mei Mei Chen (Li).

In a film which is sometimes fascinating, sometimes deadly dull, Keith Gordon has invented an unusual TV. Sometimes it picks up heaven.

2847. *Staying Alive* (1983, Paramount, 96m, c). P Robert Stigwood & Sylvester Stallone, D Stallone, W Stallone & Norman Wexler (based on characters created by Nik Cohn), PH Nick McLean, M The Bee Gees, Frank Stallone & Johnny Mandel, ED Don Zimmerman & Mark Warner, PD Robert F. Boyle.

LP John Travolta (Tony Manero), Cynthia Rhodes (Jackie), Finola Hughes (Laura), Steve Inwood (Jesse), Julie Bovasso (Mrs. Manero), Charles Ward (Butler), Steve Bickford (Sound Technician), Patrick Brady (Derelict).

Sylvester Stallone almost ended John Travolta's career with this horrible sequel to *Saturday Night Live.* Sly has John sweating à la Rocky as a supposed star dancer in a hit musical. Fred Astaire always insisted that full body shots of his dancing be shown so that audiences could see what he was doing. Travolta is not so much dancing as moving from one pose to another with the camera doing the dancing. It's one of the all-time turkeys.

2848. *Staying Together* (1989, Hemdale, 91m, c). P Joseph Feury, D Lee Grant, W Monte Merrick, PH Dick Bush, ED Katherine Wenning, PD Stuart Wurtzel, AD W. Steven Graham.

LP Sean Astin (Duncan McDermott), Stockard Channing (Nancy Trainer), Melinda Dillon (Eileen McDermott), Jim Haynie (Jake McDermott), Levon Helm (Denny Stockton), Dinah Manoff (Lois Cook), Dermot Mulroney (Kit McDermott), Tim Quill (Brian McDermott).

The McDermott clan, Mom, Dad and three strapping boys run a home-cooked chicken restaurant in a small South Carolina town. Everything is just ducky until yuppies move into the area with their condos and unlimited supply of money. Dad sells the restaurant when he is offered an almost obscene profit. The three lads are now forced to re-evaluate their lives, learning that there is more to life than good times.

2849. *Stealing Heaven* (1989, Scotti Bros., GB/Yugo., 116m, c). P Simon

MacCorkindale, D Clive Donner, W Chris Bryant (based on the novel by Marion Meade), PH Mikael Salomon, M Nick Bicat, ED Michael Ellis, PD Voytek Roman.

LP Derek de Lint (Pierre Abelard), Kim Thompson (Heloise), Denholm Elliott (Fulbert), Mark Jax (Jourdain), Rachel Kempson (Prioress), Angela Pleasence (Sister Cecilia), Bernard Hepton (Bishop Martin), Kenneth Cranham (Vice Chancellor Suger).

This modest production is surprisingly well done. It is the true story of 12th-century philosopher Pierre Abelard and his beautiful gifted student Heloise. They become lovers, have a child and are secretly married. This does not set well with Heloise's powerful uncle, who had other plans for her. He has Abelard castrated. The latter becomes a monk, while Heloise reluctantly retires to a convent.

2850. *Stealing Home* (1988, Warner, 98m, c). P Thom Mount & Hank Moonjean, D&W Steven Kampmann & Will Aldis, PH Bobby Byrne, M David Foster, ED Antony Gibbs, AD Vaughan Edwards, SD Robert Franco.

LP Mark Harmon (Billy Wyatt as an adult), Blair Brown (Ginny Wyatt), Jodie Foster (Katie Chandler), Jonathan Silverman (Alan Appleby as a teen), Harold Ramis (Alan Appleby as an adult), John Shea (Sam Wyatt), William McNamara (Billy Wyatt as a teen), Thatcher Goodwin (Billy Wyatt as a child), Judith Kahan (Laura Appleby).

Flashbacks tell the story of minor league baseball player Mark Harmon's bittersweet relationship with Jodie Foster, an older woman who was both his lover and mentor.

2851. *Steaming* (1985, Columbia, GB, 95m, c). P Paul Mills, D Joseph Losey, W Patricia Losey (based on the play by Nell Dunn), PH Christopher Challis, M Richard Harvey, ED Reginald Beck, PD Maurice Fowler.

LP Vanessa Redgrave (Nancy), Sarah Miles (Sarah), Diana Dors (Violet), Patti Love (Josie), Brenda Bruce (Mrs. Meadows), Felicity Dean (Dawn Meadows), Sally Sagoe (Celia).

The performances are better than average in this story of the interactions of a group of women in a run-down London steam bath. The film could use a bit more humor to make it palatable.

2852. *Steel* (1980, World/Northal, 99m, c, aka *Look Down and Die; Men of Steel*). P Peter S. Davis & William N. Panzer, D Steven Carver, W Leigh Chapman (based on a story by Rob Ewing, Davis & Panzer), PH Roger Shearman, M Michel Colombier, ED David Blewitt, PD Ward Preston.

LP Lee Majors (Mike Catton), Jennifer O'Neill (Cass Cassidy), Art Carney (Pignose Moran), George Kennedy (Lew Cassidy), Harris Yulin (Eddie Cassidy), Redmond Cleason (Harry), Terry Kiser (Valentino).

When construction boss George Kennedy is killed, his daughter Jennifer O'Neill vows to complete his last project. It's harmless hokum.

2853. *Steel Dawn* (1987, Vestron/Silver Lion, 100m, c). P Lance Hool & Conrad Hool, D L. Hool, W Doug Lefler, PH George Tirl, M Brian May, ED Mark Conte, PD Alex Tavoularis.

LP Patrick Swayze (Nomad), Lisa Niemi (Kasha), Christopher Neame (Sho), Brion James (Tark), John Fujioka (Cord), Brett Hool (Jux), Anthony Zerbe (Damnil), Marcel Van Heerden (Lann), Arnold Vosloo (Makker).

In a modern version of *Shane,* Patrick Swayze is a sword-wielding martial arts expert who wanders the desert wasteland, becoming Lisa Niemi and her son's champion against the evil Anthony Zerbe and his men.

2854. *Steel Magnolias* (1989, Tri-Star, 118m, c). P Ray Stark, D Herbert Ross, W Robert Harling (based on his play), PH John A. Alonzo, M Georges Delerue, ED Paul Hirsch, PD Gene Callahan & Edward Pisoni.

LP Sally Field (M'Lynn Eatenton), Dolly Parton (Truvy Jones), Shirley MacLaine (Ouiser Boudreaux), Daryl Hannah (Annelle Dupuy Desoto), Olympia Dukakis (Clairee Belcher), Julia Roberts† (Shelby Eatenton Latcherie), Tom Skerritt (Drum Eatenton), Sam Shepard (Spud Jones), Dylan McDermott (Jackson Latcherie), Kevin J. O'Connor (Sammy Desoto), Bill McCutcheon (Owen Jenkins).

Here's the one to see at the end of the 1980s. It's a superb cast which makes audiences laugh and cry and cheer a bit. The movie differs from the still-running play, in that it opens up and introduces the men (only talked about on stage) of the wild, lively group of Southern women who meet in a beauty parlor to gossip, crack jokes and help each other. Each of the six women stars check their egos at the door of the beauty parlor and work surprisingly well together. It's tough to say which one gives the best performance, but if forced to vote, we'd say Olympia Dukakis squeaks by Shirley MacLaine by an eyelash. Others may choose Sally Field, who handles the chores of the mother of doomed Julia Roberts with a sure sense.

2855. *Steele Justice* (1987, Atlantic, 95m, c). P John Strong, D&W Robert Boris, PH John M. Stephens, M Misha Segal, ED John O'Connor & Steve Rosenblum, PD Richard N. McGuire.

LP Martin Kove (John Steele), Sela Ward (Tracy), Ronny Cox (Bennett), Bernie Casey (Reese), Joseph Campanella (Harry), Soon-Teck Oh (Gen. Bon Soong Kwan), Jan Gan Boyd (Cami Van Minh), David Froman (Kelso), Sarah Douglas (Kay).

Vietnam vet Martin Kove's investigation of the murders of the family of a Vietnamese friend in L.A. puts him on the trail of former Vietnam general Soon-Teck Oh, who's now a druglord in the U.S.

2856. *The Stepfather* (1987, New Century/Vista, 90m, c). P Jay Benson, D Joseph Ruben, W Donald E. Westlake (based on a story by Carolyn Lefcourt, Brian Garfield & Westlake), PH John W. Lindley, M Patrick Moraz, ED George Bowers, PD James William Newport.

LP Terry O'Quinn (Jerry Blake, the Stepfather/Henry Morrison/Bill Hodgkins), Jill Schoelen (Stephanie Maine), Shelley Hack (Susan Blake), Charles Lanyer (Dr. Bondurant), Stephen Shellen (Jim Ogilvie), Stephen E. Miller (Al Brennan), Robyn Stevan (Karen), Jeff Schultz (Paul Baker).

Terry O'Quinn's stepdaughter Jill Schoelen has good instincts in not liking him. He's been married before, with a family. When he grew tired of them, he killed them and assumed a new identity. Will Schoelen and her mother Shelley Hack be next?

2857. *Stepfather II: Make Room for Daddy* (1989, Millimeter Films, 88m, c). P William Burr & Darin Scott, D Jeff Burr, W John Auerbach, PH Jacek Kaskus, M Jim Manzie, ED Pasquale A. Buba.

LP Terry O'Quinn (The Stepfather), Meg Foster (Carol Grayland), Jonathan Brandis (Todd Grayland), Caroline Williams (Matty Crimmins), Henry Brown (Dr. Joseph Danvers), Mitchell Laurance (Phil Grayland).

Terry O'Quinn reprises his role of what appears to be an average middleclass male. However, his tight little smile suggests a menace which doesn't stay hidden. The film appears to miss the hand of director Joseph Ruben, who has gone on to better things.

2858. *Stephen King's Silver Bullet* (1985, Paramount, 95m, c). P Martha Schumacher, D Daniel Attias, W Stephen King (based on his novelette *Cycle of the Werewolf*), PH Armando Nannuzzi, M Jay Chattaway, ED Daniel Loewenthal, PD Giorgio Postiglione.

LP Gary Busey (Uncle Red), Everett McGill (Rev. Lowe/Werewolf), Corey Haim (Marty Coslaw), Megan Follows (Jane Coslaw), Robin Groves (Nan Coslaw), Leon Russom (Bob Coslaw), Terry O'Quinn (Sheriff Joe Haller).

Once again, our contention is that if moviemakers use the name of a popular writer *in the title,* they are advertising that the film is a stinker and needs the boost of a well-known name. Plucky, handicapped, young Corey Haim, with the help of his drunken uncle Gary Busey, his disbelieving sister Megan Follows, and a silver bullet put an end to the rampage of a nasty werewolf ravaging their small town.

2859. *Stewardess School* (1987, Columbia, 87m, c). P Phil Feldman, D&W Ken Blancato, PH Fred J. Koenekamp, M Robert Folk, ED Lou Lombardo & Kenneth C. Paonessa, PD Daniel A. Lomino.

LP Brett Cullen (Philo Henderson), Mary Cadorette (Kelly Johnson), Donald

Most (George Bunkle), Sandahl Bergman (Wanda Polanski), Wendie Jo Sperber (Jolean Winters), Judy Landers (Sugar Dubois).

The curriculum of this school features a lot of foolin' around. The interiors of airplanes apparently are aphrodisiacs.

2860. *Stick* (1985, Universal, 109m, c). P Jennings Lang, D Burt Reynolds, W Elmore Leonard & Joseph C. Stinson (based on the novel by Leonard), PH Nick McLean, M Barry De Vorzon & Joseph Conlan, ED William Gordean, PD James Shanahan.

LP Burt Reynolds (Stick), Candice Bergen (Kyle), George Segal (Barry), Charles Durning (Chucky), Jose Perez (Rainy), Richard Lawson (Cornell), Castulo Guerra (Nestor), Dar Robinson (Moke), Alex Rocco (Firestone).

Director Burt Reynolds should have canned actor Burt Reynolds, who seems to be just going through the motions. He's an ex-con who wants to start a new life in Miami, but keeps running into various bad guys who make him mad enough to seek revenge. Actor Reynolds should have insisted on a new director, one who knew something about pacing and actors working together.

2861. *Sticky Fingers* (1988, Spectrafilm, 97m, c). P Catlin Adams & Melanie Mayron, D Adams, W Adams & Mayron, PH Gary Thieltges, M Gary Chang, ED Bob Reitano, PD Jessica Scott-Justice.

LP Helen Slater (Hattie), Melanie Mayron (Lolly), Danitra Vance (Evanston), Eileen Brennan (Stella), Carol Kane (Kitty), Loretta Devine (Diane), Stephen McHattie (Eddie), Christopher Guest (Sam), Gwen Welles (Marcie), Shirley Stoller (Reeba).

Helen Slater and Melanie Mayron are charmless as two struggling musicians who discover a suitcase containing $900,000 left in their care by a friendly dope dealer. They spend, spend, spend.

2862. *Stitches* (1985, Intl. Film Marketing, 89m, c). P William B. Kerr & Robert P. Marcucci, D Alan Smithee [Rod Holcomb], W Michel Choquette & Michael Paseornek, PH Hector R. Figueroa, M Bob Floke, ED John Duffy, AD Diane Campbell.

LP Parker Stevenson (Bobby Stevens), Geoffrey Lewis (Ralph Rizzo), Brian Tochi (Sam Boon Tong), Robin Dearden (Nancy McNaughton), Bob Dubac (Al Rosenberg), Tommy Koenig ("Barfer" Bogan), Sidney Lassick (Sheldon Mendelbaum), Eddie Albert (Dean Bradley), Susanne Wasson (Judith Bradley).

Didn't the British have a string of hits on their hands a decade or so ago about the hijinks of medical students and their amorous times with sexy nurses? Why can't nice American boys like Parker Stevenson, Bob Dubac and Brian Tochi make a successful American version? Because they are untalented clods who smirk and giggle like horny 13 year olds while carrying off unfunny sexist and scatological practical jokes, most at the expense of poor old Eddie Albert.

2863. *Still of the Night* (1982, MGM/United Artists, 91m, c). P Arlene Donovan, D&W Robert Benton (based on a story by David Newman & Benton), PH Nestor Almendros, M John Kander, ED Jerry Greenberg, PD Mel Bourne.

LP Roy Scheider (Sam Rice), Meryl Streep (Brooke Reynolds), Jessica Tandy (Grace Rice), Joe Grifasi (Joseph Vitucci), Sara Botsford (Gail Phillips), Josef Sommer (George Bynum), Rikke Borge (Heather Wilson).

Manhattan psychiatrist Roy Scheider is suspected of having killed one of his patients or at least knowing more about the death than he's telling. He claims doctor-patient confidentiality. The deceased's mistress Meryl Streep is also a likely candidate as the murderer. Director Robert Benton is trying to play like Alfred Hitchcock, but he's out of his league.

2864. *Still Smokin'* (1983, Paramount, 91m, c, aka *Cheech and Chong's Still Smokin'*). P Peter MacGregor-Scott, D Thomas Chong, W Chong & Cheech Marin, PH Harvey Harrison, M George S. Clinton, ED David Ramirez & James Coblentz, AD Ruud Van Dijk.

LP Cheech Marin, Tommy Chong (Themselves), Hans Van In't Veld (Promoter), Carol Van Herwijen (Hotel Manager), Shireen Strooker (Assn't Manager), Susan Hahn (Maid), Arjan Ederveen & Kees Prins (Bellboys), Mariette

Bout (Waitress), Fabiola (Barge Lady), Carla Van Amstel (Queen Beatrix).

Cheech and Chong travel to Amsterdam to raise money for a film festival by holding a dope-a-thon. They're dopes for sure and even their staunchest fans will be hard pressed to follow their hallucinations in this one.

2865.   *A Sting in the Tale* (1989, Rosa Colosimo Films, Australia, 96m, c). P Rosa Colosimo & Reg McLean, D Eugene Schlusser, W Patrick Edgeworth, PH Nicholas Sherman, M Allan Zavod, ED Zbigniew Friedrich, PD Lisa Blitz Brennan.

LP Diane Craig (Diane Lane), Gary Day (Barry Robbins), Lynne Williams (Louise Parker), Edwin Hodgeman (Roger Monroe), Don Barker (Prime Minister Falcon), Jon Noble (P.M.'s minder), Tony Mack (Michael Meadows).

In a corny Australian soap opera, Diane Craig becomes Australia's first female prime minister and ruins a powerful media baron at the same time.

2866.   *The Sting II* (1983, Universal, 102m, c). P Jennings Lang, D Jeremy Paul Kagan, W David S. Ward, PH Bill Butler, M Lalo Schifrin†, ED David Garfield, PD Edward C. Carfagno.

LP Jackie Gleason (Henry Gondorff), Mac Davis (Johnny Hooker), Teri Garr (Veronica), Karl Malden (Macalinski), Oliver Reed (Doyle Lonnegan), Bert Remsen (Kid Colors), Jose Perez (Carlos), Larry Bishop (Gallecher).

The competition is stiff, but this film definitely is in the running for worst sequel to a good movie. Jackie Gleason and Mac Davis play the Paul Newman and Robert Redford roles, respectively. They come up with a boxing scam involving nightclub owner Karl Malden, but also must deal with Oliver Reed who as Doyle Lonnegan is still steamed at the pair for the sting they pulled on him in the original. Only Teri Garr is worth seeing in this dull film.

2867.   *Stir Crazy* (1980, Columbia, 111m, c). P Hannah Weinstein, D Sidney Poitier, W Bruce Jay Friedman, PH Fred Schuler, M Tom Scott, ED Harry Keller, PD Alfred Sweeney.

LP Gene Wilder (Skip Donahue), Richard Pryor (Harry Monroe), Georg Stanford Brown (Rory Schultebrand), JoBeth Williams (Meredith), Miguelangel Suarez (Jesus Ramirez), Craig T. Nelson (Deputy Ward Wilson).

New Yorkers Gene Wilder and Richard Pryor, heading for California to change their luck, are wrongly convicted of a bank robbery. Once in prison they plan their escape. There are a number of amusing moments in the film, but overall it's disappointing.

2868.   *The Stone Boy* (1984, 20th Century–Fox, 93m, c). P Joe Roth & Ivan Bloch, D Chris Cain, W Gina Berriault (based on her short story), PH Juan Ruiz Anchia, M James Horner, ED Paul Rubell, PD Joseph G. Pacelli.

LP Robert Duvall (Joe Hillerman), Frederic Forrest (Andy Jansen), Glenn Close (Ruth Hillerman), Wilford Brimley (George Jansen), Jason Presson (Arnold Hillerman), Gail Youngs (Lu Jansen), Dean Cain (Eugene Hillerman).

In a film which easily could have been called "Ordinary People," the lives of poor farmer Robert Duvall, his wife Glenn Close, and their family is torn asunder when their two sons, Jason Presson and Dean Cain (the director's son) go out early one morning duck hunting, with the result that the former accidentally kills the latter. Immediately Presson retreats into a shell, which Duvall misreads as either being uncaring or not realizing the enormity of his deed. Left out of his parents' grief, Presson withdraws even more, becoming completely silent, a "stone boy." It isn't easy for these simple folks, without the means to hire any professional help to sort out their problems and unite as a family once more.

2869.   *Stone Cold Dead* (1980, Ko-Zak/Dimension, Canada, 97m, c). P George Mendeluk & John Ryan, D&W Mendeluk (based on the novel *The Sin Sniper* by Hugh Garner), PH Dennis Miller, ED Martin Pepler, AD Ted Watkins.

LP Richard Crenna (Sgt. Boyd), Paul Williams (Julius Kurtz), Linda Sorenson (Monica Page), Belinda J. Montgomery (Sandy MacAuley), Charles Shamata

(Sgt. Tony Colabre), Alberta Watson (Olivia Page).

Police sergeant Richard Crenna hunts a sniper who only shoots prostitutes. He taunts the police with photographs of the girls at their moments of death.

2870. *Stoogemania* (1986, Atlantic, 83m, c/b&w). P Chuck Workman & James Ruxin, D Workman, W Jim Geoghan & Workman, PH Christopher Tufty, M Hummie Mann & Gary Tigerman, ED Ruxin.

LP Josh Mostel (Howard F. Howard), Melanie Chartoff (Beverly), Mark Holton (Son of Curly), Sid Caesar (Dr. Fixyer Minder), Patrick DeSantis (Moe, Jr.), Armin Shimermann (Larry II), Thom Sharp (Bob), Josh Miller (Young Howard), Victoria Jackson (Nurse Grabatit), Ron House (Stooge Hills Director).

Nerdish Josh Mostel becomes so obsessed with the Three Stooges that they begin to take over and ruin his life.

2871. *Storm* (1987, Cannon, Canada, 81m, c). P,D&W David Winning, PH Tim Hollings, M Amin Bhatia, ED Bill Campbell.

LP David Palfy (Lowell), Stan Kane (Jim), Tom Schioler (Booker), Harry Freedman (Burt), Lawrence Elion (Stanley), Stacy Christensen (Corbi), Tibi (Lisa), Sean O'Byrne (Danny), James Hutchison (Hostage).

This dull rip-off of *Gotcha* has two college students playing assassination tag with paint-pellet guns.

2872. *Stormy Monday* (1988, Atlantic, GB, 93m, c). P Nigel Stafford-Clark, D&W Mike Figgis, PH Roger Deakins, M Figgis, ED David Martin, PD Andrew McAlpine.

LP Melanie Griffith (Kate), Tommy Lee Jones (Cosmo), Sting (Finney), Sean Bean (Brendan), James Cosmo (Tony), Mark Long (Patrick), Brian Lewis (Jim), Heathcote Williams (Peter Reed), Prunella Gee (Mrs. Finney), Alison Steadman (Mayor), Al Matthews (Radio DJ), Guy Manning.

In this interesting thriller, unlikely lovers Melanie Griffith and Sean Bean work to prevent self-serving American business magnate/gangster Tommy Lee Jones from taking over a Newcastle jazz club owned by Sting.

2873. *Straight to Hell* (1987, Island, GB, 86m, c). P Eric Fellner, D Alex Cox, W Dick Rude & Cox, PH Tom Richmond, M The Pogues & Pray for Rain, ED Dave Martin, PD Andrew McAlpine, SE Juan Ramon Molina.

LP Sy Richardson (Norwood), Joe Strummer (Simms), Dick Rude (Willy), Courtney Love (Velma), Zander Schloss (Karl), Del Zamora (Poncho), Luis Contreras (Sal), Jim Jarmusch (Mr. Amos Dade), Miguel Sandoval (George).

This spoof of spaghetti westerns is about as digestible as two-week old pasta with clam sauce.

2874. *Stranded* (1987, New Line, 80m, c). P Scott Rosenfelt & Mark Levinson, D Tex Fuller, W Alan Castle, PH Jeff Jur, M Stacy Widelitz, ED Stephen E. Rivkin, SE Allen Hall.

LP Ione Skye (Deirdre Clark), Joe Morton (Sheriff McMahon), Maureen O'Sullivan (Grace Clark), Susan Barnes (Helen Anderson), Cameron Dye (Lt. Scott), Michael Greene (Vernon Burdett), Brendan Hughes (Prince).

Aliens land on earth and take Ione Skye and her grandmother Maureen O'Sullivan hostage. It's science fiction all right, but it owes more to *The Desperate Hours* than fantasy writers.

Strange Behavior see Dead Kids

2875. *Strange Brew* (1983, MGM/United Artists, 90m, c). P Louis M. Silverstein, D Dave Thomas & Rick Moranis, W Thomas, Moranis & Steven DeJarnatt, PH Steven Poster, M Charles Fox, ED Patrick McMahon, PD David L. Snyder.

LP Dave Thomas (Doug McKenzie), Rick Moranis (Bob McKenzie), Max von Sydow (Brewmeister Smith), Paul Dooley (Claude Elsinore), Lynne Griffin (Pam Elsinore), Agnus MacInnes (Jean LaRose), Tom Harvey (Inspector).

Dave Thomas and Rick Moranis bring their "SCTV" comedy skit of the beer-swilling, plaid-shirted Canadian brothers to the big screen. The hoseheads must stop mad brewmaster Max von Sydow from taking control of the world.

2876. *Strange Invaders* (1983, Orion, 94m, c). P Walter Coblenz, D Michael Laughlin, W William Condon & Laughlin, PH Louis Horvath, M John Addison, ED John W. Wheeler, PD Susanna Moore.

LP Paul LeMat (Charles Bigelow), Nancy Allen (Betty Walker), Diana Scarwid (Margaret), Michael Lerner (Willie Collins), Louise Fletcher (Mrs. Benjamin), Wallace Shawn (Earl), Fiona Lewis (Waitress/Avon Lady), Kenneth Tobey (Arthur Newman), June Lockhart (Mrs. Bigelow).

During the 1950s a small Illinois town is invaded by aliens that replace the townspeople whom they beam by small blue spheres to their spaceship. After three decades the aliens decide to go home, but must take all of their race with them including the half-alien, half-human daughter of earthling Paul LeMat and alien Diana Scarwid. Mixed marriages can be a problem.

2877. *The Stranger* (1987, Columbia, US/Arg., 88m, c). P Hugo Lamonica, D Adolfo Aristarain, W Dan Gurskis, PH Horacio Maira, M Craig Safan, ED Eduardo Lopez.

LP Bonnie Bedelia (Alice Kildee), Peter Riegert (Dr. Harris Kite), Barry Primus (Sgt. Drake), David Spielberg (Hobby), Marcos Woinski (Macaw), Julio de Grazia (Jay), Cecilia Roth (Anita).

Bonnie Bedelia witnesses some killings and then develops amnesia with the murderers on her trail.

2878. *A Stranger Is Watching* (1982, MGM/United Artists, 92m, c). P Sidney Beckerman, D Sean S. Cunningham, W Earl MacRauch & Victor Miller (based on the novel by Mary Higgins Clark), PH Barry Abrams, M Lalo Schifrin, ED Cunningham, AD Virginia Field.

LP Kate Mulgrew (Sharon Martin), Rip Torn (Artie Taggart), James Naughton (Steve Peterson), Shawn von Schreiber (Julie Peterson), Barbara Baxley (Lally), Stephen Joyce (Detective), James Russo (Ronald Thompson).

In this unpleasant, sadistic thriller, Rip Torn is a psychopathic killer who kidnaps and terrorizes Shawn von Schreiber and her mother Kate Mulgrew, whom he rapes and kills.

2879. *Stranger Than Paradise* (1984, Goldwyn/ZDF, US/Ger., 95m, b&w). P Sara Driver, D&W Jim Jarmusch, PH Tom Di Cillo, M John Lurie & Aaron Picht, ED Jarmusch & Melody London.

LP John Lurie (Willie), Eszter Balint (Eva), Richard Edson (Eddie), Cecilla Stark (Aunt Lottie), Danny Rosen (Billy), Rammellzee (Man with Money), Tom Di Cillo (Airline Agent), Richard Boes (Factory Worker).

Three lost souls, John Lurie, who came to New York from Hungary 10 years ago, expecting but not finding paradise, his visiting adorable cousin Eszter Balint and his friend Richard Edson, survive a comically empty life. It's a semi–avant garde film.

2880. *Strangers Kiss* (1984, Orion Classics, 93m, c). P Douglas Dilge, D Matthew Chapman, W Blaine Novak & Chapman (based on a story by Novak), PH Mikhail Suslov, M Gato Barbieri, ED William Carruth, AD Ginny Randolph.

LP Peter Coyote (Stanley the Director), Victoria Tennant (Carol Redding/ Betty). Blaine Novak (Stevie Blake), Dan Shor (Farris the Producer), Richard Romanus (Frank Silva), Linda Kerridge (Shirley), Carlos Palomino (Estoban), Vincent Palmieri (Scandelli).

Peter Coyote, the director of a 1955 film, encourages his leading lady Victoria Tennant and his leading man Blaine Novak to have an off-screen affair to bring more realism to their on-screen romance. Things are OK until Tennant's boyfriend Richard Romanus, the producer of the film, gets wind of the method acting techniques being employed.

2881. *Strapless* (1989, Granada, GB, 97m, c). P Rick McCallum, D&W David Hare, PH Andrew Dunn, M Nick Bicat, ED Edward Marnier, PD Roger Hall.

LP Blair Brown (Dr. Lillian Hempel), Bruno Ganz (Raymond Forbes), Bridget Fonda (Amy Hempel), Alan Howard (Mr. Cooper), Michael Gough (Douglas Brodie), Hugh Laurie (Colin), Suzanne Burden (Romaine Salmon).

After living in Britain for 12 years, American physician Blair Brown has come to care for British values even more so than the native born. She secretly marries apparently wealthy stranger Bruno Ganz. He has no money, but he does have a wife and son, whom he has abandoned. He also has no intention of staying with Brown. Contrasted with Brown is her flighty sister Bridget Fonda, who has many affairs but changes her attitude and behavior when she discovers she is pregnant.

2882. *Streamers* (1983, United Artists Classics, 118m, c). P Robert Altman & Nick J. Mileti, D Altman, W David Rabe (based on his play), PH Pierre Mignot, ED Norman Smith, PD Wolf Kroeger.

LP Matthew Modine (Billy), Michael Wright (Carlyle), Mitchell Lichtenstein (Richie), David Alan Grier (Roger), Guy Boyd (Rooney), George Dzundza (Cokes), Albert Macklin (Martin), B.J. Cleveland (Pfc. Bush).

This version of David Rabe's claustrophobic play about tensions at a training camp for the 83rd Airborne Division features young macho recruits baring their souls.

Street Gang see Vigilante

2883. *Street Justice* (1989, Lorimar, 94m, c). P David Witz & Michael Masciarelli, D Richard C. Sarafian, W James J. Docherty, PH Roland (Ozzie) Smith, M James Szmadzinski & Paul Hertzog, ED Mark Goldberg, AD Jo-Ann Chorney.

LP Michael Ontkean (Curt Flynn), Joanna Kerns (Katharine Watson), Catherine Bach (Tamarra), J.D. Cannon (Arthur Dante), Jeanette Nolan (Edith Chandler), Richard Cox (Sam Chandler), William Windom (Father Burke), Sondra Currie (Mandy), Richard C. Sarafian (Taxi Driver).

This drama, which went direct to video, is the story of former government agent Michael Ontkean who returns home after spending 12 years in a Soviet prison after his mission was terminated by the CIA out of expediency. He not only has a hit on him ordered by the "Company," but finds his wife remarried, and his daughter seriously injured by the powerful Chandler clan which runs his home town. He goes on the warpath.

Street Love see Scarred

2884. *Street Music* (1982, Pacificon, 92m, c). P Richard Bowen, D Jenny Bowen, PH R. Bowen, M Ed Bogas & Judy Munson, ED Lisa Fruchtman & Diana Pelligrini, AD Don De Fina.

LP Elizabeth Daily (Sadie), Larry Breeding (Eddie), Ned Glass (Sam), Mar-

jorie Eaton (Mildred), W.F. Walker (Jasper), Miriam Phillips (Hattie), D'Alan Moss (Monroe), Sam Morford (Slim), John Romano (Potts).

Singer Elizabeth Daily and her boyfriend Larry Breeding organize senior citizens in danger of losing their housing in fighting for their rights.

2885. *Street Smart* (1987, Cannon, 95m, c). P Menahem Golan & Yoram Globus, D Jerry Schatzberg, W David Freeman, PH Adam Holender, M Robert Irving, III & Miles Davis, ED Priscilla Nedd, PD Dan Leigh.

LP Christopher Reeve (Jonathan Fisher), Morgan Freeman† (Fast Black), Kathy Baker (Punchy), Mimi Rogers (Alison Parker), Jay Patterson (Leonard Pike), Andre Gregory (Ted Avery), Anna Maria Horsford (Harriet).

Christopher Reeve, an out-of-favor reporter for a Manhattan magazine, is given the assignment of writing the story of a pimp. Unable to get a cooperative subject, he fakes the story. Things boomerang when the D.A. believes Reeve knows something about a murder suspect. Morgan Freeman gives an outstanding Oscar-nominated performance in a movie that has little else to recommend it.

2886. *Street Story* (1988, Films Around the World, 90m, c). P,D,W, PH&ED Joseph B. Vasquez, M Edward W. Burrows.

LP Angelo Lopez (Junior), Cookie (Joey), Lydia Ramirez (Cecilia), Melvin Muza (T.C.), Soraya Andrade (Rosa), Zerocks (Willie), Rena Zentner (Nadia), Edward W. Burrows (Father).

Two South Bronx brothers fight the local drug-pusher gangs who demand protection money from their barber father.

2887. *A Street to Die* (1985, Mermaid Beach, Australia, 91m, c). P,D&W Bill Bennett, PH Geoff Burton, M Michael Atkinson & Michael Spicer, ED Denise Hunter, PD Igor Nay.

LP Chris Haywood (Col Turner), Jennifer Cluff (Lorraine Turner), Peter Hehir (Peter Townley), Arianthe Galani (Dr. Walsea), Peter Kowitz (Craig), Sussanah Fowle (Julie), Pat Evison (Sister Sweet).

Chris Haywood struggles to get financial compensation from the government for Australian Vietnam veterans dying of leukemia and other cancers brought on by American use of Agent Orange defoliant. When he dies of his disease, his wife continues his crusade.

2888. *Street Trash* (1987, Chaos/Lightning, 91m, c). P Roy Frumkes, D Jim Muro, W Frumkes, PH David Sperling, M Rick Ulfik, ED Dennis Werner, PD Robert Marcucci.

LP Mike Lackey (Fred), Vic Noto (Bronson), Bill Chepil (Bill the Cop), Mark Sferrazza (Kevin), Jane Arakawa (Wendy), Nicole Potter (Winette), R.L. Ryan (Frank Schnizer), Clarenze Jarmon (Burt).

Bums and winos are being killed in a Brooklyn junkyard ruled by a Vietnam vet. The cause is a fatal brand of alcohol called Tenafly Viper.

Streetfighters see Ninja Turf

2889. *Streets of Fire* (1984, Universal/RKO, 94m, c). P Lawrence Gordon & Joel Silver, D Walter Hill, W Hill & Larry Gross, PH Andrew Laszlo, M Ry Cooder, ED Freeman Davies, Michael Ripps, James Coblentz & Michael Tronick, PD John Vallone.

LP Michael Pare (Tom Cody), Diane Lane (Ellen Aim), Rick Moranis (Billy Fish), Amy Madigan (McCoy), Willem Dafoe (Raven), Deborah Van Valkenburgh (Reva), Richard Lawson (Ed Price), Rick Rossovich (Officer Cooley), Bill Paxton (Clyde).

Soldier-of-fortune Michael Pare rescues his former girlfriend, rock sensation Diane Lane, when she is kidnapped by a dangerous motorcycle gang called the "Bombers."

2890. *Streets of Gold* (1986, 20th Century-Fox, 95m, c). P Joe Roth & Harry Ufland, D Roth, W Heywood Gould, Richard Price & Tom Cole (based on a story by Dezso Magyar, PH Arthur Albert, M Jack Nitzsche, Brian Banks & Anthony Marinelli, ED Richard Chew, PD Marcos Flaksman.

LP Klaus Maria Brandauer (Alek Neuman), Adrian Pasdar (Timmy Boyle), Wesley Snipes (Roland Jenkins), Angela Molina (Elena Gitman), Elya Baskin (Klebanov), Rainbow Harvest (Brenda), Adam Nathan (Grisha), John Mahoney (Lineman).

Former Russian boxing champion Klaus Maria Brandauer, now a Brooklyn dishwasher, helps train two street kids for the U.S. boxing team, hoping to defeat his former Russian coach.

2891. *Streetwalkin'* (1985, Concorde, 86m, c). P Robert Alden, D Joan Freeman, W Freeman & Alden, PH Steven Fierberg, M Matthew Ender & Doug Timm, ED John K. Adams & Patrick Rand, PD Jeffrey Robbins.

LP Melissa Leo (Cookie), Dale Midkiff (Duke), Leon Robinson (Jason), Julie Newmar (Queen Bee), Randall Batinkoff (Tim), Annie Golden (Phoebe), Antonio Fargas (Finesse), Deborah Offner (Heather).

Melissa Leo is an innocent, seductive teenager, forced onto the streets by the advances of her lecherous stepfather. She falls for the come-on of pimp Dale Midkiff.

2892. *Strikebound* (1984, TRM/Mainline, Australia, 100m, c). P Miranda Bain & Timothy White, D&W Richard Lowenstein (based on the novel *Dead Men Don't Dig Coal* by Wendy Lowenstein), PH Andrew De Groot, M Declan Affley, ED Jill Bilcock, PD Tracy Watt.

LP Chris Haywood, Carol Burns, Hugh Keays-Byrne, Rob Steele, Nik Forster, David Kendall, Anthony Hawkins, Marion Edward, Lazar Rodic.

This familiar coal mine story is set in Australia. It features the troubles of the miners with scabs who take their jobs when the union strikes.

2893. *Striking Back* (1981, Film Ventures, 91m, c). P James Margellos, D William Fruet, W Don Enright, M FM.

LP Perry King (Kip), Tisa Farrow (Kate), Don Stroud (Buddy), George Kennedy (Capt. Fusqua), Park Jong Soo (Assassin).

Having paid George Kennedy's price to appear in this action/adventure turkey, there apparently wasn't any money left to hire a good director or screenwriter.

2894. *Stripes* (1981, Columbia, 106m, c). P Ivan Reitman & Dan Goldberg, D Reitman, W Len Blum, Goldberg & Harold Ramis, PH Bill Butler, M Elmer Bernstein, ED Eva Ruggiero, Michael Luciano & Harry Keller, PD James H. Spencer.

LP Bill Murray (John), Harold Ramis (Russell), Warren Oates (Sgt. Hulka), P.J. Soles (Stella), Sean Young (Louise), John Candy (Ox), John Larroquette (Capt. Stillman), John Voldstad (Aide), John Diehl (Cruiser), Lance LeGault (Col. Glass), Roberta Leighton (Anita).

In a sort of "Saturday Night Live meets Abbott and Costello in *Buck Privates,*" Bill Murray and Harold Ramis go through some of the usual army recruit hijinks, adding a bit of sex and hip comedy to generally dull proceedings.

2895. *Stripped to Kill* (1987, Concorde, 84m, c). P Andy Ruben, Mark Byers & Matt Leipzig, D Katt Shea Ruben, W K.S. Ruben & A. Ruben, PH John Leblanc, M John O'Kennedy, ED Zach Staenberg, AD Paul Raubertas.

LP Kay Lenz (Cody/Sunny), Greg Evigan (Sgt. Heineman), Norman Fell (Ray), Tracy Crowder (Fanny), Athena Worthey (Zeena), Carlye Byron (Cinnamon), Debbie Nassar (Dazzle), Lucia Nagy Lexington (Brandy).

A serial killer is killing dancers at a L.A. topless bar. Undercover cop Kay Lenz is the tasty bait used to catch the killer. Before this happens she has to show more than her dancing talents.

2896. *Stripped to Kill II: Live Girls* (1989, Concorde, 82m, c). P Andy Ruben, D&W Katt Shea Ruben, PH Phedon Papamichael, M Gary Stockdale, ED Stephen Mark, PD Virginia Lee.

LP Maria Ford (Shady), Eb Lottimer (Decker), Karen Mayo Chandler (Cassandra), Birke Tan (Dazzle), Marjean Holden (Something Else), Debra Lamb (Montra), Lisa Glaser (Victoria), Tommy Ruben (Ike).

Stripper Maria Ford is tormented by dreams in which she kills other strippers, slashing their throats with a razor blade held in her teeth. When strippers are found with their throat slashed and Ford awakens with blood dribbling from her lips, things look pretty grim for our girl in a G-string. There's a plethora of barely clad bodies and imaginative strip routines

for those who like their sadism with a little sex.

2897. *Stroker Ace* (1983, Universal/Warner, 96m, c). P Hank Moonjean, D Hal Needham, W Needham & Hugh Wilson (based on the novel *Stand On It* by William Neely & Robert K. Ottum), PH Nick McLean, M Al Capps, ED Carl Kress & William Gordean, AD Paul Peters.

LP Burt Reynolds (Stroker Ace), Ned Beatty (Clyde Torkle), Jim Nabors (Lugs), Parker Stevenson (Aubrey James), Loni Anderson (Pembroke Feeney), John Byner (Doc Seegle), Frank O. Hill (Dad Seegle), Bubba Smith (Arnold).

Flamboyant race car driver Burt Reynolds tries to get out of his long term contract with chicken franchise magnate Ned Beatty. It's a clucky movie with not enough yolks.

2898. *Stryker* (1983, New World, Phil./US, 84m, c). P&D Cirio H. Santiago, W Howard R. Cohen (based on a story by Leonard Hermes), PH Ricardo Remias, M Ed Gatchalian & Susan Justin, ED Bas Santos & Ruby Cabrales, PD Pol Dimalanta.

LP Steve Sandor (Stryker), Andria Savio (Delha), William Ostrander (Bandit), Michael Lane (Kardis), Julie Gray (Laurenz), Monique St. Pierre (Cerce), Ken Metcalfe (Trun), Jon Harris, III (Oiric).

In another of Philippine helmer Cirio H. Santiago's postholocaust films, bands of marauders fight each other for the scarcest resource—water.

2899. *Stuck on You* (1984, Troma, 90m, c). P Lloyd Kaufman & Michael Herz, D Herz, Samuel Weil, W Weil, ED Darren Kloomok & Richard Haines.

LP Prof. Irwin Corey (Judge), Virginia Penta (Carol), Mark Mikulski (Bill), Albert Pia (Artie), Norma Pratt (Bill's Mother), Daniel Harris (Napoleon), Denise Silbert (Cavewoman), Eddie Brill (Caveman).

Having all of the intelligence of a cancelled check, this film features looney judge Irwin Corey, presiding over a palimony case.

2900. *Stuckey's Last Stand* (1980, Royal Oak, 92m, c). P,D&W Lawrence G. Goldfarb, PH Anthony J. Fitzsimmons, M Carson Whitsett, ED Fitzsimmons & Ethan Edwards, AD Julia Norris.

LP Whit Reichert (Whit), Ray Anzalone (Russ), Will Shaw (Will), Tom Murray (Pete), Richard Cosentino (Duke), Marilyn Terschluse (Billie), Jeanne L. Austin (Marianne), John Zimmerman (Gordon), Dan Dierdorf (Angry Father).

In this Hamburger-Helper version of *Meatballs,* unhappy campers and inept counselors are played by talentless actors, stuck with an impossible script.

2901. *Student Affairs* (1988, Platinum, 94m, c). P&D Chuck Vincent, W Craig Horrall & Vincent (based on a story idea by John Weidner), PH Larry Revene, ED Vincent, James Davalos & Chip Lambert, AD D. Gary Phelps.

LP Louie Bonanno (Louie Balducci), Jim Abele (Andy Armstrong), Deborah Blaisdell [Veronica Hart] (Kelly), Beth Broderick (Alexis), Alan Fisler (Devon Wheler), Jane Hamilton (Veronica Harper), Richard Parnes (Rudy).

Former porno-movie maker Chuck Vincent is back with another effort to crack the mainstream market with several of his triple-X performers appearing in a film within a film as characters in a 50s teen movie.

2902. *Student Bodies* (1981, Paramount, 86m, c). P Allen Smithee (Michael Ritchie), D&W Mickey Rose, PH Robert Ebinger, M Gene Hobson, ED Kathryn Ruth Hope, PD Donald Nunley.

LP Kristin Ritter (Toby), Matthew Goldsby (Hardy), Richard Brando (The Breather), Joe Flood (Mr. Dumpkin), Joe Talarowski (Principal Peters), Mimi Weddell (Miss Mumsley), Carl Jacobs (Dr. Sigmund).

Here's another spoof of high school *Halloween*-like horror films. Young couples are murdered by person or persons unknown just as they are about to have sex. Funny, it's not.

2903. *Student Confidential* (1987, Troma, 94m, c). P,D&W Richard Horian, PH James Dickson, M&ED Horian, PD David Wasco.

LP Eric Douglas (Johnny Warshetsky), Marlon Jackson (Joseph Williams), Susan Scott (Susan Bishop), Elizabeth Singer (Elaine Duvat), Ronee Blakley (Jenny Selden), Richard Horian (Michael Drake), Paula Sorenson (Carla).

In a ludicrous story, millionaire Richard Horian's help to a group of troubled teens is repaid when he considers suicide.

2904. *The Stuff* (1985, New World, 93m, c). P Paul Kurta, D&W Larry Cohen, PH Paul Glickman, M Anthony Guefen, ED Armond Lebowitz, PD Larry Lurin, SE David Allen.

LP Michael Moriarty (David "Moe" Rutherford), Andrea Marcovici (Nicole Kendall), Garrett Morris (Chocolate Chip Charlie), Paul Sorvino (Col. Spears), Scott Bloom (Jason), Danny Aiello (Vickers), Alexander Scourby (Evans).

Ice cream executive Alexander Scourby hires industrial spy Michael Moriarty to discover the secret ingredients in a new yogurt-like desert sensation, known only as "The Stuff." He finds that its popularity is because it's addictive, altering consumers' minds.

2905. *The Stunt Man* (1980, 20th Century–Fox, 129m, c). P&D Richard Rush† (as director), W Lawrence B. Marcus & Rush† (based on the novel by Paul Brodeur), PH Mario Tosi, M Dominic Frontiere, ED Jack Hofstra & Caroline Ferriol, AD James Schoppe.

LP Peter O'Toole† (Eli Cross), Steve Railsback (Cameron), Barbara Hershey (Nina Franklin), Allen Goorwitz (Sam), Alex Rocco (Jake), Sharon Farrell (Denise), Adam Roarke (Raymond Bailey), Philip Bruns (Ace), Chuck Bail (Chuck Barton).

Vietnam veteran Steve Railsback, on the run from the police, takes refuge with a movie company on location, headed up by megalomaniac director Peter O'Toole, who blackmails Railsback into assuming the role of a stuntman who is killed. It's an enjoyable behind-the-scenes look at making movies.

2906. *Suburbia* (1984, New World, 99m, c, aka *The Wild Side*). P Bert Dragin, D&W Penelope Spheeris, PH

Tim Suhrstedt, M Alex Gibson, ED Ross Albert, AD Randy Moore.

LP Timothy Eric O'Brien (Tom), Grant Miner (Keef), Michael Bayer (Razzle), Bill Coyne (Evan), Andrew Pece (Ethan), Chris Pederson (Jack), Wade Walston (Joe Schmo), De Waldron (De Generate), Jennifer Clay (Sheila).

When a group of punk teens becomes squatters in a condemned suburban development, the locals form a vigilante group to evict them.

2907. *Subway Riders* (1981, Hep/Mainline, 118m, c). P Johanna Heer & Amos Poe, D&W Poe, PH Heer, M Various Artists, ED Orlando Gallini, Heer & Poe.

LP Robbie Coltrane (Detective Fritz Langley), Charlene Kaleina (Claire Smith), Cookie Mueller (Penelope Trasher), John Lurie (The Saxaphonist), Amos Poe (Writer Ant), Susan Tyrrell (Eleanor Langley), Bill Rice (Mr. Gollstone), Leigh Taylor (Susannah).

Psychopath saxophonist John Lurie draws an audience on the streets of Manhattan, first plays, then slays a listener before fleeing into the subway. The musical score by a group of avant garde artists is probably the best thing about this underground 16mm film.

2908. *Success Is the Best Revenge* (1984, Gaumont, GB, 90m, c). P&D Jerzy Skolimowski, W Michael Lyndon & Skolimowski, PH Mike Fash, M Stanley Myers & Hans Zimmer, ED Barrie Vince, PD Voytek.

LP Michael York (Alex Rodak), Janna Szerzerbic (Wife), Michael Lyndon (Adam), George Skolimowski (David), Michel Piccoli (French Official), Anouk Aimee (Monique de Fontaine), John Hurt (Dino Montecurva).

In this unusual comedy, complications abound when an expatriate Pole, George Skolimowski, attempts to direct a play.

2909. *Sudden Death* (1985, Lodestar/Marvin, 95m, c). P Steven Shore & David Greene, D&W Sig Shore, PH Benjamin Davis, M Arthur Baker, ED John Tintori, AD Charles Weaver.

LP Denise Coward (Valarie Wells), Frank Runyeon (Det. Marty Lowery), Jamie Tirelli (Willie), Robert Trumbull

(Herbert), Rebecca Hollen (Peggy), J. Kenneth Campbell (Kosakowski), Joe Maruzzo (Raphael).

In this hyper-feminist, man-hating movie, New York businesswoman Denise Coward vows to kill every rapist she can, after she is raped and beaten.

2910. *Sudden Impact* (1983, Warner, 117m, c). P&D Clint Eastwood, W Joseph C. Stinson (based on a story by Earl E. Smith & Charles B. Pierce, based on characters by Harry Julian Fink & R.M. Fink), PH Bruce Surtees, M Lalo Schifrin, ED Joel Cox, PD Edward Carfagno.

LP Clint Eastwood (Harry Callahan), Sondra Locke (Jennifer Spencer), Pat Hingle (Chief Jannings), Bradford Dillman (Capt. Briggs), Paul Drake (Mick), Audrie J. Neenan (Ray Parkins), Jack Thibeau (Kruger), Michael Currie (Lt. Donnelly), Albert Popwell (Horace King).

Clint Eastwood in his role as "Dirty Harry" tracks down revenged-obsessed murderer Sondra Locke, who is one-by-one brutally killing the guys who gang-raped her and her sister, leaving the latter in a catatonic state. Eastwood catches up with her, but as she finishes her vengeful chore, he lets her go. This is the film in which Clint delivers his classic line: "Go ahead, make my day."

2911. *The Suicide Club* (1988, Angelika, 90m, c). P&D James Bruce, W Matthew Gaddis, Susan Kouguell & Carl Caportoto (based on a story by Robert Louis Stevenson), PH Frank Prinzi, M Joel Diamond, ED Bruce & Keith Rouse, PD Stephen McCabe.

LP Mariel Hemingway (Sasha Michaels), Robert Joy (Michael Collins), Lenny Henry (Cam), Madeleine Potter (Nancy), Michael O'Donaghue (Mervin), Anne Carlisle (Catherine), Sullivan Brown (Brian), Leta McCarthy (Cowgirl).

Feeling guilty over her brother's suicide, Mariel Hemingway and other bored rich kids participate in a lethal card game in which the "winner" must swallow a fatally poisonous drink.

2912. *Sullivan's Pavilion* (1987, Adirondack Alliance, 83m, c). P,D&W Fred G. Sullivan, PH Hal Landen, M Kenneth

Higgins & James Calabrese, ED Fred G. Sullivan, AD Susan Neal.

LP Polly Sullivan, Tate Sullivan, Katie Sullivan, Kirk Sullivan, Ricky Sullivan, Fred G. Sullivan (Themselves), Jon Granik (Bear/Narrator), James R. Hogue (Conrad P. Drizzle), Jan Jalenak (The Temptress), Judith Mayes (Sister Mary Anthony).

Independent filmmaker Fred G. Sullivan makes an autobiographical film about the trials of his family and himself as he tries to make it as an independent filmmaker.

2913. *Summer Camp Nightmare* (1987, Concorde, 87m, c, aka *The Butterfly Revolution*). P Robert T. Crow, Emilia Lesniak-Crow & Andy Howard, D Bert L. Dragin, W Dragin & Penelope Spheeris (based on the novel *The Butterfly Revolution* by William Butler), PH Don Burgess, M Ted Neeley & Gary Chase, ED Michael Spence, PD Richard McGuire.

LP Chuck Connors (Mr. Warren), Charles Stratton (Franklin Reilly), Harold B. Pruett (Chris Wade), Adam Carl (Donald Poultry), Tom Fridley (John Mason), Melissa Brennan (Heather), Stuart Rogers (Stanley Runk).

In a muddled story, idealistic counselor Charles Stratton organizes a revolt of the kids at a summer camp run by despotic Chuck Connors. For good measure they also liberate a nearby girl's camp.

2914. *Summer Heat* (1987, Atlantic, 90m, c). P William Tennant, D&W Michie Gleason (based on the novel *Here to Get My Baby Out of Jail* by Louise Shivers), PH Elliot Davis, M Steve Tyrell, ED Mary Bauer, PD Marcia Hinds.

LP Lori Singer (Roxanna "Roxy" Walston), Anthony Edwards (Aaron Walston), Bruce Abbott (Jack Ruffin), Clu Gulager (Will Stanton), Kathy Bates (Ruth Stanton), Jessie Kent (Baby Walston), Noble Willingham (Strother).

This torpid romantic triangle drama involving tobacco farmer Anthony Edwards, his young wife Lori Singer and hired hand Bruce Abbott takes place in North Carolina in 1937. Things get a bit out of hand, but hardly enough to stir the audience from its nap.

2915. *Summer Job* (1989, SVS Films, 90m, c). P Josi W. Konski, D Paul Madden, W Ralph Wilson, PH Orson Ochoa, M Ike Stubblefield, ED Christopher Cibelli.

LP Amy Baxter (Susan), Sherrie Rose (Kathy), Cari Mayor (Donna), George O. (Herman), Renee Shugart (Karen), James Summer, Chantal, Dave Clouse.

Here's a loser that very few people will see or miss, even in video stores. It's filled with stupid dialogue, dumb gags, poor performances and no plot. Sherrie Rose is the supervisor of college kids working at a Florida resort one summer. The college kids do what college kids do. It doesn't look like much fun.

2916. *Summer Lovers* (1982, Filmways/Orion, 98m, c). P Mike Modor, D&W Randal Kleiser, PH Peter Collister, Timothy Galfas & Dimitri Papacostandis, M Basil Poledouris, ED Robert Gordon, PD Bruce Weintraub.

LP Peter Gallagher (Michael Papas), Daryl Hannah (Cathy Feathererst), Valerie Quennessen (Lina), Barbara Rush (Jean Feathererst), Carole Cook (Barbara Foster), Hans Van Tongeren (Jan Tolin), Lydia Lenosi (Aspa).

Rich-kid lovers Peter Gallagher and Daryl Hannah spend their summer vacation at a Greek island villa, adding archaeologist Valerie Quennessen to their exploitations of life and love. Give it an X for content, language, nudity, sex and an F for dramatic values.

2917. *Summer of the Colt* (1989, Cinema Plus, Canada, 100m, c). P Rock Demers & Lita Stantic, D Andre Melancon, W Genevieve Lefebvre & Rodolfo Otero (based on Otero's story), PH Thomas Vamos, M Osvaldo Montes, ED Andre Corriveau.

LP Hector Alterio (Federico), China Zorrilla (Ana), Alexandra London-Thompson (Laura), Juan de Benedictis (Daniel), Santiago Gonzalez (Martin), Mariano Bertolini (Felipe), Gabriela Felperin (Manuela), Manuel Callau (Luis), Emilia Farah (Damasia).

Filmed in Argentina, four children come to visit their grandfather and his sister on the former's beautiful horse ranch for the summer. Unfortunately for Alexandra London-Thompson, she reminds her grandfather of his young wife who long ago deserted him and his children. He turns against the poor 13-year-old, but everything is satisfactorily resolved before the children return to their Buenos Aires home at the end of the summer.

2918. *Summer Rental* (1985, Paramount, 88m, c). P George Shapiro, D Carl Reiner, W Jeremy Stevens & Mark Reisman, PH Ric Waite, M Alan Silvestri, ED Bud Molin & Lee Burch, PD Peter Wooley.

LP John Candy (Jack Chester), Richard Crenna (Al Pellet), Rip Torn (Scully), Karen Austin (Sandy Chester), Kerri Green (Jennifer Chester), John Larroquette (Don Moore), Joey Lawrence (Bobby Chester), Aubrey Jene (Laurie Chester), Dick Anthony Williams (Dan Gardner).

Suffering from burnout, Chicago air traffic controller John Candy takes his family to Florida for a vacation in a beach house and runs afoul of wealthy snob Richard Crenna. Candy challenges Crenna to a sailing race, with Candy's ship being a floating restaurant owned by Rip Torn. Doesn't sound very funny, does it?

2919. *Summer School* (1987, Paramount, 98m, c). P George Shapiro & Howard West, D Carl Reiner, W Jeff Franklin (based on a story by Stuart Birnbaum, Dave Dashev & Jeff Franklin), PH David M. Walsh, M Danny Elfman, ED Bud Molin, PD David L. Snyder.

LP Mark Harmon (Freddy Shoop), Kirstie Alley (Robin Bishop), Robin Thomas (Phil Gills), Patrick Laborteaux (Kevin Winchester), Courtney Thorne-Smith (Pam House), Dean Cameron (Francis "Chainsaw" Gremp), Gary Riley (Dave Frazier).

Mark Harmon is given a chance to earn a regular teaching job by working in summer school with a group of remedial students who must pass a big test. Kirstie Alley also keeps Harmon guessing.

2920. *A Summer Story* (1988, Atlantic, US/GB, 96m, c). P Danton Rissner, D Piers Haggard, W Penelope Mortimer (based on a story "The Apple Tree" by John Galsworthy), PH Kenneth Mac-

Millan, M Georges Delerue, ED Ralph Sheldon, PD Leo Austin.

LP Imogen Stubbs (Megan David), James Wilby (Frank Ashton), Kenneth Colley (Jim), Sophie Ward (Stella Halliday), Susannah York (Mrs. Narracombe), Jerome Flynn (Joe Narracombe), Lee Billett (Nick Narracombe), Oliver Perry (Rick Narracombe).

Set in rural 1902 southwest England, this beautiful film is the story of the love of farm girl Imogen Stubbs and young London lawyer James Wilby, each faced with decisions which will change their lives forever.

The Summons see *Scorpion*

2921. *Sunburn* (1980, Paramount, 99m, c). P John Daly & Gerald Green, D Richard C. Sarafian, W Daly, Stephen Oliver & James Booth (based on the novel *The Bind* by Stanley Ellin), PH Alex Phillips, Jr., M John Cameron, ED Geoff Foot, PD Ted Tester.

LP Farah Fawcett [Majors] (Ellie), Charles Grodin (Jake), Art Carney (Marcus), Joan Collins (Nera), William Daniels (Crawford), John Hillerman (Webb), Eleanor Parker (Mrs. Thoren), Keenan Wynn (Mark Elmes).

In this comedy-mystery, private eye Charles Grodin hires model Farrah Fawcett to pose as his wife as he travels to Acapulco while he investigates the violent death of an aging industrialist. Farrah looks great, but has little to do related to acting.

2922. *Sunset* (1988, Tri-Star, 107m, c). P Tony Adams, D&W Blake Edwards (based on a story by Rod Amateau), PH Anthony B. Richmond, M Henry Mancini & Duke Ellington, ED Robert Pergament, PD Rodger Maus, COS Patricia Norris.

LP Bruce Willis (Tom Mix), James Garner (Wyatt Earp), Malcolm McDowell (Alfie Alperin), Mariel Hemingway (Cheryl King), Kathleen Quinlan (Nancy Shoemaker), Jennifer Edwards (Victoria Alperin), Patricia Hodge (Christina Alperin), Richard Bradford (Capt. Blackworth), M. Emmet Walsh (Chief Marvin Dibner), Joe Dallesandro (Dutch Kieffer).

In this fictional story, legendary lawman Wyatt Earp (James Garner) and cowboy movie star Tom Mix (Bruce Willis) become fast friends. They team up to try to solve a William Desmond Taylor-like murder case.

2923. *Super Fuzz* (1981, Avco Embassy, 97m, c, aka *Supersnooper*). P Maximilian Wolkoff, D Sergio Corbucci, W Corbucci & Sabatino Ciuffini, PH Silvano Ippoliti, M La Bionda, ED Eugene Alabiso, PD Marco Dentici.

LP Terence Hill (Dave Speed), Ernest Borgnine (Willy Dunlop), Joanne Dru (Rosy Labouche), Marc Lawrence (Torpedo), Julie Gordon (Evelyn), Lee Sandman (Chief McEnroy), Herb Goldstein (Silvius).

After being exposed to radiation, rookie cop Terence Hill develops super powers which he uses to fight crime.

2924. *The Super Jocks* (1980, Brenner, 100m, c). P&W Emil Nofal, D Nofal & Ray Sargeant.

LP Joe Stewardson (Will), Ken Leach (Tony), John Higgins (Barry), Richard Loring (Paul), Jenny Meyer (Sandra), Madeleine Usher, Diane Ridler, Tony Jay.

Look if you want, but you're not likely to find this dumb film in any of your friendly video stores. A group of athletes flex their muscles for the usual assortment of adoring girls.

2925. *Supergirl* (1984, Tri-Star, GB, 114m, c). P Timothy Burrill, D Jeannot Szwarc, W David Odell (based on the comic book character), PH Alan Hume, M Jerry Goldsmith, ED Malcolm Cooke, PD Richard MacDonald.

LP Faye Dunaway (Selena), Helen Slater (Kara, Supergirl/Linda Lee), Peter O'Toole (Zaltar), Mia Farrow (Alura), Brenda Vaccaro (Bianca), Peter Cook (Nigel), Simon Ward (Zor-El), Marc McClure (Jimmy Olsen), Hart Bochner (Ethan), Maureen Teefy (Lucy Lane).

Several fine performers might like to forget this film when putting together their résumés. None is more poorly used than Faye Dunaway, whose career seems to be in one long downward spin. Cute young Helen Slater probably will survive portraying Superman's cousin, who leaves Krypton (yeah, we thought it had been destroyed, too) to recover the Omegahedron Stone.

2926. *The Supergrass* (1985, Comic Strip, GB, 105m, c). P Elaine Taylor, D Peter Richardson, W Pete Richens & Richardson, PH John Metcalfe, M Keith Tippet & Working Week Big Band, ED Geoff Hogg, AD Niki Wateridge.

LP Adrian Edmondson (Dennis), Jennifer Saunders (Lesley), Peter Richardson (Harvey Duncan), Dawn French (Andrea), Keith Allen (Wong), Nigel Planer (Gunter), Robbie Coltrane (Troy), Daniel Peacock (Jim Jarvis).

In this comedy set in England's West Country, the police are convinced that boastful young Adrian Edmondson is a drug smuggler.

2927. *Superman II* (1981, Warner, 127m, c). P Pierre Spengler, D Richard Lester, W Mario Puzo, David Newman & Leslie Newman (based on a story by Puzio, from characters created by Jerry Siegel & Joe Shuster), PH Geoffrey Unsworth & Robert Paynter, M Ken Thorne (based on original music composed by John Williams), ED John Victor Smith, PD John Barry & Peter Murton, AD Maurice Fowler, SE Colin Chilvers, Roy Field & Zoran Perisic.

LP Gene Hackman (Lex Luthor), Christopher Reeve (Clark Kent/Superman), Ned Beatty (Otis), Jackie Cooper (Perry White), Sarah Douglas (Ursa), Margot Kidder (Lois Lane), Jack O'Halloran (Non), Valerie Perrine (Eve Teschmacher), Susannah York (Lara), Clifton James (Sheriff), Marc McClure (Jimmy Olsen), Terence Stamp (General Zod).

Three renegade Kryptonians, Terence Stamp, Sarah Douglas and Jack O'Halloran threaten earth with a space bomb, while Superman is away at his North Pole retreat, becoming a mere mortal so he can become Kidder's lover. Even when he regains his powers, the trio of villains are his match in super powers. What will he do? What will he do?

2928. *Superman III* (1983, Warner, 123m, c). P Pierre Spengler, D Richard Lester, W David Newman & Leslie Newman (based on characters created by Jerry Siegel & Joe Shuster), PH Robert Paynter, M Ken Thorne & John Williams, ED John Victor Smith, PD Peter Murton, SE Roy Field, Colin Chilvers, Martin Gutteridge & Brian Warner.

LP Christopher Reeve (Clark Kent/ Superman), Richard Pryor (Gus Gorman), Jackie Cooper (Perry White), Margot Kidder (Lois Lane), Annette O'Toole (Lana Lang), Annie Ross (Vera Webster), Pamela Stephenson (Lorelei Ambrosia), Robert Vaughn (Ross Webster), Marc McClure (Jimmy Olsen).

Computer whiz Richard Pryor is employed by villainous Robert Vaughn and his nasty sister Annie Ross to manufacture some synthetic Kryptonite. The phony material warps Superman's character, but he snaps out of it just in time.

2929. Superman IV: The Quest for Peace (1987, Warner, 89m, c). P Menahem Golan & Yoram Globus, D Sidney J. Furie, W Lawrence Konner & Mark Rosenthal (based on a story by Konner, Rosenthal & Christopher Reeve), PH Ernest Day, M John Williams & Alexander Courage, ED John Shirley, PD John Graysmark.

LP Christopher Reeve (Superman/ Clark Kent), Gene Hackman (Lex Luthor), Jackie Cooper (Perry White), Marc McClure (Jimmy Olsen), Jon Cryer (Lenny), Sam Wanamaker (David Warfield), Mark Pillow (Nuclear Man), Mariel Hemingway (Lacy Warfield), Margot Kidder (Lois Lane).

It may be time to close the book on the Superman series. With this film, the man of steel becomes rather preachy as he rids the world of all nuclear weapons when asked to do so in a letter from a child. Villain Gene Hackman takes advantage of the situation to create a worthy opponent for Superman, solar energized Mark Pillow. Mariel Hemingway gives Margot Kidder some competition for Christopher Reeve, with Mariel after Clark Kent and Kidder still hot for Superduperman.

2930. The Supernaturals (1987, Republic Ent. Intl., 80m, c). P Michael S. Murphey & Joel Soisson, D Armand Mastroianni, W Michael S. Murphey & Soisson, PH Peter Collister, M Robert O. Ragland, AD Jo Ann Chorney.

LP Maxwell Caulfield (Lt. Ray Ellis), Nichelle Nichols (Sgt. Leona Hawkins), Talia Balsam (Pvt. Angela Lejune), Bradford Bancroft (Pvt. Tom Weir), LeVar Burton (Pvt. Michael Osgood), Bobby Di Cicco (Pvt. Tim Cort).

Sgt. Nichelle Nichols' present-day soldiers are troubled by a group of zombies, former Confederate soldiers forced by Union forces to cross a mine field at the time of the Civil War.

Supersnooper see Super Fuzz

2931. Superstition (1985, Almi, 84m, c, aka *The Witch*). P Ed Carlin, John D. Schwartz & Robert L.J. Lewis, D James W. Roberson, W Michael Sajbel, Bret Plate, Brad White & Donald G. Thompson (based on the story "The Witch" by Sajbel), PH Lee Madden, M David Gibney, ED Al Rabinowitz, AD Penny Hadfield.

LP James Carl Houghton (Rev. David Thompson), Albert Salmi (Inspector Sturgess), Larry Pennell (George Leahy), Lynn Carlin (Melinda Leahy), Maylo McCaslin (Sheryl Leahy), Heidi Bohay (Ann Leahy), Billy Jacoby (Justin Leahy).

Despite warnings from the locals, a reverend and his family move into a vacant house near Black Pond, where the remains of a 200-year-old witch burned at the stake refuses to rest.

2932. The Sure Thing (1985, Embassy, 94m, c). P Roger Birnbaum & Andrew Scheinman, D Rob Reiner, W Steven L. Bloom & Jonathan Roberts, PH Robert Elswit, M Tom Scott, ED Robert Leighton, PD Lily Kilvert.

LP John Cusack (Walter "Gib" Gibson), Daphne Zuniga (Alison Bradbury), Anthony Edwards (Lance), Boyd Gaines (Jason), Lisa Jane Persky (Mary Ann Webster), Viveca Lindfors (Prof. Taub), Nicollette Sheridan (The Sure Thing), Tim Robbins (Gary Cooper), Fran Ryan (Louise).

In a charming film in the same way *It Happened One Night* was charming five decades earlier, horny Yale college student John Cusack is induced to spend Christmas vacation with friend Anthony Edwards on the West Coast by the promise of a "sure thing." Somehow Cusack and Daphne Zuniga, a classmate with whom he doesn't get along, are teamed in a cross country trip and as would be expected they fall in love—demonstrating that mere casual sex isn't the prescription for happiness.

2933. *Surf Nazis Must Die* (1987, Troma, 95m, c). P Robert Tinnell, D Peter George, W Jon Ayre, PH Rolf Kesterman, M Jon McCallum, ED Craig Colton, AD Byrnadette diSanto.

LP Gail Neely (Mama Washington), Robert Harden (LeRoy Washington), Barry Brenner (Adolf), Dawn Wildsmith (Eva), Michael Sonye (Mengele), Joel Hile (Hook), Gene Mitchell (Brutus), Tom Shell (Smeg), Bobbie Bresee (Smeg's Mom).

The favorite activities of the Nazis in this movie are surfing and killing on California beaches. Gail Neely, the mother of one of their victims, uses guns, grenades and motorcycles to take revenge.

2934. *Surf II* (1984, Intl. Film Marketing, 91m, c). P George G. Braunstein & Ron Hamady, D&W Randall Badat, PH Alex Phillips, M Peter Bernstein, ED Jacqueline Cambas, PD Jeff Staggs.

LP Morgan Paull (Dad), Ruth Buzzi (Chuck's Mother), Lyle Waggoner (Chief Boyardie), Cleavon Little (Daddy-O), Linda Kerridge (Sparkle), Carol Wayne (Mrs. O'Finlay), Eddie Deezen (Menlo Schwartzer), Peter Isacksen (Beaker), Eric Stoltz (Chuck).

Bet you wonder why you can't find *Surf I*. Well, none was ever made. Bet you often wondered what had happened to the likes of Ruth Buzzi, Lyle Waggoner and Cleavon Little. Bet you don't care enough to rent this film from your local video store to watch surfers getting sick from drinking tainted soda pop.

2935. *Surrender* (1987, Warner, 96m, c). P Aaron Spelling & Alan Greisman, D&W Jerry Belson, PH Juan Ruiz Anchia, M Michel Colombier, ED Wendy Greene Briemont, PD Lilly Kilvert.

LP Sally Field (Daisy Morgan), Michael Caine (Sean Stein), Steve Guttenberg (Marty Caesar), Peter Boyle (Jay Bass), Julie Kavner (Ronnie), Jackie Cooper (Ace Morgan), Louise Lasser (Joyce), Iman (Hedy).

Wealthy writer Michael Caine, tired of being taken to the cleaners by women, pretends he's poor. Struggling artist Sally Field falls for him, but their courtship is not exactly what either hopes for.

2936. *The Surrogate* (1984, Cinepix, Canada, 99m, c). P John Dunning & Don Carmody, D Carmody, W Carmody & Robert Geoffrian, PH Francois Protat, M Daniel Lanois, ED Rit Wallace, AD Charles Dunlop.

LP Art Hindle (Frank Waite), Carole Laure (Anouk Van Derlin), Shannon Tweed (Lee Waite), Michael Ironside (George Kyber), Marilyn Lightstone (Dr. Harriet Forman), Jim Bailey (Eric), Jackie Burroughs (Fantasy Woman).

Sexually dissatisfied with their marriage, Art Hindle and Shannon Tweed seek help from sex therapist Carol Laure, who helps couples release their most hidden sexual fantasies. When a series of sexually related murders result in the couple's friends being killed one by one, the question is who has gone too far.

2937. *Survival Game* (1987, TransWorld, 91m, c). P Gideon Amir, D Herb Freed, W Freed, Susannah de Nimes & P.W. Swann (based on a story by Freed), PH Avraham Karpick, M Tom Simonec & Michael Linn, ED Charles Simmons & Karen Gebura, PD Diana Morris.

LP Mike Norris (Mike Falcon), Deborah Goodrich (C.J. Forrest), Seymour Cassel (Dave Forrest), Ed Bernard (Sugar Bear), John Sharp (Charles), Rick Grassi (Ice), Arlene Golonka (Mike's Mom), Michael Halton (Harlan).

Chuck Norris' son Mike, a survival-camp trainee, falls for Deborah Goodrich, whom he meets after a car crash. When she and her 60s drug guru are kidnapped, the martial arts chip-off-the-block takes on their abductors.

2938. *Survival Quest* (1989, MGM/United Artists, 96m, c). P Roberto Quezada, D&W Don Coscarelli, PH Daryn Okada, M Fred Myrow, ED Coscarelli, PD Andrew Siegel.

LP Lance Henriksen (Hank), Mark Rolston (Jake), Steve Antin (Raider), Michael Allen Ryder (Harper), Paul Provenza (Joey), Ben Hammer (Hal), Dominic Hoffman (Jeff), Traci Lin (Olivia), Dermot Mulroney (Gray).

This almost direct-to-video film isn't worth a rental. It deals with two separate survival course runs over the same rugged northern Rockies terrain. The two groups get into it and blood is spilled, but the good guys win.

2939. *Survival Run* (1980, Film Ventures, 90m, c). P Lance Hool, D Larry Spiegel, W Spiegel, G.M. Cahill & Fredric Shore (based on a story by Cahill & Shore), PH Alex Phillips, Jr., M Gary William Friedman, ED Chris Greenbury.

LP Peter Graves, Ray Milland, Vincent Van Patten, Pedro Armendariz, Jr., Alan Conrad, Anthony Charnota, Gonzalo Vega, Cosie Costa, Randi Meryl.

Six teenagers stranded in the desert are harrassed by Peter Graves and Ray Milland when the kids see the pair making a shady deal.

2940. *Survivor* (1988, Vestron, GB, 91m, c). P Martin Wragge, D Michael Shackleton, W Bima Stagg, PH Fred Tammes, M Andraan Strydom, ED Max Lemon.

LP Chip Mayer (Survivor), Richard Moll (Kragg), Sue Kiel, Richard Haines, John Carson, Rex Garner, Sandra Duncan, Sven Forsell, Bima Stagg.

NASA astronaut Chip Mayer returns to earth after World War III has made the world one vast desert wasteland. He comes across a subterranean society headed by crazy Richard Moll (Bull, of TV's "Night Court"). The latter, not so dumb as he looks, has gathered together all the surviving beautiful women with whom he plans to repopulate the world.

2941. *The Survivors* (1983, Columbia, 102m, c). P William Sackheim, D Michael Ritchie, W Michael Leeson, PH Billy Williams, M Paul Chihara, ED Richard A. Harris, PD Gene Callahan.

LP Walter Matthau (Sonny Paluso), Robin Williams (Donald Quinelle), Jerry Reed (Jack Locke), James Wainwright (Wes Huntley), Kristen Vigard (Candice Paluso), Annie McEnroe (Doreen), Anne Pitoniak (Betty).

Young executive Robin Williams and former gas station owner Walter Matthau find themselves the target of Jerry Reed, an out-of-work hit man, whom they disarm in a robbery attempt. Williams takes off for a survivalist camp, followed by Matthau and shortly thereafter by Reed.

2942. *Suspect* (1987, Tri-Star, 121m, c). P Daniel A. Sherkow, D Peter Yates, W Eric Roth, PH Billy Williams, M Michael Kamen, ED Ray Lovejoy, PD Stuart Wurtzel.

LP Cher (Kathleen Riley), Dennis Quaid (Eddie Sanger), Liam Neeson (Carl Wayne Anderson), John Mahoney (Judge Matthew Helms), Joe Mantegna (Charlie Stella), Philip Bosco (Paul Gray), E. Katherine Kerr (Grace Comisky), Fred Melamed (Morty Rosenthal).

Washington, D.C., public defender Cher is given the assignment of defending homeless, mentally unstable, deaf-mute Vietnam vet Liam Neeson against a charge of murdering a woman. Things look bad for her client but with the unwelcome help of juror Dennis Quaid, who becomes romantically obsessed with Cher during the trial, justice prevails.

2943. *Swamp Thing* (1982, Embassy, 90m, c). P Benjamin Melniker & Michael E. Uslan, D&W Wes Craven (based on DC comic characters), PH Robin Goodwin, M Harry Manfredini, ED Richard Bracken, PD Robb Wilson King.

LP Louis Jourdan (Arcane), Adrienne Barbeau (Alice Cable), Ray Wise (Dr. Alec Holland), David Hess (Ferret), Nicholas Worth (Bruno), Don Knight (Ritter), Al Ruban (Charlie), Dick Durock (Swamp Thing), Ben Bates (Arcane Monster).

Filmed in comic book format, the movie is the story of a group of scientists performing a top secret experiment in a swamp and their troubles with their lunatic archenemy, Louis Jourdan.

2944. *Sweet Country* (1987, Cinema Group, 147m, c). P Michael Cacoyannis & Costas Alexakis, D&W Cacoyannis (based on a novel by Caroline Richards), PH Andreas Bellis, M Starvos Xarhakos, ED Dinos Katsourides & Cacoyannis.

LP Jane Alexander (Anna Willing), John Cullum (Ben Willing), Carole Laure (Eva Araya), Franco Nero (Paul), Joanna Pettet (Monica Araya), Randy Quaid (Juan), Irene Papas (Mrs. Araya), Jean-Pierre Aumont (Mr. Araya).

In 1973, American activist Jane Alexander, her teacher husband John Cullum, and their friends, divorced sisters Carole Laure and Joanna Pettet, become involved in political intrigue in Chile when Marxist leader Salvador Allende is overthrown.

2945. *Sweet Dirty Tony* (1980, Key West, 90m, c, aka *Cuba Crossing; Kill*

Castro; Assignment: Kill Castro). P Peter J. Barton, D&W Chuck Workman.

LP Stuart Whitman (Capt. Tony Terracino), Robert Vaughn (Hudd), Raymond St. Jacques (Bell), Caren Kaye (Tracy), Woody Strode (Titi), Sybil Danning (Veronica), Mary Lou Gassen (Maria), Albert Salmi (Delgato), Michael Gazzo (Rosselini).

In a dreadful film, soldier-of-fortune Stuart Whitman gets mixed up in a plot to assassinate Castro.

2946. *Sweet Dreams* (1985, Tri-Star, 115m, c). P Bernard Schwartz, D Karel Reisz, W Robert Getchell, PH Robbie Greenberg, M Charles Gross, ED Malcolm Cooke, PD Albert Brenner.

LP Jessica Lange† (Patsy Cline), Ed Harris (Charlie Dick), Ann Wedgeworth (Hilda Hensley), David Clennon (Randy Hughes), James Staley (Gerald Cline), Gary Basaraba (Woodhouse), John Goodman (Otis), P.J. Soles (Wanda).

In a well-acted biopic, Jessica Lange shines in the story of the short turbulent life of country singer Patsy Cline. The hits of the latter lip-synched by Lange include "San Antonio Rose," "Lovesick Blues," "Foolin' Around," "Your Cheatin' Heart," "Seven Lonely Days," "Walking After Midnight," "I Fall to Pieces" and the title song.

2947. *Sweet Heart's Dance* (1988, Tri-Star, 101m, c). P Jeffrey Lurie, D Robert Greenwald, W Ernest Thompson, PH Tak Fujimoto, M Richard Gibbs, ED Robert Florio, PD James Allen.

LP Don Johnson (Wiley Boon), Susan Sarandon (Sandra Boon), Jeff Daniels (Sam Manners), Elizabeth Perkins (Adie Nims), Kate Reid (Pearne Manners), Justin Henry (Kyle Boon), Holly Marie Combs (Debs Boon), Heather Coleman (BJ Boon), Matthew Wohl (Dick Merezini), Laurie Corbin (Claire Norton).

Conflicts arise between two Vermont friends, as one, Jeff Daniels, falls in love for the first time with Elizabeth Perkins, while the other, Don Johnson, is ending a 15-year marriage to Susan Sarandon. The film isn't much but the four main performers are charming.

2948. *Sweet Liberty* (1986, Universal, 107m, c). P Martin Bregman, D&W Alan Alda, PH Frank Tidy, M Bruce Brough-

ton, ED Michael Economou, PD Ben Edwards.

LP Alan Alda (Michael Burgess), Michael Caine (Elliott James), Michelle Pfeiffer (Faith Healy), Bob Hoskins (Stanley Gould), Lise Hilboldt (Gretchen Carlsen), Lillian Gish (Cecelia Burgess), Lois Chiles (Leslie), Saul Rubinek (Bo Hodges), Linda Thorson (Grace).

Small town historian Alan Alda finds his prize-winning saga of the Revolutionary War and his hometown being ruined by the film crew making a movie based on his work. Besides everything else, the star of the movie, Michael Caine, tries to bed every female around, including Alda's love, Lise Hilboldt. Young director Saul Rubinek believes that all ages are filled with alienation and the desire to remove everyone's clothes.

2949. *Sweet Lies* (1989, Island, 96m, c). P Serge Touboul & Chris Blackwell, D Nathalie Delon, W Rob Dunn (based on Delon's story), PH Dominique Chapuis, M Trevor Jones, ED Marie-Sophie Dubus, AD Bruno Held.

LP Treat Williams (Peter Nicholl), Joanna Pacula (Joelle), Julianne Phillips (Dixie), Laura Manszky (Lisa), Marilyn Dodds Frank (Maggie), Norbert Weisser (Bill), Aina Walle (Isabelle), Gisele Casadesus (Nemo).

Joanna Pacula and Julianne Phillips make a wager as to who will be the first to bed American detective Treat Williams, in Paris to investigate insurance fraud.

2950. *Sweet Lorraine* (1987, Angelika, 91m, c). P&D Steve Gomer, W Michael Zettler & Shelly Altman (based on a story by Zettler, Altman & George Malko), PH Rene Ohashi, M Richard Robbins, ED Laurence Solomon, PD David Gropman.

LP Maureen Stapleton (Lillian Garber), Trini Alvarado (Molly), Lee Richardson (Sam), John Bedford Lloyd (Jack), Freddie Roman (Phil Allen), Giancarlo Esposito (Howie), Edith Falco (Karen), Todd Graff (Leonard).

Young Trini Alvarado pitches in to help her grandmother Maureen Stapleton keep her run-down Catskills resort, which is facing bankruptcy.

2951. *Sweet Revenge* (1987, Concorde, 78m, c). P Brad Krevoy & Steven

Stabler, D Mark Sobel, W Steven Krauzer & Tim McCoy (based on an original story by Michael Jones & Randy Kornfield), PH Shane Kelly, M Ernest Troost, ED Michael S. Murphy, PD Vic Dabao.

LP Nancy Allen (Jillian Grey), Ted Shackelford (Boone), Martin Landau (Cicero), Sal Landi (Gil), Michele Little (Lee), Gina Gershon (K.C.), Lotis Key (Sonya), Stacey Adams (Tina), Leo Martinez (Buddha).

Investigating a white slavery ring run by Martin Landau in the Far East, reporter Nancy Allen is kidnapped and finds herself the ring's latest recruit.

2952. *Sweet 16* (1983, Century Intl., 90m, c). P&D Jim Sotos, W Erwin Goldman, PH James L. Carter, M Tommy Vig, ED Drake Silliman.

LP Bo Hopkins (Dan), Susan Strasberg (Joanne), Don Stroud (Billy), Dana Kimmell (Marci), Aleisa Shirley (Melissa), Don Shanks (Jason), Steve Antin (Hank), Logan Clarke (Jimmy).

Beautiful, mysterious, promiscuous 16-year-old Aleisa Shirley finds her boyfriends always turning up dead. What a bother!

2953. *Sweet William* (1982, World Northal, GB, 92m, c). P Jeremy Watt, D Claude Whatham, W Beryl Bainbridge (based on her novel), PH Les Young, ED Peter Coulson, PD Eileen Diss.

LP Sam Waterston (William), Jenny Agutter (Ann), Anna Massey (Edna), Geraldine James (Pamela), Daphne Oxenford (Mrs. Walton), Rachel Bell (Mrs. Kershaw), David Wood (Vicar).

Londoner Jenny Agutter finds her Scottish lover Sam Waterston constantly unfaithful.

2954. *Sweetie* (1989, Filmpac, Australia, 97m, c). P John Maynard, D Jane Campion, W Campion & Gerard Lee, PH Sally Bongers, M Martin Armiger, ED Veronika Heussler, PD Peter Harris.

LP Genevieve Lemon (Dawn [Sweetie]), Karen Colston (Kay), Tom Lycos (Louis), Jon Darling (Gordon), Dorothy Barry (Flo), Michael Lake (Bob).

In this tragicomedy, Karen Colston is afraid of trees and a believer in fortunetellers. She initially figures that Tom Lycos, who has just become engaged to a coworker, is the one foretold to be the man in her life. She goes about seducing him, but after awhile she's no longer so sure he's the one. Her sister Genevieve Lemon, plump and plain, and eager for a show biz career, may be more to Lycos' liking.

2955. *Swing Shift* (1984, Warner, 113m, c). P Jerry Bick, D Jonathan Demme, W Rob Morton, PH Tak Fujimoto, M Patrick Williams, ED Craig McKay, PD Peter Jamison.

LP Goldie Hawn (Kay Walsh), Kurt Russell (Lucky Lockhart), Christine Lahti† (Hazel Zanussi), Fred Ward (Biscuits Toohey), Ed Harris (Jack Walsh), Sudie Bond (Annie), Holly Hunter (Jeannie Sherman), Patty Maloney (Laverne), Lisa Pelikan (Violet Mulligan).

In this nostalgic look at the times of World War II's "Rosie the Riveter," Goldie Hawn takes a job in an aircraft factory to make ends meet while her sailor husband Ed Harris is away at war. She has a fling with a fellow worker, 4-F Kurt Russell. This complicates things for her when her man comes home at the end of the war.

2956. *Switching Channels* (1988, Tri-Star, 105m, c). P Martin Ransohoff, D Ted Kotcheff, W Jonathan Reynolds (based on *The Front Page,* a play by Ben Hecht & Charles MacArthur), PH Francois Protat, M Michel Legrand, ED Thom Noble, PD Anne Pritchard.

LP Kathleen Turner (Christy Colleran), Burt Reynolds (John L. Sullivan, IV), Christopher Reeve (Blaine Bingham), Ned Beatty (Roy Ridnitz), Henry Gibson (Ike Roscoe), George Newbern (Siegenthaler), Al Waxman (Berger), Joe Silver (Morosini), Monica Parker (Jessica), Laura Robinson (Karen Ludlow).

While male viewers may never grow tired of seeing Kathleen Turner in another wholesomely sexy role, few will feel the same about Burt Reynolds and Christopher Reeve, who are charmless in this atrocious remake of *The Front Page* and *His Girl Friday.* The newspaper people are changed to TV news gatherers (make that inventors). For the record, ace TV reporter Turner is quitting the business to marry boring Reeve. Her ex-husband Reynolds tries anything to prevent her leaving. All is resolved as TV covers the planned execution of innocent Henry Gibson. It's hard to describe just how bad this film really is.

2957. The Sword and the Sorcerer (1982, Group 1, 100m, c). P Brandon & Marion Chase, D Albert Pyun, W Pyun, Thomas Karnowski & John Stuckmeyer, PH Joseph Mangine, M David Whittaker, ED Marshall Harvey, AD George Costello.

LP Lee Horsley (Talon), Kathleen Beller (Alana), Simon MacCorkindale (Mikah), George Maharis (Machelli), Richard Lynch (Cromwell), Richard Moll (Xusia), Anthony DeLongis (Rodrigo), Nina Van Pallandt (Malia).

Lee Horsley regains control of a kingdom seized by an evil tyrant with the help of a powerful magician.

2958. Sword of Heaven (1985, Trans-World, 85m, c). P Joseph J. Randazzo & Britt Lomond, D Byron Meyers, W James Bruno, Lomond, William P. O'Hagan & Randazzo, PH Gil Hubbs, M Christopher L. Stone, ED Warren Chadwick.

LP Tadashi Yamashita (Tadashi), Mel Novak (Dirk), Gerry Gibson (Patrick), Joe Randazzo (Cain), Mika (Satoko), Wynston A. Jones (Cal), Bill "Superfoot" Wallace (Cal), Karen Lee Shepherd, Venus Jones.

Crooked L.A. cop Wynston A. Jones and his martial arts buddy Mel Novak scheme to strip rich men of their money in order to equip a paramilitary crime-fighting unit, but they are stopped by visiting Japanese police officer Tadashi Yamashita.

2959. The Sword of the Barbarians (1983, Cannon, US/Ital., 88m, c). P Pino Burricchi, D Michael E. Lemick, W Pietro Regnoli, PH Giancarlo Ferrando, M Franco Campanino, ED Alessandro Lucidi.

LP Peter MacCoy (Sangral), Margareta Rance, Yvonne Fraschetti, Anthony Freeman, Sabrina Siani, Ziomaria Rodriguez, Al Huang.

In this routine sword-and-fantasy film, Peter MacCoy seeks the "Golden Goddess."

2960. Sword of the Valiant (1984, Cannon, GB, 101m, c). P Menahem Golan & Yoram Globus, D Stephen Weeks, W Weeks, Philip M. Breen & Howard C. Pen, PH Freddie A. Young & Peter Hurst, M Ron Geesin, ED Richard Marden & Barry Peters, PD Maurice Fowler & Derek Nice.

LP Miles O'Keeffe (Gawain), Cyrielle Claire (Linet), Leigh Lawson (Humphrey), Sean Connery (Green Knight), Trevor Howard (King Arthur), Peter Cushing (Seneschal), Ronald Lacey (Oswald), Lila Kedrova (Lady of Lyonesse), John Rhys-Davies (Baron Fortinbras), Wilfred Brambell (Porter).

Sean Connery as the Green Knight arrives in Camelot to challenge anyone to take a blow at him with a sword as long as he can return the blow. After awhile Miles O'Keeffe as Sir Gawain accepts the challenge and with a broadsword severs Connery's head from his body. At this the decapitated knight picks up his head and walks out, informing Gawain that he'll take his turn later. Readers will be relieved to learn that O'Keeffe, who was so miserable in Bo Derek's *Tarzan, the Ape Man,* is just as bad this time and required his lines to be dubbed. Unfortunately he's allowed to keep his head.

Swordkill see Ghost Warrior

2961. Sylvester (1985, Columbia, 103m, c). P Martin Jurow, D Tim Hunter, W Carol Sobieski, PH Hiro Narita, M Lee Holdridge, ED Howard Smith, Suzanne Pettit & David Garfield, PD James W. Newport.

LP Richard Farnsworth (Foster), Melissa Gilbert (Charlie), Michael Schoeffling (Matt), Constance Towers (Muffy), Pete Kowanko (Harris), Yankton Hatten (Grant), Shane Serwin (Seth), Chris Pedersen (Red).

Sixteen-year-old Melissa Gilbert and cranky stockyard boss Richard Farnsworth team up to train a battered horse named Sylvester for the National Equestrian trials. It's not *National Velvet,* but it's enjoyable.

2962. Sylvia (1985, MGM/United Artists, New Zealand, 98m, c). P Don Reynolds & Michael Firth, D Firth, W Michael Quill, F. Fairfax & Firth (based on the books *Teacher and I Passed This Way* by Sylvia Ashton-Warner), PH Ian Paul, M Leonard Rosenman, ED Michael Horton.

LP Eleanor David (Sylvia Henderson), Nigel Terry (Aden Morris), Tom Wilkinson (Keith Henderson), Mary Regan (Opal Saunders), Joseph George (Seven), Eileen Glover (Lilac), Graham Glover (Ashton), Tessa Wells (Jasmine).

Eleanor David gives an excellent portrayal of Sylvia Ashton-Warner, who in the early 40s bucked the New Zealand educational structure to offer innovative reading instructions to the Maori children.

2963. Table for Five (1983, Warner, 122m, c). P Robert Schaffel, D Robert Lieberman, W David Seltzer, PH Vilmos Zsigmond, M Miles Goodman & John Morris, ED Michael Kahn, PD Robert R. Boyle.

LP Jon Voight (J.P. Tannen), Richard Crenna (Mitchell), Marie-Christine Barrault (Marie), Millie Perkins (Kathleen), Roxana Zal (Tilde), Robby Kiger (Truman-Paul), Son Hoang Bui (Trung), Maria O'Brien (Mandy).

Trying to show that daddies make just as good parents as mommies and sometimes even better ones, this sickeningly sentimental soap opera stars Jon Voight as a divorced father. He tries to re-establish a relationship with the children he has let get away, while they all take an ocean cruise.

2964. Taffin (1988, MGM/United Artists, US/GB, 96m, c). P Peter Shaw, D Francis Megahy, W David Ambrose (based on the book by Lyndon Mallett), PH Paul Beeson, M Stanley Myers & Hans Zimmer, ED Rodney Holland, PD William Alexander.

LP Pierce Brosnan (Mark Taffin), Ray McAnally (O'Rourke), Alison Doody (Charlotte), Jeremy Child (Martin), Patrick Bergan (Mo Taffin), Ronan Wilmot (The Deacon), Alan Stanford (Sprawley), Gerald McSorley (Ed).

An ex-seminarian and now a debt-collector, Pierce Brosnan learns that the athletic field in his small Irish home town is the planned site of a dangerous chemical plant. He mounts a vigorous campaign against the plant's owners.

Things turn violent when hired thugs are turned loose on the conservationists.

2965. Tail of the Tiger (1984, Roadshow, Australia, 82m, c). P James M. Vernon, D&W Rolf de Heer, PH Richard Michalak, M Steve Arnold & Graham Tardif, ED Surresh Ayyar, PD Judi Russell.

LP Grant Navin (Orville Ryan), Gordon Poole (Harry), Caz Lederman (Lydia Ryan), Gayle Kennedy (Beryl), Peter Feeley (Spike), Dylan Lyle (Rabbit), Walter Sullivan (Stan), Basil Clarke (Jack).

The neighborhood boys won't allow airplane enthusiast Grant Navin to join them in flying model planes. He takes to hanging around old Gordon Poole who is trying to restore an ancient deHaviland Tiger in an abandoned warehouse. The efforts of the two are frequently aided by the ghosts of deceased pilots.

2966. Tainted (1989, Cardinal, 93m, c). P Orestes Matacena & Phyllis Redden, D&W Matacena, PH Ramon Suarez, M Hayden Wayne, ED Stephen Sheppard, AD Randy Barcelo.

LP Shari Shattuck (Cathy Lowell), Park Overall (Marian), Gene Tootle (Frank), Magilla Schaus (Tom), Blaque Fowler (Rapist), Ross Taylor (Principal), Ruben Rabasa (Guard).

Filmed in 1984, it was planned to release this film theatrically as *Body Passion,* but instead it went directly to video shelves. Shari Shattuck, a small-town school teacher, is raped by a prowler who in turn is killed by her mortician husband Gene Tootle. The latter promptly expires from a heart attack. Rather than call in the police, Shattuck decides to cover up the incident.

Tai-Pan see James Clavell's Tai-Pan

2967. Take This Job and Shove It (1981, Avco Embassy, 100m, c). P Greg Blackwell, D Gus Trikonis, W Barry Schneider (based on a story by Jeffrey Bernini & Schneider from a song by David Allen Coe), PH James Devis, M Billy Sherrill, ED Richard Belding, AD Jim Dultz.

LP Robert Hays (Frank Maclin), Art Carney (Charlie Pickett), Barbara Hershey (J.M. Halstead), David Keith (Harry Meade), Tim Thomerson (Ray

Binkowski), Martin Mull (Dick Ebersol), Eddie Albert (Samuel Ellison).

Robert Hays, a junior executive for a megaconglomerate, is sent to his home town to modernize a brewery. By this film's end, his disgust for his company makes him shout the title which was named after a song. That's the kiss of death for any movie.

2968.   *Take Two* (1988, Hadar/TBJ, 100m, c). P Ronnie Hadar, D Peter Rowe, W Moshe Hadar, PH James Mathers, M Donald Hulette, ED Terry Chiappe.

LP Grant Goodeve (Barry/Frank), Robin Mattson (Susan Bentley), Frank Stallone (Ted Marvin), Nita Talbot (Betty Griffith), Warren Berlinger (Apartment Manager), Mickey Morton (Det. Stratton).

A wealthy man arranges for Nita Talbot to serve as a surrogate mother. She gives birth to twins but only presents her client with one of the boys, keeping the other to raise herself. Later when the lad has grown to be Grant Goodeve, Talbot tells him of his parentage and encourages him to collect his share of his deceased father's estate. When he presents this notion to his twin (also Goodeve), Bro wants nothing to do with it. The disinherited lad seduces his brother's abused wife Robin Mattson and the two plot to do away with the unwanted twin.

2969.   *Tales from the Gimli Hospital* (1989, Extra Large/Winnipeg Film Group, Canada, 72m, b&w). D,W, PH&ED Guy Maddin, AD Jeff Solylo.

LP Kyle McCulloch (Einar), Michael Gottli (Gunnar), Angela Heck (Snjofridur), Margaret-Anne MacLeod (Amma), Heather Neale (Fjola), Caroline Bonner (Elfa Egilsdottir).

This midnight movie creation of 31-year-old Guy Maddin seems headed for cult status. It is the story of the rivalry of two men, Kyle McCulloch and Michael Gottli, who share the same dirty hospital room in turn-of-the-century Icelandic village of Gimli. They are in quarantine because of an epidemic. They pass the time regaling each other with stories of their miserable lives which involved wife-killing and grave robbing. Their surreal relationship supposedly draws upon strange ancient Icelandic customs.

2970.   *Tales of the Third Dimension* (1985, Owensby/Shapiro, 90m, c). P Earl Owensby, D Thom McIntyre ("Young Blood"), Worth Keeter ("The Guardians"), Todd Durham (Visions of Sugar-Plum"), W McIntyre, Keeter & Durham, M Dee Barton.

LP "Young Blood" — Robert Bloodworth, Kate Hunter, Fran Taylor, Kevin Campbell. "The Guardians" — William Hicks, Terry Laughlin, Leon Rippy. "Visions of Sugar-Plum" — Helene Tryon, Kathy O'Toole, Neal Powell.

Earl Owensby, the king of the Southern drive-ins, presents three comedy-horror stories. In "Young Blood" a vampire couple have a problem child who is actually a werewolf. In "The Guardians," greedy grave robbers dig up more than they bargained for. In "Visions of Sugar-Plum," visiting grandmother takes on a murderous twist.

2971.   *Tale of Two Sisters* (1989, Vista Street, 89m, b&w/c). P Lawrence Bender & Randolf Turrow, D Adam Rifkin, W Improvised by the cast, PH John F.K. Parenteau, M Marc David Decker, ED King Wilder.

LP Valerie Breiman (Phil), Claudia Christian (Liz), Sidney Lassick (Dad), Dee Coppola (Mom), Tom Hodges (Butler/Auntie Sparkle), Jeff Conaway (Taxi driver), Pete Berg (Gardener).

Surreal images are used to illustrate the feelings of two adult sisters Valerie Breiman and Claudia Christian. They have a reunion after five years and recall their childhood and their mutual resentments.

2972.   *Talk Radio* (1988, Universal, 110m, c). P Edward R. Pressman, D Oliver Stone, W Eric Bogosian & Stone (based on the play created by Bogosian & Tad Savinar, and the book *Talked to Death: The Life and Murder of Alan Berg* by Stephen Singular), PH Robert Richardson, M Stewart Copeland, ED David Brenner, PD Bruno Rubeo.

LP Eric Bogosian (Barry Champlain), Alec Baldwin (Dan), Ellen Greene (Ellen), Leslie Hope (Laura), John C.

McGinley (Stu), John Pankow (Chuck Dietz), Michael Wincott (Kent), Zach Grenier (Sid Greenberg).

Recreating his stage role, Eric Bogosian is in the mold of a Morton Downey, Jr., talk show host. His abrasive and abusive style with callers provokes the crazies in his audience, leading to a violent conclusion.

2973. *Talking to Strangers* (1988, Baltimore Film Factory, 92m, c). P J.K. Eareckson, D&W Rob Tregenza, PH Tregenza.

LP Ken Gruz (Jesse), Dennis Jordan (Red Coat), Marvin Hunter (General), Caron Tate (Ms. Taylor), Brian Constantini (Angry Man), Bill Sanders (Manager), Henry Strozier (Priest), Richard Foster (Slick).

This independent film is about a pompous artist trying to find material for a movie by "talking to strangers." Nine continuous takes are arranged in random order, so the audience never really knows the director's intentions—assuming he had any.

2974. *Talking Walls* (1987, New World, 83m, c, aka *Motel Vacancy*). P Philip A. Waxman, D&W Stephen Verona (based on the novel *The Motel Tapes* by Mike McGrady), PH Scott Miller, M Richard Glasser, ED Jonathan Lawton, AD Rick Carter.

LP Stephen Shellen (Paul Barton), Marie Laurin (Jeanne), Barry Primus (Prof. Hirsh), Karen Lee Hopkins (Luna), Sybil Danning (Bathing Beauty), Don Davis (Don), Rae Davis (Rae), Hector Elias (Roberto).

Seeking the secret of romance, intimacy and lasting relationships, sociology student Stephen Shellen videotapes trysts held at the Total Media Hotel via one-way mirrors. His incessant use of a camera just about ruins his chance to have a meaningful relationship with beautiful French art student Marie Laurin.

2975. *The Tall Guy* (1989, Vestron, GB, 92m, c). P Paul Webster, D Mel Smith, W Richard Curtis, PH Adrian Biddle, M Peter Brewis, ED Dan Rae, PD Grant Hicks.

LP Jeff Goldblum (Dexter King), Emma Thompson (Kate Lemon), Rowan Atkinson (Ron Anderson), Emil Wolk (Cyprus Charlie), Geraldine James (Carmen), Kim Thomson (Cheryl), Susan Field (Dr. Freud), Hugh Thomas (Karabekian).

American actor Jeff Goldblum has been performing as straight man for comedian Rowan Atkinson for several years in London's West End. He falls for nurse Emma Thompson and about the time the two sexually connect, Atkinson fires Goldblum. The latter turns this defeat into triumph when he is cast in the title role in a musical version of *The Elephant Man.* Is any further comment called for?

2976. *Tango and Cash* (1989, Warner, 98m, c). P Jon Peters & Peter Guber, D Andrei Konchalovsky, W Randy Feldman, PH Donald E. Thorin, M Harold Faltermeyer, ED Stuart Baird, Hubert de la Bouillerie & Robert Ferretti, PD J. Michael Riva.

LP Sylvester Stallone (Tango), Kurt Russell (Cash), Teri Hatcher (Kiki), Jack Palance (Yves Perret), Brion James (Courier/Requin), James Hong (Quan), Marc Alaimo (Lopez).

Appearing as a macho Laurel and Hardy, Sylvester Stallone and Kurt Russell are Los Angeles narcotics officers. They are framed by drugpin Jack Palance and sent to prison. This buddy picture is merely a poor excuse to show off the muscles of the two stars, but it is their ignorance that is shown to greatest advantage. There's abundant mindless violence and gore, but little that can pass for plot or acting.

2977. *Tango Bar* (1989, Zaga-Beco/Manley, 90m, b&w). P Roberto Gandara and Juan Carlos Codazzi, D Marcos Zurinaga, W Jose Pablo Feinman, Codazzi & Zurinaga, PH Zurinaga, M Atilio Stampone, ED Pablo Mari, PD Maria Julia Bertotto.

LP Raul Julia (Ricardo), Valerie Lynch (Elena), Ruben Juarez (Antonio).

In this musical, Raul Julia is the foremost tango singer in the world. Reunited in Buenos Aires with Valerie Lynch and Ruben Juarez, the three stars of the nightspot called the Tango Bar form a romantic triangle in a bones-bare plot.

2978. *Tank* (1984, Universal, 113m, c). P Irwin Yablans, D Marvin J. Chomsky, W Dan Gordon, PH Don Birnkrant, M Lalo Schifrin, ED Donald R. Rode, PD Bill Kenney.

LP James Garner (Zack), Shirley Jones (LaDonna), C. Thomas Howell (Billy), Mark Herrier (Elliott), Sandy Ward (Gen. Hubik), Jenilee Harrison (Sarah), James Cromwell (Deputy Euclid), Dorian Harewood (Sgt. Tippet), G.D. Spradlin (Sheriff Buelton).

G.D. Spradlin is a delightful villain, worthy of resounding hisses and boos. He's the tyrannical sheriff of a small Southern town outside a military base where James Garner is the top sergeant. Garner's hobby is restoring tanks. He owns a working Sherman tank. He uses it to break his son C. Thomas Howell out of a harsh prison farm. Spradlin used Howell to punish Garner for coming to the assistance of prostitute Jenilee Harrison when Deputy James Cromwell began slapping her around. Garner, Howell and Harrison try to escape by tank to the next state where they hope to get a fair shake from the authorities. Spradlin and his rednecks are intent on preventing this from happening.

2979. *Tank Malling* (1989, Pointlane Films, GB, 108m, c). P Glen Murphy & Jamie Foreman, D James Marcus, W Marcus & Mick Southworth, PH Jason Lehel, M Rick Fenn & Nick Mason, ED Brian Peachey, PD Geoffrey Sharpe.

LP Ray Winstone (Tank Malling), Amanda Donohoe (Helen Searle), Peter Wyngarde (Robert Knights), Glen Murphy (Cashman), Jason Connery (Dunboyne), Marsha Hunt (Salena), Jamie Foreman (Danny), John Bett (Campbell Sinclaire).

In this clichéd and caricature-filled crime thriller, investigative reporter Ray Winstone has just been released from prison. He had been framed for perjury. He's approached by high-priced callgirl Amanda Donohoe who has some dirt on powerful national figure Peter Wyngarde. While he's busy gathering facts on the corruption in high places, he and Donohoe are being tracked by killer Glen Murphy, not too particular whom he kills.

2980. *Tanya's Island* (1980, Intl. Film Exchange, Canada, 82m, c). P Pierre Brousseau, D Alfred Sole, W Brousseau, PH Mark Irwin, M Jean Musy, ED Michael MacLaverty, AD Angelo Stea, SE Rick Baker & Rob Bottin.

LP D.D. Winters (Tanya), Richard Sargent (Lobo), Mariette Levesque (Kelly), Don McCleod (Blue).

In a Beauty and the Beast story, beautiful D.D. Winters, abused by her artist husband Richard Sargent, dreams about living on an island where she makes friends with an ape.

2981. *Tap* (1989, Tri-Star, 110m, c). P Gary Adelson & Richard Vane, D&W Nick Castle, Jr., PH David Gribble, M James Newton Howard, ED Patrick Kennedy, PD Patricia Norris.

LP Gregory Hines (Max), Suzzanne Douglas (Amy), Sammy Davis, Jr. (Little Mo), Savion Glover (Louis), Joe Morton (Nicky), Dick Anthony Williams (Francis), Sandman Sims (Sandman), Bunny Briggs (Bunny), Steve Condos (Steve), Jimmy Slyde (Slim), Pat Rico (Spats), Arthur Duncan (Arthur), Harold Nicholas (Harold).

Talented tap dancer Gregory Hines is just out of jail after serving a robbery stretch. The plot is merely an excuse to feature his superb dancing talent. In one memorable sequence he works with seven great old-time tap dancers, each showing what made them great. Fortunately for the audience the camera is drawn back and their routines are shown in full figures.

2982. *Tapeheads* (1988, Avenue, 97m, c). P Peter McCarthy, D Bill Fishman, W Fishman & McCarthy (based on a story by Fishman, McCarthy, Jim Herzfeld & Ryan Rowe), PH Bojan Bazelli, M Fishbone, ED Mondo Jenkins, PD Catherine Hardwicke.

LP John Cusack (Ivan Alexeev), Tim Robbins (Josh Tager), Mary Crosby (Samantha Gregory), Connie Stevens (June Tager), Clu Gulager (Norman Mart), Katy Boyer (Belinda Mart), Jessica Walter (Kay Mart), Sam Moore (Billy Diamond), Junior Walker (Lester Diamond), King Cotton (Roscoe).

In this spoof of the music business, John Cusack and Tim Robbins are fired from their jobs as security guards. They move into the video production business and get their hands on a video damaging to the career of politician Clu Gulager. Thugs are sent to recover the incriminating video.

2983. *Taps* (1981, 20th Century–Fox, 119m, c). P Stanley R. Jaffe & Howard B. Jaffe, D Harold Becker, W Darryl Ponicsan, Robert Mark Kamen & James Lineberger (based on the novel *Father Sky* by Devery Freeman), PH Owen Roizman, M Maurice Jarre, ED Maury Winetrobe, AD Stan Jolley & Alfred Sweeney.

LP George C. Scott (Gen. Harlan Bache), Timothy Hutton (Brian Moreland), Ronny Cox (Col. Kerby), Sean Penn (Alex Dwyer), Tom Cruise (David Shawn), Brendan Ward (Charlie Auden), Evan Handler (Edward West), John P. Navin, Jr. (Derek Mellott), Billy Van Zandt (Bug).

When the students of an elite military school learn that the trustees plan to close the school and sell the grounds to the developer of condominiums, they arm themselves and defend their turf. The result is a bloodbath.

2984. *Target* (1985, Warner, 117m, c). P Richard D. Zanuck & David Brown, D Arthur Penn, W Howard Berk & Don Petersen (based on a story by Leonard Stern), PH Jean Tournier & Robert Jessup, M Michael Small, ED Stephen A. Rotter & Richard P. Cirincione, AD Willy Holt & Richard James.

LP Gene Hackman (Walter Lloyd), Matt Dillon (Chris Lloyd), Gayle Hunnicutt (Donna Lloyd), Victoria Fyodorova (Lise), Ilona Grubel (Carla), Herbert Berghof (Schroeder), Josef Sommer (Taber), Guy Boyd (Clay), Richard Munch (The Colonel).

When his wife Gayle Hunnicutt is kidnapped in Paris, Dallas lumberyard owner Gene Hackman and son Matt Dillon fly to France to find her. When assassins try to kill Hackman, he must reveal to Dillon his past as a CIA agent. Hackman and Dillon team up to get mom back safely.

2985. *Tarzan, The Ape Man* (1981, MGM/United Artists, 112m, c). P Bo Derek, D John Derek, W Tom Rowe & Gary Goddard (based on the characters created by Edgar Rice Burroughs), PH John Derek, M Perry Botkin, ED James B. Ling, AD Alan Roderick-Jones.

LP Bo Derek (Jane), Richard Harris (Parker), John Phillip Law (Holt), Miles O'Keeffe (Tarzan), Akushula Selayah (Africa), Steven Strong (Ivory King), Maxime Philoe (Riano), Leonard Bailey (Feathers).

Anyone who believes that a movie which features a naked Bo Derek frolicking with the animals on a beach and in the jungle can't be all bad, hasn't seen this film. Everything about the movie is amateurish, and the acting is atrocious. But Miles O'Keeffe as the Ape Man is an embarrassment to the simian parents who raised him.

2986. *The Taste of Hemlock* (1989, Intl. Artists, GB, 90m, c). P Eric Tynan Young, D Geoffrey Darwin, W Young (based on the play *The Astrakhan Coat* by Pauline Macaulay), PH Roger Tonry, M Young, ED Henry Te.

LP Randy Harrington (Claud Thatch), Eric Tynan Young (James Hattan), Anne Elizabeth Ramsey (Barbara), Reed Armstrong (Barry), David McKnight (Lt. Jordan), Barbara Pilavin (Mrs. Dobrowski), Shea Young (Sgt. Narducci).

The plot seems to be one large shaggy dog story made at the expense of both Randy Harrington, who buys an expensive coat from manipulative Eric Tynan Young, even though he can't afford it, and the audience.

2987. *A Taste of Sin* (1983, New West/Ambassador, 84m, c). P&D Ulli Lommel, W Lommel, John P. Marsh & Ron Norman, PH Lommel, Jochen Breitenstein, Jon Kranhouse, Dave Sperling & Jurg Walthers, M Joel Goldsmith, ED Terrell Tannen.

LP Suzanna Love (Olivia), Robert Walker (Michael Grant), Jeff Winchester (Richard), Bibbe Hansen (Mother), Amy Robinson (Olivia at age 6), Nicholas Love (G.I.), Ulli Lommel (Detective).

As a child Suzanna Love witnessed the

murder of her prostitute mother by a G.I. As an adult, she hears her mother's voice from the grave and becomes a killer, dressed as a hooker, hitting the pavement on London Bridge.

2988. *Tattoo* (1981, 20th Century–Fox, 103m, c). P Joseph E. Levine & Richard P. Levine, D Bob Brooks, W Joyce Bunuel (based on a story by Brooks), PH Arthur Ornitz & Michael Seresin, M Barry DeVorzon, ED Thom Noble, PD Stuart Wurtzel.

LP Bruce Dern (Karl Kinski), Maud Adams (Maddy), Leonard Frey (Halsey), Rikke Borge (Sandra), John Getz (Buddy), Peter Iacangelo (Dubin), Alan Leach (Customer), Cynthia Nixon (Cindy), Trish Doolin (Cheryl).

Maniacal tattoo artist Bruce Dern almost jumps out of his skin with his obsession of making Adams his ultimate canvas.

2989. *Teachers* (1984, MGM/United Artists, 106m, c). P Aaron Russo, D Arthur Hiller, W W.R. McKinney (based on a story by A. Russo & Irwin Russo), PH David M. Walsh, ED Don Zimmerman, MD Sandy Gibson, PD Richard MacDonald.

LP Nick Nolte (Alex), JoBeth Williams (Lisa), Judd Hirsch (Roger), Ralph Macchio (Eddie), Allen Garfield (Rosenberg), Lee Grant (Dr. Burke), Richard Mulligan (Herbert), Royal Dano (Ditto), William Schallert (Horn), Art Metrano (Troy), Laura Dern (Diane), Crispin Glover (Danny), Morgan Freeman (Lewis).

For anyone who has ever taught at the high school level, this film is a chilling reminder of all the things that are wrong with American public schools. The students aren't much interested in learning, the administration cares more for appearances than education and many of the teachers are an incompetent, frightened lot. The best teacher shown in the film is Richard Mulligan, an escapee from a looney bin who is mistaken for a substitute teacher and really turns students on to American history before he is taken away with a net. Royal Dano has developed a technique of conducting his classes which does not require any interaction with his students. It's so effective that one day he dies at his desk during the first period and no one notices all day. Nick Nolte is the obligatory caring pedagogue and Ralph Macchio is the student he wishes to salvage when he's not otherwise occupied bedding reporter JoBeth Williams.

2990. *Teen Mothers* (1980, Cannon, 90m, c, aka *Seed of Innocence*). P Yoram Globus, D Boaz Davidson, W Stuart Krieger, PH Adam Greenberg, M Shalom Chanach, ED Jon Koslowsky, PD Brent Swift.

LP Timothy Wead (Danny), Mary Cannon (Alice), Vincent Schiavelli (Leo), T.K. Carter (Captain), Azizi Johari (Denise), Julianna McCarthy (Nadine), Sonja O. Menor (Teacher), Mary Ellen O'Neill (Sister Mary).

Teenage couple Timothy Wead and Mary Cannon (she's pregnant) run away to New York City and find it an unfriendly place.

2991. *Teen Vamp* (1989, New World, 89m, c). P Jim McCullough, D&W Samuel Bradford, PH Richard Mann, M Robert Sprayberry, ED Uncredited.

LP Clu Gulager (Reverend), Karen Carlson (Mom), Angie Brown (Connie), Beau Bishop (Murphy), Mike Lane, Evans Dietz, Edd Anderson, Jude Gerard.

Nerdish Beau Bishop is turned into a hip, leather-jacketed, 50s cool-cat after he's bitten in the neck by a whore at a road house.

2992. *Teen Witch* (1989, TransWorld Ent., 105m, c). P Alana Lambros, Rafael Eisenman, D Dorian Walker, W Robin Menkin & Vernon Zimmerman, PH Marc Reshovsky, M Richard Elliot, ED Natan Zahavi, PD Stephen Rice.

LP Robyn Lively (Louise Miller), Zelda Rubinstein (Madame Serena), Dan Gauthier (Brad), Joshua Miller (Richie), Caren Kaye (Margaret), Dick Sargent (Frank), Lisa Fuller (Randa), Shelley Berman (Mr. Weaver).

In this comedy-fantasy, music and dance are incorporated into a contemporary fable about designated loser Robyn Lively, a member of the "outcrowd" at her school. She runs into fortuneteller Zelda Rubinstein, who predicts Lively will turn into a witch before her

16th birthday. She does and her attempts at "turn-about-is-fair-play" are moderately funny.

2993. *Teen Wolf* (1985, Atlantic, 91m, c). P Mark Levinson, Scott Rosenfelt & George Perkins, D Rod Daniel, W Joseph Loeb III & Matthew Weisman, PH Tim Suhrstedt, M Miles Goodman, ED Lois Freeman-Fox, AD Chester Kaczenski.

LP Michael J. Fox (Scott Howard), James Hampton (Harold Howard), Susan Ursitti (Lisa "Boof" Marconi), Jerry Levine (Rupert "Stiles" Stilinsky), James MacKrell (Russell Thorne), Lorie Griffin (Pamela Wells), Mark Arnold (Mick McAllister).

Life as a teenager is the pits for Michael J. Fox. The high school basketball team for which the short little actor plays is putrid. He can't get to first base with beauty Lorie Griffin and he can't shake persistent Susan Ursitti. Things improve when he discovers that he's a werewolf. His howl is worse than his bite, however.

2994. *Teen Wolf Too* (1987, Atlantic, 95m, c). P Kent Bateman, D Christopher Leitch, W R. Timothy Kring (based on a story by Joseph Loeb, III & Matthew Wcisman), PH Jules Brenner, M Mark Goldenberg, ED Steven Polivka, Kim Secrist, Harvey Rosenstock & Raja Gosnell.

LP Jason Bateman (Todd Howard), Kim Darby (Prof. Brooks), John Astin (Dean Dunn), Paul Sand (Coach Finstock), James Hampton (Uncle Howard), Mark Holton (Chubby), Estee Chandler (Nicki), Robert Neary (Gustavson).

Jason Bateman, the heartthrob star of television's "Valerie," plays the cousin of Michael J. Fox, who had the title role in the original film about a teenage werewolf. Bateman also has lycanthrophy ability, but this film didn't pull in the big bucks at the box office as did the Fox number.

2995. *The Telephone* (1988, New World, 82m, c). P Robert Katz & Moctesuma Esparza, D Rip Torn, W Harry Nilsson & Terry Southern, PH David Claessen, M Christopher Young, ED Sandra Adair, AD Jim Pohl.

LP Whoopi Goldberg (Vashti Blue), Severn Darden (Max), Amy Wright (Honey Boxe/Irate Neighbor), Elliott Gould (Rodney), John Heard (Telephone Man), Ronald J. Stallings (Saxaphone Player).

The movie serves as a vehicle for Whoopi Goldberg to do a variety of her monologs. She appears as an out-of-work actress with no money to pay her bills. She vents her anger on her telephone, employing various accents and personas.

2996. *Tell Me a Riddle* (1980, Filmways, 90m, c). P Mindy Affrime, Rachel Lyon & Susan O'Connell, D Lee Grant, W Joyce Eliason & Alev Lytle (based on the novella by Tillie Olsen), PH Fred Murphy, M Sheldon Shkolnik, ED Suzanne Pettit, PD Patrizia von Brandenstein.

LP Melvyn Douglas (David), Lila Kedrova (Eva), Brooke Adams (Jeannie), Lili Valenty (Mrs. Mays), Dolores Dorn (Vivi), Bob Elross (Sammy), Jon Harris (Mathew), Zalman King (Paul), Winifred Mann (Hannah).

After years of quarreling, elderly Melvyn Douglas and his dying wife of 40 years Lila Kedrova rediscover the love they once had.

2997. *Tempest* (1982, Columbia, 140m, c). P&D Paul Mazursky, W Mazursky & Leon Capetanos (based on the play by William Shakespeare), PH Donald McAlpine, M Stomu Yamashta, ED Donn Cambern, PD Pato Guzman.

LP John Cassavetes (Phillip), Gena Rowlands (Antonia), Susan Sarandon (Aretha), Vittorio Gassman (Alonzo), Raul Julia (Kalibanos), Molly Ringwald (Miranda), Sam Robards (Freddy), Paul Stewart (Phillip's Father), Jackie Gayle (Trinc), Anthony Holland (Sebastian).

In this contemporary version of Shakespeare's *The Tempest,* John Cassavetes is an architect in the mold of Gary Cooper in *The Fountainhead.* He leaves his wife Gena Rowlands, for a Greek island, taking along Susan Sarandon and his teenage daughter Molly Ringwald. Cassavetes and Sarandon have not consummated their affair. Raul Julia is the Caliban-like character. The film makes a grand effort and Cassavetes gives a peak performance, but the result is a valiant failure.

Temptation Blues see Nowhere to Run (1989)

2998. *Ten Little Indians* (1989, Cannon, 98m, c). P Harry Alan Towers, D Alan Birkinshaw, W Jackson Hunsicker & Gerry O'Hara (based on Agatha Christie's play), PH Arthur Lavia, M George C. Clinton, ED Penelope Shaw, PD Roger Orpen.

LP Donald Pleasence (Justice Wargrave), Frank Stallone (Capt. Lombard), Sarah Maur Thorp (Vera Claythorne), Herbert Lom (Gen. Romensky), Brenda Vaccaro (Marion Marshall), Warren Berlinger (Blore), Yehuda Efroni (Dr. Hans Werner), Paul L. Smith (Elmo Rodgers), Moira Lister (Ethel Rodgers), Neil McCarthy (Anthony Mardsen).

This new version of Agatha Christie's masterful mystery story is even worse than the 1965 and the 1975 versions and should not even be mentioned in the same breath with the 1945 classic directed by Rene Clair. Set in the 30s, ten disparate individuals are summoned to an African safari party where they are dispatched one-by-one by their unseen host using means corresponding to the way the little Indians died in the nursery rhyme "Ten Little Indians."

2999. *10 to Midnight* (1983, Cannon, 101m, c). P Pancho Kohner & Lance Hool, D J. Lee Thompson, W William Roberts, PH Adam Greenberg, M Robert O. Ragland, ED Peter Lee Thompson, AD Jim Freiburger.

LP Charles Bronson (Leo Kessler), Lisa Eilbacher (Laurie Kessler), Andrew Stevens (Paul McAnn), Gene Davis (Warren Stacy), Geoffrey Lewis (Dave Dante), Wilford Brimley (Capt. Malone), Robert Lyons (Nathan Zager).

In this thoroughly unpleasant movie, Charles Bronson is a cop who makes his own rules in dealing with psychopathic killer Gene Davis. The latter wearing only his birthday suit preys on young women, including Bronson's daughter Lisa Eilbacher. The film finds many ways to offend all but bloody-thirsty voyeurs.

3000. *10 Violent Women* (1982, New American/Aquarius, 95m, c). P&D Ted V. Mikels, W Mikels & James Gordon White, PH Yuval Shousterman, M Nich-

olas Carras, ED Mikels, PD Mike Mc-Clusky.

LP Sherri Vernon (Samantha), Dixie Lauren (Maggie), Georgia Morgan (Bri Terry), Jane Farnsworth (Madge), Ted V. Mikels (Leo), Anne Gaybis (Vickie), Melodie Bell, Christina de Cattani.

Bored with their jobs, ten lovely ladies embark on a million dollar jewel heist. They end up in a women's prison where the guards subject them to cruel indignities.

3001. *Tender Mercies*† (1983, Universal, 89m, c). P Philip S. Hobel, Mary-Ann Hobel, Horton Foote & Robert Duvall, D Bruce Beresford†, W Horton Foote*, PH Russell Boyd, M George Dreyfus, ED William Anderson, AD Jeannine Oppewall, SONG "Over You" by Bobby Hart & Austin Roberts†.

LP Robert Duvall* (Mac Sledge), Tess Harper (Rosa Lee), Betty Buckley (Dixie), Wilford Brimley (Harry), Ellen Barkin (Sue Anne), Allan Hubbard (Sonny), Lenny Von Dohlen (Robert).

Ex-alcoholic country-and-western singer Robert Duvall attempts a comeback after taking a job with widow Tess Harper, whom he marries. Lurking in the background is Duvall's ex-wife Betty Buckley, herself a country-and-western singer. Finally Duvall realizes that show business is not for him and that true happiness can be found with Harper and her young son Allan Hubbard.

3002. *Tennessee Nights* (1989, Nelson, US/Swiss, 95m, c). P Bernard Lang & Peter-Christian Fueter, D Nicolas Gessner, W Gessner & Laird Koenig (based on *Minnie* by Hans Werner Kettenbach), PH Pio Corradi, M Gabriel Yared, ED Marie-Therese Boiche.

LP Julian Sands (Wolfgang Leighton), Stacey Dash (Minnie), Ed Lauter, Ned Beatty, Denise Crosby, Brian McNamara, Rod Steiger.

The chaotic story sees uptight British lawyer Julian Sands, who specializes in music contracts, visiting Nashville and taking a side trip into the world of Kafka.

3003. *Tequila Sunrise* (1988, Warner, 116m, c). P Thom Mount, D Robert Towne, W Towne, PH Conrad L. Hall†, M Dave Grusin, ED Claire Simpson, PD Richard Sylbert.

LP Mel Gibson (Dale McKussic), Kurt Russell (Lt. Nick Frescia), Michelle Pfeiffer (Jo Ann Vallenari), Raul Julia (Escalante), J.T. Walsh (Maguire), Arliss Howard (Gregg Lindroff), Ann Magnuson (Shaleen).

High school friends Mel Gibson, a retired cocaine dealer, and Kurt Russell, a L.A. narcotics cop, both fall for Michelle Pfeiffer, proprietor of a trendy restaurant. That's how it seems, but maybe Russell is just using the lovely lady to implicate his old buddy in a major drug deal.

3004. Terminal Choice (1985, Magder/Almi, Canada, 95m, c). P Gary Magder, D Sheldon Larry, W Neal Bell (based on a story by Peter Lawrence), PH Zale Magder, M Brian Bennett, ED Murray Magder, PD David Jaquest.

LP Joe Spano (Dr. Frank Holt), Diane Venora (Anna Lang), David McCallum (Dr. Dodson), Robert Joy (Dr. Harvey Rimmer), Don Francks (Chauncey Rand), Nicholas Campbell (Henderson), Ellen Barkin (Mary O'Connor).

A modern computer-managed hospital has patients dying at an alarming rate. Is it human or computer error? Accident or a sinister plot?

3005. Terminal Entry (1988, TBA/International, 95m, c). P Sharyon Reis Cobe, D John Kincade, W David Mickey Evans & Mark Sobel (based on a story by Sobel), PH James L. Carter, M Gene Hobson, ED Dean Goodhill, AD Alexandra Kicenik.

LP Edward Albert (Capt. Danny Jackson), Kabir Bedi (Terrorist Commander), Heidi Helmer (Chris), Mazhar Khan (Abdul), Yaphet Kotto (Styles), Patrick Laborteaux (Bob), Yvette Nipar (Tina), Kavi Raz (Mahaddi), Paul Smith (Stewart).

Teenage computer hackers break into the Terminal Entry program and mistake it for an interactive terrorist game. Actually the program is an information source for terrorists planning to assassinate the president.

Terminal Exposure see *Double Exposure*

3006. The Terminator (1984, Orion, 108m, c). P Gale Anne Hurd, D James Cameron, W Cameron, Hurd & William Wisher, Jr., PH Adam Greenberg, M Brad Fiedel, ED Mark Goldblatt, AD George Costello.

LP Arnold Schwarzenegger (Terminator), Michael Biehn (Kyle Reese), Linda Hamilton (Sarah Connor), Paul Winfield (Traxler), Lance Henriksen (Vukovich), Rick Rossovich (Matt), Bess Motta (Ginger).

In this sf thriller Arnold Schwarzenegger is a death-dealing android sent back from the 21st century to assassinate Linda Hamilton. But he must contend with Michael Biehn, also from the future, hot on his trail.

3007. Termini Station (1989, Astral Bellevue Pathe, Canada, 108m, c). P&D Allan King, W Colleen Murphy, PH Brian Hebb, M Mychall Dama, ED Gordon McClellan, PD Lillian Sarafinchan.

LP Colleen Dewhurst (Molly Dushane), Megan Follows (Micheline), Gordon Clapp (Harvey Dushane), Norma Dell'Agnese (Val), Debra McGrath, Leon Pownall.

Boozing widow Colleen Dewhurst lives with her businessman son Gordon Clapp and his wife. Her daughter Megan Follows is a hooker in a small Ontario mining town. Everyone's problems stem from a longtime affair Dewhurst had with a businessman who is the true father of her daughter.

3008. Terms of Endearment* (1983, Paramount, 130m, c). P James L. Brooks, Penney Finkelman & Martin Jurow, D Brooks*, W Brooks* (based on the novel by Larry McMurtry), PH Andrzej Bartkowiak, M Michael Gore†, ED Richard Marks†, PD Polly Platt, AD/SD Platt, Harold Michelson, Tom Pedigo & Anthony Mondell†, SOUND Donald O. Mitchell, Rick Kline, Kevin O'Connell & Jim Alexander†.

LP Debra Winger† (Emma Horton), Shirley MacLaine* (Aurora Greenway), Jack Nicholson* (Garrett Breedlove), Danny DeVito (Vernon Dahlart), Jeff Daniels (Flap Horton), John Lithgow† (Sam Burns), Betty King (Rosie), Lisa Hart Carroll (Patsy Clark), Huckleberry Fox (Toddy), Megan Morris (Melanie), Troy Bishop (Tommy).

In a five-handkerchief weeper, eccentric Shirley MacLaine fends off suitors and interferes with her daughter Debra Winger's life and marriage. Winger develops an incurable cancer and takes about a reel to die, giving all the performers the opportunity to show off their dramatic talents.

Terror Eyes see *Night School*

The Terror Factor see *Scared to Death*

Terror in the Forest see *The Forest*

3009. *Terror Squad* (1988, Matterhorn/Manson, 92m, c). P&D Peter Maris, W Chuck Rose (based on a story by Mark Verheiden), PH Peter Jensen, M Chuck Cirino, ED Jack Tucker.

LP Chuck Connors (Chief Rawlings), Brodie Greer (Capt. Steiner), Bill Calvert (Johnny), Kerry Brennan (Jennifer), Kavi Raz (Yassir), Joseph Nasser (Gamel), Budge Threlkeld (Mr. Nero), Dennis Moynahan (Norman).

When Libyan terrorists attack a nuclear power plant in Kokomo, Indiana, sheriff Chuck Connors has his hands full.

3010. *Terror Train* (1980, 20th Century–Fox, Canada, 97m, c, aka *Train of Terror*). P Harold Greenberg, D Roger Spottiswoode, W T.Y. Drake, PH John Alcott, Rene Verzier, Peter Benison & Al Smith, M John Mills-Cockell, ED Anne Henderson, PD Glenn Bydwell.

LP Ben Johnson (Carne), Jamie Lee Curtis (Alana), Hart Bochner (Doc), David Copperfield (The Magician), Derek MacKinnon (Kenny Hampson), Sandee Currie (Mitchy), Timothy Webber (Mo), Anthony Sherwood (Jackson).

Revelers at a wild party aboard a train are killed one-by-one by a mysterious psychotic.

3011. *The Terror Within* (1989, Concorde, 86m, c). P Roger Corman, D Thierry Notz, W Thomas M. Cleaver, PH Ronn Schmidt, M Rick Conrad, ED Brent Schoenfeld, PD Kathleen B. Cooper.

LP George Kennedy (Hal), Andrew Stevens (David), Starr Andreeff (Sue), Terri Treas (Linda), John LaFayette (Andre), Tommy Hinchley (Neil), Yvonne Saa (Karen), Roren Sumner (Gargoyle).

Almost the entire human race has been killed by the plague. A group of scientists in the underground Mojave Lab for Disease Control are running out of food and must constantly fight off marauding mutants topside. They find a pregnant girl whose child, a real little monster, bursts from her chest and terrorizes everyone.

3012. *Terrorvision* (1986, Empire Pictures, 82m, c). P Albert Band, D&W Ted Nicolaou, PH Romano Albani, M Richard Band, ED Tom Meshelski, PD Giovanni Natalucci.

LP Diane Franklin (Suzy), Gerrit Graham (Stanley), Mary Woronov (Raquel), Chad Allen (Sherman), Jonathan Gries (O.D.), Jennifer Richards (Medusa), Alejandro Rey (Spiro), Bert Remsen (Gramps).

In this wacky sf/horror flick, a high-tech TV satellite turns into a real-life terror.

3013. *The Terry Fox Story* (1983, 20th Century–Fox, Canada, 98m, c). P Robert Cooper, D Ralph L. Thomas, W Edward Hume (based on a story by John & Rose Kastner), PH Richard Ciupka, M Bill Conti, ED Ron Wisman, AD Gavin Mitchell.

LP Robert Duvall (Bill Vigars), Eric Fryer (Terry Fox), Michael Zelniker (Alward), Chris Makepeace (Darrell Fox), Rosalind Chao (Rika), Elva Mai Hoover (Betty Fox), Frank Adamson (Rolly Fox), Marie McCann (Judith Fox).

Unfortunately the filming of this true story of a young Canadian who loses his leg to cancer, and runs across the country to raise money for research before he dies, is not engrossing drama.

3014. *Tess*† (1980, Columbia, France/GB, 170m, c). P Claude Berri, D Roman Polanski†, W Polanski, Gerard Brach & John Brownjohn (based on the novel *Tess of the d'Urbervilles* by Thomas Hardy), PH Geoffrey Unsworth & Ghislain Cloquet*, M Philippe Sarde†, ED Alastair McIntyre & Tom Priestley, PD Pierre Guffroy*, SD Jack Stephens*, COS Anthony Powell*.

LP Nastassja Kinski (Tess Durbeyfield), Leigh Lawson (Alec d'Urberville), Peter Firth (Angel Clare), John Collin

(John Durbeyfield), David Markham (Rev. Mr. Clare), Rosemary Martin (Mrs. Durbeyfield), Richard Pearson (Vicar of Marlott), Carolyn Pickles (Marian).

Peasant girl Nastassja Kinski attempts to prove her noble heritage but is betrayed by Leigh Lawson, a cocky young nobleman, who seduces her and sends her home pregnant. The baby dies and Kinski takes work on a dairy farm where she attracts the attention of Peter Firth. He marries her, but leaves her on their wedding night, unable to accept her past. She returns to Lawson, but Firth soon changes his mind and comes for her. Kinski lashes out at Lawson and fatally stabs him. She and Firth spend a final idyllic evening together before she is arrested and hanged for her crime.

A Test of Love see Annie's Coming Out

3015. Testament (1983, Paramount, 90m, c). P Jonathan Bernstein & Lynne Littman, D Littman, W John Sacret Young (based on the story *The Last Testament* by Carol Amen), PH Steven Poster, M James Horner, ED Suzanne Pettit, PD David Nichols.

LP Jane Alexander† (Carol Wetherly), William Devane (Tom Wetherly), Ross Harris (Brad Wetherly), Roxana Zal (Mary Liz Wetherly), Lukas Haas (Scottie Wetherly), Philip Anglim (Hollis), Lilia Skala (Fania), Leon Ames (Henry Abhart), Lurene Tuttle (Rosemary Abhart), Rebecca DeMornay (Cathy Pitkin), Kevin Costner (Phil Pitkin).

The film opens on a typical American family living in Hamlin, California. A nuclear bomb is dropped, the government issues reassuring statements, but then people begin to die. Jane Alexander's family, now minus father William Devane, who one assumes is dead because he never reappears after the bomb is dropped, relies on memories to get them through the horror.

3016. Testimony (1988, GB, 157m, c/ b&w). P,D,ED&PD Tony Palmer, W David Rudkin & Palmer (based on Memoirs of Dimitri Shostakovich as edited by Solomon Volkov), PH Nic Knowland.

LP Ben Kingsley (Dimitri Shostako-vich), Terence Rigby (Josef Stalin), Ronald Pickup (Tukhachevsky), John Shrapnel (Andrei Zhdanov), Sherry Baines (Nina Shostakovich), Robert Stephens (Meyerhold), Murray Melvin (Film Editor), Robert Urquhart (Journalist).

Although Ben Kingsley is admirable as composer Dimitri Shostakovich, this overly long biopic is a banal production. As the film concentrates on the political problems of an artist in the Soviet Union, the pretentious film makes little use of the master's music.

3017. Tex (1982, Buena Vista, 103m, c). P Tim Zinnemann, D Tim Hunter, W Hunter & Charlie Haas (based on the novel by S.E. Hinton), PH Ric Waite, M Pino Donaggio, ED Howard Smith, PD Jack T. Collis.

LP Matt Dillon (Tex McCormick), Jim Metzler (Mason McCormick), Meg Tilly (Jamie Collins), Bill McKinney (Pop McCormick), Frances Lee McCain (Mrs. Johnson), Ben Johnson (Cole Collins), Emilio Estevez (Johnny Collins), Zeljko Ivanek (Hitchhiker).

Disney treats audiences to a realistic look at adolescent growing pains in this story of young motherless brothers Matt Dillon and Jim Metzler, living by themselves in the Southwest when their father takes off. They must learn to take responsibility for their lives and settle their differences.

3018. The Texas Chainsaw Massacre Part 2 (1986, Cannon, 95m, c). P Menahem Golan & Yoram Globus, D Tobe Hooper, W L.M. Kit Carson, PH Richard Kooris, M Hooper & Jerry Lambert, ED Alain Jakybowicz, PD Cary White, SE Tom Savini.

LP Dennis Hopper (Lt. "Lefty" Enright), Caroline Williams (Vanita "Stretch" Brock), Bill Johnson (Leatherface), Jim Siedow (Cook/Drayton Sawyer), Bill Moseley (Chop-Top), Lou Perry (L.G. McPeters).

"Leatherface" returns in this sequel to the 1974 shocker, with his powerful and deadly hand tool. The blood splatters in all directions as the screaming starts up again.

Texas Chainsaw Massacre 3 see Leather-face: Texas Chainsaw 3

3019. *Texas Lightning* (1981, Film Ventures, 93m, c). P Jim Sotos, D&W Gary Graver.

LP Cameron Mitchell, Channing Mitchell, Maureen McCormick, Peter Jason, Danone Camden, J.L. Clark.

Father and son truck drivers spend their free time in a honky-tonk cowboy bar.

3020. *That Championship Season* (1982, Cannon, 110m, c). P Menahem Golan & Yoram Globus, D&W Jason Miller (based on his play), PH John Bailey, M Bill Conti, ED Richard Halsey, PD Ward Preston.

LP Bruce Dern (George Sitkowski), Stacy Keach (James Daley), Robert Mitchum (Coach Delaney), Martin Sheen (Tom Daley), Paul Sorvino (Phil Romano), Arthur Franz (Macken), Michael Bernosky (Jacks), James M. Langan (Cooney).

This Pulitzer Prize–winning play makes a boring movie. Basketball coach Robert Mitchum and four of his five former players from a championship team 20 years earlier get together for a reunion. At first they are happy to be together, but a few drinks begin to reveal the envy, bitterness and anger they really feel for each other. But it's all talk, talk, talk. Slam dunk this one.

3021. *That Summer of White Roses* (1989, Amy Intl./Jadran, GB/Yugo., 103m, c). P Simon MacCorkindale & Mike Mihalic, D Rajko Grlic, W Grlic, MacCorkindale & Borislav Pekic (based on Pekic's book *Defense and the Last Days*), PH Tomislav Pinter, M Brane Zivkovic, Junior Campbell & Mike O'Donnell, ED Damir F. German.

LP Tom Conti (Andrija Gavrilovic), Susan George (Ana), Rod Steiger (Martin), Nitzan Sharron (Danny), Alun Armstrong (Zemba), John Gill (Doctor), John Sharp (Mayor).

Simpleminded Yugoslavian lifeguard Tom Conti can't seem to do anything right when he tries to do right. In the last year of the war he hides Susan George and her son, refugees from the Germans. He plans to marry her to protect her because she has no papers. In the meantime he rescues the one and only person ever in danger of drowning in his peaceful lake.

It turns out to be the new German commandant of the area. The Germans treat Conti as a hero; the rest of the town folk consider him a collaborator.

3022. *That Was Then...This Is Now* (1985, Paramount, 102m, c). P Gary R. Lindberg & John M. Ondov, D Christopher Cain, W Emilio Estevez (based on the novel by S.E. Hinton), PH Juan Ruiz Anchia, M Keith Olsen & Bill Cuomo, ED Ken Johnson, AD Chester Kaczenski.

LP Emilio Estevez (Mark Jennings), Craig Sheffer (Byron Douglas), Kim Delaney (Cathy Carlson), Jill Schoelen (Angela Shepard), Barbara Babcock (Mrs. Douglas), Frank Howard (M&M Carlson), Frank McCarthy (Mr. Carlson), Larry B. Scott (Terry Jones), Morgan Freeman (Charlie Woods).

Emilio Estevez and Craig Sheffer are raised as brothers by the latter's widowed mother Barbara Babcock. They react differently to the challenges of growing up. Sheffer becomes responsible, determined to make something of himself. Estevez deals in drugs and steals cars.

3023. *That's Dancing* (1985, MGM, 105m, c/b&w). P David Niven, Jr. & Jack Haley, Jr., D&W Jack Haley, Jr., ADDITIONAL PH Andrew Laszlo & Paul Lohmann, ED Bud Friedgen & Michael J. Sheridan, M Henry Mancini.

LP Mikhail Baryshnikov, Ray Bolger, Sammy Davis, Jr., Gene Kelly, Liza Minnelli.

This dance compilation film features scenes from many movies starring dancing greats such as Fred Astaire, Mikhail Baryshnikov, Ray Bolger, James Cagney, Cyd Charisse, Dan Dailey, Sammy Davis, Jr., Isadora Duncan, Dame Margot Fonteyn, Bob Fosse, Carol Haney, Michael Jackson, Ruby Keeler, Gene Kelly, Paula Kelly, Michael Kidd, Shirley MacLaine, Ann Miller, The Nicholas Brothers, Rudolf Nureyev, Donald O'Connor, Anna Pavlova, Eleanor Powell, Jane Powell, Debbie Reynolds, Chita Rivera, Bill "Bojangles" Robinson, Ginger Rogers, Shirley Temple, John Travolta & Vera-Ellen.

That's Life   see   Blake Edward's That's Life

3024. *That's My Baby* (1985, Gemini, Canada, 98m, c). P Edie Yolles, D&W Jon Bradshaw & Yolles, PH W.W. Reeve, M Eric N. Robertson, ED Stephen Withrow.

LP Timothy Webber (Louis), Sonja Smits (Suzanne), Joann McIntyre (Sugar), Lenore Zann (Sally), Derek McGrath (Bob Morgan).

Career-woman Sonja Smits rejects all of Timothy Weber's urgings for paternity until he agrees to become a house-husband and free her from all domestic chores.

3025. *There Goes the Bride* (1980, Vanguard, GB, 88m, c). P Ray Cooney & Martin Schute, D Terence Marcel, W Cooney, Marcel & John Chapman (based on the play by Cooney), PH James Devis, M Harry Robinson, ED Alan Jones, PD Peter Mullins.

LP Tom Smothers (Timothy Westerby), Twiggy (Polly), Martin Balsam (Mr. Babcock), Sylvia Syms (Ursula Westerby), Michael Whitney (Bill Shorter), Geoffrey Sumner (Gerald Drimond), Graham Stark (Rossi), Hermione Baddeley (Daphne Drimond), Jim Backus (Mr. Perkins), Toria Fuller (Judy Westerby).

Since this film is one of the least funny comedies ever thrust onto unsuspecting audiences, one must conclude that either Dickie Smothers had all the talent or the film's writers are incredibly untalented hacks. Tommy Smothers is the father of bride-to-be Toria Fuller. The proceedings are interrupted by Twiggy, the ghost of a 20s model, who only Tommy can see.

3026. *They All Laughed* (1981, 20th Century–Fox/United Artists, 115m, c). P George Morfogen & Blaine Novak, D&W Peter Bogdanovich, PH Robby Muller, M Douglas Dilge, ED Scott Vickrey, AD Kert Lundell.

LP Audrey Hepburn (Angela Niotes), Ben Gazzara (John Russo), John Ritter (Charles Rutledge), Colleen Camp (Christy Miller), Patti Hansen (Deborah "Sam" Wilson), Dorothy Stratten (Dolores Martin), George Morfogen (Leon Leondopolous), Blaine Novak (Arthur Brodsky).

Three agency detectives, Ben Gazarra, John Ritter and Blaine Novak, fall in and out of love with the three women, Audrey Hepburn, Patti Hansen and Dorothy Stratten, they have been hired to trail. The film is good enough to be remembered for more than being Stratten's last picture—she was murdered by her husband after its completion (possibly because of her affair with director Peter Bogdanovich while this movie was in production).

3027. *They Call Me Bruce* (1980, Film Ventures, 88m, c, aka *A Fistful of Chopsticks*). P&D Elliott Hong, W Hong, David Randolph, Johnny Yune & Tim Clawson, PH Robert Roth, M Tommy Vig.

LP Johnny Yune (Bruce), Ralph Mauro (Freddy), Pam Huntington (Anita), Margaux Hemingway (Karmen), Tony Brande (Boss of Bosses), Bill Capizzi (Lil Pete), Martin Azarow (Big Al).

Korean comic Johnny Yune is mistaken for Bruce Lee, giving him the opportunity to emulate his martial arts hero. There are some funny bits in this story of an Oriental working as an Italian chef when he gets involved with the mob.

3028. *They Live* (1988, Universal, 93m, c). P Larry Franco, D John Carpenter, W Frank Armitage [Carpenter] (based on the short story "Eight O'Clock in the Morning" by Ray Nelson), PH Gary B. Kibbe, M Carpenter & Alan Howarth, ED Frank E. Jimenez, AD William J. Durrell, Jr.

LP Roddy Piper (John Nada), Keith David (Frank), Meg Foster (Holly), George "Buck" Flower (Drifter), Peter Jason (Gilbert), Raymond St. Jacques (Street Preacher), Jason Robards, III (Family Man), John Lawrence (Bearded Man).

When construction worker Roddy Piper comes into possession of a special pair of sunglasses, they reveal ordinary looking people to be aliens.

3029. *They Still Call Me Bruce* (1987, Shapiro, 91m, c). P,C&W Johnny Yune & James Orr, PH R. Michael Delahoussaye, M Morton Stevens, ED Roy Watts, AD Jeff McManus.

LP Johnny Yune (Bruce Won), Robert Guillaume (V.A. Officer), Pat Paulsen (Psychiatrist), David Mendenhall (Orphan), Carl Bensen (Mr. B.), Joey Travolta, Bethany Wright, Don Gibb.

Funnier and faster than the original, this martial arts comedy stars Korean comedian Johnny Yune as a bungling karate expert who takes on a bunch of baddies with a magic sock.

3030. *They're Playing with Fire* (1984, New World, 96m, c). P Howard Avedis & Marlene Schmidt, D Avedis, W Avedis & Schmidt, PH Gary Graver, M John Cacavas, ED Jack Tucker, ED Rosemary Brandenburg.

LP Sybil Danning (Dianne Stevens), Eric Brown (Jay Richards), Andrew Prine (Michael Stevens), Paul Clemens (Martin "Bird" Johnson), K.T. Stevens (Lillian Stevens), Gene Bicknell (George Johnson).

Professor Sybil Danning seduces her student Eric Brown and then enlists him in a plot to kill her husband Andrew Prine, but things don't quite follow her lesson plan.

3031. *Thief* (1981, United Artists, 122m, c, aka *Violent Streets*). P Jerry Bruckheimer & Ronnie Caan, D&W Michael Mann (based on the book *The Home Invaders* by Frank Hohimer), PH Donald Thorin, M Tangerine Dream, ED Dov Hoenig, PD Mel Bourne.

LP James Caan (Frank), Tuesday Weld (Jessie), Willie Nelson (Okla), James Belushi (Barry), Robert Prosky (Leo), Tom Signorelli (Attaglia), Dennis Farina (Carl), Nick Nickeas (Nick), Bill Brown (Mitch).

James Caan, a professional thief, enjoys working alone, but is forced to slave for a crime syndicate to bring in more money for his family.

3032. *Thief of Hearts* (1984, Paramount, 100m, c). P Don Simpson & Jerry Bruckheimer, D&W Douglas Day Stewart, PH Andrew Laszlo, M Harold Faltermeyer, ED Tom Rolf, AD Edward Richardson.

LP Steven Bauer (Scott Muller), Barbara Williams (Mickey Davis), John Getz (Ray Davis), David Caruso (Buddy Calamara), Christine Ebersole (Janie Pointer), George Wendt (Marty Morrison), Alan North (Sweeney).

San Francisco burglar Steven Bauer breaks into the house of Barbara Williams and her husband John Getz. Besides money, he takes Williams' private journals in which she describes her fantasies. Bauer becomes obsessed with fulfilling her fantasies. He arranges for them to meet and knowing what she's looking for, it's no time before they are having the affair she always dreamed of — but dreams can become nightmares.

3033. *The Thing* (1982, Universal, 108m, c). P David Foster & Lawrence Turman, D John Carpenter, W Bill Lancaster (based on the story "Who Goes There?" by John W. Campbell, Jr.), PH Dean Cundey, M Ennio Morricone, ED Todd Ramsay, PD John J. Lloyd.

LP Kurt Russell (MacReady), A. Wilford Brimley (Blair), T.K. Carter (Nauls), David Clennon (Palmer), Keith David (Childs), Richard Dysart (Dr. Copper), Charles Hallahan (Norris), Peter Maloney (Bennings).

This remake of the 1951 science fiction classic is disappointing. The filmmakers seem to have learned nothing in the intervening 30 years. While more faithful to the source work by John W. Campbell, it's not nearly as entertaining as the earlier film. Scientists at an isolated outpost in the Antarctic (is there any other kind on the southern continent?), discover the presence of an alien which can transform itself into an exact replica of any living thing, including any of the scientists.

3034. *Things and Other Stuff* (1989, Lynchpin & Tosh, Australia, 88m, c). P Michael Lynch, D&W Tony Wellington, PH Kim Batterham, M Dale Barlow, ED Marcus D'Arcy, PD Judith Harvey.

LP Kelly Dingwall (David), Rebecca Rigg (Michelle), John Polson (Billy), Barry Leane, Jan Ringrose, Kate Reid, Sylvia Coleman.

Director Tom Wellington attempts an Australian *Breakfast Club*–type film of meaningful teen interplay. Kelly Dingwall and a reluctant Rebecca Rigg, with John Polson tagging along, break into a mansion to get some money. Emotional and class barriers are torn down almost violently as complex relationships among the three are explored.

3035. *Things Are Tough All Over* (1982, Columbia, 90m, c). P Howard Brown, D Thomas K. Avildsen, W "Cheech" Marin & Thomas Chong, PH Bobby Byrne, M Gaye Delorme, ED Dennis Dolan, PD Richard Tom Sawyer.

LP Richard "Cheech" Marin (Himself/Mr. Slyman), Tommy Chong (Himself/Prince Habib), Michael Aragon (Cheech's Double), Toni Attell (Cocktail Waitress), Mike Bacarella (Cop), Billy Beck (Pop).

The comedy of Cheech and Chong is an acquired taste perhaps not worth acquiring. Playing both themselves and Arab princes, C&C are tricked into transporting money to Las Vegas to be laundered.

3036. *Things Change* (1988, Columbia, 105m, c). P Michael Hausman, D David Mamet, W Mamet & Shel Silverstein, PH Juan Ruiz Anchia, M Alaric Jans, ED Trudy Ship, PD Michael Merritt.

LP Don Ameche (Gino), Joe Mantegna (Jerry), Robert Prosky (Joseph Vincent), J.J. Johnston (Frankie), Ricky Jay (Mr. Silver), Mike Nussbaum (Mr. Green), Jack Wallace (Repair Shop Owner), Dan Conway (Butler).

Bearing a remarkable resemblance to a mobster facing a long jail term, Italian shoeshine man Don Ameche agrees to take the rap and go to prison. His none-too-reliable, mob-soldier guard, Joe Mantegna, decides to give Ameche one last hurrah at Lake Tahoe. Both performances sparkle.

3037. *Thinkin' Big* (1988, AFC/Arista, 94m, c). P Jim C. Harris, D S.F. Brownrigg, W Robert Joseph Sterling & Loretta Yeargin, PH Brian H. Hooper, M John Boy Cooke, ED Hooper.

LP Bruce Anderson (Pud), Nancy Buechler (Morgan), Darla Ralston (Liz), Kenny Sargent (The Chief), Randy Jandt (Wong), Derek Hunter (Barry), Regina Mikel (Dee-Dee), Claudia Church (Wendy), April Burrage (Georgia).

The one-joke plot of this sophomoric teen comedy is that Randy Jandt is believed to have a three-foot-long member. This makes him very popular with the buxomy bikini-clad girls on the Texas shore.

3038. *The 13th Floor* (1989, Premiere, Australia, 94m, c). P David Hannay & Charles Hannah, D Chris Roache, W Roache, PH Stephen Prime, M Mick Coleman, ED Peter McBain, PD Darrell Lass.

LP Lisa Hensley (Heather Thompson), Tim McKenzie (John Burke), Miranda Otto (Rebecca), Jeff Truman (Bert), Vic Rooney (Brenner), Michael Caton (Dr. Fletcher), Tony Blackett (Thompson), Paul Hunt (Nick).

An 8-year-old witnesses her politician father ordering the torture of a man on the 13th floor of a building under construction. The victim is accidentally electrocuted. Years later, the girl, grown to be Lisa Hensley, is estranged from her father. With druggie friend Miranda Otto, she camps out on the 13th floor of the building, still unoccupied because it is reported to be haunted. Indeed it is, by the ghost of the electrocuted lad—but he's a friendly spirit.

3039. *This Is Elvis* (1981, Warner, 101m, c/b&w). P,D&W Malcolm Leo & Andrew Solt, PH Gil Hubbs, M Walter Scharf, ED Bud Friedgen & Glenn Farr.

LP David Scott (Elvis at 18), Paul Boensch, III (Elvis at 10), Johnny Harra (Elvis at 42), Lawrence Koller (Vernon Presley), Rhonda Lyn (Priscilla Presley), Debbie Edge (Gladys Presley), Larry Raspberry (Dewey Phillips), Liz Robinson (Minnie Mae Presley), Dana MacKay (Elvis at 35).

This harmless pseudodocumentary of the king of rock 'n' roll combines film clips and dramatic reconstructions of episodes in Elvis' life. It's not very interesting or revealing. Viewers are exposed to the myth, not the man.

3040. *This Is Spinal Tap* (1984, Embassy, 82m, c, aka *Spinal Tap*). P Karen Murphy, D Rob Reiner, W Christopher Guest, Michael McKean, Harry Shearer & Reiner, PH Peter Smokler, M Guest, McKean, Shearer & Reiner, ED Kent Beyda, Kim Secrist & Robert Leighton, PD Bryan Jones.

LP Rob Reiner (Marty DiBergi), Michael McKean (David St. Hubbins), Christopher Guest (Nigel Tufnel), Harry Shearer (Derek Smalls), R.J. Parnell (Mick Shrimpton), David Kaff (Vic

Savage), Tony Hendra (Ian Faith), Bruno Kirby (Tommy Pischedda).

In this hilarious, good-natured spoof, Rob Reiner is a documentary filmmaker covering the American tour of aging British rock group "Spinal Tap." It has risen from obscurity to become England's loudest group. The film has achieved cult status.

3041. *Those Glory, Glory Days* (1986, Cinecom, 91m, c). P Chris Griffin, D Philip Saville, W Julie Welch, PH Phil Meheux, ED Max Lemon, AD Maurice Cain.

LP Julia McKenzie (Mrs. Herrick), Elizabeth Spriggs (Coalhole), Julia Goodman (Julia, journalist), Rachael Meidman (Young Danny), Zoe Nathenson (Danny), Liz Campion (Jailbird), Sara Sugarman (Toni).

Thirteen-year-old Rachael Meidman, mad about soccer, drives her parents and teachers crazy. She grows up to become sports reporter Zoe Nathenson.

3042. *Those Lips, Those Eyes* (1980, United Artists, 107m, c). P Steven-Charles Jaffe & Michael Pressman, D Pressman, W David Shaber, PH Bobby Byrne, M Michael Small, ED Millie Moore, PD Walter Scott Herndon.

LP Frank Langella (Harry Crystal), Glynnis O'Connor (Ramona), Thomas Hulce (Artie Shoemaker), Kevin McCarthy (Mickey Bellinger), Jerry Stiller (Mr. Shoemaker), Herbert Berghof (Dr. Julius Fuldauer).

Pre-med student Tom Hulce takes a summer job with an outdoor Ohio theater. He is befriended by never-has-been and never-will-be professional actor Frank Langella. The latter helps Hulce with his job and his romance with chorus girl Glynnis O'Connor.

3043. *Thou Shall Not Kill...Except* (1987, Filmworld, 94m, c). P Scott Spiegel, D Josh Becker, W Becker & Spiegel (based on a story by Becker, Sheldon Lettich & Bruce Campbell), M Joseph Lo Duca, SE Gary Jones.

LP Brian Schulz (Sgt. Jack Stryker), John Manfredi (Miller), Robert Rickman (Jackson), Tim Quill (Tyler), Sam Raimi (Cult Leader), Cheryl Hanson (Sally), Perry Mallette (Otis), Rick Hudson (Kennel Owner).

Unless you were in Detroit in September, 1987, you likely missed this feature, shown theatrically only in the Motor City where it was filmed. Brian Schulz, in the guise of Stryker (a macho name very popular with helmers of horror, action/adventure and science fiction movies) is a Vietnam vet. After his fiancée Cheryl Hanson is kidnapped by a Charlie Manson–like cult headed by Sam Raimi, he calls on his ex-army buddies to help him kick a little ass.

3044. *Thrashin'* (1986, Fries, 90m, c). P Alan Sacks, D David Winters, W Paul Brown & Sacks, PH Chuck Colwell, M Barry Goldberg, ED Nicholas Smith & Lorenzo De Stefano, PD Katheryn Hardwick.

LP Josh Brolin (Cory Webster), Robert Rusler (Tommy Hook), Pamela Gidley (Chrissy), Brooke McCarter (Tyler), Brett Marx (Bozo), Josh Richman (Radley), David Wagner (Little Stevie), Sherilyn Fenn (Velvet).

Josh Brolin, a skateboard riding fool, is newly arrived in a California neighborhood inhabited by unfriendly leather and chain clad skateboarders.

3045. *Three Amigos* (1986, Orion, 105m, c). P Lorne Michaels & George Folsey, Jr., D John Landis, W Steve Martin, Michaels & Randy Newman, PH Ronald W. Browne, M Elmer Bernstein, ED Malcolm Campbell, PD Richard Sawyer.

LP Chevy Chase (Dusty Bottoms), Steve Martin (Lucky Day), Martin Short (Ned Nederlander), Patrice Martinez (Carmen), Alfonso Arau (El Guapo), Tony Plana (Jefe), Joe Mantegna (Harry Flugelman).

Saturday Night Live alums Chevy Chase, Steve Martin and Martin Short do not cover themselves with glory in this tom-foolery about three movie cowboys faced with taking on real bandits in a Mexican town. The Magnificent Three they are not.

3046. *3:15 The Moment of Truth* (1986, Dakota Ent. Corp., 92m, c). P Dennis Brody & Robert Kenner, D Larry Gross, W Sam Bernard & Michael Jacobs, PH Misha Suslov, M Gary Chang, ED Steven Kemper.

LP Adam Baldwin (Jeff Hanna), Deborah Foreman (Sherry Haviland), Rene Auberjonois (Horner), Ed Lauter (Moran).

Filmed in 1984, this is a typical low-budget teen gang film with little to recommend it.

3047. *Three for the Road* (1987, New Century/Vista, 88m, c). P Herb Jaffe & Mort Engelberg, D B.W.L. Norton, W Richard Martini, Tim Metcalfe & Miguel Tejada-Flores (based on a story by Martini), PH Steve Posey, M Barry Goldberg, ED Christopher Greenbury, PD Linda Allen.

LP Charlie Sheen (Paul Tracy), Kerri Green (Robin Kitteridge), Alan Ruck (Tommy "T.S."), Sally Kellerman (Blanche), Blair Tefkin (Missy), Raymond J. Barry (Sen. Kitteridge), Alexa Hamilton (Virginia), Bert Remsen (Stu), James Avery (Clarence).

Young congressional aide Charlie Sheen is chosen by Senator Raymond J. Barry to accompany the latter's teenage daughter Kerri Green to a school for troubled youngsters. Sheen talks his friend Alan Ruck into going along for the ride. The guys discover that Green's father is the problem as time after time she tries to escape from her escorts. Finally Sheen and Ruck deliver Green to her mother Sally Kellerman, rather than the reformatory-like institution her father had picked out to rid himself of her.

3048. *Three Fugitives* (1989, Buena Vista, 96m, c, aka *Fugitives*). P Lauren Shuler-Donner, D&W Francis Veber, PH Haskell Wexler, M David McHugh, ED Bruce Green, PD Rick Carter.

LP Nick Nolte (Lucas), Martin Short (Perry), Sarah Rowland Doroff (Meg), James Earl Jones (Dugan), Alan Ruck (Tener), Kenneth McMillan (Horvath).

Just out of prison, Nick Nolte innocently enters a bank to open an account where he is taken hostage by novice bank robber Martin Short. The police figure Nolte is involved; so he must go on the run with Short and the latter's little daughter Sarah Rowland Doroff. This is director Francis Veber's remake of his French film *Les Fugitifs*.

3049. *Three Kinds of Heat* (1987, Cannon, 87m, c, aka *Fireworks*). P Michael J. Kagan, D&W Leslie Stevens, PH Terry Cole, M Michael Bishop & Scott Page, ED Bob Dearberg, PD Duncan Cameron.

LP Robert Ginty (Elliot Cromwell), Victoria Barrett (Sgt. Terry O'Shea), Shakti (Maj. Shan), Sylvester McCoy (Harry Pimm), Barry Foster (George Norris), Jeannie Brown (Angelica).

The film begins with a New York shoot-out between rival warring Oriental underworld factions. Interpol assigns three of its crack investigators Robert Ginty, Victoria Barrett and Shakti to track down dangerous Chinese crime boss Sylvester McCoy. There's plenty more gunfire in the final confrontation.

3050. *Three Men and a Baby* (1987, Buena Vista, 99m, c). P Ted Field, Robert W. Cort & Edward Teets, D Leonard Nimoy, W James Orr & Jim Cruickshank (based on the French film *Trois Hommes et un Couffin* by Coline Serreau), PH Adam Greenberg, M Marvin Hamlisch, ED Michael A. Stevenson, PD Peter Larkin.

LP Tom Selleck (Peter Mitchell), Steve Guttenberg (Michael Kellam), Ted Danson (Jack Holden), Nancy Travis (Sylvia), Margaret Colin (Rebecca), Lisa & Michelle Blair (Mary), Celeste Holm (Mrs. Holden), Philip Bosco (Det. Melkowitz), Derek de Lint (Jan Clopatz).

Apparently lacking confidence in their stars or having a poor opinion of American audiences, the makers of this film were not content to merely make an English-language film of the French comedy *Three Men and a Cradle*. They added a hokey subplot about a misdirected drug shipment. The real story has Nancy Travis dropping off the baby fathered by Ted Danson at the luxurious apartment he shares with two equally swinging bachelor playboys Tom Selleck and Steve Guttenberg. Although initially they are very poor at caring for an infant, they come to adore the baby.

3051. *Three O'Clock High* (1987, Universal, 97m, c). P David E. Vogel, D Phil Joanou, W Richard Christian Matheson & Thomas Szollosi, PH Barry Sonnenfeld, M Tangerine Dream, ED Joe Anne Fogle, PD Bill Matthews & Tom Bugenhaven.

LP Casey Siemaszko (Jerry Mitchell), Anne Ryan (Franny Perrins), Stacey Glick (Brei Mitchell), Jonathan Wise (Vincent Costello), Richard Tyson (Buddy Revell), Jeffrey Tambor (Mr. Rice), Liza Morrow (Karen Clarke).

It's not Casey Siemaszko's day. His car has a flat on the way to school and he's sent to the dean's office for being late. Worse yet he's incurred the wrath of mean, nasty new student Richard Tyson, with whom he has a 3 o'clock appointment for a fight.

3052. *Threshold* (1983, 20th Century-Fox, Canada, 97m, c). P Jon Slan & Michael Burns, D Richard Pearce, W James Salter, PH Michel Brault, M Micky Erbe & Maribeth Solomon, ED Susan Martin, PD Anne Pritchard.

LP Donald Sutherland (Dr. Thomas Vrain), Jeff Goldblum (Dr. Aldo Gehring), Allan Nicholls (Dr. Basil Rents), Sharon Acker (Tilla Vrain), Jana Stinson (Sally Vrain), Jessica Steen (Tracy Vrain), Mavor Moore (Usher), Mare Winningham (Carol Severance).

Donald Sutherland gives a fine performance as a surgeon who plants an artificial heart in Mare Winningham, her only chance of survival.

3053. *Thrilled to Death* (1989, Platinum, 92m, c). P&D Chuck Vincent, W Craig Horrall, PH Larry Revene, M Joey Mennonna, ED James Davalos & Marc Ubell [Vincent].

LP Blake Bahner (Cliff Jackson), Rebecca Lynn (Elaine Jackson), Richard Maris (Darryl Christie), Christine Moore (Nan Christie), Harvey Siegel (Val), Scott Baker (Bill), Karen Nielsen (Trudy).

Innocent young couple Blake Bahner and Rebecca Lynn become mixed up with sinister twosome Richard Maris and Christine Moore when Bahner researches a novel at a club for swingers. They find themselves involved with drugs, sex and murder.

3054. *Thrillkill* (1988, Brightstar, Canada, 87m, c). P Anthony Kramreither, D Kramreither & Anthony D'Andrea, W D'Andrea, PH John Clement, M Tim McCauley, ED Nick Rotundo, AD Andrew Deskin.

LP Robin Ward (Frank), Gina Massey (Bobbie Kendell), Laura Robinson (Adrian), Diana Reis (Carly), Colleen Embree (Parrish), Kurt Reis (Schofield), Eugene Clark (Grissom), Frank Moore (Caspar), Joy Boushel (Maggie).

Filmed in 1984 the movie was held up until 1988 before going directly to video. Gina Massey is featured as a young woman who finds herself caught up in a multimillion dollar theft by computer when her sister Diana Reis, a software whiz mysteriously vanishes.

3055. *Throw Momma from the Train* (1987, Orion, 88m, c). P Larry Brezner, D Danny DeVito, W Stu Silver, PH Barry Sonnenfeld, M David Newman, ED Michael Jablow, PD Ida Random.

LP Danny DeVito (Owen), Billy Crystal (Larry), Kim Greist (Beth), Anne Ramsey† (Momma), Kate Mulgrew (Margaret), Branford Marsalis (Lester), Rob Reiner (Joel).

Getting the idea from a filming of *Strangers on a Train,* Danny De Vito believes he has made a bargain with his creative writing teacher Billy Crystal to trade murders. DeVito will kill Crystal's ex-wife Kate Mulgrew, while Crystal is to reciprocate by eliminating DeVito's nasty, overbearing mother Anne Ramsey. Crystal believes Mulgrew stole his best-selling novel and is the cause of his present severe case of writer's block. DeVito is treated like a piece of garbage by his momma. The results are funnier than in the Hitchcock movie.

3056. *Thunder Alley* (1985, Cannon, 92m, c). P William R. Ewing, D&W J.S. Cardone, PH Karen Grossman, M Robert Folk, ED Daniel Wetherbee, PD Joseph T. Garrity, AD Pat Tagliaferro.

LP Roger Wilson (Richie), Jill Schoelen (Beth), Scott McGinnis (Donnie), Cynthia Eilbacher (Lorraine), Clancy Brown (Weasel), Leif Garrett (Skip), Phil Brock (Butch), Brian Cole (Wolf).

Keyboardist Scott McGinnis starts a rock 'n' roll band. Lead singer Leif Garrett and guitarist Roger Wilson don't get along, but the band seems on its way to success until McGinnis gets hooked on drugs.

3057. *Thunder Run* (1986, Lynn-Davis, Australia, 91m, c). P Carol Lynn, D Gary Hudson, W Charles Davis & Carol

Heyer (based on a story by Clifford Wenger, Sr. & Lynn), PH Harvey Genkins, M Matthew McCauley & Jay Levy, ED Burton Lee Harry, AD Heyer.

LP Forrest Tucker (Charlie Morrison), John Ireland (George Adams), John Sheperd (Chris), Jill Whitlow (Kim), Wally Ward (Paul), Cheryl M. Lynn (Jilly), Marilyn O'Connor (Maggie Morrison), Graham Ludlow (Mike).

John Ireland persuades old army buddy Forrest Tucker to act as bait to catch terrorists. It's a grade Z bomb.

3058. *Thunder Warrior* (1983, Trans-World, Italy, 91m, c). P Fabrizio De Angelis, D Larry Ludman [Fabrizio De Angelis], W David Parker, Jr. & Ludman, M Francesco De Masi, ED Eugenio Alabiso, AD & COS Massimo Lentini (based on a story by Parker), PH Sergio Salvati.

LP Mark Gregory (Thunder), Bo Svenson (Sheriff Roger), Raymund Harmstorf (Rusty), Karen Reel (Sheena), Paolo Malco (Sherman), Valerie Ross (Sheila).

Young American Indian Mark Gregory explodes with all the violence of a one-man war party against injustice to his people and himself.

3059. *Thunder Warrior II* (1987, TransWorld, Italy, 93m, c). P Larry Ludman [Fabrizio De Angelis], D David Parker, Jr. & Ludman, PH Sergio Salvati, M Walter Ritz, ED Albert Moryalty.

LP Mark Gregory (Thunder), Bo Svenson (Sheriff Roger), Raymund Harmstorf (Rusty), Karen Reel (Sheena), William Rice, Vic Roych, Clayton Tevis, Bill Rossly.

Indian Mark Gregory has been pardoned by the governor of Arizona for his exploits in the original film. He teams up with sheriff Bo Svenson to combat drug traffickers who are making life hell for the Indians.

Thursday the 12th see *Pandemonium*

3060. *Ticket to Heaven* (1981, United Artists, Canada, 107m, c). P Vivienne Leebosh, D Ralph L. Thomas, W Thomas & Anne Cameron (based on the book *Moonwebs* by Josh Freed), PH Richard Leiterman, M Micky Erbe & Maribeth Solomon, ED Ron Wisman, PD Susan Longmire.

LP Nick Mancuso (David), Saul Rubinek (Larry), Meg Foster (Ingrid), Kim

Cattrall (Ruthie), R.H. Thompson (Linc Strunk), Jennifer Dale (Lisa), Guy Bond (Eric), Dixie Seatle (Sarah), Paul Soles (Morley).

After breaking up with his girlfriend, young Canadian Nick Mancuso visits San Francisco where he is seduced into joining a religious cult by the group's Meg Foster and Kim Cattrall. Thoroughly brainwashed, Mancuso rejects his family and his past. His best friend Saul Rubinek sets out to deprogram him.

3061. *Tiger Shark* (1989, Chappell, 99m, c). P Lana Lee Jones, D Emmet Alston, W Mike Stone & Ivan Rogers, PH Robert Ebinger, M Quito Colayco, ED Uncredited, AD Lito Nicdao.

LP Mike Stone (Tava, Tiger Shark), John Quade (Dave, Cowboy), Pamela Bryant (Karen), Vic Silayan (Col. Barro), Roy Alvarez (Tony), Roland Dantes (Ponsok), Jimmy Fabrigas (Vladimir), Lana Lee Jones (Jan Carter).

Mike Stone, who runs a Hawaiian martial arts academy, is helped by his old war buddy John Quade to rescue his kidnapped girlfriend Pamela Bryant.

3062. *Tiger Warsaw* (1988, Continental/Sony, 93m, c). P&D Amin Q. Chaudhri, W Roy London, PH Robert Draper, M Ernest Troost, ED Brian Smedley-Aston, PD Tom Targownik.

LP Patrick Swayze (Chuck "Tiger" Warsaw), Piper Laurie (Frances Warsaw), Lee Richardson (Mitchell Warsaw), Mary McDonnell (Paula Warsaw), Barbara Williams (Karen), Bobby DiCicco (Tony), Jenny Chrisinger (Val).

As she plans her wedding, Mary McDonnell's black sheep brother Patrick Swayze shows up for the first time in 15 years. His mother Piper Laurie is happy to see him, but his father Lee Richardson doesn't want him around. Swayze rekindles a romance with former girlfriend Barbara Williams and chums around with his old buddy Bobby DiCicco.

3063. *A Tiger's Tale* (1988, Atlantic, 97m, c). P&D Peter Douglas, W Douglas (based on the book *Love and Other Natural Disasters* by Allen Hannay 3d), PH Tony Pierce-Roberts, M Lee Holdridge, PD Shay Austin.

LP Ann-Margret (Rose), C. Thomas Howell (Bubber), Charles Durning

(Charlie), Kelly Preston (Shirley), Ann Wedgeworth (Claudine), Angel Tompkins (La Vonne), William Zabka (Randy), Tim Thomerson (Lonny).

When Texas teen C. Thomas Howell has an affair with his ex-girlfriend Kelly Preston's divorced mother Ann-Margret, a pregnancy results because Preston punches a hole in her mom's diaphram. What a nasty kid!

3064. *Tightrope* (1984, Warner, 114m, c). P Clint Eastwood & Fritz Manes, D&W Richard Tuggle, PH Bruce Surtees, M Lennie Niehaus, ED Joel Cox, PD Edward Carfagno.

LP Clint Eastwood (Wes Block), Genevieve Bujold (Beryl Thibodeaux), Dan Hedaya (Detective Molinari), Alison Eastwood (Amanda Block), Jennifer Beck (Penny Block), Marco St. John (Leander Wolfe), Rebecca Perle (Becky Jacklin), Regina Richardson (Sarita), Randi Brooks (Jamie Cory).

New Orleans vice cop Clint Eastwood, separated from his wife and raising two daughters (one played by his own daughter Alison), searches for a serial killer whose victims are the very same prostitutes whom Eastwood now and then takes comfort and kink with.

3065. *Tim* (1981, Pisces/Satori, Australia, 90m, c). P,D&W Michael Pate (based on a novel by Colleen McCullough), PH Paul Onorato, M Eric Jupp, ED David Stiven, AD John Carroll.

LP Piper Laurie (Mary Horton), Mel Gibson (Tim Melville), Alwyn Kurts (Ron Melville), Pat Evison (Emily Melville), Peter Gwynne (Tom Ainsley), Deborah Kennedy (Dawn Melville), David Foster (Mick Harrington).

Piper Laurie is an older woman who falls in love with slightly retarded but gorgeous hunk Mel Gibson. She teaches him to read rather than how to respond to her lust for him.

3066. *Time After Time* (1985, BBC-TV Arts & Entertainment, GB, 103m, c). P Terry Coles, D Bill Hays, W Andrew Davis (based on the novel by Molly Keane), PH John McGlashan, M Jim Parker, ED Dave King, PD Don Taylor.

LP John Gielgud (Jasper Swift), Googie Withers (Leda Klein), Helen Cherry (April Grange-Gorman), Ursula Howells (May Swift), Brenda Bruce (June Swift), Mark Lambert (Christy Lucy), Trevor Howard (Brigadier Crowshawe), Freddie Jones (Ulick Uniake), Mavis Walker (Lady Alys Crowshawe).

In this witty comedy, John Gielgud lives on an estate with his three elderly and eccentric sisters. Their lives are significantly altered by the arrival of their manipulative cousin Googie Withers.

3067. *Time Bandits* (1981, Avco Embassy, 110m, c). P&D Terry Gilliam, W Michael Palin & Gilliam, PH Peter Biziou, M Mike Moran, ED Julian Doyle, PD Millie Burns.

LP John Cleese (Robin Hood), Sean Connery (King Agamemnon), Shelley Duvall (Pansy), Katherine Helmond (Mrs. Ogre), Ian Holm (Napoleon), Michael Palin (Vincent), Ralph Richardson (Supreme Being), Peter Vaughan (Ogre), David Warner (Evil Genius), David Rappaport (Randall), Kenny Baker (Fidget), Jack Purvis (Wally), Mike Edmunds (Og), Malcolm Dixon (Strutter), Tiny Ross (Vermin), Craig Warnock (Kevin).

Six dwarves and young Warnock make their way through the universe with a map that reveals gaps in time. They travel through history encountering such famous fictional and real characters as Robin Hood, King Agamemnon and Napoleon. Coming from the pen of Monty Python members it has the sharp, clever slapstick edge associated with that troupe.

3068. *Time Burst: The Final Alliance* (1989, Action Intl., 93m, c). P&D Peter Yuval, W Yuval & Michael Bogert, PH Paul Maibaum, M Todd Hayen, ED Todd Felker.

LP Scott David King (Urbane), Michiko (Jane English), Gerald Okamura (Master), Jay Richardson (Mueller), Craig Ng (Takeda/Akira), Chet Hood, Jack Vogel, Richard Rogers.

After surviving a plane crash, Scott David King develops amnesia. He becomes involved with a group of Japanese samauri of an earlier time seeking some ancient tablets.

3069. *A Time of Destiny* (1988, Columbia, 118m, c). P Anna Thomas, D Gregory Nava, W Nava & Thomas, PH

James Glennon, M Ennio Morricone, ED Betsy Blankett, PD Henry Bumstead.

LP William Hurt (Martin Larraneta), Timothy Hutton (Jack McKenna), Melissa Leo (Josie Larraneta), Francisco Rabal (Jorge Larraneta), Concha Hidalgo (Sebastiana Larraneta), Stockard Channing (Margaret Larraneta).

In this old-fashioned soap opera, Basque-American William Hurt vows revenge when his father is killed trying to prevent Timothy Hutton from eloping with Hurt's sister Melissa Leo. During World War II, Hurt is attached to Hutton's unit and tries to kill him. Neither of the two very fine actors, Hurt and Hutton, are in top form in this one.

3070. *Time of the Beast* (1989, Liberty Films, 89m, c). P Russell Markowitz, D John R. Bowey, W Lynn Rose Higgins, M Rene Veldsman, SE Robert Burman.

LP Brion James, Carolyn Ann Clark, Milton Raphael Murrill, Neil McCarthy, Brian O'Shaughnessy.

The beast of this film comes into existence as the result of a foul-up in a genetic laboratory. It's tame and routine—the movie, that is, not the beast.

Time Raiders see Warrior of the Apocalypse

3071. *Time Trackers* (1989, Concorde, 87m, c). P Roger Corman, D&W Howard R. Cohen, PH Ronn Schmidt, M Parmer Fuller, ED Brent Schoenfeld, AD Peter Flynn.

LP Ned Beatty (Harry), Wil Shriner (Charles), Kathleen Beller (R.J.), Bridget Hoffman (Madeline), Alex Hyde-White (Edgar), Lee Bergere (Zandor).

A group of young scientists travel backwards in time from the year 2033 to prevent evil scientist Lee Bergere from changing history. No one seems to note or care that their presence in the past will have a like effect.

3072. *Time Walker* (1982, New World, 83m, c). P Dimitri Villard & Jason Williams, D Tom Kennedy, W Karen Levitt & Tom Friedman, PH Robbie Greenberg, M Richard Band, ED Joseph Yanuzzi, AD R.A. Burns & Joe Garrity.

LP Ben Murphy (Doug McCadden),

Nina Axelrod (Susy Fuller), Kevin Brophy (Peter), James Karen (Wendell Rossmore), Robert Random (Parker), Austin Stoker (Dr. Ken Melrose), Shari Belafonte-Harper (Linda).

When jewels from the sarcophagus of an Egyptian mummy brought to a California university by archaeologist Ben Murphy are stolen, the mummy comes alive. Its touch is fatal to humans.

3073. *Timerider, The Adventures of Lyle Swann* (1983, Jensen-Farley, 93m, c). P Harry Gittes, D William Dear, W Dear & Michael Nesmith, PH Larry Pizer, M Nesmith, ED Suzanne Pettit, Kim Secrist & R.J. Kizer, AD Linda Pearl.

LP Fred Ward (Lyle Swann), Belinda Bauer (Clair Cygne), Peter Coyote (Porter Reese), Ed Lauter (Padre), Richard Masur (Claude Dorsett), Tracey Walter (Carl Dorsett), L.Q. Jones (Ben Potter), Chris Mulkey (Daniels).

Fred Ward, a modern motorcycle rider, passes through a time warp and finds himself and his bike on dusty plains with outlaw horsemen of the old West.

3074. *Times Square* (1980, Butterfly Valley/AFD, 111m, c). P Robert Stigwood & Jacob Brackman, D Alan Moyle, W Brackman (based on a story by Moyle & Leanne Unger), PH James A. Contner, ED Tom Priestley, PD Stuart Wurtzel.

LP Tim Curry (Johnny Laguardia), Trini Alvarado (Pamela Pearl), Robin Johnson (Nicky Marotta), Peter Coffield (David Pearl), Herbert Berghof (Dr. Huber), David Margulies (Dr. Zymabsky), Anna Maria Horsford (Rosie Washington), Michael Margotta (JoJo).

Wealthy Trini Alvarado runs away from her uncaring politician father with Robin Johnson to Times Square. There she becomes a stripper and he, a punk rock star. DJ Tim Curry turns them both into media celebrities.

3075. *Tin Man* (1983, Goldfarb, 95m, c). P&D John G. Thomas, W Bishop Holiday, PH Virgil Harper, M Holiday.

LP Timothy Bottoms, Deana Jurgens, John Phillip Law, Troy Donahue.

Born deaf and dumb, auto mechanic Timothy Bottoms invents a computer that becomes his ears and tongue.

3076. *Tin Men* (1987, Buena Vista, 110m, c). P Mark Johnson, D&W Barry Levinson, PH Peter Sova, M Fine Young Cannibals, ED Stu Linder, PD Peter Jamison.

LP Richard Dreyfuss (Bill "BB" Babowsky), Danny DeVito (Ernest Tilley), Barbara Hershey (Nora Tilley), John Mahoney (Moe), Jackie Gayle (Sam), Stanley Brock (Gil), Seymour Cassel (Cheese), Bruno Kirby (Mouse), J.T. Walsh (Wing), Richard Portnow (Carly), Matt Craven (Looney), Alan Blumenfeld (Stanley), Brad Sullivan (Masters).

In as fine a film as was made in 1987, audiences laughed at the antics of aluminum siding con-artist salesmen Richard Dreyfuss and Danny DeVito, but not at them. The film is very touching as well as amusing. The trouble begins when DeVito and Dreyfuss, "tin men" for different companies, run their new Cadillacs into each other in Baltimore of the early 60s. They spend much of the rest of the movie seeking ways to get even with each other. Dreyfuss even seduces DeVito's wife Barbara Hershey, only to find Danny glad to be rid of her. Dreyfuss falls in love with Hershey. Both men lose their licenses to sell aluminum siding because of the various crooked scams they used.

3077. *Tin Star Void* (1988, Double Helix, 95m, c). P Jean Bodon, Paul Falcone, Tom Gniazdowski & Leopold Wurm, D Gniazdowski, PH Adam Goldfine, M David Perlman, ED Michael Lang.

LP Daniel Chapman (Wade Holt), Ruth Collins (Annie), Loren Blackwell (Hawk), Karen Rizzo (Star), Phillip Nutman (Tough), John Pierce (Kid).

In this comedy crime western, Daniel Chapman is sent to a seedy prison, but returns to take revenge on the punk cowboys who framed him. The latter all drive around in 50s roadsters, rather than riding ponies.

Titan Find see *Creature*

3078. *Title Shot* (1982, Cinepax, Canada, 96m, c). P Bob Iveson, D Les Rose, W John Saxton (based on a story by Richard Gabourie), PH Henry Fiks, M Paul

James Zaza, ED Ronald Sanders, AD Karen Bromley.

LP Tony Curtis (Frank Renzetti), Richard Gabourie (Blake), Susan Hogan (Sylvia), Allan Royal (Dunlop), Robert Delbert (Rufus Taylor), Natsuko Ohama (Terry), Jack Duffy (Mr. Green), Sean McCann (Lt. Grace).

Mafia chief Tony Curtis plots to kill the heavyweight boxing champion during a match. Richard Gabourie is a tough cop out to stop him.

3079. *To All a Goodnight* (1980, IRC-IWC, 84m, c). P Sandy Gobe, D David Hess, W Alex Rebar, PH B. Godsey, M Rich Tufo, PD Joe Garrity.

LP Buck West (Weird Ralph), Sam Shamshak (Polansky), Katherine Herington (Mrs. Jensen), Jennifer Runyon, Forrest Swanson, Linda Gentile, William Lauer, J. Bridges.

Five young couples expect to have a good time during Christmas vacation at The Calvin Finishing School for Girls, but a mad Santa Claus slaughters them one by one.

3080. *To Be or Not to Be* (1983, 20th Century-Fox, 108m, c). P Mel Brooks, D Alan Johnson, W Thomas Meehan & Ronny Graham (based on the film by Ernst Lubitsch, written by Edwin Justus Mayer), PH Gerald Hirschfeld, M John Morris, ED Alan Balsam, PD Terence Marsh.

LP Mel Brooks (Frederick Bronski), Anne Bancroft (Anna Bronski), Tim Matheson (Lt. Andre Sobinski), Charles Durning† (Col. Erhardt), Jose Ferrer (Prof. Siletski), Christopher Lloyd (Capt. Shultz), James Haake (Sasha), George Gaynes (Ravitch), George Wyner (Ratkowski).

Older film fans have fond memories of the 1942 version of this film. This may be due to an appreciation of the talents of Jack Benny, the tragic conclusion of the film for Carole Lombard, killed in a plane crash before her final scenes were shot, and the comedy of the "Lubitsch touch." The material at the time seemed fresh and daring. Forty years later with Mel Brooks and Anne Bancroft it seems trite and dated.

3081. *To Die For* (1989, Skouras, 90m, c). P Barin Kumar, D Devan

Sarafian, W Leslie King, PH David Boyd, M Cliff Eidelman, ED Dennis Dolan, PD Maxine Shepard, AD Greg Oehler, SE John Carl Buechler.

LP Brendan Hughes (Vlad Tepish), Sydney Walsh (Kate Wooten), Amanda Wyss (Celia Kett), Scott Jacoby (Martin Planting), Micah Grant (Mike Dunn), Duane Jones (Simon Little), Steve Bond (Tom), Remy O'Neill (Jane).

The filmmakers attempt unsuccessfully to demonstrate that the pleasures and eroticism of a bite from a handsome vampire, such as Brendan Hughes, may be worth the consequences to a woman like Sydney Walsh, afraid she may never experience the grand passion of uncontrollable love.

To Elvis with Love *see* ***Touched by Love***

3082.   *To Kill a Priest* (1988, Columbia, US/France, 117m, c). P Jean-Pierre Alessandri, D Agnieszka Holland, W Holland & Jean-Yves Pitoun, PH Adam Holender, M Georges Delerue, ED Herve de Luze, AD Emile Ghigo.

LP Christopher Lambert (Father Alek), Ed Harris (Stefan), Joanne Whalley (Anna), Joss Ackland (The Colonel), David Suchet (The Bishop), Tim Roth (Feliks), Peter Postlethwaite (Joseph).

Polish filmmaker Agnieszka Holland presents the story of priest Christopher Lambert. He is a charismatic spokesman for the Solidarity Labor movement. He is pursued by police chief Ed Harris who believes himself to be under orders from high in the government to silence the troublesome priest. The story is a bit passé now, considering all that has happened in Poland, but is still a suspenseful chase film.

3083.   *To Kill a Stranger* (1985, Angel-Radio Video-Star World, 88m, c). P Raul Vale, D Juan Lopez-Moctezuma, W Emerich Oross, Rafael Bunuel, Michael Elliot, Lopez-Moctezuma & Morrie Ruvinsky, PH Alex Phillips, M Mort Garson, ED Carlos Savage.

LP Angelica Maria (Cristina Carver), Dean Stockwell (John Carver), Donald Pleasence (Col. Kostik), Aldo Ray (Inspector Benedict), Sergio Aragones (Maj.

Keller), Ken Grant (Tom), Jill Franklyn (Susan).

In an unidentified South American country, Angelica Maria kills unknown attacker Donald Pleasence who tries to rape her after she helps him following an accident. She and hubby discover that the deceased was a war hero and the militaristic government is not sympathetic to her actions.

3084.   *To Live and Die in L.A.* (1985, MGM/United Artists, 116m, c). P Irving H. Levin, D William Friedkin, W Friedkin & Gerald Petievich (based on Petievich's novel), PH Robby Muller, M Wang Chung, ED Scott Smith & Bud Smith, PD Lilly Kilvert.

LP William L. Petersen (Richard Chance), Willem Dafoe (Eric Masters), John Pankow (John Vukovich), Debra Feuer (Bianca Torres), John Turturro (Carl Cody), Darlanne Fluegel (Ruth Lanier), Dean Stockwell (Bob Grimes), Steve W. James (Jeff Rice), Robert Downey (Thomas Bateman).

Filmed in the style of a music video, director William Friedkin attempts to make a sort of West Coast *French Connection*. Secret Service agent William L. Petersen is out to nab counterfeiter Willem Dafoe. The characters are vulgar and the story is trite. A hair-raising car chase is the best thing in an otherwise unappealing film.

3085.   *Toby McTeague* (1986, Spectrafilm, Canada, 95m, c). P Nicolas Clermont, D Jean-Claude Lord, W Jeff Maguire, Djordje Milicevic & Jamie Brown, PH Rene Verzier, M Claude Demers, ED Yves Langlois.

LP Winston Rekert (Tom McTeague), Yannick Bisson (Toby McTeague), Timothy Webber (Edison Crowe), Stephanie Morgenstern (Sara), Andrew Bednarski (Sam McTeague), Liliane Clune (Jenny Lessard), George Clutesi (Chief George Wild Dog).

In this children's story, Canadian teenager Yannick Bisson must take over the reins of his father Winston Rekert's dog team for the big race.

3086.   *Tom Horn* (1980, Warner, 98m, c). P Fred Weintraub, D William Wiard, W Thomas McGuane & Bud Shrake (based on *Life of Tom Horn,*

Government Scout and Interpreter by Tom Horn), PH John Alonzo, M Ernest Gold, ED George Grenville, AD Ron Hobbs.

LP Steve McQueen (Tom Horn), Linda Evans (Glendolene Kimmel), Richard Farnsworth (John Coble), Billy Green Bush (Joe Belle), Slim Pickens (Sam Creedmore), Peter Canon (Assistant Prosecutor), Elisha Cook (Stable Hand).

It's based on the true story of Old West gunman Tom Horn. By the age of 40 he had already been a railroad worker, stagecoach driver, U.S. Cavalry scout, silver miner, Rough Rider with Teddy Roosevelt at Sam Juan Hill and a Pinkerton detective. The movie picks up with Steve McQueen as Horn invited by Wyoming ranchers to put an end to rustling on their lands.

3087. The Tomb (1986, TransWorld, 84m, c). P Fred Olen Ray & Ronnie Hadar, D Ray, W Kenneth J. Hall, PH Paul Elliott, M Drew Neumann, ED Miriam L. Preissel, AD Maxine Shepard.

LP Cameron Mitchell (Prof. Phillips), John Carradine (Mr. Androheb), Sybil Danning (Jade), Susan Stokey (Helen), Richard Alan Hench (David Manners), Michelle Bauer (Nefratis), David Pearson (John Banning).

Long dead Egyptian princess Michelle Bauer wreaks havoc in the modern world. Don't look for sparkling dialogue.

3088. Tomboy (1985, Crown, 91m, c). P Marilyn J. Tenser & Michael D. Castle, D Herb Freed, W Ben Zelig (based on an idea by Mark Tenser), PH Daniel Yarussi, ED Richard E. Westover, AD Randy Ser.

LP Betsy Russell (Tommy Boyd), Jerry Dinome (Randy Starr), Kristi Somers (Seville Ritz), Richard Erdman (Chester), Philip Sterling (Earl Delarue), Eric Douglas (Ernie Leeds, Jr.), Paul Gunning (Frankie).

Baby-faced, neatly built Betsy Russell has a hard-edged sexiness which seems appropriate for the S&M scenes. In this film she's a female mechanic determined to win the love of Jerry Dinome, a pretty boy superstar race driver. Just in case he's confused by her name and tomboy behavior, she frequently takes off her shirt to reassure him.

3089. Too Much (1987, Cannon, 89m, c). P Menahem Golan & Yoram Globus, D Eric Rochat, W Rochat & Joan Laine, PH Daisaku Kimura, M George S. Clinton, ED Alain Jakubowicz, AD Tsuneo Kantake, SE Osamu Kung.

LP Bridgette Andersen (Suzy/Narrator), Masato Fukazama (Too Much), Hiroyuki Watanabe ("Uncle" Tetsuro), Char Fontana (Prof. Finkel), Uganda (Bernie).

Not even the most easily-pleased dull child will be able to stomach this comedy about adorable little Bridgette Andersen, her robot friend Masato Fukazama and their experiences in Japan.

3090. Too Outrageous (1987, Spectrafilm, Canada, 105m, c). P Roy Krost, D&W Dick Benner, PH Fred Guthe, M Russ Little, ED George Appleby, AD Andris Hausmanis.

LP Craig Russell (Robin Turner), Hollis McLaren (Liza Connors), David McIlwraith (Bob), Ron White (Luke), Lynn Cormack (Betty Treisman), Michael J. Reynolds (Lee Sturges), Timothy Jenkins (Rothchild).

Female inpersonator Craig Russell becomes a smash in the Big Apple. His story isn't interesting, but he sure can make you believe he's Barbra Streisand, Mae West, etc.

3091. Too Scared to Scream (1985, Movie Store, 104m, c). P Mike Connors, D Tony Lo Bianco, W Neal Barbera & Glenn Leopold, PH Larry Pizer, M George Garvarentz, ED Ed Beyer & Michael Economou, PD Lilly Kilvert.

LP Mike Connors (Lt. Dinardo), Anne Archer (Kate), Leon Isaac Kennedy (Frank), Ian McShane (Hardwick), Ruth Ford (Irma), John Heard (Lab Technician), Carrie Nye (Graziella), Maureen O'Sullivan (Mother).

New York police detective Mike Connors teams up with female undercover cop Anne Archer to solve a series of bizarre murders of females in a Manhattan apartment building. The prime suspect is Shakespeare-quoting doorman Ian McShane who lives with his invalid mother Maureen O'Sullivan in a luxurious brownstone.

3092. *Tootsie*† (1982, Columbia, 116m, c). P Sydney Pollack & Dick Richards, D Pollack†, W Larry Gelbart, Murray Schisgal & Don McGuire† (uncredited, Elaine May, based on a story by Don McGuire & Gelbert), PH Owen Roizman†, M Dave Grusin, ED Fredric Steinkamp & William Steinkamp†, PD Peter Larkin, SD Tom Tonery, SONG "It Might Be You" by Dave Grusin, Alan & Marilyn Bergman, SOUND Arthur Plantadosi, Les Fresholtz, Dick Alexander & Les Lazarowitz†.

LP Dustin Hoffman† (Michael Dorsey/Dorothy Michaels), Jessica Lange* (Julie), Teri Garr† (Sandy), Dabney Coleman (Ron), Charles Durning (Les), Bill Murray (Jeff), Sydney Pollack (George Fields), George Gaynes (John Van Horn), Geena Davis (April), Doris Belack (Rita), Ellen Foley (Jacqui).

Unable to find work, actor Dustin Hoffman dresses up as a woman and wins a pivotal role on a soap opera. He falls for Jessica Lange, who sees "her" as a confidant. How to win the girl of his dreams and remain employed is his problem. Oh, that and the fact that Lange's father Charles Durning has the hots for "her."

3093. *Top Gun* (1986, Paramount, 109m, c). P Don Simpson & Jerry Bruckheimer, D Tony Scott, W Jim Cash & Jack Epps, Jr., PH Jeffrey Kimball, M Harold Faltermeyer, ED Billy Weber & Chris Lebenzon†, SOUND EFFECTS EDITING Cecelia Hall & George Walters, II†, PD John F. De Cuir, Jr., M/L "Take My Breath Away" by Giorgio Moroder & Tom Whitlock*, SOUND Donald O. Mitchell, Kevin O'Connell, Rick Kline & William B. Kaplan†.

LP Tom Cruise (Maverick), Kelly McGillis (Charlie), Val Kilmer (Ice), Anthony Edwards (Goose), Tom Skerritt (Viper), Michael Ironside (Jester), John Stockwell (Cougar), Barry Tubb (Wolfman), Rick Rossovich (Slider), Tim Robbins (Merlin), Clarence Gilyard, Jr. (Sundown), Whip Hubley (Hollywood), Meg Ryan (Carole).

The film is a long winded tribute to naval fighter pilots. The story isn't much and beautiful Kelly McGillis is wasted, but the scenes in the sky almost make it worth the price of admission.

3094. *Top Secret!* (1984, Paramount, 90m, c). P Jon Davison & Hunt Lowry, D Jim Abrahams, David Zucker & Jerry Zucker, W Abrahams, D. & J. Zucker & Martyn Burke, Ph Christopher Challis, M Maurice Jarre, ED Bernard Gribble, PD Peter Lamont.

LP Omar Sharif (Cedric), Jeremy Kemp (Gen. Streck), Warren Clarke (Col. Von Horst), Tristram Jellinek (Maj. Crumpler), Val Kilmer (Nick Rivers), Billy J. Mitchell (Martin), Major Wiley (Porter), Gertan Klauber (Mayor).

The creators of the disaster spoofs *Airplane* and *Airplane II* try their hands at a satire featuring Val Kilmer as an Elvis-like entertainer. They find time for surf, spy and cold war intrigue in their zany script.

3095. *Torch Song Trilogy* (1988, New Line, 120m, c). P Howard Gottfried, D Paul Bogart, W Harvey Fierstein (based on his play), PH Mikael Salomon, M Peter Matz, ED Nicholas C. Smith, PD Richard Hoover.

LP Anne Bancroft (Ma), Matthew Broderick (Alan), Harvey Fierstein (Arnold Beckoff), Brian Kerwin (Ed), Karen Young (Laurel), Eddie Castrodad (David), Ken Page (Murray), Charles Pierce (Bertha Venation), Axel Vera (Marina Del Rey).

Gay female impersonator Harvey Fierstein falls in love with bisexual teacher Brian Kerwin but loses him to Karen Young. Fierstein takes up with Matthew Broderick, a young model, in what seems to be a permanent relationship, but Broderick is beaten to death by a gang of gay bashers, just as the couple are about to adopt troubled teen Eddie Castrodad. Fierstein takes his role as "father" to Castrodad very seriously and renews his relationship with Kerwin, who has broken with his wife Young.

3096. *Torchlight* (1984, Film Ventures, 91m, c). P Joel Douglas & Michael Schroeder, D Tom Wright, W Pamela Sue Martin & Eliza Moorman, PH Alex Phillips, M Michael Cannon, AD Craig Stearns.

LP Pamela Sue Martin (Lillian Gregory), Steve Railsback (Jake Gregory), Ian McShane (Sidney), Al Corley (Al), Rita Taggart (Rita), Arnie Moore (Richard).

Artist Pamela Sue Martin marries Steve Railsback, the rich owner of an L.A. construction firm. Wealthy art dealer Ian McShane introduces them to free-basing cocaine and their life begins to crumble.

3097. *Torment* (1986, New World, 90m, c). P,D&W Samson Aslanian & John Hopkins, PH Stephen Carpenter, M Christopher Young, ED John Penney, Earl Ghaffari, Bret Shelton, AD Chris Hopkins.

LP Taylor Gilbert (Jennifer), William Witt (Father), Eve Brenner (Mrs. Courtland), Warren Lincoln (Michael), Najean Cherry (Helen), Stan Weston (Bogartis), Doug Leach (Officer Tilman), Lisa Ramirez (Dianne).

Middle-aged William Witt becomes a psychopathic killer when he's rejected by a young woman. He preys on single San Francisco women. Taylor Gilbert appears to be his next intended victim.

3098. *Touch and Go* (1980, Mutiny/Great Union, Australia, 92m, c). P John Pellatt, D Peter Maxwell, W Peter Yeldham (based on a story by Maxwell & Yeldham), PH John McLean, ED Sara Bennett & Paul Maxwell.

LP Wendy Hughes (Eva Gilmour), Chantal Contouri (Fiona Latham), Carmen Duncan (Millicent Hoffman), Jeanie Drynan (Gina Tesoriero), Liddy Clark (Helen Preston), Christine Amor (Sue Fullerton), Jon English (Frank Butterfield).

Three beautiful women turn to grand larceny to keep the local kindergarten in operation.

3099. *Touch and Go* (1987, Tri-Star, 101m, c). P Stephen Friedman, D Robert Mandel, W Alan Ormsby, Bob Sand & Harry Colomby, PH Richard H. Kline, M Sylvester Levay, ED Walt Mulconery, PD Charles Rosen.

LP Michael Keaton (Bobby Barbato), Maria Conchita Alonso (Denise DeLeon), Ajay Naidu (Louis DeLeon), John Reilly (Jerry Pepper), Maria Tucci (Dee Dee), Richard Venture (Gower), Max Wright (Lester), Michael Zelniker (McDonald).

Self-centered and emotionally isolated hockey player Michael Keaton becomes involved with Maria Conchita Alonso and her 11-year-old prospective juvenile delinquent son Ajay Naidu in this "feel-good" movie.

3100. *Touched* (1983, Lorimar, 93m, c). P Dick Petersmann & Barclay Lottimer, D John Flynn, W Lyle Kessler, PH Fred Murphy, M Shirley Walker, ED Harry Keramidas, PD Patrizia von Brandenstein.

LP Robert Hays (Daniel), Kathleen Beller (Jennifer), Ned Beatty (Herbie), Gilbert Lewis (Ernie), Lyle Kessler (Timothy), Farnham Scott (Thomas), Meg Myles (Jennifer's Mother), Mady Kaplan (Arlene).

In a well-meaning but dramatically emotionless story, Robert Hays and Kathleen Beller leave a mental institution and struggle against all odds to set up a normal household.

3101. *Touched by Love* (1980, Columbia, 95m, c, aka *To Elvis, with Love*). P Michael Viner, D Gus Trikonis, W Hesper Anderson (based on the story "To Elvis, with Love" by Lena Canada), PH Richard H. Kline, M John Barry, ED Fred Chulack, AD Claudio Guzman.

LP Deborah Raffin (Lena Canada), Diane Lane (Karen), Michael Learned (Dr. Bell), John Amos (Tony), Christina Raines (Amy), Mary Wickes (Margaret), Clu Gulager (Don Fielder), Twyla Volkins (Monica).

The film is based on the true story of a girl suffering from cerebral palsy, here played by Diane Lane, who learns the power of love from a dedicated teacher played by Deborah Raffin. The two write a letter to Elvis Presley. He responds and they begin a correspondence that brings great joy to the girl.

3102. *Tough Enough* (1983, 20th Century–Fox, 107m, c). P William S. Gilmore, D Richard O. Fleischer, W John Leone, PH James A. Contner, M Michael Lloyd & Steve Wax, ED Dann Cahn, PD Bill Kenney.

LP Dennis Quaid (Art Long), Carlene Watkins (Caroline Long), Stan Shaw (P.T. Coolidge), Pam Grier (Myra), Warren Oates (James Neese), Bruce McGill (Tony Fallon), Wilford Brimley (Bill Long), Fran Ryan (Gert Long).

Hoping to raise money to finance his

country-western singing career, Dennis Quaid enters the boxing ring and finds himself developing into an up-and-coming contender.

3103. *Tough Guys* (1986, Buena Vista, 102m, c). P Joe Wizan, D Jeff Kanew, W James Orr & Jim Cruickshank, PH King Baggot, M James Newton Howard, ED Kaja Fehr, PD Todd Hallowell.

LP Burt Lancaster (Harry Doyle), Kirk Douglas (Archie Long), Charles Durning (Deke Yablonski), Alexis Smith (Belle), Dana Carvey (Richie Evans), Darlanne Fluegel (Skye Foster), Eli Wallach (Leon B. Little).

Seventy-two year old Burt Lancaster and 69-year-old Kirk Douglas don't embarrass themselves portraying two flamboyant train robbers released from prison after serving a thirty year stretch. Unable to adjust to the modern world, they return to what they know best. Douglas does look a wee bit out of place with swinging young Darlanne Fluegel as his main squeeze. Lancaster has the better sense to take up with Alexis Smith, someone more nearly his age.

3104. *Tough Guys Don't Dance* (1987, Cannon, 108m, c). P Menahem Golan & Yoram Globus, D&W Norman Mailer (based on his novel), PH John Bailey, M Angelo Badalamenti, ED Debra McDermott, PD Armin Ganz.

LP Ryan O'Neal (Tim Madden), Isabella Rossellini (Madeline), Debra Sandlund (Patty Lareine), Wings Hauser (Regency), John Bedford Lloyd (Wardley Meeks, III), Clarence Williams, III (Bolo), Lawrence Tierney (Dougy Madden), Penn Jillette (Big Stoop), Frances Fisher (Jessica Pond).

Loser Ryan O'Neal may have committed murder but he can't remember. Look for a sparkling performance from Lawrence Tierney as O'Neal's no-nonsense father in this tribute to film noir.

3105. *Tougher Than Leather* (1988, New Line, 92m, c). P Vincent Giordano, D Rick Rubin, W Ric Menello & Rubin (based on a story by Bill Adler, Lyor Cohen & Menello), PH Feliks Parnell, ED Steven Brown.

LP Joseph Simmons (Run), Darryl McDaniels (DMC), Jason Mizell (Jam Master Jay), Richard Edson (Bernie), Jenny Lumet (Pam), Rick Rubin (Vic), Lois Ayer (Charlotte), George Godfrey (Nathan), Russell Simmons (Russell).

If you didn't get enough of rap music stories with *Wild Style, Beat Street, Breakin', The Disorderlies* and *Krush Groove,* this subpar action picture features Run DMC doing their thing.

Tower of Evil see Beyond the Fog

3106. *The Toxic Avenger* (1985, Troma, 81m, c). P Lloyd Kaufman & Michael Herz, D Herz & Samuel Weil, W Joe Ritter (additional material by Kaufman, Gay Terry & Stuart Strutin), PH James London & Kaufman, ED Richard Haines & Alan J. Polyniak, AD Barry Shapiro & Alexandra Mazur, SE Jennifer Aspinall & Tom Lauten.

LP Andree Maranda (Sara), Mitchell Cohen (The Toxic Avenger), Jennifer Baptist (Wanda), Cindy Manion (Julie), Robert Prichard (Slug), Gary Schneider (Bozo), Pat Ryan, Jr. (Mayor Belgoody), Mark Torgl (Melvin), Dick Martinsen (Officer O'Clancy), Chris Liano (Walter Harris).

Despite some sick humor, this film, about a nerdish pool attendant thrown into a tub of toxic waste, only to emerge with special powers which he uses as a crimefighter, has some very funny moments.

3107. *The Toxic Avenger: Part II* (1989, Troma, 95m, c). P&D Lloyd Kaufman & Michael Herz, W Gay Partington Terry (based on an original story by Kaufman), PH James London, M Barrie Guard, ED Michael Schweitzer, AD Alex Grey, SE Pericles Lewnes.

LP Ron Fazio & John Altamura (The Toxic Avenger), Phoebe Legere (Claire), Rick Collins (Apocalypse Inc. Chairman), Rikiya Yasuoka (Big Mac), Tsutomu Sekine (Announcer), Shinoburyu (Shockikuyama), Lisa Gaye (Malfaire).

While the original had a few laughs, this sequel has jokes so bad five-year-olds will groan. Toxic makes it to Japan to seek out his father Big Mac, the head cheese in an underworld gang—you know, Big Mac with cheese. Terrible!

3108. *The Toxic Avenger Part III: The Last Temptation of Toxie* (1989, Troma, 89m, c). P&D Michael Herz & Lloyd Kaufman, W Gay Partington Terry & Kaufman (based on a story by Kaufman), PH James London, M Christopher DeMarco (based on music by Antonin Dvorak), ED Joseph McGirr.

LP Ron Fazio & John Altamura (The Toxic Avenger), Phoebe Legere (Claire), Rick Collins (Chairman/The Devil), Lisa Gaye (Malfaire), Jessica Dublin (Mrs. Junko).

The former nerd who became a deformed superhero after emerging from a vat of toxic waste is back in a stupid second sequel which unfortunately may not be the last. Not so long as there are young people with a limited imagination and a weird notion of what's funny. Among other things Toxie, played by both Ron Fazio and John Altamura, attempts to raise money needed for an operation to restore the sight of his "beautiful blind buxom bimbo" Phoebe Legere (that's how she's frequently referred to in the film).

3109. *The Toy* (1982, Columbia, 99m, c). P Phil Feldman, D Richard Donner, W Carol Sobieski (based on the film *Le Jouet* by Francis Veber), PH Laszlo Kovacs, M Patrick Williams, ED Richard Harris & Michael A. Stevenson, PD Charles Rosen.

LP Richard Pryor (Jack Brown), Jackie Gleason (U.S. Bates), Ned Beatty (Mr. Morehouse), Scott Schwartz (Eric Bates), Teresa Ganzel (Fancy Bates), Wilfrid Hyde-White (Barkley), Annazette Chase (Angela), Tony King (Clifford), Don Hood (O'Brien).

Janitor Richard Pryor finds himself the new "toy" of Scott Schwartz, the son of department store owner Jackie Gleason. Pryor gets to play a modern day slave in this not very funny movie.

3110. *Toy Soldiers* (1984, New World, 91m, c). P E. Darrell Hallenbeck, D David A. Fisher, W Fisher & Walter Fox, PH Francisco Bojorquez, M Leland Bond, ED Geoffrey Rowland.

LP Jason Miller (Sarge), Cleavon Little (Buck), Rodolfo De Anda (Col. Lopez), Terri Garber (Amy), Tracy Scoggins (Monique), Willard Pugh (Ace), Jim Greenleaf (Tom), Mary Beth Evans (Buffy), Tim Robbins (Boe).

A group of kids from Beverly Hills are on a relaxing cruise off Central America when they are taken captive and held for ransom. They escape and join-up with a seasoned mercenary who turns them into a vigilante force.

3111. *Track 29* (1988, Island, GB, 90m, c). P Rick McCallum, D Nicolas Roeg, W Dennis Potter, PH Alex Thomson, M Stanley Myers, ED Tony Lawson, PD David Brockhurst.

LP Theresa Russell (Linda Henry), Gary Oldman (Martin), Sandra Bernhard (Nurse Stein), Christopher Lloyd (Dr. Henry Henry), Colleen Camp (Arlanda), Seymour Cassel (Dr. Bernard Fairmont), Leon Rippy (Trucker).

Texas housewife Theresa Russell's husband Christopher Lloyd is more interested in model trains and nurse Sandra Bernhard than in her. Russell encounters mysterious Englishman Gary Oldman: Is he the son she abandoned years ago? It's a bewildering story.

3112. *Trading Hearts* (1988, Cineworld, 88m, c). P Herb Jaffe & Mort Engelberg, D Neil Leifer, W Frank Deford, PH Karen Grossman, M Stanley Myers, ED Rick Shaine, PD George Goodridge.

LP Raul Julia (Vinnie), Beverly D'Angelo (Donna), Jenny Lewis (Yvonne), Parris Buckner (Robert), Robert Gwaltney (Ducky), Ruben Rabasa (Pepe), Mark Harris (Ralph).

Set in 1957 Miami, Raul Julia, a washed-up pitcher with the Boston Red Sox, is released during spring training. Cute tomboy Jenny Lewis believes that Julia would make a neat new father, but her mother, lounge singer Beverly D'Angelo, isn't buying him.

3113. *Trading Places* (1983, Paramount, 106m, c). P Aaron Russo, D John Landis, W Timothy Harris & Herschel Weingrod, PH Robert Paynter, M Elmer Bernstein†, ED Malcolm Campbell, PD Gene Rudolf.

LP Dan Aykroyd (Louis Winthorpe, III), Eddie Murphy (Billy Ray Valentine), Ralph Bellamy (Randolph Duke), Don Ameche (Mortimer Duke), Denholm Elliott (Coleman), Jamie Lee Curtis (Ophelia), Kristin Holby (Penelope Witherspoon), Paul Gleason (Clarence Beeks).

Eddie Murphy establishes himself as a major star in this movie in which all participants deserve praise for their comedy work. Rich fat cat brothers Ralph Bellamy and Don Ameche make a bet about what will happen if Dan Aykroyd, who has had all the advantages that money and class can bring him, is forced to change places with poor black beggar Murphy. Ultimately, Aykroyd and Murphy turn the tables on Bellamy and Ameche, with the help of butler Denholm Elliott and prostitute Jamie Lee Curtis.

3114.   Trail of the Pink Panther (1982, MGM/United Artists, 97m, c). P Blake Edwards & Tony Adams, D Edwards, W Frank Waldman, Tom Waldman, B. Edwards & Geoffrey Edwards, Friz Freleng (based on a story by B. Edwards and characters created by David H. DePatie & Frelang, PH Dick Bush, M Henry Mancini, ED Alan Jones, PD Peter Mullins.

LP Peter Sellers (Inspector Clouseau), David Niven (Sir Charles Litton), Herbert Lom (Dreyfus), Richard Mulligan (Clouseau Sr.), Joanna Lumley (Marie Jouvet), Capucine (Lady Litton), Robert Loggia (Bruno), Harvey Korman (Prof. Balls), Burt Kwouk (Cato), Graham Stark (Hercule), Peter Arne (Col. Bufoni).

As this movie clearly demonstrates, there is no respect for the dead in Hollywood. Using outtakes of earlier Pink Panther movies and peppering the scenes with characters who appeared in them, director Blake Edwards gets one last sick laugh from the late Peter Sellers. Clouseau is reported missing after falling from a ship at sea. TV reporter Joanna Lumley interviews all who knew him including a ghastly looking David Niven, then suffering from Lou Gehrig's disease which would soon take his life.

Train of Terror   see   Terror Train

Trancers   see   Future Cop

3115.   The Transformers—The Movie (1986, DeLaurentiis, animated, 86m, c). P Joe Bacal & Tom Griffin, D Nelson Shin, W Ron Friedman, M Vince DiCola.

VOICES Eric Idle (Wreck Gar), Judd Nelson (Hot Rod/Rodimus Prime), Leonard Nimoy (Galvatron), Robert Stack (Ultra Magnus), Lionel Stander (Kup), Orson Welles (Unicorn), Scatman Crothers (Jazz), Clive Revill (Kickback).

The popular TV characters, who convert to cars and dinosaurs to fight evil, face their biggest challenge in combatting the sinister forces of Orson Welles.

3116.   Transylvania 6-5000 (1985, New World, 93m, c). P Mace Neufeld & Thomas H. Brodek, D&W Rudy De-Luca, PH Tom Pinter, M Lee Holdridge & Alfie Kabiljo, ED Harry Keller, PD Zeljko Senecic.

LP Jeff Goldblum (Jack Harrison), Joseph Bologna (Dr. Malavaqua), Ed Begley, Jr. (Gil Turner), Carol Kane (Lupi), Jeffrey Jones (Lepescu), John Byner (Radu), Geena Davis (Odette), Donald Gibb (Wolfman).

In a film that can only be described as dumb, dumb and dumb, klutzy reporters Jeff Goldblum and Ed Begley, Jr., go to modern day Transylvania where they encounter an array of comedic monsters. The wolfman has all the best lines.

3117.   Trapper County War (1989, Noble Ent. Group/Alpine, 95m, c). P Michael W. Leighton, D Worth Keeter, W Russel V. Manzatt, PH Irl Dixon, M Shuki Levy, ED Miriam L. Preisel, PD R. Clifford Searcy.

LP Robert Estes (Ryan Cassidy), Betsy Russell (Lacey Luddigger), Bo Hopkins (Sheriff Sam Frost), Don Swayze (Walt Luddigger), Noah Black (Bobby Keal), Sarah Hunley (Mom Luddigger), R.G. Armstrong (Pop Luddigger).

This city folks vs. rednecks story is better than most of its kind. Robert Estes and Noah Black are young New Jersey musicians who run into trouble in a small North Carolina community when they strike up a friendship with bored waitress Betsy Russell, who'd like to become a singer. The violent climax looks like the start of another civil war.

3118.   The Traveller (1989, BLP/ Lighthouse, Canada, 96m, c). P Bruno Lazaro Pacheco & Raymond Massey, D Pacheco, W Pacheco & Jean Pierre Lefebvre (based on an original story and

French screenplay by Guy P. Buckholtzer), PH Thomas H. Turnbull, M Daniel Ross, ED Pacheco & Patricia Lambkin.

LP R. Lewis Morrison (Robert Braun), Ginette St. Denis (Ginette), Denise Brillon, Phillip Stewart, James Stevens, Arlen Jones.

Wooden performances and direction doom this story of businessman R. Lewis Morrison who is in Vancouver to buy Pacific Northwest Indian masks. He has sort of a mid-life crisis because he's torn between his lucrative business exploiting the Indians and the fact that he was raised by the Indians and married one of their maidens.

3119. *Travelling North* (1988, View Pictures, Australia, 97m, c). P Ben Gannon, D Carl Schultz, W David Williamson (based on his play), PH Julian Penney, M Alan John, Beethoven, Mozart & Vivaldi, ED Henry Dangar, PD Owen Paterson.

LP Leo McKern (Frank), Julia Blake (Frances), Graham Kennedy (Freddie), Henri Szeps (Saul), Michele Fawdon (Helen), Diane Craig (Sophie), Andrea Moor (Joan), Drew Forsythe (Martin), John Gregg (Jim), Rob Steele (Syd).

Crusty seventyish Melbourne civil engineer Leo McKern retires. He convinces much younger widow Julie Blake to join him in starting a new life in subtropical northern Australia.

3120. *Traxx* (1988, DEG, 84m, c). P Gary De Vore & Richard McWhorter, D Jerome Gary, W Gary De Vore, PH Giuseppe Maccari, M Jay Gruska, ED Michael Kahane, PD Jack Poplin.

LP Shadoe Stevens (Traxx), Priscilla Barnes (Mayor Alexandria Cray), Willard E. Pugh (Deeter), John Hancock (Chief Emmett Decker), Hugh Gillin (Comm. R.B. Davis), Hershal Sparber, Jonathan Lutz & Lucius Houghton (Guziks), Darrow Igus (Wendall).

Ex-cop turned mercenary Shadoe Stevens starts a cookie business in a Texas town. Hoping for reward money from sexy mayor Priscilla Barnes, he teams with black sidekick Willard E. Pugh to take on the local Mafia and clean up a crime-ridden neighborhood.

3121. *Treasure of the Yankee Zephyr* (1984, Film Ventures, 90m, c, AKA *Race for the Yankee Zephyr*). P Anthony I. Ginnane, John Barnett & David Hemmings, D Hemmings, W Everett de Roche, PH Vincent Morton, M Brian May, ED John Laing, PD Bernard Hides.

LP Ken Wahl (Barney), Lesley Ann Warren (Sally), Donald Pleasence (Gibbie), George Peppard (Theo Brown), Bruno Lawrence & Robert Bruce (Barkers), Grant Tilly (Coin Collector), Harry Rutherford-Jones (Harry).

Wahl, Warren and Pleasence set off across New Zealand to find a plane that went down 40 years earlier carrying a cache of gold bars worth $50 million.

3122. *Tree of Hands* (1989, Greenpoint Film, GB, 90m, c). P Ann Scott, D Giles Foster, W Gordon Williams (based on the novel by Ruth Rendell), PH Kenneth MacMillan, M Richard Hartley, ED David Martin, PD Adrian Smith.

LP Helen Shaver (Benet Archdale), Lauren Bacall (Marsha Archdale), Malcolm Stoddard (Dr. Ian Raeburn), Peter Firth (Terence), Paul McGann (Barry), Kate Hardie (Carol).

Set in contemporary London, bestselling author Helen Shaver lives with her young son. Her mother Lauren Bacall, with a history of mental illness, arrives from the United States, intent on mending fences between her daughter and herself, and building a relationship with her grandson. When the boy dies unexpectedly, Bacall brings home a youngster she's found in the streets, beaten and abandoned by his parents. The two women decide to keep the child for a while. Shaver, posing as a journalist, gets to know his bickering parents, who are into kinky sex. There seems to be more plot here than director Giles Foster can handle.

3123. *Trenchcoat* (1983, Buena Vista, 91m, c). P Jerry Leider, D Michael Tuchner, W Jeffrey Price & Peter Seaman, PH Tonino Delli Colli, M Charles Fox, ED Frank J. Urioste, PD Rodger Maus.

LP Margot Kidder (Mickey Raymond), Robert Hays (Terry Leonard), David Suchet (Inspector Stagnos), Gila Von Weitershausen (Eva Werner), Daniel Faraldo (Nino Tenucci), Ronald Lacey (Princess Aida), John Justin (Marquis DePina).

In this detective spoof, aspiring mystery writer Margot Kidder heads to Malta to write a story and finds herself drawn into a real-life conspiracy.

3124. *Trespasses* (1987, Shapiro, 100m, c). P Loren Bivens & Richard Rosetta, D Adam Roarke & Bivens, W Bivens & Lou Diamond Phillips & Jo Carol Pierce, PH Monte Dhooge & Phil Curry, M Wayne Bell & Chuck Pennell, ED Sherri Galloway, AD Becky Block & Lisa Knight.

LP Robert Kuhn (Franklin Ramsey), Van Brooks (Richard), Mary Pillot (Sharon Rae), Adam Roarke & Lou Diamond Phillips (Drifters), Ben Johnson (August Klein), Deborah Neumann (Catherine), Thom Meyer (Johnny Ramsey).

Shot in 1983, this is the inane story of the relationship of cattleman Robert Kuhn and married rape victim Mary Pillot.

3125. *Tribute* (1980, 20th Century–Fox, Canada, 123m, c). P Joel B. Michaels & Garth B. Drabinsky, D Bob Clark, W Bernard Slade (based on his stage play), PH Reginald H. Morris, M Kenn Wannberg, Barry Manilow, Jack Feldman, Bruce Sussman, Jack Lemmon & Alan Jay Lerner, ED Richard Halsey, PD Trevor Williams.

LP Jack Lemmon† (Scottie Templeton), Robby Benson (Jud Templeton), Lee Remick (Maggie Stratton), Kim Cattrall (Sally Haines), Colleen Dewhurst (Gladys Petrelli), John Marley (Lou Daniels), Gale Garnett (Hilary).

Dying Broadway press agent Jack Lemmon is determined to achieve a reconciliation with his son Robby Benson. With the help of his ex-wife Lee Remick, he succeeds. Benson arranges for a testimonial dinner for his father before he dies.

3126. *Trick or Treat* (1986, DeLaurentiis, 97m, c). P Michael S. Murphey & Joel Soisson, D Charles Martin Smith, W Murphey, Soisson & Rhet Topham (based on a story by Topham), PH Robert Elswit, M Christopher Young & Fastway, ED Jane Schwartz Jaffe, PD Curt Schnell.

LP Marc Price (Eddie Weinbauer),

Tony Fields (Sammi Curr), Lisa Orgolini (Leslie Graham), Doug Savant (Tim Hainey), Elaine Joyce (Angie Weinbauer), Glen Morgan (Roger Mockus), Gene Simmons (Nuke), Ozzy Osbourne (Rev. Aaron Gilstrom).

High school nerd and school scapegoat Marc Price conjures up the disfigured ghost of his late rock idol Tony Fields to help him take revenge on his numerous tormentors. The film is a comical homage to heavy-metal horror.

3127. *Trick or Treats* (1982, Lone Star, 91m, c). P,D,W,PH&ED Gary Graver, SD Michael Railsback.

LP Jackelyn Giroux (Linda), Peter Jason (Malcolm), Chris Graver (Christopher), David Carradine (Richard), Carrie Snodgress (Joan), Jillian Kesner (Andrea), Dan Pastorini & Tim Rossovich (Men in White Shorts).

The film is another of the many *Halloween* rip-offs, no better or worse than the average. It's a strange tribute to a moneymaker that has its own poorly produced clones.

3128. *The Trip to Bountiful* (1985, Island, 105m, c). P Sterling VanWagenen & Horton Foote, D Peter Masterson, W Foote† (based on his play), PH Fred Murphy, M J.A.C. Redford, ED Jay Freund, PD Neil Spisak.

LP Geraldine Page* (Mrs. Watts), John Heard (Ludie Watts), Carlin Glynn (Jessie Mae Watts), Richard Bradford (Sheriff), Rebecca De Mornay (Thelma), Kevin Cooney (Roy), Norman Bennett & Harvey Lewis (Bus Ticket Men), Kirk Sisco (Ticket Agent, Houston Train Station), Dave Tanner (Billy Davis).

Geraldine Page is perfection as an old woman in 1947 living in cramped quarters in a Houston Texas apartment with her wimpy son John Heard and his shrewish wife Carlin Glynn. Page's heart is not strong and the only dream she has left in life is to return to the small town of Bountiful where she was born and grew up. She hides her pension check from Glynn and escapes to the bus station when her daughter-in-law is away. The town is a ruin and her ex-home is an abandoned shack, but the sheriff of the region allows her one last look at the place which means so much to her. She sees it as it was and doesn't mind so much when her son and his wife come for her to take her back to Houston.

3129. *Triumph of the Spirit* (1989, Nova Intl., 120m, c). P Arnold Kopelson & Shimon Arama, D Robert M. Young, W Andrzej Krakowski & Laurence Heath (based on a story by Arama & Zion Haen), PH Curtis Clark, M Cliff Eidelman, ED Arthur Coburn, PD Jerzy Maslowska.

LP Willem Dafoe (Salamo Arouch), Edward James Olmos (Gypsy), Robert Loggia (Poppa), Wendy Gazelle (Allegra), Kelly Wolf (Elena), Costas Mandylor (Avram), Kario Salem (Jacko), Edward Zentara (Janush), Hartmut Becker (Maj. Rauscher).

Filmed almost entirely inside the Auschwitz/Birkenau Nazi death camps, the film presents the true story of a Greek boxing champion (Willem Dafoe) who saved his life by entertaining Nazi officers by defeating opponents in a ring at Auschwitz. The vanquished were sent to the gas chamber and the contestants were aware that was to be the fate of the losers. The film fails to be great drama because it is so obvious and sentimental. Then too, the director doesn't explore the moral anguish that the boxer must have felt.

3130. *Triumphs of a Man Called Horse* (1984, Redwing/Jensen Farley, US/Mex., 86m, c). P Derek Gibson, D John Hough, W Ken Blackwell & Carlos Aured (based on a story by Jack DeWitt and a character created by Dorothy M. Johnson), PH John Alcott & John Cabrera, M George Garvarentz, ED Roy Watts, PD Alan Roderick-Jones.

LP Richard Harris (Man Called Horse), Michael Beck (Koda), Ana De Sade (Redwing), Vaughn Armstrong (Capt. Cummings), Anne Seymour (Elk Woman), Buck Taylor (Sgt. Bridges), Simon Andreu (Gance), Lautaro Murua (Perkins).

In this dumb rip-off of the "Man Called Horse" series, Richard Harris appears very briefly as the white man who has led a Sioux tribe for 30 years. It is his half-breed son Michael Beck who must save his people from prospectors and once more bring peace to his land.

3131. *Troll* (1986, Marvin Films, 86m, c). P Albert Band, D John Buechler, W Ed Naha, PH Romano Albani, M Richard Band, ED Lee Percy.

LP June Lockhart (Eunice St. Clair), Jenny Beck (Wendy Potter), Anne Lockhart (Young Eunice St. Clair), Shelley Hack (Mrs. Potter), Michael Moriarty (Mr. Potter), Sonny Bono (Peter Dickenson).

In this fantasy, a malevolent troll haunts an apartment building. It plans to turn all humans into trolls.

3132. *Troma's War* (1988, Troma, 99m, c). P Lloyd Kaufman & Michael Herz, D Herz & Samuel Weil, W Mitchell Dana & Kaufman (based on a story by Kaufman), PH Jane London, PD Alexis Grey.

LP Carolyn Beauchamp (Lydia), Sean Bowen (Taylor), Michael Ryder (Parker), Patrick Weathers (Kirkland), Jessica Dublin (Dottie), Steven Crossley (Marshall), Lorayn Lane DeLuca (Maria), Charles Kay Hune (Hardwick).

A group of survivors of an air crash find themselves fighting terrorists with plans of infecting the people of the U.S. with an AIDS virus. Timely, but dumb.

3133. *Tron* (1982, Buena Vista, 96m, c). P Donald Kushner, D&W Steven Lisberger (based on a story by Lisberger & Bonnie MacBird), PH Bruce Logan, M Wendy Carlos, ED Jeff Gourson, PD Dean Edward Mitzner, COS Elois Jenssen & Rosanna Norton†, SOUND Michael Minkler, Bob Minkler, Lee Minkler & Jim La Rue.

LP Jeff Bridges (Kevin Flynn/Clu), Bruce Boxleitner (Alan Bradley/Tron), David Warner (Ed Dillinger/Sark), Cindy Morgan (Lora/Yori), Barnard Hughes (Dr. Walter Gibbs/Dumont), Dan Shor (Ram), Peter Jurasik (Crom).

Video game designer Jeff Bridges is scientifically transformed into a component of a computer and must battle his own creations in the "Tron" dimension in order to survive. It's the old western good guys wear white, bad guys wear black shtick with a science fiction twist.

3134. *Troop Beverly Hills* (1989, Columbia, 100m, c). P Ava Ostern Fries, D

Jeff Kanew, W Pamela Norris & Margaret Grieco Oberman, PH Donald E. Thorin, M Randy Edelman, ED Mark Melnick, PD Robert F. Boyle, AD Jack G. Taylor, Jr.

LP Shelley Long (Phyllis Nefler), Craig T. Nelson (Freddy Nefler), Betty Thomas (Velda Plendor), Mary Gross (Annie Herman), Stephanie Beacham (Vicki Sprantz), Audra Lindley (Frances Temple), Carla Gugino (Chica Barnfell).

How can you not like spoiled princess Shelley Long? Well, it's possible if she doesn't soon add some other facets to her act. Still tossing her hair, wearing smart clothes and being the know-it-all that we came to love on TV's "Cheers" and in a few movies, Long is den mother to a group of Beverly Hills girls scouts. Somehow the fancy locale is supposed to make a difference. OK Shelley, we'll let you get away with it one more time—but for goodness' sake grow up!

3135. *Tropical Snow* (1989, PSM Ent., 88m, c). P J.D. Leif, D&W Ciro Duran, PH Eduardo Serra, M Alan DerMarderosian, ED Duncan Burns, Oscar Alzate.

LP Nick Corri (Gustavo [Tavo]), Madeleine Stowe (Marina), David Carradine (Oskar), Argermiro Catiblanco, Alfonso Ortiz, Merena Dimont, Libia Tenorio, Roger Melo, Celmira Yepes, William Mesa, Sonia Ceballos, Antonio Corral.

In view of Colombia's attempted crackdown on druglords, this movie filmed in Bogotá and Barranquilla in 1986 is at least timely. Colombian couple Nick Corri and Madeleine Stowe want to leave their country for New York to find a better life. They are offered free passage by David Carradine if they will do him a little favor— smuggle a lot of cocaine into the States.

3136. *Trouble in Mind* (1985, Raincity/Alive, 111m, c). P Carolyn Pfeiffer & David Blocker, D&W Alan Rudolph, PH Toyomichi Kurita, M Mark Isham, ED Sally Coryn Allen & Tom Walls, PD Steven Legler.

LP Kris Kristofferson (Hawk), Keith Carradine (Coop), Lori Singer (Georgia), Genevieve Bujold (Wanda), Joe Morton (Solo), Divine (Hilly Blue), George Kirby (Lt. Gunther), John Considine (Nate Nathanson), Dirk Blocker (Rambo), Albert Hall (Leo).

Former detective Kris Kristofferson returns home after serving a prison term for killing a mobster. He moves into an apartment over a seedy diner run by his former lover Genevieve Bujold. Small-time hood Keith Carradine and girlfriend Lori Singer move their camper next door to the diner. Kristofferson falls for Singer. When Crime boss Divine (in his only nondrag role) orders a hit on Carradine, Kristofferson intervenes for Singer's sake.

3137. *The Trouble with Dick* (1987, Frolix, 93m, c). P Gary Walkow & Leslie Robins, D&W Walkow, PH Daryl Studebaker, M Roger Bourland, ED G.A. Walkowishky, PD Eric Jones.

LP Tom Villard (Dick Kendred), Susan Dey (Diane), Elaine Giftos (Sheila Dibble), Elizabeth Gorcey (Haley Dibble), David Clennon (Lars), Jack Carter (Samsa), Marianne Muellerleile (Betty).

Tom Villard, a struggling writer of "literary science fiction," is suffering from writer's block. While he would like to renew a romance with Susan Dey, she's not interested so he seeks his muse with his divorced landlady Elaine Giftos and her hot-to-trot daughter Elizabeth Gorcey, but this only earns him a nervous breakdown.

3138. *The Trouble with Spies* (1987, DEG-HBO, 91m, c). P,D&W Burt Kennedy (based on the novel *Apple Pie in the Sky* by Marc Lovell), PH Alex Phillips, M Ken Thorne, ED Warner E. Leighton, PD Jose Maria Tapiador.

LP Donald Sutherland (Appleton Porter), Ned Beatty (Harry Lewis), Ruth Gordon (Mrs. Arkwright), Lucy Gutteridge (Mona Smith), Michael Hordern (Jason Lock), Robert Morley (Angus Watkins), Gregory Sierra (Capt. Sanchez).

Made for HBO in 1984 but never shown on cable, Donald Sutherland appears as a bumbling British agent sent to the Mediterranean isle of Ibiza to find Soviet spies who have developed a truth serum. Sutherland is no Peter Sellers in this poor attempt to imitate an Inspector Clouseau/Pink Panther film.

3139. *True Believer* (1989, Columbia, 104m, c). P Walter F. Parkes & Lawrence

Lasker, D Joseph Ruben, W Wesley Strick, PH John W. Lindley, M Brad Fiedel, ED George Bowers, PD Lawrence Miller.

LP James Woods (Eddie Dodd), Robert Downey, Jr. (Roger Baron), Margaret Colin (Kitty Greer), Yuji Okumoto (Shu Kai Kim), Kurtwood Smith (Robert Reynard), Tom Bower (Cecil Skell), Miguel Fernandes (Art Esparza).

Woods, a 60s-style liberal, idealistic lawyer, is still taking cases for the underdog in the 80s. He's hired by a Japanese woman to defend her son in prison for murder. As part of a prison gang he has become implicated in another murder. Lawyers like Woods are adept at espousing conspiracy theories against their clients. They often defend clients that the general public already believe guilty from reading and listening to news stories about the cases. We need such attorneys, even if we don't always relish their working methods.

3140. *True Blood* (1989, Fries Ent., 97m, c). P Peter Maris, D&W Frank Kerr, PH Mark H.L. Morris, M Scott Roewe, ED Mac Haight.

LP Jeff Fahey (Ray Trueblood), Chad Lowe (Donny Trueblood), Sherilyn Fenn (Jennifer), James Tolkan (Lt. Joe Hanley), Billy Drago (Spider Masters), Ken Foree (Charlie).

The film is a predictable crime drama about street gangs and rumbles. It's violent enough but for no noticeable purpose.

3141. *True Confessions* (1981, United Artists, 108m, c). P Irwin Winkler & Robert Chartoff, D Ulu Grosbard, W John Gregory Dunne & Joan Didion (based on the novel by Dunne), PH Owen Roizman, M Georges Delerue, ED Lynzee Klingman, PD Stephen S. Grimes.

LP Robert De Niro (Des Spellacy), Robert Duvall (Tom Spellacy), Charles Durning (Jack Amsterdam), Ed Flanders (Dan T. Champion), Burgess Meredith (Seamus Fargo), Rose Gregorio (Brenda Samuels), Cyril Cusack (Cardinal Danaher), Kenneth McMillan (Frank Crotty), Dan Hedeya (Howard Terkel).

In 1948 L.A. homicide detective Robert Duvall clashes with his brother Robert De Niro, a bright young monsignor with quite a future in the Catholic Church.

The bone of contention is former pimp and hood Charles Durning, striving desperately for respectability, trying to buy his way to heaven with his contributions to the church. Duvall wants to burn Durning for the murder of a "Black Dahlia"-like whore, while De Niro is forced to award Durning the title "Catholic Layman of the Year." Duvall wins out and the scandal ruins De Niro's career, condemning him to a life as the pastor of a tiny run-down church in the desert. DeNiro and Duvall, two of the best "star" characters actors in the business, are both superb.

3142. *True Love* (1989, United Artists, 104m, c). P Richard Guay & Shelley Houis, D Nancy Savoca, W Savoca & Guay, PH Lisa Rinzler, M Various Composers, ED John Tintori, PD Lester W. Cohen.

LP Annabella Sciorra (Donna), Ron Eldard (Michael), Aida Turturro (Grace), Roger Rignack (Dom), Star Jasper (J.C.), Michael J. Wolfe (Brian), Kelly Cinnante (Yvonne), Rick Shapiro (Kevin).

Hollywood brought audiences *Moonstruck,* the story of a romance in New York's Little Italy. Now director Nancy Savoca invites us to a large, rambunctious Italian-American wedding — and anyone who has attended one knows how much fun they can be. This one doesn't disappoint and neither does this touching, amusing and memorable film.

3143. *True Stories* (1986, Warner, 111m, c). P Gary Kurfirst, D David Byrne, W Stephen Tobolowsky, Beth Henley & Byrne, PH Ed Lachman, M Talking Heads, ED Caroline Biggerstaff, PD Barbara Ling.

LP John Goodman (Louis Fyne), Annie McEnroe (Kay Culver), Jo Harvey Allen (The Lying Woman), Spalding Gray (Earl Culver), Alix Elias (The Cute Woman), Roebuck "Pops" Staples (Mr. Tucker), Humberto "Tito" Larriva (Ramon), John Ingle (The Preacher), Swoosie Kurtz (The Lazy Woman), David Byrne (Narrator).

This is a long-rock video with head Talking Head David Byrne presenting audiences who care with the eccentric lives of the weird folks who reside in the fictional town of Virgil, Texas. For Talking

Head fans, ignore the movie; listen to the soundtrack LP.

3144. *Trust Me* (1989, Cinecom, 104m, c). P George Edwards, D Bobby Houston, W Houston & Gary Rigdon, PH Thomas Jewett, M Pray for Rain, ED Barry Zetlin.

LP Adam Ant (James Callendar), David Packer (Sam Brown), Talia Balsam (Catherine Walker), William DeAcutis (Billy Brawthwaite), Joyce Van Patten (Nettie Brown), Barbara Bain (Mary Casal), Brooke Da Vida (Denise Tipton), Simon McQueen (Holly Windsor), Alma Beltran (Imelda), Marilyn Tokuda (Chic Girl).

Adam Ant stars as an art gallery owner who doesn't know much about art, but does know that a dead painter's work brings in more money than a live one. He tries to drive artist David Packer over the brink so he'll leave this vale of tears, which will quickly be followed by a markup of his cute little cherubs in flight.

3145. *Tuck Everlasting* (1981, Vestron, animated, 100m, c). P Howard Kling, W Stratton Rawson, Fred A. Keller, F.K. Keller, Jim Bisco, M Malcolm Dalglish, Grey Larson, AD Michael Bucur, D Frederick King Keller (based on the novel by Natalie Babbitt).

VOICES Margaret Chamberlain, Paul Flessa, Fred A. Keller, James McGuire, Sonia Raimi, Bruce D'Auria.

Dreamy young Margaret Chamberlain befriends a family with an incredible secret in this entertaining fable.

3146. *Tucker: The Man and His Dream* (1988, Paramount, 111m, c). P Fred Roos & Fred Fuchs, D Francis Ford Coppola, W Arnold Schulman & David Seidler, PH Vittorio Storaro, M Joe Jackson, ED Priscilla Nedd, PD Dean Tavoularis†, AD Alex Tavoularis, SD Armin Ganz†, COS Milena Canonero.

LP Jeff Bridges (Preston Tucker), Joan Allen (Vera Tucker), Martin Landau† (Abe Karatz), Frederic Forrest (Eddie Dean), Mako (Jimmy Sakuyama), Lloyd Bridges (Senator Homer Ferguson), Elias Koteas (Alex Tremulis), Christian Slater (Junior), Nina Siemaszko (Marilyn Lee Tucker), Dean Stockwell (Howard Hughes).

In the late 1940s, Preston Tucker, part visionary, part conman, has a dream of building the best car possible, with aerodynamic design, seat belts, rear engine, fuel injection, disc brakes, pop-out windows, etc., features which only in recent years found their ways into cars. In the late 1940s, he attempts to make that dream a reality, with the Tucker automobile, "The Car of Tomorrow—Today!" Unfortunately, he tries to sell the cars even before he had a working model. This minor drawback, combined with the opposition of the major automobile makers of the time and the politicians they have in their pockets, is enough to grease the skids for the exuberant world-beater-to-be, and destroy his dream.

3147. *Tuff Turf* (1985, New World, 112m, c). P Donald P. Borchers, D Fritz Kiersch, W Jette Rinck (based on a story by Greg Collins O'Neill & Murray Michaels), PH Willy Kurant, M Jonathan Elias, ED Marc Grossman, AD Craig Stearns.

LP James Spader (Morgan Hiller), Kim Richards (Frankie Croyden), Paul Mones (Nick Hauser), Matt Clark (Stuart Hiller), Claudette Nevins (Page Hiller), Robert Downey, Jr. (Jimmy Parker), Olivia Barash (Ronnie).

The new kid in a lowerclass section of L.A., tough but brainy James Spader engages local gang leader Paul Mones in a bitter turf dispute.

3148. *Tulips* (1981, Avco Embassy, Canada, 92m, c). P Don Carmody, D Stan Ferris (Mark Warren, Rex Bromfield, Al Waxman), W Fred Sappho (Bromfield, Waxman, Henry Olek & Gabe Kaplan), PH Francois Protat, M Eddie Karam, ED Alan Collins & Yurij Lohovy, AD Ted Watkins.

LP Gabe Kaplan (Leland Irving), Bernadette Peters (Rutanya Wallace), Al Waxman (Bert Irving), Henry Gibson (Maurice "Boom Boom" Avocado), David Boxer (Dr. Carl Walburn), Jazzmine Lauzane (Metermaid).

Believing that he has nothing to live for but unable to commit suicide, Gabe Kaplan takes out a contract on his life, then meets Bernadette Peters, who makes him want to live—but how do they cancel his "hit"?

Tunnels see *Criminal Act*

3149. *Turk 182!* (1985, 20th Century–Fox, 98m, c). P Ted Field & Rene Dupont, D Bob Clark, W James Gregory Kingston, Denis Hamill & John Hamill (based on a story by Kingston), PH Reginald H. Morris, M Paul Zaza, ED Stan Cole, PD Harry Pottle.

LP Timothy Hutton (Jimmy Lynch), Robert Urich (Terry Lynch), Kim Cattrall (Danny Boudreau), Robert Culp (Mayor Tyler), Darren McGavin (Detective Kowalski), Steven Keats (Jockamo), Paul Sorvino (Himself), Peter Boyle (Detective Ryan), James S. Tolkan (Hanley).

When New York fireman Robert Urich is disabled rescuing a little girl from a burning building, he is denied his pension because he was off duty and drunk at the time. His angry brother Timothy Hutton takes on City Hall to win back his brother's rights.

3150. *Turkey Shoot* (1983, Hemdale, Australia, 92m, c, aka *Escape 2000*). P Anthony I. Ginnane & William Fayman, D Brian Trenchard-Smith, W Jon George & Neill Hicks (based on a story by George Schenck, Robert Williams & David Lawrence), PH John McLean, M Brian May, ED Alan Lake, PD Bernard Hides.

LP Steve Railsback (Paul Anders), Olivia Hussey (Chris Walters), Michael Craig (Charles Thatcher), Carmen Duncan (Jennifer), Noel Ferrier (Mallory), Lynda Stoner (Rita Daniels), Roger Ward (Ritter), Michael Petrovich (Tito).

In this sadistic, futuristic bloodbath, individuality is considered a crime and those who fail to conform are hunted down like animals in a jungle.

3151. *Turner and Hooch* (1989, Touchstone, 98m, c). P Raymond Wagner, D Roger Spottiswoode, W Dennis Shryack, Michael Blodgett, Daniel Petrie, Jr., Jim Cash & Jack Epps, Jr. (based on a story by Shryack, Blodgett and Petrie), PH Adam Greenberg, M Charles Gross, ED Paul Seydor, Mark Conte, Kenneth Morrisey & Lois Freeman-Fox, PD John De Cuir, Jr.

LP Tom Hanks (Scott Turner), Mare Winningham (Emily Carson), Beasley (Hooch), Craig T. Nelson (Chief Hyde), Reginald VelJohnson (David Sutton), Scott Paulin (Zack Gregory), J.C. Quinn (Walter Boyett), John McIntire (Amos Reed).

Tom Hanks has worked with many funny partners including John Candy, Dan Aykroyd, Shelley Long and Jackie Gleason, but none were any more appealing than his canine partner Beasley. Fussy police detective Hanks is investigating the murder of the master of the massive, ugly creature with huge floppy jowls and a constantly drooling mouth.

3152. *Turtle Diary* (1985, Goldwyn, GB, 97m, c). P Richard Johnson, D John Irvin, W Harold Pinter (based on a novel by Russell Hoban), PH Peter Hannan, M Geoffrey Burgon, ED Peter Tanner, PD Leo Austin.

LP Glenda Jackson (Neaera Duncan), Ben Kingsley (William Snow), Richard Johnson (Mr. Johnson), Michael Gambon (George Fairbairn), Rosemary Leach (Mrs. Inchcliff), Eleanor Bron (Miss Neap), Jeroen Krabbe (Sandor).

In this witty, eccentric comedy, writer-artist Glenda Jackson and bookstore clerk Ben Kingsley, both self-admitted "characters," take it upon themselves to release turtles from captivity in the London Zoo.

3153. *Twice Dead* (1988, Concorde, 85m, c). P Guy J. Louthan & Robert McDonnell, D Bert Dragin, W Bert Dragin & Robert McDonnell, PH Zoran Hochstatter, M David Bergeaud, ED Patrick Rand, PD Stephan Rice.

LP Tom Breznahan (Scott), Jill Whitlow (Robin/Myrna), Jonathan Chapin (Crip/Tyler), Christopher Burgard (Silk), Sam Melville (Harry), Brooke Bundy (Sylvia), Todd Bridges (Petie), Shawn Player (Stony).

When an All-American family moves into a home that a street gang has been using for a clubhouse, the punks aren't happy and terrorize the family. A ghost in the home helps the family foil the gang.

3154. *Twice in a Lifetime* (1985, Yorkin, 117m, c). P&D Bud Yorkin, W Colin Welland, PH Nick McLean, M Pat Metheny, ED Robert C. Jones & Catherine L. Peacock, PD William J. Creber.

LP Gene Hackman (Harry MacKenzie), Ann-Margret (Audrey Minelli), Ellen Burstyn (Kate MacKenzie), Amy Madigan† (Sunny Sobel), Ally Sheedy

(Helen MacKenzie), Brian Dennehy (Nick), Stephen Lang (Keith Sobel), Darrell Larson (Jerry MacKenzie), Chris Parker (Tim).

Gene Hackman turns fifty and decides to make a clean break with his family and start a new life with busty barmaid Ann-Margret. His self-sacrificing wife Ellen Burstyn puts aside her despair at being deserted to plan her daughter's wedding. It's just another midlife-crisis comedy drama with no new insights into the problem.

3155. *Twice Upon a Time* (1983, Warner, animated, 75m, c). P Bill Couturie, D John Korty & Charles Swenson, W Korty, Swenson, Suella Kennedy & Couturie (based on a story by Korty, Couturie & Kennedy), M Dawn Atkinson & Ken Melville, ED Jennifer Gallagher, AD Harley Jessup.

VOICES Lorenzo Music (Ralph), Judith Kahan Kampmann (Fairy Godmother), Marshall Elfron (Synonamess Botch), James Cranna (Rod Rescueman/ Scuzzbopper), Julie Payne (Flora Fauna), Hamilton Camp (Greensleeves), Paul Frees (Narrator/Chief of Stage/ Judge/Bailiff).

Using a pseudo-cutout style called "Lumage," this animated feature pits a silly bunch of would-be heroes against the evil bosses of Murkworks who wish to doom the world to perpetual darkness. Young kids aren't going to get it, older kids and adults probably won't care.

3156. *Twilight Zone — The Movie* (1983, Warner, 102m, c). P Steven Spielberg & John Landis, D&W Landis (Segment 1 & Prologue); D Spielberg, W George Clayton Johnson, Richard Matheson & Josh Rogan (Segment 2); D Joe Dante, W Matheson (based on a story by Jerome Bixby) (Segment 3); D George Miller, W Matheson (based on his story) (Segment 4) (All based on stories which appeared on Rod Serling's TV series "Twilight Zone"), PH Stevan Larner, Allen Daviau & John Hora, M Jerry Goldsmith, ED Malcolm Campbell, Michael Kahn, Tina Hirsch & Howard Smith, PD James D. Bissell.

LP Segment 1 and Prolog: Dan Aykroyd (Passenger), Albert Brooks (Driver), Vic Morrow (Bill), Doug McGrath (Larry), Charles Hallahan (Ray); Segment 2: Scatman Crothers (Bloom), Bill Quinn (Conroy), Martin Garner (Weinstein), Selma Diamond (Mrs. Weinstein), Helen Shaw (Mrs. Dempsey), Murray Matheson (Agee); Segment 3: Kathleen Quinlan (Helen), Jeremy Licht (Anthony), Kevin McCarthy (Uncle Walt), Patricia Barry (Mother), William Schallert (Father); Segment 4: John Lithgow (Valentine), Abbe Lane (Senior Stewardess), Donna Dixon (Junior Stewardess), Larry Cedar (Creature).

In the only segment not based on an original episode of TV's "Twilight Zone," Vic Morrow portrays a big-mouthed bigot who is transported in time to Nazi-occupied France where he is a persecuted Jew, to the South as a black being tracked by the KKK, and then to Vietnam where he is a "gook" hunted by American soldiers. Tragically, Morrow and two Vietnamese children were killed in an accident during the making of this segment. In the second segment, based on "Kick the Can," Scatman Crothers arrives at a retirement home, where he gets the old folks to play a game of kick-the-can; they are transformed into youthful incarnations of themselves, but only briefly. In the third segment, based on the episode "It's a Good Life," Jeremy Licht is a little boy who has everyone in the house where he lives terrified of him because he is able to turn them into cartoon characters on TV. In the final segment, based on "Nightmare at 20,000 Feet," John Lithgow appears as a plane passenger deathly afraid of flying. His phobia causes him to see a menacing creature standing on the wing of the plane in flight. Of course no one else sees the creature — save the audience, that is.

3157. *Twinkle, Twinkle, "Killer" Kane* (1980, Warner, 105m, c, aka *The Ninth Configuration*). P,D&W William Peter Blatty (based on his novel), PH Gerry Fisher, M Barry DeVorzon, ED T. Battle Davis, Peter Lee Thompson & Roberto Silvi, PD Bill Malley & J. Dennis Washington.

LP Stacy Keach (Col. Kane), Scott Wilson (Capt. Cutshaw), Jason Miller (Lt. Reno), Ed Flanders (Col. Fell), Neville Brand (Groper), George DiCenzo

(Capt. Fairbanks), Moses Gunn (Maj. Nammack), Robert Loggia (Lt. Bennish), Joe Spinell (Spinell), Alejandro Rey (Lt. Gomez).

Stacy Keach, the new psychiatrist at a military mental institution, may be crazier than his patients.

3158. *Twins* (1988, Universal, 112m, c). P&D Ivan Reitman, W William Davies, William Osborne, Timothy Harris & Herschel Weingrod, PH Andrzej Bartkowiak, M Georges Delerue & Randy Edelman, ED Sheldon Kahn & Donn Cambern, PD James D. Bissell.

LP Arnold Schwarzenegger (Julius Benedict), Danny DeVito (Vincent Benedict), Kelly Preston (Marnie Mason), Chloe Webb (Linda Mason), Bonnie Bartlett (Mary Ann Benedict), Marshall Bell (Webster), Trey Wilson (Beetroot McKinley), David Caruso (Al Greco), Hugh O'Brien (Granger), Nehemiah Persoff (Mitchell Traven).

Danny DeVito is a very droll little man. Arnold Schwarzenegger has a way to go before he can be considered intentionally funny. In this outlandish comedy, DeVito carries his musclebound partner, with the two playing twins, their difference the result of a genetic experiment. They are separated after birth, Arnie raised by a scientist, not only to be a perfect physical specimen, but a perfect man. DeVito is—well, DeVito, kicked out of his orphanage for corrupting a nun, grown to being a womanizing, thieving conman. Things get going when the two are reunited.

The Twisted Legend of Dr. Hunter S. Thompson see Where the Buffalo Roam

3159. *Twisted Nightmare* (1988, United Filmmakers, 94m, c). P Sandy Horowitz, D Paul Hunt, W Hunt, PH Hunt & Gary Graver, ED Allen Persselin, SE Cleve Hall.

LP Rhonda Gray (Laura), Cleve Hall, Brad Bartrum, Robert Padillo, Heather Sullivan, Scott King, Juliet Martin.

Seven young couples are murdered one-by-one at a secluded backwoods camp by an unseen killer. If it sounds like dozens of other slasher films—that's because it is.

3160. *Twister* (1989, Vestron, 94m, c). P Wieland Schulz-Keil, D&W Michael Almereyda (based on the novel *Oh* by Mary Robison), PH Renato Berta, M Hans Zimmer, ED Roberto Silvi, PD David Wasco.

LP Harry Dean Stanton (Eugene Cleveland), Suzy Amis (Maureen Cleveland), Crispin Glover (Howdy Cleveland), Dylan McDermott (Chris), Jenny Wright (Stephanie), Charlaine Woodard (Lola), Lois Chiles (Virginia), William S. Burroughs (Man in Bar).

Retired soda pop tycoon Harry Dean Stanton presides over a fruitcake Kansas family consisting of his do-nothing daughter, Suzy Amis, his would-be-but-probably-never-will-be artist son, Crispin Glover, the latter's fiancé, Jenny Wright, an uppity black maid, Charlaine Woodard, and his own fiancée, Lois Chiles. Arriving just ahead of an impending twister is Amis' estranged husband Dylan McDermott, who for some weird reason would like to once more be part of this oddball group.

3161. *Two for the Money* (1985, Bonner Films, 75m, c). P Mary Holland, D Lee Bonner, W Bonner & Leif Elsmo, PH David Insley, M John Palumbo, ED Bonner & Randy Aitken, PD Vincent Peranio.

LP Ronald Hunter (Walter), Sean Murphy (Betsy), Steve Beauchamp (Skipper), Peter Walker (Oliver), Hans Kramm (Bartender), Joseph Cimino, Art Donovan, Marcello Rollando & George Stover (Gangsters).

In this routine crime thriller Ronald Hunter is in trouble with the mob. It's pay up or be shut up, for good.

3162. *Two Moon Junction* (1988, Lorimar, 104m, c). P Donald P. Borchers, D Zalman King, W King (based on a story by King & MacGregor Douglas), PH Mark Plummer, M Jonathan Elias, ED Marc Grossman, PD Michelle Minch.

LP Sherilyn Fenn (April Delongpre), Richard Tyson (Perry), Louise Fletcher (Belle), Kristy McNichol (Patti-Jean), Martin Hewitt (Chad Douglas Fairchild), Burl Ives (Sheriff Earl Hawkins), Juanita Moore (Delilah), Don Galloway (Senator Delongpre), Millie Perkins (Mrs. Delongpre), Herve Villechaize (Smiley).

In this softcore porn movie, wealthy engaged Southern girl Sherilyn Fenn gets an itch, which she scratches, to take off with Richard Tyson, a Conan-like hunk working with a carnival. Her grandma Louise Fletcher and sheriff Burl Ives conspire to ruin her fun. No one in this movie ever restrains themselves when it comes to sex. Clothes come off often in great sensual frenzies.

3163. *Two of a Kind* (1983, 20th Century–Fox, 87m, c). P Roger M. Rothstein & Joe Wizan, D&W John Herzfeld, PH Fred Koenekamp, M Patrick Williams, ED Jack Hofstra, PD Albert Brenner.

LP John Travolta (Zack), Olivia Newton-John (Debbie), Charles Durning (Charlie), Beatrice Straight (Ruth), Scatman Crothers (Earl), Castulo Guerra (Gonzales), Oliver Reed (Beazley), Richard Bright (Stuart).

Four angels propose to an angry God that the earth be spared from a second flood if two arbitrarily chosen human beings can be seen to perform a great sacrifice for each other. The makers of this film must have hoped that John Travolta and Olivia Newton-John would recapture some of the magic of *Grease*. They didn't and we could understand God's opening up the skies and letting the rain begin to fall, if the world depends on these two.

3164. *2010* (1984, MGM/United Artists, 114m, c). P,D&W Peter Hyams (based on the novel *2010: Odyssey Two* by Arthur C. Clarke), PH Hyams, M David Shire, Richard Strauss & Gyorgi Ligeti, ED James Mitchell & Mia Goldman, PD Albert Brenner†, SD Rick Simpson†, COS Patricia Norris†, SOUND Michael J. Kohut, Aaron Rochin, Carlos de Larios & Gene S. Cantamessa†, VE Richard Edlund, Neil Krepela, George Jensen & Mark Stetson†, MK Michael Westmore†.

LP Roy Scheider (Heywood Floyd), John Lithgow (Walter Curnow), Helen Mirren (Tanya Kirbuk), Bob Balaban (R. Chandra), Keir Dullea (Dave Bowman), Douglas Rain (Voice of HAL 9000), Madolyn Smith (Caroline Floyd), Dana Elcar (Dimitri Moisevitch), Taliesin Jaffe (Christopher Floyd).

With Earth on the brink of war, the U.S. and the U.S.S.R. reluctantly join forces to reclaim the spaceship *Discovery* before its decaying orbit around Jupiter causes it to crash on the planet. Scientists seek the meaning of the black monolith. It's a tame sequel to 2001, offering little in the way of story or spectacular special effects.

3165. *The Two Worlds of Angelita* (1983, First Run Features, 73m, c). P&D Jane Morrison, W Jose Manuel Torres Santiago, Rose Rosenblatt & Jane Morrison (based on the novel *Angelita* by Wendy Kesselman), PH Affonso Beato, M Dom Salvador, ED Suzanne Fenn, PD Randy Barcelo.

LP Marien Perez Riera (Angelita), Rosalba Rolon (Fela), Angel Domenech Soto (Chuito), Delia Esther Quinones (Dona Angela), Roberto Rivera Negron (Don Curro), Pedro Juan Texidor (Manolo), Idalia Perez Garay (Fortuna).

The problems of Puerto Rican families who have moved into the barrios of New York City are seen through the eyes of nine-year-old Marien Perez Riera.

3166. *Two Wrongs Make a Right* (1989, Paradigm, 83m, c). P Ivan Rogers, D Robert Brown, W Rogers, PH David Yosha, M Tony Byrne, ED Sheri J. Galloway, AD Yosha.

LP Ivan Rogers (Fletcher Quinn), Eva Wu (Jayna), Rick Komenich (Lake), R. Michael Pyle (Lt. Zander), Michael G. Rizk (Sgt. Vellosi), Ron Blackstone (Jack Balantine).

The film is a low-key blaxploitation film, starring Ivan Rogers as a nightclub owner whose club is shot up by gangsters when he refuses to sell. They also beat up his Asian-American girlfriend Eva Wu, making him extremely irritated and turning this mild-mannered man into a vigilante.

3167. *Uforia* (1985, Universal, 100m, c). P Gordon Wolf & Susan Spinks, D&W John Binder, PH David Myers, M Richard Baskin, ED Dennis M. Hill, PD Bill Malley.

LP Cindy Williams (Arlene), Harry Dean Stanton (Brother Bud), Fred Ward (Sheldon), Beverly Hope Atkinson (Naomi), Harry Carey, Jr. (George Martin), Diane Diefendorf (Delores), Robert Gray (Emile).

Filmed in 1981, this quirky little film is the story of born-again Christian Cindy

Williams who believes that salvation will come to earth in the form of a flying saucer. Crooked evangelist Harry Dean Stanton pumps all he can out of this notion.

3168.   UHF (1989, Orion, 96m, c). P Gene Kirkwood & John Hyde, D Jay Levey, W Al Yankovic & Levey, PH David Lewis, M John Du Prez, ED Dennis O'Connor, PD Ward Preston.

LP Weird Al Yankovic (George Newman), Victoria Jackson (Teri), Kevin McCarthy (R.J. Fletcher), Michael Richards (Stanley Spadowski), David Bowie (Bob), Stanley Brock (Uncle Harvey), Anthony Geary (Philo), Trinidad Silva (Raul Hernandez), Gedde Watanabe (Kuni), Billy Barty (Noodles), Sue Ane Langdon (Aunt Esther).

That particular breed of musical madness fan — those who adore Weird Al Yankovic's music parodies — may find this movie a scream. Their hero inherits a dinky little TV station and makes it a success by appealing to the wackos in TV land. Even though Yankovic's dream sequences, in which he parodies some Steven Spielberg movies, are fun, the film just won't make it with most audiences.

3169.   *The Ultimate Solution of Grace Quigley* (1984, MGM/UA/Cannon, 102m, c, aka *Grace Quigley*). P Menahem Golan & Yoram Globus, D Anthony Harvey, W A. Martin Zweiback, PH Larry Pizer, M John Addison, ED Robert Raetano, PD Gary Weist.

LP Katharine Hepburn (Grace Quigley), Nick Nolte (Seymour Flint), Elizabeth Wilson (Emily Watkins), Chip Zien (Dr. Herman), Kit Le Fever (Muriel), William Duell (Mr. Jenkins), Walter Abel (Homer).

Dotty old Katharine Hepburn convinces hit man Nick Nolte to kill off her elderly friends who don't want to live anymore. It's a tender little comedy, filled with love. But if you're one of the victims to be, don't change your mind.

The Umbrella Woman see ***The Good Wife***

3170.   *The Unbearable Lightness of Being* (1988, Orion, 171m, c). P Saul Zaentz, D Philip Kaufman, W Jean-Claude Carriere & Kaufman† (based on the novel by Milan Kundera), PH Sven Nykvist†, M Mark Adler, Keith Richards & Leos Janacek, ED Walter Murch, PD Pierre Guffroy.

LP Daniel Day-Lewis (Tomas), Juliette Binoche (Tereza), Lena Olin (Sabina), Derek de Lint (Franz), Erland Josephson (The Ambassador), Pavel Landovsky (Pavel), Donald Moffat (Chief Surgeon), Daniel Olbrychski (Interior Ministry Official), Stellan Skarsgard (The Engineer), Tomek Bork (Jiri), Bruce Myers (Czech Editor).

Director Philip Kaufman provides a fascinating production of Czech writer Milan Kundera's story of Daniel Day-Lewis, a free-spirited brain surgeon, who has romantic interludes with shy waitress Juliette Binoche and assertive Lena Olin. The complex saga of sex, love, and fidelity takes place in Prague in 1968, shortly after Soviet tanks invade the country to prevent deviation from communist unity. The mixture of sex and politics is extremely well-handled in this provocative but sometimes confusing film. It's a delight, as are the three leading performers.

3171.   *The Unbelievable Truth* (1989, Action Features, 98m, c). P Bruce Weiss & Hal Hartley, D&W Hartley, PH Michael Spiller, M Jim Coleman, ED Hartley, PD Cara Gerona.

LP Adrienne Shelly (Audry Hugo), Robert Burke (Josh Hutton), Christopher Cooke (Victor Hugo), Julia McNeal (Pearl), Gary Sauer (Emmett), Mark Bailey (Mike), Katherine Mayfield (Liz).

Adrienne Shelly, a contrary 17-year-old sexpot, dumps her long-time boyfriend, passes on college, makes it big as a model in Manhattan, shacks up with a photographer and puts the make on Robert Burke, an ex-con who works as a mechanic in the small-town garage owned by her father. It's a full life.

3172.   *Uncle Buck* (1989, Universal, 100m, c). P John Hughes & Tom Jacobson, D&W Hughes, PH Ralf D. Bode, M Ira Newborn, ED Lou Lombardo, Tony Lombardo & Peck Prior, PD John W. Corso.

LP John Candy (Buck Russell), Amy Madigan (Chanice Kobolowski), Jean Louisa Kelly (Tia Russell), Gaby Hoffman (Maizy Russell), Macaulay Culkin (Miles Russell), Elaine Bromka (Cindy Russell),

Garrett M. Brown (Bob Russell), Laurie Metcalf (Marcie), Jay Underwood (Bug).

John Candy is quite good portraying men who are strangely appealing despite numerous faults or defects. In this comedy he's a ne'er-do-well, uncouth, unwelcome member of the family, pressed into service to stay with three kids when their parents rush from suburban Chicago to be at the side of Elaine Bromka's father, who has suffered a heart attack, From this point on the film is a typical TV situation comedy, dealing rather poorly with the generation gap. The kids are mortified by Candy's coarse behavior and furious with his crude meddling in their affairs. We hope the very funny Mr. Candy will find better vehicles than those he was stuck with in 1989.

3173. Uncle Scam (1981, New World Pictures of Philadelphia, 105m, c). P&D Tom Pileggi & Michael Levanios, Jr., W Pileggi, Levanios, Jr., Tom Pilong & Joe Ryan, PH John Burke, M Michael Levanios, III, ED Levanios, Jr.

LP Tom McCarthy (Tom Ryan), Maxine Greene (Ginger), John Russell (Art), James E. Myers (Steve Vitali), Sharon Victoria (Linda), David Cassling (Herbie), Matt Myers (Governor Jones), Pat Cooper (Agency Chief).

Federal agents attempt to solicit bribes à la the Abscam scandal. They do but the cameras catch the feds in some extramarital activities. It was meant to be funny — we think.

3174. Uncommon Valor (1983, Paramount, 105m, c). P John Milius & Buzz Feitshans, D Ted Kotcheff, W Joe Gayton, PH Stephen H. Burum & Ric Waite, M James Horner, ED Mark Melnick, PD James L. Schoppe.

LP Gene Hackman (Col. Rhodes), Robert Stack (MacGregor), Fred Ward (Wilkes), Reb Brown (Blaster), Randall "Tex" Cobb (Sailor), Patrick Swayze (Scott), Harold Sylvester (Johnson), Tim Thomerson (Charts), Alice Lau [Lau Nga Lai] (Lai Fun), Kwan Hi Lim (Jiang).

Retired Colonel Gene Hackman goes to Vietnam to locate his son declared missing in action. There's about an even mix of suspense and clichés.

3175. Under Cover (1987, Cannon, 94m, c). P Menahem Golan & Yoram

Globus, D John Stockwell, W Stockwell & Scott Fields, PH Alexander Gruszynski, M Todd Rundgren, ED Sharyn L. Ross, PD Becky Block.

LP David Neidorf (Sheffield), Jennifer Jason Leigh (La Rue), Barry Corbin (Sgt. Irwin Lee), David Harris (Lucas), Kathleen Wilhoite (Corrine), Brad Leland (Drug Dealer).

Baltimore cop David Neidorf goes undercover in a South Carolina high school in order to organize a mass bust on kids using drugs.

3176. Under Fire (1983, Orion, 127m, c). P Jonathan Taplin, D Roger Spottiswoode, W Ron Shelton & Clayton Frohman (based on a story by Frohman), PH John Alcott, M Jerry Goldsmith†, ED John Bloom, AD Augustin Ytuarte & Toby Rafelson.

LP Nick Nolte (Russell Price), Ed Harris (Oates), Gene Hackman (Alex Grazier), Joanna Cassidy (Claire), Alma Martinez (Isela), Holly Palance (Journalist), Ella Laboriel (Nightclub Singer), Hamilton Camp (Regis Seydor), Jean-Louis Trintignant (Jazy), Richard Masur (Hub Kittle).

Journalists in Nicaragua become involved in the revolutionary cause when they encounter double-dealing in the political regime. This raises serious ethical concerns for them.

3177. Under the Boardwalk (1988, New World, 104m, c, aka *Wipeout*). P Steven H. Chanin & Gregory S. Blackwell, D Fritz Kiersch, W Robert King (based on a story by Matthew Irmas & King), PH Don Burgess, M David Kitay, ED Daniel Gross, PD Maxine Shepard.

LP Keith Coogan (Andy), Danielle Von Zerneck (Allie), Richard Joseph Paul (Nick Rainwood), Roxana Zal (Gitch).

Two teenagers from different backgrounds find romance and love amidst the world of surfing.

3178. Under the Cherry Moon (1986, Warner, 98m, c). P Robert Cavallo, Joseph Ruffalo & Steven Fargnoli, D Prince, W Becky Johnston, PH Michael Ballhaus, M Prince, ED Eva Gardos, PD Richard Sylbert.

LP Prince (Christopher Tracy), Jerome Benton (Tricky), Kristin Scott Thomas (Mary Sharon), Steven Berkoff

(Mr. Sharon), Emmanuelle Sallet (Katy), Alexandra Stewart (Mrs. Sharon), Francesca Annis (Mrs. Wellington).

In this vanity piece, Prince portrays an American gigolo/entertainer in the south of France who women find irresistible.

3179.   *Under the Gun* (1989, Marquis Picture, 89m, c). P Warren Stein, D James Sbardellati, W Almer John Davis, James Devney & Sbardellati (based on Devney's story), PH Gary Thieltges, M Edna Sterling, ED George Copanas, PD James Shumaker.

LP Sam Jones (Mike Braxton), Vanessa Williams (Samantha Richards), John Russell (Stone), Michael Halsey (Frank), Nick Cassavetes (Tony), Steven Williams (Gallagher), Bill McKinney (Miller).

Dethroned Miss America Vanessa Williams makes her film debut as the lawyer of plutonium thief John Russell. His henchmen have killed St. Louis cop Sam Jones' brother Nick Cassavetes. Jones wants revenge and Williams has the information which can put Russell away for good.

3180.   *Under the Rainbow* (1981, Warner, 98m, c). P Fred Bauer, D Steve Rash, W Pat McCormick, Harry Hurwitz, Martin Smith, Pat Bradley & Bauer (based on a story by Bradley & Bauer), PH Frank Stanley, M Joe Renzetti, ED David Blewitt, PD Peter Wooley.

LP Chevy Chase (Bruce Thorpe), Carrie Fisher (Annie Clark), Billy Barty (Otto Kriegling), Eve Arden (Duchess), Joseph Maher (Duke), Robert Donner (Assassin), Mako (Nakamuri), Cork Hubbert (Rollo Sweet), Pat McCormick (Tiny), Adam Arkin (Henry Hudson), Richard Stahl (Lester).

Set in 1938, this is purported to be the story of the hundreds of midgets brought to Hollywood to appear in *The Wizard of Oz*. The film concentrates on their destructive, drunken carousing at the hotel where they are staying. It's all done in extremely bad taste.

3181.   *Under the Volcano* (1984, Universal, 112m, c). P Moritz Borman & Wieland Schulz-Keil, D John Huston, W Guy Gallo (based on the novel by Malcolm Lowry), PH Gabriel Figueroa, M Alex North†, ED Roberto Silvi, PD Gunther Gerzso.

LP Albert Finney† (Geoffrey Firmin), Jacqueline Bisset (Yvonne Firmin), Anthony Andrews (Hugh Firmin), Ignacio Lopez Tarso (Dr. Vigil), Katy Jurado (Senora Gregoria), James Villiers (Brit), Dawson Bray (Quincey), Carlos Riquelme (Bustamante), Jim McCarthy (Gringo).

Set in 1938, the film is a superb production of Malcolm Lowry's masterpiece about the last day in the life of alcoholic ex-consul Albert Finney in Mexico. Finney's alcoholism, aggravated by his wife Jacqueline Bisset's infidelity with his half-brother Anthony Andrews, is the device used to liken his descent into a personal hell with the self-destruction taking place in the world at the time.

3182.   *The Underachievers* (1988, PMS/Lightning, 90m, c). P&D Jackie Kong, W Kong, Tony Rosato & Gary Thompson (based on a story by Rosato), PH Chuck Colwell, M Don Preston, ED Tom Meshelski, PD Jay Burkhardt.

LP Edward Albert (Danny Warren), Barbara Carrera (Katherine), Michael Pataki (Murphy), Susan Tyrrell (Mrs. Grant), Mark Blankfield (Kline), Garrett Morris (Dummont), Vic Tayback (Coach), Jesse Aragon (Carlos).

This tepid comedy is set in a night school, where various society rejects gather.

3183.   *Underground Aces* (1981, Filmways, 95m, c). P Jay Weston, D Robert Butler, W Jim Carabatsos, Lenore Wright & Andrew Peter Marin, PH Tom Del Ruth, M Pete Rugolo, ED Argyle Nelson.

LP Dirk Benedict (Huff), Melanie Griffith (Lucy), Robert Hegyes (Tico), Jerry Orbach (Penlitter), Frank Gorshin (Kruger), Rick Podell (Joe), Randi Brooks (Ollie), T.K. Carter (DeeJay), Joshua Daniel (Wally).

A group of parking attendants at a large hotel amuse themselves with sex, carousing and wrecking the vehicles of the guests.

3184.   *Underground Terror* (1989, SVS Film, 90m, c). P Steven Mackler, D James McCalmont, W Robert Zimmerman & Brian O'Hara (based on O'Hara's story), PH Anghel Deca, M Taj, ED Keith Reamer, PD Mikhail Fishgoyt.

LP Doc Dougherty (John Willis), Lennie Loftin (Boris), B.J. Geordan (Kim Knowles), Ric Siler (Weasel), Joe Bachana, James Davies, Alan L. Rickman.

A ruthless gang lives in the subway, preying on unsuspecting travelers.

3185. *Underground U.S.A.* (1980, New Cinema, 85m, c). P Eric Mitchell & Erdner Rauschalle, D&W Mitchell, PH Tom DiCillo, M Various Artists, ED J.P. Roland-Levy.

LP Patti Astor (Vickie), Eric Mitchell (Hustler), Rene Ricard (Kenneth), Tom Wright (Frank), Jackie Curtis (Roommate), Cookie Mueller, Taylor Mead, Duncan Smith, Steve Mass.

Hustler Eric Mitchell takes up with Patti Astor, a film star whose career is almost all behind her. The film gives audiences a peek at the underground art scene.

3186. *The Understudy: Graveyard Shift II* (1989, Cinema Ventures, 88m, c). P Stephen R. Flaks & Arnold H. Bruce, D&W Gerard Ciccoritti, PH Barry Stone, M Philip Stern, ED Neil Grieve, PD Ciccoritti.

LP Wendy Gazelle (Camilla/Patti), Mark Soper (Matthew), Silvio Oliviero (Baissez), Ilse Von Glatz (Ash), Tim Kelleher (Duke/Larry).

Real vampire Silvio Oliviero takes the place of an actor who is to appear as a vampire in a movie.

3187. *Underworld* (1985, Limehouse Pictures, GB, 100m, c). P Kevin Attew, Don Hawkins & Graham Ford, D George Pavlou, W Clive Barker & James Caplin, PH Sydney Macartney, M Freur, ED Chris Ridsdale.

LP Denholm Elliott (Dr. Savary), Steven Berkoff (Hugo Motherskille), Larry Lamb (Roy Bain), Miranda Richardson (Oriel), Art Malik (Fluke), Nicola Cowper (Nicole), Ingrid Pitt (Pepperdine), Irina Brook (Bianca).

Mad scientist Denholm Elliott develops a serum which allows a user to experience his or her fantasies in real life. The catch is that there's an aftereffect which horribly disfigures the users, forcing them to hide underground.

3188. *Uneasy Silence* (1989, Full Circle, 90m, c). P Wanda Rohm & Robert Rothman, D John Strysik, W Rothman & Strysik, PH Michael Goi, M Elliott Delman, ED Strysik, PD Thomas B. Mitchell.

LP Robert Rothman (Sam), Kathleen Sykora (Sarah), Michael Bacarella (Astro), Carolyn Kodes (Terry Quinn), Charles Gerace (T.J.).

Robert Rothman and Kathleen Sykora are not very believable as Chicago vagrants trying to eke out an existence, in this downbeat movie.

3189. *Unfaithfully Yours* (1984, 20th Century–Fox, 96m, c). P Marvin Worth & Joe Wizan, D Howard Zieff, W Valerie Curtin, Barry Levinson & Robert Klane (based on the screenplay by Preston Sturges), PH David M. Walsh, M Bill Conti, Tchaikovsky violin concerto, ED Sheldon Kahn, PD Albert Brenner.

LP Dudley Moore (Claude Eastman), Nastassja Kinski (Daniella Eastman), Armand Assante (Maxmillian Stein), Albert Brooks (Norman Robbins), Cassie Yates (Carla Robbins), Richard Libertini (Giuseppe), Richard B. Shull (Jess Keller), Jan Triska (Jerzy Czyrek).

This a modernized version of Preston Sturges' 1948 film, which starred Rex Harrison as an orchestral conductor who believes his wife is being unfaithful. While he's conducting he imagines three different ways of dealing with the situation. In the remake, conductor Dudley Moore wrongly believes wife Nastassja Kinski is having an affair with guest violinist Armand Assante. The little actor imagines a perfect scheme to have his revenge, but it goes awry when he tries to put his plan into practice.

3190. *Unfinished Business* (1985, Unfinished Business Pty., Australia, 78m, c). P Rebel Penfold-Russell, D&W Bob Ellis, PH Andrew Lesnie, ED Amanda Robson, PD Jane Johnston.

LP John Clayton (Geoff), Michele Fawdon (Maureen), Norman Kaye (George), Bob Ellis (Geoff's Flatmate), Andrew Lesnie (Telegraph Boy).

After leaving his wife and three children in the U.S., John Clayton returns to Australia, where he encounters old flame Michele Fawdon. She's now married but unfulfilled because she has no children. She suggests that Clayton impregnate her. He's delighted, but the process isn't all the fun he was hoping for.

3191. *Unfinished Business* (1987, American Film Institute, 65m, c). P Dale Ann Stieber, Chrisann Verges & Suzanne Kent, D&W Viveca Lindfors, PH Sean McLin, M Patricia Lee Stotter, Don Rebic & Matt Sullivan, ED Dale Ann Stieber & Sharyn G. Blumenthal, PD Johanna Leovey.

LP Viveca Lindfors (Helena), Peter Donat (Ferenzy), Gina Hecht (Vickie), James Morrison (Jonathan), Anna Devere Smith (Anna), Haley Taylor-Block (Kristina), Herriett Guiar (Cynthia).

Actress Viveca Lindfors is preparing to appear in a production of "Brecht on Brecht." Her former lover Peter Donat, who left her 15 years earlier, resurfaces in her life, dragging along his mistress. He'd like to get back with Lindfors, and by the end of the film this seems as certain as that the film is dull.

Unforgettable see Chances Are

3192. *The Unholy* (1988, Vestron, 100m, c). P Mathew Hayden, D Camilo Vila, W Philip Yordan & Fernando Fonseca, PH Henry Vargas, M Roger Bellon, ED Mark Melnick, PD Fonseca.

LP Ben Cross (Father Michael), Ned Beatty (Lt. Stern), Jill Carroll (Millie), William Russ (Luke), Hal Holbrook (Archbishop Mosely), Trevor Howard (Father Silva), Peter Frechette (Claude), Claudia Robinson (Teresa Montez), Nicole Fortier (Demon).

In this confusing horror nonsense, Ben Cross is a priest who has mysteriously survived a fall. He's assigned to a parish in New Orleans where he unravels the mystery of the death of two priests who previously prayed before the altar of the church. He must resist beautiful naked redheaded demon Nicole Fortier, who attempts to seduce him.

3193. *The Uninvited* (1988, Heritage, 89m, c). P,D&W Greydon Clark, PH Nicholas Von Sternberg, M Dan Slider, ED Travis Clark, PD Peter Paul Raubertas.

LP George Kennedy (Mike Harvey), Alex Cord (Walter Graham), Clu Gulager (Albert), Toni Hudson (Rachel), Eric Larson (Martin), Clare Carey (Bobbie),

Rob Estes (Corey), Shari Shattuck (Suzanne).

The "uninvited" in this film is a cat that shows up now and then, spits out a puppet head which gnaws people to death, and disappears. All of this takes place on dishonest Alex Cord's yacht, skippered by Toni Hudson. Along for the ride are guests Clare Carey and Shari Shattuck, and three guys that they invited along for a trip to Bimini.

3194. *Union City* (1980, Kinesis, 87m, c). P Graham Belin, D&W Mark Reichert (based on the short story "The Corpse Next Door" by Cornell Woolrich), PH Edward Lachman, M Chris Stein, ED Eric Albertson, Lana Tokel & J. Michaels, AD George Stavrinos.

LP Dennis Lipscomb (Harlan), Deborah Harry (Lillian), Irina Maleeva (Contessa), Everett McGill (Larry Longacre), Sam McMurray (Young Vagrant), Terina Lewis (Evelyn), Pat Benatar (Jeanette).

In this gloomy film, Deborah Harry, the lead singer with the defunct New Wave band Blondie, is a mousy-looking brunette married to neurotic Dennis Lipscomb. His obsession is to trap vagrant Sam McMurray, who steals a drink of milk out of a bottle delivered to Lipscomb's door each day. Things escalate into madness and murder.

3195. *The Unnamable* (1988, Yankee Classic, 87m, c). P Dean Ramser & Jean-Paul Ouellette, D&W Ouellette (based on a story by H.P. Lovecraft), PH Tom Fraser, M David Bergeaud, ED Wendy J. Plump, PD Gene Abel.

LP Charles King (Howard Damon), Mark Kinsey Stephenson (Randolph Carter), Alexandra Durrell (Tanya), Laura Albert (Wendy), Katrin Alexandre (Alyda Winthrop), Eben Ham (Bruce), Blane Wheatley (John Babcock), Mark Parra (Joel Manton).

This direct-to-video horror film takes place in a small college town where two young couples spend the night in an ancient mansion. The 17th century owner, a warlock, was horribly murdered by a creature that he kept chained in the attic. Well, it's still there.

3196. *Unni* (1989, Malabar, 113m, c). P Kitty Morgan & Bill Rothman, D G.

Aravindan, W Rothman & Morgan, PH Sunny Joseph, M Aravindan, ED Beena Venugopal, AD Aravindan.

LP Tara Johannessen (Tara), Gijie Abraham (Unni), Sethu (Sethu), Elizabeth Anthony (Mary), Vivian Colodro (Maggie), Bill Swotes (Bill).

This meandering film follows the adventures of American student Tara Johannessen in Kerala, a section of southern India.

3197. *An Unremarkable Life* (1989, SVS/Continental, 92m, c). P&D Amin Q. Chaudhri, W Marcia Dinneen, PH Alan Hall, M Avery Sharpe, ED Sandi Gerling, PD Norman B. Dodge, Jr.

LP Patricia Neal (Frances McEllany), Shelley Winters (Evelyn), Mako (Max Chin), Rochelle Oliver, Charles Dutton, Lily Knight, Jenny Chrisinger.

Patricia Neal and Shelley Winters portray two aging sisters who share a household and live with their memories. When Neal takes up with Mako, a happy Asian auto mechanic, Winters, who doesn't care for foreigners, makes her opinions known. It's a rather drab movie about drab, unremarkable lives, but the leads Neal and Winters give solid performances.

3198. *The Unseen* (1981, World Northal, 89m, c). P Anthony Unger & Don P. Behrns, D Peter Foleg, W Michael L. Grace, PH Roberto Quezada, Irv Goodnoff & James Carter, M Michael J. Lewis, ED Jonathan Braun, AD Dena Roth, SE Harry Woolman.

LP Barbara Bach (Jennifer), Sidney Lassick (Ernest Keller), Stephen Furst (Junior), Lelia Goldoni (Virginia Keller), Karen Lamm (Karen), Doug Barr (Tony), Lois Young (Vicki).

When three female reporters are forced to take lodging in a private home because all the hotels are completely booked during a festival they are covering, they find that their host is not what he seems. In addition there is living in the cellar a monster who gets out to torment them.

3199. *An Unsuitable Job for a Woman* (1985, Castle Hill, GB, 90m, c). P Michael Relph & Peter McKay, D Christopher Petit, W Elizabeth McKay, Brian Scobie & Petit (based on the novel by

P.D. James), PH Martin Schafer, M Chaz Jankel, Philip Bagenal & Peter Van-Hooke, ED Mick Audsley.

LP Billie Whitelaw (Elizabeth Leaming), Paul Freeman (James Calender), Pippa Guard (Cordelia Gray), Dominic Guard (Andrew Lunn), Elizabeth Spriggs (Miss Markland), David Horovitch (Sgt. Maskell), Dawn Archibald (Isobel).

Twenty-three year old novice detective Pippa Guard is hired to investigate the apparent suicide of a wealthy young man. She becomes obsessed with him, living in his cottage, wearing his clothes and speaking to him using tape recordings.

3200. *Until September* (1984, MGM/United Artists, 95m, c). P Michael Gruskoff, D Richard Marquand, W Janice Lee Graham, PH Philippe Welt, M John Barry, ED Sean Barton, PD Hilton McConnico.

LP Karen Allen (Mo Alexander), Thierry Lhermitte (Xavier De La Perouse), Christopher Cazenove (Philip), Hutton Cobb (Andrew), Michael Mellinger (Col. Viola), Nitza Saul (Sylvia), Rochelle Robertson (Carol).

Stranded in Paris, American Karen Allen meets and falls in love with married banker Thierry Lhermitte. She accepts his suggestion that they be lovers until summer is over. It's a little hard to believe that she'd buy the arrangement, particularly since his attitude and behavior doesn't mark him as Mr. Wonderful.

3201. *The Untouchables* (1987, Paramount, 119m, c). P Art Linson, D Brian DePalma, W David Mamet, PH Stephen H. Burum, M Ennio Morricone†, ED Jerry Greenberg & Bill Pankow, AD William A. Elliott, Patrizia Von Brandenstein†, SD Hal Gausman†, COS Marilyn Vance-Straker†.

LP Kevin Costner (Eliot Ness), Sean Connery* (James Malone), Charles Martin Smith (Oscar Wallace), Andy Garcia (George Stone), Robert De Niro (Al Capone), Richard Bradford (Mike), Jack Kehoe (Walter Payne), Brad Sullivan (George), Billy Drago (Frank Nitti), Patricia Clarkson (Catherine Ness).

Kevin Costner is the naive, incorruptible T-man, brought into Chicago to find some means of putting away notorious Al

Capone. With the help of Sean Connery as a tough Irish cop, marksman Andy Garcia and tax expert Charles Martin Smith, the Untouchables are able to send Scarface to prison for tax evasion. The film has plenty of bloodshed and killings for those seeking that kind of action, but it is the relationship between Connery as grizzled mentor and the unemotional Costner that makes the film special.

3202. *Up the Academy* (1980, Warner, 88m, c, aka *Mad Magazine's Up the Academy; The Brave Young Men of Weinberg*). P Marvin Worth & Danton Rissner, D Robert Downey, W Tom Patchett & Jay Tarses, PH Harry Stradling, Jr., M Jody Taylor Worth, ED Bud Molin, PD Peter Wooley.

LP Ron Leibman (Major), Wendell Brown (Ike), Tom Citera (Hash), J. Hutchinson (Oliver), Ralph Macchio (Chooch), Harry Teinowitz (Ververgaert), Tom Poston (Sisson), Ian Wolfe (Commandant Caseway), Stacey Nelkin (Candy), Barbara Bach (Bliss).

In this tasteless teenage sexual comedy, Ron Leibman runs the Sheldon R. Weinberg Military Academy with an iron fist. But four new students lay waste timeless traditions and enrage their talentless teachers. The film was sponsored by *Mad* magazine, but even they have disowned it.

3203. *Up the Creek* (1984, Orion, 95m, c). P Michael L. Metzer & Fred Baum, D Robert Butler, W Jim Kouf (based on a story by Kouf, Jeff Sherman & Douglas Grossman), PH James Glennon, M William Goldstein, ED Bill Butler, PD William M. Hiney.

LP Tim Matheson (Bob McGraw), Jennifer Runyon (Heather Merriweather), Stephen Furst (Gonzer), Dan Monahan (Max), Sandy Helberg (Irwin), Jeff East (Rex), Blaine Novak (Braverman), James B. Sikking (Tozer).

The boys from Lepetomane University (named after a performer in turn-of-the-century French theaters whose specialty was passing gas in rhythm at various pitches), are off to a raft-race. It's a vulgar, scatological, violent but funny film.

3204. *Up Your Alley* (1989, Unknown Film Co., 88m, c). P Murray Langston, D Bob Logan, W Langston & Logan, PH Mark Melville, M Paul Ventimiglia, ED Tom Siiter.

LP Linda Blair (Vickie Adderly), Murray Langston (David), Bob Zany (Sonny), Ruth Buzzi (Marilyn), Johnny Dark (Nick), Jack Hanrahan (Joe), Glen Vincent (Lance), Melissa Shear (Pauline).

Unknown comic Murray Langston is responsible for this stinker, presenting the story of street people, who, as if they didn't have enough to contend with, are being knocked off by some madman.

3205. *Uphill All the Way* (1986, New World, 86m, c). P Burr Smidt & David L. Ford, D&W Frank Q. Dobbs, PH Roland Smith, M Dennis M. Pratt, ED Chuck Weiss, PD Hal Matheny.

LP Roy Clark (Ben), Mel Tillis (Booger Skaggs), Burl Ives (Sheriff), Glen Campbell (Capt. Hazleton), Trish Van Devere (Widow Quinn), Richard Paul (Dillman), Burt Reynolds (Poker Player), Elaine Joyce (Jesse), Jacque Lynn Colton (Lucinda).

Country singers Roy Clark and Mel Tillis portray inept robbers in the old West in a film filled with cameo appearances and pitifully short on laughs.

The Upstate Murders see Savage Weekends

3206. *Urban Cowboy* (1980, Paramount, 135m, c). P Robert Evans & Irving Azoff, D James Bridges, W Bridges & Aaron Latham (based on a story by Latham), PH Ray Villalobos, M Ralph Burns, ED Dave Rawlins, PD Stephen Grimes.

LP John Travolta (Bud), Debra Winger (Sissy), Scott Glenn (Wes), Madolyn Smith (Pam), Barry Corbin (Uncle Bob), Brooke Alderson (Aunt Corene), Cooper Huckabee (Marshall), James Gammon (Steve Strange).

Texas oil-field worker John Travolta seeks love and adventure in Gilley's country and western bar, which features a mechanical bull to ride. He falls for Debra Winger, but their romance goes sour once they are married. Dumb blond hussy Madolyn Smith separates Travolta from Winger. She takes up with rat Scott Glenn. Travolta and Winger get together again, but it really doesn't matter for those who have had enough of the bull in this film, mechanical or otherwise.

3207. *Used Cars* (1980, Columbia, 113m, c). P Bob Gale, D Robert Zemeckis, W Zemeckis & Galc, PH Donald M. Morgan, M Patrick Williams, ED Michael Kahn, PD Peter M. Jamison.

LP Kurt Russell (Rudy Russo), Jack Warden (Roy L. Fuchs/Luke Fuchs), Gerrit Graham (Jeff), Frank McRae (Jim), Deborah Harmon (Barbara Fuchs), Joseph P. Flaherty (Sam Slaton), David L. Lander (Freddie Paris), Michael McKean (Eddie Winslow).

Jack Warden portrays two brothers with competing used car lots. Kurt Russell is the head salesman, for the less successful lot. He and his partner Gerrit Graham will try any scam to sell a car.

3208. *Utilities* (1983, New World, Canada, 91m, c, aka *Getting Even*). P Robert Cooper, D Harvey Hart, W David Greenwalt & M. James Kouf, Jr., PH Richard Leiterman, M John Erbe & Mickey Solomon, ED John Kelly, PD Bill Boeton.

LP Robert Hays (Bob), Brooke Adams (Marion), John Marley (Roy), James Blendick (Kenneth), Ben Gordon (Eddie), Jane Mallet (Dr. Rogers), Toby Tarnow (Gilda), Helen Burns (Ruby), Lee Broker (Jack).

Crusading social worker Robert Hays teams up with beautiful lady cop Brooke Adams to take on a local utilities company.

3209. *Utu* (1984, Glitteron, New Zealand, 104m, c). P Geoff Murphy & Don Blakeney, D Murphy, W Murphy & Keith Aberdein, PH Graeme Cowley, M John Charles, ED Michael Horton & Ian John, PD Ron Highfield.

LP Anzac Wallace (Te Wheke), Bruno Lawrence (Williamson), Kelly Johnson (Lt. Scott), Wi Kuki Kaa (Wiremu), Tim Elliot (Col. Elliot), Ilona Rodgers (Emily), Tania Bristowe (Kura), Martyn Sanderson (Vicar).

In a New Zealand "western," in 1870 the Maoris seek retribution after the colonials have squeezed them off their land.

3210. *The Vacant Lot* (1989, Picture Plant, Canada, 100m, c). P Terry Greenlaw, D&W William D. MacGillivray, PH Lionel Simmons, ED Angela Baker & MacGillivray, AD Angela Murphy.

LP Trudi Petersen (Trudi), Grant Fullerton (David), Barbara Nicholson, Rick Mercer, Caitlyn Colquhoun, Cheryl Reid, Tara Wilde.

"The Vacant Lot" is the name of a female punk rock band, featuring Trudi Petersen as the rhythm guitarist. She takes up with Grant Fullerton, an older ex-guitar great of the 60s. He joins the band when Petersen breaks her arm in a car accident. They go on a mini roadtrip — but nothing very interesting happens.

3211. *Valentino Returns* (1989, Skouras, 88m, c). P Peter Hoffman & David Wisnievitz, D Hoffman, W Leonard Gardner (based on his story "Christ Has Returned to Earth and Preaches Here Nightly"), PH Jerzy Zielinski, ED Denine Rowan, AD Woody Romine.

LP Barry Tubb (Wayne Gibbs), Frederic Forrest (Sonny Gibbs), Veronica Cartwright (Patricia Gibbs), Jenny Wright (Sylvia), David Packer (Count Messner), Seth Isler (Harry Ames), Miguel Ferrer (The Biker), Kit McDonough (Ruth Fuller).

In this bit of Americana, small-town teen Barry Tubb's rites of passage in the 50s are not smooth. We follow one important night in his life when everything goes wrong.

3212. *Valet Girls* (1987, Lexyn/Empire, 82m, c). P Dennis Murphy, D Rafal Zielinski, W Clark Carlton, PH Nicholas Von Sternberg, M Robert Parr, ED Akiko B. Metz, AD Dins Danielsen.

LP Meri D. Marshall (Lucy), April Stewart (Rosalind), Mary Kohnert (Carnation), Christopher Weeks (Dirk Zebra), Patricia Scott Michel (Tina Zebra), John Sharp (Lindsay Brawnsworth), Michael Karm (Alvin Sunday).

Three shapely, enterprising girls put themselves through school running a parking service. Their uniforms on the job include high heels, hot pants and not much else.

3213. *Valley Girl* (1983, Atlantic, 95m, c). P Wayne Crawford & Andrew Lane, D Martha Coolidge, W Crawford & Lane, PH Frederick Elmes, M Scott Wilk & Marc Levinthal, ED Eva Gardos, PD Mary Delia Javier.

LP Nicolas Cage (Randy), Deborah Foreman (Julie Richman), Elizabeth Daily (Loryn), Michael Bowen (Tommy), Cameron Dye (Fred), Heidi Holicker (Stacey), Michelle Meyrink (Suzie), Tina Theberge (Samantha), Lee Purcell (Beth Brent), Colleen Camp (Sarah Richman), Frederic Forrest (Steve Richman).

This is the Romeo and Juliet tale of Valley Girl (i.e., L.A. valley as in the Frank & Moon Zappa hit song) Deborah Foreman and Hollywood punker Nicolas Cage. Her friends try to get her back with an old flame, while his pals crash Valley parties to cause trouble. Director Martha Coolidge deserves praise for giving audiences a cute film about clashing cultures, even though few viewers can identify with either of them.

3214. *Valmont* (1989, Orion, 134m, c). P Paul Rassam & Michael Hausman, D Milos Forman, W Jean-Claude Carrière (based on the novel *Les Liaisons Dangereuses* by Choderlos de Laclos), PH Miroslav Ondricek, M Christopher Palmer, ED Alan Heim & Nena Danevic, PD Pierre Guffroy, COS Theodor Pistek†.

LP Colin Firth (Valmont), Annette Bening (Mme. de Merteuil), Meg Tilly (Mme. de Tourvel), Fairuza Balk (Cecile), Sian Phillips (Mme. de Volanges), Fabia Drake (Mme. de Rosemonde), Jeffrey Jones (Gercourt), Henry Thomas (Danceny), T.P. McKenna (Baron).

This adaptation of the familiar story of sex and love used as weapons to gain power over others is at a disadvantage in following Stephen Frear's very popular version, *Dangerous Liaisons,* by only a year. Yet it is a lovely production with a beautiful performance by Annette Bening which easily rivals that of Glenn Close in the 1988 film. Colin Firth as the title character and Meg Tilly as his virtuous conquest are less compelling than John Malkovich and Michelle Pfeiffer. Young Fairuza Balk as 15-year-old Cecile is different in every way than Uma Thurman, but no less impressive.

3215. *The Vals* (1985, Sundowner, 100m, c). P&D James Polakof, W Polakof & Deborah Amelon (based on a story by Polakof), PH G.W. "Dink" Read, M Daphne Edwards, ED Millie Paul.

LP Jill Carroll (Samantha), Elena Stratheros (Trish), Michelle Laurita (Beth), Gina Calabrase (Annie), Chuck Connors (Trish's Father), Tiffany Bolling (Samantha's Mother), Sue Ane Langdon (TV Star), Sonny Bono (Spaced-out Guest), John Carradine (Mr. Stanton).

Scheduled for a 1983 release to take advantage of the popularity of California's "Valley Girls," popularized by Frank and Moon Zappa in 1982, instead this loser sat on the shelf for a couple of years until it was decided that it might make back some of its cost from videocassettes. The Vals of the title are four teen girls trying to save an orphanage by conning the needed funds from drug dealers.

3216. *Vamp* (1986, New World, 93m, c). P Donald P. Borchers, D&W Richard Wenk (based on a story by Borchers & Wenk), PH Elliot Davis, M Jonathan Elias, ED Marc Grossman, PD Alan Roderick-Jones.

LP Chris Makepeace (Keith), Sandy Baron (Vic), Robert Rusler (A.J.), Dedee Pfeiffer (Amaretto), Gedde Watanabe (Duncan), Grace Jones (Katrina), Billy Drago (Snow), Brad Logan (Vlad), Lisa Lyon (Cimmaron).

In order to be taken into a college fraternity, Chris Makepeace and Robert Rusler must arrange for a stripper to appear at the frat's big party. Together with weirdo Gedde Watanabe, the boys make their way to the After Dark Club where they engage Grace Jones for the job, unaware that she is a bloodsucking vampire.

3217. *Vamping* (1984, Atlantic, 107m, c). P Howard Kling & Stratton Rawson, D Frederick King Keller, W Michael Healy & Robert Seidman (based on a story by Keller), PH Skip Roessel, M Ken Kaufman, ED Darren Kloomok, PD Kling, Karen Morse & Rawson.

LP Patrick Duffy (Harry Baranski), Catherine Hyland (Diane Anderson), Rod Arrants (Raymond O'Brien), Fred A. Keller (Fat Man), David Booze (Benjamin), Jed Cooper (Lennie), Steve Gilborn (Jimmy).

Down-on-his-luck saxophonist Patrick Duffy moonlights as a burglar to raise money. He falls for one of his victims.

3218. *Vampire at Midnight* (1988, Skouras, 93m, c). P Jason Williams & Tom Friedman, D Gregory McClatchy,

W Dulhany Ross Clements (based on a story by Williams & Friedman), PH Daniel Yarussi, M Robert Etoll, ED Kaye Davis.

LP Jason Williams (Det. Roger Stutter), Gustav Vintas (Victor Radkoff), Lesley Milne (Jenny Carlon), Jeanie Moore (Amalia), Esther Alise (Lucia), Ted Hamaguchi (Capt. Takato), Robert Random (Childress).

Police detective Jason Williams is on the trail of a fiendishly clever serial killer who may be a vampire.

3219. *Vampire's Kiss* (1989, Hemdale, 105m, c). P Barbara Zitwer & Barry Shils, D Robert Bierman, W Joseph Minion, PH Stefan Czapsky, M Colin Towns, ED Angus Newton, PD Christopher Nowak.

LP Nicolas Cage (Peter Loew), Maria Conchita Alonso (Alva Restrepo), Jennifer Beals (Rachel), Elizabeth Ashley (Dr. Glaser), Kasi Lemmons (Jackie), Bob Lujan (Emilio), Jessica Lundy (Sharon).

Literary agent Nicolas Cage is fearful of romantic commitments. When he does find the perfect woman, Jennifer Beals, she's a vampire. Once again Cage demonstrates his limitations as an actor.

3220. *Variety* (1984, Horizon, 100m, c). P Renee Schafransky, D Bette Gordon, W Kathy Acker (based on a story by Gordon), PH Tom Di Cillo & John Foster, M John Lurie, ED Ila Von Hasperg.

LP Sandy McLeod (Christine), Will Patton (Mark), Richard Davidson (Louie), Luis Guzman (Jose), Nan Goldin (Nan), Lee Tucker (Projectionist), Peter Rizzo (Driver).

Despite an initial aversion to porno films, Sandy McLeod, a ticket-taker at the Variety, one of the oldest theaters in New York, and now a triple-X rated movie theater, becomes fascinated with the patrons. She follows one around after working hours. The message about women, pornography and power that the independent filmmakers are trying to make is garbled.

3221. *Vasectomy: A Delicate Matter* (1986, Vandom International, 90m, c). P Robert Burge & Lou Wills, D Burge, W Robert Hilliard & Burge, PH Gary Thieltges, M Fred Karlin, ED Beth Conwell.

LP Paul Sorvino (Gino), Cassandra Edwards (Anna), Abe Vigoda (Detective Edwards), Ina Balin (Regine), Lorne Greene (Theo Marshall), June Wilkinson, William Marshall.

This comedy about a man whose wife wishes him to have the title operation is about as funny as a knee in the groin.

3222. *Vendetta* (1986, Concorde, 88m, c). P Jeff Begun, Ken Solomon & Ken Dalton, D Bruce Logan, ED Glenn Morgan, W Emil Farkas, Simon Maskell, Laura Cavestani & John Adams, PH Robert New, M David Newman, AD Chris Clarens.

LP Sandy Martin (Kay), Kin Shriner (Steve Nelson), Greg Bradford (Joe-Bob), Holly Butler (Movie Star), Karen Chase (Laurie), Lisa Clarson (Bobo), Roberta Collins (Miss Dice), Pilar Delano (Inmate), Eugene Rogert Glazer (David Greene).

Stuntwoman Karen Chase deliberately commits crimes which will get her sent to the same prison where her younger sister was killed by a prison gang, so she may take vengeance.

Vengeance: The Demon see *Pumpkinhead*

3223. *Venom* (1982, Paramount, GB, 93m, c). P Martin Bregman, D Piers Haggard, W Robert Carrington (based on the novel by Alan Scholefield), PH Gilbert Taylor & Denys Coop, M Michael Kamen, ED Michael Bradsell, SE Alan Whibley & Richard Dean.

LP Klaus Kinski (Jacmel), Oliver Reed (Dave), Nicol Williamson (Cmdr. William Bulloch), Sarah Miles (Dr. Marion Stowe), Sterling Hayden (Howard Anderson), Corelia Sharpe (Ruth Hopkins), Mike Gwilym (Det. Constable Dan Spencer), Lance Holcomb (Philip Hopkins).

A big game hunter and his asthmatic grandson are held for ransom in a house where a black mamba, one of the most deadly of snakes, is loose.

3224. *Venus Peter* (1989, Atlantic, GB, 92m, c). P Christopher Young, D Ian Sellar, W Sellar & Christopher Rush, PH Gabriel Beristain, M Jonathan Dove, ED David Spiers, PD Andy Harris.

LP George R. Strachan (Peter), Ray McAnally (Grandfather), David Hayman (Kinnear), Sinead Cusack (Miss Balsilbie), Caroline Paterson (Peter's Mother),

Peter Caffrey (Peter's Father), Alex Mc-Avoy (Beadle), Emma Dingwall (Jenny).

Set in the windswept Orkney Islands north of Scotland, the film is the story of young George R. Strachan who lives with his mother and grandfather. His father is missing. The boy likes to imagine he's a ship's captain. Things in this family film slowly reach a moving climax after the father, who had grown tired of living on the island, returns.

3225. The Verdict† (1982, 20th Century–Fox, 129m, c). P Richard D. Zanuck & David Brown, D Sidney Lumet†, W David Mamet† (based on the novel by Barry Reed), PH Andrzej Bartkowiak, M Johnny Mandel, ED Peter Frank, PD Edward Pisoni.

LP Paul Newman† (Frank Galvin), Charlotte Rampling (Laura Fischer), Jack Warden (Mickey Morrissey), James Mason† (Ed Concannon), Milo O'Shea (Judge Hoyle), Lindsay Crouse (Kaitlin Costello Price), Edward Binns (Bishop Brophy), Julie Bovasso (Maureen Rooney), Roxanne Hart (Sally Doneghy), James Handy (Kevin Doneghy).

Aging, alcoholic attorney Paul Newman is unexpectedly given a case of medical malpractice and successfully sues a hospital. It's an interesting examination of legal and medical ethics, with Newman giving another of his first rate performances, as does James Mason.

3226. Verne Miller (1988, Three Aces/Alive, 95m, c). P Ann Broke Ashley, D&W Ron Hewitt, PH Misha Suslov, M Tom Chase & Steve Rucker, ED John O'Connor, PD Victoria Paul.

LP Scott Glenn (Verne Miller), Barbara Stock (Vi Miles), Thomas G. Waites (Al Capone), Lucinda Jenney (Bobby), Sonny Carl Davis (Frank "Baldy" Nash), Diane Salinger (Mortician's wife), Ed O'Ross (Ralph Capone), Vyto Rugins (Fitzsimmons), Andrew Robinson (Pretty Boy Floyd), Joseph Carberry (Hymie Ross).

Former lawman Scott Glenn has two talents, killing and bedding any woman he wants. He develops his skills in both areas, then moves to Chicago to offer half of his services to Al Capone. He's given several assignments to "hit" opponents of the South Side mob chief, but ultimately finds a contract has been put out on him when he becomes too ambitious. Don't wonder why you missed this film. It's so poorly done, it went directly to video.

3227. Vibes (1988, Columbia, 99m, c). P Deborah Blum & Tony Ganz, D Ken Kwapis, W Lowell Ganz (based on a story by Blum, Lowell Ganz & Babaloo Mandel), PH John Bailey, M James Horner, ED Carol Littleton, PD Richard Sawyer.

LP Cyndi Lauper (Sylvia Pickel), Jeff Goldblum (Nick Deezy), Julian Sands (Dr. Harrison Steele), Googy Gress (Ingo Swedlin), Peter Falk (Harry Buscafusco), Michael Lerner (Burt Wilder), Ramon Bieri (Eli Diamond), Elizabeth Pena (Consuela).

In her feature film debut, psychic Cyndi Lauper joins psychometric (one who can tell an object's history merely by touching it) Jeff Goldblum and conman Peter Falk to seek a lost city of gold in Ecuador.

3228. Vice Squad (1982, Avco Embassy/Hemdale, 97m, c). P Brian Frankish, D Gary A. Sherman, W Sandy Howard, Kenneth Peters & Robert Vincent O'Neil, PH John Alcott, M Keith Rubinstein, ED Roy Watts, PD Lee G. Fischer.

LP Season Hubley (Princess), Gary Swanson (Tom Walsh), Joseph DiGiroloma (Kowalski), Wings Hauser (Ramrod), Pepe Serna (Pete Mendez), Beverly Todd (Louise Williams), Maurice Emmanuel (Edwards).

It's the sleazy story of L.A.'s underbelly, featuring a whore helping the police capture a vicious wire-hanger-wielding pimp.

3229. Vice Versa (1988, Columbia, 98m, c). P Dick Clement & Ian La Frenais, D Brian Gilbert, W Clement & La Frenais, PH King Baggot, M David Shire, ED David Garfield, PD Jim Schoppe.

LP Judge Reinhold (Marshall Seymour), Fred Savage (Charlie Seymour), Corinne Bohrer (Sam), Swoosie Kurtz (Tina), David Proval (Turk), Jane Kaczmarek (Robyn), Gloria Gifford (Marcie), William Prince (Avery).

The device of a preadolescent boy or a teen exchanging bodies with an adult has been overworked recently and this entry is the least effective. Overworked businessman Judge Reinhold and his neglected son Fred Savage develop a greater respect for each other after spending some time in the other's world and body.

3230. *Vicious* (1988, SVS, Australia, 88m, c). P David Hannay & Charles Hannah, D Karl Zwicky, W Paul J. Hogan & Zwicky (based on an original idea by Hogan), PH John Stokes, M Robert Scott & John Sleith, ED Roy Mason.

LP Tambly Lord (Damon Kennedy), Craig Pearce (Terry), Tiffiny Dowe (Sondra Price), John Godden (Felix), Kelly Dingwall (Benny), Leather (Claire), Joanna Lockwood (Diane Kennedy), Frank McNamara (Gerry).

In a terrible exploitation film, Tambly Lord is a rich youngster who becomes a ruthless killer after falling in with a trio of juvenile delinquents.

3231. *Victor/Victoria* (1982, MGM/United Artists, GB, 133m, c). P Blake Edwards & Tony Adams, D Edwards, W Edwards† (based on the film *Viktor und Viktoria* by Rheinhold Schuenzel & Hans Hoemburg), PH Dick Bush, M Henry Mancini, ED Ralph E. Winters, PD Rodger Maus, AD Maus, Tim Hutchinson & William Craig Smith†, SD Harry Cordwell†, COS Patricia Norris†, M/L Mancini & Leslie Bricusse*.

LP Julie Andrews† (Victor/Victoria), James Garner (King), Robert Preston† (Toddy), Lesley Ann Warren† (Norma), Alex Karras (Squash), John Rhys-Davies (Cassell), Graham Stark (Waiter), Peter Arne (Labisse), Sherloque Tanney (Bovin).

This delightful sex-farce did not become the box-office success it deserved to be. Set in Paris during the Depression, British singer Julie Andrews and aging homosexual performer Robert Preston both have hit rock bottom. Things start to turn around when Preston convinces Andrews to pose as a female impersonator singer-dancer. She becomes the toast of the town. Entering the picture is James Garner, a Chicago gangster, travelling with his cheap blonde mistress Lesley Ann Warren and his bodyguard Alex Karras. He is attracted to Andrews, suspecting she really is a woman. When he discovers that he is right, he must go along with the masquerade because of her career. Now everyone believes that he's gay, something he's discovered is true of Karras. It all works out in the end. Preston and Warren are excellent in their roles, as is Graham Stark as a waiter who has seen it all.

3232. *Victory* (1981, Paramount, 117m, c, aka *Escape to Victory*). P Freddie Fields, D John Huston, W Evan Jones & Yabo Yablonsky (based on a story by Yablonsky, Djordje Milicevic & Jeff Maguire, PH Gerry Fisher, M Bill Conti, ED Roberto Silvi, PD J. Dennis Washington.

LP Sylvester Stallone (Robert Hatch), Michael Caine (John Colby), Pele (Luís Fernández), Bobby Moore (Terry Brady), Osvaldo Ardiles (Carlos Rey), Paul Van Himst (Michel Fileu), Kazimierz Deyna (Paul Wolchek), Hallvar Thorensen (Gunnar Hilsson), Max von Sydow (Maj. Karl Von Steiner).

Various international soccer stars including Pele appear in this routine prisoner-of-war film with a sports connection. Both the Germans and the prisoners have their own reasons for wanting a soccer match between a team of "all-star" prisoners and the German National Team. The Germans see it as a public relations opportunity and the prisoners plan to use it as a chance to escape.

3233. *The Video Dead* (1987, Interstate 5-Highlight, 90m, c). P,D&W Robert Scott, PH Greg Becker, M Stuart Rabinowitsk, Kevin McMahon & Leonard Marcel, ED Bob Sarles, PD Katalin Rogers, SE Dale Hall, Jr.

LP Roxanna Augeson (Zoe Blair), Rocky Duvall (Jeff Blair), Michael St. Michaels (Henry Jordan), Al Millan (Taxi Driver), Sam David McClelland (Joshua Daniels), Jennifer Miro (The Woman), Libby Russler (Maria).

An old TV set gets only one channel, which plays the same horror film over and over. The set also releases zombies and evil monsters to do their damnedest on a quiet tree-lined street.

Video Madness see Joysticks

3234. *Videodrome* (1983, Unviersal, Canada, 88m, c). P Claude Heroux, D&W David Cronenberg, PH Mark Irwin, M Howard Shore, ED Ronald Sanders, PD Carol Spier.

LP James Woods (Max Renn), Sonja Smits (Bianca O'Blivion), Deborah Harry (Nicki Brand), Peter Dvorsky (Harlan),

Les Carlson (Barry Convex), Jack Creley (Prof. Brian O'Blivion), Lynne Gorman (Masha).

Ambitious cable TV programmer James Woods schedules programs with soft-porn and S&M content whose signals he has pirated from satellite disks. When he tries to find out where the programs come from, he discovers he has bitten off more than he can chew.

3235. *A View to a Kill* (1985, MGM/United Artists, GB, 131m, c). P Albert R. Broccoli & Michael G. Wilson, D John Glen, W Richard Maibaum & Wilson (based on characters created by Ian Fleming), PH Alan Hume, M John Barry, ED Peter Davies, PD Peter Lamont.

LP Roger Moore (James Bond), Christopher Walken (Max Zorin), Tanya Roberts (Stacey Sutton), Grace Jones (May Day), Patrick Macnee (Tibbett), Patrick Bauchau (Scarpine), David Yip (Chuck Lee), Fiona Fullerton (Pola Ivanova), Manning Redwood (Bob Conley).

In what we trust will be Roger Moore's last venture as 007, he is teamed with lovely Tanya Roberts, a woman who moves so fluidly but acts so woodenly. Their adversary is mean-spirited Christopher Walken, who seems to be playing the role in his sleep. The latter's "right-hand man" is Grace Jones, who chews up the scenery to a fair-thee-well. But as Bond cannot be resisted by any woman, she gives her life in the end to save our hero when Walken has found it prudent to sacrifice her so he may escape.

3236. *Vigil* (1984, Enterprise, New Zealand, 90m, c). P John Maynard, D Vincent Ward, W Ward & Graeme Tetley, PH Alun Bollinger, M Jack Body, ED Simon Reece, PD Kai Hawkins.

LP Penelope Stewart (Elizabeth), Frank Whitten (Ethan), Bill Kerr (Birdie), Fiona Kay (Toss), Gordon Shields, Arthur Sutton, Snow Turner.

The film is seen through the eyes of 11-year-old Fiona Kay, who must learn to deal with the death of her father as well as the new man in her mother's life and hers.

3237. *Vigilante* (1983, Film Ventures, 90m, c, aka *Street Gang*). P Andrew Garroni & William Lustig, D Lustig, W Richard Vetere, PH James Lemmo, M

Jay Chattaway, ED Lorenzo Marinelli, PD Mischa Petrow.

LP Robert Forster (Eddie), Fred Williamson (Nick), Richard Bright (Burke), Rutanya Alda (Vickie), Don Blakely (Prago), Joseph Carberry (Ramon), Willie Colon (Rico), Joe Spinell (Eisenberg), Carol Lynley (D.A. Fletcher), Woody Strode (Rake).

Factory worker Robert Forster resists joining the vigilante group put together by Fred Williamson and others until a Puerto Rican gang victimizes his family, killing his son. When the leader of the gang goes free because of a corrupt judicial system, Forster joins Williamson's group and the bloodletting begins.

3238. *Vincent—The Life and Death of Vincent Van Gogh* (1988, Australia, 103m, c). P Tony Llewellyn-Jones, D,W,PH&ED Paul Cox (based on the letters of Vincent Van Gogh), M Norman Kaye, PD Neil Angwin.

VOICE John Hurt.

John Hurt reads the letters of Vincent Van Gogh to his brother Theo, providing the only text of this tribute to the passionate painter by Australian director Paul Cox, who visualizes the world of trees, sunflowers, sky and fields as he imagines Van Gogh saw them.

Vindicator see *Desert Warrior*

Violent Streets see *Thief*

3239. *Violent Zone* (1989, Arista Films, 90m, c). P&D John Garwood, W John Bushelman & Daved Pritchard, PH Roger Estrada, M Mark Josephson & Malcolm Cecil, ED Steve Bushelman.

LP John Jay Douglas (Steve Ryker), Christopher Weeks (Charles Townsend), Chard Hayward (Norman McKloskey), Cynthia Killion (Linda Blomberg), Daved Pritchard (Rick O'Brien), Michael Myracle (Doris).

In this direct-to-video movie, John Jay Douglas is recruited for a special mission 43 years after he fought the Japanese on Kao Teng Island. He will return to the island with a team he trains to rescue Christopher Weeks' son who has been held captive by the communists since 1974.

3240. *Violets Are Blue* (1986, Columbia, 90m, c). P Marykay Powell, D Jack Fisk, W Naomi Foner, PH Ralf Bode, M Patrick Williams, ED Edward Warschilka, PD Peter Jamison, M/L "One Day" by Williams & Will Jennings (sung by Laura Brannigan).

LP Sissy Spacek (Gussie Sawyer), Kevin Kline (Henry Squires), Bonnie Bedelia (Ruth Squires), John Kellogg (Ralph Sawyer), Jim Standiford (Addy Squires), Augusta Dabney (Ethel Sawyer), Kate McGregor-Stewart (Sara Mae), Adrian Sparks (George), Annalee Jefferies (Sally).

During high school, dreamers Sissy Spacek and Kevin Kline were lovers. He stayed home, taking over the family newspaper, and marrying local girl Bonnie Bedelia. She became a world-traveling photojournalist. When she returns home for R&R, the spark is still there as they team up for a news exposé.

3241. *The Violins Came with the Americans* (1987, Sun and Moon Prods., 94m, c). P David Greene, D Kevin Conway, W M. Quiros, Mila Burnette, PH Benjamin Davis, M Fred Weinberg, ED John Tintori.

LP Mila Burnette (Annie Adams), Joaquim de Almeida (David Garcia), Jose Ferrer (Don Fulhencio), Maria Norman, Kevin Conway, Norma Candal.

Disenchanted with her marriage, Mila Burnette leaves Manhattan for the South Bronx. There she falls in love with Puerto Rican lawyer Joaquim de Almeida and helps him organize the tenants of a tenement to force their absent landlord to make improvements.

3242. *Viper* (1988, Fries Distribution, 94m, c). P&D Peter Maris, W Frank Kerr, PH Gerald Wolfe, M Scott Roewe, ED Jack Tucker.

LP Linda Purl (Laura McCalla), James Tolkan (Col. Tanzer), Jeff Kober (Richard Gelb), Ken Force (Harley Trueblood), Chris Robinson (Jim McCalla), David M. Sterling (Powell), Charles Hoyes (Broadnax).

CIA agents kill members of the administration of a university, blaming it on Middle Eastern terrorists. The government then has justification for taking military action against an Arab nation. It takes the widow of an assassinated operative to unravel the circumstances surrounding her husband's death and expose the plot.

3243. *The Virgin Queen of St. Francis High* (1987, Crown International, Canada, 94m, c). D&W Francesco Lucente, PH Joseph Bitoni & Kevin Alexander, M Danny Lowe, Brad Steckel & Brian Island, ED Lucente.

LP Joseph R. Straface (Mike), Stacy Christensen (Diane), J.T. Wotton (Charles), Anna-Lisa Iapaolo (Judy), Lee Barringer (Randy), Bev Wotton (Diane's Mother).

Nicknamed "Snow White" because she's saving herself for marriage, Stacy Christensen, the prettiest, most virginal girl at St. Francis High, is the dream girl of nerdish Joseph R. Straface. Obnoxious Lee Barringer taunts Straface into accepting a bet that he can bet Christensen to go with him to the local lover's lane. He does but they don't have sex. Instead they become friends.

3244. *Vision Quest* (1985, Warner, 107m, c). P Jon Peters & Peter Guber, D Harold Becker, W Darryl Ponicsan (based on the novel by Terry Davis), PH Owen Roizman, M Tangerine Dream, ED Maury Winetrobe, PD Bill Malley.

LP Matthew Modine (Louden Swain), Linda Fiorentino (Carla), Michael Schoeffling (Kuch), Ronny Cox (Louden's Dad), Harold Sylvester (Tanneran), Charles Hallahan (Coach), J.C. Quinn (Elmo), Daphne Zuniga (Margie Epstein), R.H. Thompson (Kevin).

Wanting to compete against the city's best wrestler, high school athlete Matthew Modine goes on a starvation diet to get himself down from 190 to 168 pounds so he can be matched with the champ.

3245. *Visiting Hours* (1982, 20th Century–Fox, Canada, 105m, c, aka *The Fright; Get Well Soon*). P Claude Heroux, D Jean Claude Lord, W Brian Taggert, PH Rene Verzier, M Jonathan Goldsmith, ED Lord & Lise Thouin.

LP Michael Ironside (Colt Hawker), Lee Grant (Deborah Ballin), Linda Purl (Sheila Munroe), William Shatner (Gary Baylor), Lenore Zann (Lisa), Harvey Atkin (Vinnie Bradshaw), Helen Hughes (Louise Shepherd), Michael J. Reynolds (Porter Halstrom).

In another of the many slasher movies, a killer stalks the corridors of a major medical center.

3246. *Volunteers* (1985, Tri-Star, 106m, c). P Richard Shepherd & Walter F. Parkes, D Nicholas Meyer, W Ken Levine & David Isaacs (based on a story by Keith Critchlow), PH Ric Waite & Jack Green, M James Horner, ED Ronald Roose & Steven Polivka, PD James L. Schoppe.

LP Tom Hanks (Lawrence Bourne, III), John Candy (Tom Tuttle from Tacoma), Rita Wilson (Beth Wexler), Tim Thomerson (John Reynolds), Gedde Watanabe (At Toon), George Plimpton (Lawrence Bourne, Jr.), Ernest Harada (Chung Mee).

Faced with elimination by gangsters when his father won't bail him out from his gambling debts, filthy-rich Ivy League graduate Tom Hanks trades his convertible for a friend's seat on a plane to Bangkok where he is to work in the Peace Corps (Hanks is forced to throw in his fiancée as well). If you think that Thailand and the experience of helping others will change him, making him more humble, think again.

3247. *Vortex* (1982, B Movies, 90m, c). D&W Scott B., Beth B., PH Steven Fierberg, M Adele Bertei, Richard Edson, Lydia Lunch, Scott B. & Beth B., ED Scott B. & Beth B.

LP James Russo (Anthony Demmer), Lydia Lunch (Angel Powers), Bill Rice (Frederick Fields), Ann Magnuson (Pamela Fleming), Brent Collins (Peter), Bill Corsair (John Allen), Tom Webber (Ron Gavers).

Detective Lydia Lunch becomes involved in corporate wars and the manipulation of politicians by companies seeking defense contracts.

3248. *Voyage of the Rock Aliens* (1988, Inter Planetary Curb, 95m, c). P Micheline H. Keller & Brian Russell, D James Fargo & Bob Giraldi, W S. James Guidotti, Edward Gold & Charles Hairston, PH Gil Taylor & Dante Spinotti, M Jack White, ED Billy Williams & Malcolm Campbell, PD Ninkey Dalton.

LP Pia Zadora (Dee Dee), Tom Nolan (Abed), Craig Sheffer (Frankie), Alison LaPiaca (Diane), Michael Berryman (Chainsaw), Ruth Gordon (Sheriff), Jermaine Jackson (Rain).

This stupid spoof combines the worst elements of science fiction, musicals and beach party movies. Alien Tom Nolan and his rock band search the universe for signs of intelligent life—which is recognized as any world which plays rock music.

3249. *Wacko* (1983, Jensen Farley, 84m, c). P&D Greydon Clark, W Dana Olsen, Michael Spound, M. James Kouf, Jr. & David Greenwalt, PH Nicholas von Sternberg, M Arthur Kempel, ED Earl Watson & Curtis Burch.

LP Joe Don Baker (Harbinger), Stella Stevens (Marg Graves), George Kennedy (Dr. Graves), Julia Duffy (Mary Graves), Scott McGinnis (Norman), Andrew Clay (Tony), Elizabeth Daily (Bambi), Michele Tobin (Rosie).

Greydon Clark, struggling to maintain his reputation as among the worst directors presently working, gives audiences an *Airplane*-like parody of slasher movies; they want to give it back.

3250. *Wagner* (1983, London Trust Cultural, GB/Hung./Austria, 300m, c). P Alan Wright, D Tony Palmer, W Charlie Wood, PH Vittorio Storaro, M Richard Wagner, ED Graham Bunn, PD Kenneth Carey.

LP Richard Burton (Richard Wagner), Vanessa Redgrave (Cosima Wagner), Gemma Craven (Minna), Laszlo Galffi (King Ludwig II of Bavaria), John Gielgud (Pfistermeister), Ralph Richardson (Pfordten), Laurence Olivier (Pfeufer), Ekkerhard Schall (Franz Liszt), Ronald Pickup (Friedrich Nietzsche), Miguel Herz-Kestranek (Hans von Bulow).

Originally filmed to run nine hours, this epic movie biography of the great German composer attempts to touch on every important event in his life. This being the case, nothing is presented in a satisfactory manner. The photography is excellent and the supporting cast impressive, but as a whole, it disappoints.

3251. *Wait Until Spring, Bandini* (1989, Orion Classics, Bel./Fr./Ital./US, 100m, c). P Erwin Provoost, Tom Luddy & Fred Roos, D Dominique Deruddere, W Deruddere (based on a novel by John Fante), PH Jean-Francois Robin, M Angelo Badalmenti, ED Ludo Troch, PD Robert Ziembicki.

LP Joe Mantegna (Svevo Bandini), Ornella Muti (Maria Bandini), Faye Dunaway (Mrs. Effi Hildegarde), Michael Bacall (Arturo Bandini), Burt Young (Rocco Saccone), Tanya Lopert (Sister Celia).

The film features a family of Italian immigrants in Colorado in 1925. Bricklayer Joe Mantegna wastes his money in pool halls before becoming a handyman in more ways than one for wealthy widow Faye Dunaway. He moves in with her, leaving his wife Ornella Muti and family to fend for themselves. His 12-year-old son Michael Bacall is finally able to bring his parents back together.

3252. *Waiting for the Moon* (1987, Skouras, 88m, c). P Sandra Schulberg, D Jill Godmilow, W Mark Magill (based on a story by Godmilow & Magill), PH Andre Neau, M Michael Sahl, ED Georges Klotz, PD Patrice Mercier.

LP Linda Hunt (Alice B. Toklas), Linda Bassett (Gertrude Stein), Bernadette Lafont (Fernande Olivier), Bruce McGill (Ernest Hemingway), Jacques Boudet (Guillaume Apollinaire), Andrew McCarthy (Henry Hopper).

This witty biography explores the 39-year relationship of Alice B. Toklas and American writer Gertrude Stein.

3253. *Waitress* (1982, Troma, 88m, c, aka *Soup to Nuts*). P Lloyd Kaufman & Michael Herz, D Samuel Weil & Herz, W Michael Stone & Charles Kaufman, PH L. Kaufman, ED Dan Lowenthal, AD Barry Shapiro.

LP Carol Drake (Andrea), Jim Harris (Jerry), Carol Bevar (Jennifer), Renata Majer (Lindsey), David Hunt (Bill), Anthony Sarrero (Moe), Ed Fenton (Mr. Bellerman), Augie Grompone (Piebalt), Bonnie Horan (Mrs. Bellerman).

There isn't much of a plot to the story of three women working as waitresses in a New York restaurant, hoping for something better in their lives.

3254. *Walk Like a Man* (1987, MGM/United Artists, 86m, c). P Leonard Kroll, D Melvin Frank, W Robert Klane, PH Victor J. Kemper, M Lee Holdridge, ED Bill Butler & Steve Butler, PD Bill Malley.

LP Howie Mandel (Bobo Shand), Christopher Lloyd (Reggie Henry), Cloris Leachman (Margaret Shand), Colleen Camp (Rhonda Shand), Amy Steel (Penny).

Weird stand-up comedian Howie Mandel portrays a young man separated from his family as an infant and raised in the wilderness by a pack of wolves. When this innocent rejoins his family, he finds that two-legged wolves are far more dangerous.

3255. *A Walk on the Moon* (1987, Benenson-Midwest, 95m, c). P Diane Silver, D Raphael Silver, W William B. Mai, PH Adam Greenberg, M Paul Chihara, ED Peter Frank, PD Holger Gross.

LP Kevin Anderson (Everett Jones), Terry Kinney (Lew Ellis), Laila Robins (Marty Ellis), Patrice Martinez (India), Pedro Armendariz, Jr. (Doctor), Roberto Sosa (Candy).

At the time of the Vietnam war, after the death of Bobby Kennedy and Martin Luther King, new Peace Corpsman Kevin Anderson, assigned to a village in Colombia, still has his idealism. Not so for the married couple Terry Kinney and Laila Robins, whose two year stint and marriage are both about finished. Before long, Anderson has a nervous breakdown, the village is almost destroyed by a torrential downpour and Kinney and Robins renew their love.

3256. *Walker* (1987, Universal, 95m, c). P Lorenzo O'Brien & Angel Flores Marini, D Alex Cox, W Rudy Wurlitzer, PH David Bridges, M Joe Strummer, ED Carlos Puente Ortega & Cox, PD Bruno Rubeo.

LP Ed Harris (William Walker), Richard Masur (Ephraim Squier), Rene Auberjonois (Maj. Siegried Henningson), Keith Szarabajka (Timothy Crocker), John Diehl (Stebbins), Peter Boyle (Commodore Cornelius Vanderbilt), Marlee Matlin (Ellen Martin), Alfonso Arau (Raousset), Pedro Armendariz, Jr. (Munoz).

In what is meant to be a farcical parable of the current U.S. policy in Latin America, Ed Harris portrays the 19th century American soldier-of-fortune who declares himself president of Nicaragua. Marlee Matlin, as Harris' militant deaf girlfriend, dies early in the movie, but the film dies even earlier.

3257. *Walking the Edge* (1985, Empire, 93m, c). P Sergei Goncharoff, D Norbert Meisel, W Curt Allen, PH Ernie Poulos, M Jay Chattaway, ED Warren Chadwick, AD Dena Roth.

LP Robert Forster (Jason Walk), Nancy Kwan (Christine), Joe Spinell (Brusstar), A. Martinez (Tony), Aarika Wells (Julia), Wayne Woodson (McKee), James McIntire (Jimmy), Russ Courtney (Leon).

Unhappy cabdriver Robert Forster innocently becomes involved with guntoting Nancy Kwan's plans to blow away Joe Spinell, the man who killed her husband and son.

3258. *Wall Street* (1987, 20th Century-Fox, 124m, c). P Edward R. Pressman & A. Kitman Ho, D Oliver Stone, W Stone & Stanley Weiser, PH Robert Richardson, M Stewart Copeland, ED Claire Simpson, PD Stephen Hendrickson.

LP Charlie Sheen (Bud Fox), Michael Douglas* (Gordon Gekko), Martin Sheen (Carl Fox), Terence Stamp (Sir Larry Wildman), Sean Young (Kate Gekko), Daryl Hannah (Darien Taylor), Sylvia Miles (Realtor), James Spader (Roger Barnes), Hal Holbrook (Lou Mannheim), Saul Rubinek (Harold Salt).

Michael Douglas and Charlie Sheen star in an effective morality tale about movers and shakers in a world of stocks and bonds. Douglas manipulates companies and people, but produces nothing except money. Douglas argues that greed is good and young Sheen buys the whole spiel, despite warnings from his hardworking father Martin Sheen and decent stockbroker Hal Holbrook. In the end Charlie goes to jail for his insider dealings, taking Douglas with him, but the "crime doesn't pay" ending seems out of place in a day and age where on the contrary it seems quite lucrative.

3259. *Walter and June* (1986, Film Forum, GB, 110m, c, aka *Loving Walter*). P Richard Creasey, D Stephen Frears, W David Cook (based on his book *Winter Doves*), PH Chris Menges, M George Fenton, ED Mick Audsley, AD Michael Minas.

LP Ian McKellen (Walter), Sarah Miles (June), Barbara Jefford, Arthur Whybrow.

Ian McKellan is excellent as an unloved mentally retarded man. His bleak existence is briefly interrupted when mentally ill Sarah Miles seduces him.

3260. *Waltz Across Texas* (1982, Atlantic, 99m, c). P Martin Jurow & Scott Rosenfelt, D Ernest Day, W Bill Svanoe (based on a story by Terry Jastrow & Anne Archer), PH Robert Elswit, M Steve Dorff, ED Jay Lash Cassidy, PD Michael Erler.

LP Anne Archer (Gail Weston), Terry Jastrow (John Taylor), Noah Beery, Jr. (Joe Locker), Mary Kay Place (Kit Peabody), Josh Taylor (Luke Jarvis), Richard Farnsworth (Frank Walker), Ben Piazza (Bill Wrather).

Husband and wife team Anne Archer and Terry Jastrow try to resurrect the romantic comedies of the 30s with this story of two people whose mutual dislike for each other turns to love when they join a quest to discover oil in West Texas. Unfortunately the resurrection doesn't take.

3261. *Wanted: Dead or Alive* (1987, New World, 104m, c). P Robert C. Peters, D Gary Sherman, W Michael Patrick Goodman, Brian Taggert & Sherman, PH Alex Nepomniaschy, M Joseph Renzetti, ED Ross Albert, PD Paul Eads.

LP Rutger Hauer (Nick Randall), Gene Simmons (Malak Al Rahim), Robert Guillaume (Philmore Walker), Mel Harris (Terry), William Russ (Danny Quintz), Susan McDonald (Louise Quintz), Jerry Hardin (John Lipton).

Former CIA career agent Rutger Hauer is a sort of modern-day bounty hunter, collecting society's scum for very good prices. But the tables are turned when an FBI-CIA conspiracy uses him as bait, with the quarry an international terrorist.

3262. *War* (1988, Troma, 99m, c). P Lloyd Kaufman & Michael Herz, D Herz & Samuel Weil, W Mitchell Dana, Eric Hattler, Thomas Martinek & Kaufman (based on a story by Kaufman), PH James London, M Christopher De Marco, SE William Jennings & Pericles Lewnes.

LP Carolyn Beauchamp (Lydia), Sean Bowen (Taylor), Michael Ryder (Parker), Patrick Weathers (Kirkland), Jessica

Dublin (Dottie), Steven Crossley (Marshall), Charles Kay Hune (Hardwick), Lorayn Lane DeLuca (Maria).

A planeload of New Jersey residents crashland on a remote tropical island overrun with terrorists plotting attacks on the U.S. The survivors band together to frustrate the terrorists' plans.

3263. War and Love (1985, Cannon, 112m, c). P Jack P. Eisner, D Moshe Mizrahi, W Abby Mann (based on the book *The Survivor* by Eisner), PH Adam Greenberg, M Gustav Mahler, ED Peter Zinner.

LP Sebastian Keneas (Jacek), Kyra Sedgwick (Halina), David Spielberg (Aron), Cheryl Gianini (Zlatka), Eda Reiss-Merin (Masha), Brita Youngblood (Hela), Reuel Schiller (Lutek), Eric Faber (Yankele).

The film is based on the experiences of producer Jack P. Eisner, who as a young man survived the horrors of the Warsaw ghetto and Nazi concentration camps.

3264. War Birds (1989, Vidmark, 88m, c). P Kurt Eggert & Joanne Watkins, D Ulli Lommel, W Clifford B. Wellman & Lommel, PH Deland Nuse, M Jerry Lambert, ED Joe Negron, PD Angela Allaire.

LP Jim Eldert (Billy Hawkins), Timothy Hicks (Jim Harris), Bill Brinsfield (Lt. Col. Ronson), Cully Holland (Vince Costello), David Schroeder (Van Dam), Joanne Watkins (Carolyn), Rick Anthony Monroe (Salim).

Bill Brinsfield recruits some "Top Gun" school graduates to fly into El Alahaim, a U.S. ally to aid the pro–American sheik fight some nasty rebels.

3265. War of the Roses (1989, 20th Century–Fox, 116m, c). P James L. Brooks & Arnon Milchan, D Danny DeVito, W Michael Leeson (based on the novel by Warren Adler), PH Stephen H. Burum, M David Newman, ED Lynzee Klingman, PD Ida Random.

LP Michael Douglas (Oliver Rose), Kathleen Turner (Barbara Rose), Danny DeVito (Gavin D'Amato), Marianne Sagebrecht (Susan), Sean Astin (Josh at 17), Heather Fairfield (Carolyn at 17), G.D. Spradlin (Harry Thurmont), Peter Donat (Larrabee).

This witty black comedy is the story of the dissolution of the marriage of Michael Douglas and Kathleen Turner. After all the years of scrimping and saving have paid off and they have both made it big, Turner wants out. All that she demands from the divorce is their luxuriously and tastefully furnished home. Douglas wants it also. Both are advised by their lawyers not to vacate their shared home. As a result the home becomes an emotional and physical battlefield with no holds barred. Douglas and Turner have never been better, separately or as a team, and Danny DeVito is proving he's a damn good director as well as a very funny man. It's to his credit and writer Michael Leeson's that the film doesn't wimp out in the end, although not everyone is going to be happy with the outcome.

3266. War Party (1989, Hemdale, 96m, c). P John Daly, Derek Gibson & Bernard Williams, D Franc Roddam, W Spencer Eastman, PH Brian Tufano, M Chaz Jankel, ED Sean Barton, PD Michael Bingham.

LP Billy Wirth (Sonny Crowkiller), Kevin Dillon (Skitty Harris), Tim Sampson (Warren Cutfoot), Jimmie Ray Weeks (Jay Stivic), Kevyn Major Howard (Calvin Morrisey), Jerry Hardin (Sheriff), Tantoo Cardinal (Sonny's Mother), Bill McKinney (Mayor).

This fictional account of a group of modern young Indians, who say "enough is enough" and violently rise up against the government in Montana, snuck into theaters for the briefest of stays and left without much attention. The filmmakers maintain the fiction that they are showing concern for the treatment of the redman but really they only want to exploit conditions in order to show a bloodbath as in the good old days of racist westerns.

3267. Wargames (1983, MGM/United Artists, 113m, c). P Harold Schneider, D John Badham, W Lawrence Lasker & Walter F. Parkes†, PH William A. Fraker†, M Arthur B. Rubinstein, ED Tom Rolf, PD Angelo P. Graham, SOUND Michael J. Kohut, Carlos de Larios, Aaron Rochin & Willie D. Burton†.

LP Matthew Broderick (David), Dahney Coleman (McKittrick), John Wood (Falken), Ally Sheedy (Jennifer), Barry Corbin (Gen. Beringer), Juanin Clay (Pat Healy), Kent Williams (Cabot), Dennis Lipscomb (Watson).

Teenage computer whiz Matthew Broderick taps into a top-secret Pentagon computer and sets in motion "Global Thermonuclear War" which he thinks is a video game, but it's the real thing.

3268. *Warlock* (1989, New World, GB, 102m, c). P&D Steve Miner, W David Twohy, PH David Eggby, ED David Finfer, PD Roy Forge Smith.

LP Richard E. Grant (Giles Redferne), Julian Sands (The Warlock), Lori Singer (Kassandra), Kevin O'Brien (Chas), Richard Kuse (Mennonite), Juli Burkhart (Daughter-in-law), Chip Johnson (Farmer), David Carpenter (Pastor), Anna Levine (Pastor's Wife).

While being prepared for execution in the Massachusetts Bay Colony of 1691, warlock Julian Sands and witch hunter Richard E. Grant are transported to 1988 L.A. From then on the film resembles *Time After Time* (1980), in which Jack the Ripper escaped to the 20th century, only to be pursued by H.G. Wells.

3269. *Warlords* (1989, American-Independent, 85m, c). P Harel Goldstein & Fred Olen Ray, D Fred Olen Ray, W Scott Ressler, PH Laslo Regos, M William Belote, ED William Shaffer, AD Corey Kaplan.

LP David Carradine (Dow), Dawn Wildsmith (Danny), Sid Haig (Warlord), Ross Hagen (Beaumont), Fox Harris (Col. Cox), Robert Quarry (Dr. Mathers), Brinke Stevens (Dow's wife), Victoria Sellers (Desert Girl).

In a tongue-in-cheek "Mad Max"–type film, David Carradine is the clone of a famous warrior. After a nuclear war and an uprising by mutants, he seeks his wife, being held by powerful warlord Sid Haig.

Warlords of the 21st Century see *Battletruck*

3270. *Warning Sign* (1985, 20th Century–Fox, 100m, c). P Jim Bloom, D Hal Barwood, W Barwood & Matthew Robbins, PH Dean Cundey, M Craig Safan, ED Robert Lawrence, PD Henry Bumstead.

LP Sam Waterston (Cal Morse), Kathleen Quinlan (Joanie Morse), Yaphet Kotto (Maj. Connolly), Jeffrey De Munn (Dan Fairchild), Richard Dysart (Dr. Nielsen), G.W. Bailey (Tom Schmidt), Jerry Hardin (Vic Flint), Rick Rossovich (Bob).

When an experiment in gene-splicing headed by fanatical scientist Richard Dysart goes awry in a secret germ warfare lab in Utah, workers are turned into homicidal zombies.

3271. *The Warrior and the Sorceress* (1984, New World, 81m, c). P Frank Isaac & John Broderick, D&W Broderick (based on a story by Broderick & William Stout), PH Leonard Solis, M Louis Saunders, ED Silvia Ripoll, SE Chris Biggs.

LP David Carradine (Kain), Luke Askew (Zeg), Maria Socas (Naja), Anthony DeLongis (Kief), Harry Townes (Bludge), William Marin (Bal Caz), Arthur Clark (Burgo), Daniel March (Blather).

In this sword and sorcery flop, wandering warrior David Carradine sells his services to both sides in a dispute over a well.

3272. *Warrior Queen* (1987, Seymour Borde, 69m, c). P Harry Alan Towers, D Chuck Vincent, W Rick Marx (based on a story by Peter Welbeck [Towers]), PH Lorenzo Battaglia, M Ian Shaw & Kai Joffe, ED Vincent, Joel Bender & Tony Delcampo, PD Lucio Parisi.

LP Sybil Danning (Berenice), Donald Pleasence (Claudius), Richard Hill (Marcus), Josephine Jacqueline Jones (Chloe), Tally Chanel (Vespa), Stasia Micula [Samantha Fox] (Philomena/Augusta), Suzanna Smith (Veneria).

This softcore sword and sorcery film has no plot that is readily apparent. It's set in Pompeii, a Roman brothel and a gladiator ring. Somehow or other these are supposed to be related, but it's not clear how.

3273. *Warriors of the Apocalypse* (1987, Film Concept, 95m, c, aka *Time Raiders; Searchers of the Voodoo Mountain*). P&D Bobby A. Suarez, W Ken Metcalfe (based on a story by Suarez), PH Juanito Pereira, M Ole Hoyer, PD Ruben Arthur Nicado.

LP Michael James (Trapper), Deborah Moore (Sheba), Franco Guerrero

(Anouk), Ken Metcalfe (Goruk), Robert Marius, Charlotte Cain, David Light, Mike Cohen.

About 150 years in the future, Michael James and his nomadic followers come across 100-year-old Franco Guerrero. They travel with him in search of Voodoo Mountain, ruled by Ken Metcalfe and his queen, Deborah Moore. The mountain hides a nuclear power plant, operated by slave labor. The battle lines are drawn.

3274. *The Wash* (1988, Skouras/Exclusive, 93m, c). P Calvin Skaggs, D Michael Toshiyuki Uno, W Philip Kan Gotanda (based on his play), PH Walt Lloyd, M John Morris, ED Jay Freund, PD David Wasco.

LP Mako (Nobu), Nobu McCarthy (Masi), Patti Yasutake (Marsha), Marian Yue (Judy), Sab Shimono (Sadao), Shizuko Hoshi (Kiyoko), Danny Kamekona (Blackie), Takayo Fischer (Chiyo), Ken Narasaki (Brad).

San Francisco is the setting for this admirable off-beat romantic comedy. Sour old codger Mako never sweetens up as the movie progresses. His 60-year-old wife Nobu McCarthy, who has left him, makes a weekly visit to bring him clean laundry. She finally comes out of her shell, finding happiness with a pleasant widower. Mako can't understand why she should want a divorce and upset their arrangement.

3275. *The Watcher in the Woods* (1980, Disney/Buena Vista, GB, 100m, c). P Ron Miller, D John Hough & Vincent McEveety (uncredited), W Brian Clemens, Harry Spalding & Rosemary Anne Sisson (based on the novel by Florence Engel Randall), PH Alan Hume, M Stanley Myers, ED Geoffrey Foot, PD Elliot Scott.

LP Bette Davis (Mrs. Aylwood), Carroll Baker (Helen Curtis), David McCallum (Paul Curtis), Lynn-Holly Johnson (Jan Curtis), Kyle Richards (Ellie Curtis), Ian Bannen (John Keller), Richard Pasco (Tom Colley).

In this Gothic horror story, the Curtis family rents a woodland mansion. Their teenage daughter is haunted by visions. Bette Davis, the owner of the mansion, lives in a small guest house on the grounds and seeks her daughter who was lost 30 years ago as a child and is trapped in another dimension.

3276. *Watchers* (1988, Universal, Canada, 92m, c). P Damian Lee & David Mitchell, D Jon Hess, W Bill Freed & Lee (based on the novel by Dean R. Koontz), PH Richard Leiterman, M Joel Goldsmith, Rick Fields, ED Bill Freda & Carolle Alain, PD Richard Wilcox Kent.

LP Corey Haim (Travis), Barbara Williams (Nora), Michael Ironside (Lem), Lala Sloatman (Tracey), Duncan Fraser (Sheriff Gaines), Blue Mankuma (Cliff), Colleen Winton (Deputy Porter), Norman Browning (Hockney).

We're not sure who's watching whom in this ridiculous sf/horror film about a hairy orange monster named Oxcom who hates a very bright, loveable little dog. Both are part of a government secret project that has gone awry. It doesn't really matter, because the film hasn't had many watchers.

3277. *Water* (1986, Atlantic, GB, 91m, c). P Ian La Frenais, D Dick Clement, W Clement, La Frenais & Bill Persky (based on a story by Persky), PH Douglas Slocombe, M Mike Moran, ED John Victor Smith, PD Norman Garwood.

LP Michael Caine (Baxter), Valerie Perrine (Pamela), Brenda Vaccaro (Bianca), Billy Connolly (Delgado), Leonard Rossiter (Sir Malcolm), Dennis Dugan (Rob), Fulton MacKay (Eric), Chris Tummings (Garfield).

This satire about the discovery of a delicious mineral water source in a British colony doesn't do much more than give Michael Caine another paycheck in one of his busier years.

3278. *Wavelength* (1983, New World, 88m, c). P James Rosenfield, D&W Mike Gray, PH Paul Goldsmith, M Tangerine Dream, ED Mark Goldblatt & Robert Leighton, AD Linda Pearl.

LP Robert Carradine (Bobby Sinclaire), Cherie Currie (Iris Longacre), Keenan Wynn (Dan), Cal Bowman (Gen. Milton Ward), James Hess (Col. James MacGruder), Terry Burns (Capt. Hinsdale), Eric Morris (Dr. Vernon Cottrell).

In this thriller military advisors and scientists perform an autopsy on an alien creature while three others are stored in frozen containers. It turns out that Cherie

Currie can communicate telepathically with the creatures.

3279. *The Way It Is* (1986, Spring Films, Inc., 80m, b&w). P Daniel Sales & Eric Mitchell, D&W Mitchell, PH Bobby Bukowski, M Vincent Gallo, ED Bob Gould & Sue Graef.

LP Kai Eric (Orpheus), Boris Major (Eurydice), Vincent Gallo (Vic), Jessica Stutchbury (Vera), Mark Boone, Jr. (Hank), Steve Buscemi (Willy), Rockets Redglare (Frank), Daniel Rosen (Dave).

East Village artists bore audiences with their production of Cocteau's "Orpheus."

3280. *Waxwork* (1988, Vestron, 97m, c/b&w). P Staffan Ahrenberg, D&W Anthony Hickox, PH Gerry Lively, M Roger Bellon, ED Christopher Cibelli, PD Gianni Quaranta, SE Bob Keen.

LP Zach Galligan (Mark), Deborah Foreman (Sarah), Michelle Johnson (China), David Warner (Mr. Lincoln), Dana Ashbrook (Tony), Patrick Macnee (Sir Wilfred), Charles McCaughan (Det. Roberts), J. Kenneth Campbell (Marquis De Sade), Miles O'Keeffe (Count Dracula), John Rhys-Davies (Anton Weber).

In a horror story loosely based on Paul Leni's 1924 classic *Waxworks,* David Warner is the proprietor of a wax museum featuring movie monsters and real-looking horrors. He is able to revive them and turn them loose on an unsuspecting mankind. It's up to a bunch of dimwitted teens to thwart his plans.

3281. *We of the Never Never* (1983, Triumph, Australia, 132m, c). P Greg Tepper & John B. Murray, D Igor Auzins, W Peter Schreck (based on the book by Jane Taylor Gunn), PH Gary Hansen, M Peter Best, ED Clifford Hayes, PD Josephine Ford.

LP Angela Punch-McGregor (Jeannie), Arthur Dignam (Aeneas Gunn), Tony Barry (Mac), Tommy Lewis (Jackeroo), Lewis Fitz-Gerald (Jack), Martin Vaughan (Dan), John Jarratt (Dandy), Tex Morton (Landlord).

It's the story of the first white woman ever to travel to the aborigine wilderness known as the "Never Never."

3282. *We Think the World of You* (1988, Cinecom, GB, 94m, c). P Tommaso Jandelli & Paul Cowan, D Colin Gregg, W Hugh Stoddart (based on the novel by J.R. Ackerley), PH Mike Garfath, M Julian Jacobson, ED Peter Delfgou, PD Jamie Leonard.

LP Alan Bates (Frank Meadows), Gary Oldman (Johnny), Frances Barber (Megan), Liz Smith (Millie), Max Wall (Tom), Kerry Wise (Rita).

Set in the mid-50s, this off-beat comedy about love and obsession centers on a friendship between Alan Bates and Gary Oldman, the latter's wife Frances Barber and a beautiful dog, Evie.

3283. *Weeds* (1987, Kingsgate, 115m, c). P Bill Badalato, D John Hancock, W Dorothy Tristan & Hancock, PH Jan Weincke, M Angelo Badalamenti, ED Dennis O'Connor, PD Joseph T. Garrity.

LP Nick Nolte (Lee Umstetter), Lane Smith (Claude), William Forsythe (Burt the Booster), John Toles-Bey (Navarro), Joe Mantegna (Carmine), Ernie Hudson (Bagdad), Mark Rolston (Dave), J.J. Johnson (Lazarus).

Prisoner Nick Nolte develops a love for theater while in the joint. After winning a pardon, he forms a group of traveling actors who perform in prisons.

3284. *Weekend at Bernie's* (1989, 20th Century–Fox, 97m, c). P Victor Drai, D Ted Kotcheff, W Robert Klane, PH Francois Protat, M Andy Summers, ED Joan E. Chapman, PD Peter Jamison.

LP Andrew McCarthy (Larry Wilson), Jonathan Silverman (Richard Parker), Catherine Mary Stewart (Gwen Saunders), Terry Kiser (Bernie Lomax), Don Calfa (Paulie), Catherine Parks (Tina), Eloise Broady (Tawny), Gregory Salata (Marty), Louis Giambalvo (Vito), Ted Kotcheff (Jack Parker).

Insurance go-getters Andrew McCarthy and Jonathan Silverman show up for a weekend at the island home of their slimy boss Terry Kiser, only to find he's been bumped off by the mob. No one else visiting that weekend seems to notice that Kiser is deceased for reasons not adequately explained to the audience. McCarthy and Silverman feel they must get Kiser's body off the island, before it's discovered he's expired.

3285. *Weekend Pass* (1984, Crown, 92m, c). P Marilyn J. Tenser & Michael

D. Castle, D&W Lawrence Bassoff (based on a story by Tenser), PH Bryan England, M John Baer, ED Harry B. Miller, III.

LP D.W. Brown (Paul Fricker), Peter Ellenstein (Lester Gidley), Patrick Hauser (Webster Adams), Chip McAllister (Bunker Hill), Pamela G. Kay (Tina Wells), Hilary Shapiro (Cindy Hazard), Graem McGavin (Tawny Ryatt).

Four wiseguy rookie sailors just having finished boot camp are off on a fun-filled amorous weekend pass.

3286. *Weekend Warriors* (1986, The Movie Store, 85m, c). P Hannah Hempstead, D Bert Convy, W Bruce Belland & Roy M. Rogosin (based on a story by Belland), PH Charles Minsky, M Perry Botkin, ED Raja Gosnell, PD Chester Kaczenski.

LP Chris Lemmon (Vince Tucker), Vic Tayback (Sgt. Burge), Lloyd Bridges (Col. Archer), Graham Jarvis (Congressman Balljoy), Daniel Greene (Phil McCracken), Marty Cohen (Decola), Brian Bradley (Cory Seacomb).

In an effort to avoid the draft, a group of young men join the National Guard. Lots of guys did that before the Korean War and found themselves cannon fodder when hostilities broke out. Nothing like that happens here; it's a sloppy comedy.

3287. *Weird Science* (1985, Universal, 94m, c). P Joel Silver, D&W John Hughes, PH Matthew F. Leonetti, M Ira Newborn, ED Mark Warner, Christopher Lebenzon & Scott Wallace, PD John W. Corso.

LP Anthony Michael Hall (Gary), Kelly LeBrock (Lisa), Ilan Mitchell-Smith (Wyatt), Bill Paxton (Chet), Suzanne Snyder (Deb), Judie Aronson (Hilly), Robert Downey (Ian), Robert Rusler (Max), Vernon Wells (Lord General).

Anthony Michael Hall and Ilan Mitchell-Smith are like car-chasing dogs; once they catch one, they don't know what to do with it. Brilliant nerds, the boys use their computer expertise to create the perfect women, Kelly LeBrock. She's a bit much for our heroes. Before the film is out the boys are happy to settle for some teenage girls who are more their speed.

3288. *Welcome Home* (1989, Columbia, 87m, c). P Martin Ransohoff, D Franklin J. Schaffner, W Maggie Kleinman, PH Fred J. Koenekamp, ED Bob Swink, PD Dan Yarhi & Dennis Davenport.

LP Kris Kristofferson (Jake Robbins), JoBeth Williams (Sarah), Brian Keith (Jake's Father), Sam Waterston (Woody), Trey Wilson (Col. Barnes), J.J. [John Marshall Jones, Jr.] (Dwayne), Thomas Wilson Brown (Tyler), Kieu Chinh [Nguyen] (Leang).

Kris Kristofferson portrays an American officer who returns to his Vermont home after 17 years in Cambodia. He is married to Kieu Chinh who has borne him two children. The military wishes he had stayed put, and at least initially so does JoBeth Williams, the wife he left so long ago. She's now living with her new husband Sam Waterston, Kristofferson's son and Kris' widower father Brian Keith.

3289. *Welcome to Canada* (1989, National Film Board, Canada, 88m, c). D John N. Smith, W Sam Grana & Smith, PH David de Volpi & Roger Martin, ED Smith, Grana & Martial Ethier.

LP Noreen Power, Brendan Foley, Madonna Hawkins, Kasivisanathan Kathrigasoo, Kumasraselvy Kathrigasoo, Pathanjali Prasad.

Using nonprofessional actors, the film explores what might have happened to the 1987 Tamil refugees from Sri Lanka who were dropped off the coast of Newfoundland where they were detained by Immigration officers. In this fictional account the Newfies are able to make personal contact with the refugees.

3290. *Welcome to 18* (1986, American Distribution Group, 91m, c). P David C. Thomas, D Terry Carr, W Judith Sherman Wolin & Carr, PH Stephen L. Posey, M Tony Berg, ED Lois Freeman-Fox, PD Steven Legler.

LP Courtney Thorne-Smith (Lindsey), Mariska Hargitay (Joey), Jo Ann Willette (Robin), Cristen Kaufman (Talia), E. Erich Anderson (Roscoe), Jeff MacGregor (Cliff), John Putch (Corey).

Three teenage girls learn something about the hard cruel world in the summer between graduation from high school and beginning college.

3291. *We're No Angels* (1989, Paramount, 108m, c). P Art Linson, D Neil Jordan, W David Mamet (loosely based on the 1955 movie *We're No Angels*, screenplay by Ranald MacDougall, adapted from the play *My Three Angels* by Sam and Bella Spewak and the play *La Cuisine de Anges* by Albert Husson), PH Philippe Rousselot, M George Fenton, ED Mick Audsley & Joke Van Wijk, PD Wolf Kroeger.

LP Robert DeNiro (Ned), Sean Penn (Jim), Demi Moore (Molly), Hoyt Axton (Father Levesque), Bruno Kirby (Deputy), Ray McAnally (Warden), James Russo (Bobby), Wallace Shawn (Translator), John C. Reilly (Young Monk), Jay Brazeau (Sheriff), Ken Buhay (Bishop Nogulich).

The time is 1935. The place is a state somewhere near the Canadian border. Robert DeNiro and Sean Penn are small-time, dimwitted hoods sentenced to hard labor. Forced to take part in a prison breakout, they take refuge in a small border town where the local monastery is celebrated for a shrine of "the Weeping Madonna." They are mistaken for visiting ecclesiastical monks and they gleefully go along with the deception. The two are redeemed in spite of themselves. Based loosely on the 1955 film, starring Humphrey Bogart, Aldo Ray and Peter Ustinov, this version isn't as funny. Maybe it misses Aldo Ray's accommodating poisonous snake "Adolphe."

3292. *Wetherby* (1985, MGM/United Artist Classics, GB, 102m, c). P Simon Relph, D&W David Hare, PH Stuart Harris, M Nick Bicat, ED Chris Wimble, PD Hayden Griffin.

LP Vanessa Redgrave (Jean Travers), Ian Holm (Stanley Pilborough), Judi Dench (Marcia Pilborough), Marjorie Yates (Verity Braithwaite), Tom Wilkinson (Roger Braithwaite), Tim McInnerny (John Morgan), Suzanna Hamilton (Karen Creasy), Stuart Wilson (Mike Langdon).

Wetherby is a small town in Yorkshire. There a stranger kills himself in school teacher Vanessa Redgrave's home in surely one of the most surprising and shocking suicides to be filmed. Police investigations reveal some secrets in Redgrave's past.

3293. *The Whales of August* (1987, Alice-Circle-Nelson, 90m, c/b&w). P Carolyn Pfeiffer & Mike Kaplan, D Lindsay Anderson, W David Berry (based on his play), PH Mike Fash, M Alan Price, ED Nicolas Gaster, MD Derek Wadsworth, PD Jocelyn Herbert.

LP Bette Davis (Libby Strong), Lillian Gish (Sarah Webber), Vincent Price (Mr. Nikolai Maranov), Ann Sothern† (Tisha Doughty), Harry Carey, Jr. (Joshua Brackett), Frank Grimes (Mr. Beckwith), Frank Pitkin (Old Randall), Mike Bush (Young Randall).

In her last film role Bette Davis appears as an elderly blind woman, tenderly cared for by her sister Lillian Gish. Art may be imitating life as Davis is quarrelsome, embittered and always willing to pass judgment on the failings of others, while Gish is saintly patient. It's always a pleasure to see these giants of the silver screen — and come to think of it, now that Bette is gone, isn't it time the Academy of Arts and Sciences presented Gish with a special Oscar for lifetime achievement before it's too late?

3294. *What Comes Around* (1986, A.W.O. Associates, 86m, c). P Ted Evanson, D Jerry Reed, W Peter Herrecks (based on a story by Gary Smith & Dave Franklin), PH James Pergola, M Al Delory, ED William Carruth, PD Don K. Ivey.

LP Jerry Reed (Joe Hawkins), Barry Corbin (Leon), Bo Hopkins (Tom Hawkins), Arte Johnson (Malone), Ernest Dixon (Big Jay), Hugh Jarrett (Ralph), Buck Ford (Chester).

Bo Hopkins kidnaps his older brother, country-western singer Jerry Reed, who is hooked on booze and drugs, in an attempt to save him from his self-destruction.

3295. *What You Take for Granted* (1984, Iris Feminist Collective, 75m, c). P,D&W Michelle Citron, PH Frances Reid, M Karen Pritikin, ED Citron.

LP Belinda Cloud (Dianna the Doctor), Donna Blue Lachman (Anna the Truck Driver), Mosetta Harris (Cable Splicer), Fran Hart (Philosophy Professor), Helen Larimore (Sculptor).

In this tedious pseudodocumentary, interviews are held with women doing jobs not ordinarily associated with women. These are intercut with fictional scenes of such women relating to each other.

3296. *Whatever It Takes* (1986, Aquarius Films, 93m, c). P,D&ED Bob Demchuk, W Chris Weatherhead & Demchuk, PH John Drake, M Garry Sherman.

LP Tom Mason (Jeff Perchick), Martin Balsam (Hap Pershicksky), Chris Weatherhead (Lee Bickford), James Rebhorn (Michael Manion), Maura Shea (Eren Haberfield), Bill Bogert (Timothy Shaughnessy), Rosetta LeNoire (Millie), Joey Ginza (Curley), Fred Morsell (Mr. Bunyon), Edward Binns (Mr. Kingsley).

Tom Mason is a cartoonist trying anything to make it to syndication and all the perks which go with it.

3297. *What's Up, Hideous Sun Demon* (1989, Greystone, 71m, b&w/c). P Greg Brown, Jeff Montgomery, Hadi Salem, D Craig Mitchell, W Mitchell, PH John Lambert & Steve Dubin, M Fred Myrow, ED Glenn Morgan.

LP Robert Clarke (Gil/Pitnik), Patricia Manning (Polly), Nan Petersen (Trudy/Bunny), Patrick Whyte (Major), Del Courtney, Fred La Porta, Bill Hampton.

This is a revamped version of Robert Clarke's 1959 monster film with voice dubbings of Jay Leno, Susan Tyrrell, Barbara Goodson and Bernard Behrens. The laughs will guarantee the film plenty of midnight showings. For those who don't recall the 1959 pic, Clarke is a research scientist exposed to radioactive poisoning. It turns him into a humanoid reptilian monster with a bad temper.

Wheels of Fire   see   Desert Warrior

3298. *When Harry Met Sally . . .* (1989, Columbia, 95m, c). P Rob Reiner & Andrew Scheinman, D Reiner, W Nora Ephron†, PH Barry Sonnenfeld, M Marc Shaiman, ED Robert Leighton, PD Jane Musky.

LP Billy Crystal (Harry Burns), Meg Ryan (Sally Albright), Carrie Fisher (Marie), Bruno Kirby (Jess), Steven Ford (Joe), Lisa Jane Persky (Alice), Michelle Nicastro (Amanda).

Director Rob Reiner and writer Nora Ephron owe a great deal to Woody Allen movies, starring Allen and Diane Keaton, such as *Annie Hall* and *Manhattan*. This romantic comedy presents Billy Crystal and Meg Ryan as friends enjoying a platonic relationship, but it doesn't stay that way. It's a cute summer movie — if one can be satisfied with that and not look for any messages or new insights into relationships between men and women.

3299. *When Nature Calls* (1985, Troma, 85m, c). P Frank Vitale & Charles Kaufman, D Kaufman, W Kaufman & Straw Weisman, PH Mike Spera, M Arthur Custer, ED Michael Jacobi, PD Susan Kaufman.

LP David Orange (Greg), Barbara Marineau (Barb), Nicky Beim (Little Billy), Tina Marie Staiano (Bambi), David Strathairn (Weejun), Silas Davis (O'Malley), Mike Brancato (Milos), Patricia Clement (Cleaning Lady).

This screwball comedy features a typical American family, grown tired of city living, that takes to the great outdoors. It's merely an excuse for a scattergun series of gags, including one about a telethon to raise money to cure the Jerry Lewis disease.

3300. *When the Whales Came* (1989, 20th Century–Fox, GB, 99m, c). P Simon Channing Williams, D Clive Rees, W Michael Morpurgo (based on his novel *Why the Whales Came*), PH Robert Paytner, M Christopher Gunning, ED Andrew Boulton, PD Bruce Grimes.

LP Paul Scofield (The Birdman), David Threlfall (Jack Jenkins), Helen Mirren (Clemmie Jenkins), David Suchet (Will), Helen Pearce (Grace Jenkins), Max Rennie (Daniel Pender), Jeremy Kemp (Mr. Wellbeloved).

Mysterious Paul Scofield seems to be the only one to know why in 1844 the island of Samson in the Scilly Isles was abandoned by its inhabitants. A whale washed up on the beach, which the locals killed. After this their wells dried up and they left their homes believing the island to be cursed. Now in 1914, a neighboring isle may experience the same fate. When a whale beaches itself Scofield convinces the people to carry the whale back to the seas and drive off a herd of narwhals heading for shore.

3301. *When the Wind Blows* (1988, Kings Road, GB, animated, 81m, c). P

John Coates, D Jimmy T. Murakami, W Raymond Briggs (based on his novel), ED John Cary, MD Ray Williams, AD/ANIM Richard Fawdry, M Roger Waters.

VOICES Dame Peggy Ashcroft (Hilda Bloogs), Sir John Mills (James Bloggs), Robin Houston (Announcer), James Russell, David Dundas, Matt Irving.

This brutal animated black comedy shows an elderly British couple who foolishly follow the advice of the government on surviving a nuclear attack. A very effective and thought-provoking film.

3302. *When Time Ran Out* (1980, Warner, 121m, c). P Irwin Allen, D James Goldstone, W Carl Foreman & Stirling Silliphant (based on the novel *The Day the World Ended* by Gordon Thomas & Max Morgan Witts), PH Fred J. Koenekamp, M Lalo Schifrin, ED Edward Biery & Freeman A. Davies, PD Philip M. Jefferies, COS Paul Zastupnevich†.

LP Paul Newman (Hank Anderson), Jacqueline Bisset (Kay Kirby), William Holden (Shelby Gilmore), Edward Albert (Brian), Red Buttons (Francis Fendly), Barbara Carrera (Iolani), Valentina Cortesa (Rose Valdez), Veronica Hamel (Nikki), Alex Karras (Tiny Baker), Burgess Meredith (Rene Valdez), Ernest Borgnine (Tom Conti), James Franciscus (Bob Spangler).

In this disaster spectacular, an assortment of familiar names and faces are staying at a splendid resort on a beautiful tropical Polynesian island. A long-dormant volcano unexpectedly explodes, turning the paradise into a hell cut off from the outside world.

3303. *Where Are the Children* (1986, Columbia, 92m, c). P Zev Braun, D Bruce Malmuth, W Jack Sholder (based on the novel by Mary Higgins Clark), PH Larry Pizer, M Sylvester Levay, ED Roy Watts, PD Robb Wilson King.

LP Jill Clayburgh (Nancy Eldridge), Max Gail (Clay Eldridge), Harley Cross (Michael Eldridge), Elisabeth Harnois (Missy Eldridge), Elizabeth Wilson (Dorothy Prentiss), Barnard Hughes (Jonathan Knowles), Frederic Forrest (Courtney Parrish).

Having survived the trauma of being cleared of murdering her kids, Jill Clayburgh is hit with more heartbreak when her mate from a previous marriage kidnaps her children from her present marriage.

3304. *Where Is Parsifal?* (1984, Terence Young, GB, 84m, c). P Daniel Carrillo, D Henri Helman, W Berta Dominguez D, PH Norman Langley, M Hubert Rostaing & Ivan Jullien, ED Russell Lloyd & Peter Hollywood, PD Malcolm Stone.

LP Tony Curtis (Parsifal Katzenellenbogen), Cassandra Domenica "Dominguez D. Berta" (Elba), Erik Estrada (Henry Board, II), Peter Lawford (Montague Chippendale), Ron Moody (Beersbohm), Donald Pleasence (Mackintosh), Orson Welles (Klingsor).

Tony Curtis, a wild hypochondriac, has invented a laser skywriter which he hopes will provide him with the money he needs to pay for his unusual life style and the crazies who live with him.

3305. *Where the Boys Are '84* (1984, Tri-Star, 97m, c). P Allan Carr, D Hy Averback, W Stu Krieger & Jeff Burkhart (based on the novel *Where the Boys Are* by Glendon Swarthout), PH James A. Contner, M Sylvester Levay, ED Melvin Shapiro & Bobbie Shapiro, PD Michael Baugh.

LP Lisa Hartman (Jennie), Wendy Schaal (Sandra), Lorna Luft (Carol), Lynn-Holly Johnson (Laurie), Russell Todd (Scott), Christopher McDonald (Tony), Howard McGillian (Chip), Daniel McDonald (Camden), Alana Stewart (Maggie), Louise Sorel (Barbara).

How times have changed. In the 1960 movie, the girls flocked to Florida to be where the boys were, but they were seeking a wedding band before going to bed. Doing it in the other order brought tragedy to one girl. In 1984, sexual abstinence is not even a consideration for the females pouring into the sunny south for Spring Break. They know exactly the effect their openness and bikini-clad bodies have on the male population.

3306. *Where the Buffalo Roam* (1980, Universal, 96m, c). P&D Art Linson, W John Kaye (based on the writings of Hunter S. Thompson), PH Tak Fujimoto, M Neil Young, ED Christopher Greenbury, PD Richard Sawyer.

LP Peter Boyle (Lazlo), Bill Murray (Hunter S. Thompson), Bruno Kirby (Marty Lewis), Rene Auberjonois (Harris), R.G. Armstrong (Judge Simpson), Danny Goldman (Porter), Rafael Campos (Rojas).

Bill Murray portrays psychotic journalist Hunter S. Thompson, who attempts to cover everything from the Superbowl to Nixon's reelection campaign. It's a strangely quirky film. Murray really gets into his role as the Gonzo journalist but the script is a stinker.

3307. *Where the River Runs Black* (1986, MGM, 100m, c). P Joe Roth & Harry Ufland, D Christopher Cain, W Peter Silverman & Neal Jimenez (based on the book *Lazaro* by David Kendall), PH Juan Ruiz Anchia, M James Horner, ED Richard Chew, PD Marcos Flaksman.

LP Charles Durning (Father O'Reilly), Alessandro Rabelo (Lazaro), Ajay Naidu (Segundo), Divana Brandao (Eagle Woman), Peter Horton (Father Mahoney), Castulo Guerra (Orlando Santos), Conchata Ferrell (Mother Marta), Dana Delany (Sister Ana).

Born of a mysterious Indian woman, Alessandro Rabelo is a child of nature, living along the Rio Negro in an Amazon rain forest. When his mother is killed, he is taken to an orphanage by Charles Durning, a priest determined to save his soul. It's a difficult adjustment for the youngster.

3308. *Where the Spirit Lives* (1989, CBC, Canada, 97m, c). P Heather Goldin, Eric Jordan & Mary Young Leckie, D Bruce Pittman, W Keith Ross Leckie, PH Rene Ohashi, M Buffy Sainte Marie, ED Michael Todd.

LP Michelle St. John (Komi/Amelia), Clayton Julian (Pita/Abraham), Heather Hess (Rachel), Ann-Marie MacDonald (Kathleen), Ron White (Taggert), Chapelle Jaffe (Miss Appleby), David Hemblen (Rev. Buckley), Patricia Collins (Mrs. Barrington).

The film tells a fictitious story about the former Canadian Federal government's actual practice of kidnapping Indian children from their reserves and keeping them virtual prisoners in religious schools. There, all vestiges of their Indian heritage are beaten out of them.

3309. *A Whisper to a Scream* (1989, Distant Horizon, Canada, 96m, c). P&W Gerard Ciccoritti & Robert Bergman, D Bergman, PH Paul Witte, M Barry Fasman & Dana Walden, ED Richard Bond, PD Ciccoritti.

LP Nadia Capone (Gabrielle), Silvio Oliviero (Frank), Yaphet Kotto (Det. Taillard), Lawrence Bayne (Ohwyn Peters), Michael Lebovic (Tullio), Denise Ryan (Mia), Soo Garay (Mimi).

In this Canadian horror film, an obsessed soundman kills strippers.

3310. *The Whistle Blower* (1987, Hemdale, GB, 104m, c). P Geoffrey Reeve, D Simon Langton, W Julian Bond (based on the novel by John Hale), PH Fred Tammes, M John Scott, ED Robert Morgan, PD Morley Smith.

LP Michael Caine (Frank Jones), James Fox (Lord), Nigel Havers (Robert Jones), Felicity Dean (Cynthia Goodburn), John Gielgud (Sir Adrian Chapple), Gordon Jackson (Bruce), Barry Foster (Charles Greig), Kenneth Colley (Bill Pickett), Dinah Stabb (Rose).

Michael Caine searches for the answers to why his only son is killed, in a thriller which abounds with spies and counterspies.

3311. *White Elephant* (1984, Worldoc, GB, 99m, c). P&D Werner Grusch, W Grusch & Ashley Pharoah (based on an idea by Grusch), PH Tom D. Hurwitz, M Various Artists, ED Thomas Schwalm.

LP Peter Firth (Peter Davidson), Peter Sarpong (Bishop of Kumasi), Nana Seowg (High Priestess), Ejissu Jasantua (Fetish Priest), Frederick Lawluwi (Reverend in Angola).

White businessman Peter Firth arrives in Ghana with plans of modernizing the country through high tech. He is met with resistance, finally succumbing to the charm of simpler ways of life.

3312. *White Ghost* (1988, Gibralter, 93m, c). P Jay Davidson & William Fay, D B.J. Davis, W Gary Thompson, PH Hans Kuhle, M Parmer Fuller, ED Ettie Feldman.

LP William Katt (Steve Shepard), Rosalind Chao (Thi Hau), Martin Hewitt (Waco), Wayne Crawford (Capt.

Walker), Reb Brown (Major Cross), Raymond Ma (Camp Commander), Karl Johnson (Brownie), Graham Clark (Doc).

Fifteen years after all other American troops pulled out of Southeast Asia, William Katt, wearing spooky white kabuki makeup, is still fighting on in a Vietnam/Cambodia border war. Katt signals for some help and Reb Brown sends in a band of mercenaries to find him.

3313. *White Mischief* (1988, Columbia, GB, 107m, c). P Simon Perry, D Michael Radford, W Radford & Jonathan Gems (based on the book by James Fox), PH Roger Deakins, M George Fenton, ED Tom Priestley, PD Roger Hall.

LP Sarah Miles (Alice de Janze), Joss Ackland (Sir John "Jock" Delves Broughton), John Hurt (Gilbert Colvile), Greta Scacchi (Diana Caldwell), Charles Dance (Josslyn Hay, Earl of Erroll), Susan Fleetwood (Gwladys, Lady Delamere), Alan Dobie (Harragin), Jacqueline Pearce (Lady Idina Gordon).

Based on fact, this film is the story of decadence in the British upper class in Kenya around 1940 and the suspected murder of notorious playboy Charles Dance by a jealous husband. It's tedious stuff.

3314. *White Nights* (1985, Columbia, 136m, c). P Taylor Hackford & William S. Gilmore, D Hackford, W James Goldman, Eric Hughes & Nancy Dowd (based on a story by Goldman), PH David Watkin, M Michel Colombier, ED Fredric Steinkamp & William Steinkamp, PD Philip Harrison, SONG "Say You, Say Me" by Lionel Richie*, SONG "Separate Lives" by Stephen Bishop†.

LP Mikhail Baryshnikov (Nikolai "Kolya" Rodchenko), Gregory Hines (Raymond Greenwood), Jerzy Skolimowski (Col. Chaiko), Helen Mirren (Galina Ivanova), Geraldine Page (Anne Wyatt), Isabella Rossellini (Darya Greenwood), John Glover (Wynn Scott).

Former Soviet ballet star Mikhail Baryshnikov, a defector to the West, survives a plane crash in Russia. He is captured and is put in the care of Gregory Hines, an American tap dancer. The latter is supposed to convince Baryshnikov

to once again dance with the Kirov Ballet Company. Before long the two become friends and together plot an escape from the U.S.S.R.

3315. *White of the Eye* (1988, Cannon, 111m, c). P Cassian Elwes & Brad Wyman, D Donald Cammell, W China Cammell & Donald Cammell (based on the novel *Mrs. White* by Margaret Tracy), PH Larry McConkey, M Nick Mason & Rick Fenn, ED Terry Rawlings, PD Philip Thomas.

LP David Keith (Paul White), Cathy Moriarty (Joan White), Art Evans (Detective Charles Mendoza), Alan Rosenberg (Mike Desantos), Michael Greene (Phil Ross), Danielle Smith (Danielle White), Alberta Watson (Ann Mason).

Philandering married audio expert David Keith is cop Art Evans' number one suspect in a series of local housewife murders. Keith's wife Cathy Moriarty and daughter Danielle Smith are menaced by the killer.

3316. *White Phantom* (1987, Spectrum, 89m, c). P Roy McAree & K.L. Lim, D Dusty Nelson, W David Hamilton & Chris Gallagher (based on a story by Nelson), PH Alan Brennecke, M Robert J. Resetar, Kevin Klingler & Bob Mamet, ED Carole A. Kenneally.

LP Jay Roberts, Jr. (Willi), Page Leong (Mai Lin), Jimmy Lee (Hanzo), Bo Svenson (Col. Slater), H.F. Chiang (Bookstore Owner), Kathy McClure (Daughter).

This straight to video package takes audiences into the world of the ninja fighters. It represents a modernday battle between good and evil. Such films are above—or below—criticism.

3317. *White Water Summer* (1987, Columbia, 90m, c). P Mark Tarlov, D Jeff Bleckner, W Manya Starr & Ernest Kinoy, PH John Alcott, M Michael Boddicker, ED David Ray.

LP Kevin Bacon (Vic), Sean Astin (Alan Block/Narrator), Jonathan Ward (Mitch), K.C. Martel (George), Matt Adler (Chris), Caroline McWilliams (Virginia Block), Charles Siebert (Jerry Block), Joseph Passarelli (Storekeeper).

Gung-ho Kevin Bacon leads a group of teens on a three week camping trip. He's particularly tough on city-kid Sean Astin, who doesn't want to be there and isn't too crazy about strenuous activities. When Bacon is injured, this least-likely kid takes charge. Sounds like John Wayne and John Agar in *Sands of Iwo Jima.*

3318. *Whiteforce* (1989, Eastern, Australian/Philippines, 85m, c). P Lope V. Juban & Marilyn G. Ong, D Eddie Romero, W Henry Tefay, PH Jose Batac, M Ryan Cayabyab, ED Gervacio Santos.

LP Sam Jones (Johnny Quinn), Kimberley Pistone (Nicki), Timothy Hughes (Alex Korda), Raoul Aragonn (Briggs), Jimmy Fabregas (Wizard), Vic Diaz, Rubin Rustia, Ken Metcalfe, Mike Monty.

Accused of murdering his partner Ken Metcalfe, Sam Jones, with some help from Kimberly Pistone, Metcalfe's daughter, dodges bullets as he tries to prove that the real villain is druglord Timothy Hughes.

3319. *Who?* (1982, Lorimar, GB/Ger., 93m, c, aka *A Man Without a Face; Prisoner of the Skull; The Man in the Skull Mask*). P Barry Levinson, D Jack Gold, W John Gould [Jack Gold] (based on the novel by Algis Budrys), PH Petrus Schloemp, M John Cameron, ED Norman Wanstall.

LP Elliott Gould (Sean Rogers), Trevor Howard (Col. Azarin), Joe Bova (Dr. Lucas Martino), Ed Grover (Finchley), James Noble (Gen. Deptford), John Lehne (Haller), Kay Tornborg (Edith), Lyndon Brook (Dr. Barrister).

Shot in 1975 this production underwent many title changes before reaching U.S. theaters. American scientist Joe Bova is nearly killed in an accident along the Soviet border. Russian doctors perform life-saving surgery that makes him half-man, half-machine. But who is he going to work for?

Who Dares Win see The Final Option

3320. *Who Framed Roger Rabbit?* (1988, Buena Vista, part-animated, 103m, c). P Robert Watts & Frank Marshall, D Robert Zemeckis, W Jeffrey Price & Peter S. Seaman (based on the book *Who Censored Roger Rabbit?* by Gary K. Wolf), PH Dean Cundey†, M Alan Silvestri, ED

Arthur Schmidt*, PD Elliot Scott & Roger Cain, AD Stephen Scott†, SD Peter Howitt†, SOUND Robert Knudson, John Boyd, Don Digiroamo & Tony Dawe†, SOUND EFFECTS Charles L. Campbell*, VE Ken Ralston, Richard Williams, Edward Jones & George Gibbs*, ANIM Richard Williams.

LP Bob Hoskins (Eddie Valiant), Christopher Lloyd (Judge Doom), Joanna Cassidy (Dolores), Stubby Kaye (Marvin Acme), Charles Fleischer (Roger Rabbit/Greasy/Psycho/Benny the Cab), Lou Hirsch (Baby Herman), Kathleen Turner (Jessica Rabbit), Amy Irving (Jessica Rabbit's Singing Voice), Alan Tilvern (R.K. Maroon), Richard le Parmentier (Lt. Santino).

In an amazing blending of live-action and animation, Robert Zemeckis brings forth a 40s comical film noir. Set in 1947 Hollywood, cartoon characters, second class citizens, are relegated to a Toon Town ghetto. Private eye Bob Hoskins reluctantly agrees to help slapstick Toon Roger Rabbit, the major suspect when a despised producer is murdered. Kathleen Turner, the speaking voice of Roger's glamorous wife Jessica, just about walks away with the honors in this truly remarkable movie breakthrough. It must be seen to be believed.

3321. *Who Has Seen the Wind* (1980, Cinema World, Canada, 100m, c). P Pierre Lamy, D Allan King, W Patricia Watson (based on the novel by W.O. Mitchell), PH Richard Leiterman, M Eldon Rathburn, ED Arla Saare, AD Anne Pritchard.

LP Brian Painchaud (Brian), Douglas Junor (The Young Ben), Gordon Pinsent (Gerald O'Connal), Chapelle Jaffe (Maggie), Jose Ferrer (The Ben), Charmion King (Mrs. Abercrombie), David Gardner (Rev. Powelly).

Brian Painchaud stars in this production of a classic Canadian children's novel. He's sort of a Tom Sawyer growing up with his father and assorted pets in Depression-era Saskatchewan.

3322. *Wholly Moses* (1980, Columbia, 109m, c). P Freddie Fields, D Gary Weis, W Guy Thomas, PH Frank Stanley, M Patrick Williams, ED Sidney Levin, PD Dale Hennesy.

LP Dudley Moore (Harvey/Herschel), Laraine Newman (Zoe/Zerelda), James Coco (Hyssop), Paul Sand (Angel of the Lord), Jack Gilford (Tailor), Dom DeLuise (Shadrach), John Houseman (Archangel), Madeline Kahn (Sorceress), Richard Pryor (Pharaoh), John Ritter (Devil).

This comedy is so sophomoric, you'd swear it was written and directed by Mel Brooks. But no, it's a bunch of other chaps slinging the crap. Dudley Moore portrays Herschel, who mistakenly believes that he, rather than Moses, is the man chosen by God to lead the Israelites out of Egypt.

3323. *The Whoopee Boys* (1986, Paramount, 88m, c). P Adam Fields & Peter MacGregor-Scott, D John Byrum, W Steve Zacharias, Jeff Buhai & David Obst, PH Ralf Bode, M Jack Nitzsche, ED Eric Jenkins, PD Charles Rosen.

LP Michael O'Keefe (Jake), Paul Rodriguez (Barney), Denholm Elliott (Col. Phelps), Carole Shelley (Henrietta Phelps), Andy Bumatai (Roy Raja), Eddie Deezen (Eddie), Marsha Warfield (Officer White), Elizabeth Arlen (Shelley).

Michael O'Keefe's problem is that he's in love with a Palm Beach heiress who must marry a wealthy, refined gentleman in order to earn her own inheritance. Being neither rich nor refined, he has his work cut out for him.

3324. *Whoops Apocalypse* (1987, MGM, GB, 89m, c). P Brian Eastman, D Tom Bussmann, W Andrew Marshall & David Renwick, PH Ron Robson, M Patrick Gowers, ED Peter Boyle, PD Tony Noble.

LP Loretta Swit (President Barbara Adams), Peter Cook (Sir Mortimer Chris), Michael Richards (Lacrobat), Rik Mayall (Specialist Catering Commander), Ian Richardson (Rear Adm. Bendish), Alexei Sayle (Himself), Herbert Lom (Gen. Mosquera), Joanne Pearce (Princess Wendy).

Based on a successful British TV series, this comedy consists of news coverage of the events leading up to World War III. It's filled with wit, expletives included,

zinging one-liners, manic energy and nontopical garbage.

3325. *Who's Harry Crumb?* (1989, Tri-Star, 87m, c). P Arnon Milchan, D Paul Flaherty, W Robert Conte & Peter Martin Wortmann, PH Stephen M. Katz, M Michel Colombier, ED Danford B. Greene, PD Trevor Williams.

LP John Candy (Harry Crumb), Jeffrey Jones (Eliot Draisen), Annie Potts (Helen Downing), Tim Thomerson (Vince), Barry Corbin (P.J. Downing), Shawnee Smith (Nikki Downing), Wesley Mann (Tim).

Teddy bear John Candy plays a bumbling, know-it-all private eye so dumb that he takes an incriminating photograph of his own client rather than of the woman's husband. He's called to L.A. by his family's detective firm to investigate the kidnapping of a beautiful heiress. He's given lines so stupid that one almost flinches. Still as expected he somehow manages to get the detecting job done—but hasn't got a clue how to get some laughs out of the script.

3326. *Who's That Girl?* (1987, Warner, 94m, c). P Rosilyn Heller & Bernard Williams, D James Foley, W Andrew Smith & Ken Finkleman (based on a story by Andrew Smith), PH Jan DeBont, M Stephen Bray & Patrick Leonard, ED Pembroke Herring, PD Ida Random.

LP Madonna (Nikki Finn), Griffin Dunne (Loudon Trutt), Haviland Morris (Wendy Worthington), John McMartin (Simon Worthington), Robert Swan (Detective Bellson), Drew Pillsbury (Detective Doyle), Coati Mundi (Raoul), Dennis Burkley (Benny).

In this screwy comedy, straitlaced lawyer Griffin Dunne and zany parolee Madonna seek out the nasty guy who framed her.

3327. *Whose Life Is It Anyway?* (1981, MGM/United Artists, 119m, c). P Lawrence P. Bachmann, D John Badham, W Brian Clark & Reginald Rose (based on the play by Clark), PH Mario Tosi, M Arthur B. Rubinstein, ED Frank Morriss, PD Gene Callahan.

LP Richard Dreyfuss (Ken Harrion), John Cassavetes (Dr. Michael Emerson), Christine Lahti (Dr. Clare Scott), Bob

Balaban (Carter Hill), Kenneth McMillan (Judge Wyler), Kaki Hunter (Mary Jo).

Totally paralyzed after a car accident, talented, successful, married sculptor Richard Dreyfuss uses the only part of his body not injured, his brain, to decide he wishes to die. He hires a lawyer to fight for his right to terminate his life. It's a thought-provoking film.

3328. **Why Not Stay for Breakfast** (1985, Artgrove, GB, 95m, c). P Martin Schute & Alan Cluer, D Terence Martel, W Martel & Ray Cooney (based on the play by Gene Stone & Cooney), PH James Devis, M Harry Robinson, ED Alan Jones.

LP George Chakaris (George Clark), Gemma Craven (Louise Hamilton), Yvonne Wilder (Helen), Ray Charleson (Davey), David Baxt (Boy), Carinthia West (Girl), Vic Gallucci (Neighbor), Baby Dale (Baby).

Produced in 1979, the film was not released until 1985. Divorced New York postal clerk George Chakaris assumes the role of protector of English girl Gemma Craven and her baby, Baby Dale.

3329. **Why Would I Lie?** (1980, MGM/United Artists, 105m, c). P Pancho Kohner, D Larry Peerce, W Peter Stone (based on the novel *The Fabricator* by Hollis Hodges), PH Gerald Hirschfeld, M Charles Fox, ED John C. Howard.

LP Treat Williams (Cletus), Lisa Eichhorn (Kay), Gabriel Swann (Jeorge), Susan Heldfond (Amy), Anne Byrne (Faith), Valerie Curtin (Mrs. Bok), Jocelyn Brando (Mrs. Crumpe), Nicolas Coster (Walter).

Thoroughly unlikeable social worker Treat Williams is a confirmed and colorful liar. He romances feminist Lisa Eichhorn while espousing his half-baked philosophical ideas.

3330. **The Wicked Lady** (1983, MGM/United Artists, GB, 99m, c). P Menahem Golan & Yoram Globus, D Michael Winner, W Winner & Leslie Arliss (based on the novel *The Life and Death of the Wicked Lady Skelton* by Magdalen King-Hall), PH Jack Cardiff, M Tony Banks, ED Arnold Crust, AD John Blezard, COS John Bloomfield.

LP Faye Dunaway (Lady Barbara Skelton), Alan Bates (Capt. Jerry Jackson), John Gielgud (Hogarth), Denholm Elliott (Sir Ralph Skelton), Prunella Scales (Lady Kingsclere), Oliver Tobias (Kit Locksby), Glynis Barber (Caroline), Joan Hickson (Aunt Agatha Trimble).

This remake of the 1946 film starring Margaret Lockwood and James Mason features Faye Dunaway in constant danger of falling out of the bodice of her dress. Her breasts and those of the other "ladies" in the film are in a constant jiggle. But all of the mammary glands and nude lovemaking don't make audiences forget that there is almost no plot to this story of a bored aristocratic lady who becomes a highway robber. Dunaway chews up the sets to a fare-thee-well, looking more than a little deranged most of the time.

3331. **Wicked Stepmother** (1989, MGM/United Artists, 92m, c). P Robert Littman, D&W Larry Cohen, PH Bryan England, M Robert Folk, ED David Kern.

LP Bette Davis (Miranda), Barbara Carrera (Priscilla), Colleen Camp (Jenny), David Rasche (Steve), Lionel Stander (Sam), Tom Bosley (Lt. MacIntosh), Shawn Donahue (Mike), Richard Moll (Nat), Evelyn Keyes (Witch Mistress).

Colleen Camp and David Rasche return from vacation to find that dad Lionel Stander has taken a new wife, Bette Davis. Seems Davis is a witch being tracked by detective Tom Bosley. About halfway through the film Bette disappears without explanation. Barbara Carrera shows up claiming to be Davis' daughter. It's sad to see Davis reduced to appearing in such crap. (The film was made before Davis' appearance in *The Whale of August*). Come to think of it, it's a shame to see Bosley, Stander and Evelyn Keyes in the same boat.

3332. **The Wild Duck** (1983, Orion, Australia, 96m, c). P Phillip Emanuel & Basil Appleby, D Henri Safran, W Safran, Peter Smalley & John Lind (based on the play by Henrik Ibsen), PH Peter James, M Simon Walker, ED Don Saunders, PD Darrell Lass.

LP Liv Ullmann (Gina), Jeremy Irons (Harold), Lucinda Jones (Henrietta), John Meillon (Maj. Ackland), Arthur Dignam (Gregory), Michael Pate

(George), Colin Croft (Mollison), Rhys McConnochie (Dr. Roland).

Henrik Ibsen's play is not dull but this needless update is. It's the story of young Pollyannaish Lucinda Jones, whose birth is kept a secret, straining the relationship between mother Liv Ullmann and her egotistical husband Jeremy Irons.

3333. *Wild Geese II* (1986, Universal, 125m, c). P Euan Lloyd, D Peter Hunt, W Reginald Rose (based on the book *The Square Circle* by Daniel Carney), PH Michael Reed, M Roy Budd, ED Keith Palmer, PD Syd Cain.

LP Scott Glenn (John Haddad), Barbara Carrera (Kathy Lukas), Edward Fox (Alex Faulkner), Laurence Olivier (Rudolf Hess), Robert Webber (Robert McCann), Robert Freitag (Heinrich Stroebling), Kenneth Haigh (Col. Reed-Henry), Stratford Johns (Mustapha El Ali).

This film has nothing to do with *Wild Geese* (1978). Its strange plot deals with an attempt to kidnap imprisoned Nazi Rudolf Hess, played by Laurence Olivier. At the end of his film career, the latter seemed willing to do anything for a paycheck.

3334. *Wild Horses* (1984, Satori, New Zealand, 90m, c). P John Barnett, D Derek Morton, W Kevin O'Sullivan [Kevin J. Wilson], PH Doug Milsome, M Dave Fraser, ED Simon Reece, PD Jose Bleakley.

LP Keith Aberdein (Dan "Mitch" Mitchell), John Bach (Jack Sullivan), Kevin J. Wilson (Harry Sullivan), Kathy Rawlings (Mary Mitchell), Helena Wilson (Anne Mitchell), Robyn Gibbes (Sara), Tom Poata (Sam Richardson).

In this New Zealand "western," horse wranglers in a national park are at odds with deerhunters. The scenery is beautiful, the story is routine.

3335. *The Wild Life* (1984, Universal, 96m, c). P Art Linson, Cameron Crowe & Don Phillips, D Linson, W Crowe, PH James Glennon, M Edward Van Halen & Donn Landee, ED Michael Jablow, PD William Sandell.

LP Christopher Penn (Tom Drake), Ilan Mitchell-Smith (Jim Conrad), Eric Stoltz (Bill Conrad), Jenny Wright (Eileen), Lea Thompson (Anita), Brin

Berliner (Tony), Rick Moranis (Harry), Hart Bochner (David Curtiss).

Many of the same people who brought us *Fast Times at Ridgemont High* are responsible for this disappointing follow-up. Christopher Penn is the leader of a bunch of teens trying to grow up too fast. Life seems to revolve around getting laid, with little else being of any importance.

3336. *The Wild Pair* (1987, Trans-World Ent., 88m, c, aka *Devil's Odds*). P Paul Mason & Randall Torno, D Beau Bridges, W Joseph Gunn (based on a story by Gunn & John Crowther), PH Peter Stein, M John Debney, ED Christopher Holmes & Scott Conrad, PD Stephen Berger.

LP Beau Bridges (Joe Jennings), Bubba Smith (Benny Avalon), Lloyd Bridges (Col. Hester), Gary Lockwood (Capt. Kramer), Raymond St. Jacques (Ivory), Danny De La Paz (Tucker), Lela Rochon (Debby), Ellen Geer (Fern Willis).

Beau Bridges and Bubba Smith challenge a private army led by Lloyd Bridges. This action-adventure film is for those who like exciting buddy-films but aren't concerned with plots.

The Wild Side see Suburbia

3337. *Wild Style* (1983, First Run Features, 85m, c). P,D&W Charlie Ahearn, PH Clive Davidson & John Foster, M Chris Stein, ED Steve Brown.

LP Lee George Quinones (Raymond), Frederick Brathwaite (Phade), Sandra Pink Fabara (Rose), Patti Astor (Virginia), Andrew Zephyr Witten (Zroc), Carlos Morales (Raymond's Brother).

In this semidocumentary, featuring rap singing and break dancing, a promoter helps graffiti artist Lee George Quinones escape the ghetto and find a place in the art world.

3338. *Wild Thing* (1987, Atlantic, US/Canada, 92m, c). P David Calloway & Nicolas Clermont, D Max Reid, W John Sayles (based on a story by Sayles & Larry Stamper), PH Rene Verzier, M George S. Clinton, ED Battle Davis & Steven Rosenblum, PD John Meighen & Jocelyn Joli.

LP Rob Knepper (Wild Thing), Kathleen Quinlan (Jane), Robert Davi (Chopper), Maury Chaykin (Det. Trask), Betty Buckley (Leah), Guillaume Lemay-Thivierge (Wild Thing 10 Years Old), Clark Johnson (Winston), Sean Hewitt (Father Quinn).

Orphaned at age three, Rob Knepper has learned to survive on his own into adulthood. He becomes a legend as "Wild Thing," protector of Montreal's ghetto people from villains.

3339. *Wildcats* (1986, Warner, 107m, c). P Anthea Sylbert, D Michael Ritchie, W Ezra Sacks, PH Donald E. Thorin, M Hawk Wolinski & James Newton Howard, ED Richard A. Harris, PD Boris Leven.

LP Goldie Hawn (Molly), Swoosie Kurtz (Verna), Robyn Lively (Alice), Brandy Gold (Marian), James Keach (Frank), Jan Hooks (Stephanie), Bruce McGill (Darwell), Nipsy Russell (Edwards), Mykel T. Williamson (Bird).

The Wildcats, a high school football team, get no respect and no wins until Goldie Hawn is made coach. It's as predictable as the smell of sweaty gym clothes.

3340. *Wildfire* (1988, Zupnik Cinema Group, 98m, c). P Jerry Tokofsky & Hunt Lowry, D Zalman King, W Matthew Bright & King (based on a story by Bright), PH Bill Butler, M Maurice Jarre, ED Caroline Biggerstaff, PD Geoffrey Kirkland.

LP Steven Bauer (Frank), Linda Fiorentino (Kay), Will Patton (Mike), Marshall Bell (Lewis), Sandra Seacat, Richard Bradford, Alisha Byrd-Pena, Jonah Ellers-Isaacs, Michelle Mayberry.

Steven Bauer and Linda Fiorentino meet in an orphanage. They break out and hit the road. Broke, Bauer robs a bank, is caught and sent to prison, while Fiorentino is adopted by a middleclass family. She marries yuppie Will Patton and is happy until Bauer shows up again, wishing to renew their relationship. The result is violence.

3341. *Wildrose* (1985, Troma, 95m, c). P Sandra Schulberg, D John Hanson, W Hanson & Eugene Corr (based on a story by Schulberg & Hanson), PH Peter Stein, M Bernard Krause, Gary S. Remal & Cris Williamson, ED Arthur Coburn.

LP Lisa Eichhorn (June Lorich), Tom Bower (Rick Ogaard), Jim Cada (Pavich), Cinda Jackson (Karen), Dan Nemanick (Ricotti), Lydia Olsen (Katri Sippola), Bill Schoppert (Timo Maki), James Stowell (Doobie).

Feisty Lisa Eichhorn, a female heavy-machine operator in the Mesabi Range of Minnesota, is at odds with her coworkers, experiencing sexist attitudes when reassigned to an otherwise all male crew. Recently divorced from a drunken wife-beater, she has an unexpected love affair with Tom Bower, the only one of her crew not to harrass her.

3342. *Willie and Phil* (1980, 20th Century–Fox, 116m, c). P Paul Mazursky & Tony Ray, D&W Mazursky, PH Sven Nykvist, M Claude Bolling & Georges Delerue, ED Donn Cambern, PD Pato Guzman.

LP Michael Ontkean (Willie Kaufman), Margot Kidder (Jeanette Sutherland), Ray Sharkey (Phil D'Amico), Jan Miner (Mrs. Kaufman), Tom Brennan (Mr. Kaufman), Julie Bovasso (Mrs. D'Amico), Louis Guss (Mr. D'Amico), Kathleen Maguire (Mrs. Sutherland), Kaki Hunter (Patti Sutherland).

In this attempt to film an American *Jules et Jim,* friends Michael Ontkean and Ray Sharkey share Margot Kidder in a veritable ménage-à-trois throughout the 70s.

3343. *Willow* (1988, MGM/United Artists, 125m, c). P Nigel Wooll, D Ron Howard, W Bob Dolman (based on a story by George Lucas), PH Adrian Biddle, M James Horner, ED Daniel Hanley & Michael Hill, PD Allan Cameron, SOUND EFFECTS ED Ben Burtt & Richard Hymns†, VE Dennis Muren, Michael McAlister, Phil Tippett & Chris Evans†.

LP Val Kilmer (Madmartigan), Joanne Whalley (Sorsha), Warwick Davis (Willow), Jean Marsh (Queen Bavmorda), Patricia Hayes (Fin Raziel), Billy Barty (High Aldwin), Pat Roach (Gen. Kael), Gavan O'Herlihy (Airk Thaughbaer), David Steinberg (Meegosh), Phil Fondacaro (Vohnkar).

In this sword and sorcery tale, evil queen Jean Marsh is determined to destroy the baby which prophecy claims will destroy her. The baby falls into the hands of amicable dwarf Warwick Davis, who with the reluctant help of mercenary Val Kilmer, sorceress Patricia Hayes and Marsh's own daughter Joanne Whalley, is able to defeat the evil one.

3344.   *Wills and Burke* (1985, Greater Union, Australia, 101m, c). P Bob Weis & Margot McDonald, D Weis, W Philip Dalkin, PH Gaetano Nino Martinetti, M Red Symonds & Paul Grabowsky, ED Edward McQueen Mason, PD Tracy Watt.

LP Garry McDonald (Robert O'Hara Burke), Kim Gyngell (William John Wills), Jonathan Hardy (John Macadam), Peter Collingwood (Sir William Stawell), Mark Little (John King), Roy Baldwin (Charley Gray).

Familiar to every Aussie schoolboy, the epic and tedious comedy tells the story of Burke and Wills, intrepid explorers, who set out to cross the Australian continent and return. They die on the way home. It is a weak piece, with little hope of attracting an audience away from Down Under.

Willy Milly *see* ***Something Special***

3345.   *Wilt* (1989, Rank, GB, 91m, c). P Brian Eastman, D Michael Tuchner, W Andrew Marshall & David Renwick (based on the novel by Tom Sharpe), PH Norman Langley, M Anne Dudley, ED Chris Blunden, PD Leo Austin.

LP Griff Rhys Jones (Wilt), Mel Smith (Flint), Alison Steadman (Eva), Diana Quick (Sally), Jeremy Clyde (Hugh), Roger Allam (Dave), David Ryall (Rev. Froude), Roger Lloyd-Pack (Dr. Pittman).

Disillusioned college lecturer Griff Rhys Jones spends much of his time walking his dog and daydreaming about murdering his domineering wife Alison Steadman. When she disappears after a night in which Rhys Jones gets dead drunk, police inspector Mel Smith is put on the case. The banter between the two British TV comedians is moderately amusing, but not enough to make this movie a commercial success.

3346.   *Wimps* (1987, Vestron, 84m, c). P&D Chuck Vincent, W Vincent & Craig Horrall, PH Larry Revene, M Ian Shaw & Kai Joffe, ED Marc Ubell [Vincent] & James Davalos, AD D. Gary Phelps.

LP Louis Bonanno (Francis), Deborah Blaisdell (Roxanne), Jim Abele (Charles Conrad), Jane Hamilton [Veronica Hart] (Tracy), Eddie Prevot, Derrick R. Roberts, Philip Campanero, Michael Heintzman.

In this updating of *Cyrano de Bergerac,* nerd Louis Bonanno helps star college quarterback Jim Abele woo fetching librarian Deborah Blaisdell. See *Roxanne* instead.

3347.   *The Wind* (1987, Omega, 93m, c). P&D Nico Mastorakis, W Mastorakis & Fred C. Perry (based on a story by Mastorakis), PH Andreas Bellis, M Stanley Myers & Hans Zimmer, ED Mastorakis & Bruce Cannon, PD Lester Gallagher.

LP Meg Foster (Sian Anderson), Wings Hauser (Phil), David McCallum (John), Robert Morley (Elias Appleby), Steve Railsback (Kesner), Michael Yannatos (Policeman), Summer Thomas (Sian's Friend).

Mystery writer Meg Foster rents a house on a Greek Island from eccentric Robert Morley, despite the latter's warnings of the dangerous winds in the region and the presence of creepy caretaker Wings Hauser. When she begins to write about the characters of the island in a new mystery story, life begins to imitate art.

3348.   *Windows* (1980, United Artists, 96m, c). P Michael Lobell, D Gordon Willis, W Barry Siegel, PH Willis, M Ennio Morricone, ED Barry Malkin, PD Melvin Bourne.

LP Talia Shire (Emily Hollander), Joseph Cortese (Bob Luffrono), Elizabeth Ashley (Andrea Glassen), Kay Medford (Ida Marx), Michael Gorrin (Sam Marx), Russell Horton (Steven Hollander), Michael Lipton (Dr. Marin).

Cinematographer Gordon Willis *(Manhattan)* makes his directorial debut with pretty pictures but an ugly psychological thriller about the unhealthy relationship between mousey Talia Shire and crazed lesbian Elizabeth Ashley.

3349.   *Windrider* (1987, MGM/United Artists, Australia, 92m, c). P Paul Barron, D Vincent Monton, W Everett De Roche & Bonnie Harris, PH Joe Pickering, M Kevin Peak, ED John Scott, AD Steve Jodrell.

LP Tom Burlinson (P.C. Simpson), Nicole Kidman (Jade), Charles Tingwell (Simpson, Sr.), Jill Perryman (Miss Dodge), Simon Chilvers, Kim Bullad, Matt Parkinson, Penny Brown.

Windsurfer Tom Burlinson and rock star Nicole Kidman become romantically involved in a little bit of nothing.

3350. Windwalker (1981, Pacific International, 108m, c). P Arthur R. Dubs & Thomas E. Ballard, D Keith Merrill, W Ray Goldrup (based on the novel by Blaine M. Yorgason), PH Reed Smoot, M Merrill Jensen, ED Stephen L. Johnson, Janice Hampton & Peter L. McCrea, PD Thomas Pratt.

LP Trevor Howard (Windwalker), Nick Ramus (Smiling Wolf/Twin Brother/Narrator), James Remar (Windwalker as a young man), Serene Hedin (Tashina), Dusty Iron Wing McCrea (Dancing Moon), Silvana Gallardo (Little Feather), Billy Drago (Crow Scout).

This is an interesting presentation of the life of American Indians of the late 18th century before the white man arrived. Except for Trevor Howard and James Remar the cast consists of Indian actors speaking in the dialects of the Crow and Cheyenne with English subtitles.

3351. Windy City (1984, Warner, 102m, c). P Alan Greisman, D&W Armyan Bernstein, PH Reynaldo Villalobos, M Jack Nitzsche, ED Clifford Jones & Christoher Rouse, PD Bill Kenney.

LP John Shea (Danny Morgan), Kate Capshaw (Emily Reubens), Josh Mostel (Sol), Jim Borrelli (Mickey), Jeffrey DeMunn (Bobby), Eric Pierpoint (Pete), Lewis J. Stadlen (Marty), James Sutorius (Eddie).

It's an uneven but ambitious attempt to make something meaningful of the last hurrah of some South Side Chicago adults who have known and cared for each other since childhood. Their lives and dreams haven't turned out quite as they planned.

Winged Serpent see *Q: Quetzalcoatl*

3352. Winners Take All (1987, Apollo/Embassy, 105m, c). P Christopher W. Knight & Tom Tatum, D Fritz Kiersch, W Ed Turner (based on a story by Tatum & Knight), PH Fred V. Murphy, II, M Doug Timm, ED Lorenzo De Stefano, PD Steve P. Sardanis.

LP Don Michael Paul (Rick Melon), Kathleen York (Judy McCormick), Robert Krantz ("Bad" Billy Robinson), Deborah Richter (Cindy Wickes), Peter DeLuise (Wally Briskin), Courtney Gains (Goose Trammel).

Top motorcycle racer Robert Krantz rides for a corporate sponsored team. He returns to his hometown for a race and once again finds himself in competition with Don Michael Paul, both on the track and with Krantz's old girlfriend Deborah Richter.

3353. Winter Flight (1984, Enigma/Goldcrest, GB, 103m, c). P Susan Richards & Robin Douet, D Roy Battersby, W Alan Janes, PH Chris Menges, M Richard Harvey, ED Lesley Walker.

LP Reece Dinsdale (Mal Stanton), Nicola Cowper (Angie), Gary Olsen (Dave), Sean Benn (Hooker), Beverly Hewitt (Lara), Shelagh Stephenson (Kel), Michael Percival (Doctor), Anthony Trent (Sgt. Bowyer).

In a routine story, Reece Dinsdale's job is to keep seagulls off a Royal Air Force runway. He becomes romantically involved with Nicola Cowper, an unmarried mother-to-be.

3354. Winter of Our Dreams (1982, Vega Enterprises/Satori, Australia, 89m, c). P Richard Mason, D&W John Duigan, PH Tom Cowan, M Sharon Calcraft, ED Henry Dangar, PD Lee Whitmore.

LP Judy Davis (Lou), Bryan Brown (Rob), Cathy Downes (Fretel), Baz Luhrmann (Pete), Peter Mochrie (Tim), Mervyn Drak (Mick), Margie McCrae (Lisa), Mercie Deane-Johns (Angela).

Sidney prostitute Judy Davis tries desperately to escape her life of drugs and degradation.

3355. Winter People (1989, Columbia, 110m, c). P Robert H. Solo, D Ted Kotcheff, W Carol Sobieski (based on the novel by John Ehle), PH Francois Protat, M John Scott, ED Thom Noble, PD Ron Foreman.

LP Kurt Russell (Wayland Jackson), Kelly McGillis (Collie Wright), Lloyd

Bridges (William Wright), Jeffrey Meek (Cole Campbell), Mitchell Ryan (Drury Campbell), Amelia Burnette (Paula Jackson), Eileen Ryan (Annie Wright), Lanny Flaherty (Gudger Wright).

Clockmaker widower Kurt Russell sets off with his young daughter, Amelia Burnette, and her pet pig, in search of a better life. His car breaks down near the cabin of unwed mother Kelly McGillis. She allows Russell and his daughter to live in a tiny shack near hers, scandalizing her family and the neighbors once again. Russell wants to be part of McGillis' life but first everyone has to deal with a Hatfield and McCoy–like feud.

Wipeout see Under the Boardwalk

3356. *Wired* (1989, Taurus, 108m, c). P Edward S. Feldman & Charles R. Meeker, D Larry Peerce, W Earl Mac Rauch (based on the book by Bob Woodward), PH Tony Imi, M Basil Poledouris, ED Eric Sears, PD Brian Eatwell.

LP Michael Chiklis (John Belushi), Ray Sharkey (Angel Velasquez), J.T. Walsh (Bob Woodward), Patti D'Arbanville (Cathy Smith), Lucinda Jenney (Judy Belushi), Alex Rocco (Arnie Fromson), Gary Groomes (Dan Aykroyd), Jere Burns (Lou).

Don't blame Michael Chiklis for the failure of this movie about the life of comedian John Belushi. Although he seems a little young for the role he gives it all he's got. Unfortunately, the director and screenwriter provide him very little to work with. The film opens with Belushi already dead, but not quite down. He escapes from his body bag in the morgue and is picked up by cabbie Ray Sharkey who turns out to be the funny man's guardian angel. The rest of the movie jumps around in time and place with no apparent goal in mind, except not to offend any of Belushi's pals or acquaintances who might sue if they were shown in the wrong light or perhaps even mentioned.

3357. *Wired to Kill* (1986, American Distribution Group, 96m, c). P Jim Buchfuehrer, D&W Franky Schaeffer, PH Tom Fraser, M Russell Ferrante & The Yellow Jackets, ED Daniel Agulian & Schaeffer.

LP Emily Longstreth (Rebecca), Devin Hoelscher (Steve), Merritt Butrick (Reegus), Frank Collison (Sly), Garth Gardner (Loady), Kim Milford (Rooster), Michael Wollet (Zero).

In the year 1998, a deadly virus has wiped out most of the population of the United States. Mutant gangs victimize the survivors. But when they kill Devin Hoelscher's girlfriend, he invents deadly booby traps to take revenge.

3358. *Wisdom* (1986, 20th Century–Fox, 108m, c). P Bernard Williams, D&W Emilio Estevez, PH Adam Greenberg, M Danny Elfman, ED Michael Kahn, PD Dennis Gassner.

LP Demi Moore (Karen Simmons), Emilio Estevez (John Wisdom), Tom Skerritt (Lloyd Wisdom), Veronica Cartwright (Samantha Wisdom), William Allen Young (Williamson), Richard Minchenberg (Cooper).

Emilio Estevez becomes the youngest person ever to write, direct and star in a movie, but he can't claim the result is much to brag about. He is a modern day Robin Hood, with pretty Demi Moore as his Maid Marian, but such shenanigans are not allowed today. He dies in a hail of bullets which he deliberately calls down on himself. Not so wise!

3359. *Wise Blood* (1980, New Line, 108m, c). P Michael Fitzgerald & Kathy Fitzgerald, D John Huston, W Benedict Fitzgerald (based on the novel by Flannery O'Connor), PH Gerald Fisher, M Alex North, ED Roberto Silvi.

LP Brad Dourif (Hazel Motes), Ned Beatty (Hoover Shoates), Harry Dean Stanton (Asa Hawks), Daniel Shor (Enoch Emery), Amy Wright (Sabbath Lilly), Mary Nell Santacroce (Landlady), John Huston (Grandfather).

The film traces the strange career of religious fanatic Brad Dourif. He attempts to found a church without salvation in retaliation for his past sufferings at the hands of his hellfire-and-brimstone preaching grandfather.

3360. *Wise Guys* (1986, MGM/United Artists, 92m, c). P Aaron Russo, D Brian DePalma, W George Gallo, PH Fred Schuler, M Ira Newborn, ED Jerry Greenberg, PD Edward Pisoni.

LP Danny DeVito (Harry Valentini),

Joe Piscopo (Moe Dickstein), Harvey Keitel (Bobby DiLea), Ray Sharkey (Marco), Dan Hedaya (Anthony Castelo), Capt. Lou Albano (Frank "The Fixer"), Julie Bovasso (Lil Dickstein), Patti LuPone (Wanda Valentini), Antonia Rey (Aunt Sadie), Mimi Cecchini (Grandma Valentini).

You have to enjoy Danny DeVito to enjoy this movie. He and Joe Piscopo are two lamebrain minor gangsters working for Ray Sharkey. When they make the wrong wager at the racetrack for their boss, their futures don't look very bright. To add to the fun, these best friends are told to "hit" each other. How they get around that is somewhat amusing.

3361.   *Wish You Were Here*   (1987, Atlantic, GB, 92m, c). P Sarah Radclyffe, D&W David Leland, PH Ian Wilson, M Stanley Myers, ED George Akers, PD Caroline Amies.

LP Emily Lloyd (Lynda), Tom Bell (Eric), Clare Clifford (Mrs. Parfitt), Barbara Durkin (Valerie), Geoffrey Hutchings (Hubert), Charlotte Barker (Gillian), Chloe Leland (Margaret), Trudy Cavanagh (Tap Dancing Lady), Jesse Birdsall (Dave).

Emily Lloyd makes a triumphant debut as a spunky but troubled British teen, living at a seaside resort during the 50s. Still grieving over the death of her mother, Lloyd rebels against her father. She has ill-fated sexual encounters, including one with sleazy but oddly magnetic Tom Bell, a friend of her father. Her favorite expression is "Up your bum."

The Witch   see   Superstition

3362.   *Witchboard*   (1987, Cinema Group, 98m, c). P Gerold Geoffray, D&W Kevin S. Tenney, PH Roy H. Wagner, M Dennis Michael Tenney, ED Daniel Duncan & Stephen J. Waller, AD Sarah Burdick.

LP Todd Allen (Jim Morar), Tawny Kitaen (Linda Brewster), Steven Nichols (Brandon Sinclair), Kathleen Wilhoite (Zarabeth), Burke Byrnes (Lt. Dewhurst), Rose Marie (Mrs. Moses), James W. Quinn (Lloyd).

The witchboard can turn an innocent player into a righteous person or a possessed murderer.

3363.   *The Witches of Eastwick*   (1987, Warner, 118m, c). P Neil Canton, Peter Guber & Jon Peters, D George Miller, W Michael Cristofer (based on a novel by John Updike), PH Vilmos Zsigmond, M John Williams†, ED Richard Francis-Bruce & Hubert C. De La Bouillerie, PD Polly Platt, SOUND Wayne Artman, Tom Beckett, Tom Dahl & Art Rochester†.

LP Jack Nicholson (Daryl Van Horne), Cher (Alexandra Medford), Susan Sarandon (Jane Spofford), Michelle Pfeiffer (Sukie Ridgemont), Veronica Cartwright (Felicia Alden), Richard Jenkins (Clyde Alden), Keith Jochim (Walter Neff), Carel Struycken (Fidel).

The first half of this film is intriguing. Three recently divorced women, sculptor Cher, high school music teacher Susan Sarandon and newspaper writer Michelle Pfeiffer, find their quiet and boring lives in the small New England town of Eastwick drastically changed by the arrival of that "horny little devil" Jack Nicholson. He takes all three as lovers and apparently knows how to satisfy women. The second half is a typical exploitation sex and horror film, gross and disgusting.

3364.   *Witchtrap*   (1989, Cinema Plus/GCO, 90m, c). P Kevin S. Tenney & Dan Duncan, D&W Tenney, PH Thomas Jewett, M Dennis Michael Tenney, ED William O. Sullivan.

LP James W. Quinn (Tony Vicente), Kathleen Bailey (Whitney), Judy Tatum (Agnes), Rob Zapple (Felix), Jack W. Thompson (Frank Murphy), Clyde Talley, 2d (Levi Jackson), Linnea Quigley (Ginger), Keith S. Tenney (Devin Lauter).

Kevin S. Tenney calls in a team of paranormal experts to exorcise the haunted house he's inherited from his uncle.

3365.   *Withnail and I*   (1987, Cineplex Odeon, GB, 108m, c). P Paul M. Heller, D&W Bruce Robinson (based on his novel), PH Peter Hannan, M David Dundas, ED Alan Strachan, PD Michael Pickwoad.

LP Richard E. Grant (Withnail), Paul McGann (Marwood [I]), Richard Griffiths (Monty), Ralph Brown (Danny), Michael Elphick (Jake), Daragh O'Mallery (Irishman), Michael Wardle (Isaac Parkin), Una Brandon-Jones (Mrs. Parkin).

In this hilarious black comedy-drama, Richard E. Grant and Paul McGann are two struggling actors of the late 60s. They share drugs, alcohol and their failures in a seedy London flat. Looking for some recuperative cure, the two decide to spend a weekend in the country and find this just as taxing and terrifying as their city life.

3366. *Without a Clue* (1988, Orion, 106m, c). P Marc Stirdivant, D Thom Eberhardt, W Gary Murphy & Larry Strawther, PH Alan Hume, M Henry Mancini, ED Peter Tanner, PD Brian Ackland-Snow.

LP Michael Caine ("Sherlock Holmes"/Reginald Kincaid), Ben Kingsley (Dr. Watson), Jeffrey Jones (Inspector Lestrade), Lysette Anthony (Fake Leslie), Matthew Sim (Real Leslie), Paul Freeman (Dr. Moriarty), Nigel Davenport (Lord Smithwick), Pat Keen (Mrs. Hudson), Peter Cook (Greenhough).

Suppose Sherlock Holmes was merely an invention of Dr. Watson, who was the true brilliant sleuth. Suppose further that the time has come for Watson to produce Holmes. Then suppose that Watson hires a drunken, none-too-bright actor to portray Holmes. And suppose further that the pair actually has to track down the nefarious Dr. Moriarty with the phony sleuth starting to believe his press clippings and his supposed brilliance in deduction. With all these suppositions, one must come to the conclusion that this film is less interesting than the least exciting tale written by Arthur Conan Doyle.

3367. *Without a Trace* (1983, 20th Century–Fox, 121m, c). P&D Stanley R. Jaffe, W Beth Gutcheon (based on her novel *Still Missing*), PH John Bailey, M Jack Nitzsche, ED Cynthia Scheider, PD Paul Sylbert.

LP Kate Nelligan (Susan Selky), Judd Hirsch (Al Menetti), David Dukes (Graham Selky), Stockard Channing (Jocelyn Norris), Jacqueline Brookes (Margaret Mayo), Keith McDermott (Phillippe), Kathleen Widdoes (Ms. Hauser), Daniel Bryan Corkill (Alex Selky).

When Kate Nelligan's son disappears, she and New York detective Judd Hirsch search all over the city until they find the child.

3368. *Without Warning* (1980, Filmways, 89m, c, aka *It Came...Without Warning*). P&D Greydon Clark, W Lyn Freeman, Daniel Grodnik, Ben Nett & Steve Mathis, PH Dean Cundey, M Dan Wyman, ED Curtis Burch, PD Jack DeWolf.

LP Jack Palance (Taylor), Martin Landau (Fred Dobbs), Tarah Nutter (Sandy), Christopher S. Nelson (Greg), Cameron Mitchell (Hunter), Neville Brand (Leo), Sue Ane Langdon (Aggy), Larry Storch (Scoutmaster), Ralph Meeker (Dave).

A small town is taken over by space invaders who resemble giant leeches. Prospective viewers have now been warned.

3369. *Witness*† (1985, Paramount, 112m, c). P Edward S. Feldman, D Peter Weir†, W Earl W. Wallace & William Kelley (based on a story by Kelley, Earl W. Wallace & Pamela Wallace*), PH John Seale†, M Maurice Jarre†, ED Thom Noble*, PD Stan Jolley, AD Stan Jolley†, SD John Anderson†.

LP Harrison Ford† (John Book), Kelly McGillis (Rachel), Josef Sommer (Schaeffer), Lukas Haas (Samuel), Jan Rubes (Eli Lapp), Alexander Godunov (Daniel Hochleitner), Patti LuPone (Elaine), Danny Glover (McFee), Brent Jennings (Carter).

Amish lad Lukas Haas witnesses a murder committed by crooked cop Danny Glover. Harrison Ford is a tough police detective who takes it on himself to flee with the boy and the lad's beautiful widowed mother Kelly McGillis to the Pennsylvania Dutch country to hide from the murderers. Ford and McGillis have time to fall in love before the bad guys show up and there is one hell of a shoot-out.

Wits End see The G.I. Executioners

3370. *The Wizard* (1989, Universal, 97m, c). P David Chisholm & Ken Topolsky, D Todd Holland, W Chisholm, PH Robert Yeoman, M J. Peter Robinson, ED Tom Finan, PD Michael Mayer.

LP Fred Savage (Corey), Luke Edwards (Jimmy), Jenny Lewis (Haley), Christian Slater (Nick), Beau Bridges (Sam).

Warning to all adults. Do not accompany your children to this kiddie knockoff of *Rain Man*. Just drop them off at the theater and pick them up about an hour-and-a-half later. Television's "Wonder Years" star, 13-year-old Fred Savage leads his troubled, uncommunicative younger half-brother Luke Edwards on a cross-country journey. They end up in the world's video game championship, where Edwards shows his stuff. The entire film is one giant advertisement for Nintendo and Universal Studio Tours.

3371. *The Wizard of Loneliness* (1988, Skouras, 110m, c). P Thom Tyson & Philip Porcella, D Jenny Bowen, W Nancy Larson & Bowen (based on the novel by John Nichols), PH Richard Bowen, M Michel Colombier, ED Lisa Day, PD Jeffrey Beecroft.

LP Lukas Haas (Wendall Olet), Lea Thompson (Sybil), Lance Guest (John T.), John Randolph (Doc), Dylan Baker (Duffy), Anne Pitoniak (Cornelia), Jeremiah Warner (Tom), Steve Hendrickson (Fred).

Set in Vermont during World War II, Lukas Haas is a spoiled kid from Los Angeles. He is sent to live with his grandparents after his mother dies and his father is shipped overseas. He is greatly affected by his disabled Uncle Lance Guest and Aunt Lea Thompson, who gives birth to an illegitimate child.

3372. *Wizards of the Lost Kingdom* (1985, Concorde, US/Arg., 75m, c). P Frank Isaac & Alex Sessa, D Hector Olivera, W Tom Edwards, PH Leonard Solis, M James Horner & Chris Young, ED Silvia Roberts, PD Mary Bertram.

LP Bo Svenson (Kor), Vidal Peterson (Simon), Thom Christopher (Shurka), Barbara Stock (Udea), Maria Socas (Acrasia), Dolores Michaels (Aura), Edward Morrow (Wulfrick/Old Simon/Gulfax), August Larreta (King Tylor).

Great warrior Bo Svenson helps boy magician Vidal Peterson battle monsters, mermaids and other mystical beings in order to restore justice to the magical kingdom.

3373. *Wolfen* (1981, Warner, 115m, c). P Rupert Hitzig, D Michael Wadleigh, W David Eyre & Wadleigh (based on the novel by Whitley Strieber), PH Gerry Fisher, M James Horner, ED Chris Leb-

enzon, Dennis Dolan, Martin Bram & Marshall M. Borden, PD Paul Sylbert, MK Carl Fullerton.

LP Albert Finney (Dewey Wilson), Diane Venora (Rebecca Neff), Edward James Olmos (Eddie Holt), Gregory Hines (Whittington), Tom Noonan (Ferguson), Dick O'Neill (Warren), Dehl Berti (Old Indian).

Mutilation murders in New York City are discovered to be the work of savage beasts. They have descended from Indian hunters who went underground, despairing of the future of the human race.

3374. *Wolfman* (1980, Omni, 101m, c). P Earl Owensby, D&W Worth Keeter, PH Darrell Cathcart, M Arthur Smith & David Floyd, ED Richard Aldridge, AD David Cadell, SE Al Yehoe, MK Sandy Barber & Keeter.

LP Earl Owensby (Colin Glasgow), Ed L. Grady (Rev. Leonard), Julian Morton (Edwin Glasgow), Kristine Reynolds (Lynn Randolph), Richard Dedmon (Uncle Clement), Maggie Lauterer (Aunt Elizabeth), Sid Rancer (Dr. Tate).

Earl Owensby slowly comes to the realization that he has inherited the family curse and will become a wolfman.

3375. *The Wolves of Willoughby Chase* (1988, Atlantic, GB, 98m, c). P Mark Forstater, D Stuart Orme, W William M. Akers (based on the novel by Joan Aiken), PH Paul Beeson, M Colin Towns, ED Martin Walsh, PD Christopher Hobbs.

LP Stephanie Beacham (Slighcarp), Mel Smith (Grimshaw), Geraldine James (Mrs. Brisket), Emily Hudson (Bonnie), Aleks Darowska (Sylvia), Lynton Dearden (Simon), Richard O'Brien (James), Jane Horrocks (Pattern).

When her parents go abroad, Emily Hudson and her timid cousin Aleks Darowska are left in the care of sinister governess Stephanie Beacham. The latter has plans to claim Willoughby Chase manor for herself. She commands a pack of wolves. It takes all of the wit and courage of the two girls to foil the evil governess in this fantasy-adventure film set in Victorian England.

3376. *The Woman in Red* (1984, Orion, 87m, c). P Victor Drai, D&W

Gene Wilder (based on the screenplay *Pardon Mon Affair* by Jean-Loup Dabadie & Yves Robert), PH Fred Schuler, M John Morris, ED Christopher Greenbury, PD David L. Snyder.

LP Gene Wilder (Theodore Pierce), Charles Grodin (Buddy), Joseph Bologna (Joe), Judith Ivey (Didi), Michael Huddleston (Michael), Kelly LeBrock (Charlotte), Gilda Radner (Ms. Milner), Kyle T. Heffner (Richard), Michael Zorek (Shelly).

Kelly LeBrock is a knock-out. Charles Grodin and Joseph Bologna are outstanding character actors who can always be counted on to please. Stevie Wonder's "I Just Called to Say I Love You" is one of his best songs. Everything else about this film is disappointingly dumb and sexist. The premise is that married Gene Wilder spies LeBrock dancing over an air vent in a parking garage. As the wind swirls up her sexy red dress, showing her very fine legs and panties, Wilder is a goner. Unfortunately, as is the case with Dudley Moore in *10,* he gets a chance to meet and bed his mysterious lady—but it's not as good as he imagines. Still the ending of the film suggests that Wilder has learned nothing from his experiences.

3377. *The Woman Inside* (1981, 20th Century-Fox, 94m, c). P Sidney H. Levine, D&W Joseph Van Winkle, PH Ron Johnson, M Eddy Lawrence Manson, ED John Duffy.

LP Gloria Manon (Holly/Hollis), Dane Clark (Dr. Rassner), Joan Blondell (Aunt Coll), Michael Champion (Nolan), Marlene Tracy (Dr. Parris), Michael Mancini (Marco), Luce Morgan (Maggie), Terri Haven (Agnes).

Joan Blondell makes her final film appearance in this story of wounded veteran Gloria Manon, who wants a sex change operation so "he" can become a woman.

3378. *A Woman Obsessed* (1989, Platinum, 105m, c). P&D Larry Vincent, W Craig Horrall, PH Larry Revene, M Joey Mennonna, ED James Davalos, AD Hilary Wright.

LP Ruth Raymond (Arlene Bellings), Linda Blair (Evie Barnes), Gregory Patrick (Ted Barnes), Troy Donahue (Jack Barnes), Carolyn Van Bellinghen (Wanda Barnes), Frank Stewart (Bobby Trumbal).

Yuppie lawyer Gregory Patrick discovers that what appears to be a nude portrait of him, for which he never posed, is actually the work of Ruth Raymond, who claims to be Patrick's mother. Her model was Patrick's father. Momma Raymond is not too stable and she's talented in mixing poison as well as paints.

3379. *The Women's Club* (1987, Lightning Pictures, 89m, c). P Fred Weintraub, D&W Sandra Weintraub, PH Kent Wakeford, M David Wheatley & Paul F. Antonelli, ED Martin Cohen, AD Tim Duffey.

LP Michael Pare (Patrick), Maud Adams (Angie), Eddie Velez (Carlos).

In this comedy, what seems a perfect job for young stud Michael Pare, servicing Adams' friends, becomes a nightmare.

3380. *Wonderland* (1989, Vestron, GB, 103m, c). P Steve Morrison, D Philip Saville, W Frank Clarke, PH Dick Pope, M Hans Zimmer, ED Richard Bedford, PD David Brockhurst.

LP Emile Charles (Eddie), Tony Forsyth (Michael), Robert Stephens (Vincent), Clare Higgins (Eve), Bruce Payne (Echo), Robbie Coltrane (Annabelle), Carsten Norgaard (Dolphin Man).

Emile Charles and Tony Forsyth are two gay Liverpool teenagers who dream of finding someplace where they can be happy. The film doesn't seem to suggest that they will ever find it. Charles identifies with the performing dolphins at Wonderland, even sneaking in to swim with them.

3381. *Working Girl*† (1988, 20th Century-Fox, 113m, c). P Douglas Wick, D Mike Nichols†, W Kevin Wade, PH Michael Ballhaus, M Carly Simon, ED Sam O'Steen, PD Patrizia Von Brandenstein, AD Doug Kraner, SD George De Titta, M/L "Let the River Run" by Simon & Phil Collins*.

LP Melanie Griffith† (Tess McGill), Harrison Ford (Jack Trainer), Sigourney Weaver† (Katherine Parker), Joan Cusack† (Cyn), Alec Baldwin (Mick Dugan), Philip Bosco (Oren Trask), Nora Dunn (Ginny), Oliver Platt (Lutz), James

Lally (Turkel), Kevin Spacey (Bob Spreck), Robert Easton (Armbrister), Olympia Dukakis (Personnel Director).

Melanie Griffith is a delight as a sweet, scrappy and sexy secretary who makes the most of the opportunity presented to her when her boss Sigourney Weaver has a skiing accident. Griffith not only shows she's a Wall Street whiz, she also snags Weaver's gentleman friend Harrison Ford in the bargain. When she tells off the obnoxious Weaver, audiences cheer, although some may object to the reference to Weaver's "bony ass." An excellent performance is given by Joan Cusack as Griffith's gum-chewing, bouffant-hairdo, clunky jewelry and gobs of eyeshadow girlfriend. She will never be anything more than a member of the steno pool, but she's there to cheer her friend on.

3382. *Working Girls* (1986, Miramax, 90m, c). P Lizzie Borden & Andi Gladstone, D Borden, W Borden & Sandra Kay (based on a story by Borden), PH Judy Irola, M David van Tieghem & Roma Baran, ED Borden, PD Kurt Ossenfort.

LP Louise Smith (Molly), Ellen McElduff (Lucy), Amanda Goodwin (Dawn), Marusia Zach (Gina), Janne Peters (April), Helen Nicholas (Mary).

The film follows a group of prostitutes through a day (or night) in their work at a high class brothel. The notorious documentary-like film is an interesting examination of sexual politics in action.

3383. *The World According to Garp* (1982, Warner, 136m, c). P George Roy Hill & Robert L. Crawford, D Hill, W Steve Tesich (based on the novel by John Irving), PH Miroslav Ondricek, ED Ronald Roose & Stephen A. Rotter, PD Henry Bumstead.

LP Robin Williams (T.S. Garp), Marybeth Hurt (Helen Holm), Glenn Close† (Jenny Fields), John Lithgow† (Roberta Muldoon), Hume Cronyn (Mr. Fields), Jessica Tandy (Mrs. Fields), Swoosie Kurtz (Hooker), James McCall (Young Garp), Peter Michael Goetz (John Wolfe).

Based on John Irving's novel, which many believed could not be filmed, the result is an episodic adaptation which perhaps shouldn't have been filmed. It is the comical and tragic life of Robin Williams, a man deliberately conceived by his nurse mother Glenn Close, using a dying, insane soldier as an unaware source of sperm. The performances of Close and John Lithgow as a transsexual former professional football player are very good.

3384. *A World Apart* (1988, Atlantic, GB, 113m, c). P Sarah Radclyffe, D Chris Menges, W Shawn Slovo, PH Peter Biziou, M Hans Zimmer, ED Nicolas Gaster, PD Brian Morris.

LP Barbara Hershey (Diana Roth), Jodhi May (Molly Roth), Jeroen Krabbe (Gus Roth), Carolyn Clayton-Cragg (Miriam Roth), Merav Gruer (Jude Roth), Yvonne Bryceland (Bertha), Albee Lesotho (Solomon), Linda Mvusi (Elsie), Rosalie Crutchley (Mrs. Harris).

In 1963, a crackdown on antiapartheid protests causes dissident Jeroen Krabbe to flee South Africa, leaving behind his wife Barbara Hershey and two daughters, Carolyn Clayton-Cragg and Jodhi May. The latter's resentment towards her mother grows in direct proportion to the continuing fight Hershey makes against apartheid, leaving little time for her daughters.

3385. *World Gone Wild* (1988, Lorimar, 94m, c). P Robert L. Rosen, D Lee H. Kazin, W Jorge Zamacona, PH Don Burgess, M Laurence Juber, ED Gary A. Griffen, PD Donald L. Harris.

LP Bruce Dern (Ethan), Michael Pare (George Landon), Catherine Mary Stewart (Angie), Adam Ant (Derek Abernathy), Anthony James (Ten Watt), Rick Podell (Exline), Julius Carry, III (Nitro), Alan Autry (Hank).

In a postapocalyptic world, survivors, jealously guarding their precious supply of water, are attacked by white-clad thugs led by androgynous Adam Ant, who quotes from Charles Manson as inspiration for the carnage of his cult.

3386. *The World Is Full of Married Men* (1980, New Line, GB, 106m, c). P Malcolm Fancey & Oscar S. Lerman, D Robert Young, W Jackie Collins & Terry Howard (based on her novel), PH Ray Parslow, M Frank Musker & Dominic Bugatti, ED David Campling.

LP Anthony Franciosa (David Cooper), Carroll Baker (Linda Cooper), Gareth Hunt (Jay Grossman), Georgina Hale (Lori Grossman), Anthony Steel

(Conrad Lee), Sherrie Cronn (Claudia Parker), Paul Nicholas (Gem Gemini), Jean Gilpin (Miss Field), John Nolan (Joe).

In this tedious production of Jackie Collins' trashy novel, the wife of advertising executive Anthony Franciosa decides to pay him back in kind for his frequent infidelities.

3387. *The Worm Eaters* (1981, New American, 94m, c). P Ted V. Mikels, D&W Herb Robins (based on a story by Nancy Kapner), PH Willis Hawkins, M Theodore Stern, ED Soly Bina, PD Jack DeWolf.

LP Herb Robins (Hermann Umgar), Lindsay Armstrong Black, Joseph Sacket, Robert Garrison, Muriel Cooper, Mike Garrison, Barry Hostetler.

An eccentric, club-footed hermit attempts to settle the score with a nearby small California community by setting loose a horde of worms to destroy their food supply.

3388. *Worth Winning* (1989, 20th Century–Fox, 102m, c). P Gil Friesen & Dale Pollock, D Will Mackenzie, W Josann McGibbon & Sara Parriott (based on the novel by Dan Lewandowski), PH Adam Greenberg, M Patrick Williams, ED Sidney Wolinsky, PD Lilly Kilvert.

LP Mark Harmon (Taylor Worth), Madeleine Stowe (Veronica Briskow), Lesley Ann Warren (Eleanor Larimore), Maria Holvoe (Erin Cooper), Mark Blum (Ned Braudy), Andrea Martin (Claire Braudy), Tony Longo (Terry Childs), Alan Blumenfeld (Howard Larimore).

The sexual innuendoes in this lost-in-space comedy are not so much tasteless as they are childish. TV weatherman Mark Harmon is very, very popular with the ladies — at least the ladies of great pulchritude and little brains, the only type to appear in the film. Harmon's friends bet him he can't get three women to agree to marry him and the lout accepts the bet, wins, but finds true love. Who cares?

3389. *The Wraith* (1986, New Century, 92m, c). P John Kemeny, D&W Mike Marvin, PH Reed Smoot, M Michael Hoenig & J. Peter Robinson, ED Scott Conrad & Gary Rocklin.

LP Charlie Sheen (The Wraith/Jake), Nick Cassavetes (Packard), Sherilyn Fenn (Keri), Randy Quaid (Loomis), Matthew Barry (Billy), David Sherrill (Skank), Jamie Bozian (Gutterboy), Clint Howard (Rughead).

Charlie Sheen is a hero sent from the skies to challenge the evil forces in a rural community.

3390. *The Wrong Guys* (1988, New World, 86m, c). P Chuck Gordon & Ronald E. Frazier, D Danny Bilson, W Bilson & Paul de Meo, PH Frank Byers, M Joseph Conlan, ED Frank J. Jimenez, PD George Costello.

LP Louie Anderson (Louie), Richard Lewis (Richard), Richard Belzer (Belz), Franklyn Ajaye (Franklyn), Tim Thomerson (Tim), Brion James (Glen Grunski), Biff Manard (Mark Grunski), John Goodman (Duke Earl).

Louie Anderson is the leader of a group of stand-up comedians appearing as members of a former Boy Scout troop on a camping trip. They encounter escaped convict John Goodman who mistakes them for the CIA. Dumb! Dumb! Dumb!

3391. *Wrong Is Right* (1982, Columbia, 117m, c, aka *The Man with the Deadly Lens*). P,D&W Richard Brooks (based on the novel *The Better Angels* by Charles McCarry), PH Fred J. Koenekamp, M Artie Kane, ED George Grenville, PD Edward Carfagno.

LP Sean Connery (Patrick Hale), George Grizzard (President Lockwood), Robert Conrad (Gen. Wombat), Katharine Ross (Sally Blake), G.D. Spradlin (Philindros), John Saxon (Homer Hubbard), Henry Silva (Rafeeq), Leslie Nielsen (Mallory), Robert Webber (Harvey), Rosalind Cash (Mrs. Ford), Hardy Kruger (Helmut Unger), Dean Stockwell (Hacker), Ron Moody (King Awad).

International TV commentator Sean Connery discovers that the world is being manipulated by the CIA. So what else is news?

3392. *Xanadu* (1980, Universal, 93m, c). P Lawrence Gordon, D Robert Greenwald, W Richard Christian Danus, Marc Reid Rubel & Michael Kane, PH Victor J. Kemper, M Barry DeVorzon, ED Dennis Virkler, PD John W. Corso.

LP Olivia Newton-John (Kira), Gene Kelly (Danny McGuire), Michael Beck (Sonny Malone), James Sloyan (Simpson), Dimitra Arliss (Helen), Katie Hanley (Sandra), Fred McCarren (Richie), Ren Woods (Jo).

This attempt to prove that 40s musicals could succeed in the 80s fell flat on its face. The muse Terpsichore (Olivia Newton-John) comes to earth to inspire artist Michael Beck who wants to open a rock 'n' roll hall. Poor Gene Kelly finds himself at the twilight of his career in possibly the worst of all musicals, after having appeared in many of the best. The story seems inspired by the not very good 1947 film *Down to Earth*.

3393. *Xtro* (1983, New Line, GB, 80m, c). P Mark Forstater, D Harry Bromley Davenport, W Iain Cassie, Robert Smith & Jo Ann Kaplan (based on a screenplay by Michel Parry & Davenport), PH John Metcalfe & John Simmons, M Davenport & Shelton Leigh Palmer, ED Nick Gaster & Kaplan, AD Andrew Mollo & Peter Body, SE Tom Harris.

LP Philip Sayer (Sam Phillips), Bernice Stegers (Rachel Phillips), Danny Brainin (Joe Daniels), Simon Nash (Tony Phillips), Maryam D'Abo (Analisc), David Cardy (Michael), Anna Wing (Miss Goodman).

In a vile film filled with grotesque special effects, mostly involving a series of repulsive bladder problems, father Philip Sayer is abducted by aliens. He returns to his family three years later in the form of a crablike monster. He infects his son, kills any number of people and turns the family's au pair into an alien breeding machine.

The XYZ Murders see *Crimewave*

3394. *The Year My Voice Broke* (1988, Avenue, Australia, 103m, c). P Terry Hayes, Doug Mitchell & George Miller, D&W John Duigan, PH Geoff Burton, M Christine Woodruff, ED Neil Thumpston, PD Roger Ford.

LP Noah Taylor (Danny), Loene Carmen (Freya), Ben Mendelsohn (Trevor), Graeme Blundell (Nils Olson), Lynette Curran (Anne Olson), Malcolm Robertson (Bruce Embling), Judi Farr (Sheila Embling).

This coming of age film is set in New South Wales in 1962. Long-time pals Noah Taylor and Loene Carmen begin to experience their first feelings of sexual desire, he for her, she for an older, wilder lad. Carmen scandalizes the town when she becomes pregnant, miscarries and must leave her home, never to be seen again by her friend Taylor.

3395. *The Year of Living Dangerously* (1983, MGM, Australia, 115m, c). P James McElroy, D Peter Weir, W David Williamson, Weir & C.J. Koch (based on the novel by Koch), PH Russell Boyd, M Maurice Jarre, ED Bill Anderson, AD Herbert Pinter.

LP Mel Gibson (Guy Hamilton), Sigourney Weaver (Jill Bryant), Linda Hunt* (Billy Kwan), Michael Murphy (Pete Curtis), Bembol Roco (Kumar), Domingo Landicho (Hortono), Hermono De Guzman (Immigration Officer), Noel Ferrier (Wally O'Sullivan), Paul Sonkkila (Kevin Condon), Ali Nur (Ali).

Young Australian journalist Mel Gibson has his first international assignment in Indonesia in 1965 when the Sukarno regime was toppling. The film belongs to diminutive Linda Hunt, playing a man who plays cupid for Gibson and British diplomatic attaché Sigourney Weaver.

3396. *Year of the Dragon* (1985, MGM/United Artists, 136m, c). P Dino De Laurentiis, D Michael Cimino, W Cimino & Oliver Stone (based on the novel by Robert Daley), PH Alex Thomson, M David Mansfield, ED Francoise Bonnot, PD Wolf Kroeger.

LP Mickey Rourke (Stanley White), John Lone (Joey Tai), Ariane (Tracy Tzu), Leonard Termo (Angelo Rizzo), Raymond Barry (Louis Bukowski), Caroline Kava (Connie White), Eddie Jones (William McKenna), Joey Chin (Ronnie Chang), Victor Wong (Harry Yung).

In a violent, racist, sexist film, Mickey Rourke portrays a police officer trying to break up Chinese youth gangs in New York's Chinatown.

3397. *Yellow Hair and the Fortress of Gold* (1984, Crown, US/Spain, 102m, c). P John Ghaffari & Diego G. Sempre, D Matt Cimber, W Cimber & John Kershaw (based on characters and story by

Cimber), PH John Cabrera, M Franco Piersanti, ED Claudio Cutry.

LP Laurene Landon (Yellow Hair), Ken Roberson (Pecos Kid), John Ghaffari (Shayowteewah), Luis Lorenzo (Col. Torres), Claudia Gravi (Grey Cloud), Aldo Sambrel (Flores), Eduardo Fajardo (Man-Who-Knows).

Seeking a fortress of gold, princess Laurene Landon looks for help from a strange man who lives in an elk's horn.

3398. *Yellowbeard* (1983, Orion, 101m, c). P Carter De Haven, D Mel Damski, W Graham Chapman, Peter Cook & Bernard McKenna, PH Gerry Fisher, M John Morris, ED William Reynolds, PD Joseph R. Jennings.

LP Graham Chapman (Yellowbeard), Peter Boyle (Moon), Richard "Cheech" Marin (El Segundo), Tommy Chong (El Nebuloso), Peter Cook (Lord Lambourn), Marty Feldman (Gilbert), Martin Hewitt (Dan), Michael Hordern (Dr. Gilpin), Eric Idle (Cmdr. Clement), Madeline Kahn (Betty), James Mason (Capt. Hughes), John Cleese (Blind Pew), Kenneth Mars (Crisp/Verdugo), Spike Milligan (Flunkie), Susannah York (Lady Churchill), Beryl Reid (Lady Lambourn).

This directionless farce follows the adventures of a 17th century pirate captain, Graham Chapman. It is the useless tasteless stuff expected from Monty Python but without the wit. Marty Feldman makes his final screen appearance, having died during production.

3399. *Yentl* (1983, MGM/United Artists, GB, 134m, c). P Barbra Streisand & Rusty Lemorande, D Streisand, W Streisand & Jack Rosenthal (based on the short story "Yentl the Yeshiva Boy" by Isaac Bashevis Singer), PH David Watkin, M Michel Legrand, Alan & Marilyn Bergman†, ED Terry Rawlings, PD Roy Walker, AD Walker & Leslie Tomkins†, SD Tessa Davies, M/L "Papa Can You Hear Me?" and "The Way He Makes Me Feel" by Legrand, Alan & Marilyn Berman†.

LP Barbra Streisand (Yentl), Mandy Patinkin (Avigdor), Amy Irving† (Hadass), Nehemiah Persoff (Papa), Steven Hill (Reb Alter Vishkower), Allan Corduner (Shimmele), Ruth Goring (Esther Rachel), David DeKeyser (Rabbi Zalman).

Many years ago in Poland, a young woman, played by Barbra Streisand, has a thirst for knowledge which is denied to one of her sex. Not to be denied she cuts her hair, puts on men's clothes and attends a yeshiva as a male. She falls in love with fellow student Mandy Patinkin, but through a series of misunderstandings, finds herself married to Amy Irving. It's a heavy-handed personal statement by Streisand which most of the industry ignored, as did audiences.

3400. *Yes, Giorgio* (1982, MGM/United Artists, 110m, c). P Peter Fetterman, D Franklin J. Schaffner, W Norman Steinberg (based on the novel by Anne Piper), PH Fred J. Koenekamp, M John Williams, ED Michael F. Anderson, PD William J. Creber, SONG "If We Were in Love" by John Williams, Alan & Marilyn Bergman*.

LP Luciano Pavarotti (Giorgio Fini), Kathryn Harrold (Pamela Taylor), Eddie Albert (Henry Pollack), Paola Borboni (Sister Teresa), James Hong (Kwan), Beulah Quo (Mei Ling), Norman Steinberg (Dr. Barmen).

Luciano Pavarotti is a magnificent tenor. He is not an accomplished actor, but even if he was, he'd be defeated by this ridiculous story in which he is asked to be a caricature of himself. His character's overbearing ego and male chauvinistic attitudes barely gets in the way of his romance with beautiful throat specialist Kathryn Harrold. She is called in when he unexpectedly loses his voice while on a U.S. tour.

You Better Watch Out see ***Christmas Evil***

3401. *You Can't Hurry Love* (1988, Lightning Pictures, 92m, c). P Jonathan D. Krane, D&W Richard Martini, PH Peter Lyons Collister & John Schwartzman, M Bob Esty, ED Richard Candib.

LP David Packer (Eddie Hayes), Scott McGinnis (Skip), Bridget Fonda (Peggy), David Leisure (Newcomb), Luana Anders (Macie Hayes), Judy Balduzzi (Glenda), Frank Bonner (Chuck Hayes), Anthony Geary (Tony), Charles Grodin (Mr. Glerman), Sally Kellerman (Kelly Bones), Kristy McNichol (Rhonda).

In a very dim comedy, David Packer is

a hick from Akron who finds life in Los Angeles to be rather unsettling. He employs a dating service, which gives the filmmakers a reason to show a number of underdressed and undressed pretty young women. Charles Grodin, Sally Kellerman and Kristy McNichol make throwaway cameo appearances.

3402. *You Talkin' to Me?* (1987, MGM/United Artists, 97m, c). P Michael Polaire, D&W Charles Winkler, PH Paul Ryan, M Joel McNeely, ED David Handman.

LP Jim Youngs (Bronson Green), James Noble (Peter Archer), Mykel T. Williamson (Thatcher Marks), Faith Ford (Dana Archer), Bess Motta (Judith Margolis), Rex Ryon (Kevin), Brian Thompson (James), Alan King (Himself).

Jim Youngs is a Robert DeNiro fan, inspired by watching *Taxi Driver* over and over. He goes to Southern California where he confronts a white supremacy group and rescues his friend, black male model Mykel T. Williamson.

3403. *Young Doctors in Love* (1982, 20th Century–Fox, 95m, c). P Jerry Bruckheimer, D Garry Marshall, W Michael Elias & Rich Eustis, PH Don Peterman, M Maurice Jarre, ED Dov Hoenig, PD Polly Platt.

LP Michael McKean (Dr. Simon August), Sean Young (Dr. Stephanie Brody), Harry Dean Stanton (Dr. Oliver Ludwig), Patrick Macnee (Dr. Jacobs), Hector Elizondo (Angelo/Angela), Dabney Coleman (Dr. Joseph Prang), Pamela Reed (Norine Sprockett), Taylor Negron (Dr. Phil Burns), Saul Rubinek (Dr. Floyd Kurtzman), Patrick Collins (Dr. Walter Rist).

This comedy about a team of new interns at a big city hospital is an *Airplane*-like spoof both of medical films and TV soap operas (to insure this point is made, several soap opera stars make cameo appearances). The jokes are hit and miss, some cruel, some obscene, some gross, some scatological, some sexist, some even funny.

3404. *Young Einstein* (1989, Warner, Australia, 90m, c). P Yahoo Serious, Warwick Ross & David Roach, D Ser-

ious, W Serious & Roach, PH Jeff Darling, M William Motzing, Martin Armiger & Tommy Tycho, ED Roach, Neil Thumpston, Peter Whitmore & Amanda Robson.

LP Yahoo Serious (Albert Einstein), Odile Le Clezio (Marie Curie), John Howard (Preston Preston), Pee Wee Wilson (Mr. Einstein), Su Cruickshank (Mrs. Einstein), Lulu Pinkus (The Blonde).

One has to be in a zany mood to appreciate this weird import from down under. It's merely a series of uneven sketches featuring Yahoo Serious as a none-too-serious Albert Einstein. Those who enjoy Monty Python might find this fun.

3405. *Young Guns* (1988, 20th Century–Fox, 97m, c). P Joe Roth & Christopher Cain, D Cain, W John Fusco, PH Dean Semler, M Anthony Marinelli & Brian Banks, ED Jack Hofstra, PD Jane Musky.

LP Emilio Estevez (William H. Bonney, aka "Billy the Kid"), Kiefer Sutherland (Josiah "Doc" Scurlock), Lou Diamond Phillips (Chevez Y Chavez), Charlie Sheen (Dick Brewer), Dermot Mulroney ("Dirty Steve" Stephens), Casey Siemaszko (Charley Bowdre), Terence Stamp (John Henry Tunstall), Jack Palance (Lawrence G. Murphy), Terrance O'Quinn (Alex McSween), Sharon Thomas (Susan McSween), Brian Keith (Buckshot Roberts), Patrick Wayne (Pat Garrett), Cody Palance (Baker).

Westerns appear to be a dead genre and this attempt to bring it back to life raised only the slightest pulse in the cadaver. It's the story of the Lincoln County War. Kindly British rancher Terence Stamp gathers together a group of scruffy young men to act as hired guns for his battle with evil beef baron Jack Palance. When Stamp is killed the war is on, with Emilio Estevez finding that he really enjoys killing people.

Young Lady Chatterley II see *Private Property*

3406. *Young Nurses in Love* (1989, Platinum Pictures, 76m, c). P&D Chuck Vincent, W Vincent & Craig Horrall, PH Larry Revene, M Bill Heller, ED "Marc Ubell" (Vincent) & James Davalos.

LP Jeanne Marie (Nurse Ellis), Alan

Fisler (Dr. Reilly), Jane Hamilton (Francesca), Jamie Gillis (Dr. Spencer), Harv Siegel (Dr. Young), James Davies, Barbara Robb, Jennifer Delora, Beth Broderick, Annie Sprinkle.

This answer to *Young Doctors in Love* (1982) is a cheap sex comedy about Soviet spy Jeanne Marie who infiltrates a hospital posing as an American nurse. Her assignment is to steal the sperm deposits of geniuses such as Einstein and Edison being stored at the hospital.

3407. *Young Sherlock Holmes* (1985, Paramount, 109m, c). P Mark Johnson, D Barry Levinson, W Chris Columbus (based on the characters created by Sir Arthur Conan Doyle), PH Stephen Goldblatt, M Bruce Broughton, ED Stu Linder, PD Norman Reynolds, VE Dennis Muren, Kit West, John Ellis & David Allen†.

LP Nicholas Rowe (Sherlock Holmes), Alan Cox (John H. Watson), Sophie Ward (Elizabeth), Anthony Higgins (Rathe), Susan Fleetwood (Mrs. Dribb), Freddie Jones (Cragwitch), Nigel Stock (Waxflatter), Roger Ashton-Griffiths (Lestrade), Earl Rhodes (Dudley).

The notion of making a picture about a precocious lad who will grow up to be the world's most famous fictional detective seems like a capital idea. Unfortunately Chris Columbus is no Conan Doyle and the story shows more the influence of co-executive producer Steven Spielberg than an author who lived and wrote during the Victorian era. It will probably appeal more to those who have never read any of the Holmes stories than to Baker Street Irregulars.

3408. *Young Warriors* (1983, Cannon, 105m, c). P Victoria Paige Meyerink, D Lawrence D. Foldes, W Foldes & Russell W. Colgin, PH Mac Ahlberg, M Rob Walsh, ED Ted Nicolaou, PD Karl Pogany.

LP Ernest Borgnine (Lt. Bob Carrigan), Richard Roundtree (Sgt. John Austin), Lynda Day George (Beverly Carrigan), James Van Patten (Kevin Carrigan), Anne Lockhart (Lucy), Tom Reilly (Scott), Ed De Stefane (Stan), Mike Norris (Fred).

In this *Death Wish* clone, cop Ernest Borgnine cooperates with authorities when his daughter is raped and killed by a gang of young punks. But his son James Van Patten organizes a bunch of his fraternity brothers into a vigilante group who roam the streets looking for the killers. They take on any criminals they encounter during their patrols.

3409. *Youngblood* (1986, MGM/United Artists, 110m, c). P Peter Bart & Patrick Wells, D&W Peter Markle (based on a story by Markle & John Whitman), PH Mark Irwin, M William Orbit/Torchsong & Chris Boardman, ED Stephen E. Rivkin & Jack Hofstra, AD Alicia Keywan & Alta Louise Doyle.

LP Rob Lowe (Dean Youngblood), Cynthia Gibb (Jessie Chadwick), Patrick Swayze (Derek Sutton), Ed Lauter (Murray Chadwick), Jim Youngs (Kelly Youngblood), Eric Nesterenko (Blane Youngblood), George Finn (Racki), Fionnula Flanagan (Miss Gill), Ken James (Frazier).

Meant to be the *Rocky* of hockey, this puck doesn't make it across the blue line. Rob Lowe, no Wayne Gretzky, lacks the killer instinct needed to become a real star. Everyone in the film acts as if they fell on the ice when they weren't wearing their helmets.

3410. *Zadar! Cow from Hell* (1989, Stone Peach Production, 87m, c). P&D Robert C. Hughes, W Merle Kessler (based on the story by Duck's Breath Mystery Theater), PH James Mathers, M Greg Brown, ED Michael Ruscio, AD Ginni Barr.

LP Bill Allard (Mr. Nifty), Dan Coffey (Rex), Merle Kessler (Sleepless Walker), Leon Martell (Dan Tension), Jim Turner (Max), Deborah Gwinn (Amy Walker), Eric Topham (Ralph, Jr.), Ned Holbrook (Chip).

This film within a film is the story of a movie crew returning to the director's home in Iowa to make a horror film about an enormous cow. It is meant to be a comedy, but it's a long time between clever ideas, let alone laughs.

3411. *Zapped!* (1982, Embassy, 96m, c). P Jeffrey D. Apple, D Robert J. Rosenthal, W Rosenthal & Bruce Rubin, PH Daniel Pearl, M Charles Fox, ED Bob Bring & Robert Ferretti, SE Robert Blalack, Dick Albain & Ron Nary.

LP Scott Baio (Barney), Willie Aames (Peyton), Robert Mandan (Walter Johnson), Felice Schachter (Bernadette), Scatman Crothers (Dexter Jones), Roger Bowen (Mr. Springboro), Marya Small (Mrs. Springboro), Sue Ane Langdon (Rose), Heather Thomas (Jane).

In another teenage exploitation film, a chemistry experiment explosion gifts Scott Baio with telekinetic powers. He uses these in the best tradition of such movies to get girls stripped to the buff. Stupid stuff!

3412. *A Zed and Two Noughts* (1985, Skouras, GB/Netherlands, 115m, c). P Peter Sainsbury & Kees Kasander, D&W Peter Greenaway, PH Sacha Vierny, M Michael Nyman, ED John Wilson, PD Ben van Os.

LP Andrea Ferreol (Alba Bewick), Brian Deacon (Oswald Deuce), Eric Deacon (Oliver Deuce), Frances Barber (Venus De Milo), Joss Ackland (Van Hoyten), Jim Davidson (Joshua Plate), Agnes Brulet (Beta Bewick).

Dutch zoologist twin brothers, Brian & Eric Deacon, become obsessed with the decay of animals after their wives are both killed in an automobile accident in which the driver Andrea Ferreol loses a leg. The brothers plan to set free all the animals in the zoo. They also have a ménage à trois with Ferreol. As a result she gives birth to twin sons. She has her remaining leg amputated and takes up with another double amputee, whom she names as the legal father of her sons before she dies. The brothers commit joint suicide. It's certainly an unusual film.

3413. *Zelig* (1983, Warner, 80m, c/b&w). P Robert Greenhut, D&W Woody Allen, PH Gordon Willis†, M Dick Hyman, ED Susan E. Morse, PD Mel Bourne, COS Santo Loquasto†.

LP Woody Allen (Leonard Zelig), Mia Farrow (Dr. Eudora Fletcher), John Buckwalter (Dr. Sindell), Marvin Chatinover (Glandular Diagnosis Doctor), Paul Nevens (Dr. Birsky), Sol Lomita (Martin Geist), Mary Louise Wilson (Sister Ruth), Sharon Ferrol (Miss Baker).

Director-writer Woody Allen produces a parody documentary about a chameleon-like nonentity. Played by Allen, the little man manages to show up at every major event of the 20th century. The remarkable recreations of old newsreels in which Allen's character is introduced is a cinematic breakthrough. Gordon Willis deserves special praise.

3414. *Zelly and Me* (1988, Columbia, 87m, c). P Sue Jett & Tony Mark, D Tina Rathborne, W Rathborne, PH Mikael Salomon, M Pino Donaggio & Jeremiah Clarke, ED Cindy Kaplan Rooney, PD David Morong.

LP Alexandra Johnes (Phoebe), Isabella Rossellini (Joan "Zelly"), Glynis Johns (CoCo), Kaiulani Lee (Nora), David Lynch (Willie), Joe Morton (Earl), Courtney Vickery (Dora), Lindsay Dickon (Kitty).

The film is the story of the struggle between orphaned eight-year-old Alexandra Johnes and her saintly but rather strange grandmother Glynis Johns. Only equally strange nanny Isabella Rossellini can referee their differences.

3415. *The Zero Boys* (1987, Omega, 89m, c). P&D Nico Mastorakis, W Mastorakis & Fred C. Perry (based on a story by Mastorakis), PH Steve Shaw, M Stanley Myers & Hans Zimmer, ED George Rosenberg.

LP Daniel Hirsch (Steve), Kelli Maroney (Jamie), Nicole Rio (Sue), Tom Shell (Larry), Jared Moses (Rip), Crystal Carson (Trish), Joe Phelan (Killer), Gary Jochimsen (Killer No. 2), John Michaels (Casey), Elise Turner (Victim), T.K. Webb (Killer No. 3).

When three survival-game champions and their girlfriends are invited to a party in the backwoods, they find themselves in a murderous plot which will really test their survival skills.

3416. *Zilch* (1989, Park Avenue Prods./Vardex, New Zealand, 95m, c). P Amanda Hocquard & Richard Riddiford, D Riddiford, W Riddiford & Jonathan Dowling, PH Murray Milne, M Chris Knox, ED Chris Todd.

LP Michael Mizrahi (Sam), Lucy Sheehan (Anna).

Telephone toll operator Michael Mizrahi listens in and tapes phone conversations. This is how he learns of a blackmail plot against a government minister by operators of a construction company (they want the pol's support for their efforts to get the contract for building a harbor crossing). Also, the politician seems fond of standing naked in a shower while Lucy Sheehan, an occasional lover of Mizrahi, pelts him with tomatoes.

3417. *Zina* (1985, Hemdale, GB, 92m, c/b&w). P&D Ken McMullen, W McMullen & Terry James, PH Bryan Loftus, M David Cunningham, Barrie Guard & Simon Heyworth, ED Robert Hargreaves, PD Paul Cheetham.

LP Domiziana Giordano, Ian McKellen, Philip Madoc, Ron Anderson, Micha Bergese, Gabrielle Dellal, Paul Geoffrey, William Hootkins, Leonie Mellinger, Maureen O'Brien.

Domiziana Giordano portrays the daughter of Leon Trotsky. The film examines her problems and obsessions while in psychoanalysis in pre–World War II Berlin.

3418. *Zombie High* (1987, Cinema Group, 91m, c).P Marc Toberoff & Aziz Ghazai, D Ron Link, W Tim Doyle, Elizabeth Passerelli & Ghazai, PH David Lux & Brian Coyne, M Daniel May, ED Shawn Hardin & James Whitney, PD Matthew Kozinets.

LP Virginia Madsen (Andrea Miller), Richard Cox (Prof. Philo), Kay Kuter (Dean Eisner), James Wilder (Barry), Sherilyn Fenn (Suzi), Paul Feig (Emerson), T. Scott Coffey (Felner), Paul Williams (Ignatius).

Virginia Madsen is one of the first coeds to enroll at a previously all male prep school. The girls find all the boys to be nerdish bores, only interested in studying. Madsen discovers the reason: the instructors have lobotomized the boys to make a serum that gives everlasting life.

3419. *Zombie Island Massacre* (1984, Troma, 95m, c). P David Broadnax, D&ED John N. Carter, W William Stoddard & Logan O'Neill (based on a story by Broadnax), M Harry Manfredini, SE Dennis Eger.

LP David Broadnax, Rita Jenrette, Tom Cantrell, Diane Clayre Holub, Ian MacMillan, George Peters, Dennis Stephenson.

Rita Jenrette, the former wife of a real-life Abscam congressman, appears nude in three early scenes. This seems to have nothing to do with the plot about bad things happening on a zombie-infested island.

3420. *Zombie Nightmare* (1987, Gold-Gems, 83m, c). P Pierre Grise, D John Bravman, W David Wellington, PH Robert Racine, M Jon-Miki Thor, ED David Franko, AD David Blanchard.

LP Adam West (Capt. Churchman), Jon-Miki Thor (Tony Washington), Tia Carrere (Amy), Manuska Rigaud (Molly), Frank Dietz (Frank), Linda Singer (Maggie), Francesca Bonacorsa (Tony's Wife).

Rock singer Jon-Miki Thor portrays a man killed by some irresponsible teenagers. He is brought back to life as a zombie by his widow and a Haitian woman who wants to use him to take revenge on those who raped her years before. Thor beats everyone he can catch with a baseball bat.

3421. *Zone Troopers* (1986, Empire, 88m, c). P Paul DeMeo, D Danny Bilson, W Bilson & DeMeo, PH Mac Ahlberg, M Richard Band, ED Ted Nicolaou, SE John Buechler.

LP Tim Thomerson (Sarge), Timothy Van Patten (Joey), Art LaFleur (Mittens), Biff Manard (Dolan), William Paulson (Alien).

What a dumb idea! During World War II a troop of American soldiers lost behind German lines encounter space aliens.

3422. *The Zoo Gang* (1985, New World, 96m, c). P Pen Densham, John Watson & Richard Barton Lewis, D&W Densham & Watson (based on a story by Stuart Birnbaum, David Dashev, Densham & Watson), PH Robert New, M Patrick Gleeson, ED James Symons, PD Steve Legler.

LP Ben Vereen (Leatherface), Jack Earle Haley (Little Joe), Tiffany Helm (Kate), Jason Gedrick (Hardin), Eric Gurry (Danny), Marc Price (Val), Gina Battist (Bobbi), Darwyn Swalve (Goose).

A group of youngsters want to start their own nightclub for teens, but other adolescents spoil their plans. Isn't that always the way?

3423. *Zoot Suit* (1982, Universal, 103m, c). P Peter Burrell, Kenneth Brecher & William P. Wingate, D&W Luis Valdez (based on his play), PH

David Myers, M Daniel Valdez & Shorty Rogers, ED Jacqueline Cambas, PD Tom H. John.

LP Daniel Valdez (Henry Reyna), Edward James Olmos (El Pachuco), Charles Aidman (George), Tyne Daly (Alice), John Anderson (Judge), Abel Franco (Enrique), Mike Gomez (Joey), Alma Rose Martinez (Lupe).

This film is based on the true story of a group of Chicanos who in 1942 were convicted of murder on some trumped-up charges. Attempts to free them were to no avail.

3424. *Zorro, the Gay Blade* (1981, 20th Century–Fox, 93m, c). P George Hamilton & C.O. Erickson, D Peter Medak, W Hal Dresner (based on a story by Dresner, Greg Alt, Don Moriarty & Bob Randall), PH John A. Alonzo, M Ian Fraser, ED Hillary Jane Kranze, PD Herman A. Blumenthal.

LP George Hamilton (Don Diego Vega/Bunny Wigglesworth), Lauren Hutton (Charlotte), Brenda Vaccaro (Florinda), Ron Leibman (Esteban), Donovan Scott (Paco), James Booth (Velasquez), Helen Burns (Consuela), Clive Revill (Garcia), Carolyn Seymour (Dolores), Eduardo Noriega (Don Francisco).

Having parodied *Dracula* with *Love at First Bite,* George Hamilton is back to take on another legendary movie, *Zorro.* He apparently thought it would be a scream if the dashing masked California hero of the oppressed had a twin brother with a limp wrist. He was wrong.

3425. *Zulu Dawn* (1980, Warner, GB, 117m, c). P Nate Kohn, D Douglas Hickox, W Cy Endfield & Anthony Storey (based on a story by Endfield), PH Ousama Rawi, M Elmer Bernstein, ED Malcolm Cooke, PD John Rosewarne.

LP Burt Lancaster (Col. Durnford), Peter O'Toole (Lord Chelmsford), Simon Ward (William Vereker), John Mills (Sir Bartle Frere), Nigel Davenport (Col. Hamilton-Brown), Michael Jayston (Col. Crealock), Ronald Lacey (Norris Newman), Denholm Elliott (Lt. Col. Pulleine), Freddie Jones (Bishop Colenso), Anna Calder-Marshall (Fanny Colenso).

This film is a prequel to *Zulu* (1964), the exciting action film about an 1879 British stand against the Zulu at Rorke's Drift. This film deals with the battle which preceded the one at Rorke's Drift. In it, 1300 British soldiers are massacred at Ulundi by Zulu warriors led by King Cetshwayo.

Index

Numbers refer to the entry number, not page number.

A

A&A Special Effects 2068
Aames, Angela 166, 1746
Aames, Willie 2212, 3411
Aanensen, Peter 400, 2663
Aaron, Caroline 545, 591
Aaron, Jack 942
Aaron, Paul 686, 1837, 1932, 2126
Aaron, Sidney 52
Aaron, Temple 1422
Abbott, Bruce 152, 2432, 2914
Abbott, Diahnne 1523, 1589, 1755
Abbott, John 2729
Abbott, Margaret 1755
Abbott, Philip 1220, 2587
Abdallah, Bassem 1054
Abdul-Jabbar, Kareem 26
Abdulla, Raficq 326
Abe, Mitzie 1714
Abed-Alnouz, Youssef 1031
Abel, Gene 2449, 3195
Abel, Liane 2522
Abel, Walter 3169
Abele, Jim 2901, 3346
Abeles, Jordan 2789
Abella, Helena 967
Abercrombie, Ian 981
Aberdein, Keith 2754, 3209, 3334
Abernathy, Lewis 721
Abernathy, Ric 2822
Abernathy, Tom 2716
Abigail 1850
Able, Sheri 890
Abraham, Dawn 691
Abraham, F. Murray 55, 1468, 2001, 2253, 2597
Abraham, Ken 586, 684

Abraham, Gijie 3196
Abraham, Valerie 1919
Abrahams, Jim 26, 228, 1998, 2558, 3094
Abrahams, Mort 2647
Abramoff, Jack 2443
Abrams, Barry 475, 1060, 2878
Abrams, Celia 825
Abrams, Jeffrey 2060
Abrams, Jesse 475
Abrams, Marilyn 2199
Abrams, Peter 1581
Abramson, Richard 1496, 2237
Abril, Victoria 549, 2149
Abroms, Edward 301, 473, 535, 2177, 2287
AC/DC 1838
Acciari, Paul 2034
Acey, Robert 90, 2720
Acharya, Anil 1487
Acheson, James 643, 1640, 2316, 2712
Achorn, John 2046
Achtman, Arnie 1268
Acierto, Tony 1535
Acker, Kathy 3220
Acker, Sharon 3052
Ackerly, J.R. 3282
Ackerman, Leslie 264
Ackerman, Thomas E. 144, 189, 1135, 1692, 2004, 2514
Ackland, Joss 109, 642, 1493, 1626, 1671, 2539, 2687, 3082, 3313, 3412
Ackland-Snow, Brian 2533, 3366
Ackland-Snow, Terry 168, 1777, 1834
Ackley, James 1347
Ackridge, Bill 1780, 2693

Ackroyd, David 1853, 1944
Acomba, David 2044
Acovone, Jay 540, 609
Acquisto, Luigi 1412
Actor, Allen 819
Acuff, Charles Kirkpatrick 2484
Adair, Hazel 1102
Adair, Sandra 2995
Adalist, Jack 1695
Adam, Adolphe 637
Adam, Ken 25, 593, 665, 718, 1586
Adames, Juan 1143
Adams, Bill 442
Adams, Brooke 48, 678, 1561, 2996, 3208
Adams, Catlin 1515, 2861
Adams, Daniel 2450
Adams, David 2773
Adams, Don 1520, 2116
Adams, Edie 1229
Adams, Jeb Stuart 1012, 2155
Adams, John 713, 2891, 3222
Adams, Julia 257
Adams, Julius 1109
Adams, Lynne 429
Adams, Marla 1177
Adams, Mason 1094
Adams, Maud 93, 1509, 2127, 2988, 3379
Adams, Peter 293
Adams, Philip 1192
Adams, Richard 1132, 2286
Adams, Stacey 2951
Adams, Tony 262, 268, 620, 971, 1802, 1860, 2723, 2765, 2922, 3114, 3231

653

D